CLYMER®
HARLEY-DAVIDSON
FLH/FLT TOURING SERIES • 2006-2009

The world's finest publisher of mechanical how-to manuals

CLYMER®

P.O. Box 12901, Overland Park, Kansas 66282-2901

Copyright ©2010 Penton Business Media, Inc.

FIRST EDITION
First Printing December, 2010

Printed in U.S.A.

CLYMER and colophon are registered trademarks of Penton Business Media, Inc.

ISBN-10: 1-59969-334-8

ISBN-13: 978-1-59969-334-7

Library of Congress: 2010941722

AUTHOR: Ed Scott.

TECHNICAL PHOTOGRAPHY: Ed Scott, with technical assistance from Jordan Engineering, Oceanside, CA. Motorcycles courtesy by Carlos Ramirez and Erik M. Steele, Oceanside, CA.

TECHNICAL ILLUSTRATIONS: Errol and Mitzi McCarthy.

WIRING DIAGRAMS: Bob Meyer.

EDITORS: Richard Arens.

PRODUCTION: Adriane Roberts.

TOOLS AND EQUIPMENT: K&L Supply Co. at klsupply.com, Engine and transmission tools provided by JIMS Tools at jimsusa.com and Boars Nest Choppers, Inc. Oceanside, CA at boarsnestchoppers.com. Twin Cam engine provided by Partick Racing, Garden Grove, CA. at patrickracing.com.

COVER: Mark Clifford Photography at markclifford.com. 2007 FLHTCU Ultra Classic Electra Guide courtesy of Pomona Valley Harley-Davidson Montclair, CA.

All rights reserved. Reproduction or use, without express permission, of editorial or pictorial content, in any manner, is prohibited. No patent liability is assumed with respect to the use of the information contained herein. While every precaution has been taken in the preparation of this book, the publisher assumes no responsibility for errors or omissions. Neither is any liability assumed for damages resulting from use of the information contained herein. Publication of the servicing information in this manual does not imply approval of the manufacturers of the products covered.

All instructions and diagrams have been checked for accuracy and ease of application; however, success and safety in working with tools depend to a great extent upon individual accuracy, skill and caution. For this reason, the publishers are not able to guarantee the result of any procedure contained herein. Nor can they assume responsibility for any damage to property or injury to persons occasioned from the procedures. Persons engaging in the procedure do so entirely at their own risk.

Chapter One
General Information

Chapter Two
Troubleshooting

Chapter Three
Lubrication, Maintenance and Tune-up

Chapter Four
Engine Top End and Exhaust System

Chapter Five
Engine Lower End

Chapter Six
Clutch and Primary Drive

Chapter Seven
Five Speed Transmission (2006 Models)

Chapter Eight
Six Speed Transmission (2007-2009 Models)

Chapter Nine
Air/Fuel and Emission Control Systems (Carbureted Models)

Chapter Ten
Air/Fuel and Emission Control Systems (Fuel-Injected Models)

Chapter Eleven
Electrical System

Chapter Twelve
Wheels, Hubs and Tires

Chapter Thirteen
Front Suspension and Steering

Chapter Fourteen
Rear Suspension

Chapter Fifteen
Brakes

Chapter Sixteen
Cruise Control

Chapter Seventeen
Body and Frame

Index

CLYMER®

Publisher Ron Rogers

EDITORIAL

Editorial Director
James Grooms

Editor
Steven Thomas

Associate Editor
Rick Arens

Authors
Michael Morlan
George Parise
Ed Scott
Ron Wright

Technical Illustrators
Steve Amos
Errol McCarthy
Mitzi McCarthy
Bob Meyer

SALES

Sales Manager–Marine
Jay Lipton

Sales Manager–Powersport/I&T
Matt Tusken

CUSTOMER SERVICE

Customer Service Manager
Terri Cannon

Customer Service Representatives
Karen Barker
Dinah Bunnell
April LeBlond
Suzanne Myers
Sherry Rudkin

PRODUCTION

Director of Production
Dylan Goodwin

Production Manager
Greg Araujo

Production Editors
Holly McComas
Adriane Roberts

Associate Production Editor
Ashley Bally

PENTON

P.O. Box 12901, Overland Park, KS 66282-2901 • 800-262-1954 • 913-967-1719

CLYMER®   **CLYMER® ProSeries**   **I&T SHOP SERVICE**

More information available at *clymer.com*

CONTENTS

QUICK REFERENCE DATA XI

CHAPTER ONE
GENERAL INFORMATION 1
    Manual organization
    Warnings, cautions and notes
    Safety
    Serial numbers
    Fasteners
    Shop supplies
    Tools
    Measuring tools
    Electrical system fundamentals
    Service methods
    Storage
    Specifications

CHAPTER TWO
TROUBLESHOOTING 31
    Engine starting
    Engine performance
    Engine noises
    Electrical testing
    Starting system
    Charging system
    Ignition system
    Fuel system (carbureted models)
    Fuel system (electronic fuel injection)
    Engine lubrication
    Clutch
    Transmission
    Lighting system
    Excessive vibration
    Front suspension and steering
    Brake problems
    Electronic diagnostic system
    Cruise control system diagnostic trouble codes
    Specifications

CHAPTER THREE
LUBRICATION, MAINTENANCE AND TUNE-UP 67

Maintenance intervals
Pre-ride inspection
Tires and wheels
Screamin' Eagle lubrication
Engine oil and filter
Transmission oil
Primary chaincase oil
Front fork oil
Control cables
Primary chain and drive belt
Brake system

Clutch system
Fuel system
Air filter
Suspension and fasteners
Compression test
Spark plugs
Ignition timing
Idle speed adjustment
Vehicle alignment (2006-2008 models)
Specifications

CHAPTER FOUR
ENGINE TOP END AND EXHAUST SYSTEM 105

Engine service precautions
Servicing engine in frame
Rocker arms, pushrods and valve lifters
Cylinder head
Valves and valve components
Cylinder

Pistons and piston rings
Pushrods
Exhaust system
Active exhaust
Specifications

CHAPTER FIVE
ENGINE LOWER END 164

Engine
Oil pump
Oil filter mount (2006 models except
  Screamin' Eagle)
Oil cooler, oil filter mount and thermostat

Camshaft support plate
Crankcase and crankshaft
Crankcase bearing replacement
Engine break-in
Specifications

CHAPTER SIX
CLUTCH AND PRIMARY DRIVE 224

Primary chaincase cover
Primary chaincase housing
Clutch assembly
Clutch pushrod and release plate
  inspection (Screamin' Eagle models)
Primary drive assembly (2006 models)
Primary chain alignment (2006 models)
Primary drive assembly (2007-2009 models)
Clutch shell, hub and sprocket
Primary chain and tensioner inspection
  (all models)
Compensating sprocket inspection
Starter jackshaft (2006 models)
Clutch cable replacement (all models except
  Screamin' Eagle)
Clutch lever assembly (all models except
  Screamin' Eagle)

Clutch release cover (all models except
  Screamin' Eagle)
Clutch service (Screamin' Eagle models)
Clutch master cylinder (Screamin'
  Eagle models)
Clutch release cover (Screamin'
  Eagle models)
Clutch secondary actuator (Screamin'
  Eagle models)
Clutch hydraulic hose replacement
  (Screamin' Eagle models)
Clutch system flushing (Screamin' Eagle
  models)
Clutch system draining (Screamin' Eagle models)
Clutch system bleeding (Screamin' Eagle
  models)
Specifications

CHAPTER SEVEN
FIVE SPEED TRANSMISSION (2006 MODELS) 279

Shift assembly
External shift mechanism
Transmission cover
Shift cam
Shift arm assembly
Shift forks
Transmission side door assembly

Transmission shafts
Side door bearings
Main drive gear
Drive sprocket
Transmission case
Oil pan
Specifications

CHAPTER EIGHT
SIX SPEED TRANSMISSION (2007-2009 MODELS) 312

Shift assembly
External shift mechanism
Transmission cover
Shift arm assembly
Shift forks and shift cam
Transmission side door assembly
Transmission shafts

Side door bearings
Main drive gear
Transmission drive sprocket
Transmission case
Oil pan
Specifications

CHAPTER NINE
AIR/FUEL AND EMISSION CONTROL SYSTEMS (CARBURETED MODELS). 348

Air filter and backplate
Carburetor
Intake manifold
Throttle and idle cables (2006-2007
 non-cruise control models)
Starting enrichment valve (choke) cable
 replacement

Fuel tank console
Fuel tank
Fuel shutoff valve
Fuel level sender (canopy)
Evaporative emission control system
 (carbureted and fuel-injected models)
Specifications

CHAPTER TEN
AIR/FUEL AND EMISSION CONTROL SYSTEMS (FUEL-INJECTED MODELS) 380

Air filter and backplate (all models except 2007
 FLHRSE3 and 2009 FLTRSE3)
Air filter and backplate (2007 FLHRSE3 and 2009
 FLTRSE3 domestic models)
Depressurizing the fuel system
Fuel tank
Fuel supply check valve
Fuel pump/level sender assembly
 (2006-2007 models)
Fuel pump and fuel filter (2008-2009 models)
Fuel pressure test (2008-2009 models)
Fuel tank console
Electronic fuel injection (EFI)
Throttle and idle cables (2006 and 2007
 non-cruise control models)

Throttle and idle cables (2006 and 2007
 cruise control models)
Throttle control actuator (TCA) (2008-2009
 models)
Throttle or twist grip sensor
 (2008-2009 models)
Twist grip sensor jumper wire
 (2008-2009 models)
Induction module
Fuel injectors
Induction module sensors
Evaporative emission control system
 (all California models)
Specifications

CHAPTER ELEVEN
ELECTRICAL SYSTEM 437

Electrical component replacement
Fuses
Maxi-Fuse
Battery
Battery tray
Charging system
Alternator
Voltage regulator
Ignition system
Ignition coil
Ignition control module (ICM) (carbureted models)
Electronic control module (ECM)
 (fuel injected models)
Electrical bracket (2006-2007 models)
Electrical caddies (2008-2009 models)
Sensors
Starting system
Starter
Lighting system
Headlight
Passing lights and front turn signals
Turn signals
Taillight/brake light
Fender tip light
Rear fascia light

License plate light
Tour-pak
Instruments
Automatic compression release solenoid
 (2006-2009 Screamin' Eagle models)
Switches
Horn
Turn signal security module (TSM, TSSM
 and HFSM)
Security siren (optional on 2007-2009 models)
Radio (storage box)
Radio antenna
Front fairing speakers
Front headset receptacle (2008-2009
 FLHTCUSE models)
Rear passenger switches
Rear speakers
CB module (FLHTCU models)
Relays
Electrical connector location and identification
Electrical connector service
Autofuse electrical connectors
Sealed butt connectors
Wiring diagrams
Specifications

CHAPTER TWELVE
WHEELS, HUBS AND TIRES 543

Motorcycle stands
Front wheel
Rear wheel
Front and rear hubs
Driven sprocket assembly
Drive sprocket
Drive belt

Laced wheel service
Wheel balance
Tire changing (laced wheels)
Tire changing (alloy wheels)
Tire repairs
Specifications

CHAPTER THIRTEEN
FRONT SUSPENSION AND STEERING 577

Handlebar
Front fork
Steering head and stem

Steering head bearing race replacement
Steering play inspection and adjustment
Specifications

CHAPTER FOURTEEN
REAR SUSPENSION 600

Shock air pressure adjustment
Air pressure loss inspection
Shock absorbers

Rear swing arm
Specifications

CHAPTER FIFTEEN
BRAKES 609

Brake service
Front brake pad replacement
Front brake caliper
Front master cylinder
Rear brake pad replacement
Rear brake caliper
Rear master cylinder and rear brake pedal (all models)
Rear master cylinder service
Brake hose and line replacement (non-ABS models)
ABS brake system
ABS wheel speed sensors
ABS brake module
ABS diode pack
Brake line replacement (ABS models)
Brake disc
Brake bleeding
Flushing the brake system
Specifications

CHAPTER SIXTEEN
CRUISE CONTROL 665

System components and operation
Control cables adjustment (2006-2007 models)
Control cables replacement (2006-2007 models)
Cruise control module (2006-2007 models)
Cruise control switches
Specifications

CHAPTER SEVENTEEN
BODY AND FRAME. 672

Seats
Rider and passenger backrests
Rear frame rails
Front fender
Rear fender
Rear fender fascia
License plate bracket
Windshield
Front fairing
Frame side covers
Saddlebags
Saddlebag supports/guards
Engine guard
Jiffy stand
Tour-pak
Footboards and highway foot pegs
Specifications

INDEX 739

WIRING DIAGRAMS .... See CD

QUICK REFERENCE DATA

MODEL: _____ YEAR: _____
VIN NUMBER: _____
ENGINE SERIAL NUMBER: _____
CARBURETOR SERIAL NUMBER OR I.D. MARK: _____

TIRE INFLATION PRESSURE (COLD)*

	kPa	PSI
Front wheels		
Rider only	248	36
Rider and one passenger	248	36
Rear wheels		
Rider only	248	36
Rider and passenger	275	40

*Tire pressure for OE equipment tires. Aftermarket tires may require different inflation pressure.

FUEL, ENGINE AND DRIVE FLUID CAPACITIES

Item	Capacity
Fuel tank, total	
2006-2007 models	5.0 gal. (18.9 L)
2008-2009 models	6.0 gal. (22.7 L)
Fuel tank, reserve*	
2006-2007 models	0.9 gal. (3.4 L)
2008-2009 models	1.0 gal. (3.8 L)
Oil tank with filter	1.0 gal. (3.8 L)
Transmission (approximate)	
2006-2007 models	20-24 oz. (591-710 ml)
2008-2009 models	32 oz. (946 ml)
Primary chaincase (approximate)	
2006 models	32 oz. (946 ml)
2007-2009 models	45 oz. (1331 ml)

*Low fuel warning light on.

FORK OIL CAPACITY AND OIL LEVEL SPECIFICATIONS

Model	Capacity – each fork leg U.S. oz. (cc)	Oil level height* in. (mm)
2006-2008 models (including Screamin' Eagle)		
FLHT, FLHX and FLTR models	10.8 (319)	5.59 (142)
FLHR models	11.1 (328)	5.24 (133)
2009 models (including Screamin' Eagle)		
FLHT, FLHX and FLTR models	10.7 (316)	4.92 (125)
FLHR models	11.0 (325)	5.92 (134)

*Measured from the top of the fork tube with the fork spring removed and the fork leg fully compressed.

RECOMMENDED ENGINE OIL

Type	Viscosity	H-D Rating	Ambient operating temperature
H-D Multi-grade	SAE 10W40	HD 360	Below 40° F (4° C)
H-D Multi-grade	SAE 20W50	HD 360	Above 40° F (4° C)
H-D Regular Heavy	SAE 50	HD 360	Above 60° F (16° C)
H-D Extra Heavy	SAE 60	HD 360	Above 80° F (16° C)
Screamin' Eagle models SYN3 Synthetic Motorcycle Lubricant	SAE 20W50	HD 360	Above 40° F (4° C)

RECOMMENDED LUBRICANTS AND FLUIDS

Brake fluid	DOT 4 hydraulic fluid
Clutch fluid (Screamin' Eagle models)	DOT 4 hydraulic fluid
Front fork oil	H-D Type E fork oil
Fuel	91 pump octane or higher
Transmission oil	
All models except Screamin' Eagle models	H-D Formula+ Transmission and Primary Chaincase Lubricant
Screamin' Eagle models	Screamin' Eagle SYN3 Synthetic Motorcycle Lubricant
Primary chaincase oil	
All models except Screamin' Eagle models	H-D Formula+ Transmission and Primary Chaincase Lubricant
Screamin' Eagle models	Screamin' Eagle SYN3 Synthetic Motorcycle Lubricant

MAINTENANCE SPECIFICATIONS

Item	Specification
Brake pad minimum thickness (front and rear)	
2006-2007 models	0.04 in. (1.2 mm)
2008-2009 models	0.016 in. (0.41 mm)
Clutch cable free play	1/16-1/8 in. (1.6-3.2 mm)
Drive belt deflection	
FLHX models	1/4-5/16 in. (6.4-7.9 mm)
All other models	3/8-7/16 in. (9.5-11.1 mm)
Engine compression	
All models except Screamin' Eagle	125 psi (862 kPa)
Screamin' Eagle (2007-2009 models)[1]	
ARC valve connected	130-170 psi (896-1172 kPa)
ARC valve disconnected	200-220 psi (1379-1517 kPa)
Idle speed	950-1050 rpm
Ignition timing	Non-adjustable
Primary chain free play (2006 models)	
Cold engine	5/8-7/8 in. (15.9-22.2 mm)
Hot engine	3/8-5/8 in. (9.5-15.9 mm)
Rear axle alignment	1/32 in. (0.8 mm)
Spark plugs	
Gap	0.038-0.043 in. (0.97-1.09 mm)
Type	HD No. 6R12[2]

1. The 2006 Screamin' Eagles are not fitted with the ARC valve. The manufacturer does not provide the specification of the 2006 Screamin' Eagle without the ARC valve.
2. Harley-Davidson recommends that no other type of spark plug be substituted.

MAINTENANCE AND TUNE-UP TORQUE SPECIFICATIONS

Item	ft.-lb.	in.-lb.	N•m
Air filter			
All models except 2007 FLHRSE3 and 2009 FLTRSE3			
Cover screw			
All models except Screamin' Eagle	36-60	–	4.0-6.8
Screamin' Eagle	27-32	–	3.1-3.6

(continued)

MAINTENANCE AND TUNE-UP TORQUE SPECIFICATIONS (continued)

Item	ft.-lb.	in.-lb.	N•m
Air filter (continued)			
All models except 2007 (continued)			
Mounting bracket	–	40-60	4.5-6.8
2007 FLHRSE3 and 2009 FLTRSE3			
Filter element mounting screws	–	55-60	6.2-6.8
Standoff bolts	–	55-60	6.2-6.8
Cover screw	–	36-60	4.1-6.8
Trim plate screws	–	27-32	3.1-3.6
Clutch adjusting screw locknut	–	72-120	8.1-13.6
Clutch cover screws	–	84-108	9.5-12.2
Engine oil drain plug	14-21	–	19-28.5
Primary chaincase			
Inspection cover screws	–	84-108	9.5-12.2
Chain adjuster shoe nut*	21-29	–	28.5-39.3
Oil drain plug	14-21	–	19-28.5
Jiffy stand leg stop bolt	12-15	–	16.3-20.3
Rear axle nut	95-105	–	128.8-142.4
Spark plug	12-18	–	16.3-24.4
Transmission oil drain plug	14-21	–	19-28.5
Transmission oil filler cap/dipstick	–	25-75	2.8-8.5
Vehicle alignment (2006-2008 models)			
Lower mounting bracket			
Engine bolts	36-40	–	48.8-54.2
Engine mount (rubber mount-to-frame)	15-20	–	20.3-27.1
Engine mount (rubber mount-to-lower bracket)	15-20	–	20.3-27.1
Lower stabilizer link			
Frame weldment bolt	18-22	–	24.4-29.8
Engine mounting bracket bolt	18-22	–	24.4-29.8
Upper mounting bracket–to–cylinder head bolts	35-40	–	47.5-54.2
Upper stabilizer link			
Frame weldment bolt	18-22	–	24.4-29.8
Frame mounting bracket	18-22	–	24.4-29.8
Voltage regulator flange nut	–	70-100	7.9-11.3

*2006 models only.

CHAPTER ONE

GENERAL INFORMATION

This detailed and comprehensive manual covers 2006-2009 Harley-Davidson FLT and FLR Touring models, including all Twin Cam 88, 96, 103 and 110 cubic inch engines. The text provides complete information on maintenance, tune-up, repair and overhaul. Hundreds of photos and drawings guide the reader through every job. Each procedure is in step-by-step format and designed for the reader who may be working on the motorcycle for the first time.

MANUAL ORGANIZATION

A shop manual is a tool and, as in all Clymer manuals, the chapters are thumb-tabbed for easy reference. Main headings are listed in the table of contents and the index. Frequently-used specifications and capacities from the tables at the end of each individual chapter are listed in the *Quick Reference Data* section at the front of the manual. Specifications and capacities are provided in U.S. standard and metric units of measure.

During some of the procedures there will be references to headings in other chapters or sections of the manual. When a specific heading is called out in a step it will be *italicized* as it appears in the manual. If a sub-heading is indicated as being "in this section" it is located within the same main heading. For example, the sub-heading *Handling Gasoline Safely* is located within the main heading *SAFETY*.

This chapter provides general information on shop safety, tools and their usage, service fundamentals and shop supplies. **Tables 1-10** at the end of the chapter provide general motorcycle, mechanical and shop information.

Chapter Two provides methods for quick and accurate diagnosis of problems. Troubleshooting procedures present typical symptoms and logical methods to pinpoint and repair the problem.

Chapter Three explains all routine maintenance necessary to keep the motorcycle running well. Chapter Three also includes recommended tune-up procedures, eliminating the need to constantly consult the chapters on the various assemblies.

Subsequent chapters describe specific systems such as engine, exhaust system, clutch and primary drive system, transmission, fuel system, suspension and brakes. Each disassembly, repair and assembly procedure is discussed step-by-step.

WARNINGS, CAUTIONS AND NOTES

The terms WARNING, CAUTION and NOTE each have specific meanings in this manual.

A WARNING emphasizes areas where injury or even death could result from negligence. Mechanical damage may also occur. WARNINGS are to be taken seriously.

A CAUTION emphasizes areas where equipment damage could result. Disregarding a CAUTION could cause permanent mechanical damage, though injury is unlikely.

A NOTE provides additional information to make a step or procedure easier or clearer. Disregarding a NOTE could cause inconvenience, but would not cause equipment damage or injury.

SAFETY

Follow these guidelines and practice common sense to safely service the motorcycle.

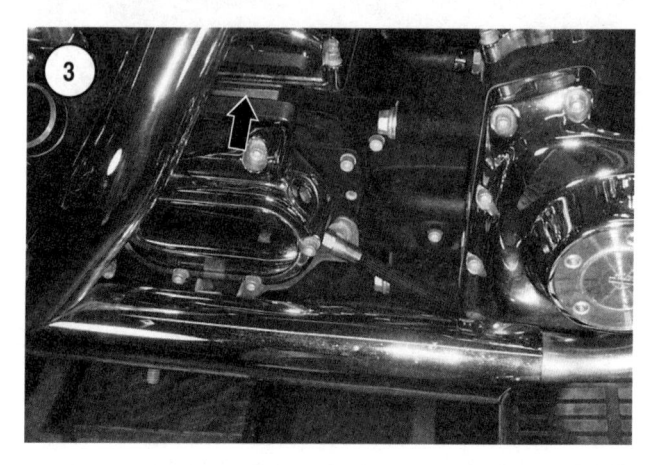

1. Do not operate the motorcycle in an enclosed area. The exhaust gases contain carbon monoxide, an odorless, colorless and tasteless poisonous gas. Carbon monoxide levels build quickly in small enclosed areas and can cause unconsciousness and death in a short time. Make sure to properly ventilate the work area or operate the motorcycle outside.
2. Never use gasoline or any extremely flammable liquid to clean parts. Refer to *Cleaning Parts* and *Handling Gasoline Safely* in this section.
3. Never smoke or use a torch in the vicinity of flammable liquids, such as gasoline or cleaning solvent.
4. If welding or brazing on the motorcycle, remove the fuel tank to a safe distance at least 50 ft. (15 m) away.
5. Use the correct type and size of tools to avoid damaging fasteners.
6. Keep tools clean and in good condition. Replace or repair worn or damaged equipment.
7. When loosening a tight fastener, be guided by what would happen if the tool slips.
8. When replacing fasteners, make sure the new fasteners are the same size and strength as the original ones.
9. Keep the work area clean and organized.
10. Wear eye protection anytime the safety of the eyes is in question. This includes procedures that involve drilling, grinding, hammering, compressed air and chemicals.
11. Wear the correct clothing for the job. Tie up or cover long hair so it does not get caught in moving equipment.
12. Do not carry sharp tools in clothing pockets.
13. Always have an approved fire extinguisher available. Make sure it is rated for gasoline (Class B) and electrical (Class C) fires.
14. Do not use compressed air to clean clothes, the motorcycle or the work area. Debris may be blown into the eyes or skin. Never direct a compressed air hose at anyone. Do not allow children to use or play with any compressed air equipment.
15. When using compressed air to dry rotating parts, hold the part so it does not rotate. Do not allow the force of the air to spin the part. The air jet is capable of rotating parts at extreme speed. The part may disintegrate or become damaged, causing serious injury.
16. Do not inhale the dust created by brake pad and clutch wear. These particles may contain asbestos. In addition, some types of insulating materials and gaskets may contain asbestos. Inhaling asbestos particles is hazardous to health.
17. Never work on the motorcycle while someone is working under it.
18. When placing the motorcycle on a stand, make sure it is secure before walking away.

Handling Gasoline Safely

Gasoline is a volatile flammable liquid and is one of the most dangerous items in the shop. Because gasoline is used so often, many people forget it is hazardous. Only use gasoline as fuel for internal combustion gas engines. Keep in mind when working on the machine that gasoline is always present in the fuel tank, fuel line and throttle body. To avoid a disastrous accident when working around the fuel system, carefully observe the following precautions:

1. Never use gasoline to clean parts. Refer to *Cleaning Parts* in this section.
2. When working on the fuel system, work outside or in a well-ventilated area.
3. Do not add fuel to the fuel tank or service the fuel system while the motorcycle is near open flames, sparks or where someone is smoking. Gasoline vapor is heavier than air; it collects in low areas and is more easily ignited than liquid gasoline.
4. Allow the engine to cool completely before working on any fuel system component.

GENERAL INFORMATION

3. Work in a well-ventilated area.
4. Wear chemical-resistant gloves.
5. Wear safety glasses.
6. Wear a vapor respirator if the instructions call for it.
7. Wash hands and arms thoroughly after cleaning parts.
8. Keep chemical products away from children and pets.
9. Thoroughly clean all oil, grease and cleaner residue from any part that must be heated.
10. Use a nylon brush when cleaning parts. Metal brushes may cause a spark.
11. When using a parts washer, only use the solvent recommended by the manufacturer. Make sure the parts washer is equipped with a metal lid that will lower in case of fire.

Warning Labels

Most manufacturers attach information and warning labels to the motorcycle. These labels contain instructions that are important to personal safety when operating, servicing, transporting and storing the motorcycle. Refer to the owner's manual for the description and location of labels. Order replacement labels from the manufacturer if they are missing or damaged.

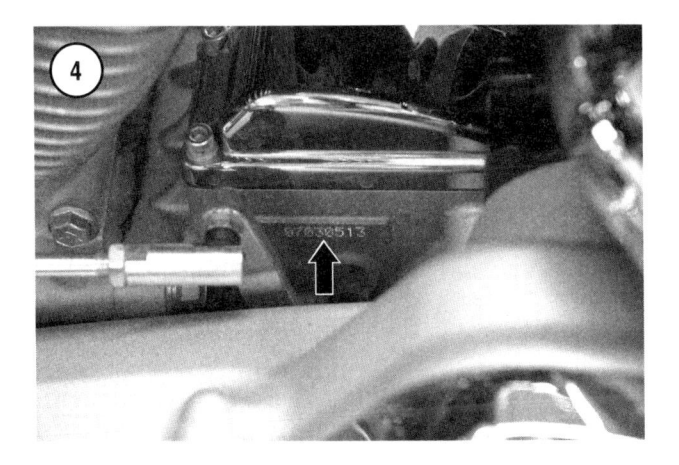

5. Do not store gasoline in glass containers. If the glass breaks, a serious explosion or fire may occur.
6. Immediately wipe up spilled gasoline with rags. Store the rags in a metal container with a lid until they can be properly disposed of, or place them outside in a safe place for the fuel to evaporate.
7. Do not pour water onto a gasoline fire. Water spreads the fire and makes it more difficult to put out. Use a class B, BC or ABC fire extinguisher to extinguish the fire.
8. Always turn off the engine before refueling. Do not spill fuel onto the engine or exhaust system. Do not overfill the fuel tank. Leave air space at the top of the tank to allow room for the fuel to expand due to temperature fluctuations.

Cleaning Parts

Cleaning parts is one of the more tedious and difficult service jobs performed in the home garage. Many types of chemical cleaners and solvents are available for shop use. Most are poisonous and extremely flammable. To prevent chemical exposure, vapor buildup, fire and serious injury, observe each product warning label and note the following:
1. Read and observe the entire product label before using any chemical. Always know what type of chemical is being used and whether it is poisonous and/or flammable.
2. Do not use more than one type of cleaning solvent at a time. If mixing chemicals is required, measure the proper amounts according to the manufacturer.

SERIAL NUMBERS

Serial numbers are stamped in various locations on the frame, engine, transmission and carburetor or throttle body. Record these numbers in the *Quick Reference Data* section in the front of the book. Have these numbers available when ordering parts.

The VIN number label (**Figure 1**) is located on the left side of the frame next to the steering head.

The engine serial number is stamped on the raised pad on the left side of the crankcase (**Figure 2**).

The 2006 model transmission serial number is stamped on a pad on the right side of the transmission case (**Figure 3**) next to the side door. The 2007-2009 model transmission serial number is stamped on a pad (**Figure 4**) on the left side of the transmission case next to the shift lever.

The carburetor serial number (**Figure 5**) is located on the side of the carburetor body next to the accelerator pump linkage.

Record these numbers in the *Quick Reference Data* section at the front of this manual and have these numbers available when ordering parts.

FASTENERS

WARNING
Do not use replacement fasteners with a lower strength classification than the originals.

Make sure replacement fasteners meet all the same requirements as the originals; failure to do so may cause equipment failure and/or damage.

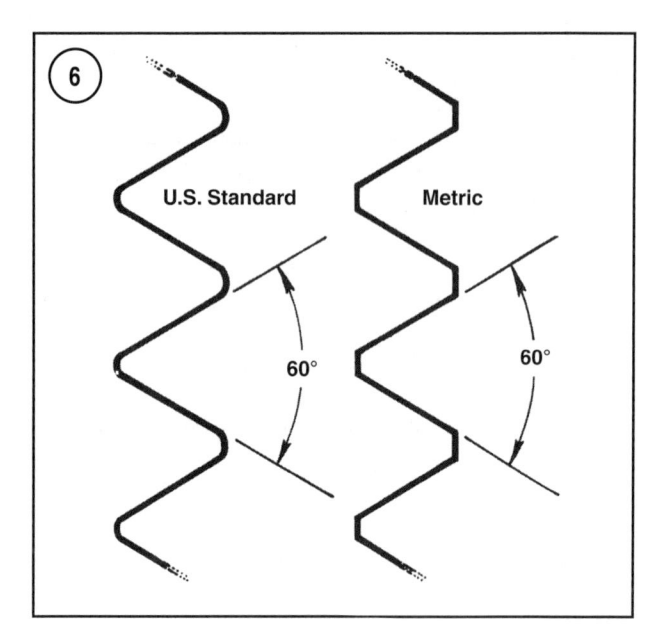

Threaded Fasteners

CAUTION
To ensure that the fastener threads are not mismatched or cross-threaded, start all fasteners by hand. If a fastener is hard to start or turn, determine the cause before tightening with a wrench.

Pay particular attention when working with unidentified fasteners; mismatched thread types can damage threads. Both Standard and metric fasteners (**Figure 6**) are used on the engine and chassis.

Threaded fasteners secure most of the components on the motorcycle. Most fasteners are tightened by turning them clockwise (right-hand threads). If the normal rotation of the component being tightened would loosen the fastener, it may have left-hand threads. If a left-hand threaded fastener is used, it is noted in the text.

Two dimensions are required to match the thread size of the fastener: the number of threads in a given distance and the outside diameter of the threads.

The length (L, **Figure 7**), diameter (D) and pitch (T), or distance between thread crests, classify metric screws and bolts. A typical bolt may be identified by the numbers, 8–1.25 × 130. This indicates the bolt has a diameter of 8 mm, the distance between thread crests is 1.25 mm and the length is 130 mm. Always measure bolt length as shown in L, **Figure 7** to avoid purchasing replacements of the wrong length.

The numbers on the top of the fastener (**Figure 7**) indicate the strength of metric screws and bolts. The higher the number, the stronger the fastener is. Typically, unnumbered fasteners are the weakest.

Many screws, bolts and studs are combined with nuts to secure particular components. To indicate the size of a nut, manufacturers specify the internal diameter and the thread pitch.

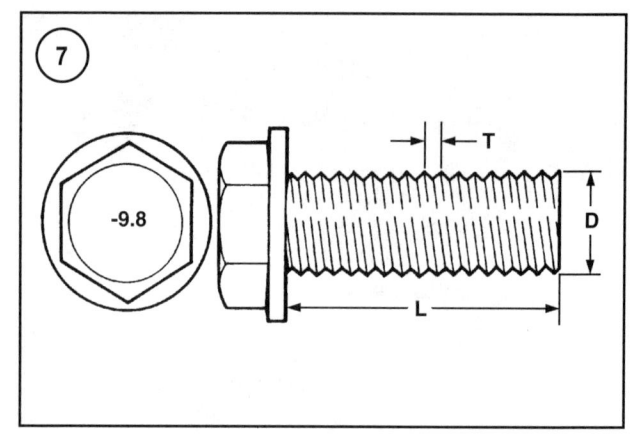

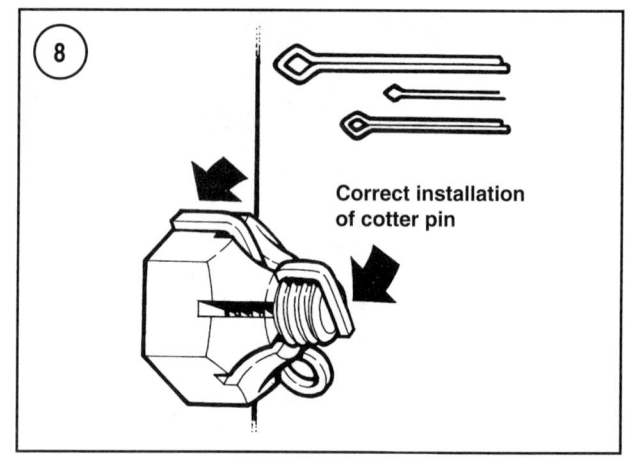

The measurement across two flats on a nut or bolt indicates the wrench size.

Torque Specifications

The materials used in the manufacturing of the motorcycle may be subjected to uneven stresses if the fasteners of the various subassemblies are not installed and tightened correctly. Fasteners that are improperly installed or work loose can cause extensive damage. It is essential to use an accurate torque wrench as described in this chapter.

Specifications for torque are provided in Newton-meters (N•m), foot-pounds (ft.-lb.) and inch-pounds (in.-lb.). Refer to **Table 5** for general torque recommendations. To determine the torque requirement, first determine the size of the fastener as described in *Threaded Fasteners* (this section). Torque specifications for specific components are listed at the end of the appropriate chapters. Torque wrenches are covered in *Basic Tools* (this chapter).

Self-Locking Fasteners

Several types of bolts, screws and nuts incorporate a system that creates interference between the two fasteners. Interference is achieved in various ways. The most common types are the nylon insert nut and a dry adhesive coating on the threads of a bolt.

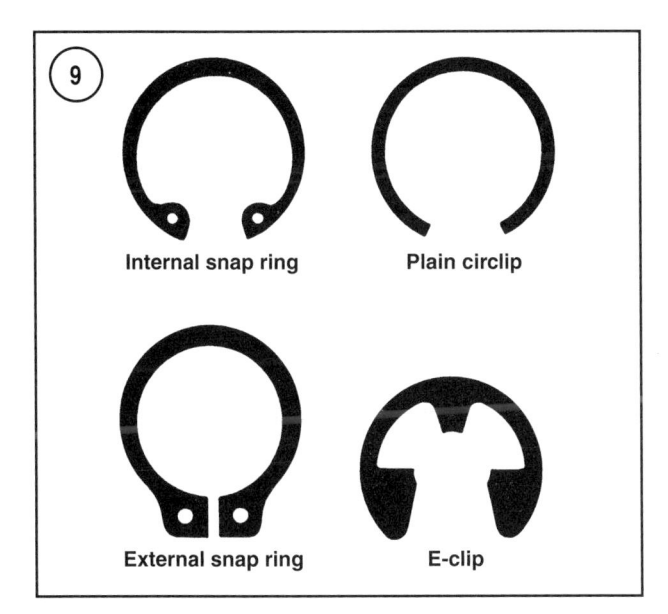

GENERAL INFORMATION

Figure 9: Internal snap ring, Plain circlip, External snap ring, E-clip

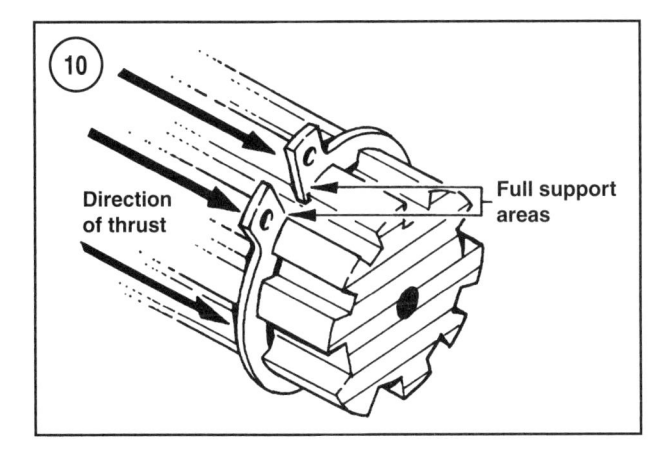

Figure 10: Direction of thrust, Full support areas

Figure 11: Rounded edges, Sharp edges, Direction of thrust

Self-locking fasteners offer greater holding strength than standard fasteners, which improves their resistance to vibration. Self-locking fasteners cannot be reused. The materials used to form the lock become distorted after the initial installation and removal. Discard and replace self-locking fasteners after removing them. Do not replace self-locking fasteners with standard fasteners.

Washers

The two basic types of washers are flat washers and lockwashers. Flat washers are simple discs with a hole to fit a screw or bolt. Lockwashers are used to prevent a fastener from working loose. Washers can be used as spacers and seals, or can help distribute fastener load and prevent the fastener from damaging the component.

As with fasteners, when replacing washers make sure the replacement washers are of the same design and quality.

Cotter Pins

A cotter pin is a split metal pin inserted into a hole or slot to prevent a fastener from loosening. In certain applications, such as the rear axle on an ATV or motorcycle, the fastener must be secured in this way. For these applications, a cotter pin and castellated (slotted) nut is used.

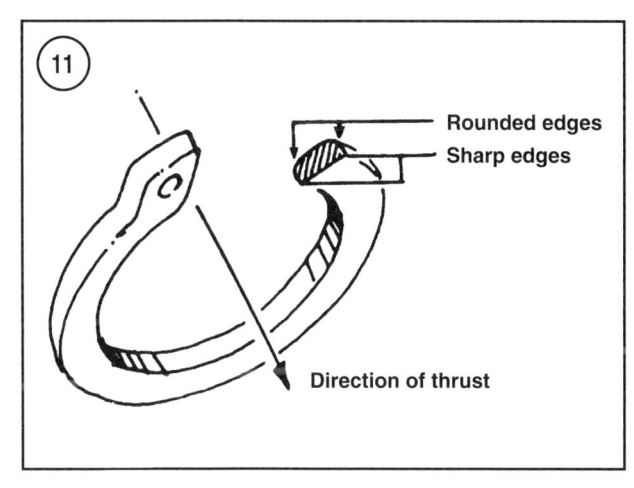

To use a cotter pin, first make sure the diameter is correct for the hole in the fastener. After correctly tightening the fastener and aligning the holes, insert the cotter pin through the hole and bend the ends over the fastener (**Figure 8**). Unless instructed to do so, never loosen a tightened fastener to align the holes. If the holes do not align, tighten the fastener just enough to achieve alignment.

Cotter pins are available in diameters and lengths. Measure the length from the bottom of the head to the tip of the shortest pin.

Snap Rings and E-clips

Snap rings (**Figure 9**) are circular-shaped metal retaining clips. They are required to secure parts and gears in place on parts such as shafts, pins or rods. External type snap rings are used to retain items on shafts. Internal type snap rings secure parts within housing bores. In some applications, in addition to securing the component(s), snap rings of varying thickness also determine endplay. These are usually called selective snap rings.

The two basic types of snap rings are machined and stamped snap rings. Machined snap rings (**Figure 10**) can be installed in either direction, because both faces have sharp edges. Stamped snap rings (**Figure 11**) are manufactured with a sharp and a round edge. When installing a stamped snap ring in a thrust application, install the sharp edge facing away from the part producing the thrust.

E-clips are used when it is not practical to use a snap ring. Remove E-clips with a flat blade screwdriver by prying between the shaft and E-clip. To install an E-clip, center it over the shaft groove and push or tap it into place.

Observe the following when installing snap rings:
1. Remove and install snap rings with snap ring pliers. Refer to *Basic Tools* (this chapter).
2. In some applications, it may be necessary to replace snap rings after removing them.
3. Compress or expand snap rings just enough to install them. If overly expanded, they lose their retaining ability.

4. After installing a snap ring, make sure it seats completely.
5. Wear eye protection when removing and installing snap rings.

SHOP SUPPLIES

Lubricants and Fluids

Periodic lubrication helps ensure a long service life for any type of equipment. Using the correct type of lubricant is as important as performing the lubrication service, although in an emergency the wrong type is better than not using one. The following section describes the types of lubricants most often required. Make sure to follow the manufacturer's recommendations for lubricant types.

Engine oils

Engine oil for four-stroke motorcycle engine use is classified by three standards: the American Petroleum Institute (API) service classification, the Society of Automotive Engineers (SAE) viscosity rating and the Japanese Automobile Standards Organization (JASO) T 903 Standard classification. Always use a oil with a classification recommended by the manufacturer. Using oil with a different classification can cause engine damage.

The API service classification and the SAE viscosity index are not indications of oil quality. The API service classification indicates that the oil meets specific lubrication standards. The first letter in the classification S indicates that the oil is for gasoline engines. The second letter indicates the standard the oil satisfies. Do not use automotive oil with an SJ or higher classification. They are designed for automotive applications and contain friction modifiers that reduce frictional losses. Oils with this classification can cause engine wear in a motorcycle.

The JASO information is for oil manufactured specifically for motorcycle use.

Viscosity is an indication of the oil's thickness. Thin oils have a lower number while thick oils have a higher number. Engine oils fall into the 5- to 50-weight range for single-grade oils. The number or sequence of numbers and letter (10W-40 for example) is the viscosity rating.

Most manufacturers recommend multi-grade oil. These oils perform efficiently across a wide range of operating conditions. Multi-grade oils are identified by a W after the first number, which indicates the low-temperature viscosity.

Greases

Grease is lubricating oil with thickening agents added to it. The National Lubricating Grease Institute (NLGI) grades grease. Grades range from No. 000 to No. 6, with No. 6 being the thickest. Typical multipurpose grease is NLGI No. 2. For specific applications, manufacturers may recommend a water-resistant grease or one with an additive such as molybdenum disulfide (MoS_2).

Brake fluid

WARNING
Use of the incorrect brake fluid may cause component damage and brake failure. Make sure the correct brake fluid is being used at all times.

Brake fluid is the hydraulic fluid used to transmit hydraulic pressure (force) to the wheel brakes. Brake fluid is classified by the Department of Transportation (DOT) to meet particular specifications. The DOT classification, DOT 4 for example, appears on the brake fluid container.

When adding brake fluid, use only the brake fluid type recommended by the manufacturer. All models covered in this manual require DOT 4 brake fluid for the brake system, and, on Screamin' Eagle models, for the hydraulic clutch system as well.

Do not intermix different types of brake fluid. Silicone-based (DOT 5) brake fluid is not compatible with any other types or for use in systems not designed for it and may cause brake failure if so used.

Brake fluid will damage any plastic, painted or plated surface it contacts. Use extreme care when working with brake fluid and remove any spills immediately with soap and water.

Hydraulic brake systems require clean and moisture-free brake fluid. Never reuse brake fluid. Keep containers and reservoirs properly sealed.

Cleaners, Degreasers and Solvents

Many chemicals are available to remove oil, grease and other residue from the motorcycle. Before using cleaning solvents, consider how they will be used and disposed of, particularly if they are not water-soluble. Local ordinances may require special procedures for the disposal of many types of cleaning chemicals. Refer to *Safety* (this chapter).

Use brake parts cleaner to clean brake system components. Brake system parts cleaner leaves no residue. Use electrical contact cleaner to clean electrical connections and components without leaving any residue. Carburetor cleaner is a powerful solvent used to remove fuel deposits and varnish from fuel system components. Do *not* use this cleaner on any of the fuel injection components, as it may damage them.

Generally, degreasers are strong cleaners used to remove heavy accumulations of grease from engine and frame components.

Most solvents are designed to be used with a parts washing cabinet for individual component cleaning. For safety, use only nonflammable or high flashpoint solvents.

Gasket Sealant

Sealant is used in combination with a gasket or seal. In other applications, such as between crankcase halves, only

GENERAL INFORMATION

a sealant is used. Follow the manufacturer's recommendation when using a sealant. Use extreme care when choosing a sealant different from the type originally recommended. Choose a sealant based on its resistance to heat, various fluids and its sealing capabilities.

A common sealant is room temperature vulcanization sealant, or RTV. This sealant cures at room temperature over a specific time period. This allows the repositioning of components without damaging gaskets.

Moisture in the air causes the RTV sealant to cure. Always install the tube cap as soon as possible after applying RTV sealant. RTV sealant has a limited shelf life and will not cure properly if the shelf life has expired. Keep partial tubes sealed and discard them if they have passed the expiration date.

Removing RTV sealant

Silicone sealant is used on some engine gasket surfaces. When cleaning parts after disassembly, a single-sided razor blade or gasket scraper is required to remove silicone residue that cannot be pulled off by hand from the gasket surface. To avoid damaging gasket surfaces, use Permatex Silicone Stripper (part No. 80647) to help soften the residue before scraping.

Applying RTV sealant

Clean all old gasket residue from the mating surfaces. Remove all gasket material from blind threaded holes to avoid inaccurate bolt torque. Spray the mating surfaces with aerosol parts cleaner and then wipe with a lint-free cloth. The area must be clean for the sealant to adhere.

Apply RTV sealant in a continuous bead 0.08-0.12 in. (2-3 mm) thick. Circle all the fastener holes with sealant unless otherwise specified. Do not allow any sealant to enter these holes. Assemble the components and tighten the fasteners to the specified torque within the time frame recommended by the sealant manufacturer.

Gasket Remover

Aerosol gasket remover can help remove stubborn gaskets. This product can speed up the removal process and prevent damage to the mating surface that may be caused by using a scraping tool. Most of these types of products are very caustic. Follow the gasket remover manufacturer's instructions for use.

Threadlock

CAUTION
Threadlock is anaerobic and will damage plastic parts. Use caution when using these products near plastic components.

Threadlock is a fluid applied to the threads of fasteners. After tightening the fastener, the fluid dries and becomes a solid filler between the threads. This makes it difficult for the fastener to work loose from vibration or heat expansion and contraction. Some types of threadlock also provide a seal against fluid leaks.

Before applying threadlock, remove any residue from both thread areas and clean them with aerosol parts cleaner. Use the threadlock sparingly. Excess fluid can run into adjoining parts.

Harley-Davidson recommends the use of Loctite Threadlocker No. 222 (purple), Loctite Threadlocker 243 (blue), Loctite 246 Medium Strength/High Temperature Threadlocker (blue) and Loctite RC/620 (green) High Temperature Retaining Compound. Use these products, or equivalent threadlock, where called for in this manual.

TOOLS

Most of the procedures in this manual can be carried out with simple hand tools and test equipment familiar to the home mechanic. Always use the correct tools for the job at hand. Keep tools organized and clean. Store them in a tool chest with related tools organized together.

Quality tools are essential. The best are constructed of high-strength alloy steel. These tools are light, easy to use and resistant to wear. Their working surface is devoid of sharp edges and carefully polished. They have an easy-to-clean finish and are comfortable to use. Quality tools are a good investment.

If purchasing tools to perform the procedures covered in this manual, consider the tool's potential frequency of use and purchase accordingly. If a tool kit is just now being started, consider purchasing a basic tool set from a quality tool supplier. These sets are available in many tool combinations and offer substantial savings when compared to individually purchased tools. As work experience grows and tasks become more complicated, specialized tools can be added.

Some of the procedures in this manual specify special tools. In many cases the tool is illustrated in use. Those with a large tool kit may be able to use a suitable substitute or fabricate a suitable replacement. However, in some cases, the specialized equipment or expertise may make it impractical for the home mechanic to attempt the procedure. When necessary, such operations come with the recommendation to have a dealership or specialist perform the task. It may be less expensive to have a professional perform these jobs, especially when considering the cost of equipment.

Refer to **Table 10** at the end of this chapter for a list of tools, their manufacturer and part number. The tools throughout this manual are either Harley-Davidson (H-D), Motion Pro (MP) or JIMS tools. Motion Pro and JIMS tools are available from dealerships and many aftermarket tool suppliers. The publisher cannot guarantee tool availability now or in the future, or that the part numbering system will remain the same. Contact the tool manufacturer for additional information.

Screwdrivers

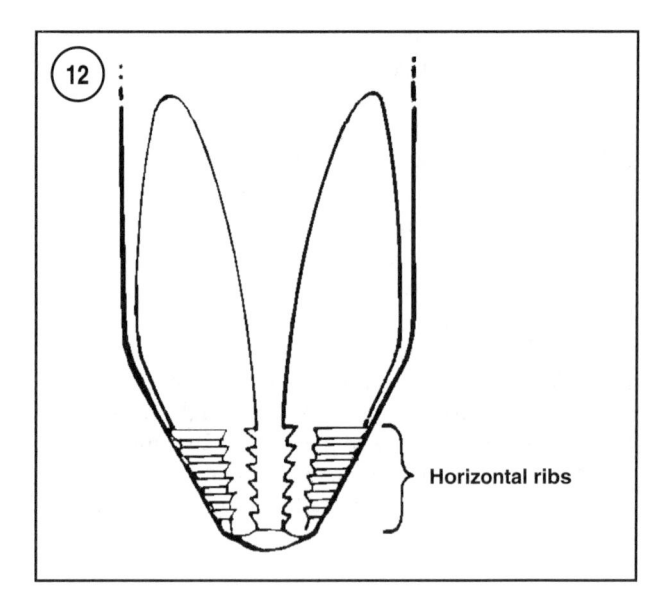

Screwdrivers of various lengths and types are mandatory for the simplest tool kit. The two basic types are the slotted tip (flat blade) and the Phillips tip. These are available in sets that often include an assortment of tip sizes and shaft lengths.

As with all tools, use a screwdriver designed for the job. Make sure the size of the tip conforms to the size and shape of the fastener. Use them only for driving screws. Never use a screwdriver for prying or chiseling metal. Repair or replace worn or damaged screwdrivers. A worn tip may damage the fastener, making it difficult to remove.

Phillips-head screws are often damaged by incorrectly fitting screwdrivers. Quality Phillips screwdrivers are manufactured with their crosshead tip machined to Phillips Screw Company specifications. Poor quality or damaged Phillips screwdrivers can back out (camout) and round over the screw head. In addition, weak or soft screw materials can make removal difficult.

An effective screwdriver to use on Phillips screws is the ACR Phillips II screwdriver. ACR stands for the horizontal anti-camout ribs found on the driving faces or flutes of the screwdriver's tip (**Figure 12**).

Designed to be used with ACR Phillips II screws, they also work well on common Phillips screws.

Another way to prevent camout and to increase the grip of a Phillips screwdriver is to apply valve grinding compound or Permatex Screw & Socket Gripper onto the screwdriver tip. After loosening/tightening the screw, clean the screw recess to prevent engine oil contamination.

Wrenches

Box-end, open-end and combination wrenches (**Figure 13**) are available in a variety of types and sizes.

The number stamped on the wrench refers to the distance between the work areas that grip the nut or bolt. This size must match the size of the fastener head.

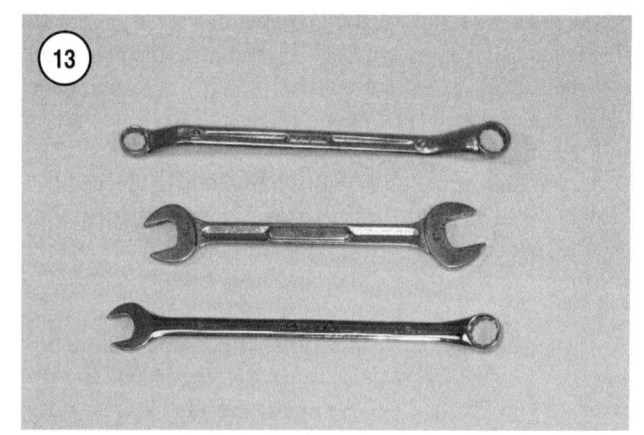

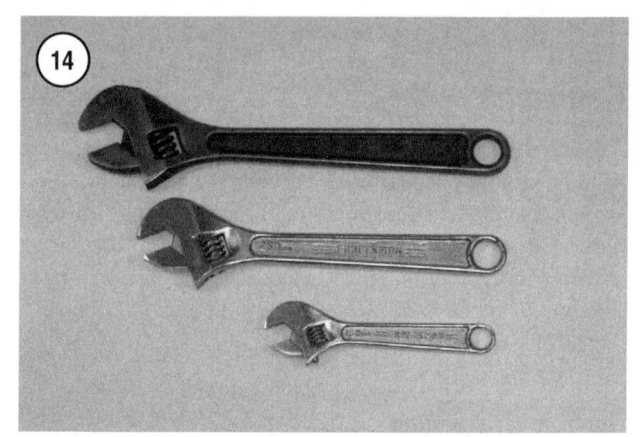

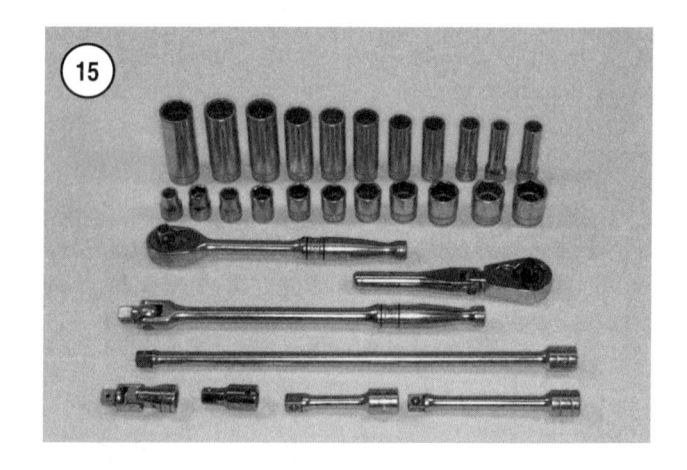

The box-end wrench is an excellent tool because it grips the fastener on all sides. This reduces the chance of the tool slipping. The box-end wrench is designed with either a 6 or 12-point opening. For stubborn or damaged fasteners, the 6-point provides superior holding because it contacts the fastener across a wider area at all six edges. For general use, the 12-point works well. It allows the wrench to be removed and reinstalled without moving the handle over such a wide arc.

An open-end wrench is fast and works best in areas with limited overhead access. It contacts the fastener at only two points and is subject to slipping if under heavy force, or if the tool or fastener is worn. A box-end wrench is preferred

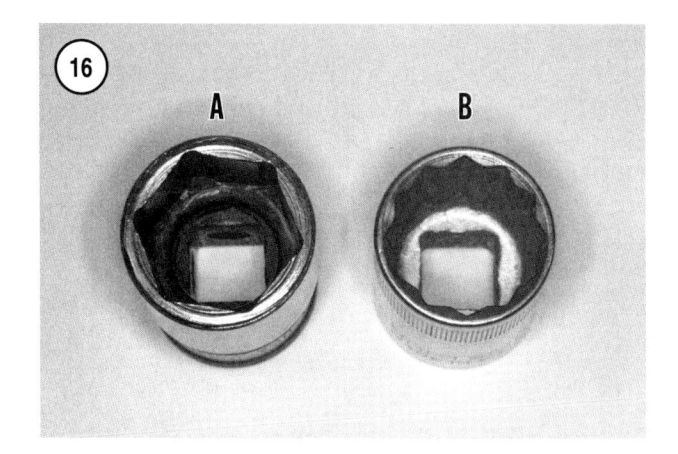

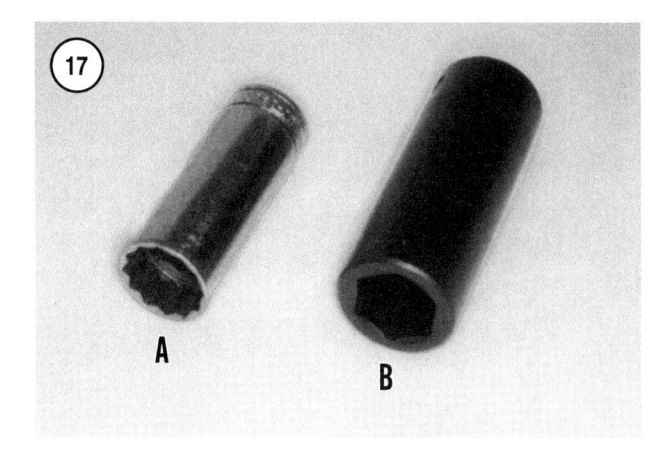

GENERAL INFORMATION

in most instances, especially when breaking loose and applying the final tightening force to a fastener.

The combination wrench has a box-end on one end and an open-end on the other. This combination makes it a convenient tool.

Adjustable Wrenches

An adjustable wrench or Crescent wrench (**Figure 14**) can fit nearly any nut or bolt head that has clear access around its entire perimeter. An adjustable wrench is best used as a backup wrench to keep a large nut or bolt from turning while the other end is being loosened or tightened with a box-end or socket wrench.

Adjustable wrenches contact the fastener at only two points, which makes them more subject to slipping off the fastener. Because one jaw is adjustable and may become loose, this tendency is increased. Make certain the solid jaw is the one transmitting the force.

Socket Wrenches, Ratchets and Handles

WARNING
Do not use hand sockets with air or impact tools because they may shatter and cause injury. Always wear eye protection when using impact or air tools.

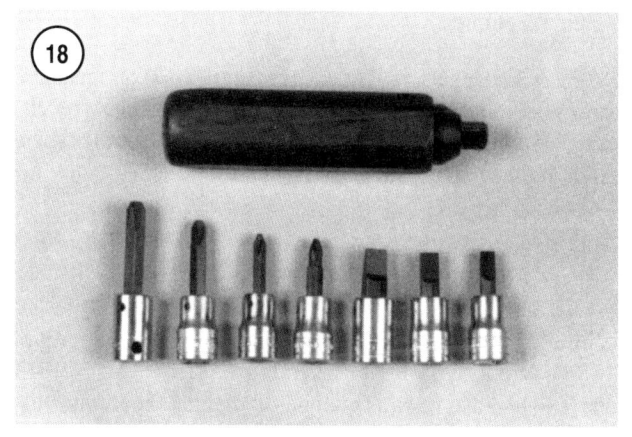

Sockets that attach to a ratchet handle (**Figure 15**) are available with 6-point (A, **Figure 16**) or 12-point openings (B). As with wrenches, a 6-point socket provides superior-holding ability, while a 12-point socket needs to be moved only half as far to reposition it on the fastener. Sockets are also available in different drive sizes. The drive size indicates the size of the square hole that accepts the ratchet handle. The number stamped on the socket is the size of the work area and must match the fastener head.

Sockets are designated for either hand or impact use. Impact sockets are made of thicker material for more durability. Compare the size and wall thickness of a 19-mm hand socket (A, **Figure 17**) and the 19-mm impact socket (B). Use impact sockets when using an impact driver or air tools. Use hand sockets with hand-driven attachments.

Various handles are available for sockets. Use the speed handle for fast operation. Flexible ratchet heads in varying lengths allow the socket to be turned with varying force and at odd angles. Extension bars allow the socket setup to reach difficult areas. The ratchet is the most versatile. It allows the user to install or remove the nut without removing the socket.

Sockets combined with any number of drivers make them undoubtedly the fastest, safest and most convenient tool for fastener removal and installation.

Impact Drivers

WARNING
Do not use hand sockets with air or impact tools because they may shatter and cause injury. Always wear eye protection when using impact or air tools.

An impact driver provides extra force for removing fasteners by converting the impact of a hammer into a turning motion. This makes it possible to remove stubborn fasteners without damaging them. Impact drivers and interchangeable bits (**Figure 18**) are available from most tool suppliers. When using a socket with an impact driver, make sure the socket is designed for impact use. Refer to *Socket Wrenches, Ratchets and Handles* in this section.

Allen Wrenches

Use Allen or setscrew wrenches (**Figure 19**) on fasteners with hexagonal recesses in the fastener head. These wrenches are available in L-shaped bar, socket and T-handle types. Allen bolts are sometimes called socket bolts.

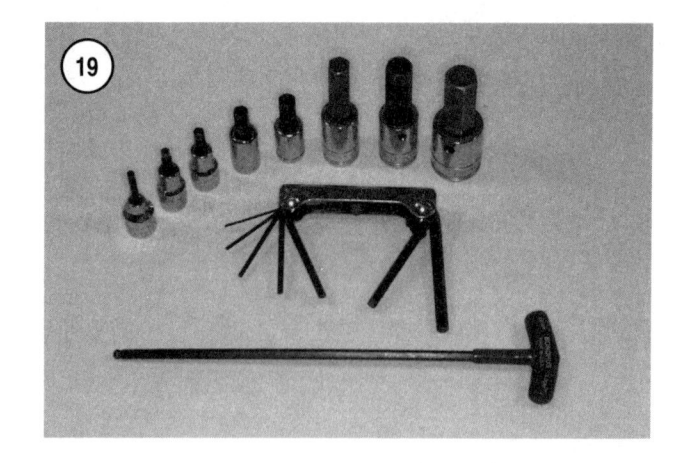

Torque Wrenches

Use a torque wrench with a socket, torque adapter or similar extension to tighten a fastener to a measured torque. Torque wrenches come in several drive sizes (1/4, 3/8, 1/2 and 3/4) and use various methods to display the torque value. The drive size indicates the size of the square drive that accepts the socket, adapter or extension. Common methods of displaying the torque value are the deflecting beam, the dial indicator and the audible click type of torque wrench (**Figure 20**).

When choosing a torque wrench, consider the torque range, drive size and accuracy needed. The torque specifications in this manual provide an indication of the range required.

A torque wrench is a precision tool that must be properly cared for to remain accurate. Store torque wrenches in cases or separate padded drawers within a toolbox. Follow the manufacturer's instructions for their care and calibration.

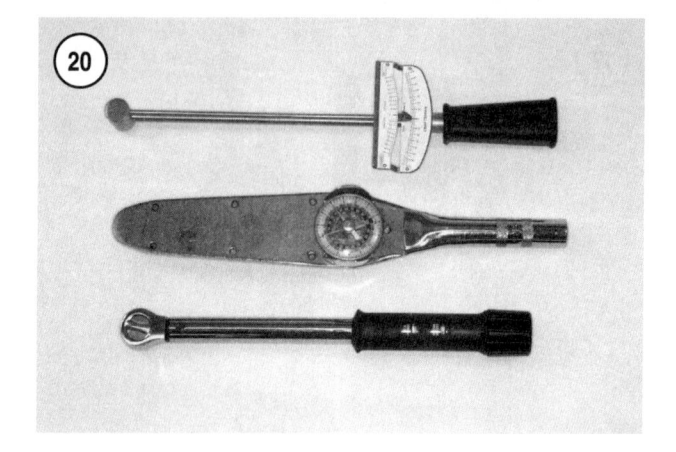

Torque Adapters

Torque adapters or extensions extend or reduce the reach of a torque wrench. The torque adapter is used to tighten a fastener that cannot be reached because of the size of the torque wrench head, drive and socket. If a torque adapter changes the effective lever length (**Figure 21**), the torque reading on the wrench will not equal the actual torque applied to the fastener. It is necessary to recalibrate the torque setting on the wrench to compensate for the change of lever length. When using a torque adapter at a right angle to the drive head, calibration is not required, because the effective length has not changed.

To recalculate a torque reading when using a torque adapter, use the following formula and refer to **Figure 21**.

$$TW = \frac{TA \times L}{L + A}$$

TW is the torque setting or dial reading on the wrench.

TA is the torque specification and the actual amount of torque that is applied to the fastener.

A is the amount that the adapter increases (or in some cases reduces) the effective lever length as measured along the centerline of the torque wrench.

L is the lever length of the wrench as measured from the center of the drive to the center of the grip.

The effective length is the sum of L and A.
Example:
TA = 20 ft.-lb.
A = 3 in.
L = 14 in.
$TW = \frac{20 \times 14}{14 + 3} = \frac{280}{17} = 16.5$ ft.-lb.

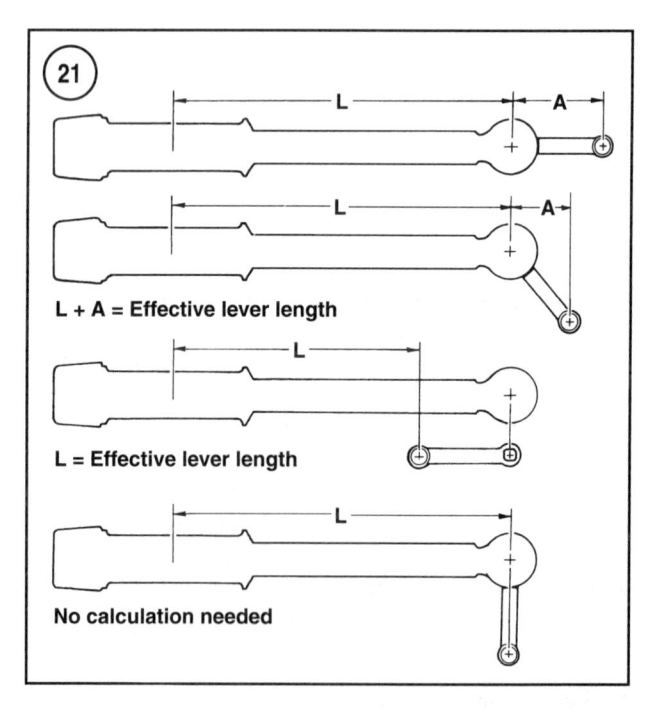

In this example, the torque wrench would be set to the recalculated torque value (TW = 16.5 ft.-lb.). When using a beam-type wrench, tighten the fastener until the pointer aligns with 16.5 ft.-lb. In this example, although the torque wrench is pre set to 16.5 ft.-lb., the actual torque applied to the fastener is 20 ft.-lb.

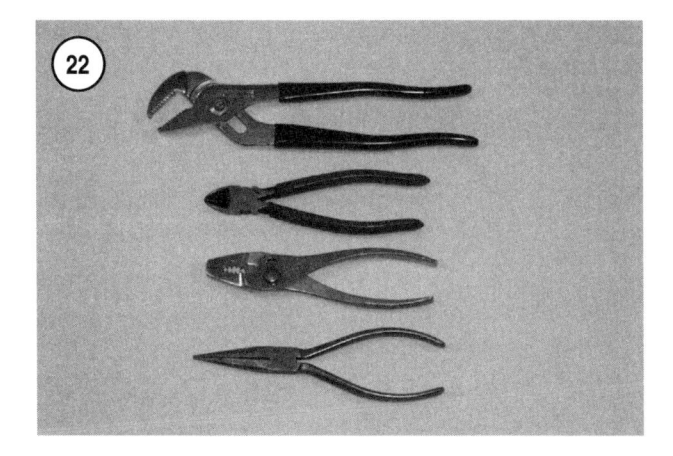

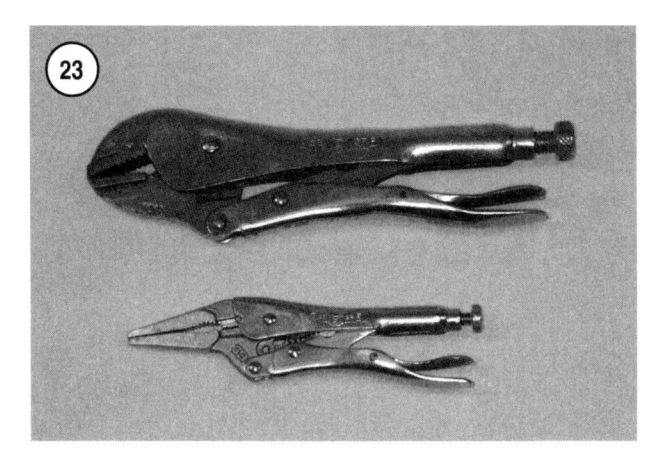

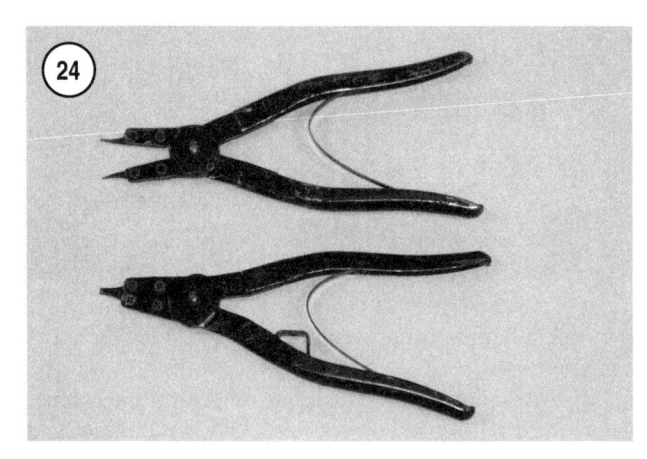

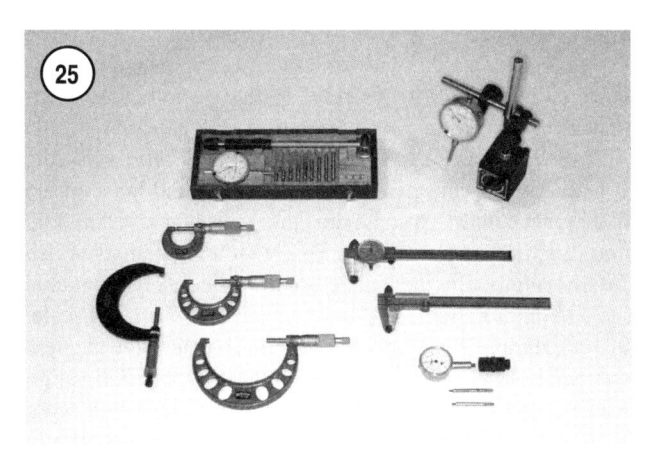

Pliers

Pliers come in a wide range of types and sizes. Pliers are useful for holding, cutting, bending and crimping. Do not use them to turn fasteners. **Figure 22** shows several types of useful pliers. Each design has a specialized function. Slip-joint pliers are general-purpose pliers used for gripping and bending. Diagonal cutting pliers are needed to cut wire and can be used to remove cotter pins. Use needlenose pliers to hold or bend small objects. Locking pliers (**Figure 23**), sometimes called Vise-Grips, are used to hold objects very tightly. They have many uses ranging from holding two parts together, to gripping the end of a broken stud. Use caution when using locking pliers, as the sharp jaws will damage the objects they hold.

Snap Ring Pliers

WARNING
Snap rings can slip and fly off when removing and installing them or the plier tips may break. Always wear eye protection when using snap ring pliers.

Snap ring pliers are specialized pliers with tips that fit into the ends of snap rings to remove and install them.

Snap ring pliers (**Figure 24**) are available with a fixed action (either internal or external) or convertible (one tool works on both internal and external snap rings). They may have fixed tips or interchangeable ones of various sizes and angles. For general use, select convertible-type pliers with interchangeable tips.

Hammers

Various types of hammers are available to fit a number of applications. Use a ball-peen hammer to strike another tool, such as a punch or chisel. Use soft-faced hammers when a metal object must be struck without damaging it. Never use a metal-faced hammer on engine or suspension components because damage will occur.

Always wear eye protection when using hammers. Make sure the hammer face is in good condition and the handle is not cracked. Select the correct hammer for the job and make sure to strike the object squarely. Do not use the handle or the side of the hammer to strike an object.

MEASURING TOOLS

The ability to accurately measure components is essential to perform many of the procedures described in this manual. Equipment is manufactured to close tolerances and obtaining consistently accurate measurements is essential to determine which components require replacement or further service.

Each type of measuring instrument (**Figure 25**) is designed to measure a dimension with a certain degree of accuracy and within a certain range. When selecting the measuring tool, make sure it is applicable to the task.

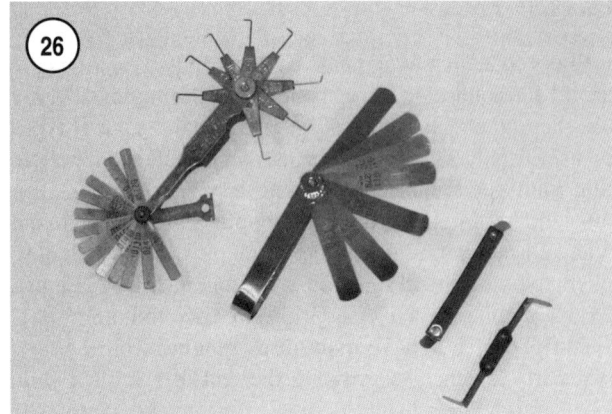

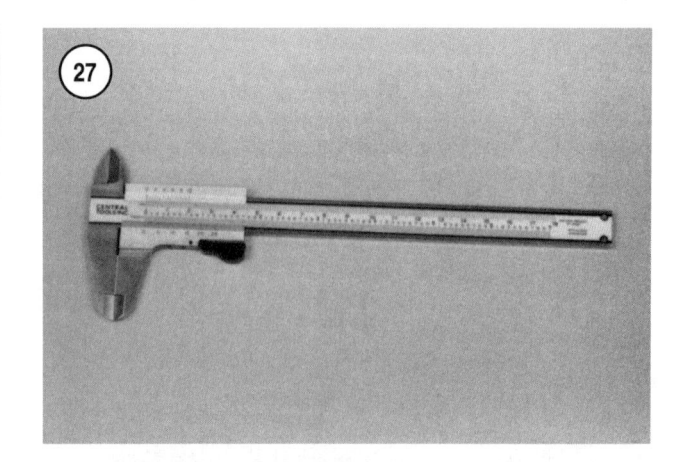

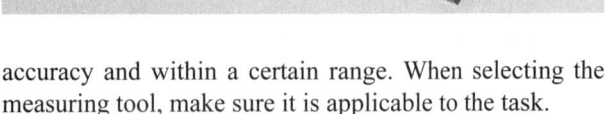

As with all tools, measuring tools provide the best results if cared for properly. Improper use can damage the tool and cause inaccurate results. If any measurement is questionable, verify the measurement using another tool. A standard gauge is usually provided with micrometers to check accuracy and calibrate the tool if necessary.

Precision of measurements can vary according to the experience of the person performing the procedure. Accurate results are only possible if the mechanic possesses a feel for using the tool. Heavy-handed use of measuring tools produces less accurate results. Hold the tool gently by the fingertips to easily feel the point at which the tool contacts the object. A feel for the equipment produces more accurate measurements and reduces the risk of damaging the tool or component. Refer to the following sections for specific measuring tools.

Feeler Gauge

Feeler or thickness gauges (**Figure 26**) are required to measure the distance between two surfaces.

A feeler gauge set consists of an assortment of steel strips of graduated thickness. Each blade is marked with its thickness. Blades can be of various lengths and angles for different procedures.

A common use for a feeler gauge is to measure valve clearance. Use wire (round) type gauges to measure spark plug gap.

Calipers

Calipers (**Figure 27**) are excellent tools for obtaining inside, outside and depth measurements. Although not as precise as a micrometer, they allow reasonable precision, typically to within 0.05 mm (0.001 in.). Most calipers have a range up to 150 mm (6 in.).

Calipers are available in dial, vernier or digital versions. Dial calipers have a dial readout that provides convenient reading. Vernier calipers have marked scales that must be compared to determine the measurement. The digital caliper uses a liquid-crystal display (LCD) to show the measurement.

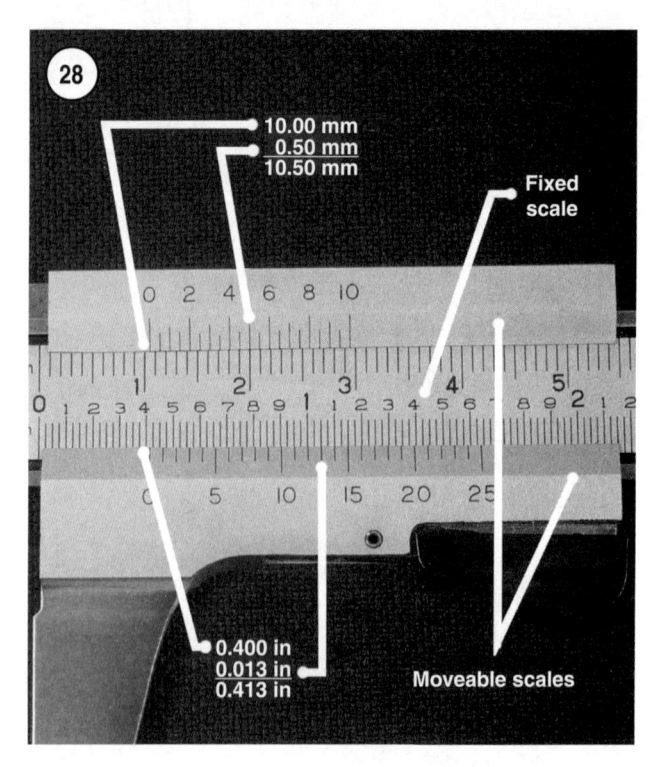

Properly maintain the measuring surfaces of the caliper. There must not be any dirt or burrs between the tool and the object being measured. Never force the caliper to close around an object. Close the caliper around the highest point so it can be removed with a slight drag. Some calipers require calibration. Always refer to the manufacturer's instructions when using a new or unfamiliar caliper.

To read a vernier caliper refer to **Figure 28**. The fixed scale is marked in 1-mm increments. Ten individual lines on the fixed scale equal 1 cm. The movable scale is marked in 0.05 mm (hundredth) increments. To obtain a reading, establish the first number by the location of the 0 line on the movable scale in relation to the first line to the left on the fixed scale. In this example, the number is 10 mm. To determine the next number, note which of the lines on the movable scale align with a mark on the fixed scale. A number of lines will seem close, but only one will align exactly. In this case, 0.50 mm

GENERAL INFORMATION

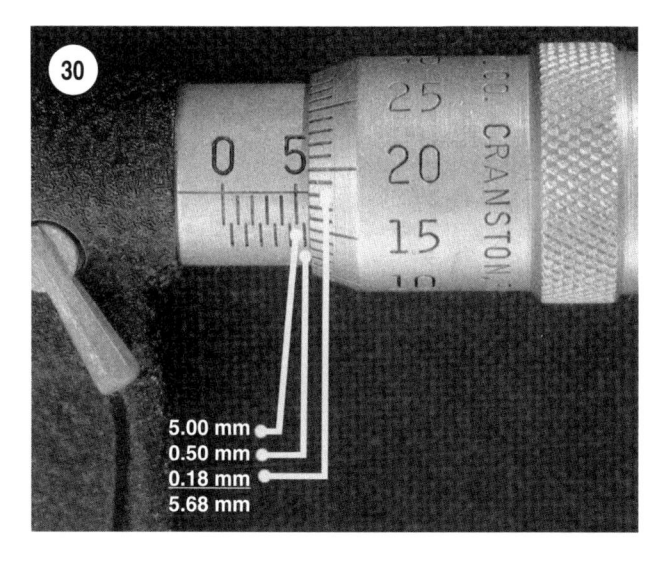

is the reading to add to the first number. Adding 10 mm and 0.50 mm equals a measurement of 10.50 mm.

Micrometers

A micrometer is an instrument designed for linear measurement using the decimal divisions of the inch or meter. While there are many types and styles of micrometers (**Figure 29**), most of the procedures in this manual call for an outside micrometer. Use the outside micrometer to measure the outside diameter of cylindrical forms and the thickness of materials.

A micrometer's size indicates the minimum and maximum size of a part that it can measure. The usual sizes are 0-25 mm (0-1 in.), 25-50 mm (1-2 in.), 50-75 mm (2-3 in.) and 75-100 mm (3-4 in.).

Micrometers that cover a wider range of measurements are available. These use a large frame with interchangeable anvils of various lengths. This type of micrometer offers a cost savings, but its overall size may make it less convenient.

Adjustment

Before using a micrometer, check its adjustment as follows:

1. Clean the anvil and spindle faces.
2A. To check a 0-1 in. or 0-25 mm micrometer:
   a. Turn the thimble until the spindle contacts the anvil. If the micrometer has a ratchet stop, use it to ensure that the proper amount of pressure is applied.
   b. If the adjustment is correct, the 0 mark on the thimble will align exactly with the 0 mark on the sleeve line. If the marks do not align, the micrometer is out of adjustment.
   c. Follow the manufacturer's instructions to adjust the micrometer.
2B. To check a micrometer larger than 1 in. or 25 mm use the standard gauge supplied by the manufacturer. A standard gauge is a steel block, disc or rod that is machined to an exact size.
   a. Place the standard gauge between the spindle and anvil and measure its outside diameter or length. If the micrometer has a ratchet stop, use it to ensure that the proper amount of pressure is applied.
   b. If the adjustment is correct, the 0 mark on the thimble will align exactly with the 0 mark on the sleeve line. If the marks do not align, the micrometer is out of adjustment.
   c. Follow the manufacturer's instructions to adjust the micrometer.

Care

Micrometers are precision instruments. They must be used and maintained with great care. Note the following:
1. Store micrometers in protective cases or in separate padded drawers of a toolbox.
2. When in storage, make sure the spindle and anvil faces do not contact each other or an other object. If they do, temperature changes and corrosion may damage the contact faces.
3. Do not clean a micrometer with compressed air. Dirt forced into the tool will cause wear.
4. Lubricate micrometers with WD-40 to prevent corrosion.

Reading

When reading a micrometer, numbers are taken from different scales and added together. The following sections describe how to read the measurements of various types of outside micrometers.

For accurate results, properly maintain the measuring surfaces of the micrometer. There cannot be any dirt or burrs between the tool and the measured object. Never force the micrometer to close around an object. Close the micrometer around the highest point so it can be removed with a slight drag.

The standard metric micrometer (**Figure 30**) is accurate to one one-hundredth of a millimeter (0.01 mm). The sleeve line is graduated in millimeter and half millimeter increments. The marks on the upper half of the sleeve line equal 1.00 mm. Each fifth mark above the sleeve line is identified with a number. The number sequence depends on the size of the micrometer. A 0-25 mm micrometer, for example, will have sleeve marks numbered 0 through 25 in 5 mm increments. This numbering sequence continues with larger micrometers. On all metric micrometers, each mark on the lower half of the sleeve equals 0.50 mm.

The tapered end of the thimble has 50 lines marked around it. Each mark equals 0.01 mm. One complete turn of the thimble aligns its 0 mark with the first line on the lower half of the sleeve line or 0.50 mm.

When reading a metric micrometer, add the number of millimeters and half-millimeters on the sleeve line to the number of one one-hundredth millimeters on the thimble. Perform the following steps while referring to **Figure 30**.

1. Read the upper half of the sleeve line and count the number of lines visible. Each upper line equals 1 mm.
2. See if the half-millimeter line is visible on the lower sleeve line. If so, add 0.50 mm to the reading in Step 1.
3. Read the thimble mark that aligns with the sleeve line. Each thimble mark equals 0.01 mm.
4. If a thimble mark does not align exactly with the sleeve line, estimate the amount between the lines. For accurate readings in two-thousandths of a millimeter (0.002 mm), use a metric vernier micrometer.
5. Add the readings from these steps together to get the final measurement.

Telescoping and Small Bore Gauges

Use telescoping gauges (**Figure 31**) and small bore gauges (**Figure 32**) to measure bores. Neither gauge has a scale for direct readings. Use an outside micrometer to determine the reading.

To use a telescoping gauge, select the correct size gauge for the bore. Compress the movable post and carefully insert the gauge into the bore. Carefully move the gauge in the bore to make sure it is centered. Tighten the knurled end of the gauge to hold the movable post in position. Remove the gauge and measure the length of the posts. Telescoping gauges are typically used to measure cylinder bores.

To use a small bore gauge, select the correct size gauge for the bore. Carefully insert the gauge into the bore. Tighten the knurled end of the gauge to carefully expand the gauge fingers to the limit within the bore. Do not overtighten the gauge because there is no built-in release. Excessive tightening can damage the bore surface and damage the tool. Remove the gauge and measure the outside dimension (**Figure 33**). Small bore gauges are typically used to measure valve guides.

Dial Indicator

A dial indicator (**Figure 34**) is a gauge with a dial face and needle used to measure variations in dimensions and movements. Measuring brake rotor runout is a typical use for a dial indicator.

Dial indicators are available in various ranges and graduations. They can come with any of three basic types of mounting bases: magnetic, clamp, or screw-in stud.

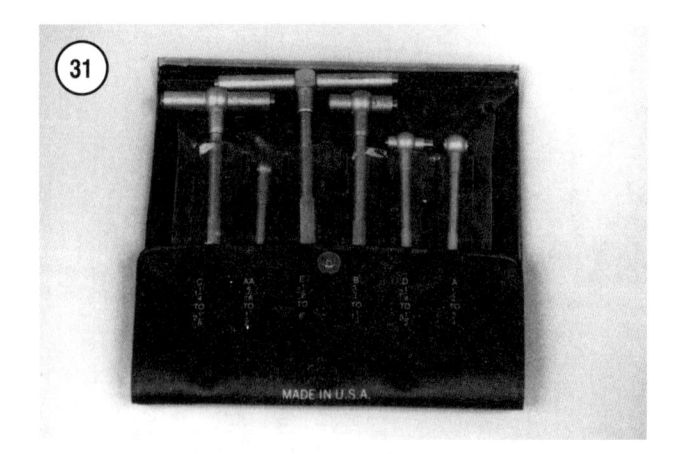

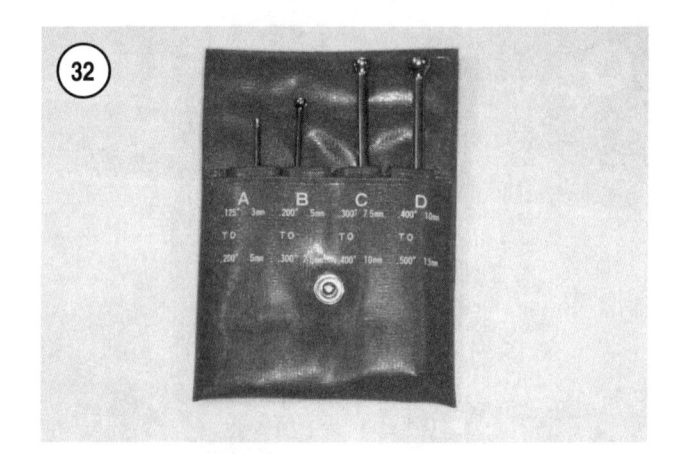

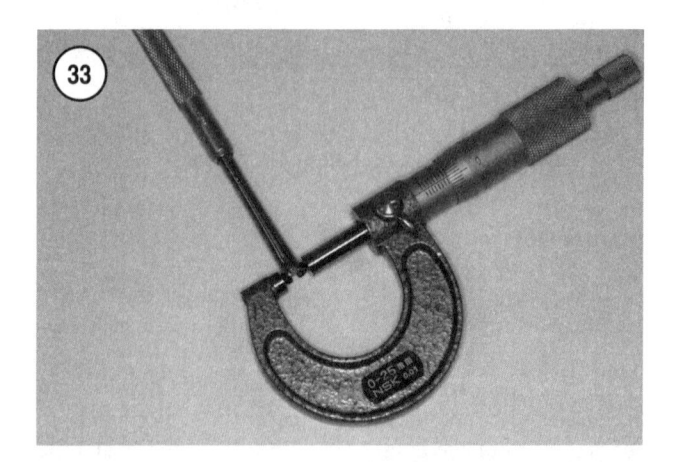

GENERAL INFORMATION

gauge adapter is either inserted or screwed into the spark plug hole to obtain the reading. Disable the engine so it will not start and hold the throttle in the wide-open position when performing a compression test. An engine that does not have adequate compression cannot be properly tuned. Refer to Chapter Three for compression test procedures.

Multimeter

A digital multimeter (**Figure 37**) is an essential tool for electrical system diagnosis. The voltage function indicates the voltage applied or available to various electrical components. The ohmmeter function tests circuits for continuity, or lack of continuity and measures the resistance of a circuit.

Some manufacturers' specifications for electrical components are based on results using a specific test meter. Results may vary if a meter not recommended by the manufacturer is used. Such requirements are noted when applicable.

If an analog ohmmeter is used, it must be calibrated. Refer to the meter manufacturer's instructions.

ELECTRICAL SYSTEM FUNDAMENTALS

Refer to *Electrical Testing* and *Electrical Troubleshooting* in Chapter Two for typical test procedures and equipment. Refer to Chapter Eleven for specific system test procedures.

Refer to the following for electrical basics necessary to perform simple diagnostic tests.

Voltage

Voltage is the electrical potential or pressure in an electrical circuit and is expressed in volts. The more pressure (voltage) in a circuit, the more work can be performed.

Direct current (DC) voltage means the electricity flows in one direction. All circuits powered by a battery are DC circuits.

Alternating current (AC) means the electricity flows in one direction momentarily and then switches to the opposite direction. Alternator output is an example of AC voltage. This voltage must be changed or rectified to direct current to operate in a battery powered system.

Resistance

Resistance is the opposition to the flow of electricity within a circuit or component and is measured in ohms. Resistance causes a reduction in available current and voltage.

Measure resistance in an inactive circuit with an ohmmeter. An ohmmeter, although useful, is not always a good indicator of a circuit's actual ability under operating conditions. This is because of the low voltage (6-9 volts) the meter uses to test the circuit. The voltage in an ignition

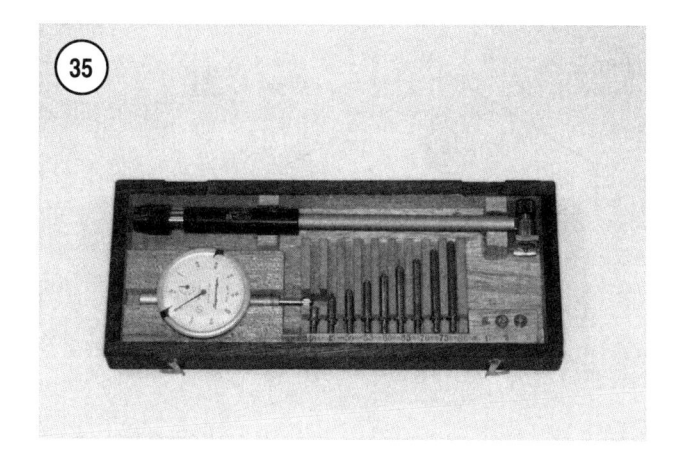

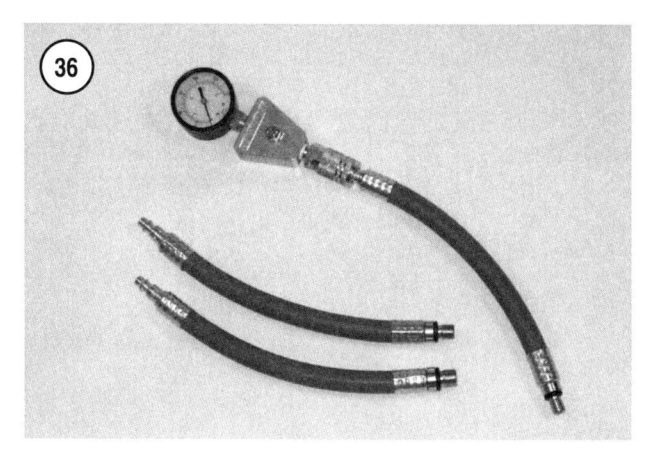

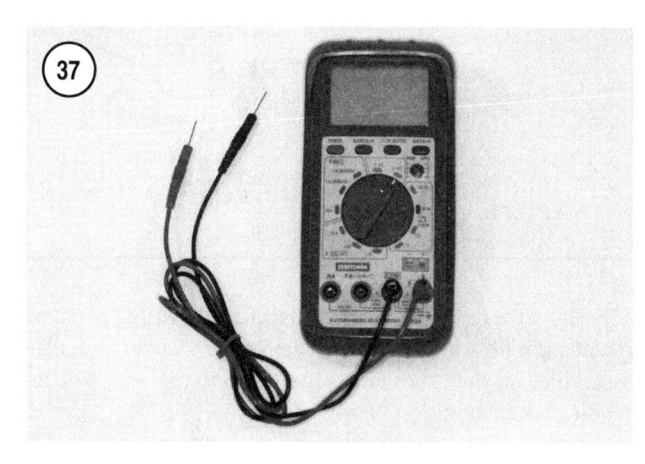

Cylinder Bore Gauge

A cylinder bore gauge is similar to a dial indicator. The gauge set shown in **Figure 35** consists of a dial indicator, handle and different length adapters (anvils) to fit various bore sizes. The bore gauge is used to measure bore size, taper and out-of-round. When using a bore gauge, follow the manufacturer's instructions.

Compression Gauge

A compression gauge (**Figure 36**) measures combustion chamber (cylinder) pressure, usually in psi or kg/cm^2. The

coil secondary winding can be several thousand volts. Such high voltage can cause the coil to malfunction, even though it tests acceptable during a resistance test.

Resistance generally increases with temperature. Perform all testing with the component or circuit at room temperature. Resistance tests performed at high temperatures may indicate high resistance readings and cause unnecessary replacement of a component.

Amperage

Amperage is the unit of measurement for the amount of current within a circuit. Current is the actual flow of electricity. The higher the current, the more work can be performed up to a given point. If the current flow exceeds the circuit or component capacity, it will damage the system.

SERVICE METHODS

Most of the procedures in this manual are straightforward and can be performed by anyone reasonably competent with tools. However, consider personal capabilities carefully before attempting any operation involving major disassembly.

1. *Front*, in this manual, refers to the front of the motorcycle. The front of any component is the end closest to the front of the motorcycle. The left and right sides refer to the position of the parts as viewed by the rider sitting on the seat facing forward.
2. Whenever servicing an engine or suspension component, secure the motorcycle in a safe manner.
3. Tag all similar parts for location and mark all mating parts for position. Record the number and thickness of any shims when removing them. Identify parts by placing them in sealed and labeled plastic sandwich bags.
4. Tag disconnected wires and connectors with masking tape and a marking pen. Do not rely on memory alone.
5. Protect finished surfaces from physical damage or corrosion. Keep gasoline and other chemicals off painted surfaces.
6. Use penetrating oil on frozen or tight bolts. Avoid using heat where possible. Heat can warp, melt or affect the temper of parts. Heat also damages the finish of paint and plastics.
7. When a part is a press fit or requires a special tool to remove, the information or type of tool is identified in the text. Otherwise, if a part is difficult to remove or install, determine the cause before proceeding.
8. To prevent objects or debris from falling into the engine, cover all openings.
9. Read each procedure thoroughly and compare the illustrations to the actual components before starting the procedure. Perform the procedure in sequence.
10. Recommendations are occasionally made to refer service to a dealership or specialist. In these cases, the work can be performed more economically by the specialist than by the home mechanic.

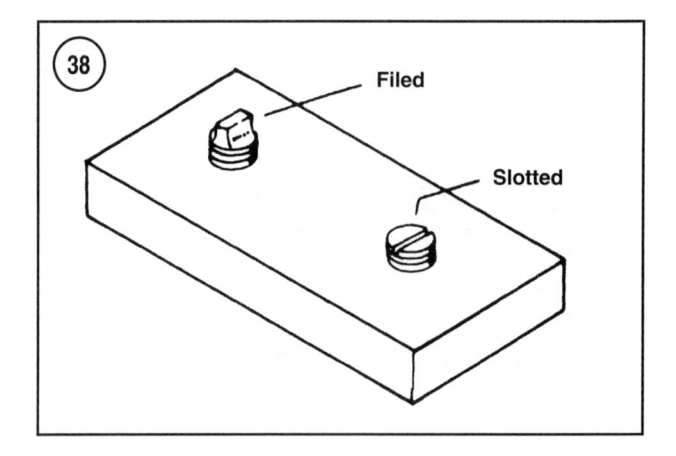

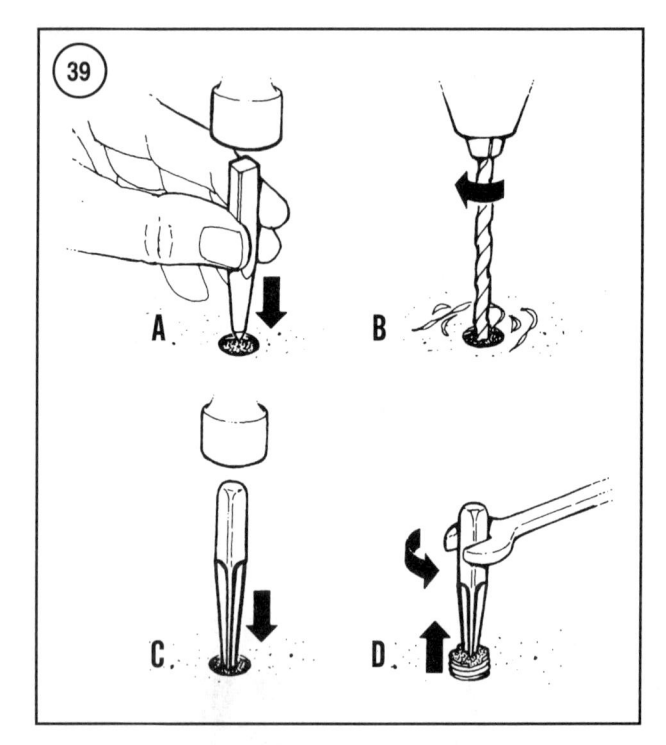

11. The term replace means to discard a defective part and replace it with a new part. Overhaul means to remove, disassemble, inspect, measure, repair and/or replace parts as required to recondition an assembly.
12. Some operations require using a hydraulic press. If a press is not available, have these operations performed by a shop equipped with the necessary equipment. Do not use makeshift equipment that may damage the motorcycle.
13. Repairs are much faster and easier if the motorcycle is clean before starting work. Degrease the motorcycle with a commercial degreaser; follow the directions on the container for the best results. Clean all parts with cleaning solvent when removing them.

CAUTION
Do not direct high-pressure water at steering bearings, fuel hoses, transmission vent hose, wheel bearings, suspension and electrical components. Water may force grease out of the bearings and possibly damage the seals.

GENERAL INFORMATION

Wrench or WD-40. Apply it liberally and let it penetrate for 10-15 minutes. Rap the fastener several times with a small hammer. Do not hit it hard enough to cause damage. Reapply the penetrating oil if necessary.

For frozen screws, apply penetrating oil as described, and then insert a screwdriver in the slot and rap the top of the screwdriver with a hammer. This loosens the rust so the screw can be removed in the normal way. If the screw head is too damaged to use this method, grip the head with locking pliers and twist the screw out.

Avoid applying heat unless specifically instructed. Heat may melt, warp or remove the temper from parts.

Removing Broken Fasteners

If the head breaks off a screw or bolt, several methods are available for removing the remaining portion. If a large portion of the remainder projects out, try gripping it with locking pliers. If the projecting portion is too small, file it to fit a wrench or cut a slot in it to fit a screwdriver (**Figure 38**).

If the head breaks off flush, use a screw extractor. To do this, center punch the exact center of the remaining portion of the screw or bolt (A, **Figure 39**). Drill a small hole in the screw (B, **Figure 39**) and tap the extractor into the hole (C). Back the screw out with a wrench on the extractor (D, **Figure 39**).

Repairing Damaged Threads

Occasionally, threads are stripped through carelessness or impact damage. Often the threads can be repaired by running a tap (for internal threads on nuts) or die (for external threads on bolts) through the threads (**Figure 40**). To clean or repair spark plug threads, use a spark plug tap.

If an internal thread is damaged, it may be necessary to install a Helicoil or some other type of thread insert. Follow the insert manufacturer's instructions when installing it.

If it is necessary to drill and tap a hole, refer to **Table 8** or **Table 9** for the applicable tap and drill sizes.

Stud Removal/Installation

A stud removal tool is available from most tool suppliers. This tool makes the removal and installation of studs easier. If one is not available, thread two nuts onto the stud and tighten them against each other. Remove the stud by turning the lower nut (**Figure 41**). Remove and install studs as follows:

1. Measure the height of the stud above the surface.
2. Thread the stud removal tool onto the stud and tighten it, or thread two nuts onto the stud.
3. Remove the stud by turning the stud remover or the lower nut.
4. Remove any threadlock residue from the threaded hole. Clean the threads with a aerosol parts cleaner.

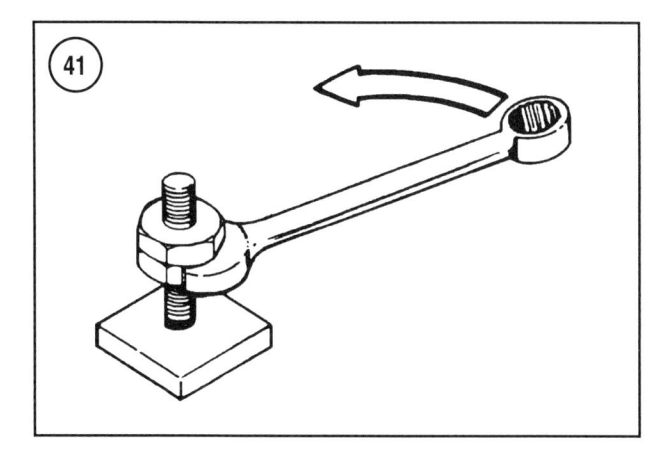

14. If special tools are required, have them available before starting the procedure. When special tools are required, they are described at the beginning of the procedure.
15. Make diagrams of similar-appearing parts. For instance, crankcase bolts are often not the same lengths. Do not rely on memory alone. Carefully laid out parts can become disturbed, making it difficult to reassemble the components correctly.
16. Make sure all shims and washers are reinstalled in the same location and position.
17. Whenever rotating parts contact a stationary part, look for a shim or washer.
18. Use new gaskets if there is any doubt about the condition of old ones.
19. If using self-locking fasteners, replace them with new ones. Do not install standard fasteners in place of self-locking ones.
20. Use grease to hold small parts in place if they tend to fall out during assembly. Do not apply grease to electrical or brake components.

Removing Frozen Fasteners

If a fastener cannot be removed, several methods may be used to loosen it. First, apply penetrating oil such as Liquid

42

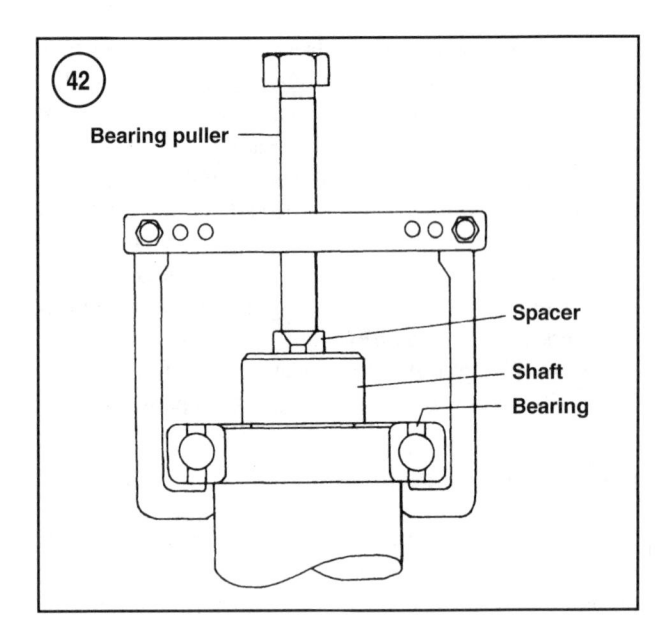

Bearing puller
Spacer
Shaft
Bearing

43

Spacer
Shaft
Bearing
Blocks

44

Press ram
Shaft
Bearing
Spacer
Press bed

5. Install the stud removal tool onto the new stud or thread two nuts onto the stud.
6. Apply threadlock to the threads of the stud.
7. Install the stud and tighten with the stud removal tool or the top nut.
8. Install the stud to the height noted or tighten to its torque specification.
9. Remove the stud removal tool or the two nuts.

Removing Hoses

Do not exert excessive force on the hose or fitting when removing stubborn hoses. Remove the hose clamp and carefully insert a small screwdriver or pick tool between the fitting and hose. Apply a spray lubricant under the hose and carefully twist the hose off the fitting. Clean the fitting of any corrosion or rubber hose material with a wire brush. Clean the inside of the hose thoroughly. Do *not* use any lubricant when installing the new or old hose. The lubricant may allow the hose to come off the fitting, even with the clamp secure.

Bearings

Bearings are used in the engine and transmission assembly to reduce power loss, heat and noise resulting from friction. Because bearings are precision parts, they must be maintained with proper lubrication and maintenance. If a bearing is damaged, replace it immediately. When installing a new bearing, take care to prevent damaging it. Bearing replacement procedures are included in the individual chapters where applicable; however, use the following sections as a guideline.

NOTE
Unless otherwise specified, install bearings with the manufacturer's mark or number facing outward.

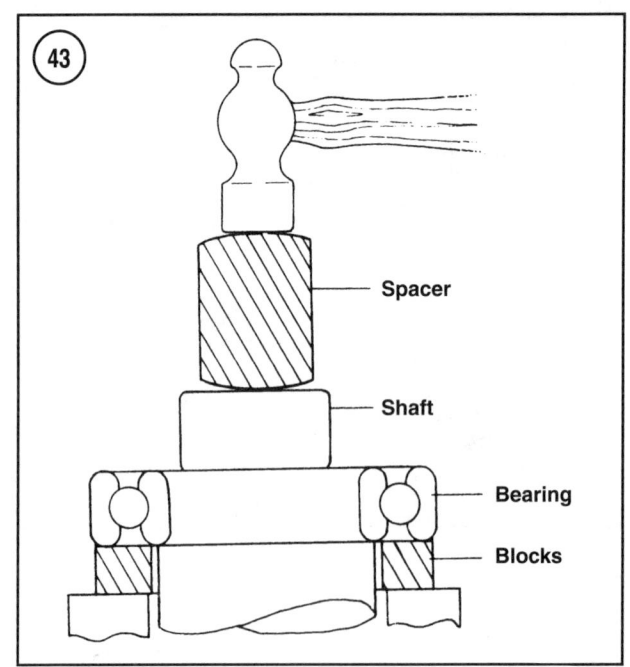

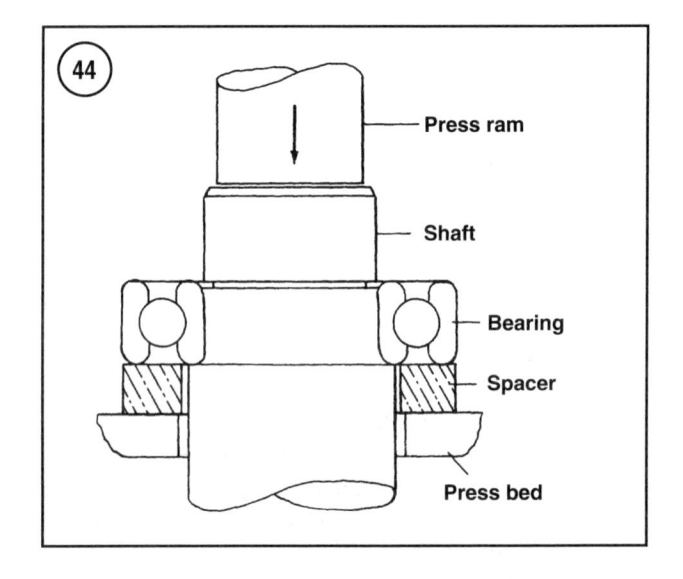

Removal

While bearings are normally removed only when damaged, there may be times when it is necessary to remove a bearing that is in good condition. However, improper bearing removal will damage the bearing and possibly the shaft or case. Note the following when removing bearings:
1. When using a puller to remove a bearing from a shaft, take care that the shaft is not damaged. Always place a piece of metal between the end of the shaft and the puller screw. In addition, place the puller arms next to the inner bearing race as shown in **Figure 42**.
2. When using a hammer to remove a bearing from a shaft, do not strike the hammer directly against the shaft. Instead, use a brass or aluminum rod between the hammer and shaft and make sure to support both bearing races with wooden blocks as shown in **Figure 43**.

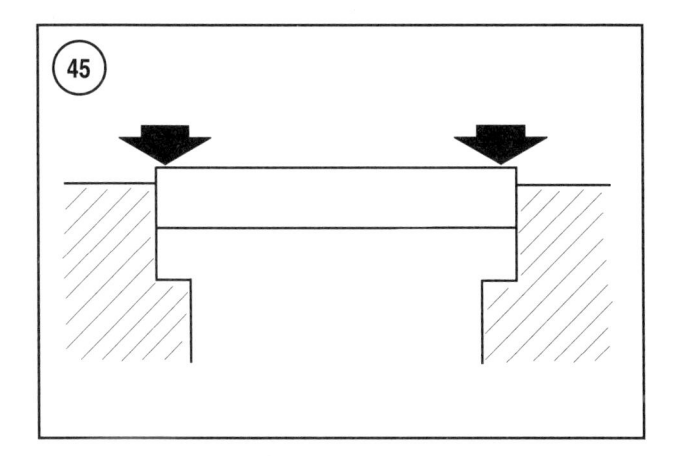

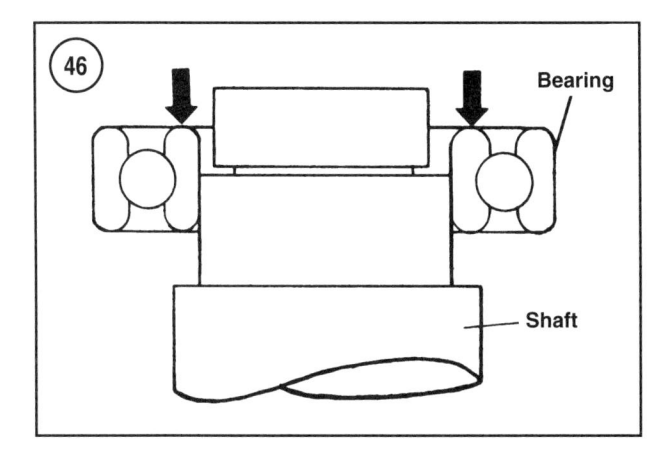

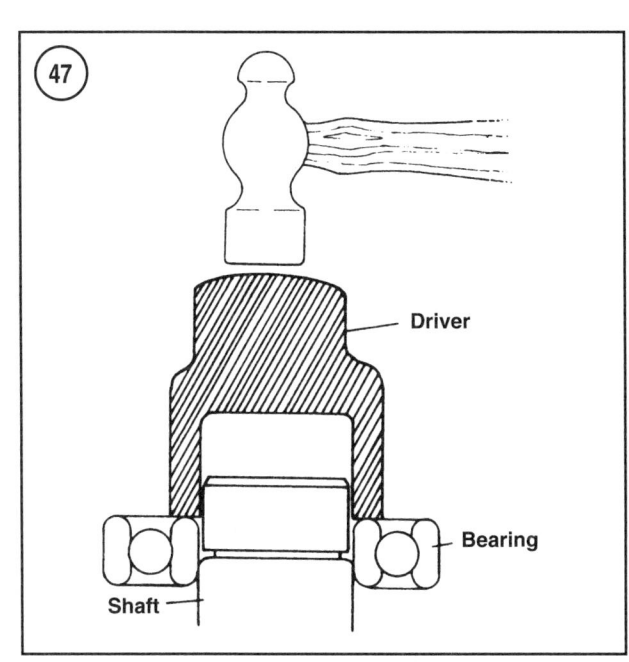

GENERAL INFORMATION

3. The ideal method of bearing removal is with a hydraulic press. Note the following when using a press:
   a. Always support the inner and outer bearing races with a suitable size wooden or aluminum spacer (**Figure 44**). If only the outer race is supported, pressure applied against the balls and/or the inner race will damage them. 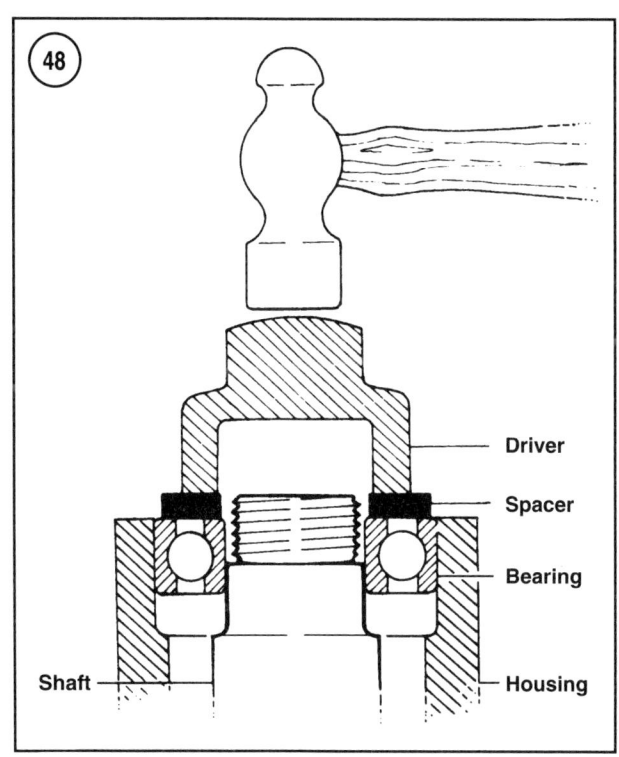
   b. Always make sure the press arm (**Figure 44**) aligns with the center of the shaft. If the arm is not centered, it may damage the bearing and/or shaft.
   c. The moment the shaft is free of the bearing, it drops to the floor. Secure or hold the shaft to prevent it from falling.

Installation

1. When installing a bearing into a housing, apply pressure to the outer bearing race (**Figure 45**). When installing a bearing on a shaft, apply pressure to the inner bearing race (**Figure 46**).
2. When installing a bearing, some type of driver is required. Never strike the bearing directly with a hammer or it will damage the bearing. When installing a bearing, use a piece of pipe or a driver with a diameter that matches the bearing inner race. **Figure 47** shows the correct way to use a driver and hammer to install a bearing.
3. This procedure describes how to install a bearing in a case half or over a shaft. However, when installing a bearing over a shaft and into the housing at the same time, a tight fit is required for both outer and inner bearing races. In this situation, install a spacer underneath the driver tool so that pressure is applied evenly across both races as shown in **Figure 48**. If the outer race is not supported as shown, the balls will push against the outer bearing race and damage it.

Interference fit

1. Follow this procedure when installing a bearing over a shaft. When a tight fit is required, the bearing inside diam-

eter is smaller than the shaft. In this case, driving the bearing on the shaft using normal methods may cause bearing damage. Instead, heat the bearing before installation. Note the following:

   a. Secure the shaft so it is ready for bearing installation.
   b. Clean all residue from the bearing surface of the shaft. Remove burrs with a file or sandpaper.
   c. Fill a suitable pot or beaker with clean mineral oil. Place a thermometer rated above 120° C (248° F) in the oil. Support the thermometer so it does not rest on the bottom or side of the pot.
   d. Remove the bearing from its wrapper and secure it with a piece of heavy wire bent to hold it in the pot. Hang the bearing in the pot so it does not touch the bottom or sides of the pot.
   e. Turn the heat on and monitor the thermometer. When the oil temperature rises to approximately 120° C (248° F), remove the bearing from the pot and quickly install it. If necessary, place a socket on the inner bearing race and tap the bearing into place. As the bearing chills, it will tighten on the shaft, so installation must be done quickly. Make sure the bearing is installed completely.

2. Follow this step when installing a bearing in a housing. Bearings are generally installed in a housing with a slight interference fit. Driving the bearing into the housing using normal methods may damage the housing or cause bearing damage. Instead, heat the housing before the bearing is installed. Note the following:

CAUTION
Before heating the housing in this procedure, wash the housing thoroughly with detergent and water. Rinse and rewash the cases as required to remove all traces of oil and other chemical deposits.

   a. Heat the housing to approximately 100° C (212° F) in an oven or on a hot plate. An easy way to check that it is the proper temperature is to place tiny drops of water on the housing; if they sizzle and evaporate immediately, the temperature is correct. Heat only one housing at a time.

CAUTION
Do not heat the housing with a propane or acetylene torch. Never bring a flame into contact with the bearing or housing. The direct heat will destroy the case hardening of the bearing and will likely warp the housing.

   b. Remove the housing from the oven or hot plate and hold onto the housing with welding gloves. It is hot!

NOTE
Remove and install the bearings with a suitable size socket and extension.

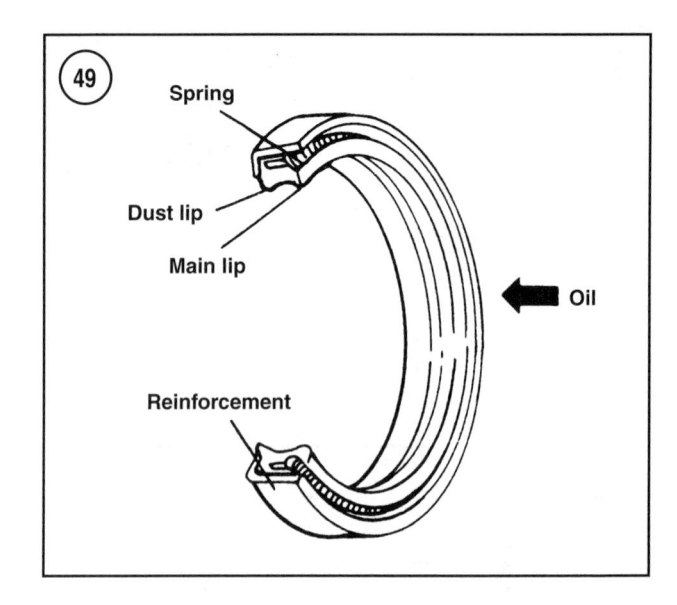

   c. Hold the housing with the bearing side down and tap the bearing out. Repeat for all bearings in the housing.
   d. Before heating the bearing housing, place the new bearing in a freezer if possible. Chilling a bearing slightly reduces its outside diameter while the heated bearing housing assembly is slightly larger due to heat expansion. This makes bearing installation easier.

NOTE
Always install bearings with the manufacturer's mark or number facing outward.

   e. While the housing is still hot, install the new bearing(s) into the housing. Install the bearings by hand, if possible. If necessary, lightly tap the bearing(s) into the housing with a driver placed on the outer bearing race (**Figure 45**). Do not install new bearings by driving on the inner-bearing race. Install the bearing(s) until it seats completely.

Seal Replacement

Seals (**Figure 49**) contain oil, water, grease or combustion gases in a housing or shaft. Improperly removing a seal can damage the housing or shaft. Improperly installing the seal can damage the seal. Note the following:

1. Prying is generally the easiest and most effective method of removing a seal from the housing. However, always place a rag underneath the pry tool to prevent damage to the housing. Note the seal's installed depth or if it is installed flush.

2. On small seals, screw a sheet metal screw (A, **Figure 50**) into the seal (B), being careful not to damage the bearing beneath it. Pull straight up on the screw and remove the seal.

3. Pack waterproof grease in the seal lips before the new seal is installed.

GENERAL INFORMATION 21

4. In most cases, install seals with the manufacturer's numbers or marks facing out.
5. Install seals with a socket or driver placed on the outside (**Figure 51**) of the seal. Drive the seal squarely into the housing until it is seated to the correct depth or flush as noted during removal. Never install a seal by hitting against the top of it with a hammer.

STORAGE

Several months of non-use can cause a general deterioration of the motorcycle. This is especially true in areas of extreme temperature variations. This deterioration can be minimized with careful preparation for storage. A properly stored motorcycle is much easier to return to service.

Storage Area Selection

When selecting a storage area, consider the following:
1. The storage area must be dry. A heated area is best, but not necessary. It should be insulated to minimize extreme temperature variations.
2. If the building has large window areas, mask them to keep sunlight off the motorcycle.
3. Avoid buildings in industrial areas where corrosive emissions may be present. Avoid areas close to saltwater.
4. Consider the area's risk of fire, theft or vandalism. Check with an insurer regarding motorcycle coverage while in storage.

Preparing the Motorcycle for Storage

The amount of preparation a motorcycle should undergo before storage depends on the expected length of non-use, storage area conditions and personal preference. Consider the following list the minimum requirement:
1. Wash the motorcycle thoroughly. Make sure all dirt, mud and road debris are removed.
2. Fill the fuel tank with a mixture of fuel and fuel stabilizer. Mix the fuel and stabilizer in the ratio recommended by the stabilizer manufacturer. Run the engine for a few minutes so the stabilized fuel can enter the fuel system. If the motorcycle will be stored for a long period, consider draining the fuel system.
3. Start the engine and allow it to reach operating temperature. Drain the engine oil regardless of the riding time since the last service. Fill the engine with the recommended type of oil.
4. Fill the fuel tank completely. There is no need to try to empty the fuel delivery or return lines since they are not vented to the atmosphere.
5. Remove the spark plugs and pour a teaspoon of engine oil into the cylinders. Place a rag over the openings and slowly turn the engine over to distribute the oil. Reinstall the spark plugs.
6. Remove the battery. Store the battery in a cool and dry location. Charge the battery once a month.
7. Cover the exhaust and intake openings.
8. Apply a protective substance to the plastic and rubber components. Make sure to follow the manufacturer's instructions for each type of product being used.
9. Place the motorcycle on blocks with the wheels off the ground.
10. Cover the motorcycle with old bed sheets or something similar that can breathe. Do not cover it with any plastic material that will trap moisture.

Returning the Motorcycle to Service

The amount of service required when returning a motorcycle to service after storage depends on the length of non-use and storage conditions. In addition to performing the reverse of the above procedure, make sure the brakes, clutch, throttle and engine run/stop switch work properly before operating the motorcycle. Refer to Chapter Three and evaluate the service intervals to determine which areas require service.

Table 1 MODEL DESIGNATIONS

FLHT Electra Glide Standard (2006-2009)
FLHTI Electra Glide Standard (2006)
FLHTC Electra Glide Classic (2007-2009)
FLHTCI Electra Glide Standard (2006)
FLHTCU Ultra Classic Electra Glide (2007-2009)
FLHTCUI Ultra Classic Electra Glide (2006)
FLHTCUSE Screamin' Eagle Ultra Classic Electra Glide (2006)
FLHTCUSE2 Screamin' Eagle Ultra Classic Electra Glide (2007)
FLHTCUSE3 Screamin' Eagle Ultra Classic Electra Glide (2008)
FLHTCUSE4 Screamin' Eagle Ultra Classic Electra Glide (2009)
FLHR Road King (2006-2009)
FLHRI Road King (2006)
FLHRS Road King Custom (2006-2007)
FLHRSI Road King Custom (2006)
FLHRC Road King Classic (2007-2009)
FLHRCI Road King Classic (2006)
FLHRSE3 Screamin' Eagle Road King (2007)
FLHRSE4 Screamin' Eagle Road King (2008)
FLHX Street Glide (2006-2009)
FLHXI Street Glide (2006)
FLTR Road Glide (2007-2009)
FLTRI Road Glide (2006)
FLTRSE3 Screamin' Eagle Road Glide (2009)

*The *I* designation indicates models equipped with fuel injection.

Table 2 GENERAL MOTORCYCLE DIMENSIONS

Item/model	in.	mm
Wheel base	63.5	1612.9
Overall length		
FLHT/FLHTCI*	93.7	2380.0
FLHTC/FLHTCI*	97.5	2476.5
FLHTCU/FLHTCUI*	98.3	2497.0
FLHTCUSE		
2006 models	97.01	2464.1
2007 models	96.7	2456.2
2008 models	97.6	2478.3
2009 models	98.2	2494.3
FLHX/FLHXI* series		
2006-2008 models	94.5	2400.3
2009 models	95.8	2433.3
FLHR/FLHRI*		
2006-2008 models	93.7	2380.0
2009 models	95.2	2418.1
FLHRC/FLHRCI*		
2006-2008 models	93.7	2380.0
2009 models	94.2	2393.2
FLHRS/FLHRSI*		
2006-2007 models	93.7	2380.0
FLHRSE	93.5	2374.9
FLTR/FLTRI* series		
2006-2008 models	93.7	2380.0
2009 models	94.1	2390.1
FLTRSE	95.6	2428.3
Overall width		
All models except for Screamin' Eagle		
2006-2008 models	39.0	990.6
2009 models	38.0	965.2
FLHTCUSE		
2006 models	38.5	977.9
2007-2009 models	38.2	970.3
FLHRSE	40.2	1021.1
FLTRSE	39.1	993.9

(continued)

GENERAL INFORMATION

Table 2 GENERAL MOTORCYCLE DIMENSIONS (continued)

Item/model	in.	mm
Road clearance		
FLHT/FLHTI* series models	5.1	129.5
FLHX/FLHXI* series models	4.7	119.4
FLHR/FLHRI* series models	5.1	129.5
FLTR/FLTRI* series models	5.1	129.5
FLHTCUSE		
2006 models	5.1	129.5
2007 models	6.0	152.4
2008 models	4.9	124.5
2009 models	5.1	129.5
FLHRSE	5.5	139.7
FLTRSE	5.1	129.5
Overall height		
FLHT/FLHTI* series	61.0	1549.4
FLHX/FLHXI* series	52.2	1325.9
FLHR/FLHRI*, FLHRC/FLHRCI*	55.1	1399.5
FLHRS/FLHRSI*	46.4	1178.6
FLTR/FLTRI* series	55.0	1397.0
FLHTCUSE		
2006 models	54.1	1374.1
2007-2009 models	57.1	1450.3
FLHRSE	52.5	1333.5
FLTRSE	49.1	1246.1
Saddle height		
FLHT/FLHTI* series	27.3	693.4
FLHX/FLHXI* series	26.3	668.0
FLHR/FLHRI*	27.3	693.4
FLHRC/FLHRCI*	26.9	683.1
FLHRS/FLHRSI*	26.1	662.9
FLHTCUSE		
2006 models	27.3	693.4
2007 models	28.1	713.7
2008 models	28.7	729.0
2009 models	27.4	696.0
FLTRSE	26.3	668.0

*The I indicates 2006 fuel-injected models.

Table 3 MOTORCYCLE WEIGHT

Model	Dry weight lb. (kg)	Gross vehicle weight lb. (kg)	Gross axle weight front lb. (kg)	Gross axle weight rear lb.(kg)
FLHT/FLHTI*				
2006 models	758 (344)	1259 (571)	500 (227)	827 (375)
2007 models	859 (390)	1259 (571)	500 (227)	827 (375)
2008 models	864 (392)	1259 (571)	500 (227)	827 (375)
2009 models	887 (402)	1360 (617)	500 (227)	927 (420)
FLHTC/FLHTCI*				
2006 models	776 (352)	1259 (571)	500 (227)	827 (375)
2007 models	784 (356)	1259 (571)	500 (227)	827 (375)
2008 models	791 (359)	1259 (571)	500 (227)	827 (375)
2009 models	827 (375)	1360 (617)	500 (227)	927 (420)
FLHTCU/FLHTCUI*				
2006 models	788 (357)	1259 (571)	500 (227)	827 (375)
2007 models	808 (367)	1259 (571)	500 (227)	827 (375)
2008 models	814 (369)	1259 (571)	500 (227)	827 (375)
2009 models	852 (386)	1360 (617)	500 (227)	927 (420)
FLHTCUSE				
2006 models	845 (383)	1259 (571)	500 (227)	827 (375)
2007 models	859 (390)	1259 (571)	500 (227)	827 (375)
2008 models	864 (392)	1259 (571)	500 (227)	827 (375)
2009 models	887 (402)	1360 (617)	500 (227)	927 (420)

(continued)

Table 3 MOTORCYCLE WEIGHT (continued)

Model	Dry weight lb. (kg)	Gross vehicle weight lb. (kg)	Gross axle weight front lb. (kg)	Gross axle weight rear lb.(kg)
FLHX/FLHXI*				
2006 models	745 (338)	1259 (571)	500 (227)	827 (375)
2007 models	733 (333)	1259 (571)	500 (227)	827 (375)
2008 models	749 (340)	1259 (571)	500 (227)	827 (375)
2009 models	773 (351)	1360 (617)	500 (227)	927 (420)
FLHR/FLHRI*				
2006 models	723 (328)	1259 (571)	500 (227)	827 (375)
2007 models	737 (334)	1259 (571)	500 (227)	827 (375)
2008 models	740 (336)	1259 (571)	500 (227)	827 (375)
2009 models	775 (352)	1360 (617)	500 (227)	927 (420)
FLHRC/FLHRCI*				
2006 models	710 (322)	1259 (571)	500 (227)	827 (375)
2007 models	732 (332)	1259 (571)	500 (227)	827 (375)
2008 models	738 (335)	1259 (571)	500 (227)	827 (375)
2009 models	773 (351)	1360 (617)	500 (227)	927 (420)
FLHRS/FLHRSI*				
2006 models	721 (327)	1259 (571)	500 (227)	827 (375)
2007 models	726 (329)	1259 (571)	500 (227)	827 (375)
FLHRSE				
2007 models	754 (342)	1259 (572)	500 (227)	827 (375)
2008 models	774 (351)	1259 (572)	500 (227)	827 (375)
FLTR/FLTRI*				
2006 models	731 (332)	1259 (571)	500 (227)	827 (375)
2007 models	761 (345)	1259 (571)	500 (227)	827 (375)
2008 models	752 (341)	1259 (571)	500 (227)	827 (375)
2009 models	783 (355)	1360 (617)	500 (227)	927 (420)
FLTRSE	847 (384)	1360 (617)	500 (227)	927 (420)

*The I indicates 2006 fuel-injected models.

Table 4 DECIMAL AND METRIC EQUIVALENTS

Fractions	Decimal in.	Metric mm	Fractions	Decimal in.	Metric mm
1/64	0.015625	0.39688	33/64	0.515625	13.09687
1/32	0.03125	0.79375	17/32	0.53125	13.49375
3/64	0.046875	1.19062	35/64	0.546875	13.89062
1/16	0.0625	1.58750	9/16	0.5625	14.28750
5/64	0.078125	1.98437	37/64	0.578125	14.68437
3/32	0.09375	2.38125	19/32	0.59375	15.08125
7/64	0.109375	2.77812	39/64	0.609375	15.47812
1/8	0.125	3.1750	5/8	0.625	15.87500
9/64	0.140625	3.57187	41/64	0.640625	16.27187
5/32	0.15625	3.96875	21/32	0.65625	16.66875
11/64	0.171875	4.36562	43/64	0.671875	17.06562
3/16	0.1875	4.76250	11/16	0.6875	17.46250
13/64	0.203125	5.15937	45/64	0.703125	17.85937
7/32	0.21875	5.55625	23/32	0.71875	18.25625
15/64	0.234375	5.95312	47/64	0.734375	18.65312
1/4	0.250	6.35000	3/4	0.750	19.05000
17/64	0.265625	6.74687	49/64	0.765625	19.44687
9/32	0.28125	7.14375	25/32	0.78125	19.84375
19/64	0.296875	7.54062	51/64	0.796875	20.24062
5/16	0.3125	7.93750	13/16	0.8125	20.63750
21/64	0.328125	8.33437	53/64	0.828125	21.03437
11/32	0.34375	8.73125	27/32	0.84375	21.43125
23/64	0.359375	9.12812	55/64	0.859375	22.82812
3/8	0.375	9.52500	7/8	0.875	22.22500
25/64	0.390625	9.92187	57/64	0.890625	22.62187
13/32	0.40625	10.31875	29/32	0.90625	23.01875
27/64	0.421875	10.71562	59/64	0.921875	23.41562
7/16	0.4375	11.11250	15/16	0.9375	23.81250
29/64	0.453125	11.50937	61/64	0.953125	24.20937
15/32	0.46875	11.90625	31/32	0.96875	24.60625
31/64	0.484375	12.30312	63/64	0.984375	25.00312
1/2	0.500	12.70000	1	1.00	25.40000

GENERAL INFORMATION

Table 5 TORQUE RECOMMENDATIONS

Type2	1/4	5/16	3/8	7/16	1/2	9/16	5/8	3/4	7/8	1
SAE 2	6	12	20	32	47	69	96	155	206	310
SAE 5	10	19	33	54	78	114	154	257	382	587
SAE 7	13	25	44	71	110	154	215	360	570	840
SAE 8	14	29	47	78	119	169	230	380	600	700

1. Convert ft.-lb. specification to N•m by multiplying by 1.3558.
2. Fastener strength of SAE bolts can be determined by the bolt head grade markings. Unmarked bolt heads and cap screws are usually mild steel. More grade markings indicate higher fastener quality.

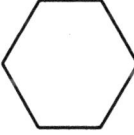

SAE 2   SAE 5   SAE 7   SAE 8

Table 6 CONVERSION FORMULAS

Multiply:	By:	To get the equivalent of:
Fluid volume		
U.S. quarts	0.9463	Liters
U.S. gallons	3.785	Liters
U.S. ounces	29.573529	Milliliters
Liters	0.2641721	U.S. gallons
Liters	1.0566882	U.S. quarts
Liters	33.814023	U.S. ounces
Milliliters	0.033814	U.S. ounces
Milliliters	1.0	Cubic centimeters
Milliliters	0.001	Liters
Torque		
Foot-pounds	1.3558	Newton-meters
Foot-pounds	0.138255	Meters-kilograms
Inch-pounds	0.11299	Newton-meters
Newton-meters	0.7375622	Foot-pounds
Newton-meters	8.8507	Inch-pounds
Meters-kilograms	7.2330139	Foot-pounds
Volume		
Cubic inches	16.387064	Cubic centimeters
Cubic centimeters	0.0610237	Cubic inches
Temperature		
Fahrenheit	(°F − 32) × 0.556	Centigrade
Centigrade	(°C × 1.8) + 32	Fahrenheit
Weight		
Ounces	28.3495	Grams
Pounds	0.4535924	Kilograms
Grams	0.035274	Ounces
Kilograms	2.2046224	Pounds
Pressure		
Pounds per square inch	0.070307	Kilograms per square centimeter
Kilograms per square centimeter	14.223343	Pounds per square inch
Kilopascals	0.1450	Pounds per square inch
Pounds per square inch	6.895	Kilopascals
Speed		
Miles per hour	1.609344	Kilometers per hour
Kilometers per hour	0.6213712	Miles per hour

Table 7 TECHNICAL ABBREVIATIONS

A	Ampere
ABS	Anti-lock brake system
AC	Alternating current
ACR	Automatic compression release
	(continued)

Table 7 TECHNICAL ABBREVIATIONS (continued)

A.h	Ampere hour
BAS	Bank angle sensor
C	Celsius
cc	Cubic centimeter
CDI	Capacitor discharge ignition
CKP sensor	Crank position sensor
cid	cubic inch displacement
cm	Centimeter
cu. in.	Cubic inch and cubic inches
cyl.	Cylinder
DC	Direct current
ECM	Electronic control module
ECU	Electronic control unit
ET sensor	Engine temperature sensor
F	Fahrenheit
fl. oz.	Fluid ounces
ft.	Foot
ft.-lb.	Foot pounds
gal.	Gallon and gallons
H/A	High altitude
HFSM	Hands-free security module
hp	Horsepower
Hz	Hertz
IAC	Idle air control
IAT sensor	Intake air temperature sensor
ICM	Ignition control module
ID	Inside diameter
in.	Inch and inches
in.-lb.	Inch-pounds
in. Hg	Inches of mercury
k	One-thousand ohms (2k = 2000 ohms)
kg	Kilogram
kg/cm^2	Kilogram per square centimeter
kgm	Kilogram meter
km	Kilometer
km/h	Kilometer per hour
kPa	Kilopascals
kW	Kilowatt
L	Liter and liters
L/m	Liters per minute
lb.	Pound and pounds
m	Meter
MAP sensor	Manifold absolute pressure sensor
mL	Milliliter
mm	Millimeter
N•m	Newton meter
O$_2$ sensor	Oxygen sensor
OD	Outside diameter
oz.	Ounce and ounces
psi	Pounds per square inch
pt.	Pint and pints
qt.	Quart and quarts
rpm	Revolution per minute
TCA	Throttle control actuator
TDC	Top dead center
TGS	Throttle grip sensor
TMAP sensor	Temperature and manifold absolute pressure sensor
TP sensor	Throttle position sensor
TSM	Turn signal module
TSSM	Turn signal and security module
V	Volt
VSS	Vehicle speed sensor
W	Watt

GENERAL INFORMATION

Table 8 U.S. TAP AND DRILL SIZES

Tap thread	Drill size	Tap thread	Drill size
#0-80	3/64	1/4-28	No. 3
#1-64	No. 53	5/16-18	F
#1-72	No. 53	5/16-24	I
#2-56	No. 51	3/8-16	5/16
#2-64	No. 50	3/8-24	Q
#3-48	5/64	7/16-14	U
#3-56	No. 46	7/16-20	W
#4-40	No. 43	1/2-13	27/64
#4-48	No. 42	1/2-20	29/64
#5-40	No. 39	9/16-12	31/64
#5-44	No. 37	9/16-18	33/64
#6-32	No. 36	5/8-11	17/32
#6-40	No. 33	5/18-18	37/64
#8-32	No. 29	3/4-10	21/32
#8-36	No. 29	3/4-16	11/16
#10-24	No. 25	7/8-9	49/64
#10-32	No. 21	7/8-14	13/16
#12-24	No. 17	1-8	7/8
#12-28	No. 15	1-14	15/16

Table 9 METRIC TAP AND DRILL SIZES

Metric size	Drill equivalent	Decimal fraction	Nearest fraction
3 × 0.50	No. 39	0.0995	3/32
3 × 0.60	3/32	0.0937	3/32
4 × 0.70	No. 30	0.1285	1/8
4 × 0.75	1/8	0.125	1/8
5 × 0.80	No. 19	0.166	11/64
5 × 0.90	No. 20	0.161	5/32
6 × 1.00	No. 9	0.196	13/64
7 × 1.00	16/64	0.234	15/64
8 × 1.00	J	0.277	9/32
8 × 1.25	17/64	0.265	17/64
9 × 1.00	5/16	0.3125	5/16
9 × 1.25	5/16	0.3125	5/16
10 × 1.25	11/32	0.3437	11/32
10 × 1.50	R	0.339	11/32
11 × 1.50	3/8	0.375	3/8
12 × 1.50	13/32	0.406	13/32
12 × 1.75	13/32	0.406	13/32

Table 10 SPECIAL TOOLS

Tool Description	Part No.	Manufacturer
Alternator rotor puller	HD-41771	H-D
ARC solenoid socket		
2007-2008 models	HD-48498	H-D
2009 models	HD-48498-A	H-D
Belt tension gauge	HD-355381	H-D
	923	JIMS
Bushing reamer tool	1726-3	JIMS
Camshaft assembly tool	990	JIMS
	HD-47956	H-D
Camshaft bearing puller	1280	JIMS
Camshaft locking tool	994	JIMS
	HD-47941	H-D
Camshaft chain tensioner tool	1283	JIMS
	HD-42313	H-D
Camshaft inner bearing installer		
2006 models	1278	JIMS
2007-2009 models	991	JIMS

(continued)

Table 10 SPECIAL TOOLS (continued)

Tool Description	Part No.	Manufacturer
Camshaft inner bearing remover tool		
2006 models	1279	JIMS
2007-2009 models	993	JIMS
Camshaft inner bearing remover/installer tool (2006-2009)	HD-42325A	H-D
Camshaft remover and installer	1277	JIMS
Camshaft/crankshaft sprocket lock	1285	JIMS
	HD-42314	H-D
Center stand jack	904	JIMS
Connecting rod bushing tool	1051	JIMS
Connecting rod bushing hone	HD-422569	H-D
Connecting rod clamp tool	1284	JIMS
	HD-95952-33C	H-D
Crankcase bearing snap ring remover and installer	1710	JIMS
Crankshaft bearing support tube	HD-42720-5	H-D
Crankshaft bearing support tube pilot/driver	HD-B-45655	H-D
Crankshaft bearing remover and installer	1146	JIMS
Crankshaft bushing tool	1281	JIMS
	HD-42315	H-D
Crankcase stud installer	08-0148	Motion Pro
	HD-42315	H-D
Crankshaft bushing reamer tool	1101	JIMS
	HD-42316	H-D
Crankcase disassembly/removing tool		
2006 models	1047-TP	JIMS
2007-2009 models	995	JIMS
Crankshaft guide	1288	JIMS
Crankshaft hard cap	1048	JIMS
Crankshaft seal installation tool	39361-69	JIMS
Crankshaft/camshaft sprocket lock	1285	JIMS
	HD-42314	H-D
Crankshaft support fixture	HD-44358	H-D
Cylinder chamfering cone	2078	JIMS
Cylinder head support stand	HD-39782-A-D	
Cylinder head holding fixture	HD-39786-A	H-D
Cylinder stud steel ball	HD-8860	H-D
Cylinder torque plates	1287	JIMS
Driver handle and remover	HD-34740	H-D
Electrical connector terminal remover (Molex)	HD-48114	H-D
Electrical terminal pick	GA500A	Snap-On
Electrical terminal pick tool (Deutsch)	114008	Deutsch
Electrical terminal remover (Packard)	HD-45928	H-D
Electrical socket terminal tool (AMP)	HD-39621-27	H-D
Electrical receptacle extractor	1764	JIMS
Engine stand/Twin Cam 88B		
Base stand	1138	JIMS
Engine stand	1142	JIMS
Exhaust oxygen sensor socket	969	JIMS
Exhaust seat adapter		
2006 models except Screamin' Eagle	HD-39782A-4	H-D
Screamin' Eagle and all 2007-2009 models	HD-39782-4	H-D
Final drive sprocket shaft bearing cone installer	HD-997225-55C	H-D
Final drive sprocket shaft bearing installation tool	97225-55	JIMS
Final drive sprocket locker	2260	JIMS
	HD-46282	H-D
Final drive sprocket shaft seal installer	39361-69	JIMS
Flywheel support fixture	HD-44358	H-D
Fork oil level gauge	08-0121	Motion Pro
Fork seal driver/installer	2046	JIMS
Fork stem bearing remover	HD-48262	H-D
Fuel pressure gauge	HD-41182	H-D
Fuel pressure gauge adapters	HD-44061	H-D
Fuel pump cam ring tool (2008-2009 models)	954	JIMS
	HD-48646	H-D
Handle/drive socket	1414	JIMS
	HD-43645	H-D
Hose clamp pincer tool	1171	JIMS

(continued)

GENERAL INFORMATION

Table 10 SPECIAL TOOLS (continued)

Tool Description	Part No.	Manufacturer
Hose clamp pliers	1171	JIMS
	HD-97087-65B	H-D
Hub bearing removal set	08-0410	Motion Pro
Hydraulic brake bleeder	MV8020	Mityvac
Hydraulic tensioner compression tool	HD-44063	H-D
Hydraulic tensioner retainer	HD-44408	H-D
Ignition switch alignment tool	943	JIMS
	HD-45962	H-D
Ignition switch connector remover	HD-45961	H-D
Intake manifold wrench	35-3975	K&L
	HD-47250	H-D
Intake seat adapter		
2006 models except Screamin' Eagle	HD-39782A-3	H-D
Screamin' Eagle and all 2007-2009 models	HD-39782-3	H-D
Long shank ball-end socket (turn signal bracket)	FABL5	Snap-On
Motor sprocket shaft seal installer tool	39361-69	JIMS
Passing lamp flare nut socket	FRX181	Snap-On
Piston ring compressor		
2006-2007 models	HD-96333-51D	H-D
2008-2009 models	HD-96333-51E	H-D
Primary drive locking tool		
2006 models	2234	JIMS
	HD-41214	H-D
2007-2009 models	2312	JIMS
	HD-47977	H-D
Pushrod tool	08-0225	Motion Pro
Radio support bracket bolt remover (ball end socket)	FABL6E	Snap-On
Retaining ring pliers	J-5586	H-D
Rear wheel alignment tool	928	JIMS
Rocker arm shaft reamer	94804-57	JIMS
Scissor jack	904	JIMS
Shift fork shaft remover (2007-2009 models)	985	JIMS
Small pick	TT600-3	Snap-On
Snap ring pliers	HD-J-5586	H-D
Snap ring remover and installer	1710	JIMS
Socket–hand drive	HD-43643	H-D
Spark tester	08-0122	Motion Pro
Sprocket shaft bearing cone installer	97225-55C	JIMS
Sprocket shaft seal installer	39361-69	JIMS
Steering stem bearing race remover	1414	JIMS
Steering head bearing race installer	1725	JIMS
Swing arm bearing installer	HD-45327	H-D
Threaded cylinders	HD-95952-1	H-D
Timken bearing race installer	2246	JIMS
Transmission bearing and race installer tool handle	33416-80	JIMS
Transmission drive sprocket locker tool	2260	JIMS
	HD-47910	H-D
Transmission main drive gear tool set		
(2006 models)	35316-80	JIMS
Transmission main drive gear bearing tool		
(2006 models)	37842-91	JIMS
Transmission main bearing remover set		
(2006 models)	1720	JIMS
Transmission mainshaft bearing race remove/install	34902-84	JIMS
Transmission mainshaft pulley locknut socket	989	JIMS
	HD-47910	H-D
Transmission mainshaft pulley locknut socket pilot	HD-94660-2	H-D
Transmisison mainshaft sprocket pulley locknut socket	94660-37A	JIMS
Transmission side door bearing remover and installer (2006 models)	1078	JIMS
Transmission side door remover		
2006 models	2283	JIMS
2007-2009 models	984	JIMS
Transmission mainshaft bearing race puller/installer	34902-84	JIMS
	HD-34902-C	H-D

(continued)

Table 10 SPECIAL TOOLS (continued)

Tool Description	Part No.	Manufacturer
Transmission main drive gear installer		
(2007-2009 models)	981	JIMS
Transmission main drive gear/bearing remover		
and installer (2007-2009 models)	HD-35316-C	H-D
Transmission main drive gear bearing installer		
(2007-2009 models)	987	JIMS
Transmission main drive gear large seal installer	972	JIMS
	HD-47856	H-D
Transmission main drive gear wedge attachment	HD-95637-46B	H-D
Transmission main drive gear bearing and		
seal installer		
(2007-2009 models)	986	JIMS
	HD-47933	H-D
Transmission shaft installer	2189	JIMS
Vacuum hose identifier kit	74600	Lisle
Valve guide cleaning brush	HD-34751-A	H-D
Valve guide driver		
All models except Screamin' Eagle	B-45524-1	H-D
Screamin' Eagle models	HD-34740	H-D
Valve guide hone		
All models except Screamin' Eagle	B-45525	H-D
Screamin' Eagle models	HD-34723-A	H-D
Valve guide installer sleeve		
All models except Screamin' Eagle	HD-34731	H-D
Screamin' Eagle models	HD-48628	H-D
Valve guide reamer		
All models except Screamin' Eagle models	B-45523	H-D
Screamin' Eagle models	HD-39932	H-D
Valve guide reamer T-handle	HD-39847	H-D
Valve guide reamer and honing lubricant	HD-39964	H-D
Valve guide seal installer (Screamin' Eagle models)	HD-48644	H-D
Valve seat cutter set, Neway		
2006-2007 models	HD-35758-A	H-D
2008-2009 models	HD-35758-C	H-D
Valve seat installation tool	HD-34643A	H-D
Valve seat driver handle	HD-34740	H-D
Valve spring compressor	HD-34736-B	H-D
Valve spring tester	HD-96796-47	H-D
Wheel alignment tool	08-0368	Motion Pro
Wheel bearing race remover and installer	33461	JIMS
	08-0410	Motion Pro
Wheel (rear) compensator bearing remover/installer	HD-48921	H-D
Wrist pin bushing reamer tool	1726	JIMS

CHAPTER TWO

TROUBLESHOOTING

This chapter describes troubleshooting procedures. Each procedure provides typical symptoms and logical methods for isolating the cause(s). Gather as much information as possible to aid in diagnosis. Never assume anything and do not overlook the obvious. Follow a systematic approach to eliminate each possibility and avoid unnecessary parts replacement.

In most cases, complicated test equipment is not required for basic troubleshooting.

However, some procedures require specialized test equipment. In such cases, eliminate all possible causes by performing any basic test(s) first, if possible. Be realistic and do not start procedures that are beyond the experience and equipment available. Many service departments will not take work that involves the re-assembly of damaged or abused equipment; if they do, expect the cost to be high. If the motorcycle does require the attention of a professional, describe symptoms and conditions accurately and fully. The more information a technician has available, the easier it will be to diagnose the problem.

Refer to **Tables 1-8** at the end of this chapter for troubleshooting specifications and diagnostic trouble codes.

ENGINE STARTING

NOTE
On fuel-injected models, do not open the throttle when starting either a cold or warm engine. The ignition control module (ICM) or electronic control module (ECM) takes throttle position into consideration during the starting procedure.

Engine Fails to Start (Spark Test)

1. Shift the transmission into neutral and confirm that the engine run/stop switch (**Figure 1**) is in the RUN position.

WARNING
To prevent fuel from being injected into the cylinders when the engine is turned over, remove the fuel pump fuse or disconnect the fuel pump electrical connector.

2. On fuel-injected models, disconnect the fuel pump (Chapter Ten).
3. Disconnect the spark plug wire and remove the spark plug as described in Chapter Three.

NOTE
*A spark tester (Motion Pro part No. 08-0122) is a useful tool for testing spark output. The tester (**Figure 2**) is inserted into the spark plug cap and its base is grounded against the cylinder head. The tester's air gap is adjustable, and it allows the visual inspection of the spark while testing the intensity of the spark.*

4. Cover the spark plug hole with a clean shop cloth to lessen the chance of gasoline vapors being emitted from the hole.

5. Insert the spark plug (**Figure 3**), or spark tester (**Figure 4**), into a plug cap and ground the base against the cylinder head. Position the spark plug or tester so the electrode is visible.

6. On 2007-2009 models, pull the clutch lever in (even with the transmission in neutral).

> *WARNING*
> *Do **not** hold the spark plug, tester, plug wire or connector. A serious electrical shock may result.*

> *WARNING*
> *Position the spark plug, or tester, away from the spark plug hole in the cylinder so that the spark or tester cannot ignite the gasoline vapors in the cylinder. If the engine is flooded, do not perform this test. The firing of the spark plug can ignite fuel that is ejected through the spark plug hole.*

7. Turn the engine over with the starter. A crisp blue spark should be evident across the spark plug electrode or spark tester terminals. Repeat for the remaining cylinder.

8. If the spark is good, check for one or more of the following possible malfunctions:
   a. Faulty fuel system component.
   b. Low engine compression or engine damage.
   c. Flooded engine.
   d. Incorrect ignition timing.

9. If the spark is weak or if there is no spark, refer to *Engine is Difficult to Start* in this chapter.

10. Install the spark plugs as described in Chapter Three.

11. On fuel-injected models, connect the fuel pump electrical connector (Chapter Ten).

Engine Is Difficult to Start

1. After attempting to start the engine, remove one of the spark plugs (Chapter Three) and check for the presence of fuel on the plug tip. Note the following:
   a. On fuel-injected models, if there is no fuel visible on the plug, remove the other spark plug. If there is no fuel on this plug, perform Step 2.
   b. If there is fuel present on the plug tip, go to Step 4.
   c. If there is an excessive amount of fuel on the plug, check for a clogged air filter, or for incorrect throttle operation (throttle plate stuck open).

2. On fuel-injected models, perform the *Fuel Pressure Test* in Chapter Ten. Note the following:
   a. If the fuel pump pressure is correct, go to Step 3B.
   b. If the fuel pump pressure is incorrect, replace the fuel pump and retest the fuel system.

3A. On carbureted models, check for an improperly adjusted carburetor float level as described in Chapter Nine.

3B. On fuel-injected models, inspect the fuel injectors as described in Chapter Ten.

4. Check for a clogged fuel line and/or contaminated fuel system.

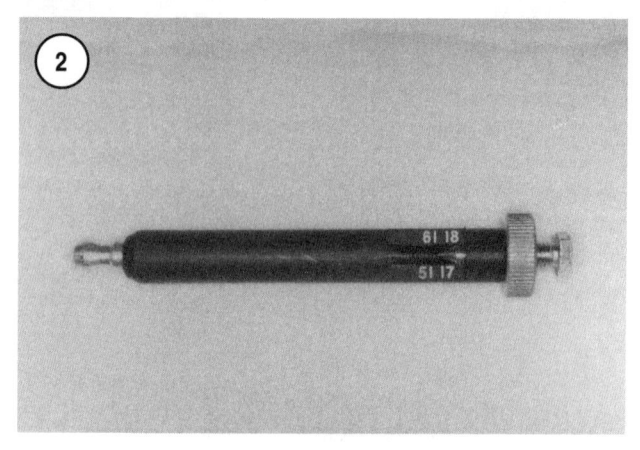

5. Perform the spark test as described in this section. Note the following:
   a. If the spark is weak or if there is no spark, go to Step 6.
   b. If the spark is good, go to Step 7.

6. If the spark is weak or if there is no spark, check the following:
   a. Fouled spark plug(s).
   b. Damaged spark plug(s).
   c. Loose or damaged ignition coil wire(s).
   d. Damaged ignition control module (ICM); carbureted models.
   e. Damaged electronic control module (ECM); fuel-injected models.
   f. Damaged crankshaft position sensor.
   g. Damaged ignition coil.
   h. Damaged engine run/stop switch.
   i. Damaged ignition switch.
   j. Damaged clutch interlock switch (2007-2009 models).
   k. Dirty or loose-fitting terminals.

7. If the engine turns over but does not start, the engine compression is probably low. Check for the following possible malfunctions:
   a. Leaking cylinder head gasket(s).
   b. Bent or stuck valve(s).
   c. Incorrect valve timing.
   d. Worn cylinders and/or pistons rings.

TROUBLESHOOTING

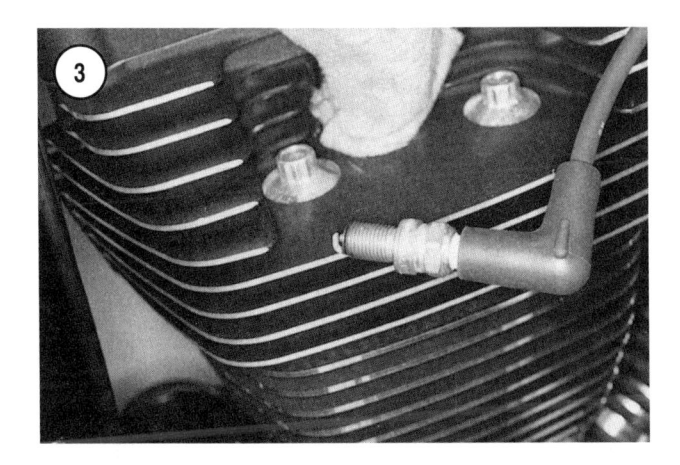

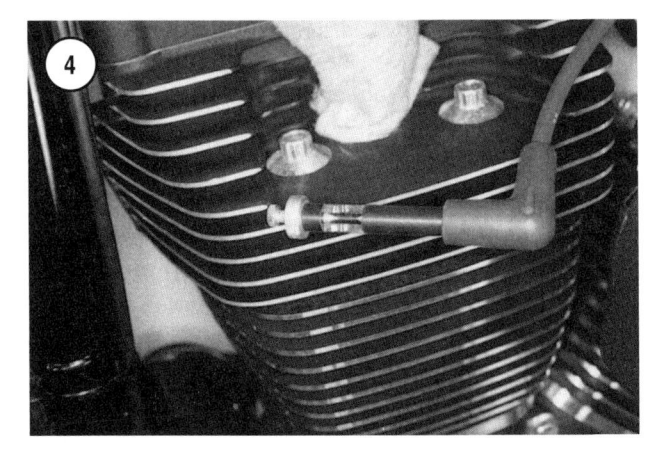

8. If the spark is good, try starting the engine by following normal starting procedures. If the engine starts but then stops, check the following conditions:
   a. Leaking or damaged rubber intake boot.
   b. Contaminated fuel.
   c. Incorrect ignition timing due to a damaged ignition coil.

Engine Does Not Crank

If the engine will not turn over, check for one or more of the following possible malfunctions:
1. Blown Maxi-Fuse (Chapter Eleven).
2. Discharged battery (Chapter Eleven).
3. Defective starter and/or starter relay (Chapter Eleven).
4. Seized piston (Chapter Five).
5. Seized crankshaft bearings (Chapter Five).
6. Broken connecting rod (Chapter Five).
7. Locked-up transmission or clutch assembly (Chapter Six, Seven or Eight).

ENGINE PERFORMANCE

If the engine runs, but performance is unsatisfactory, refer to the following procedure(s) that best describes the symptom(s).

NOTE
The ignition timing is not adjustable. If incorrect ignition timing is suspected as being the cause of a malfunction, a defective ignition system component is indicated. Refer to **Ignition System** *(this chapter).*

Engine Will Not Idle

1. Clogged air filter element.
2. Poor fuel flow.
3. Fouled or improperly gapped spark plug(s).
4. Leaking head gasket(s) or vacuum leak.
5. Leaking or damaged rubber intake boot(s).
6. Incorrect ignition timing: damaged ignition control module (ICM), electronic control module (ECM), or crankshaft position sensor.
7. Obstructed or defective carburetor or fuel injector(s).
8. Low engine compression.

Poor Overall Performance

1. Support the motorcycle with the rear wheel off the ground, and then spin the rear wheel by hand. If the wheel spins freely, perform the next step. If the wheel does not spin freely, check for the following conditions:
   a. Dragging rear brake.
   b. Damaged rear axle/bearing holder assembly.
   c. Damaged drive belt.
   d. Damaged drive or driven sprockets.
2. Check the clutch operation. If the clutch slips, refer to *Clutch* (this chapter).
3. If the previous steps did not locate the problem, test ride the motorcycle and accelerate lightly. If the engine speed increased according to throttle position, perform the next step. If the engine speed did not increase, check for one or more of the following problems:
   a. Clogged air filter.
   b. Restricted fuel flow.
   c. Clogged or damaged muffler(s).
4. Check for one or more of the following problems:
   a. Low engine compression.
   b. Worn spark plug(s).
   c. Fouled spark plug(s).
   d. Incorrect spark plug heat range.
   e. Clogged or defective carburetor or fuel injector(s).
   f. Incorrect oil level (too high or too low).
   g. Contaminated oil.
   h. Worn or damaged valve train assembly.
   i. Engine overheating. Refer to *Engine Overheating* (this section).
   j. Incorrect ignition timing: damaged ignition control module (ICM), electronic control module (ECM) or crankshaft position sensor.
5. If the engine knocks when it is accelerated or when running at high speed, check for one or more of the following possible malfunctions:
   a. Incorrect type of fuel.

b. Lean fuel mixture.
c. Advanced ignition timing: damaged ignition control module (ICM), or electronic control module (ECM),
d. Excessive carbon buildup in combustion chamber.
e. Worn pistons and/or cylinder bores.

Poor Idle or Low Speed Performance

1. Check for damaged rubber intake boots, a loose carburetor or throttle body, or loose air filter housing hose clamps.
2. On fuel-injected models, check the fuel flow and the fuel injectors as described in Chapter Ten.
3. Perform the spark test (this section). Note the following:
   a. If the spark is good, test the fuel system as described in this chapter.
   b. If the spark is weak, test the ignition system as described in this chapter.

Poor High Speed Performance

1. Check the fuel flow and the fuel injectors as described in Chapter Ten on fuel-injected models.
2. Incorrect valve timing and worn or damaged valve springs can cause poor high-speed performance. If the camshafts were timed just prior to experiencing this type of problem, the cam timing may be incorrect. If the cam timing was not set or changed, and all of the other inspection procedures in this section failed to locate the problem, remove the cylinder heads and inspect the camshafts and valve assembly.

Engine Overheating

1. Improper spark plug heat range.
2. Oil not circulating properly.
3. Valves leaking.
4. Heavy engine carbon deposits in combustion chamber(s).
5. Dragging brake(s).
6. Clutch slipping.

Engine Backfires

1. Incorrect ignition timing (due to loose or defective ignition system component).
2. Incorrect carburetor or throttle body adjustment.

Engine Misfires During Acceleration

1. Incorrect ignition timing (due to loose or defective ignition system component).
2. Incorrect carburetor or throttle body adjustment.

ENGINE NOISES

1. A knocking or pinging during acceleration is typically caused by using a lower octane fuel than recommended or poor quality fuel. Incorrect carburetor jetting (carbureted models) and an incorrect (hot) spark plug heat range can cause pinging. Refer to *Spark Plug Heat Range* in Chapter Three. Check also for excessive carbon buildup in the combustion chamber or a defective ignition module.
2. If a slapping or rattling noises at low speed or during acceleration is heard, consider excessive piston-to-cylinder wall clearance as a possible cause. Also check also for a bent connecting rod, a worn piston pin and/or a worn piston pin hole in the piston.
3. A knocking or rapping while decelerating is usually caused by excessive rod bearing clearance.
4. A persistent knocking and vibration is usually caused by worn main bearings and/or excessive crankshaft runout. Connecting rod and piston (stuck/broken rings) problems can also exhibit this condition. However, rule out the following first:
   a. Loose engine mounts.
   b. Cracked frame.
   c. Leaking cylinder head gasket(s).
   d. Exhaust pipe leaks at cylinder head(s).
5. A rapid on-off squeal indicates a compression leak around the cylinder head gasket or spark plug.
6. If the valve train is noisy, check for the following:
   a. Bent pushrod(s).
   b. Defective lifter(s).
   c. Valve sticking in guide.
   d. Worn cam gears and/or cam.
   e. Damaged rocker arm or shaft. Rocker arm may be binding on shaft.

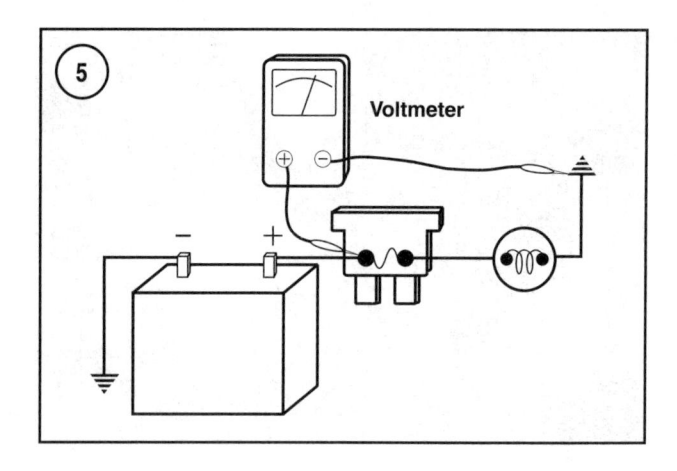

ELECTRICAL TESTING

This section describes general electrical test procedures and equipment use. Subsequent sections cover the starting, charging and ignition systems.

After determining which system requires testing, start with the first inspection in the list and perform the indicated test(s). Each test presumes that the component tested in the prior step is working properly. The test can yield invalid results if they are performed out of sequence. If a test indicates that a component is working properly, reconnect the electrical connections and proceed to the next step.

TROUBLESHOOTING

Systematically work through the procedure until the problem is found. Repair or replace faulty parts as described in the appropriate section of this manual.

If necessary, refer to the wiring diagrams located on the CD inserted into the back cover of the manual for component and connector identification. Trace the current paths from the power source through the circuit components to ground. Check any circuits that share the same fuse, ground or switch. If the other circuits work properly and the shared wiring is good, the cause must be in the wiring used only by the suspect circuit. If all related circuits are faulty at the same time, the probable cause is a poor ground connection or a blown fuse(s).

Electrical connections are often the weak link in the electrical system. Dirty, loose-fitting electrical connectors cause numerous electrical-related problems, especially on high-mileage motorcycles. When troubleshooting an electrical problem, carefully inspect the connectors and wiring harness.

As with all troubleshooting, analyze typical symptoms in a systematic manner. Never assume anything, and do not overlook the obvious, like a blown fuse or an electrical connector that has separated.

Electrical Component Replacement

Most dealerships and parts suppliers will not accept the return of any electrical part. Consider any test results carefully before replacing a component that tests only slightly out of specification, especially for resistance. A number of variables can affect test results dramatically. These include: the testing meter's internal circuitry, ambient temperature and conditions under which the machine has been operated. All instructions and specifications have been checked for accuracy; however, successful test results depend to a great degree upon individual accuracy. If the exact cause of any electrical system malfunction cannot be determined, have a dealership retest that specific system to verify the test results before purchasing a non-returnable part.

Preliminary Checks and Precautions

Prior to starting any electrical troubleshooting procedure perform the following:
1. Check the Maxi-Fuse as described in Chapter Eleven. If the Maxi-Fuse is blown, replace it.
2. Check the individual fuses mounted in the fuse box as described in Chapter Eleven. Remove the suspected fuse and replace if blown.
3. Inspect the battery as described in Chapter Eleven. Make sure it is fully charged, and that the battery leads are clean and securely attached to the battery terminals.
4. Disconnect each electrical connector in the suspect circuit and check that there are no bent terminals on either side of the connector.
5. Make sure all electrical terminals are clean and free of corrosion. Clean, if necessary, and pack the connectors with dielectric grease.
6. Make sure the terminals are pushed all the way into the connector. If not, carefully push them in with a narrow blade screwdriver.
7. Check the wires where they enter the individual connectors.
8. Push the connectors together and make sure they are fully engaged and locked together.
9. Never pull on the electrical wires when disconnecting an electrical connector.

Test Light or Voltmeter

Use a test light to check for voltage in a circuit by attaching one lead to ground and the other lead to various points along the circuit. Where battery voltage is present the light bulb will light.

Use a voltmeter in the same manner as the test light to determine if battery voltage is present in any given circuit. When using a voltmeter, attach the positive lead to the component or wire to be checked and the negative lead to a good ground (**Figure 5**).

Voltage Test

Make all voltage tests with the electrical connectors still connected, unless otherwise specified. Insert the test leads into the backside of the connector and make sure the test lead touches the electrical wire or metal terminal within the connector housing. Touching the wire insulation will yield a false reading.

Always check both sides of the connector as one side may be loose or corroded thus preventing electrical flow through the connector. This type of test can be performed with a test light or a voltmeter. A voltmeter gives the best results.

NOTE
When using a test light, either lead can be attached to ground.

1. Attach the voltmeter negative test lead to a good ground. Make sure the part used for ground is not insulated with a rubber gasket or rubber grommet.
2. Attach the voltmeter positive test lead to the point (electrical connector, etc.) to be checked.
3. Turn the ignition switch to IGN. When using a test light, the test light will come on if voltage is present. When using a voltmeter, note the voltage reading. The reading should be within 1 volt of battery voltage. If the voltage is significantly less than battery voltage, there is a problem in the circuit.

Voltage Drop Test

Since resistance causes voltage to drop, a voltmeter can be used to determine resistance in an active circuit. This is called a voltage drop test. A voltage drop test measures the difference between the voltage at the beginning of the circuit and the available voltage at the end of the circuit while the circuit is operating. If the circuit has no resistance, there is no voltage drop so the voltmeter indicates 0 volts. The greater the resistance in the circuit will result in a greater the voltage drop reading. A voltage drop of 1 or more volts indicates that a circuit has excessive resistance.

Remember a 0 reading on a voltage drop test is good. Battery voltage, on the other hand, indicates an open circuit. A voltage drop test is an excellent way to check the condition of solenoids, relays, battery cables and other high-current electrical components.
1. Connect the voltmeter positive test lead to the end of the wire or device closest to the battery.
2. Connect the voltmeter negative test lead to the ground side of the wire or device (**Figure 6**).
3. Turn the components on in the circuit.
4. The voltmeter should indicate 0 volts. If there is a drop of 1 volt or more, there is a problem within the circuit. A voltage drop reading of 12 volts indicates an open in the circuit.

Ammeter

An ammeter measures the flow of current (amps) in a circuit (**Figure 7**). When connected in series in the circuit, the ammeter determines whether current is flowing in the circuit, and whether the current flow is excessive because of a short in the circuit. This current flow is usually referred to as current draw. Comparing actual current draw in the circuit or component to the manufacturer's specified current draw rating provides useful diagnostic information.

Ohmmeter

CAUTION
Never connect an ohmmeter to a circuit that has power applied to it. Always disconnect the negative battery cable before using the ohmmeter.

An ohmmeter reads resistance in ohms to current flow in a circuit or component. Ohmmeters may be an analog type (needle scale) or a digital type (LCD or LED readout). Both types of ohmmeters have a switch that allows the selection of different ranges of resistance for accurate readings. The analog ohmmeter also has a set-adjust control which is used to zero or calibrate the meter needle for accurate adjustments. Digital ohmmeters do not require calibration.

Use an ohmmeter by connecting its test leads to the terminals or leads of the circuit or component being tested. When using an analog meter, calibrate it by crossing the test leads and turning the set-adjust knob until the meter needle reads zero. When the leads are uncrossed, the needle should move to the other end of the scale, indicating infinite resistance.

During a continuity test, a reading of infinite indicates that there is an open in the circuit or component. A reading of zero indicates continuity, which means there is no measurable resistance in the circuit or component being tested. If the meter needle falls between the two ends of the scale, this indicates the actual resistance to current flow that is present. To determine the resistance, multiply the meter reading by the ohmmeter scale. For example, a meter reading of 5 multiplied by the R × 1000 scale is 5000 ohms of resistance.

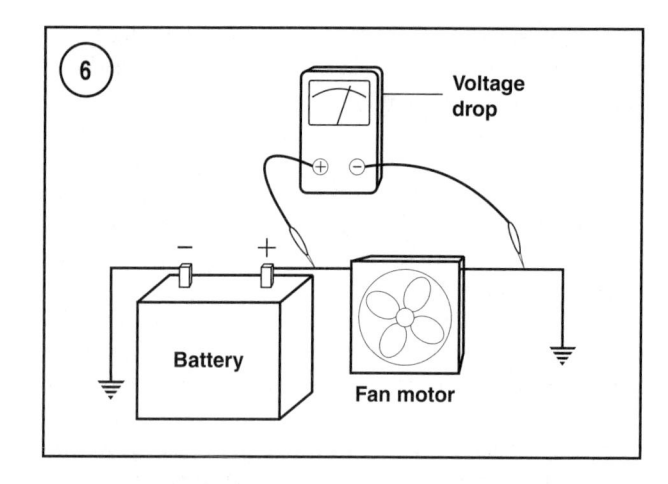

Self-Powered Test Light

CAUTION
Never use a self-powered test light on circuits that contain solid-state devices. The solid-state device may be damaged.

A self-powered test light can be constructed of a 12-volt light bulb, a pair of test leads and a 12-volt battery. When the test leads are touched together, the light bulb illuminates.

Use a self-powered test light as follows:
1. Touch the test leads together to make sure the light bulb goes on. If not, correct the problem prior to using it in a test procedure.
2. Disconnect the motorcycle's battery or remove the fuse(s) that protects the circuit to be tested. Refer to Chapter Eleven.
3. Select two points within the circuit that should have continuity.
4. Attach one lead of the self-powered test light to each point.
5. If there is continuity, the self-powered test light bulb will come on.
6. If there is no continuity, the self-powered test light bulb will not come on. This indicates an open, or a break, in the circuit.

Continuity Test

A continuity test is used to determine the integrity of a circuit, wire or component. A circuit has continuity if it forms a complete circuit; if there are no opens, or breaks, in either the electrical wires or components within the circuit. A circuit with an open or break in it has no continuity.

TROUBLESHOOTING

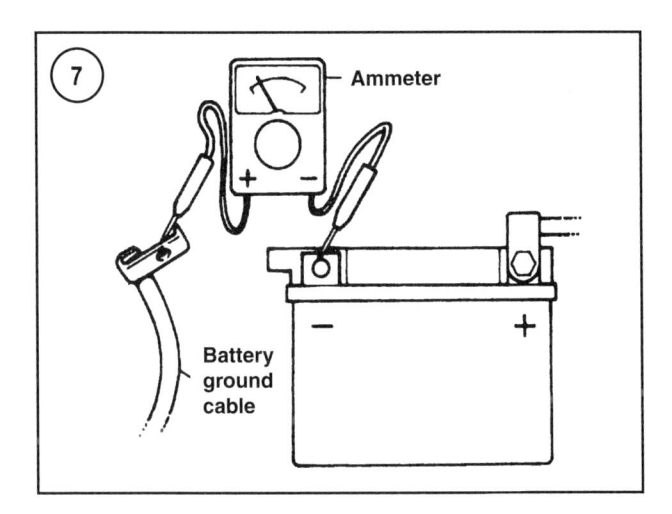

This type of test can be performed with a self-powered test light or an ohmmeter. An ohmmeter gives the best results. When using an analog ohmmeter, calibrate the meter by touching the leads together and turning the set-adjust knob until the meter needle reads zero.

1. Disconnect the battery negative cable.
2. Attach one test lead (test light or ohmmeter) to one end of the part of the circuit to be tested.
3. Attach the other test lead to the other end of the part or the circuit to be tested.
4. The self-powered test light comes on if there is continuity. An ohmmeter reads 0 or very low resistance if there is continuity. A reading of infinite resistance indicates no continuity; the circuit has an open, or a break, in it.

Jumper Wire

A jumper wire is a simple way to bypass a potential problem and isolate it to a particular point in a circuit. If a faulty circuit works properly with a jumper wire installed, an open exists between the two jumper points in the circuit.

To troubleshoot with a jumper wire, first use the wire to determine if the problem is on the ground side or the load side of a device. Test the ground by connecting the wire between the device and a good ground. If the device comes on, the problem is the connection between the device and ground. If the device does not come on with the jumper installed, the device's connection to ground is good so the problem is between the device and the power source.

To isolate the problem, connect the jumper between the battery and the device. If it comes on, the problem is between these two points. Next, connect the jumper between the battery and the fuse side of the switch. If the device comes on, the switch is good. By moving the jumper from one point to another, the problem can be isolated to a particular place in the circuit.

Note the following when using a jumper wire:
1. A jumper wire is a temporary test measures only. Do not leave a jumper wire installed as a permanent solution. This creates a severe fire hazard that could easily lead to complete loss of the motorcycle.
2. Never use a jumper wire across any load (a component that is connected and turned on). This would result in a direct short and will blow the fuse(s).
3. Install an inline fuse/fuse holder (available at most automotive supply stores or electronic supply stores) to the jumper wire.
4. Make sure the jumper wire gauge (thickness) is the same as that used in the circuit being tested. Smaller gauge wire will rapidly overhead and could melt.
5. Install insulated boots over alligator clips. This prevents accidental grounding, sparks or possible shock when working in cramped quarters.

Testing For a Short With an Ohmmeter

1. Disconnect the battery negative cable.
2. Remove the blown fuse from the fuse panel.
3. Connect one test lead of the ohmmeter (or self-powered test light) to the load side (battery side) of the fuse terminal in the fuse panel.
4. Connect the other test lead to a good ground. Make sure the part used for a ground is not insulated with a rubber gasket or rubber grommet.
5. With the ohmmeter attached to the fuse terminal and ground, wiggle the wiring harness of the suspect circuit at 6 in. (15.2 cm) increments. Start next to the fuse panel and work away from the fuse panel.
6. Watch the ohmmeter as you progress along the harness. If the ohmmeter moves when the harness is wiggled, there is a short-to-ground at that point in the harness.

Testing For a Short With a Test Light

1. Remove the blown fuse from the fuse panel.
2. Connect the test light (or voltmeter) across the fuse terminals in the fuse panel. Turn the ignition switch to IGN and check for battery voltage.
3. With the test light attached to the fuse terminals, wiggle the wiring harness of the suspect circuit at 6 in. (15.2 cm) intervals. Start next to the fuse panel and work away from the panel.
4. Watch the test light as you progress along the harness. If the test light blinks or if the needle on the voltmeter moves when the harness is wiggled, there is a short-to-ground at that point in the harness.

Wiggle Test

The wiggle test locates intermittent problems within a circuit.
1. Connect a digital volt/ohmmeter between two points within a suspected circuit.
2. Start the engine, let it idle and note the voltage.
3. Shake the harness while observing the meter. If a large change in voltage occurs, an intermittent short or open exists between the two tested points.

4. To narrow the search, move one probe closer to the other point and repeat the test until the intermittent has been isolated to a place in the circuit.

STARTING SYSTEM

The starting system consists of the battery, starter, starter relay, solenoid, starter switch, starter mechanism and related wiring.

When the ignition switch is turned to IGN and the starter switch is pushed in, current is transmitted from the battery to the starter relay. When the relay is activated, it allows electricity to flow from the battery to the starter.

Before troubleshooting the starting system, perform the following:
1. Make sure the battery is fully charged.
2. Replace damaged or undersize cables.
3. Make sure all electrical connections are clean and tight.
4. Inspect the wiring harness for worn or frayed insulation or loose harness sockets.
5. Verify fuel tank is filled with an adequate supply of fresh gasoline.

Voltage Drop Test

Before performing the steps listed in *Starter Troubleshooting* (this section), perform this voltage drop test. These steps will help find weak or damaged electrical components that may be causing the starting system problem.

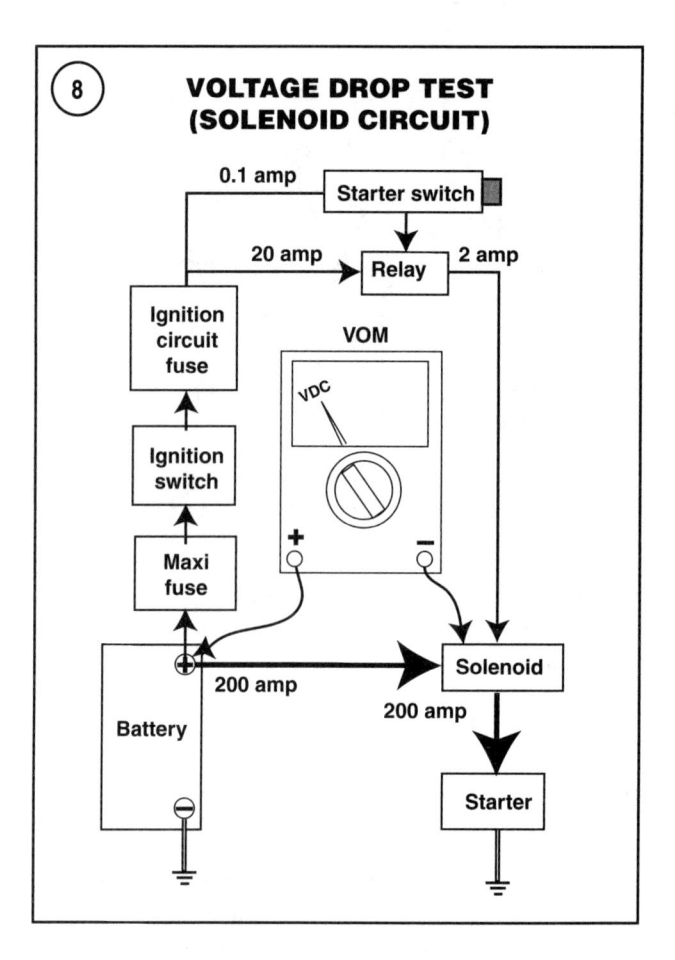

1. Connect the positive voltmeter lead to the positive battery terminal, and then connect the negative voltmeter lead to the solenoid (**Figure 8**). The voltmeter lead must not touch the starter-to-solenoid terminal.
2. Shift the transmission into neutral. On 2007-2009 models, pull the clutch lever in (even with the transmission in neutral).
3. Turn the ignition switch to IGN and push the starter switch while reading the voltmeter scale. Note the following:
   a. The circuit is operating correctly if the voltmeter reading is 2 volts or less. A voltmeter reading of 12 volts indicates an open circuit.
   b. A voltage drop of more than 2 volts shows a problem in the solenoid circuit.
   c. If the voltage drop reading is correct, continue with the test procedure.

NOTE
This procedure checks the voltage drop across the starter ground circuit. To check any other ground in the starting circuit, repeat this test but leave the negative voltmeter lead connected to the battery and connect the positive voltmeter lead to the ground that is being tested.

4. To check the starter ground circuit, connect the negative voltmeter lead to the negative battery terminal, and then

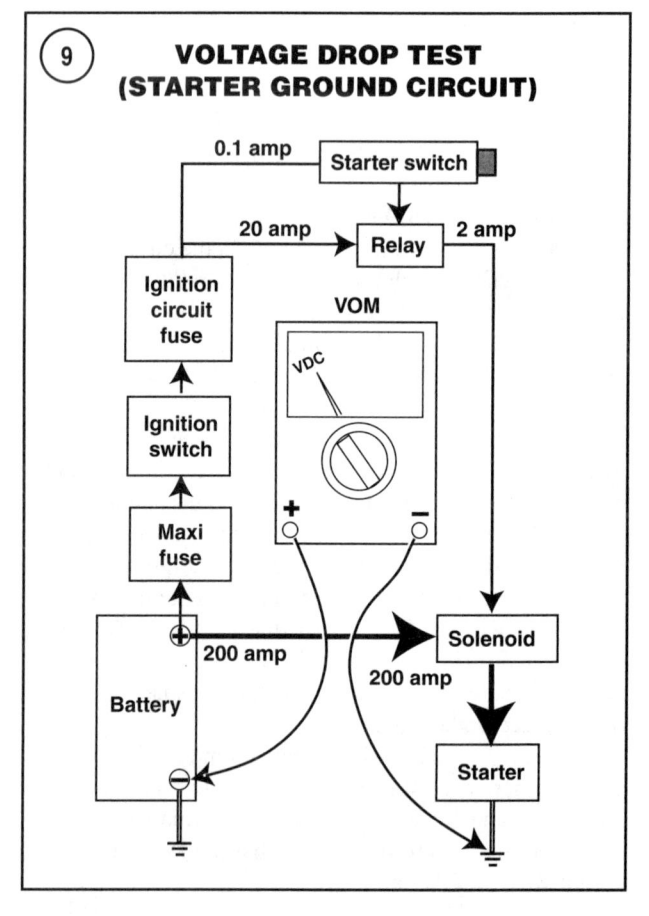

TROUBLESHOOTING

STARTER JUMP TEST

2006 MODELS

2007-2009 MODELS

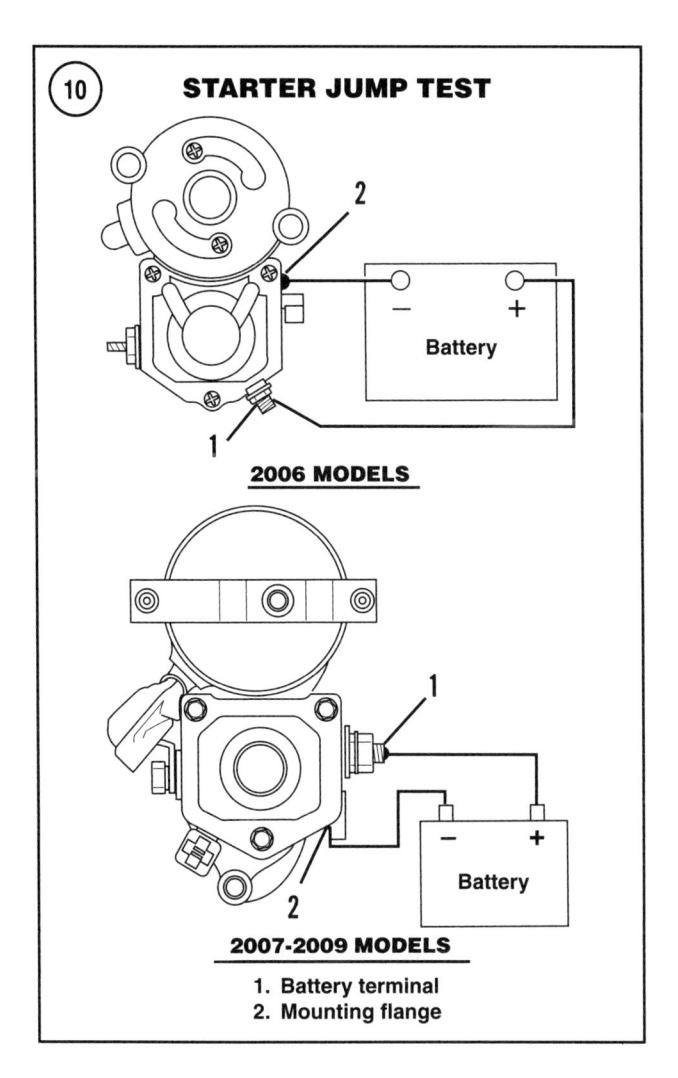

1. Battery terminal
2. Mounting flange

connect the positive voltmeter lead to the starter housing (**Figure 9**).

5. Turn the ignition switch to IGN and push the starter switch while reading the voltmeter scale. The voltage drop must not exceed 0.2 volts. If it does, check the ground connections between the meter leads.
6. If the problem is not located, refer to *Starter Troubleshooting* in this section.

Starter Troubleshooting

The basic starter-related troubles are:
1. Starter does not spin.
2. Starter spins but does not engage.
3. The starter will not disengage after the starter switch is released.
4. Loud grinding noise when starter turns.
5. Starter stalls or spins to slowly.

CAUTION
Never operate the starter for more than 30 seconds at as time. Allow the starter to cool before reusing it. Failure to allow the starter to cool after continuous starting attempts can damage the starter.

Starter does not spin

1. Turn the ignition switch to IGN and push the starter switch while listening for a click at the starter relay in the electrical panel. Turn the ignition switch off and note the following:
   a. If the starter relay clicks, test the starter relay as described in this section. If the starter relay test readings are correct, continue with Step 2.
   b. If the solenoid clicks, go to Step 3.
   c. If there was no click, go to Step 6.
2. Check the wiring connectors between the starter relay and solenoid. Note the following:
   a. Repair any dirty, loose fitting or damaged connectors or wiring.
   b. If the wiring is in good condition, remove the starter as described in Chapter Eleven. Perform the solenoid tests and starter current draw tests described in this section.
3. Perform a voltage drop test between the battery and solenoid terminals as described in *Voltage Drop Test (*this section). The normal voltage drop is less than 2 volts. Note the following:
   a. If the voltage drop is less than 2 volts, perform Step 4.
   b. If the voltage drop is more than 2 volts, check the solenoid and battery wires and connections for dirty or loose fitting terminals; clean and repair as required.
4. Remove the starter as described in Chapter Eleven. Momentarily connect a fully charged 12-volt battery to the starter. Refer to **Figure 10**. If the starter is operational, it will turn when connected to the battery. Disconnect the battery and note the following:
   a. If the starter turns, perform the solenoid pull-in and hold-in tests as described in *Solenoid Tests (*this section).
   b. If the starter does not turn, disassemble the starter as described in Chapter Eleven, and check for opens, shorts and grounds.
5. On 2006 models, if the problem is not evident after performing Steps 3 and 4, check the starter shaft to see if it is binding at the jackshaft. Check the jackshaft for binding or damage. Refer to *Starter Jackshaft* in Chapter Six.
6. If there is no click when performing Step 1, measure voltage between the starter switch and the starter relay. The voltmeter must read battery voltage. Note the following:
   a. If battery voltage is noted, continue with Step 7.
   b. If there is no voltage, go to Step 8.
7. Check the starter relay ground at the starter relay. Note the following:
   a. If the starter relay is properly grounded, test the starter relay as described in this section.
   b. If the starter relay is not grounded, check the ground connection. Repair the ground connection, and then retest the relay.
8. Check for voltage at the starter switch. Note the following:

a. If there is voltage at the starter switch, test the starter relay as described in this section.
b. If there is no voltage at the starter switch, check continuity across the switch. If there is voltage leading to the starter switch, but no voltage leaving the switch, replace the switch and retest. If there is no voltage leading to the starter switch, check the switch wiring for dirty or loose-fitting terminals or damaged wiring. Clean and/or repair the terminals or wiring as required.

Starter spins but does not engage

If the starter spins but the pinion gear does not engage the ring gear, perform the following:
1. Remove the outer primary cover as described in Chapter Six.
2A. On 2006 models, inspect the pinion gear (A, **Figure 11**) mounted on the end of the jackshaft. If the teeth are chipped or worn, inspect the clutch ring gear (B, **Figure 11**) for the same problems. Note the following:
   a. If the pinion gear and ring gear are damaged, service these parts as described in Chapter Six.
   b. If the pinion gear and ring gear are not damaged, continue with Step 3.
2B. On 2007-2009 models, inspect the starter pinion gear (**Figure 12**). If the teeth are chipped or worn, inspect the clutch ring gear (**Figure 13**) for the same problems.
   a. If the pinion gear and ring gear are damaged, service the parts as described in Chapter Six or Chapter Eleven.
   b. If the pinion gear and ring gear are not damaged, continue with Step 3.
3. Remove and disassemble the starter as described in Chapter Eleven. Then, check the overrunning clutch assembly (**Figure 14**) for:
   a. Roller damage (**Figure 15**).
   b. Compression spring damage (A, **Figure 16**).
   c. Excessively worn or damaged pinion teeth.
   d. Pinion does not run in overrunning direction.
   e. Damaged clutch shaft splines (B, **Figure 16**).
   f. On 2006 models, damaged drive assembly (**Figure 17**).
4. Replace worn or damaged parts as required.

Starter will not disengage after the starter switch is released

1. A sticking solenoid, caused by a worn solenoid compression spring (A, **Figure 16**), can cause this problem. Replace the solenoid if damaged.
2. On high-mileage 2006 models, the pinion gear (A, **Figure 11**) can bind on a worn clutch ring gear (B). Unable to return, the starter will continue to run. This condition usually requires ring gear replacement.
3. Check the starter switch and starter relay for internal damage. Test the starter switch as described in *Switches* (Chapter Eleven). Test the starter relay as described in this chapter.

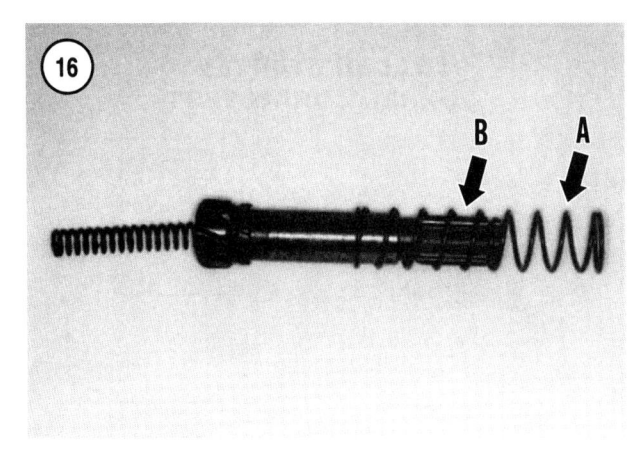

TROUBLESHOOTING

a. If the voltage drop is less than 2 volts, continue with Step 2.
b. If the voltage drop exceeds 2 volts, check the solenoid and battery wires and connections for dirty or loose-fitting terminals. Clean and/or repair the terminals or wiring as required.

2. Perform a voltage drop test between the solenoid terminals and the starter as described in *Voltage Drop Test* (this section). The normal voltage drop is less than 2 volts. Note the following:
   a. If the voltage drop is less than 2 volts, continue with Step 3.
   b. If the voltage drop exceeds 2 volts, check the solenoid and starter wires and connections for dirty or loose-fitting terminals. Clean and/or repair the terminals or wiring as required.

3. Perform a voltage drop test between the battery ground wire and the starter as described in *Voltage Drop Test* (this section). The normal voltage drop is less than 2 volts. Note the following:
   a. If the voltage drop is less than 2 volts, continue with Step 4.
   b. If the voltage drop exceeds 2 volts, check the battery ground wire connections for dirty or loose-fitting terminals. Clean and/or repair the terminals or wiring as required.

4. Perform the *Loaded Current Draw Test* (this section). Note the following:
   a. If the loaded current draw is excessive, check for a damaged starter or starter drive assembly. Remove the starter as described in Chapter Eleven and perform the *Free-Running Current Draw Test* (this section).
   b. If the current draw reading is correct, continue with Step 5.

5A. On 2006 models, remove the outer primary cover as described in Chapter Six. Check the pinion gear (A, **Figure 11**). If the teeth are chipped or worn, inspect the clutch ring gear (B, **Figure 11**) for the same problem.
   a. If the pinion gear and ring gear are damaged, service these parts as described in Chapter Six.
   b. If the pinion gear and ring gear are not damaged, continue with Step 6.

5B. On 2007-2009 models, remove the outer primary cover as described in Chapter Six. Check the clutch ring gear (**Figure 13**). If the teeth are chipped or worn, service this part as described in Chapter Six. Disassemble the starter and check the starter pinion gear (**Figure 12**). If the teeth are chipped or worn, service this part as described in Chapter Eleven.

6. Remove and disassemble the starter as described in Chapter Eleven. Check the disassembled starter for opens, shorts and grounds.

Loud grinding noises when the starter turns

Incorrect pinion gear and clutch ring gear engagement (B, **Figure 11**), or a damaged overrunning clutch drive assembly (**Figure 17**) on 2006 models can cause this problem. Remove and inspect the starter as described in Chapter Eleven.

Starter stalls or spins too slowly

1. Perform a voltage drop test between the battery and solenoid terminals as described in *Voltage Drop Test* (this section). The normal voltage drop is less than 2 volts. Note the following:

Starter Relay
Testing

Check starter relay operation with an ohmmeter, jumper wires and a fully charged 12-volt battery.

1. Carefully remove the starter relay from the fuse block assembly (**Figure 18**) as described in Chpater Eleven.

CAUTION
The battery negative lead must be connected to starter relay terminal No. 85 to avoid internal diode damage.

2. Connect an ohmmeter and 12-volt battery between the relay terminals shown in **Figure 19**. This setup will energize the relay for testing.
3. Check for continuity through the relay contacts using an ohmmeter while the relay coil is energized. The correct reading is 0 ohm. If resistance is excessive or if there is no continuity, replace the relay.
4. If the starter relay passes this test, reconnect and install the starter relay as described in Chapter Eleven.

Starter Current Draw Tests

The battery must be fully charged for these tests. Refer to *Battery* in Chapter Eleven. An inductive ammeter is required.

Loaded Current draw test (starter installed)

1. Shift the transmission into neutral.
2. Disconnect the spark plug caps from both spark plugs, and ground the plug caps with two extra spark plugs. Do *not* remove the spark plugs from the cylinder heads.
3. Connect an inductive ammeter between the starter terminal and positive battery terminal (**Figure 20**). Connect a jumper cable from the negative battery terminal to ground.
4. Turn the ignition switch to IGN and press the starter switch for approximately 10 seconds. Note the ammeter reading.

NOTE
The current draw is high when the starter switch is first pressed, and then it will drop and stabilize at a lower reading. Refer to the lower stabilized reading during this test.

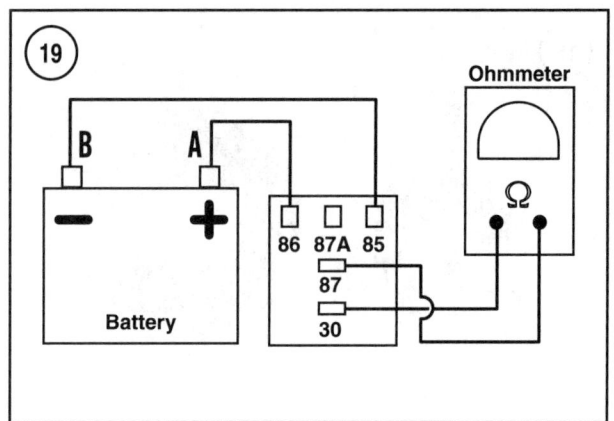

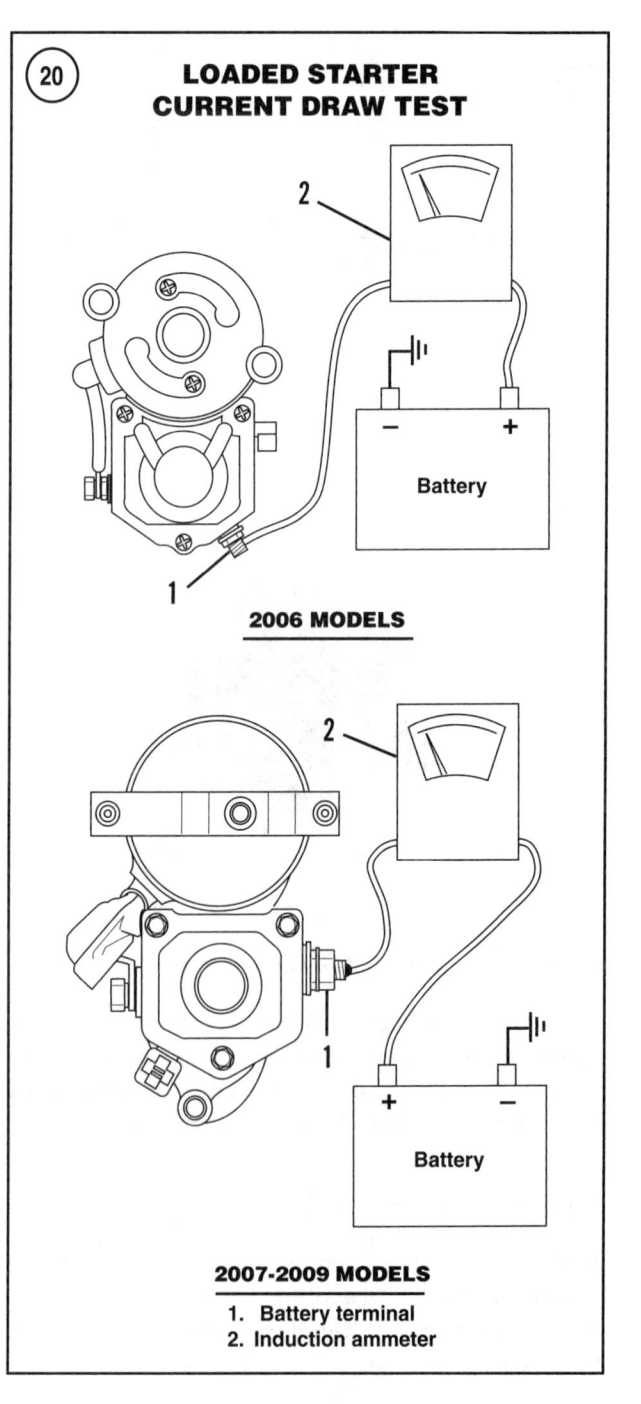

TROUBLESHOOTING

STARTER FREE-RUNNING CURRENT DRAW TEST (Figure 21)

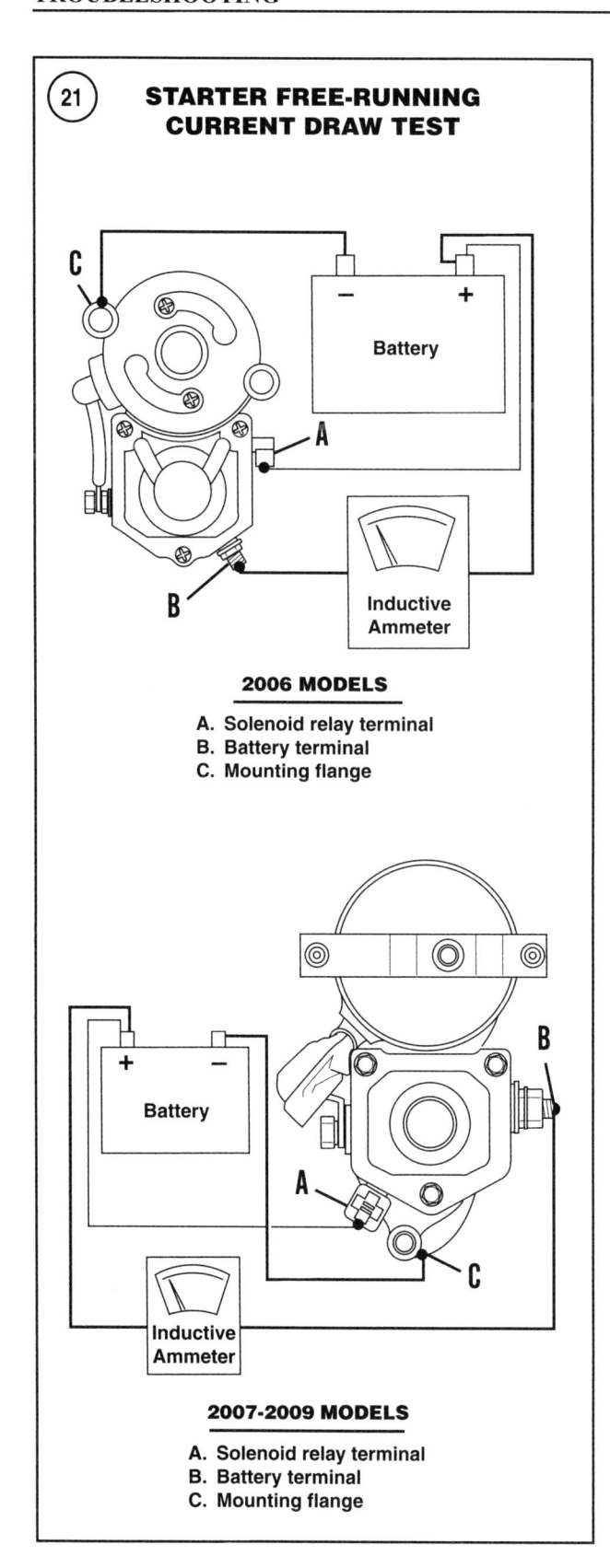

2006 MODELS
A. Solenoid relay terminal
B. Battery terminal
C. Mounting flange

2007-2009 MODELS
A. Solenoid relay terminal
B. Battery terminal
C. Mounting flange

5. If the current draw exceeds the current draw specification in **Table 1**, check for a defective starter or starter drive mechanism. Remove and service these components as described in Chapter Eleven.
6. Disconnect the ammeter and jumper cables.

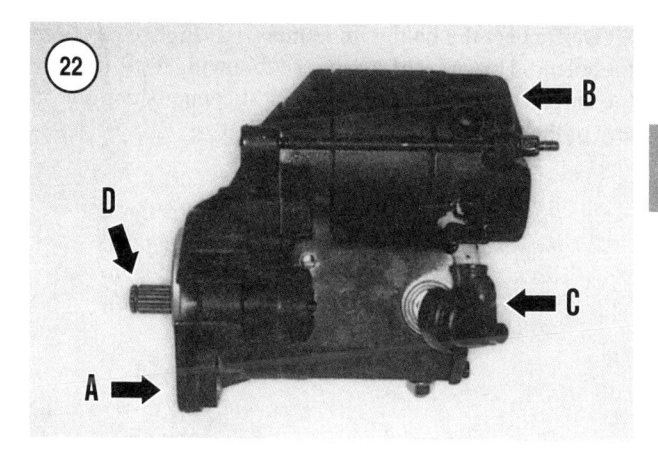

Free-running current draw test (starter removed)

A jumper wire (14 gauge minimum) and 3 jumper cables (6-gauge minimum) are required for this test.
1. Remove the starter as described in Chapter Eleven.

NOTE
The solenoid must be installed on the starter during the following tests.

2. Mount the starter in a vise with soft jaws.
3. Connect the 14-gauge jumper wire between the positive battery terminal and the solenoid relay terminal (A, **Figure 21**).
4. Connect a jumper cable between the positive battery terminal and the ammeter (**Figure 21**).
5. Connect the second jumper cable between the ammeter and the starter battery terminal (B, **Figure 21**) on the starter solenoid.
6. Connect the third jumper cable between the battery ground terminal and the starter mounting flange (C, **Figure 21**).
7. Read the ammeter; the correct ammeter reading is 90 amps. A damaged pinion gear assembly will cause an excessively high current draw reading. If the current draw reading is low, check for an undercharged battery or an open field winding or armature in the starter.

Solenoid Tests

The battery must be fully charged for this test. Refer to *Battery* in Chapter Eleven.

Three jumper wires are also required.

NOTE
The following procedure is shown on a 2006 model starter; 2007-2009 models are similar.

1. Remove the starter (A, **Figure 22**, typical) as described in Chapter Eleven.

NOTE
*The solenoid (B, **Figure 22**) must be installed on the starter during the following tests. Do not remove it.*

2. Disconnect the field wire terminal (C, **Figure 22**) from the solenoid before performing the following tests. Insulate the end of the wire terminal so that it cannot short out on any of the test connectors.

CAUTION
Battery voltage is being applied directly to the solenoid and starter in the following tests. Do not leave the jumper cables connected to the solenoid for more than 3-5 seconds; otherwise, the solenoid will be damaged.

NOTE
Thoroughly read the following procedure to familiarize and understand the procedures and test connections. Perform the tests in the order listed and without interruption.

3. Perform the solenoid pull-in test as follows:
    a. Connect one jumper wire from the negative battery terminal to the solenoid housing ground (A, **Figure 23**).
    b. Connect one jumper wire from the negative battery terminal to the solenoid motor terminal (B, **Figure 23**).
    c. Touch a jumper wire from the positive battery terminal to the starter relay terminal (C, **Figure 23**). The pinion shaft (D, **Figure 22**) must extend from the housing.
    d. Leave the jumper wires connected and continue with Step 4.
4. To perform the solenoid hold-in test, perform the following:
    a. With the pinion shaft retracted, disconnect the solenoid motor terminal jumper wire (**Figure 24**) from the negative battery terminal and connect it to the positive battery terminal. The pinion shaft will remain extended from the housing. If the pinion shaft returns to its normal position, replace the solenoid.
    b. Leave the jumper wires connected and continue with Step 5.
5. To perform the solenoid return test, perform the following:
    a. Disconnect the jumper wire from the starter relay terminal (**Figure 25**). The pinion shaft must return to its original position.
    b. Disconnect all of the jumper wires from the solenoid and battery.
6. Replace the solenoid as described in Chapter Eleven if the starter shaft failed to operate properly during these tests.

CHARGING SYSTEM

The charging system consists of the battery, alternator and a voltage regulator/rectifier. Alternating current generated by the alternator is rectified to direct current. The voltage regulator maintains the voltage to the battery and additional electrical loads, like the lights and ignition system, at a constant voltage regardless of variations in engine speed and load.

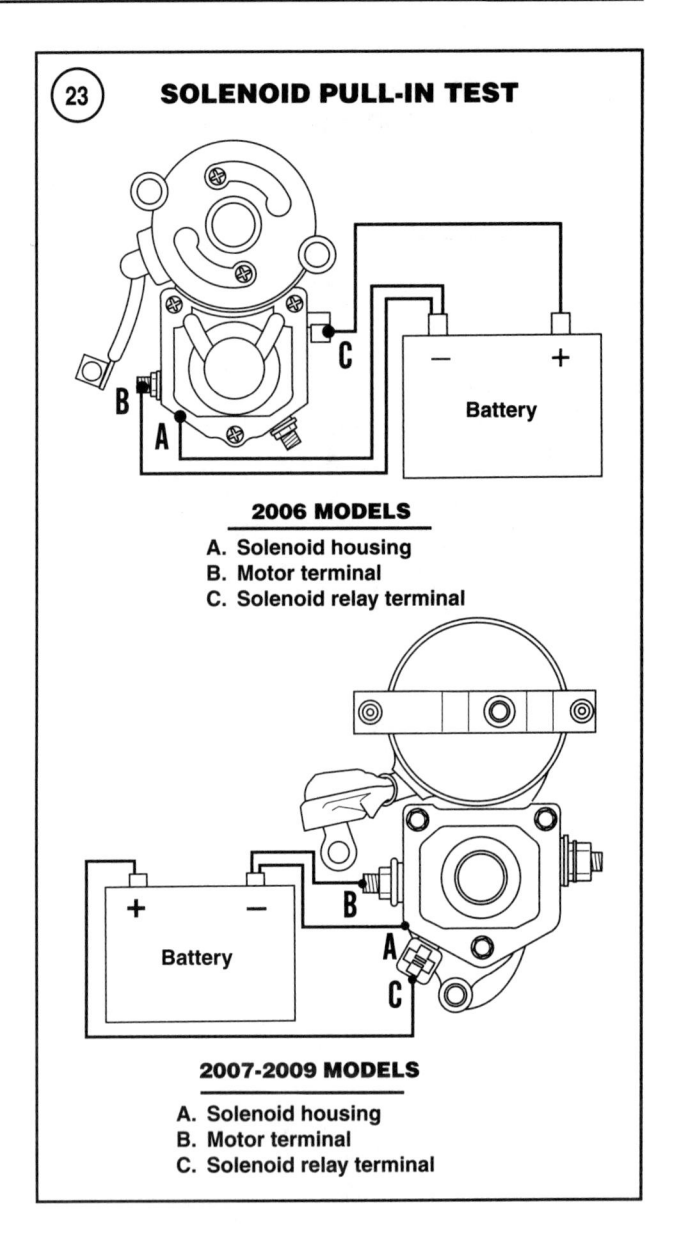

23 SOLENOID PULL-IN TEST

2006 MODELS
A. Solenoid housing
B. Motor terminal
C. Solenoid relay terminal

2007-2009 MODELS
A. Solenoid housing
B. Motor terminal
C. Solenoid relay terminal

Milliamp Draw Test

1. Turn the ignition switch off. Make sure all accessories are in the off position.
2. Disconnect the Maxi-Fuse as described in Chapter Eleven.

CAUTION
Before connecting the ammeter into the circuit, set the meter to its highest amperage scale. This prevents a large current flow from damaging the meter or blowing the meter's fuse.

NOTE
*Even with the ignition in the off position, an initial current draw of up to 200mA will occur directly after connecting the ammeter. This should drop to the values shown in **Table 1** within one minute.*

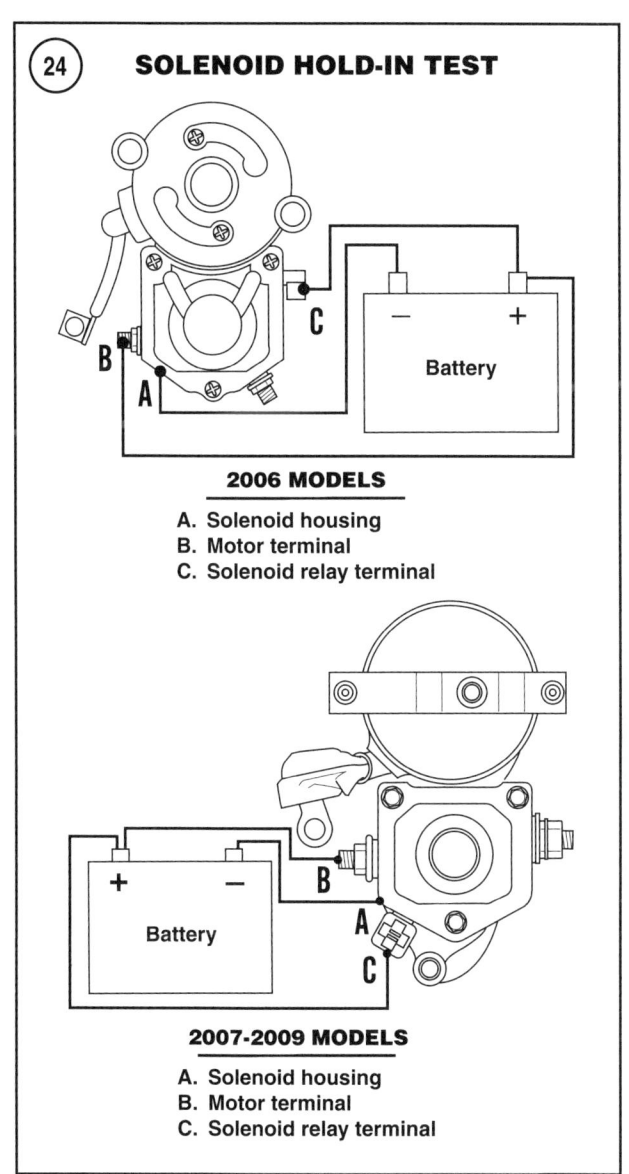

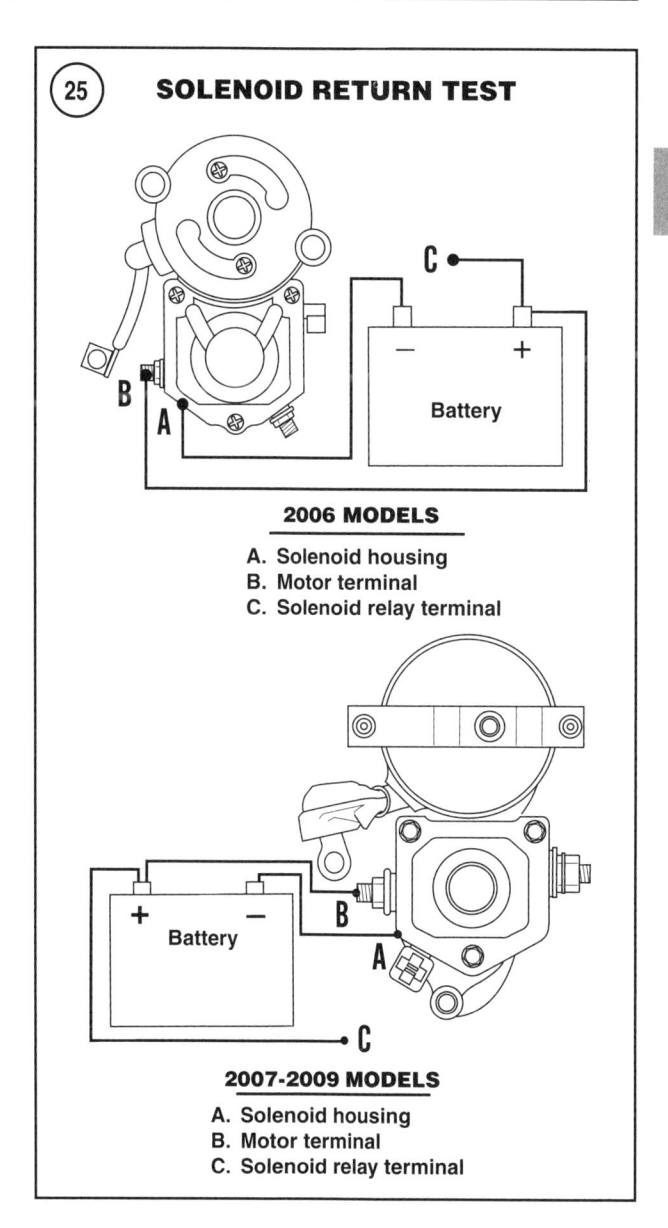

TROUBLESHOOTING

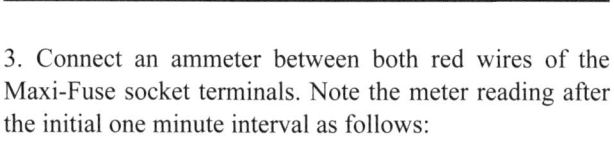

24 **SOLENOID HOLD-IN TEST**

2006 MODELS
A. Solenoid housing
B. Motor terminal
C. Solenoid relay terminal

2007-2009 MODELS
A. Solenoid housing
B. Motor terminal
C. Solenoid relay terminal

25 **SOLENOID RETURN TEST**

2006 MODELS
A. Solenoid housing
B. Motor terminal
C. Solenoid relay terminal

2007-2009 MODELS
A. Solenoid housing
B. Motor terminal
C. Solenoid relay terminal

3. Connect an ammeter between both red wires of the Maxi-Fuse socket terminals. Note the meter reading after the initial one minute interval as follows:
   a. Add the current draw (0.5mA) to the approximate values of the TSM/TSSM/HFSM/ECM and additional components listed in **Table 1**. If this total is less than the ammeter reading, then the current draw is within limits.
   b. If there is a higher reading, this indicates an excessive draw and all accessories must be checked for excessive current drain.
4. Dirt and/or electrolyte on top of the battery or a crack in the battery case can create a path for battery current to flow. If excessive current draw is noted, remove and clean the battery (Chapter Eleven), and then repeat the test.
5. If the current draw is still excessive, consider the following probable causes:
   a. Faulty voltage regulator.
   b. Damaged battery.
   c. Short circuit in the system.
   d. Loose, dirty or faulty electrical connectors in the charging circuit.
6. To find the short circuit that is causing excessive current draw, refer to the wiring diagrams located on the CD inserted into the back cover of this manual. Then, continue to measure the current draw while disconnecting different connectors in the electrical system one by one. If the current draw returns to an acceptable level, the problem circuit is indicated. Test the circuit further to find the fault.
7. Disconnect the ammeter.
8. Connect the Maxi-Fuse as described in Chapter Eleven.

Total Current Draw Test

This test, requiring a load tester, measures the total current load of the electrical system and any additional accessories while the engine is running. Perform this test if the battery keeps being discharged, yet the charging system output is within specifications.

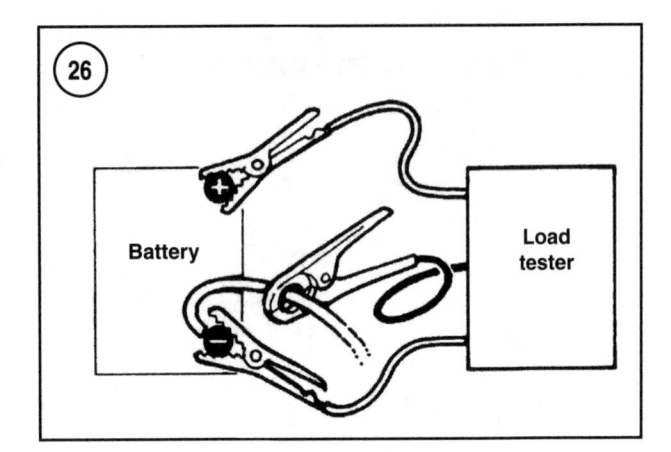

If aftermarket accessories have been installed on the motorcycle, the increased current demand may exceed the charging system's capacity and result in a discharged battery.

NOTE
When using a load tester, refer to the manufacturer's instructions. To prevent tester damage caused by overheating, do not leave the load switch on for more than 20 seconds at a time.

1. Connect a load tester to the battery as shown in **Figure 26**.
2. Turn the ignition switch to IGN, but do not start the engine. Then, turn on *all* electrical accessories and switch the headlight beam to HIGH.
3. Read the ampere reading (current draw) on the load tester and compare it to the test results obtained in the *Current Output Test* (this section). The current output test results must exceed the current draw by 3.5 amps for the battery to remain sufficiently charged.
4. If aftermarket accessories have been added to the motorcycle, disconnect them and repeat the test. If the current draw is now within specification, the problem is with the additional accessories.
5. If no accessories have been added to the motorcycle, a short circuit may be causing the battery to discharge.

Current Output Test

This test requires a load tester.
1. The battery must be fully charged for this test. Refer to *Battery* in Chapter Eleven.

NOTE
When using the load tester, read and follow the manufacturer's instructions. To prevent tester damage caused by overheating, do not leave the load switch on for more than 20 seconds at a time.

2. Connect the load tester negative and positive leads to the battery terminals. Then, place the induction pickup of the load tester around the positive voltage regulator wire (**Figure 27**).
3. Start the engine and bring the speed up to 3000 rpm while reading the load tester scale. With the engine running at 3,000 rpm, operate the load tester switch until the voltage scale reads 13.0 volts. The correct current output reading is 45-60 amps.
4. Turn the engine off and disconnect the load tester.
5. Perform the *Stator Tests* described in this section. If the results of the stator tests are acceptable, a defective voltage regulator/rectifier or a wiring short circuit is indicated. Make sure to eliminate the possibility of a poor connection or damaged wiring before replacing the voltage regulator/rectifier.

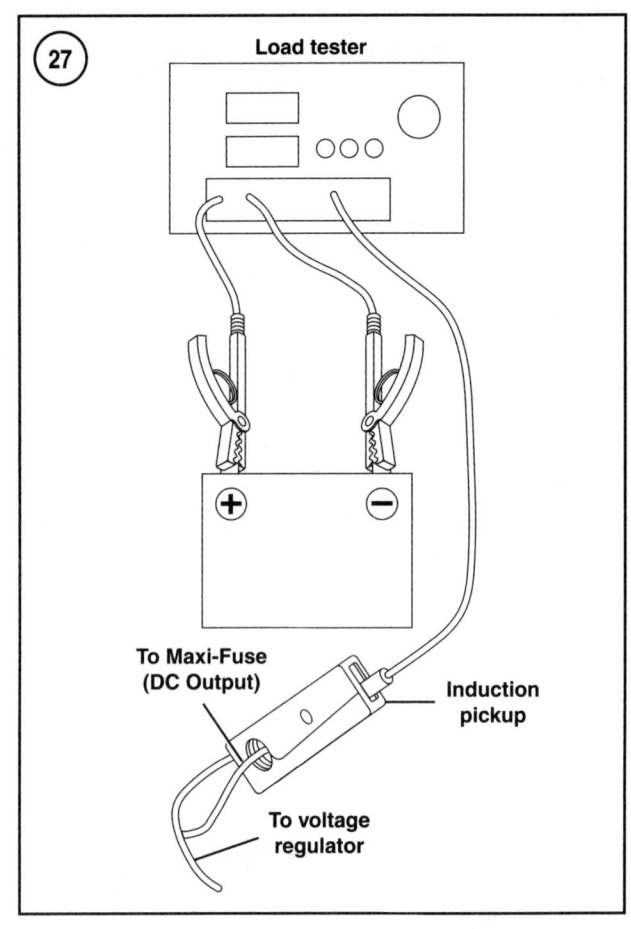

Stator Tests

Grounded stator

1. Turn the ignition switch off. Partially remove the voltage regulator (Chapter Eleven) and disconnect the round connector (**Figure 28**) from the left side of the regulator.
2. Insert one of the ohmmeter probes into any of the three connector sockets and connect the other probe to ground. The correct reading is infinity. Any other reading indicates a grounded stator. Repeat this test for the other two stator sockets. Again, the correct ohmmeter reading is infinity.
3. If resistance is not as specified, replace the stator assembly as described in Chapter Eleven.

TROUBLESHOOTING

Figure 28

Figure 29 — Electrical connector

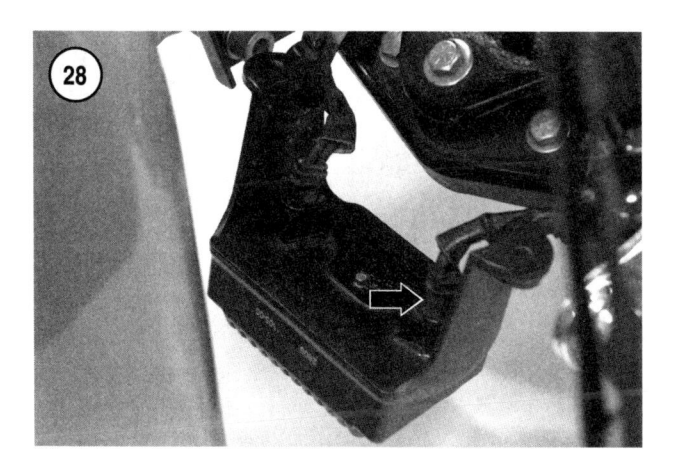

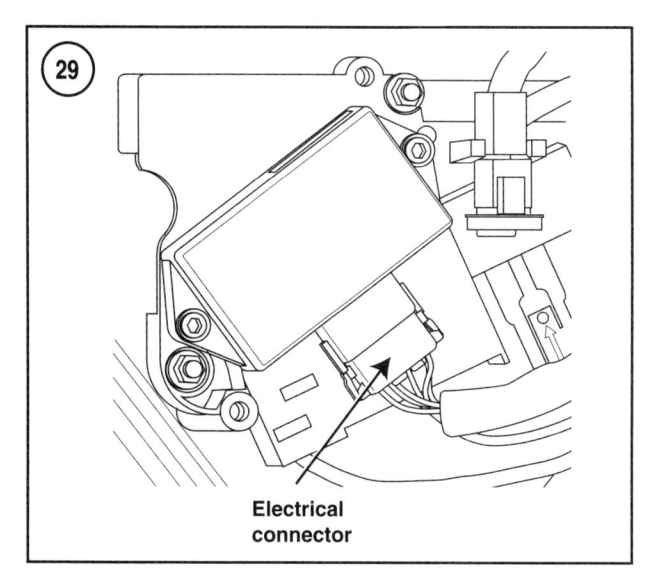

Figure 30

4. Reconnect the round connector (**Figure 28**) and install the voltage regulator (Chapter Eleven).

Open stator

1. Turn the ignition switch off, partially remove the voltage regulator (Chapter Eleven), and disconnect the round connector (**Figure 28**) from the left side of the regulator.
2. Insert the ohmmeter probes between all three sockets (1-2, 2-3, 1-3). The correct reading should be less than 1 ohm (typically 0.1-0.3 ohm). If resistance is not as specified, replace the stator assembly as described in Chapter Eleven.
3. Reconnect the round connector (**Figure 28**) and install the voltage regulator (Chapter Eleven).

AC output

1. Turn the ignition switch off, and then disconnect the round connector (**Figure 28**) from the regulator/rectifier.
2. Connect an AC voltmeter across any two terminals.
3. Start the engine and slowly increase engine speed until the engine is running at 2000 rpm. The AC output should be 30-40 VAC for 2006-2007 models or 32-46 VAC for 2008-2009 models.

4. If the AC voltage output reading is below the specified range, replace the stator assembly as described in Chapter Eleven.
5. Reconnect the round regulator/rectifier connector (**Figure 28**).

Voltage Regulator Ground Test

The voltage regulator base must be grounded to the frame for proper operation.

1. Connect one ohmmeter lead to a good engine or frame ground and the other ohmmeter lead to the regulator base. Read the ohmmeter scale. The correct reading is 0 ohm. Note the following:
   a. If there is low resistance (0 ohm), the voltage regulator is properly grounded.
   b. If there is high resistance, remove the voltage regulator and clean its frame mounting points.
2. Remove the voltage regulator and check the connectors on the backside of the voltage regulator. They must be tight and free of corrosion.

IGNITION SYSTEM

Precautions

Before testing the ignition system, observe the following precautions to prevent damage to protect the system:
1. Never disconnect any of the electrical connectors while the engine is running.
2. Apply dielectric grease to all electrical connectors prior to reconnecting them. This will help seal out moisture.
3. Make sure all electrical connectors are free of corrosion and are securely fastened to each other.
4A. On carbureted models, the ignition control module (ICM) must always be mounted securely to the electrical mounting bracket and the electrical connector (**Figure 29**) must be securely fastened.
4B. On fuel-injected models, the electronic control module (ECM) must always be mounted securely to the electrical mounting bracket and the electrical connector (**Figure 30**) must be securely fastened.

Troubleshooting Preparation

1. Refer to the wiring diagrams located on the CD inserted into the back cover of this manual for the specific model.
2. Check the wiring harness for visible signs of damage.
3. Make sure all connectors are fastened securely to each other and locked in place.
4. Check all electrical components for a good ground to the engine.
5. Check all wiring for short circuits or open circuits.
6. Remove the left side frame cover and saddlebag as described in Chapter Seventeen.
7. To check for a blown fuse, perform the following:
   a. Depress both latches (A, **Figure 31**) on the Maxi-Fuse holder, slide the holder (B) toward the rear and disengage the tongue from groove on the fuse holder.
   b. Pull the fuse block (**Figure 32**) straight out and release it from the tabs on the frame mounting bracket.

NOTE
*Fuse description and location is printed on the fuse block cover (**Figure 33**, typical).*

   c. Locate the blown fuse and install a new *fuse with the same amperage.*

Ignition Coil Testing

Use an ohmmeter to check the ignition coil secondary and primary resistance. Test the coil twice: first when it is cold (room temperature) and then at normal operating temperature. If the engine will not start, heat the coil with a hair dryer, and test it with the ohmmeter.

1. Remove the ignition coil as described in Chapter Eleven.
2. Disconnect the primary wire connector (A, **Figure 34**) and the secondary wires (B) from the ignition coil.
3A. On carbureted models, measure the primary coil resistance between terminals (**Figure 35**) as follows:
   a. Front coil: Terminal 2 and 3.
   b. Rear coil: Terminal 1 and 2.
3B. On fuel-injected models, measure the primary coil resistance between terminals (**Figure 36**) as follows:
   a. Front coil: Terminal A and D.
   b. Rear coil: Terminal A and C.
4. Set the ohmmeter on its highest scale. Measure the resistance between the secondary terminals.
5. Compare the primary coil resistance reading to the specification in **Table 1**. Replace the ignition coil if the reading is not within specification.
6. If the resistance values are less than specified, there is most likely a short in the coil windings. Replace the coil.
7. If the resistance values are more than specified, this may indicate corrosion or oxidation of the coil's terminals. Thoroughly clean the terminals, and spray with an aerosol

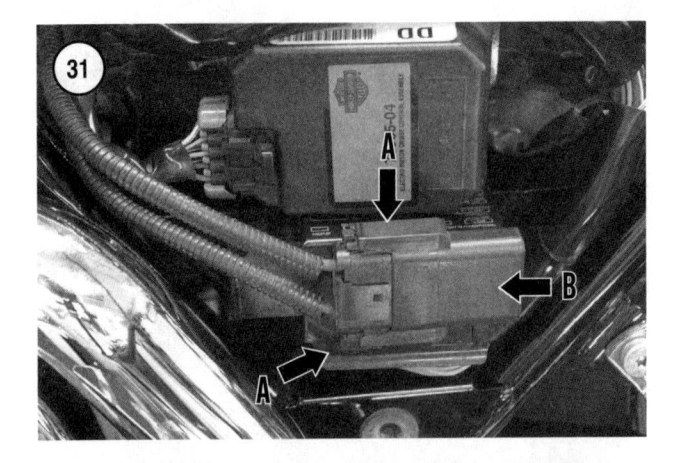

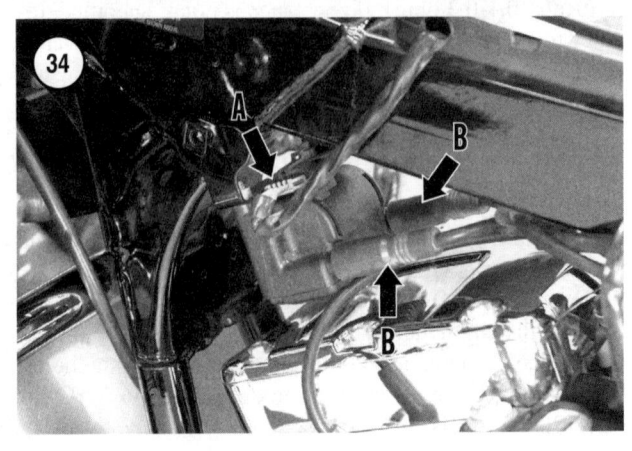

TROUBLESHOOTING

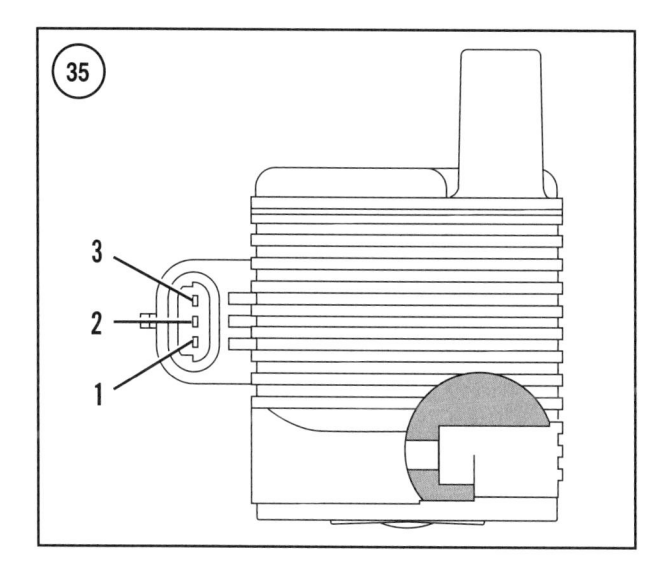

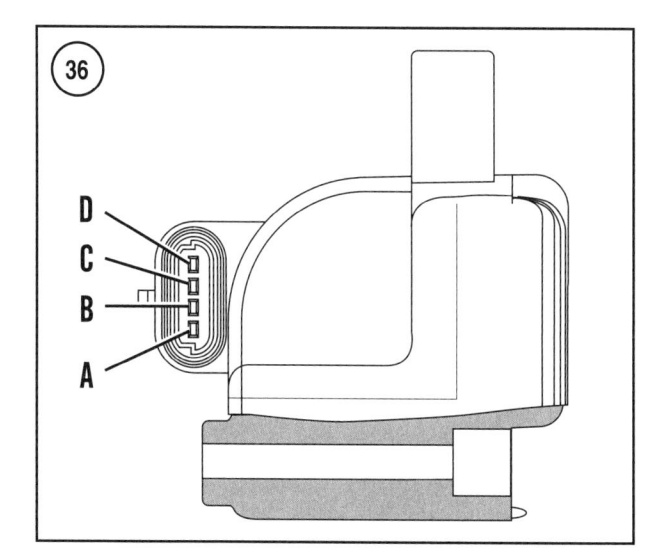

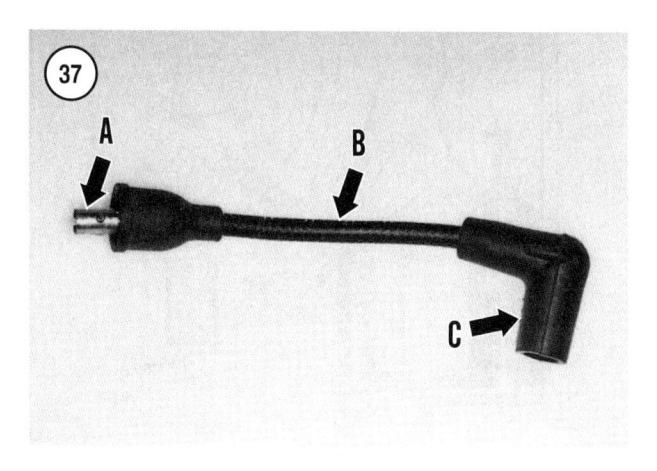

35

36

37

electrical contact cleaner. Repeat the test and if the resistance value is still high, replace the coil.
8. If the coil resistance does not meet (or come close to) either of these specifications, the coil must be replaced. If the coil exhibits visible damage, replace it as described in Chapter Eleven.
9. Install the ignition coil as described in Chapter Eleven.

Spark Plug Cable Resistance Test and Inspection

1. Remove the ignition coil as described in Chapter Eleven.
2. Disconnect the cables from the spark plug and ignition coil.
3. Measure the resistance of each spark plug cable (**Figure 37**) from end to end.
4. Compare the reading to the specification in **Table 1**. Replace the spark plug cable if the reading is not within specification.
5. Inspect the spark plug cables for:
   a. Corroded or damaged connector ends (A, **Figure 37**).
   b. Breaks in the cable insulation (B, **Figure 37**) that could allow arcing.
   c. Split or damaged plug caps (C, **Figure 37**) that could allow arcing to the cylinder heads.
6. Connect the cables onto the spark plugs and ignition coil.
7. Install ignition coil as described in Chapter Eleven.

FUEL SYSTEM (CARBURETED MODELS)

Begin fuel system troubleshooting with the fuel tank and work through the system, reserving the carburetor as the final point. Most fuel system problems result from an empty fuel tank, a plugged fuel filter or fuel valve, sour fuel, a dirty air filter or clogged carburetor jets. Do not assume that the carburetor is the problem. Unnecessary carburetor adjustments can compound the problem.

Identifying Carburetor Conditions

Refer to the following conditions to identify whether the engine is running lean or rich.

Rich

1. Fouled spark plugs.
2. Engine misfires and runs rough under load.
3. Excessive exhaust smoke as the throttle is increased.
4. An extreme rich condition results in a choked or dull sound from the exhaust and an inability to clear the exhaust with the throttle held wide open.

Lean

1. Blistered or very white spark plug electrodes.
2. Engine overheats.
3. Slow acceleration, engine power is reduced.
4. Flat spots on acceleration that are similar in feel to when the engine starts to run out of gas.
5. Engine speed fluctuates at full throttle.

Fuel Level System

The fuel level system is shown in **Figure 38**. Proper carburetor operation depends on a constant and correct carburetor fuel level. The float level in the bowl drops as fuel is drawn from the float bowl during engine operation. As the float drops, the fuel valve moves away from its seat and allows fuel to flow through the seat into the float bowl. Fuel entering the float bowl will cause the float to rise and push against the fuel valve. When the fuel level reaches a predetermined level, the fuel valve is pushed against the seat to prevent the float bowl from overfilling.

If the fuel valve fails to close, the engine will run too rich or flood with fuel. Symptoms of this problem are rough running, excessive black smoke and poor acceleration. This condition will sometimes clear up when the engine is run at wide-open throttle, as the fuel is being drawn into the engine before the float bowl can overfill. As the engine speed is reduced, however, the rich running condition returns.

Several things can cause fuel overflow. In most instances, it can be as simple a small piece of dirt trapped between the fuel valve and seat or an incorrect float level. If fuel is flowing out of the overflow tube connected to the bottom of the float bowl, the fuel valve inside the carburetor is being held open. First, check the position of the fuel shutoff valve lever. Turn the fuel shutoff valve lever off. Then, lightly tap on the carburetor float bowl and turn the fuel shutoff valve lever on. If the fuel flow stops running out of the overflow tube, whatever was holding the fuel valve off of its seat now has been dislodged. If fuel continues to flow from the overflow tube, remove and service the carburetor. Refer to Chapter Nine.

NOTE
Fuel will not flow from the vacuum-operated fuel shutoff valve until the engine is running.

Starting Enrichment (Choke) System

A cold engine requires a rich mixture to start and run properly. On all models, a cable-actuated starter enrichment valve is used for cold starting.

If the engine is difficult to start when cold, check the starting enrichment (choke) cable adjustment described in Chapter Three.

Accelerator Pump System

During sudden throttle openings the diaphragm-type accelerator pump system (**Figure 39**) provides additional fuel to the engine. Without this system, the carburetor would not be able to provide a sufficient amount of fuel.

The system consists of a spring-loaded neoprene diaphragm that is compressed during sudden acceleration by the pump lever. This movement causes the diaphragm to force fuel from the pump chamber, through a check valve and into the carburetor venturi. The diaphragm spring returns the diaphragm to the uncompressed position, which allows the chamber to refill with fuel.

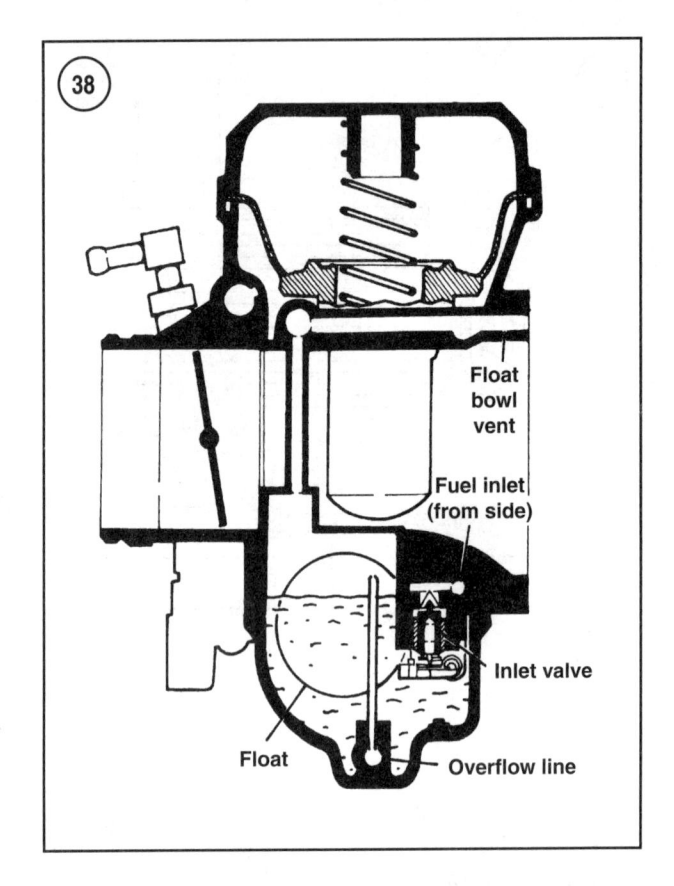

If the engine hesitates during sudden acceleration, check the operation of the accelerator pump system. Carburetor service is covered in Chapter Nine.

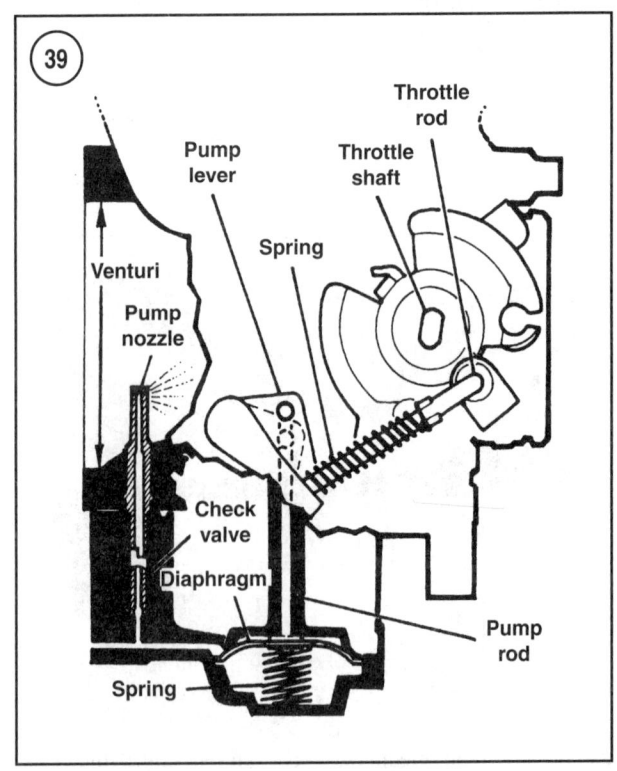

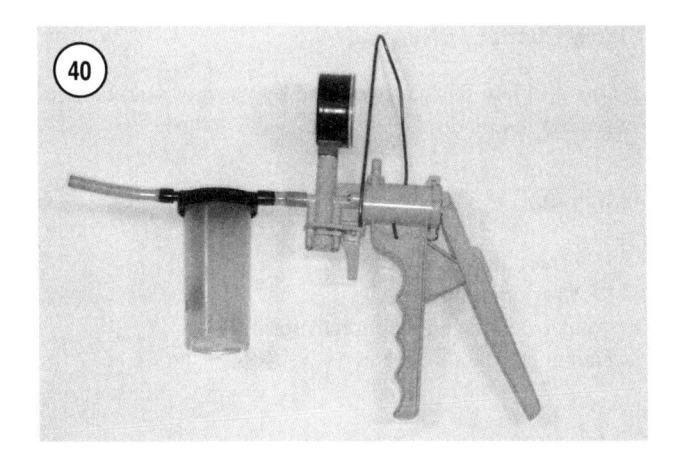

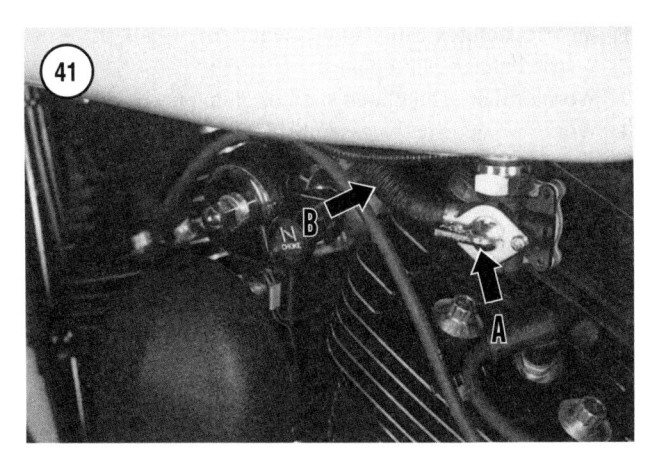

TROUBLESHOOTING

4. Connect the drain hose to the fuel shutoff valve and secure it with a hose clamp. Insert the end of the drain hose into a gas can.

WARNING
Do not perform this test if there are open flames or sparks in the area.

5. Disconnect the vacuum hose from the fuel shutoff valve.
6. Connect a hand-operated vacuum pump to the fuel shutoff valve vacuum hose nozzle.
7. Turn the fuel shutoff valve lever on.

CAUTION
Do not apply more than 25 in. (635 mm) Hg vacuum or the fuel shutoff valve diaphragm will be damaged.

8. Apply 25 in. Hg vacuum to the valve. Fuel must flow through the fuel shutoff valve when the vacuum is applied.
9. With the vacuum still applied, turn the fuel shutoff valve lever to the RES position. Fuel must continue to flow through the valve.
10. Release the vacuum and check that fuel flow stops.
11. Repeat the test five times and check that fuel flows with vacuum applied and stops flowing when the vacuum is released.
12. Turn the fuel shutoff valve off. Disconnect the vacuum pump and drain hose.
13. Reconnect the fuel hose (B, **Figure 41**) onto the fuel shutoff valve.
14. If the fuel valve failed this test, replace the fuel shutoff valve as described in Chapter Nine.

Vacuum-Operated Fuel Shutoff Valve Testing

All models are equipped with a vacuum-operated fuel shutoff valve. A vacuum hose is connected between the fuel shutoff valve diaphragm and the carburetor. When the engine is running, vacuum is applied to the fuel shutoff valve through this hose. For fuel to flow through the fuel valve, a vacuum must be present with the fuel shutoff valve in the on or reserve positions. The following steps troubleshoot the fuel shutoff valve by applying a vacuum from a separate source. A hand-operated vacuum pump (**Figure 40**), a gas can, a drain hose long enough to reach from the fuel valve to the gas can, and a hose clamp are required for this test.

WARNING
Gasoline is highly flammable. When servicing the fuel system, work in a well-ventilated area. Do not expose gasoline and gasoline vapors to sparks or other ignition sources.

1. Disconnect the negative battery cable from the battery as described in Chapter Eleven.
2. Visually check the amount of fuel in the tank. Add fuel if necessary.
3. Turn the fuel shutoff valve (A, **Figure 41**, typical) off and disconnect the fuel hose (B) from the fuel shutoff valve. Plug the open end of the hose.

FUEL SYSTEM (ELECTRONIC FUEL INJECTION)

Start troubleshooting the fuel system at the fuel tank and work throughout the fuel system reserving the fuel injecting system to the final point. Check for an empty fuel tank, a plugged filter, fuel pump failure, sour fuel or a clogged air filter element. Refer to *Starting the Engine* and *Engine Performance* in this chapter.

The fuel injection system is controlled by the electronic control module (ECM) component of the engine management system.

ENGINE LUBRICATION

An improperly operating engine lubrication system will quickly lead to engine damage. Check the engine oil level weekly as described in Chapter Three. Oil pump service is covered in Chapter Five.

Low Oil Warning Light

The low oil warning light, mounted on the indicator light panel, will come on when the ignition switch is turned to IGN before starting the engine. After the engine is started, the oil light will turn off when the engine speed is above idle.

If the low oil warning light does not come on when the ignition switch is turned to IGN and the engine is not running, check for a burned out low oil indicator light bulb as described in Chapter Eleven. If the bulb is working, check the oil pressure switch, or sender, (**Figure 42**) as described in Chapter Eleven.

On 2006 models, if the oil light remains on when the engine speed is above idle, turn the engine off and check the oil level in the oil tank. If the oil level is satisfactory, oil may not be returning to the oil tank through the return line. Check for a clogged or damaged return line or a damaged oil pump. If the bike is being operated in conditions where the ambient temperature is below freezing, ice and sludge may be blocking the oil feed pipe. This condition will prevent the oil from circulating properly.

Oil Consumption High or Engine Smokes Excessively

1. Worn valve guides.
2. Worn valve guide seals.
3. Worn or damaged piston rings.
4. Oil pan overfilled.
5. Oil filter restricted.
6. Leaking cylinder head surfaces.

Oil Fails to Return to Oil Pan

1. Oil lines or fittings restricted or damaged (2006 models only).
2. Oil pump damaged or operating incorrectly.
3. Oil pan empty.
4. Oil filter restricted.
5. Damaged oil feed pump.

Engine Oil Leaks

1. Clogged air filter breather hose.
2. Restricted or damaged oil return line to oil pan.
3. Loose engine parts.
4. Damaged gasket sealing surfaces.
5. Oil pan overfilled.
6. Restricted oil filter.
7. Plugged air filter-to-breather system hose.

CLUTCH

All clutch troubles, other than adjustments (except Screamin' Eagle models), require partial clutch disassembly to identify and cure the problem. Refer to Chapter Six for clutch service procedures.

Clutch Chatter or Noise

This problem is usually caused by worn or warped friction and plain plates.

Clutch Slip

1. Incorrect clutch adjustment.
2. Worn friction plates.
3. Weak or damaged diaphragm spring.
4. Damaged pressure plate.

Clutch Drag

1. Incorrect clutch cable adjustment.
2. Warped clutch plain plates.
3. Worn or damaged clutch shell or clutch hub.
4. Worn or incorrectly assembled clutch ball and ramp mechanism.
5. Incorrect primary chain alignment.
6. Weak or damaged diaphragm spring.

TRANSMISSION

Transmission symptoms are sometimes hard to distinguish from clutch symptoms. Refer to Chapter Seven or Chapter Eight for transmission service procedures.

Gears Will Not Stay Engaged

1. Worn or damaged shifter parts.
2. Incorrect shifter rod adjustment.
3. Severely worn or damaged gears and/or shift forks.

Difficult Shifting

1. Worn or damaged shift forks.
2. Worn or damaged shifter clutch dogs.
3. Weak or damaged shifter return spring.
4. Clutch drag.

Excessive Gear Noise

1. Worn or damaged bearings.
2. Worn or damaged gears.
3. Excessive gear backlash.

LIGHTING SYSTEM

If bulbs burn out frequently, check for excessive vibration, loose connections that permit sudden current surges, or the installation of the wrong type of bulb.

Most light and ignition problems are caused by loose or corroded ground connections. Check these prior to replacing a bulb or electrical component.

TROUBLESHOOTING

EXCESSIVE VIBRATION

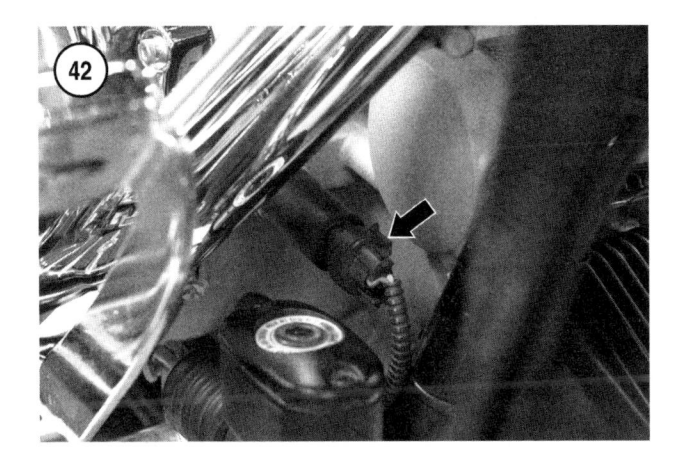

Excessive vibration is usually caused by loose engine mounting hardware. A bent axle shaft or loose suspension component will cause high-speed vibration problems. Vibration can also be caused by the following conditions:

1. Cracked or broken frame.
2. Severely worn primary chain.
3. Tight primary chain links.
4. Loose, worn or damaged engine stabilizer link(s).
5. Loose or damaged rubber mounts.
6. Improperly balanced wheel(s).
7. Defective or damaged wheel(s).
8. Defective or damaged tire(s).
9. Internal engine wear or damage.
10. Loose or worn steering head bearings.
11. Loose swing arm pivot shaft nut.

FRONT SUSPENSION AND STEERING

Poor handling may be caused by improper tire inflation pressure, a damaged or bent frame or front steering components, worn wheel bearings or dragging brakes. Possible causes for suspension and steering malfunctions are listed below.

Irregular or Wobbly Steering

1. Loose wheel axle nut(s).
2. Loose or worn steering head bearings.
3. Excessive wheel bearing play.
4. Damaged cast wheel.
5. Laced wheel out of alignment.
6. Unbalanced wheel assembly.
7. Incorrect wheel alignment.
8. Incorrect vehicle alignment.
9. Bent or damaged steering stem or frame at steering neck.
10. Tire incorrectly seated on rim.
11. Excessive front end loading from non-standard equipment.

Stiff Steering

1. Low front tire air pressure.
2. Bent or damaged steering stem or frame.
3. Loose or worn steering head bearings.

Stiff or Heavy Fork Operation

1. Incorrect fork springs.
2. Incorrect fork oil viscosity.
3. Excessive amount of fork oil.
4. Bent fork tubes.
5. Incorrect fork air pressure.

Poor Fork Operation

1. Worn or damaged fork tubes.
2. Fork oil capacity low due to leaking fork seals.
3. Bent or damaged fork tubes.
4. Contaminated fork oil.
5. Incorrect fork springs.
6. Excessive front end loading from non-standard equipment.

Poor Rear Shock Absorber Operation

1. Weak or worn springs.
2. Damper unit leaking.
3. Shock shaft worn or bent.
4. Incorrect rear shock springs.
5. Rear shocks adjusted incorrectly.
6. Excessive rear end loading from non-standard equipment.
7. Incorrect loading.
8. Incorrect rear shock air pressure.

BRAKE PROBLEMS

Perform the maintenance specified in Chapter Three to minimize brake system problems. Brake system service is covered in Chapter Fifteen. When refilling the front and rear master cylinders, use only DOT 4 brake fluid.

Insufficient Braking Power

Worn brake pads or disc, air in the hydraulic system, glazed or contaminated pads, low brake fluid level, or a leaking brake line or hose can cause this problem. Visually check for leaks. Check for worn brake pads. Check also for a leaking or damaged primary cup seal in the master cylinder. Bleed the brakes. Rebuild a leaking master cylinder or brake caliper. Brake drag will result in excessive heat and brake fade. Refer to *Brake Drag* in this section.

Spongy Brake Feel

This problem is generally caused by air in the hydraulic system. Bleed the brakes as described in Chapter Fifteen.

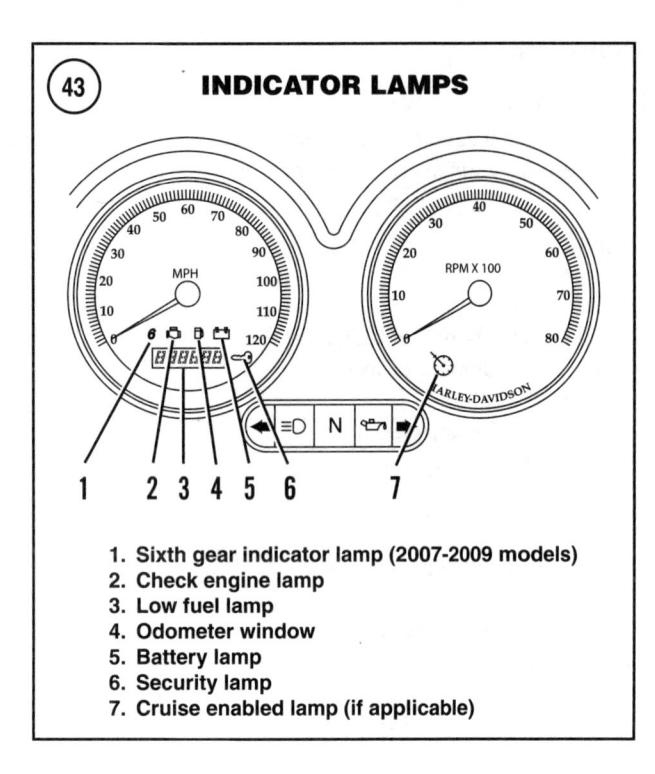

43 INDICATOR LAMPS

1. Sixth gear indicator lamp (2007-2009 models)
2. Check engine lamp
3. Low fuel lamp
4. Odometer window
5. Battery lamp
6. Security lamp
7. Cruise enabled lamp (if applicable)

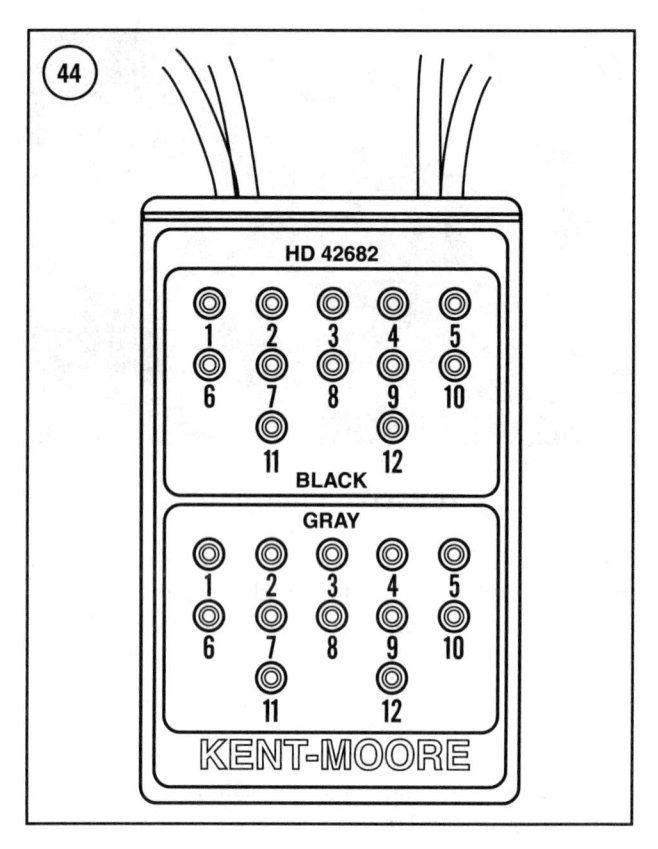

44 HD 42682 / KENT-MOORE

Brake Drag

Check for insufficient brake pedal and/or hand lever free play. Also check for worn, loose or missing parts in the brake calipers. Check the brake disc(s) for excessive runout.

Brakes Squeal or Chatter

Check brake pad thickness and disc condition. Check that the caliper anti-rattle springs are properly installed and in good condition. Clean off any dirt on the pads. Loose components can also cause this. Check for:
1. Warped brake disc.
2. Loose brake disc.
3. Loose caliper mounting bolts.
4. Loose front axle nut.
5. Worn wheel bearings.
6. Damaged hub.

ELECTRONIC DIAGNOSTIC SYSTEM (EXCEPT 2006-2007 CRUISE CONTROL)

All models are equipped with an electronic diagnostic system that monitors the operating condition of the starting, charging, instruments, TSM/TSSM, and engine management components. A serial data bus connects these components. If a malfunction occurs, a diagnostic trouble code (DTC) may be generated by the system.

The trouble code is retained in the memory of the ICM, ECM, TSM/TSSM/HFSM and speedometer. A current DTC identifies a problem that is affecting motorcycle operation now. A historic DTC identifies a problem that has been resolved either through servicing or a changed condition. Historic DTCs are retained to provide information should an intermittent problem exist. A historic DTC is retained in memory until fifty start/run cycles have occurred, at which time the DTC is erased.

Not all malfunctions cause the generation of a DTC. Refer to *No-DTC Fault* in this section.

Startup Check

The diagnostic system indicates a normal condition or an operating problem each time the ignition switch is turned to IGN.

1. During normal startup, the following occurs after the ignition switch is turned to IGN:
   a. The *check engine* lamp (2, **Figure 43**) illuminates for four seconds, and then goes out.
   b. The *security* lamp (6, **Figure 43**) illuminates for four seconds, and then goes out.
2. Note the following indications of potential problems during startup:
   a. If the check engine lamp or security lamp does not illuminate, the speedometer may be faulty. Refer to the *Initial Diagnostic Checks* DTC flow chart (located on CD inserted into back cover of manual).
   b. If the check engine lamp or security lamp illuminates after 8 seconds, a serial data bus problem may exist. Check for a DTC.
   c. If the check engine lamp or security lamp stays on, the speedometer may be faulty or a DTC exists. Refer to the *Initial Diagnostic Checks* DTC flow chart (located on CD inserted into back cover of manual).

TROUBLESHOOTING

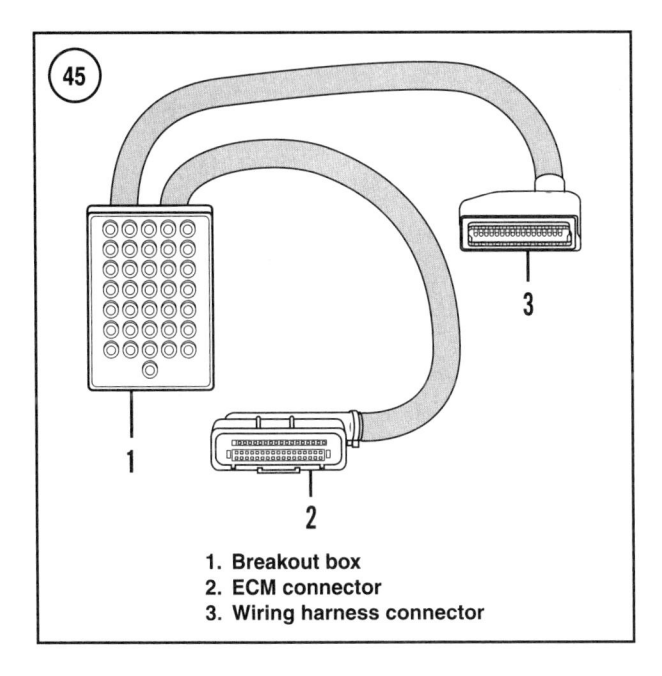

45

1. Breakout box
2. ECM connector
3. Wiring harness connector

DTC Retrieval

Trouble codes consist of a letter prefix followed by four numbers. Retrieve trouble codes by either performing the retrieval sequence with the speedometer display or by using the H-D digital technician.

The message *BusEr* is a trouble code which may appear during diagnostic troubleshooting. *BusEr* indicates a problem in the serial bus data circuit.

1. With the engine run/stop switch in the RUN position, turn the ignition switch to IGN. The following should occur:
   a. The speedometer backlighting comes on.
   b. The speedometer needle rotates to full deflection position.

NOTE
The security lamp may come on even though the motorcycle is not equipped with a security system.

   c. The indicator lamps controlled by the serial bus (battery, security and check engine) should illuminate.
2. Push and hold in the odometer reset switch on the back of the speedometer.
3. The message *diag* appears in the odometer window on the speedometer.
4. Press and release the odometer reset switch. The letter *P* will flash indicating that information concerning the ECM/ICM is obtainable. Letters are used to identify the following components:
   a. The letter *P* identifies the ECM/ICM.
   b. The letter *S* identifies the TSM/TSSM/HFSM.
   c. The letter *SP* identifies the speedometer.
   d. The letter *t* identifies the tachometer (on models so equipped).
   e. The letter *b* identifies the ABS system (on models so equipped).

5. To cycle through the *P* letter identifiers, push and quickly release the odometer reset switch. The selected component letter identifier will flash.
6. To obtain a DTC, select a component (letter identifier flashes), and then push and hold in the odometer reset switch for more than 5 seconds. Release the switch. The code will appear in the odometer window, or *none*. Record the DTC.

NOTE
When reading additional codes, push in and release the reset switch only long enough to retrieve the next code. Holding in the reset switch for more than 5 seconds will erase the codes.

7. If *none* appears, pushing and releasing the reset button causes the speedometer to diplay the part number of the selected device. As an example, the display may read *Pn 34246-08A* for the ECM.
8. Press and release the reset switch as needed to read additional trouble codes until *end* appears.
9. Turn the ignition switch off to exit the diagnostic program.

Diagnostic Tools

The Harley-Davidson digital technician (part No. HD-44750) or digital technician II (part No. HD-48650), is needed to obtain or erase historic DTCs and to reprogram a new ICM/ECM or TSM/TSSM/HFSM. At the time of publication, these tools were not available to the general public. However, many of the test procedures can be performed and provide valuable diagnostic information without the H-D digital technician. A number of aftermarket devices are available; however, we did not test them nor are the procedures written for their use. The wiring checks can be performed with commercial pin connectors that connect to the terminals and VOM meter leads. Use caution to prevent damage to the connectors.

The troubleshooting steps in some of the flowcharts require different H-D breakout boxes, harness connector test kits and harness adapters. Harness test kits allow the test lead probes to be inserted into the various terminals without damaging them.

Note the following tools:
1. 2006 carbureted models:
   a. Breakout box, part No. HD-42682 (panel colors relate to the colors of the box connectors: one pair of black and one pair of gray [**Figure 44**]).
   b. Harness connector test kit, part No. 41404A.
2. 2006 fuel-injected models:
   a. Breakout box, part No. HD-43876.
   b. Harness connector test kit, part No. 41404A.
3. 2007 models:
   a. Breakout box, part No. HD-42682 (speedometer test).
   b. Breakout box part, No. HD-43876 (EFI test [**Figure 45**]).
   c. Harness connector test kit, part No. 41404B.

d. Harness adapters, part No. 46601.
4. 2008-2009 models:
   a. Breakout box, part No. HD-42682 (speedometer test).
   b. Breakout box, part No. HD-48637 (EFI test).
   c. Breakout box, part No. HD-48642 (ABS test).
   d. Harness connector test kit, part No. 41404B.
   e. Harness adapters, part No. 46601.

Data Link Connector

The data link connector provides access to the data bus and provides a testing terminal when troubleshooting. Remove the frame right side cover as described in Chapter Seventeen, and release the data link connector (A, **Figure 46**) from the mounting bracket. Remove the cover (B, **Figure 46**) from the data link connector.

DTC Troubleshooting

A list of DTCs is found at the end of this chapter in **Table 3**, which also identifies the possible problem and a troubleshooting flowchart. Refer to the applicable flow chart in **Figures 47-181**. Procedures in the flow charts relate to all models and years unless otherwise specified. Note the following before beginning troubleshooting:
1. Before retrieving DTCs, read the information in *Initial Diagnostic Check* (this section).
2. Not all malfunctions set a DTC. If the motorcycle is not operating properly and no DTC has been set, refer to **Table 4**. Select the symptom that best describes the problem, and turn to the indicated diagnostic flow chart.
3. Check for obvious causes before undertaking what may be a complicated troubleshooting procedure. Look for loose or disconnected connectors, damaged wiring, etc.
4. The DTCs are prioritized according to importance. If multiple DTCs occur, correct the DTC with the highest priority (**Table 5**) first and continue through the list. It is possible for one fault to trigger more than one DTC.
5. Refer to the wiring diagrams located on the CD inserted into the back cover of this manual to identify connector numbers referred to in the charts. Refer to the appropriate sections in this chapter and Chapter Eleven for additional component testing.

No-DTC fault

Some malfunctions, such as fuel and starting system problems, will not trigger the generation of a DTC. In these cases, the troubleshooting guidelines found in this chapter will help locate the problem. However, there are some faults that can be diagnosed by using the procedures implemented when diagnosing a DTC. These faults may not generate a DTC, but the specified flow chart will help identify the problem. Refer to **Table 4** for a list of symptoms that do not set fault codes.

Speedometer DTC Display Inspection

Because the speedometer displays the DTCs, it may be necessary to troubleshoot it before initiating a diagnostic sequence.

Initial diagnostic check

NOTE
Be sure the engine run/stop switch is in the RUN position.

Check speedometer operation as follows:
1. During normal operation, when the ignition switch is turned to IGN, the speedometer should operate as follows:
   a. The speedometer backlighting comes on.

NOTE
The security lamp may come on even though the motorcycle is not equipped with a security system.

   b. The check engine and security lamps illuminate.
   c. The odometer display illuminates.
2. If the speedometer operates abnormally, then refer to **Figures 47-49** and follow the *Initial Diagnostic Checks* DTC flow chart.

WOW test

To ensure the speedometer is functioning correctly, perform the following procedure:
1. Push in the odometer reset switch on the back of the speedometer.
2. Turn the ignition switch to IGN, and release the odometer reset switch. Check for the following:
   a. The speedometer backlighting should come on.
   b. The speedometer needle should rotate to the full deflection position.

NOTE
The security lamp may come on even though the motorcycle is not equipped with a security system.

TROUBLESHOOTING

c. The check engine, battery and security lamps should illuminate.
d. The message *diag* should appear in the odometer window on the speedometer.

3. If the speedometer fails this test, check the wiring for the battery, ground, ignition, odometer reset switch and accessories.

CRUISE CONTROL SYSTEM DIAGNOSTIC TROUBLE CODES (2006-2007 MODELS)

The cruise control on-board diagnostic system identifies faults within the system and stores this information as a three-digit diagnostic trouble code. If more than one fault is found, it also stores any other noted codes up to the maximum of eleven trouble codes that can be set.

Diagnostic trouble codes are displayed as a series of flashes at the cruise control engaged lamp (*C*) on the face of tachometer. To retrieve the diagnostic trouble code(s), perform the following:

1. Turn the engine off.
2. On the front fairing cap, turn the cruise ON/OFF power switch off. The light in the power switch is extinguished.
3. On the right side handlebar switch, push the cruise SET/RESUME switch to SET and hold it in this position.
4. Turn the ignition switch to IGN, but do not start the engine.
5. On the right side handlebar switch, release the cruise SET/RESUME switch from the SET position while looking at the cruise control engaged lamp (*C*). The lamp will begin transmitting the stored cruise diagnostic trouble codes. Each code consists of three digits.
6. The system will flash the first digit of the stored diagnostic trouble code. The cruise control engaged lamp (*C*) will illuminate for about 1/4 of a second and then turn off for about 1/4 of a second. Count the number of flashes and record the number. For example, two blinks indicate the first digit is two.
7. The system will pause for one second and then flash the second digit of the diagnostic trouble code. Count the number of flashes, and record this number. For example, five blinks indicate the second digit is five.
8. The system will again pause for one second and then flash the third digit of the diagnostic trouble code. Count the number of flashes, and record this number. For example, three blinks indicate the third digit is three. This indicates that the first trouble code is two hundred fifty three, or an internal failure.
9. If more than one trouble code is present, the system will pause for two seconds and then flash the ready signal, which is a series of six rapid flashes. It is now ready to flash the next trouble code.
10. Refer to **Table 8** for diagnostic trouble codes to determine where the problem is located.
11. To exit the diagnostic mode, turn the ignition off.
12. The trouble codes can only be cleared by a dealership.

CRUISE CONTROL SYSTEM DIAGNOSTIC TROUBLE CODES (2008-2009 MODELS)

The cruise control on-board diagnostic system identifies faults within the system and stores this information as a diagnostic trouble code (DTC). A serial data bus connects the cruise control components and if a malfunction occurs, a diagnostic trouble code (DTC) may be generated.

Refer to *Electronic Diagnostic System (Except 2006-2007 Cruise Control)* in this chapter to identify the trouble code(s).

Table 1 ELECTRICAL SYSTEM SPECIFICATIONS

Item	Specification
ACR solenoid compression	
ACR-connector connected	130-170 psi (896-1172 kPa)
ACR-connector disconnected	200-220 psi (1379-1517 kPa)
Current draw[1]	
ECM	1.0 milliamperes
Speedometer	
2006-2006 models	0.5 milliamperes
2007-2009 models	1.0 milliamperes
Tachometer	
2006-2006 models	0.5 milliamperes
2007-2009 models	1.0 milliamperes
TSM (non-security models)	
2006-2006 models	0.5 milliamperes
2007-2009 models	1.0 milliamperes
TSSM/HFSM–disarmed	3.0 milliamperes
TSSM/HFSM–armed	3.0 milliamperes
TSSM/HSFM–storage mode	
2006-2006 models	0.5 milliamperes
2007-2009 models	1.0 milliamperes
HFSM	1.0 milliamperes
Security siren–optional	20.0 milliamperes[2]
(continued)	

Table 1 ELECTRICAL SYSTEM SPECIFICATIONS (continued)

Item	Specification
Current draw[1] (continued)	
Voltage regulator	2.0 milliamperes
Radio	2.0 milliamperes
High output amplifier	0.2 milliamperes
CB module	
2006-2006 models	0.4 milliamperes
2007-2009 models	1.0 milliamperes
XM module	
2006-2006 models	0.1 milliamperes
2007-2009 models	1.0 milliamperes
Ignition coil	
Primary resistance	
Carbureted models	0.5-0.7 ohm
EFI models	0.3-0.5 ohm
Secondary resistance	2500-3500 ohms
Sensor operational values	
ET sensor	
-4° F (-20° C)	28,144 ohms, 4.4 volts
14° F (-10° C)	15,873 ohms, 4.0 volts
32° F (0° C)	9255 ohms, 3.5 volts
50° F (10° C)	5571 ohms, 3.0 volts
68° F (20° C)	3457 ohms, 2.4 volts
77° F (25° C)	2750 ohms, 2.1 volts
86° F (30° C)	2205 ohms, 1.8 volts
104° F (40° C)	1442 ohms, 1.3 or 4.1 volts[3]
122° F (50° C)	965 ohms, 1.0 or 3.7 volts[3]
140° F (60° C)	661 ohms, 3.3 volts
158° F (70° C)	462 ohms, 2.9 volts
176° F (80° C)	329 ohms, 2.5 volts
194° F (90° C)	238 ohms, 2.1 volts
212° F (100° C)	175 ohms, 1.7 volts
IAT sensor (2006-2008 models)	
-4° F (-20° C)	29,121 ohms, 4.9 volts
14° F (-10° C)	16,599 ohms, 4.8 volts
32° F (0° C)	9750 ohms, 4.6 volts
50° F (10° C)	5970 ohms, 4.3, volts
68° F (20° C)	3747 ohms, 4.0 volts
77° F (25° C)	3000 ohms, 3.8 volts
86° F (30° C)	2417 ohms, 3.6 volts
104° F (40° C)	1598 ohms, 3.1 volts
122° F (50° C)	1080 ohms, 2.6 volts
140° F (60° C)	746 ohms, 2.2 volts
158° F (70° C)	526 ohms, 1.7 volts
176° F (80° C)	377 ohms, 1.4 volts
194° F (90° C)	275 ohms, 1.1 volts
212° F (100° C)	204 ohms, 0.9 volts
IAT/TMAP sensor (2009 models)	
-4° F (-20° C)	15,614 ohms, 4.7 volts
14° F (-10° C)	9426 ohms, 4.5 volts
32° F (0° C)	5887 ohms, 4.3 volts
50° F (10° C)	3791 ohms, 4.0, volts
68° F (20° C)	2511 ohms, 3.6 volts
77° F (25° C)	2063 ohms, 3.4 volts
86° F (30° C)	1715 ohms, 3.2 volts
104° F (40° C)	1200 ohms, 2.7 volts
122° F (50° C)	851 ohms, 2.3 volts
140° F (60° C)	612 ohms, 1.9 volts
158° F (70° C)	446 ohms, 1.5 volts
176° F (80° C)	330 ohms, 1.2 volts
194° F (90° C)	246 ohms, 1.0 volts
212° F (100° C)	186 ohms, 0.8 volts
Spark plug cable resistance	5000-11,666 ohms

1. Average reading.
2. Siren will draw for 2-24 hours from time motorcycle battery is connected and 0.05 milliamperes once siren battery is charged. Disconnect siren during milliampere draw test. Siren will draw up to 20.0 milliamperes.
3. The ECM changes scaling between 40-50° C. Voltage for the ET sensor shifts scales in that range. This provides proper sensor resolutions for all temperatures.

TROUBLESHOOTING

Table 2 TYPICAL ENGINE SCAN VALUES (EFI MODELS ONLY)

Item	Minimum value	Maximum value	Hot idle
MAP sensor (2006-2007 models)	2.95 in. Hg. (10 kPa) 0 volts	30.71 in. Hg (104 kPa) 5.1 volts	10.3-13.3 in. Hg (35-45 kPa)
TMAP sensor (2008-2009 models)	3.04 in. Hg (10.3 kPa) 0 volts	30.71 in. Hg (104 kPa) 5.1 volts	10.3-13.3 in. Hg (35-45 kPa)
TP sensor (2006-2007 models)[1]	0 0.2 volts	100 4.5 volts	0% 0.2-1.0 volts
IAC pintle (2006-2007 models)[2]	0	155	30-45 steps
RPM	800	5600	975
ECT sensor	3° F (-16° C) 0 volts	464° F (240° C) 5.0 volts	230-300° F (110-149° C) 0.5-1.5 volts
IAT sensor (2006-2007 models)[3]	3° F (-16° C) 0 volts	248° F (120° C) 5.1 volts	104-140° F (40-60° C) 2.2-3.7 volts
Front injector pulse width	0	50 millisecond	2-4 millisecond
Rear injector pulse width	0	50 millisecond	2-4 millisecond
Ignition timing			
Advance			
Front			
2006-2007 models	0	50°	10-15°
2008-2009 models	-4	45°	12-24°
Rear			
2006-2007 models	0	50°	10-15°
2008-2009 models	-4	45°	12-24°
VSS	0	120	0 mph
Battery voltage	10 volts	15 volts	14.5 volts
Idle speed			
2006-2007 models	800 rpm	1300 rpm	940-975 rpm
2008-2009 models	975 rpm	1450 rpm	975-1025 rpm

1. The throttle position is controlled by the twist grip, therefore no specification.
2. Not equipped on 2008-2009 models
3. IAT is part of TMAP sensor on 2008-2009 models.

Table 3 DIAGNOSTIC TROUBLE CODES

DTC	Problem	Diagnostic Flow Chart
BUS Er	Engine starts, and then stalls (2006 carbureted models)	Figure 64
BUS Er	Engine starts, and then stalls (2006-2007 EFI models)	Figure 63
BUS Er	Engine starts, and then stalls (2008-2009 EFI models)	Figure 65
B0563	Battery voltage high. Replace the TSM/TSSM/HFSM*	
B1004	Fuel level sender low (2006-2007 models)	Figure 51
B1004	Fuel level sender low (2008-2009 models)	Figure 52
B1005	Fuel level sender unit high/open (2006-2007 models)	Figure 53
B1005	Fuel level sender unit high/open (2008-2009 models)	Figure 54
B1006	Accessory or ignition line over voltage	Figure 55
B1007	Accessory or ignition line over voltage	Figure 55
B1008	Odometer reset switch closed	Figure 56
B1121	Turn signals will not flash; 4-way flasher inoperable	Figure 72
B1122	Turn signals will not flash; 4-way flasher inoperable	Figure 72
B1123	Left or tight turn signal short to ground	Figure 75
B1124	Left or tight turn signal short to ground	Figure 75
B1125	Left or right turn signal short to voltage	Figure 76
B1126	Left or right turn signal short to voltage	Figure 76
B1131	Alarm output low	Figure 77
B1132	Alarm output high	Figure 77
B1134	Starter output high	Figure 78
B1141	Turn signals will not flash; 4-way flasher inoperable	Figure 72
B1141	Turn signals will not flash, no codes (HFSM models only)	Figure 73
B1143	Security antenna short to ground	Figure 79
(continued)		

Table 3 DIAGNOSTIC TROUBLE CODES (continued)

DTC	Problem	Diagnostic Flow Chart
B1144	Security antenna short to voltage	Figure 80
B1145	Security antenna open	Figure 81
B1154	Clutch switch short to ground	Figure 82
B1155	Neutral switch short to ground	Figure 83
C0562	ABS device voltage low (2008-2009 models)	Figure 167
C0563	ABS device voltage high (2008-2009 models)	Figure 168
C1014	ABS ECU internal fault (2008-2009 models)	Figure 181
C1017	ABS brake pump motor power circuit open (2008-2009 models)	Figure 169
C1018	ABS brake pump motor ground high resistance (2008-2009 models)	Figure 170
C1021	ABS brake wheel sensor equals zero–front wheel (2008-2009 models)	Figure 171
C1023	ABS brake wheel sensor equals zero–rear wheel (2008-2009 models)	Figure 171
C1025	ABS brake wheel sensor intermittent or frequency out of range (front wheel) (2008-2009 models)	Figure 172
C1027	ABS brake wheel sensor intermittent or frequency out of range (rear wheel) (2008-2009 models)	Figure 172
C1032	ABS brake wheel sensor circuit open or shorted–front and rear (2008-2009 models)	Figure 173
C1034	ABS brake wheel sensor circuit open or shorted–front and rear (2008-2009 models)	Figure 173
C1055-1066	ABS ECU internal fault (2008-2009 models)	Figure 181
C1094	ABS front brake switch always on (2008-2009 models)	Figure 174
C1095	ABS front brake switch open (2008-2009 models)	Figure 175
C1118	ABS ECU internal fault (2008-2009 models)	Figure 181
C1121	ABS ECU internal fault (2008-2009 models)	Figure 181
C1151	ABS front wheel release too long (2008-2009 models)	Figure 176
C1153	ABS rear wheel release too long (2008-2009 models)	Figure 177
C1206	ABS brake wheel sensor intermittent or frequency out of range–front wheel (2008-2009 models)	Figure 172
C1208	ABS brake wheel sensor intermittent or frequency out of range–rear wheel (2008-2009 models)	Figure 172
C1212	ABS front and rear brake not applied on deceleration (2008-2009 models)	Figure 178
C1214	ABS rear brake switch always on (2008-2009 models)	Figure 179
C1216	ABS rear brake switch open (2008-2009 models)	Figure 180
P0106	MAP sensor error (carbureted models)	Figure 90
P0106	MAP sensor error (2006-2007 EFI models)	Figure 91
P0107	MAP sensor failed open/low (carbureted models)	Figure 90
P0107	MAP sensor failed open/low (2006-2007 EFI models)	Figure 91
P0107	MAP portion of TMAP sensor open/low (2008-2009 EFI models)	Figure 92
P0107	MAP portion of TMAP sensor high (2008-2009 EFI models)	Figure 92
P0108	MAP sensor failed high (carbureted models)	Figure 90
P0108	MAP sensor failed high (2006-2007 EFI models)	Figure 91
P0112	IAT sensor voltage low (2006-2007 models)	Figure 114
P0112	IAT portion of TMAP sensor low (2008-2009 models)	Figure 115
P0113	IAT sensor open/high (2006-2007 models)	Figure 115
P0113	IAT portion of TMAP sensor open/high (2008-2009 models)	Figure 115
P0117	ET sensor voltage low	Figure 116
P0118	ET sensor open/high	Figure 116
P0120	TP sensor TPS1/TPS2 range error (2008-2009 models)	Figure 118
P0122	TP sensor open/low (2006-2007 models)	Figure 117
P0122	Throttle position (TP) sensor TPS1/TPS2 low/open (2008-2009 models)	Figure 120
P0123	Throttle position (TP) sensor TPS1/TPS2 high (2008-2009 models)	Figure 119
P0131	O2 sensor (front) fault low or engine running lean	Figure 122
P0132	Engine running rich	Figure 122
P0134	O2 sensor (front) open/not responding/high	Figure 122
P0151	O2 sensor (rear) low or engine running lean	Figure 122
P0152	Engine running rich	Figure 122
P0154	O2 sensor (rear) open/not responding/high	Figure 122
P0220	TP sensor TPS1/TPS2 range error (2008-2009 models)	Figure 118
P0222	Throttle position (TP) sensor TPS1/TPS2 low/open (2008-2009 models)	Figure 120
P0223	Throttle position (TP) sensor TPS1/TPS2 high (2008-2009 models)	Figure 119
P0261	Front injector–front open/low	Figure 121
P0262	Fuel injector–front high	Figure 121
P0263	Fuel injector–rear open/low	Figure 121
P0264	Fuel injector–rear high	Figure 121
P0371	Crankshaft position sensor (CKP) sensor shorted high (carbureted models)	Figure 93
P0372	Crankshaft position sensor (CKP) sensor shorted low (carbureted models)	Figure 93

(continued)

TROUBLESHOOTING

Table 3 DIAGNOSTIC TROUBLE CODES (continued)

DTC	Problem	Diagnostic Flow Chart
P0374	Crankshaft position sensor (CKP) SYNC error (carbureted models)	Figure 93
P0373	Crankshaft position sensor (CKP) intermittent (2006-2007 EFI models)	Figure 94
P0374	Crankshaft position sensor (CKP) SYN error (2006-2007 EFI models)	Figure 94
P0373	Crankshaft position sensor (CKP) intermittent (2008-2009 EFI models)	Figure 95
P0374	Crankshaft position sensor (CKP) SYN error (2008-2009 EFI models)	Figure 95
P0501	VSS sensor low (carbureted models)	Figure 96
P0502	VSS sensor high/open (carbureted models)	Figure 96
P0501	VSS sensor low (2006-2007 EFI models)	Figure 97
P0502	VSS sensor high/open (2006-2007 EFI models)	Figure 97
P0501	VSS sensor low (2008-2009 EFI models)	Figure 98
P0502	VSS sensor high/open (2008-2009 EFI models)	Figure 98
P0505	Loss of idle speed control (2006-2007 models)	Figure 112
P0562	Battery voltage low (carbureted models)	Figure 99
P0563	Battery voltage high (carbureted models)	Figure 99
P0562	Battery voltage low (EFI models)	Figure 100
P0563	Battery voltage high (EFI models)	Figure 100
P0572	Brake switch input error (2008-2009 models)	Figure 101
P0577	Cruise control inoperative (2008 models)	Figure 163
P0577	Cruise control inoperative (2009 models)	Figure 164
P0602	Calibration memory error	Replace the ICM1
P0603	EE-PROM error	Replace the ICM or ECM1
P0604	RAM failure	Replace the ICM1
P0605	Flash memory error	Replace the ICM or ECM1
P0607	A to D converter error	Replace the ICM1
P0661	Active intake solenoid open/low (2007 HDI models)	Figure 123
P0662	Active intake solenoid high/shorted (2007 HDI models)	Figure 123
P1001	System relay coil open/low (EFI models)	Figure 108
P1002	System relay coil high/shorted (EFI models)	Figure 109
P1003	System relay contacts open (EFI models)	Figure 108
P1004	System relay contacts closed (EFI models)	Figure 110
P1009	Incorrect password	Figure 102
P1010	Missing password	Figure 102
P1351	Ignition coil open/low (carbureted models)	Figure 103
P1351	Ignition coil open/low (2006-2007 EFI models)	Figure 104
P1351	Ignition coil open/low (2008-2009 EFI models)	Figure 105
P1352	Ignition coil high/shorted (carbureted models)	Figure 103
P1352	Ignition coil high/shorted (2006-2007 EFI models)	Figure 104
P1352	Ignition coil high/shorted (2008-2009 EFI models)	Figure 105
P1353	Combustion absent–front cylinder (EFI models)	Figure 113
P1354	Ignition coil open/low (carbureted models)	Figure 103
P1354	Ignition coil open/low (2006-2007 EFI models)	Figure 104
P1354	Ignition coil high/shorted (2008-2009 EFI models)	Figure 105
P1355	Ignition coil high/shorted (carbureted models)	Figure 103
P1355	Ignition coil high/shorted (2006-2007 EFI models)	Figure 104
P1355	Ignition coil high/shorted (2008-2009 EFI models)	Figure 105
P1356	Combustion absent–rear cylinder (EFI models)	Figure 113
P1357	Combustion intermittent–front cylinder (EFI models)	Figure 113
P1358	Combustion intermittent–rear cylinder (EFI models)	Figure 113
P1475	Exhaust actuation position error (2007-2009 HDI models)	Figure 124
P1477	Exhaust actuator open/low (2007-2009 HDI models)	Figure 124
P1478	Exhaust actuator high (2007-2009 HDI models)	Figure 124
P1501	Jiffy stand sensor low (2008-2009 HDI models)	Figure 126
P1502	Jiffy stand sensor high (2008-2009 HDI models)	Figure 127
P1510	Throttle actuation control management (limited performance mode)	Figure 128
P1511	Throttle actuation control management (power management mode)	Figure 128
P1512	Throttle actuation control (forced idle mode)	Figure 128
P2100	Throttle actuation control/motor open (2008-2009 models)	Figure 129
P2101	Throttle actuation control/motor circuit (actuation error) (2008-2009 models)	Figure 129
P2102	Throttle actuation control motor control circuit shorted low (2008-2009 models)	Figure 129
P2103	Throttle actuation control motor control circuit shorted high (2008-2009 models)	Figure 129
P2105	Throttle actuation control/forced engine shutdown (2008-2009 models)	Figure 130
P2107	Throttle actuation control diagnosis (2008-2009 models)	Figure 131
P2122	Throttle twist grip sensor TSG1–open/low (2008-2009 models)	Figure 135
P2123	Throttle twist grip sensor TSG1–high (2008-2009 models)	Figure 135
P2127	Throttle twist grip sensor TSG2–open/low (2008-2009 models)	Figure 135
P2128	Throttle twist grip sensor TSG2–high (2008-2009 models)	Figure 135

(continued)

Table 3 DIAGNOSTIC TROUBLE CODES (continued)

DTC	Problem	Diagnostic Flow Chart
P2135	Throttle actuation control correlation error (2008-2009 models)	Figure 132
P2138	Throttle actuation control correlation error (2008-2009 models)	Figure 132
P2170	Twist grip sensor validation error (2008-2009 models)	Figure 133
P2176	Throttle actuation control: close position not learned (2008-2009 models)	Figure 134
U1016	Loss of ICM/ECM serial data or serial data error (2006-2007 models)	Figure 57
U1016	Loss of ECM serial data or serial data error (2008-2009 models)	Figure 58
U1064	Loss of TSM/TSSM/HFSM serial data or serial data error	Figure 59
U1097	Loss of speedometer serial data (EFI models)	Figure 62
U1255	Loss of speedometer serial data or serial data error (carbureted models)	Figure 60
U1255	Loss of speedometer serial data or serial data error (EFI models)	Figure 61
U1255	ECM serial data error/missing	Figure 57, Figure 58
U1255	TSM/TSSM/HFSM serial data error/missing	Figure 59
U1255	Speedometer serial data error/missing (carbureted models)	Figure 60, Figure 61
U1300	Engine starts then stalls (2006-2007 EFI models)	Figure 63
U1300	Engine starts then stalls (2006 carbureted models)	Figure 64
U1300	Engine starts then stalls (2008-2009 EFI models)	Figure 65
U1301	Engine starts then stalls (2006-2007 EFI models)	Figure 63
U1301	Engine starts then stalls (2006 carbureted models)	Figure 64
U1301	Engine starts then stalls (2008-2009 EFI models)	Figure 65

*The code indicates a failure that requires replacement of this device.

Table 4 SYMPTOMS THAT DO NOT SET DTC CODES

Item	Diagnostic Flow Chart
ABS initial diagnostic check (2008-2009 models)	Figure 165
ABS indicator always on or inoperative (2008-2009 models)	Figure 166
ACR diagnostics (2007-2008 Screamin' Eagle models)	Figure 145
ARC solenoid low or open (2009 Screamin' Eagle models)	Figure 146
ARC solenoid high or shorted (2009 Screamin' Eagle models)	Figure 147
Charging system test: battery discharged	Figure 136
Cruise control (2006-2007 models)	
No front or rear brake lights (FLHRC models)	Figure 162
No front or rear brake lights (FLHTCU and FLTR models)	Figure 161
Cruise engaged lamp power	Figure 157
Resume switch	Figure 158
Cruise control unique codes other than DTC (2006-2007 models)	
Code 112: Throttle switch	Figure 159
Code 113: Cruise control enable (FLHRC models)	Figure 152
Code 113: Cruise control enable (FLHTCU and FLTR models)	Figure 153
Code 121, 211, 212: Initial diagnosis (FLHRC models)	Figure 150
Code 121, 211, 212: Initial diagnosis (FLHTCU and FLTR models)	Figure 151
Code 122: Brake light on	Figure 160
Code 213, 221, 222, 223: Speedometer input	Figure 154
Code 231, 232, 242: Tachometer input (models so equipped)	Figure 155
Code 341: Cruise power	Figure 156
Engine cranks, but will not start (carbureted models)	Figure 88
Engine cranks, but will not start (EFI models)	Figure 89
Fuel pressure check (EFI models)	Figure 111
Fuel system electrical test (2006 EFI models)	Figure 106
Fuel system electrical test (2007-2009 EFI models)	Figure 107
Heated handgrip diagnosis (Screamin' Eagle models)	Figure 149
Heated seat diagnosis (Screamin' Eagle models)	Figure 148
HFSM fails to disarm (HFSM models only)	Figure 69
High beam or turn signal indicator does not function	Figure 50
Initial diagnostic check	Figure 47
No ECM power (EFI models)	Figure 85
No spark/no ICM power (carbureted models)	Figure 84
Misfire at idle or under load (carbureted models)	Figure 86
Misfire at idle or under load (EFI models)	Figure 87
Oil pressure or neutral indicator does not function	Figure 49
Speedometer self diagnosis	Figure 48
Security symbol does not light when ignition key is turned on (2006 models)	Figure 66
Security lamp on continuously (2006 models)	Figure 67
Side Stand displayed in odometer (2008-2009 HDI models)	Figure 125

(continued)

TROUBLESHOOTING

Table 4 SYMPTOMS THAT DO NOT SET DTC CODES (continued)

Item	Diagnostic Flow Chart
Starter Test 1: initial	Figure 137
Starter Test 2: solenoid clicks	Figure 138
Starter Test 3: relay clicks	Figure 139
Starter Test 4: nothing clicks (2006 models)	Figure 140
Starter Test 4: nothing clicks (2007-2009 models)	Figure 141
Starter Test 5: starter spins, but does not engage	Figure 142
Starter Test 6: starter stalls or spins too slowly	Figure 143
Tachometer inoperative	Figure 144
Turn signals flash at double normal rate; all bulbs work.	Figure 71
Turn signals cancel erratically or do not cancel upon completion of a turn	Figure 70
Weak or no key fob signal to TSM/TSSM (2006 models)	Figure 68

Table 5 MULTIPLE DTC PRIORITY*

Ranking	Speedometer	TSM	TSSM/HFSM	ICM	ECM
1	BUS Er	BUS Er	U1300	P0605	P0605
2	U1300	U1300	U1301	P0603	P0603
3	U1301	U1301	U1016	P0602	BUS Er
4	U1016	U1016	U1255	P0604	U1300 (ECM serial data low)
5	U1064	U1097	B1142	P0607	U1301 (ECM serial data open/high)
6	U1255	U1255	B1135	BUS Er	U1300 (TSM/TSSM/HFSM serial data low)
7	B1007	B1135	B1136	U1300	U1301 (TSM/TSSM/HFSM serial data open/high)
8	B1006	B1151	B1154	U1301	U1300 (Speedometer serial data low)
9	B1008	B1152	B1154	U1064	U1301 (Speedometer serial data open/high)
10	B1004	B1153	B1134	U1097	U1064 (Loss of TSM/TSSM/HFSM serial data at ECM)
11	B1005	B1134	B1121	U1255 (missing response at TSM/TSSM)	U1064 (Loss of TSM/TSSM/HFSM serial data at speedometer)
12		B1121	B1122	U1255 (missing response at speedometer)	U1016
13		B1122	B1123	P1009	U1097
14		B0563	B1124	P1010	U1255 (Missing response at TSM/TSSM/HFSM)
15		B1131	B1125	P0371	U1255 (Missing response at speedometer)
16		B1132	B1126	P0372	P1003
17		B1141	B1143	P0374	P1002
18			B1144	P0106	P1001

(continued)

Table 5 MULTIPLE DTC PRIORITY* (continued)

Ranking	Speedometer	TSM	TSSM/HFSM	ICM	ECM
19			B1145	P0107	P1004
20			B0563	P0108	P1009
21			B1131	P1351	P1010
22			B1132	P1354	P0373
23			B1141	P1352	P0374
24				P1355	P0122
25				P0562	P0123
26				P0563	P0107
27				P0501	P0108
28				P0502	P1501
29					P1502
30					P0117
31					P0118
32					P0112
33					P0113
34					P1351
35					P1354
36					P1352
37					P1355
38					P1357
39					P1358
40					P0261
41					P0263
42					P0262
43					P0264
44					P0562
45					P0563
46					P0501
47					P0502
48					P1365
49					P1353
50					P0505
51					P1475
52					P1477
53					P1478
54					P0661
55					P0662
56					P0131
57					P0151
58					P0132
59					P0152
60					P0134
61					P0154

*Does not include ABS or cruise control codes.

Table 6 ABS DTC PRIORITY (2008-2009 MODELS)

Ranking	DTC	Fault condition
8	C1118	ECU internal fault
9	C1121	ECU internal fault
10	C1014	ECU internal fault
15	C1158	Calibration programming required
16	C1018	Pump motor ground high resistance fault
17	C1017	Pump motor power circuit open fault
18	C0562	Device voltage low
19	C0563	Device voltage high
20	C1032	Front wheel speed sensor circuit open or shorted
21	C1034	Rear wheel speed sensor circuit open or shorted
22	C1021	Front wheel speed sensor equals zero
23	C1023	Rear wheel speed sensor equals zero
24	C1025	Front wheel speed signal intermittent
25	C1027	Rear wheel speed signal intermittent
26	C1206	Wheel speed sensor frequency out of range

(continued)

TROUBLESHOOTING

Table 6 ABS DTC PRIORITY (2008-2009 MODELS) (continued)

Ranking	DTC	Fault condition
27	C1208	Wheel speed sensor frequency out of range
28	C1094	Front brake switch always on
29	C1095	Front brake switch open
30	C1214	Rear brake switch always on
31	C1216	Rear brake switch open
32	C1212	Front or rear brake not applied with deceleration
33	C1151	Front wheel release too long
34	C1153	Rear wheel release too long

Table 7 DEVICE PART NUMBERS

Device	2006	2007	2008	2009
TSM/HFSM	68921-01C	68920-07	68920-07	68920-07
TSSM (HDI)	68924-00C	68924-07	68924-07	68922-07
		68922-07	68922-07	68924-07
Remote control fob	68926-00	68926-07	68926-07	68926-07
Remote control fob (HDI)	68927-00	68926-07	68939-00	68939-00
Security system	68922-00C	68922-07	68924-07	68926-07
Siren (HDI)	68958-00	68958-00	68958-07A	68958-07A
ICM	32622-04A	–	–	–
ECM	32534-05A	32534-05B	34246-08	34246-08A

Table 8 CRUISE INOPERATIVE DIAGNOSIS (2006-2007 MODELS)*

NO	ACTION	CORRECT FUNCTION	INCORRECT FUNCTION
1.	Enter the diagnostic code: Turn CRUISE/OFF switch on. Turn SET/RESUME switch to set. Turn ignition on.	The cruise engaged lamp will illuminate and remain on as song as the SET/RESUME switch is held in the SET position. Continue to Step 2.	If the cruise engaged lamp remains illuminated after the switch is released, then eight the switch or related wiring is shorted
2.	Turn SET/RESUME switch to RESUME and hold in this position.	The cruise engaged lamp will illuminate and remain on as long as the SET/RESUME switch is held in the RESUME position. Continue to Step 3.	If the cruise engaged lamp does not illuminate at all, check for one or more of the following conditions: • Resume switch wired incorrectly. • Broken or pinch wire to RESUME switch or cruise control module. Refer to **Figure 158**.
3.	Turn the throttle grip tightly closed. Check the throttle switch.	The cruise engaged lamp will illuminate as the throttle switch is closed, and then it goes out when the throttle grip returns to the free position. Continue to Step 4.	If the cruise engaged lamp does not illuminate at all, check for one or more of the following conditions: • Throttle grip switch wired incorrectly. • Broken or pinched wire to throttle grip switch or cruise control module. • Throttle grip switch not working correctly. Refer to **Figure 159**.
4.	Apply front brake lever.	The cruise engage lamp will illuminate and remain on until the brake lever is released. Continue to Step 5.	If the cruise engaged lamp does not illuminate at all, check for one or more of the following conditions: • Front brake switch wired incorrectly. • Broken or pinched wire to front brake switch or cruise control module.

(continued)

Table 8 CRUISE INOPERATIVE DIAGNOSIS (2006-2007 MODELS)* (continued)

NO	ACTION	CORRECT FUNCTION	INCORRECT FUNCTION
4. (continued)			• Front brake switch not working properly. Refer to **Figure 160** or **Figure 161**.
5.	Apply the rear brake pedal and hold for at least 5 seconds.	The cruise engage lamp will illuminate while the brake pedal is applied for 5 seconds and will then go out. Release the brake pedal. The cruise control module will momentarily pull the throttle open slightly and then release. Continue to Step 6.	The cruise engaged lamp will not illuminate if any of the following conditions are present: • Rear brake light wired incorrectly. • Broken or pinched wire to front brake switch or cruise control module. • Rear brake switch not working properly. The throttle will not open if the following conditions are present: • Throttle cables not adjusted correctly. • Faulty cruise control module. Refer to **Figure 160** or **Figure 161**.
6.	Rotate rear wheel.	The cruise engaged lamp will flash on and off indicating the vehicle speed signal is wired correctly and working correctly. Continue to Step 7.	The cruise engaged lamp will not illuminate if any of the following conditions are present: • Vehicle speed signal is wired incorrectly. • Broken or pinched wire to speedometer. • Vehicle speed signal disconnected. Refer to **Figure 154**.
7.	Turn cruise ON/OFF switch off. Turn the ignition switch off. Disconnect both spark plug wires.	Continue to Step 8.	
8.	Turn the SET/RESUME switch to RESUME and hold it in this position.	Continue to Step 9.	
9.	Turn ignition switch to IGN. Turn the SET/RESUME switch to RESUME and hold it in this position. Crank the engine (battery must be fully charged to provide accurate test results).	The cruise engaged lamp will flash with the input of the engine RPM. Continue to Step 10.	The cruise engaged lamp does not flash with engine rpm input. Refer to **Figure 154**.
10.	Turn the SET/RESUME switch to RESUME and hold it in this position. Turn cruise ON/OFF switch on. Release the SET/RESUME switch.	Cruise engaged lamp blinks twice. NOTE: Lamp may go on for 3 seconds. If RPM signal was above cranking speed. Diagnostic routine exited.	
11.	To restart or repeat the diagnostic sequence, return to Step 1.		

*Correctly adjust the throttle cables (Chapter Three) prior to starting this diagnostic procedure. If the throttle roll off switch is *not* continually closed, the results may be inaccurate.

CHAPTER THREE

LUBRICATION, MAINTENANCE AND TUNE-UP

This chapter describes lubrication, maintenance and tune-up procedures.

During the inspection procedures in this chapter, compare the measurements taken to the maintenance and tune-up specifications in the tables at the end of this chapter. Replace any part that is damaged, worn or out of specification. During assembly, tighten fasteners as specified.

Refer to **Tables 1-7** located at the end of this chapter for specifications.

MAINTENANCE INTERVALS

Refer to **Table 1** for the maintenance intervals. Adherence to these recommendations helps ensure a long service life from the motorcycle. If the motorcycle is operated in high humidity, extreme temperatures, continuous stop and go traffic, areas of blowing dirt or other extreme elements, consider performing service more frequently.

PRE-RIDE INSPECTION

1. Check wheel and tire condition. Check tire pressure. Refer to *Tires and Wheels* in this chapter.
2. Check engine for oil leaks. If necessary, add oil as described in this chapter.
3. Check brake fluid level and condition. If necessary, add fluid as described in this chapter.
4. On Screamin' Eagle models, check clutch fluid level and condition. If necessary, add fluid as described in this chapter.
5. Check the operation of the front and rear brakes.
6A. On all models except Screamin' Eagle, check clutch operation. If necessary, adjust the clutch as described in this chapter.
6B. On Screamin' Eagle models, check clutch operation. If necessary, bleed the clutch hydraulic system as described in Chapter Six.
7. Check the throttle operation. The throttle should move smoothly and return quickly when released. On 2006-2007 models, adjust throttle cable free play as described in this chapter if necessary.
8. Inspect the front and rear suspension. They should have a solid feel with no looseness.
9. Check the exhaust system for leaks or damage.
10. Inspect the fuel system for leaks.
11. Check drive belt deflection as described in this chapter.
12. With the ignition switch turned to IGN, check the following.
    a. Pull the front brake lever and check that the brake light comes on.
    b. Push the rear brake pedal down and check that the brake light comes on soon after the pedal has been depressed.
    c. Make sure the headlight and taillight are on.
    d. Press the dimmer switch and make sure the headlight elements are working in both the high and low positions.
    e. Push the right and left turn signal switches and make sure all four turn signal lights are working.
    f. Check that all accessory lights work properly, if so equipped.
    g. Check the horn switch operation.

h. If the horn or any light fails to work properly, refer to Chapter Eleven.

TIRES AND WHEELS

Tire Pressure

Check the tire pressure often to maintain tire performance and prevent unnecessary tire wear.

Refer to **Table 2** for original equipment tire pressure.

Tire Inspection

Inspect the tires periodically for excessive wear, deep cuts and imbedded objects such as stones or nails. If a nail or other object is found in a tire, mark its location with a light crayon prior to removing the object.

Measure the depth (**Figure 1**) with a tread depth gauge or a small ruler. As a guideline, replace tires when the tread wear indicator bars appear on the tread surface and when the tread depth is 1/32 in. (0. 8 mm.) or less. Locate the arrows on the sidewall indicating the location of the tread wear indicators. Refer to Chapter Twelve for tire changing and repair information.

Spoke Tension

Check laced wheels for loose or damaged spokes. Refer to Chapter Twelve for wheel service.

Wheel Inspection

Check the wheel for cracks and other damage. Refer to Chapter Twelve for wheel service.

SCREAMIN' EAGLE LUBRICATION

Engine, Transmission and Primary Chaincase Oil Recommendations

All new Screamin' Eagle models use Screamin' Eagle SYN3 synthetic motorcycle lubricant. If additional oil must be added to correct oil level, and the SYN3 oil is not available, *temporarily* add the correct viscosity of HD-360 motor oil. Although both types of lubricant are compatible, the intermixed lubricant should be changed as soon as possible. If SYN3 is not going to be used permanently, completely drain the engine, transmission or primary chaincase oil and use in another type of oil recommended in **Table 4**.

ENGINE OIL AND FILTER

Oil Level Check

Check the engine oil level with the dipstick/oil filler cap located in the transmission/oil tank case cover.

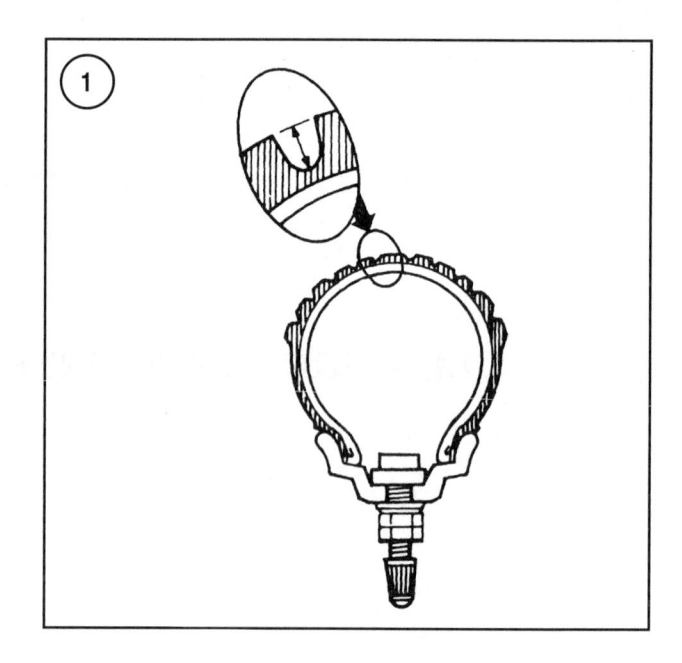

CAUTION
On 2006 models, if the oil level is overfilled, the oil filler cap/dipstick will pop out when the oil becomes hot.

NOTE
On 2006 models, check the vent hose and interconnecting hoses for swelling, cracks or damage and replace immediately. Make sure the interconnecting hose clamps are secure.

Engine hot

1. Ride the motorcycle until the engine is at normal operating temperature.
2. Place the motorcycle on a level surface and park it on the jiffy stand, and allow the engine to idle for 1-2 minutes. Turn off the engine and leave the motorcycle resting on the jiffy stand.

CAUTION
Holding the motorcycle straight up will result in an incorrect oil level reading.

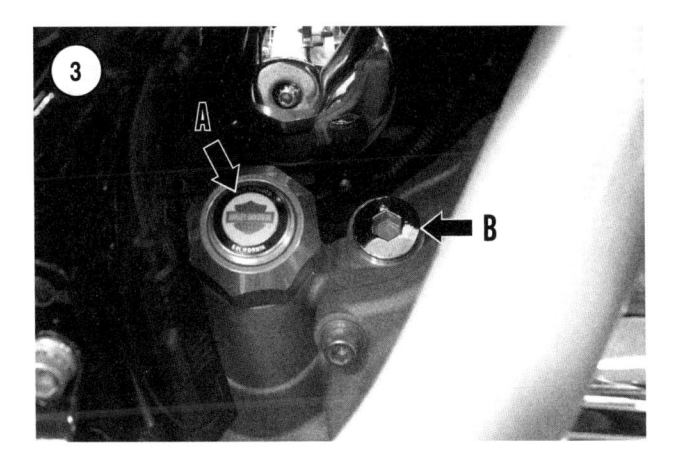

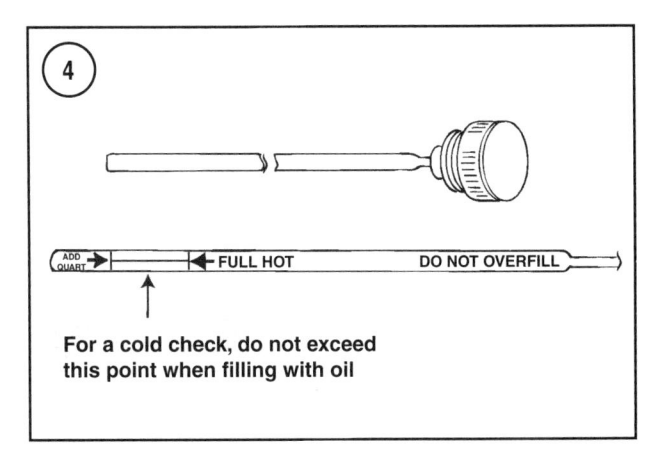

LUBRICATION, MAINTENANCE AND TUNE-UP

is below the FULL HOT mark, adjust the oil level as described in this section.

5. To adjust the oil level, add the correct type of engine oil listed in **Table 4** to bring the oil to the FULL HOT mark on the dipstick.

6. Check the O-ring (**Figure 5**) for cracks or other damage. Replace the O-ring if necessary.

7A. On 2006 models, reinstall the oil filler cap/dipstick and push it in until it bottoms in the fill spout.

7B. On 2007-2009 models, thread the oil filler cap/dipstick into the fill spout and tighten completely.

Engine cold

NOTE
Oil level cannot be accurately measured on a cold engine. Do not add oil to bring the oil level on a cold engine to the FULL HOT mark on the dipstick.

1. Place the motorcycle on a level surface and park it on its jiffy stand.

2A. On 2006 models, wipe the area around the oil filler cap with a clean rag. Pull up and remove the oil filler cap/dipstick (**Figure 2**) from the transmission case. Wipe the dipstick off with a clean rag and reinsert the oil filler cap/dipstick, and push it in until it bottoms in the fill spout.

2B. On 2007-2009 models, wipe the area around the oil filler cap with a clean rag. Unscrew the oil filler cap/dipstick (A, **Figure 3**) from of the transmission case. Wipe the dipstick off with a clean rag and reinsert the oil filler cap/dipstick, and tighten completely into the fill spout.

3. Pull up (2006 models) or unscrew (2007-2009 models) and withdraw the oil filler cap/dipstick again and check the oil level on the dipstick. The oil level should be between the ADD QUART arrow and FULL HOT arrow on the dipstick (**Figure 4**). If the oil level is below the lower ADD QUART arrow, add only enough of the oil type listed in **Table 3** to bring the level *between the two arrows*.

4. Check the O-ring (**Figure 5**) for cracks or other damage. Replace the O-ring if necessary.

5A. On 2006 models, reinstall the oil filler cap/dipstick and push it in until it bottoms in the fill spout.

5B. On 2007-2009 models, thread the oil filler cap/dipstick into the fill spout and tighten completely.

6. Verify correct oil level by performing *Engine Hot* check described in this section.

Oil and Filter Change

Refer to **Table 1** for the recommended oil and filter change interval, which assumes that the motorcycle is operated in moderate climates. If the motorcycle is operated under dusty conditions, the oil becomes contaminated more quickly and should be changed more frequently.

Use a motorcycle oil with a classification recommended by the manufacturer and one specifically designated

3A. On 2006 models, wipe the area around the oil filler cap with a clean rag. Pull up and remove the oil filler cap/dipstick (**Figure 2**) from the transmission case. Wipe the dipstick off with a clean rag and reinsert the oil filler cap/dipstick, and push it in until it bottoms in the fill spout.

3B. On 2007-2009 models, wipe the area around the oil filler cap with a clean rag. Unscrew the oil filler cap/dipstick (A, **Figure 3**) from the transmission case. Wipe the dipstick off with a clean rag and reinsert the oil filler cap/dipstick, and tighten completely into the fill spout.

4. Pull up (2006 models) or unscrew (2007-2009 models) and withdraw the oil filler cap/dipstick again and check the oil level on the dipstick. The oil level should be at the FULL HOT mark on the dipstick (**Figure 4**). If the oil level

for motorcycle applications. Always try to use the same brand of oil at each change. Refer to **Table 4** for correct oil viscosity to use under anticipated ambient temperatures. Using oil additives is not recommended as they may cause clutch damage.

WARNING
Contact with oil may cause skin cancer. Wash oil from hands with soap and water as soon as possible after handling engine oil.

CAUTION
Do not use automotive oils in motorcycle engines. These oils typically contain friction modifiers that reduce frictional losses on engine components. Specifically designed for automotive engines, these oils can cause damage to motorcycle engine and clutch assemblies.

NOTE
Never dispose of motor oil in the trash, on the ground or down a storm drain. Many service stations and oil retailers will accept used oil for recycling. Do not combine other fluids with motor oil to be recycled.

1. Ride the motorcycle until engine is at normal operating temperature.
2. Turn off the engine and allow the oil to settle in oil pan. Support the motorcycle on level ground on a swing arm stand.
3A. On 2006 models, wipe the area around the oil filler cap with a clean rag. Pull up and remove the oil filler cap/dipstick (**Figure 2**) from of the transmission case.
3B. On 2007-2009 models, wipe the area around the oil filler cap with a clean rag. Unscrew the oil filler cap/dipstick (A, **Figure 3**) from of the transmission case.

NOTE
*The oil pan is equipped with two drain plugs. Remove only the engine oil drain plug (A, **Figure 6**) located at the front left side of the oil pan. Do not remove the transmission drain plug (B, **Figure 6**) at the base of the oil pan.*

4. Place a drain pan underneath the oil pan and remove the engine oil drain plug (A, **Figure 6**) and O-ring from the front left side of the oil pan.
5. Allow the engine oil to drain completely.
6. To replace the oil filter (A, **Figure 7**), perform the following:
    a. Temporarily install the drain bolt and O-ring finger-tight. Then, move the drain pan underneath the oil filter. Place a shop cloth (B, **Figure 7**) over the voltage regulator, and under the oil filter to catch residual oil drips after the oil filter (A) is removed.
    b. Install a socket-type oil filter wrench squarely over the oil filter (A, **Figure 7**) and turn it *counterclockwise* to loosen it. Place another shop cloth on the filter as it is hot and quickly remove the oil filter as oil will begin to run out.
    c. Position the oil filter so the open end faces up.
    d. Place the oil filter over the drain pan, turn it over and pour out the remaining oil. Place the filter in a plastic bag, seal it and dispose of it properly.
    e. Remove the shop cloth and dispose of it properly. Wipe all spilled oil from the surrounding area.
    f. Coat the new oil filter gasket with clean engine oil.

CAUTION
Tighten the oil filter by hand. Do not overtighten.

    g. Screw the oil filter onto its mount and tighten it by hand until the filter gasket just touches the sealing surface. Then, tighten the filter by hand an additional 1/2 to 3/4 turn.
7. Install a *new* O-ring (**Figure 8**) onto the engine oil drain plug.
8. Lubricate the O-ring with clean engine oil before installing it. Install the engine oil drain plug and new O-ring and tighten the drain plug to 14-21 ft.-lb. (19-28.5 N•m).
9. While the engine is drained of oil, inspect the pipe plug at the front right side crankcase for leaks. If leaks have occurred, remove the pipe plug and clean the threads thoroughly in solvent and dry. Apply Loctite Pipe Sealant, or an equivalent, to the threads, and then reinstall the pipe plug and tighten it securely.

LUBRICATION, MAINTENANCE AND TUNE-UP

10. Add the correct type (**Table 4**) and quantity (**Table 3**) of oil into the oil pan.

11A. On 2006 models, reinstall the oil filler cap/dipstick and push it in until it bottoms in the fill spout.

11B. On 2007-2009 models, thread the oil filler cap/dipstick into the fill spout and tighten completely.

NOTE
*After oil has been added, the oil level will register above the FULL HOT dipstick mark (**Figure 4**) until the engine runs and the filter fills with oil. To obtain a correct reading after installing a new oil filter and adding oil, follow the procedure described here.*

12. After changing the engine oil and filter, check the oil level as follows:
    a. Start and run the engine for 1 minute, and then shut it off.
    b. Check the oil level on the dipstick as described in this section.
    c. If the oil level is correct, it will register in the dipstick's safe operating level range. If so, *do not* top off or add oil to bring it to the FULL HOT level on the dipstick.
    d. Ride the motorcycle until engine is at normal operating temperature.
    e. Place the motorcycle on a level surface and park it on its jiffy stand and allow the engine to idle for 1-2 minutes. Turn off the engine and recheck the oil level; adjust if necessary.

13. Check the oil filter and drain plug for leaks.
14. Dispose of the used oil properly.

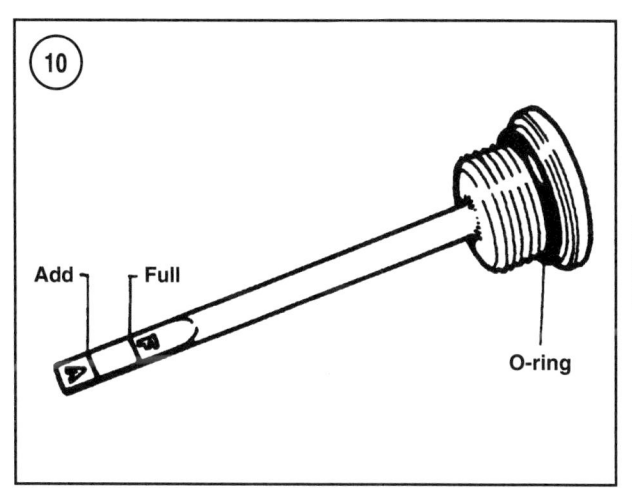

TRANSMISSION OIL

Oil Level Check

Table 1 lists the recommended transmission oil inspection intervals. When checking the transmission oil level, do not allow any dirt or debris to enter the clutch release cover housing opening (2006 models) or transmission case opening (2007-2009 models).

WARNING
Contact with oil may cause skin cancer. Wash oil from hands with soap and water as soon as possible after handling transmission oil.

1. Ride the motorcycle for approximately 10 minutes and shift through all gears until the transmission oil has reached normal operating temperature. Turn off the engine and allow the oil to settle. Park the motorcycle on a level surface and have an assistant support it in an upright position.

CAUTION
Do not check the oil level with the motorcycle supported on its jiffy stand or the reading will be incorrect.

2A. On 2006 models, clean the area around the transmission filler cap/dipstick (**Figure 9**) on the clutch release cover housing and unscrew it.

2B. On 2007-2009 models, clean the area around the transmission filler cap/dipstick (B, **Figure 3**) on top of the transmission case and unscrew it.

3. Wipe the dipstick and reinsert it back into the clutch release cover housing, or into the transmission case; do not screw the cap/dipstick into place. Rest it on the opening and then withdraw it. The oil level is correct when it registers between the two dipstick marks (**Figure 10**).

CHAPTER THREE

CAUTION
*Do not add engine oil. Add only the recommended type of transmission oil listed in **Table 5**.*

4. If the oil level is low, add the recommended type of transmission oil, or equivalent, listed in **Table 5**. Do not overfill.
5. Inspect the filler cap O-ring. Replace if worn or damaged.
6. Install the transmission oil filler cap/dipstick and tighten it to 25-75 in.-lb. (2.8-8.5 N•m).
7. Wipe any spilled oil off the clutch release cover housing or transmission case.

Oil Change

Table 1 lists the recommended transmission oil change intervals.
1. Ride the motorcycle for approximately 10 minutes and shift through all gears until the transmission oil has reached normal operating temperature. Turn off the engine and allow the oil to settle in the tank. Park the motorcycle on a level surface and have an assistant support it in an upright position.
2A. On 2006 models, clean the area around the transmission filler cap/dipstick (**Figure 9**) on the clutch release cover housing and unscrew it.
2B. On 2007-2009 models, clean the area around the transmission filler cap/dipstick (B, **Figure 3**) on top of the transmission case and unscrew it.

NOTE
*The oil pan is equipped with two drain plugs. Make sure to remove the transmission oil drain plug on the base of the oil pan (B, **Figure 6**) not the engine oil drain plug (A) at the front left side.*

3. Place a drain pan underneath the transmission/oil tank pan and remove the transmission oil drain plug (B, **Figure 6**) and O-ring on the base of the oil pan.

WARNING
If any oil spills onto the ground, wipe it up immediately before it contacts the rear tire.

4. Check the drain plug O-ring (**Figure 8**) for damage and replace if necessary.
5. The drain plug is magnetic. Check the plug for metal debris that may indicate transmission damage, and wipe the plug off. Replace the plug if damaged.
6. Install the transmission drain plug (B, **Figure 6**) and tighten to 14-21 ft.-lb. (19-28.5 N•m).

CAUTION
*Add only the recommended type of transmission oil listed in **Table 5**; do not add engine oil. Make sure to add the oil to the correct oil filler hole.*

7. Refill the transmission through the oil filler cap/dipstick hole with the recommended quantity (**Table 3**) and type (**Table 5**) of transmission oil.
8. Install the transmission oil filler cap/dipstick and tighten it to 25-75 in.-lb. (2.8-8.5 N•m).
9. Wipe any spilled oil off the clutch release cover housing or transmission case.
10. Dispose of the used oil properly.
11. Ride the motorcycle until the transmission oil reaches normal operating temperature. Shut off the engine.
12. Check the transmission drain plug for leaks.
13. Check the transmission oil level as described in this section. Readjust the level if necessary.

PRIMARY CHAINCASE OIL

Oil Level Check

The primary chaincase oil lubricates the clutch, primary chain and sprockets. **Table 1** lists the intervals for checking the chaincase oil level. When checking the primary chaincase oil level, do not allow any dirt or debris to enter the housing.
1. Ride the motorcycle for approximately 10 minutes and shift through all gears until the primary chaincase oil has reached normal operating temperature. Turn off the engine and allow the oil to settle in the case. Park the motorcycle on a level surface and have an assistant support it in an upright position. Do not support it on the jiffy stand.

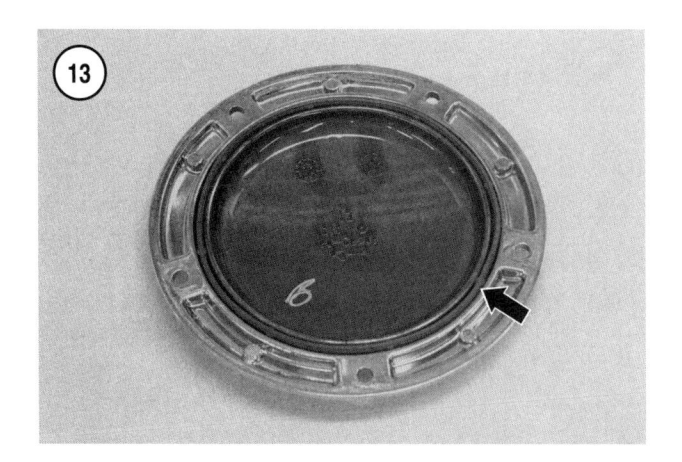

LUBRICATION, MAINTENANCE AND TUNE-UP

CAUTION
Do not check the oil level with the motorcycle supported on its jiffy stand or the reading will be incorrect.

2. Remove the Torx screws (T27) securing the clutch cover (**Figure 11**) and gasket, or seal ring. Then, remove the cover.
3. The oil level is correct when it is even with the bottom of the clutch opening (**Figure 12**) or at the bottom of the clutch diaphragm spring.

CAUTION
Do not add engine oil. Add only the recommended type of primary chaincase lubricant listed in Table 5.

4. If necessary, add the recommended type of lubricant, or its equivalent, through the opening to correct the level.
5. Refer to *Oil Change* in this section to correctly install the seal ring (**Figure 13**), clutch cover and screws.

Oil Change

Table 1 lists the recommended primary chaincase lubricant replacement intervals.
1. Ride the motorcycle for approximately 10 minutes and shift through all gears until the primary chaincase oil has reached normal operating temperature. Turn off the engine and allow the oil to settle in the case. Park the motorcycle on a level surface. 
2. Place a drain pan under the chaincase and remove the drain plug (**Figure 14**).
3. Allow the oil to drain for at least 10 minutes.
4. The drain plug is magnetic. Check the plug for metal debris that may indicate drive component or clutch damage, and then wipe the plug off. Replace the plug if damaged.
5. Reinstall the drain plug and tighten to 14-21 ft.-lb. (19-28.5 N•m).
6. Remove the Torx screws (T27) securing the clutch cover (**Figure 11**) and gasket, or seal ring (**Figure 13**). Then, remove the cover.

CAUTION
Add only the recommended type of primary chaincase lubricant listed in Table 5. Do not add engine oil.

7. Position a funnel (**Figure 15**) into the clutch opening, and refill the primary chaincase with the recommended quantity (**Table 3**) and type (**Table 5**) of primary chaincase oil. Do not overfill. The oil level must be even with the bottom of the clutch opening (**Figure 12**) or at the bottom of the clutch diaphragm spring.
8A. On 2006 models, perform the following:
   a. Position the *new* gasket with the rubber molding and the words *Toward Clutch* facing the engine.
   b. Align the triangular-shaped hole in the *new* gasket with the top hole in the clutch cover.

CAUTION
Do not push the screw through the triangular-shaped hole in the new gasket as the sealing qualities of the gasket will be damaged.

   c. Insert the screw, with captive washer, though the clutch cover and carefully *thread it* all the way through the triangular-shaped hole in the new gasket.
   d. Install the clutch cover and new gasket onto the chaincase cover. Then, thread the top screw part way in.

e. Make sure the clutch cover is correctly aligned with the chaincase cover and install the remaining four screws with captive washers.
f. Use a Torx driver and tighten the screws (T27) in a crossing pattern to 84-108 in.-lb. (9.5-12.2 N•m).

8B. On 2007-2009 models, perform the following:

NOTE
All lubricant must be removed from the seal ring and its mounting groove prior to installation. If any lubricant remains, there will be temporary lubricant seepage around the clutch cover.

a. Remove the seal ring (**Figure 13**) from the clutch cover. Wipe all lubricant from the seal ring and inspect it for cuts or deterioration; replace if necessary. Wipe all lubricant from the seal ring groove and install the seal ring onto the cover. Push the nibs into the ring groove walls.
b. Install the clutch cover and seal ring (**Figure 13**) onto the primary chaincase cover.
c. Install the clutch cover screws and tighten them to 84-108 in.-lb. (9.5-12.2 N•m).

9. Ride the motorcycle until the primary chaincase oil reaches normal operating temperature. Then, shut the engine off.

10. Check the primary chaincase drain plug and clutch cover for leaks.

FRONT FORK OIL

The front fork must be removed and partially disassembled in order to change the oil. Refer to Chapter Thirteen.

CONTROL CABLES

Control Cable Lubrication

Lubricate the control cables at the intervals in **Table 1** or sooner if they become stiff. At this time, inspect each cable for fraying and cable sheath damage. Replace any faulty cable(s). Lubricate the cables with a cable lubricant.

CAUTION
If the original equipment cables have been replaced with nylon-lined cables, do not lubricate them as described in this procedure. Oil and most cable lubricants will cause the cable liner to expand, pushing the liner against the cable sheath and binding the cable. Nylon-lined cables are normally used dry. Follow the manufacturer's instructions when servicing nylon-lined and other aftermarket cables.

CAUTION
Do not use chain lube to lubricate control cables.

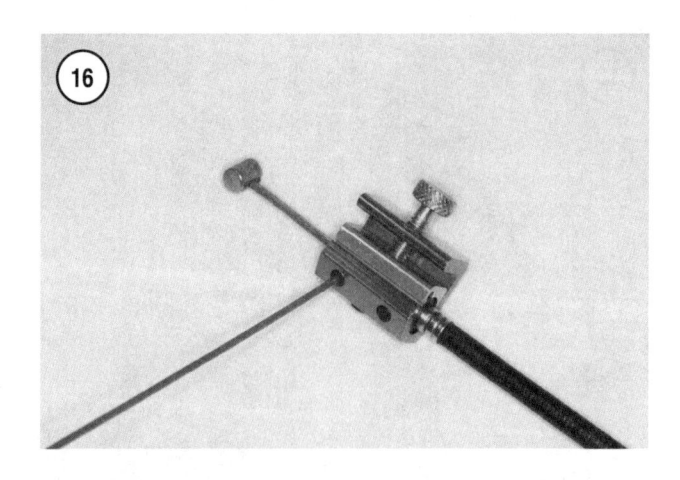

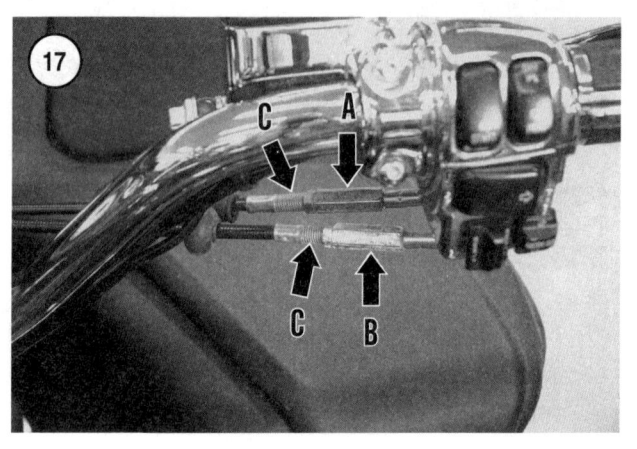

CAUTION
*On carbureted models, the enrichment valve (choke) cable is designed to operate with a certain amount of cable resistance. Do **not** lubricate the enrichment cable or its conduit.*

NOTE
The major cause of cable damage is improper lubrication. Maintaining the cables as described in this section will ensure long service life.

1. On all models except Screamin' Eagle, disconnect the clutch cable ends as described in *Clutch Cable Replacement* (Chapter Six).
2. On 2006-2007 models, disconnect both throttle cable ends as described in *Throttle and Idle Cables* (Chapter Nine or Chapter Ten).
3. Attach a cable lubricator (**Figure 16**) to the cable following its manufacturer's instructions.

NOTE
Place a shop cloth at the opposite end of the cable to catch all excess lubricant.

4. Insert the lubricant nozzle tube into the lubricator, press the button on the can and hold it down until the lubricant begins to flow out of the other end of the cable. If the lubricant squirts out from around the lubricator, it is not

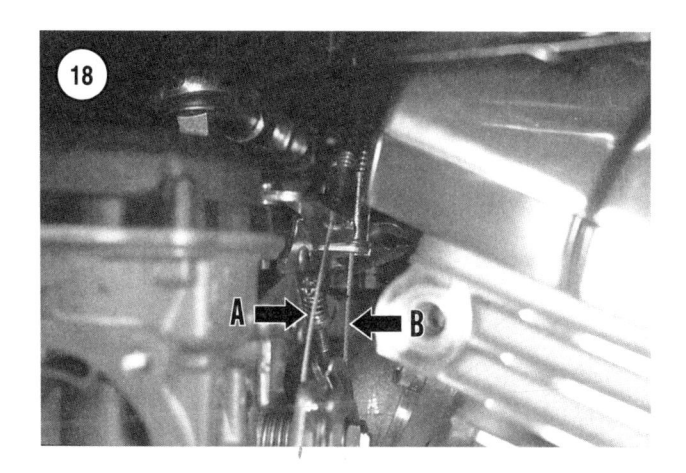

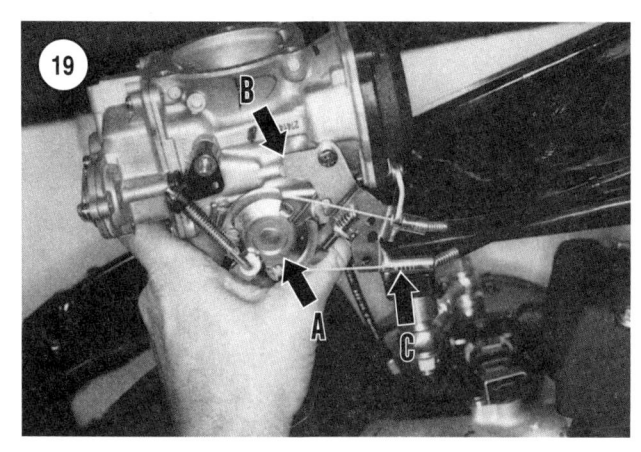

LUBRICATION, MAINTENANCE AND TUNE-UP

clamped to the cable properly. Loosen and reposition the cable lubricator.

NOTE
If the lubricant does not flow out of the other end of the cable, check the cable for fraying, bending or other damage. Replace damaged cables.

5. Remove the lubricator and wipe off both ends of the cable.
6. Reconnect the clutch cable ends as described in *Clutch Cable Replacement* (Chapter Six).
7. Reconnect both cable ends as described in *Throttle and Idle Cable Replacement* (Chapter Nine or Chapter Ten).
8. Adjust the cables as described in this section.

Throttle Cable Inspection
(2006-2007 Models)

Inspect the throttle cables from grip to carburetor or induction module. Make sure they are not kinked or chafed. If necessary, replace them as described in Chapter Nine or Chapter Ten.

Make sure that the throttle grip rotates smoothly from fully closed to fully open. Check with the handlebar at center, full left and full right positions.

Throttle Cable Adjustment
(2006-2007 Non-Cruise Control Models)

NOTE
The throttle is controlled by the ECM on 2008-2009 models. There are no cables requiring adjustment.

There are two different throttle cables. At the throttle grip, the front cable is the throttle control cable (A, **Figure 17**) and the rear cable is the idle control cable (B).

At the throttle valve, the outer cable is the throttle control cable (A, **Figure 18**) and the inner cable is the idle control cable (B).

1. Remove the air filter and backplate as described in Chapter Nine or Chapter Ten.
2. At the handlebar, loosen both control cable adjuster locknuts. Then, turn the cable adjusters (C, **Figure 17**) *clockwise* as far as possible to increase cable slack.
3. Turn the handlebars so the front wheel points straight ahead. Then, turn the throttle grip to open the throttle valve completely and hold it in this position.

NOTE
***Figure 19** is shown with the carburetor body removed to better illustrate the steps.*

4A. On carbureted models, turn the throttle control cable adjuster (C, **Figure 17**) at the handlebar counterclockwise until the throttle cam (A, **Figure 19**) stop just touches the stop boss (B) on the carburetor body. Then, tighten the throttle cable adjuster locknut and release the throttle grip.
4B. On fuel-injected models, turn the throttle control cable adjuster (C, **Figure 17**) at the handlebar counterclockwise until the throttle cam (A, **Figure 20**) stop just touches the cam stop (B) on the throttle body. Then, tighten the throttle cable adjuster locknut and release the throttle grip.
5. Turn the front wheel all the way to the full right lock position and hold it there.
6A. On carbureted models, turn the idle cable adjuster (C, **Figure 17**) at the handlebar until the lower end of the idle control cable just contacts the spring in the carburetor cable guide (C, **Figure 19**). Tighten the idle cable locknut.
6B. On fuel-injected models, turn the idle cable adjuster (C, **Figure 17**) at the handlebar until the lower end of the idle control cable housing just contacts the spring in the cable support sleeve (C, **Figure 20**). Tighten the idle cable locknut.
7. Install the backplate and the air filter as described in Chapter Nine or Chapter Ten.
8. Shift the transmission into neutral and start the engine.
9. Increase engine speed several times. Release the throttle and make sure the engine speed returns to idle. If the engine speed does not return to idle, at the handlebar, loosen the idle control cable adjuster locknut and turn the cable adjuster *clockwise* as required. Tighten the idle control cable adjuster locknut.

10. Allow the engine to idle in neutral and apply the rear brake. Then, turn the handlebar from side to side. Do not operate the throttle. If the engine speed increases when the handlebar assembly is turned, the throttle cables are routed incorrectly or damaged. Turn off the engine. Recheck cable routing and adjustment.

11. Carefully rotate the throttle control *counterclockwise* to the wide open position and release it. The throttle must return to the idle position freely. If it does not, check for improper cable routing, a damaged cable, or a binding throttle control.

**Throttle Cable Adjustment
(2006-2007 Cruise Control Models)**

Refer to Chapter Sixteen for throttle cable adjustment.

**Starting Enrichment Valve (Choke) Cable Adjustment
(Carbureted Models)**

The starting enrichment (choke) knob (**Figure 21**) must move from fully open to fully closed without any sign of binding. The knob must also stay in its fully closed or fully open position without creeping. If the knob does not stay in position, adjust tension on the cable by turning the knurled plastic nut behind the knob (**Figure 22**) as follows:

*CAUTION
The starting enrichment (choke) cable must have sufficient cable resistance to work properly. Do not lubricate the enrichment cable or its conduit.*

1. Loosen the hex nut behind the mounting bracket. Then, move the cable to free it from its mounting bracket slot.
2. Hold the cable across its flats with a wrench and turn the knurled plastic nut *counterclockwise* to reduce cable resistance. The knob must slide inward freely.
3. Turn the knurled plastic nut (**Figure 22**) *clockwise* to increase cable resistance. Continue adjustment until the knob remains stationary when pulled all the way out. The knob must move without any roughness or binding.
4. Reinstall the cable into the slot in its mounting bracket with the star washer located between the bracket and hex nut. Tighten the hex nut securely.
5. Recheck the knob movement and readjust if necessary.

**Throttle Control Grip Lubrication
(2006-2007 Models)**

Table 1 lists the recommended throttle control grip lubrication intervals. To remove and install the throttle grip, refer to *Throttle and Idle Cable Replacement* in Chapter Nine or Chapter Ten. Lubricate the throttle control grip where it contacts the handlebar with graphite.

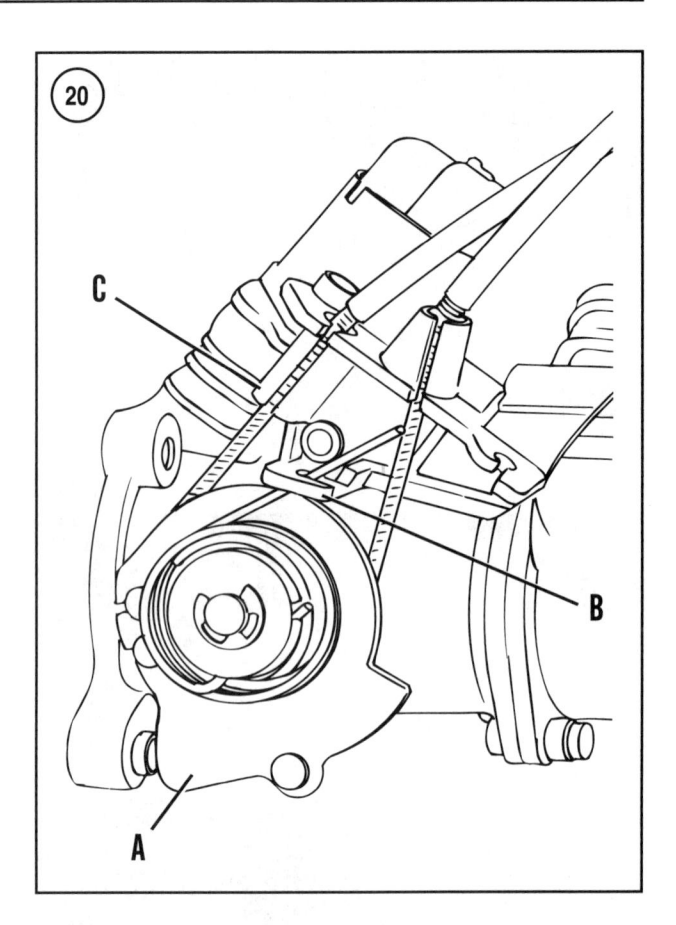

PRIMARY CHAIN AND DRIVE BELT

**Primary Chain Adjustment
(2006 Models)**

*NOTE
The primary chain is adjusted automatically on 2007-2009 models.*

As the primary chain stretches and wears, its free play movement increases. Excessive free play will cause premature wear on the chain and sprocket, and increase chain noise. If the free play is adjusted too tight, the chain will wear prematurely. Check primary chain deflection at the intervals listed in **Table 1**.

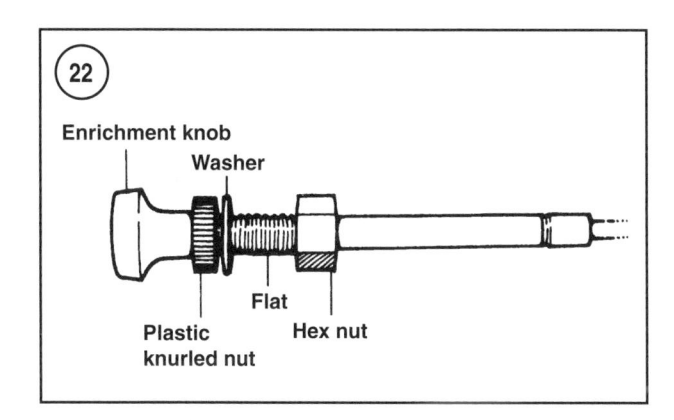

LUBRICATION, MAINTENANCE AND TUNE-UP

3. Remove the primary chain inspection cover (**Figure 23**) and gasket.
4. Turn the primary chain to find the tightest point on the chain. Measure the chain free play at this point.

NOTE
Figure 24 is shown with the primary chain cover removed to better illustrate the procedure.

5. Check primary chain free play at the upper chain run midway between the sprockets (**Figure 24**). The correct primary chain free play specifications are:
   a. Cold engine: 5/8 to 7/8 in. (15.9-22.2 mm).
   b. Hot engine: 3/8 to 5/8 in. (9.5-15.9 mm).
6. If the primary chain free play is incorrect, loosen the primary chain adjuster shoe nut (**Figure 25**).
7. Move the adjuster shoe assembly up or down to obtain the correct amount of free play.
8. Tighten the primary chain adjuster shoe nut (**Figure 25**) to 21-29 ft.-lb. (28.5-39.3 N•m) and recheck free play.
9. Align the holes in the *new* gasket with the inspection cover, and then install the cover (**Figure 23**). Using a crossing pattern, tighten the cover screws to 84-108 in.-lb. (9.5-12.2 N•m).
10. Lower the motorcycle to the ground.
11. Connect the negative battery cable as described in Chapter Eleven.

Final Drive Belt
Deflection and Alignment

Inspect drive belt deflection and rear axle alignment at the intervals specified in **Table 1**. If the drive belt is severely worn, or if it is wearing incorrectly, refer to Chapter Twelve for inspection and replacement procedures.

The drive belt deflection can be inspected with the rear wheel off the ground or with the motorcycle resting on the jiffy stand without rider or luggage. A belt tension gauge (JIMS part No. 923 or H-D part No. HD-35381), or the equivalent, is needed to check drive belt defection.

NOTE
Always disarm the optional TSM/TSSM security system prior to disconnecting the battery or pulling the Maxi-Fuse so the siren will not sound.

1. Disconnect the negative battery cable as described in Chapter Eleven.
2. Support the motorcycle with the rear wheel off the ground.

NOTE
Note the location of the inspection cover screws. There are two different length screws and they must be reinstalled in the correct location.

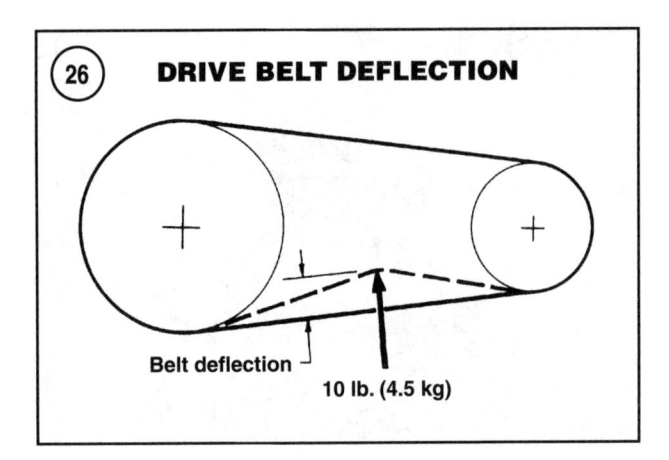

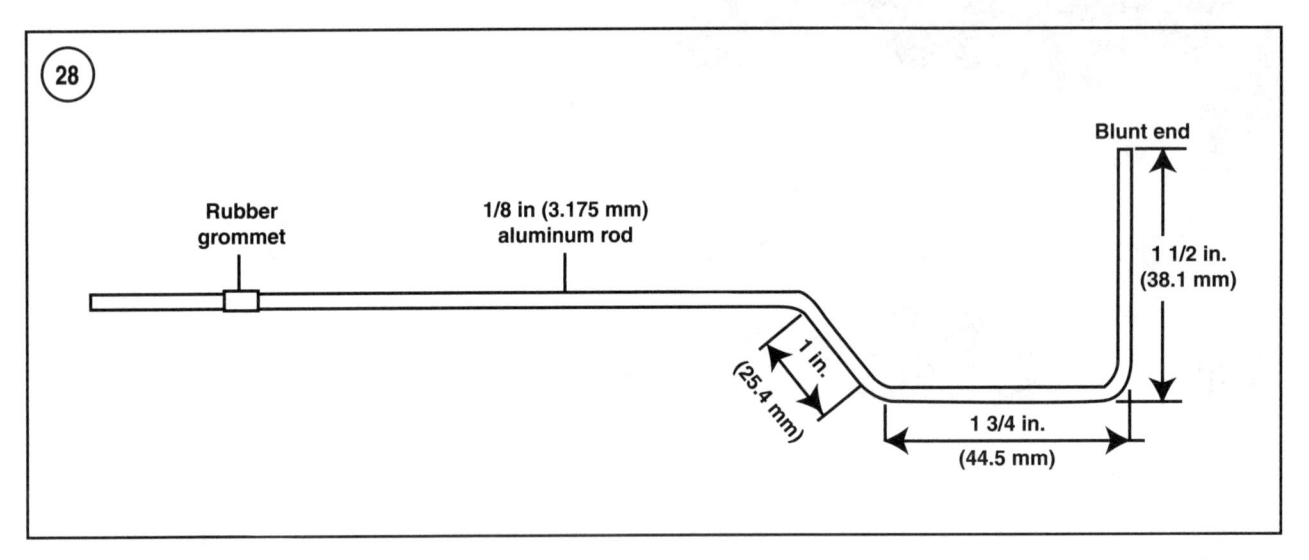

78 CHAPTER THREE

26 DRIVE BELT DEFLECTION

Belt deflection
10 lb. (4.5 kg)

28

Rubber grommet
1/8 in (3.175 mm) aluminum rod
Blunt end
1 1/2 in. (38.1 mm)
1 in. (25.4 mm)
1 3/4 in. (44.5 mm)

NOTE
Check drive belt deflection and axle alignment when the belt is at room temperature, not after a ride.

1. Remove the left side saddlebag as described in Chapter Seventeen.
2. Support the motorcycle with the rear wheel off the ground, or position it on the Jiffy stand.
3. Shift the transmission into neutral.
4. If the rear wheel is off the ground, turn the rear wheel and check the drive belt for its tightest point. If positioned on the Jiffy stand, move the motorcycle forward for the tightest point. When this point is located, move the wheel so that the belt's tight spot is on the lower belt run, midway between the front and rear sprockets.
5. Slide the O-ring on the gauge toward the 0 lb. (0 kg) mark on the gauge.
6. Position the gauge on the lower belt strand half way between the transmission drive sprocket and rear wheel driven sprocket.
7. Push up on the gauge until the O-ring slides to the 10 lb. (4.5 kg) mark while measuring the belt deflection at the same point (**Figure 26**).
8. Rotate the rear wheel and measure the deflection at different locations on the belt.

9. Compare the belt deflection measurement with the correct specification in **Table 6**. If the belt deflection measurement is correct, install the left side saddlebag. If the deflection measurement is incorrect, continue the procedure to adjust the belt tension.
10. Remove the right side muffler as described in Chapter Four.
11. Remove the e-clip (A, **Figure 27**) and loosen the rear axle nut (B).
12. Support the motorcycle with the rear wheel off the ground, if it is not already in this position.
13. Rotate the rear axle in either direction to adjust belt deflection while maintaining rear wheel alignment. Recheck drive belt deflection as described in this section.
14. After the drive belt deflection measurement is correct, check axle alignment as follows:
    a. Make the alignment tool as shown in **Figure 28** or use a wheel alignment tool (Motion Pro part No. 08-0368), or an equivalent.
    b. Support the motorcycle with the rear wheel off the ground.
    c. Insert the alignment tool into the swing arm index holes. Then, hold it parallel to the rear axle and slide the grommet on the tool until it aligns with the axle center point.

LUBRICATION, MAINTENANCE AND TUNE-UP

17. Install the right side muffler as described in Chapter Four.
18. Lower the rear wheel to the ground.

BRAKE SYSTEM

Front Brake Lever Pivot Pin Lubrication

Inspect the front brake lever pivot pin for lubrication at the intervals specified in **Table 1**. If the pin is dry, lubricate it with light weight oil. To service the pivot pin, refer to *Front Master Cylinder* in Chapter Fifteen.

Brake Pad Inspection

1. Without removing either brake caliper, inspect the brake pads for damage.
2. If the pad material appears marginal; remove the brake pads as described in Chapter Fifteen.
3. Measure the thickness of each brake pad lining (**Figure 30**) with a ruler. Replace the brake pads if worn to the minimum specification in **Table 6**. Replace the brake pads as described in Chapter Fifteen. Always replace both brake pads as a set.

Brake Fluid Level

WARNING
Use only DOT 4 brake fluid. Do not intermix different types of brake fluids, as they are not compatible. DOT 5 is silicone-based and the mistaken use of silicone brake fluid in these models can cause brake failure.

WARNING
If the brake fluid level is low enough to allow air in the hydraulic system, bleed the brakes as described in Chapter Fifteen.

CAUTION
Be careful when handling brake fluid. Do not spill it on painted or plastic surfaces, as it damages them. Wash the area immediately with soap and water and thoroughly rinse it.

Front master cylinder

1. Support the motorcycle on level ground with a swing arm stand.
2. Block the front wheel so the motorcycle will not roll in either direction while on the swing arm stand.
3. Turn the handlebars to the straight ahead position to level the front master cylinder.

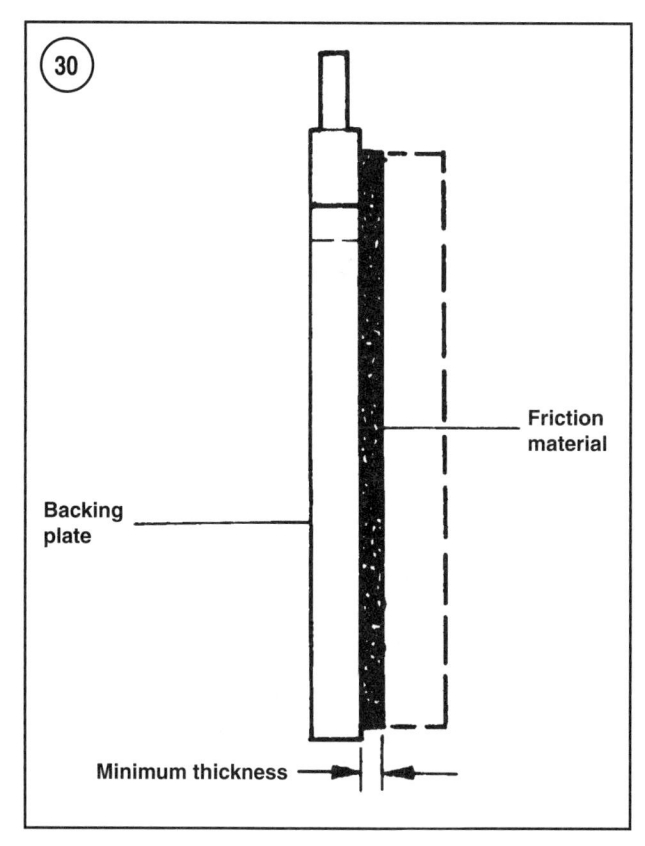

d. Without repositioning the grommet, remove the tool and check the opposite side of the swing arm, comparing this position with the opposite side. Axle alignment is correct if the two measurements are identical or within 1/32 in. (0.8 mm) of each other.
e. If the axle alignment is incorrect, adjust the axle while maintaining the correct drive belt deflection measurement.

15. Verify that the axle adjuster cam (C, **Figure 27**) contacts the swing arm boss (**Figure 29**) on each side.
16. When the drive belt deflection and axle alignment adjustments are correct, secure the axle on the left side and tighten the axle nut (B, **Figure 27**) to 95-105 ft.-lb. (128.8-142.4 N•m). Position the e-clip with the flat side facing out and install (A, **Figure 27**) around the axle. Make sure it is correctly seated.

4. Remove the screws, cover, and diaphragm from the master cylinder. Refer to (**Figure 31**) for 2006-2007 models or (**Figure 32**) for 2008-2009 models.
5A. On 2006-2007 models, the brake fluid level should be 1/4 in. (6.4 mm) from the top edge (**Figure 33**) of the master cylinder body.
5B. On 2008-2009 models, the brake fluid level should be flush with the top ledge cast into the front of the master cylinder body.
6. Add fresh DOT 4 brake fluid to correct the level. Reinstall the diaphragm and top cover. Tighten the screws securely.

Rear master cylinder

1. Support the motorcycle on level ground.
2. Remove the screws, cover, and diaphragm from the master cylinder (**Figure 34**).
3A. On 2006-2007 models, the brake fluid level should be 1/4 in. (6.4 mm) from the top edge of the master cylinder body.
3B. On 2008-2009 models, the brake fluid level should be flush with the top ledge cast into the front of the master cylinder body.
4. Add fresh DOT 4 brake fluid to correct the level. Reinstall the diaphragm and top cover. Tighten the screws securely.

Front and Rear Brake Disc Inspection

Inspect the front and rear brake discs (**Figure 35**) for scoring, cracks or other damage. Measure the brake disc thickness, and if necessary, service the brake discs as described in Chapter Fifteen.

Brake Lines and Seals

Check the brake lines between each master cylinder and each brake caliper and at the control module on ABS models. If there are any leaks, tighten the connections and bleed the brakes as described in Chapter Fifteen.

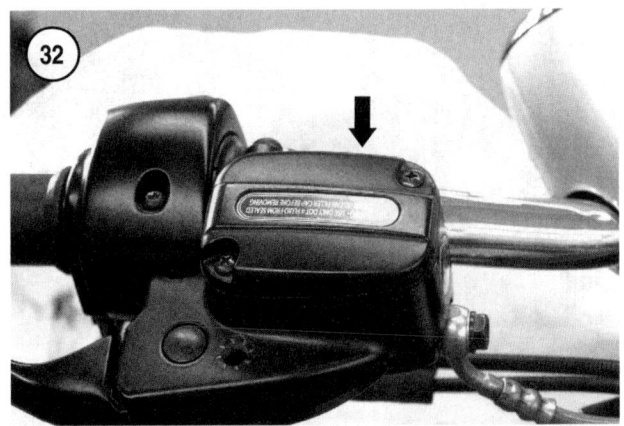

LUBRICATION, MAINTENANCE AND TUNE-UP

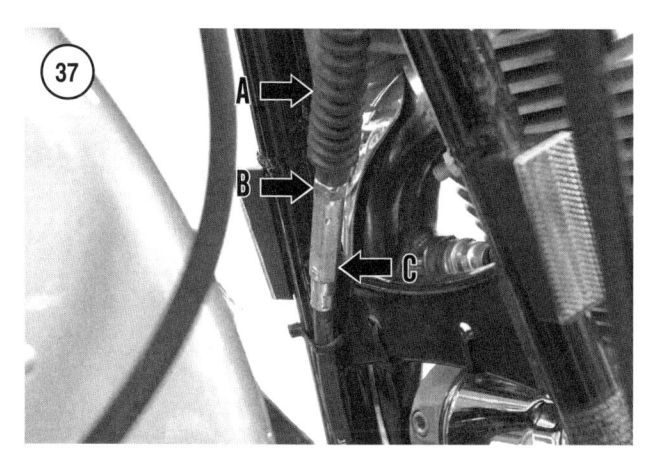

Brake Fluid Change

To change brake fluid, follow the brake bleeding procedure in Chapter Fifteen.

CLUTCH SYSTEM

Clutch Lever Pivot Pin Lubrication

Inspect the clutch lever pivot pin at the intervals specified in **Table 1**. Lubricate the pin with light weight oil or silicone brake grease on Screamin' Eagle models. To service the pivot pin, refer to Chapter Six.

Clutch Adjustment
(All Models Except Screamin' Eagle)

CAUTION
Because the clutch cable adjuster clearance increases with engine temperature, adjust the clutch when the engine is cold. If the clutch is adjusted when the engine is hot, insufficient pushrod clearance can cause the clutch to slip.

1. Remove the Torx screws (T27) securing the clutch cover (**Figure 36**) and gasket, or seal ring. Then, remove the cover.
2. Slide the rubber boot (A, **Figure 37**) away from the clutch cable in-line adjuster.
3. Loosen the adjuster locknut (B, **Figure 37**) and turn the adjuster (C) to provide maximum cable slack.
4. Check that the clutch cable seats squarely in its perch (**Figure 38**) at the handlebar.
5. At the clutch mechanism, loosen the clutch adjusting screw locknut (A, **Figure 39**) and turn the adjusting screw (B) *clockwise* until it is lightly seated.
6. Apply the clutch lever three times to verify the clutch balls are seated in the ramp release mechanism located behind the transmission side cover.
7. Back out the adjusting screw (A, **Figure 40**) *counter-clockwise* 1/2 to 1 turn. Then, hold the adjusting screw (A, **Figure 40**) and tighten the locknut (B) to 72-120 in.-lb. (8.1-13.6 N•m).

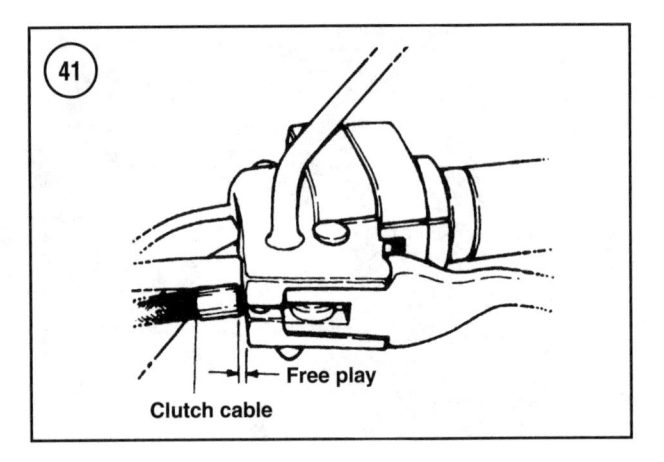

8. Once again, apply the clutch lever to its maximum limit three times to set the clutch balls and ramp release mechanism.
9. Check the free play as follows:
   a. At the clutch cable in-line adjuster, turn the adjuster away from the locknut until slack is eliminated at the clutch lever.
   b. Pull the clutch cable sheath away from the clutch lever, and turn the clutch cable adjuster to obtain the clearance gap (**Figure 41**) of 1/16-1/8 in. (1.6-3.2 mm).
   c. When the adjustment is correct, secure the adjuster and tighten the locknut. Slide the rubber boot back over the cable adjuster.
10A. On 2006 models, perform the following:
   a. Position the *new* gasket with the rubber molding and the words *Toward Clutch* facing the engine.
   b. Align the triangular-shaped hole in the *new* gasket with the top hole in the clutch cover.

CAUTION
Do not push the screw through the triangular-shaped hole in the new gasket as the sealing qualities of the gasket will be damaged.

   c. Insert the screw, with captive washer, though the clutch cover and carefully *thread it* all the way through the triangular-shaped hole in the new gasket.
   d. Install the clutch cover and new gasket onto the chaincase cover. Then, thread the top screw part way in.
   e. Make sure the clutch cover is correctly aligned with the chaincase cover and install the remaining four screws with captive washers.
   f. Use a Torx driver and tighten the screws (T27) in a crossing pattern to 84-108 in.-lb. (9.5-12.2 N•m).
10B. On 2007-2009 models, perform the following:

NOTE
All lubricant must be removed from the seal ring and its groove prior to installation. If any lubricant remains, there will be a temporary lubricant leak around the clutch cover.

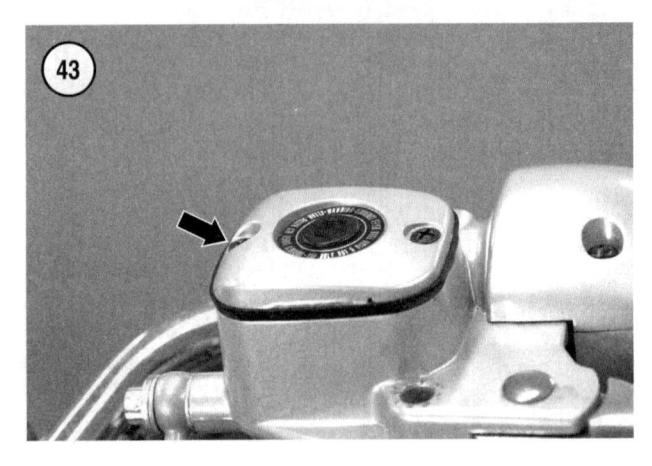

   a. Remove the seal ring (**Figure 42**) from the clutch cover. Wipe all lubricant from the seal ring and inspect it for cuts or deterioration; replace if necessary. Wipe all lubricant from the seal ring groove and install the seal ring onto the cover. Push the nibs into the ring groove walls.
   b. Install the clutch cover and seal ring (**Figure 36**) onto the primary chaincase cover.
   c. Install the clutch cover screws and tighten them to 84-108 in.-lb. (9.2-12.2 N•m).

Clutch Fluid Level
(Screamin' Eagle Models)

WARNING
Use only DOT 4 brake fluid in the clutch system. Do not intermix DOT4 with DOT 5 brake fluids, as they are not compatible. DOT 5 is silicone-based and the mistaken use of silicone brake fluid in these models can cause clutch failure.

CAUTION
Be careful when handling brake fluid. Do not spill it on painted or plastic surfaces, as it damages them. Wash the area immediately with soap and water, and thoroughly rinse it.

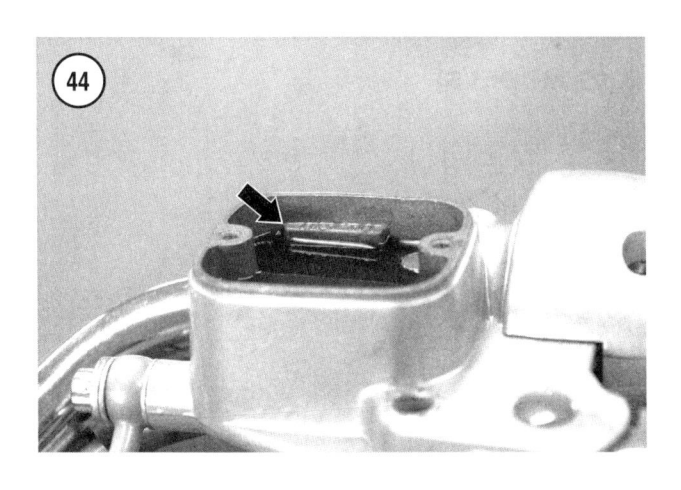

LUBRICATION, MAINTENANCE AND TUNE-UP

NOTE
If the clutch fluid level is low enough to allow air in the hydraulic system, bleed the clutch as described in Chapter Six.

1. Turn the handlebars to the straight ahead position to level the clutch master cylinder.
2. Clean any dirt from the master cylinder cover prior to removing it.
3. Remove the screws, cover, and diaphragm from the master cylinder (**Figure 43**).
4A. On 2006-2007 models, the clutch fluid level should be 1/4 in. (6.4 mm) from the top edge of the clutch master cylinder body.
4B. On 2008-2009 models, the clutch fluid level should be flush with the top ledge (**Figure 44**) cast into the front of the clutch master cylinder body.
5. Add enough fresh DOT 4 brake fluid to correct the level. Reinstall the diaphragm and top cover. Tighten the screws securely.

Clutch Hoses and Seals (Screamin' Eagle Models)

Check the clutch hose between the master cylinder and the release cylinder. If there is any leak, tighten the connections and bleed the clutch as described in Chapter Six. If this does not stop the leak or if a line is obviously damaged, cracked, or chafed, replace the hose and/or the master cylinder or release cylinder(s). Then, bleed the clutch as described in Chapter Six.

Clutch Fluid Change (Screamin' Eagle Models)

A small amount of dirt and moisture enters the clutch fluid each time the reservoir cap is removed. The same thing happens if a leak occurs or when any part of the hydraulic system is loosened or disconnected. Dirt can clog the system and cause unnecessary wear. Water in the fluid vaporizes at high temperatures, impairing the hydraulic action and reducing clutch performance.

To change the clutch fluid, drain the fluid from the clutch system as described in Chapter Six. Add new fluid to the master cylinder, and bleed the clutch at the release cylinder until the fluid leaving the release cylinder is clean and free of contaminants and air bubbles. Refer to the clutch bleeding procedure in Chapter Six.

FUEL SYSTEM

WARNING
Do not ride the motorcycle until the throttle cables are properly adjusted. Also, the cables must not catch or pull when the handlebar is turned from side to side. Improper cable routing and adjustment can cause the throttle to stick open. This could cause loss of control and a possible crash. Recheck this adjustment before riding the motorcycle.

Fuel Line Inspection

Inspect the fuel lines from the fuel tank to the carburetor or fuel injection module, and the cross over hose at the front of the fuel tank. Replace leaking or damaged fuel lines. Make sure the hose clamps are in place and holding securely. Check the hose fittings for looseness.

WARNING
A damaged or deteriorated fuel line can cause a fire or explosion if fuel spills onto a hot engine or exhaust pipe.

Fuel Shutoff Valve Filter (Carbureted Models)

Refer to Chapter Nine for the service procedure.

AIR FILTER

Remove and clean the air filter at the interval in **Table 1**. Replace the element whenever it is damaged or starts to deteriorate.

Removal/Installation (All Models Except 2007 FLHRSE3 and 2009 FLTRSE3)

Refer to **Figure 45** and **Figure 46**.
1A. On all models except Screamin' Eagle, remove the air filter cover Allen screw (A, **Figure 47**), and then remove the cover (B).
1B. On Screamin' Eagle models, remove the trim plate screws and trim plate. Remove the air filter cover Allen screw, and then remove the cover.
2. Remove the Torx screws (T27) and bracket (A, **Figure 48**) from the air filter element (B).
3. Gently pull the air filter element away from the backplate and disconnect the two breather hoses (A, **Figure 49**) from the breather hollow bolts on the backplate. Remove the air filter element (B, **Figure 49**).

CHAPTER THREE

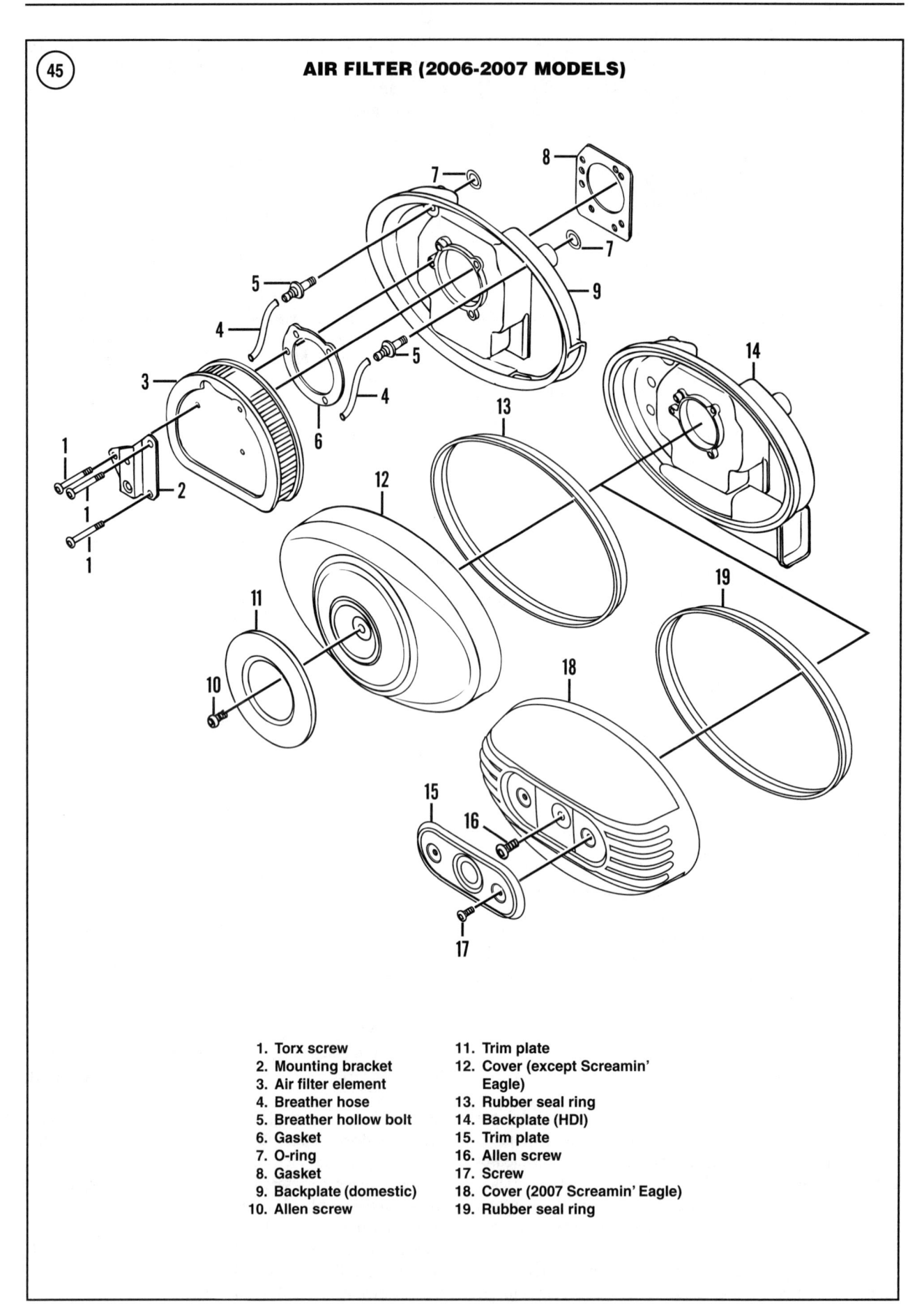

(45) AIR FILTER (2006-2007 MODELS)

1. Torx screw
2. Mounting bracket
3. Air filter element
4. Breather hose
5. Breather hollow bolt
6. Gasket
7. O-ring
8. Gasket
9. Backplate (domestic)
10. Allen screw
11. Trim plate
12. Cover (except Screamin' Eagle)
13. Rubber seal ring
14. Backplate (HDI)
15. Trim plate
16. Allen screw
17. Screw
18. Cover (2007 Screamin' Eagle)
19. Rubber seal ring

LUBRICATION, MAINTENANCE AND TUNE-UP

㊻ **AIR FILTER (2008-2009 MODELS AND 2007-2009 SCREAMIN' EAGLE MODELS EXCEPT 2007 FLHRSE3 AND 2009 FLTRSE3)**

1. Torx screw
2. Mounting bracket
3. Air filter element
4. Gasket
5. Breather hose
6. Breather hollow bolt
7. Backplate
8. Gasket
9. Allen screw
10. Trim plate
11. Cover (Screamin' Eagle shown)
12. Rubber seal ring
13. Screw

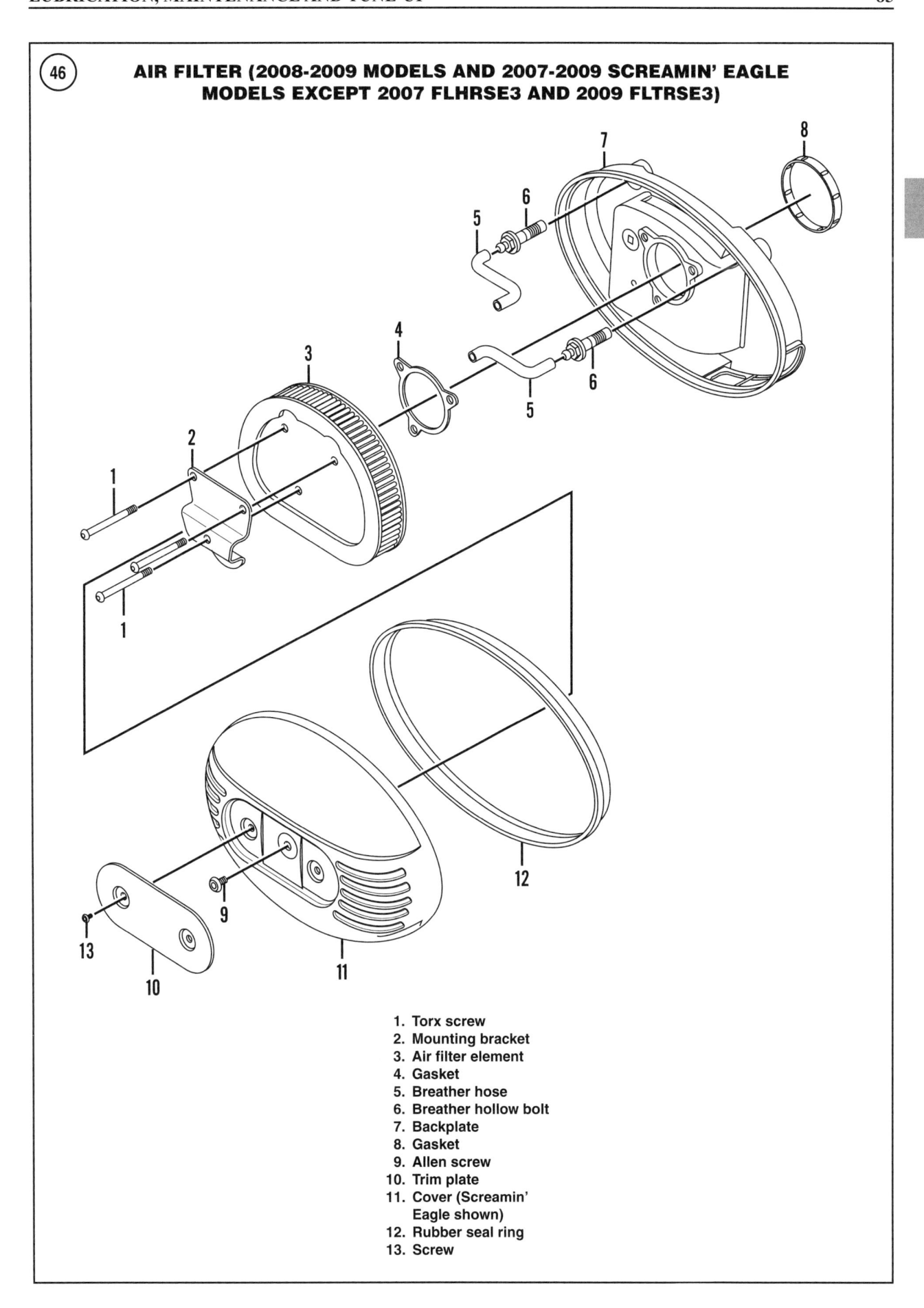

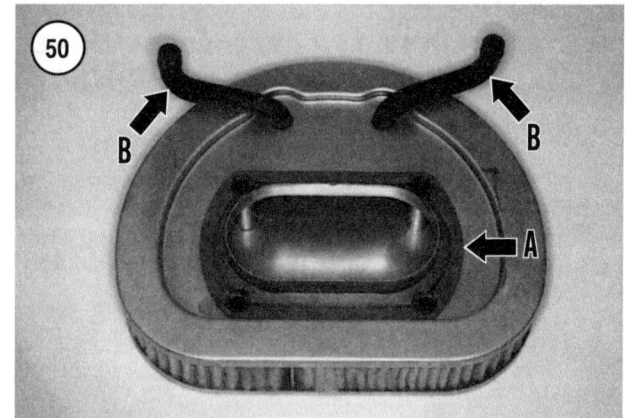

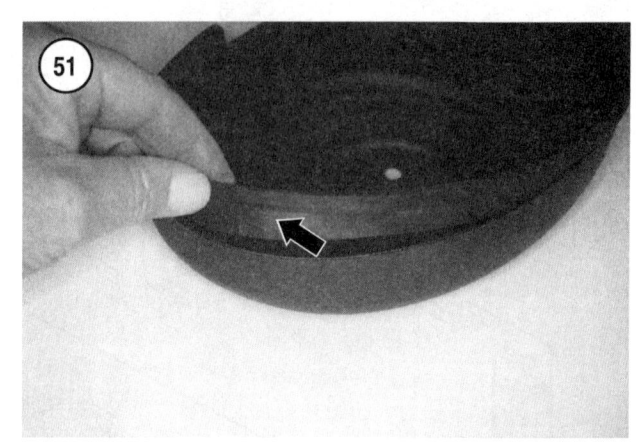

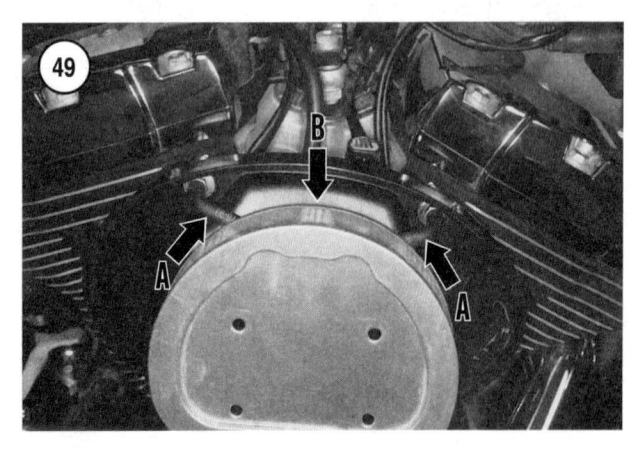

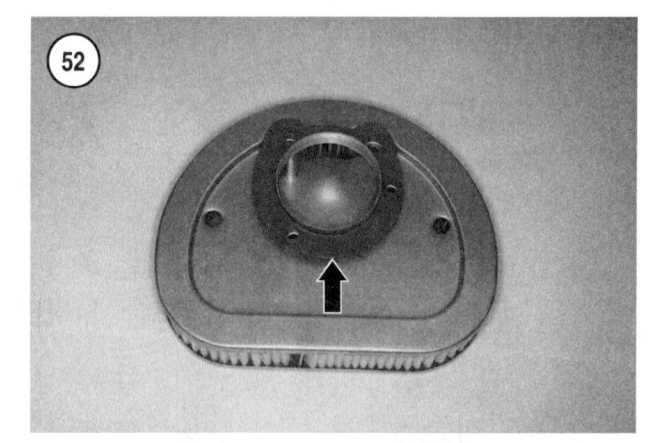

4. Remove the gasket (A, **Figure 50**) from the inboard side of the element. Discard the gasket.
5. Clean the air filter as described in the following procedure.
6. Inspect the breather hoses (B, **Figure 50**) for tears or deterioration. Replace if necessary.
7. Inspect the seal ring (**Figure 51**) on the air filter cover for hardness or deterioration. Replace if necessary.
8. Install a *new* gasket (**Figure 52**) on the inboard side of the element.
9. Position the filter element with the flat side facing down.
10. Insert the breather hoses (**Figure 53**) about 1/4 inch (6.4 mm) onto the breather hollow bolts located on the backside of the element.

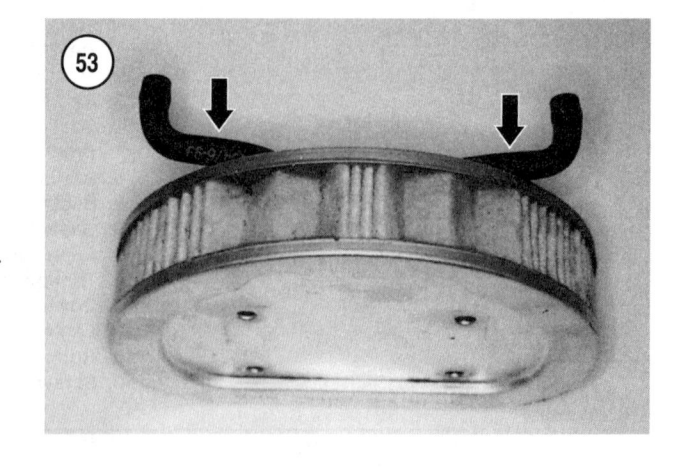

LUBRICATION, MAINTENANCE AND TUNE-UP

AIR FILTER (2007 FLHRSE3 SCREAMIN' EAGLE)

1. Screw
2. Trim plate
3. Allen screw
4. Cover
5. Gasket
6. Screw
7. Air filter element
8. Breather tube
9. Breather hollow bolt
10. Backplate
11. O-ring
12. Standoff bolt
13. Gasket

AIR FILTER (2009 FLTRSE3 SCREAMIN' EAGLE)

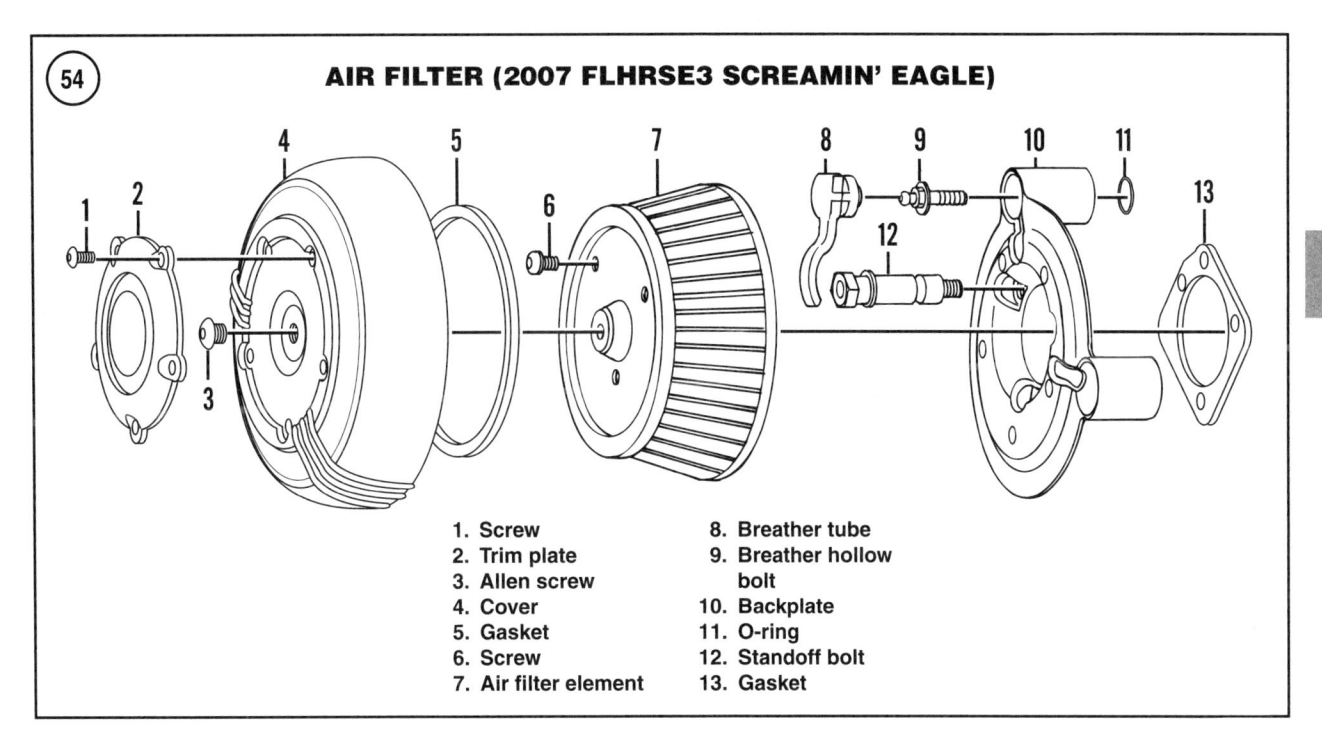

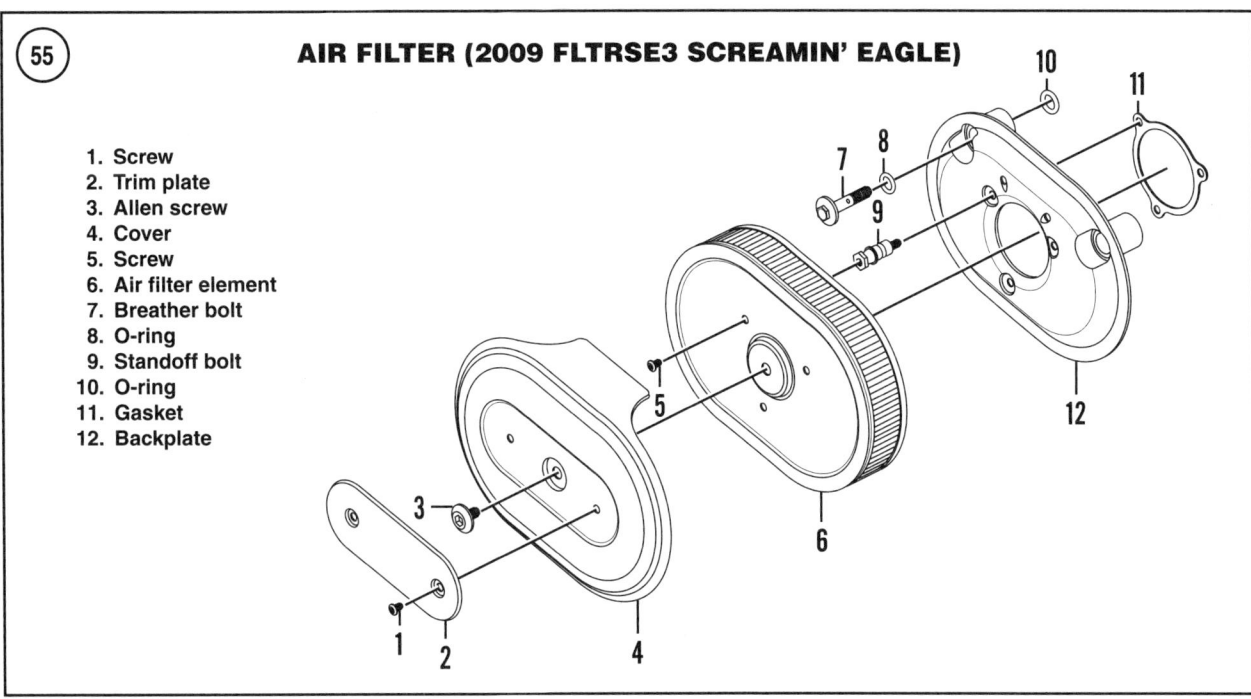

1. Screw
2. Trim plate
3. Allen screw
4. Cover
5. Screw
6. Air filter element
7. Breather bolt
8. O-ring
9. Standoff bolt
10. O-ring
11. Gasket
12. Backplate

11. Move the element into position and install the mounting bracket (A, **Figure 48**). Install the Torx screws through the mounting bracket and element (B, **Figure 48**). Align the screw holes and tighten the Torx screws (T27) to 40-60 in.-lb. (4.5-6.8 N•m).

12. Apply a drop of Loctite 243 (blue), or an equivalent, threadlock to the cover screw prior to installation.

13A. On all models except Screamin' Eagle, install the air filter cover (B, **Figure 47**) and Allen screw (A). Tighten the screw to 36-60 in.-lb. (4.0-6.8 N•m).

13B. On Screamin' Eagle models, perform the following:

   a. Install the cover and tighten the Allen screw to 36-60 in.-lb. (4.1-6.8 N•m).

   b. Install the trim plate and screws, and tighten to 27-32 in.-lb. (3.1-3.6 N•m).

Removal/Installation (2007 FLHRSE3 and 2009 FLTRSE3 models)

Refer to **Figure 54** and **Figure 55**.

1A. On 2007 FLHRSE3 models, remove the air filter cover Allen screw and remove the cover.

1B. On 2009 FLTRSE3 models, remove the trim plate screws and trim plate. Remove the air filter cover Allen screw and remove the cover.

2. Remove the screws (A, **Figure 56**) from the air filter element (B).

3. Gently pull the air filter element away from the backplate and remove it.

4. Clean the air filter as described in this section.

5. On models so equipped, inspect the seal ring on the air filter cover for hardness or deterioration. Replace if necessary.

6. Check the tightness of the standoff bolts (**Figure 57**). If loose, tighten the bolts to 55-60 in.-lb. (6.3-6.7 N•m).

7. Install the element onto the backplate and align the screw holes.

8. Install filter screws (A, **Figure 56**) through the element (B). Tighten the screws to 55-60 in.-lb. (6.2-6.8 N•m).

9. Apply a drop of Loctite 243 (blue), or an equivalent, threadlock to the cover screw prior to installation.

10. Install the air filter cover (B, **Figure 47**) and Allen screw (A). Tighten the Allen screw to 36-60 in.-lb. (4.0-6.8 N•m).

11. If removed, install the trim plate and screws. Tighten the screws to 27-32 in.-lb. (3.1-3.6 N•m).

Element Cleaning

WARNING
Do not clean the air filter in any type of solvent. Never clean the air filter element in gasoline or any type of low flash-point solvent. The residual solvent or vapors left by these chemicals may cause a fire or explosion after the filter is reinstalled.

CAUTION
Do not tap or strike the air filter element on a hard surface to dislodge dirt. Do not use high air pressure to dry the filter. Doing so will damage the element.

1. Remove the air filter element as described in this section.

2. Place the air filter in a pan filled with lukewarm water and mild detergent. Move the air filter element back and forth to help dislodge trapped dirt. Thoroughly rinse in clean water to remove all detergent residue.

3. Remove the air filter and hold it up to a strong light. Check the filter pores for dirt and oil. Repeat the cleaning process until there is no longer dirt and oil in the filter pores. If the air filter cannot be cleaned, or if the filter is saturated with oil or other chemicals, replace it.

CAUTION
Do not blow compressed air through the outer surface of the air filter element. Doing so can force dirt trapped on the outer filter surface deeper into the air filter element, restricting airflow and damaging the air filter element.

4. Gently apply compressed air from the inside of the air filter element to remove loosened dirt and dust trapped in the filter.

5. Inspect the air filter element. Replace if torn or damaged. Do not ride the motorcycle with a damaged filter element as it may allow dirt to enter the engine.

6. Clean the breather hoses in the same solution used for the filter. Make sure both hoses are clean and clear. Clean out with a pipe cleaner if necessary.

7. Wipe the inside of the cover and backplate with a clean, damp shop rag.

LUBRICATION, MAINTENANCE AND TUNE-UP

CAUTION
Air will not pass through a wet or damp filter. Make sure the filter is thoroughly dry before installing it.

8. Allow the filter to dry completely, and reinstall it as described in this section.

SUSPENSION AND FASTENERS

Steering Play

Check the steering head play as described in Chapter Thirteen at the intervals specified in **Table 1**. Adjust the bearings as necessary.

Rear Swing Arm Pivot Bolt

Check the rear swing arm pivot bolt tightness as described in Chapter Fourteen at the intervals specified in **Table 1**.

Rear Shock Absorbers

Check the rear shock absorbers for oil leaks or damaged bushings. Check the shock absorber mounting bolts and nuts for tightness. Refer to *Shock Absorbers* in Chapter Fourteen for procedures.

Engine Mounts and Stabilizer

Check the stabilizers and the engine and frame mounts for loose or damaged parts. Refer to Chapter Five for procedures.

Exhaust System

Check all fittings, including the crossover pipe connections, for exhaust leaks at the intervals specified in **Table 1**. Tighten all bolts and nuts to the specifications listed in Chapter Four. Replace gaskets as necessary.

Fasteners

CAUTION
*To accurately check cylinder head mounting bolts for tightness, refer to **Cylinder Head Installation** in Chapter Four. Tightening these bolts incorrectly can cause an oil leak or cylinder head damage.*

Check the tightness of all fasteners at the intervals specified in **Table 1**, especially those on:
1. Engine mounting hardware.
2. Engine and primary covers.
3. Handlebar and front fork.
4. Gearshift levers.
5. Sprocket bolts and nuts.
6. Brake pedal and lever.
7. Exhaust system.
8. Lighting equipment.
9. Fairing and saddlebag components.

Electrical Equipment and Switches

Check all electrical equipment and switches for proper operation at the intervals specified in **Table 1**. Refer to Chapter Eleven.

COMPRESSION TEST

A compression test is one of the most effective ways to check the condition of the engine. If possible, check the compression at each tune-up, record it, and then compare the readings at subsequent tune-ups. This will help identify any developing problems.

All Models Except Screamin' Eagle

1. Prior to starting the compression test, make sure the following are correct:
   a. The cylinder head bolts (**Figure 58**) are tightened to the specified torque as described in Chapter Four.
   b. The battery is fully charged to ensure proper engine cranking speed.
2. Ride the motorcycle until engine is at normal operating temperature.
3. Place the motorcycle on a level surface and park it on the jiffy stand. Turn off the engine.
4. Shift the transmission into neutral.
5. Remove the spark plugs (**Figure 59**) as described in this chapter. Reinstall the caps onto the spark plugs and place the spark plugs against the cylinder heads to ground them.
6. Connect the compression tester (**Figure 60**) to the front cylinder following the manufacturer's instructions.
7. On carbureted models, make sure the starting enrichment (choke) knob (**Figure 21**) is off.
8. Rotate the throttle to the wide-open position and keep it there.

9. Crank the engine over continuously through 5-7 full revolutions until there is no further rise in pressure.
10. Record the reading and remove the tester. The standard compression pressure is 125 psi (862 kPa).
11. Repeat the procedure for the rear cylinder.
12. Reinstall the spark plugs and reconnect their caps.

2007-2008 Screamin' Eagle Models

1. Prior to starting the compression test, make sure the following are correct:
    a. The cylinder head bolts (**Figure 58**) are tightened to the specified torque as described in Chapter Four.
    b. The battery is fully charged to ensure proper engine cranking speed.
2. Ride the motorcycle until engine is at normal operating temperature.
3. Place the motorcycle on a level surface and park it on the jiffy stand. Turn off the engine.
4. Shift the transmission into neutral.
5. Remove the spark plugs (**Figure 59**) as described in this chapter. Reinstall the caps onto the spark plugs and place the spark plugs against the cylinder heads to ground them.
6. Connect the compression tester (**Figure 60**) to the front cylinder following the manufacturer's instructions.
7. Rotate the throttle to the wide-open position and keep it there.
8. Crank the engine over continuously through 5-7 full revolutions until there is no further rise in pressure. Record the reading and remove the tester. The standard compression pressure is 130-170 psi (896-1172 kPa).
9. Repeat the tester procedure for the rear cylinder.
10. Disconnect the automatic compression release (ACR) 2-pin AMP electrical connector (No. 203FB) with one yellow/green wire and one violet/grey wire from the main harness between the cylinder heads. Also disconnect the identical ACR 2-pin AMP electrical connector (No.201RB) for the rear cylinder head.
11. Repeat the test procedure for both cylinders with the ACR disconnected. The standard compression pressure at this time is 200-220 psi (1379-1517 kPa).
12. Reinstall the spark plugs and reconnect their caps.
13. Connect both automatic compression release (ACR) 2-pin AMP electrical connectors to the main harness.

2009 Screamin' Eagle Models

1. Prior to starting the compression test, make sure the following is correct:
    a. The cylinder head bolts (**Figure 58**) are tightened to the specified torque as described in Chapter Four.
    b. The battery is fully charged to ensure proper engine cranking speed.
2. Ride the motorcycle until engine is at normal operating temperature.
3. Place the motorcycle on a level surface and park it on the jiffy stand. Turn off the engine.

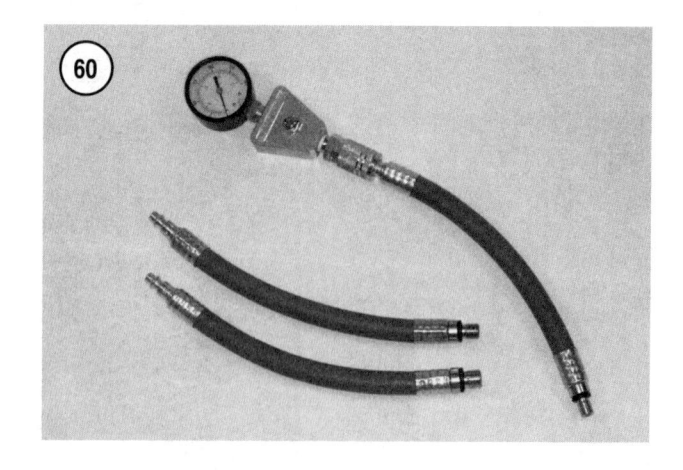

4. Remove the air filter cover and filter element as described in this chapter.
5. Remove the spark plugs (**Figure 59**) as described in this chapter. Reinstall the caps onto the spark plugs and place the spark plugs against the cylinder heads to ground them.
6. Disconnect the throttle control actuator (TCA) 6-pin electrical connector (No. 211) from the induction module (**Figure 61**).

CAUTION
To avoid damage to the induction module and/or the throttle plate, do not use any metallic object to hold the throttle plate open.

7. Carefully open throttle plate. Then, *very carefully* insert a wood or plastic dowel into the throttle plate area of the induction module to hold the throttle plate in the wide open position. Use a dowel about 12 in. (305 mm) long and by 0.75 in. (19 mm) in diameter.
8. Connect the compression tester (**Figure 60**) to the front cylinder following its manufacturer's instructions.
9. Crank the engine over continuously through 5-7 full revolutions until there is no further rise in pressure.
10. Record the reading and remove the tester. The standard compression pressure is 130-170 psi (896-1172 kPa).
11. Disconnect the system relay (**Figure 62**) from the left side electrical caddy as described in Chapter Eleven.
12. Repeat the test procedure for the front cylinder with the system relay removed. The standard compression pressure at this time is 200-220 psi (1379-1517 kPa).
13. Connect the system relay onto the left side electrical caddy as described in Chapter Eleven.
14. Repeat the test procedure for the rear cylinder with the system relay connected and again with it disconnected. Record the readings.
15. Carefully open the throttle plate. Then, *very carefully*, withdraw the wood or plastic dowel from the throttle plate area of the induction module.

NOTE
The removal of the system relay may set a diagnostic trouble code. Clear the diagnostic trouble code(s) as described in Chapter Two, if necessary.

LUBRICATION, MAINTENANCE AND TUNE-UP

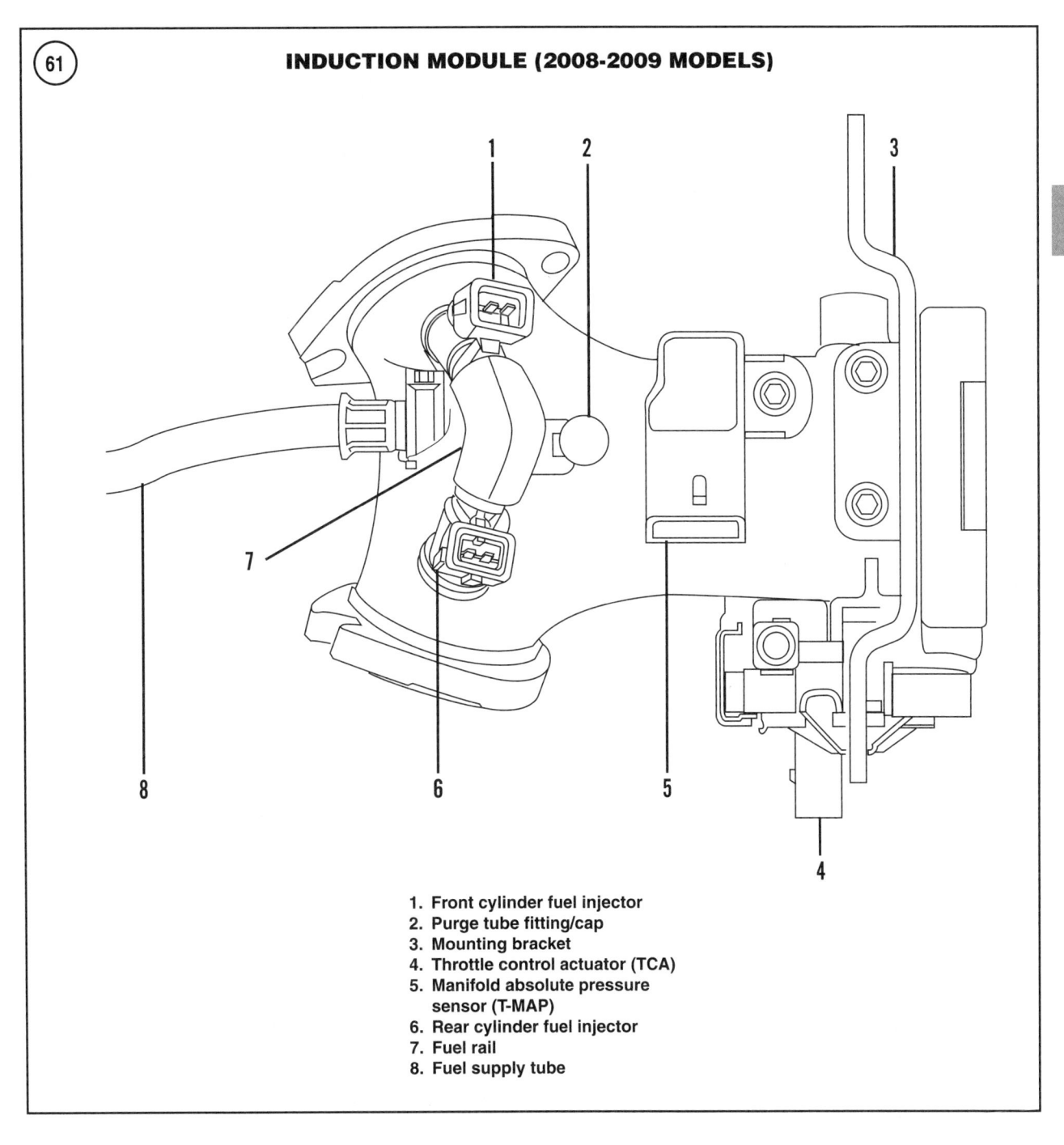

⑥ INDUCTION MODULE (2008-2009 MODELS)

1. Front cylinder fuel injector
2. Purge tube fitting/cap
3. Mounting bracket
4. Throttle control actuator (TCA)
5. Manifold absolute pressure sensor (T-MAP)
6. Rear cylinder fuel injector
7. Fuel rail
8. Fuel supply tube

16. Connect the throttle control actuator (TCA) 6-pin electrical connector (No. 211) onto the induction module (**Figure 61**).

17. Reinstall the spark plugs and reconnect their caps as described in this chapter.

18. Install the filter element and air filter cover as described in this chapter.

Results

Table 6 lists the standard engine compression reading. When interpreting the results, also note any difference between the cylinder readings. The pressure must not vary between the cylinders by more than 10 percent. If a low reading is obtained or greater differences are indicated, consider worn or broken rings and/or leaky or sticky valves. Do not rule out a blown head gasket also.

If a low reading (10 percent or more) is obtained, pour about a teaspoon of engine oil into the spark plug hole. Then, perform another compression test and record the reading. If the compression increases significantly, the valves are good but the rings are defective on that cylinder. If compression does not increase, the valves require servicing.

SPARK PLUGS

Removal

CAUTION
Whenever the spark plug is removed, dirt around it can fall into the plug hole.

1. Blow away any loose dirt or debris that may have accumulated around the base of the spark plug and could fall into the cylinder head.
2. Grasp the spark plug cable (**Figure 63**), and twist from side to side to break the seal loose. Then, pull the cap off the spark plug. If the cap is stuck to the plug, twist it slightly to break it loose.

NOTE
Use a spark plug socket equipped with a rubber insert that holds the spark plug. This type of socket is necessary for both removal and installation.

3. Install the spark plug socket onto the spark plug. Make sure it is correctly seated and install an open-end wrench or ratchet handle and remove the spark plug. Mark which cylinder it was removed from on the spark plug.
4. Repeat for the remaining spark plug.
5. Thoroughly inspect each plug. Look for broken center porcelain, excessively eroded electrodes and excessive carbon or oil fouling.
6. Inspect the spark plug caps and secondary wires for damage, or hardness. If any portion is damaged, the cap and secondary wire must be replaced as an assembly. The front and rear cylinder plug wire assemblies are different.

Service and Installation

Carefully gap the spark plugs to ensure a reliable, consistent spark. Use a spark plug gapping tool and a wire feeler gauge.
1. Insert a wire feeler gauge (**Figure 64**) between the center and side electrode of the plug. The correct gap is listed in **Table 6**. If the gap is correct, a slight drag will be felt as the wire gauge is pulled through. If there is no drag, or the gauge will not pass through, bend the side electrode with a gapping tool (**Figure 65**) to adjust the gap to the proper one listed in **Table 6**.
2. Install the terminal nut (A, **Figure 66**).
3. Apply a *light coat* of antiseize lubricant on the threads of the spark plug before installing it. Do *not* use engine oil on the plug threads.

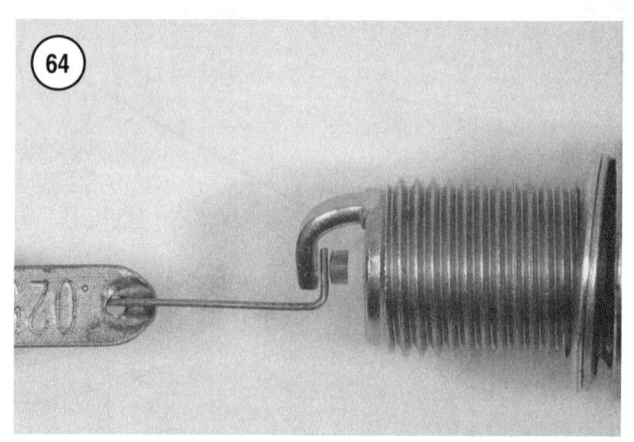

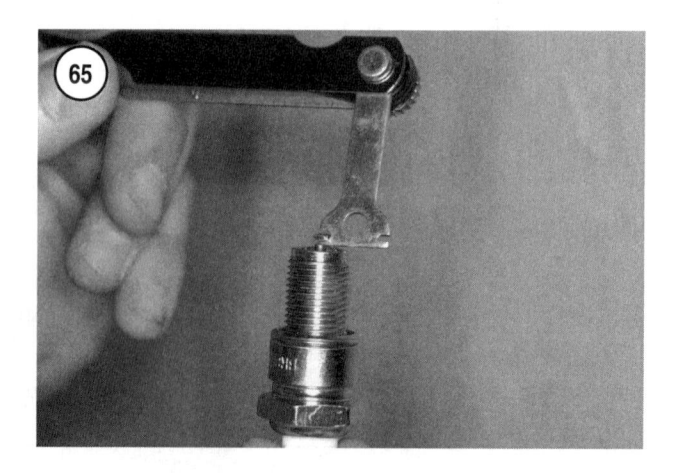

CAUTION
The aluminum cylinder head is easily damaged by cross-threading the spark plug.

4. Slowly screw the spark plug into the cylinder head by hand until it seats. Very little effort is required. If force is necessary, the plug is cross-threaded; unscrew it and try again.

LUBRICATION, MAINTENANCE AND TUNE-UP

A plug with an incorrect heat range can foul, overheat and cause piston damage.

In general, use a hot plug for low speeds and low temperatures. Use a cold plug for high speeds, high engine loads and high temperatures. The plug should operate hot enough to burn off unwanted deposits, but not so hot that it is damaged or causes preignition. To determine if plug heat range is correct, remove each spark plug and examine the insulator.

Do not change the spark plug heat range to compensate for adverse engine or carburetion conditions.

When replacing plugs, make sure the reach (B, **Figure 66**) of the plug is correct. A longer than standard plug could interfere with the piston, causing engine damage.

Refer to **Table 6** for recommended spark plugs.

Spark Plug Reading

Reading the spark plugs can provide a significant amount of information regarding engine performance. Reading plugs that have been in use will give an indication of spark plug operation, air/fuel mixture composition and engine conditions (such as oil consumption or pistons). Before checking the spark plugs, operate the motorcycle under a medium load for approximately 6 miles (10 km). Avoid prolonged idling before shutting off the engine. Remove the spark plugs as described in this chapter. Examine each plug and compare it to those in **Figure 67** while referring to the following sections to determine the operating conditions.

On carbureted models, if the plugs are being read to determine if carburetor jetting is correct, start with *new* plugs and operate the motorcycle at the load that corresponds to the jetting information desired. For example, if the main jet is in question, operate the motorcycle at full throttle and shut the engine off and coast to a stop.

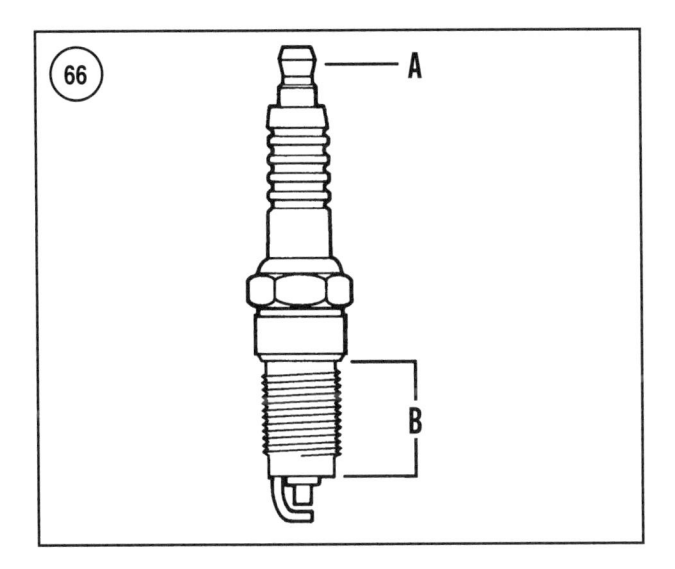

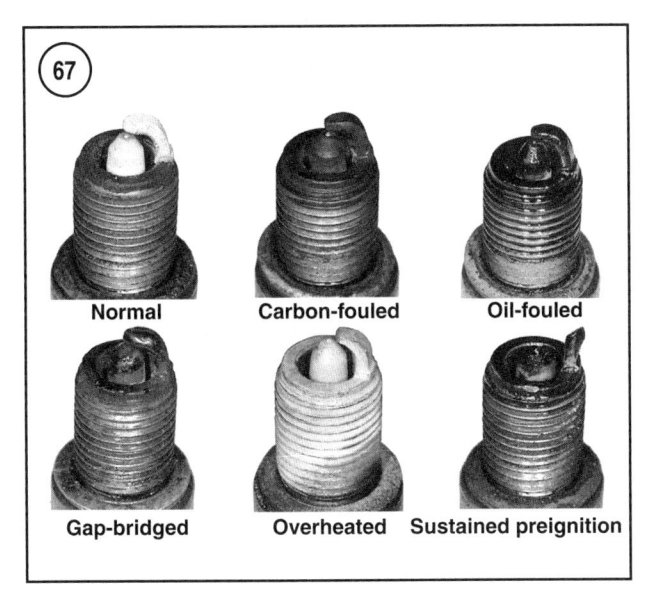

5. Hand-tighten the spark plug until it seats against the cylinder head, and then tighten to 12-18 ft.-lb. (16.3-24.4 N•m).
6. Install the spark plug cap and lead to the correct spark plug. Rotate the cap slightly in both directions and make sure it is attached to the spark plug.
7. Repeat the procedure for the other spark plug.

Spark Plug Heat Range

NOTE
The manufacturer only recommends using HD-6R12 spark plugs. This specific resistor spark plug reduces radio interference created by the ignition system and also maintains optimal performance.

Spark plugs are available in heat ranges hotter or colder than the plugs originally installed by the manufacturer.

Select a plug with a heat range designed for the loads and conditions under which the motorcycle will be operated.

Spark Plug Reading

Normal condition

If the plug has a light tan- or gray-colored deposit and no abnormal gap wear or erosion, good engine, air/fuel mixture and ignition conditions are indicated. The plug in use is of the proper heat range and may be serviced and returned to use.

Carbon fouled

Soft, dry, sooty deposits covering the entire firing end of the plug are evidence of incomplete combustion. Even though the firing end of the plug is dry, the plug's insulation decreases when in this condition. An electrical path is formed that bypasses the electrodes, resulting in a misfire condition. Carbon fouling can be caused by one or more of the following:
1. Rich fuel mixture (carbureted models).
2. Cold spark plug heat range.
3. Clogged air filter.

4. Improperly operating ignition component.
5. Ignition component failure.
6. Low engine compression.
7. Prolonged idling.

Oil fouled

The tip of an oil-fouled plug has a black insulator tip, a damp oily film over the firing end and a carbon layer over the entire nose. The electrodes are not worn. Oil-fouled spark plugs may be cleaned in an emergency, but it is better to replace them. It is important to correct the cause of fouling before the engine is returned to service. Common causes for this condition are:
1. Incorrect air/fuel mixture (carbureted models).
2. Low idle speed or prolonged idling.
3. Ignition component failure.
4. Cold spark plug heat range.
5. Engine still being broken in.
6. Valve guides worn.
7. Piston rings worn or broken.

Gap bridging

Plugs with this condition exhibit gaps shorted out by combustion deposits between the electrodes. If this condition is encountered, check for excessive carbon or oil in the combustion chamber. Be sure to locate and correct the cause of this condition.

Overheating

Badly worn electrodes and premature gap wear are signs of overheating, along with a gray or white blistered porcelain insulator surface. The most common cause for this condition is using a spark plug of the wrong heat range (too hot). If spark plug is the correct heat range and is overheated, consider the following causes:
1. Lean air/fuel mixture (carbureted models).
2. Improperly operating ignition component.
3. Engine lubrication system malfunction.
4. Cooling system malfunction (clogged cooling fins).
5. Engine air leak.
6. Improper spark plug installation (over-tightening).
7. No spark plug gasket.

Worn out

Corrosive gases formed by combustion and high voltage sparks have eroded the electrodes. A spark plug in this condition requires more voltage to fire under hard acceleration. Replace with a new spark plug.

Preignition

If the electrodes are melted, preignition is almost certainly the cause. Check for intake air leaks at the intake manifold, carburetor, or throttle body, and for advanced ignition timing. It is also possible that a plug of the wrong heat range (too hot) is being used. Find the cause of the preignition before returning the engine to service.

IGNITION TIMING

The ignition system is controlled by the ignition control module (ICM) or electronic control module (ECM). There are no means of adjusting ignition timing. The manufacturer does not provide any procedure for checking the ignition timing. If an ignition related problem is suspected, inspect the ignition components as described in Chapter Eleven.

Incorrect ignition timing can cause a loss of engine performance. It may also cause overheating.

IDLE SPEED ADJUSTMENT

Carbureted Models

1. Start the engine and warm it to normal operating temperature. Shut off the engine.
2. Make sure the starting enrichment (choke) valve is off.
3. Connect a portable tachometer to the engine following the manufacturer's instructions.

LUBRICATION, MAINTENANCE AND TUNE-UP

NOTE
Figure 68 is shown with the air filter assembled removed to better illustrate the step.

4. Start the engine and with the engine idling, compare the tachometer reading to the idle speed specification in **Table 6**. If the tachometer reading is incorrect, adjust the idle speed with the carburetor throttle stop screw (**Figure 68**).

NOTE
The idle mixture is set by the manufacturer and is not adjustable.

5. Accelerate the engine a couple of times and release the throttle. The idle speed must return to the set speed.
6. If installed, disconnect and remove the portable tachometer.

Fuel-Injected Models

Idle speed adjustment must be performed by a dealership. Do not tamper with the throttle stop screw as it will not permanently change idle speed.

VEHICLE ALIGNMENT (2006-2008 MODELS)

This procedure checks the alignment of the rear axle with the swing arm pivot shaft. It also checks the engine stabilizer adjustment that aligns the engine in the frame. These inspections determine the condition and alignment of the components that hold the motorcycle together: steering stem, front axle, engine, swing arm pivot shaft and rear axle. If any of these items are out of alignment, the motorcycle will not handle properly. Bad handling will increase the motorcycle's vibration level while reducing its overall performance and driveability.

NOTE
There is no alignment procedure for the 2009 models due to the all new frame and engine mounting system.

Preliminary Inspection

Before checking vehicle alignment, make the following checks to spot problems caused from normal wear. Adjust, repair or replace any component as required.
1. On 2006-2007 models, the upper stabilizer, mounted between the cylinder heads (**Figure 69**) and upper frame weldment (**Figure 70**), aligns the top portion of the engine in the frame.
2. On 2008 models, the front upper stabilizer, mounted on the front cylinder head and upper frame tube, aligns the top portion of the engine in the frame.
3. The lower stabilizer link, connecting the lower mounting bracket (A, **Figure 71**) to the lower frame weldment (B), aligns the bottom portion of the engine in the frame.
4. Check both engine stabilizers every 10,000 miles (16,000 km) for loose or damaged parts. To service or replace the engine stabilizer, refer to Chapter Four. To adjust the engine stabilizer, perform the *Alignment* procedure in this section.
5. Check the steering head bearing adjustment as described in Chapter Thirteen. Adjust the steering play if necessary.
6. Check the runout of each wheel as described in Chapter Twelve. True or replace the wheel(s) as necessary.
7. Check the tightness of the engine mounting bolts; tighten if necessary as described in Chapter Five.

Alignment

Refer to **Figure 72** and **Figure 73**.
Each alignment step, inspection and adjustment, affects the next one. Work carefully and accurately when performing the following steps.
1. Perform all of the checks listed in *Preliminary Inspection* (this section). When all of the settings are within the specifications, continue with the procedure. If the motorcycle has been involved in a crash, refer frame alignment to a dealership.

NOTE
Always disarm the optional TSSM/HFSM security system prior to disconnecting the battery or pulling the Maxi-Fuse so the siren will not sound.

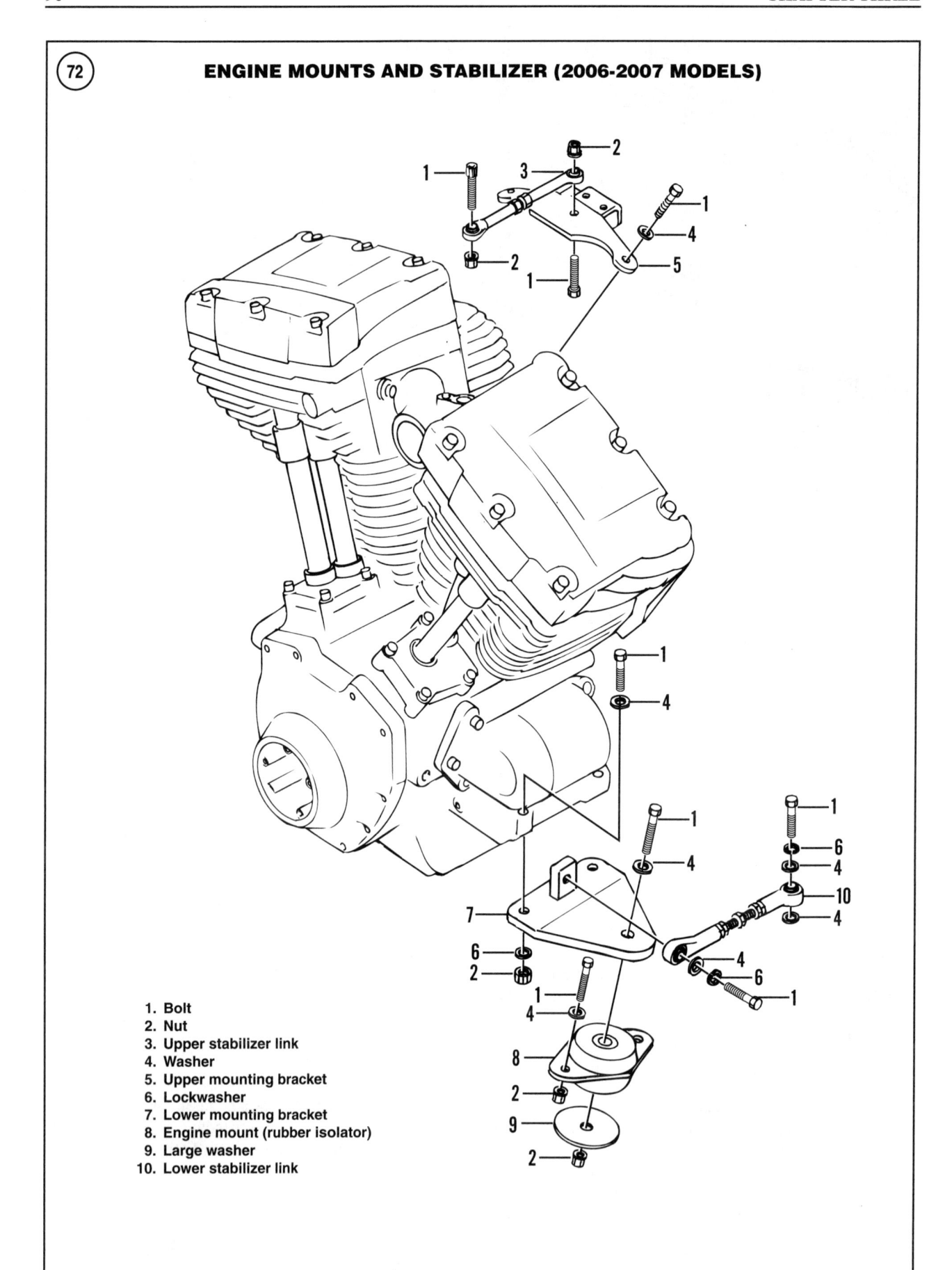

CHAPTER THREE

72 ENGINE MOUNTS AND STABILIZER (2006-2007 MODELS)

1. Bolt
2. Nut
3. Upper stabilizer link
4. Washer
5. Upper mounting bracket
6. Lockwasher
7. Lower mounting bracket
8. Engine mount (rubber isolator)
9. Large washer
10. Lower stabilizer link

LUBRICATION, MAINTENANCE AND TUNE-UP

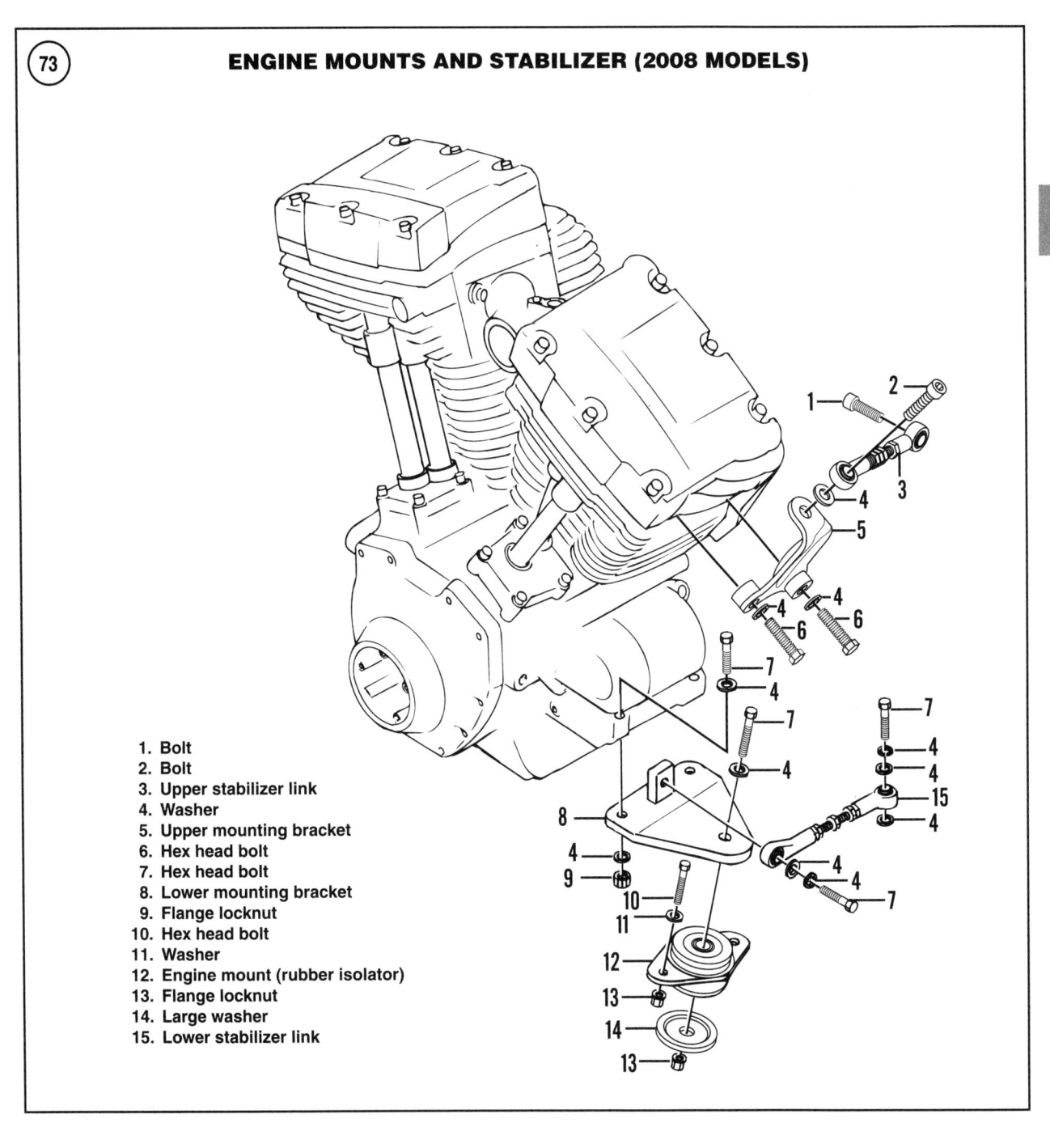

73 ENGINE MOUNTS AND STABILIZER (2008 MODELS)

1. Bolt
2. Bolt
3. Upper stabilizer link
4. Washer
5. Upper mounting bracket
6. Hex head bolt
7. Hex head bolt
8. Lower mounting bracket
9. Flange locknut
10. Hex head bolt
11. Washer
12. Engine mount (rubber isolator)
13. Flange locknut
14. Large washer
15. Lower stabilizer link

2. Disconnect the negative battery cable as described in Chapter Eleven.
3. Remove the seat and both saddlebags as described in Chapter Seventeen.
4. Remove the fuel tank as described in Chapter Nine or Chapter Ten.
5. Remove the mufflers as described in Chapter Four.
6. Remove both passenger footboards as described in Chapter Seventeen.
7. Remove the chrome trim cap from the swing arm brackets.
8. Remove the flange locknuts (A, **Figure 74**) securing the voltage regulator (B) to the frame. Remove the voltage regulator from the mounting studs and move it out of the

75

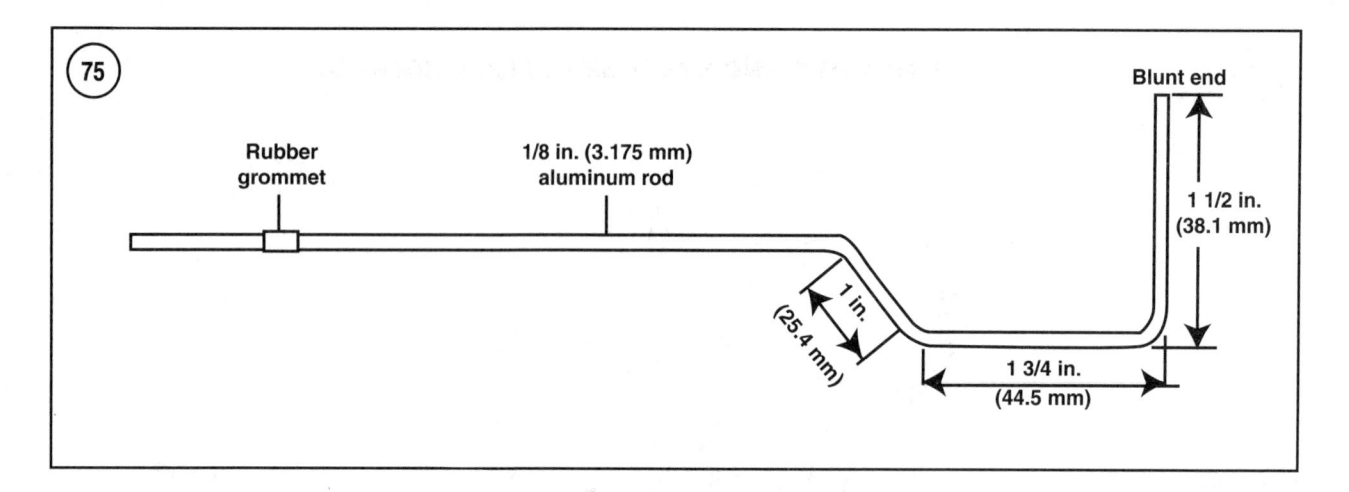

Rubber grommet — 1/8 in. (3.175 mm) aluminum rod — Blunt end — 1 1/2 in. (38.1 mm) — 1 in. (25.4 mm) — 1 3/4 in. (44.5 mm)

way. Suspend it with a length of wire; do not suspend it by the electrical harness.

9. Use a rear wheel alignment tool (JIMS part No. 928) or fabricate a special tool from 1/8 in. (3.176 mm) aluminum, or drill, rod as shown in **Figure 75**.

10. Insert the blunt end of the alignment tool (**Figure 75**) into the center of the swing arm pivot shaft (**Figure 76**). Slide the rubber grommet down the length of the tool until it is aligned with the center of the rear axle.

11. Without repositioning the grommet, remove the tool and repeat the process for the opposite swing arm side, comparing this position with the first measurement. The measurements must be equal. If the alignment is incorrect, perform the *Final Drive Belt Deflection and Alignment* procedure as described in this chapter. When the drive belt adjustment is correct, continue with the procedure.

NOTE
The remainder of the procedure must be performed with the rear wheel off the ground.

12. Support the motorcycle with the rear wheel off the ground. Refer to *Motorcycle Stands* in Chapter Twelve.

13. If loose, tighten the upper mounting bracket bolts as follows:
    a. On 2006-2007 models, tighten the bolts (**Figure 69**) securing the upper mounting bracket to both cylinders heads to 35-40 ft.-lb. (47.5-54.2 N•m).
    b. On 2008 models, tighten the bolts securing the upper mounting bracket to the front cylinder head to 35-40 ft.-lb. (47.5-54.2 N•m).
    c. Tighten the bolt securing the upper stabilizer link eyelet (**Figure 70**) to the frame weldment to 18-22 ft.-lb. (24.4-29.8 N•m).

14. Use an open-end crowfoot wrench and loosen both upper stabilizer link jam nuts (**Figure 77**).

15. Remove the bolt and nut (**Figure 78**) securing the upper stabilizer link eyelet to the upper mounting bracket.

NOTE
Refer to Figure 79 for the location of various fasteners.

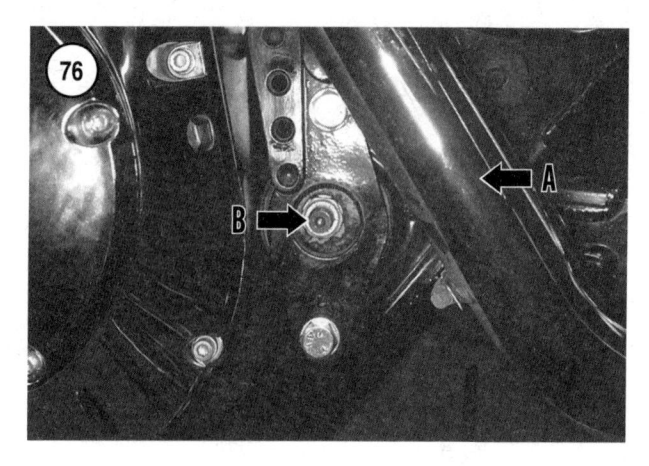

16. If loose, tighten both bolts (A, **Figure 80**) and nuts securing the lower mounting bracket to the engine. Tighten the fasteners to 36-40 ft.-lb. (48.8-54.2 N•m).

17. If loose, tighten the bolt (B, **Figure 80**) securing the lower stabilizer link eyelet to the lower mounting bracket. Tighten the bolt to 18-22 ft.-lb. (24.4-29.8 N•m).

18. Loosen both lower stabilizer link jam nuts (C, **Figure 71**).

19. Remove the bolt (**Figure 81**) securing the lower stabilizer link eyelet to the frame weldment.

20. Remove the bolt (C, **Figure 80**), washers and nut securing the lower mounting plate to the engine mount.

21. At the upper stabilizer, use an open-end crowfoot wrench and rotate the center hex nut to achieve equal thread engagement at both stabilizer eyelets to allow the bolt (**Figure 78**) to pass through the eyelet without any stress or engine movement. Install the bolt (**Figure 78**) and nut securing the stabilizer link eyelet to the upper mounting bracket. Tighten finger tight at this time.

22. At the lower stabilizer, rotate the center hex nut to achieve equal thread engagement at both stabilizer eyelets to allow the bolt (**Figure 81**) to pass through the eyelet without any stress or engine movement. Install the bolt (**Figure 81**) and nut securing the stabilizer link eyelet to the frame weldment. Tighten finger tight at this time.

23. Alternately tighten the bolts on the upper (**Figure 78**) and lower (**Figure 81**) stabilizer links to 18-22 ft.-lb. (24.4-29.8 N•m).

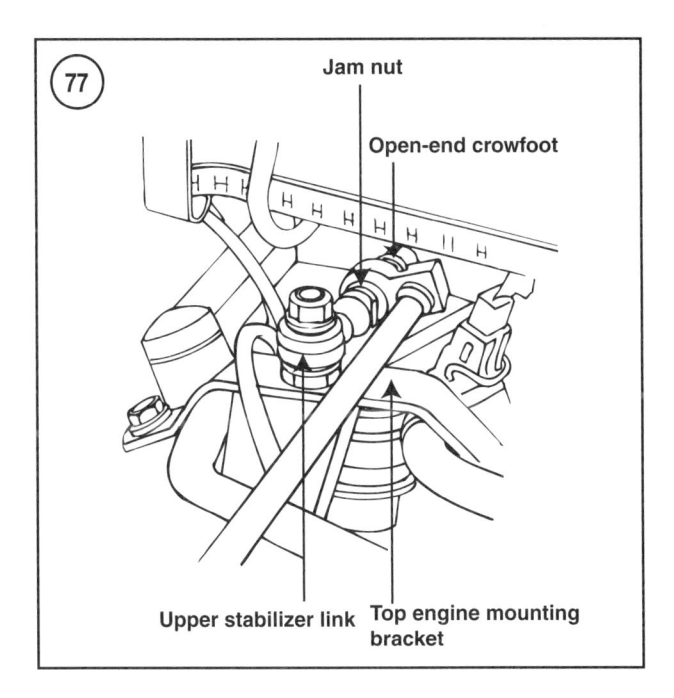

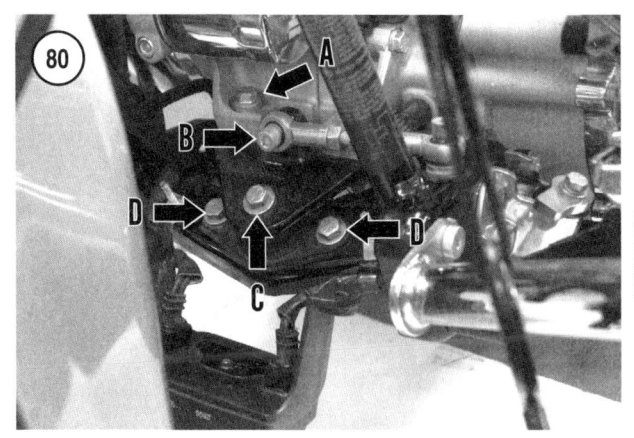

LUBRICATION, MAINTENANCE AND TUNE-UP

77
Jam nut
Open-end crowfoot
Upper stabilizer link
Top engine mounting bracket

78

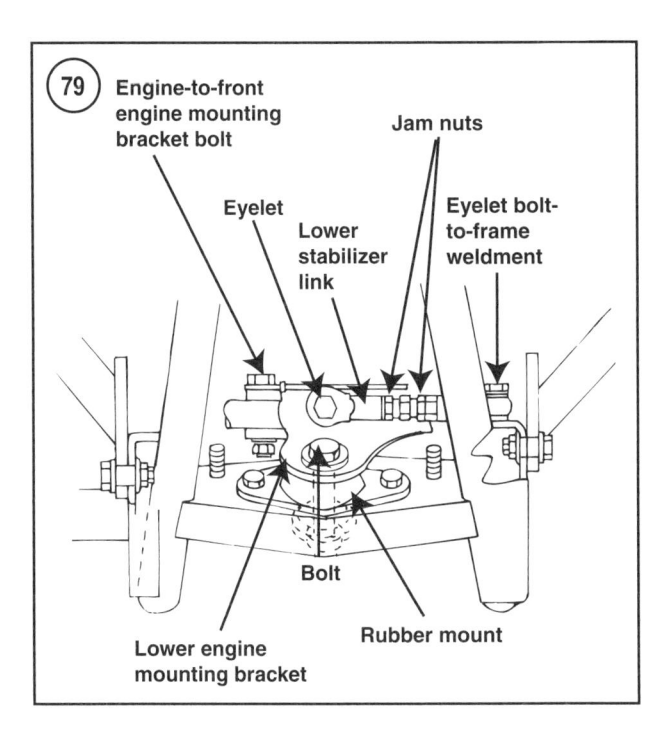

79
Engine-to-front engine mounting bracket bolt
Jam nuts
Eyelet
Lower stabilizer link
Eyelet bolt-to-frame weldment
Bolt
Rubber mount
Lower engine mounting bracket

80

81

24. Secure the stabilizer link adjuster and mounting eyelets to prevent movement or binding. Tighten the jam nuts securely on both stabilizers.

25. With the engine weight on the front rubber mount, verify that the front rubber mount is centered under the engine mounting bolt hole (C, **Figure 80**). If not centered, perform the following:

   a. Loosen the bolts (D, **Figure 80**) securing the engine mount to the frame.
   b. Push the engine mount plate from side to side to center it under the lower mounting bracket bolt hole. Bounce or wiggle the engine if necessary to unload any stress on the rubber isolator portion of the engine mount to achieve alignment.
   c. Tighten the two engine mount-to-frame mount bolts (D, **Figure 80**) to 15-20 ft.-lb. (20.3-27.1 N•m).

26. Install the bolt (C, **Figure 80**), and small washer through the lower mounting bracket and engine mount. Install the large washer and nut securing the lower mounting plate to the engine mount.

27. Tighten the bolt (C, **Figure 80**) and lower nut securing the engine lower mounting bracket to the engine mount (rubber isolator). Tighten the fasteners to 15-20 ft.-lb. (20.3-27.1 N•m).

28. Move the voltage regulator (B, **Figure 74**) onto the frame mounting studs. Install the flange locknuts (A, **Figure 74**) securing the voltage regulator (B) to the frame and tighten to 70-100 in.-lb. (7.9-11.3 N•m).

29. Install the chrome trim cap onto each swing arm bracket.

30. Install both passenger footboards as described in Chapter Seventeen.
31. Install the mufflers as described in Chapter Four.
32. Install the fuel tank as described in Chapter Nine or Chapter Ten.
33. Install the seat and both saddlebags as described in Chapter Seventeen.
34. Connect the negative battery cable as described in Chapter Eleven.
35. Test ride the motorcycle.

Table 1 MAINTENANCE AND LUBRICATION SCHEDULE[1]

Pre-ride check
  Check tire condition and inflation pressure.
  Check wheel rim condition.
  Check light and horn operation.
  Check engine oil level; add oil if necessary.
  Check brake fluid level and condition; add fluid if necessary.
  Check clutch fluid level and condition (Screamin' Eagle models); add fluid if necessary.
  Check the operation of the front and rear brakes.
  Check throttle operation.
  Check clutch lever operation.
  Check fuel level in fuel tank; top off if necessary.
  Check fuel system for leaks.
First Service
  Change engine oil and filter.
  Check the oil lines, brake lines, and clutch lines (Screamin' Eagle models) for leaks.
  Inspect air filter element.
  Check tire condition and inflation pressure.
  Check the wheel spokes; tighten as necessary.
  Change the primary chaincase lubricant.
  Change transmission lubricant.
  Check clutch operation; adjust if necessary.
  Check primary chain deflection; adjust if necessary (2006 models).
  Check drive belt deflection; adjust if necessary.
  Check drive belt and sprockets condition.
  Check battery condition; clean cable connections if necessary.
  Check front and rear brake pads and discs for wear.
  Check brake fluid level and condition; add fluid if necessary.
  On Screamin' Eagle models, check clutch fluid level and condition; add fluid if necessary.
  Inspect spark plugs.
  Lubricate front brake and clutch lever pivot pin.
  Check throttle cable operation. Adjust and lubricate the cable as necessary (2006-2007 models).
  Check the clutch cable operation. Adjust and lubricate the cable as necessary (except Screamin' Eagle models).
  On Screamin' Eagle models, check the clutch release system.
  On carbureted models, check enrichment (choke) cable operation. Adjust the cable as necessary.
  Check engine idle speed (carbureted models); adjust if necessary.
  Check fuel system for leaks.
  Check electrical switches and equipment for proper operation.
  Check the jiffy stand. Lubricate as necessary.
  Adjust the steering head bearings.
  Lubricate the hinges and latches on the fuel door, Tour-Pak and saddlebags.
  Check the exhaust system for leaks, cracks or loose fasteners.
  Check all fasteners for tightness[2].
  Road test the motorcycle.
Every 5000 miles (8000 km)
  Change engine oil and filter.
  Check the oil lines, brake lines, and clutch lines (Screamin' Eagle models) for leaks.
  Clean and inspect air filter element.

(continued)

LUBRICATION, MAINTENANCE AND TUNE-UP

Table 1 MAINTENANCE AND LUBRICATION SCHEDULE[1] (continued)

Every 5000 miles (8000 km) (continued)
  Check tire condition and inflation pressure.
  Check the wheel spokes; tighten as necessary.
  Check clutch operation; adjust if necessary.
  Check primary chain deflection; adjust if necessary.
  Check drive belt deflection; adjust if necessary.
  Check throttle cable operation. Adjust and lubricate the cable and throttle grip as necessary (2006-2007 models).
  Check the clutch cable operation. Adjust and lubricate the cable as necessary.
  On Screamin' Eagle models, check the clutch release system.
  On carbureted models, check enrichment (choke) cable operation. Adjust the cable as necessary.
  Check cruise control disengage switch and components (2006-2007 models).
  Check fuel system for leaks.
  Check fuel shutoff valve operation (carbureted models).
  Check brake fluid level and condition; add fluid if necessary.
  Check clutch fluid level and condition (Screamin' Eagle models); add fluid if necessary.
  Check transmission oil level; add fluid if necessary.
  Check primary chaincase oil level; add fluid if necessary.
  Inspect spark plugs.
  Check air suspension for pressure, proper operation and leaks.
  Check battery condition; clean cable connections if necessary.
  Check electrical switches and equipment for proper operation.
  Check engine idle speed; adjust if necessary.
  Inspect and lubricate front brake lever pivot pin.
  Inspect and lubricate clutch lever pivot pin.
  Lubricate the hinges and latches on the fuel door, Tour-Pak and saddlebags.
  Check the exhaust system for leaks, cracks or loose fasteners.
  Check steering play; adjust if necessary.
  Road test the motorcycle.
Every 10,000 miles (16,000 km)
  Check the oil lines, brake lines, and clutch lines (Screamin' Eagle models) for leaks.
  Clean and inspect air filter element.
  Check tire condition and inflation pressure.
  Change the primary chaincase lubricant.
  Check clutch operation; adjust if necessary.
  Check primary chain deflection; adjust if necessary.
  Check drive belt deflection; adjust if necessary.
  Check drive belt and drive sprockets condition.
  Check battery condition; clean cable connections if necessary.
  Check throttle cable operation. Adjust and lubricate the cable and throttle grip as necessary (2006-2007 models).
  Check the clutch cable operation. Adjust and lubricate the cable as necessary.
  On Screamin' Eagle models, check the clutch release system.
  On carbureted models, check enrichment (choke) cable operation. Adjust the cable as necessary.
  Check fuel system for leaks.
  Check electrical switches and equipment for proper operation.
  Check windshield bushings (models so equipped).
  Check the jiffy stand. Lubricate as necessary.
  Check front and rear brake pads and discs for wear.
  Check brake fluid level and condition; add fluid if necessary.
  Check clutch fluid level and condition (Screamin' Eagle models); add fluid if necessary.
  Replace spark plugs (2006-2007 models).
  Lubricate and adjust the steering head bearings.
  Inspect the windshield bushings.
  Check all fasteners for tightness[2].
  Check rear swing arm pivot bolt tightness.
  Check engine mounts and stabilizer links.
  Road test the motorcycle.
Every 20,000 miles (32,000 km)
  Replace spark plugs (2008-2009 models).
  Clean and repack the swing arm bearings.
  Change the transmission lubricant.
  Disassemble, inspect, and lubricate the steering head bearings.
  Check the wheel spokes; tighten as necessary.
Every 25,000 miles (40,000 km)
  Replace the fuel tank filter screen (carbureted models).
  Adjust the steering head bearings.
Every 50,000 miles (80,000 km)
  Change front fork oil.

(continued)

Table 1 MAINTENANCE AND LUBRICATION SCHEDULE[1] (continued)

Every year
  Check battery condition; clean cable connections if necessary.
  Check the exhaust system for leaks, cracks, broken heat shields and/or loose fasteners.
Every 2 years
  Flush and replace the hydraulic fluid in the brake system.
  Flush and replace the fluid in the clutch system (Screamin' Eagle models).
Routine
  Inspect the rear wheel compensator isolators at every tire change (2008-2009 models).

1. Consider this maintenance schedule a guide to general maintenance and lubrication intervals. If the motorcycle is ridden harder than normal or if it is exposed to mud, water or high humidity; perform most of these maintenance items more frequently than indicated.
2. Except cylinder head bolts. Cylinder head bolts must be tightened following the procedure listed in Chapter Four. Improper tightening of the cylinder head bolts may cause cylinder gasket damage and/or cylinder head leaks.

Table 2 TIRE INFLATION PRESSURE (COLD)*

	kPa	psi
Front wheels		
Rider only	248	36
Rider and one passenger	248	36
Rear wheels		
Rider only	248	36
Rider and passenger	275	40

*Tire pressure for OE equipment tires. Aftermarket tires may require different inflation pressure.

Table 3 FUEL, ENGINE AND DRIVE FLUID CAPACITIES

Item	Capacity
Fuel tank, total	
2006-2007 models	5.0 gal. (18.9 L)
2008-2009 models	6.0 gal. (22.7 L)
Fuel tank, reserve*	
2006-2007 models	0.9 gal. (3.4 L)
2008-2009 models	1.0 gal. (3.8 L)
Oil tank with filter	1.0 gal. (3.8 L)
Transmission (approximate)	
2006-2007 models	20-24 oz. (591-710 ml)
2008-2009 models	32 oz. (946 ml)
Primary chaincase (approximate)	
2006 models	32 oz. (946 ml)
2007-2009 models	45 oz. (1331 ml)

*Low fuel warning light on.

Table 4 RECOMMENDED ENGINE OIL

Type	Viscosity	H-D Rating	Ambient operating temperature
H-D Multi-grade	SAE 10W40	HD 360	Below 40° F (4° C)
H-D Multi-grade	SAE 20W50	HD 360	Above 40° F (4° C)
H-D Regular Heavy	SAE 50	HD 360	Above 60° F (16° C)
H-D Extra Heavy	SAE 60	HD 360	Above 80° F (16° C)
Screamin' Eagle models SYN3 Synthetic Motorcycle Lubricant	SAE 20W50	HD 360	Above 40° F (4° C)

Table 5 RECOMMENDED LUBRICANTS AND FLUIDS

Brake fluid	DOT 4 hydraulic fluid
Clutch fluid (Screamin' Eagle models)	DOT 4 hydraulic fluid
Front fork oil	H-D Type E fork oil

(continued)

LUBRICATION, MAINTENANCE AND TUNE-UP

Table 5 RECOMMENDED LUBRICANTS AND FLUIDS (continued)

Fuel	91 pump octane or higher
Transmission oil	
All models except Screamin' Eagle models	H-D Formula+ Transmission and Primary Chaincase Lubricant
Screamin' Eagle models	Screamin' Eagle SYN3 Synthetic Motorcycle Lubricant
Primary chaincase oil	
All models except Screamin' Eagle models	H-D Formula+ Transmission and Primary Chaincase Lubricant
Screamin' Eagle models	Screamin' Eagle SYN3 Synthetic Motorcycle Lubricant

Table 6 MAINTENANCE SPECIFICATIONS

Item	Specification
Brake pad minimum thickness (front and rear)	
2006-2007 models	0.04 in. (1.2 mm)
2008-2009 models	0.016 in. (0.41 mm)
Clutch cable free play	1/16-1/8 in. (1.6-3.2 mm)
Drive belt deflection	
FLHX models	1/4-5/16 in. (6.4-7.9 mm)
All other models	3/8-7/16 in. (9.5-11.1 mm)
Engine compression	
All models except Screamin' Eagle	125 psi (862 kPa)
Screamin' Eagle (2007-2009 models)[1]	
ARC valve connected	130-170 psi (896-1172 kPa)
ARC valve disconnected	200-220 psi (1379-1517 kPa)
Idle speed	950-1050 rpm
Ignition timing	Non-adjustable
Primary chain free play (2006 models)	
Cold engine	5/8-7/8 in. (15.9-22.2 mm)
Hot engine	3/8-5/8 in. (9.5-15.9 mm)
Rear axle alignment	1/32 in. (0.8 mm)
Spark plugs	
Gap	0.038-0.043 in. (0.97-1.09 mm)
Type	HD No. 6R12[2]

1. The 2006 Screamin' Eagles are not fitted with the ARC valve. The manufacturer does not provide the specification of the 2006 Screamin' Eagle without the ARC valve.
2. Harley-Davidson recommends that no other type of spark plug be substituted.

Table 7 MAINTENANCE AND TUNE-UP TORQUE SPECIFICATIONS

Item	ft.-lb.	in.-lb.	N•m
Air filter			
All models except 2007 FLHRSE3 and 2009 FLTRSE3			
Cover screw			
All models except Screamin' Eagle	36-60	–	4.0-6.8
Screamin' Eagle	27-32	–	3.1-3.6
Mounting bracket	–	40-60	4.5-6.8
2007 FLHRSE3 and 2009 FLTRSE3			
Filter element mounting screws	–	55-60	6.2-6.8
Standoff bolts	–	55-60	6.2-6.8
Cover screw	–	36-60	4.1-6.8
Trim plate screws	–	27-32	3.1-3.6
Clutch adjusting screw locknut	–	72-120	8.1-13.6
Clutch cover screws	–	84-108	9.5-12.2
Engine oil drain plug	14-21	–	19-28.5
Primary chaincase			
Inspection cover screws	–	84-108	9.5-12.2
Chain adjuster shoe nut*	21-29	–	28.5-39.3
Oil drain plug	14-21	–	19-28.5
Jiffy stand leg stop bolt	12-15	–	16.3-20.3
Rear axle nut	95-105	–	128.8-142.4
Spark plug	12-18	–	16.3-24.4
Transmission oil drain plug	14-21	–	19-28.5
Transmission oil filler cap/dipstick	–	25-75	2.8-8.5

(continued)

Table 7 MAINTENANCE AND TUNE-UP TORQUE SPECIFICATIONS (continued)

Item	ft.-lb.	in.-lb.	N•m
Vehicle alignment (2006-2008 models)			
Lower mounting bracket			
Engine bolts	36-40	–	48.8-54.2
Engine mount (rubber mount-to-frame)	15-20	–	20.3-27.1
Engine mount (rubber mount-to-lower bracket)	15-20	–	20.3-27.1
Lower stabilizer link			
Frame weldment bolt	18-22	–	24.4-29.8
Engine mounting bracket bolt	18-22	–	24.4-29.8
Upper mounting bracket–to–cylinder head bolts	35-40	–	47.5-54.2
Upper stabilizer link			
Frame weldment bolt	18-22	–	24.4-29.8
Frame mounting bracket	18-22	–	24.4-29.8
Voltage regulator flange nut	–	70-100	7.9-11.3

*2006 models only.

CHAPTER FOUR

ENGINE TOP END AND EXHAUST SYSTEM

The engine is an air-cooled four-stroke, overhead-valve V-twin. Viewed from the engine's right side, engine rotation is clockwise.

Both cylinders fire once in 720° of crankshaft rotation. The rear cylinder fires 315° after the front cylinder. The front cylinder fires again in another 405°. Note that one cylinder is always on its exhaust stroke when the other fires on its compression stroke.

Refer to **Tables 1-5** at the end of the chapter for specifications.

ENGINE SERVICE PRECAUTIONS

Before working on the engine, note the following:
1. Review *Service Methods* and *Measuring Tools* in Chapter One.
2. The text frequently mentions the left and right side of the engine. This refers to the engine as it is mounted in the frame, not how it may sit on the workbench.
3. Always replace worn or damaged fasteners with those of the same size, type and torque requirements. Clearly identify each bolt before replacing it. Lubricate bolt threads with engine oil, unless otherwise noted, before tightening them. If a torque specification is not listed in **Table 5**, refer to the general torque recommendations table in Chapter One.
4. Use the correct tools as noted. Refer to Chapter One for a list of tools and their part numbers.
5. Store parts in boxes, plastic bags and containers. Use masking tape and a permanent, waterproof marking pen to label parts.
6. Use a set of assorted size and color vacuum hose identifiers (Lisle part No. 74600) to identify hoses and fittings during engine removal and disassembly.
7. Use a vise with protective jaws to hold parts.
8. Use a press and/or the specific tools listed when force is required to remove and install parts. Do not try to pry, hammer or otherwise force them on or off.
9. Replace all gaskets, O-rings and oil seals during reassembly. Lubricate new O-rings with the lubricant that is being sealed. Apply a small amount of grease to the inner lips of each new seal to prevent damage when the engine is first started. Thoroughly clean all gasket, O-ring or seal mating surfaces before installation.
10. Record the location, position and thickness of all shims as they are removed.
11. Always disarm the optional security system (TSSM/HFSM) before disconnecting the battery or pulling the Maxi-Fuse so the siren will not sound.

SERVICING ENGINE IN FRAME

The following components can be accessed while the engine is mounted in the frame:
1. Rocker arm cover and rocker arms.
2. Cylinder heads.
3. Cylinders and pistons.
4. Camshafts.
5. Gearshift mechanism.
6. Clutch and primary drive assembly.
7. Transmission.
8. Carburetor or fuel-injection induction module.
9. Starter and gears.
10. Alternator and electrical systems.

ROCKER ARMS, PUSHRODS AND VALVE LIFTERS

Refer to **Figure 1** and **Figure 2**.

CHAPTER FOUR

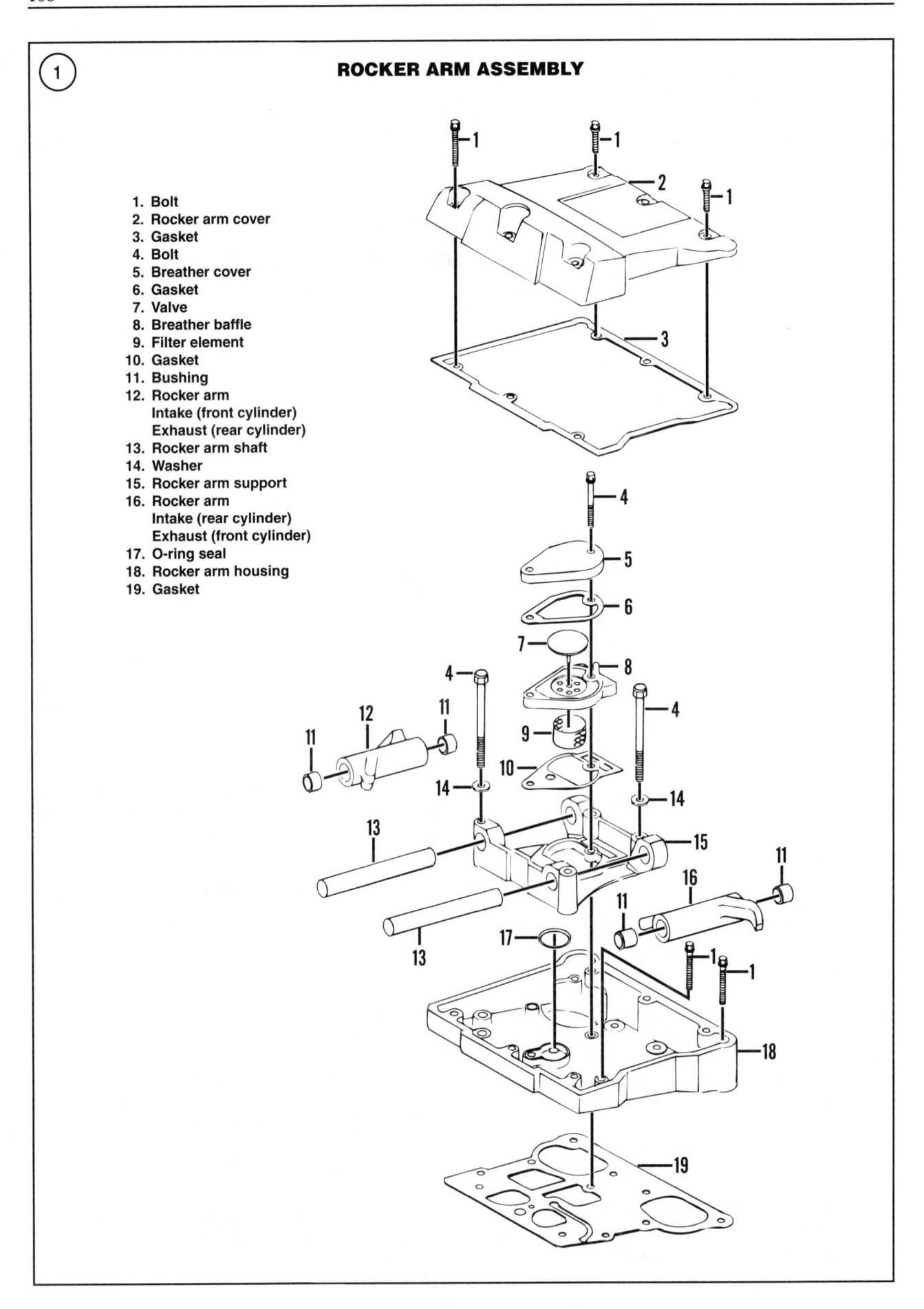

ROCKER ARM ASSEMBLY

1. Bolt
2. Rocker arm cover
3. Gasket
4. Bolt
5. Breather cover
6. Gasket
7. Valve
8. Breather baffle
9. Filter element
10. Gasket
11. Bushing
12. Rocker arm
    Intake (front cylinder)
    Exhaust (rear cylinder)
13. Rocker arm shaft
14. Washer
15. Rocker arm support
16. Rocker arm
    Intake (rear cylinder)
    Exhaust (front cylinder)
17. O-ring seal
18. Rocker arm housing
19. Gasket

ENGINE TOP END AND EXHAUST SYSTEM

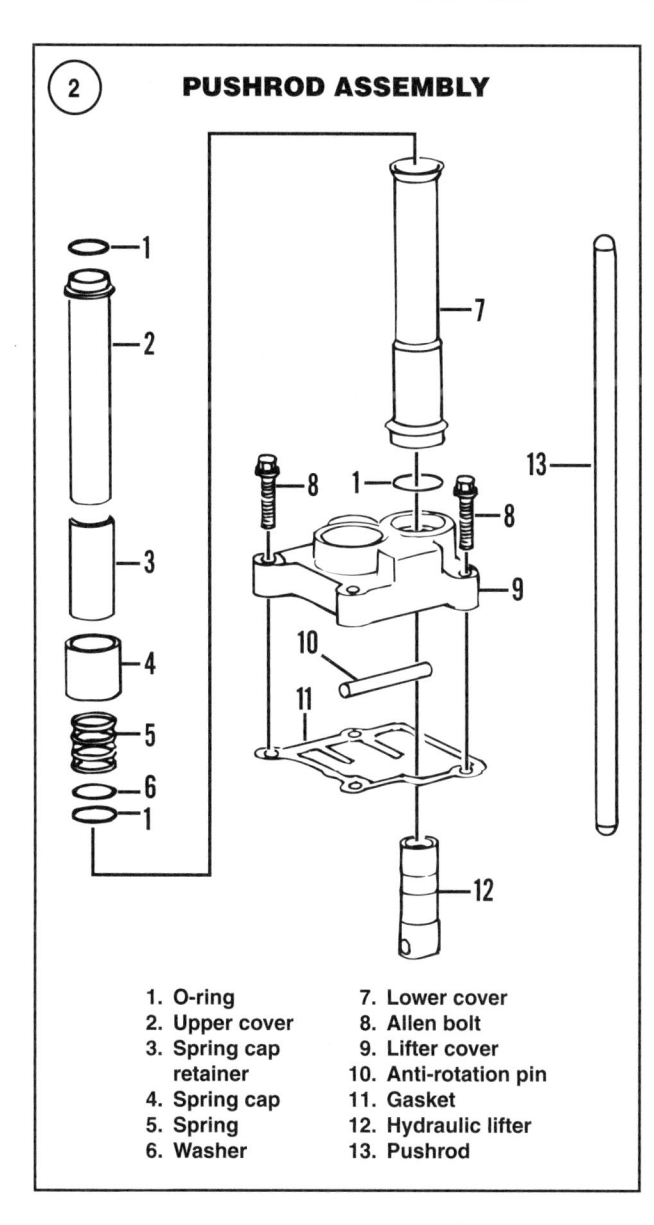

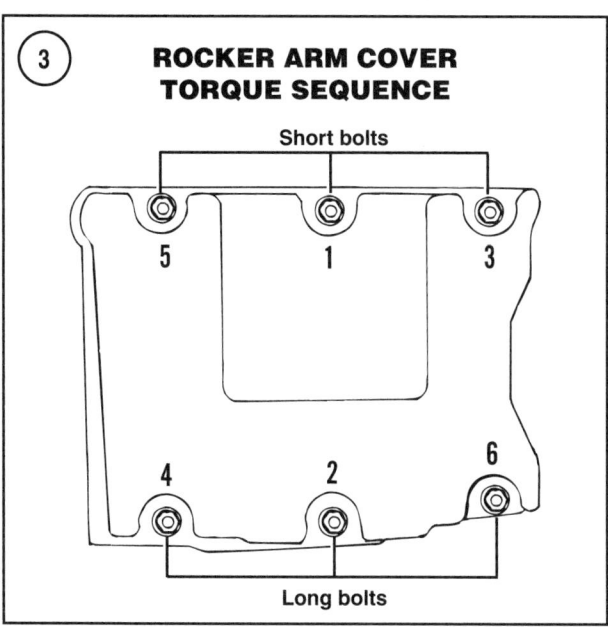

② PUSHROD ASSEMBLY

1. O-ring
2. Upper cover
3. Spring cap retainer
4. Spring cap
5. Spring
6. Washer
7. Lower cover
8. Allen bolt
9. Lifter cover
10. Anti-rotation pin
11. Gasket
12. Hydraulic lifter
13. Pushrod

③ ROCKER ARM COVER TORQUE SEQUENCE

Short bolts: 5, 1, 3
Long bolts: 4, 2, 6

The rocker arm, pushrod and valve lifter procedures are shown performed on the rear cylinder. The same procedures also apply to the front cylinder. Any differences are noted.

The rear cylinder head is closer to the frame backbone than the front cylinder. In some cases it may be possible to completely remove some the rocker arm mounting bolts on the front cylinder that are not possible on achieve on the rear cylinder.

Removal

1. If the engine is mounted in the frame, perform the following:
   a. Securely support the motorcycle on a level surface. Refer to *Motorcycle Stands* in Chapter Twelve.
   b. Thoroughly clean the engine of all dirt and debris.
   c. Remove the seat and right footboard as described in Chapter Seventeen.
   d. Disconnect the negative battery cable (Chapter Eleven).
   e. Drain the engine oil and remove the spark plugs as described in Chapter Three.
   f. Remove the fuel tank as described in Chapter Nine or Chapter Ten.
   g. Remove the air filter and backplate as described in Chapter Nine or Chapter Ten.
   h. Remove the exhaust system as described in this chapter.
   i. Remove the carburetor (Chapter Nine) or the fuel induction module (Chapter Ten).

2. Following the sequence shown in **Figure 3**, evenly loosen the rocker arm cover bolts. Remove each bolt and its captive washer. Note and record the location of the short and long bolts during removal.

3. Remove the rocker arm cover (**Figure 4**) and gasket. Discard the gasket.

4. If not already performed, remove both spark plugs as described in Chapter Three to make it easier to rotate the engine by hand.

5A. Use the pushrod tool (Motion Pro part No. 08-0255) and compress the upper and lower pushrod covers. Insert a screwdriver (**Figure 5**) and pry the spring cap retainer free and remove it.

5B. If special tool is not available, using a screwdriver, pry the spring cap retainer (**Figure 6**) from between the cylinder head and spring cap. Compress the upper (A, **Figure 7**) and lower (B) push rod covers.

CAUTION
The piston must be at top dead center (TDC) on the compression stroke to avoid damage to the pushrods and rocker arms.

6A. *With the primary chain cover in place*, position the piston for the cylinder being worked on at top dead center (TDC) on the compression stroke as follows:
   a. Support the motorcycle on a stand with the rear wheel off the ground. Refer to *Motorcycle Stands* in Chapter Twelve.
   b. Shift the transmission into fifth or sixth gear.
   c. Rotate the rear wheel in the direction of normal rotation.
   d. Stop rotating the rear wheel when the intake and exhaust valves are closed.
   e. Look into the spark plug hole with a flashlight and verify that the piston is at TDC.
   f. Wiggle both rocker arms. There should be free play that indicates that both valves are closed and that the piston is at top dead center (TDC) on the compression stroke. Also, the push rods are in the unloaded position.

6B. *With the primary chain cover removed*, position the piston for the cylinder being worked on at top dead center (TDC) on the compression stroke as follows:
   a. Shift the transmission into neurtral.
   b. Place a socket or wrench on the compensating sprocket shaft nut.
   c. Rotate the compensating sprocket shaft *counterclockwise* until the intake and exhaust valves are closed.
   d. Look into the spark plug hole with a flashlight and verify that the piston is at TDC.
   e. Wiggle both rocker arms. There should be free play that indicates that both valves are closed and that the piston is at top dead center (TDC) on the compression stroke. Also, the push rods are in the unloaded position.

ENGINE TOP END AND EXHAUST SYSTEM

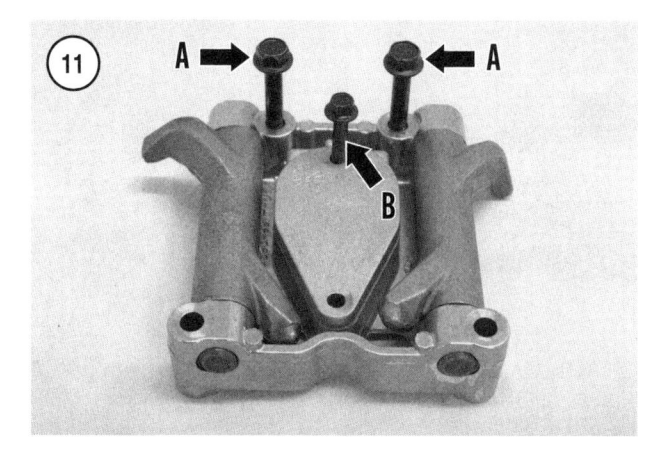

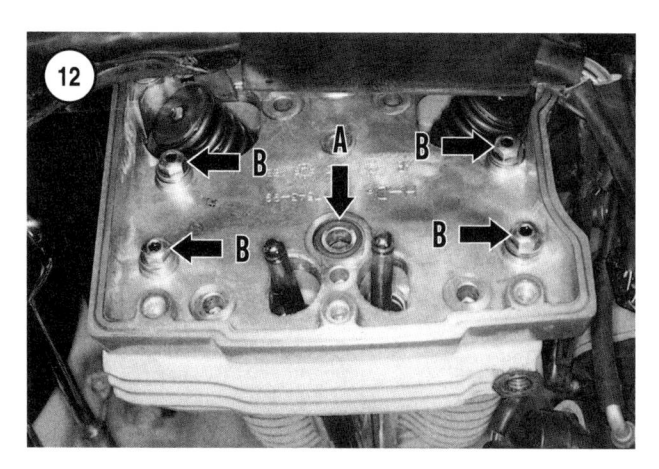

7. Using a crossing pattern, completely loosen the four bolts (A, **Figure 8**) securing the rocker arm support plate. The bolts cannot be removed at this time.

8. Completely loosen the bolts securing the breather assembly (B, **Figure 8**).

9. Remove the two *right side* rocker arm support bolts (A, **Figure 9**) and the *right side* breather assembly bolt (B).

NOTE
The two left side rocker arm support bolts and left side breather assembly bolt cannot be removed until the rocker arm support plate is removed from the cylinder head.

10. Lift the right side of the rocker arm support plate (A, **Figure 10**) sufficiently to clear the push rods (B).

11. Carefully slide the rocker arm support plate out through the right side and remove it from the cylinder head.

12. Remove the two *left side* rocker arm support bolts (A, **Figure 11**) and the *left side* breather assembly bolt (B). Remove the breather assembly from the rocker arm support plate.

13. Remove the O-ring seal (A, **Figure 12**) from the rocker arm housing.

CAUTION
When removing the pushrods, do not mix the parts from each set. When reinstalling the original pushrods, install them so each end faces in its original operating position. The pushrods develop a set wear pattern and installing them upside down may cause rapid wear to the pushrod, lifter and rocker arm.

14. Lift the silver (A, **Figure 13**) intake and black (B) exhaust pushrods from the cylinder head. Mark the top and bottom of each pushrod, and mark its operating location in the cylinder head.

15. Remove the pushrod covers.
   a. Slide the upper cover (A, **Figure 14**) down, and remove the pushrod cover assembly (B) from the cylinder head and the lifter cover.
   b. Label the cover assembly so it can be reinstalled in its original location.

c. Repeat the process to remove the remaining pushrod cover(s) on the opposite cylinder.

NOTE
*To clear the cylinder's lower cooling fins, loosen the lifter cover's two inner Allen bolts with a short 90° Allen wrench (**Figure 15**).*

16. Remove the lifter cover mounting bolts (**Figure 16**) and captive washers. Then, remove the cover.
17. Remove and discard the lifter cover gasket.

CAUTION
Do not mix the valve lifters when removing them. Mark them so they can be installed in their original positions.

18. Remove the anti-rotation pin (A, **Figure 17**), and then remove both valve lifters (B). Store the lifters upright in a container filled with clean engine oil until installation or inspection.
19. Cover the crankcase openings with duct tape (**Figure 18**) to prevent the entry of debris.
20. Loosen the six rocker arm housing bolts in 1/8-turn increments in the sequence shown in **Figure 19**. Remove the rocker arm housing bolts and their captive washers. Note that the two bolts on the left side of the engine are longer than the other four interior bolts (B, **Figure 12**). Mark the bolts for proper reinstallation.
21. Tap the rocker arm housing with a rubber mallet, and then lift it off the cylinder head.
22. Remove and discard the rocker arm housing gasket.
23. Disassemble and inspect the rocker arm assembly, pushrod covers or breather as described in this section.

Installation

NOTE
***Figure 20** and **Figure 21** are shown with the engine removed to clearly illustrate the steps.*

1. Position a *new* rocker arm housing gasket (**Figure 20**) onto the cylinder head so the breather channel (**Figure 21**) is covered and install the gasket.
2. Install the rocker arm housing onto the cylinder head.
3. Apply Loctite Threadlocker 243 (blue) to the bolt threads, and install the six rocker arm housing bolts along with their captive washer. Install the two long rocker arm housing bolts into the left side. Tighten all bolts by hand until snug. Following the sequences shown in **Figure 19**, evenly tighten the bolts in 1/8-turn increments. Tighten the rocker arm housing bolts to 10-14 ft.-lb. (13.6-19.0 N•m).

CAUTION
The valve springs must not contact any part of the rocker arm housing.

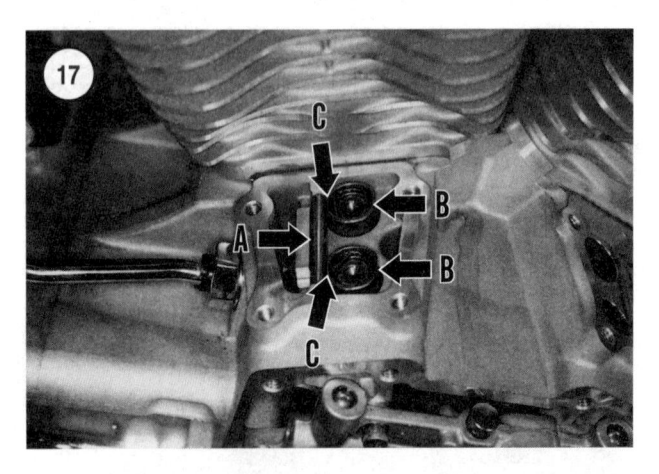

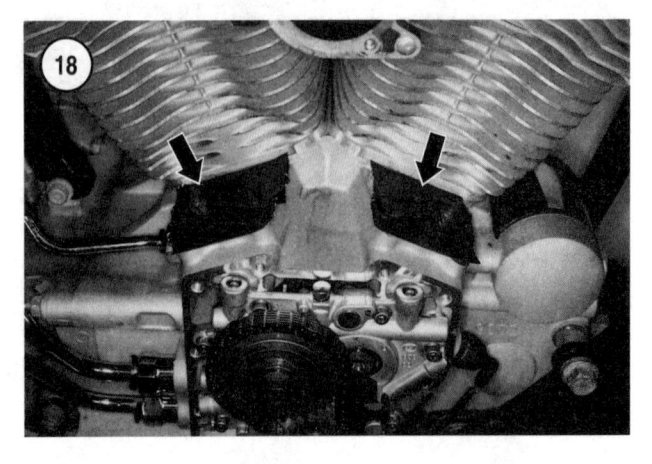

ENGINE TOP END AND EXHAUST SYSTEM

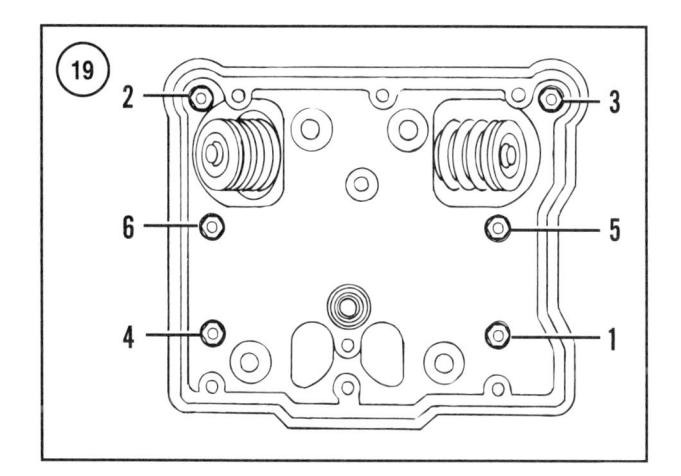

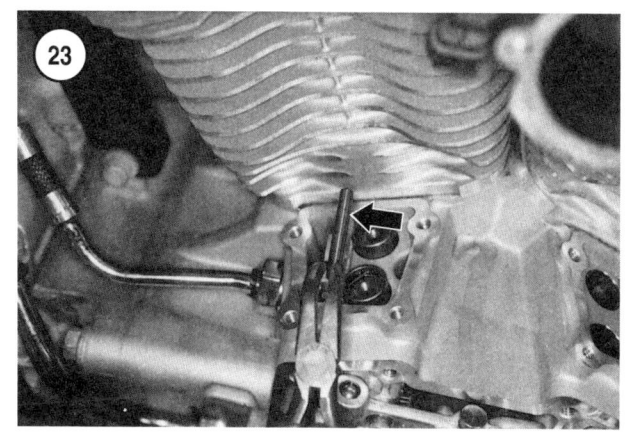

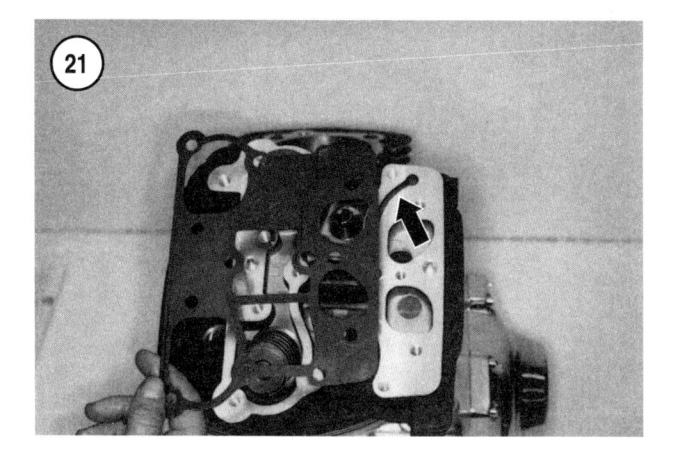

8. Remove the duct tape from the crankcase openings.
9. Install each valve lifter into the correct crankcase bore. The oil hole of each lifter (**Figure 22**) must face the inboard side of its bore and the lifter flats must face the front and rear of the engine. This is necessary for installation of the anti-rotation pin in the next step.

CAUTION
Failure to install the anti-rotational pin will allow the lifter to rotate off the camshaft lobe and cause severe internal engine damage.

10. Completely seat the anti-rotation pin (**Figure 23**) within the crankcase slot. Make sure the pin (A, **Figure 17**) rests against the flats (C) of both hydraulic lifters (B).
11. If the engine's position has been disturbed since the rocker arm components were removed, rotate the engine until both lifters for the cylinder being serviced sit on the lowest point (base circle) of the cam. The lifter's top surface should be flush with the top surface of the crankcase as shown in **Figure 24**.
12. Install a *new* lifter cover gasket (**Figure 25**) onto the crankcase.

NOTE
To clear the cylinder's lower cooling fins, tighten the lifter cover two inner Allen bolts with a short 90° Allen wrench.

4. Install a *new* O-ring seal (A, **Figure 12**) onto the rocker arm housing. Apply a light coat of clean engine oil to the O-ring.
5. Check for clearance between each valve spring and the rocker arm housing. If necessary, loosen the housing bolts, and adjust the position of the rocker arm housing. Retighten the bolts as described in this section.
6. Install the breather assembly onto the rocker arm support plate, if removed.
7. Apply Loctite Threadlocker 243 (blue) to the bolt threads and install the two left side bolts (A, **Figure 11**) and left side breather assembly bolt (B) onto the rocker arm housing.

112　CHAPTER FOUR

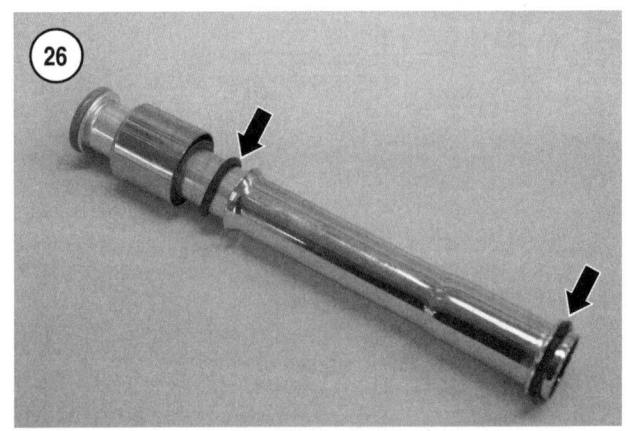

13. Install the lifter cover and the mounting bolts (**Figure 16**). Tighten the lift cover bolts to 90-120 in.-lb. (10.2-13.6 N•m).

14. Install a *new* O-ring (**Figure 26**) onto each end of the pushrod covers. Apply a light coat of clean engine oil to each O-ring.

15. If the pushrod cover assembly was disassembled, reassemble it as described in this section.

CAUTION
The pushrod covers and the pushrods must be installed in the correct locations on the cylinder head and lifter cover as indicated in **Table 4**.

16. Install the pushrod covers by performing the following:
    a. Compress the pushrod cover assembly, and fit the lower cover into the correct lifter cover bore (**Figure 27**).
    b. Slide the upper cover (**Figure 28**) up into the cylinder head bore. Do not install the spring cap retainer at this time.
    c. Repeat this process to install the remaining pushrod cover.

17. Install the pushrods as follows:

CAUTION
Two different length pushrods are used in the Twin Cam engines. The black exhaust push-

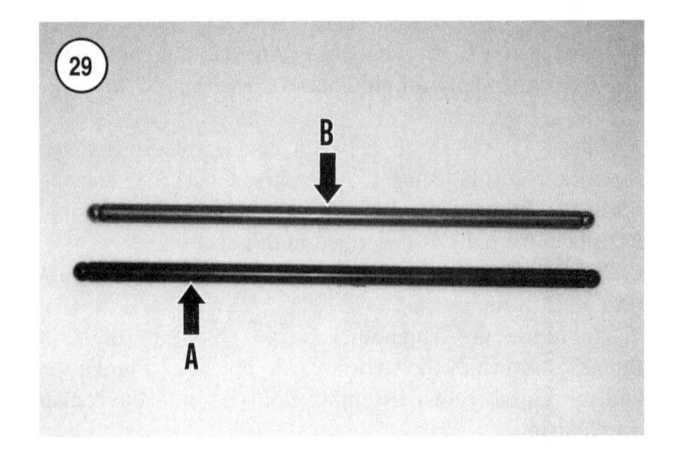

ENGINE TOP END AND EXHAUST SYSTEM 113

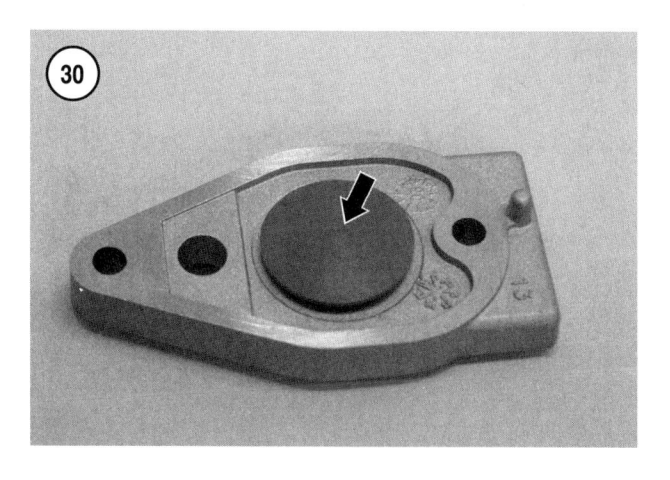

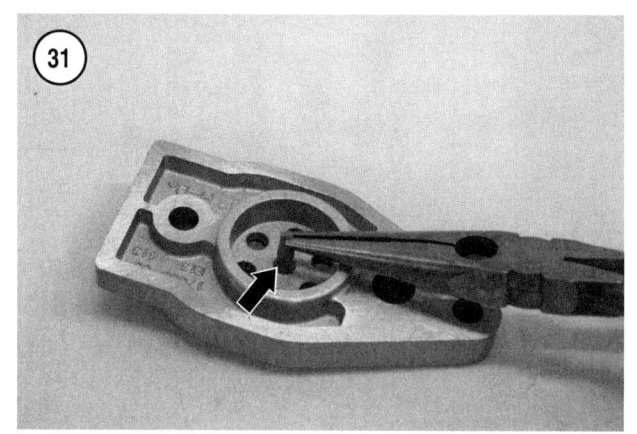

rods (A, **Figure 29**) are longer than the silver intake pushrods (B).

a. When installing the existing pushrods, install each pushrod in its original position and with the correct orientation. Refer to A, **Figure 13** for an intake pushrod, and B, **Figure 13** for an exhaust pushrod.

NOTE
Because new pushrods are symmetrical, they can be installed with either end facing up.

b. Make sure the pushrod is centered in its respective lifter.

18. If disassembled, install the breather assembly by performing the following:

a. If removed, install a new valve (**Figure 30**) onto the breather baffle. Lubricate the valve stem with denatured alcohol or glass cleaner, insert the valve stem through the center hole in the top of the breather baffle and pull the stem (**Figure 31**) through from the other side to seat the valve.

b. Align the hole in a new filter (**Figure 32**) with the valve stem, and press the filter into the bore (**Figure 33**) on the bottom of the baffle.

c. Install a *new* breather baffle gasket (**Figure 34**).

d. Hold the filter element in place and install the breather baffle (**Figure 35**).

e. Install a *new* cover gasket (**Figure 36**).

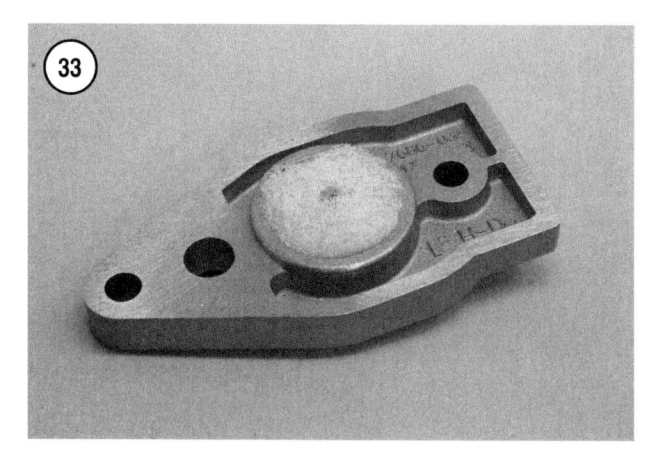

f. Install the cover (A, **Figure 37**) and *left side* cover bolt (B).

19. Install the two *left side* bolts (**Figure 38**).
20. From the right side, slide the rocker arm support plate (A, **Figure 39**) onto the rocker arm housing, and past the pushrods (B). Do not forget to install the breather assembly left side bolt (B, **Figure 37**). This bolt cannot be installed after the rocker arm support plate is in place on the cylinder head.
21. Lift the left side of the rocker arm support plate, and install the two right side bolts (A, **Figure 40**) and the right side breather assembly bolt (B). Do not tighten the bolts at this time.

CAUTION
To avoid damaging a pushrod, the rocker arms or the valves, follow a crossing pattern and tighten the rocker arm support plate bolts evenly in 1/4-turn increments. When tightening the mounting bolts, spin each pushrod by hand to ensure the rocker arm support plate is being tightened evenly. If one or both pushrods cannot be rotated, loosen the mounting bolts and determine the cause.

22. Install the rocker arm support plate bolts and finger-tighten them. Using a crossing pattern, tighten the rocker arm support plate bolts evenly to 18-22 ft.-lb. (24.4-29.8 N•m).
23. Lift each lower pushrod cover and confirm that each pushrod rotates freely.
24. Make sure the pushrod cover O-rings are correctly seated in the cylinder head and lifter cover.
25A. Use the pushrod tool (Motion Pro part No. 08-0255) to compress the upper and lower pushrod covers (**Figure 41**) and install the spring cap retainer. Repeat the process to install the remaining pushrod cover.
25B. If the pushrod tool is not available, compress the spring cap with a thin open end wrench (A, **Figure 42**), or an equivalent, and install the spring cap retainer (B). Make sure the spring cap retainer is positioned correctly on both the upper cover and the spring cap (**Figure 43**). Repeat the process to install the remaining pushrod cover.

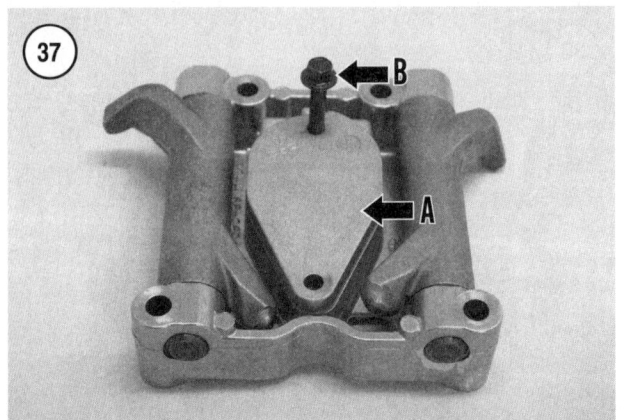

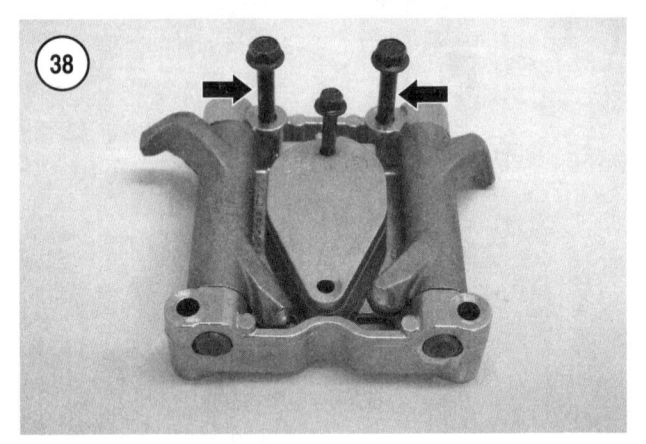

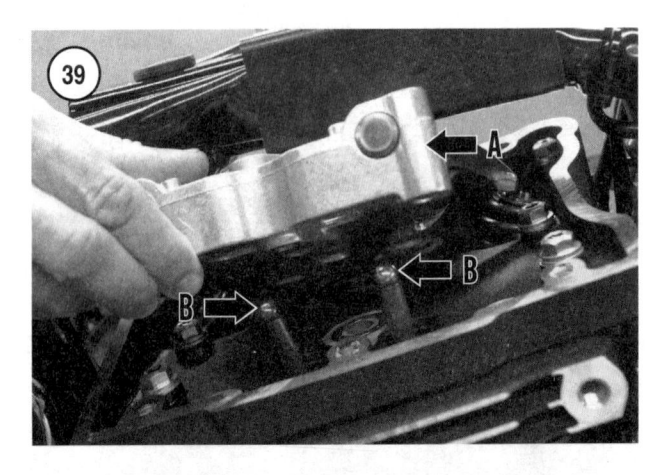

ENGINE TOP END AND EXHAUST SYSTEM

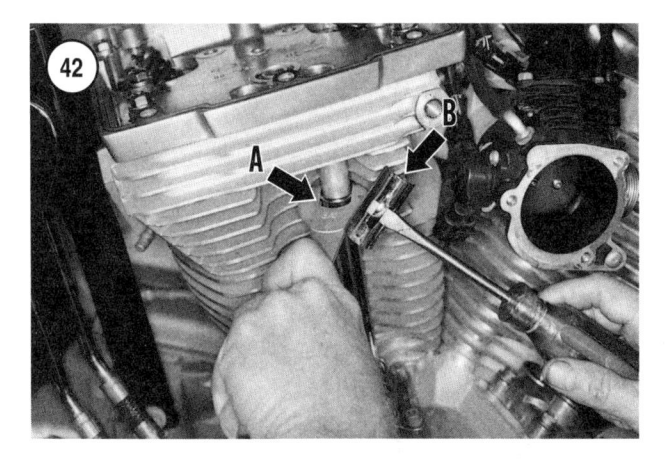

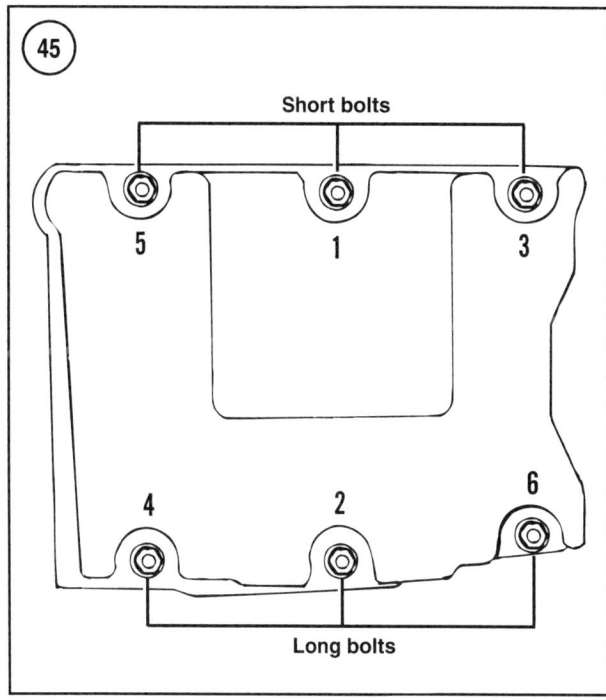

26. Tighten the breather assembly bolts evenly to 90-120 in.-lb. (10.2-13.6 N•m).
27. Install a *new* rocker arm cover gasket (**Figure 44**), and rocker arm cover.

NOTE
*There are two different length bolts (**Figure 45**) securing the rocker arm cover.*

28. Apply Loctite Threadlocker 243 (blue) to the bolt threads, and then install each rocker arm cover bolt with its captive washer. Using the sequence shown in **Figure 45**, tighten the bolts in 1/8-turn increments to 15-18 ft.-lbs. (20.3-24.4 N•m).
29. Install both spark plugs as described in Chapter Three.
30. If the engine is mounted in the frame, perform the following:
   a. Install the carburetor (Chapter Nine) or induction module (Chapter Ten).
   b. Install the exhaust system as described in this chapter.
   c. Install the air filter and backplate as described in Chapter Nine or Chapter Ten.
   d. Install the fuel tank as described in Chapter Nine or Chapter Ten.
   e. Refill the engine oil and install the spark plugs as described in Chapter Three.
   f. Connect the negative battery cable (Chapter Eleven).
   g. Install the seat and right footboard as described in Chapter Seventeen.

Rocker Arm Disassembly/Assembly

1. Before removing the rocker arms (**Figure 46**), measure the rocker arm end clearance as follows:

ROCKER ARM ASSEMBLY

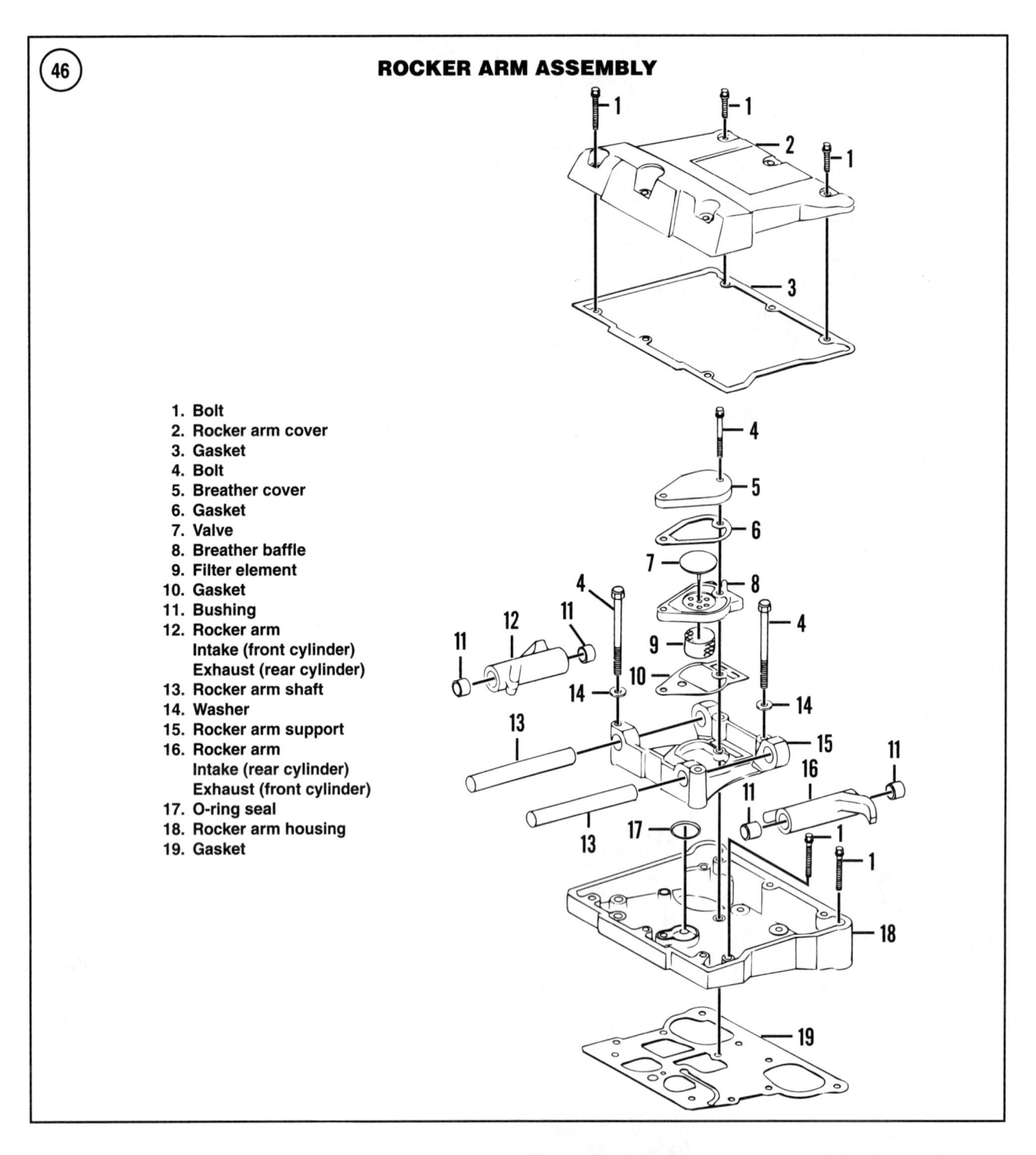

1. Bolt
2. Rocker arm cover
3. Gasket
4. Bolt
5. Breather cover
6. Gasket
7. Valve
8. Breather baffle
9. Filter element
10. Gasket
11. Bushing
12. Rocker arm
    Intake (front cylinder)
    Exhaust (rear cylinder)
13. Rocker arm shaft
14. Washer
15. Rocker arm support
16. Rocker arm
    Intake (rear cylinder)
    Exhaust (front cylinder)
17. O-ring seal
18. Rocker arm housing
19. Gasket

   a. Insert a feeler gauge between the rocker arm and the inside of the rocker arm support plate (**Figure 47**).
   b. Record the measurement.
   c. Repeat for each end of both rocker arms.
   d. Replace the rocker arm and/or the rocker arm support if end clearance exceeds the service limit (**Table 2** or **Table 3**).
2. Prior to disassembling the rocker arms, mark each one with an IN for intake or an EX for exhaust (**Figure 48**) to ensure they are installed in their original positions.
3. Use a hammer and drift, and tap the left side of each rocker shaft so the notched ends come out first. Remove the rocker arm shafts (A, **Figure 49**), and then remove the rocker arms (B).
4. Clean all parts in solvent, blow compressed air through all oil passages, and inspect the components as described in this section.
5. Install the rocker arm shaft (A, **Figure 50**) part way into the rocker arm support plate (B) in its original position.
6. Install a rocker arm (C, **Figure 50**) into its original position and push the shaft part way through the rocker arm.
7. Align the notch (A, **Figure 51**) in the rocker arm shaft with the corresponding mounting bolt hole (B) in the rock-

ENGINE TOP END AND EXHAUST SYSTEM

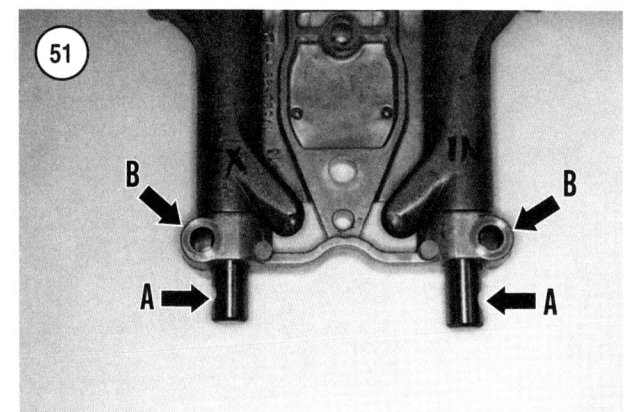

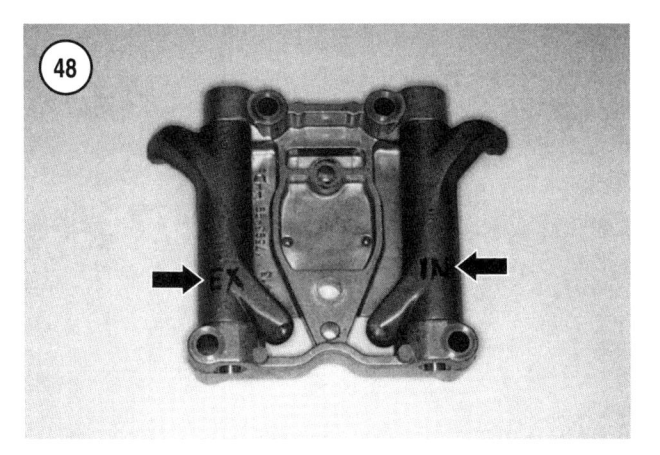

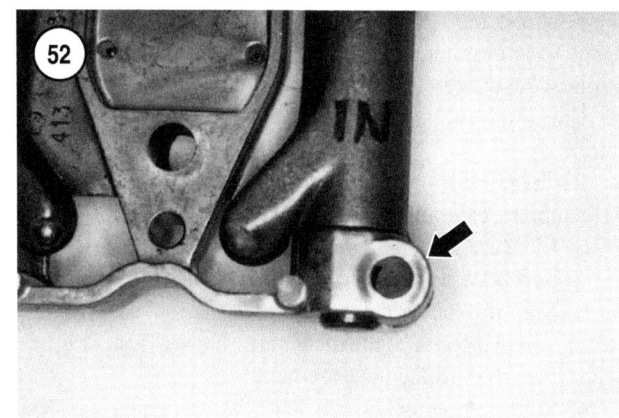

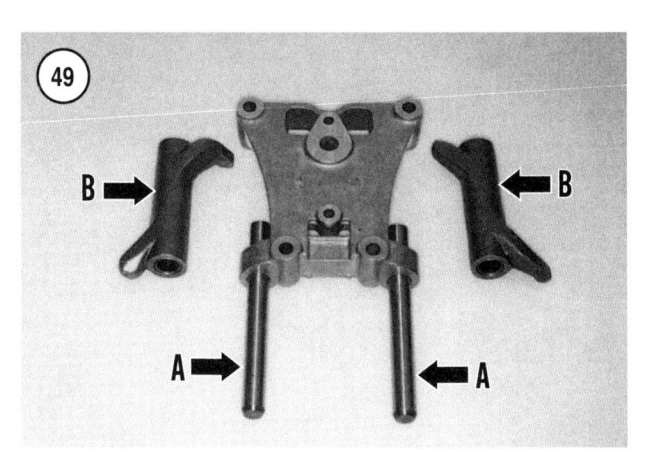

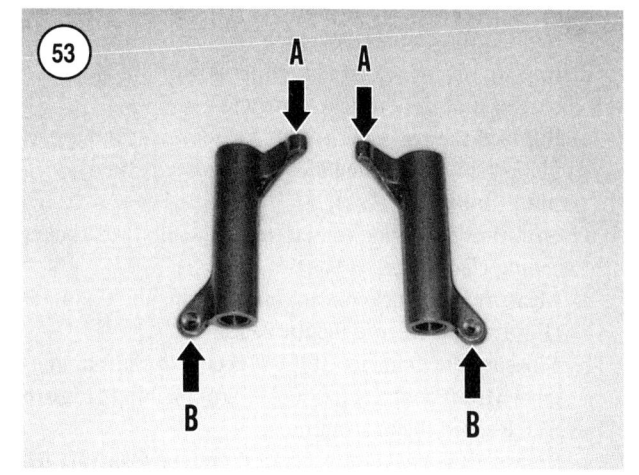

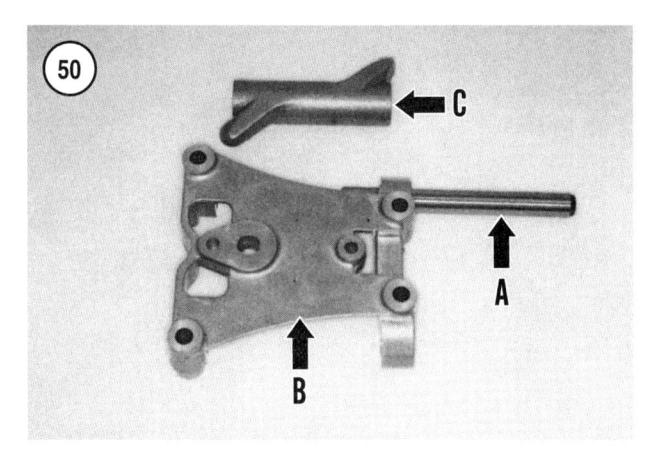

er arm support and install the shaft all the way. Check for correct alignment (**Figure 52**).

8. Repeat the proccess to install the remaining rocker arm and shaft.

Rocker Arm Component Inspection

During inspection, compare any measurements to the specifications in **Table 2** or **Table 3**. Replace any part that is worn, damaged or out of specification.

1. Inspect the rocker arm pads (A, **Figure 53**) and ball sockets (B) for pitting and excessive wear.

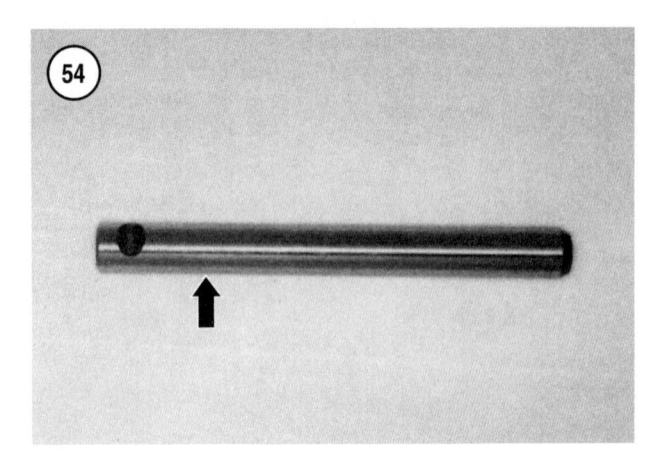

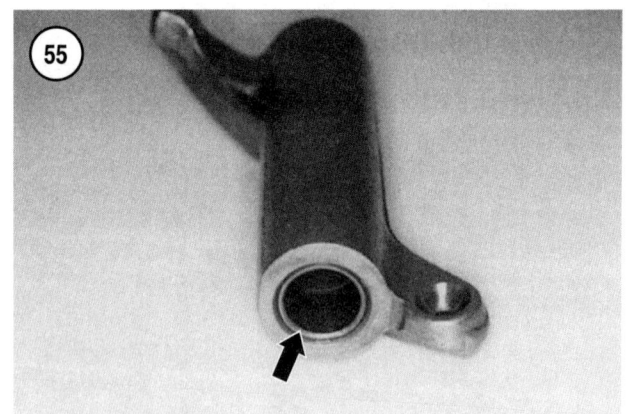

2. Examine the rocker arm shaft (**Figure 54**) for scoring, ridge wear or other damage. If these conditions are present, replace the rocker arm shaft.
3. Check the rocker arm bushing (**Figure 55**) for wear or scoring.
4. Perform the following to determine the shaft-to-rocker arm support clearance.
    a. Measure the inside diameter of the rocker arm support bore (**Figure 56**). Record the measurement.
    b. Measure the outside diameter of the rocker arm shaft where it contacts the rocker arm support bore (**Figure 57**). Record the measurement.
    c. Subtract the rocker arm shaft diameter measurement from the rocker arm support bore inside diameter measurement. The difference equals the shaft-to-rocker arm support clearance.
    d. Repeat the measurement process for the opposite side of the support plate bore and shaft.
    e. Replace the rocker arm shaft or rocker arm support plate if any calculated clearance exceeds the service limit (**Table 2** or **Table 3**).
5. Perform the following to determine the shaft-to-rocker arm bushing clearance:
    a. Measure the rocker arm bushing inside diameter (**Figure 58**). Record the measurement.
    b. Measure the diameter of the rocker arm shaft diameter where it contacts the rocker arm bushing (**Figure 57**). Record the measurement.
    c. Subtract the rocker arm shaft diameter from the inside diameter of the bushing.
    d. Repeat the measurement process for the opposite side of the rocker arm and shaft.
    e. Replace the shaft or bushing if any clearance exceeds the specified service limit (**Table 2** or **Table 3**).
6. Inspect the rocker arm support plate bores (**Figure 58**) for wear or elongation.
7. Inspect the gasket surface of the rocker arm cover for damage or warp.
8. Inspect the rocker arm support plate (**Figure 59**) for damage or warp.
9. Inspect both gasket surfaces of the rocker arm housing for damage or warp.

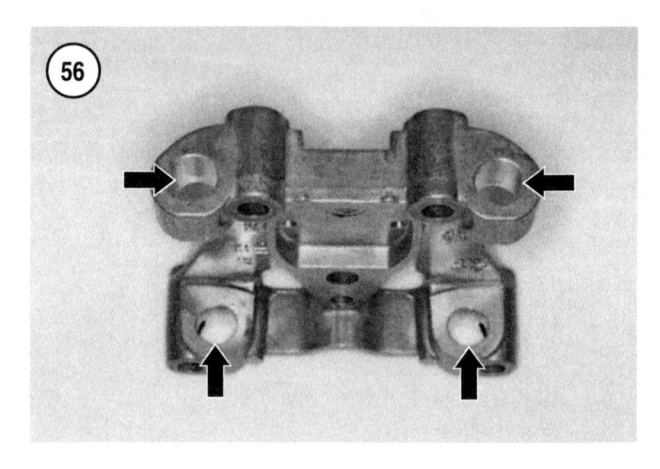

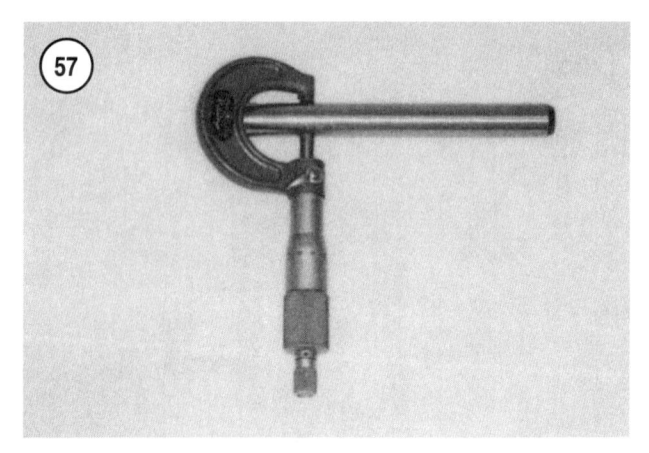

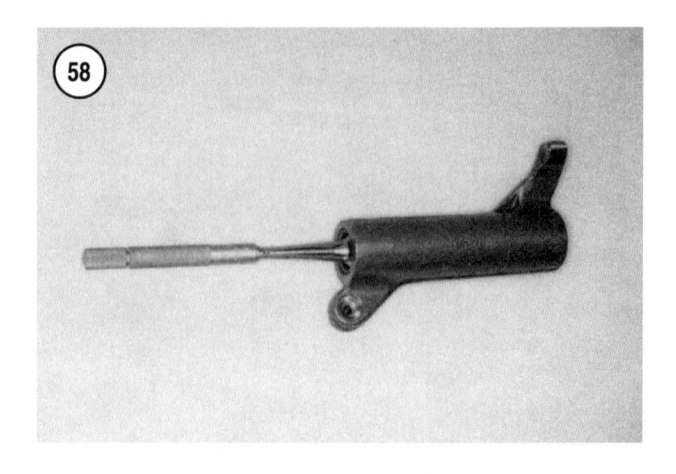

ENGINE TOP END AND EXHAUST SYSTEM

PUSHROD ASSEMBLY

1. O-ring
2. Upper cover
3. Spring cap retainer
4. Spring cap
5. Spring
6. Washer
7. Lower cover
8. Allen bolt
9. Lifter cover
10. Anti-rotation pin
11. Gasket
12. Hydraulic lifter
13. Pushrod

NOTE
Since the new bushings must be reamed, just remove one bushing at a time. The opposite bushing is then used as a guide to ream the first bushing.

1. Press one bushing (**Figure 55**) out of the rocker arm. Do not remove the second bushing. If the bushing is difficult to remove, perform the following:
   a. Thread a 9/16 × 18 tap into the bushing.
   b. Support the rocker arm in a press so the tap is at the bottom.
   c. Insert a mandrel through the top of the rocker arm and seat it on top of the tap.
   d. Press on the mandrel to force the bushing and tap out of the rocker arm.
   e. Remove the tap from the bushing and discard the bushing.
2. Position the new bushing with the split portion facing toward the top of the rocker arm.
3. Press the new bushing into the rocker arm until the bushing's outer surface is flush with the end of rocker arm bore.
4. Ream the new bushing with the bushing reamer as follows:
   a. Mount the rocker arm in a vise with soft jaws so the new bushing is at the bottom.

CAUTION
Only turn the reamer clockwise. Do not rotate the reamer counterclockwise or the reamer and bushing will be damaged.

   b. Mount a tap handle on top of the reamer and insert the reamer into the bushing. Turn the reamer *clockwise* until it passes through the new bushing and remove it from the bottom side.
5. Remove the rocker arm from the vise and repeat the procedure to replace the opposite bushing.
6. Ream the second bushing. The first bushing now serves as a guide.
7. After installing and reaming both bushings, clean the rocker arm assembly in solvent. Then, clean it with hot, soapy water and rinse it with clear water. Dry it with compressed air.
8. Calculate the shaft-to-rocker arm bushing clearance at each end of the rocker arm as described in *Rocker Arm Component Inspection*. Each clearance must be within specification.

Valve Lifter Inspection

Figure 60 shows a valve lifter in relation to the pushrod and valve lifter cover. The valve lifters and covers are installed on the right side of the engine. During engine operation, the lifters are pumped full with engine oil, thus taking up all play in the valve train. When the engine is turned off, the lifters leak down after a period of time as some of the oil drains out. When the engine is started, the lifters click

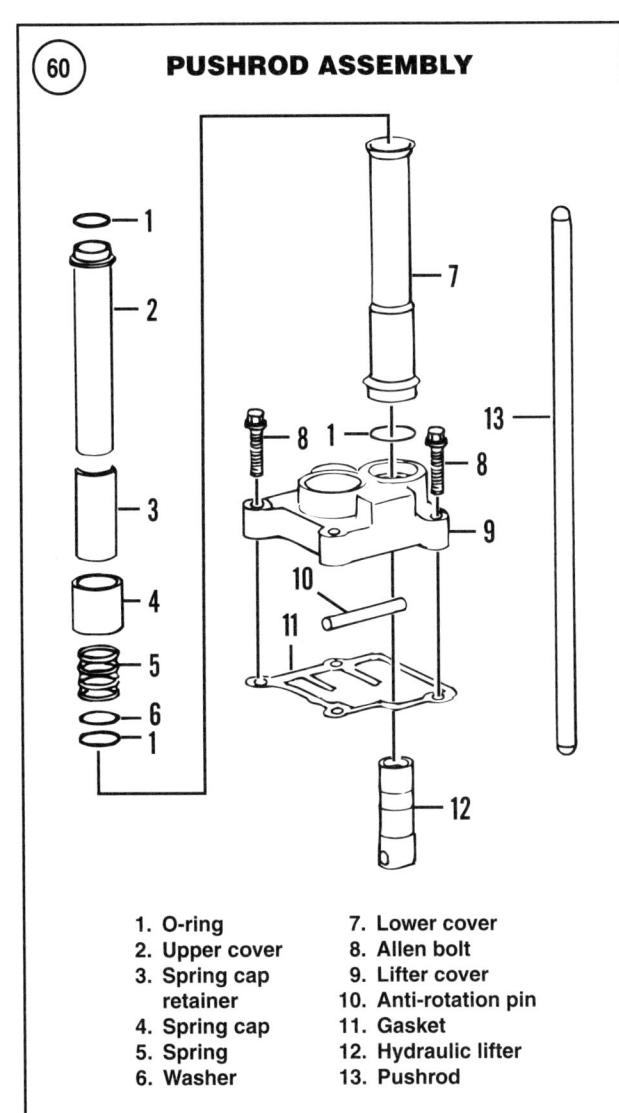

Rocker Arm Bushing Replacement

Each rocker arm is equipped with two bushings (**Figure 55**). Replacement bushings must be reamed after installation. Use the rocker arm bushing reamer (JIMS part No. 94804-57). If the correct size reamer is unavailable, have the bushings replaced by a dealership.

until they completely refill with oil. The lifters are working properly when they stop clicking after the engine is run for a few minutes. If the clicking persists, a problem may exist with the lifter(s).

CAUTION
Place the lifters on a clean, lint-free cloth during inspection.

1. Check the pushrod socket (**Figure 61**) in the top of the lifter for wear or damage.
2. Check the lifter roller (A, **Figure 62**) for pitting, scoring, galling or excessive wear. If the roller is excessively worn, check the mating cam lobe for the same condition.
3. Clean the lifter roller. Measure the radial play of the roller pin and the roller end clearance. Replace the lifter if either measurement clearance exceeds the wear limit.
4. Determine the lifter-to-bore clearance as follows:
    a. Use an inside micrometer or a bore gauge to measure the inside diameter of the lifter bore in the crankcase.
    b. Use outside micrometers to measure the lifter outside diameter (B, **Figure 62**).
    c. Calculate the lifter-to-bore clearance by subtracting the lifter outside diameter from the lifter bore inside diameter.
    d. Replace the lifter and/or crankcase if the lifter-to-bore clearance exceeds the service limit.
5. If a lifter does not show visual damage, it may be contaminated with dirt or have internal damage. If so, replace it. The lifters are not serviceable and must be replaced as a unit.
6. After inspecting the lifters, store them upright in a container filled with clean engine oil until installation.
7. If most of the oil has drained out of the lifter, refill it with a pump-type oil can through the oil hole in the side of the lifter.
8. Clean all gasket material from the mating surfaces of the crankcase and the lifter cover.
9. Inspect the lifter cover (**Figure 63**) for cracks or damage.

Pushrod Inspection

1. Clean the pushrods in solvent and dry them with compressed air.
2. Check the pushrods for cracks and worn or damaged ball heads (**Figure 64**).
3. Roll the pushrods on a surface plate or on a piece of glass, and check for bending.
4. Replace any damaged pushrods.

Pushrod Cover Disassembly/Inspection/Assembly

Refer to **Figure 60**.
1. Remove and discard the O-rings from their seats on the upper and lower pushrod covers.
2. Pull the lower pushrod cover (**Figure 65**) from the upper cover.

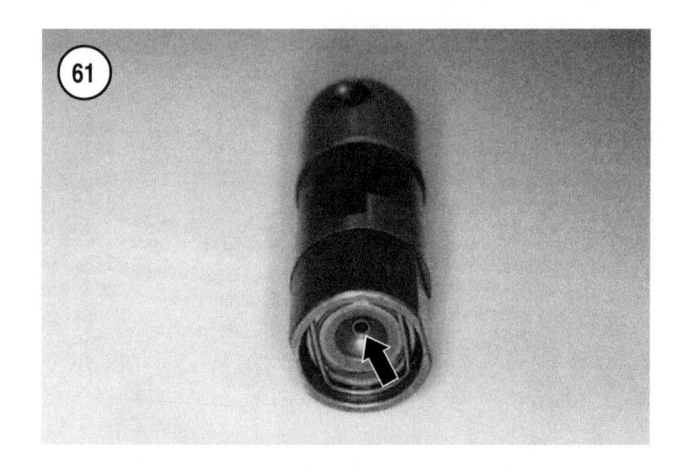

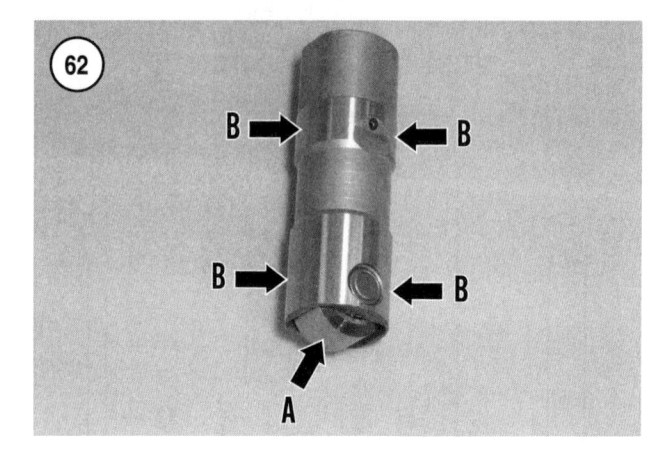

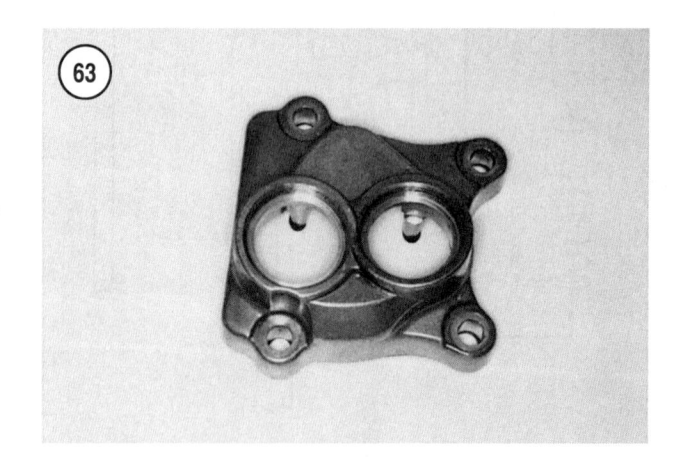

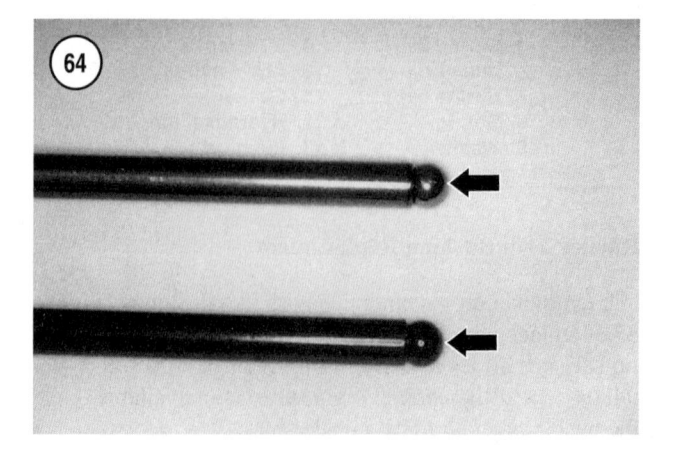

ENGINE TOP END AND EXHAUST SYSTEM

Breather Disassembly/Inspection

Refer to **Figure 68**.
1. Remove the breather fasteners, and lift the breather assembly from the rocker arm support plate.
2. Remove the breather cover and gasket. Discard the gasket.
3. Remove the filter element from the breather baffle, and then remove the valve. Discard both.
4. Clean all parts in solvent. Blow them dry with compressed air.
5. Inspect the breather by performing the following:
    a. Place a straightedge diagonally across the breather cover so the straightedge crosses opposite corners of the cover.
    b. Check breather cover warp by inserting a feeler gauge at several places between the straightedge and the cover.
    c. Repeat the process and check for warp across the opposite diagonal.
    d. Replace the breather cover if any measurement exceeds the specified service limit.
    e. Repeat the measurement procedure, and check the breather baffle for warp.
6. Reassemble the breather assembly as described in *Installation* (this section).

CYLINDER HEAD

The cylinder head procedures shown here are performed on the rear cylinder (**Figures 69-71**). The same procedures apply to the front cylinder. Any differences are noted.

NOTE
The following procedures are shown with the engine removed to clearly illustrate the steps.

Removal

1. Remove the rocker arm support plate, rocker arm housing, pushrods and pushrod covers as described in this chapter.
2. Disconnect the breather hose from the fitting on the cylinder head.
3. On Screamin' Eagle models, loosen the set screw, and then remove each cylinder head bolt cover from the bolt head. *Do not* remove the set screws.
4. Following the sequence shown in **Figure 72**, loosen the cylinder head bolts (**Figure 73**) in 1/4-turn increments until they are loose. Remove the four bolts. Note and mark the position of the short and long bolts.
5. Tap the cylinder head with a rubber mallet to free it, and lift it off the cylinder.
6. Remove the cylinder head gasket.
7. Remove the cylinder head dowels (**Figure 74**) and O-rings. Discard each O-ring.
8. Repeat the procedure to remove the opposite cylinder head.

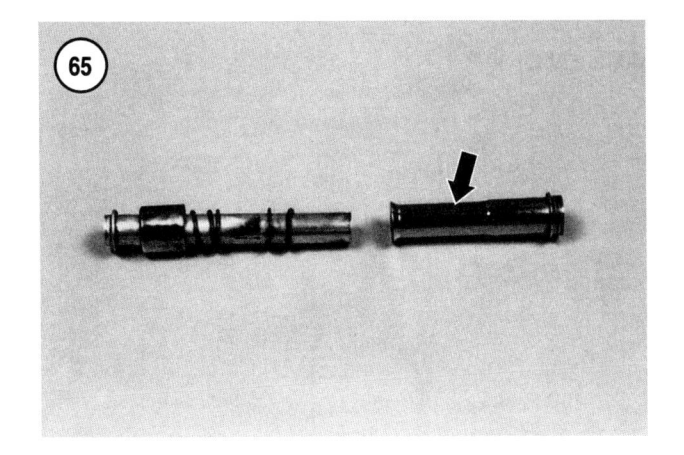

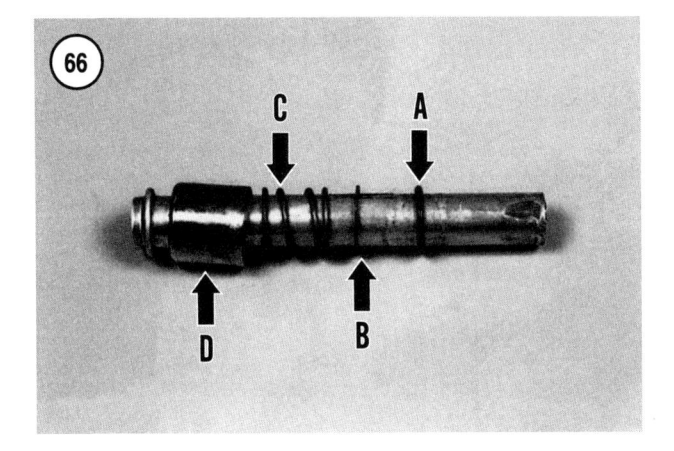

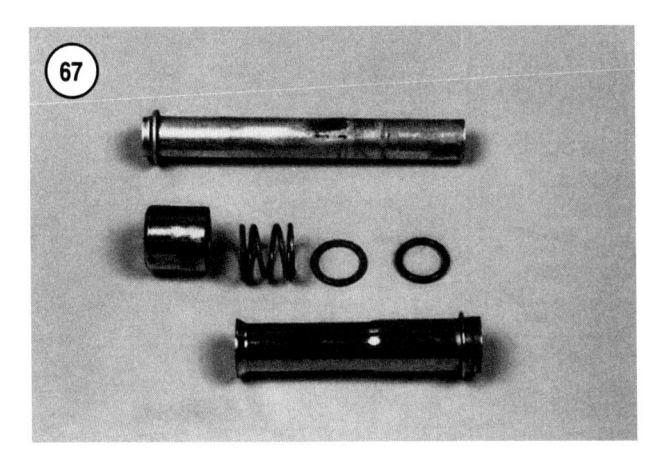

3. Slide the O-ring (A, **Figure 66**), washer (B), spring (C) and spring cap (D) from the upper pushrod cover. Discard the O-ring.
4. Clean all parts in solvent, and blow them dry with compressed air. Make sure the O-ring seats and contact surfaces of the covers are clean.
5. Check the pushrod cover assembly (**Figure 67**) as follows:
    a. Check the spring for sagging or cracking.
    b. Check the washer for deformation or damage.
    c. Check the pushrod covers for cracking or damage.
6. Replace all worn or damaged parts.
7. Assembly is the reverse of disassembly. Install new O-rings. Lubricate each O-ring with clean engine oil.

CHAPTER FOUR

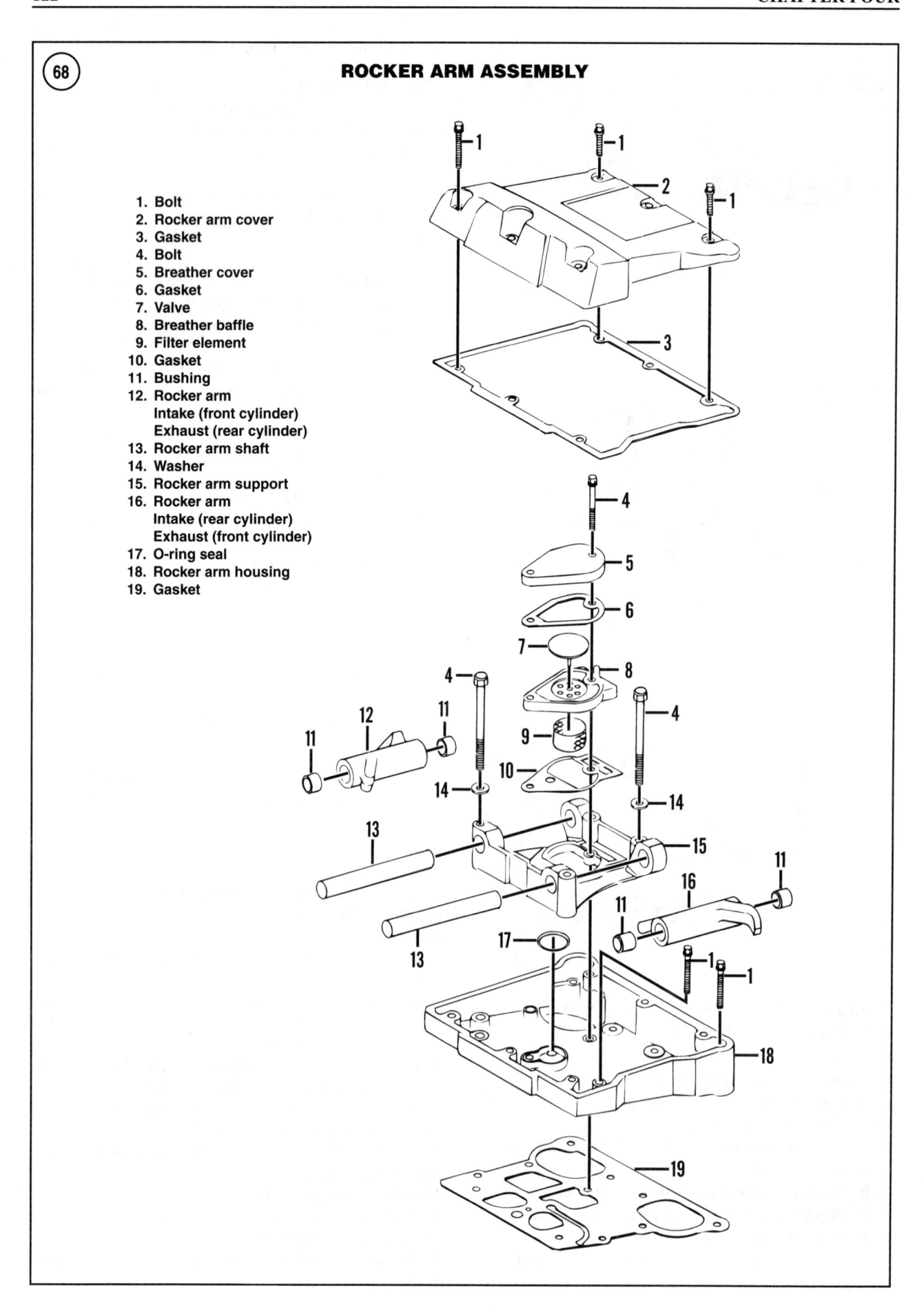

ROCKER ARM ASSEMBLY

1. Bolt
2. Rocker arm cover
3. Gasket
4. Bolt
5. Breather cover
6. Gasket
7. Valve
8. Breather baffle
9. Filter element
10. Gasket
11. Bushing
12. Rocker arm
    Intake (front cylinder)
    Exhaust (rear cylinder)
13. Rocker arm shaft
14. Washer
15. Rocker arm support
16. Rocker arm
    Intake (rear cylinder)
    Exhaust (front cylinder)
17. O-ring seal
18. Rocker arm housing
19. Gasket

ENGINE TOP END AND EXHAUST SYSTEM

⑥⑨ CYLINDER HEAD (2006-2009 MODELS EXCEPT SCREAMIN' EAGLE)

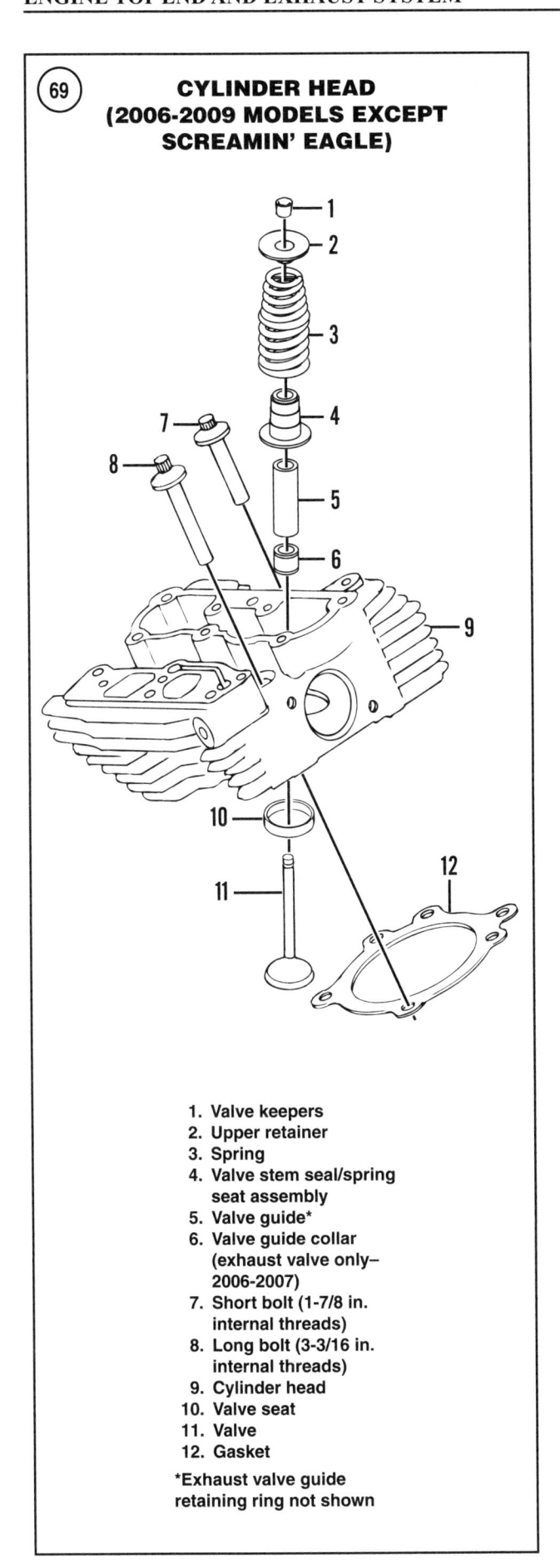

1. Valve keepers
2. Upper retainer
3. Spring
4. Valve stem seal/spring seat assembly
5. Valve guide*
6. Valve guide collar (exhaust valve only– 2006-2007)
7. Short bolt (1-7/8 in. internal threads)
8. Long bolt (3-3/16 in. internal threads)
9. Cylinder head
10. Valve seat
11. Valve
12. Gasket

*Exhaust valve guide retaining ring not shown

⑦⓪ CYLINDER HEAD (2006 SCREAMIN' EAGLE MODELS)

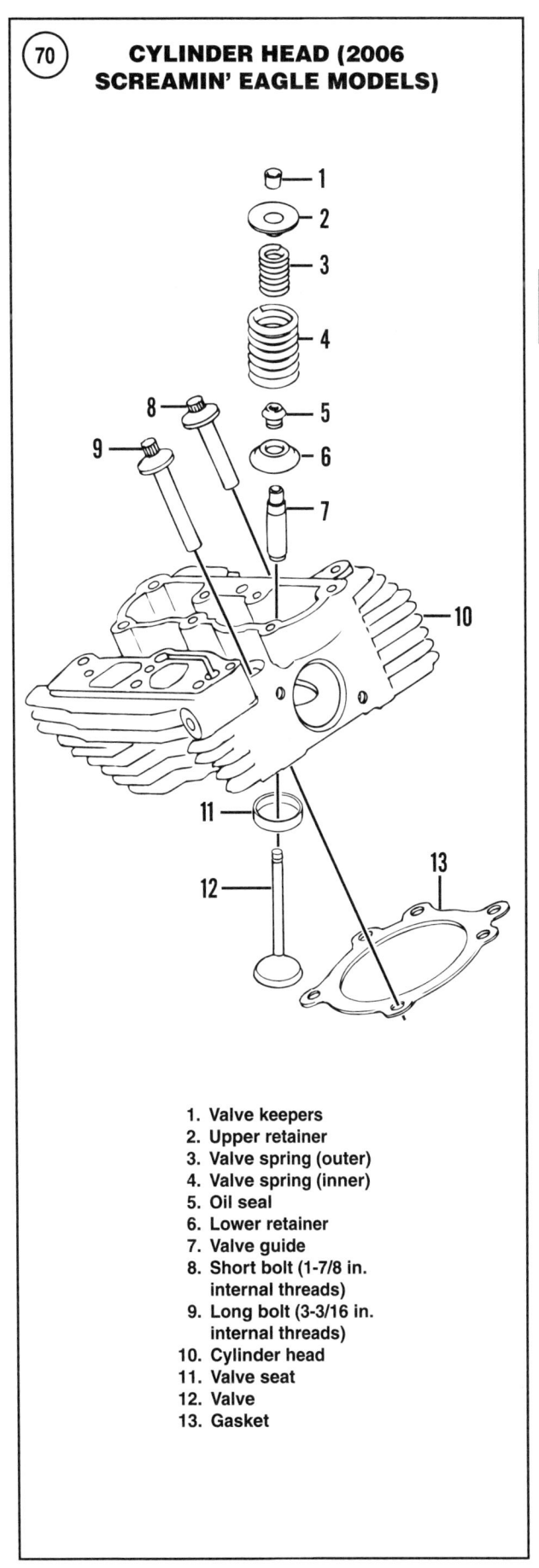

1. Valve keepers
2. Upper retainer
3. Valve spring (outer)
4. Valve spring (inner)
5. Oil seal
6. Lower retainer
7. Valve guide
8. Short bolt (1-7/8 in. internal threads)
9. Long bolt (3-3/16 in. internal threads)
10. Cylinder head
11. Valve seat
12. Valve
13. Gasket

124 CHAPTER FOUR

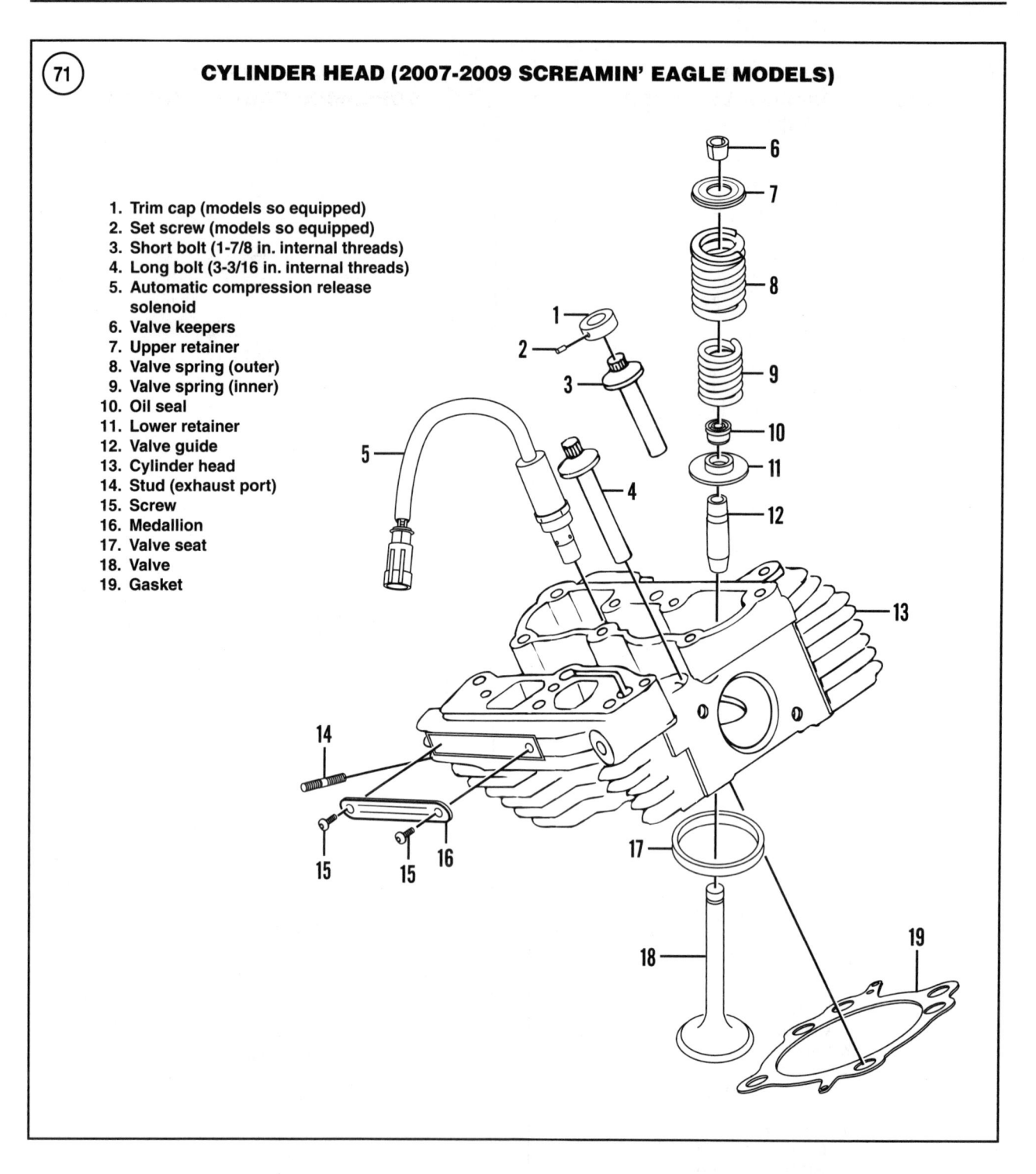

⑦ CYLINDER HEAD (2007-2009 SCREAMIN' EAGLE MODELS)

1. Trim cap (models so equipped)
2. Set screw (models so equipped)
3. Short bolt (1-7/8 in. internal threads)
4. Long bolt (3-3/16 in. internal threads)
5. Automatic compression release solenoid
6. Valve keepers
7. Upper retainer
8. Valve spring (outer)
9. Valve spring (inner)
10. Oil seal
11. Lower retainer
12. Valve guide
13. Cylinder head
14. Stud (exhaust port)
15. Screw
16. Medallion
17. Valve seat
18. Valve
19. Gasket

Installation

1. If removed, install the piston and cylinder as described in this chapter.
2. Lubricate the cylinder head bolts as follows:
    a. Clean the cylinder head bolts in solvent and dry with compressed air.
    b. Apply clean engine oil to the cylinder head bolt threads and to the flat shoulder surface on each bolt (**Figure 75**). Wipe excess oil from the bolts, leaving only an oil film on these surfaces.
3. Install the dowels (**Figure 74**) into the top of the cylinder.
4. Install a *new* O-ring (**Figure 74**) over each dowel. Apply a light coat of clean engine oil to the O-rings.

CAUTION
Because the O-rings center the head gasket on the cylinder, install them before installing the head gasket.

5. Install a *new* cylinder head gasket (**Figure 76**) onto the cylinder.

ENGINE TOP END AND EXHAUST SYSTEM

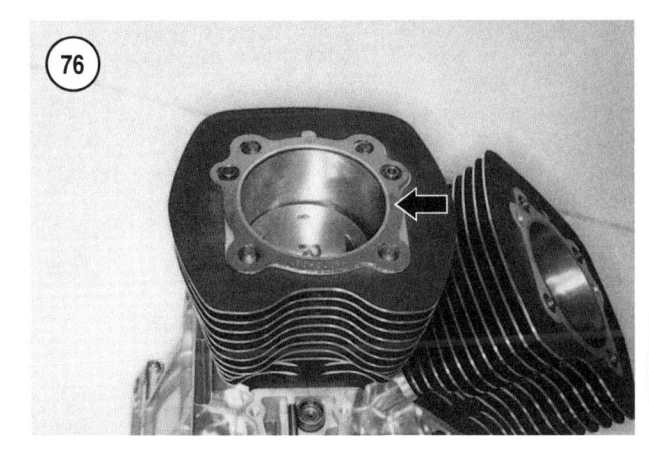

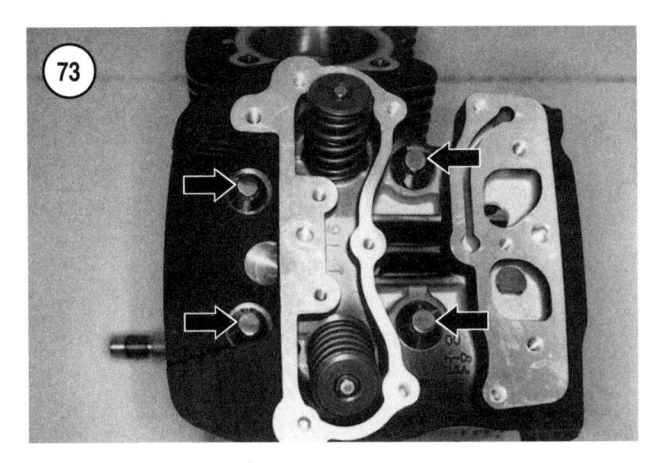

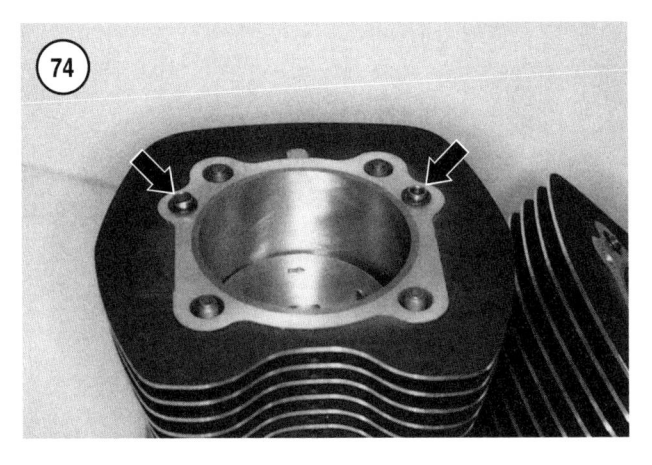

72

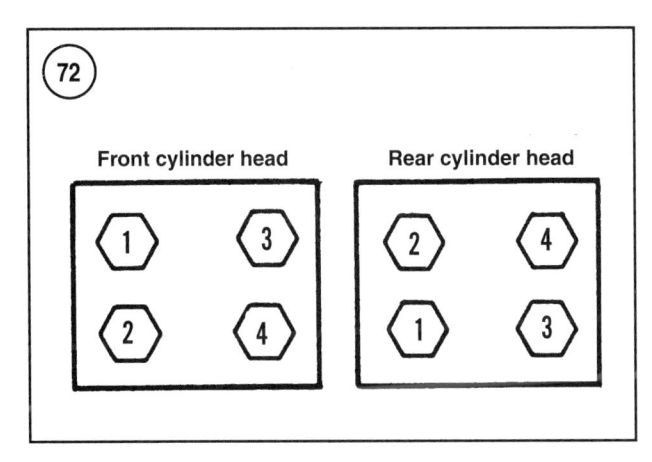

Front cylinder head | Rear cylinder head
1 3 | 2 4
2 4 | 1 3

CAUTION
Do not use sealer on the cylinder head gasket. For an aftermarket head gasket, follow the gasket manufacturer's instructions for installation.

NOTE
*The cylinder heads are **not** identical. Refer to the **FRONT** or **REAR** (**Figure 77**) identifier cast into top surface of the cylinder head.*

6. Lower the cylinder head (**Figure 78**) onto the cylinder and the dowels. Position the head carefully to avoid moving the head gasket out of alignment.

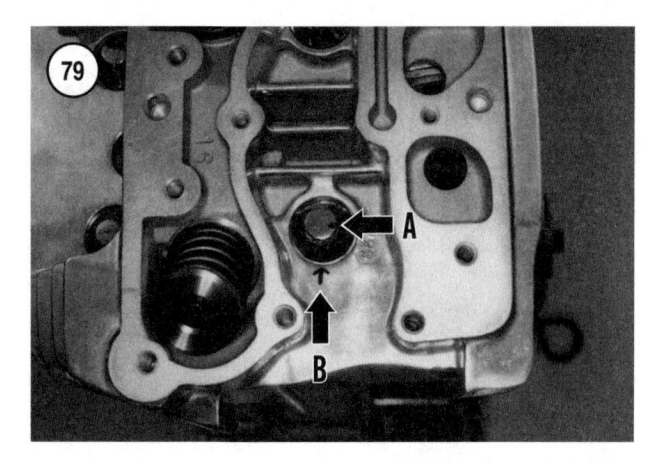

7. Install and lightly finger-tighten the cylinder head bolts. Make sure the short bolts are on the spark plug side of the head.

CAUTION
Failure to follow the proper torque sequence may distort the cylinder head, allowing the gasket to leak.

8. Following the torque sequence shown in **Figure 72**, tighten the cylinder head bolts as follows:
   a. Starting with bolt No. 1, evenly finger-tighten the cylinder head bolts in order.
   b. Tighten each bolt in order to 10-12 ft.-lb. (13.6-16.3 N•m).
   c. Tighten each bolt in order to 15-17 ft.-lb. (20.3-23.0 N•m).
   d. Make a vertical mark (A, **Figure 79**) with a permanent marker on each bolt head. Make another mark (B, **Figure 79**) on the cylinder head at a 90° angle or 1/4-turn from the mark on the bolt head.
   e. Following the torque sequence, tighten each bolt an additional 90° or 1/4-turn using the marks as a guide (**Figure 80**).
9. On Screamin' Eagle models, install the cylinder head bolt caps. Tighten the set screws to 60-84 in.-lb. (6.8-9.5 N•m). Make sure each set screw sits in a notch between the bolt points.
10. Connect the breather hose to its fitting.
11. Install the rocker arm assemblies, pushrods and pushrod covers as described in this chapter.

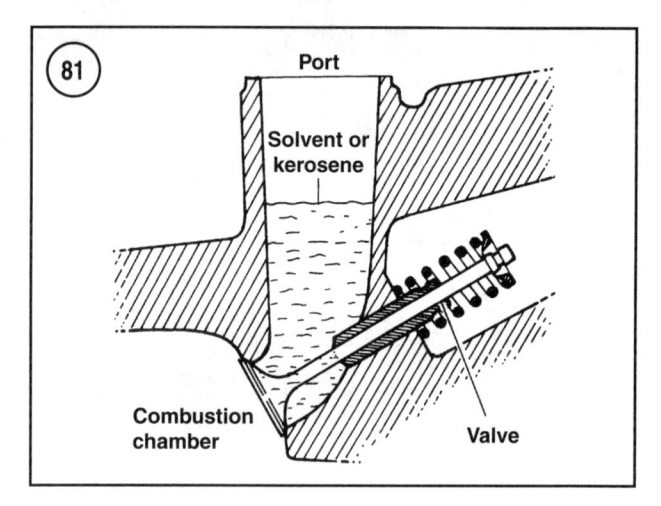

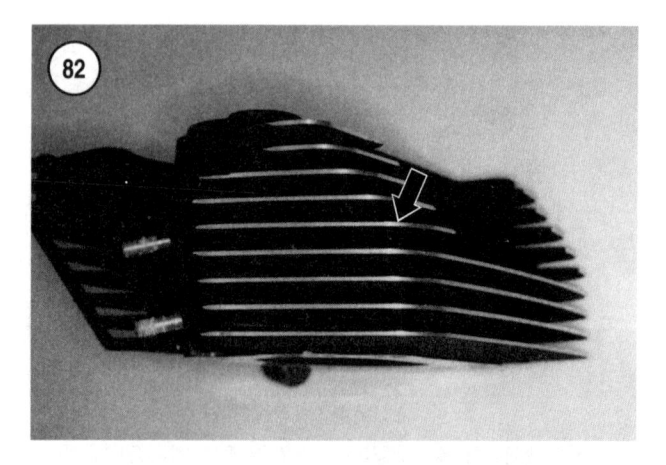

Leak Test

Before removing the valves or cleaning the cylinder head, perform the cylinder head leak test.
1. Position the cylinder head so the exhaust port faces up. Pour solvent or kerosene into each exhaust port opening (**Figure 81**).
2. After at least ten seconds, turn the head over slightly and check each exhaust valve area on the combustion chamber side. If the valves and seats are in good condition, no fluid will be found and the valve seat area will be dry. If any area is wet, the valve seat is not sealing correctly. The valve seat or face may be damaged or the valve may be bent or damaged. Remove the valve, and inspect the valve and seat as decribed in this section.
3. Pour solvent into the intake port and repeat the procedure to check the intake valve for leaks.

Inspection

During inspection, compare any measurements taken to the specifications listed in **Table 2** or **Table 3**. Replace any part that is worn, damaged or out of specification.

ENGINE TOP END AND EXHAUST SYSTEM

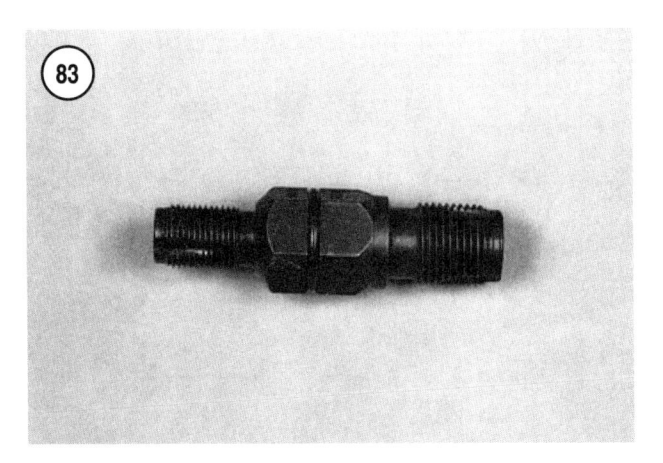

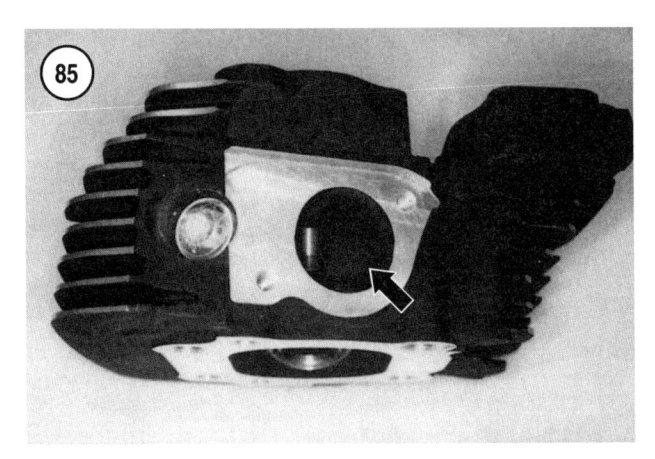

1. Perform the *Leak Test* (this section).
2. Thoroughly clean the outside of the cylinder head. Use a stiff brush, soap and water to remove all debris from the cooling fins (**Figure 82**). If necessary, use a piece of wood and scrape away any lodged dirt. Clogged cooling fins can cause overheating and lead to engine damage.

CAUTION
Cleaning the combustion chamber with the valves removed can damage the valve seat surfaces. A damaged or even slightly scratched valve seat will cause poor valve seating.

3. *Without removing the valves*, use a wire brush to remove all carbon deposits from the combustion chamber. Use a fine wire brush and dip it in solvent or make a scraper from hardwood. Be careful not to damage the cylinder head, valves or spark plug threads.

NOTE
If there is severe thread damage, restore the threads by installing a thread insert. If necessary, have this done by a machine shop.

4. Examine the spark plug threads in the cylinder head for damage. If there is minor damage or if the threads are dirty or clogged with carbon, use a spark plug thread tap (**Figure 83**) and kerosene or cutting fluid to clean the threads.
5. After all carbon is removed from the combustion chambers and valve ports, and the spark plug thread hole has been repaired, clean the entire head in solvent. Dry it with compressed air.
6. Examine the crown on the piston (**Figure 84**). The crown should show no signs of wear or damage. If the crown appears pecked or spongy-looking, also check the spark plug, valves and combustion chamber for aluminum deposits. If these deposits are found, the cylinder has overheated. Check for a lean fuel mixture or other conditions that could cause preignition.
7. Check for cracks in the combustion chamber, the intake port (**Figure 85**) and the exhaust port (**Figure 86**). Replace a cracked head if welding cannot repair it.
8. Inspect the exhaust pipe mounting studs (**Figure 87**) for damage. Repair the threads with a die if they are damaged.

CAUTION
If the cylinder head is bead-blasted, clean the head thoroughly with solvent, and then with hot soapy water. Residual grit seats in small crevices and other areas, and can be hard to get out. Also, run a tap through each exposed thread to remove grit from the threads. Any grit left in the engine will cause premature wear.

9. Thoroughly clean the cylinder head.
10. Measure the head for warp by placing a straightedge across the gasket surface at several points and attempting to insert a feeler gauge between the straightedge and the cylinder head at each location (**Figure 88**). Distortion or nicks in the cylinder head surface could cause an air leak and overheating. If warp exceeds the specified service limit, replace the cylinder head.
11. Repeat the procedure to check the rocker arm housing mating surfaces (**Figure 89**) for warp.
12. Make sure the breather channel (**Figure 90**) is clear at each end.
13. Check the valves and valve guides as described in *Valves and Valve Components* (this chapter).

VALVES AND VALVE COMPONENTS

The following procedures describe how to check the valve components for wear and how to determine what type of valve service is required.

Refer to **Figures 91-93**.

Tools

The following tools, or their equivalents, are needed for valve removal and installation:
1. Valve spring compressor (H-D part No. HD-34736-B).
2. Valve guide cleaning brush (H-D part No. HD-34751-A).
3. Valve guide seal installer (H-D part No. HD-48644); Screamin' Eagle models only.
4. Cylinder head holding fixture (H-D part No. HD-39786-A).
5. ACR solenoid socket (H-D part No. HD-48498).

Valve Removal

1. Remove the cylinder head as described in this chapter.
2. If using the cylinder head holding fixture, install the 12-mm end of the tool into the spark plug hole. Secure the fixture in a vise.
3. On 2007-2009 Screamin' Eagle models, use the ACR solenoid socket to remove the ACR solenoid from the cylinder head.
4. Install the valve spring compressor (**Figure 94**) squarely over the valve spring upper retainer (**Figure 95**) and against the valve head.

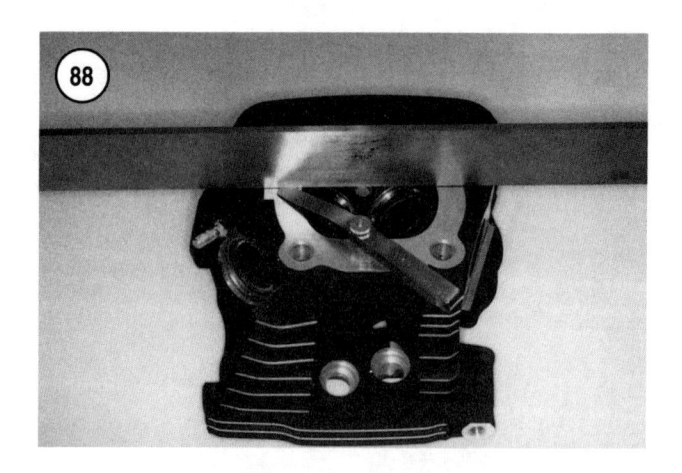

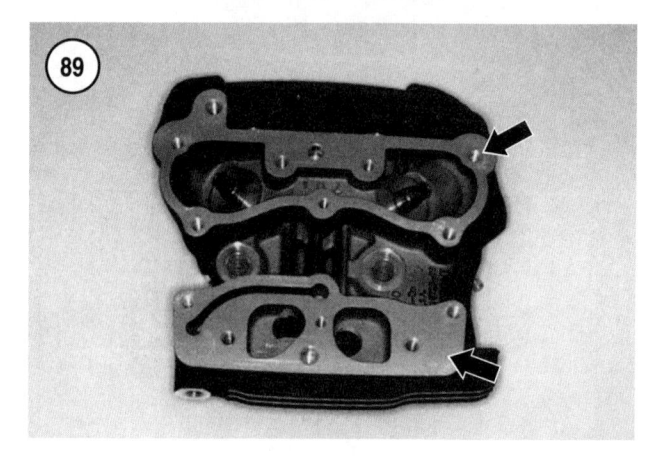

CAUTION
To avoid loss of spring tension, compress the spring just enough to remove the valve keepers.

5. Tighten the valve spring compressor until the valve keepers separate from the valve stem. Lift the valve keepers out through the valve spring compressor with a magnet or needlenose pliers.
6. Gradually loosen the valve spring compressor and remove it from the cylinder head.
7. Remove the spring retainer and the valve spring. On Screamin' Eagle models, remove both the outer and inner springs.

ENGINE TOP END AND EXHAUST SYSTEM

91. CYLINDER HEAD (2006-2009 MODELS EXCEPT SCREAMIN' EAGLE)

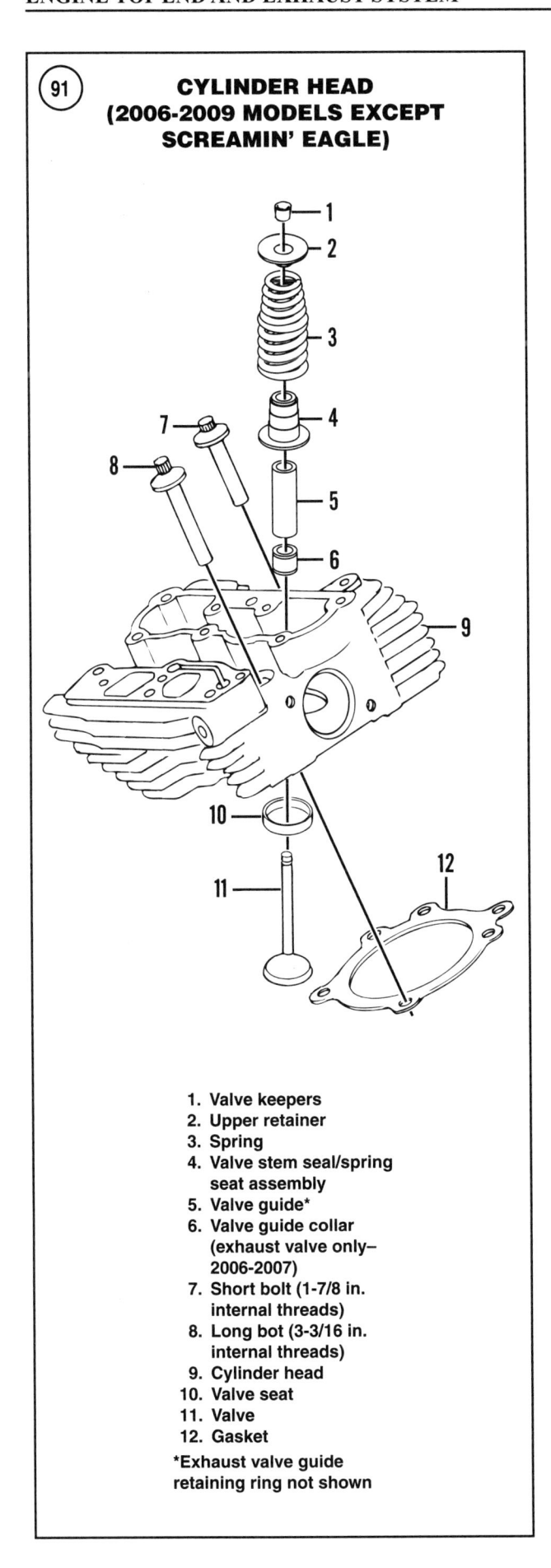

1. Valve keepers
2. Upper retainer
3. Spring
4. Valve stem seal/spring seat assembly
5. Valve guide*
6. Valve guide collar (exhaust valve only– 2006-2007)
7. Short bolt (1-7/8 in. internal threads)
8. Long bot (3-3/16 in. internal threads)
9. Cylinder head
10. Valve seat
11. Valve
12. Gasket

*Exhaust valve guide retaining ring not shown

92. CYLINDER HEAD (2006 SCREAMIN' EAGLE)

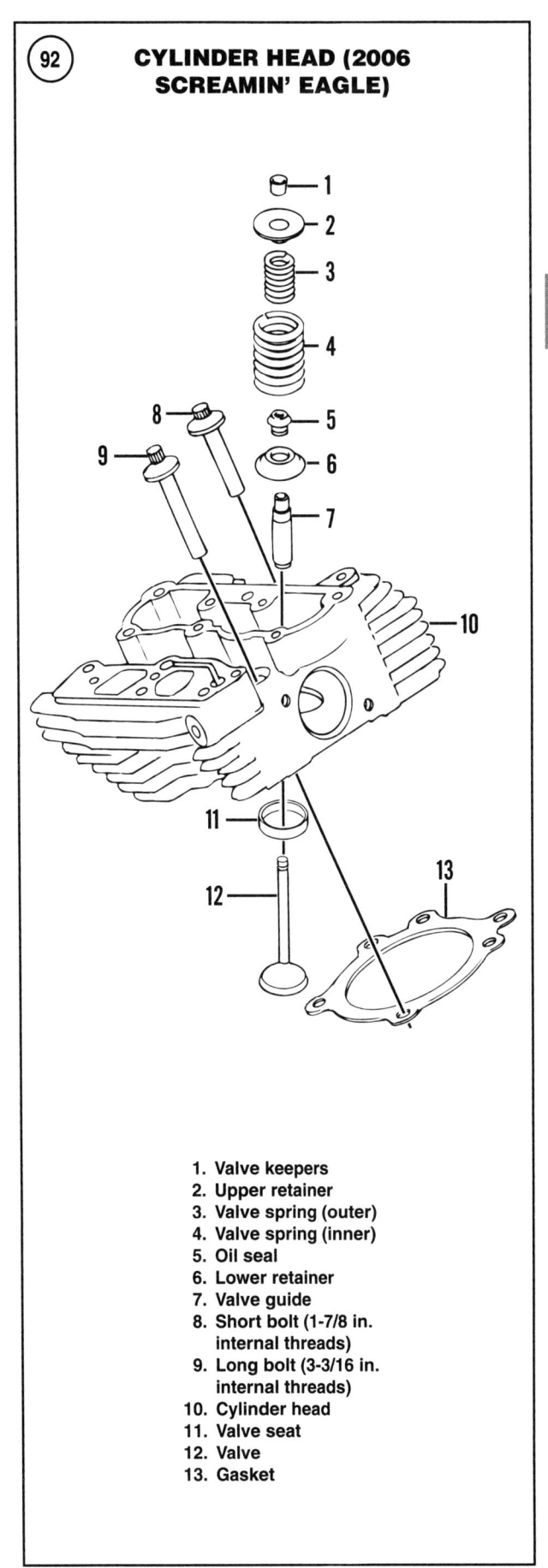

1. Valve keepers
2. Upper retainer
3. Valve spring (outer)
4. Valve spring (inner)
5. Oil seal
6. Lower retainer
7. Valve guide
8. Short bolt (1-7/8 in. internal threads)
9. Long bolt (3-3/16 in. internal threads)
10. Cylinder head
11. Valve seat
12. Valve
13. Gasket

CHAPTER FOUR

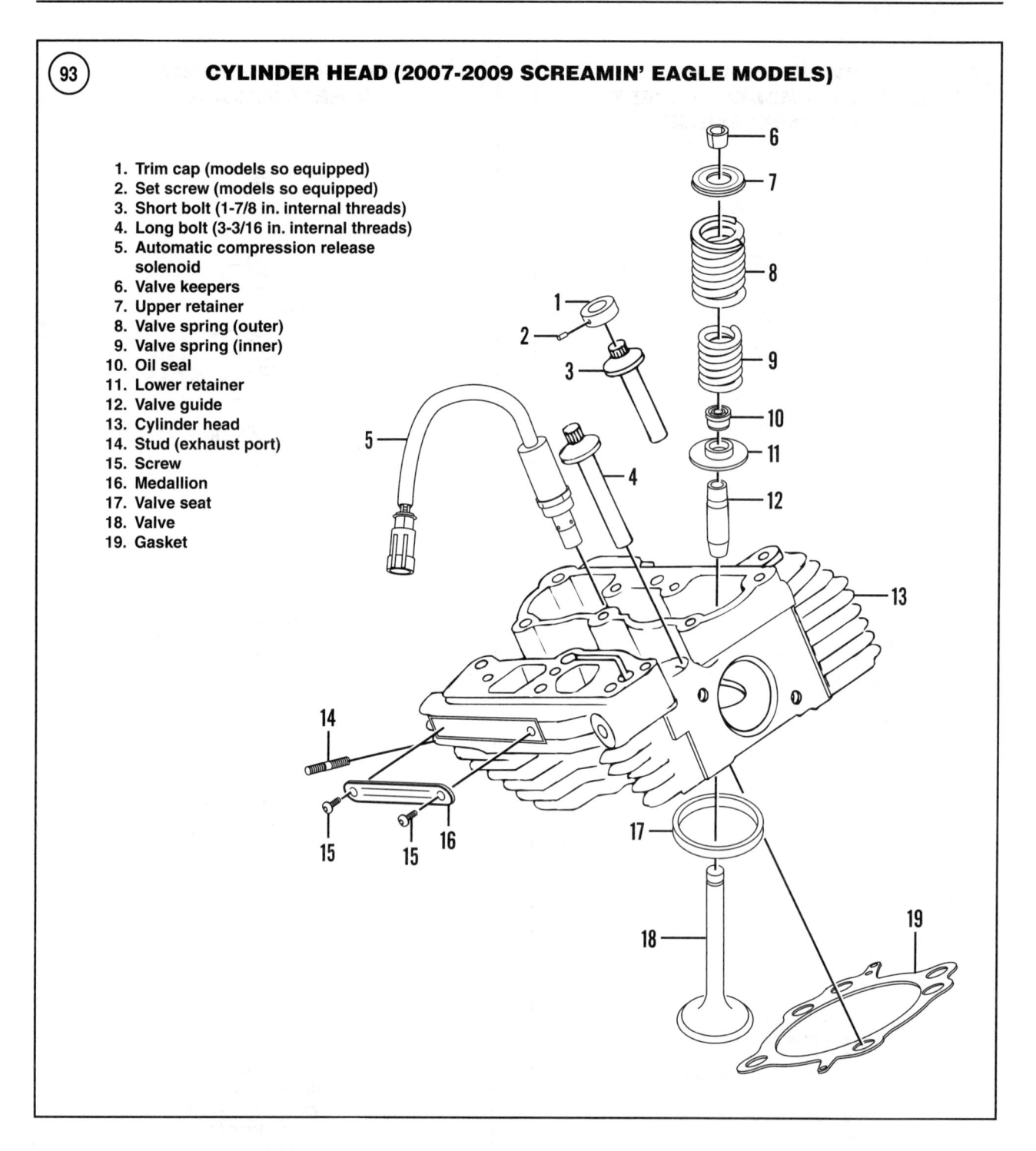

93 **CYLINDER HEAD (2007-2009 SCREAMIN' EAGLE MODELS)**

1. Trim cap (models so equipped)
2. Set screw (models so equipped)
3. Short bolt (1-7/8 in. internal threads)
4. Long bolt (3-3/16 in. internal threads)
5. Automatic compression release solenoid
6. Valve keepers
7. Upper retainer
8. Valve spring (outer)
9. Valve spring (inner)
10. Oil seal
11. Lower retainer
12. Valve guide
13. Cylinder head
14. Stud (exhaust port)
15. Screw
16. Medallion
17. Valve seat
18. Valve
19. Gasket

CAUTION
*Remove any burrs from the valve stem keeper groove (**Figure 96**) before removing the valve; otherwise the valve guide will be damaged as the valve stem passes through it.*

8. Remove the valve from the cylinder head while rotating it slightly.

9A. On all models except Screamin' Eagle, use needlenose pliers to carefully twist and remove the valve stem seal/spring seat assembly from the valve guide. Discard the valve stem seal/spring seat assembly.

9B. On Screamin' Eagle models:
 a. Use needlenose pliers to carefully twist and remove the valve stem seal from the valve guide. Discard the seal.
 b. Remove the spring seat from the cylinder head.

CAUTION
Keep the components of each valve assembly together. Identify the components as either intake or exhaust. If both cylinders are disassembled, also label the components front or rear. Do not mix components from the valve assemblies. Excessive wear may result.

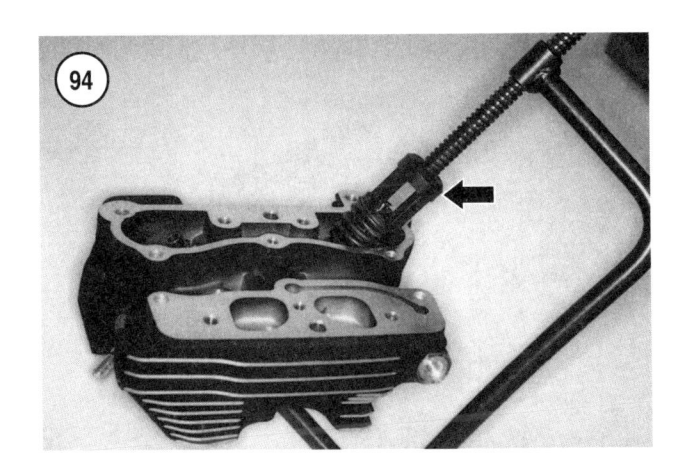

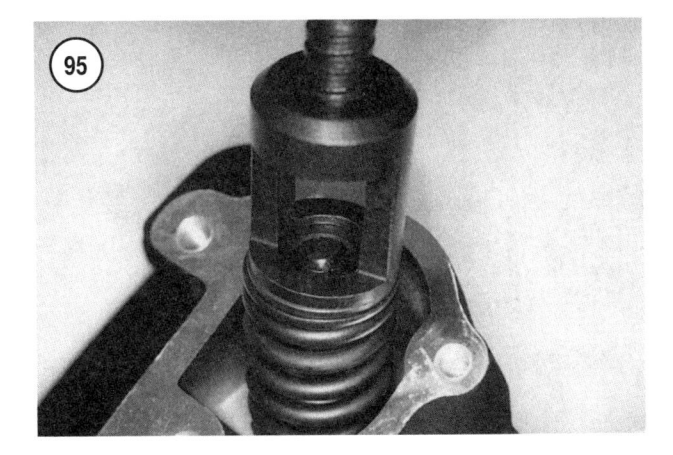

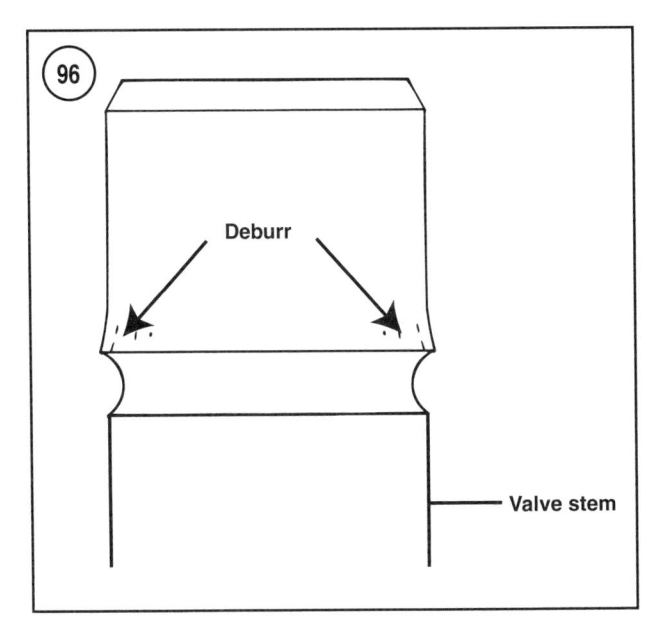

ENGINE TOP END AND EXHAUST SYSTEM

10. Repeat the procedure to remove the remaining valve.

Valve Installation

1. Run the valve cleaning brush through the valve guide to make sure it is clean.
2. Coat a valve stem with Torco MPZ, molybdenum disulfide paste or an equivalent lubricant. Install the valve part way into the guide. Slowly turn the valve as it enters the oil seal and continue turning it until the valve is installed all the way.
3. Work the valve back and forth in the valve guide to ensure the lubricant is distributed evenly within the valve guide.
4. Withdraw the valve and apply an additional coat of lubricant.
5. On 2006 models except Screamin' Eagle, assemble the valve seal/spring seat components as follows:
    a. Apply engine oil to a new valve seal (A, **Figure 97**) and the spring seat (B).
    b. Insert the valve seal into the spring seat so the spring end of the seal faces out (C, **Figure 97**).
    c. Press the valve seal until it completely seats within the spring seat (D, **Figure 97**).
6A. On all models except Screamin' Eagle, perform the following:

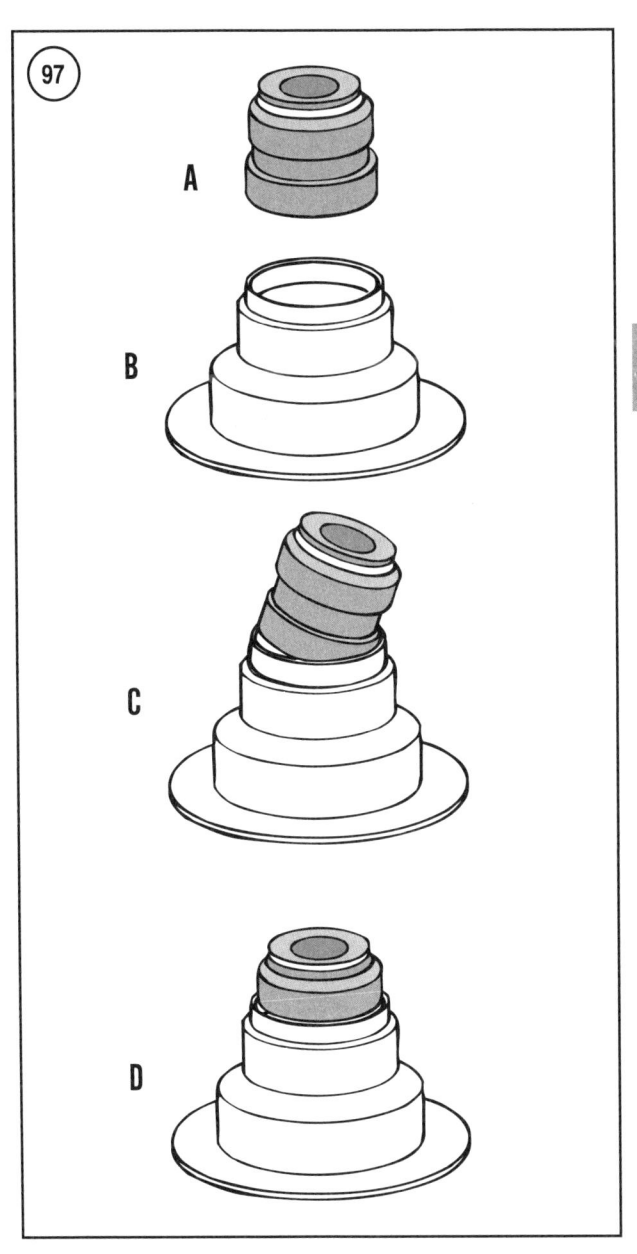

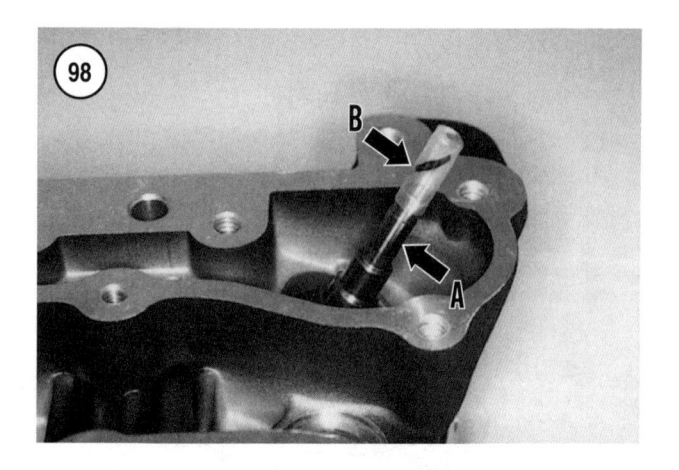

a. Reinstall the valve into the valve guide, and push the valve (A, **Figure 98**) all the way into the cylinder head until it bottoms.

CAUTION
The valve seal will be torn as it passes the valve stem keeper groove if the plastic capsule is not installed. The capsule is included in the top end gasket set.

b. Hold the valve in place and install the plastic capsule (B, **Figure 98**) onto the end of the valve stem. Apply a light coat of clean engine oil to the outer surface of the capsule.

NOTE
On 2007-2009 models except Screamin' Eagle, the valve seal/spring seat assembly is sold as a unit. Always install a new valve seal/spring seat assembly on 2007-2009 models.

c. Hold the valve in place, and slowly slide the valve seal/spring seat assembly (**Figure 99**) onto the valve stem. Push the assembly down until it bottoms on the machined surface of the cylinder head (**Figure 100**).
d. Remove the plastic capsule from the valve stem, but keep it. The capsule will be used on the remaining valves.

6B. On Screamin' Eagle models, perform the following:
  a. Install the spring seat over the valve guide and into the cylinder head.
  b. Reinstall the valve into the valve guide, but do not push the valve past the top of the valve guide.
  c. Use isopropyl alcohol, or its equivalent, to thoroughly clean all grease from the outside surface of the valve guide.

CAUTION
Do not apply the retaining compound to the top or inside of the valve guide.

  d. Carefully apply Loctite RC620 (green) to the valve seal seating surface on the outside of the valve guide.

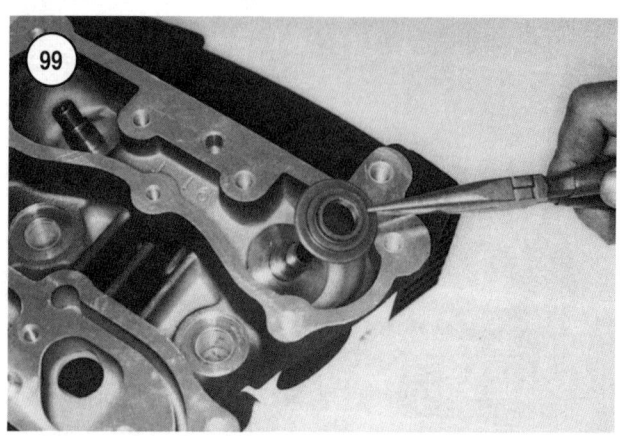

ENGINE TOP END AND EXHAUST SYSTEM

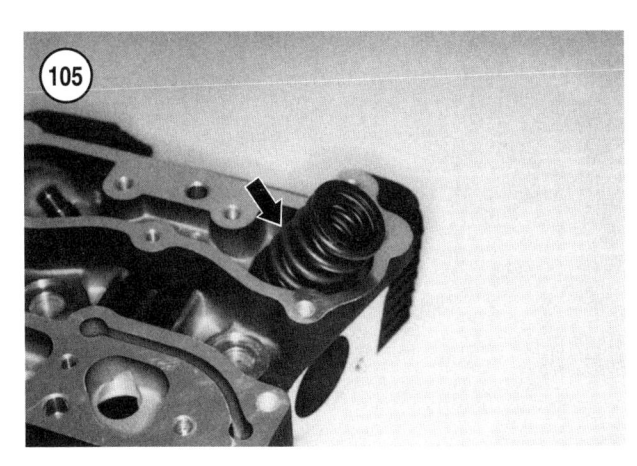

e. Push the valve (A, **Figure 98**) all the way into the cylinder head until it bottoms.

CAUTION
The valve seal will be torn as it passes the valve stem keeper groove if the plastic capsule is not installed. The capsule is included in the top end gasket set.

f. Hold the valve in place and install the plastic capsule (B, **Figure 98**) onto the end of the valve stem. Apply a light coat of clean engine oil to the outer surface of the capsule.
g. Slide a new valve seal (**Figure 101**) over the capsule and down the valve stem until the seal contacts the valve guide.
h. Remove the plastic capsule from the valve stem, but keep it. The capsule will be used on the remaining valves.
i. Slide the valve guide seal installer (**Figure 102**) over the seal. Use a small hammer to gently tap the seal installer until the valve seal lightly bottoms on the valve guide.

7A. On all 2006-2009 models except Screamin' Eagle, position the valve spring (**Figure 103**) with the tapered end going on last and install the valve spring.

7B. On Screamin' Eagle models, perform the following:
 a. Install the inner valve spring (**Figure 104**) and make sure it is properly seated on the lower spring retainer.
 b. Install the outer valve spring (**Figure 105**) and make sure it is properly seated on the lower spring retainer. The larger diameter flange must separate the inner and outer springs.
 c. Install the spring retainer (**Figure 106**).

CAUTION
To avoid loss of spring tension, compress the springs just enough to install the valve keepers.

8. Compress the valve spring with a valve spring compressor (**Figure 94**) and install the valve keepers (**Figure 107**).

134 CHAPTER FOUR

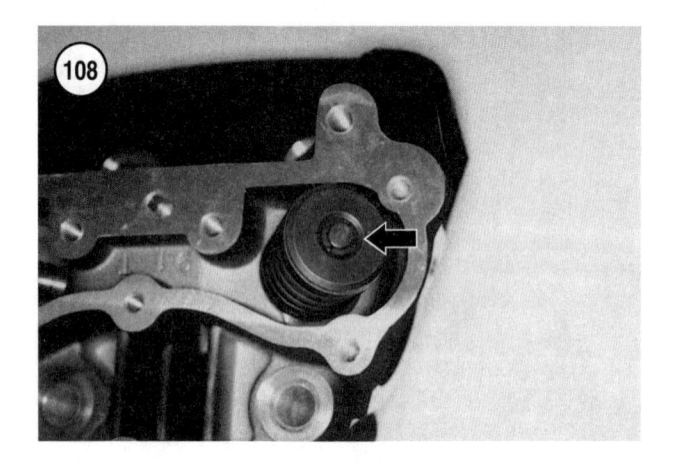

9. Make sure both keepers are seated around the valve stem prior to releasing the compressor.
10. Slowly release tension from the compressor and remove it. After removing the compressor, inspect the valve keepers to make sure they are properly seated (**Figure 108**). Tap the end of the valve stem with a *soft-faced* hammer to ensure the keepers are properly seated.
11. Repeat the procedure to install the remaining valves.
12. On Screamin' Eagle models, install the ACR solenoid as follows:
    a. Make sure the copper washer is in place on the ACR solenoid.
    b. Apply three dots of Loctite 246 Threadlocker Medium Strength/High Temperature to the lower 1/3 of the solenoid threads. Evenly space the dots of threadlock around the circumference of the threads.
    c. Install the ACR solenoid into the cylinder head. Using the solenoid socket, tighten the ACR solenoid to 11-15 ft.-lb. (14.9-20.3 N•m).
13. Install the cylinder head as described in this chapter.

Valve Inspection

During inspection, compare any measurements taken to the specifications listed in **Table 2** or **Table 3**. Replace any part that is worn, damaged or out of specification.
1. Clean valves in solvent. Do not gouge or damage the valve seating surface.
2. Inspect the valve face. Minor roughness and pitting (**Figure 109**) can be removed by lapping the valve as described in this section. Excessive unevenness of the valve contact surface indicates the valve is not serviceable.
3. Inspect the valve stem for wear and roughness. Then, measure the valve stem outside diameter (**Figure 110**) with a micrometer.
4. Remove all carbon and varnish from the valve guides with a stiff spiral wire brush before measuring wear.
5. Measure the valve guide inside diameter with a small bore gauge (**Figure 111**) at the top, center and bottom positions. Then, measure the small bore gauge with a micrometer.
6. Determine the valve stem-to-valve guide clearance by subtracting the valve stem outside diameter from the valve guide inside diameter.

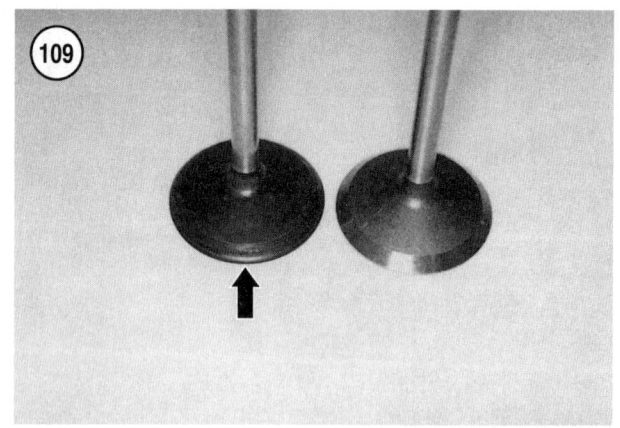

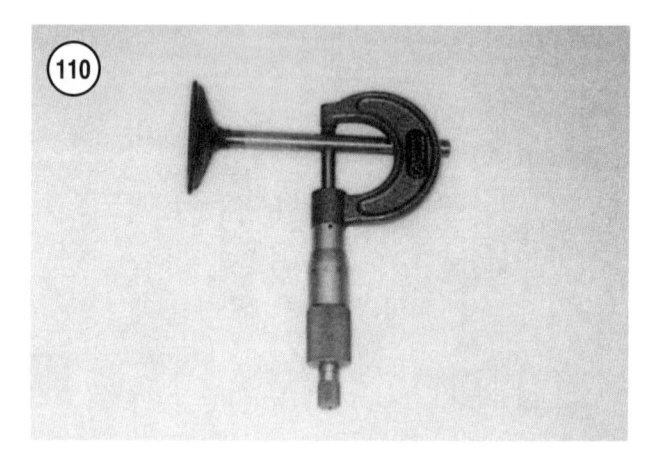

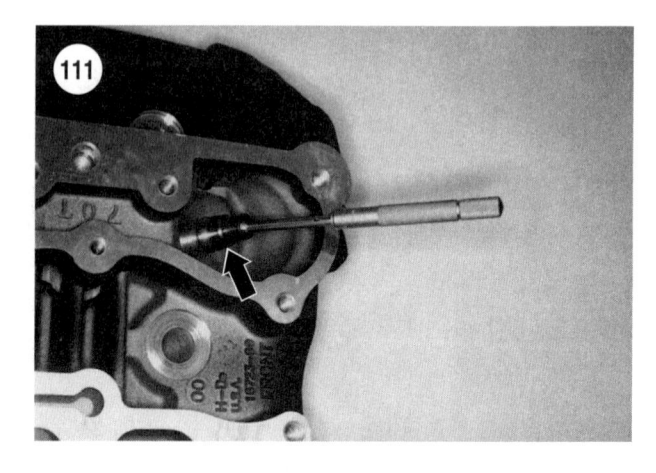

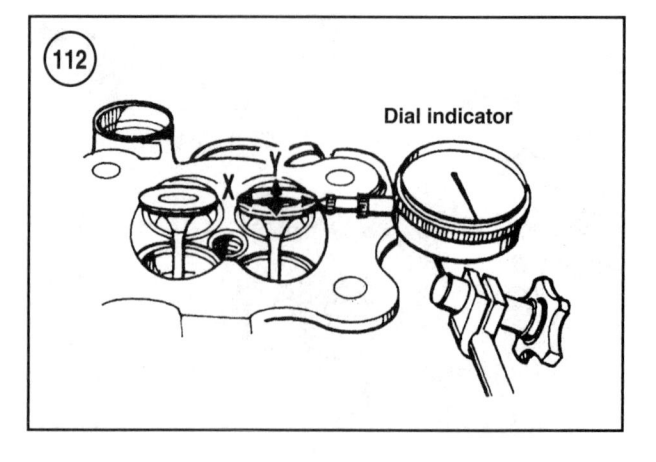

ENGINE TOP END AND EXHAUST SYSTEM

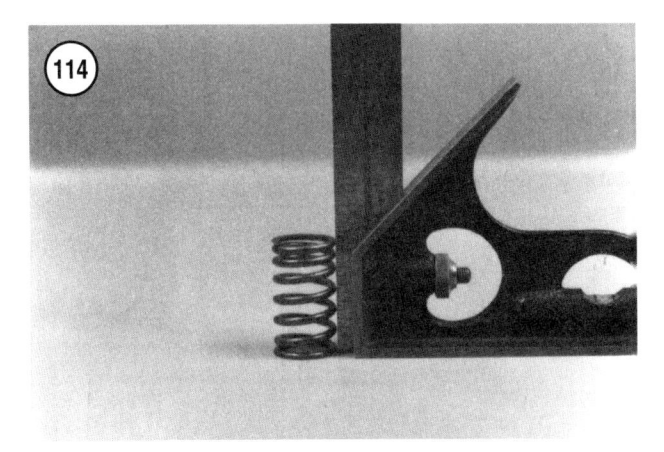

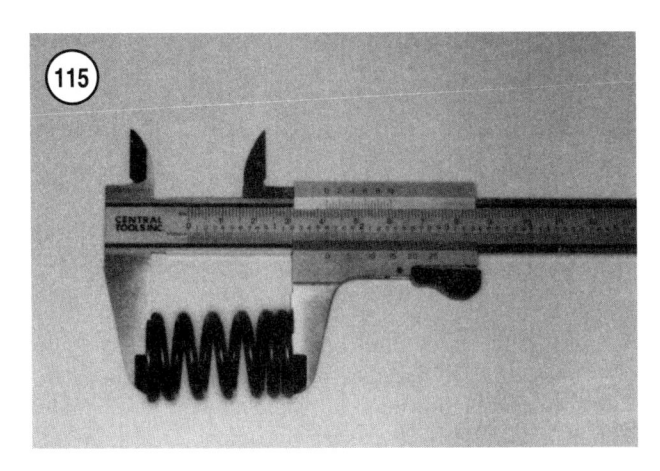

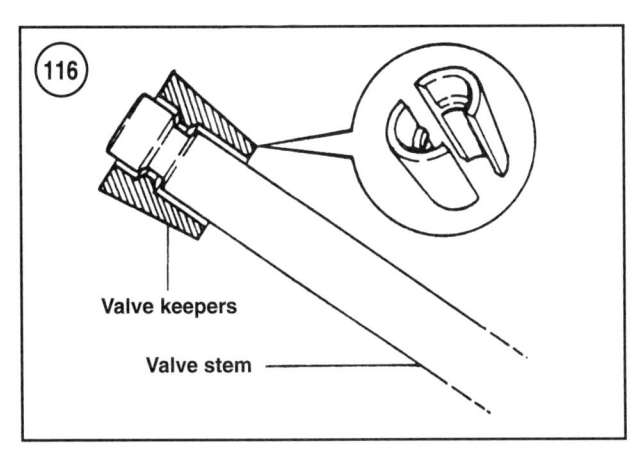

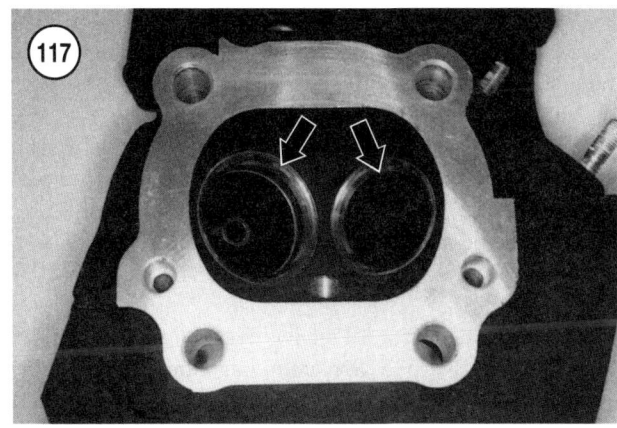

7. If a small bore gauge is not available, insert each valve into its guide. Attach a dial indicator to the valve stem next to the head (**Figure 112**). Hold the valve slightly off its seat and rock it sideways in both directions 90° to each other. If the valve rocks more than slightly, the guide is probably worn. Take the cylinder head to a dealership or machine shop and have the valve guides measured.
8. Check the valve spring as follows:
    a. Inspect the valve spring(s) (**Figure 113**) for visible damage.
    b. Use a square (**Figure 114**) to visually check the spring for distortion or tilt.
    c. Measure the valve spring free length with a caliper (**Figure 115**).
    d. Repeat the measurements for each valve spring.
    e. Replace the defective spring(s).
9. Check the valve spring retainer and seat for cracks or other damage.
10. Check the valve keepers fit on the valve stem end (**Figure 116**). They should index tightly into the valve stem groove.
11. Inspect the valve seats (**Figure 117**) in the cylinder head. If they are worn or burned, they can be reconditioned as described in this section. Seats and valves in near-perfect condition can be reconditioned by lapping as described in this section.

Valve Guide Replacement

Tools

The following tools, or their equivalents, are required to replace the valve guides.
1. Cylinder head stand (H-D part No. HD-39782-A).
2. Intake seat adapter (2006 models except Screamin' Eagle: H-D part No. HD-39782A-3; Screamin' Eagle and all 2007-2009 models: H-D part No. HD-39782-3).
3. Exhaust seat adapter (2006 models except Screamin' Eagle: H-D part No. HD-39782A-4; Screamin' Eagle and all 2007-2009 models: H-D part No. HD-39782-4).
4. Valve guide driver (All models except Screamin Eagle: H-D part No. B-45524-1; Screamin' Eagle models: H-D part No. HD-34740).

5. Valve guide installer sleeve (All models except Screamin' Eagle: H-D part No HD-34731; Screamin' Eagle models: H-D part No. HD-48628).
6. Valve guide brush (H-D part No. HD-34751-A).
7. Valve guide reamer (All models except Screamin' Eagle: H-D part No. B-45523; Screamin' Eagle models: H-D part No. HD-39932).
8. Valve guide reamer T-handle (H-D part No. HD-39847).
9. Valve guide reamer honing lubricant (H-D part No. HD-39964).
10. Valve guide hone (All models except Screamin' Eagle: H-D part No. B-45525; Screamin' Eagle models: H-D part No. HD-34723-A).
11. Hydraulic press.

Procedure

CAUTION
The valve guides must be removed and installed using the proper tools to avoid damage to the cylinder head. Use the correct size valve guide removal tool to remove the valve guides or the tool may expand the end of the guide. An expanded guide will widen and damage the guide bore in the cylinder head as it passes through it.

1. Remove the old valve guide (**Figure 118**) as follows:

NOTE
Retaining rings are used on the exhaust valve guides of all 2006 and 2007 models except Screamin' Eagle. Retaining rings are used on the intake and exhaust valve guides of all 2008-2009 models except Screamin' Eagle.

  a. When removing a valve guide that uses a retaining ring, remove the retaining ring from the top of the cylinder head.
  b. Install the intake (A, **Figure 119**) or exhaust (B) valve seat adapter into the tube at the top of the cylinder head support stand (C).
  c. Set the support stand onto a hydraulic press table.
  d. Install the cylinder head (A, **Figure 120**) onto the support stand (B) *centering* the cylinder head valve seat on the seat adapter.
  e. Insert the valve guide driver (C, **Figure 120**) into the valve guide bore until the driver stops on the valve guide shoulder.
  f. Center the valve guide driver under the press ram. Make sure the driver is perpendicular to the press table.
  g. Support the cylinder head, and then slowly apply ram pressure and drive the valve guide out through the combustion chamber. Discard the old valve guide.
  h. Remove the cylinder head and tools from the press bed.
  i. Repeat the process to remove for the remaining valve guides.

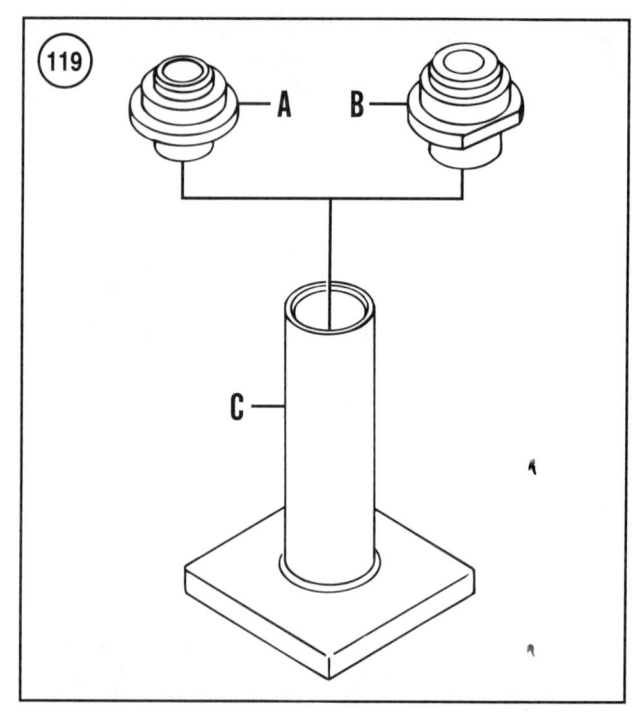

2. Clean the valve guide bores in the cylinder head.
3. Because the valve guide bores in the cylinder head may have been enlarged during removal of the old guides, measure each valve guide bore. Purchase the new valve guides to match their respective bore diameters. Determine the bore diameter as follows:
  a. Measure the valve guide bore diameter in the cylinder head with a small bore gauge. Record the bore diameter.
  b. The outside diameter of the *new* valve guide must be 0.0020-0.0033 in. (0.051-0.084 mm) larger than the valve guide bore in the cylinder head. When purchasing new valve guides, measure the new guide's outside diameter with a micrometer. If the new guide's outside diameter is not within this specification, install oversize valve guide(s). Refer to a dealership for available sizes and part numbers.
4. Apply a thin coat of Vaseline to the entire outer surface of the new valve guide before installing it in the cylinder head.

ENGINE TOP END AND EXHAUST SYSTEM

Figure 120

Figure 121

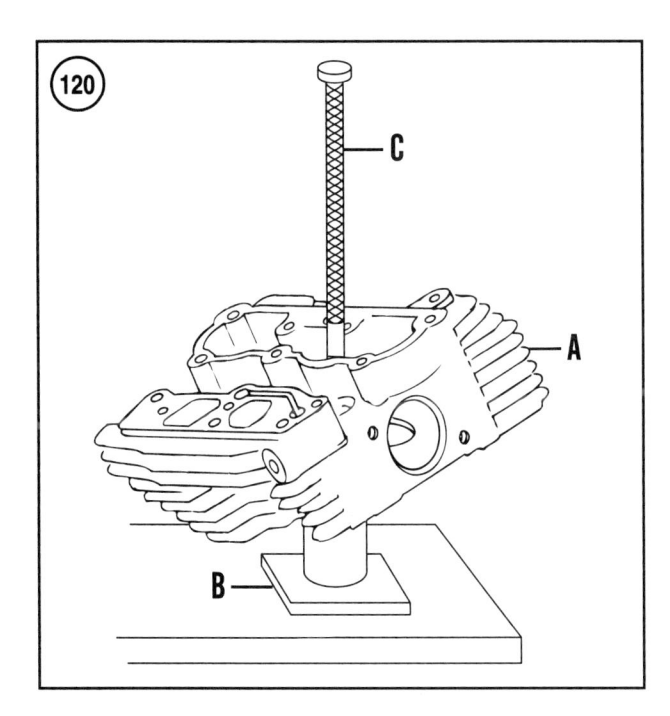

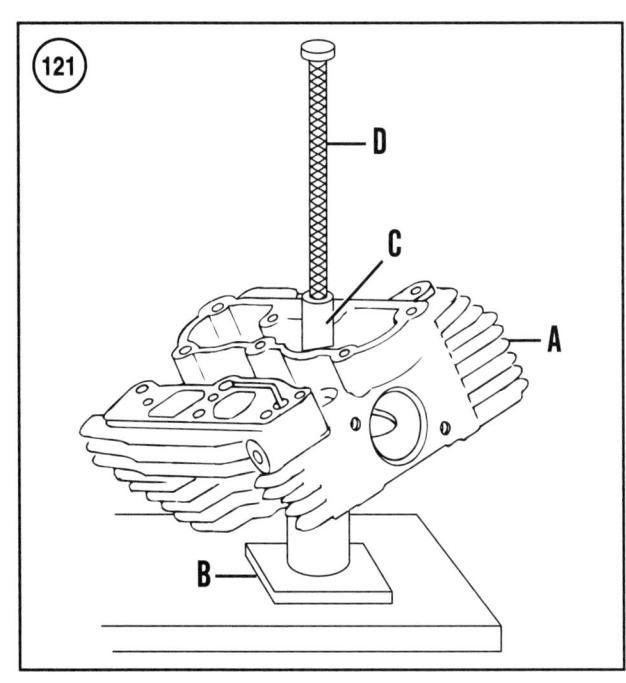

CAUTION
When installing oversize valve guides, make sure to match each guide to its respective bore in the cylinder head.

5. Install the *new* valve guide as follows:
   a. Install the intake (A, **Figure 119**) or exhaust (B) seat adapter into the tube at the top of the cylinder head support stand (C).
   b. Install the support stand onto the hydraulic press table.
   c. Install the cylinder head (A, **Figure 121**) onto the support stand (B) *centering* the cylinder head valve seat on the seat adapter.

NOTE
Retaining rings are used on the exhaust valve guides of all 2006 and 2007 models except Screamin' Eagle models. Retaining rings are used on the intake and exhaust valve guides of all 2008-2009 models except Screamin' Eagle models.

   d. Install the valve guide over its bore in the cylinder head. On guides that use retaining rings, make sure the valve guide retaining ring groove faces out away from the cylinder head.
   e. Install the valve guide installer sleeve (C, **Figure 121**) over the valve guide, and insert the tapered end of the valve guide driver (D) into the installer sleeve.
   f. Center the valve guide driver under the press ram. Make sure the driver is perpendicular to the press table.
   g. Support the cylinder head. Slowly apply ram pressure, and then start to drive the valve guide into the cylinder head receptacle. Stop and back off the press ram to allow the valve guide to center itself.
   h. Verify that the support stand (B, **Figure 121**) and valve guide driver (D) are square with the press table.
   i. Apply ram pressure and continue to drive the valve guide part way into the cylinder head receptacle. Once again, stop and back off the press ram to allow the valve guide to center itself.
   j. Apply ram pressure again and drive the valve guide into the bore until the installer sleeve (C, **Figure 121**) contacts the machined surface of the cylinder head. Remove the valve guide driver and installer sleeve.
   k. Install a *new* retaining ring into the groove of a valve guide that uses a retaining ring. Make sure the retaining ring is completely seated in the valve guide groove.
   l. Remove the cylinder head and tools from the press bed.
   m. Repeat the process to install the remaining valve guides.

6. Replacement valve guides are sold with a smaller inside diameter than the valve stem. Ream the guide to within 0.0005-0.0001 in (0.013-0.0025 mm) of its finished size as followed:
   a. Install the valve guide reamer onto the T-handle.
   b. Apply a liberal amount of reamer lubricant to the ream bit and to the valve guide bore.
   c. Start the reamer straight into the valve guide bore at the top of the cylinder head.

CAUTION
Only apply pressure to the end of the drive socket. If pressure is applied to the T-handle, the bore will be uneven, rough cut and tapered.

   d. Apply thumb pressure to the end of the drive socket portion of the T-handle while rotating the T-handle *clockwise*. Only *light* pressure is required. Apply additional lubricant to the reamer and into the valve guide while rotating the reamer.

e. Continue to rotate the reamer until the entire bit has traveled through the valve guide and the shank of the reamer rotates freely.

CAUTION
Never back the reamer out through the valve guide as the guide will be damaged.

f. Remove the T-handle from the reamer. Remove the reamer from the combustion chamber side of the cylinder head.

g. Apply low-pressure compressed air to remove the small shavings from the valve guide bore. Clean the valve guide bore with a valve guide brush.

7. Hone the valve guide as follows:
   a. Install the valve guide hone into a high-speed electric drill.
   b. Lubricate the valve guide bore and hone stones with reamer lubricant–*do not use motor oil*.
   c. Carefully insert the hone stones into the valve guide bore.
   d. Start the drill and move the hone back and forth in the valve guide bore for 10 to 12 complete strokes to obtain a 60° degree crosshatch pattern.

8. Repeat the reaming and honing process for each valve guide.

9. Soak the cylinder head in a container filled with hot, soapy water. Then, clean the valve guides with a valve guide brush or an equivalent bristle brush. *Do not use a steel brush*. Do not use cleaning solvent, kerosene or gasoline as these chemicals will not remove all of the abrasive particles produced during the honing operation. Repeat this step until all of the valve guides are thoroughly cleaned. Then, rinse the cylinder head and valve guides in clear water and dry them with compressed air.

10. After cleaning and drying the valve guides, apply clean engine oil to the guides to prevent rust.

11. Resurface the valve seats as described in *Valve Seat Reconditioning* (this section).

Valve Seat Inspection

1. Remove all carbon residue from each valve seat. Then, clean the cylinder head as described in *Valve Inspection* (this section).

2. Check the valve seats in their original locations with machinist's dye as follows:
   a. Thoroughly clean the valve face and valve seat with contact cleaner.
   b. Spread a thin layer of machinist's dye evenly on the valve face.
   c. Insert the valve into its guide.
   d. Support the valve by hand (**Figure 122**) and tap the valve up and down in the cylinder head. Do not rotate the valve or the reading will be false.
   e. Remove the valve and examine the impression left by the machinist's dye. The impressions on the valve and the seat should be even around their circumferences and the width (**Figure 123**) should be within the specification in **Table 2** or **Table 3**. If the width is beyond the specification or if the impression is uneven, recondition the valve seats.

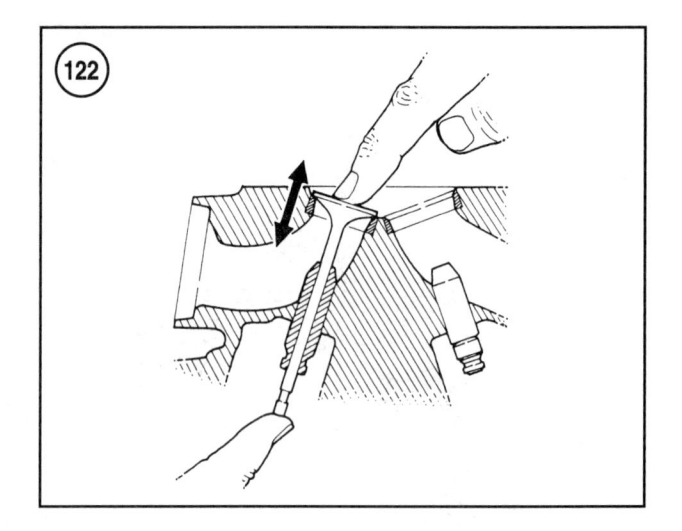

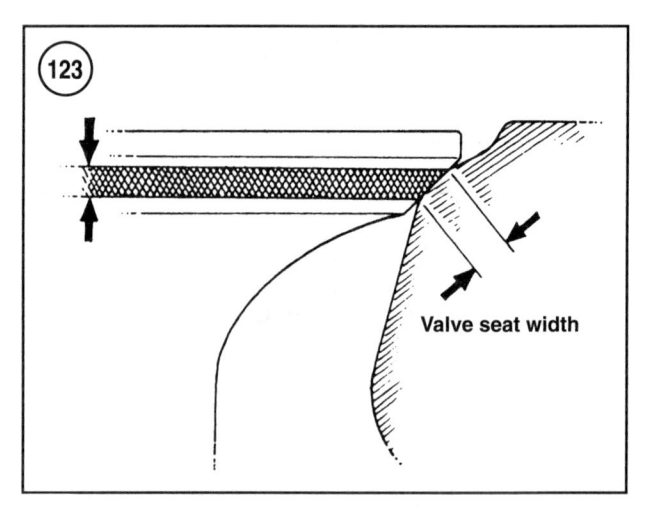

3. Closely examine the valve seat in the cylinder head (**Figure 117**). It should be smooth and even with a polished seating surface.

4. If the valve seat is in good condition, install the valve as described in this section.

5. If the valve seat is not correct, recondition the valve seat as described in this section.

Valve Seat Reconditioning

Valve seat reconditioning requires experience and a number of tools. In most cases, it is more practical to have these procedures performed by a machinist.

A valve seat cutter set (2006-2007 models: H-D part No. HD-35758-A; 2008-2009 models: H-D part No. HD-35758-C), or an equivalent, is required.

Refer to **Figure 124** for valve seat angles.

ENGINE TOP END AND EXHAUST SYSTEM

Figure 124: Cylinder head, Seat, Valve, Seat width, 60°, 31°, 46° cutting, 45° grinding, Margin

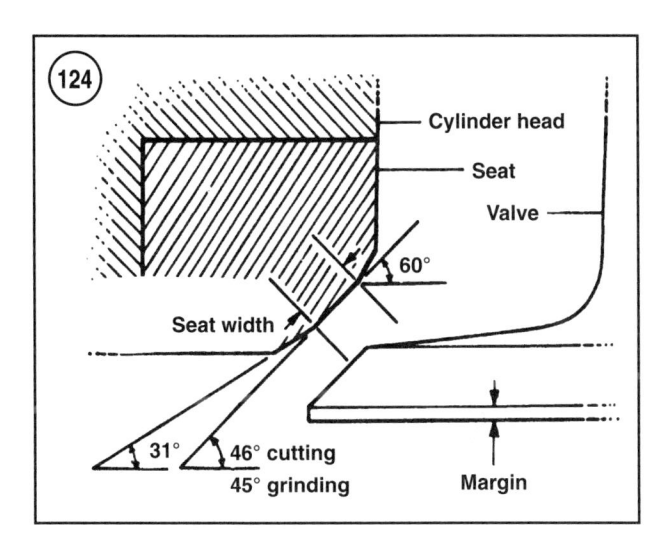

1. Clean the valve guides as described in *Valve Inspection* (this section).
2. Measure the valve stem protrusion by performing the following:
   a. Insert the valve stem into the valve guide from the combustion chamber side of the cylinder head.
   b. Use a caliper to measure the distance from the top of the valve stem to the cylinder head's machined surface.
   c. If the measured valve stem protrusion exceeds the service limit (**Table 2** or **Table 3**), replace the valve seat or cylinder head as necessary.
3. Carefully rotate and insert the solid pilot into the valve guide. Make sure the pilot is correctly seated.

CAUTION
Valve seat cutting accuracy depends on a correctly sized and installed pilot.

4. Using the proper 46° cutter (intake or exhaust), descale and clean the valve seat with one or two turns.

CAUTION
*Measure the valve seat contact area in the cylinder head (**Figure 124**) after each cut to make sure its size and area are correct. Overgrinding will lower the valves into the cylinder head and off the valve seat far enough that the seat will have to be replaced.*

5. If the seat is still pitted or burned, turn the cutter until the surface is clean. Work slowly and carefully to avoid removing too much material from the valve seat.
6. Remove the pilot from the valve guide.
7. Apply a small amount of valve lapping compound to the valve face and install the valve. Rotate the valve against the valve seat using a valve lapping tool. Remove the valve.
8. Measure the valve seat with a caliper (**Figure 123** and **Figure 124**). Record the measurement to use as a reference point when performing the following steps.

CAUTION
The 31° cutter removes material quickly. Work carefully and check the progress often.

9. Reinsert the solid pilot into the valve guide. Make sure the pilot is properly seated. Install the 31° cutter onto the solid pilot and lightly cut the seat to remove 1/4 of the existing valve seat.
10. Install the 60° cutter onto the solid pilot and lightly cut the seat to remove the lower 1/4 of the existing valve seat.
11. Measure the valve seat width with a caliper. Fit the 46° cutter onto the solid pilot, and cut the valve seat to the specified seat width in **Table 2** or **Table 3**.
12. Remove the solid pilot from the cylinder head.
13. Inspect the valve seat-to-valve face impression as described in *Valve Seat Inspection* (this section).
14. If the contact area is too high or too wide on the valve, cut the seat with the 31° cutter. This will remove part of the top valve seat area to lower or narrow the contact area.
15. If the contact area is too low or too narrow on the valve, cut the seat with the 60° degree cutter. This will remove part of the lower area to raise and widen the contact area.
16. After obtaining the desired valve seat position and angle, use the 46° cutter and *lightly* clean off any burrs caused by the previous cuts.
17. When the contact area is correct, lap the valve as described in this section.
18. Repeat this procedure to recondition the remaining valve seats.
19. Thoroughly clean the cylinder head and all valve components in solvent. Then, wash them with detergent and hot water, and rinse them in cold water. Dry them with compressed air.
20. After cleaning and drying the cylinder head and valve components, apply a light coat of engine oil to all non-aluminum surfaces to prevent rust formation.

Valve Lapping

If valve wear or distortion is not excessive, restore the valve's sealing ability by lapping the valve to the seat.
1. Smear a light coat of fine-grade valve lapping compound on the seating surface of the valve.
2. Insert the valve into the head.
3. Wet the suction cup of the lapping tool, and stick it onto the head of the valve. Lap the valve to the seat by spinning the tool between both hands while lifting and moving the valve around the seat 1/4-turn at a time.
4. Wipe off the valve and seat frequently to check progress. Lap the valve just enough to achieve a precise seating ring around the valve head.
5. Closely examine the valve seat in the cylinder head. The seat must be smooth and even with a polished seating ring.
6. Thoroughly clean the valves and cylinder head in solvent to remove all lapping compound residue. Compound left on the valves or the cylinder head will cause rapid engine wear.
7. After installing the valves into the cylinder head, test each valve for proper seating by performing the *Leak Test* as described in this section. If solvent leaks past any valve,

140

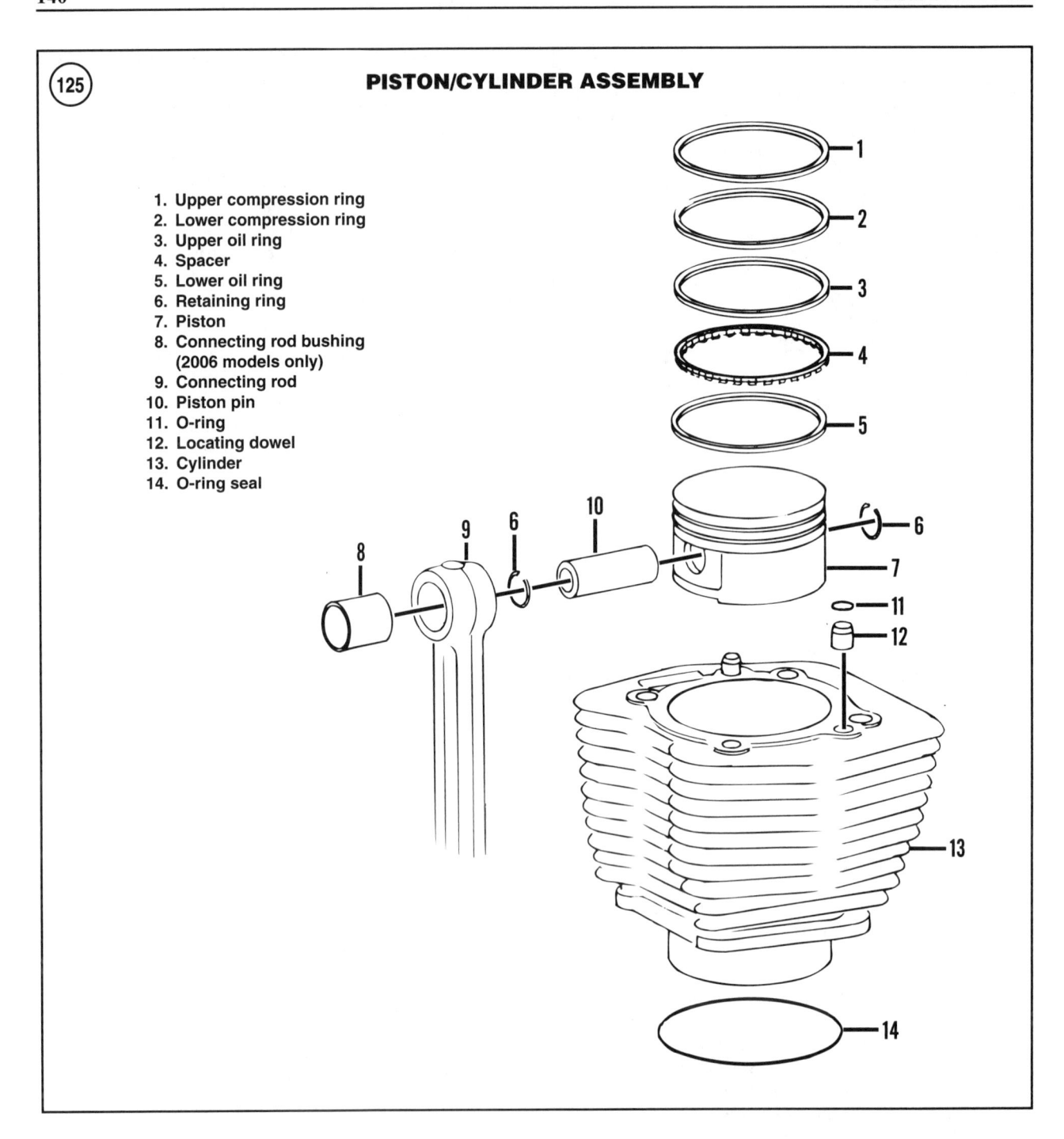

PISTON/CYLINDER ASSEMBLY

1. Upper compression ring
2. Lower compression ring
3. Upper oil ring
4. Spacer
5. Lower oil ring
6. Retaining ring
7. Piston
8. Connecting rod bushing (2006 models only)
9. Connecting rod
10. Piston pin
11. O-ring
12. Locating dowel
13. Cylinder
14. O-ring seal

disassemble the leaking valve and repeat the lapping procedure or recondition the valve seat as described in this section.

Valve Seat Replacement

Valve seat replacement requires considerable experience and equipment. Refer this work to a dealership or machine shop.

CYLINDER

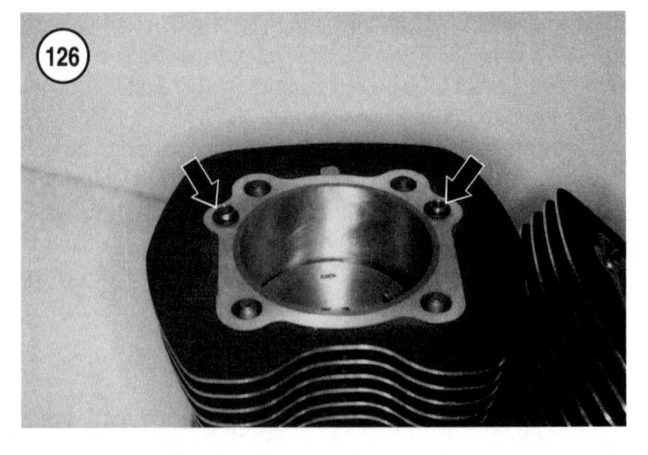

Refer to **Figure 125**.

ENGINE TOP END AND EXHAUST SYSTEM

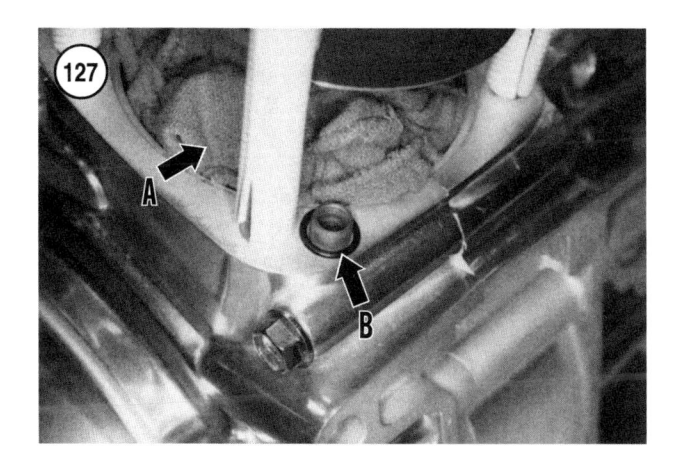

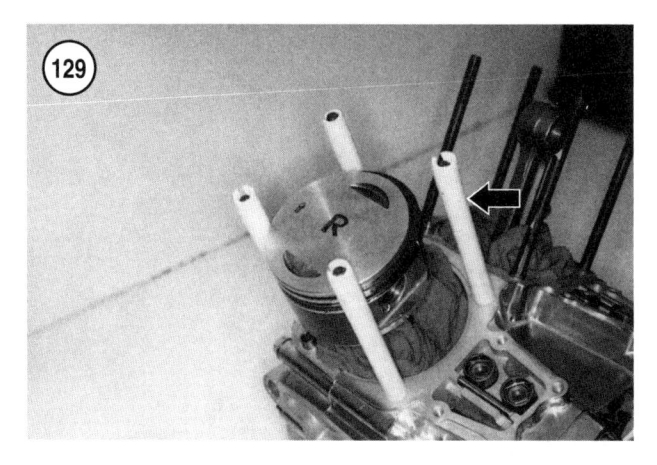

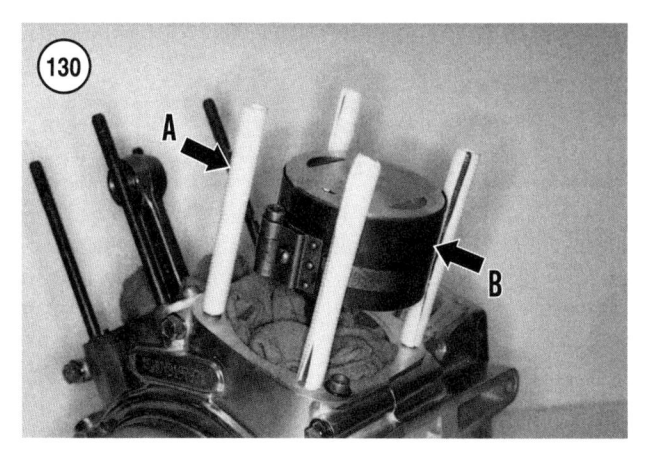

Removal

1. Remove the cylinder head as described in this chapter.
2. Remove all debris from the cylinder base.
3. Remove the dowels (**Figure 126**) and their O-rings from the top of the cylinder if they are still in place.
4. Turn the crankshaft until the piston is at bottom dead center (BDC).

CAUTION
The front and rear cylinders are identical (same part number). Mark each cylinder so it can be reinstalled in its original position.

5. Pull the cylinder straight up and off the piston and cylinder studs. If necessary, tap around the perimeter of the cylinder with a rubber or plastic mallet.
6. Place clean shop rags (A, **Figure 127**) into the crankcase opening to prevent objects from falling undetected into the crankcase.
7. Remove the O-rings (B, **Figure 127**) from the locating dowels in the crankcase. Leave the dowels in place unless they are loose.
8. Remove and discard the O-ring (A, **Figure 128**) from the base of the cylinder.
9. Install a hose (**Figure 129**) over each stud to protect the piston.

CAUTION
After removing the cylinder, be careful when working around the cylinder studs to avoid bending or damaging them. The slightest bend could cause the stud to fail.

10. Repeat the procedure to remove the other cylinder.

Installation

CAUTION
*When a cylinder has been bored oversize, the inner lead-in angle (B, **Figure 128**) at the base of the bore skirt has been eliminated. This lead-in angle is necessary for the piston rings to safely enter the cylinder bore. If necessary, use a cylinder chamfering cone (JIMS part No. 2078) or a hand grinder with a fine stone to make a new lead-in angle. The finished surface must be smooth so it will not catch and damage the piston rings during installation.*

1. If removed, install the pistons and rings as described in this chapter.
2. Remove gasket residue and clean the cylinder as described in *Inspection* (this section).
3. Remove the rubber hose (A, **Figure 130**) from each stud.
4. Install a *new* O-ring (**Figure 128**) onto the base of the cylinder. Apply a light coat of clean engine oil to the O-ring.

5. If removed, install the locating dowels (**Figure 131**) into the crankcase.
6. Install a *new* O-ring (B, **Figure 127**) onto each dowel. Apply a light coat of clean engine oil to each O-ring.
7. Turn the crankshaft until the piston is at top dead center (TDC).
8. Lubricate the cylinder bore, piston and piston rings liberally with clean engine oil.
9. Position the top compression ring gap so it is facing the intake port. Then, stagger the remaining piston ring end gaps as shown in **Figure 132**.
10. Compress the piston rings with a ring compressor (B, **Figure 130**).

NOTE
Install the cylinder in its original position as noted during removal.

11. Position the cylinder so the indents in the cooling fins face the right side (front facing forward). Carefully align the cylinder with the studs, and slowly slide the cylinder down (**Figure 133**) the studs until it sits over the top of the piston. Continue sliding the cylinder down past the rings. Remove the ring compressor (A, **Figure 134**) once the piston rings enter the cylinder bore. Remove the shop rag (B, **Figure 134**) from the crankcase opening.
12. Continue to slide the cylinder down until it bottoms out on the crankcase.
13. Repeat the process to install the other cylinder.
14. Install the cylinder heads as described in this chapter.

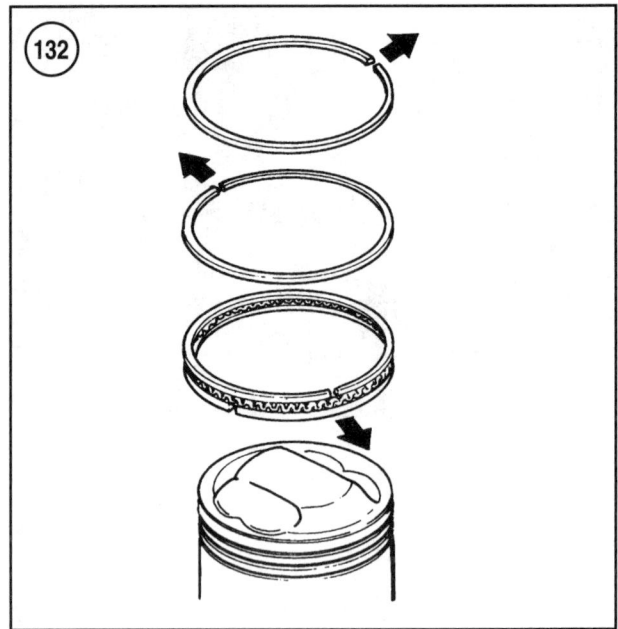

Inspection

During inspection, compare all measurements taken to the specifications listed in **Table 2** or **Table 3**. Replace any part that is worn, damaged or out of specification.

To obtain an accurate cylinder bore measurement, the cylinder must be tightened between cylinder torque plates (JIMS part No. 1287). Measurements made without the torque plates will be inaccurate and may vary by as much as 0.001 in. (0.025 mm). Refer this procedure to a shop equipped and experienced with this procedure if the tools are not available. The cylinder bore must be thoroughly clean and at room temperature to obtain accurate measurements. Do not measure the cylinder immediately after it has been honed as it will still be warm. Measurements can vary by as much as 0.002 in. (0.051 mm) if the cylinder block is not at room temperature.

1. Thoroughly clean the outside of the cylinder. Use a stiff brush, soap and water to clean all debris from the cool-

ENGINE TOP END AND EXHAUST SYSTEM

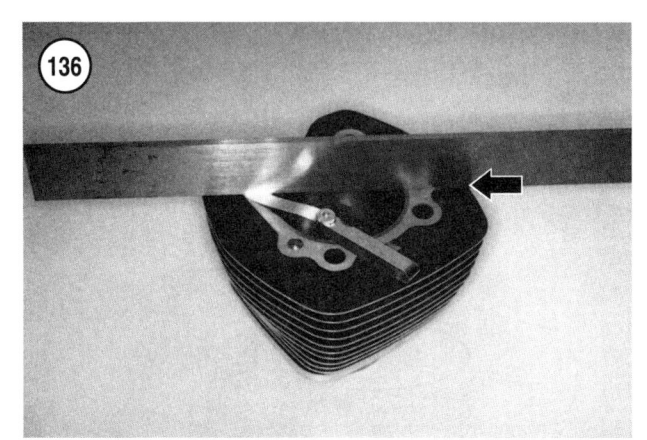

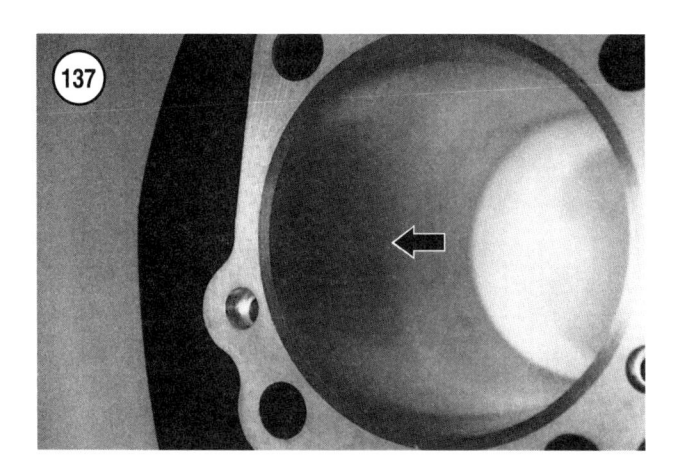

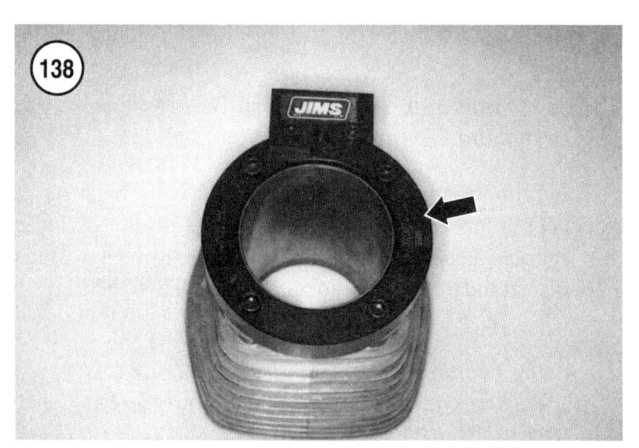

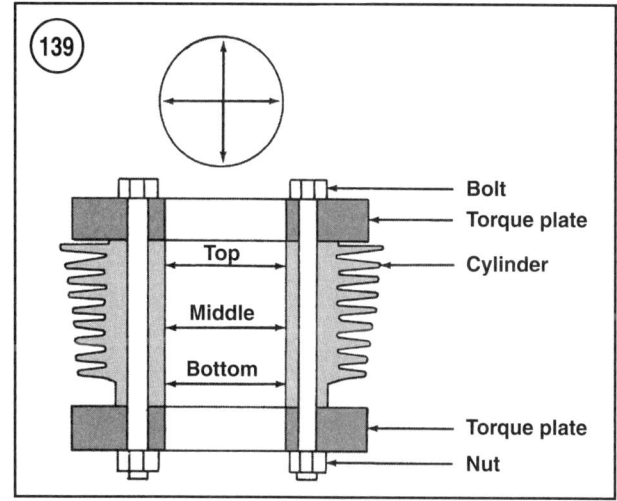

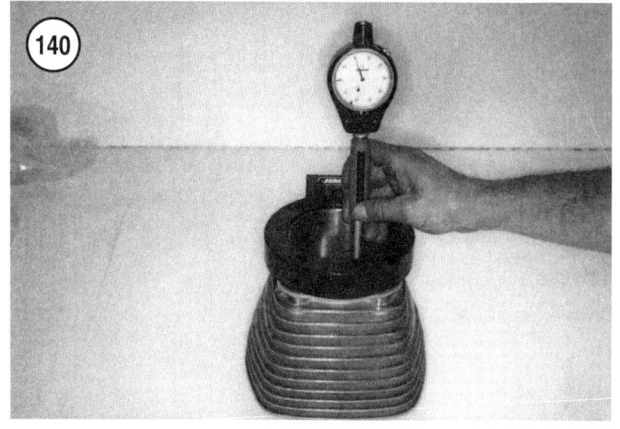

ing fins (**Figure 135**). If necessary, use a piece of wood to scrape away any dirt lodged between the fins. Clogged cooling fins can cause overheating and lead to possible engine damage.

2. Carefully remove all gasket residue from the top and bottom cylinder gasket surfaces.

3. Thoroughly clean the cylinder with solvent, and dry it with compressed air. Lightly oil the cylinder block bore to prevent rust.

4. Check the top and bottom cylinder gasket surfaces for warp with a straightedge and feeler gauge (**Figure 136**). If warp exceeds the service limit in **Table 2** or **Table 3**, replace the cylinder.

5. Check the cylinder bore (**Figure 137**) for scuff marks, scratches or other damage.

6. Install the cylinder torque plates onto the cylinder (**Figure 138**) following the tool manufacturer's instructions.

7. Measure the cylinder bore inside diameter with a bore gauge or inside micrometer at the positions indicated in **Figure 139**. Perform the first measurement 0.500 in. (12.7 mm) below the top of the cylinder (**Figure 140**). Do not measure areas where the rings do not travel.

8. Measure the bore in two axes aligned with the piston pin and at 90° to the pin. If the taper or out-of-round measurements exceed the service limits, bore both cylinders

PISTON/CYLINDER ASSEMBLY

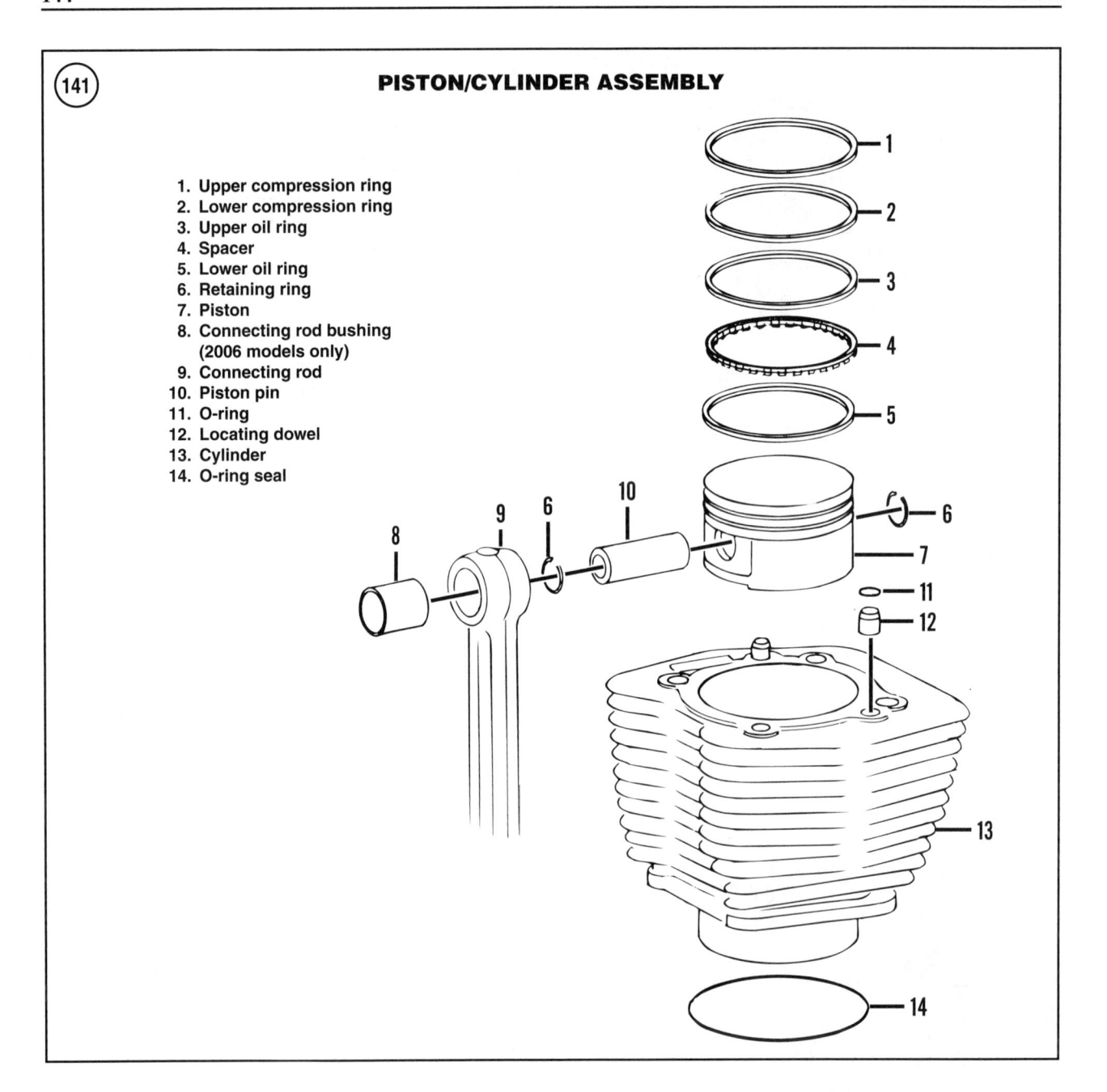

1. Upper compression ring
2. Lower compression ring
3. Upper oil ring
4. Spacer
5. Lower oil ring
6. Retaining ring
7. Piston
8. Connecting rod bushing (2006 models only)
9. Connecting rod
10. Piston pin
11. O-ring
12. Locating dowel
13. Cylinder
14. O-ring seal

to the next oversize and install oversize pistons and rings. Confirm the accuracy of all measurements and consult with a parts supplier on the availability of replacement parts before having the cylinder serviced.

9. Remove the torque plates.
10. If the cylinders were serviced, wash each cylinder in hot, soapy water to remove the fine grit material left from the boring or honing process. Run a clean white cloth through the cylinder bore. If the cloth shows traces of grit or oil, the bore is not clean. Wash the cylinder until the cloth passes through cleanly. When the bore is clean, dry it with compressed air, and then lubricate it with clean engine oil to prevent rust.

CAUTION
Only hot, soapy water will completely clean the cylinder bore. Solvent and kerosene cannot wash fine grit out of the cylinder crevices. Abrasive grit left in the cylinder will cause premature engine wear.

Cylinder Studs and Cylinder Head Bolts Inspection and Cleaning

The cylinder studs and cylinder head bolts must be in good condition and properly cleaned before the cylinder and cylinder heads are installed. Damaged or dirty studs may distort the cylinder head and cause gasket leaks.

CAUTION
The cylinder studs, cylinder head bolts and washers consist of hardened material. Do not use a substitute.

ENGINE TOP END AND EXHAUST SYSTEM

Figure 142

Figure 143

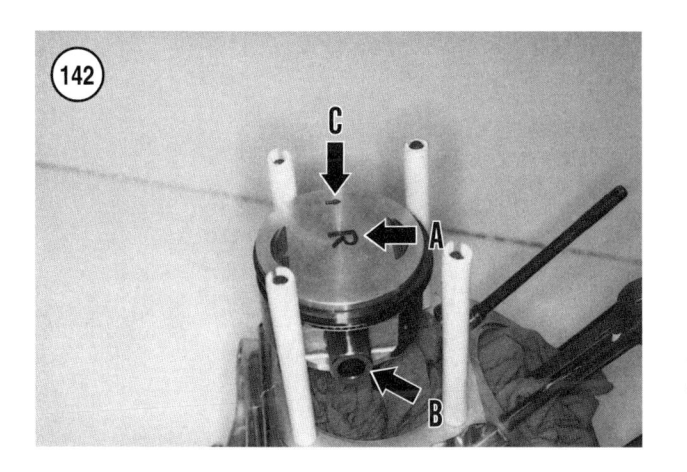

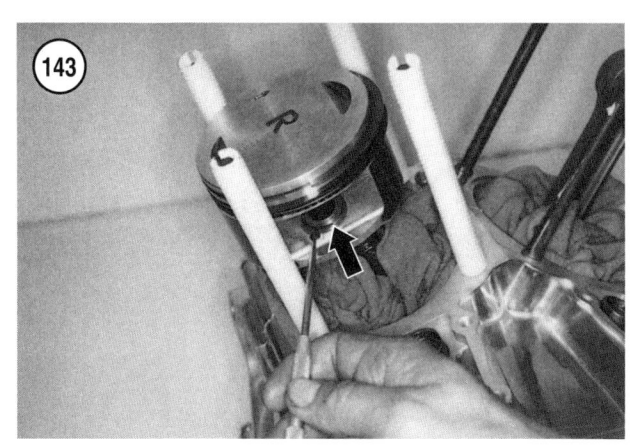

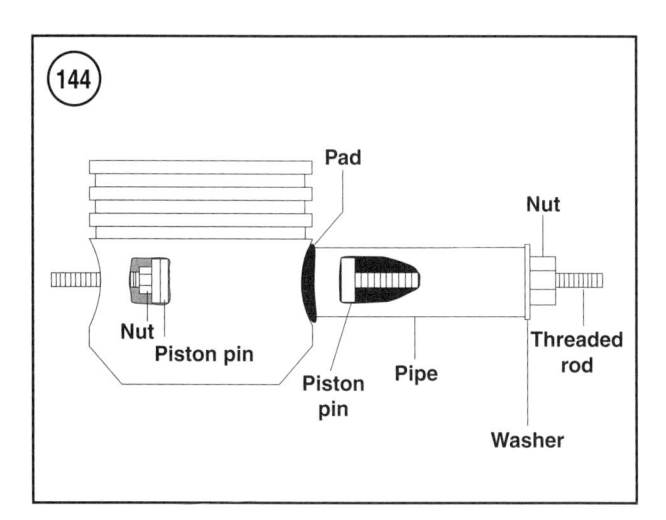

Figure 144 — Pad, Nut, Piston pin, Nut, Pipe, Piston pin, Threaded rod, Washer

1. Inspect the cylinder head bolts. Replace any that are damaged.
2. Examine the cylinder studs for bending, looseness or damage. Replace studs as described in *Cylinder Stud Replacement* in Chapter Five.
3. Cover both crankcase openings with shop rags to prevent debris from falling into the engine.
4. Remove all carbon residue from the cylinder studs and cylinder head bolts as follows:
    a. Apply solvent to the cylinder stud and mating cylinder head bolt threads, and thread the bolt onto the stud.
    b. Turn the cylinder head bolt back and forth to loosen and remove the carbon residue from the threads. Remove the bolt from the stud. Wipe off the residue with a shop rag moistened in cleaning solvent.
    c. Repeat the process until both thread sets are free of carbon residue.
    d. Spray the cylinder stud and cylinder head bolt with an aerosol parts cleaner and allow them to dry.
    e. Set the clean bolt aside and install it on the same stud when installing the cylinder head.
5. Repeat the carbon removal procedure for each cylinder stud and cylinder head bolt set.

PISTONS AND PISTON RINGS

Refer to **Figure 141**.

Piston Removal

1. Remove the cylinder as described in this chapter.
2. Cover the crankcase with clean shop rags.
3. Lightly mark the pistons with a F for front or a R (A, **Figure 142**) for rear so they can be reinstalled onto their original connecting rods.

WARNING
The piston pin retaining rings may spring out of the piston during removal. Wear safety glasses when removing them.

4. Use an awl, and pry the piston pin retaining rings (**Figure 143**) out of the piston. Place a thumb over the hole for the piston pin to help keep the retaining rings from flying out during removal.
5. Support the piston and push out the piston pin (B, **Figure 142**). If the piston pin is difficult to remove, use a piston pin removal tool (**Figure 144**).
6. Remove the piston from the connecting rod. Keep the connecting rod propped upright so it does not hit the crankcase.
7. Fit a long piece of hose or some foam pipe insulation over each connecting rod stud so it will not be damaged.
8. If necessary, remove the piston rings as described in this section.
9. Inspect the pistons, piston pins and piston rings as described in this section.

Piston Installation

1. Cover the crankcase openings to avoid dropping a retaining ring into the engine.
2. If removed, install the piston rings as described in this section.
3. Install a *new* piston pin retaining ring into one groove in the piston. Make sure the ring seats in the groove completely.
4. Coat the connecting rod bushing and piston pin with clean engine oil.

5. Slide the piston pin (**Figure 145**) into the piston until its end is flush with the piston pin boss.

6. Place the piston over the connecting rod with the arrow mark (C, **Figure 142**) on the piston facing toward the front of the engine. Seat a used piston onto its original connecting rod. Refer to the marks made on the pistons during removal.

7. Push the piston pin (B, **Figure 142**) through the connecting rod bushing and into the other side of the piston. Push the piston pin in until it bottoms against the retaining ring.

8. Install the other *new* piston pin retaining ring (**Figure 146**) into the piston groove. Make sure it seats properly in the piston groove (**Figure 147**).

9. Repeat the process to install for the remaining piston.

10. Install the cylinders as described in this chapter.

Piston Inspection

During inspection, compare all measurements taken to the specifications listed in **Table 2** or **Table 3**. Replace any part that is worn, damaged or out of specification.

1. If necessary, remove the piston rings as described in this section.

CAUTION
Be very careful not to gouge or otherwise damage the piston when removing carbon. Never use a wire brush to clean the piston ring grooves. Do not attempt to remove carbon from the sides of the piston above the top ring or from the cylinder bore near the top. Removal of carbon from these two areas may cause increased oil consumption.

2. Carefully clean the carbon from the piston crown (**Figure 148**) with a soft scraper. Large carbon accumulations reduce piston cooling and cause detonation and piston damage. Make sure the piston remains properly identified.

3. After cleaning the piston, examine the crown. The crown should show no signs of wear or damage. If the crown appears pecked or spongy-looking, check the spark plug, valves and combustion chamber for aluminum deposits. If aluminum deposits are found, the engine is overheating.

4. Remove all carbon buildup and oil residue from the ring grooves with a broken piston ring. Do not gouge or remove any aluminum from the ring grooves as this will increase side clearance. Replace the piston if necessary.

5. Examine each ring groove for burrs, dented edges or other damage. Pay particular attention to the top compression ring groove as it usually wears more than the others. The oil rings and grooves generally wear less than compression rings and their grooves. If the oil ring groove is worn or if the oil ring assembly is tight and difficult to remove, the piston skirt may have collapsed due to excessive heat and is permanently deformed. Replace the piston.

6. Check the oil control holes (**Figure 149**) in the piston for carbon or oil sludge buildup. Clean the holes with wire and blow them out with compressed air.

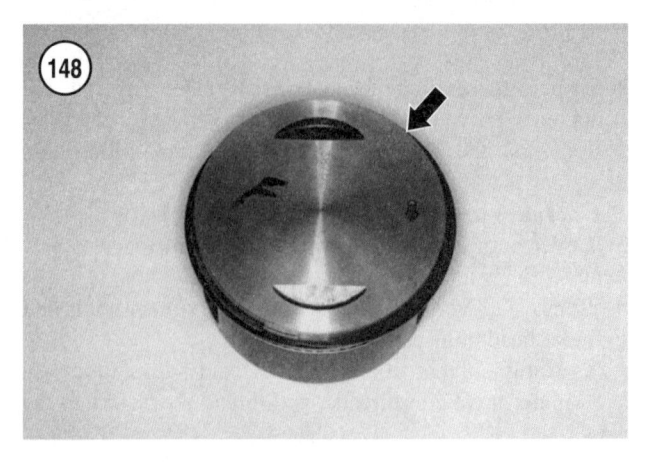

ENGINE TOP END AND EXHAUST SYSTEM

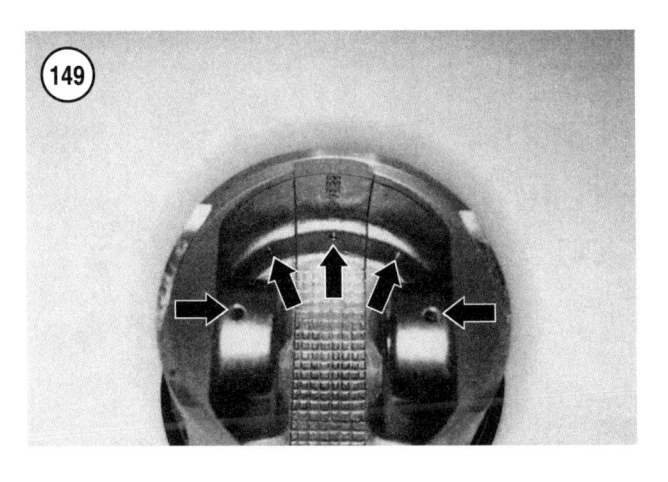

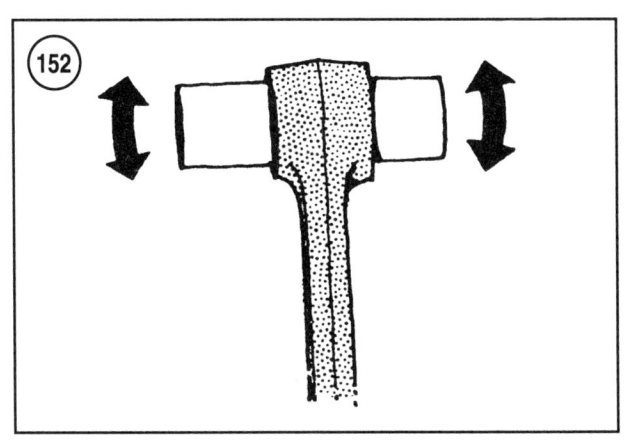

CAUTION
*The pistons have a special coating on the skirt (**Figure 150**). Do not scrape or use any type of abrasive on this surface as it will be damaged.*

NOTE
If the piston skirt is worn or scuffed unevenly from side-to-side, the connecting rod may be bent or twisted.

7. Check the piston skirt (**Figure 150**) for cracks or other damage. If a piston shows signs of partial seizure such as aluminum build-up on the piston skirt, replace the piston to reduce the possibility of engine noise and further piston seizure.

8. Check the circlip groove (**Figure 151**) on each side for wear, cracks or other damage. If the grooves are questionable, check the circlip fit by installing a new circlip into each groove, and then attempt to move the circlip from side-to-side. If the circlip has any side play, the groove is worn and the piston must be replaced.

9. Measure piston-to-cylinder clearance as described in *Piston Clearance* (this section).

10. If the piston needs to be replaced, select a new piston as described in *Piston Clearance* (this section). If the piston and cylinder are not damaged and are dimensionally correct, they can be reused. The manufacturer recommends that *new* piston rings be installed every time the piston is removed.

Piston Pin Inspection and Clearance

1. Clean the piston pin in solvent and dry it thoroughly.
2. Inspect the piston pin for chrome flaking or cracks. Replace it if necessary.
3. Oil the piston pin and install it in the connecting rod. Slowly rotate the piston pin and check for radial play (**Figure 152**).
4. Oil the piston pin and install it in the piston (**Figure 153**). Check the piston pin for excessive play.
5. To measure piston pin-to-piston clearance, perform the following:
    a. Measure the piston pin outside diameter with a micrometer (**Figure 154**).

b. Measure the inside diameter of the piston pin bore (**Figure 155**) with a small bore gauge. Measure the small bore gauge with a micrometer.

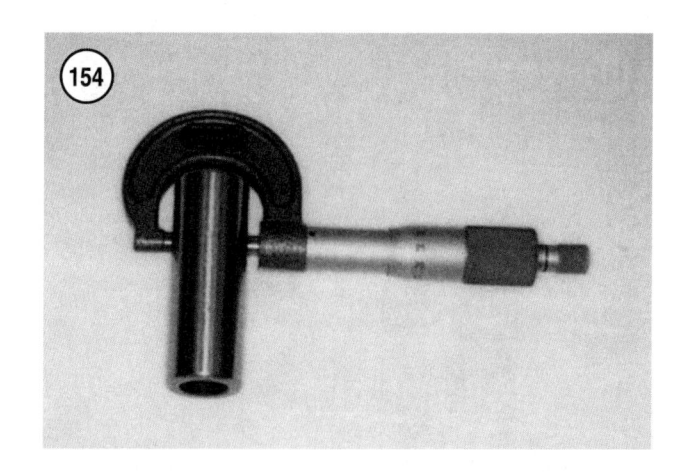

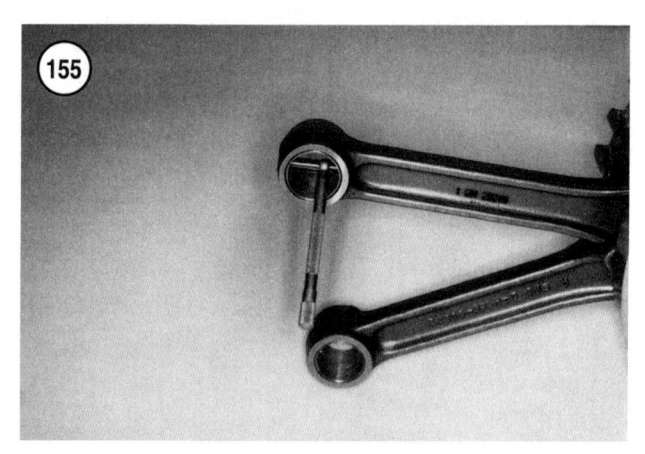

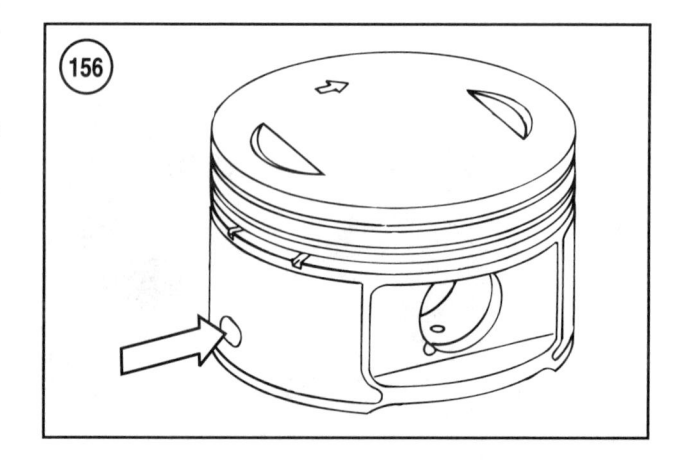

c. Subtract the piston pin outside diameter from the piston pin bore inside diameter to obtain the piston pin clearance.

6. If the piston pin clearance exceeds the service limit (**Table 2** or **Table 3**), replace the piston and/or the piston pin.

Piston Clearance

The piston has a small oval-shaped opening (**Figure 156**) on the piston skirt coating. This opening is used to locate the micrometer for an accurate outer diameter measurement. This small oval-shaped opening is too small for the standard flat anvil micrometer to obtain an accurate measurement. Use a 3-4 inch blade or ball anvil style micrometer, or a 4-5 inch micrometer with spherical ball adapters to achieve a correct measurement (**Figure 157**).

1. Make sure the piston skirt (**Figure 150**) and cylinder bore (**Figure 137**) are clean and dry.
2. Measure the cylinder bore inside diameter (**Figure 140**) as described in *Cylinder Inspection* in this chapter.
3A. On all models except Screamin' Eagle models, measure the piston diameter with a micrometer as follows:
   a. Use the previously described special micrometer and correctly position it on the bare aluminum spot on each side of the piston as shown in **Figure 157**.
   b. Measure the piston at this location only (**Figure 156**).
3B. On Screamin' Eagle models, measure the piston diameter with a micrometer as follows:
   a. Set the piston on a flat surface.
   b. Mark the center of each side of the skirt at a point 0.394 in. (10 mm) up from the skirt bottom.
   c. Fit a micrometer onto these marks, and measure the piston diameter.
4. Subtract the piston diameter from the largest bore inside diameter; the difference is piston-to-cylinder clearance. If the clearance exceeds the service limit in **Table 2** or **Table 3**, replace the pistons and have the cylinders bored oversize, and then honed. Purchase the new pistons first. Measure their diameter and add the specified clearance to determine the proper cylinder bore diameter.

Piston Pin Bushing Inspection

The piston pin bushings are reamed to provide correct piston pin-to-connecting rod clearance. This clearance is critical in preventing pin knock and top end damage.

1. Inspect the piston pin bushings (**Figure 158**) for excessive wear or damage such as pit marks, scoring or wear grooves. Then, make sure the bushings are not loose. The bushings must be a tight fit in the connecting rods.
2. Measure the piston pin outside diameter (**Figure 154**) where it contacts the bushing.
3. Measure the piston pin bushing inside diameter using a small bore gauge (**Figure 155**).

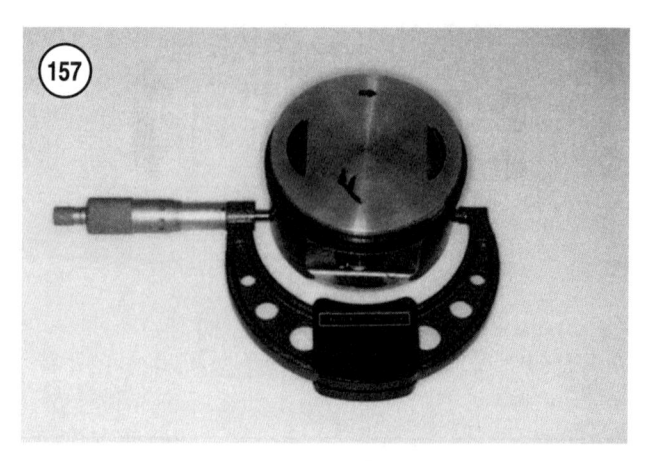

ENGINE TOP END AND EXHAUST SYSTEM

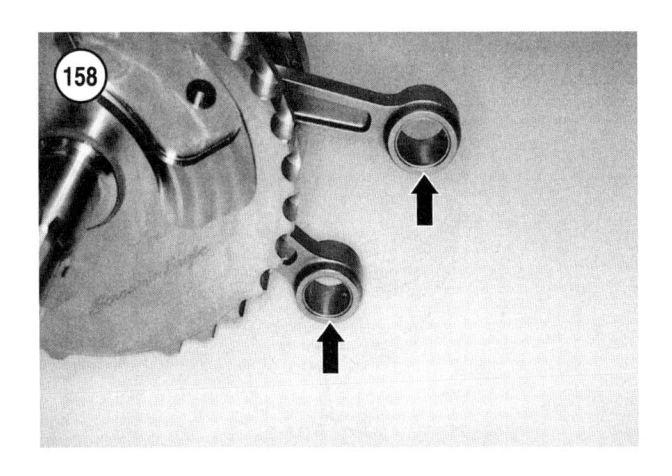

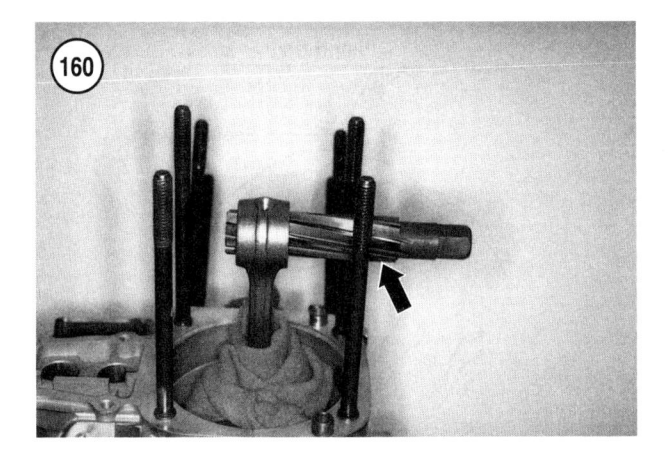

4. Subtract the piston pin outer diameter from the bushing inner diameter to determine piston pin-to-connecting rod clearance.

NOTE
*The connecting rod upper bushings are not serviceable on all 2007-2009 models. Replace the piston pin and/or crankshaft assembly if the clearance equals or exceeds the service limit (**Table 2** or **Table 3**).*

5. On all 2006 models, replace the piston pin and bushing if the clearance equals or exceeds the service limit (**Table 2**).

Piston Pin Bushing Replacement (2006 Models Only)

Tools

The following tools are required to replace and ream the piston pin bushings on 2006 models. The clamp tool is only required if the bushing is being replaced with the crankcase assembled. If these tools are not available, have a shop with the proper equipment perform the procedure.

1. Connecting rod clamp tool (JIMS part No. 1284) or (H-D part No. HD-95952-33C).
2. Connecting rod bushing tool (JIMS part No. 1051).
3. Bushing reamer tool (JIMS part No. 1726-3).
4. Connecting rod bushing hone (H-D part No. HD-422569).
5. Threaded cylinders (H-D part No. HD-95952-1).

Procedure

1. Remove two of the plastic hoses protecting the cylinder studs.
2. Install the connecting rod clamp tool as follows:
   a. Install the clamp portion of the connecting rod clamp tool over the connecting rod so the slots engage the cylinder head studs. Do not scratch or bend the studs.
   b. With the knurled end of the threaded cylinder facing up, and turn the threaded cylinders onto the studs. Tighten them securely against the clamp.
   c. Alternately tighten the thumbscrews on the side of the connecting rod. Do not turn only one thumbscrew, as this will move the connecting rod off center and tightening the other thumbscrew will cause the connecting rod to flex or bend.
3. Cover the crankcase opening to keep bushing particles from falling into the engine.

CAUTION
When installing the new bushing, align the oil slot in the bushing with the oil hole in the connecting rod.

4. Replace the bushing using the connecting rod bushing tool (**Figure 159**) by following the tool manufacturer's instructions. The new bushing must be flush with both sides of the connecting rod.
5. Ream the piston pin bushing with the bushing reamer tool (**Figure 160**) by following the tool manufacturer's instructions.
6. Hone the new bushing to obtain the final specified piston pin-to-connecting rod clearance (**Table 2** or **Table 3**). Use honing oil, not engine oil, when finish-honing the bushing to size.
7. Install the piston pin through the bushing. The pin should move through the bushing smoothly. Confirm pin clearance using a micrometer and small bore gauge.
8. Carefully remove all metal debris from the crankcase.

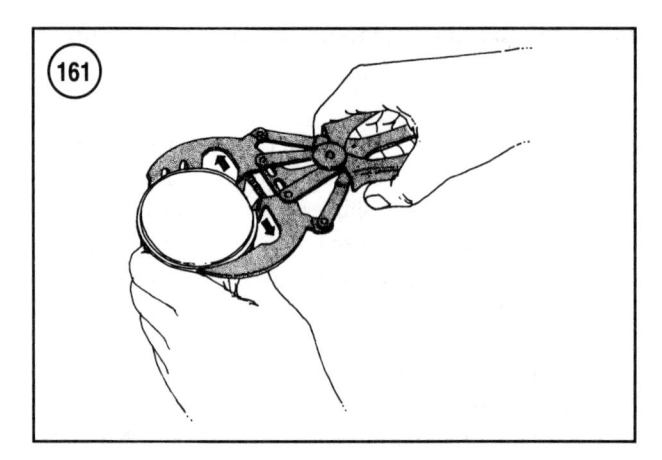

Piston Ring Removal/Inspection

During inspection, compare any measurements taken to the specifications listed in **Table 2** or **Table 3**. Replace any part that is worn, damaged or out of specification.

1. Remove the piston rings by using a ring expander tool (**Figure 161**) or by spreading them by hand (**Figure 162**)
2. Clean the piston ring grooves as described in *Piston Inspection* (this section).
3. Inspect the ring grooves for burrs, nicks, or broken or cracked lands. Replace the piston if necessary.
4. Insert one piston ring into the top of its cylinder, and tap it down approximately 1/2 in. (12.7 mm), using the piston to square it in the bore. Measure the ring end gap (**Figure 163**) with a feeler gauge and compare it with the specification in **Table 2** or **Table 3**. Replace the piston rings as a set if any one ring end gap measurement is excessive. Repeat this process for each ring.
5. Roll each compression ring around its piston groove as shown in **Figure 164**. The ring should move smoothly with no binding. If a ring binds in its groove, check the groove for damage. Replace the piston if necessary.

Piston Ring Installation

Each piston is equipped with three piston rings: two compression rings and one oil ring assembly. The top compression ring is not marked. The lower compression ring (**Figure 165**) is marked with a dot.

The manufacturer recommends that *new* piston rings be installed every time the piston is removed. Always lightly hone the cylinder before installing new piston rings.

1. Wash the piston in hot, soapy water. Rinse it with clear water, and dry it with compressed air. Make sure the oil control holes in the lower ring groove are clear.
2. Install the oil ring assembly as follows:
    a. The oil ring assembly consists of three rings: a ribbed spacer ring (A, **Figure 166**) and two steel rings (B).
    b. Install the spacer ring into the lower ring groove. Butt the spacer ring ends together. Do not overlap the ring ends.
    c. Insert one end of the first steel ring into the lower groove so it is below the spacer ring. Then, spiral the

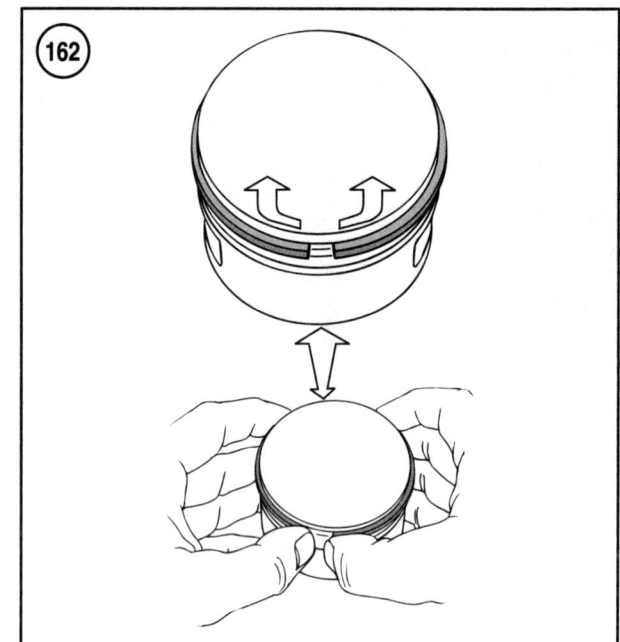

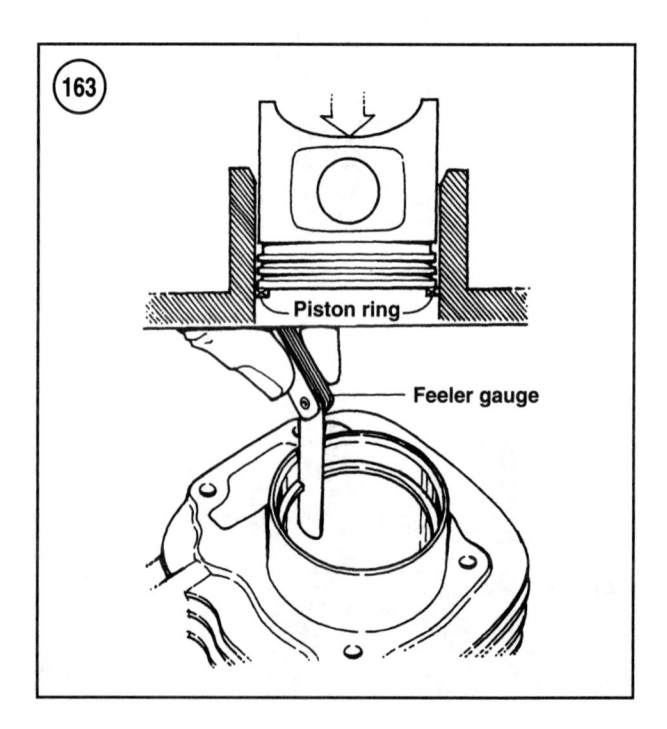

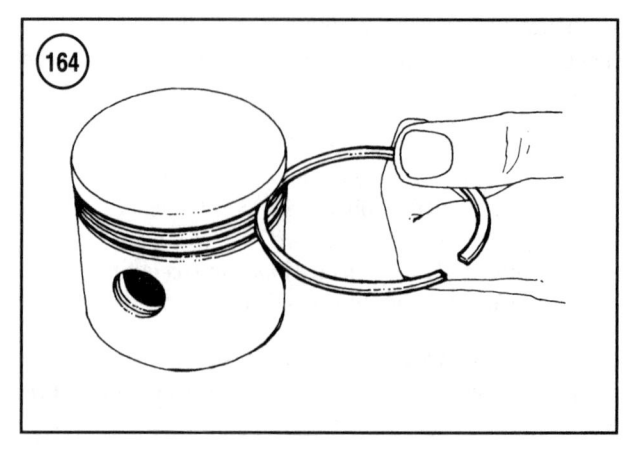

ENGINE TOP END AND EXHAUST SYSTEM

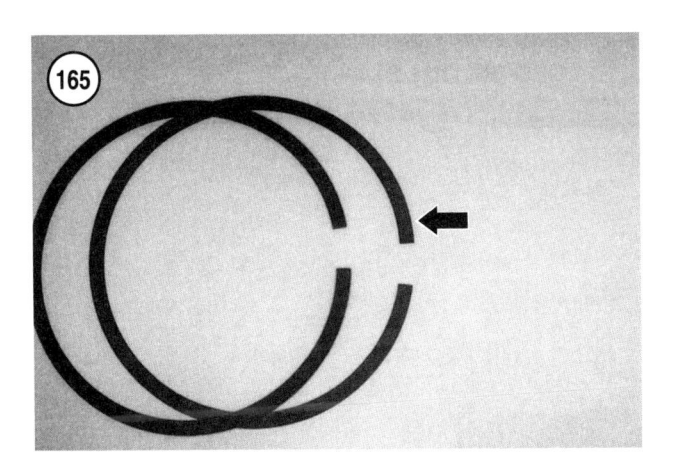

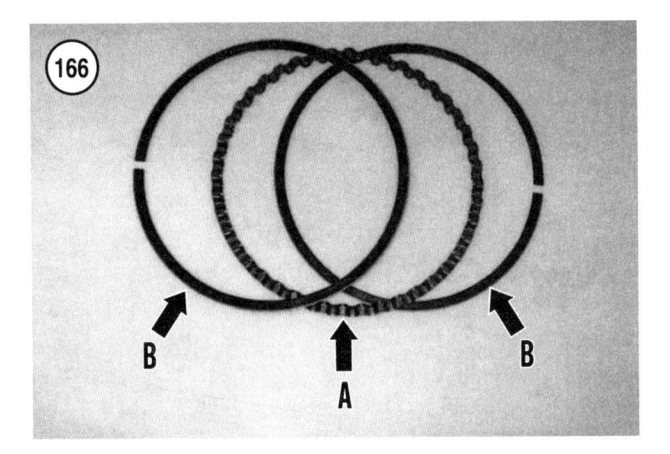

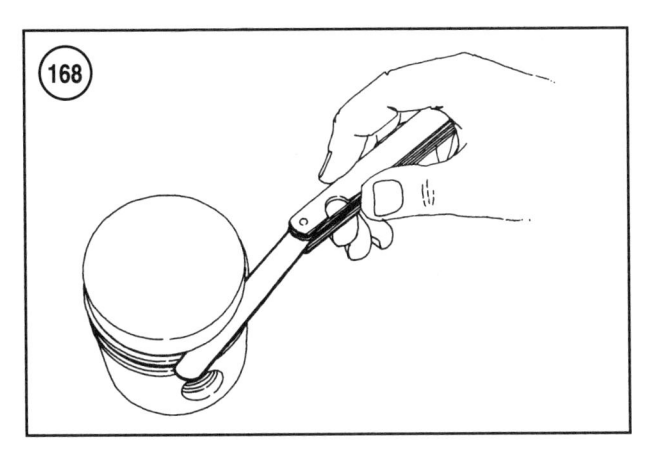

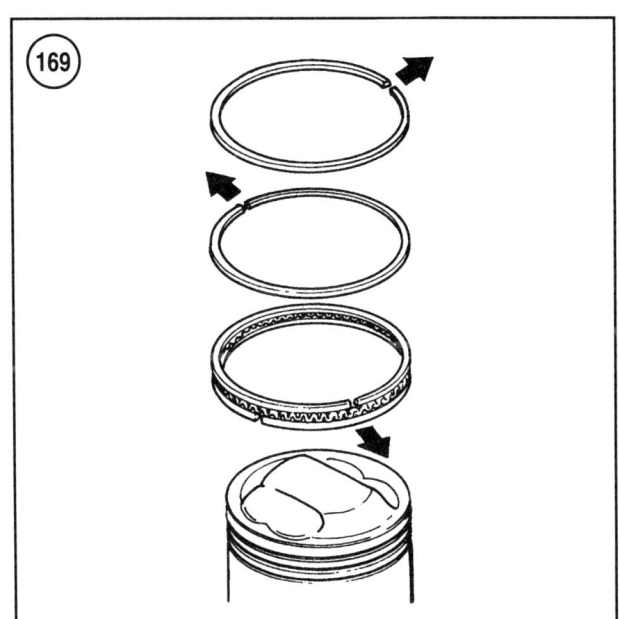

other end over the piston crown and into the lower groove. To prevent the ring end from scratching the side of the piston, place a piece of shim stock or a thin, flat feeler gauge between the ring and piston.

d. Repeat the process to install the other steel ring above the spacer ring.

CAUTION
*To install the compression rings, use a ring expander as shown in **Figure 161**. Do not expand the rings any more than necessary to install them.*

3. Install the *new* lower compression ring with the dot (**Figure 167**) facing up.
4. Install the *new* top compression ring with either side facing up.
5. Check the ring side clearance with a feeler gauge as shown in **Figure 168**. Check the side clearance in several spots around the piston. If the clearance is larger than the service limit in **Table 2** or **Table 3**, replace the piston.
6. Stagger the ring gaps around the piston as shown in **Figure 169**.

PUSHRODS

Removal/Installation

Remove and install the pushrods as described in *Rocker Arms Pushrods and Valve Lifters* (this chapter).

EXHAUST SYSTEM

2006-2008 Models

Removal

Refer to **Figure 170**.

CHAPTER FOUR

EXHAUST SYSTEM (2006-2008 MODELS)

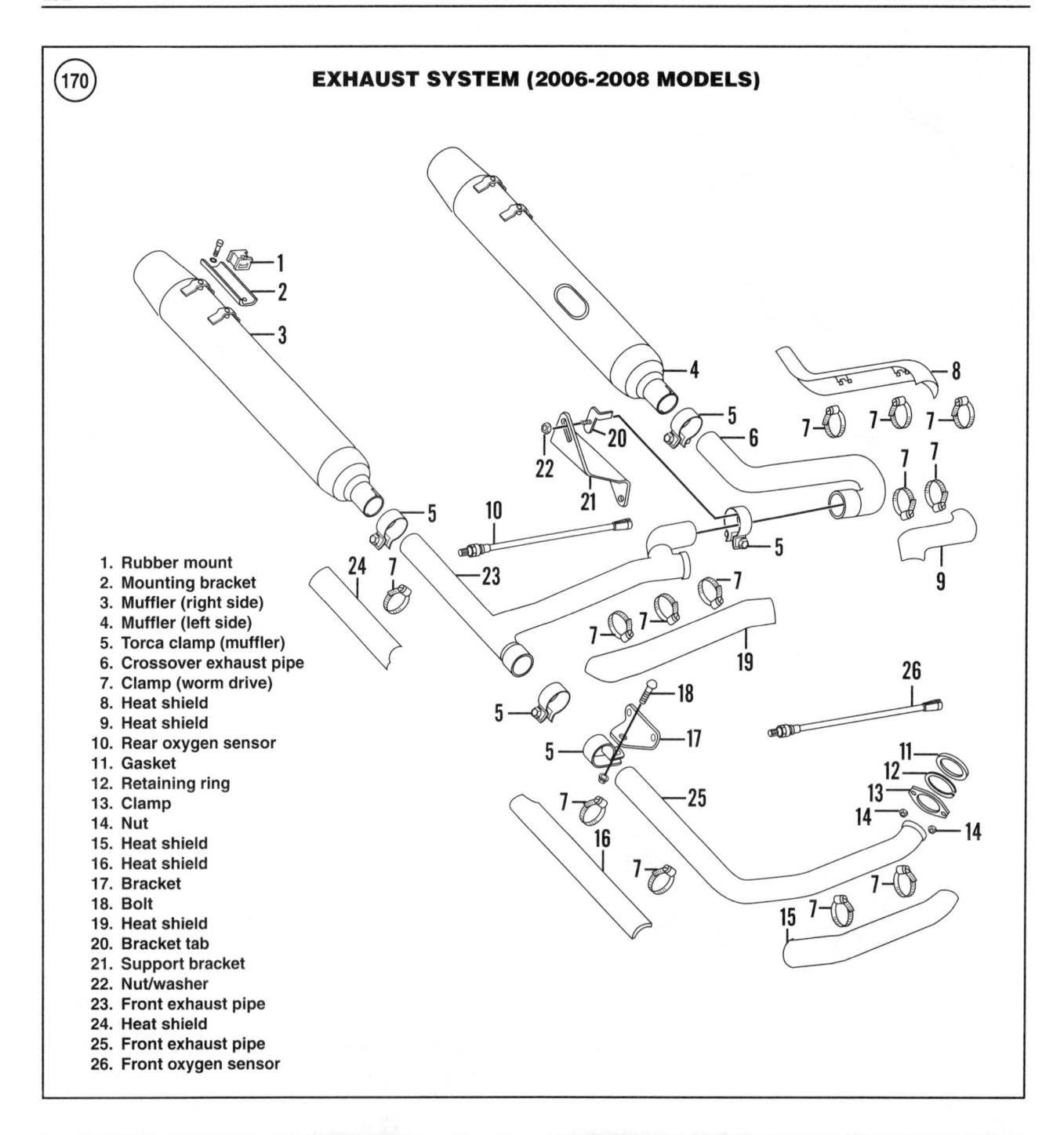

1. Rubber mount
2. Mounting bracket
3. Muffler (right side)
4. Muffler (left side)
5. Torca clamp (muffler)
6. Crossover exhaust pipe
7. Clamp (worm drive)
8. Heat shield
9. Heat shield
10. Rear oxygen sensor
11. Gasket
12. Retaining ring
13. Clamp
14. Nut
15. Heat shield
16. Heat shield
17. Bracket
18. Bolt
19. Heat shield
20. Bracket tab
21. Support bracket
22. Nut/washer
23. Front exhaust pipe
24. Heat shield
25. Front exhaust pipe
26. Front oxygen sensor

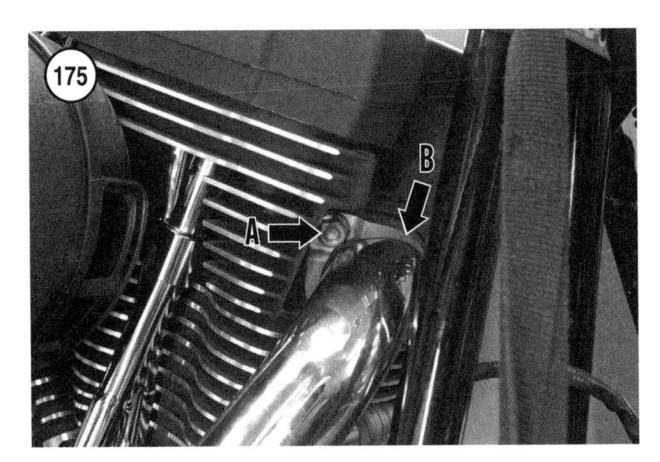

ENGINE TOP END AND EXHAUST SYSTEM

NOTE
If the system joints are corroded or rusty, spray all connections with PB Blaster, WD-40, or an equivalent. Allow the penetrating oil to soak in sufficiently to free the rusted joints.

1. Support the motorcycle on a work stand. Refer to *Motorcycle Stands* in Chapter Twelve.
2. Remove the seat as described in Chapter Seventeen.
3. Remove both saddlebags as described in Chapter Seventeen.
4. Remove both footboards as described in Chapter Seventeen.
5. Remove the engine guard and lower fairing assemblies on both sides (Chapter Seventeen), on models so equipped.
6. On HDI models, disconnect the cable from the valve actuator as described in this chapter.
7. Disconnect the 02 sensors as follows:
   a. Cut the strap securing the wiring to the back of the cross brace between the frame down tubes on the left side.
   b. Disconnect the 2-pin front oxygen sensor (**Figure 171**) connector.
   c. Disconnect the 2-pin rear oxygen sensor (**Figure 172**) connector, located under the starter cover.
8. Identify and mark the heat shields prior to removal as this will aid during installation. They look very similar but all have slight differences. Use the numbers assigned to these parts in **Figure 170** to aid identification.
9. Protect the finish, and then secure each muffler to the saddlebag mounting bracket with a Bungee cord or rope.
10. Release clamps on crossover heat shield above starter. Remove the heat shield.
11. Loosen the Torca clamp (**Figure 173**) between the rear exhaust pipe and the crossover pipe.
12. Remove the nut and pull the bracket tab and stud from the slots in the Torca clamp and the support bracket.
13. Remove the bolts and lockwashers (**Figure 174**) securing the left side muffler to the saddlebag support rail.
14. Remove the Bungee cord, or rope, and release the left side muffler.
15. Carefully pull and twist on the crossover pipe and disconnect the crossover pipe and left side muffler from the rear exhaust pipe. Remove the assembly from the frame. Remove the Torca clamp and discard it.
16. Release clamps on front exhaust pipe heat shield. Remove the heat shield.
17. At front cylinder head, loosen and remove the two flange nuts (A, **Figure 175**) securing the front exhaust pipe to the cylinder head.
18. Slide the exhaust flange (B, **Figure 175**) off the cylinder head studs.
19. Release clamps (A, **Figure 176**) on rear exhaust pipe heat shield (B). Remove the heat shield.

20. At rear cylinder head, loosen and remove the two flange nuts (A, **Figure 177**) securing the rear exhaust pipe to the cylinder head.
21. Slide the exhaust flange (B, **Figure 177**) off the cylinder head studs.
22. Adjacent to the transmission side door, release clamps (A, **Figure 178**) on front exhaust pipe-to-rear exhaust pipe heat shield (B). Remove the heat shield.
23. Remove the bolt securing the clamp to the bracket on the transmission. Open the clamp with channel lock pliers.
24. Carefully pull and twist on the front exhaust pipe and disconnect it from the rear exhaust pipe.
25. Remove the screws and lockwashers securing the right side muffler to the saddlebag support rail.
26. Depress the rear brake pedal and secure it to the frame in this position.
27. Remove the Bungee cord, or rope, and release the right side muffler.
28. Remove the rear exhaust pipe and muffler assembly from the frame.
29. Remove the snap ring and gasket (**Figure 179**) from each cylinder head exhaust port. Discard the gaskets.
30. Inspect the exhaust system as described in this chapter.
31. Store the exhaust system components in a safe place until they are reinstalled.

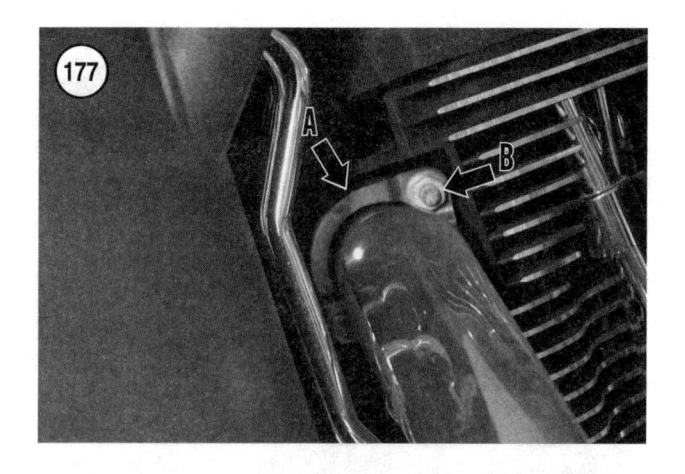

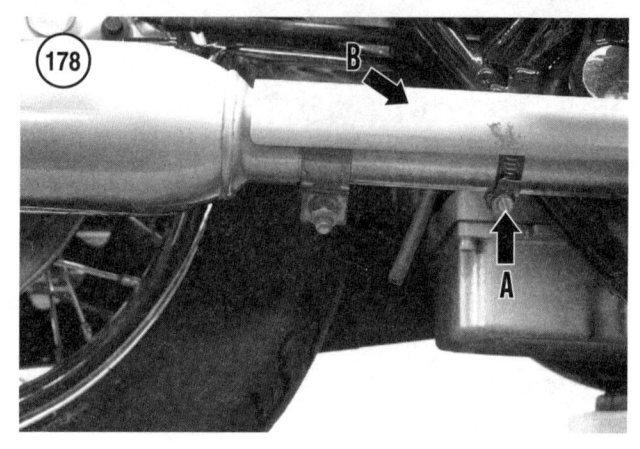

Installation

NOTE
New Torca clamps must be installed to ensure correct sealing integrity. The new Torca clamps eliminate the need for graphite or silicone tape during installation of the mufflers.

NOTE
To eliminate exhaust leaks, do not tighten any of the mounting bolts and nuts or the Torca clamps until all of the exhaust components are in place.

1. Before installing the *new* exhaust port gaskets, scrape the exhaust port surfaces to remove all carbon residue. Then, wipe the port with a rag.
2. Install a *new* exhaust port gasket (**Figure 180**) into each exhaust port with the tapered side facing out. Install the snap ring and secure the gasket in place.
3. Depress the rear brake pedal and secure it in this position.
4. Install the rear exhaust pipe and muffler assembly onto the frame and engine.
5. Install the rear exhaust pipe onto the rear cylinder head exhaust port.
6. Slide the exhaust flange (A, **Figure 177**) onto the rear cylinder head studs.
7. Install the flange nuts (B, **Figure 177**) finger-tight.
8. Install the bolts and lockwashers securing the right side muffler to the saddlebag support rail. Tighten the bolts finger-tight.
9. Install the clamp and *new* Torca clamp onto both exhaust pipes at the joint, if removed.
10. Install the front exhaust pipe onto the frame and engine.
11. Carefully push and twist on the front exhaust pipe and connect it onto the rear exhaust pipe and front cylinder exhaust port.
12. Slide the exhaust flange (B, **Figure 175**) onto the front cylinder head studs.
13. Install the flange nuts (A, **Figure 175**) finger-tight.
14. Install the bolt and locknut securing the clamp to the bracket on the transmission. Close the clamp with channel lock pliers.
15. Install front exhaust pipe-to-rear exhaust pipe heat shield (B, **Figure 178**) adjacent to the transmission side door. Tighten the clamps (A, **Figure 178**) finger-tight.
16. Install a *new* Torca clamp (**Figure 173**) onto the crossover pipe, if removed.
17. Install the crossover pipe and left side muffler onto the frame and onto the rear exhaust pipe. Carefully push and twist on the crossover pipe and connect the crossover pipe onto the rear exhaust pipe and rear cylinder exhaust port.

ENGINE TOP END AND EXHAUST SYSTEM

18. Install the bolts and lockwashers (**Figure 174**) securing the left side muffler to the saddlebag support rail. Tighten the bolts finger-tight.
19. Push the bracket tab and stud into the slots in the Torca clamp and the support bracket. Install and tighten the nut to 12-15 ft.-lbs. (16.3-20.3 N•m).
20. Install the crossover heat shield above starter. Tighten the clamps finger-tight.
21. Check the entire exhaust system to make sure none of the exhaust components are touching the frame. If necessary, make slight adjustments to avoid any contact with the frame that would transmit vibrations to the rider.
22. Check the exhaust assembly alignment, and then tighten the mounting bolts, nuts and Torca clamps as follows:
    a. Front cylinder head flange nuts. Tighten the upper nut to 9-18 in.-lbs. (1-2 N•m), and then tighten the lower nut to 110-120 in.-lbs. (11.3-13.6 N•m). Re-tighten the upper nut to 120 in.-lbs. (13.6 N•m).
    b. Rear cylinder head flange nuts. Tighten the upper nut to 9-18 in.-lbs. (1-2 N•m), and then tighten the lower nut to 110-120 in.-lbs. (11.3-13.6 N•m). Re-tighten the upper nut to 120 in.-lbs. (13.6 N•m).
    c. Tighten the transmission clamp bolt securely.
    d. On each side, tighten the muffler-to-saddlebag support rail mounting bracket bolts to 96-144 in.-lbs. (10.8-16.3 N•m).
    e. Tighten the crossover pipe to the rear exhaust pipe and the rear exhaust pipe to the front exhaust pipe Torca clamps to 45-60 ft.-lbs. (61-81.3 N•m). Then, tighten the left side muffler to the crossover pipe and the right side muffler to the rear exhaust pipe Torca clamps to 45-60 ft.-lbs. (61-81.3 N•m).
23. Release the depressed rear brake pedal from the frame.
24. Connect the 02 sensors as follows:
    a. Connect the 2-pin rear oxygen sensor connectors, located under the starter cover.
    b. Connect the 2-pin front oxygen sensor connectors.
    c. Secure the wiring to the back of the cross brace between the frame down tubes on the left side with a new cable strap.
25. On HDI models, connect the cable onto the valve actuator as described in this chapter.
26. Start the engine and check for exhaust leaks.
27. Install the engine guard and lower fairing assemblies on both sides (Chapter Seventeen), on models so equipped.
28. Install both footboards as described in Chapter Seventeen.
29. Install both saddlebags as described in Chapter Seventeen.
30. Install the seat as described in Chapter Seventeen.

2009 Models

Removal

Refer to **Figure 181**.

NOTE
If the system joints are corroded or rusty, spray all connections with PB Blaster, WD-40, or an equivalent. Allow the penetrating oil to soak in sufficiently to free the rusted joints.

1. Support the motorcycle on a work stand. Refer to *Motorcycle Stands* in Chapter Twelve.
2. Remove the seat as described in Chapter Seventeen.
3. Remove both saddlebags as described in Chapter Seventeen.
4. Remove both footboards as described in Chapter Seventeen.
5. Remove the engine guard and lower fairing assemblies on both sides (Chapter Seventeen), on models so equipped.
6. On HDI models, disconnect the cable from the valve actuator as described in this chapter.
7. Disconnect the 02 sensors as follows:
    a. Cut the strap securing the wiring to the back of the cross brace between the frame down tubes on the left side.
    b. Disconnect the 2-pin front oxygen sensor (**Figure 171**) connector.
    c. Disconnect the 2-pin rear oxygen sensor (**Figure 172**) connector, located under the starter cover.
8. Remove the mufflers as follows:

CHAPTER FOUR

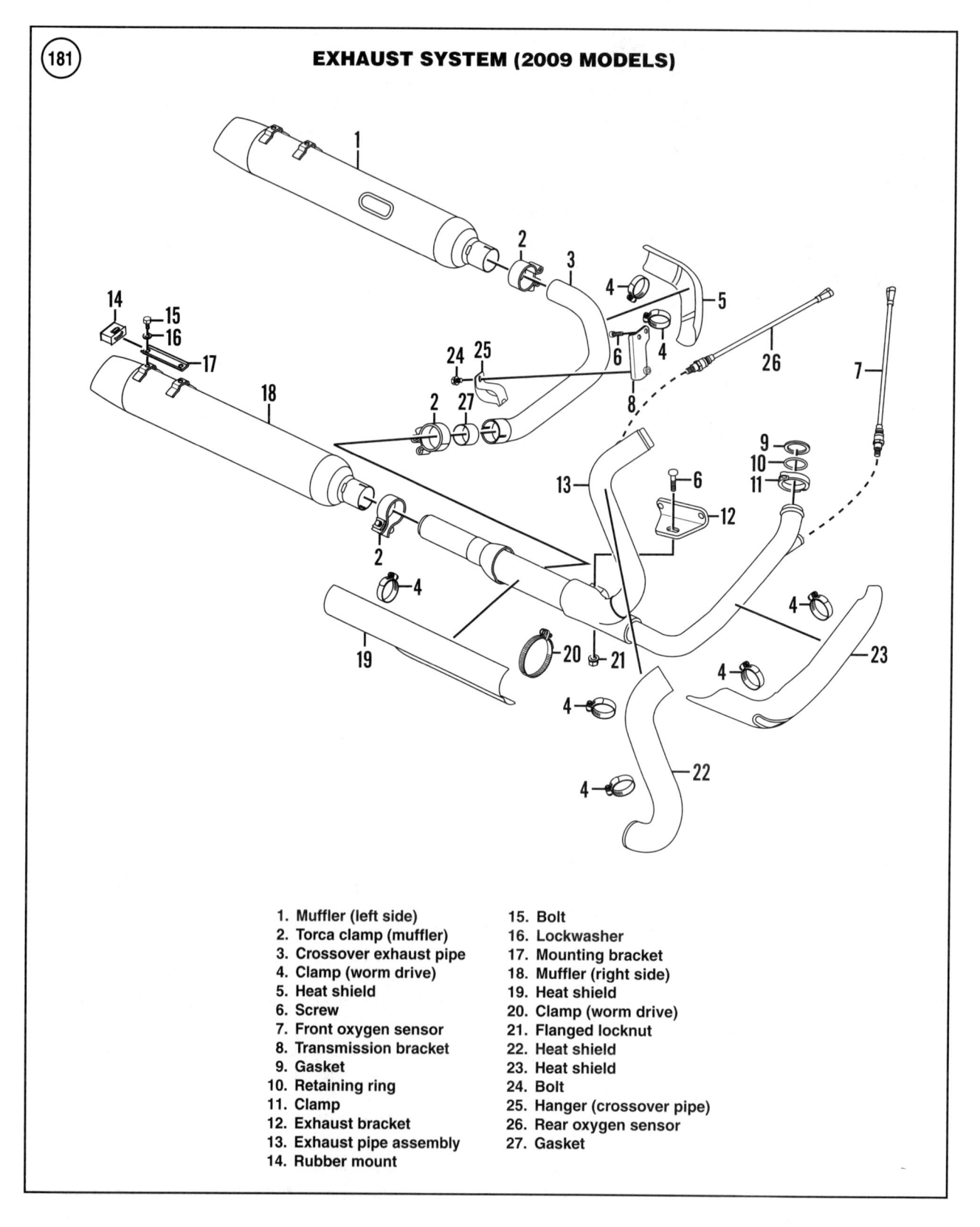

EXHAUST SYSTEM (2009 MODELS)

1. Muffler (left side)
2. Torca clamp (muffler)
3. Crossover exhaust pipe
4. Clamp (worm drive)
5. Heat shield
6. Screw
7. Front oxygen sensor
8. Transmission bracket
9. Gasket
10. Retaining ring
11. Clamp
12. Exhaust bracket
13. Exhaust pipe assembly
14. Rubber mount
15. Bolt
16. Lockwasher
17. Mounting bracket
18. Muffler (right side)
19. Heat shield
20. Clamp (worm drive)
21. Flanged locknut
22. Heat shield
23. Heat shield
24. Bolt
25. Hanger (crossover pipe)
26. Rear oxygen sensor
27. Gasket

a. Loosen the Torca clamp securing the muffler(s) to the exhaust pipe assembly or crossover exhaust pipe.
b. Remove the bolts, lockwashers and mounting bracket securing the muffler(s) to the saddle bag guard.
c. Twist and pull straight back, and remove the right side muffler from the exhaust pipe assembly.
d. Twist and pull straight back, and remove the left side muffler from the crossover exhaust pipe.

9. Identify and mark the heat shields prior to removal as this will aid during installation. Use the numbers assigned to these parts in **Figure 181** to aid identification.
10. Loosen the clamps and remove all four heat shields.

ENGINE TOP END AND EXHAUST SYSTEM

11. Loosen the Torca clamp between the exhaust pipe assembly and the crossover pipe.
12. Remove the locknut securing the crossover hanger to the frame bracket. Open the hanger from around the crossover pipe.
13. Carefully pull and twist on the crossover pipe and disconnect the crossover pipe from the exhaust pipe assembly, and remove from the frame.
14. At the front cylinder head, loosen and remove the two flange nuts securing the front portion of exhaust pipe assembly to the front cylinder head.
15. Slide the exhaust flange off the front cylinder head studs.
16. At the rear cylinder head, loosen and remove the two flange nuts securing the rear portion of the exaust pipe assembly to the rear cylinder head.
17. Slide the exhaust flange off the rear cylinder head studs.
18. Remove the bolt and flanged locknut securing the exhaust pipe assembly to the frame bracket.
19. Remove the exhaust pipe assembly from the exhaust ports on both cylinder heads.
20. Remove the snap ring and gasket from each cylinder head exhaust port. Discard the gaskets.
21. Inspect the exhaust system as described in this section.
22. Store the exhaust system components in a safe place until they are reinstalled.

Installation

NOTE
New Torca clamps must be installed to ensure correct sealing integrity. The new Torca clamps eliminate the need for graphite or silicone tape during installation of the mufflers.

NOTE
To eliminate exhaust leaks, do not tighten any of the mounting bolts and nuts or the Torca clamps until all of the exhaust components are in place.

1. Before installing the *new* exhaust port gaskets, scrape the exhaust port surfaces to remove all carbon residue. Then, wipe the ports with a rag.
2. Install a *new* exhaust port gasket into each exhaust port with the tapered side facing out. Install the snap ring and secure the gasket in place.
3. Install the exhaust pipe assembly onto the exhaust ports on both cylinder heads.
4. Slide the exhaust flange onto the front cylinder head studs.
5. At the front cylinder head, install the two flange nuts securing the front portion of the exhaust pipe assembly to the front cylinder head. Finger-tighten the nuts.
6. Slide the exhaust flange onto the rear cylinder head studs. Install the two flange nuts securing the rear portion of the exhaust pipe assembly to the rear cylinder head. Finger-tighten the nuts.
7. Install the bolt and flanged locknut securing the exhaust pipe assembly to the exhaust bracket. Finger-tighten the nut.
8. Install a *new* Torca clamp onto the crossover pipe.
9. Install the crossover pipe onto the frame. Carefully push and twist on the crossover pipe and connect it onto the exhaust pipe assembly.
10. Finger-tighten the Torca clamp between the exhaust pipe assembly and the crossover pipe.
11. Close the hanger around the crossover pipe and install the locknut securing the crossover hanger to the frame bracket. Finger-tighten the locknut.
12. Install the mufflers as follows:
    a. Install the left side muffler and Torca clamp onto the crossover pipe.
    b. Install the right side muffler and Torca clamp onto the exhaust pipe assembly.
    c. Install the bolts, lockwashers and mounting brackets onto the saddlebag guards. Finger-tighten the bolts.
13. Check the entire exhaust system to make sure none of the exhaust components are touching the frame. If necessary, make slight adjustments to avoid any contact that would transmit any vibrations to the rider via the frame.
14. Install the four heat shields. Position the crossover heat shield with the longer straight portion facing the muffler. Finger-tighten the clamps.
15. Check the exhaust assembly alignment, and tighten the mounting bolts, nuts and Torca clamps as follows:
    a. Front cylinder head flange nuts. Tighten the upper nut to 9-18 in.-lbs. (1-2 N•m), and then tighten the lower nut to 110-120 in.-lbs. (11.3-13.6 N•m). Re-tighten the upper nut to 120 in.-lbs. (14 N•m).
    b. Rear cylinder head flange nuts. Tighten the upper nut to 9-18 in.-lbs. (1-2 N•m), and then tighten the lower nut to 110-120 in.-lbs. (11.3-13.6 N•m). Re-tighten the upper nut to 120 in.-lbs. (14 N•m).
    c. Crossover hanger bolt to 14-18 ft.-lbs. (19-24.4 N•m).
    d. Tighten the exhaust bracket flange locknut to 20-25 ft.-lbs. (27.1-33.9 N•m).
    e. Tighten the transmission bracket bolt to 84-132 in.-lbs. (9.5-14.9 N•m).
    f. On each side, tighten the muffler to saddlebag mounting bracket bolts to 96-144 in.-lbs. (10.8-16.3 N•m).
    g. Tighten all Torca clamps to 38-43 ft.-lbs. (51.5-58.3 N•m) in this order. Tighten the crossover pipe and the rear exhaust pipe assembly three clamps.
16. Connect the 02 sensors as follows:
    a. Secure the wiring to the back of the cross brace between the frame down tubes on the left side. Install a new cable clamp.
    b. Connect the 2-pin front oxygen sensor connectors.
    c. Connect the 2-pin rear oxygen sensor connectors, located under the starter cover.
17. On HDI models, connect the cable onto the valve actuator as described in this chapter.

18. Start the engine and check for exhaust leaks.
19. Install the engine guard and lower fairing assemblies on both sides (Chapter Seventeen), on models so equipped.
20. Install both footboards as described in Chapter Seventeen.
21. Install both saddlebags as described in Chapter Seventeen.
22. Install the seat as described in Chapter Seventeen.

Exhaust System Inspection (All Models)

Replace any rusted or damaged exhaust system components.
1. Inspect all pipes for rust or corrosion. Remove all rust from exhaust pipes and muffler mating surfaces.
2. Replace damaged exhaust pipe flanges.
3. Replace worn or damaged heat shield clamps as required.
4. Check the mounting bracket bolts and nuts for tightness. The Torca clamps are not reusable.

Oxygen sensor removal/installation

To replace the oxygen sensor, perform the following:
1. Disconnect the 2-pin electrical connector from the sensor.
2. Carefully cut all cable clamps securing the sensor wiring harness to the frame.

NOTE
Figure 182 is show with the exhaust pipe removed for photo clarity.

3. Carefully install the oxygen sensor socket (JIMS part No. 969) over the sensor. Use a ratchet with a socket extension to turn the sensor socket *counterclockwise* and loosen it from the exhaust pipe (**Figure 182**).
4. Remove the sensor socket and unthread the sensor from the exhaust pipe by hand.
5. Install the oxygen sensor into the exhaust pipe by hand, and then tighten it with the sensor socket to 30-44 ft.-lb. (40.7-59.7 N•m).

ACTIVE EXHAUST (2007-2009 HDI MODELS, EXCEPT JAPAN)

Refer to **Figure 183**.

Cable Disconnect/Connect

1. Push on the metal sleeve at the end of the cable housing and release the plastic insert from the cable guide slot.
2. Release the cable from the groove at the center of the actuator wheel. Gently pull the barrel end from the hole.
3. Release the cable housing from the cable clip on the crankcase and remove the cable from the frame.

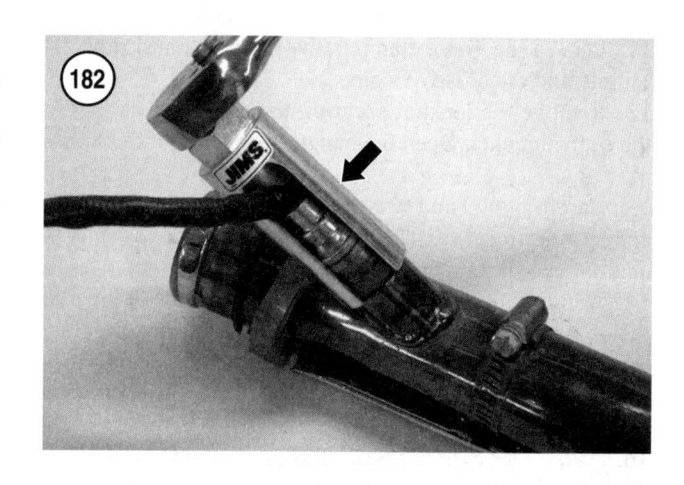

4. Gently push the barrel end of the cable into hole in the actuator wheel until the cable has engaged the groove at the center.
5. Push on the metal sleeve at the end of the cable housing and engage the plastic insert in the cable guide slot.
6. Gently pull on the cable to ensure the cable is secure in the cable housing.

Actuator Removal/ Installation (2007 Models)

1. Remove the right side frame cover as described in Chapter Seventeen.
2. Remove the battery as described in Chapter Eleven.
3. Remove the starter as described in Chapter Eleven.
4. Disconnect the rear end of the cable from the actuator as described in this section.
5. Remove the cable clip from the slotted flange on the front of the active exhaust valve.
6. Release the cable from the J-clamp on the swing arm bracket.
7. At the front edge of the actuator, remove the two flange nuts securing the actuator and the spacer to the base of the battery tray.
8. Remove the stud plate from the top surface of the battery tray.
9. Underneath the battery tray, remove the spacer and lower the actuator.
10. Disconnect the 5-pin electrical connector (179B) from the actuator.
11. Remove the actuator and cable from the frame.
12. Installation is the reverse of removal.

Actuator Removal/ Installation (2008-2009 Models)

1. Remove the right side frame cover as described in Chapter Seventeen.
2. Disconnect the rear end of the cable from the actuator as described in this section.
3A. On 2008 models, perform the following:

ENGINE TOP END AND EXHAUST SYSTEM

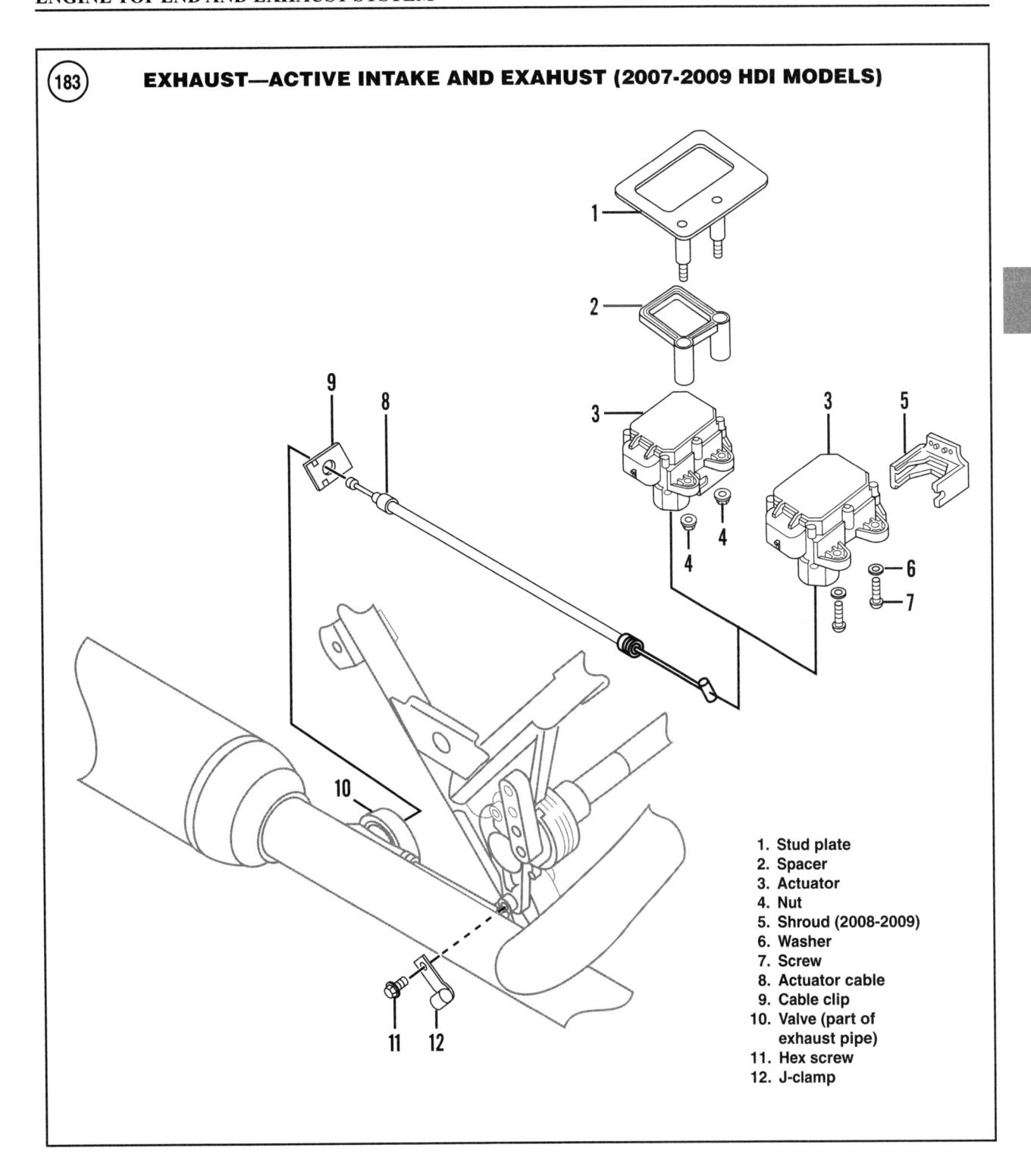

183 EXHAUST—ACTIVE INTAKE AND EXAHUST (2007-2009 HDI MODELS)

1. Stud plate
2. Spacer
3. Actuator
4. Nut
5. Shroud (2008-2009)
6. Washer
7. Screw
8. Actuator cable
9. Cable clip
10. Valve (part of exhaust pipe)
11. Hex screw
12. J-clamp

a. Remove the electrical caddy as described in Chapter Eleven.
b. Remove the two Torx screws (T27) and flat washers securing the actuator to the base of the caddy, and lower the actuator.

3B. On 2009 models, remove the two screws and flat washers securing the actuator to the base of the battery tray, and lower the actuator.

4. Disconnect the 5-pin electrical connector (179B) from the actuator.

5. Remove the actuator and cable from the frame.
6. Installation is the reverse of removal.

Active Exhaust valve

The active exhaust valve is an integral part of the rear exhaust pipe on 2007-2008 models, or the exhaust pipe assembly on 2009 models. The valve is not repairable and the exhaust pipe, or assembly, must be replaced if the valve is faulty or damaged.

Table 1 GENERAL ENGINE SPECIFICATIONS

Item	Specifications
Engine type	4-stroke, 45°, OHV V-twin, Twin Cam 88, 96, 103 and 110
Bore and stroke	
88 models	3.75 × 4.00 in. (95.25 × 101.6 mm)
96 models	3.75 × 4.375 in. (95.25 × 111.13 mm)
103 models	3.875 × 4.375 in. (98.43 × 111.13 mm)
110 models	4.00 × 4.375 in. (101.6 × 111.13 mm)
Displacement	
88 models	88 cubic inch (1450 cc)
96 models	96 cubic inch (1584 cc)
103 models	103 cubic inch (1690 cc)
110 models	110 cubic inch (1800 cc)
Compression ratio	
88 models	9.0 to 1
96 models	
2007-2008 models	9.0 to 1
2009 models	9.2 to 1
103 models	9.0 to 1
110 models	9.3 to 1
Torque	
88 models	85 ft.-lb. (115.2 N•m) @ 3000 rpm
96 models	
2007-2008 models	91 ft.-lb. (123.4 N•m) @ 3000 rpm
2009 models	
North America	93 ft.-lb. (125.6 N•m) @ 3500 rpm
International (except Japan)	90 ft.-lb. (122.3 N•m) @ 3400 rpm
Japan	87 ft.-lb. (118.0 N•m) @ 2500 rpm
103 models	100 ft.-lb. (135.6 N•m) @ 3500 rpm
110 models	
North America	113 ft.-lb. (153.2 N•m) @ 3750 rpm
International	110 ft.-lb. (149.1 N•m) @ 3500 rpm
Maximum sustained engine speed	5500 rpm
Idle speed	950-1050 rpm
Cooling system	Air-cooled

Table 2 ENGINE TOP END SPECIFICATIONS (ALL MODELS EXCEPT SCREAMIN' EAGLE)

Item	New in. (mm)	Service limit in. (mm)
Breather cover warp		0.005 (0.13)
Breather baffle warp		0.005 (0.13)
Cylinder head		
Warp limit	–	0.006 (0.15)
Valve guide fit in head	0.0022-0.0033 (0.056-0.084)	0.002 (0.051)
Valve seat fit in head	0.0030-0.0045 (0.076-0.114)	0.002 (0.051)
Rocker arm		
Bushing fit in rocker arm	0.002-0.004 (0.051-0.102)	–
End clearance	0.003-0.013 (0.076-0.330)	0.025 (0.635)
Shaft-to-rocker arm bushing clearance	0.0005-0.0020 (0.013-0.051)	0.0035 (0.089)
Shaft-to-rocker arm support clearance	0.0007-0.0022 (0.018-0.056)	0.0035 (0.089)
Valves		
Valve stem-to-guide clearance		
Intake	0.001-0.003 (0.025-0.076)	0.0038 (0.097)
Exhaust	0.001-0.003 (0.025-0.076)	0.0038 (0.097)
Seat width	0.040-0.062 (1.02-1.58)	–
Valve stem protrusion from cylinder head boss	2.012-2.032 (51.11-51.61)	2.069 (52.55)
Valve springs		
Free length	2.325 (59.1)	–
Spring rate		
Closed	135 lbs. @ 1.85 in. (61.2 kg @ 47.0 mm)	–
Open	312 lbs. @ 1.30 in. (141.5 kg @ 33.0 mm)	–

(continued)

ENGINE TOP END AND EXHAUST SYSTEM

Table 2 ENGINE TOP END SPECIFICATIONS (ALL MODELS EXCEPT SCREAMIN' EAGLE) (continued)

Item	New in. (mm)	Service limit in. (mm)
Piston-to-cylinder clearance	0.0014-0.0025 (0.036-0.064)	0.003 (0.076)
Piston pin-to-connecting rod clearance	0.0007-0.0012 (0.018-0.031)	0.002 (0.051)
Piston pin clearance (fit in piston)	0.0002-0.0005 (0.005-0.013)	0.0008 (0.020)
Piston rings		
Ring end gap		
Top ring	0.010-0.020 (0.25-0.51)	0.003 (0.0762)
Second ring	0.014-0.024 (0.36-0.61)	0.034 (0.864)
Oil control ring end gap	0.010-0.050 (0.254-1.27)	0.050 (1.27)
Ring side clearance		
Top ring	0.0012-0.0037 (0.031-0.094)	0.0045 (0.114)
Second ring	0.0012-0.0037 (0.031-0.094)	0.0045 (0.114)
Oil control ring	0.0031-0.0091 (0.079-0.231)	0.010 (0.254)
Cylinder		
Taper	–	0.002 (0.051)
Out of round	–	0.002 (0.051)
Warp		
At top (cylinder head)	–	0.006 (0.152)
At base (crankcase)	–	0.004 (0.102)
Cylinder bore		
All models except FLSTFSE2		
Standard	3.7500-3.7505 (95.250-95.263)	3.752 (95.301)
Oversize 0.005 in	3.7550-3.7555 (95.377-95.390)	3.757 (95.428)
Oversize 0.010 in.	3.7600-3.7605 (95.504-95.517)	3.762 (95.555)
Hydraulic lifters		
Lifter-to-bore clearance	0.0008-0.0020 (0.020-0.051)	0.0030 (0.076)
Radial play	–	0.0015 (0.0381)
Roller end clearance	–	0.026 (0.660)

Table 3 ENGINE TOP END SPECIFICATIONS (SCREAMIN' EAGLE MODELS)

Item	New in. (mm)	Service limit in. (mm)
Breather cover warp	–	0.005 (0.127)
Breather baffle warp	–	0.005 (0.127)
Cylinder head		
Warp limit	–	0.006 (0.152)
Valve guide fit in head	0.0020-0.0033 (0.051-0.084)	0.002 (0.051)
Valve seat fit in head		
2006 models		
Intake and exhaust	0.0030-0.0045 (0.076-0.114)	0.002 (0.051)
2007-2009 models		
Intake	0.0040-0.0055 (0.102-0.140)	0.002 (0.051)
Exhaust		
2007-2008 models	0.0030-0.0045 (0.076-0.114)	0.002 (0.051)
2009 models	0.0040-0.0055 (0.102-0.140)	0.004 (0.102)
Rocker arm		0.002 (0.0051)
Bushing fit in rocker arm	0.0020-0.004 (0.051-0.102)	–
End clearance	0.0030-0.0130 (0.076-0.330)	0.025 (0.635)
Shaft-to-rocker arm bushing clearance	0.0005-0.0020 (0.013-0.051)	0.0035 (0.089)
Shaft-to rocker arm support clearance	0.0007-0.0022 (0.018-0.056)	0.0035 (0.089)
Valves		
Valve stem-to-guide clearance		
2006 models		
Intake	0.0008-0.0026 (0.020-0.066)	0.0035 (0.089)
Exhaust	0.0015-0.0033 (0.038-0.084)	0.0038 (0.097)
2007-2009 models		
Intake	0.0011-0.0029 (0.028-0.074)	0.0038 (0.097)
Exhaust	0.0011-0.0029 (0.028-0.074)	0.0038 (0.097)
Seat width		
2006 models	0.040-0.062 (1.02-1.58)	–
2007-2009 models	0.034-0.062 (0.86-1.58)	–
Valve stem protrusion from cylinder head boss	1.990-2.024 (50.55-51.41)	–

(continued)

Table 3 ENGINE TOP END SPECIFICATIONS (SCREAMIN' EAGLE MODELS) (continued)

Item	New in. (mm)	Service limit in. (mm)
Valve springs		
Free length	N.A.	–
Spring rate		
2006 models		
Closed	165 lbs @ 1.820 in	
	(75 kg @ 46.2 mm)	–
Open	416 lbs @ 1.290 in.	
	(189 kg @ (32.8 mm)	–
2007-2009 models		
Closed	175 lbs @ 1.800 in	
	(79 kg @ 45.7 mm)	–
Open	432 lbs @ 1.250 in.	
	(196 kg @ (31.8 mm)	–
Piston-to-cylinder clearance		
2006 models	0.0018-0.0027 (0.046-0.069)	0.003 (0.076)
2007-2009 models	0.0014-0.0025 (0.036-0.064)	0.003 (0.076)
Piston pin-to-connecting rod clearance		
2006 models	0.0006-0.0012 (0.015-0.030)	0.002 (0.051)
2007-2009 models	0.0003-0.0007 (0.008-0.018)	0.001 (0.025)
Piston pin-to-piston clearance		
(fit in piston)		
2006 models	0.0005-0.0009 (0.013-0.023)	0.0009 (0.023)
2007-2009 models	0.0002-0.0005 (0.005-0.013)	0.0008 (0.020)
Piston rings		
Ring end gap		
Top ring		
2006 models	0.010-0.020 (0.254-0.508)	0.030 (0.762)
2007-2009 models	0.016-0.024 (0.406-0.610)	0.034 (0.864)
Second ring	0.014-0.024 (0.356-0.610)	0.034 (0.864)
Oil control ring end gap		
2006 models	0.0031-0.0091 (0.079-0.231)	0.050 (1.27)
2007-2009 models	0.010-0.030 (0.254-0.762)	0.030 (0.762)
Ring side clearance		
Top ring		
2006 models	0.0012-0.037 (0.031-0.940)	0.0045 (0.114)
2007-2009 models	0.00098-0.0024 (0.025-0.061)	0.0032 (0.081)
Second ring		
2006 models	0.0012-0.037 (0.031-0.094)	0.0045 (0.114)
2007-2009 models	0.00098-0.0024 (0.025-0.061)	0.0032 (0.081)
Oil control ring		
2006 models	0.0031-0.0091 (0.079-0.231)	0.010 (0.254)
2007-2009 models	0.002-0.004 (0.051-0.102)	0.004 (0.102)
Cylinder		
Taper	–	0.002 (0.051)
Out of round	–	0.002 (0.051)
Warp		
At top (cylinder head)	–	0.006 (0.152)
At base (crankcase)	–	0.004 (0.102)
Cylinder bore		
Standard	4.0000-4.0005 (101.6-101.613)	4.002 (101.65)
Oversize 0.005 in	4.0050-4.0055 (101.727-101.740)	4.007 (101.78)
Oversize 0.010 in.	4.0100-4.0105 (101.854-101.867)	4.012 (101.91)
Hydraulic lifters		
Lifter-to-bore clearance	0.0008-0.0020 (0.020-0.051)	0.0030 (0.076)
Radial play	–	0.0015 (0.038)
Roller end clearance	–	0.026 (0.660)

N.A.-Specification not available from the manufacturer.

ENGINE TOP END AND EXHAUST SYSTEM

Table 4 PUSHROD AND LIFTER LOCATION

Cylinder	Lifter bore	Cylinder head/rocker housing
Front		
Intake	Inside	Rear
Exhaust	Outside	Front
Rear		
Intake	Inside	Front
Exhaust	Outside	Rear

Table 5 ENGINE TOP END AND EXHAUST TORQUE SPECIFICATIONS

Item	ft.-lb.	in.-lb.	N•m
Automatic compression release			
(ACR) solenoid (Screamin' Eagle models)	11-15	–	14.9-20.3
Breather assembly bolts		90-120	10.2-13.6
Cylinder head bolts			
Initial	10-12	–	13.6-16.3
Secondary	15-17	–	20.3-23.0
Final	additional 90°		
Cylinder head bracket bolts	35-40	–	47.5-54.2
Cylinder stud	10-20	–	13.6-27.1
Cylinder-head bolt-cover set			
screw (Screamin' Eagle models)	–	60-84	6.8-9.5
Exhaust system fasteners			
Bracket tab and stud mounting nut			
(slotted Torca clamp)	12-15	–	16.3-20.3
Crossover hanger locknut			
(2009 models)	14-18	–	19.0-24.4
Cylinder head flange nuts			
Upper nut			
Preliminary	–	9-18	1-2
Final	–	120	13.6
Lower nut	–	110-120	12.4-13.6
2009 Models			
Exhaust bracket flange locknut	20-25	–	27.1-33.9
Crossover hanger bolt	14-18	–	19-24.4
Transmission bracket bolt	–	84-132	9.5-14.9
Saddlebag mounting bracket bolt	–	96-144	10.8-16.3
Muffler-to-saddlebag support rail			
mounting bracket bolt (2006 models)	–	96-144	10.8-16.3
Oxygen sensor	30-44	–	40.7-59.7
Torca clamp nut (2006-2008 models)	45-60	–	61.0-81.3
Torca clamps (2009 models)	38-43	–	51.5-58.3
Torca clamp support bracket nut	12-15	–	16.3-20.3
Lifter cover bolts	–	90-120	10.2-13.6
Rocker arm cover bolt	15-18	–	20.3-24.4
Rocker arm housing bolt	10-14	–	13.6-19.0
Rocker arm support plate bolts	18-22	–	24.4-29.8
Spark plug	12-18	–	16.3-24.4

CHAPTER FIVE

ENGINE LOWER END

This chapter provides service and overhaul procedures for the lower end, including engine removal and installation.

Specifications are located at the end of the chapter in **Tables 1-3**.

ENGINE

WARNING
The engine assembly is heavy. Have one, or preferably two, others assist with its removal and installation.

Removal

Refer to **Figures 1-3**.

NOTE
Always disarm the optional TSSM/HFSM security system prior to disconnecting the battery or pulling the Maxi-Fuse so the siren will not sound.

1. Thoroughly clean all dirt and debris from the engine.
2. Support the motorcycle frame and transmission with a floor jack. Also, tie the motorcycle down for additional stability.
3. Remove the fuel tank as described in Chapter Nine or Chapter Ten.
4. Remove both frame side covers and both saddlebags as described in Chapter Seventeen.
5. Remove both footboards as described in Chapter Seventeen.
6. Remove the lower fairing assemblies on both sides (Chapter Seventeen), on models so equipped.
7. Remove the engine guard (Chapter Seventeen), on models so equipped.
8. Remove the air filter and backplate as described in Chapter Nine or Chapter Ten.
9A. On carbureted models, remove the carburetor as described in Chapter Nine.
9B. On fuel-injected models, remove the fuel induction module as described in Chapter Ten.
10. Remove the purge control solenoid as described in Chapter Nine, on models so equipped.
11. Remove the exhaust system as described in Chapter Four.
12. Remove the rear brake pedal as described in Chapter Fifteen.
13. Drain the engine oil and remove the oil filter as described in Chapter Three.
14. On 2006 models, perform the following:
    a. Remove the bolts securing the oil line cover and remove the cover (**Figure 4**).
    b. Remove the clamps and disconnect the three oil lines from the crankcase. Plug the oil lines to prevent dirt from entering the hoses.
    c. Straighten the locking tabs away from the oil filter mount top and bottom mounting bolts.
    d. Remove the three bolts and washers securing the mount to the crankcase. Remove the lockplate.
    e. Remove the oil filter mount from the crankcase and discard the O-ring seals.
15. Remove the crankshaft position sensor mounting bolt (A, **Figure 5**) and the sensor (B) from the crankcase.

ENGINE LOWER END

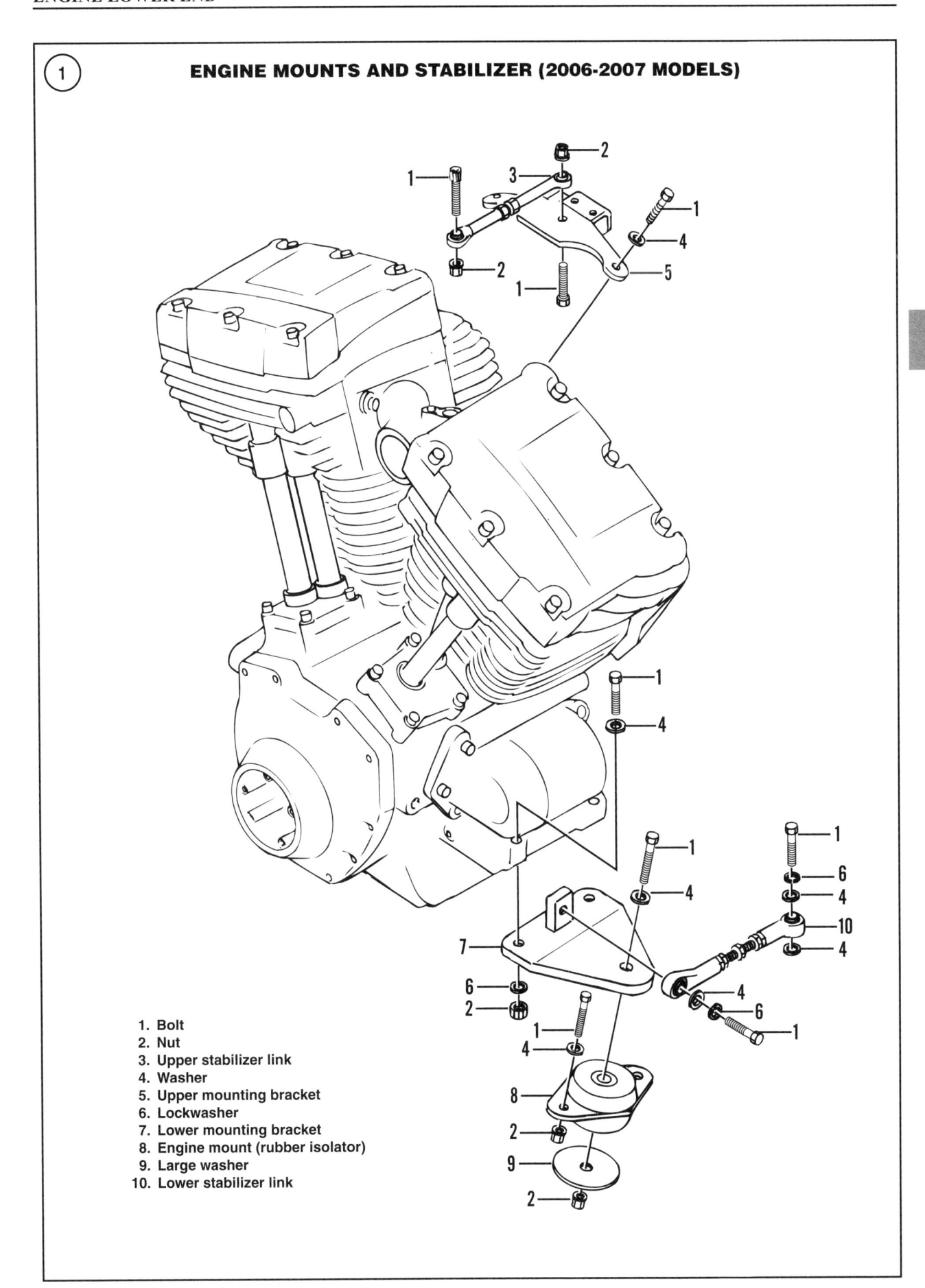

① **ENGINE MOUNTS AND STABILIZER (2006-2007 MODELS)**

1. Bolt
2. Nut
3. Upper stabilizer link
4. Washer
5. Upper mounting bracket
6. Lockwasher
7. Lower mounting bracket
8. Engine mount (rubber isolator)
9. Large washer
10. Lower stabilizer link

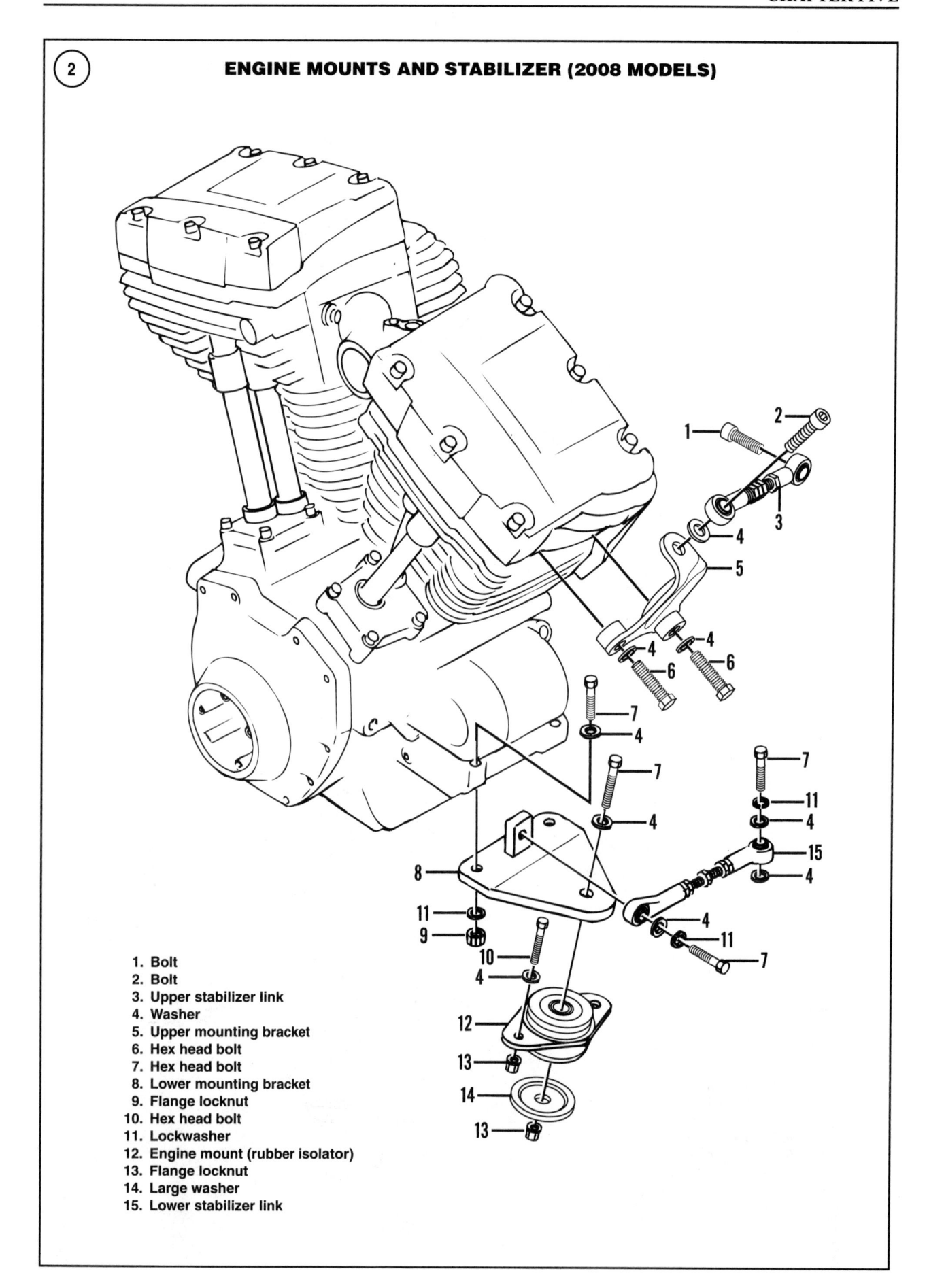

CHAPTER FIVE

② ENGINE MOUNTS AND STABILIZER (2008 MODELS)

1. Bolt
2. Bolt
3. Upper stabilizer link
4. Washer
5. Upper mounting bracket
6. Hex head bolt
7. Hex head bolt
8. Lower mounting bracket
9. Flange locknut
10. Hex head bolt
11. Lockwasher
12. Engine mount (rubber isolator)
13. Flange locknut
14. Large washer
15. Lower stabilizer link

ENGINE LOWER END

③ **ENGINE MOUNTS AND STABILIZER (2009 MODELS)**

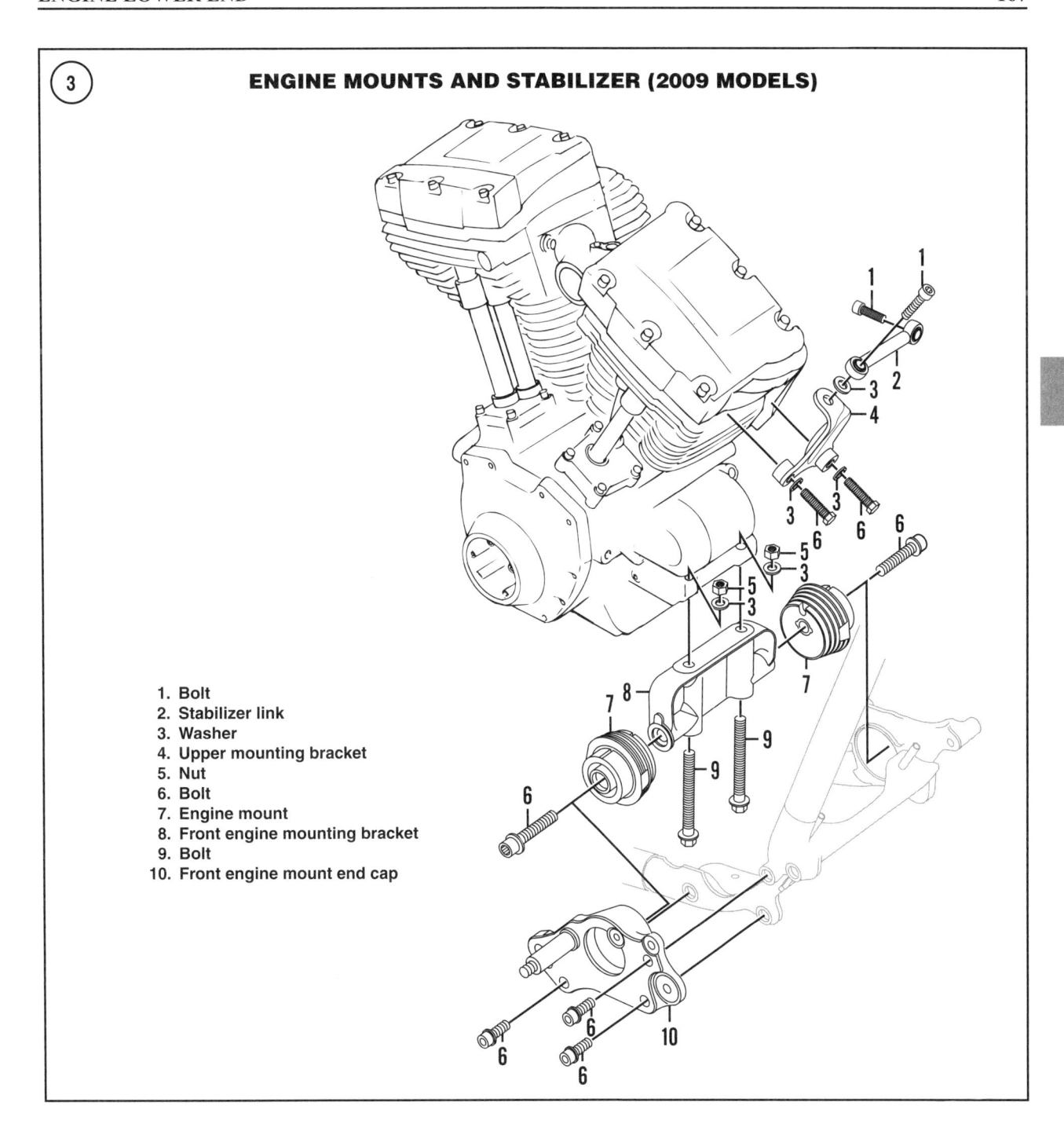

1. Bolt
2. Stabilizer link
3. Washer
4. Upper mounting bracket
5. Nut
6. Bolt
7. Engine mount
8. Front engine mounting bracket
9. Bolt
10. Front engine mount end cap

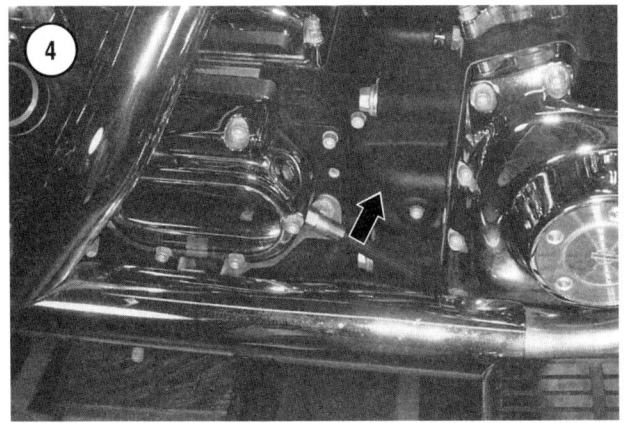

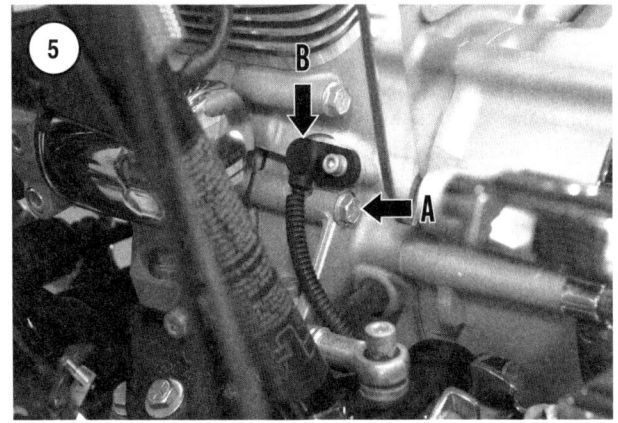

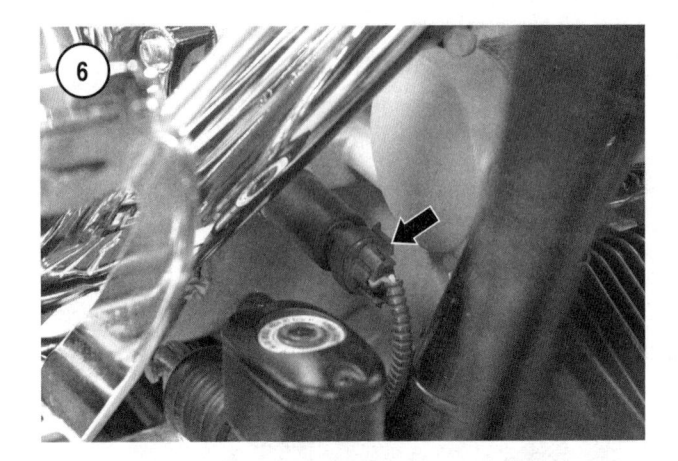

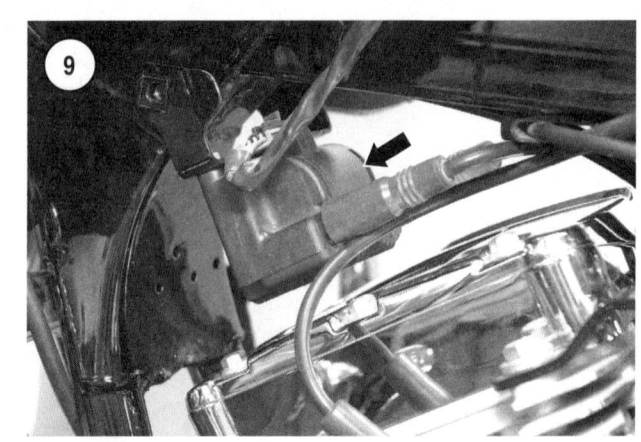

16. Disconnect the electrical connectors from the following:
   a. Oil pressure sender (**Figure 6**).
   b. Engine temperature sensor (**Figure 7**).
   c. Speed sensor (located under the starter).
   d. Neutral indicator switch (**Figure 8**).

17. Disconnect the connector from the TSSM/HFSM as described in Chapter Eleven. Disconnect the siren connector on models so equipped.

18. Remove the horn assembly as described in Chapter Eleven.

19. Remove the primary chaincase assembly, including the inner housing, as described in Chapter Six.

20. Remove the alternator rotor and stator as described in Chapter Eleven.

21. Remove the ignition coil assembly (**Figure 9**) as described in Chapter Eleven.

22. Remove the voltage regulator from the frame as described in Chapter Eleven.

23. Disconnect the hose from the breather cover (**Figure 10**) and move the hose behind the transmission flange.

24A. On all models except Screamin' Eagle, remove the clutch cable from the lower portion of the crankcase as described in Chapter Six.

24B. On Screamin Eagle models, disconnect the hydraulic fluid line from the clutch release cover as described in Chapter Six.

ENGINE LOWER END

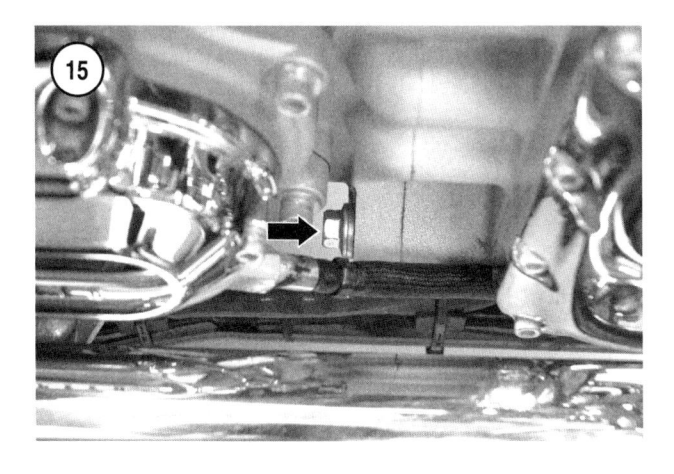

25. Support the engine with a floor or scissor jack (JIMS part No. 904).
26. Apply enough floor jack pressure on the transmission oil pan to support its weight prior to removing the engine mounting bolts.
27A. On 2006-2007 models, perform the following:
   a. On the right side, remove the bolt and nut securing the inboard end (A, **Figure 11**) of the upper stabilizing link to the frame.
   b. On the left side, remove the two bolts (B, **Figure 11**) and washers securing the upper mounting bracket to the cylinder heads.
   c. Remove the stabilizer link and upper mounting bracket assembly from the frame and engine.
27B. On 2008 models, perform the following:
   a. On the left side, remove the two bolts (A, **Figure 12**) and flat washers securing the upper mounting bracket to the cylinder heads.
   b. On the right side, remove the bolt (**Figure 13**) securing the stabilizer link to the frame weld.
   c. Remove the mounting bracket (B, **Figure 12**) assembly from the frame.
27C. On 2009 models, perform the following:
   a. Remove the bolts and washers securing the upper mounting bracket to the cylinder head.
   b. Remove the Allen bolt securing the stabilizer link to the frame weld.
   c. Remove the upper mounting bracket assembly from the engine and frame.
28. Wrap the front frame down tubes and the lower tubes in protective foam padding to protect them from surface damage.
29. Cover both rocker covers with foam padding to protect the finish.
30A. On 2006-2008 models, perform the following:
   a. Remove the short (1/2 in.) upper bolts (**Figure 14**) and the long (9/16 in.) lower bolts (**Figure 15**), along with their washers, that secure the engine to the transmission on each side.
   b. Remove the two bolts and washers (A, **Figure 16**) securing the engine to the lower mounting bracket (B).
30B. On 2009 models, remove the short (1/2 in.) upper bolts (**Figure 14**) and the long (9/16 in.) lower bolts

(**Figure 15**), along with their washers, that secure the engine to the transmission on each side.

31. On 2009 models, remove the front engine mount as follows:
    a. Loosen, *but do not remove*, the two long Allen bolts securing each engine mount to the front engine mounting bracket.
    b. Remove the two hex head bolts, washers and nuts securing the front engine mounting bracket to the engine.
    c. On the right side, remove the three short Allen bolts securing the end cap to the frame. Remove the end cap from the frame and the right side engine mount.
    d. Remove the front engine mounting bracket and both engine mounts as an assembly from the frame receptacle on the left side.

32. Check the engine to make sure all electrical wiring, hoses and other related components have been disconnected from the engine. Make sure nothing will interfere with the removal of the engine from the right side of the frame.

33. Move the engine far enough forward to clear the clear the locating dowels on the front of the transmission. The dowels stick out approximately 1/2 in. (12.7 mm).

34. Raise the engine up, slightly rotate it toward the right side, and remove the engine from the right side of the frame. Carefully avoid the rear brake line and reservoir and the main wiring harness.

35. Carry the engine to the workbench and mount the engine in an engine stand (JIMS part No. 1142) and base stand (JIMS part No. 1138), or an equivalent holding fixture (**Figure 17**).

36. Remove the locating dowels from the engine or transmission mounting surface.

37. On 2007-2009 models, remove the gasket from the transmission case and discard it.

38. Clean all engine mounting bolts and washers in solvent and dry thoroughly. Do not allow solvent to contact the engine mount rubber isolators.

Installation

1. Remove engine from the engine stand and base stand, if used.
2. Cover both rocker covers with foam padding to protect the finish.
3. Secure the transmission to the frame ratchet strap, if removed.
4. If removed, install the two lower locating dowels into the transmission case. Refer to **Figure 18** and **Figure 19**.
5. On 2007-2009 models, perform the following:
    a. Thoroughly clean the gasket mating surface of the transmission case.
    b. Apply a light coat of gasket sealer to the transmission side of the *new* gasket.
    c. Position the gasket with the alignment pins facing the transmission and install it onto the transmission case. Press the gasket into place until the alignment pins have seated onto the transmission case receptacles.

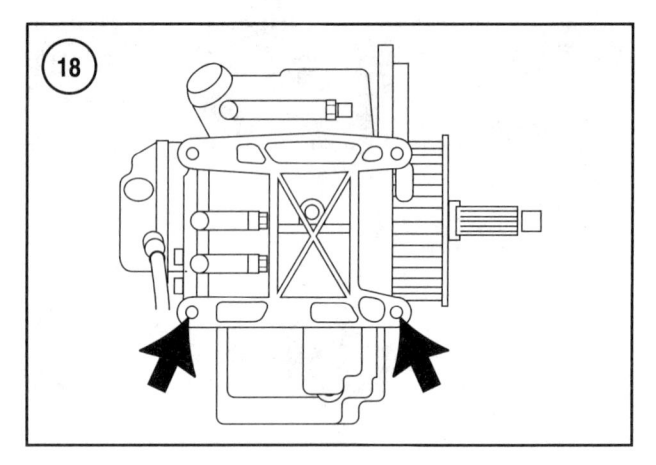

6. Make sure all electrical wiring, hoses and other related components are out of the way and will not interfere with engine installation.

7. Correctly position the floor or scissor jack (JIMS part No. 904) to accept the engine as it is moved into position in the frame.

8. Install the engine from the right side of the frame and place it on a piece of wood laid across the jack. Apply enough jack pressure on the crankcase to support its weight prior to installing the engine mounting bolts.

9. Slide the engine toward the rear and onto the two transmission locating dowels. The engine may have to be rotated slightly to accept the dowels.

10. Install the short (1/2 in.) upper bolts (**Figure 14**) and the long (9/16 in.) lower bolts (**Figure 15**), along with their washers, securing the engine to the transmission on each side. Finger-tighten the bolts at this time.

NOTE
The engine mounting bracket, both engine mounts and the long Allen bolts must be assembled as a unit prior to installation onto the frame.

11. On 2009 models, install the front engine mount as follows:
    a. Install the engine front mounting bracket and both engine mounts as an assembly from the right side. Index it into the frame receptacle on the left side.

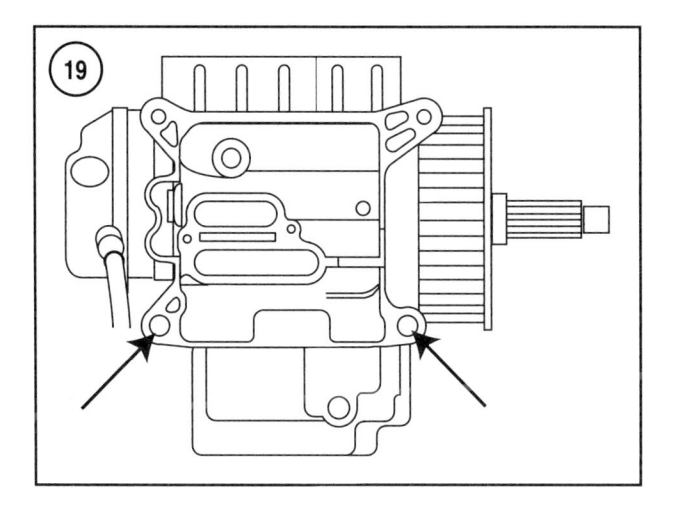

b. On the right side, thread the three short Allen bolts securing the end cap to the frame. Do not tighten the bolts at this time.
c. Install the two hex head bolts through the mounting bracket and into the bolt holes in the engine.
d. Apply Loctite Threadlocker 243 (blue) to the nut threads. Install the washers and nuts onto the two hex bolts. Finger-tighten the fasteners at this time.
e. Tighten the three short Allen bolts securing the end cap to 42-48 ft.-lb. (56.9-65.2 N•m).
f. Tighten the two long engine mount Allen bolts to 40-50 ft.-lb. (53.4-67.8 N•m).

12A. On 2006-2008 models, use a crossing pattern to tighten the engine-to-transmission bolts in the following sequence:
   a. Preliminary: 15 ft.-lb. (20.3 N•m).
   b. Final: 30-35 ft.-lb. (40.7-47.5 N•m).

12B. On 2009 models, use a crossing pattern to tighten the engine-to-transmission bolts in the following sequence:
   a. Preliminary: 15 ft.-lb. (20.3 N•m).
   b. Final: 34-39 ft.-lb. (46.1-52.9 N•m).

13. On 2009 models, tighten the front engine mounting bracket hex head bolts and nuts to 36-40 ft.-lb. (48.8-54.2 N•m).

14. On 2006-2007 models, thread the two bolts (A, **Figure 16**) and washers securing the lower mounting bracket (B) to the engine. Tighten the bolts to 33-38 ft.-lb. (44.7-51.5 N•m).

15A. On 2006-2007 models, perform the following:
   a. Install the stabilizer link and upper mounting bracket assembly onto the frame and cylinder head.
   b. Install the two bolts (B, **Figure 11**) and washers securing the upper mounting bracket to the cylinder heads, and finger-tighten the bolts.
   c. Install the bolt and nut securing the inboard end (A, **Figure 11**) of the stabilizing link to the frame, and finger-tighten the fasteners.
   d. Tighten the bolts securing the upper mounting bracket to the cylinder heads to 18-22 ft.-lb. (24.4-29.8 N•m).
   e. Tighten the bolt and nut securing the stabilizing link to the frame to 30-35 ft.-lb. (40.7-47.5 N•m).

15B. On 2008 models, perform the following:
   a. Install the mounting bracket assembly onto the frame and cylinder head.
   b. Install the bolt (**Figure 13**) securing the stabilizer link to the frame weldment, and finger-tighten the bolt.
   c. Install the two bolts (A, **Figure 12**) and flat washers securing the upper mounting bracket (B) to the cylinder heads and finger-tighten the bolts.
   d. Tighten the bolt securing the stabilizer link to the frame weldment to 18-22 ft.-lb. (24.4-29.8 N•m).
   e. Tighten the bolts securing the upper mounting bracket to the cylinder head to 30-35 ft.-lb. (40.7-47.5 N•m).

15C. On 2009 models, perform the following:
   a. Install the upper mounting bracket assembly onto the engine and frame.
   b. Install the bolts securing the upper mounting bracket to the cylinder head and tighten to 18-22 ft.-lb. (24.4-29.8 N•m).
   c. Install the Allen bolt securing the stabilizer link to the frame weldment and tighten the bolt to 30-35 ft.-lb. (40.7-47.5 N•m).

16. Remove the floor jack or scissor jack from under the crankcase and the transmission.
17. Remove the protective foam padding from the front frame down tubes and lower tubes.
18. Remove the foam padding from the rocker covers.
19A. On all models, except Screamin' Eagle models, install the clutch cable as described in Chapter Six.
19B. On Screamin Eagle models, connect the hydraulic fluid line to the clutch release cover as described in Chapter Six.
20. Connect the hose (**Figure 10**) onto the breather cover.
21. Install the voltage regulator as described in Chapter Eleven.
22. Install the ignition coil assembly (**Figure 9**) as described in Chapter Eleven.
23. Install the alternator rotor and stator as described in Chapter Eleven.
24. Install the primary chaincase assembly, including the inner housing, as described in Chapter Six.
25. Install the horn assembly as described in Chapter Eleven.
26. Connect the connector onto the TSM/TSSM/HFSM. Connect the siren connector on models so equipped.
27. Connect the following electrical connectors:
   a. Neutral indicator switch (**Figure 8**).
   b. Speed sensor (located under the starter).
   c. Engine temperature sensor (**Figure 7**).
   d. Oil pressure sender (**Figure 6**).
28. Install the crankshaft position sensor (B, **Figure 5**) and install the screw (A) into the crankcase. Tighten the screw to 90-120 in.-lb. (10.2-13.6 N•m).

NOTE
The following shows the engine removed from the frame to better illustrate the procedure.

29. On 2006 models, perform the following:

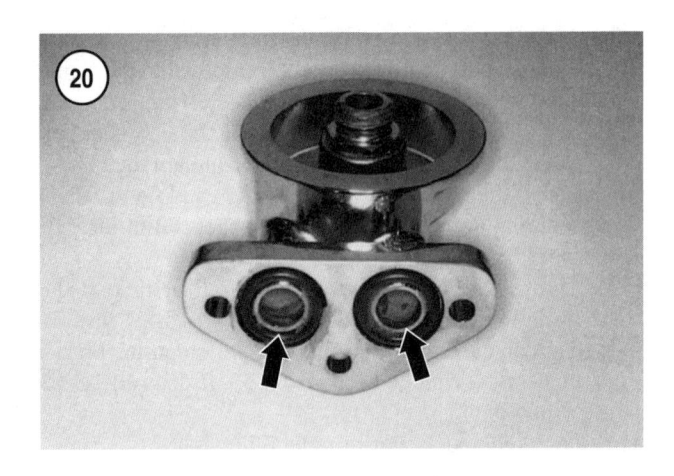

a. Install *new* O-ring seals (**Figure 20**) onto the oil filter mount.
b. Apply Loctite Threadlocker 243 (blue), or an equivalent, to the mounting bolt threads prior to installing them into the *new* lockplate.
c. Install the oil filter mount onto the crankcase, and then install the lockplate with its three mounting bolts (**Figure 21**) and washers.
d. Tighten the oil filter mounting bracket bolts to 12-16 ft.-lb. (16.3-21.7 N•m).
e. Bend the locking tabs down against the top and bottom mounting bolt heads.
f. Install the oil filter.
g. Connect the three oil lines onto the crankcase fittings and install *new* hose clamps.
h. Install the bolts securing the oil line cover (**Figure 4**) and tighten securely.

30. Refill the engine oil as described in Chapter Three.
31. On Screamin' Eagle models, refill and bleed the clutch hydraulic system as described in Chapter Six.
32. Install the rear brake pedal as described in Chapter Fifteen.
33. Install the exhaust system as described in Chapter Four.
34. Install the purge control solenoid as described in Chapter Nine, on models so equipped.
35A. On carbureted models, install the carburetor as described in Chapter Nine.
35B. On fuel-injected models, install the fuel induction module as described in Chapter Ten.
36. Install the air filter and backplate as described in Chapter Nine or Chapter Ten.
37. Install the engine guard and lower fairing assemblies on both sides (Chapter Seventeen), on models so equipped.
38. Install the footboards as described in Chapter Seventeen.
39. Install both frame side covers as described in Chapter Seventeen.
40. Install both saddlebags as described in Chapter Seventeen.
41. Install the fuel tank as described in Chapter Nine or Chapter Ten.
42. Remove the stand from under the motorcycle and place the motorcycle on the jiffy stand.
43. Connect the negative battery cable as described in Chapter Eleven.
44. Install the seat as described in Chapter Seventeen.
45. Start the engine and check for leaks.

OIL PUMP

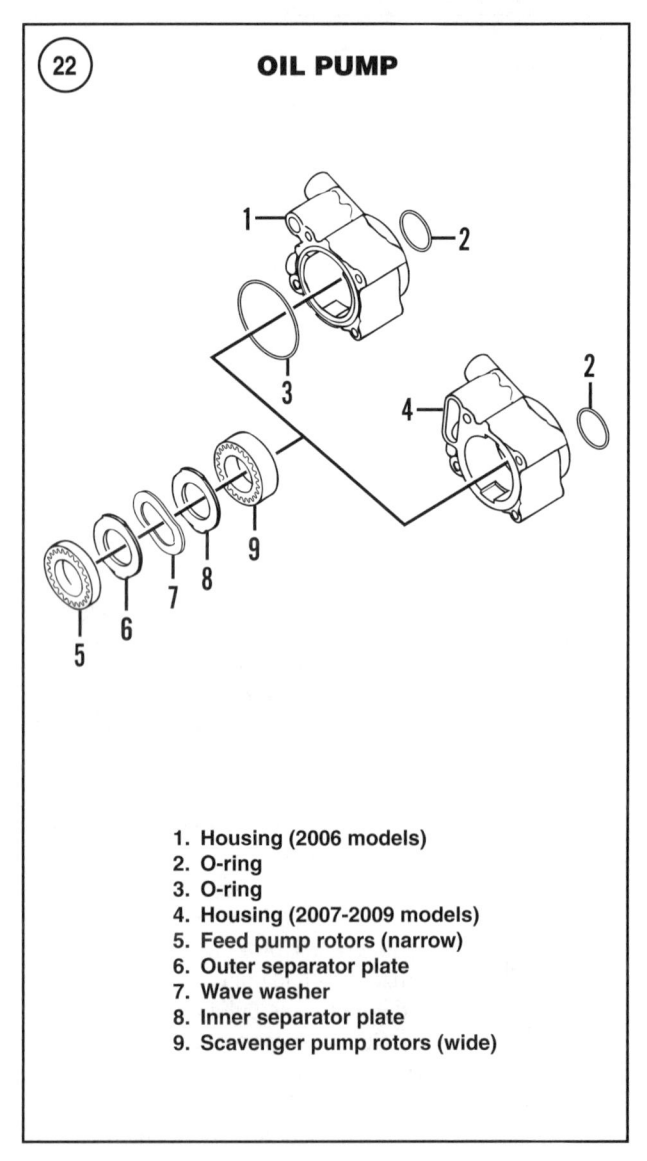

1. Housing (2006 models)
2. O-ring
3. O-ring
4. Housing (2007-2009 models)
5. Feed pump rotors (narrow)
6. Outer separator plate
7. Wave washer
8. Inner separator plate
9. Scavenger pump rotors (wide)

ENGINE LOWER END

Cleaning and Inspection

1. Remove any corrosion from the engine mount bolts with a wire wheel.
2. Clean and dry the engine mount bolts.
3. Clean and inspect the engine mounting bolt threads and the threads in the frame for damage.
4. Replace damaged fasteners.
5. Inspect the jiffy stand bracket for cracks and fractures.
6. Check the wire harness routing in the frame. Check the harness cover and wires for chafing or other damage. Replace harness cable guides and clips as required.
7. Clean the electrical connectors with contact cleaner.
8. On Screamin' Eagle models, check the clutch hydraulic line for kinks or damage. Check the fasteners for damage.

OIL PUMP

The oil pump is located on the right side of the crankcase under the camshaft support plate. The oil pump consists of two sections: a feed pump (narrow rotors) which supplies oil under pressure to the engine components and a scavenger pump (wide rotors) which returns the oil from the engine to the oil pan in the base of the transmission case. On 2006 models, oil travels from the engine to the transmission case through two interconnecting hoses. On 2007-2009 models, there are no external oil lines. The oil travels directly from the engine to the transmission case via oil flow channels within both components.

Disassembly/Removal

The oil pump can be removed with the engine in the frame. Refer to **Figure 22**.

1. Drain the engine oil as described in Chapter Three.
2. Remove the camshaft support plate assembly as described in this chapter.
3. Remove the feed pump outer (**Figure 23**) and inner (**Figure 24**) rotors.
4. Remove the outer separator plate (A, **Figure 25**), wave washer (**Figure 26**) and the inner separator plate (A, **Figure 27**).

5. Remove the scavenger pump outer (**Figure 28**) and inner (**Figure 29**) rotors.
6. Carefully pull the oil pump body (**Figure 30**) straight off the crankshaft.
7. Remove the O-ring (A, **Figure 31**) from the backside of the oil pump housing.

Assembly/Installation

NOTE
*Position both inner and outer rotor sets with the punch marks (**Figure 32**, typical) facing out. If the rotor set is not marked, position the rotors in either orientation.*

1. Install a *new* O-ring (A, **Figure 31**) onto the backside of the oil pump. Apply clean engine oil to the O-ring.
2. Carefully push the oil pump body (**Figure 30**) straight onto the crankshaft. Align the O-ring and fitting to the crankcase fitting (B, **Figure 31**). Push it on until it bottoms. Make sure the O-ring seats correctly in the crankcase fitting.
3. Align the flat on the scavenger inner rotor with the flat on the crankshaft, and install the inner rotor (**Figure 29**).
4. Install the scavenger outer rotor (**Figure 28**) into the oil pump. Push it on until it is meshed with the inner rotor and the oil pump housing.

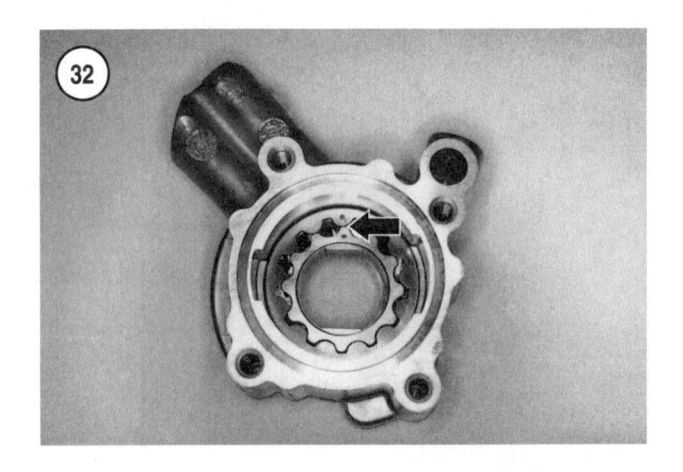

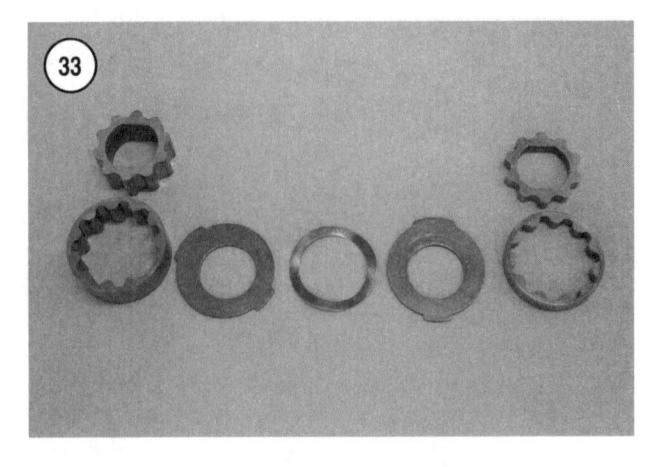

ENGINE LOWER END

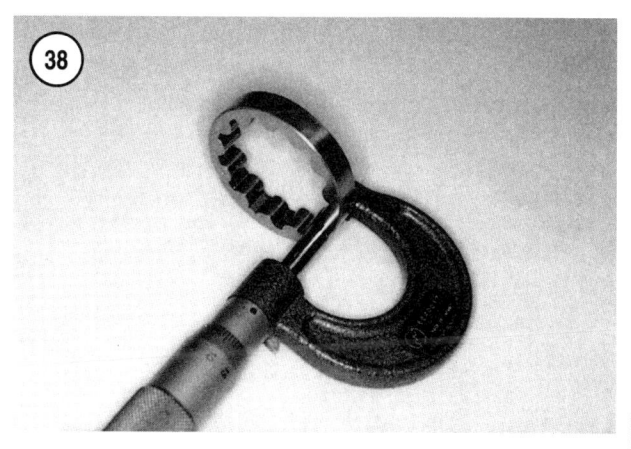

5. Align the tangs on the inner separator plate with the oil pump grooves (B, **Figure 27**), and install the inner separator plate (A).
6. Install the wave washer (**Figure 26**).
7. Align the tangs on the outer separator plate with the oil pump grooves (B, **Figure 25**), and install the outer separator plate (A).
8. Align the flat on the feed pump inner rotor with the flat on the crankshaft and install the inner rotor (**Figure 24**).
9. Install the feed pump outer rotor (**Figure 23**) into the oil pump housing. Push in on the outer rotor until it is meshed with the inner rotor and the oil pump housing.
10. Install the camshaft support plate assembly as described in this chapter.
11. Refill the engine oil as described in Chapter Three.

Inspection

1. Clean all parts thoroughly in solvent and place them on a clean, lint-free cloth (**Figure 33**).
2. Inspect both sets of inner and outer rotors (**Figure 34**) for scratches and abrasion.
3. Inspect the oil pump housing (**Figure 35**) for scratches caused by the rotors.
4. Inspect the interior passageways of the oil pump housing. Make sure all oil sludge and debris are removed. Blow low-pressure compressed air through all passages in the pump housing.
5. Install an inner rotor into its outer rotor. Use a flat feeler gauge to measure the clearance (**Figure 36**) between the tips of the inner and outer rotors. Replace the rotors as a set if the clearance exceeds the service limit (**Table 1**). Also measure the other set of rotors.
6. Measure the thickness of the inner (**Figure 37**) and outer (**Figure 38**) rotors. Compare the two measurements. If the difference exceeds 0.001 in. (0.025 mm), replace the rotors as a complete set. Also measure the other set of rotors.
7. Perform the following to check the feed rotor height:
   a. Assemble the oil pump (**Figure 22**).
   b. Set the pump on the bench with the feed rotors facing up.
   c. Place a straightedge across the feed rotors. Use a feeler gauge to measure the distance from the pump

176

CHAPTER FIVE

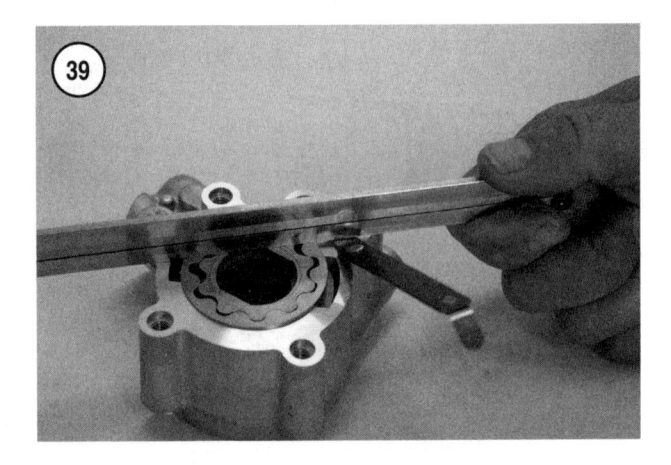

housing to the bottom of the straightedge (**Figure 39**).

d. If this measurement is less than the service limit (**Table 1**), replace the wave washer.

e. Assemble the pump with the new wave washer, and measure the feed rotor height. If it is still out of specification, replace the pump.

OIL FILTER MOUNT (2006 MODELS EXCEPT SCREAMIN' EAGLE)

The oil filter mount is located on the right side of the crankcase and can be removed with the engine in the frame.

Removal

1. Park the motorcycle on a level surface.
2. Remove the front exhaust pipe as described in Chapter Four.
3. Drain the engine oil and remove the oil filter as described in Chapter Three.
4. Place several shop cloths under the oil filter mount to catch any residual oil that drains out.
5. Straighten the lockplate tabs and remove the three bolts (**Figure 40**) and washers. Remove the oil filter mount from the crankcase.

Installation

1. Thoroughly clean the crankcase mounting surface.
2. Install *new* O-ring seals (**Figure 41**) onto the filter mount.
3. Apply Loctite Threadlocker 243 (blue) to the threads of the three mounting bolts prior to installation.
4. On the exterior of the mount, place flat washers in the top and bottom recessed bolt holes.
5. Align the lockplate bolt holes with the two flat washers.
6. Insert the two bolts through the lockplate, the two flat washers and the mounting flange.
7. Install the oil filter mount, lockplate and washers assembly onto the crankcase. Carefully install the two bolts into the crankcase, and finger-tighten the bolts.

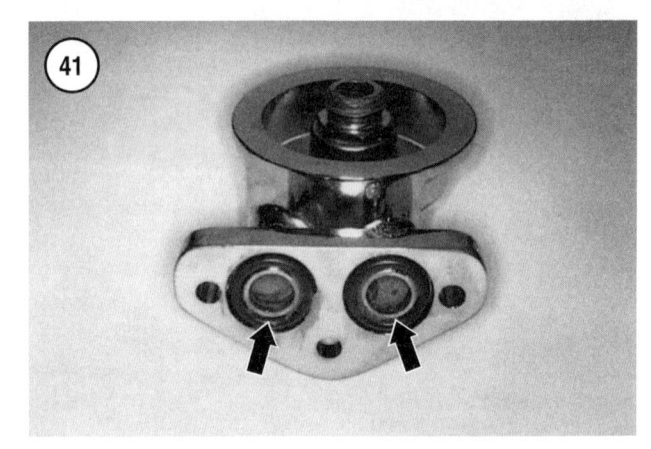

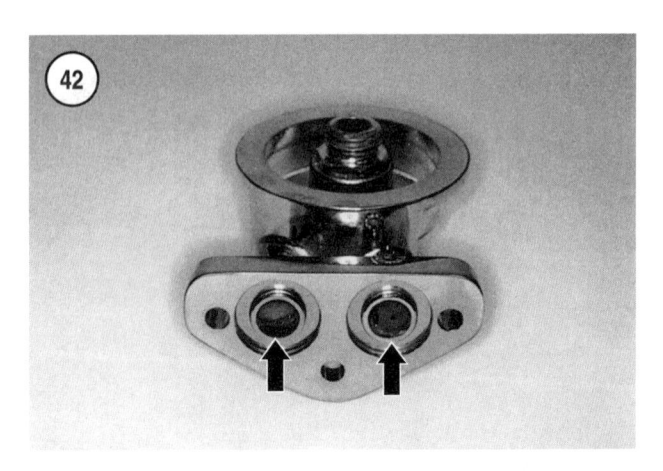

ENGINE LOWER END

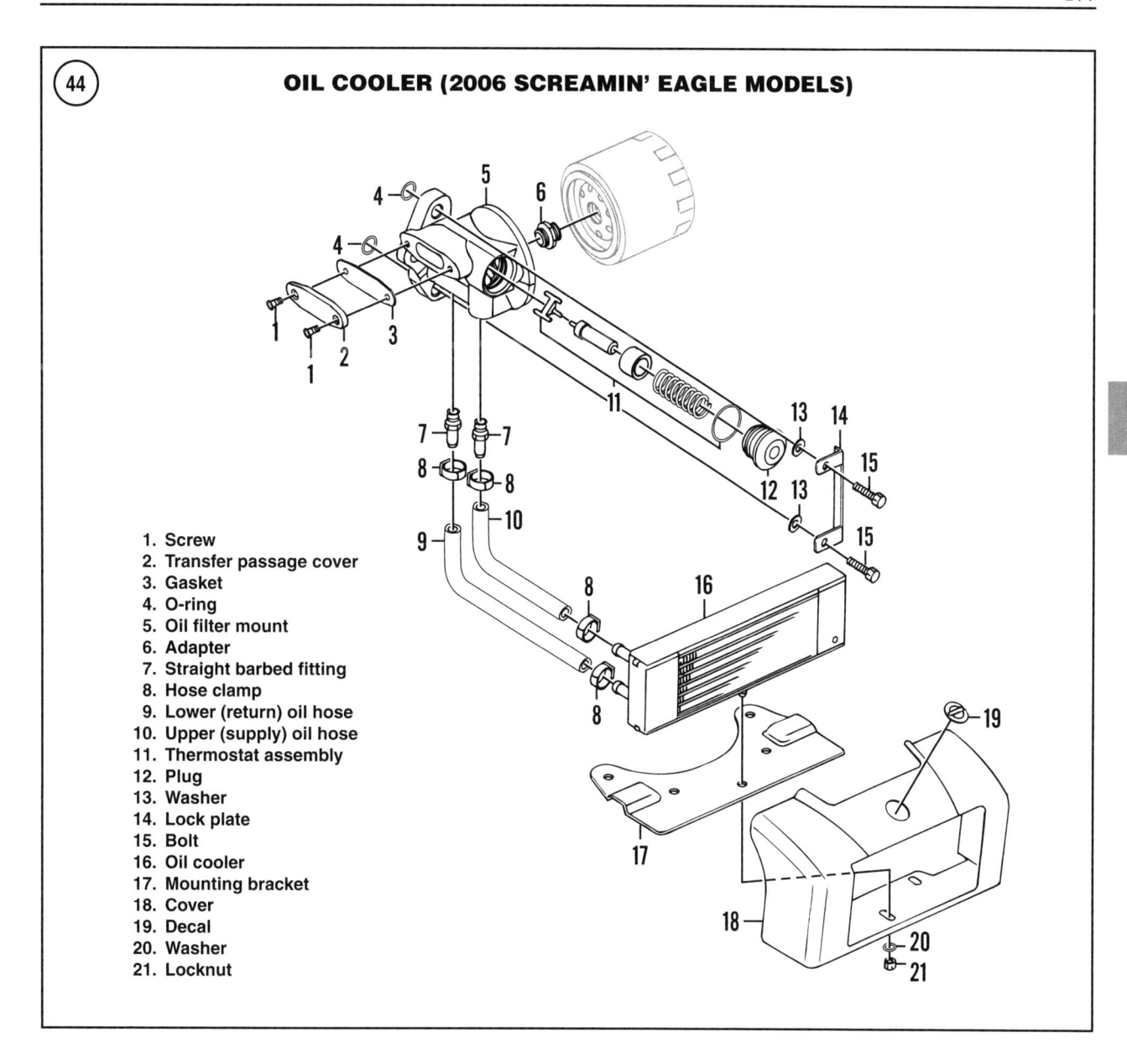

OIL COOLER (2006 SCREAMIN' EAGLE MODELS)

Figure 44

1. Screw
2. Transfer passage cover
3. Gasket
4. O-ring
5. Oil filter mount
6. Adapter
7. Straight barbed fitting
8. Hose clamp
9. Lower (return) oil hose
10. Upper (supply) oil hose
11. Thermostat assembly
12. Plug
13. Washer
14. Lock plate
15. Bolt
16. Oil cooler
17. Mounting bracket
18. Cover
19. Decal
20. Washer
21. Locknut

8. Install the remaining bolt and washer and finger-tighten the bolt.
9. Starting at the top bolt, alternately tighten the three mounting bolts to 12-16 ft.-lb. (16.3-21.7 N•m).
10. Install the front exhaust pipe as described in Chapter Four.
11. Install a new oil filter and refill the engine oil as described in Chapter Three.
12. Start the engine and check for oil leaks.

Inspection

1. Clean the oil filter mount in solvent and dry with compressed air.
2. Check the oil filter mount for damage that could result in an oil leak.
3. Make sure the oil passageways (**Figure 42**) are clear.
4. Check the oil filter mounting surface (A, **Figure 43**) and oil filter mounting threads (B) for wear or damage.

OIL COOLER, OIL FILTER MOUNT AND THERMOSTAT (2006 SCREAMIN' EAGLE MODELS)

The oil cooler and oil filter mount are located on the front of the crankcase and can be removed with the engine in the frame.

NOTE
The original equipment hose clamps will be damaged when they are removed. A quality screw-type hose clamp can be used in place of the original clamp. The original equipment hose clamps must be installed using JIMS hose clamp pincer tool (part No. 1171), or an equivalent.

Oil Cooler and Cover Removal/Installation

Refer to **Figure 44**.

1. Place the motorcycle on level ground.
2. Cover the front fender to protect the finish.
3. Remove the front exhaust pipe as described in Chapter Four.
4. Remove the front fairing lower panel assembly as described in the Chapter Seventeen.
5. Place a drain pan under the oil cooler assembly.
6. Remove the locknut and washer securing the oil cooler and cover assembly to the mounting bracket.
7. Carefully move the assembly forward, and then use side-cutting pliers to cut the ties securing the assembly to both oil hoses.
8. Remove the original hose clamps with pliers. Then, label and disconnect the hoses from the oil cooler. Plug the end of the hoses to prevent the entry of debris.
9. Remove the oil cooler assembly and drain any residual oil from the oil cooler.
10. If necessary, carefully separate the cover from the oil cooler. The cover is held in place with adhesive tape.
11. Install by reversing the removal steps. Note the following:
    a. Connect the oil filter mount rear hose to the lower fitting on the oil cooler and the front hose to the upper hose fitting.
    b. Install *new* hose clamps securing the oil hoses to the oil cooler. Use hose clamp pliers to crimp the *new* hose clamps in place if using original style of clamps.
    c. Tighten the oil cooler mounting locknuts to 80-110 in.-lb. (9.0-12.4 N•m).
    d. Check engine oil level and add additional oil to the correct level as described in Chapter Three.
    e. Start the engine and check for oil leaks.

Oil Filter Mount and Hoses

Removal

1. Remove the oil cooler and cover assembly as described in this section.
2. Remove the oil filter as described in Chapter Three.
3. Remove the rubber boot and disconnect the electrical connector from the oil pressure switch.
4. Use a 1-1/16 in. open-end crowfoot wrench and unscrew the oil pressure switch from the engine.
5. If the oil filter adapter is going to be replaced, unscrew it from the mount at this time.
6. Remove the original hose clamps with pliers. Then, label and remove the oil hoses connected to the oil filter mount.
7. If necessary, loosen but do not remove the thermostat plug.
8. Bend the locking tabs away from the mounting bolts.
9. Remove the two mounting bolts, lock plate and washers securing the oil filter mount to the crankcase.
10. Remove the center mounting bolt and washer and remove the oil filter mount. Remove the O-rings from oil filter mount and discard them.

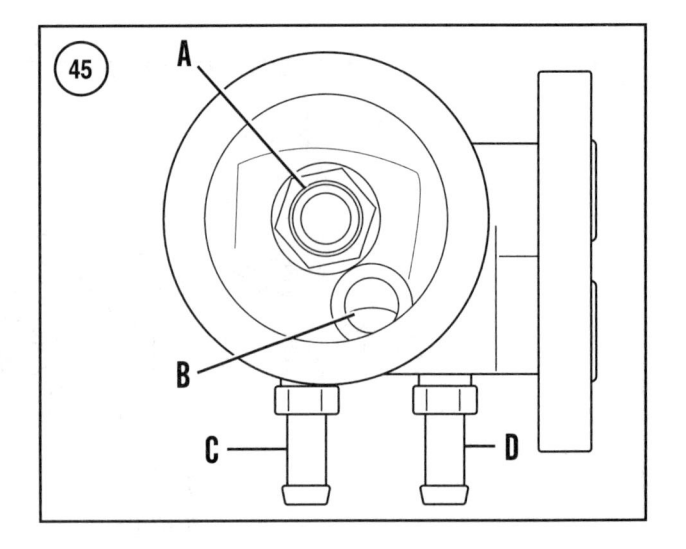

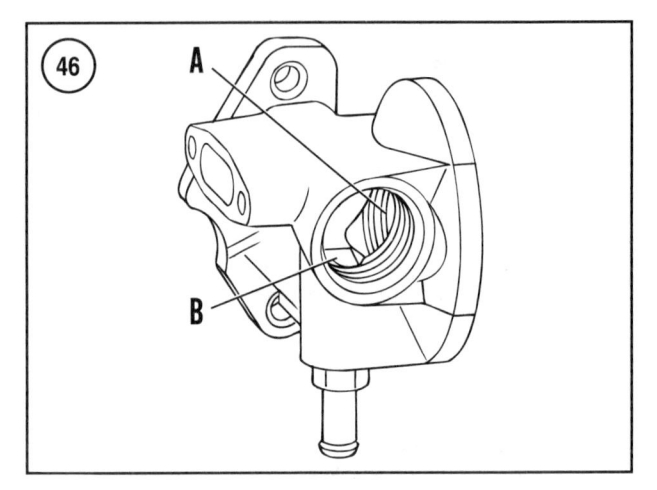

Installation

1. Install *new* O-ring seals (**Figure 41**) onto the filter mount.
2. On the exterior of the mount, place flat washers in the top and bottom recessed bolt holes.
3. Align the lockplate bolt holes with the two flat washers.
4. Insert the two bolts through the lockplate, the two flat washers and the mounting flange.
5. Apply Loctite Threadlocker 246 (red) to the threads of the bolts prior to installation.
6. Install the oil filter mount, lockplate and washers assembly onto the crankcase. Carefully install the two bolts into the crankcase and finger-tighten them.
7. Install the remaining center mounting bolt and washer and finger-tighten it at this time.
8. Starting at the top bolt, alternately tighten the three mounting bolts to 12-16 ft.-lb. (16.3-21.7 N•m).
9. Install *new* clamps onto the hoses and install the hoses onto the mount. Tighten the hose clamps securely. Use hose clamp pliers to crimp the *new* hose clamps in place if using original style of clamps.
10. Bend the locking tabs against the top and bottom mounting bolts.

ENGINE LOWER END

47

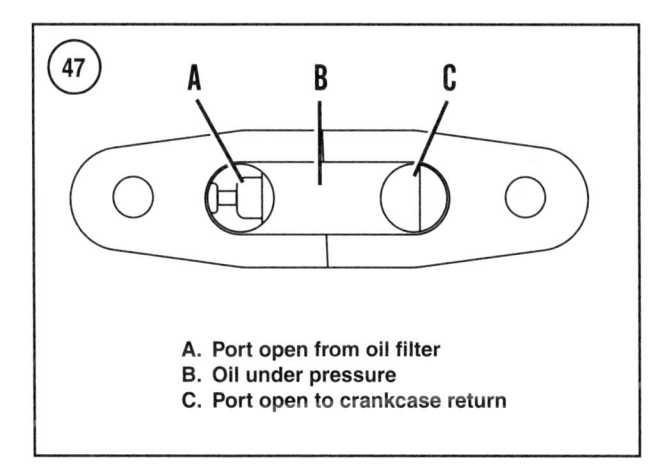

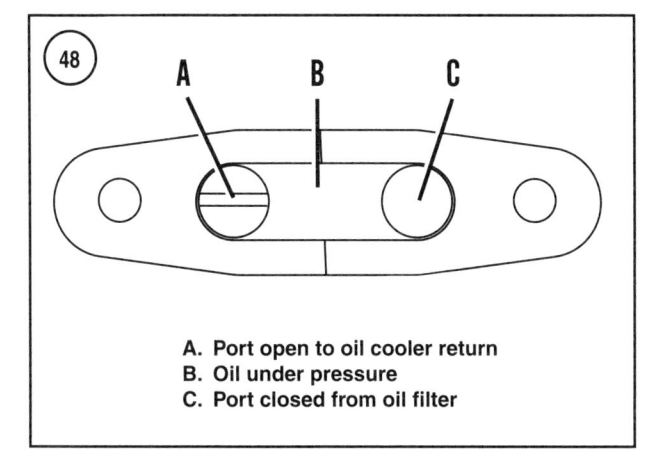

A. Port open from oil filter
B. Oil under pressure
C. Port open to crankcase return

48

A. Port open to oil cooler return
B. Oil under pressure
C. Port closed from oil filter

11. If the oil filter adapter (A, **Figure 45**) was removed, install it as follows:
   a. Remove all old threadlock reside from the adapter and the mount.
   b. Apply a medium-strength threadlock to the adapter.
   c. Install it into the mount and tighten to 12-16 ft.-lb. (16.3-21.7 N•m).
12. Apply Loctite Thread sealant to the oil pressure switch and install the switch. Use a 1-1/16 in. open-end crowfoot wench and tighten the oil pressure switch to 96-144 in.-lb. (10.9-16.3 N•m).
13. Install the electrical connector onto the oil pressure switch and rubber boot.
14. Install the oil filter as described in Chapter Three.
15. Install the oil cooler and cover assembly as described in this section.
16. Install the front exhaust pipe as described in Chapter Four.
17. Start the engine and check for oil leaks.

Inspection

1. If still in place, remove the O-rings from the oil filter mount.
2. Remove the screws securing the transfer passage cover. Remove the cover and gasket from the mount. Discard the gasket.
3. Thoroughly clean the oil filter mount in solvent and dry with compressed air.
4. At the oil filter mount, inspect the oil passageways to the oil filter (B, **Figure 45**), from the oil filter (A, **Figure 46**) and to the oil cooler (B). Make sure there is no residual oil sludge, especially in the thermostat area.
5. If necessary, unscrew the straight, barbed oil supply hose (C, **Figure 45**) and oil return hose (D) fittings from the mount.
6. Install a *new* gasket on the transfer passage cover, and then install the cover and screws. Tighten the screws to 90-120 in.-lb. (10.2-13.6 N•m).
7. Apply pipe sealant or Teflon tape to the oil hose straight barbed fittings. Install the fittings and tighten securely.

Thermostat Test Procedure

When the engine is cool, the thermostat is in its closed position as shown in **Figure 47**. The spring holds the piston over the return passageway from the oil cooler, blocking off the oil flow to the crankcase.

When the engine warms, the thermostat moves to the open position as shown in **Figure 48**. This allows the oil to flow from the oil cooler to the crankcase.

NOTE
This test procedure requires the use of an infrared thermometer in order to test the oil temperature at both the oil pan and at the oil cooler while the engine is operating.

1. Ride the motorcycle a short distance to achieve normal operating temperature. Shut off the engine.
2. Remove the lower fairing assemblies on both sides as described in Chapter Seventeen.
3. Start the engine and let it idle. Aim the thermometer at the engine oil pan and note the reading.
4. Aim the thermometer at the oil cooler and note the reading.
5. Shut off the engine.
6. The thermostat may be stuck open if the oil cooler temperature is the same as the oil pan temperature and both are below 180°F (82°C).
7. The thermostat is operating correctly if the oil cooler temperature is below 180°F (82°C), and lower than the oil pan temperature.
8. The thermostat is stuck closed if the oil pan temperature exceeds 210°F (99°C) and the oil cooler is well below this temperature.
9. If the temperatures are incorrect, then test the plunger as describeed in this section.
10. Allow the engine to cool to room temperature, and remove the thermostat assembly from the oil filter mount as described in the following procedure.
11. Test the plunger operation as follows:

NOTE
Do not allow the thermometer or the plunger to touch the sides or bottom of the pan or a false reading will result.

OIL COOLER THERMOSTAT

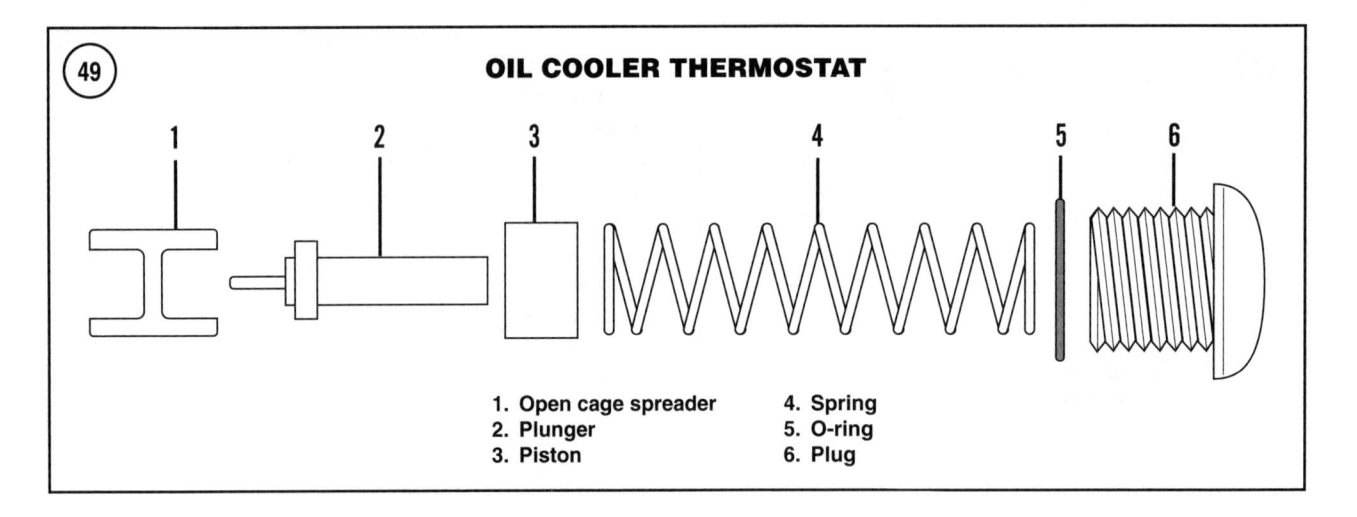

49

1. Open cage spreader
2. Plunger
3. Piston
4. Spring
5. O-ring
6. Plug

a. Suspend the plunger in a container of water and place a thermometer in the pan of water. Use a thermometer that is rated higher than the test temperature.
b. With the water at room temperature, verify that the plunger is not extended.
c. Gradually heat the water and continue to gently stir the water until it reaches the *Start To Open* temperature of 180°F (82°C). Verify that the plunger starts to extend.
d. Continue to heat the water past the *Start To Open* temperature to the *Full Open* temperature of 210°F (99°C). Verify that the plunger is fully extended.
e. If the plunger does not extend as specified, replace the thermostat assembly as described in this section.

12. Install the lower fairing assemblies as described in Chapter Seventeen.

Thermostat Replacement

Refer to **Figure 49**.
1. Place the motorcycle on level ground.
2. Remove the lower fairing assemblies on both sides as described in Chapter Seventeen.
3. The engine must be at room temperature.
4. Place several shop cloths under the thermostat plug to catch the residual oil that will drain out.
5. Use a ball-end Allen wrench and remove the plug from the thermostat.
6. Use needlenose pliers and remove the spring and the plunger assembly from the port in the oil filter mount.
7. Use a pick and remove the open cage spreader from the receptacle.
8. Clean the thermostat housing receptacle in the oil filter mount with a lint-free shop cloth and solvent, and wipe dry.
9. Insert the open cage spreader part way into the receptacle.
10. Install the plunger into piston.
11. Position the pointed end of the plunger onto the open cage spreader. Slowly push the plunger/piston assembly and the open cage spreader into the port until they bottom.
12. Install the spring onto the piston.

13. Install a *new* O-ring onto the plug and install the plug. Slowly tighten the plug to 15-20 ft.-lb. (20.3-27.1 N•m).
14. Install the lower fairing assemblies on both sides as described in Chapter Seventeen.

OIL COOLER, OIL FILTER MOUNT AND THERMOSTAT (2007-2009 SCREAMIN' EAGLE MODELS)

The oil cooler and oil filter mount are located on the front of the crankcase and can be removed with the engine in the frame.

NOTE
The original equipment hose clamps will be damaged when they are removed. A quality screw-type hose clamp can be used in place of the original clamp. The original equipment hose clamps must be installed using JIMS hose clamp pincer tool (part No. 1171).

Oil Cooler and Cover Removal/Installation

Refer to **Figure 50**.
1. Place the motorcycle on level ground.
2. Cover the front fender to protect the finish.
3. Remove the front exhaust pipe as described in Chapter Four.
4. Remove the left side front fairing lower panel assembly as described in Chapter Seventeen.
5. Place a drain pan under the oil cooler assembly.
6. Remove the flanged locknut(s) and washer(s) securing the oil cooler and cover assembly to the mounting bracket.
7. Carefully move the assembly forward and remove the cover.
8. Use side-cutting pliers to cut the ties securing both oil hoses to the cooler.
9. Remove the original hose clamps with pliers. Then, label and disconnect the hoses from the oil cooler adapter. Plug the end of the hoses to prevent the entry of debris.

ENGINE LOWER END

50 — OIL COOLER (2007-2009 SCREAMIN' EAGLE MODELS)

1. Oil cooler adapter
2. Oil filter adapter
3. Hose clamp
4. Return hose
5. Supply hose
6. Fitting hose
7. Oil cooler (2007-2008 models)
8. Oil cooler (2009 models)
9. Mounting bracket
10. Flange locknut
11. Cover

51 — OIL COOLER ADAPTER (2007-2009 SCREAMIN' EAGLE MODELS)

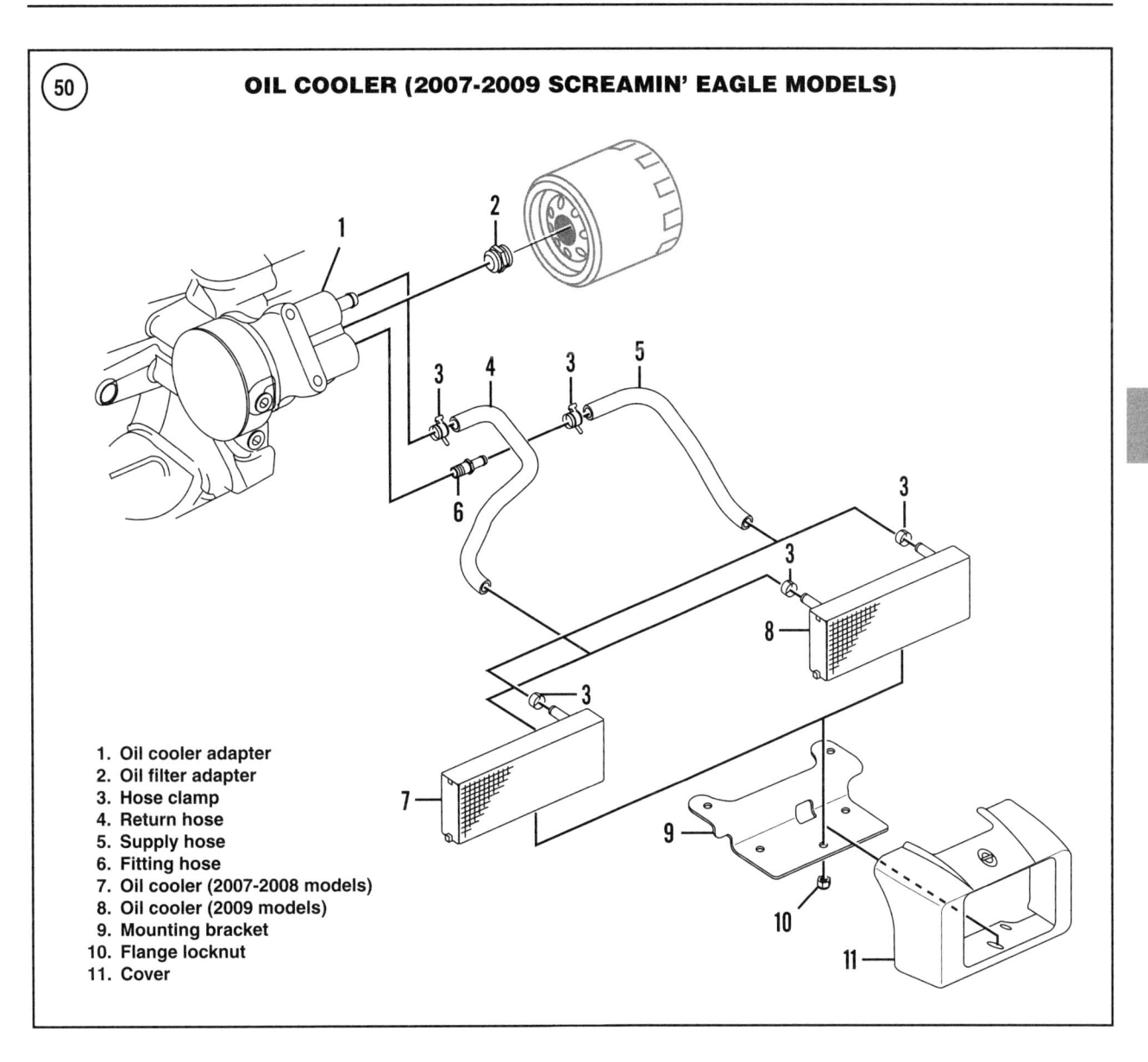

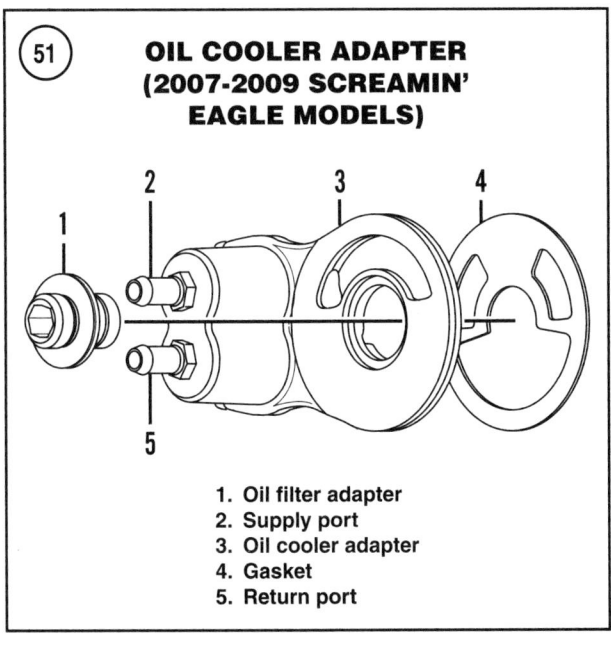

1. Oil filter adapter
2. Supply port
3. Oil cooler adapter
4. Gasket
5. Return port

10. Remove the oil cooler and drain any residual oil from the oil cooler.

11. If necessary, use side-cutting pliers cut the ties securing both oil hoses to the oil cooler adapter. Disconnect the hoses and drain any residual oil.

12. Install by reversing the removal steps. Note the following:
   a. Install *new* hose clamps securing the oil hoses to the oil cooler and adapter. Use hose clamp pliers to crimp the *new* hose clamps in place if using original style clamps.
   b. Tighten the oil cooler mounting flange locknuts to 70-100 in.-lb. (7.9-11.3 N•m).
   c. Check engine oil level and add additional oil to the correct level as described in Chapter Three.
   d. Start the engine and check for oil leaks.

Oil Cooler Adapter
Removal/Inspection/Installation

Refer to **Figure 51**.

CHAPTER FIVE

CAMSHAFTS AND COVER (2006 MODELS)

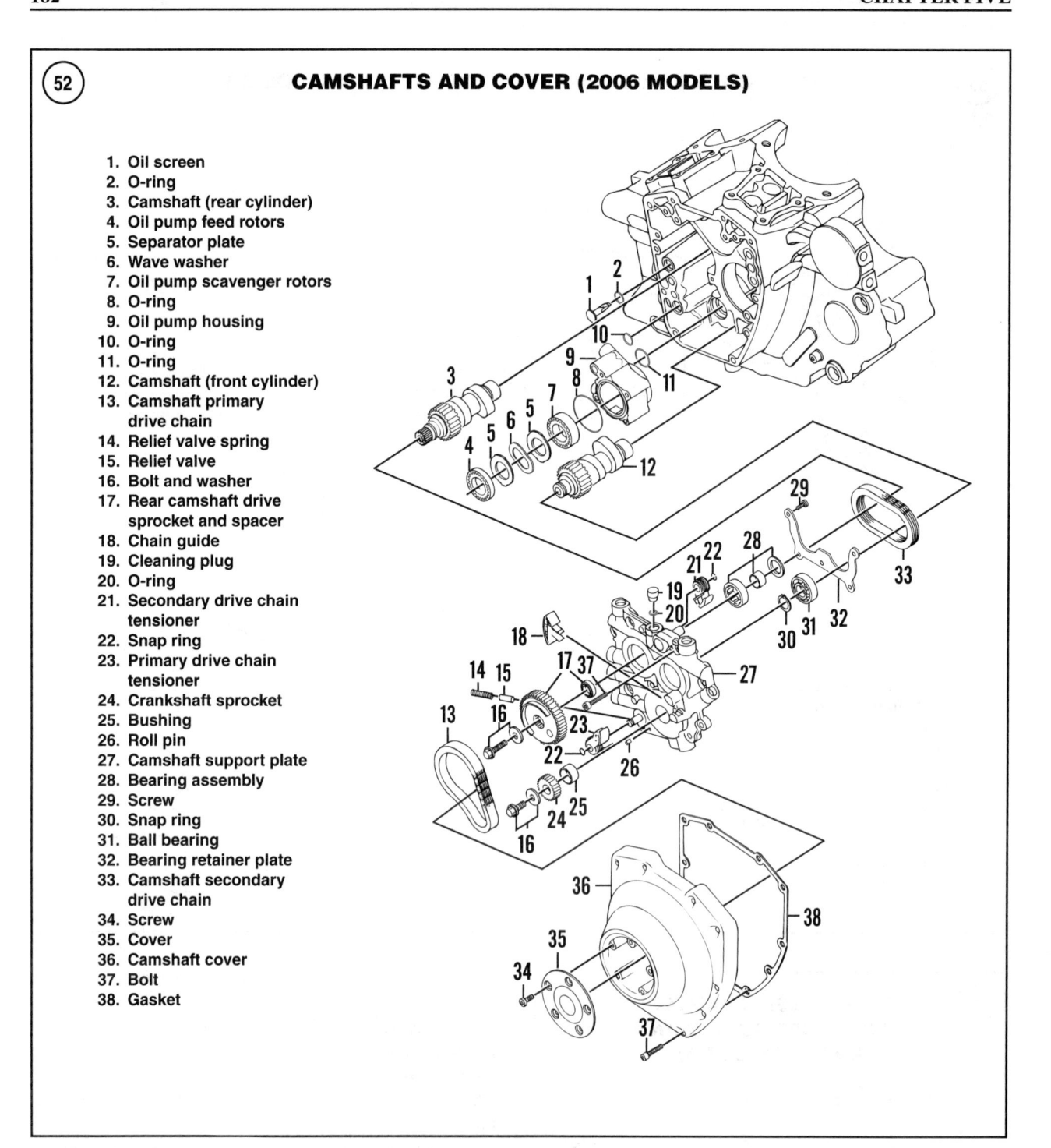

1. Oil screen
2. O-ring
3. Camshaft (rear cylinder)
4. Oil pump feed rotors
5. Separator plate
6. Wave washer
7. Oil pump scavenger rotors
8. O-ring
9. Oil pump housing
10. O-ring
11. O-ring
12. Camshaft (front cylinder)
13. Camshaft primary drive chain
14. Relief valve spring
15. Relief valve
16. Bolt and washer
17. Rear camshaft drive sprocket and spacer
18. Chain guide
19. Cleaning plug
20. O-ring
21. Secondary drive chain tensioner
22. Snap ring
23. Primary drive chain tensioner
24. Crankshaft sprocket
25. Bushing
26. Roll pin
27. Camshaft support plate
28. Bearing assembly
29. Screw
30. Snap ring
31. Ball bearing
32. Bearing retainer plate
33. Camshaft secondary drive chain
34. Screw
35. Cover
36. Camshaft cover
37. Bolt
38. Gasket

1. Remove the oil filter as described in Chapter Three.
2. Remove the hoses from the oil cooler adapter as described in this section.
3. Unscrew and remove the oil filter adapter from the crankcase.
4. Remove the oil cooler adapter and gasket from the crankcase.
5. Inspect the gasket, and replace if damaged or there is evidence of oil leaks.
6. Thoroughly clean the oil cooler adapter in solvent and dry with compressed air, especially through the oil hose fitting ports.
7. Clean off all gasket residue from the gasket surface on the oil cooler adapter and crankcase.
8. Install a *new* gasket onto the oil cooler adapter, if necessary.
9. Align the positioning bosses on the oil cooler adapter to those on the crankcase mounting surface, and install the oil cooler adapter and gasket onto the crankcase. Make sure it is positioned correctly; readjust if necessary.
10. Apply Loctite Threadlocker 246 (red) to the threads of the oil filter adapter prior to installation.
11. Make sure the oil cooler adapter is positioned correctly and hold it in place.

ENGINE LOWER END

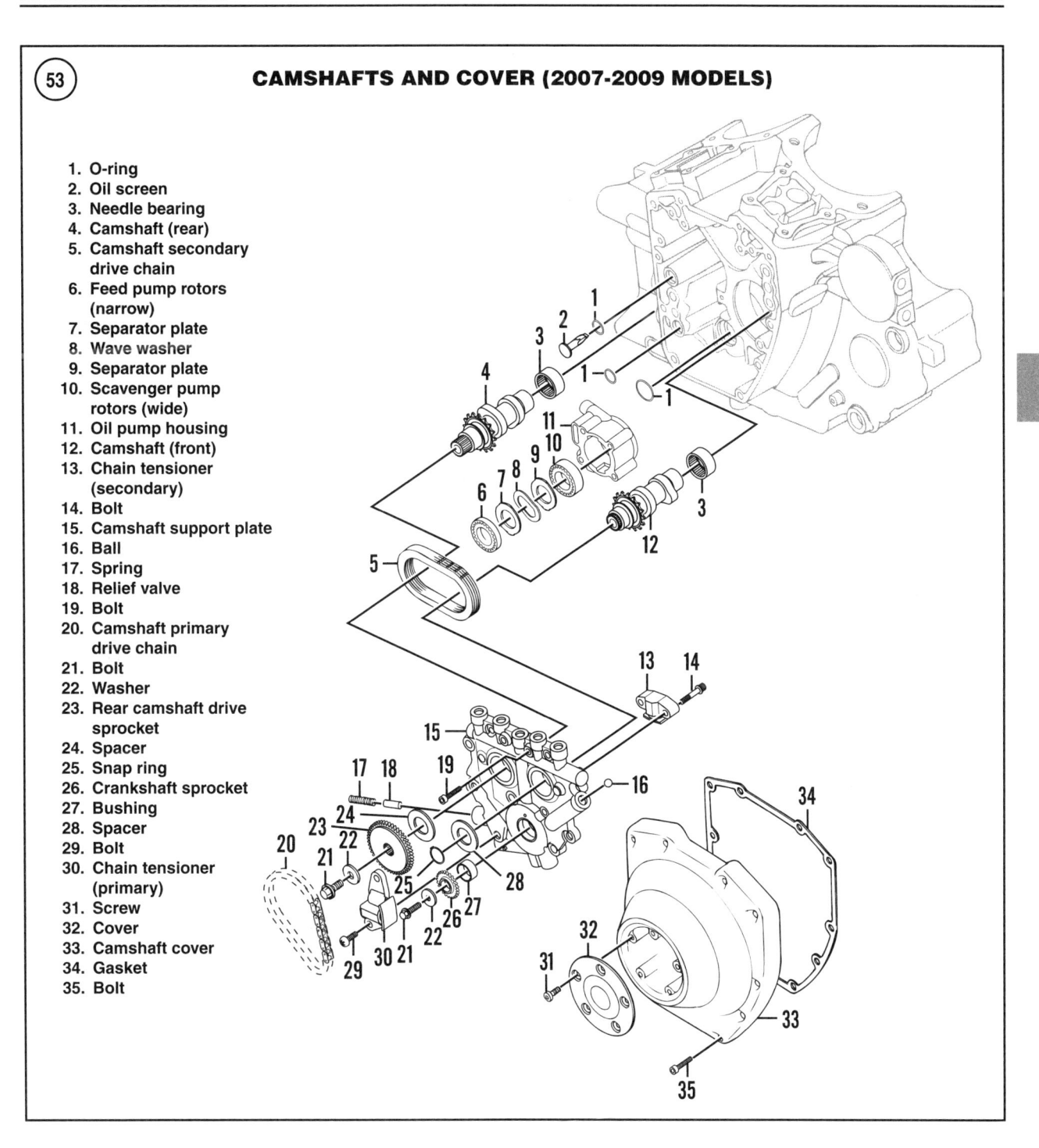

53 CAMSHAFTS AND COVER (2007-2009 MODELS)

1. O-ring
2. Oil screen
3. Needle bearing
4. Camshaft (rear)
5. Camshaft secondary drive chain
6. Feed pump rotors (narrow)
7. Separator plate
8. Wave washer
9. Separator plate
10. Scavenger pump rotors (wide)
11. Oil pump housing
12. Camshaft (front)
13. Chain tensioner (secondary)
14. Bolt
15. Camshaft support plate
16. Ball
17. Spring
18. Relief valve
19. Bolt
20. Camshaft primary drive chain
21. Bolt
22. Washer
23. Rear camshaft drive sprocket
24. Spacer
25. Snap ring
26. Crankshaft sprocket
27. Bushing
28. Spacer
29. Bolt
30. Chain tensioner (primary)
31. Screw
32. Cover
33. Camshaft cover
34. Gasket
35. Bolt

CAUTION
The threaded area of the oil filter adapter is small and easily damaged.

12. Position the oil filter adapter with the Allen bolt receptacle facing out and carefully install the adapter into the crankcase. Tighten the oil filter adapter to 18-22 ft.-lb. (24.4-27.3 N•m).
13. Attach the hoses to the oil cooler adapter as described in this section.
14. Install a *new* oil filter as described in Chapter Three.
15. Check engine oil level and add additional oil to the correct level as described in Chapter Three.
16. Start the engine and check for oil leaks.

CAMSHAFT SUPPORT PLATE

On 2006 models, a camshaft and crankshaft sprocket lock (JIMS part No. 1285 or H-D part No. HD-42314), and a camshaft chain tensioner tool (JIMS part No. 1283 or H-D part No. HD-42313), or equivalent tools, are required to remove and install the camshaft support plate. On 2007-2009 models, a camshaft locking tool (JIMS part No. 994 or H-D part No. HD-47941), or an equivalent, is needed.

Refer to **Figure 52** or **Figure 53**.

CHAPTER FIVE

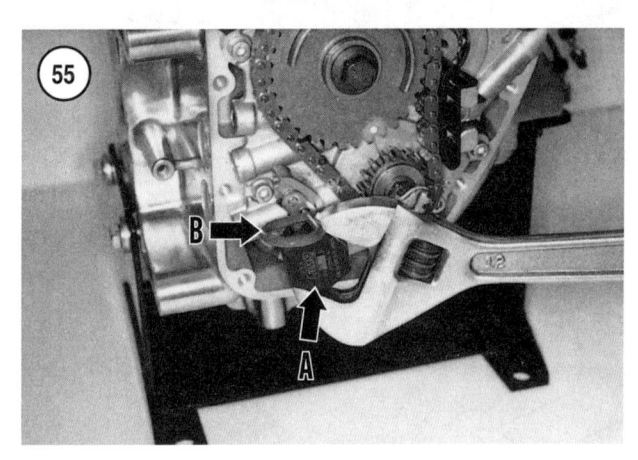

Removal

1. Remove the exhaust system as described in Chapter Four.
2. Drain the engine oil as described in Chapter Three.
3. Remove the rocker arm support plate, pushrods, pushrod covers and valve lifters as described in *Rocker Arms, Pushrods, and Valve Lifters* (Chapter Four).
4. Using a crossing pattern, evenly loosen, and then remove the camshaft cover bolts and their captive washers. Remove the cover (**Figure 54**, typical) and its gasket. Discard the gasket.
5. To ensure the camshaft primary drive chain is reinstalled with its original direction of travel, mark one of the link plates with a permanent marking pen or a scribe.
6A. On 2006 models, perform the following:
   a. Install the camshaft chain tensioner tool (A, **Figure 55**) onto the primary chain tensioner.
   b. Using a wrench, rotate the tool *counterclockwise* until the tensioner hole aligns with the hole in the support plate. Insert the hold pin (B, **Figure 55**) through the holes until the pin bottoms.
   c. Remove the wrench and tensioner tool.
   d. Install and mesh the camshaft and crankshaft sprocket locking tool (**Figure 56**) between the camshaft and crankshaft sprockets.
6B. On 2007-2009 models, perform the following:

ENGINE LOWER END

CAUTION
*The rear camshaft sprocket bolt comes from the manufactuer secured with threadlock. Attempt to loosen the bolt with an impact driver or air impact wrench. If this is not successful, evenly heat the bolt head with a propane torch, or high temperature heat gun. Use caution, as excessive heat may damage the tensioner assembly. Do **not** use excessive force to remove the bolt. If necessary, have a dealership remove the bolt.*

8. Loosen the rear camshaft sprocket bolt (C, **Figure 58**, typical).
9. Remove the sprocket locking tool (A, **Figure 58**).
10. Remove camshaft sprocket bolt (C, **Figure 58**) and crankshaft sprocket bolt (B) along with their washers.

NOTE
If it is difficult to loosen either sprocket from its respective shaft, use a small pry bar to gently loosen the sprocket from its shaft.

11. Remove the rear camshaft drive sprocket (A, **Figure 59**), the crankshaft sprocket (B), and the primary camshaft drive chain (C) as an assembly. Pull the assembly straight off the shafts.
12. Remove the sprocket spacer (**Figure 60**) from the rear camshaft.
13. On 2006 models, squeeze the tabs and remove the camshaft chain guide (**Figure 61**).
14. Remove the camshaft support plate bolts in the following sequence:
    a. Evenly loosen the four center camshaft support plate bolts in the sequence shown in **Figure 62**, and then remove the bolts.
    b. Evenly loosen the remaining six perimeter camshaft support plate bolts in the order shown in **Figure 63**, and then remove the bolts.
15. Withdraw the camshaft support plate assembly from the crankcase. If necessary, carefully pry the plate loose

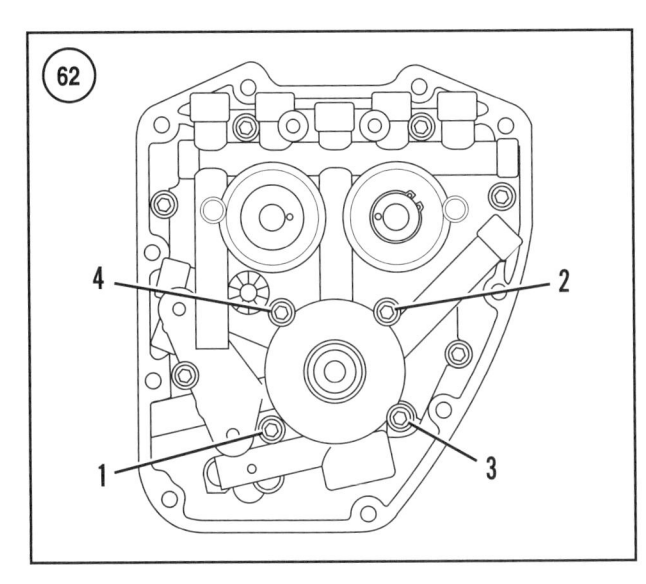

a. Insert a wire into the hole (A, **Figure 57**) in the primary chain tensioner to keep the tensioner parts assembled.
b. Remove the primary chain tensioner bolts (B, **Figure 57**), and remove the tensioner (C).
c. Install the camshaft locking tool (A, **Figure 58**, typical) so it engages the teeth of the rear camshaft sprocket and the crankshaft sprocket.

7. Loosen the crankshaft sprocket bolt (B, **Figure 58**, typical).

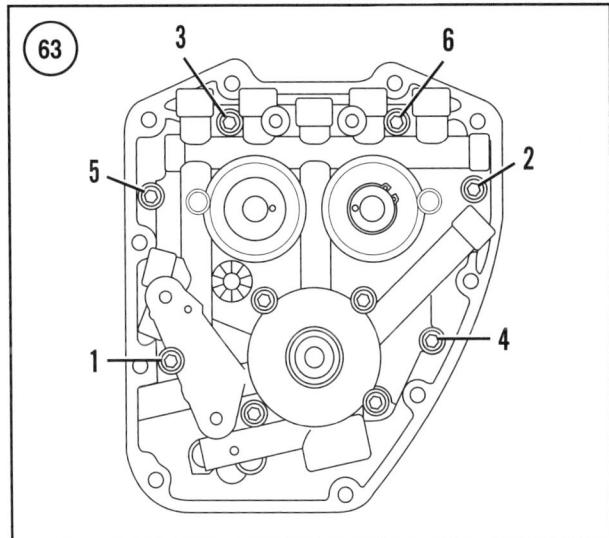

186

from the crankcase in the areas where the dowels are located (**Figure 64**).

16. On 2006 models, remove the O-ring (A, **Figure 65**) from the oil pump assembly.

17. Remove the lower O-ring (B, **Figure 65**) from the left crankcase flange.

18. Remove the upper O-ring (C, **Figure 65**) and the oil screen (**Figure 66**) behind the O-ring.

19. Remove the dowels (D, **Figure 65**).

20. If necessary, disassemble and remove the camshafts as described in this section.

Installation

NOTE
*On 2006 models, release the tension on the camshaft secondary chain tensioner in order to install the camshaft inboard journals into the crankcase bearings (E, **Figure 65**). If the tension is not released, the inner ends of the camshafts will be pulled together and out of alignment with the bearings, making installation difficult, if not impossible.*

1. On 2006 models, release the tension on the secondary chain tensioner as follows:
   a. Install the camshaft chain tensioner tool onto the camshaft secondary chain tensioner.
   b. Use a wrench to rotate the tool (**Figure 67**) *counterclockwise*, and insert the hold pin (A, **Figure 68**) through the hole in the outer surface of the support plate and through the hole in the tensioner. Push the hold pin in until it bottoms.
   c. Remove the wrench and tensioner tool.

2. Press on the oil pump assembly to make sure it is correctly seated against the crankcase.

3. On 2006 models, install a *new* O-ring (A, **Figure 65**) onto the oil pump assembly. On all models, install a *new* O-ring (B, **Figure 65**) into the left crankcase flange. Apply a light coat of clean engine oil to the O-rings.

4. Install the oil screen (**Figure 66**) and a *new* O-ring (C, **Figure 65**). Apply a light coat of clean engine oil to the O-ring.

ENGINE LOWER END

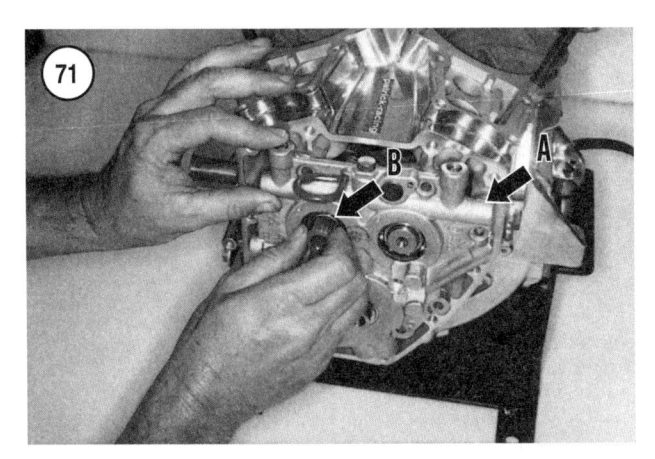

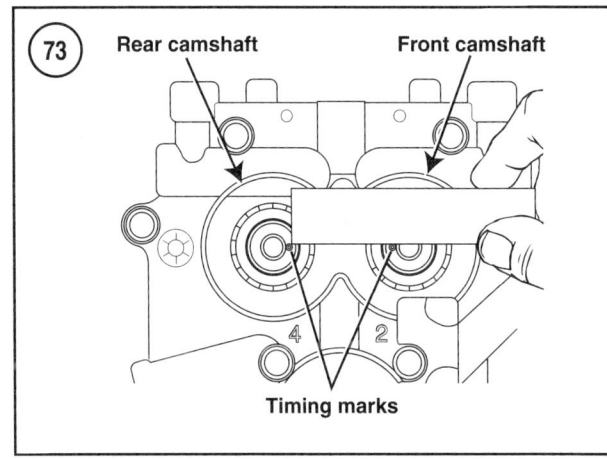

5. Lubricate the camshaft needle bearings (**Figure 69**) in the crankcase and the camshaft journals (B, **Figure 68**) with clean engine oil.

6. Make sure the timing marks (**Figure 70**) on the camshafts align with each other. If the marks are not aligned, reposition the camshafts before installing the assembly into the crankcase.

7. If removed, install the two locating dowels (D, **Figure 65**) onto the crankcase.

CAUTION
Do not force the camshaft support plate assembly into the crankcase. During installation the camshaft ends may not be correctly aligned with the needle bearings. If force is applied, the needle bearing(s) will be damaged.

8. Slowly install the camshaft support plate assembly (A, **Figure 71**) into the crankcase. Guide the camshaft ends into the crankcase needle bearings (**Figure 69**). If necessary, slightly rotate and/or wiggle the end of the rear cylinder camshaft (B, **Figure 71**) to assist in the alignment.

CAUTION
When properly aligned, the camshaft support plate assembly fits snugly against the crankcase mating surface. If they do not meet correctly, do not attempt to pull the parts together with the mounting bolts. Remove the camshaft support plate assembly and determine the cause of the interference.

9. Push the camshaft support plate assembly into the crankcase until it engages the dowels and bottoms against the crankcase mating surface.

10. Make sure the timing marks (**Figure 72**) on each camshaft are still aligned. If they are not aligned (**Figure 73**), correct the problem at this time.

11. Tighten the six perimeter camshaft support plate bolts in the following sequence:
    a. Install and finger-tighten the six Allen bolts.
    b. Using the sequence shown in **Figure 63**, tighten the six bolts to 90-120 in.-lb. (10.2-13.6 N•m).

12. Tighten the four center camshaft support plate bolts in the following sequence:
    a. Loosely install the four bolts around the oil pump housing. Evenly tighten the bolts until they just contact the support plate, and then back them out 1/4 turn.
    b. Rotate the engine until the oil pump finds its neutral center with no load on it.
    c. Tighten bolts 1 and 2 until they are snug against the support plate.
    d. Tighten bolts 3 and 4 until each is snug against the support plate.
    e. Using the sequence shown in **Figure 62**, tighten the bolts to 40-45 in.-lb. (4.5-5.1 N•m). Then, tighten them again, using the same sequence, to 90-120 in.-lb. (10.2-13.6 N•m).
13. Check the outer edge of the support plate to make sure it is evenly seated against the crankcase mating surface.
14. On 2006 models, perform the following:
    a. Install an angled pick (A, **Figure 74**) into the crankcase opening, and press it against the secondary camshaft chain tensioner shoe. *Slowly* release the hold pin (B, **Figure 74**) and allow the tensioner shoe to gradually contact the chain surface. If it is released too quickly, the shoe surface will slam against the chain and be damaged.
    b. Squeeze the camshaft chain guide tabs and install it (**Figure 61**) onto the two posts.

CAUTION
Alignment of parts is not necessary if the original camshaft support plate, both camshafts, rear camshaft sprocket, crankshaft drive sprocket and the crankshaft assembly are reused. If any of these components have been replaced, performing the alignment procedure is necessary to ensure correct alignment between the rear camshaft sprocket and the crankshaft drive sprocket. If the alignment is incorrect, the primary drive chain and both sprockets will bind and cause premature wear.

15A. If new parts have been installed, perform the alignment procedure described in *Rear Camshaft Sprocket and Crankshaft Drive Sprocket Alignment* (this section) now.
15B. If the original parts are being re-installed, continue with installation procedure.
16. On 2006 models, relieve the tension on the camshaft primary drive chain as follows:
    a. Install the camshaft chain tensioner tool (**Figure 75**) onto the primary chain tensioner.
    b. Use a wrench (A, **Figure 76**), rotate the tool *counterclockwise* and insert the hold pin (B) through the hole in the tensioner and into the hole in the support plate. Push the hold pin in until it bottoms.
    c. Remove the wrench and tensioner tool from the tensioner.

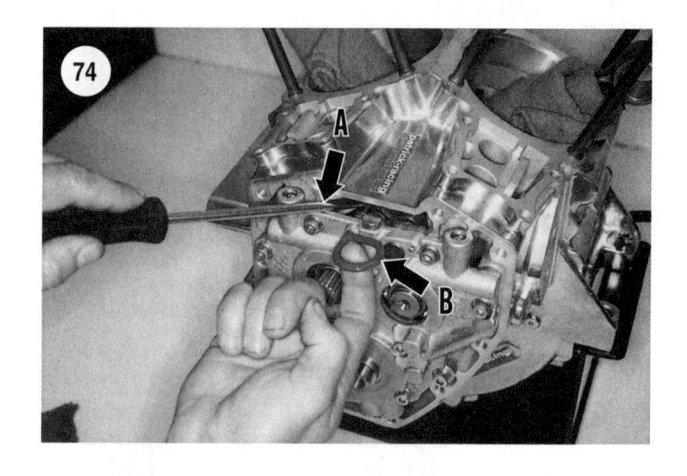

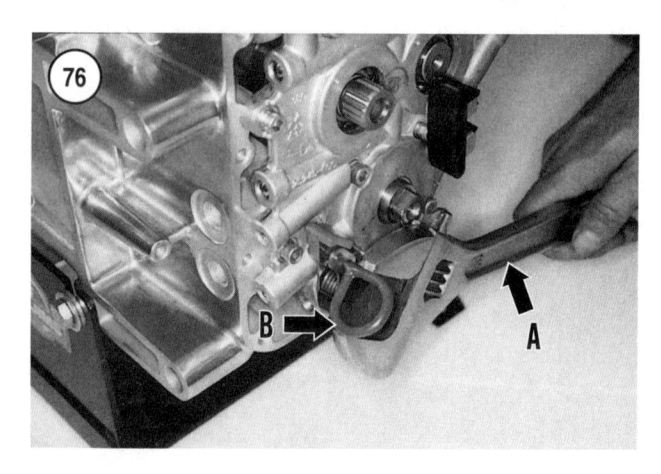

ENGINE LOWER END

18. Assemble the rear camshaft sprocket, the crankshaft drive sprocket and the primary drive chain as an assembly. Align the index mark on both sprockets so they face each other as shown in **Figure 77**.

19. Install the rear camshaft drive sprocket (A, **Figure 59**), the crankshaft sprocket (B), and the primary camshaft drive chain (C) as an assembly. Align the camshaft sprocket key with the keyway on the rear camshaft, align the flat on the crankshaft sprocket with the flat on the crankshaft (A, **Figure 78**), and seat each sprocket on its shaft. Check the alignment (**Figure 79**) of the index mark on both sprockets. They must still face each other as shown in B, **Figure 78** (2006 models) or **Figure 79** (2007-2009 models). Remove the chain/sprocket assembly and realign the sprocket index marks as necessary to achieve the correct alignment.

20. Install *new* crankshaft and rear-camshaft sprocket bolts as follows:
   a. Apply clean engine oil beneath the flange of the sprocket bolts.

   NOTE
   If new sprocket bolts are unavailable, oil the flange of the bolts and apply a small amount of Loctite Threadlocker 262 (red) to the threads of each sprocket bolt.

   b. Install the correct flat washer onto each sprocket bolt. The washers are not interchangeable.
   c. Install the rear camshaft sprocket bolt and crankshaft sprocket bolt. Finger-tighten the bolts snugly at this time.

21. Install the camshaft/crankshaft sprocket lock tool (A, **Figure 58**) between the camshaft and crankshaft sprockets.

22. Tighten both sprocket bolts as follows:
   a. Tighten both bolts to 15 ft.-lb. (20.3 N•m).
   b. Loosen both bolts one complete revolution (360°).
   c. Tighten the rear camshaft sprocket bolt (C, **Figure 58**) to 34 ft.-lb. (46.1 N•m).
   d. Tighten the crankshaft sprocket bolt to (B, **Figure 58**) 24 ft.-lb. (32.5 N•m).

23. Remove the sprocket lock tool (A, **Figure 58**).

24A. On 2006 models, place a flat blade screwdriver (A, **Figure 80**) between the primary camshaft drive chain and the tensioner. Slowly release the hold pin (B, **Figure 80**), and then slowly withdraw the screwdriver so the tensioner to gradually contacts the chain surface. If it is released too fast, the shoe surface will slam against the chain and be damaged.

24B. On 2007-2009 models, install the primary chain tensioner (C, **Figure 57**). Tighten the cam chain tensioner mounting bolts (B, **Figure 57**) to 100-120 in.-lbs. (11.3-13.6 N•m). Remove the wire (A, **Figure 57**) from the tensioner.

25. Install a *new* camshaft cover gasket onto the crankcase.

26. Install the camshaft cover (**Figure 81**) onto the crankcase, and then install the cover bolts. Following the sequence shown in **Figure 82**, tighten the camshaft cover bolts to 125-155 in.-lb. (14.1-17.5 N•m).

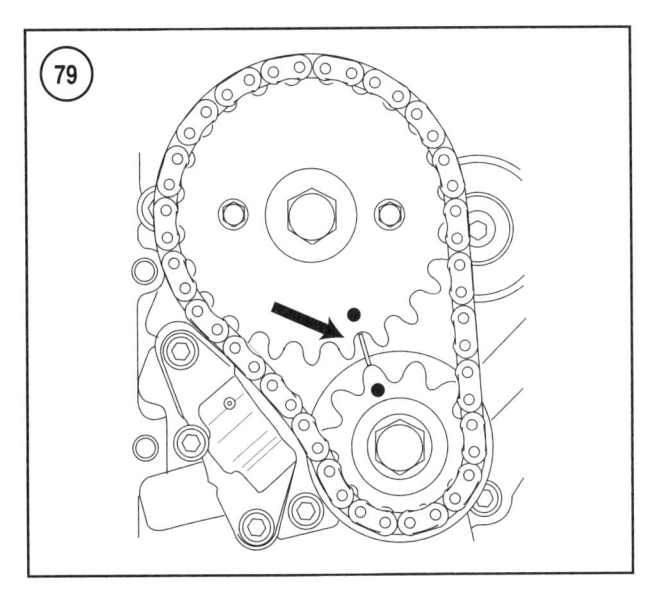

17. Install the sprocket spacer (**Figure 60**) onto the rear camshaft with the manufacturer's marks facing the crankcase.

CAUTION
Refer to the mark made before removal and position the camshaft primary drive chain so it will travel in the original direction. If it is installed incorrectly, the drive chain will wear prematurely.

27. Install the valve lifters, pushrod covers, pushrods, and the rocker arm support plate as described in *Rocker Arms, Pushrods, and Valve Lifters* (Chapter Four).
28. Refill the engine oil as described in Chapter Three.
29. Install the exhaust system as described in Chapter Four.

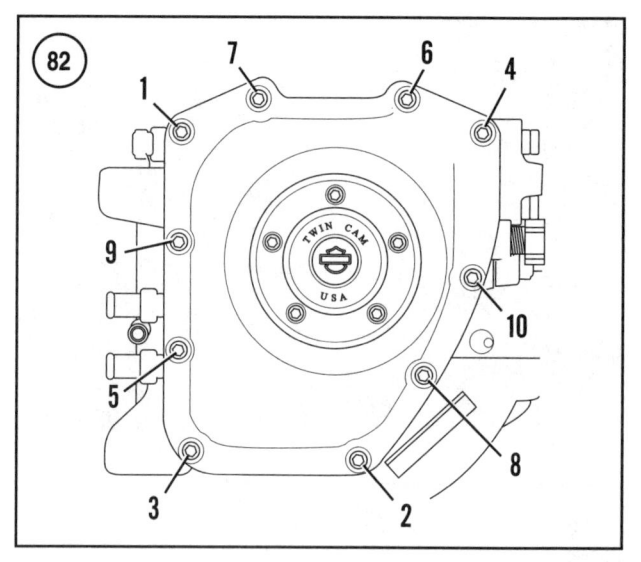

Rear Camshaft Sprocket and Crankshaft Drive Sprocket Alignment

This procedure is required if the camshaft support plate, one or both camshafts, the rear camshaft sprocket, the crankshaft drive sprocket and/or the crankshaft assembly have been replaced.

If alignment between the rear camshaft sprocket and the crankshaft drive sprocket is incorrect, the primary drive chain and both sprockets will bind and cause premature wear.

1. Install the sprocket spacer (**Figure 83**) onto the rear camshaft with the manufacturer's marks facing toward the crankcase.
2. Apply clean engine oil to the camshaft splines and to the rear camshaft sprocket splines.
3. Install the rear camshaft sprocket onto the camshaft. Install the *used* rear camshaft sprocket bolt (A, **Figure 84**) and flat washer. Finger-tighten the bolt at this time.

NOTE
Use a washer with a smaller outside diameter than the original washer installed on the crankshaft sprocket bolt. This creates room for a straightedge to be placed against the flat surface of the crankshaft sprocket face.

4. Install the crankshaft sprocket onto the crankshaft. Install the *used* crankshaft sprocket bolt and a washer (B, **Figure 84**) with a smaller outside diameter than the original washer (see previous note). Finger-tighten the bolt at this time.
5. Install the camshaft/crankshaft sprocket lock (A, **Figure 58**) between the camshaft and crankshaft sprockets.
6. Tighten both crankshaft and rear camshaft sprocket bolts as follows:
   a. Tighten both bolts to 15 ft.-lb. (20.3 N•m).
   b. Loosen both bolts one complete revolution (360°).
   c. Tighten the rear camshaft sprocket bolt (C, **Figure 58**) to 34 ft.-lb. (46.1 N•m).
   d. Tighten the crankshaft sprocket bolt to (B, **Figure 58**) 24 ft.-lb. (32.5 N•m).
   e. Remove the sprocket lock tool (A, **Figure 58**).
7. If the engine was not removed from the engine, install the compensating sprocket (Chapter Six) to pull the crankshaft to the left side.
8. Press the crankshaft and rear camshaft into the crankcase to eliminate any end play.

ENGINE LOWER END

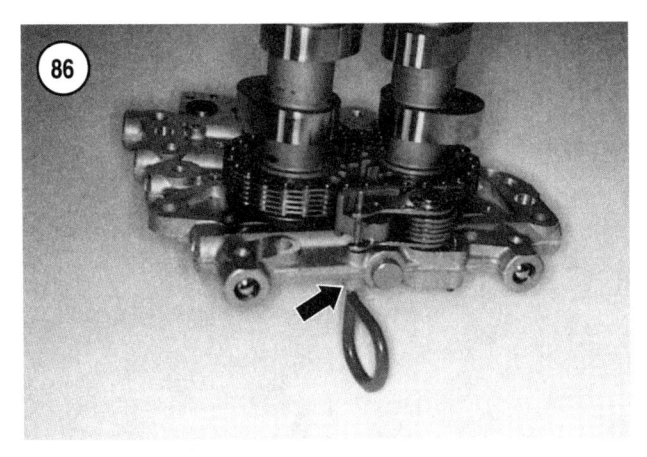

9. Place a straightedge (C, **Figure 84**) against the face of both sprockets.

10. Try to insert a 0.010 in. (0.254mm) feeler gauge (D, **Figure 84**) between the straightedge and the each sprocket face.

11A. If the 0.010 in. (0.254 mm) feeler gauge cannot be inserted at either location, the sprockets are correctly aligned. Remove both sprockets and complete installation of the components as described in *Camshaft Support Plate Installation* (this section).

11B. If a different thickness feeler gauge can be inserted, indicating a height difference other than 0.010 in. (0.254 mm), the rear camshaft spacer must be changed. Continue to insert feeler gauges of different thicknesses until the offset dimension is determined. Record this dimension. It will be used to choose a new spacer.

12. Remove the rear camshaft sprocket bolt, washer and sprocket.

13. Remove the existing sprocket spacer (**Figure 83**) from the rear camshaft. Compare the part number stamped on the spacer with the part numbers in **Table 2** to determine its thickness.

14A. If the crankshaft sprocket sits more than 0.010 in. (0.254 mm) above the rear camshaft sprocket, install the next *thicker* size spacer behind the camshaft sprocket.

14B. If the rear camshaft sprocket sits more than 0.010 in. (0.254 mm) above the crankshaft sprocket, install the next *thinner* size spacer behind the rear camshaft sprocket.

15. Install a new spacer and repeat the measurement process until the sprockets are correctly aligned.

16. After the correct spacer thickness is established, remove the sprockets from the rear camshaft and crankshaft, and complete installation of the components as described in *Camshaft Support Plate Installation* (this section).

Camshaft Removal (2006 Models)

A hydraulic press, camshaft chain tensioner tool (JIMS part No. 1283) and camshaft remover and installer (JIMS part No. 1277), or their equivalents, are required to perform the following procedure.

1. Remove the camshaft support plate as described in this section.
2. Remove the snap ring (**Figure 85**) from the front cylinder camshaft.
3. Release the tension on the camshaft secondary chain tension as follows:
   a. Install the camshaft chain tensioner tool onto the camshaft secondary chain tensioner.
   b. Using a wrench, rotate the tool *counterclockwise* and insert the hold pin (**Figure 86**) through the hole in the outer surface of the support plate and into the hole in the tensioner. Push the hold pin in until it bottoms.
   c. Remove the wrench and tensioner tool.
4. Loosen and remove the bearing retainer plate Torx screws (**Figure 87**), and remove the bearing retainer plate (**Figure 88**).

5. Press the camshafts and secondary drive chain out of the camshaft support plate as follows:
   a. Turn the camshaft support cover face up on two support blocks in a press bed. Make sure the support blocks are tall enough to allow the complete removal of the camshafts from the cover.
   b. Install the cups of the camshaft remover and installer onto the top of the camshafts (**Figure 89**) following the manufacturer's instructions.
   c. Center the press ram over the center of the tool (**Figure 90**).
   d. Slowly press the camshaft assembly out of the support cover.
   e. Remove the assembly, cover and tool from the press bed.
6. To ensure the camshaft secondary drive chain is reinstalled in the same direction of travel, mark one of the link plates (**Figure 91**) on the bearing side with a permanent marking pen or scribe.
7. Remove each camshaft from the secondary drive chain.

Camshaft Installation (2006 Models)

1. Install a new ball bearing and new roller bearing into the camshaft support plate as described in this section.
2. Set the bearing retainer plate (**Figure 88**) into place so the hole in the retainer aligns with the secondary cam chain oiler. Apply Loctite Threadlocker 243 (blue) to the threads

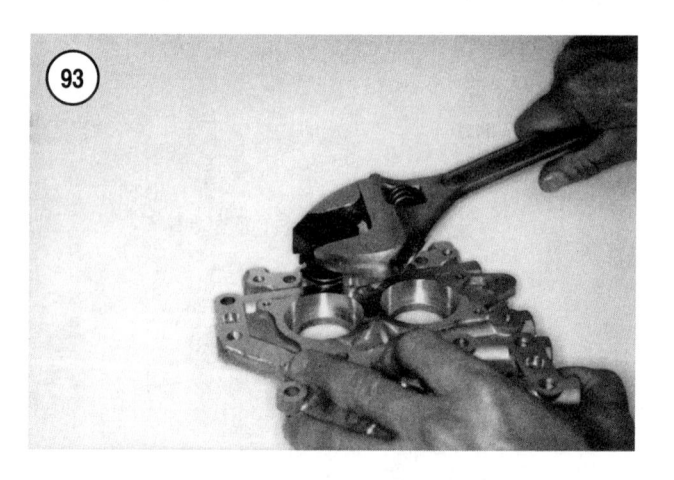

ENGINE LOWER END

95 Rear camshaft / Front camshaft

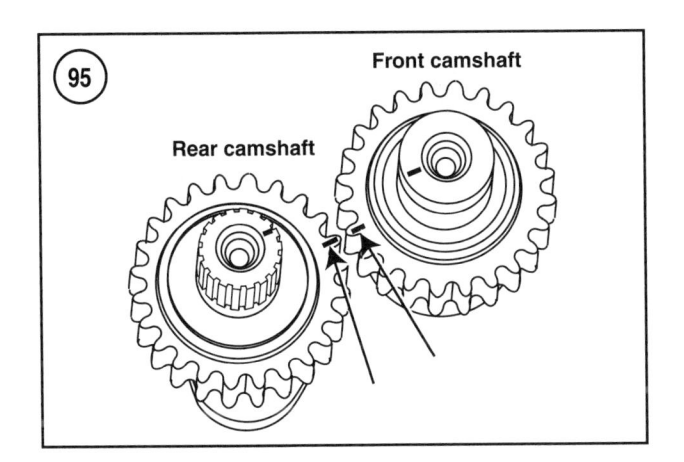

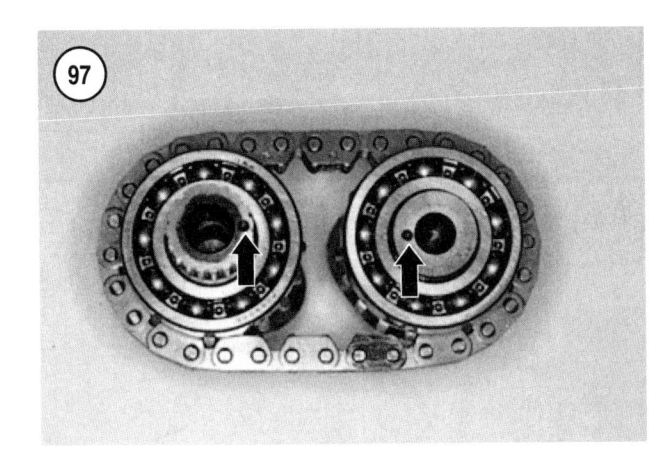

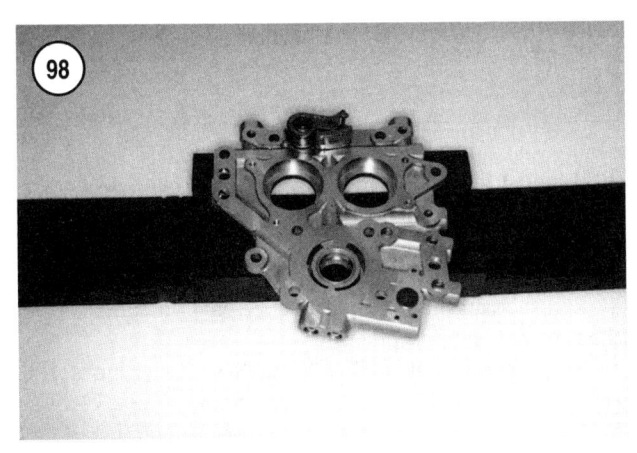

96

97

98

of the retainer plate Torx screws (**Figure 87**), and tighten the bearing retainer plate screws (T20) to 20-30 in.-lb. (2.3-3.4 N•m).

3. Before installing the camshaft assembly into the camshaft support plate, relieve the tension on the secondary chain tensioner as follows:
   a. Install the camshaft chain tensioner tool (**Figure 92**) onto the camshaft secondary chain tensioner.
   b. Using a wrench, rotate the tool *counterclockwise* (**Figure 93**). Insert the hold pin through the hole in the tensioner and into the hole in the support plate. Push the hold pin in until it bottoms (**Figure 94**).
   c. Remove the wrench and tensioner tool from the tensioner.

4. Assemble the camshafts and the secondary drive chain as follows:

NOTE
*On some models, the index marks are lines as shown in **Figure 95**. On others, these marks are dots.*

   a. Locate the index marks (**Figure 95**) on the front of the camshafts. Transfer these marks (**Figure 96**) to the same location on the backside of the sprockets with a permanent marking pen or scribe. These marks will be used for proper alignment of the camshaft as it is pressed into the camshaft support plate.

CAUTION
Refer to the mark made on one of the link plates during disassembly, and position the camshaft secondary drive chain so it travels in the same direction as noted prior to removal. If it is installed incorrectly, the drive chain will wear prematurely.

   b. Position the camshafts so the index marks (**Figure 97**) on the sprockets align with each other.
   c. Position the secondary chain with the marked link plate facing up (**Figure 91**), and install the secondary chain onto both camshafts.
   d. Rotate the camshafts in either direction several times, and check the alignment of the index marks. If necessary, adjust one of the camshafts to attain correct alignment (**Figure 97**).

5. Apply a light coat of clean engine oil, or press lube, to the camshaft ends and to the bearings in the camshaft support plate.

6. Place the camshaft support plate on support blocks on the press bed with the bearing receptacles facing up (**Figure 98**). Make sure the blocks support the bearing bores.

7. Set the sprocket ends of the camshaft assembly into the bearings in the support plate.

8. Position the camshaft assembly on the camshaft support plate with the rear cylinder camshaft (**Figure 99**) located toward the back of the support plate. Align the bearings with the support plate receptacles and hold the assembly in place.

CAUTION
*Before pressing the camshaft assembly into place, check the alignment of the camshaft index marks on the backside of the sprockets (**Figure 100**). If they are out of alignment, remove the assembly and correct this alignment.*

9. Install one cup of the camshaft remover and installer tool (A, **Figure 101**) onto the top of the *front* camshaft (B) only.
10. Center the front camshaft under the press ram (C, **Figure 101**).
11. Slowly press the front camshaft to *start* the front camshaft into its bearing. Wiggle the rear camshaft as needed to guide the inner race between the bearing rollers.
12. Once the inner race on the rear camshaft starts to enter in its bearing, apply pressure until front camshaft is complete seated in its bearing. If necessary, maintain finger pressure atop the rear camshaft to keep the assembly square.
13. Remove the assembly and tool from the press bed.
14. Turn the assembly over, and use a straightedge to confirm that the camshaft index marks are still correctly aligned (**Figure 102**). If necessary, remove the camshafts and realign the index marks.
15. Rotate the camshafts several complete revolutions and check for binding.
16. Install the snap ring (**Figure 103**) onto the front camshaft so the sharp edge of the snap ring faces out. Make sure the snap ring is correctly seated in the camshaft groove.
17. Place a flat blade screwdriver between the secondary camshaft drive chain and the tensioner. Slowly release the hold pin (**Figure 94**), and then slowly withdraw the screwdriver so the tensioner gradually contacts the chain surface. If it is released too fast, the shoe surface will slam against the chain and be damaged.
18. Install the camshaft support plate as described in this section.

Camshaft Removal (2007-2009 Models)

1. Remove the camshaft support plate as described in this section.
2. Remove the tensioner bolts (A, **Figure 104**) and remove the secondary chain tensioner (B). 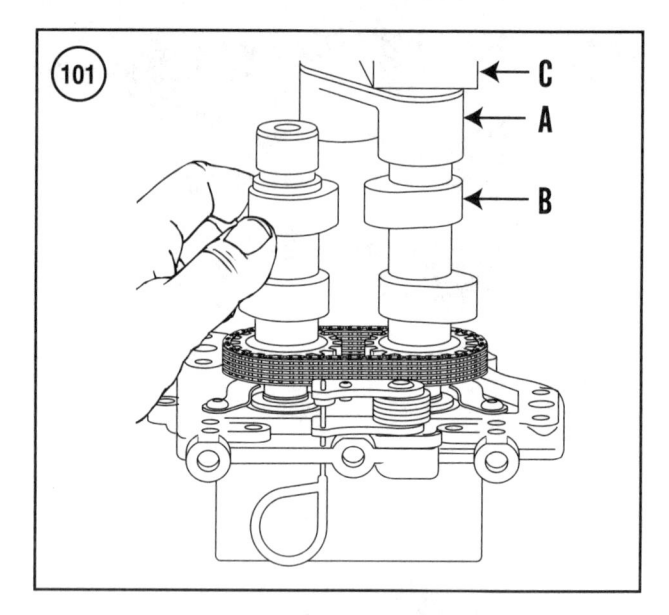 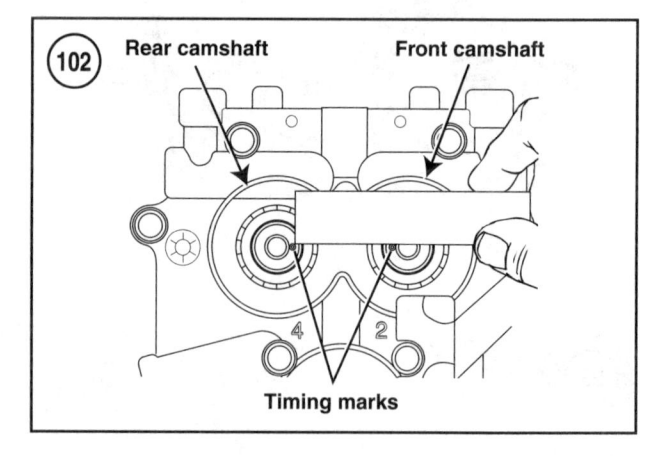
3. Remove the snap ring (A, **Figure 105**) and spacer (B) from the front cylinder camshaft. Mark the spacer so it will not be confused with the rear camshaft spacer. They are not interchangeable.
4. Pull the camshaft and secondary chain assembly from the camshaft support plate.
5. Use a permanent marker to mark a link (**Figure 106**, typical) on the outboard side of the secondary cam chain so the chain can be installed with the same orientation.

ENGINE LOWER END 195

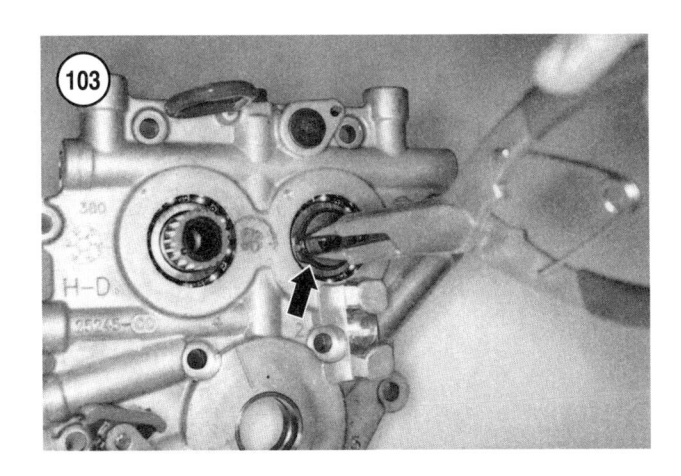

6. Remove each camshaft from between the runs of the secondary chain.

Camshaft Installation (2007-2009 Models)

The camshaft assembly tool (JIMS part No. 990 or H-D part No. HD-47956), or an equivalent, is needed for this procedure.

NOTE
On some models, the index marks are lines as shown in Figure 95. On others, these marks are dots.

1. Position the camshafts so the index marks (**Figure 95**) on the sprockets align with each other.
2. Position the secondary chain with the marked link plate facing up (**Figure 106**, typical), and install the secondary chain onto both camshafts.
3. Rotate the camshafts in either direction several times, and check the alignment of the index marks. If necessary, adjust one of the camshafts to attain correct alignment (**Figure 95**).
4. Set the inboard end of each camshaft into the camshaft assembly tool base (A, **Figure 107**). Make sure the timing marks (B, **Figure 107**) still align.
5. Place the small guide (A, **Figure 108**) onto the rear camshaft and the large guide (B) over the front camshaft.

CHAPTER FIVE

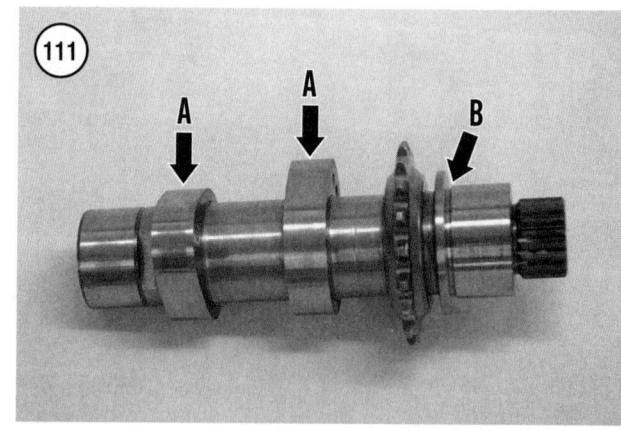

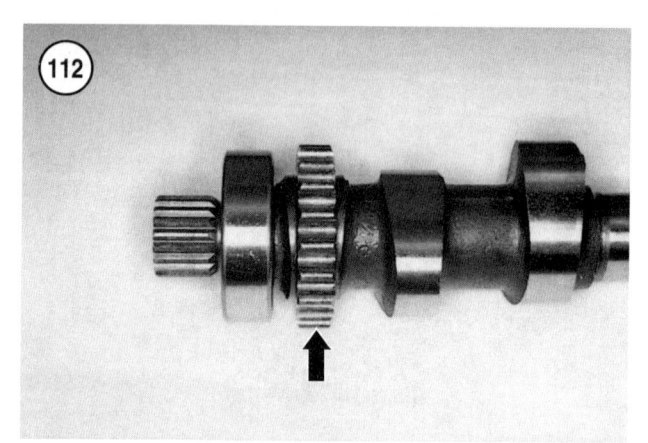

6. Apply engine oil to the camshaft bores in the camshaft support plate, and lower the support plate (A, **Figure 109**) over the guides (B) and onto the camshafts.
7. Remove the guides (B, Figure109) and base (A, **Figure 107**) from the assembly.
8. Use a straightedge (**Figure 110**) to confirm that the camshaft index marks are still correctly aligned (**Figure 102**). If necessary, remove the camshafts and realign the index marks.
9. Install the front camshaft spacer (B, **Figure 105**) onto the front camshaft, and install a *new* snap ring (A) so its sharp edge faces out. Make sure the snap ring is completely seated in the camshaft groove.
10. Rotate the camshafts several complete revolutions and check for binding.
11. Install the secondary chain tensioner (B, **Figure 104**). Tighten the camshaft chain tensioner mounting bolts (A, **Figure 104**) to 100-120 in.-lb. (11.3-13.6 N•m).

Camshaft and Sprocket Inspection (All Models)

The manufacturer does not provide camshaft specifications. Visually inspect the camshafts to determine if they require replacement.
1. Check the camshaft lobes (A, **Figure 111**) for wear. The lobes should not be scored and the edges should be square.
2. Inspect the camshaft secondary drive chain sprocket for broken or chipped teeth. Refer to **Figure 112** for 2006

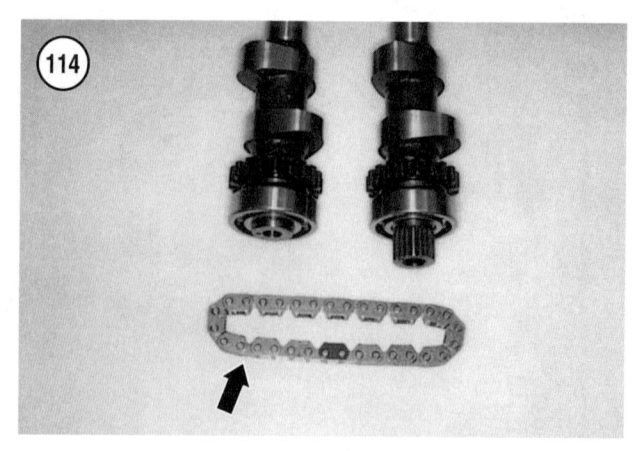

ENGINE LOWER END

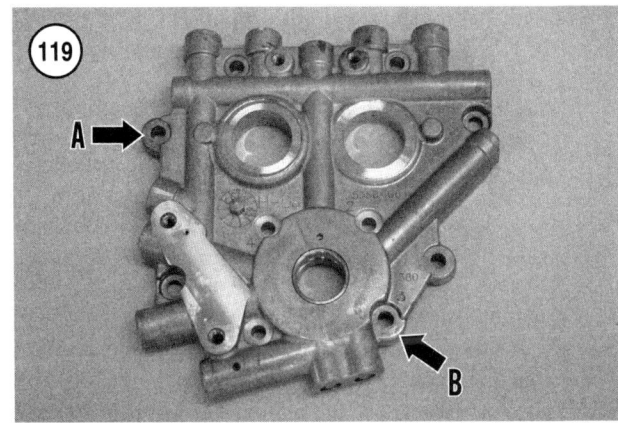

models or to **Figure 113** for 2007-2009 models. Also check the teeth for cracking or rounding. If the sprocket is damaged or severely worn, replace the camshaft.

3. If the camshaft secondary drive chain sprockets are worn, check the camshaft secondary drive chain. Refer to **Figure 114** for 2006 models or **Figure 115** for 2007-2009 models.

4. Inspect the external splines (A, **Figure 116**) on the rear cylinder's camshaft and the internal splines (B) on the rear camshaft primary drive chain sprocket. Check for worn or damaged splines and replace either or both parts as necessary. The sprocket must fit tightly on the camshaft.

5. Inspect the crankshaft and rear camshaft primary drive chain sprockets for broken or chipped teeth. Also check the teeth for cracking or rounding. Replace a damaged or severely worn sprocket. Inspect the primary drive chain for damage if the rear camshaft primary drive chain sprocket is worn or damaged.

6. Check the snap ring groove (B, **Figure 111**) on the front camshaft for wear or damage.

7. On 2006 models, inspect and rotate the bearing (**Figure 117**) on each camshaft. The front camshaft uses a ball bearing; the rear camshaft, a roller bearing. Each bearing should rotate smoothly with no roughness. Replace worn bearing(s) as described in this section.

8. Inspect the crankshaft bushing (**Figure 118**) for wear or damage.

Camshaft Support Plate Inspection

1. Check the six perimeter (A, **Figure 119**) and the four center (B) mounting bolt holes on the camshaft support plate for cracks or fractures. Replace the support plate as necessary.

2. Check the crankcase mating surface (**Figure 120**) for warping and/or surface damage, and replace as necessary.

Crankshaft Bushing Replacement (2006 Models)

Tools

The following tools, or their equivalents, are needed to replace the crankshaft bushing (**Figure 118**):

1. A crankshaft bushing tool (JIMS part No. 1281 or H-D part No. HD-42315) is required to remove and install the crankshaft bushing.
2. Crankshaft bushing reamer (JIMS part No. 1101 or H-D part No. HD-42316).
3. Handle/drive socket (H-D part No. HD-43645).

Procedure

1. Place the bushing support tool on the press bed.
2. Position the camshaft support plate with the primary chain side facing up. Place the camshaft support plate onto the bushing support tool and center the bushing over the tool (**Figure 121**).
3. Install the *remove side* of the driver (**Figure 122**) through the bushing and into the support tool until the shoulder of the driver contacts the edge of the bushing.
4. Center the assembly under the press ram, and press the bushing out of the support plate until the driver collar contacts the support plate.
5. If the bushing support tool was removed, center it beneath the press ram.
6. Position the camshaft support plate with the secondary chain side facing up. Place the camshaft support plate onto the bushing support tool.
7. Apply a light coat of clean engine oil, or press lube, to the outer surface of the bushing and to the support plate bushing bore.
8. Position the bushing into the bore with the knurled side facing up. Make sure the hole in the bushing aligns with the hole in the bushing bore.
9. Fit the *install side* of the driver (**Figure 123**) through the bushing and into the support tool until the driver contacts the edge of the bushing.
10. Center the camshaft support plate under the press ram, and press the bushing into the support plate until the driver collar contacts the support plate.
11. Remove the tools and the support plate from the press bed.

NOTE
A new bushing must be reamed to size. The crankcase must be split or a spare right crankcase half must be used to properly ream the bushing.

12. Ream the bushing by performing the following.
   a. Press the camshaft support plate onto its dowels in the right crankcase half.
   b. Install the six perimeter camshaft support plate bolts. Evenly snug them down to secure the plate in place.
   c. From the inboard side of the case half, inert the tapered end of the reamer pilot (A, **Figure 124**) into the bearing until the pilot bottoms on the bearing.
   d. Slide the reamer (B, **Figure 124**) through the pilot and into the crankshaft bushing. Do not apply any lubricant.

ENGINE LOWER END

124

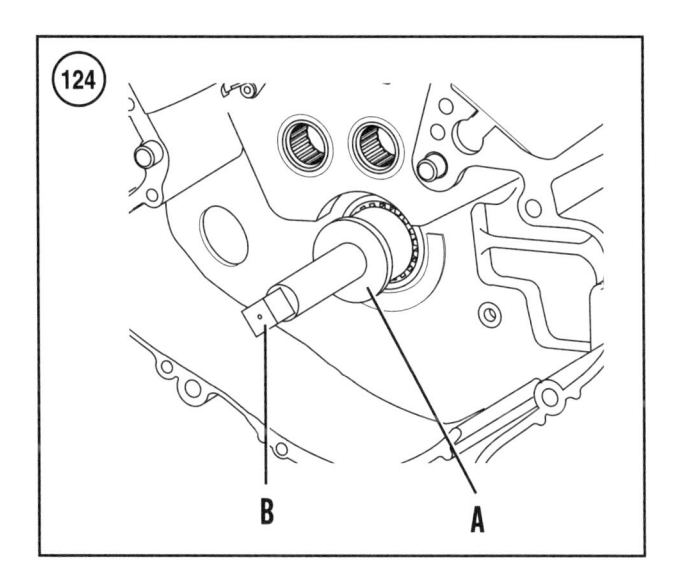

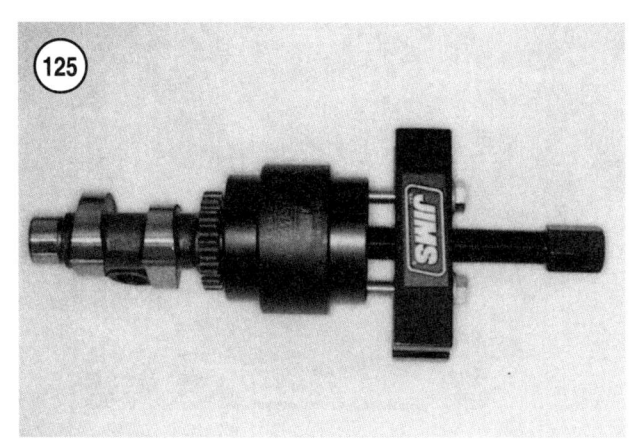

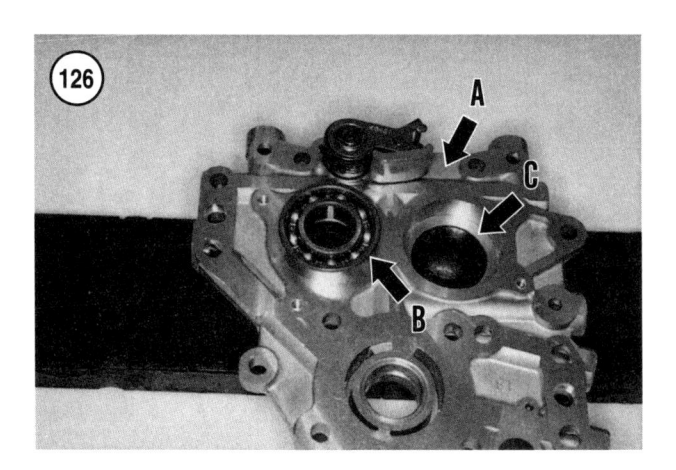

125

126

e. Install the handle/driver socket onto the end of the reamer.
f. While rotating the handle *clockwise*, use a thumb to apply slight pressure to the driver socket.
g. Rotate the reamer until its entire length has passed through the bushing, and the reamer rotates freely.
h. Remove the handle/driver socket, and carefully pull the reamer from camshaft support plate.
i. Remove the pilot, and remove the camshaft support plate from the crankcase half.

127

Camshaft Bearing Replacement

Ball bearing (2006 models)

A camshaft bearing puller (JIMS part No 1280), and a camshaft remover and installer (JIMS part No. 1277), or equivalent tools, are required to remove and install the camshaft ball bearings.

1. Install the camshaft bearing puller tool (**Figure 125**) onto the front camshaft ball bearing, and remove the camshaft ball bearing following the manufacturer's instructions.

NOTE
The ball bearing is installed in the camshaft support plate, not on the camshaft(s).

2. Install a new ball bearing into the camshaft support plate using the camshaft remover and installer as follows:
   a. Place the support block onto the press bed.
   b. Place the camshaft support plate (A, **Figure 126**) onto the support block so the bearing bores face up. Make sure the support plate is indexed correctly into the support block.
   c. Apply a light coat of clean engine oil, or press lube, to the outer surface of the ball bearing and to the support plate bearing bore.
   d. Place the ball bearing into the front camshaft bearing bore (B, **Figure 126**) so the side with the manufacturer's marks faces out.
   e. Install the bearing pilot (**Figure 127**) into the ball bearing.
   f. Press the bearing straight into the support plate until it bottoms.
   g. Remove the pilot from the bearing and remove the support plate from the press bed.

Roller bearing (2006 models)

A camshaft bearing puller (JIMS part No 1280), or an equivalent tool, is needed to remove the bearing inner race from the camshaft.

1. Slide the roller bearing from the end of the rear camshaft. The bearing inner race remains on the camshaft.

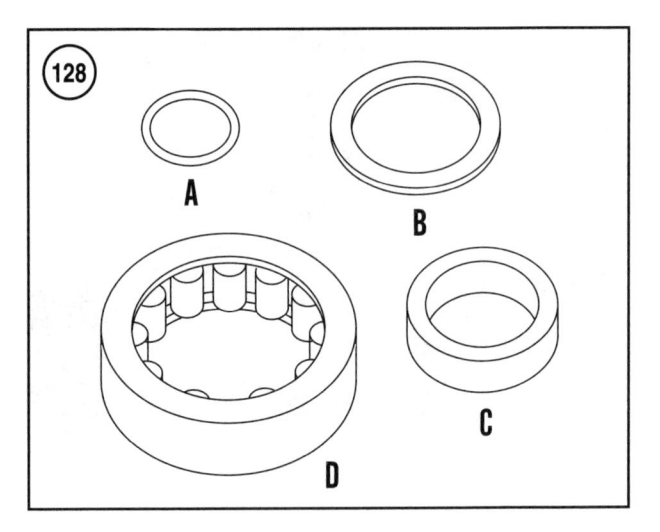

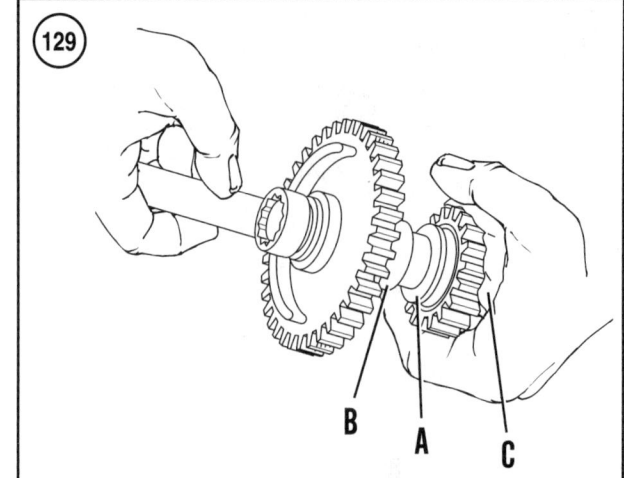

2. Install the camshaft bearing puller onto the rear camshaft so the tool sits against the inboard side of the bearing inner race.
3. Wrap a cloth around the camshaft, and firmly grasp the camshaft.
4. Use a wrench to turn the puller screw, and pull the bearing inner race and thrust washer from the rear camshaft.
5. Remove the O-ring from the rear camshaft relief groove.

CAUTION
Do not damage the O-ring during installation. This O-ring is only available as part of the roller bearing kit (Figure 128) and is not available separately. If the O-ring is damaged, a second roller bearing kit must be purchased.

a. Oil a new O-ring (A, **Figure 128**), and carefully install it onto the rear camshaft so the O-ring is completely seated within the relief groove. The groove sits between the machined area of the camshaft and the secondary cam sprocket.
b. Install the thrust washer (B, **Figure 128**) and center it over the O-ring.
c. Install the inner race (C, **Figure 128**) down the rear camshaft until it rests on the shoulder of the shaft's machined area.
d. Install the cam sprocket spacer (A, **Figure 129**) and the rear camshaft drive sprocket (B). Install a long flange bolt with a thick flat washer.
e. Wrap a cloth (C, **Figure 129**) around the camshaft, and firmly grasp the camshaft.
f. Use a wrench to turn the bolt until the inner race firmly seats against the thrust washer. Check that the thrust washer is locked in place and cannot be rotated. If necessary, secure the rear camshaft in a vise with soft jaws, and tighten the flange bolt until the thrust washer cannot turn.
g. Install the new roller bearing (D, **Figure 128**) into the camshaft support plate as described in *Camshaft Bearing Replacement, Ball Bearing* (this section).

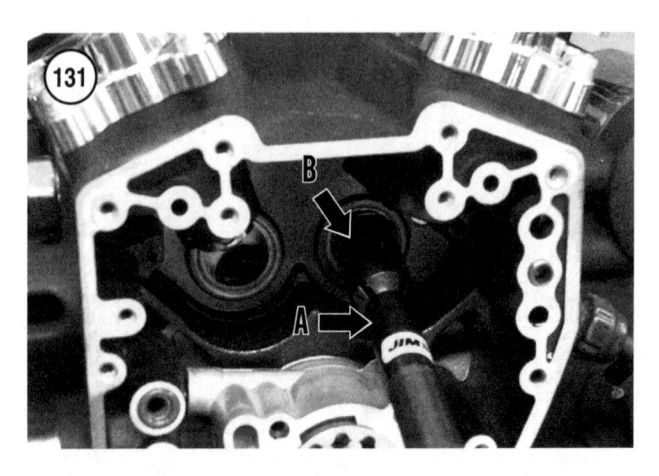

Install the roller bearing into the rear camshaft bearing bore (C, **Figure 126**).

Needle bearings (all models)

A camshaft inner bearing installer (JIMS part No. 1278 for 2006 models, or JIMS part No. 991 for 2007-2009 models) and a camshaft inner bearing remover (JIMS part No. 1279 for 2006 models or JIMS part No. 993 for 2007-2009 models), or equivalent tools, are needed for this procedure.

ENGINE LOWER END

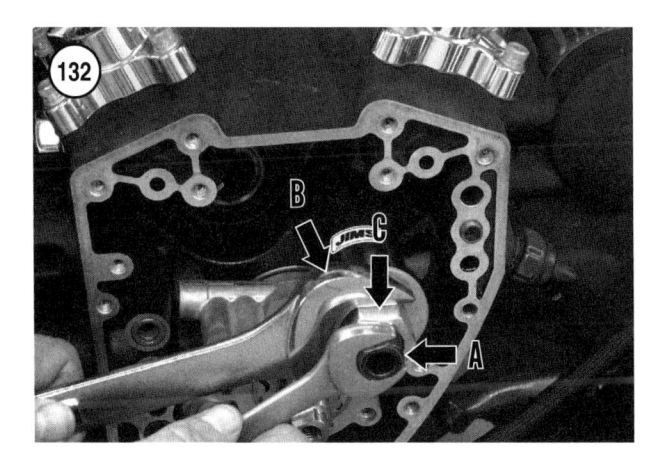

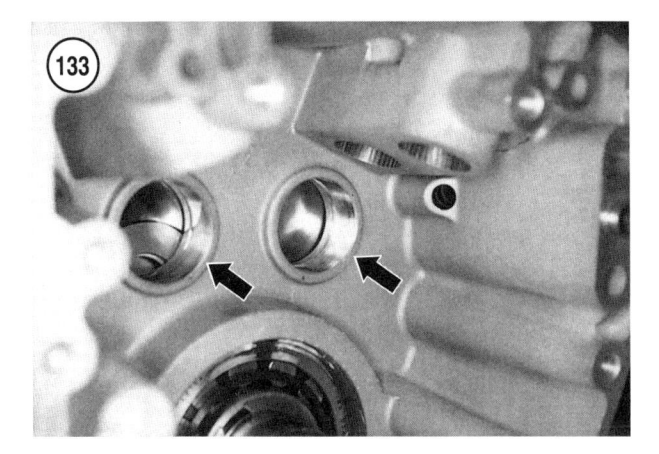

NOTE
*The camshaft needle bearings (**Figure 130**) can be removed with the engine mounted in the frame after the camshaft support plate is removed.*

NOTE
Replace both needle bearings as a set even if only one requires replacement.

1. Remove the camshaft support plate assembly from the engine as described in this section.
2. Install the puller portion of the tool set (A, **Figure 131**) part way into the needle bearing. Install a small hose clamp onto the end that is closest to the needle bearing (B, **Figure 131**) and tighten it. This closes the end of the tool so it can pass through the needle bearing. Push the puller all the way through the needle bearing and remove the hose clamp.
3. Assemble the remainder of the tool components onto the puller following the manufacturer's instructions.
4. Place a 5/8 in. wrench on the flats of the puller (A, **Figure 132**).
5. Place a 1-1/8 in. wrench, or an adjustable wrench, on the large nut (B, **Figure 132**).

CAUTION
Do not turn the 5/8 in. wrench as this will damage the tool and the crankcase receptacle.

6. Hold the 5/8 in. wrench (A, **Figure 132**) to keep the puller from rotating. Turn the 1-1/8 in. wrench (B, **Figure 132**) *clockwise* on the large nut (C). Tighten the large nut and pull the needle bearing out of the crankcase bore.
7. Disassemble the tool, and remove the needle bearing from it.
8. Repeat the process to remove the other needle bearing.
9. Apply a light coat of clean engine oil, or press lube, to the outer surface of the *new* needle bearing(s) and to the crankcase needle bearing bore(s) (**Figure 133**, typical).
10. Apply a light coat of clean engine oil to the threads of the screw portion and to the installer plate.
11. Insert the screw portion of the tool part way into the installer plate.
12. Push the installer onto the screw until it locks into place.
13. Position the *new* bearing (A, **Figure 134**) on the installer (B) with the manufacturer's marks facing out on the installer.
14. Postition the installer plate on the crankcase, aligning the tool to the bearing bore.
15. Install the thumb screws (A, **Figure 135**) through the installer plate and into the crankcase threaded holes. Tighten the thumb screws securely.
16. Slowly tighten the installer screw (B, **Figure 135**) until the bearing starts to enter the crankcase bore. Continue to tighten it until the installer contacts the crankcase surface. This correctly positions the needle bearing within the crankcase.

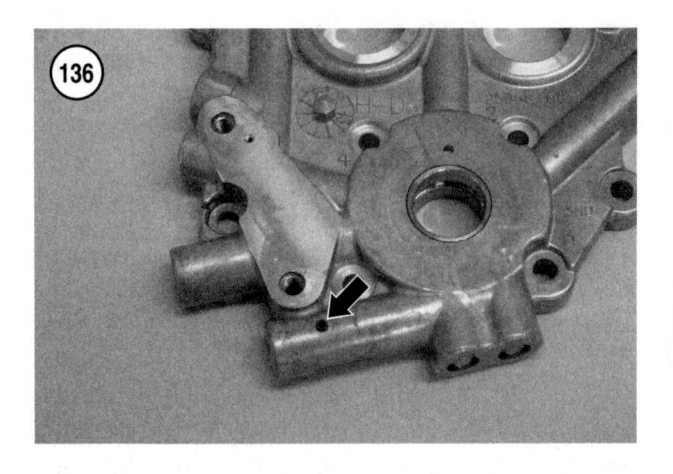

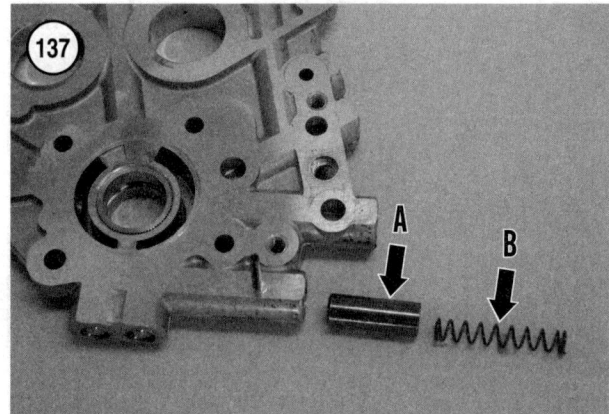

17. Remove the tools.
18. Repeat the process to install the remaining needle bearing.

Oil Pressure Relief Valve (All Models) Removal/Inspection/Installation

NOTE
This procedure is shown with the camshaft assembly removed to clearly illustrate the steps.

1. Remove the camshaft support plate assembly from the engine as described in this section.
2A. If the camshafts are still in place, secure the camshaft support plate in a vise with soft jaws.
2B. If the camshafts have been removed, place the camshaft support plate on a piece of soft wood.
3. Before disassembling the valve, measure the seated depth of the valve body in the bore by performing the following:
    a. Insert a stiff wire down through the valve spring until it reaches bottom inside the valve body.
    b. Mark the wire where it aligns with the outside edge of the bore.
    c. Remove the wire and measure the distance from the end of the wire to the mark. It should approximately equal the valve seated depth (**Table 1**).
    d. If the measurement is out of specification, the spring is fatigued. Replace the spring.
4. Use a 1/8 in. punch to drive the roll pin (**Figure 136**) from the camshaft support plate. Discard the roll pin.
5. Remove the valve body (A, **Figure 137**) and spring (B) from the relief-valve port of the camshaft support plate.
6. Inspect the spring for signs of stretching, cracks or wear. Replace it if worn.
7. Inspect the valve body and the relief-valve port (**Figure 138**) for burrs, scoring or metal chips. If found, replace the valve body and the support plate.
8. Determine the running clearance by performing the following:
    a. Measure the outside diameter of the valve body (**Figure 139**).

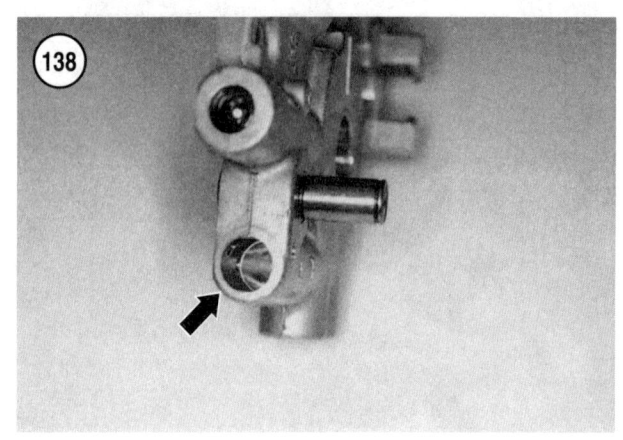

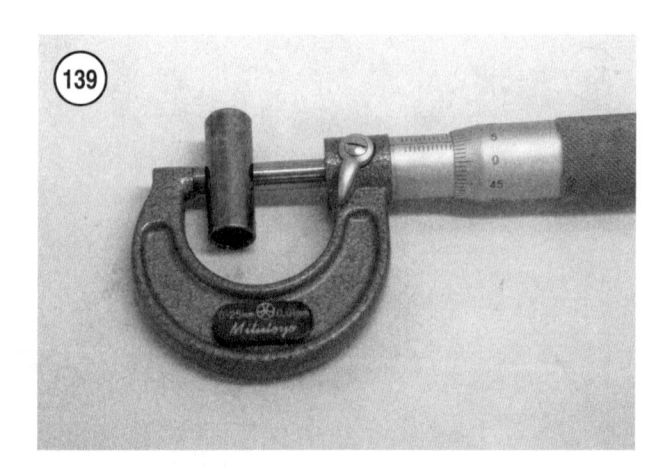

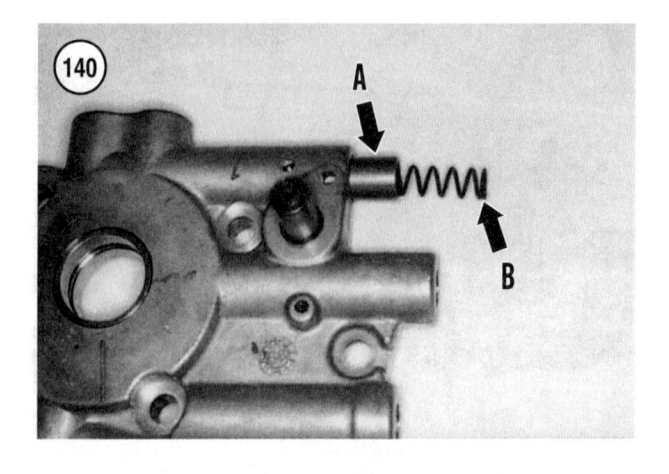

ENGINE LOWER END

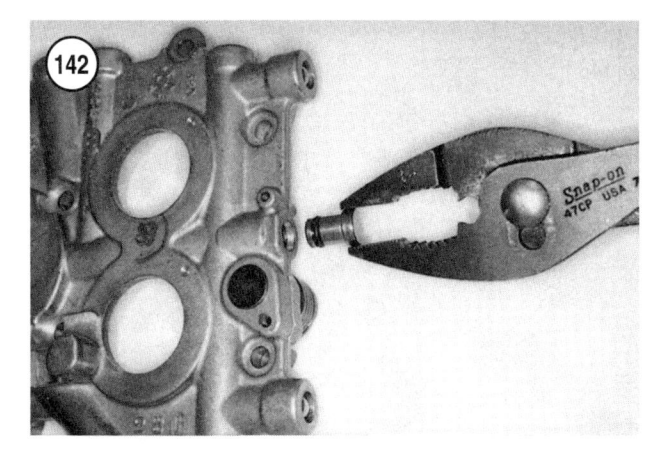

b. Measure the inside diameter of the relief-valve port in the camshaft support plate.
c. Subtract the valve body outside diameter from the relief-valve port inside diameter. This is the running clearance.
d. If running clearance exceeds specification (**Table 1**), replace the valve body. Measure the outside diameter of the new valve body and recalculate the running clearance. If the running clearance still exceeds specification, replace the valve body and camshaft support plate.

9. Apply a light coat of clean engine oil to the bypass port and to the valve body.
10. Install the valve body (A, **Figure 140**) so its closed end goes into the bypass port first.
11. Install the spring (B, **Figure 140**) into the valve body.
12. Push the valve body and spring into the bypass port. Hold them in place (A, **Figure 141**) and install a *new* roll pin (B). Tap the roll pin in until it sits flush with the support plate (**Figure 136**).

Cleaning Plug (2006 Models)
Removal/Installation

NOTE
This procedure is shown with the camshaft assembly removed to clearly illustrate the steps.

1. Remove the camshaft support plate from the engine as described in this section.
2A. If the camshafts are still in place, secure the camshaft support plate in a vise with soft jaws.
2B. If the camshafts have been removed, place the camshaft support plate on piece of soft wood.
3. Use a pair of pliers to carefully remove the cleaning plug (**Figure 142**) from the camshaft support plate. Remove the O-ring.
4. Thoroughly clean the cleaning plug receptacle and support plate in solvent. Dry them with compressed air.
5. Apply low-pressure compressed air to the cleaning plug port (**Figure 143**) to blow out any debris. Make sure the oil hole is clear.
6. Install a *new* O-ring onto the cleaning plug, and install the cleaning plug. Press it in until it bottoms.

Chain Tensioner (2006 Models)
Removal/Inspection/Installation

NOTE
This procedure is pictured being performed on a primary chain tensioner. These steps also apply to the secondary chain tensioner.

1. Remove the camshaft primary and/or secondary drive chain as described in this section.
2. Remove the snap ring (**Figure 144**) securing the chain tensioner to the mounting post.

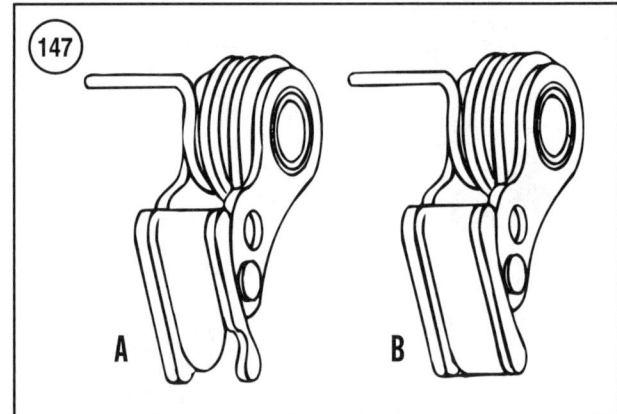

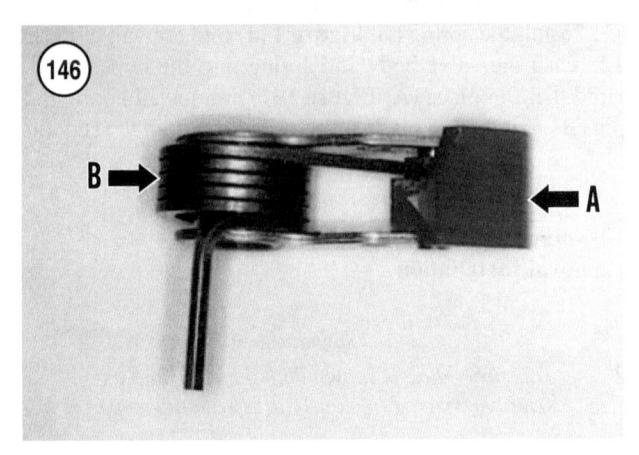

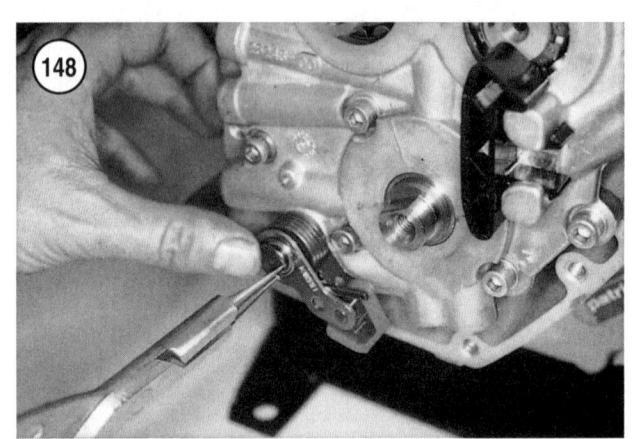

3. Slide the chain tensioner (A, **Figure 145**) off the mounting post.
4. Inspect the chain tensioner shoe (A, **Figure 146**) for wear. If the shoe surface is chipped (A, **Figure 147**) or worn halfway through (B), replace the tensioner. Check the tensioner spring (B, **Figure 146**) for sagging or damage. Replace the chain tensioner assembly if necessary.
5. Install the chain tensioner onto the mounting post, and insert the spring end (B, **Figure 145**) into the receptacle in the cover. Push the chain tensioner until it bottoms.
6. Install a *new* snap ring (**Figure 148**). Make sure it is correctly seated in the mounting post groove.

Chain Tensioner Inspection
(2007-2009 Models)

1. Visually inspect the tensioner shoe (A, **Figure 149**). Replace the tensioners if the contact surface of the shoe is less than 0.060 in. (1.52 mm) thick.
2. If tensioner was disassembled, assemble it by performing the following:
    a. Insert the piston (A, **Figure 150**) and spring (B) into the tensioner housing.
    b. Align the shoe (C, **Figure 150**) with the cutouts in the housing, and press the shoe into the housing (D).
    c. Insert a wire (B, **Figure 149**) through the hole in the tensioner housing to hold the assembly together.

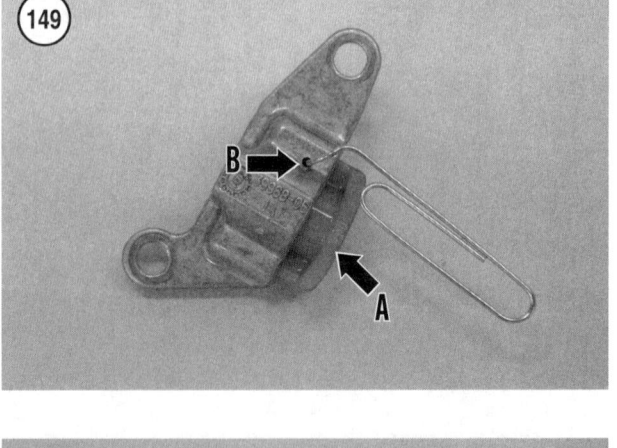

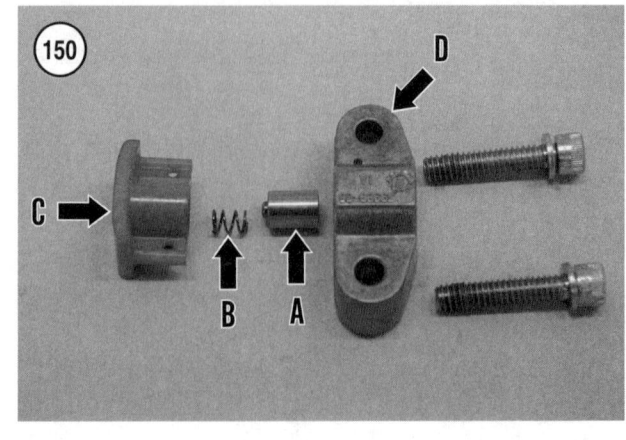

ENGINE LOWER END

CRANKCASE ASSEMBLY (2006 MODELS)

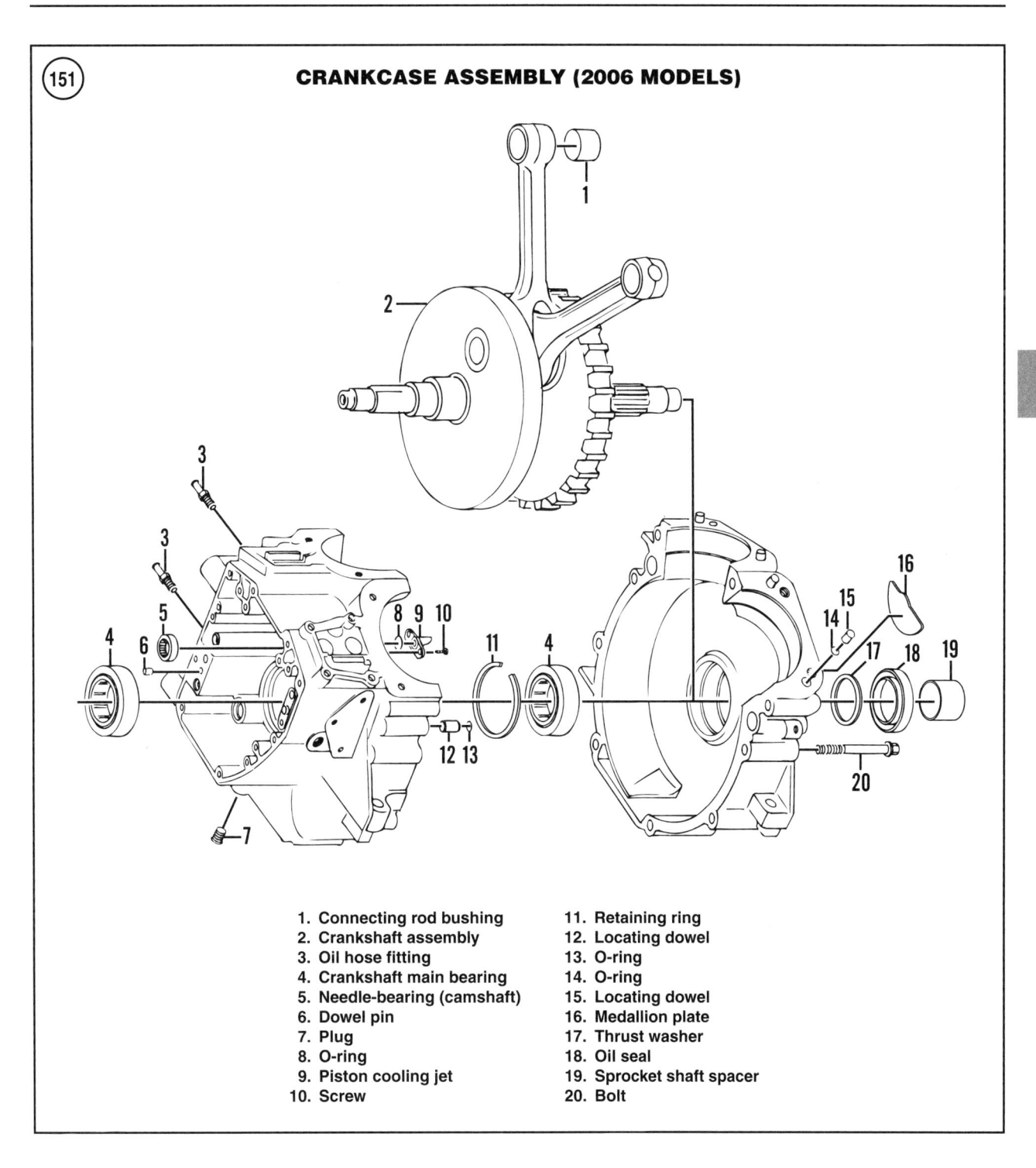

1. Connecting rod bushing
2. Crankshaft assembly
3. Oil hose fitting
4. Crankshaft main bearing
5. Needle-bearing (camshaft)
6. Dowel pin
7. Plug
8. O-ring
9. Piston cooling jet
10. Screw
11. Retaining ring
12. Locating dowel
13. O-ring
14. O-ring
15. Locating dowel
16. Medallion plate
17. Thrust washer
18. Oil seal
19. Sprocket shaft spacer
20. Bolt

CRANKCASE AND CRANKSHAFT

Crankcase Disassembly

An engine stand (JIMS part No. 1142), base stand (JIMS part No. 1138) and a crankshaft disassembly/removing tool (JIMS part No. 1047-TP for 2006 models or JIMS part No. 995 for 2007-2009 models) are used in some of the following procedures.

Refer to **Figures 151-153**.

1. Remove the engine as described in this chapter.

CAUTION
Do not lift the crankcase assembly by the cylinder studs. Bent or damaged cylinder studs may cause an oil leak.

2. Remove the following components:
   a. Rocker arms, pushrods and valve lifters as described in Chapter Four.
   b. Cylinder heads, pistons and cylinders as described in Chapter Four.
   c. Camshaft support plate and oil pump as described in this chapter.

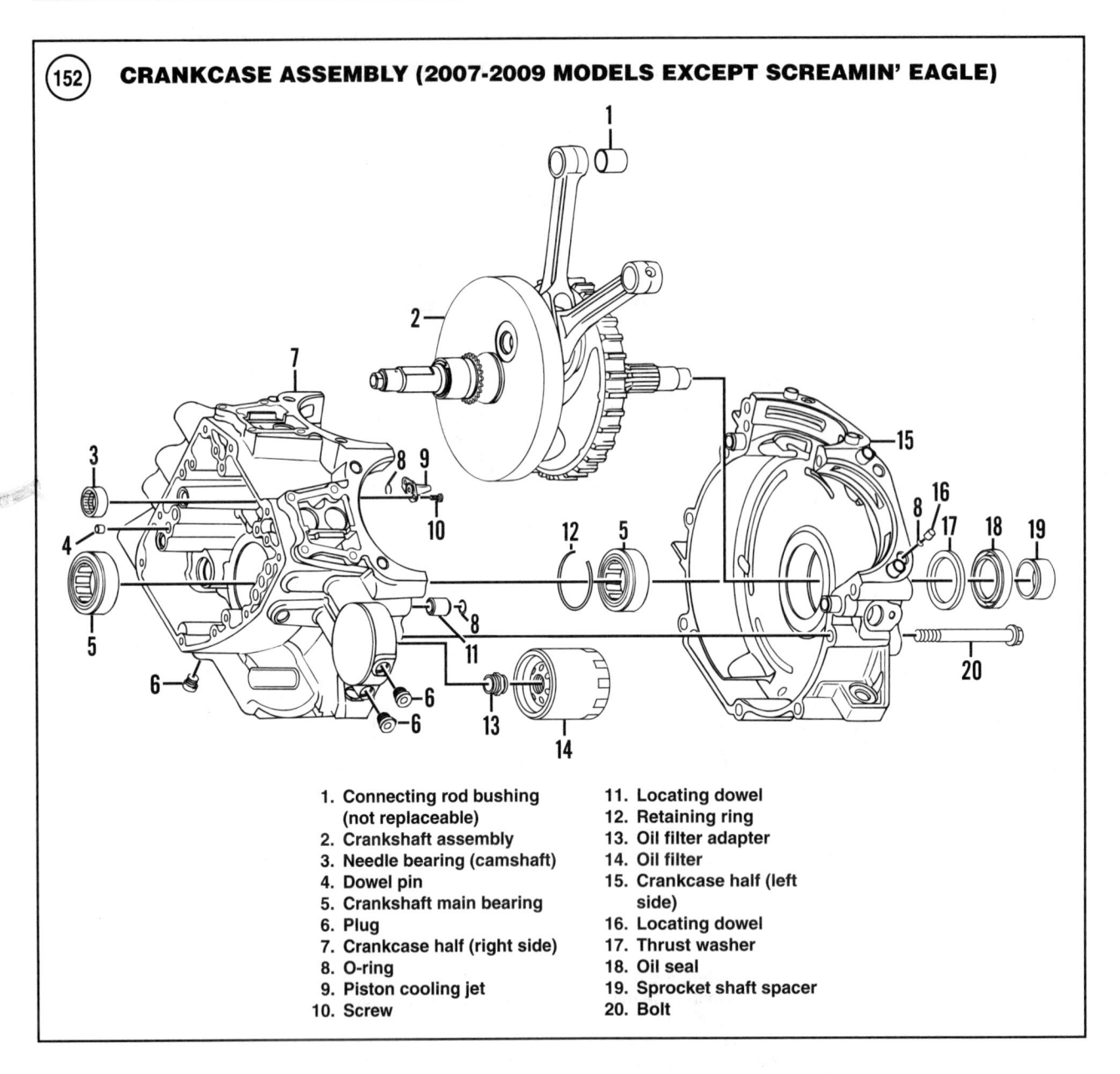

152 CRANKCASE ASSEMBLY (2007-2009 MODELS EXCEPT SCREAMIN' EAGLE)

1. Connecting rod bushing (not replaceable)
2. Crankshaft assembly
3. Needle bearing (camshaft)
4. Dowel pin
5. Crankshaft main bearing
6. Plug
7. Crankcase half (right side)
8. O-ring
9. Piston cooling jet
10. Screw
11. Locating dowel
12. Retaining ring
13. Oil filter adapter
14. Oil filter
15. Crankcase half (left side)
16. Locating dowel
17. Thrust washer
18. Oil seal
19. Sprocket shaft spacer
20. Bolt

d. Alternator rotor and stator assembly as described in Chapter Eleven.

NOTE
Leave the bolts for the left side off so the case halves can be separated in the following steps.

3. Attach the crankcase assembly to an engine stand (**Figure 154**) following the manufacturer's instructions.
4. Secure the engine stand to the workbench.
5. Following the sequence shown in **Figure 155**, loosen the bolts (**Figure 156**) from the left side of the crankcase in two to three stages. Then, remove the bolts.
6. Place the crankcase assembly on wooden blocks with the camshaft cover (left side) facing up. Use wooden blocks thick enough so the right side of the crankshaft clears the workbench surface (**Figure 157**).
7. Tap around the perimeter of the crankcase with a plastic mallet and remove the left crankcase half (**Figure 158**).

8. If the crankcase halves will not separate easily, perform the following:
   a. Install the separation tool(s) (A, **Figure 159**) onto the left side of the crankcase following the manufacturer's instructions.
   b. Make sure the right side engine stand bolts (A, **Figure 160**) are *not* installed onto the crankcase half.
   c. Apply clean engine oil, or press lube, to the end of the center screw and install it into the tool.

CAUTION
Do not use a hand impact driver or air impact wrench on the center screw. These will damage the crankcase halves and the tool(s).

   d. Slowly turn the center screw (B, **Figure 159**) with a wrench 1/2 turn at a time. After each turn, tap on the end of the center screw with a brass mallet to relieve the stress on the center screw and the tool.

ENGINE LOWER END

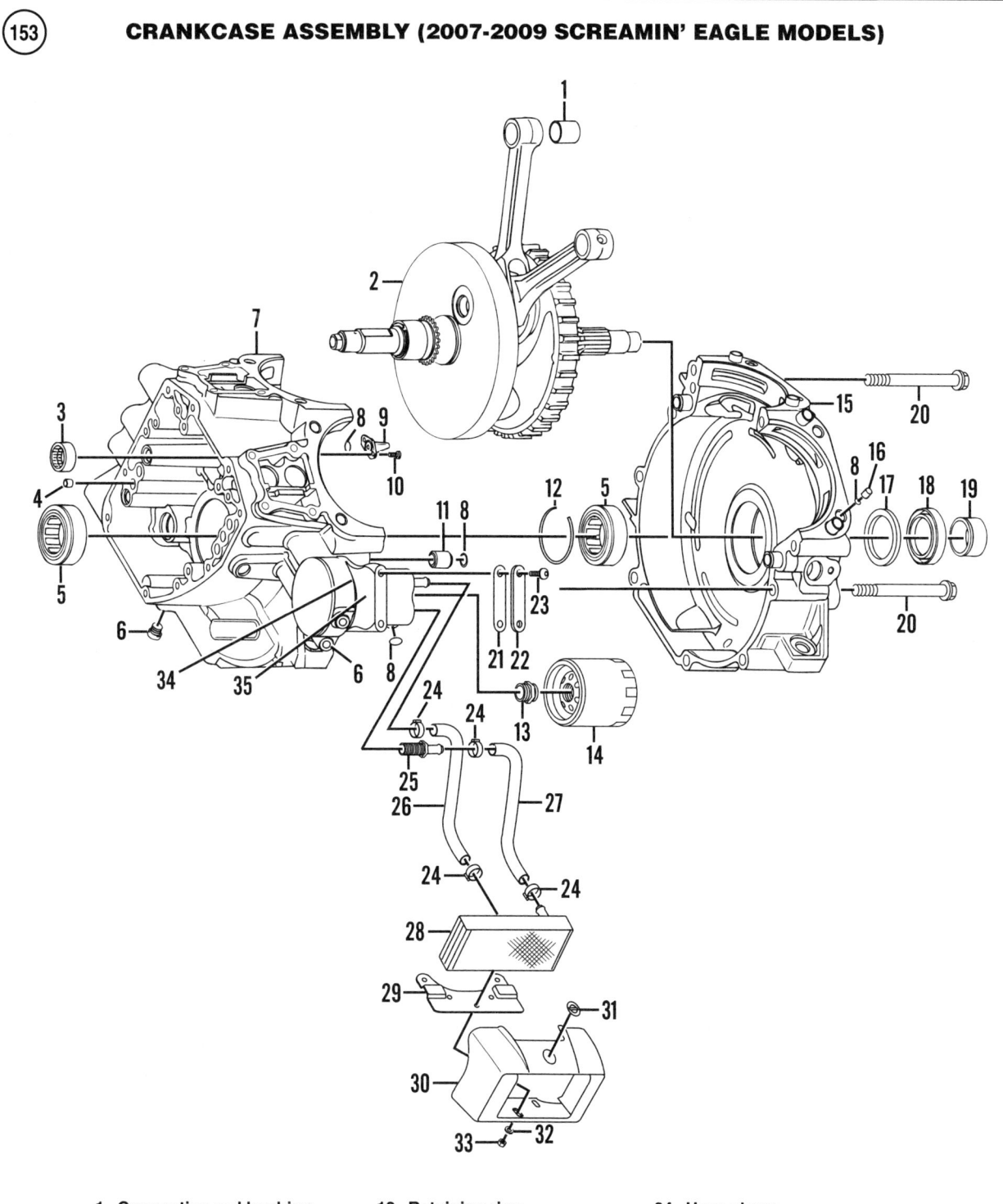

CRANKCASE ASSEMBLY (2007-2009 SCREAMIN' EAGLE MODELS)

1. Connecting rod bushing (not replaceable)
2. Crankshaft assembly
3. Needle bearing (camshaft)
4. Dowel pin
5. Crankshaft main bearing
6. Plug
7. Crankcase half (right side)
8. O-ring
9. Piston cooling jet
10. Screw
11. Locating dowel
12. Retaining ring
13. Oil filter adapter
14. Oil filter
15. Crankcase half (left side)
16. Locating dowel
17. Thrust washer
18. Oil seal
19. Sprocket shaft spacer
20. Bolt
21. Gasket
22. Cover
23. Screw
24. Hose clamp
25. Fitting (hose)
26. Return hose
27. Supply hose
28. Oil cooler (2009 models shown)
29. Mounting plate
30. Cover
31. Trim plate
32. Washer
33. Flange locknut
34. Gasket
35. Adapter assembly

CHAPTER FIVE

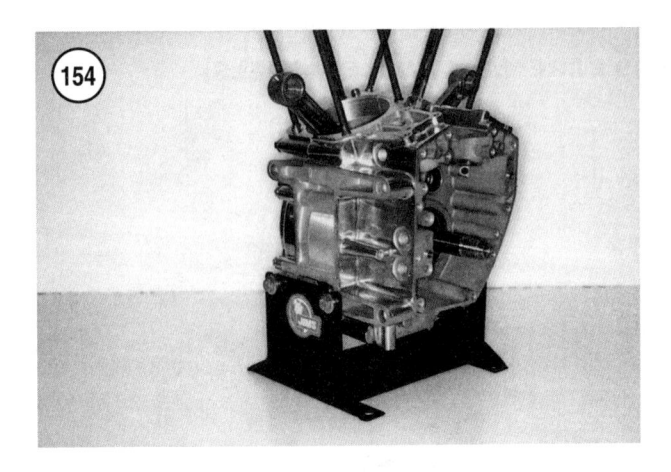

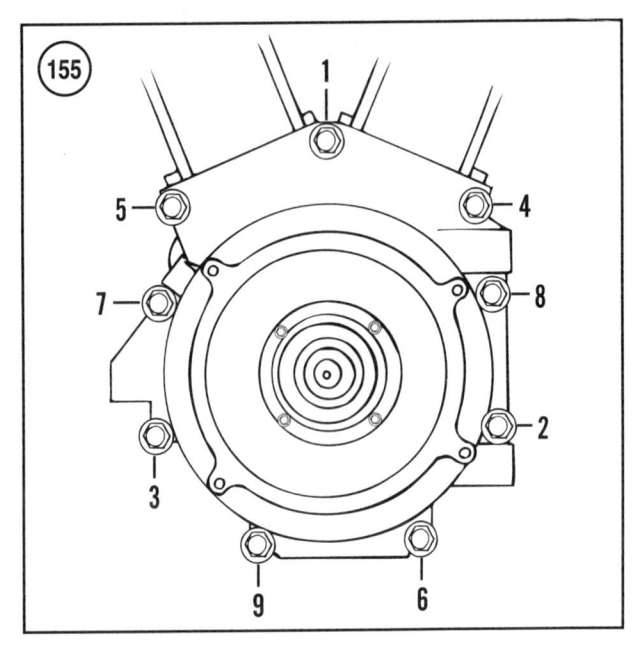

e. Repeat the process until the center screw turns freely and the crankcase halves begin to separate (B, **Figure 160**).
f. Remove the crankcase from the engine stand.
g. Remove the right side crankcase half (**Figure 161**).
h. Remove the separation tool from the left side crankcase half unless the crankshaft is going to be removed.

9. Remove the locating dowels (**Figure 162**) and O-rings from the right side crankcase half.

CAUTION
Do not drive the crankshaft out of the crankcase half with a hammer.

10A. If a hydraulic press is available, press the crankshaft out of the right crankcase half as follows:
a. Support the right crankcase half in a press on wooden blocks with the outer surface facing up.
b. Center the press ram onto the end of the crankshaft, and then press the crankshaft out of the right crankcase half. Have an assistant support the crankshaft as it is being pressed out.
c. Remove the crankshaft.

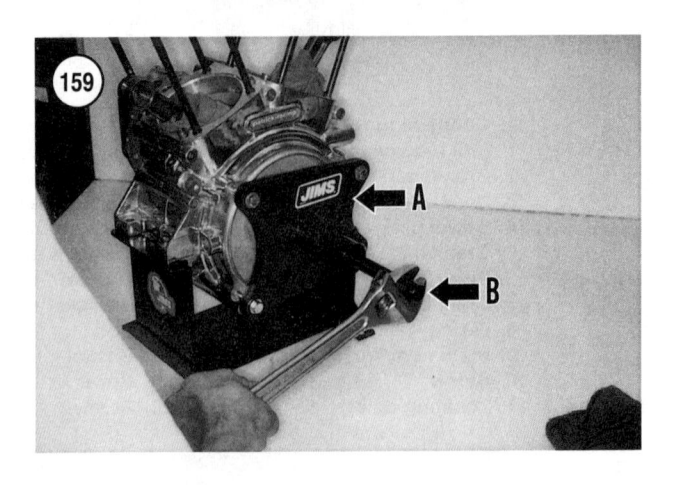

ENGINE LOWER END

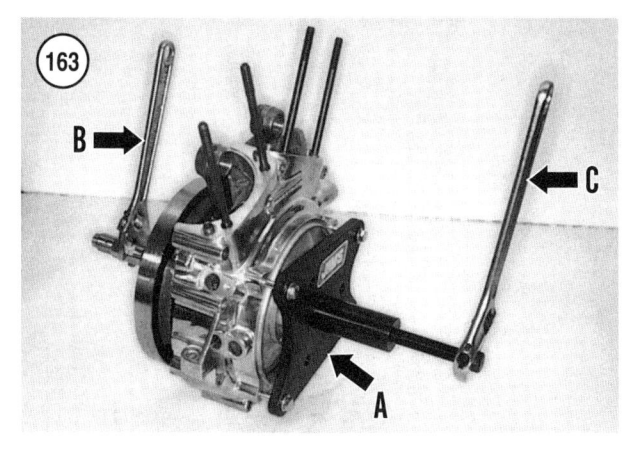

d. Remove the right crankcase half from the press bed and move it to workbench for further service.

10B. If a hydraulic press is not available, perform the following:

a. Install the crankshaft disassembly/removing tool (A, **Figure 163**) onto the left side of the crankcase following the manufacturer's instructions.

b. Apply clean engine oil, or press lube, to the end of the center screw and install it into the tool.

CAUTION
Do not use a hand impact driver or air impact wrench on the center screw, as these will damage the crankcase and the tool(s).

c. Secure the right side of the crankshaft with a wrench (B, **Figure 163**) to prevent it from rotating.

d. Slowly turn the center screw with a wrench (C, **Figure 163**) 1/2 turn at a time. After each turn, tap on the end of the center screw with a brass mallet to relieve the stress on the center screw and the tool.

e. Repeat the process until the center screw pushes the crankshaft out of the left side crankcase half.

f. Remove the tool from the left side crankcase half.

11. To remove the crankshaft outer roller bearing and oil seal assembly from the left crankcase half, perform the following:

a. Place the left crankcase half on the workbench with the outer surface facing up.

b. Carefully pry the sprocket shaft spacer out of the oil seal.

c. Carefully pry the oil seal out of the crankcase using a wide-blade screwdriver. Support the screwdriver with a rag to prevent damage to the crankcase.

d. Lift the outer roller bearing from the crankcase.

Crankcase Assembly

A crankshaft guide (JIMS part No. 1288), or an equivalent tool, is required to assemble the crankcase halves.

1. Perform Steps 1-9 of *Crankcase Cleaning and Inspection* (this section).

2. Support the left crankcase half on wooden blocks (**Figure 164**) so the inboard side faces up. Make sure the

blocks are thick enough so the left side of the crankshaft will clear the workbench surface.

3. Install the locating dowels (**Figure 165**) and *new* O-rings in both locations in the right crankcase half. Apply clean engine oil to the O-rings (**Figure 166**).

4. Fit the crankshaft guide (**Figure 167**) onto the crankshaft sprocket shaft (left side), and install the crankshaft into the left crankcase half. Make sure each connecting rod sits in the correct cylinder cutout.

5. Thoroughly clean and dry the crankcase gasket surface of each crankcase half.

6. Apply a thin coat of a non-hardening gasket sealant to the crankcase mating surfaces. Use High Performance Sealant, Gray (H-D part No. HD-99650-02), or an equivalent.

7. Align the crankcase halves and carefully lower the right crankcase half over the crankshaft and onto left crankcase half (**Figure 168**). Press it down until it is seated correctly on the locating dowels. If necessary, carefully tap around the perimeter of the right crankcase half until it is completed seated on the left half (**Figure 169**).

CAUTION
When properly aligned, the crankcase halves will fit snugly against each other around the entire perimeter. If they do not meet correctly, do not attempt to pull the case halves together with the mounting bolts. Separate the crankcase assembly and investigate the cause of the interference.

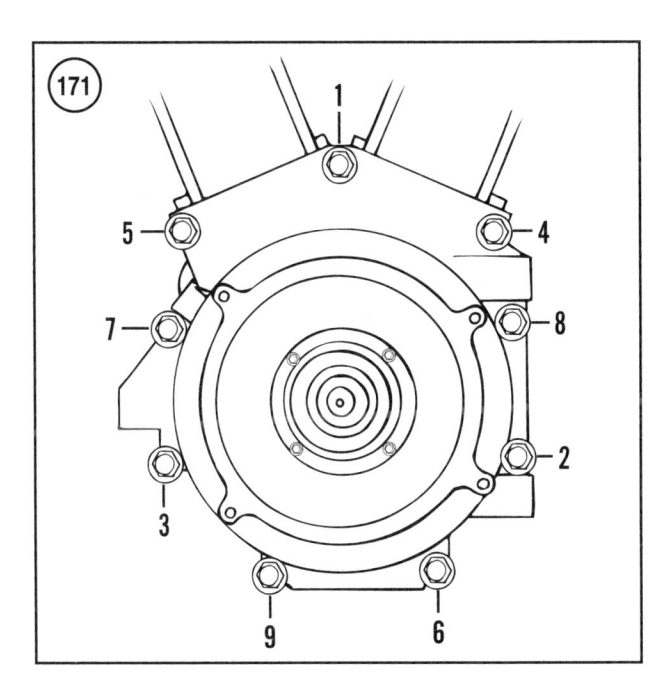

ENGINE LOWER END

171

172

173

174

175

b. Following the torque sequence shown in **Figure 171**, tighten the bolts to 10 ft.-lb. (13.6 N•m).
c. Following the same sequence, tighten the crankcase bolts to 15-19 ft.-lb. (20.3-25.8 N•m).

11. Apply clean engine oil to the outer surface of the sprocket shaft spacer (**Figure 172**) and install it onto the crankshaft and into the new oil seal.

12. Install the following components:
    a. Alternator rotor and stator assembly as described in Chapter Eleven.
    b. Camshaft support plate and oil pump as described in this chapter.
    c. Cylinder heads, pistons and cylinders as described in Chapter Four.
    d. Rocker arms, pushrods and valve lifters as described in Chapter Four.

Crankcase Cleaning and Inspection

1. Clean both crankcase halves in solvent and dry with compressed air.
2. Apply a light coat of oil to the races to prevent rust.
3. Inspect the right (**Figure 173**) and left (**Figure 174**) crankcase halves for cracks or other damage.
4. Inspect the case studs (**Figure 175**) for bending, cracks or other damage. Check the exposed stud threads for damage. If necessary, replace studs as described in *Cylinder Stud Replacement* (this section).

8. Pull the crankshaft guide from the crankshaft.
9. If available, place the crankcase assembly in an engine stand (A, **Figure 170**). Secure the engine stand to the workbench.
10. Install the crankcase bolts into the left crankcase half (B, **Figure 170**) and tighten them as follows:
    a. Alternately finger-tighten the bolts.

5. Inspect the left side main bearing races. Refer to **Figure 176** for the outer bearing race and **Figure 177** for the inner bearing race. Also, check the roller bearings for wear or damage. The bearings must turn smoothly with no roughness. If any of these parts are worn, replace the bearing assembly as described in *Left Side Main Bearing Assembly Replacement* (this chapter).

6. Inspect the right side main roller bearing (**Figure 178**) for wear or damage. The bearing must turn smoothly with no roughness. If damaged, replace the bearing assembly as described in *Right Side Main Bearing Replacement* (this chapter).

7. Inspect the camshaft needle bearings (**Figure 179**) in the right crankcase half for damage. To replace one or both of these bearings, refer to *Camshaft Support Plate* (this chapter).

8. Inspect the valve lifter bore receptacles (**Figure 180**) for wear or damage. Refer to *Valve Lifter Inspection* (Chapter Four).

NOTE
If the original piston cooling jets are being reinstalled, apply Loctite No. 222 (purple), or an equivalent threadlock, to the screw threads prior to installation.

9. Make sure the piston cooling jets (**Figure 181**) are clear. If necessary, remove the Torx mounting screws (T20), and then remove the cooling jets and O-rings. Clean the oil jets

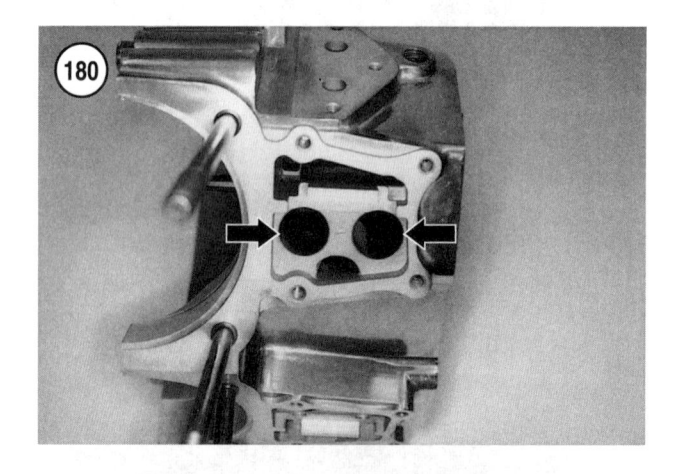

ENGINE LOWER END

with compressed air. Install *new* O-rings and tighten the mounting screws securely.

Crankshaft and Connecting Rods Cleaning and Inspection

If any portion of the crankshaft and/or connecting rods are worn or damaged, they must be replaced as one assembly. If necessary, have the crankshaft overhauled by a dealership.

1. Clean the crankshaft assembly in solvent and dry thoroughly with compressed air.
2. Hold the shank portion of each connecting rod where it attaches to the crankshaft (**Figure 182**). Pull up and down on each connecting rod. Any slight amount of up and down movement indicates excessive lower bearing wear. If there is movement, the crankshaft must be overhauled.
3. Measure connecting rod side play with a feeler gauge (**Figure 183**). Compare the results with the service limit in **Table 2**.
4. Inspect the pinion shaft (**Figure 184**) on the right side and the sprocket shaft (**Figure 185**) on the left side for excessive wear or damage.
5. Support the crankshaft on a truing stand or in a lathe and check runout with a dial indicator at the flywheel outer rim (A, **Figure 186**) and at the shaft adjacent to the flywheel (B). If the runout exceeds the service limit in **Table 2**, have the crankshaft trued or overhauled.
6. Inspect the crankshaft position sensor timing teeth (**Figure 187**) on the left side flywheel for damaged or missing teeth.
7. Inspect the connecting rod bushings (**Figure 188**) for wear. If necessary, replace the bushings on 2006 models as described in *Piston Pin Bushing Replacement* (Chapter Four). The bushings are not serviceable on 2007-2009 models.

Cylinder Stud Replacement

Replace bent or otherwise damaged cylinder studs (**Figure 175**) to prevent cylinder block and cylinder head leaks.

187

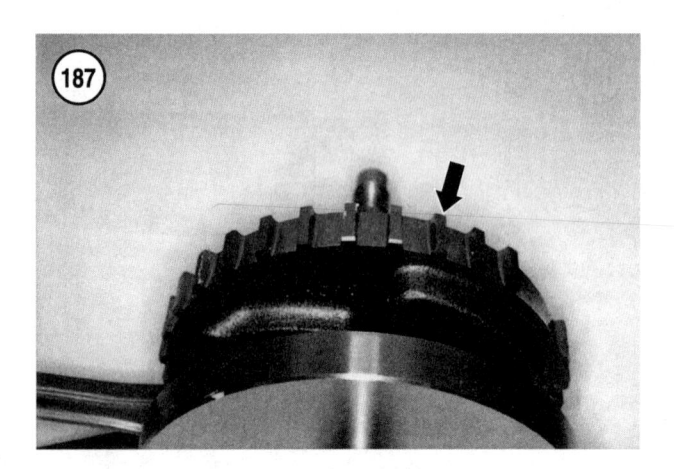

188

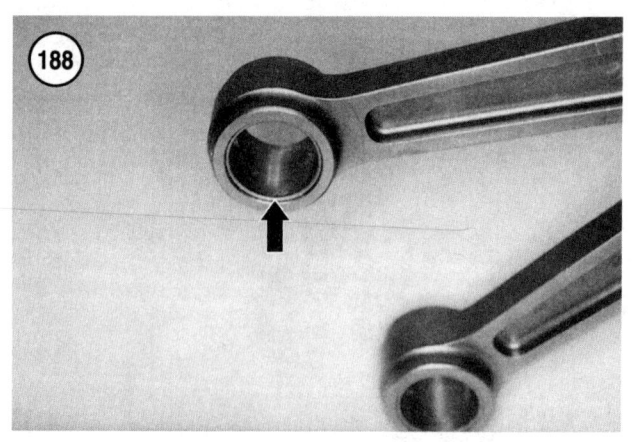

189

CRANKCASE ASSEMBLY (2006 MODELS)

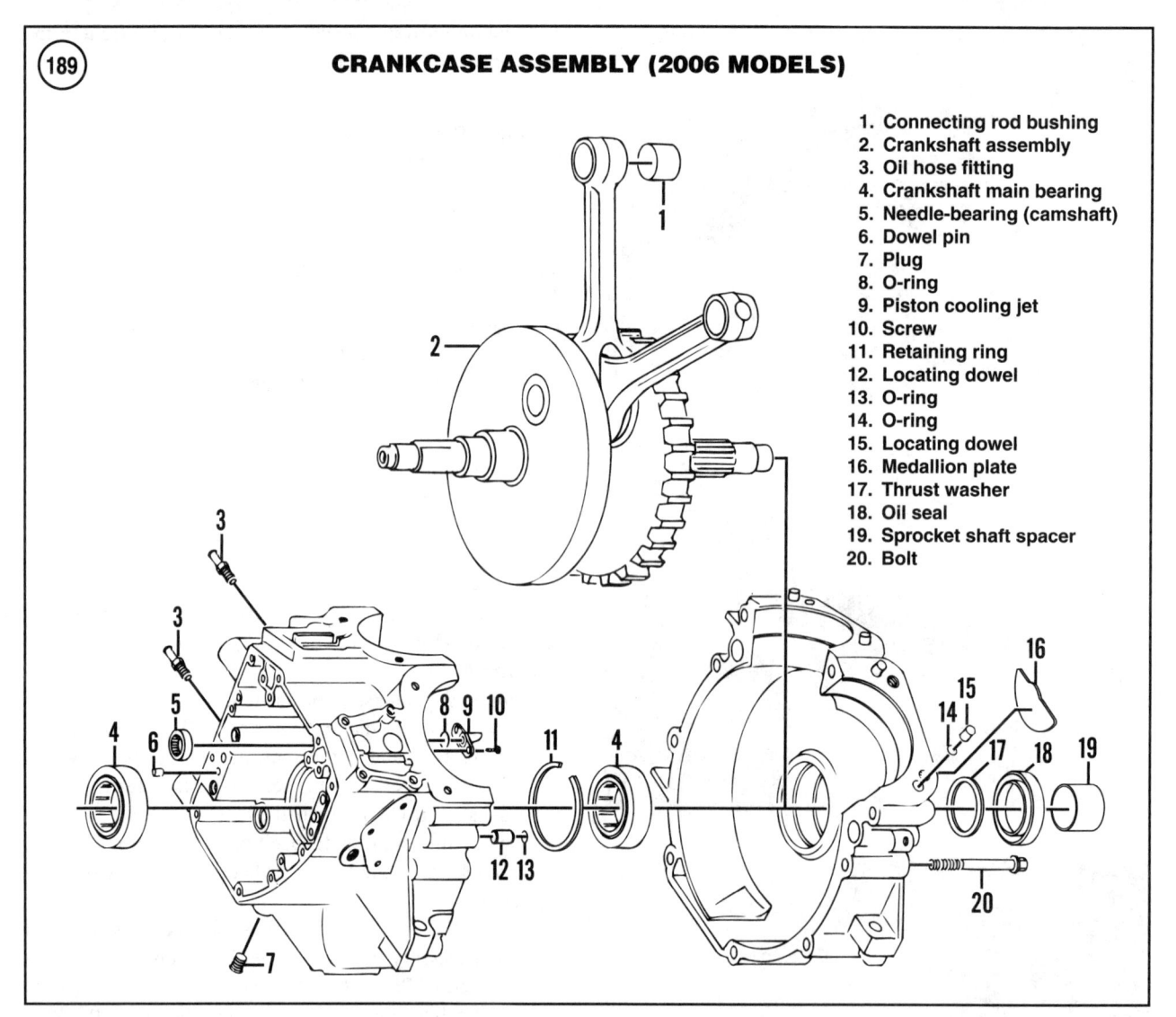

1. Connecting rod bushing
2. Crankshaft assembly
3. Oil hose fitting
4. Crankshaft main bearing
5. Needle-bearing (camshaft)
6. Dowel pin
7. Plug
8. O-ring
9. Piston cooling jet
10. Screw
11. Retaining ring
12. Locating dowel
13. O-ring
14. O-ring
15. Locating dowel
16. Medallion plate
17. Thrust washer
18. Oil seal
19. Sprocket shaft spacer
20. Bolt

1. If the engine lower end is assembled, block off the lower crankcase opening with clean shop cloths.

2A. If the stud has broken off flush with the top surface of the crankcase, remove it as described in Chapter One.

2B. If the whole stud is still in place, perform the following:

   a. Thread a 3/8-16 nut onto the top of the stud.

   b. Thread an additional nut onto the stud and tighten it against the first nut so that they are locked.

   c. Turn the bottom nut *counterclockwise* and unscrew the stud.

3. Clean the stud threads in the crankcase with a spiral brush, and then clean with an aerosol parts cleaner. If necessary, clean the threads with an appropriate size tap.

ENGINE LOWER END

CRANKCASE ASSEMBLY (2007-2009 MODELS)

1. Connecting rod bushing (not replaceable)
2. Crankshaft assembly
3. Needle bearing (camshaft)
4. Dowel pin
5. Crankshaft main bearing
6. Plug
7. Crankcase half (right side)
8. O-ring
9. Piston cooling jet
10. Screw
11. Locating dowel
12. Retaining ring
13. Oil filter adapter
14. Oil filter
15. Crankcase half (left side)
16. Locating dowel
17. Thrust washer
18. Oil seal
19. Sprocket shaft spacer
20. Bolt

NOTE
New studs may have a patch of threadlock already applied to the lower stud threads. If so, do not apply any additional threadlock to these studs.

4. If the new stud does not have the patch of threadlock already applied, apply ThreeBond TB1360, or an equivalent, to the lower stud threads.

NOTE
The cylinder studs have a shoulder on one end and this end must be installed next to the crankcase surface.

5. To protect the threaded end of the stud, place a 0.313 in. (7.95 mm) diameter steel ball (H-D part No. 8860) into a cylinder head hollow bolt. Then, thread the bolt onto the end of the new stud.

6. Position the stud with the shoulder end going in first and hand-thread the new stud into the crankcase.

CAUTION
Do not use a breaker bar, ratchet or similar tool to install the studs. These tools may bend the stud and cause the engine to leak oil.

7. Hold an air impact wrench directly in-line with the stud. *Slowly* tighten the new stud with an air impact wrench until the stud shoulder contacts the top surface of the crankcase.

8. Use a torque wrench and hand-tighten the stud to 10-20 ft.-lb. (13.6-27.1 N•m).

9. Remove the cylinder head bolt and steel ball from the cylinder stud.

10. Repeat the procedure to install any additional studs.

CRANKCASE BEARING REPLACEMENT

Right Side Main Bearing Replacement

Refer to **Figures 189-191**.

Tools

The following tools, or their equivalents, are required to remove and install the right side main bearing:

1. Hydraulic press.
2. Crankshaft bearing support tube (H-D part No. 42720-5) marked with either *A* or *B*.
3. Pilot/driver (H-D part No. B-45655).

CHAPTER FIVE

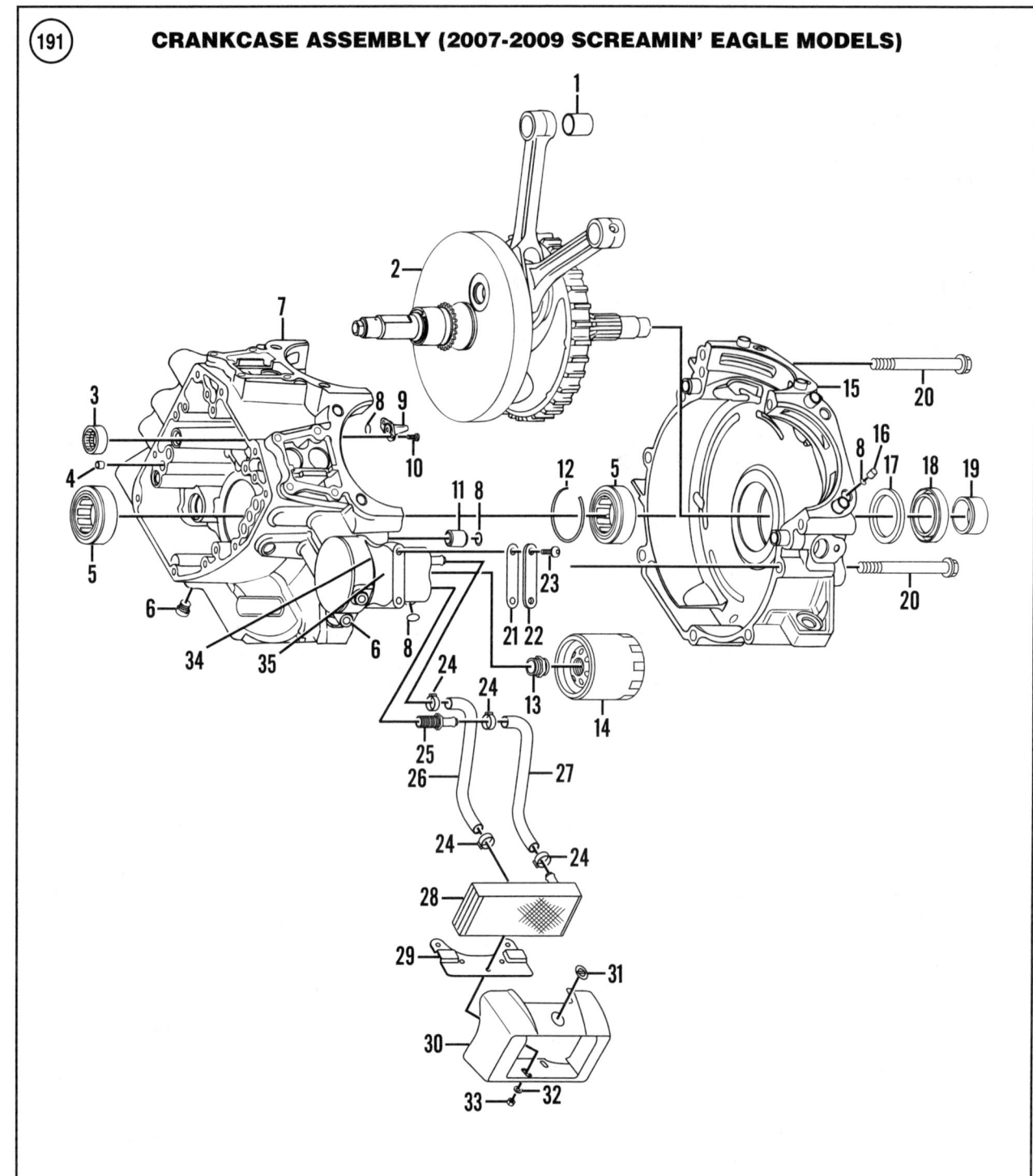

CRANKCASE ASSEMBLY (2007-2009 SCREAMIN' EAGLE MODELS)

1. Connecting rod bushing (not replaceable)
2. Crankshaft assembly
3. Needle bearing (camshaft)
4. Dowel pin
5. Crankshaft main bearing
6. Plug
7. Crankcase half (right side)
8. O-ring
9. Piston cooling jet
10. Screw
11. Locating dowel
12. Retaining ring
13. Oil filter adapter
14. Oil filter
15. Crankcase half (left side)
16. Locating dowel
17. Thrust washer
18. Oil seal
19. Sprocket shaft spacer
20. Bolt
21. Gasket
22. Cover
23. Screw
24. Hose clamp
25. Fitting (hose)
26. Return hose
27. Supply hose
28. Oil cooler (2009 models shown)
29. Mounting plate
30. Cover
31. Trim plate
32. Washer
33. Flange locknut
34. Gasket
35. Adapter assembly

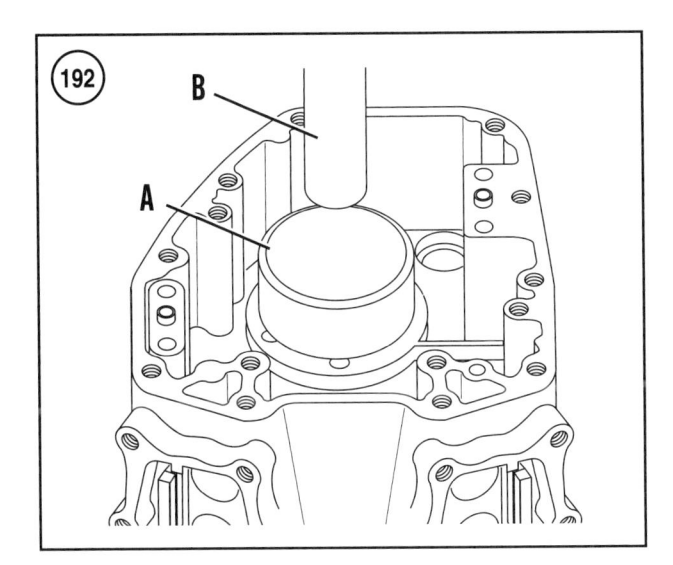

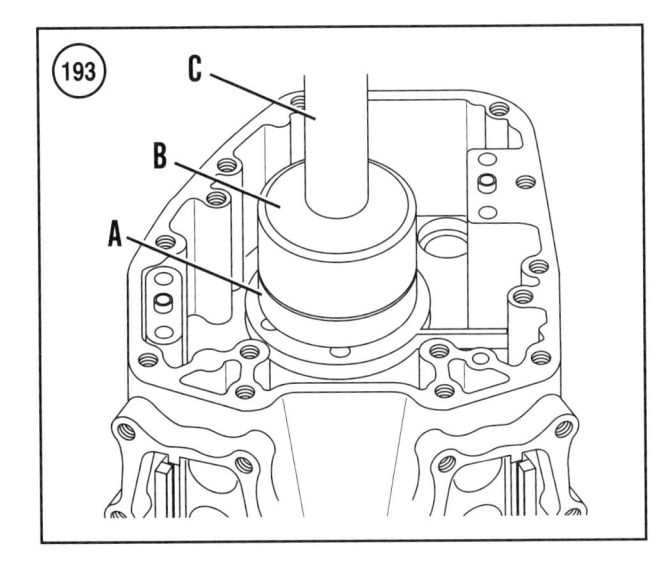

ENGINE LOWER END

(192)

(193)

3. Position the right crankcase half onto the press bed with the outboard side facing up. Position the crankshaft bearing bore over the support tube. Correctly align the two parts.
4. Position the *new* bearing (A, **Figure 193**) with the manufacturer's marks facing up and place it over the crankcase bearing bore.
5. Install the pilot/driver (B, **Figure 193**) through the bearing and into the support tube.
6. Center the press ram (C, **Figure 193**) over the pilot driver.
7. Slowly apply ram pressure on the pilot driver, pressing the bearing into the crankcase half. Apply pressure until resistance is felt and the bearing bottoms in the support tube. This will correctly locate the bearing within the crankcase half. Remove the pilot driver.
8. Remove the right crankcase half and the support tube from the press bed.
9. Check on each side of the crankcase half to make sure the bearing is centered within the receptacle. If not, reposition the bearing until it is centered correctly.
10. Spin the bearing to make sure it rotates smoothly with no binding.

Left Side Main Bearing Replacement

Refer to **Figures 189-191**.

Tools

The following tools, or their equivalents, are required to remove and install the left side main bearing:
1. Hydraulic press.
2. Crankshaft bearing support tube (H-D part No. HD-42720-5) marked with either *A* or *B*.
3. Pilot/driver (H-D part No. B-45655).

Bearing removal

1. Place the left crankcase half on the workbench with the inner surface facing up.
2. If still in place, remove the crankshaft spacer from the bearing bore.
3. Carefully pull the thrust washer from the outboard side of the crankcase past the oil seal.
4. Place the support tube on the workbench with the *A* side facing up.
5. Position the crankcase half with the outer surface facing up and place the bearing bore over the support tube.
6. Use a suitable size drift and tap the oil seal out of the bearing bore. Discard the oil seal.
7. Turn the crankcase half over with the inner surface facing up.

CAUTION
Do not damage the crankcase retaining ring groove with the screwdriver. The groove must remain sharp to correctly seat the retaining ring.

Removal

1. Place the support tube on the press bed with the *A* side facing up.
2. Position the right crankcase half with the outboard side facing up and position the bearing directly over the support tube on the press bed.
3. Install the pilot/driver shaft (A, **Figure 192**) through the bearing and into the support tube.
4. Center the press driver (B, **Figure 192**) over the pilot/driver shaft.
5. Hold the crankcase half parallel to the press bed and have an assistant slowly apply ram pressure on the pilot shaft until the bearing is free from the crankcase half.
6. Remove the crankcase half and tools from the press bed.

Installation

1. Apply a light coat of clean engine oil to the outer surface of the *new* bearing and to the crankcase bearing bore.
2. Place the support tube on the press bed with the *B* side facing up.

8. The roller bearing (A, **Figure 194**) is secured in the crankcase half with a retaining ring (B) fit into a groove on the inner surface of the bearing bore. Remove the retaining ring as follows:
   a. Use a flat-bladed screwdriver (C, **Figure 194**) and place it under the retaining ring. Carefully lift the edge of the retaining ring up and out of the crankcase groove.
   b. Slide the tip of the screwdriver around the edge of the bearing and continue to lift the retaining ring out of the crankcase groove.
   c. Remove the retaining ring.
9. Position the support tube (A, **Figure 195**) on the press bed with the *A* side facing up.
10. Position the left crankcase half onto the press bed with the outboard side facing up. Position the crankshaft's bearing bore over the support tube. Correctly align the two parts.
11. Slide the pilot/driver (B, **Figure 195**) through the crankcase bearing and into the support.
12. Center the press ram (C, **Figure 195**) directly over the pilot/driver (B) and slowly press the bearing out of the crankcase half.
13. Remove the crankcase half and tools from the press bed.
14. Clean the crankcase half in solvent and dry it with compressed air.

Bearing installation

1. Apply clean engine oil, or press lube, to the bearing receptacle in the crankcase half and to the outer race of the *new* bearing.
2. Position the support tube (A, **Figure 196**) on the press bed with the *A* side facing up.
3. Position the crankcase half with the inboard side facing up and position the crankshaft bearing bore over the support tube. Correctly align the two parts.
4. Correctly position the *new* bearing (B, **Figure 196**) over the crankcase bearing bore with the manufacturer's marks facing down.
5. Slide the pilot/driver (C, **Figure 196**) through the new bearing and crankcase half and into the support tube.
6. Center the press ram (D, **Figure 196**) directly over the pilot/driver (C) and slowly press the bearing into the crankcase half until it *lightly* bottoms in the crankshaft bearing bore.
7. Remove the crankcase half and tools from the press.
8. Make sure the bearing has been pressed in past the retaining ring groove. If the groove is not visible above the bearing, repeat the installation process until the groove is visible.
9. Position the crankcase half on the workbench with the inboard side facing up.

CAUTION
Do not damage the crankcase retaining ring groove with the screwdriver. The groove must remain sharp to correctly seat the retaining ring. If the retaining ring will not correctly

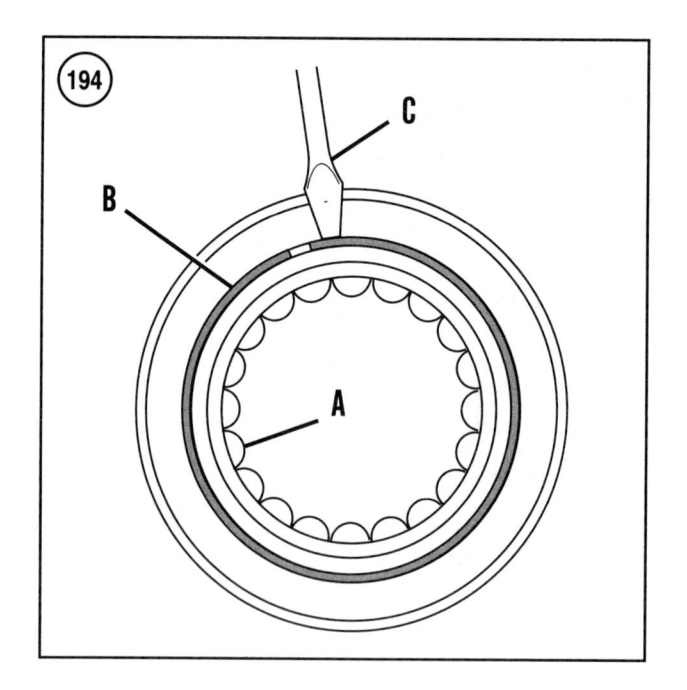

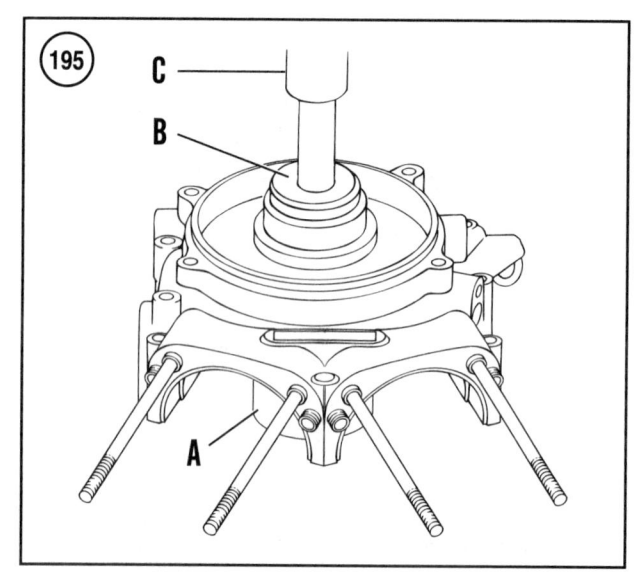

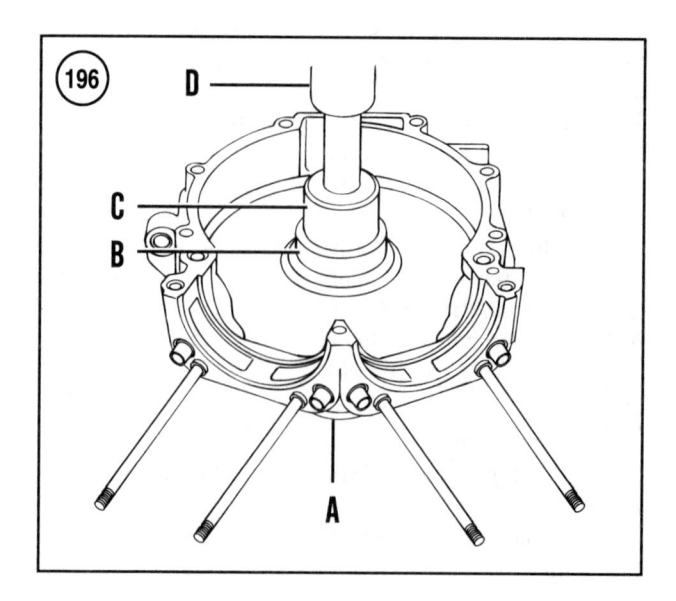

ENGINE LOWER END

Figure 197

Figure 198

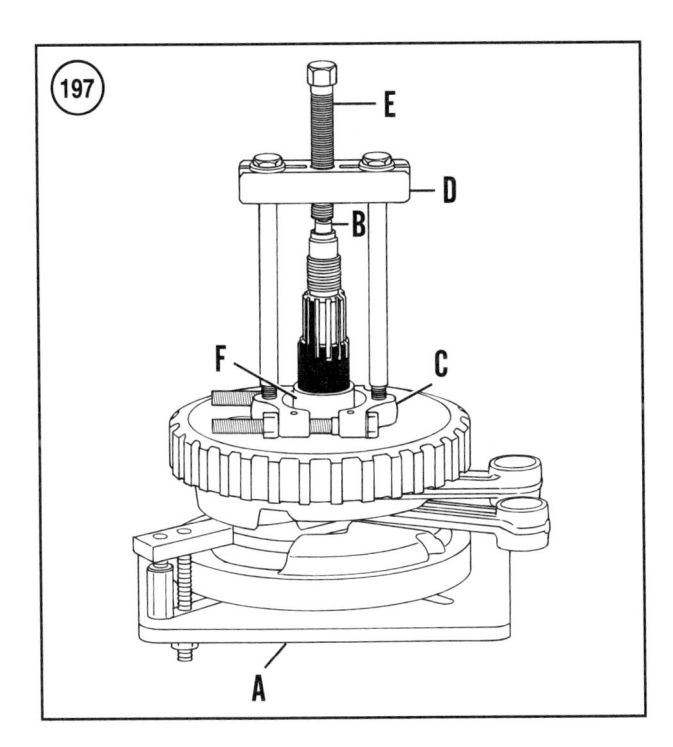

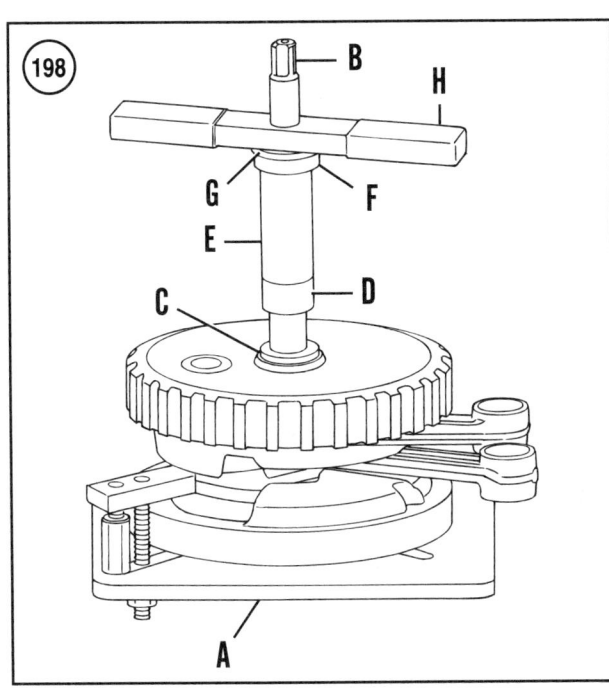

seat in the crankcase groove, the bearing is not correctly seated in the crankcase bore. Repeat the installation process until the retaining ring groove is accessible.

10. Install a *new* bearing retaining ring as follows:
   a. Work the retaining ring into the crankcase groove, being careful not to damage the crankcase groove.
   b. Use a flat-bladed screwdriver and push the retaining ring into the groove. Continue to push the retaining ring into the crankcase until it fully engages the groove. Make sure it is correctly seated in the groove.

Crankshaft Left Side Main Bearing Inner Race Replacement

Refer to **Figures 189-191**.

Removal

1. Support the crankshaft in a support fixture (H-D part No. HD-44358), or an equivalent (A, **Figure 197**), with the bearing side facing up.
2. Place a hardened plug (B, **Figure 197**) between the bearing puller and the end of the crankshaft.
3. Install the bearing splitter (C, **Figure 197**) under the bearing inner race.
4. Attach a bearing puller (D, **Figure 197**) to the splitter. Apply graphite lubricant to the bearing puller center screw before installing it.

WARNING
Never use the heat gun in conjunction with the penetrating oil. The heat from the gun may ignite the oil resulting in a fire.

5A. Use a high temperature heat gun and apply heat uniformly to the bearing inner race for approximately 30 seconds.
5B. If a heat gun is not available, apply penetrating oil to the inner race and crankshaft and allow the oil to penetrate for 30 minutes.
6. Make sure the bearing puller is square to the crankshaft so the bearing inner race is not out of alignment with the crankshaft shoulder.
7. Slowly tighten the bearing puller center screw (E, **Figure 197**) and withdraw the bearing inner race (F) from the crankshaft shoulder.
8. Remove the bearing puller, splitter and bearing inner race from the crankshaft.
9. Remove the thrust washer from the crankshaft. Discard the thrust washer, it cannot be re-used.
10. Clean the sprocket shaft with contact cleaner. Check the sprocket shaft for cracks or other damage. If it is damaged, refer service to a dealership.

Installation

The sprocket shaft bearing cone installer (H-D part No. HD-97225-55C) is required to install the sprocket shaft bearing inner race.

1. Support the crankshaft in a support fixture (H-D part No. HD-44358), or an equivalent (A, **Figure 198**), with the bearing side facing up.
2. Thread the tool pilot shaft (B, **Figure 198**) onto the crankshaft until it contacts the crankshaft.
3. Slide the *new* thrust washer (C, **Figure 198**) over the sprocket shaft.

WARNING
Never use the heat gun in conjunction with the penetrating oil. The heat from the gun may ignite the oil resulting in a fire.

4A. Place the *new* bearing race on the workbench. Use a heat gun and uniformly heat the bearing race for approximately 60 seconds. Wear heavy duty gloves and install the new inner race (D, **Figure 198**) onto the crankshaft.

4B. If a heat gun is not available, apply penetrating oil to the inner surface of the bearing race and to the crankshaft shoulder. Install the new inner race (D, **Figure 198**) onto the crankshaft.

5. Apply graphite lubricant to the threads of the pilot shaft and flat washer.

6. Slide the tool sleeve (E, **Figure 198**) onto the crankshaft until it contacts the bearing inner race.

7. Slide the tool installer bearing (F, **Figure 198**) and flat washer (G) over the pilot shaft until it contacts the top of the sleeve.

8. Thread the tool handle (H, **Figure 198**) onto the pilot shaft (B).

9. Slowly tighten the handle *clockwise* until the bearing inner race bottoms on the crankshaft shoulder.

10. Unscrew and remove all parts of the tool.

Crankcase Left Side Oil Seal Replacement

Refer to **Figures 189-191**.

Tools

The following tools, or their equivalent, are required to install the oil seal.

1. Sprocket shaft seal installer tool (JIMS part No. 39361-69).
2. Sprocket shaft bearing cone installer (H-D part No. HD-97225-55C).

Removal

1. Remove the sprocket shaft spacer (**Figure 199**) from the crankshaft and the oil seal.

2. Carefully pry the old oil seal (**Figure 200**) out of the bearing bore and discard it.

3. Position the *new* oil seal so the side with the manufacturer's marks faces out.

ENGINE LOWER END

the large nut slowly and make sure the oil seal (**Figure 203**) is entering straight into the bearing bore.

9. Tighten the large nut until the shaft seal installer tool contacts the crankcase surface (**Figure 204**).

10. Remove the tools.

11. Apply clean engine oil to the outer surface of the sprocket shaft spacer (**Figure 199**), and install it onto the crankshaft and into the oil seal.

4. Install the oil seal (A, **Figure 201**) onto the crankshaft and center it within the bearing bore.

5. Apply clean engine oil or press lube to the installer tool threads, both washers and the radial bearing.

6. Install the main tool body (B, **Figure 201**) onto the crankshaft and screw it on until it stops.

7. Install the rest of the shaft seal installer tool following the manufacturer's instructions.

8. Hold the handle (A, **Figure 202**) of the main tool body and slowly tighten the large nut (B) with a wrench. Tighten

ENGINE BREAK-IN

Following cylinder service (boring, honing, new rings) and major lower end work, the engine must be broken in just as though it were new. The service and performance life of the engine depends on a careful and sensible break-in.

1. For the first 50 mi. (80 km), maintain engine speed below 2500 rpm in any gear. However, do not lug the engine. Do not exceed 50 mph during this period.

2. From 50-500 mi. (80-805 km), vary the engine speed. Avoid prolonged steady running at one engine speed. During this period, increase engine speed to 3000 rpm. Do not exceed 55 mph during this period.

3. After the first 500 mi. (805 km), the engine break-in is complete.

Table 1 ENGINE LOWER END SPECIFICATIONS

Item	New in. (mm)	Service limit in. (mm)
Breather assembly		
Cover warp	–	0.005 (0.13)
Baffle warp	–	0.005 (0.13)
Camshaft support plate		
Camshaft chain tensioner shoe		
2006 models	–	1/2 thickness of shoe
2007-2009 models (primary and secondary)	–	0.060 (1.524)
Camshaft bushing fit (2006 models)	–	0.0008 (0.020)
Camshaft bushing maximum inside diameter		
(2007-2009 models)	–	0.08545 (2.1704)
Camshaft bore in plate (2007-2009 models)	–	1.1023 (27.998)
Connecting rod		
Connecting rod-to-crankpin clearance	0.0004-0.0017 (0.010-0.043)	0.002 (0.051)
Piston pin clearance in connecting rod		
All models except Screamin' Eagle	0.0007-0.0012 (0.018-0.030)	0.002 (0.051)
Screamin' Eagle models		
2006 models	0.0003-0.0007 (0.008-0.018)	0.001 (0.025)
2007-2009 models	0.0006-0.0012 (0.015-0.030)	0.002 (0.051)
Side play	0.005-0.015 (0.13-0.38)	0.020 (0.508)
Oil pump pressure		
[at 110° C (230° F)]	30-38 psi (207-262 kPa) @ 2000 rpm	
Oil pump rotor tip-to-tip clearance	–	0.004 (0.10)
Oil pump feed rotor height		
2006-2008 models	0.080-0.090 (2.03-2.29)	Less than 0.080 (2.03)
2009 models	0.015-0.025 (0.38-0.64)	Less than 0.015 (0.38)
(continued)		

Table 1 ENGINE LOWER END SPECIFICATIONS (continued)

Item	New in. (mm)	Service limit in. (mm)
Crankshaft		
Runout (2006-2007 models)		
Flywheel at rim	0.000-0.010 (0.00-0.25)	0.015 (0.381)
Shaft at flywheel		
2006 models	0.000-0.002 (0.00-0.051)	0.003 (0.076)
2007 models	0.000-0.003 (0.00-0.076)	0.010 (0.254)
Runout (2008-2009 models)		
Measured on truing stand	0.000-0.004 (0.00-0.102)	0.005 (0.127)
End Play	0.003-0.010 (0.076-0.254)	0.010 (0.254)
Crankshaft/sprocket shaft bearings		
Roller bearing fit (loose)	0.0002-0.0015 (0.005-0.038)	greater than 0.0015 (0.038)
Bearing in crankcase	0.0038-0.0054 (0.097-0.137)	less than 0.0038 (0.097)
Crankshaft to inner face clearance	0.0004-0.0014 (0.010-0.036)	less than 0.0004 (0.010)
Oil pressure relief valve		
Running clearance	0.003 (0.076)	–
Seated depth	2.25 (57.15)	–

Table 2 REAR CAMSHAFT SPROCKET SPACERS

Part No.	in.	mm
2006 models		
25717-00	0.327	8.31
25719-00	0.317	8.05
25721-00	0.307	7.80
25722-00	0.287	7.29
25723-00	0.297	7.54
25725-00	0.337	8.56
2007-2009 models		
25731-06	0.110	2.79
25734-06	0.120	3.05
25736-06	0.130	3.30
25737-06	0.140	3.56
25738-06	0.150	3.81

Table 3 ENGINE LOWER END TORQUE SPECIFICATIONS

Item	ft.-lb.	in.-lb.	N•m
Breather cover bolts	–	90-120	10.2-13.6
Camshaft cover bolts	–	125-155	14.1-17.5
Camshaft support plate bolt			
Perimeter six bolts	–	90-120	10.2-13.6
Center four bolts (adjacent to oil pump)			
Preliminary		40-45	4.5-5.1
Final	–	90-120	10-2-13.6
Sprocket bolts			
Preliminary	15	–	20.3
Rear camshaft sprocket bolt	34	–	46.1
Crankshaft sprocket bolt	24	–	32.5
Camshaft cover bolts	–	125-155	14.1-17.5
Camshaft primary chain tensioner bolts	–	100-120	11.3-13.6
Camshaft bearing retainer Torx screws (2006 models)	–	20-30	2.3-3.4
Camshaft chain tensioner mounting bolts (2007-2009 models)	–	100-120	11.3-13.6
Crankshaft position sensor screw	–	90-120	10.2-13.6

(continued)

Table 3 ENGINE LOWER END TORQUE SPECIFICATIONS (continued)

Item	ft.-lb.	in.-lb.	N·m
Crankshaft sprocket bolt	24	–	32.5
Crankcase bolts			
Preliminary	10	–	13.6
Final	15-19	–	20.3-25.8
Cylinder studs	10-20	–	13.6-27.1
Engine mounting fasteners			
Engine-to-transmission bolt	70-80	–	94.9-108.5
Preliminary	15	–	20.3
Final			
2006-2008 models	30-35	–	40.7-47.5
2009 models	34-39	–	46.1-52.9
2006-2007 models			
Lower mounting bracket-			
to-engine bolts	33-38	–	44.7-51.5
Upper bracket-to-cylinder			
head bolts	18-22	–	24.4-29.8
Upper stabilizer link-to-frame			
weldment bolt	30-35	–	40.7-47.5
2008 models			
Upper bracket-to-cylinder			
head bolts	18-22	–	24.4-29.8
Upper stabilizer link-to-frame			
weldment bolt	30-35	–	40.7-47.5
2009 models			
Front mounting bracket			
hex bolts/nuts	36-40	–	48.8-54.2
Upper bracket-to-cylinder			
head bolts	18-22	–	24.4-29.8
Upper stabilizer link-to-frame			
weldment Allen bolt	30-35	–	40.7-47.5
End cap Allen bolts			
Short bolts	42-48	–	56.9-65.1
Long engine mount bolts	40-50	–	54.2-67.8
Oil filter mounting bracket bolts			
(2006 models except Screamin' Eagle)	12-16	–	16.3-21.7
Oil cooler (2006 Screamin' Eagle models)			
Mounting locknuts	–	80-110	9.0-12.4
Oil filter mount bolts	12-16	–	16.3-21.7
Oil filter adapter-to-filter mount	12-16	–	16.3-21.7
Oil pressure switch	–	96-144	10.8-16.3
Oil filter passage cover screws	–	90-120	10.2-13.6
Thermostat plug	15-20	–	20.3-27.1
Oil cooler (2007-2009 Screamin' Eagle models)			
Mounting flange locknuts	–	70-100	7.9-11.3
Adapter-to-crankcase	18-22	–	24.4-29.8

CHAPTER SIX

CLUTCH AND PRIMARY DRIVE

This chapter describes service procedures for the clutch and primary drive assemblies.

Specifications are in **Tables 1-3** at the end of this chapter.

PRIMARY CHAINCASE COVER

Removal

Refer to **Figure 1** or **Figure 2**.

WARNING
Disconnect the negative battery cable or pull the Maxi-Fuse before working on the clutch or any primary drive component to avoid accidentally activating the starter.

NOTE
Always disarm the optional TSSM/HFSM security system before disconnecting the battery or pulling the Maxi-Fuse so the alarm will not sound.

1. Disconnect the negative battery cable as described in Chapter Eleven.
2. Remove both left footboards as described in Chapter Seventeen.
3. Remove the clamp bolt (A, **Figure 3**) and remove the heel shift lever (B).
4. Drain the primary chaincase oil as described in Chapter Three.

NOTE
*The primary chaincase cover can be removed with the inspection cover (A, **Figure 4**) and clutch cover (B) in place on 2006 models.*

NOTE
*Two different length bolts secure the primary chaincase cover. Note and mark the location of the short and long bolts. They must be reinstalled in the correct location. Refer to **Figure 5** for 2006 models, or **Figure 6** for 2007-2009 models.*

5A On 2006 models, perform the following:
   a. Evenly loosen the primary chaincase cover bolts (**Figure 5**) and the inspection cover bolts.
   b. Remove the bolts along with their washers, and then remove the primary chaincase cover. Do not lose the dowel pins (**Figure 7** and **Figure 8**) behind the cover.
   c. Remove the cover gasket.
5B. On 2007-2009 models, perform the following:
   a. Evenly loosen the primary chaincase cover bolts (**Figure 5**).
   b. Pull the cover bolts along with their washers, and remove the chaincase cover and gasket. Do not lose the dowel pins (A, **Figure 9**) behind the cover.

CLUTCH AND PRIMARY DRIVE

PRIMARY CHAINCASE HOUSING (2006 MODELS)

1. Bearing
2. Outer snap ring
3. Bearing
4. Inner snap ring
5. Oil seal
6. Housing
7. Dowel pin
8. Jackshaft bushing
9. Captive washer
10. Bolt
11. Dowel pin
12. Washer
13. Shift lever bushing
14. Gasket
15. Primary chaincse cover
16. Bolt
17. Bolt
18. Clutch cover
19. O-ring
20. Screw
21. Drain screw
22. Gasket
23. Primary chaincse inspection cover
24. Screw

PRIMARY CHAINCASE HOUSING (2007-2009 MODELS)

1. Locating dowel
2. Bolt
3. Oil seal
4. Retaining ring
5. Bearing
6. Gasket
7. Bushing
8. Gasket
9. O-ring
10. Drain plug
11. Chain tensioner
12. Sleeve (HDI)
13. Cover
14. Bolt
15. Gasket
16. Clutch cover
17. Housing
18. Screw

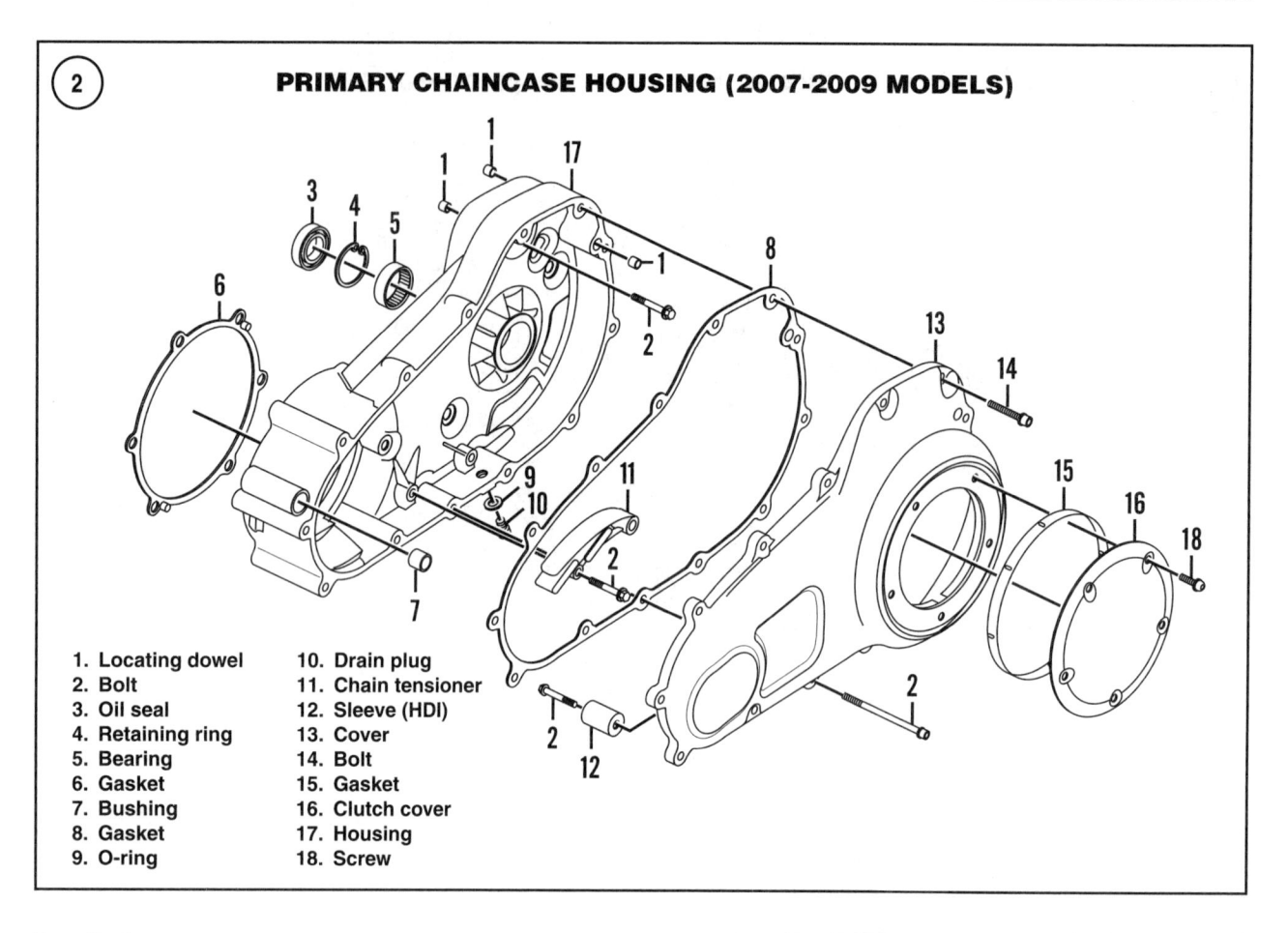

Installation

1. If removed, install the dowels into the primary chaincase housing. Refer to **Figure 7** and **Figure 8** for 2006 models or A, **Figure 9** for 2007-2009 models.

NOTE
The gasket is thin and it may shift prior to installation of the cover bolts.

2. Apply a small amount of gasket sealer to the backside of the *new* gasket in a few areas to help hold it in place on the dowels.

CAUTION
*The manufacturer specifies that a **new** gasket must be installed every time the primary chaincase cover is removed to avoid oil leaks.*

3. Install the *new* gasket over the dowels, and seat it against the gasket surface (**Figure 10**: 2006 models; B, **Figure 9**: 2007-2009 models) of the chaincase housing.

4. Slide the primary cover over the dowels, and set it securely against the gasket.

5A. On 2006 models, install the short and long primary chaincase cover bolts and inspection cover bolts, along with their washers, into the locations noted during removal. Following the torque sequence shown in **Figure 5**, tighten the primary chaincase cover bolts to 108-120 in.-lb. (12.2-

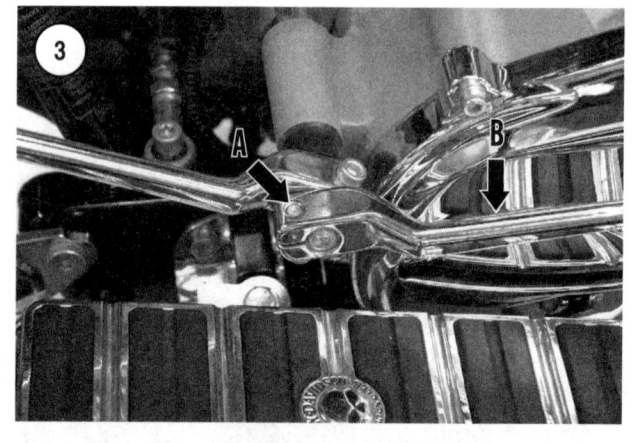

CLUTCH AND PRIMARY DRIVE

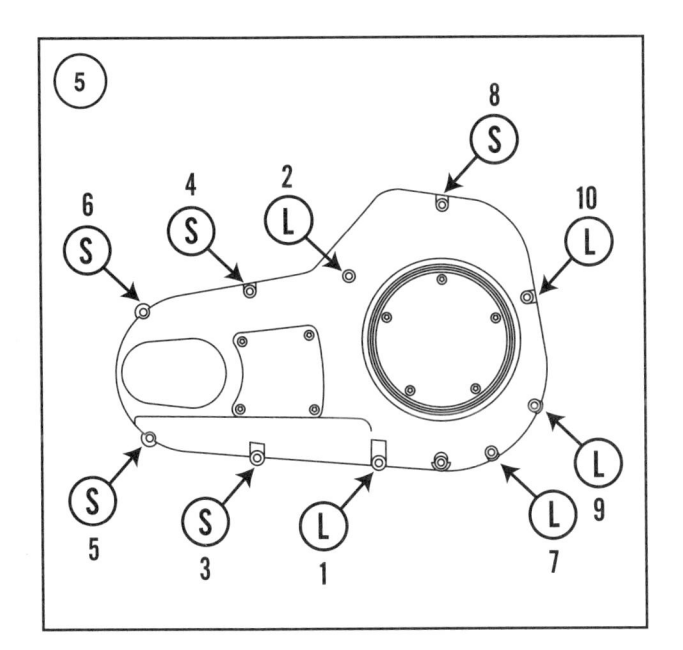

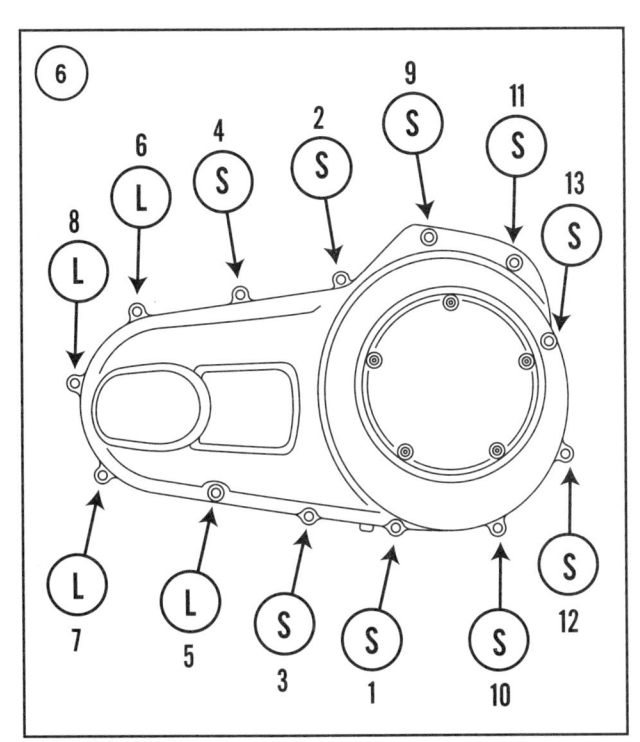

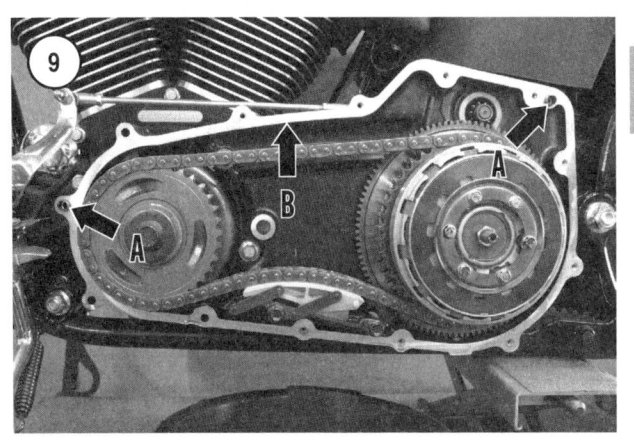

13.6 N•m). Make sure the cover gasket seats evenly around the cover.

5B. On 2007-2009 models, insert the short and long bolts, with their washers into the locations noted during removal. Following the torque sequence shown in **Figure 6**, tighten the primary chaincase cover bolts to 108-120 in.-lb. (12.2-13.6 N•m). Make sure the gasket seats flush around the cover.

6. Install the heel shift lever (B, **Figure 3**) and clamp bolt (A). Tighten the bolt securely.

7. Install both left footboards as described in Chapter Seventeen.

8. Fill the primary chaincase with the type and quantity of oil specified as described in Chapter Three.

9. Connect the negative battery cable or install the Maxi-Fuse as described in Chapter Eleven.

Inspection

1. Remove all gasket material from the chaincase cover (**Figure 11**: 2006 models; **Figure 12**: 2007-2009 models) and chaincase housing gasket (B, **Figure 9**) surfaces.
2. Clean the primary cover in solvent. Dry it with compressed air.
3. Inspect the primary chaincase cover for cracks or damage.
4. On 2006 models, inspect the starter jackshaft bushing (**Figure 13**) for excessive wear or damage. To replace the bushing, perform the following:
   a. Remove the bushing with a blind bearing removal tool.
   b. Clean the bushing bore in the housing.
   c. Press in the new bushing until its outer surface is flush with the edge of the bushing bore.

PRIMARY CHAINCASE HOUSING (2006 MODELS)

The primary chaincase inner housing mounts to both the engine and transmission. It houses the primary drive assembly, alternator rotor, starter jackshaft, and the mainshaft oil seal and bearing assembly.

Refer to **Figure 1**.

Removal

NOTE
Always disarm the optional TSSM/HFSM security system before disconnecting the battery or pulling the Maxi-Fuse so the alarm will not sound.

1. Disconnect the negative battery cable as described in Chapter Eleven.
2. Remove the primary chaincase cover as described in this chapter.
3. Remove the primary drive assembly as described in this chapter.
4. Remove the starter as described in Chapter Eleven.
5. Remove the front two housing bolts (**Figure 14**).
6. Remove the five remaining housing bolts (A and B, **Figure 15**).
7. Remove the starter jackshaft assembly from the housing as described in this chapter.
8. Tap the housing loose.
9. Remove the housing from the crankcase, transmission and gearshift shaft.
10. Remove the O-ring (**Figure 16**) from the engine crankcase shoulder, and discard it.

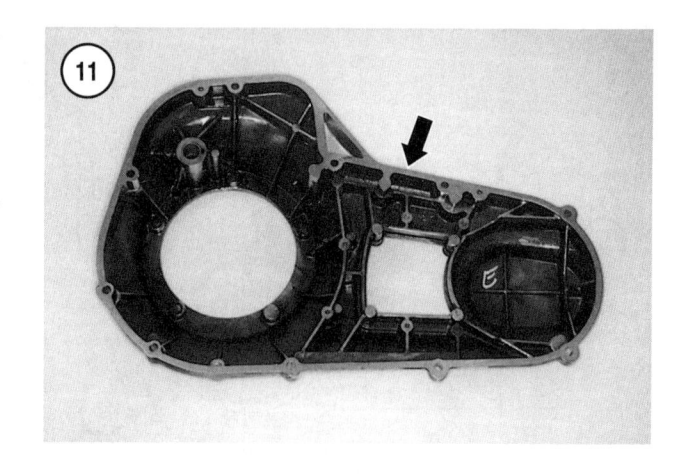

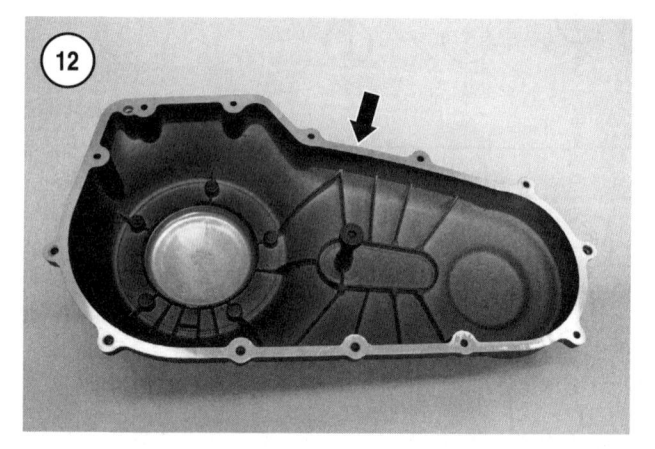

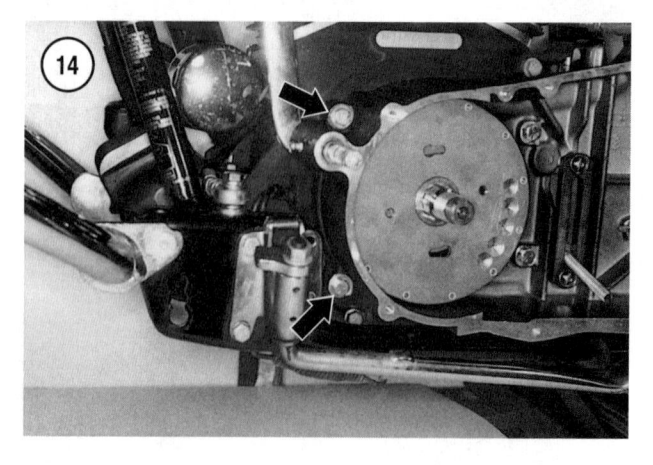

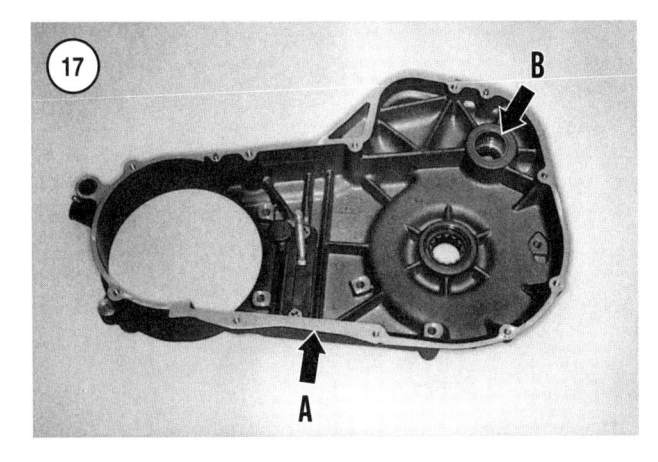

CLUTCH AND PRIMARY DRIVE

Installation

1. Thoroughly clean the *outer surface* of the five bolt holes inside the housing. Also, clean all threadlock residue from the blind bolt holes in the transmission and crankcase.
2. Thoroughly clean the mating surfaces of the housing, transmission and crankcase.
3. Install a *new* O-ring (**Figure 16**) onto the engine crankcase shoulder.
4. To prevent the transmission mainshaft splines from damaging the oil seal, wrap the mainshaft splines with 1-2 layers of smooth tape (not duct tape). Apply clean primary crankcase oil to the tape.
5. If removed, install the drive belt prior to installing the housing.
6. Align the housing with the crankcase and transmission and install it over the gearshift lever shaft. Push the housing on until stops. Remove the tape from the mainshaft splines.
7. If the existing bolts are going to be reused, apply two drops of Loctite Threadlocker 243 (blue) to each of the bolts prior to installation.
8. Install the housing bolts finger-tight as follows:
    a. Front two housing bolts (**Figure 14**) into the front of the crankcase.
    b. Two remaining housing bolts (A, **Figure 15**) into the front of the crankcase adjacent to the alternator rotor.
    c. Remaining three housing bolts (B, **Figure 15**) into the rear of the transmission housing.
9. Using a crossing pattern, tighten all seven primary chaincase housing bolts to 15-19 ft.-lb. (20.3-25.8 N•m).
10. Install the starter jackshaft assembly as described in this chapter.
11. Install the starter as described in Chapter Eleven.
12. Install the primary drive assembly as described in this chapter.
13. Install the primary chaincase cover as described in this chapter.
14. Connect the negative battery cable as described in Chapter Eleven.

Inspection

1. Remove all gasket material from the inner housing gasket surfaces (A, **Figure 17**).
2. Clean the inner housing in solvent and dry thoroughly.
3. Check the housing (**Figure 18**) for cracks or other damage.
4. Check the starter jackshaft oil seal for wear or damage. To replace the oil seal, perform the following:
    a. Note the direction the oil seal lip faces in the housing.
    b. Pry the oil seal out of the inner primary chaincase housing.
    c. Pack the new oil seal lips with grease.
    d. Carefully drive the *new* oil seal into the housing until it seats against the housing shoulder.
5. Inspect the starter jackshaft bushing (B, **Figure 17**) for wear, cracks or other damage. To replace the bushing, perform the following:

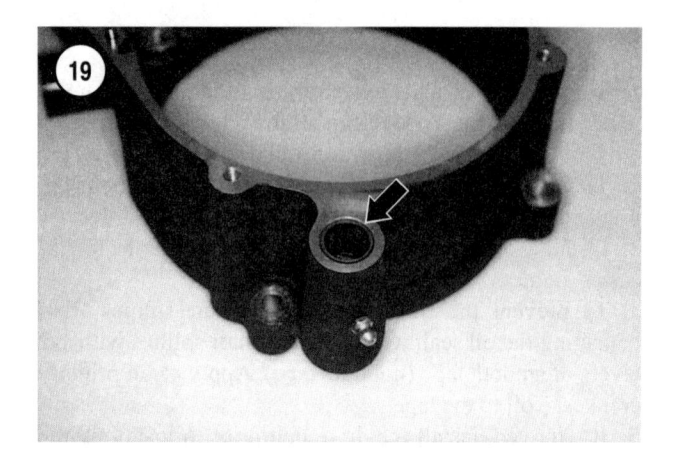

a. Remove the bushing with a blind bearing removal tool.
b. Clean the bushing bore in the housing.
c. Press in the new bushing until its outer surface is flush with the edge of the bushing bore.

6. Inspect the shift lever bushings (**Figure 19**) for wear, cracks or other damage. To replace the bushing(s), perform the following:
   a. Remove the bushing(s) with a blind bearing removal tool.
   b. Clean the bushing bore in the housing.
   c. Press in the new bushing(s) until the outer surface is flush with the edge of the bushing bore.

7. Turn the mainshaft bearing inner race (**Figure 20**) by hand. Replace the bearing as follows:
   a. Remove the oil seal (**Figure 21**) as described in this section.
   b. Remove the inner and outer bearing snap rings.
   c. Support the housing and press the bearing out.
   d. Install a *new* outer snap ring (transmission side). Align the snap ring gap with the oil hole (A, **Figure 22**) in the housing so the snap ring (B) does not block the hole. Make sure the outer snap ring is completely seated in the groove.

CAUTION
When pressing the bearing into the housing, fully support the outer snap ring. The force required to press the bearing into the inner primary housing may force the snap ring out of its groove, damaging the housing.

   e. Support the housing and outer snap ring.
   f. Press the bearing into the inner housing until it seats against the outer snap ring.
   g. Install a *new* inner snap ring. Make sure the inner snap ring is seated correctly in the groove.
   h. Install a *new* oil seal as described in this section.

8. Inspect the cover oil seal (**Figure 21**) for excessive wear, tearing or other damage. To replace the oil seal, perform the following:
   a. Remove the oil seal with a flat-bladed screwdriver.
   b. Clean the oil seal bore.
   c. Pack the oil seal lip with a waterproof bearing grease.

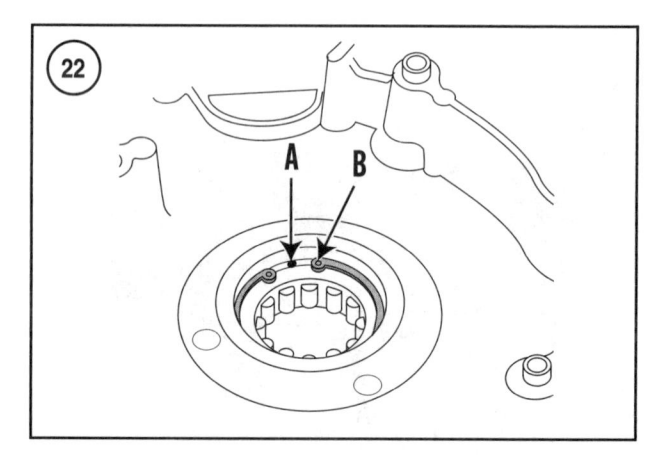

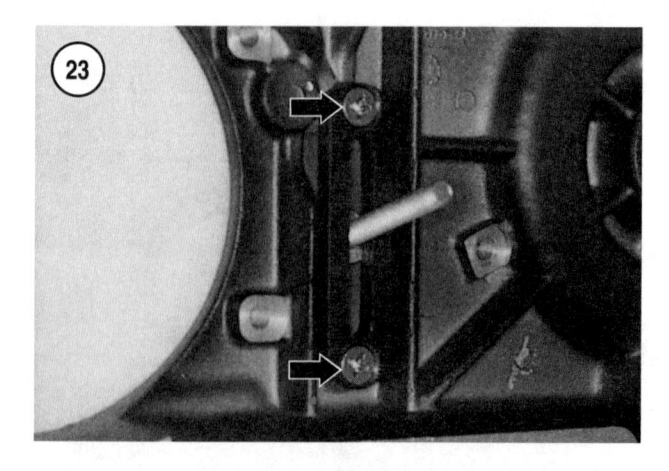

CLUTCH AND PRIMARY DRIVE

PRIMARY CHAINCASE (2007-2009 MODELS)

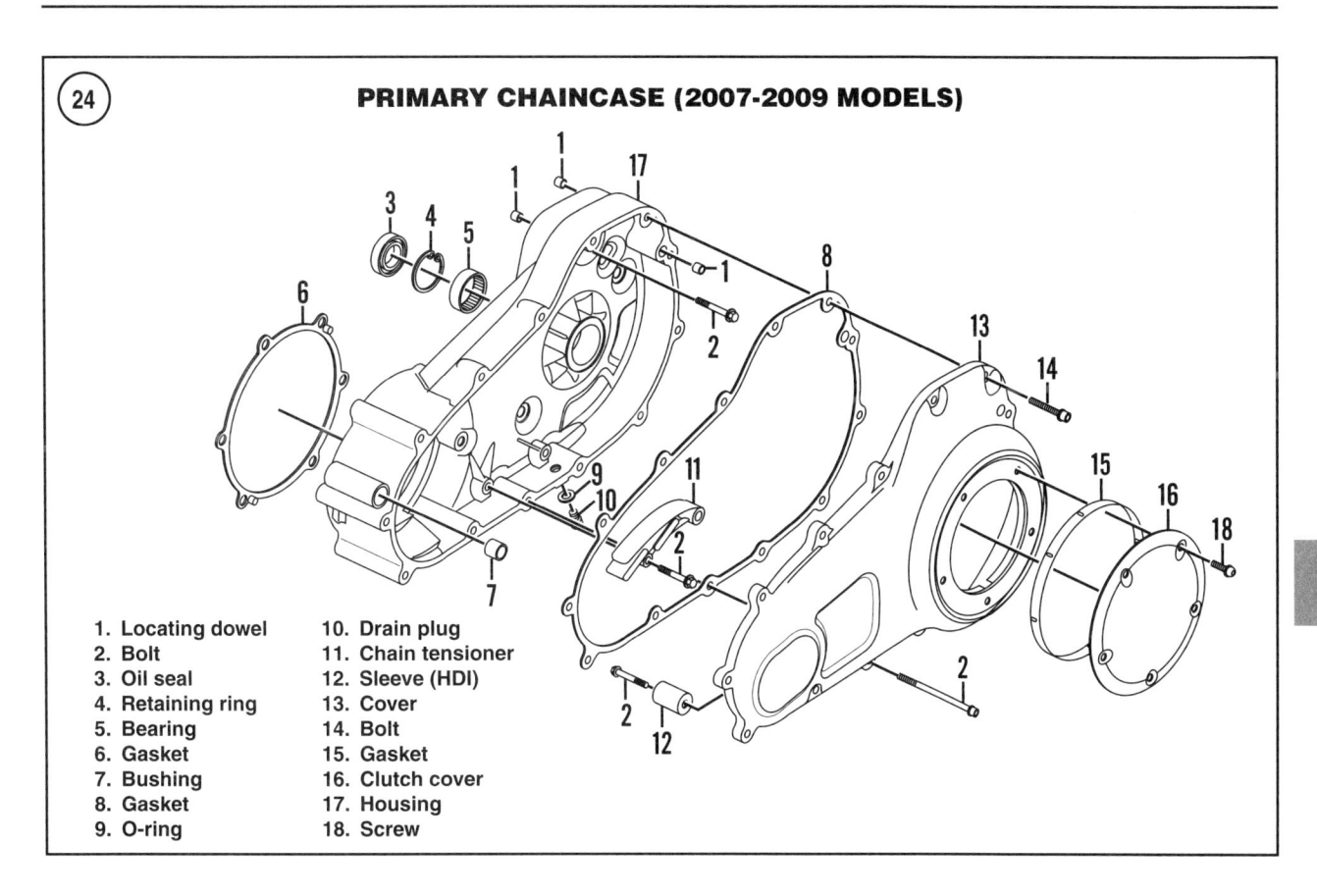

1. Locating dowel
2. Bolt
3. Oil seal
4. Retaining ring
5. Bearing
6. Gasket
7. Bushing
8. Gasket
9. O-ring
10. Drain plug
11. Chain tensioner
12. Sleeve (HDI)
13. Cover
14. Bolt
15. Gasket
16. Clutch cover
17. Housing
18. Screw

d. Position the oil seal with its closed side facing out. Press in the *new* oil seal until its outer surface is flush with the edge of the bearing bore.

9. Check the primary chain adjuster rack mounting screws (**Figure 23**) for looseness. Tighten the screws, if necessary.

PRIMARY CHAINCASE HOUSING (2007-2009 MODELS)

The primary chaincase housing mounts to both the engine and transmission. It houses the primary drive assembly, alternator rotor, and the mainshaft oil seal and bearing assembly.

Refer to **Figure 24**.

Removal

NOTE
Always disarm the optional TSSM/HFSM security system before disconnecting the battery or pulling the Maxi-Fuse so the alarm will not sound.

1. Disconnect the negative battery cable as described in Chapter Eleven.
2. Remove the primary chaincase cover and the primary drive assembly as described in this chapter.
3. Remove the starter as described in Chapter Eleven.
4. Remove the five primary chaincase housing bolts (**Figure 25**). Discard the bolts as they cannot be reused.
5. Tap the housing loose.
6. Remove the housing from the crankcase, transmission and gearshift shaft.
7. Remove the gasket (**Figure 26**) from the engine crankcase flange and discard it.
8. If still in place, remove the gasket locating pins from the crankcase flange or old gasket.
9. If still in place, remove the two locating dowels from the transmission case.

Installation

1. Confirm that the swing arm pivot shaft is properly tightened. Refer to Chapter Fifteen.

2. Thoroughly clean the *outer surface* of the five primary chaincase housing bolt holes.

3. Thoroughly clean the mating surfaces of the housing, transmission and crankcase.

4. Install the locating dowels (A, **Figure 27**) into the transmission case or the inboard side of the primary housing.

5. Ensure the two gasket locating pins (**Figure 28**) are in place on a new crankshaft gasket. Apply engine oil to the rubber portion of the gasket.

6. Install the *new* gasket (**Figure 26**) onto the engine crankcase flange so the gasket locating pins engages the crankcase flange holes.

7. To prevent the transmission mainshaft splines from damaging the oil seal in the housing, wrap the mainshaft splines with 1-2 layers of smooth tape (no duct tape) (A, **Figure 29**). Apply clean primary crankcase oil to the tape and to the lips of the oil seal (B, **Figure 29**).

8. If removed, install the drive belt before installing the housing.

9. Align the housing dowels (A, **Figure 27**) with their mating holes transmission case, install the housing and press it securely against the crankcase and transmission case. Remove the tape (A, **Figure 29**) from the mainshaft splines.

10. Install the five *new* primary chaincase bolts finger-tight. Do *not* apply lubricant to the captive rubber seal on the bolts.

11. Following the torque sequence shown in **Figure 30**, tighten the primary chaincase housing bolts evenly in two-to-three stages to 25-27 ft.-lb. (33.9-36.6 N•m) on 2007 models and to 26-28 ft.-lb. (35.3-38.0 N•m) on 2008-2009 models.

12. Install the starter as described in Chapter Eleven.

13. Install the primary drive assembly and the primary chaincase cover as described in this chapter.

14. Connect the negative battery cable or install the Maxi-Fuse as described in Chapter Eleven.

Inspection

1. Remove all gasket material from the housing gasket surfaces on the outboard (B, **Figure 27**) and inboard (**Figure 31**) sides of the primary chaincase housing.

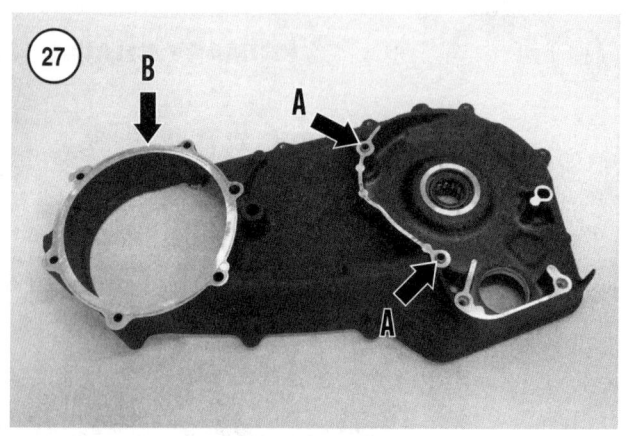

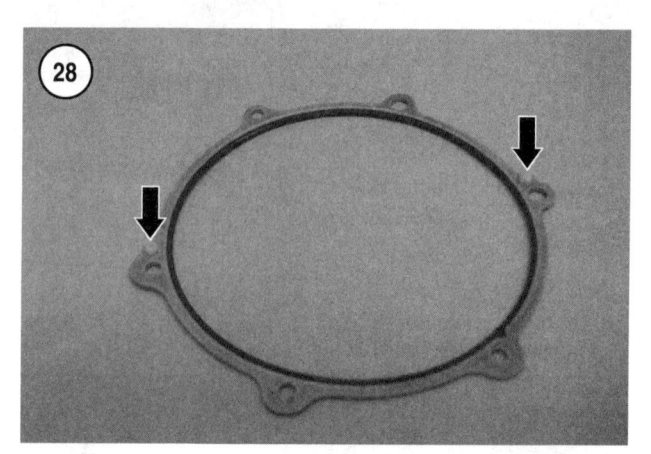

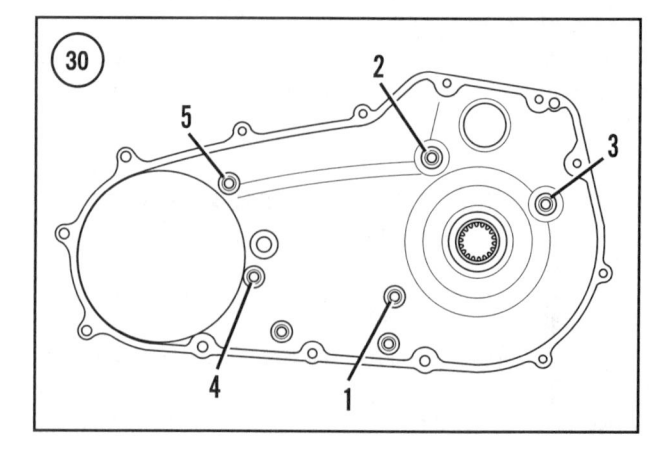

CLUTCH AND PRIMARY DRIVE

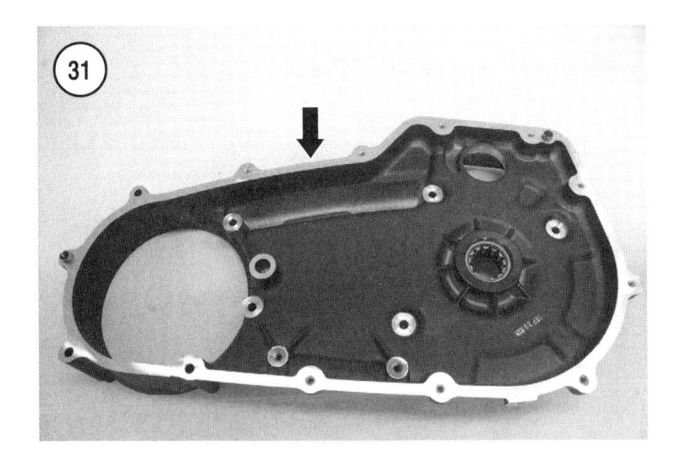

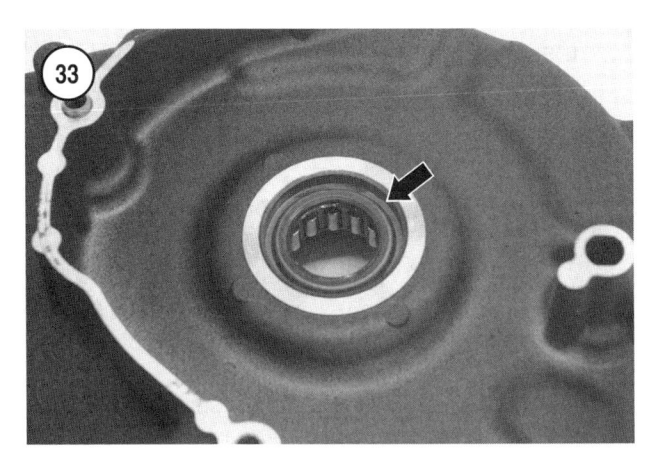

2. Clean the inner housing in solvent. Dry it thoroughly.
3. Check the housing for cracks or other damage.
4. Turn the mainshaft bearing (**Figure 32**) by hand. If necessary, replace the bearing as follows:
   a. Remove the oil seal (**Figure 33**) as described in this section.
   b. Remove the bearing snap ring (A, **Figure 22**) that sits beneath the oil seal. Discard the snap ring.
   c. Support the housing in a press with the clutch side facing up (**Figure 31**) and press the bearing from the housing.
   d. Apply engine oil to the *new* bearing and the bearing bore in the primary chaincase housing.
   e. Support the housing in the press so the transmission side faces up.
   f. Position the bearing so the side with the manufacturer's marks face up. Then, press in the bearing until it bottoms in the bearing bore. Use a driver or socket that matches the outside diameter of the bearing.
   g. Install a *new* snap ring (A, **Figure 22**) so it is completely seated within the groove in the housing. Position the snap ring so it does not block the oil hole (B, **Figure 22**).
   h. Install a *new* oil seal as described in this section.
5. If necessary, replace the mainshaft bearing inner race (**Figure 34**) as described in *Transmission Side Door Assembly* (Chapter Eight).
6. Inspect the oil seal (**Figure 33**) for excessive wear, tearing or other damage. To replace the oil seal, perform the following:
   a. Use a flat-bladed screwdriver to pry the oil seal from the transmission side (inboard) of the housing.
   b. Clean the oil seal bore.
   c. Pack the lip of the new oil seal with a waterproof bearing grease.
   d. Position the oil seal so the side marked *OIL SIDE* faces the bearing. Using a driver (**Figure 35**) or a socket that presses against the outside edge of the seal, press the *new* oil seal into the housing until its outer surface sits flush with the edge of the bearing bore.

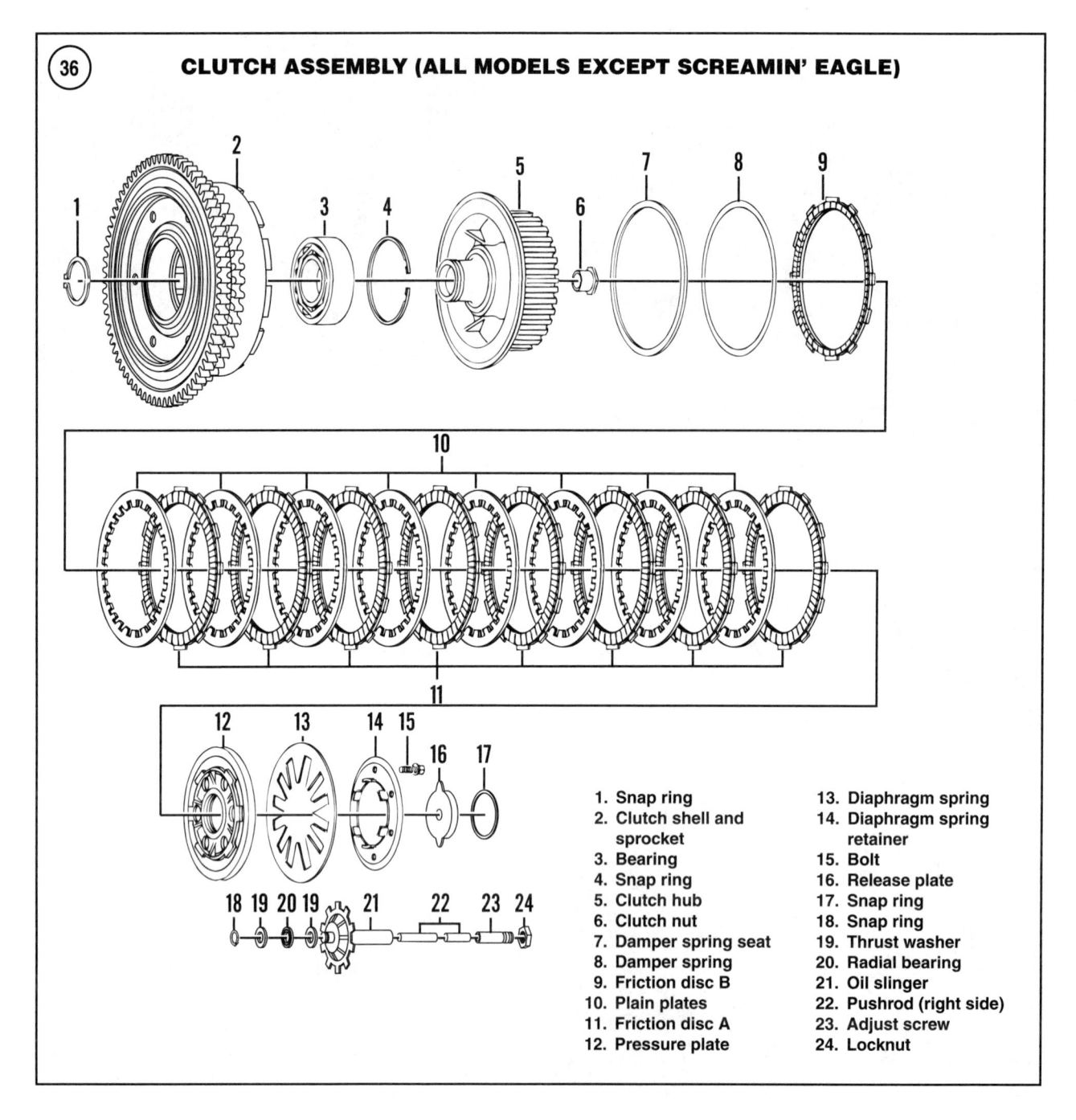

36 CLUTCH ASSEMBLY (ALL MODELS EXCEPT SCREAMIN' EAGLE)

1. Snap ring
2. Clutch shell and sprocket
3. Bearing
4. Snap ring
5. Clutch hub
6. Clutch nut
7. Damper spring seat
8. Damper spring
9. Friction disc B
10. Plain plates
11. Friction disc A
12. Pressure plate
13. Diaphragm spring
14. Diaphragm spring retainer
15. Bolt
16. Release plate
17. Snap ring
18. Snap ring
19. Thrust washer
20. Radial bearing
21. Oil slinger
22. Pushrod (right side)
23. Adjust screw
24. Locknut

CLUTCH ASSEMBLY

This section describes removal, inspection and installation of the clutch plates. If the clutch requires additional service, refer to *Clutch Shell, Hub and Sprocket* in this chapter.

Refer to **Figure 36** and **Figure 37**.

The photographs in this section show the clutch assembly used on 2007-2009 models. The procedures in this section also apply to the clutch found on 2006 models. The only difference between the clutch assemblies is the relative position of the primary drive sprocket and the starter gear on the clutch shell. On 2006 models, the primary chain sprocket (**Figure 38**) sits inboard of the starter gear. On 2007-2009 models, the primary chain sprocket (**Figure 38**) is outboard of the starter gear.

Removal

NOTE
Always disarm the optional TSSM/HFSM security system before disconnecting the battery or pulling the Maxi-Fuse so the alarm will not sound.

1. Disconnect the negative battery cable as described in Chapter Eleven.
2. Remove the primary chaincase cover (**Figure 39**) as described in this chapter.
3A. On all models except Screamin' Eagle, perform the following:

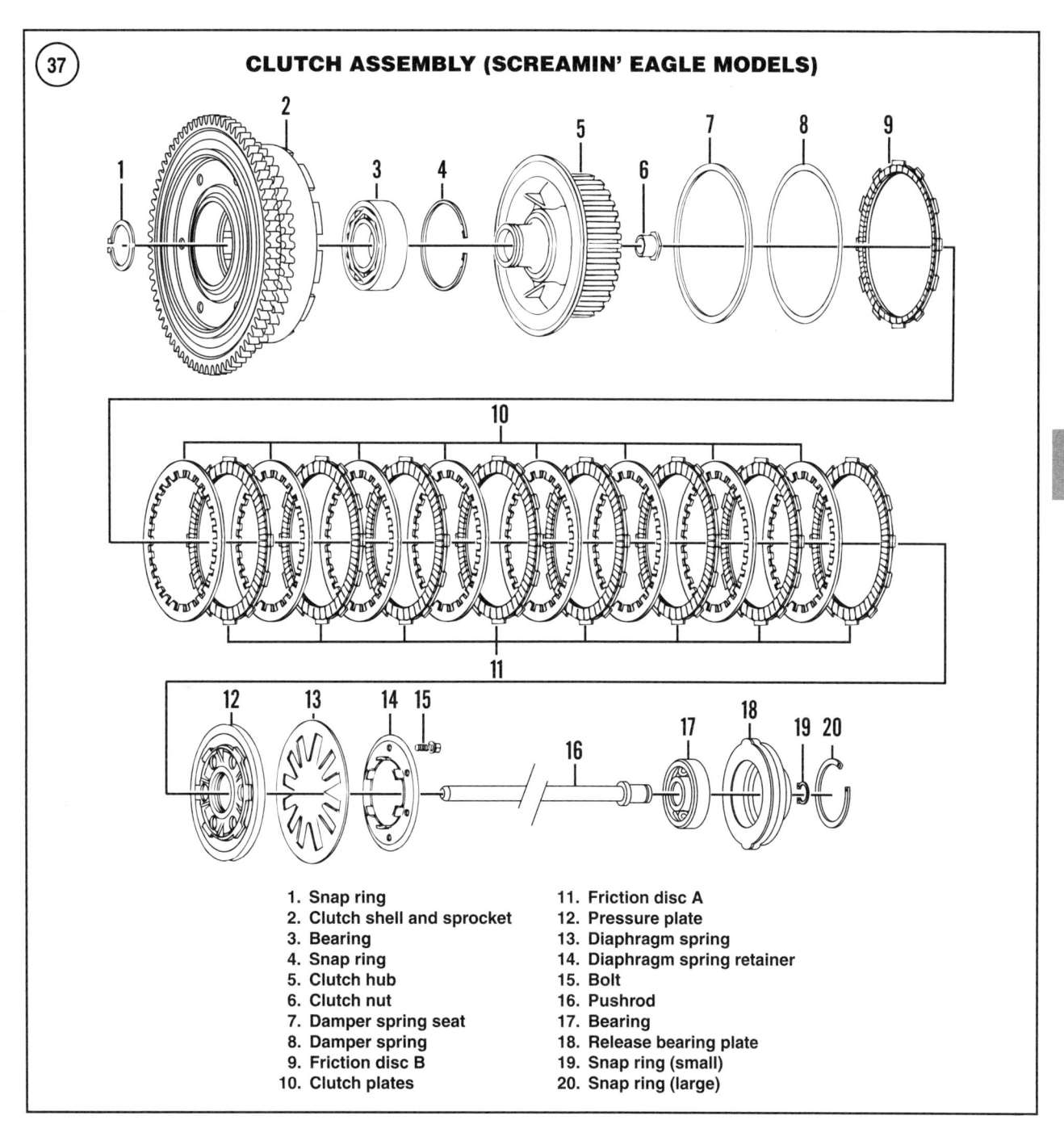

CLUTCH AND PRIMARY DRIVE

③⑦ CLUTCH ASSEMBLY (SCREAMIN' EAGLE MODELS)

1. Snap ring
2. Clutch shell and sprocket
3. Bearing
4. Snap ring
5. Clutch hub
6. Clutch nut
7. Damper spring seat
8. Damper spring
9. Friction disc B
10. Clutch plates
11. Friction disc A
12. Pressure plate
13. Diaphragm spring
14. Diaphragm spring retainer
15. Bolt
16. Pushrod
17. Bearing
18. Release bearing plate
19. Snap ring (small)
20. Snap ring (large)

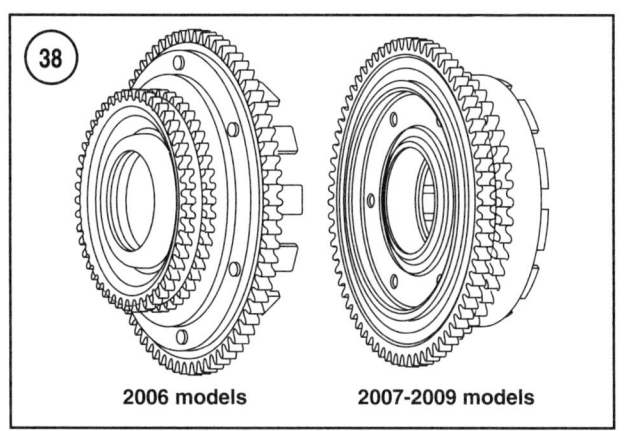

㊳
2006 models   2007-2009 models

㊴

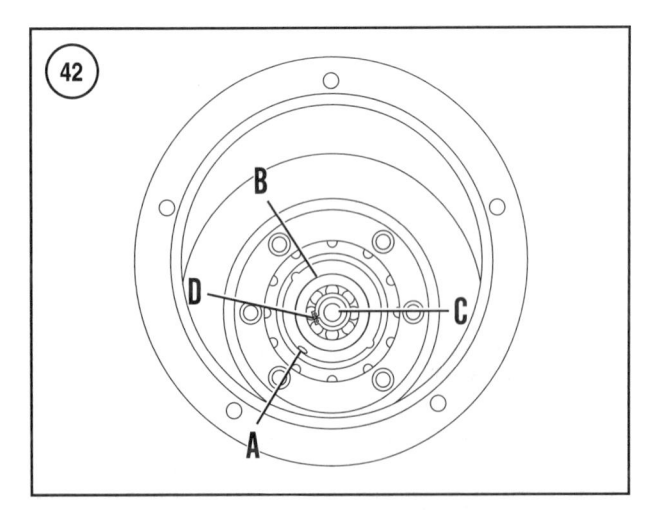

a. At the clutch, loosen the clutch adjusting screw locknut (A, **Figure 40**) and turn the adjusting screw (B) *counterclockwise* to allow slack against the diaphragm spring.
b. Remove the snap ring (C, **Figure 40**), and then remove the release plate/adjusting screw assembly (**Figure 41**).

3B. On Screamin' Eagle models, perform the following:
a. Remove the large snap ring (A, **Figure 42**) securing the release bearing plate.
b. Pull the release bearing plate (B, **Figure 42**) and the pushrod (C) from the pressure plate as an assembly.

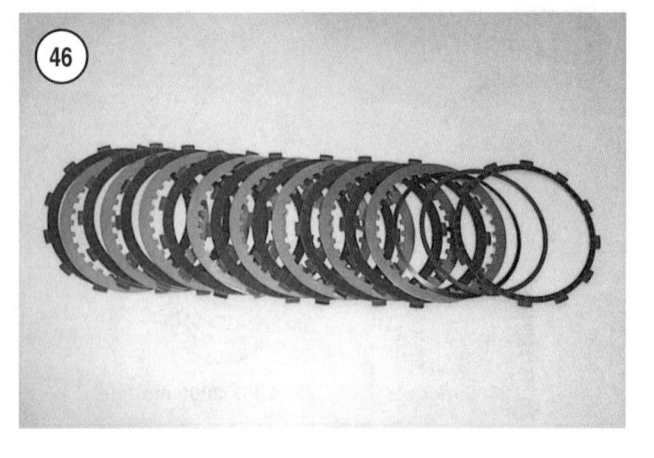

CLUTCH AND PRIMARY DRIVE

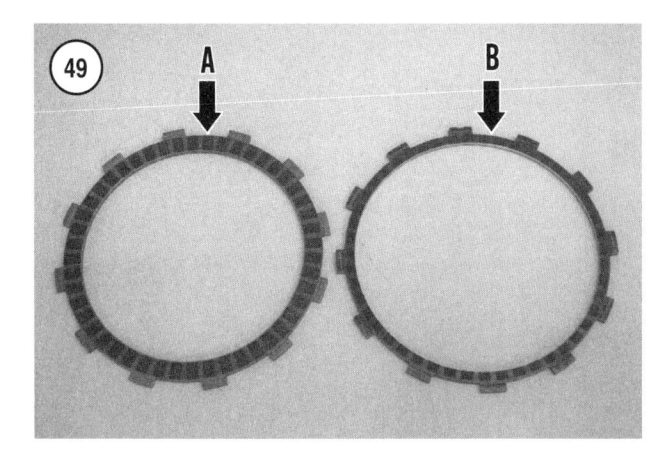

c. Remove the small snap ring (D, **Figure 42**). If necessary, pull the push rod from the release bearing.

4. Using a crossing pattern, evenly loosen the diaphragm spring retainer bolts (A, **Figure 43**). Remove the bolts and the retainer (B, **Figure 43**).

5. Remove the diaphragm spring (**Figure 44**) and pressure plate (**Figure 45**).

6. Remove each friction disc and plain plate (**Figure 46**) from the clutch shell, keeping them in the order of removal.

7. Remove the damper spring (**Figure 47**) and damper spring seat (**Figure 48**) from the clutch shell.

8. Inspect the parts as described in this section.

Installation

NOTE
*The original equipment clutch set (**Figure 46**) has nine friction discs, eight plain plates, one damper spring and one damper spring seat. Make sure each part is installed.*

1. Soak the clutch friction disc and clutch plates in new primary drive oil for approximately 5 minutes before installing them.

NOTE
*The clutch uses two different types of friction discs (**Figure 49**). The wider friction disc A (A, **Figure 49**) is the normal width disc. The narrower friction disc B (B, **Figure 49**) is installed first, as it works in conjunction with the damper spring and damper spring seat.*

2. Install friction disc B (**Figure 50**) so its tangs engage the slots in clutch shell. Push the disc all the way in until it bottoms within the clutch hub.

3. Install the damper spring seat (**Figure 48**) onto the clutch hub and push it in until it seats within friction disc B.

4. Position the damper spring (**Figure 47**) with the concave side facing out and install it onto the clutch hub against the damper spring seat.

5. Install a plain plate (**Figure 51**) so its inner teeth engage the clutch hub, and then install a friction disc A

(**Figure 52**). Continue to alternately install the clutch plates and friction discs A. The last part installed is a friction disc A (**Figure 52**).

6. Install the pressure plate (**Figure 45**) onto the clutch hub.

7. Position the diaphragm spring (**Figure 44**) with its concave side facing in, and seat it onto the pressure plate.

8. Install the diaphragm spring retainer (B, **Figure 43**) so its tabs sit between the fingers of the diaphragm spring, and then install the retainer bolts (A).

9. Using a crossing pattern, evenly tighten the diaphragm-spring-retainer bolts to 90-110 in.-lb. (10.2-12.4 N•m).

10A. On all models except Screamin' Eagle, install the release plate/adjuster assembly (**Figure 41**) so the ears of the release plate engage the cutouts (**Figure 53**) in the pressure plate. Make sure the side of the release plate marked OUT faces out.

10B. On Screamin' Eagle models, refer to **Figure 37** and perform the following:

   a. Press a new bearing into the release plate.
   b. Install the pushrod into the bearing, and install a new small snap ring into the pushrod groove.
   c. Slide the pushrod/release plate assembly into the mainshaft bore so the ears of the release plate engage the cutouts in the pressure plate.
   d. Install a new large snap ring.

11. Install the primary chaincase cover as described in this chapter.

12A. On all models except Screamin' Eagle, adjust the clutch as described in Chapter Three.

12B. On Screamin' Eagle models, inspect the clutch pushrod and release plate as described in this chapter.

13A. On 2006 models, perform the following:

   a. Position a *new* clutch cover gasket with the rubber molding and the words *Toward Clutch* facing the engine.
   b. Align the triangular-shaped hole in the *new* gasket with the top hole in the clutch cover.

CAUTION
Do not push the screw through the triangular-shaped hole in the new gasket as the gasket will be damaged.

   c. Insert the screw, with the captive washer, through the clutch cover and carefully *thread it* all the way through the triangular-shaped hole in the new gasket.
   d. Install the clutch cover and new gasket onto the chaincase cover and thread the top screw part way in.
   e. Make sure the clutch cover is correctly aligned with the chaincase cover and install the remaining four screws with captive washers.
   f. Using a crossing pattern, tighten the Torx screws (T27) to 84-108 in.-lb. (9.5-12.2 N•m).

13B. On 2007-2009 models, perform the following:

CLUTCH AND PRIMARY DRIVE

onto the cover. Push the nibs into the ring groove walls.
   b. Install the clutch cover and seal ring (**Figure 54**) onto the primary chaincase cover.
   c. Install the clutch cover screws (**Figure 55**). Then, using a crossing pattern, evenly tighten the clutch cover screws to 84-108 in.-lb. (9.5-12.2 N•m).
14. Connect the negative battery cable as described in Chapter Eleven.

Inspection

Compare any measurements taken to the specifications listed in **Table 1** when inspecting clutch components. Replace any parts that are worn, damaged or out of specification.

1. Clean all parts in solvent. Thoroughly dry them with compressed air.
2. Inspect the friction discs as follows:

NOTE
*If any friction disc need replacing, replace **all nine** friction discs as a set. Never replace only one or two discs.*

   a. Inspect the friction material (**Figure 49**) for excessive or uneven wear, cracks and other damage.

NOTE
If the friction disc tangs are damaged, inspect the clutch shell fingers carefully as described in this chapter.

   b. Check the disc tangs for surface damage. The sides of the disc tangs must be smooth where they contact the clutch shell slots; otherwise, the discs cannot engage and disengage correctly.
   c. Measure the thickness (**Figure 56**) of each friction disc with a caliper at several places around the disc.

3. Inspect the plain plates (**Figure 57**) as follows:
   a. Inspect the plain plates for cracks, damage or color change. Overheated clutch plates have a bluish discoloration.
   b. Check the plain plates for oil glaze buildup. Remove any glaze by lightly sanding both sides of each plate with 400 grit sandpaper placed on a surface plate or piece of glass.
   c. Place each plain plate on a flat surface, and check for warp (**Figure 58**) with a feeler gauge.

NOTE
If the clutch plate teeth are damaged, inspect the clutch hub splines carefully as described in this chapter.

   d. The clutch plate inner teeth mesh with the clutch hub splines. Check the clutch plate teeth for any roughness or damage. The teeth contact surfaces must be smooth; otherwise, the plates cannot engage and disengage correctly.

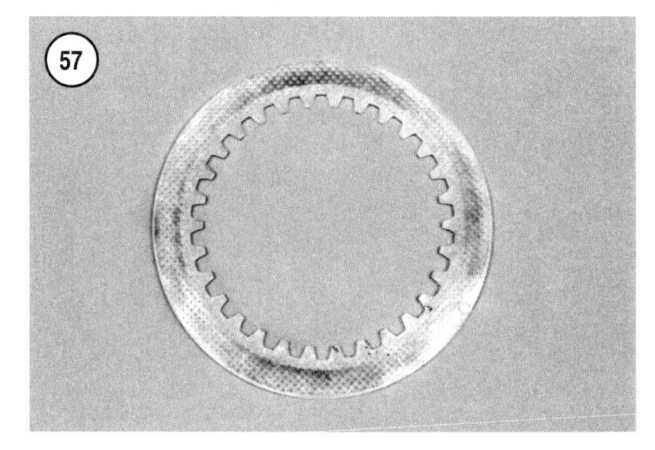

NOTE
All lubricant must be removed from the seal ring and its groove prior to installation. If any lubricant remains there will be temporary lubricant seepage around the inspection cover.

   a. Remove the seal ring from the clutch cover. Wipe all lubricant from the seal ring and inspect it for cuts or deterioration, replace if necessary. Wipe all lubricant from the seal ring groove and install the seal ring

4. Inspect the diaphragm spring (**Figure 59**) for cracks or damage.
5. Inspect the diaphragm spring retainer (**Figure 60**) for cracks or damage. Check also for bent or damaged fingers.
6. Inspect outer surface of the pressure plate (**Figure 61**) for wear caused by contact with the diaphragm spring. Check also for cracks or other damage.
7. On all models except Screamin' Eagle, perform the following:
   a. Inspect the release plate, left pushrod and locknut for wear or damage.
   b. Inspect the pressure-plate snap ring groove for damage.

CLUTCH PUSHROD AND RELEASE PLATE INSPECTION (SCREAMIN' EAGLE MODELS)

1. Remove the clutch cover (**Figure 55**) from the primary chaincase cover.
2. Mount a dial indicator to one of the clutch cover bolt holes or to a suitable stationary stand.
3. Position the dial indicator anvil against the end of the clutch pushrod (C, **Figure 42**).
4. Fully apply the clutch lever, and note the pushrod movement.
5. The pushrod must move a minimum of 0.065 in. (1.65 mm) to guarantee complete clutch disengagement.

NOTE
Correct the clutch fluid level and bleed the clutch system if pushrod movement is greater than 0.065 in. (1.65 mm).

6. If the push rod movement is less than specified, the clutch fluid level is low and the clutch system must be bled as described in this chapter.
7A. On 2006 models, perform the following:
   a. Position a *new* clutch cover gasket with the rubber molding and the words *Toward Clutch* facing the engine.
   b. Align the triangular-shaped hole in the *new* gasket with the top hole in the clutch cover.

CAUTION
Do not push the screw through the triangular-shaped hole in the new gasket as the gasket will be damaged.

   c. Insert the screw, with the captive washer through the clutch cover and carefully *thread it* all the way through the triangular-shaped hole in the new gasket.
   d. Install the clutch cover and new gasket onto the primary chaincase cover and thread the top screw part way in.
   e. Make sure the clutch cover is correctly aligned with the chaincase cover and install the remaining four screws with captive washers.
   f. Using a crossing pattern, tighten the clutch cover Torx screws (T27) evenly to 84-108 in.-lb. (9.5-12.2 N•m).
7B. On 2007-2009 models, perform the following:

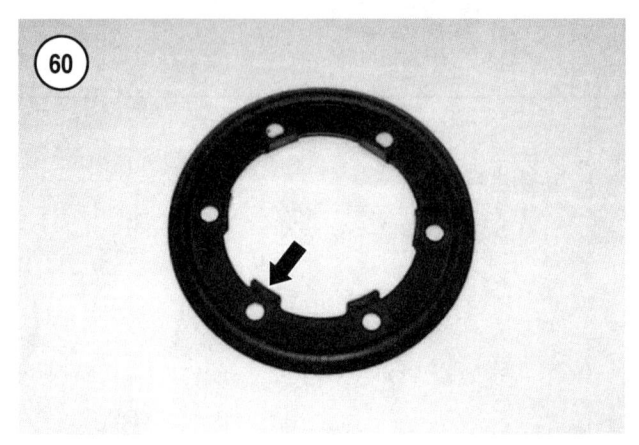

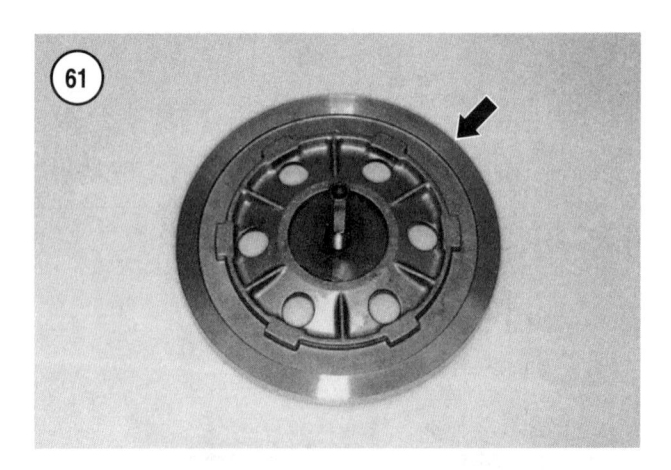

NOTE
All lubricant must be removed from the seal ring and its groove prior to installation. If any lubricant remains there will be temporary lubricant seepage around the inspection cover.

   a. Remove the seal ring from the clutch cover. Wipe all lubricant from the seal ring and inspect it for cuts or deterioration; replace if necessary. Wipe all lubricant

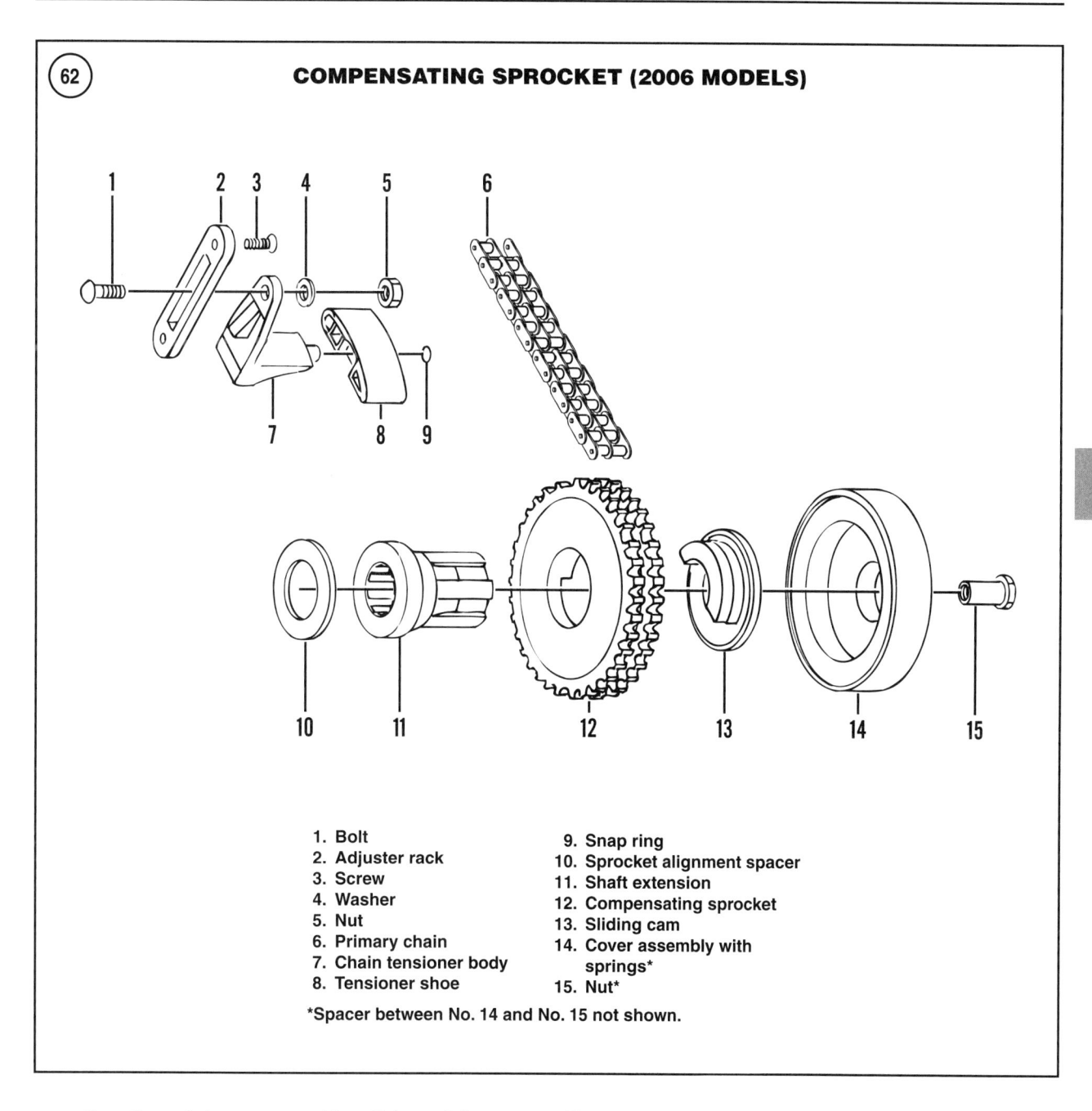

CLUTCH AND PRIMARY DRIVE

62 **COMPENSATING SPROCKET (2006 MODELS)**

1. Bolt
2. Adjuster rack
3. Screw
4. Washer
5. Nut
6. Primary chain
7. Chain tensioner body
8. Tensioner shoe
9. Snap ring
10. Sprocket alignment spacer
11. Shaft extension
12. Compensating sprocket
13. Sliding cam
14. Cover assembly with springs*
15. Nut*

*Spacer between No. 14 and No. 15 not shown.

from the seal ring groove and install the seal ring onto the cover. Push the nibs into the ring groove walls.
  b. Install the clutch cover (**Figure 55**) and seal ring (**Figure 54**) onto the primary chain case cover.
  c. Install the clutch cover screws. Then, using a crossing pattern, evenly tighten the Torx screws (T27) to 84-108 in.-lb. (9.5-12.2 N•m).

PRIMARY DRIVE ASSEMBLY (2006 MODELS)

The primary drive assembly consists of the clutch shell, compensating sprocket and primary chain (**Figure 62**). They must be removed and installed as an assembly.

The primary drive locking tool (JIMS part No. 2234 or H-D part No. HD-41214) is needed to remove and install the primary drive assembly.

Removal

NOTE
Always disarm the optional TSSM/HFSM security system before disconnecting the battery or pulling the Maxi-Fuse so the alarm will not sound.

1. Disconnect the negative battery cable as described in Chapter Eleven.
2. Remove the primary chaincase cover as described in this chapter.
3. Measure the primary chain alignment as described in this chapter. If necessary, select a new sprocket alignment spacer (**Table 2**) to install behind the compensating sprocket during installation.

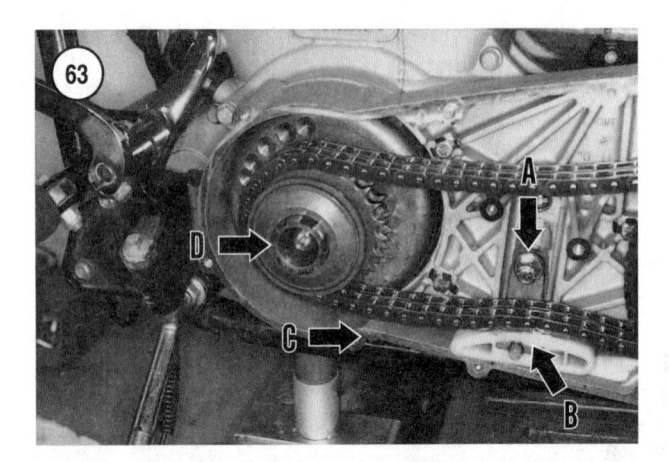

4. Loosen the chain tensioner locknut (A, **Figure 63**). Pull the tensioner shoe (B, **Figure 63**) outward, and slide it down the adjuster rack so it rests on the bottom of the primary chaincase (C).

5A. On all models except Screamin' Eagle, perform the following:
   a. Loosen the clutch adjusting screw locknut (A, **Figure 64**), and turn the adjusting screw (B) *counterclockwise* to allow slack against the diaphragm spring.
   b. Remove the snap ring (C, **Figure 64**).
   c. Make sure the locknut (A, **Figure 65**) is still on the adjusting screw, and remove the release plate (B).

5B. On Screamin' Eagle models, perform the following:
   a. Remove the large snap ring (A, **Figure 66**) securing the release bearing plate.
   b. Pull the release bearing plate (B, **Figure 66**) and the pushrod (C) from the pressure plate as an assembly.

6. Place the primary drive locking tool (**Figure 67**) between the upper run of the primary chain and the clutch housing.

CAUTION
*The clutch nut has **left-hand threads**. Turn the clutch nut clockwise to loosen it.*

7. Loosen the clutch nut (**Figure 68**) with an impact wrench. Remove the clutch nut and the locking tool.

8. Place the primary drive locking tool (**Figure 67**) between the upper run of the primary chain and the compensating sprocket.

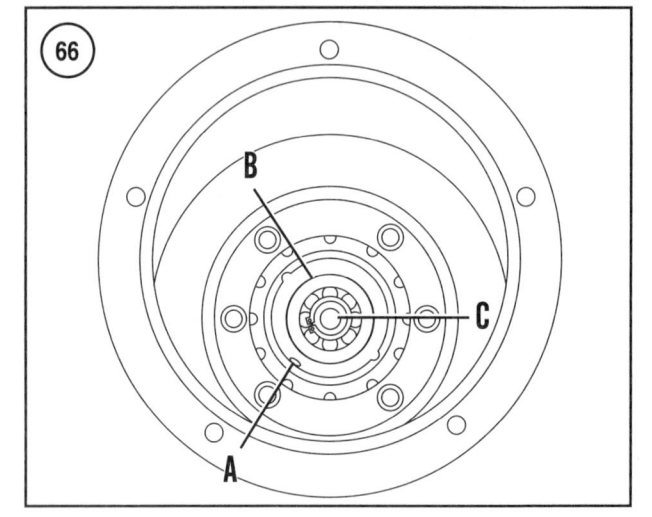

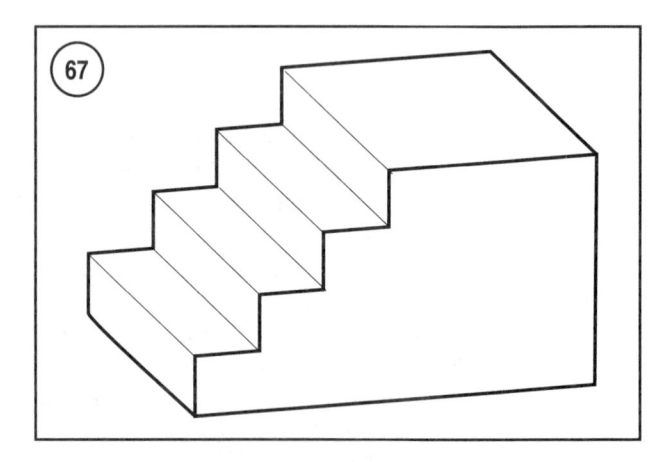

9. Loosen the compensating sprocket nut (**Figure 69**) with an impact wrench. Remove the locking tool.

10. Remove the compensating sprocket nut, cover assembly (**Figure 70**) and the sliding cam (D, **Figure 63**).

11. Remove the compensating sprocket (A, **Figure 71**), primary chain (B) and clutch shell assembly (C) at the same time.

12. Remove the shaft extension (**Figure 72**) and the sprocket alignment spacer (**Figure 73**) from the crankshaft.

13. Inspect the various components as described in this chapter.

CLUTCH AND PRIMARY DRIVE

Installation

1. Remove all threadlock residue from the threads of the crankshaft, mainshaft, compensating sprocket nut and the clutch nut.
2. Remove all gasket material from the primary housing gasket surfaces.

NOTE
If the primary chain alignment measurement taken before disassembly revealed that a new sprocket alignment spacer is needed, install the new spacer at this time.

3. Install the sprocket alignment spacer (**Figure 73**) and the shaft extension (**Figure 72**) onto the crankshaft.
4. Assemble the compensating sprocket, primary chain and clutch shell assembly.

NOTE
The compensating sprocket and clutch hub are splined. Rotate them slightly to ease installation.

5. Install the compensating sprocket (A, **Figure 71**), primary chain (B) and clutch shell assembly (C) at the same time.
6. Install the sliding cam (D, **Figure 63**) and cover assembly (**Figure 70**) onto the shaft extension.
7. Install the primary drive locking tool (**Figure 67**) between the upper run of the primary chain and the compensating sprocket.

NOTE
*The clutch nut has **left-hand threads**. Turn the nut counterclockwise to tighten it.*

8. Apply two drops of Loctite Threadlocker 262 (red), or an equivalent, to the clutch nut threads. Install and tighten the clutch nut (**Figure 68**) to 70-80 ft.-lb. (94.9-108.5 N•m).

9. Install the primary drive locking tool (**Figure 67**) between the upper run of the primary chain and the clutch shell.

10. Apply two drops of Loctite Threadlocker 262 (red), or an equivalent, to the compensating sprocket nut threads. Install the nut (**Figure 69**) and tighten it as follows:
   a. Tighten the compensating sprocket nut to 75 ft.-lb. (101.7 N•m).
   b. Tighten the compensating sprocket nut a maximum of an additional 45-50° as shown in **Figure 74**.

11A. On all models except Screamin' Eagle, perform the following:
   a. Make sure the locknut (A, **Figure 65**) is still on the adjusting screw, and install the release plate (B) so the ears of the release plate engage the cutouts (**Figure 75**) in the pressure plate.
   b. Install the snap ring (C, **Figure 64**).

11B. On Screamin' Eagle models, perform the following:
   a. Install the release bearing plate (B, **Figure 66**) and the pushrod (C) as an assembly.
   b. Install the large snap ring (A, **Figure 66**). Make sure it is completely seated.

12. Adjust the primary chain as described in Chapter Three.

13A. On all models except Screamin' Eagle, adjust the clutch (Chapter Three).

13B. On Screamin' Eagle models, inspect the clutch pushrod and release plate as described in this chapter.

14. Install the primary chaincase cover as described in this chapter.

15. Connect the negative battery cable or install the Maxi-Fuse as described in Chapter Eleven.

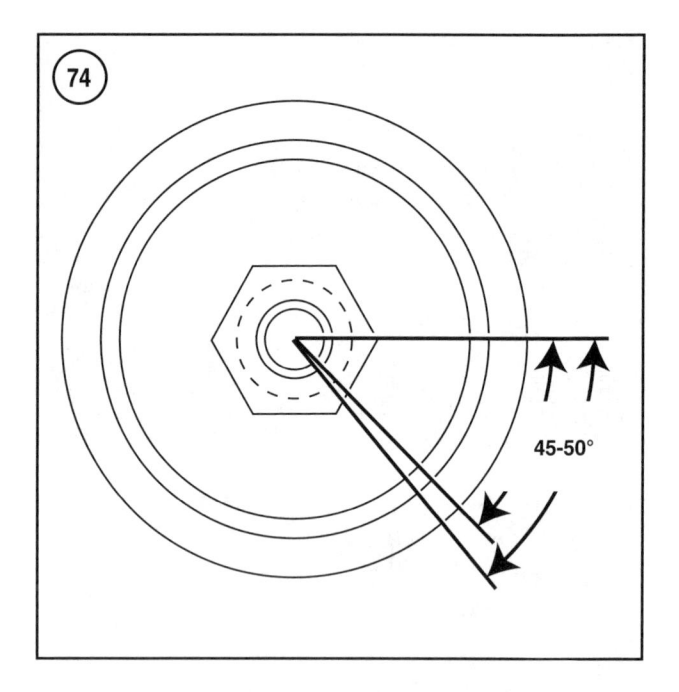

PRIMARY CHAIN ALIGNMENT (2006 MODELS)

A spacer, installed behind the compensating sprocket, aligns the compensating and clutch sprockets. Install the original spacer when reinstalling the compensating sprocket, primary chain and clutch assembly. However, if the primary chain is showing wear on one side, or if new components that could affect alignment have been installed, the alignment must be checked and corrected if necessary.

NOTE
This procedure is not required on 2007-2009 models.

1. Remove the primary chaincase cover as described in this chapter.

2. Adjust the primary chain tension so the chain is snug against both the compensating sprocket and clutch shell sprocket.

3. Push the primary chain toward the engine and transmission (at both sprockets) as far as it will go.

4. Place a straightedge across the primary chain side plates as close to the compensating sprocket as possible.

CLUTCH AND PRIMARY DRIVE

7. The difference between the two measurements should be within 0.030 in. (0.76 mm) of each other. If the difference exceeds this amount, replace the spacer (**Figure 78**) with a suitable size spacer. Refer to **Table 2** for spacer thickness and part numbers.

8. To replace the spacer, refer to *Primary Drive Assembly (2006 Models)* in this chapter.

9. Install the primary chaincase cover as described in this chapter.

10. Check and adjust the primary chain tension as described in Chapter Three.

PRIMARY DRIVE ASSEMBLY (2007-2009 MODELS)

The primary drive assembly consists of the clutch shell, compensating sprocket and primary chain. These must be removed and installed as an assembly.

The primary drive locking tool (JIMS part No. 2312 or H-D part No. HD-47977) is needed to remove and install the primary drive assembly.

Removal

Refer to **Figure 79**.

NOTE
Always disarm the optional TSSM/HFSM security system before disconnecting the battery or pulling the Maxi-Fuse so the alarm will not sound.

1. Disconnect the negative battery cable as described in Chapter Eleven.
2. Remove the primary chaincase cover as described in this chapter.
3A. On all models except Screamin' Eagles, perform the following:
   a. Loosen the clutch adjusting screw locknut (A, **Figure 64**) and turn the adjusting screw (B) *counterclockwise* to allow slack against the diaphragm spring.
   b. Remove the snap ring (C, **Figure 64**).
   c. Make sure the locknut (A, **Figure 65**) is still on the adjusting screw (B), and remove the release plate.
3B. On Screamin' Eagle models, perform the following:
   a. Remove the large snap ring (A, **Figure 66**) securing the release bearing plate.
   b. Pull the release bearing plate (B, **Figure 66**) and the pushrod (C) from the pressure plate as an assembly.

CAUTION
Failure to secure the tensioner in the compressed position will result in damage to the last 2-3 threads of the primary chain tensioner bolts during removal.

4. Secure the tensioner assembly in the compressed position with a cable strap. Insert the cable strap under the tensioner and over the top of the tensioner shoe, leaving the

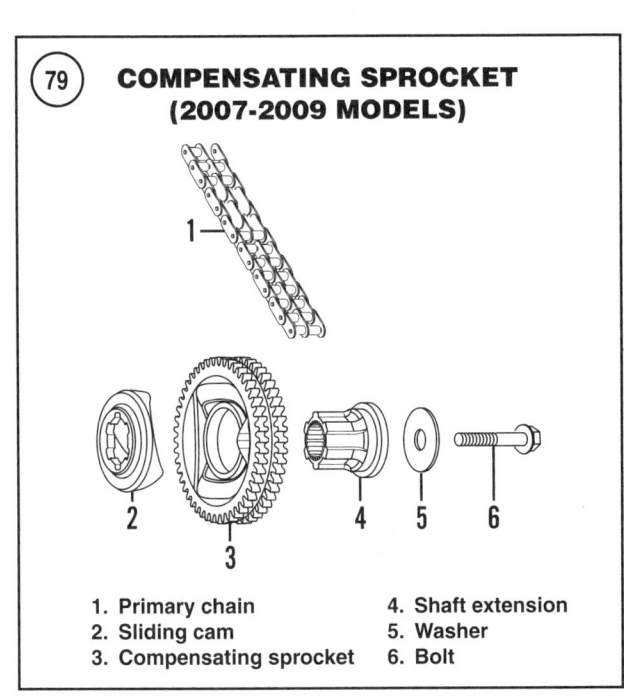

5. Measure the distance from the chain link side plates to the primary chaincase housing gasket surface (**Figure 76**). Record the measurement.

6. Repeat the process with the end of the straightedge (**Figure 77**) as close to the clutch sprocket as possible. Record the measurement.

COMPENSATING SPROCKET (2007-2009 MODELS)
1. Primary chain
2. Sliding cam
3. Compensating sprocket
4. Shaft extension
5. Washer
6. Bolt

tail of the cable strap (A, **Figure 80**) in place. It serves as a reminder to remove the cable strap during installation.

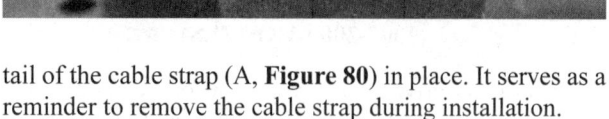

5. Remove the primary chain tensioner bolts (B, **Figure 80**), and remove the tensioner assembly.

6. Install the primary drive locking tool (A, **Figure 81**) between the teeth of the primary chain sprocket on the clutch hub and compensating sprocket to prevent the clutch from rotating.

CAUTION
*The clutch nut has **left-hand threads**. Turn the clutch nut clockwise to loosen it.*

7. Loosen the clutch nut (B, **Figure 81**) *clockwise* with an impact wrench, and remove the clutch nut.

8. Reposition the primary drive locking tool (A, **Figure 82**) to prevent the compensating sprocket from rotating.

9. Loosen the compensating sprocket bolt (B, **Figure 82**) with an impact wrench.

10. Remove the compensating sprocket bolt (**Figure 83**), washer and shaft extension (**Figure 84**).

11. Use a permanent marker pen or scribe to mark an outboard link on the primary chain. The primary chain should be reinstalled so it rotates in its original direction to prolong chain life. Refer to these marks during installation.

12. Remove the compensating sprocket (**Figure 85**), primary chain and clutch shell assembly (**Figure 86**) all at the same time.

13. Remove the sliding cam (A, **Figure 87**) located behind the compensating sprocket (B).

14. Inspect the various components as described in this chapter.

Installation

1. Remove all threadlock residue from the threads of the crankshaft, mainshaft, compensating sprocket bolt and the clutch nut.

2. Remove all gasket material from the primary housing gasket surfaces.

NOTE
If reinstalling the old primary chain tensioner, compress the tensioner.

CLUTCH AND PRIMARY DRIVE

PRIMARY CHAIN TENSIONER (2007-2009 MODELS)

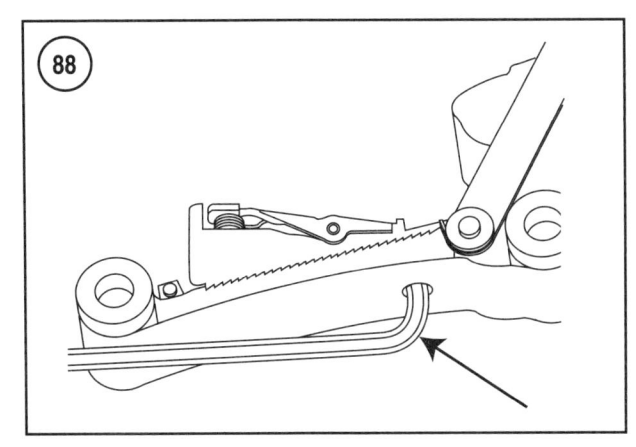

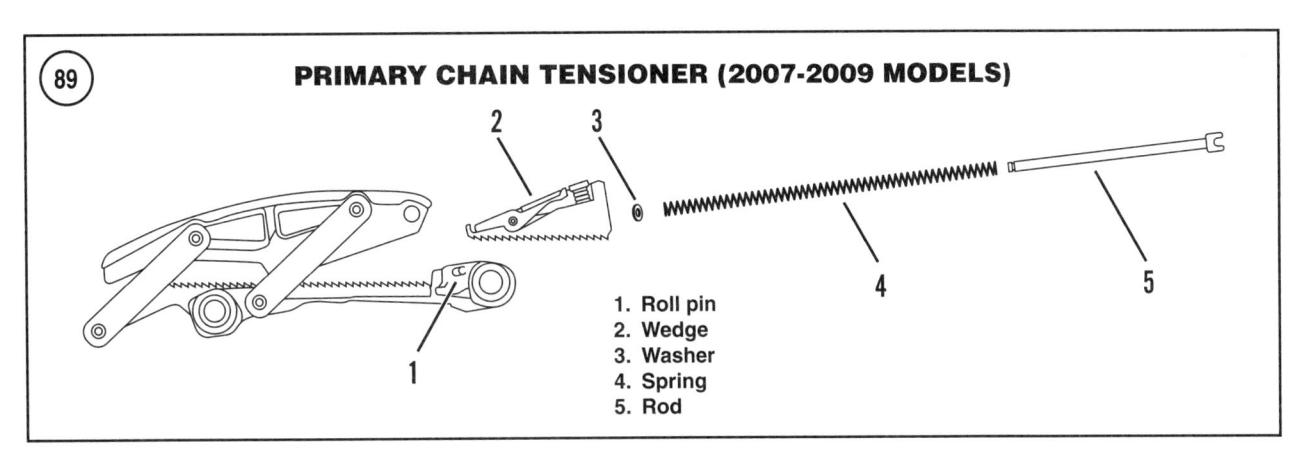

1. Roll pin
2. Wedge
3. Washer
4. Spring
5. Rod

3A. On 2007 models, compress the tensioner as follows:
   a. Cut and remove the cable strap from the tensioner and allow it to decompress slowly.
   b. Lift the wedge and release it from the serrations in the tensioner.
   c. Compress the spring and slide the wedge to the very end of the spring rod.
   d. Engage the rear most serration of the wedge with the rear most tooth on the tensioner serrations. Hold the wedge in this position.
   e. Insert the short end of a 5/32 inch Allen wrench (**Figure 88**) into the hole at the bottom of the tensioner to hold the wedge in this position.
   f. Slide the nylon shoe down over the wedge.
   g. Engage the holes in the retention plate with the index pin on the nylon shoe and the roll pin on the tensioner. If the retention plate is not available, reinstall the cable strap and secure the tensioner in this position.
   h. Remove the Allen wrench from the tensioner.

3B. On 2008-2009 models, assemble the tensioner (**Figure 89**) if necessary. Then, compress the tensioner as follows:
   a. Position the spring rod end on the roll pin.
   b. Slide the wedge (A, **Figure 90**) toward the roll pin until all travel is removed.
   c. Push tensioner shoe (B, **Figure 90**) down until it contacts the wedge and hold it in this position. Keep tension on shoe to keep wedge in place.

d. Install a cable strap around the shoe and tensioner so the end of the strap is located outboard of the tensioner assembly (**Figure 91**). The end of the strap must hang below the primary chain cover to insure it is visible after the tensioner is installed so it will be cut and removed.

NOTE
*The 2008-2009 chain tensioner is sold as an assembly, but may become disassembled during shipment as shown in **Figure 89**.*

4. If installing a new chain tensioner, assemble the tensioner, if necessary, and then compress it as follows:
   a. Compress the spring rod into the wedge, and seat the end of the spring rod onto the roll pin.
   b. Slide the wedge (A, **Figure 92**) to the very end of the spring rod (B).
   c. Lower the wedge so its rear-most tooth engages the rear-most tooth on the tensioner serrations. Hold the wedge in this position.
   d. Push the tensioner shoe (C, **Figure 92**) down against the wedge. Hold it in this position.
   e. Use a cable strap to secure the tensioner (**Figure 93**) in this compressed position. The cable strap end must sit on the outboard side of the tensioner so it can be cut and removed after tensioner installation.

5. Apply a light coat of primary chaincase oil to the inside bore of the compensating sprocket and to the splines of the shaft extension.
6. Lubricate the ramps of the sliding cam (A, **Figure 87**) and fit the sliding cam on the back of the compensating sprocket (B).
7. Slide the washer onto a *new* compensating sprocket bolt.
8. Refer to the marks made on the primary chain during removal to ensure it will rotate in the original direction. Fit the primary chain onto compensating sprocket and onto the primary chain sprocket on the clutch shell.
9. Install the compensating sprocket (**Figure 85**), primary chain and clutch assembly (**Figure 86**) all at the same time. Rotate the compensating sprocket and clutch hub slightly to ease installation.
10. Install the shaft extension (**Figure 84**) into the compensating sprocket.

CAUTION
If the primary chain tensioner is not installed, the primary chain could be pinched against the primary chain housing when the compensating sprocket bolt is tightened.

11. Insert the primary chain tensioner under the primary chain, and seat it against its mounting boss. Install the tensioner mounting bolts (B, **Figure 80**) and finger-tighten them.
12. Apply two drops of Loctite Threadlocker 262 (red) to the threads of the *new* compensating sprocket bolt. Install the bolt (**Figure 83**) and washer. Then, finger-tighten the bolt.

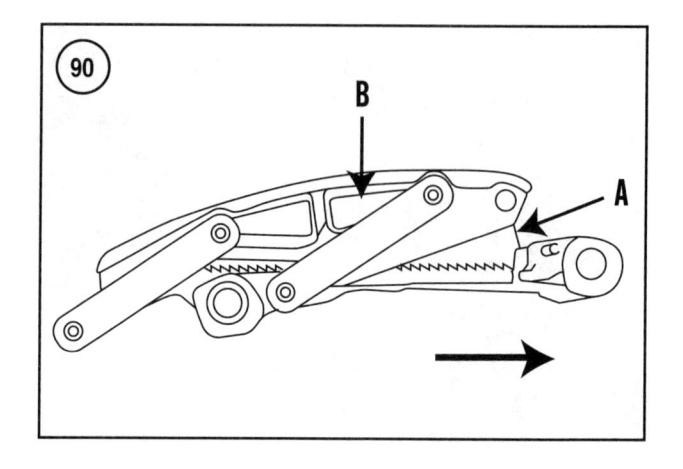

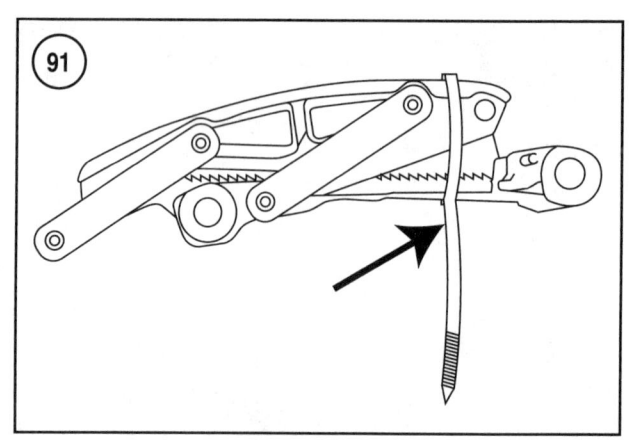

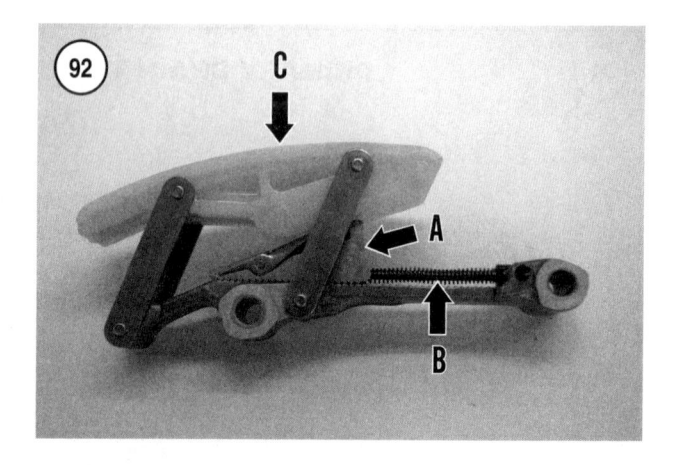

13. Position the primary drive locking tool (A, **Figure 94**) to keep the compensating sprocket from rotating.
14A. On 2007 and 2008 models, tighten the compensating sprocket bolt (B, **Figure 94**) to 155-165 ft.-lb. (210.2-223.7 N•m).
14B. On 2009 models, perform the following:
   a. Tighten the compensating sprocket bolt to 100 ft.-lb. (135.6 N•m).
   b. Loosen the bolt one full turn (360°).
   c. Re-tighten the compensating sprocket bolt to 140 ft.-lb. (189.8 N•m).
15. Position the primary drive locking tool (A, **Figure 95**) to keep the clutch from rotating.

CLUTCH AND PRIMARY DRIVE

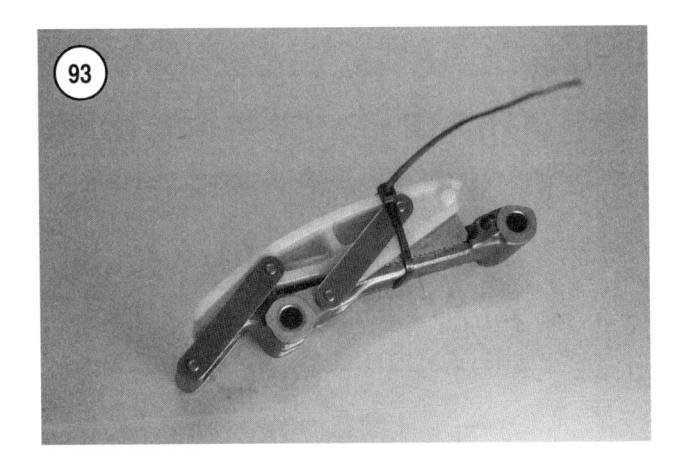

93

94

95

16. Apply two drops of Loctite Threadlocker 262 (red) to the clutch nut.

NOTE
*The clutch nut has **left-hand threads**. Turn the nut counterclockwise to tighten it.*

17. Install the clutch nut (B, **Figure 95**), and tighten it *counterclockwise* to 70-80 ft.-lb. (94.9-108.5 N•m).
18. Remove the primary drive locking tool.
19. Tighten the primary chain tensioner bolts (B, **Figure 80**) to the following specification:
   a. 2007 models: 21-24 ft.-lb. (28.5-32.5 N•m).
   b. 2008-2009 models: 15-19 ft.-lb. (20.3-25.8 N•m).

NOTE
The tensioner will not completely release and adjust the primary chain until the motorcycle has been ridden a short distance.

20. Cut and remove the cable strap (A, **Figure 80**). Make sure no portion of the strap remains in the primary chaincase.
21A. On Screamin' Eagle models, refer to **Figure 37** and perform the following:
   a. Press a new bearing into the release plate.
   b. Install the pushrod into the bearing, and install a *new* small snap ring into the pushrod groove.
   c. Slide the pushrod/release plate assembly into the mainshaft bore so the ears of the release plate engage the cutouts in the pressure plate.
   d. Install a *new* large snap ring.
21B. On all models except Screamin' Eagle, install the release plate/adjuster assembly so the ears (**Figure 41**) of the release plate engage the cutouts (**Figure 53**) in the pressure plate. Make sure the side of the release plate marked OUT faces out. Install a *new* snap ring (C, **Figure 40**) and make sure it is seated correctly.
22. If removed, install the clutch plates, friction discs, pressure plate and diaphragm spring as described in *Clutch Assembly* (this chapter).
23. Install the primary chaincase cover as described in this chapter.
24. On all models except Screamin' Eagle, adjust the clutch as described in Chapter Three.
25. Connect the negative battery cable or install the Maxi-Fuse (Chapter Eleven).

CLUTCH SHELL, HUB AND SPROCKET

Inspection
(All Models)

The clutch shell is a subassembly consisting of the clutch shell, the clutch hub, the bearing and two snap rings. Refer to **Figures 96-98**.
1. Remove the primary drive assembly as described in this chapter.
2. Remove the clutch shell assembly from the primary drive chain.
3. Hold the clutch shell and rotate the clutch hub by hand. The bearing is damaged if the clutch hub binds or turns roughly.
4. Check the primary chain sprocket (A, **Figure 99**: 2006 models; A, **Figure 100**: 2007-2009 models) and the starter gear (B) on the clutch shell for cracks, deep scoring, excessive tooth wear or heat discoloration.
5. If the sprocket or the gear are worn or damaged, replace the clutch shell. If the primary chain sprocket is worn, also check the primary chain and the compensating sprocket as described in this chapter.
6. Inspect the clutch hub for the following:

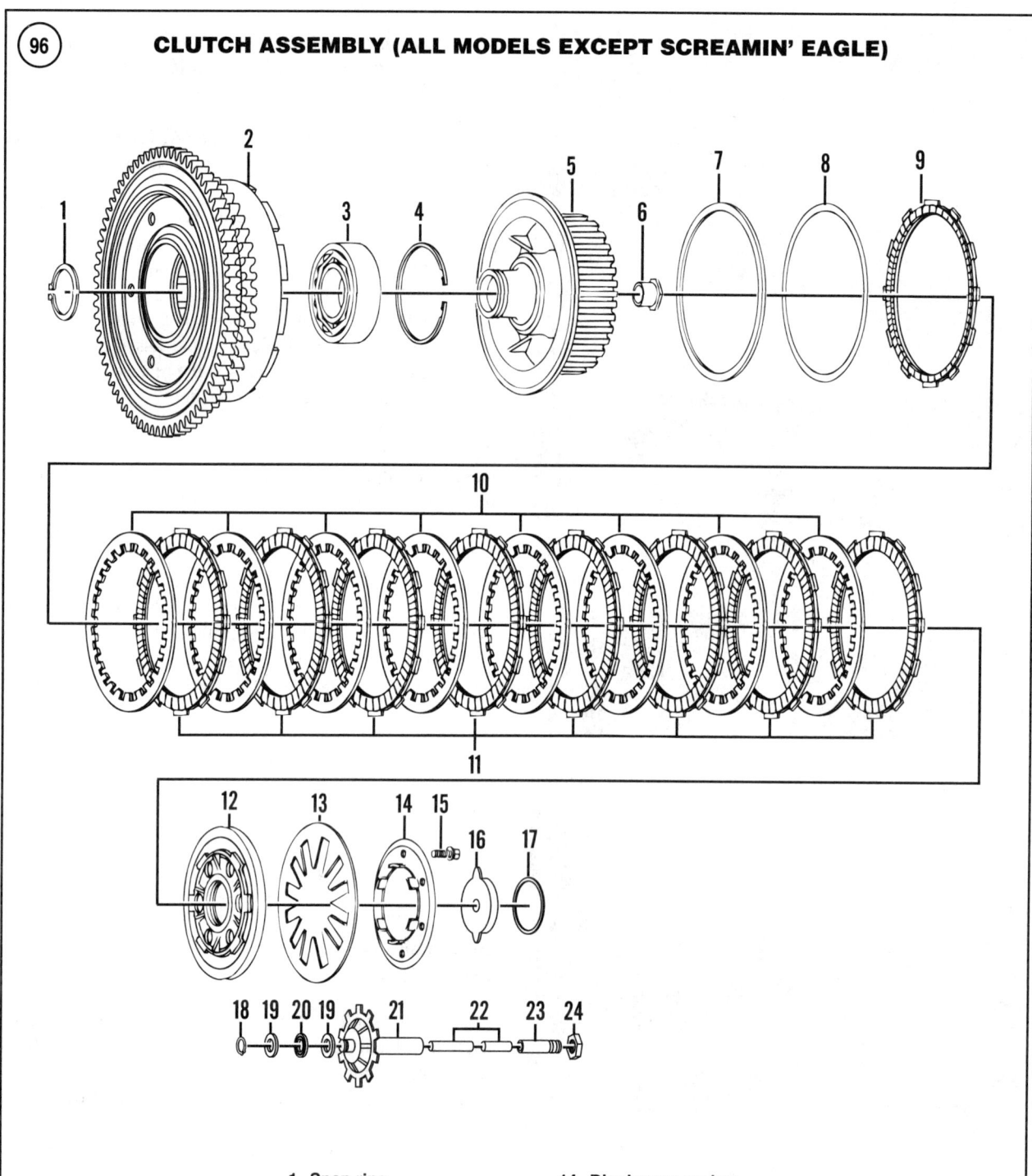

CLUTCH ASSEMBLY (ALL MODELS EXCEPT SCREAMIN' EAGLE)

1. Snap ring
2. Clutch shell and sprocket
3. Bearing
4. Snap ring
5. Clutch hub
6. Clutch nut
7. Damper spring seat
8. Damper spring
9. Friction disc B
10. Plain plates
11. Friction disc A
12. Pressure plate
13. Diaphragm spring
14. Diaphragm spring retainer
15. Bolt
16. Release plate
17. Snap ring
18. Snap ring
19. Thrust washer
20. Radial bearing
21. Oil slinger
22. Pushrod (right side)
23. Adjusting screw (left side)
24. Locknut

CLUTCH AND PRIMARY DRIVE

97 CLUTCH ASSEMBLY (SCREAMIN' EAGLE MODELS)

1. Snap ring
2. Clutch shell and sprocket (2007-2009 models shown)
3. Bearing
4. Snap ring
5. Clutch hub
6. Clutch nut
7. Damper spring seat
8. Damper spring
9. Friction disc B
10. Clutch plates
11. Friction disc A
12. Pressure plate
13. Diaphragm spring
14. Diaphragm spring retainer
15. Bolt
16. Pushrod
17. Bearing
18. Release bearing plate
19. Snap ring (small)
20. Snap ring (large)

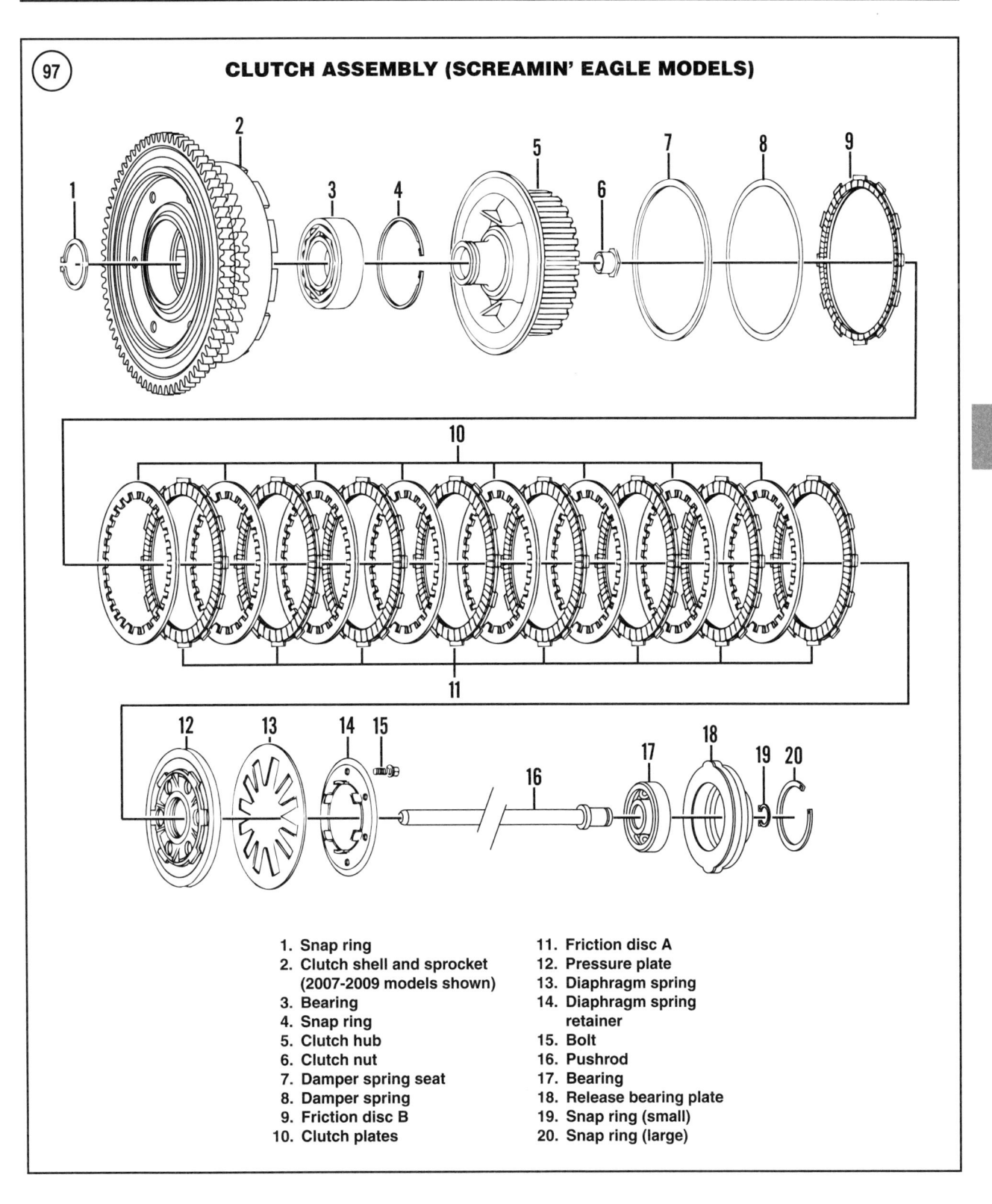

a. The clutch plate teeth must slide in the clutch hub splines. Inspect the splines (A, **Figure 101**: 2006 models; A, **Figure 102**: 2007-2009 models) for rough spots, grooves or other damage. Repair minor damage with a file or oil stone. If the damage is severe, replace the clutch hub.

b. Inspect the bolt towers (B, **Figure 101**: 2006 models; B, **Figure 102**: 2007-2009 models) for thread damage or cracks at the base of the tower. Repair any thread damage with the correct size metric tap. If a tower is cracked or damaged, replace the clutch hub.

c. The friction disc tangs must slide in the clutch shell slots (C, **Figure 101**: 2006 models; C, **Figure 102**: 2007-2009 models). Inspect the slots for cracks or galling. Repair minor damage with a file. If the damage is severe, replace the clutch housing.

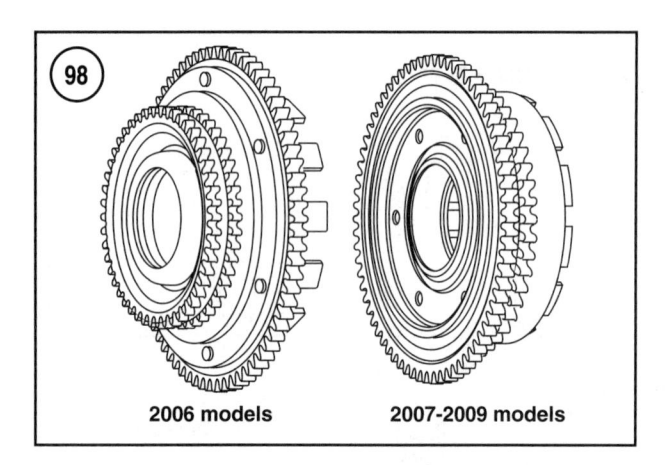

7. Inspect the clutch hub inner splines (**Figure 103**: 2006 models; **Figure 104**: 2007-2009 models). Check for galling, severe wear or other damage. Repair minor damage with a fine cut file. If damage is severe, replace the clutch hub.

8. If the clutch hub, the clutch shell or bearing are damaged, replace them as described in this section.

Disassembly/Assembly
(2006 Models)

Do not separate the clutch shell and hub unless the bearing or either part must be replaced. The bearing will be damaged when the shell and hub are separated. Removal and installation of the bearing requires the use of a hydraulic press.

1. Remove the friction discs and plain plates as described in *Clutch Assembly* (this chapter).

2. Remove the primary drive assembly as described in this chapter. Remove the clutch shell assembly from the primary drive chain.

3. Remove the snap ring (**Figure 105**) from the clutch hub groove.

4. Support the clutch shell on the press bed (**Figure 106**) with the primary chain sprocket side facing up.

5. Place a suitable size arbor or socket onto the clutch hub surface, and press the clutch hub (A, **Figure 107**) out of the bearing.

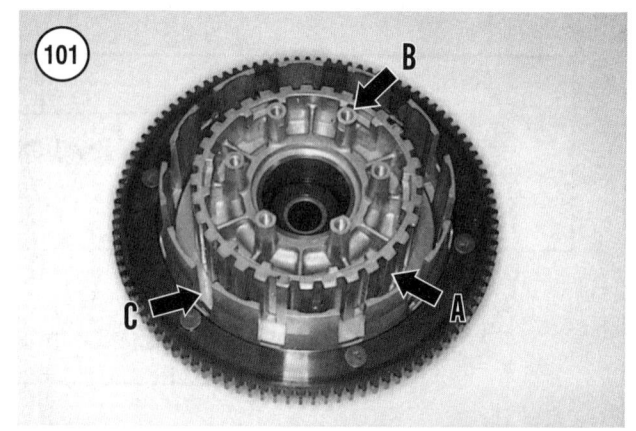

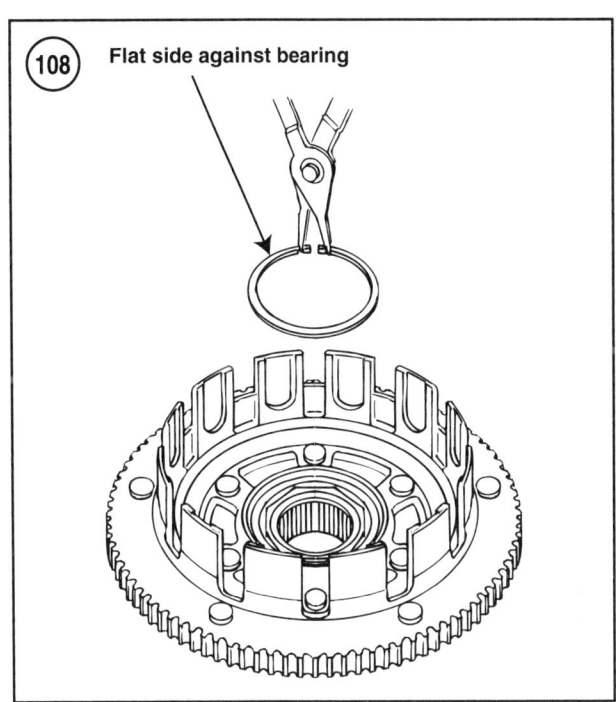

CLUTCH AND PRIMARY DRIVE

108 Flat side against bearing

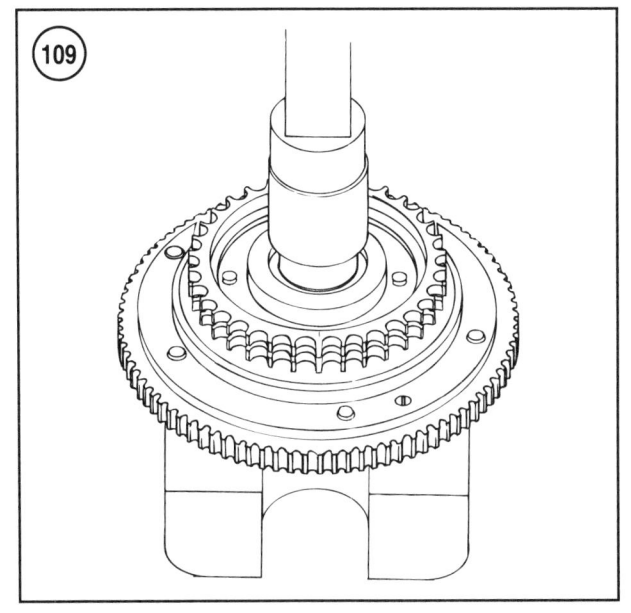

6. Remove the clutch shell (B, **Figure 107**) from the press.
7. Remove the bearing snap ring (**Figure 108**) from the groove in the middle of the clutch shell.

CAUTION
Press the bearing out from the primary chain sprocket side of the clutch shell. The bearing bore has a shoulder on the starter ring gear side.

8. Support the clutch shell in the press with the primary chain sprocket side *facing up*.
9. Place a suitable size arbor or socket on the bearing inner race (**Figure 109**), and press the bearing out of the clutch shell.

10. Thoroughly clean the clutch hub and shell in solvent. Dry them with compressed air.

11. Inspect the bearing bore in the clutch shell for damage or burrs. Clean off any burrs that would interfere with new bearing installation.

12. Support the clutch shell in the press with the primary chain sprocket side *facing down*.

13. Apply chaincase lubricant to the clutch shell bearing bore and to the outer surface of the bearing.

14. Align the bearing with the clutch shell receptacle.

15. Place a suitable size arbor on the bearing outer race, and slowly press the bearing into the clutch shell until it bottoms on the lower shoulder. Press only on the outer bearing race. Applying force to the bearing's inner race will damage the bearing. Refer to *Bearings* (Chapter One) for additional information.

16. Turn the assembly over. Position the new snap ring with its flat side facing the bearing (**Figure 108**), and install the snap ring into the clutch shell groove. Make sure the snap ring is completely seated in the clutch shell groove.

17. Press the clutch hub into the clutch shell as follows:

CAUTION
Failure to support the inner bearing race properly will cause bearing and clutch shell damage.

a. Place the clutch shell in a press. Support the inner bearing race with a sleeve as shown in **Figure 110**.
b. Align the clutch hub with the bearing, and slowly press the clutch hub into the bearing until the clutch hub shoulder seats against the bearing inner race.
c. Install a *new* snap ring (**Figure 105**) into the clutch hub. Make sure the snap ring is completely seated in the clutch hub groove.

18. After completing assembly, hold the clutch hub (A, **Figure 111**) and rotate the clutch shell (B) by hand. The shell must turn smoothly with no roughness or binding. If the clutch shell binds or turns roughly, the bearing was installed incorrectly. Repeat the assembly procedure until this problem is corrected.

Disassembly/Assembly
(2007-2009 Models)

Do not separate the clutch shell and hub unless the bearing or either part must be replaced. The bearing will be damaged when the shell and hub are separated. Removal and installation of the bearing requires the use of a hydraulic press.

1. Remove the friction discs and plain plates as described in *Clutch Assembly* (this chapter).
2. Remove the primary drive assembly as described in this chapter.
3. Remove the clutch shell assembly from the primary drive chain.
4. Place the clutch hub on the bench with the starter gear side facing up.

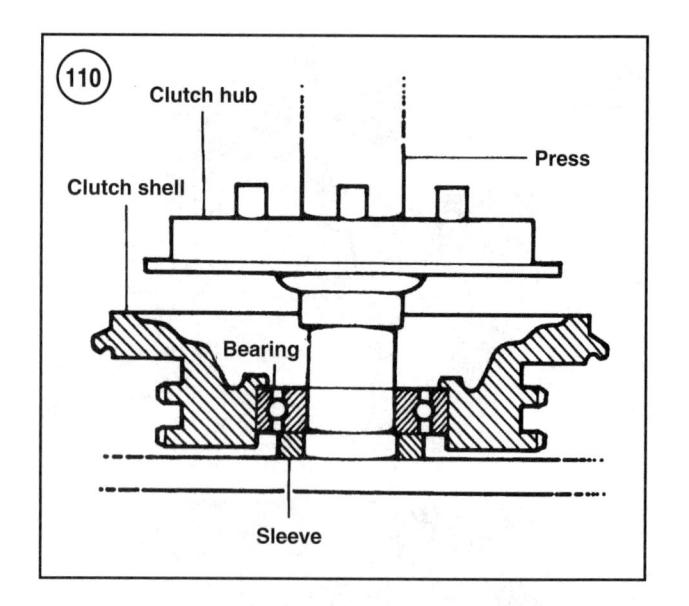

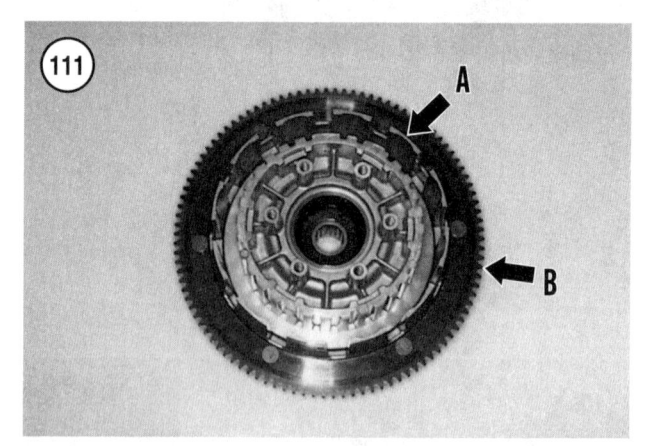

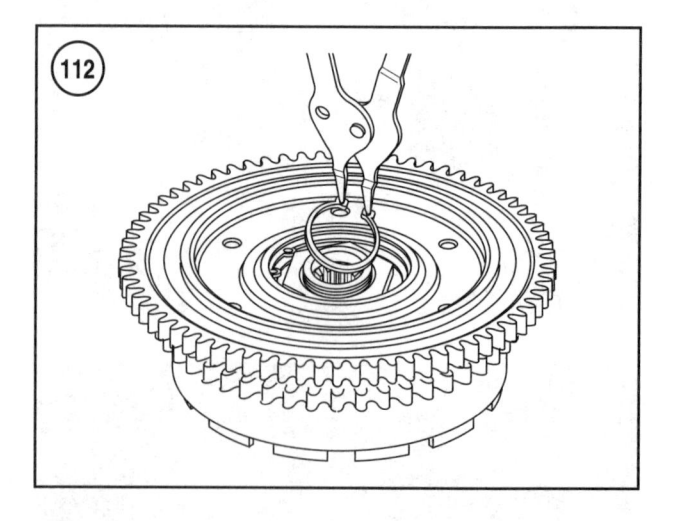

5. Remove the small snap ring (**Figure 112**) from the clutch hub groove.
6. Support the clutch shell on the press bed with the starter gear side *facing up*.
7. Place a suitable size arbor or socket on the clutch hub surface (**Figure 113**), and press the clutch hub from the bearing.
8. Remove the clutch shell from the press bed.

CLUTCH AND PRIMARY DRIVE

12. Thoroughly clean the clutch hub and shell in solvent. Dry them with compressed air.
13. Inspect the bearing bore in the clutch shell for damage or burrs. Clean off any burrs that would interfere with new bearing installation.
14. Support the clutch shell in the press with the starter gear side *facing up*.
15. Apply chaincase lubricant to the bearing bore in the clutch shell and to the outer surface of the bearing.
16. Align the bearing with the clutch shell bore.
17. Place a suitable size arbor on the bearing outer race, and slowly press the bearing into the clutch shell until it bottoms on the lower shoulder. Press only on the outer bearing race. Applying force to the bearing's inner race will damage the bearing. Refer to *Bearings* (Chapter One) for additional information.
18. Position the *new* large snap ring with its flat side against the bearing (**Figure 114**), and install the large snap ring into the clutch shell groove. Make sure the snap ring completely seats in the clutch shell groove.
19. Press the clutch hub into the clutch shell as follows:

CAUTION
Failure to support the inner bearing race properly will cause bearing and clutch shell damage.

   a. Place the clutch shell in a press so the starter gear side *faces down*. Support the inner bearing race with a sleeve that matches the bearing inner race.
   b. Align the clutch hub with the bearing, and slowly press the clutch hub into the bearing until the clutch hub shoulder seats against the bearing inner race.
   c. Turn the assembly over, and install a *new* small snap ring (**Figure 112**) into the clutch hub. Make sure the snap ring is completely seated in the clutch hub groove.

20. After completing assembly, hold the clutch hub (A, **Figure 116**) and rotate the clutch shell (B) by hand. The shell must turn smoothly with no roughness or binding. If the clutch shell binds or turns roughly, the bearing was installed incorrectly. Repeat the assembly procedure until this problem is corrected.

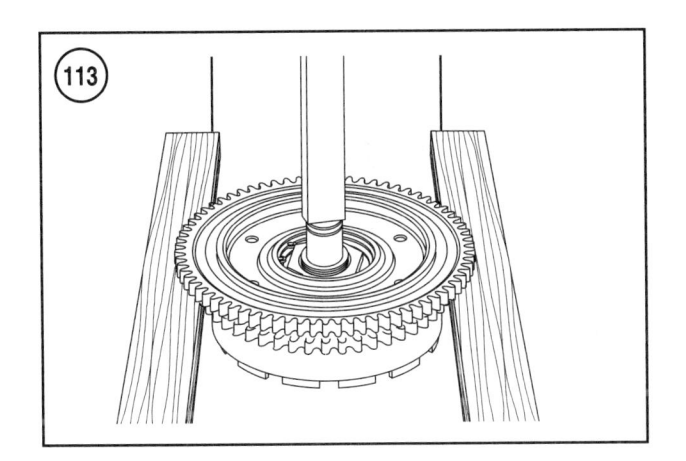

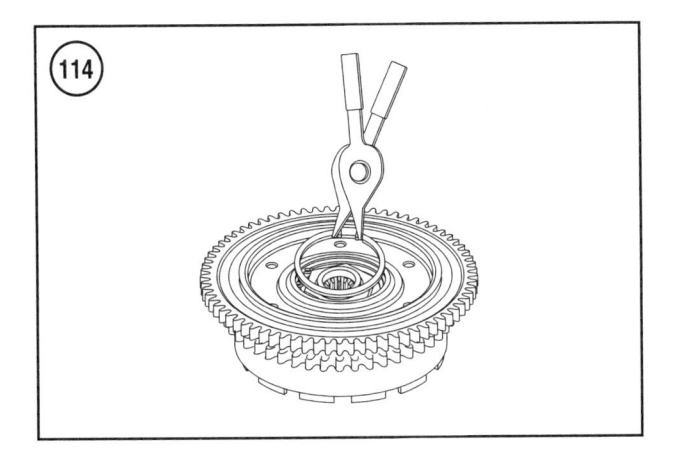

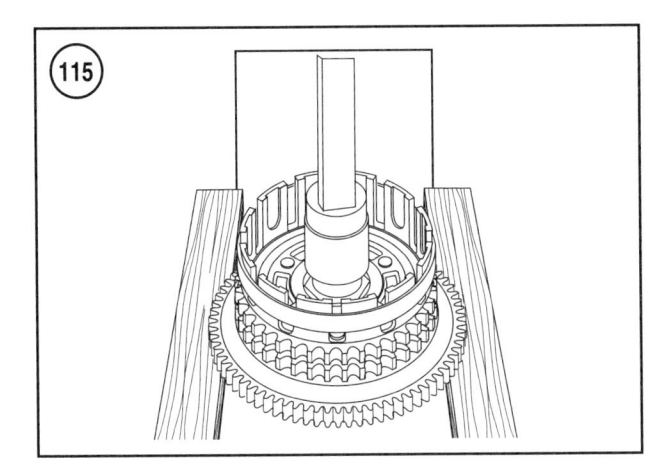

9. Remove the large snap ring (**Figure 114**) from the clutch shell groove.

CAUTION
Press the bearing out from the primary chain sprocket side of the clutch shell. The bearing bore has a shoulder on the starter ring gear side.

10. Support the clutch shell in the press with the primary chain sprocket side *facing up*.
11. Place a suitable size arbor or socket on the bearing inner race (**Figure 115**), and press the bearing out of the clutch shell.

PRIMARY CHAIN AND TENSIONER INSPECTION (ALL MODELS)

1. Remove the primary chain as described in this chapter.
2. Remove the compensating sprocket and the clutch shell from the primary chain.
3. Clean the primary chain in solvent and dry thoroughly.
4. Inspect the primary chain (**Figure 117**) for excessive wear, cracks or other damage. If the chain is worn or damaged, check both sprockets for wear and damage.

NOTE
If the primary chain is near the end of its adjustment level or if no more adjustment is available, and the tensioner shoe is not worn or damaged; the primary chain is excessively worn. Specifications for chain wear are not available.

5A. On 2006 models, inspect the tensioner shoe (A, **Figure 118**) for cracks, severe wear or other damage. If necessary, replace the tensioner shoe by performing the following:
   a. Remove the snap ring (B, **Figure 118**) from the chain tensioner post.
   b. Slide the tensioner shoe from chain tensioner boss.
   c. Reverse the removal procedure to install the new shoe and new snap ring.

NOTE
The 2007-2009 tensioner assembly cannot be serviced. It must be replaced if any portion is worn or damaged.

5B. On 2007-2009 models, inspect the chain tensioner shoe assembly (**Figure 119**) for cracks, severe wear or other damage. Replace the chain tensioner assembly if necessary.

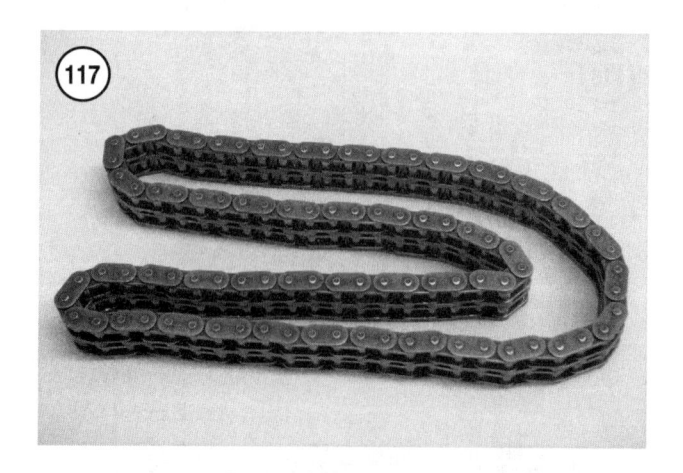

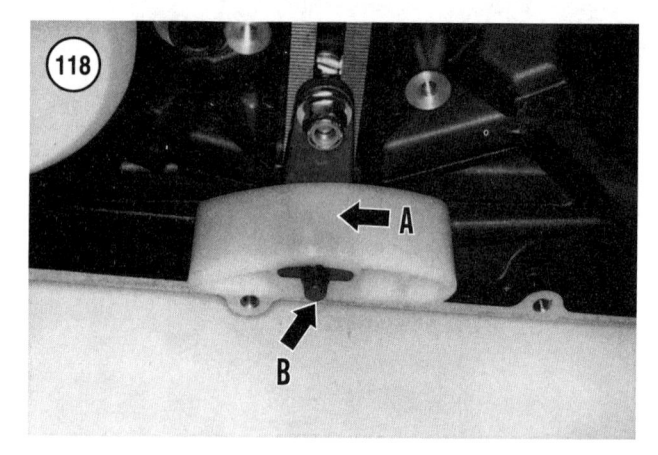

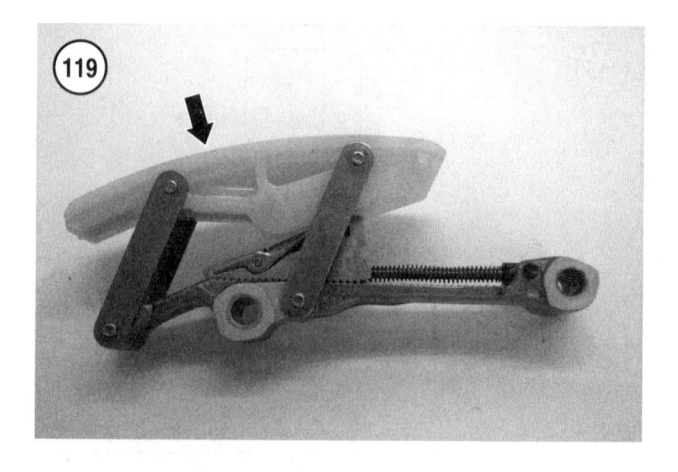

COMPENSATING SPROCKET INSPECTION

2006 Models

Refer to **Figure 120**.
1. Remove the compensating sprocket assembly as described in this chapter.
2. Clean all parts in solvent, Dry them with compressed air.
3. Check the cam surfaces (**Figure 121**) on the sliding cam and compensating sprocket for cracks, deep scoring or wear.

NOTE
If the compensating sprocket teeth are worn, also check the primary chain and the clutch-shell primary chain sprocket for wear.

4. Check the compensating sprocket gear teeth (**Figure 122**) for cracks or wear.
5. Check the compensating sprocket inner bushing (**Figure 123**) for wear.
6. Check the sliding cam inner splines (**Figure 124**) for wear.
7. Check the shaft extension splines for wear or galling.
8. Check the cover (**Figure 125**) for damage.
9. Inspect the inner threads (**Figure 126**) of the compensating sprocket nut for damage.

2007-2009 Models

Refer to **Figure 127**.
1. Remove the compensating sprocket assembly as described in this chapter.
2. Clean all parts in solvent. Dry them with compressed air.

CLUTCH AND PRIMARY DRIVE

120 COMPENSATING SPROCKET (2006 MODELS)

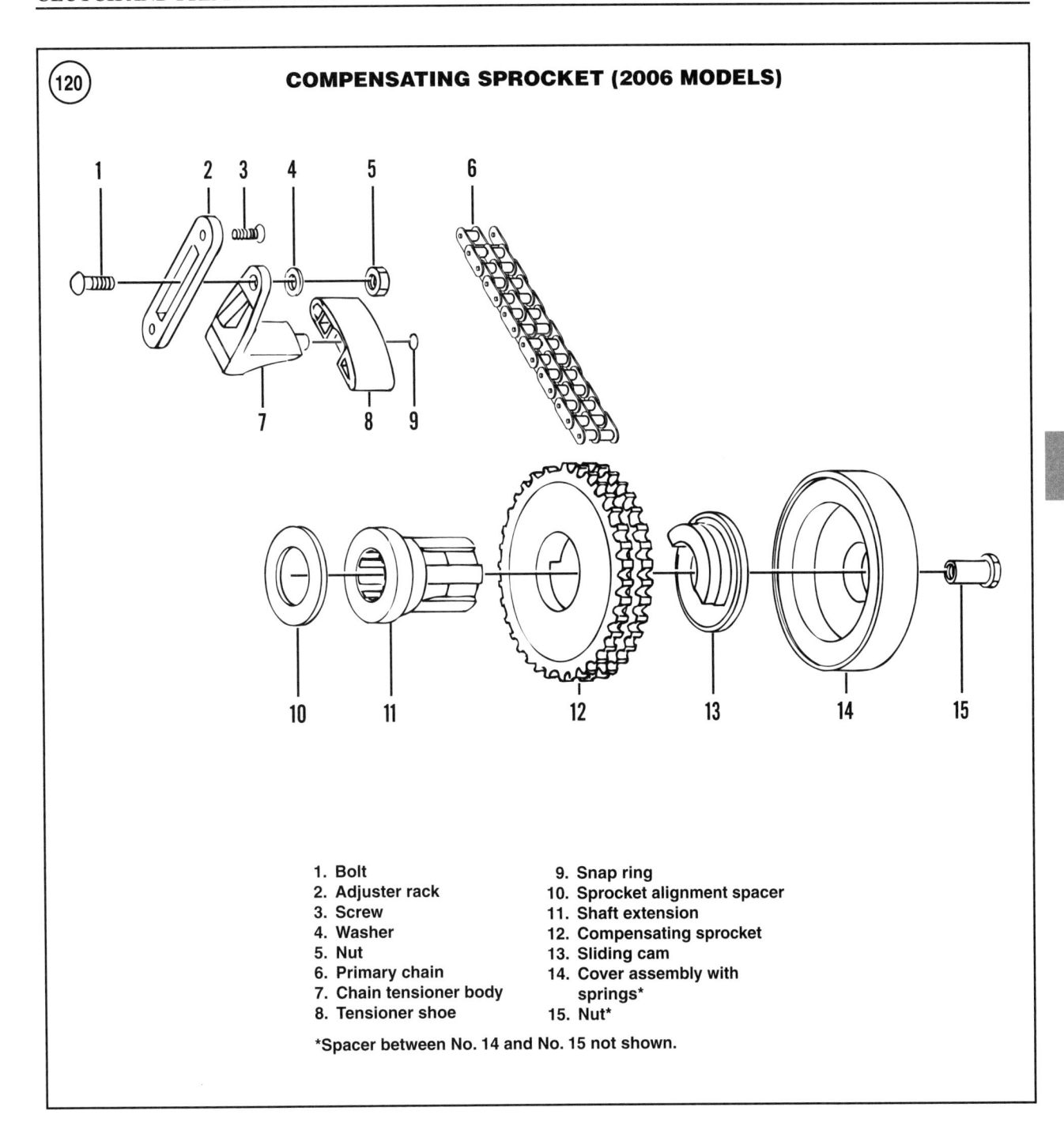

1. Bolt
2. Adjuster rack
3. Screw
4. Washer
5. Nut
6. Primary chain
7. Chain tensioner body
8. Tensioner shoe
9. Snap ring
10. Sprocket alignment spacer
11. Shaft extension
12. Compensating sprocket
13. Sliding cam
14. Cover assembly with springs*
15. Nut*

*Spacer between No. 14 and No. 15 not shown.

121

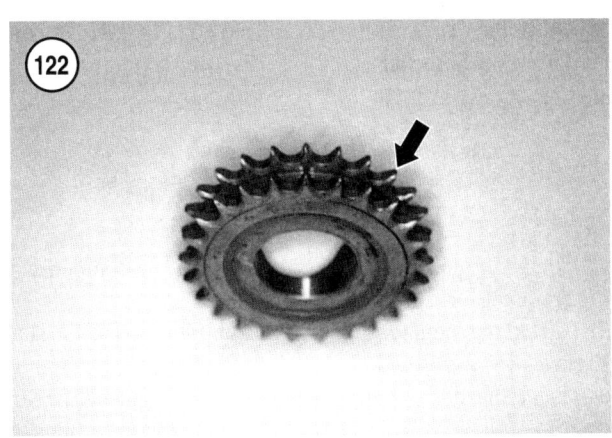

122

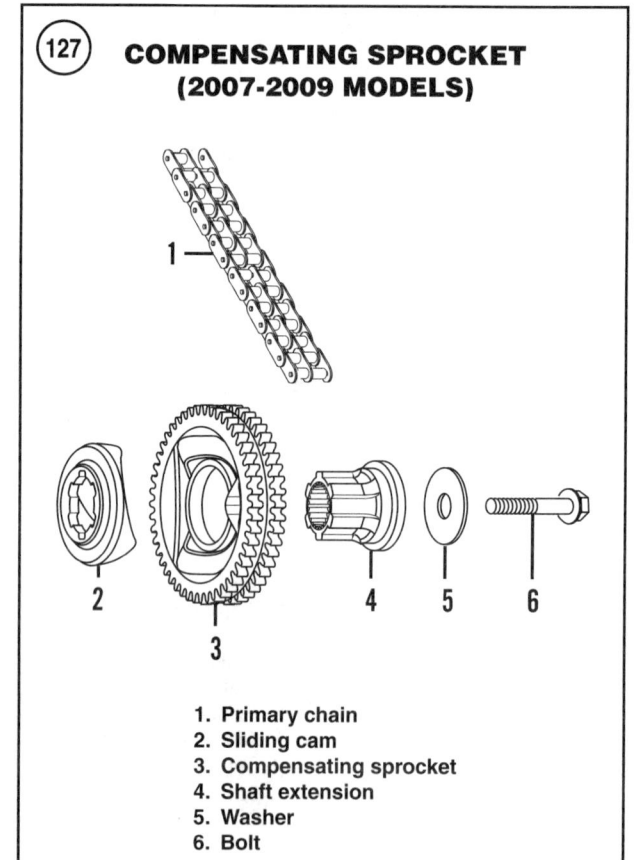

3. Check the ramps on the sliding cam (A, **Figure 128**) and compensating sprockets (B) for cracks, deep scoring or wear.

NOTE
If the compensating sprocket teeth are worn, also check the primary chain and the clutch shell gear teeth for wear.

4. Check the gear teeth (C, **Figure 128**) on the compensating sprocket for cracks or wear.
5. Check the compensating sprocket inner bushing (D, **Figure 128**) for wear.
6. Check the sliding cam inner splines (E, **Figure 128**) for wear.

COMPENSATING SPROCKET (2007-2009 MODELS)

1. Primary chain
2. Sliding cam
3. Compensating sprocket
4. Shaft extension
5. Washer
6. Bolt

CLUTCH AND PRIMARY DRIVE

STARTER JACKSHAFT (2006 MODELS)

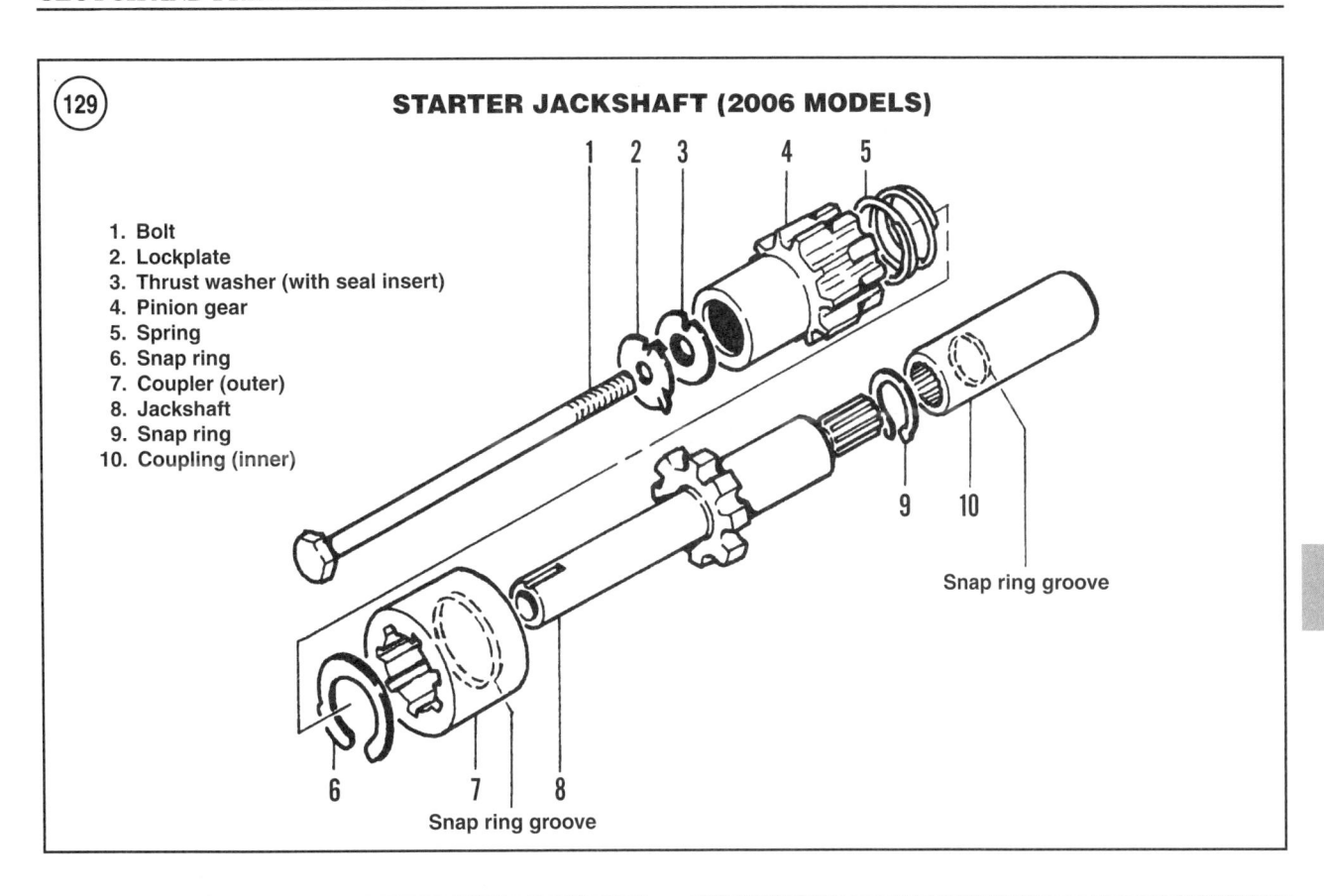

1. Bolt
2. Lockplate
3. Thrust washer (with seal insert)
4. Pinion gear
5. Spring
6. Snap ring
7. Coupler (outer)
8. Jackshaft
9. Snap ring
10. Coupling (inner)

7. Check the shaft extension splines (F, **Figure 128**) for wear or galling.
8. Inspect the bolt threads for damage.

STARTER JACKSHAFT (2006 MODELS)

Refer to **Figure 129**.

Removal

NOTE
Always disarm the optional TSSM/HFSM security system before disconnecting the battery or pulling the Maxi-Fuse so the alarm will not sound.

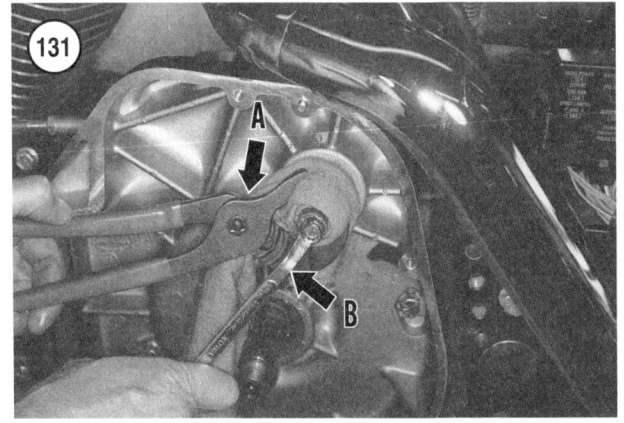

1. Disconnect the negative battery cable as described in Chapter Eleven.
2. Remove the primary chaincase cover as described in this chapter.

NOTE
*The pinion gear components (**Figure 129**) can be removed with the primary drive assembly in place. If only these parts require service, it is not necessary to remove the primary drive assembly.*

3. Remove the primary drive assembly as described in this chapter.
4. Straighten the tab (**Figure 130**) on the lockplate.
5. Wrap the pinion gear with a cloth to protect the finish, and secure it with pliers (A, **Figure 131**).

6. Loosen and remove the bolt (B, **Figure 131**), lockplate and thrust washer from the starter jackshaft assembly.
7. Remove the pinion gear (**Figure 132**) and spring from the jackshaft.

CAUTION
*Removing the inner coupling and its snap ring (**Figure 129**) from the primary housing will damage the oil seal. If the inner coupling and/or snap ring must be replaced, remove the starter (Chapter Eleven), and then remove the parts from the starter.*

8. Remove the jackshaft and the outer coupling from the primary housing.

Installation

NOTE
*Before installing the inner coupling, note the snap ring (A, **Figure 133**) installed inside the coupling. The coupling side with the snap ring closest to its end slides over the jackshaft.*

1. If removed, perform the following to install the inner coupling:
   a. Install the snap ring (A, **Figure 133**) into the inner coupling (B). Make sure it is correctly seated in the groove.
   b. Install the coupling onto the starter output shaft so the end with the snap ring (A, **Figure 133**) faces out away from the starter.
   c. Install the starter as described in Chapter Eleven.
2. Install the jackshaft (**Figure 134**) into the housing. Push it in until it stops.
3. Position the outer coupling with its counter bore facing the jackshaft, and install the coupling (**Figure 135**) into the housing bushing.
4. Install the spring (**Figure 136**) onto the jackshaft.
5. Install the pinion gear (**Figure 137**) onto the jackshaft.
6. Push the pinion gear (A, **Figure 138**) in, and then install the bolt, lockplate and thrust washer (B) onto the jackshaft.
7. Push the assembly in until it bottoms.

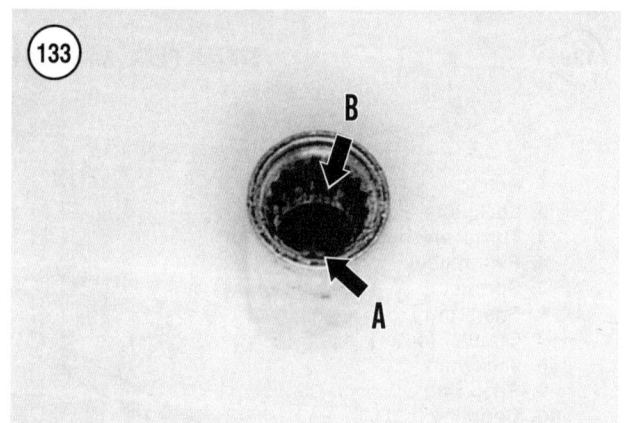

CLUTCH AND PRIMARY DRIVE

8. Align the lockplate tab with the thrust washer, and insert the tab into the notch in the end of the jackshaft.
9. Finger-tighten the bolt into the starter shaft.
10. Wrap the pinion gear with a cloth to protect the finish, and secure it with pliers (A, **Figure 131**).
11. Tighten the jackshaft bolt (B, **Figure 131**) to 60-80 in.-lb. (6.8-9.0 N•m). Bend the outer lockplate tab (**Figure 130**) against the bolt head.
12. To ensure the components have been installed correctly, perform the following:
   a. Install the clutch shell onto the transmission mainshaft.
   b. With the starter not engaged, the pinion gear (A, **Figure 139**) must *not* engage the clutch shell gear (B).
   c. To check for proper engagement, pull out on the pinion gear, and engage it with the clutch shell gear. Rotate the clutch shell in either direction and make sure the pinion gear rotates with it.
   d. If engagement is incorrect, remove the clutch shell and correct the problem.
   e. Remove the clutch shell.
13. Install the primary drive assembly and primary chaincase cover as described in this chapter.
14. Connect the negative battery cable as described in Chapter Eleven.

Inspection

1. Clean the jackshaft assembly (**Figure 140**) in solvent. Dry it with compressed air.
2. Check the snap ring installed in the inner coupling (A, **Figure 133**) and the outer coupling (**Figure 141**). Replace any loose or damaged snap rings.
3. Replace all worn or damaged parts.

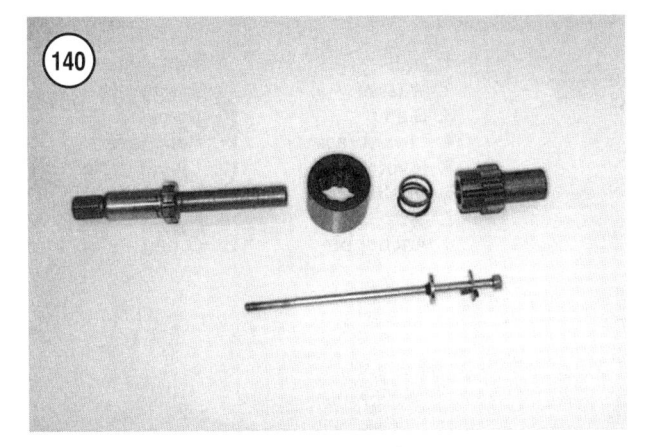

CLUTCH CABLE REPLACEMENT (ALL MODELS EXCEPT SCREAMIN' EAGLE)

Refer to **Figure 142** and **Figure 143**.
1. Before removing the clutch cable, make a drawing of the cable's path from the handlebar, down the left frame-

CHAPTER SIX

CLUTCH CABLE CONTROL (2006-2007 MODELS)

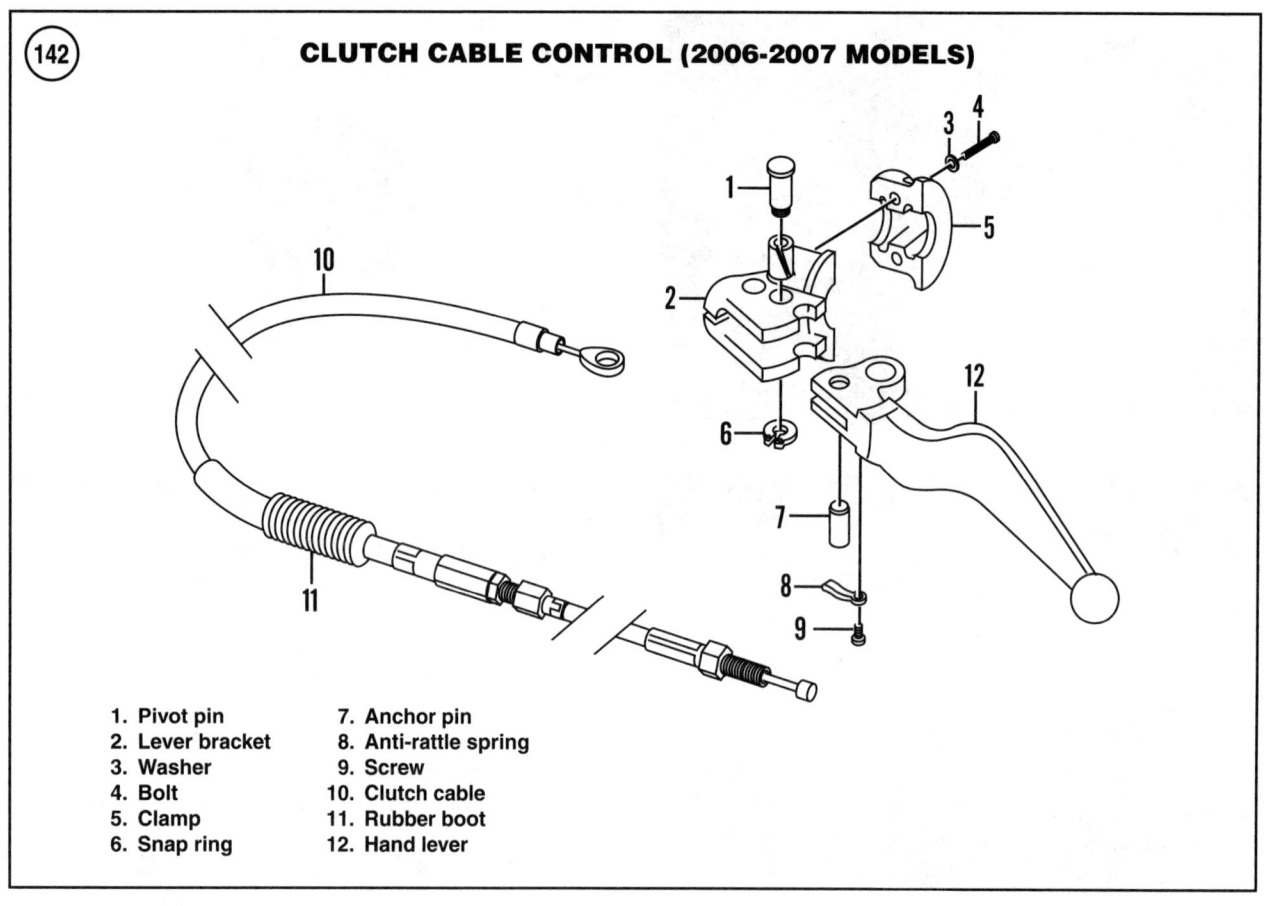

1. Pivot pin
2. Lever bracket
3. Washer
4. Bolt
5. Clamp
6. Snap ring
7. Anchor pin
8. Anti-rattle spring
9. Screw
10. Clutch cable
11. Rubber boot
12. Hand lever

CLUTCH CABLE CONTROL (2008-2009 MODELS)

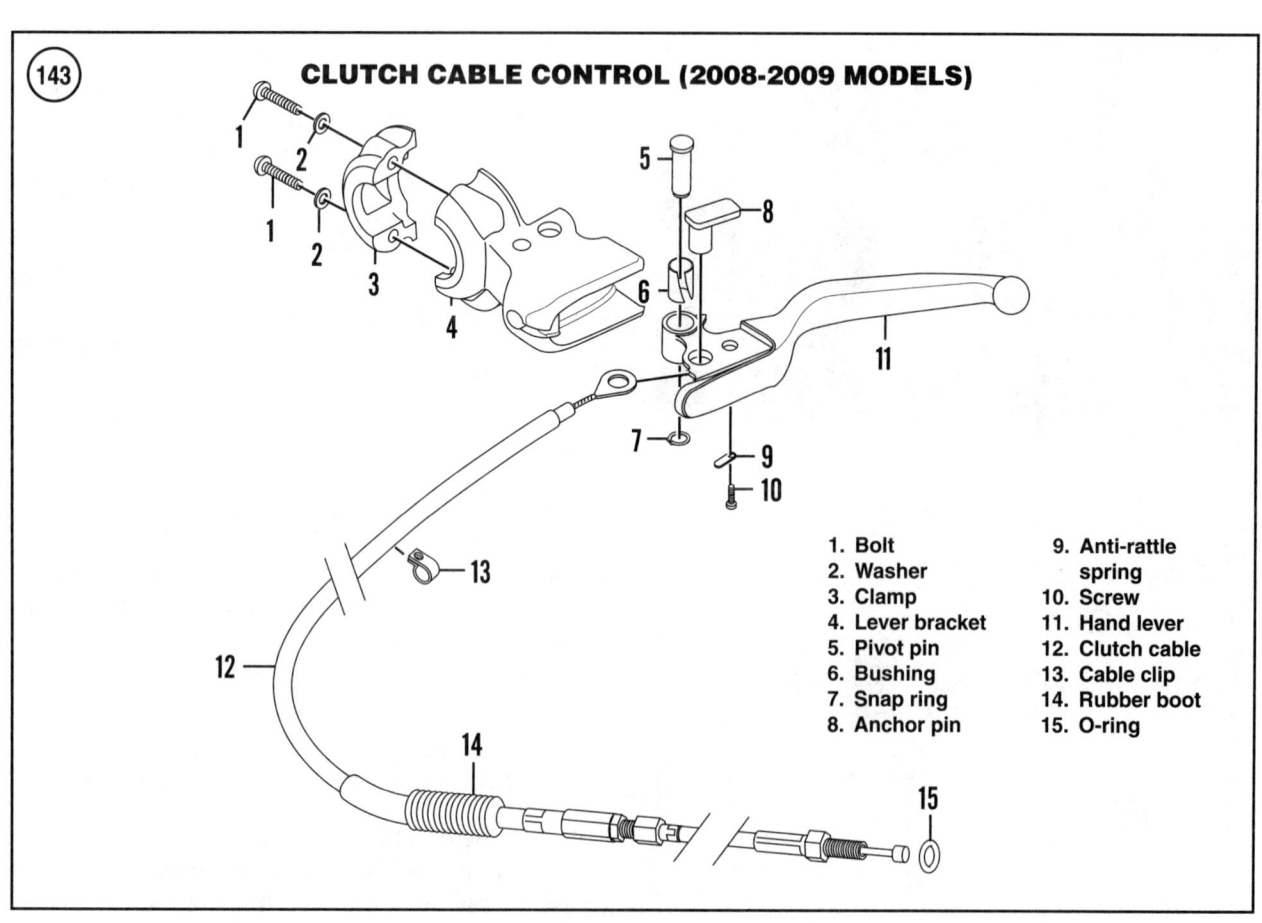

1. Bolt
2. Washer
3. Clamp
4. Lever bracket
5. Pivot pin
6. Bushing
7. Snap ring
8. Anchor pin
9. Anti-rattle spring
10. Screw
11. Hand lever
12. Clutch cable
13. Cable clip
14. Rubber boot
15. O-ring

CLUTCH AND PRIMARY DRIVE

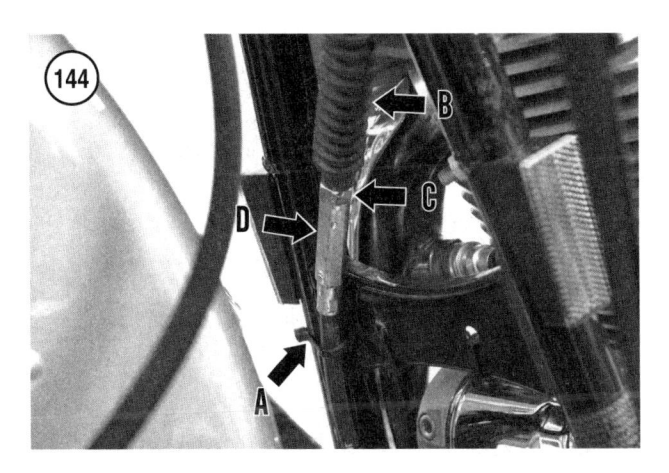

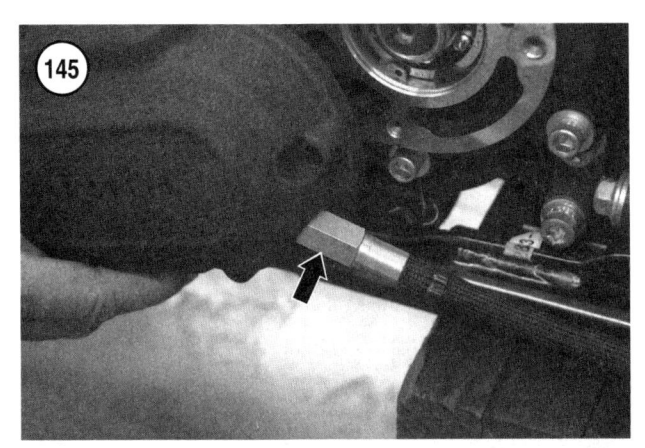

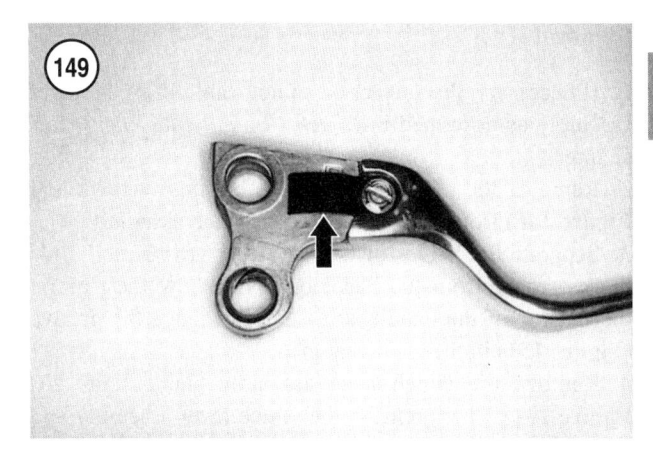

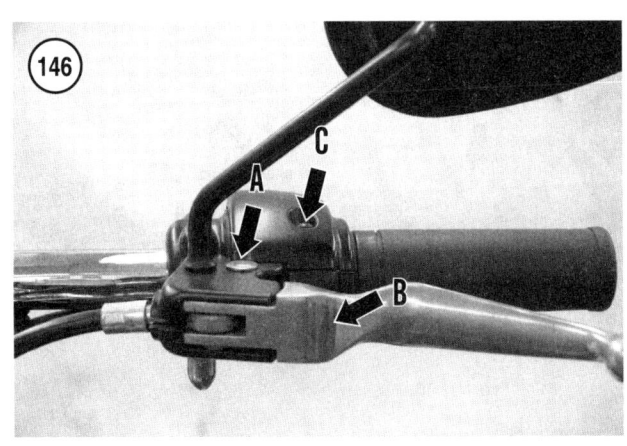

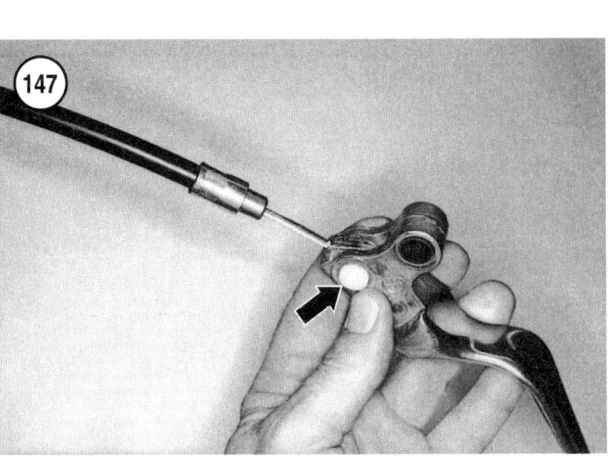

down tube, under the engine mounting spacer and on to the clutch release cover. The new cable must be routed along the same path.

2. Perform the following at the clutch cable adjuster:
   a. Release the clutch cable from the clamp (A, **Figure 144**) and slide the boot (B) away from the adjuster.
   b. Loosen the locknut (C, **Figure 144**), and turn the adjuster (D) to provide maximum slack.

3. Disconnect the clutch cable (**Figure 145**) from the clutch release mechanism and remove it from the release cover as described in *Clutch Release Cover Disassembly* (this chapter).

4. Remove the snap ring from the bottom of the clutch lever pivot pin.

5. Remove the pivot pin (A, **Figure 146**), and slide the clutch lever (B) from the lever bracket.

6. Remove the anchor pin (**Figure 147**), and disconnect the clutch cable from the lever.

7. Check the clutch lever components (**Figure 148**) for worn or damaged parts.

8. Make sure the anti-rattle spring screw (**Figure 149**) on the bottom of the clutch lever is tight.

9. On FLHT and FLHX models, withdraw the clutch cable from the inner fairing rubber grommet (**Figure 150**). Move the clutch cable forward and out of the fairing.

10. Following the path noted prior to removal, route the new clutch cable from the handlebar to the clutch release cover.

11. Fit the clutch cable end into its lever. Secure it with the anchor pin (**Figure 147**).
12. Slide the clutch lever (B, **Figure 146**) into the bracket, and install the pivot pin (A).
13. Secure the pivot pin with the snap ring.
14. Reconnect the clutch cable (**Figure 145**) to the clutch release mechanism as described in *Clutch Release Cover Assembly* (this chapter).
15. Adjust the clutch as described in Chapter Three.

CLUTCH LEVER ASSEMBLY (ALL MODELS EXCEPT SCREAMIN' EAGLE)

Removal

1. If necessary, disconnect the clutch cable from the lever assembly as described in *Clutch Cable Replacement* (this chapter).
2. Remove the handlebar switch housing screws (C, **Figure 146**) from the left handlebar switch assembly.
3. Separate the halves of the handlebar switch, and slide the assembly from the handlebar. Note how the ribs on the outside of the handlebar assembly engage the groove (**Figure 151**) in the handlebar grip.
4. Remove the clutch lever assembly clamp bolts (A, **Figure 152**). Then, remove the clutch lever assembly and its clamp (B, **Figure 152**) from the handlebar.
5. If necessary, remove the handlebar grip (C, **Figure 152**) from the handlebar.

Installation

1. If removed, install a new handlebar grip (C, **Figure 152**) by performing the following:
    a. Clean all adhesive from the handlebar.
    b. Pour adhesive into the new grip and roll the grip to evenly spread the adhesive on the grip's inner surface.
    c. Roll the new grip onto the handlebar. Clean away any excess adhesive.
2. Fit the left handlebar switch onto the handlebar so the switch ribs engage the groove (**Figure 151**) in the handlebar grip.
3. Install and finger-tighten the handlebar switch housing screws (C, **Figure 146**).
4. Position the clutch lever assembly onto the handlebar so the notch (A, **Figure 153**; typical) in the clutch lever assembly engages the tab (B) in the lower handlebar switch housing.
5. Fit the clamp (B, **Figure 152**) into position and install the clutch lever assembly clamp bolts (A).
6. Tighten the upper clutch control clamp bolt first, and then the lower bolt. Tighten each bolt as follows:
    a. 2006-2007 models: 108-132 in.-lb (12.2-14.9 N•m).
    b. 2008-2009 models: 60-80 in.-lb. (6.8-9.0 N•m).

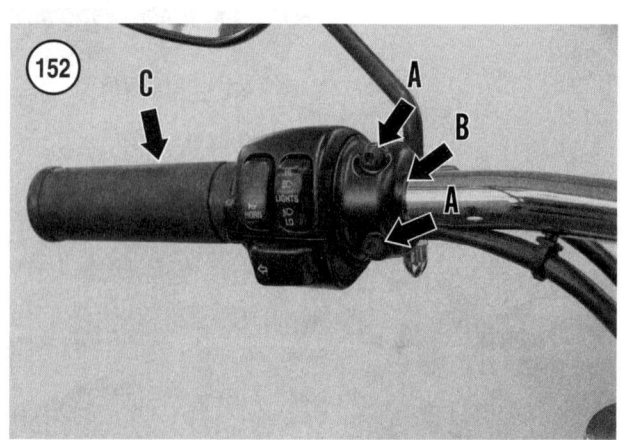

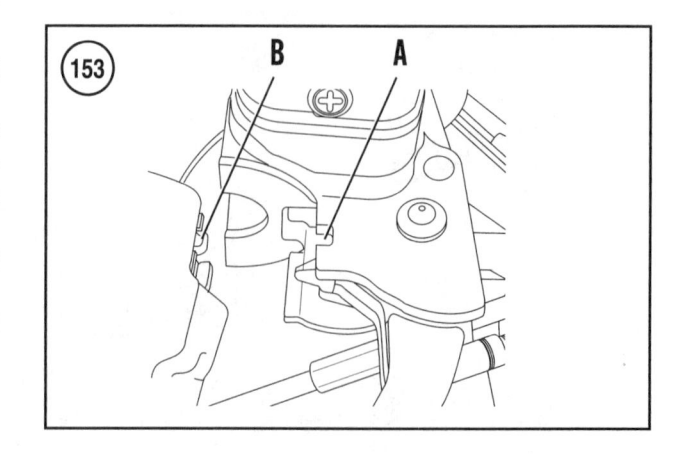

CLUTCH AND PRIMARY DRIVE

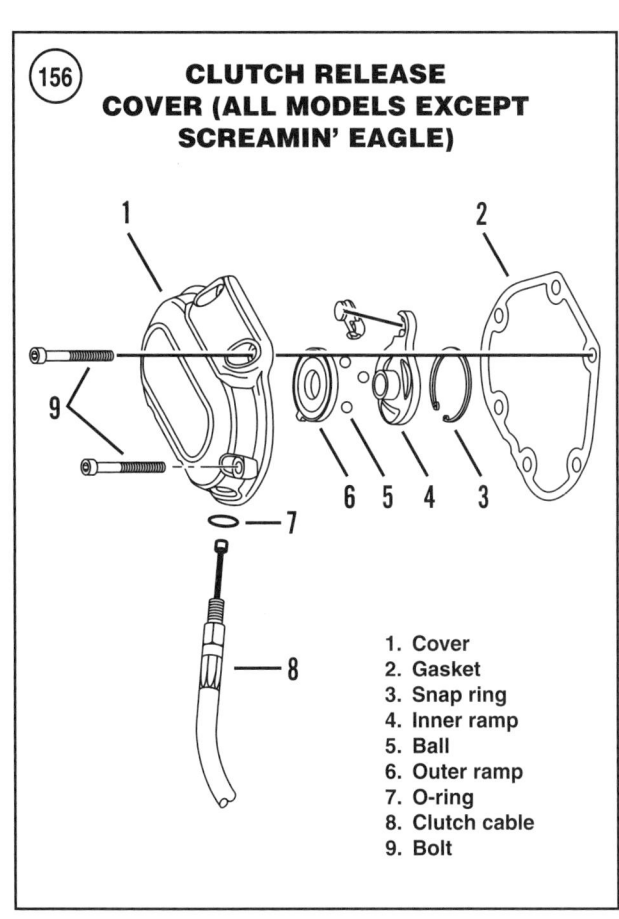

7. Starting with the bottom screw, tighten the handlebar switch housing screws (C, **Figure 146**) securely.

8. If removed, install the clutch cable as described in *Clutch Cable Replacement* (this chapter).

CLUTCH RELEASE COVER (ALL MODELS EXCEPT SCREAMIN' EAGLE)

Removal

1. Remove the exhaust system as described in Chapter Four.

2. Drain the transmission oil as described in Chapter Three.

NOTE
If the cover is difficult to remove, apply the clutch lever after the mounting bolts have been removed. This usually breaks the cover loose.

3. Remove the mounting bolts (A, **Figure 154**) securing the clutch release cover.

4. Remove the clutch release cover and gasket from the transmission side door. Discard the cover gasket.

5. Do not lose the locating dowels (**Figure 155**) behind the cover.

Installation

1. If removed, install the locating dowels (**Figure 155**) into the transmission side door.

2. Install a *new* gasket.

3. Install the clutch release cover bolts (A, **Figure 154**). Using a crossing pattern, tighten the clutch release cover bolts to 84-108 in.-lb. (9.5-12.2 N•m).

4A. On 2006-2007 models, tighten the clutch cable fitting (B, **Figure 154**) to 36-60 in.-lb. (4.1-6.8 N•m).

4B. On 2008-2009 models, tighten the clutch cable fitting to 90-120 in.-lb. (10.2-13.6 N•m).

5. Refill the transmission with oil as described in Chapter Three.

6. Install the exhaust system as described in a Chapter Four.

7. Adjust the clutch as described in Chapter Three.

Disassembly

Refer to **Figure 156**.

1. Remove the clutch release cover as described in this section.

2. Perform the following at the clutch cable adjuster:

   a. Release the clutch cable from the clamp (A, **Figure 144**), and slide the boot (B) away from the adjuster.

   b. Loosen the locknut (C, **Figure 144**), and turn the adjuster (D) to provide maximum slack.

---

156 CLUTCH RELEASE COVER (ALL MODELS EXCEPT SCREAMIN' EAGLE)

1. Cover
2. Gasket
3. Snap ring
4. Inner ramp
5. Ball
6. Outer ramp
7. O-ring
8. Clutch cable
9. Bolt

NOTE
*Before removing the snap ring, note that the snap ring opening (A, **Figure 157**) is centered on the cover slot. The snap ring must be reinstalled with the opening in the same position.*

3. Remove the snap ring (B, **Figure 157**) from the groove in the side cover.
4. Disconnect the ramp coupling (A, **Figure 158**) from the inner ramp (B).
5. Disconnect the cable end (**Figure 159**) from the ramp coupling, and remove the coupling.
6. Lift the inner ramp (**Figure 160**) from the release cover.
7. Remove the three balls (**Figure 161**) from the outer ramp.
8. Remove the outer ramp (A, **Figure 162**).
9. If necessary, loosen the clutch cable fitting (**Figure 163**), and remove the cable from the clutch release cover.

Assembly

1. If removed, insert the cable and thread the clutch cable fitting (**Figure 163**) into the clutch release cover. Do not tighten the cable fitting at this time.
2. Install the outer ramp (A, **Figure 162**) into the cover and engage the ramp's tab (B) with the cover slot. The ball sockets in the outer ramp must face up.
3. Seat a ball (**Figure 161**) into each socket in the outer ramp. Center each ball in its socket.
4. Align the inner ramp socket with the balls, and install the inner ramp (**Figure 160**) into the cover.
5. Connect the cable end (**Figure 159**) to the ramp coupling. Then, connect the ramp coupling (A, **Figure 158**) to the inner ramp (B).
6. Install the snap ring (B, **Figure 157**) into the clutch release cover groove. Position the snap ring so its opening (A, **Figure 157**) is centered on the slot in the cover. Make sure the snap ring is completely seated in the groove.
7. Tighten the cable fitting (**Figure 163**) securely.

Inspection

1. Clean the side cover and all components thoroughly in solvent, and dry them with compressed air.
2. Check the release mechanism balls (A, **Figure 164**), inner ramp sockets (B) and outer ramp sockets (C) for cracks, deep scoring or excessive wear.
3. Check the clutch release cover for cracks or damage. Check the clutch cable threads and the coupling snap ring groove for damage. Check the ramp bore in the release cover for excessive wear, or grooves that could catch and bind the ramps causing improper clutch adjustment.
4. Replace the clutch cable O-ring.
5. Replace all worn or damaged parts.

CLUTCH AND PRIMARY DRIVE

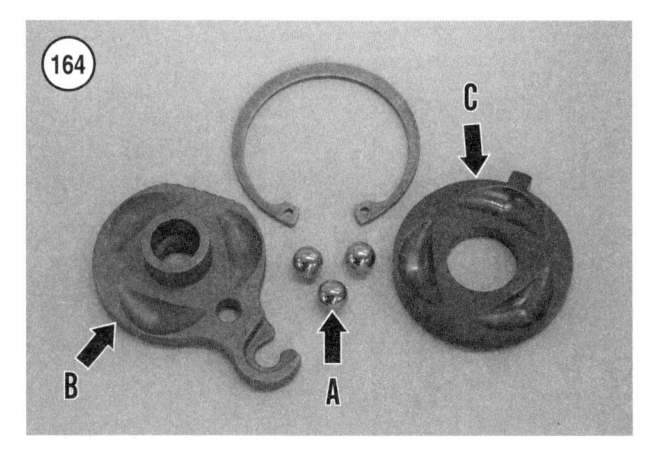

CLUTCH SERVICE (SCREAMIN' EAGLE MODELS)

The hydraulic release system transmits hydraulic pressure from the master cylinder to the clutch release mechanism in the clutch release cover. As the clutch components wear, the clutch release piston moves out. As this occurs, the fluid level in the master cylinder reservoir goes down. Occasionally adding fluid compensates for this drop.

Proper operation of the hydraulic clutch system depends on a supply of clean brake fluid (DOT 4). Always work in a clean environment when servicing this system. Even tiny particles of debris that enter the system can damage components and cause poor clutch performance.

Brake fluid is hygroscopic (easily absorbs moisture), and moisture in the system reduces clutch performance. Purchase brake fluid in small containers and properly discard any small quantities that remain. Small quantities of fluid quickly absorb moisture in the container. Use only fluid clearly marked DOT 4. Other types of brake fluid are not compatible with DOT 4. If possible, always use the same brand of brake fluid. Fluids from different manufacturers may not be compatible with one another. Do not reuse drained fluid. Properly discard all old brake fluid. Do not mix it with other fluids for recycling.

Perform clutch service procedures carefully. Do not use any sharp tools inside the master cylinder or release mechanism piston. Damage to these components could cause a loss in the system's ability to maintain hydraulic pressure. If there is any doubt about the ability to correctly and safely service the clutch system, have a professional technician perform the task.

Consider the following when servicing the hydraulic clutch system:

1. The hydraulic components rarely require disassembly. Make sure it is necessary.
2. Keep the reservoir cover in place to prevent the entry of moisture and debris.
3. Clean parts with an aerosol brake parts cleaner or isopropyl alcohol. Never use petroleum-based solvents on internal clutch system components. They will cause seals to swell and distort.
4. Do not allow brake fluid to contact plastic, painted or plated parts. It quickly damages these surfaces.
5. Dispose of used brake fluid properly.
6. If the hydraulic system, not including the reservoir cover, has been opened, bleed the system to remove air from the system. Refer to *Clutch System Bleeding* in this chapter.

CLUTCH MASTER CYLINDER (SCREAMIN' EAGLE MODELS)

Read *Clutch Service* in this chapter before servicing the clutch master cylinder.

Refer to **Figure 165** and **Figure 166**.

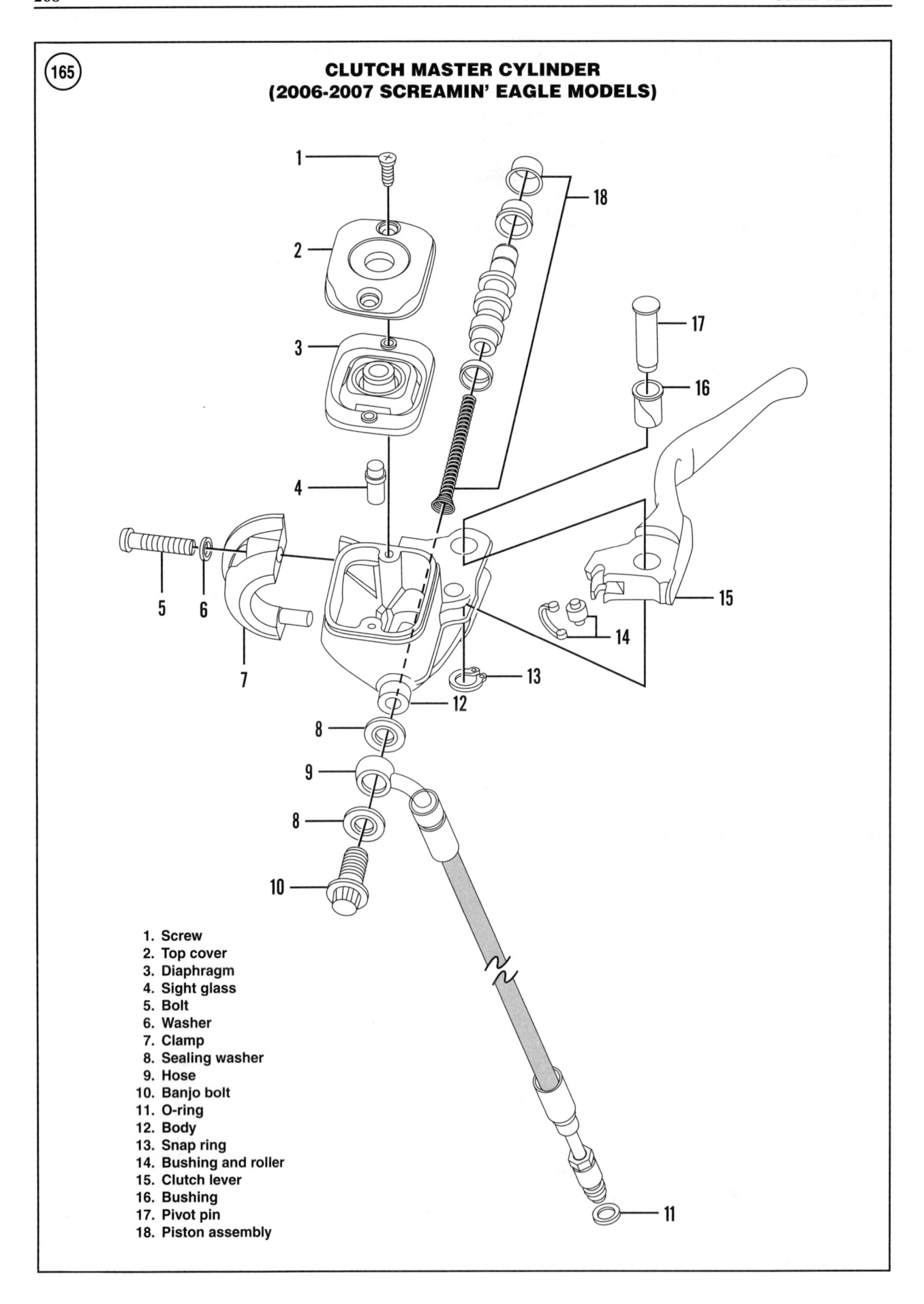

CLUTCH MASTER CYLINDER (2006-2007 SCREAMIN' EAGLE MODELS)

1. Screw
2. Top cover
3. Diaphragm
4. Sight glass
5. Bolt
6. Washer
7. Clamp
8. Sealing washer
9. Hose
10. Banjo bolt
11. O-ring
12. Body
13. Snap ring
14. Bushing and roller
15. Clutch lever
16. Bushing
17. Pivot pin
18. Piston assembly

CLUTCH AND PRIMARY DRIVE

CLUTCH MASTER CYLINDER
(2008-2009 SCREAMIN' EAGLE MODELS)

(166)

1. Bolt
2. Washer
3. Clamp
4. Screw
5. Top cover
6. Diaphragm
7. Body
8. Sight glass and gasket
9. Banjo bolt
10. Sealing washer
11. Pivot pin
12. Snap ring
13. Piston assembly
14. Bushing and roller
15. Bushing
16. Clutch lever
17. Bolt
18. Cable retainer
19. Nut
20. O-ring
21. Tubing
22. Hose

Removal/Installation

1. Use a swing arm stand to support the motorcycle on level ground.
2. Block the front wheel so the motorcycle cannot roll in either direction while on the swing arm stand.
3. If the master cylinder will be serviced, perform the following:
   a. Cover the fuel tank, front fairing and front fender with a heavy cloth or plastic tarp to protect them from accidental brake fluid spills.

CAUTION
Wash brake fluid off any surface immediately, as it damages the finish. Use soapy water and rinse completely.

   b. Drain the clutch system as described in this chapter.
   c. Remove the banjo bolt and washers securing the clutch hose to the master cylinder. Seal the clutch hose in a plastic bag so brake fluid cannot drip onto the motorcycle. Tie the loose end of the hose to the handlebar.
   d. Plug the bolt opening in the master cylinder to prevent dripping when removing the master cylinder in the following steps.
4. Remove the clutch master cylinder clamp bolts, washers and the clamp, and lower the clutch master cylinder from the handlebar.
5A. If necessary, service the master cylinder as described in this section.
5B. If the master cylinder will not be serviced, suspend it from the motorcycle. Use a bungee cord so the clutch hose is not strained, and keep the master cylinder upright.
6. Clean the handlebar, master cylinder and clamp mating surfaces.
7. Mount the master cylinder onto the handlebar and position it to rider's preference.
8. Install the master cylinder clamp, clamp bolts and washers.

NOTE
When the master cylinder clamp is correctly installed, the upper edge of the clamp touches the master cylinder mating surface, leaving a gap at the bottom.

9. Tighten the upper master cylinder clamp bolt first, and then tighten the lower bolt. Tighten each bolt to 60-80 in.-lb. (6.8-9.0 N•m).
10. If removed, install a *new* sealing washer on each side of the clutch hose and secure the clutch hose to the master cylinder with the banjo bolt. Tighten the banjo bolt to the following:
    a. 2006-2007 models: 17-22 ft.-lb. (23.0-29.8 N•m).
    b. 2008-2009 models: 12.5-14.5 ft.-lb. (16.9-19.7 N•m).
11. Bleed the clutch system as described in this chapter.
12. Test ride the motorcycle to ensure the clutch is operating correctly.

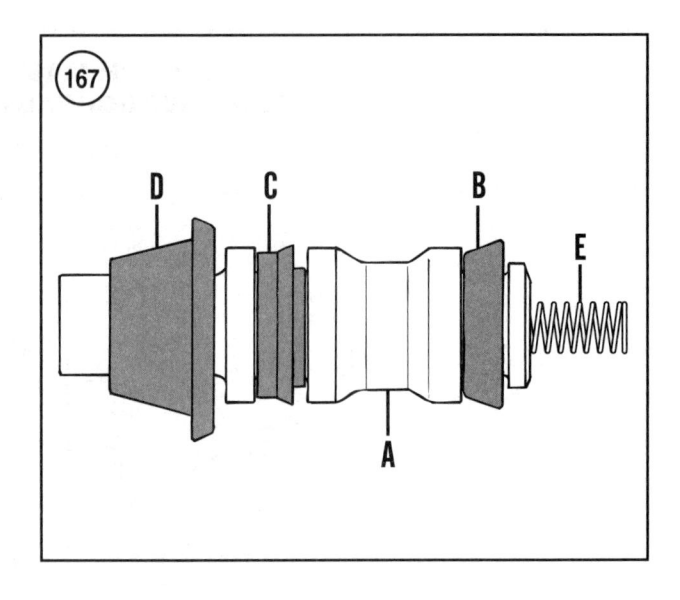

Disassembly

1. Remove the master cylinder as described in this section.
2. If still in place, remove the master cylinder cover and diaphragm. Pour out and discard any remaining brake fluid.
3. Remove the snap ring from the clutch lever pivot pin.
4. Apply slight hand pressure to the clutch lever to remove some of the spring pressure on the pivot pin.
5. Withdraw the pivot pin from the body, and then remove the clutch lever. Watch for the bushing and roller in the lever.
6. Remove the rubber boot from the groove in the body at the end of the piston.

NOTE
If brake fluid is leaking from the piston bore, the piston cups are worn or damaged. Replace the piston assembly.

7. Remove the piston assembly and spring from the master cylinder bore. Do not remove the primary and secondary cups from the piston.

Assembly

1. If installing a new piston assembly, assemble it as described in *Inspection* (this section).
2. Lubricate the piston (A, **Figure 167**), primary cup (B), secondary cup (C), rubber boot (D) and cylinder bore with DOT 4 brake fluid.
3. Install the narrow end of the spring (E, **Figure 167**) into the piston.

CAUTION
Do not allow the piston cups to tear or turn inside out when installing the piston into the master cylinder bore. Both cups are larger than the bore. To ease installation, lubricate the cups and piston with DOT 4 brake fluid.

CLUTCH AND PRIMARY DRIVE

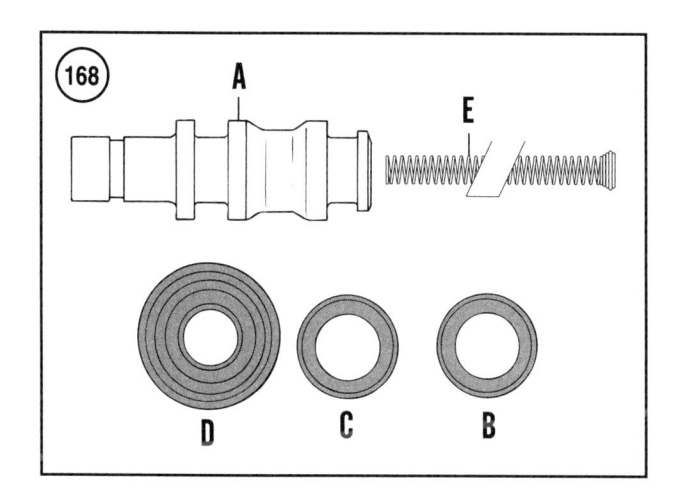

168

A E D C B

4. Insert the spring and piston assembly into the master cylinder bore. Press the end of the piston until the entire assembly sits in the bore.

CAUTION
The rubber boot must completely seat in the master cylinder groove. Slowly push and release the piston a few times to make sure it moves smoothly and that the rubber boot does not pop out.

5. Hold the piston in place, and carefully install the rubber boot into the groove in the master cylinder bore. Make sure the entire perimeter of the boot is correctly seated in the groove.
6. Lubricate the pivot pin and bushing with silicone brake grease.
7. If removed, install the bushing and roller kit into the end of the clutch lever. Position the bushing so it sits flush with both sides of the clutch lever.
8. Install the clutch lever onto the body, and install the pivot pin part way in from the top.
9. Apply slight hand pressure to the clutch lever to compress the spring, and push the piston in all the way.
10 Install a *new* snap ring onto the pivot pin. Make sure it is correctly seated in the groove.
11. Check that the clutch lever moves freely. If there is any binding or roughness, remove the pivot pin and clutch lever, and inspect the parts.
12. Temporarily install the diaphragm and cover. Install and finger-tighten the cover screws. Do not fully tighten the screws, as brake fluid will be added later.
13. Install the master cylinder as described in this chapter.

Inspection

The manufacturer does not supply specifications for the clutch master cylinder. Replace visibly worn or damaged parts as described in this section.
1. Clean and dry the master cylinder assembly as follows:
   a. Handle the brake components carefully when servicing them.

CAUTION
Do not get any oil or grease onto any of the master cylinder components. These chemicals cause the rubber parts in the brake system to swell, permanently damaging them.

b. Use only DOT 4 brake fluid or isopropyl alcohol to wash rubber parts (rubber boot and piston assembly) in the clutch system. Never allow any petroleum-based cleaner to contact the rubber parts. These chemicals cause the rubber to swell, requiring their replacement.
c. Clean the master cylinder piston rubber boot groove carefully. Use a small pick or brush to clean the groove. If a hard varnish residue has built up in the groove, soak the master cylinder in solvent to help soften the residue. Then, wash in soapy water and rinse completely.
d. Blow the master cylinder dry with compressed air to remove any solvent residue.
e. Place cleaned parts on a clean, lint-free cloth until assembly.

CAUTION
Do not remove the primary and secondary cups from the piston assembly for cleaning or inspection purposes.

2A. Check the piston assembly for the following defects:
   a. Scratched or corroded piston (A, **Figure 168**).
   b. Worn, cracked, damaged or swollen primary (B, **Figure 168**) and secondary (C) cups.
   c. Worn or damaged rubber boot (D, **Figure 168**).
   d. Broken, distorted or collapsed piston return spring (E, **Figure 168**).
2B. If any of these parts are worn or damaged, replace the piston assembly.
3. To assemble a *new* piston assembly, perform the following:
   a. Install the *new* primary and secondary cups onto the piston. Use the original piston assembly as a reference when installing the new cups onto the piston.
   b. Before installing the new piston cups, lubricate them with DOT 4 brake fluid.
   c. Clean the new piston (A, **Figure168**) in brake fluid.
   d. Install the primary cup (B, **Figure 168**) onto the spring end of the piston, and then the secondary (C) cup.
4. Inspect the master cylinder bore. Replace the master cylinder if the bore is corroded, cracked or damaged in any way. Do not hone the master cylinder bore to remove scratches or other damage.
5. Make sure the fluid passageway in the reservoir is clear. Clean it out with compressed air if necessary.
6. Check the banjo bolt threads for damage.
7. Inspect the diaphragm and cover for deterioration and other damage.
8. Check the clutch lever assembly for the following defects:

CHAPTER SIX

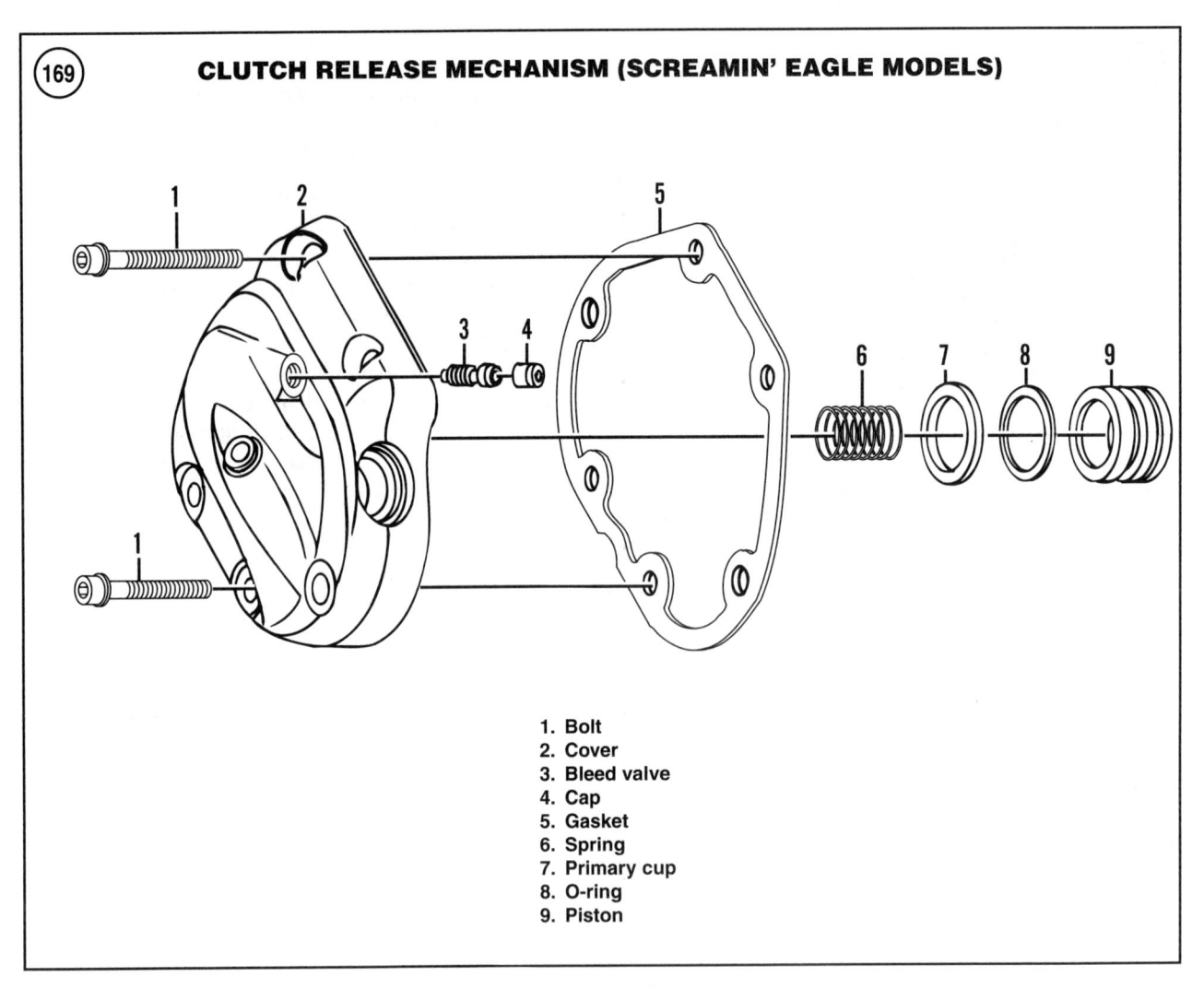

169 **CLUTCH RELEASE MECHANISM (SCREAMIN' EAGLE MODELS)**

1. Bolt
2. Cover
3. Bleed valve
4. Cap
5. Gasket
6. Spring
7. Primary cup
8. O-ring
9. Piston

a. Damaged clutch lever.
b. Excessively worn or damaged pivot pin.
c. Worn or damaged bushing.

CLUTCH RELEASE COVER (SCREAMIN' EAGLE MODELS)

Refer to **Figure 169**.

Removal

1. Use a swing arm stand to support the motorcycle on level ground.
2. Block the front wheel so the motorcycle cannot roll in either direction while on the swing arm stand.
3. Remove the exhaust system as described in Chapter Four.
4. Drain the transmission oil as described in Chapter Three.

CAUTION
Wash brake fluid off any surface immediately, as it damages the finish. Use soapy water and rinse completely.

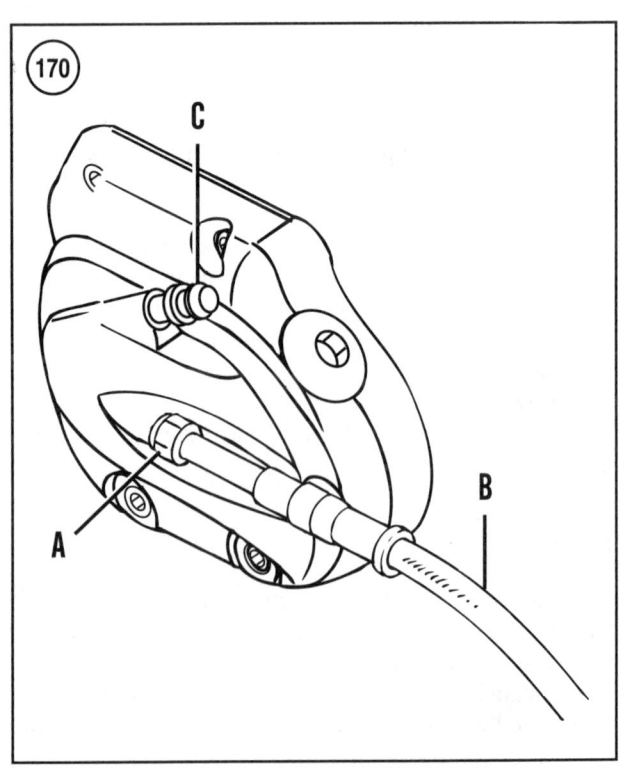

170

CLUTCH AND PRIMARY DRIVE

NOTE
Note that two different length cover bolts are used. Two short bolts are used at the top of the cover; long bolts are used at the four remaining locations.

11. Remove the clutch release cover bolts, and then remove the cover. Watch for the dowels (**Figure 155**, typical) behind the cover.
12. Remove and discard the cover gasket.

Installation

1. If removed, install the locating dowels (**Figure 155**, typical).
2. Install a *new* gasket over the locating dowels.
3. Install the clutch release cover.
4. Install the two short bolts at the top of the clutch release cover and the long bolts at the four remaining locations. Using a crossing pattern, tighten the clutch release cover bolts to 10-12 ft.-lb. (13.6-16.3 N•m).
5. Install a *new* O-ring (**Figure 171**) onto the end of the clutch hose.
6. Connect the clutch hose (B, **Figure 170**) to the cover. Manually thread the flare nut into the cover until it bottoms. Tighten the clutch hose flare nut to 80-115 in.-lb. (9-13 N•m). Do not cross thread the flare nut or scratch the cover.
7. On 2006 models, install the transmission oil level dipstick.
8. Refill the transmission oil as described in Chapter Three.
9. Install the exhaust system as described in Chapter Four.
10. Refill the clutch master cylinder and bleed the system as described under in this chapter.
11. Start the engine, check for proper clutch operation, and test ride the motorcycle.

CLUTCH SECONDARY ACTUATOR (SCREAMIN' EAGLE MODELS)

Disassembly/Assembly

1. Remove the clutch release cover as described in this chapter.
2. If removed, install the bleed valve. On 2006 models, tighten the bleed valve to 80-100 in.-lb. (9.0-11.3 N•m). On 2007-2009 models, tighten the bleed valve to 12-15 in.-lb. (1.4-1.7 N•m).
3. To remove the piston (**Figure 172**), perform the following:
    a. Place a piece of soft wood on the work bench.
    b. Position the release cover with the piston side facing toward the work bench.
    c. Apply compressed air through the clutch hose port in the cover, and force the piston part way out of the cover receptacle.

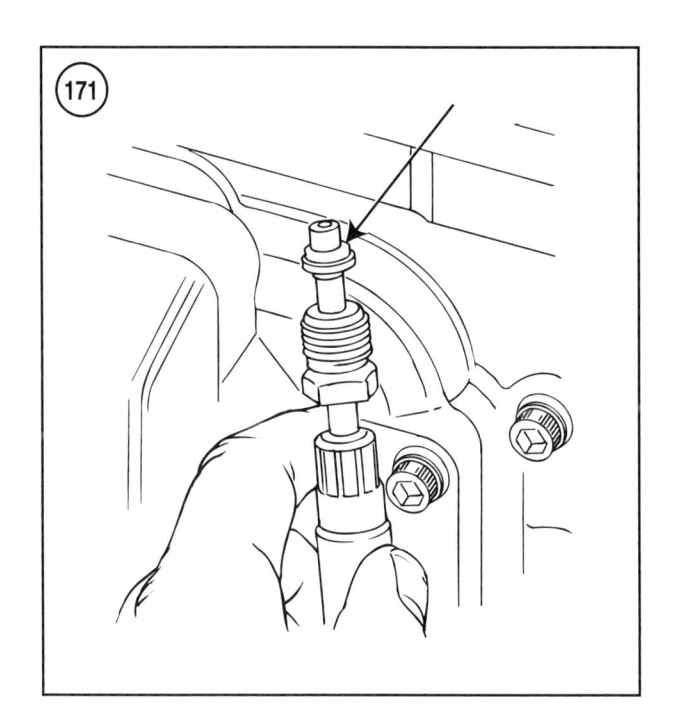

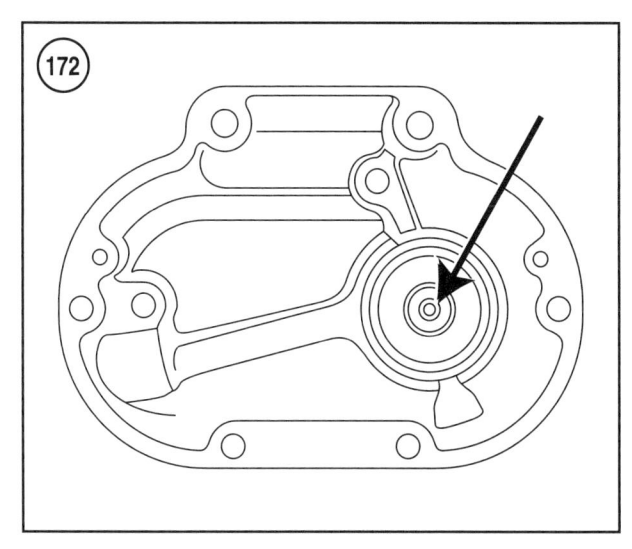

5. Cover the frame under the transmission case with a heavy cloth or plastic tarp to protect it from accidental brake fluid spills.
6. On 2006 models, remove the transmission oil level dipstick.
7. Slightly loosen the clutch release cover bolts, and apply the clutch lever. This helps break the cover loose from the transmission side door.
8. Drain the hydraulic fluid from the clutch system as described in this chapter.
9. Carefully loosen the flare nut (A, **Figure 170**, typical) securing the clutch hose (B) to the cover. Do not scratch the chrome cover.
10. Disconnect the clutch hose (B, **Figure 170**, typical) from the cover, and place the end into a plastic bag. Remove the O-ring (**Figure 171**, typical) from the end of the clutch hose, or if necessary, remove the O-ring from the threaded outlet within the cover.

4. Withdraw the piston assembly and spring (**Figure 173**) from the cover receptacle.

5. If the primary cup was removed from the piston, install the cup so its raised leading-edge lip faces the spring end of the piston.

6. Apply DOT 4 brake fluid to the *new* primary cup, O-ring and piston (**Figure 174**). Also apply DOT 4 brake fluid to the cylinder in the cover.

7. Install the spring into the piston, and install the assembly into the cover cylinder. Guide the primary cup into the receptacle to prevent the lips from turning over.

8. Push the piston and spring in until they bottom. Press the piston into the bore and check that the spring pushes it back out part way. The piston must move freely within the bore.

9. Install the clutch release cover as described in this chapter.

Inspection

Replacement parts are not available for the piston assembly (**Figure 174**). If any part is worn or damaged, replace the piston and spring as an assembly.

1. Clean the cylinder bore and piston in DOT 4 brake fluid or isopropyl alcohol. Dry them with compressed air.
2. Inspect the spring for fractures or sagging.
3. Check the O-ring and primary cup for hardness or deterioration.
4. Check the piston and cylinder bore for scratches, scoring or other damage.
5. Check the piston O-ring and primary cup grooves for damage.
6. Inspect the threaded flare nut hole in the cover. If it is worn or damaged, clean it out with a thread tap or replace the cover.
7. Inspect the threaded bleed valve hole in the cover. If it is worn or damaged, clean it out with a thread tap or replace the cover.
8. Inspect the bleed valve. Apply compressed air to the opening and make sure it is clear. Clean it out, if necessary, with brake fluid. Install the bleed valve and tighten it as follows:
    a. On 2006 models, tighten the bleed valve to 80-100 in.-lb. (9.0-11.3 N•m).
    b. On 2007-2009 models, tighten the bleed valve to 12-15 in.-lb (1.4-1.7 N•m).

CLUTCH HYDRAULIC HOSE REPLACEMENT (SCREAMIN' EAGLE MODELS)

1. Use a swing arm stand to support the motorcycle on level ground.
2. Block the front wheel so the motorcycle cannot roll in either direction while on the swing arm stand.
3. Before removing the hose, make a drawing of its path from the handlebar to the clutch release cover. The new hose must be routed along the same path.

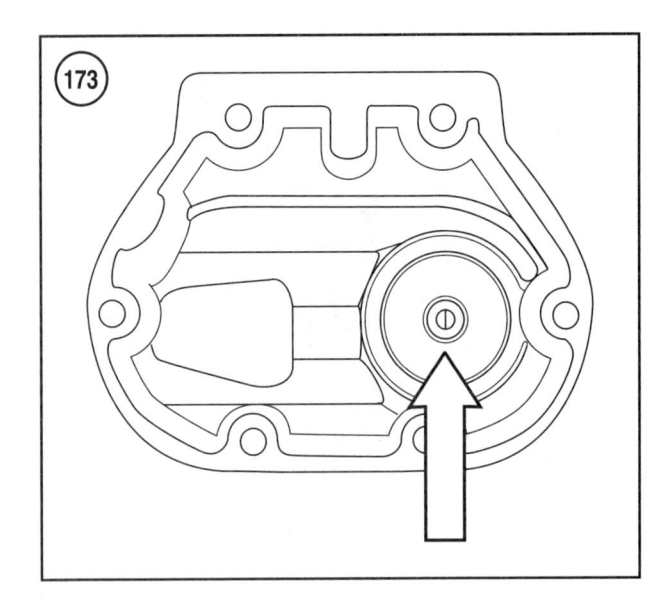

4. Remove the front exhaust pipe as described in Chapter Four.
5. Cover the frame under the transmission case with a heavy cloth or plastic tarp to protect it from accidental brake fluid spills.

CAUTION
Wash brake fluid off any surface immediately, as it damages the finish. Use soapy water and rinse completely.

6. Drain the fluid from the clutch system as described in this chapter.
7. Carefully loosen the flare nut (A, **Figure 170**, typical) securing the clutch hose to the clutch release cover. Do not scratch the chrome cover.
8. Disconnect the clutch hose (B, **Figure 170**, typical) from the cover, and place the loose end in a container.
9. Continue to apply the clutch lever and drain the brake fluid out of the clutch hose.
10. Remove the O-ring (**Figure 171**) from the end of the clutch hose, or if necessary, remove the O-ring within the cover threaded outlet.
11. Remove the banjo bolt and washers securing the clutch hose to the master cylinder. Separate the hose from the master cylinder.
12. Seal both ends of the hose in a small plastic bag and tape them closed so brake fluid does not drip onto the motorcycle.
13. Release the hose from any clamps securing it to the frame. Note the location of each hose clamp.
14. Carefully pull the clutch hydraulic hose and fitting out through the inner fairing, on models so equipped. Clean any clutch fluid from the inner fairing immediately.
15. Plug the bolt opening in the master cylinder and clutch release cover to prevent any leaks and the entry of foreign matter.
16. Install the *new* clutch hydraulic hose through the frame and along the same path noted during removal. Secure it with the hose clamps noted during removal.

CLUTCH AND PRIMARY DRIVE

174 CLUTCH PISTON ASSEMBLY (SCREAMIN' EAGLE MODELS)

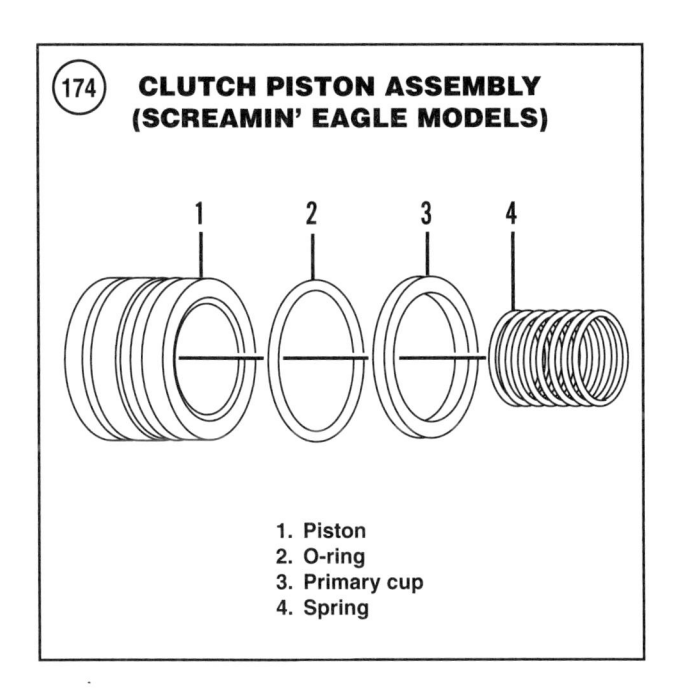

1. Piston
2. O-ring
3. Primary cup
4. Spring

17. Secure the clutch hose to the master cylinder with the banjo bolt and two *new* washers, one on each side of the clutch hose. Tighten the banjo bolt to 17-22 ft.-lb. (23.0-29.8 N•m) on 2006-2007 models or to 12.5-14.5 ft.-lb (16.9-19.7 N•m) on 2008-2009 models.

18. Install a *new* O-ring (**Figure 171**) onto the end of the clutch hose.

19. Connect the clutch hose (B, **Figure 170**) to the cover. Thread the flare nut all the way into the cover by hand until it bottoms. Tighten the clutch hose flare nut to 80-115 in.-lb. (9-13 N•m). Do not cross thread the flare nut or scratch the cover.

20. Bleed the clutch as described in *Clutch System Bleeding* (this chapter).

21. Test ride the motorcycle to ensure the clutch is operating correctly.

CLUTCH SYSTEM FLUSHING (SCREAMIN' EAGLE MODELS)

CAUTION
Never reuse old brake fluid. Properly discard all brake fluid flushed from the system.

When flushing the clutch system, use DOT 4 brake fluid as a flushing fluid. Flushing consists of pulling *new* brake fluid through the clutch system until the new fluid appears at the release cover bleed valve without the presence of any air bubbles. To flush the clutch system, follow one of the bleeding procedures described in this chapter.

CLUTCH SYSTEM DRAINING (SCREAMIN' EAGLE MODELS)

To drain the system, follow one of the bleeding procedures, but do not add fluid to the reservoir. Bleed the system until all fluid has been removed from the reservoir and hydraulic lines.

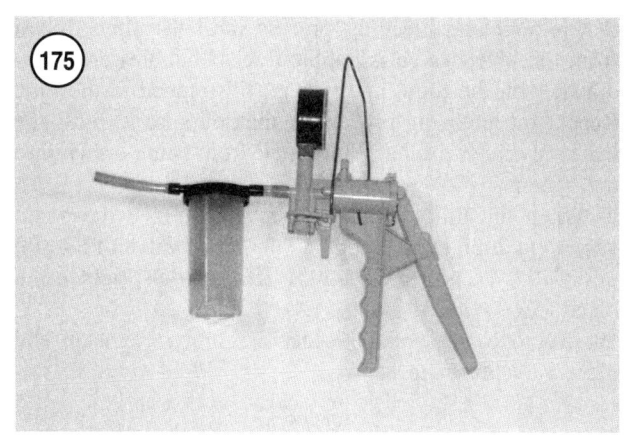

CLUTCH SYSTEM BLEEDING (SCREAMIN' EAGLE MODELS)

Brake Bleeding Process

This procedure uses a hydraulic brake bleeding kit (**Figure 175**) that is commonly available from automotive or motorcycle supply stores.

1. Remove the dust cap from the bleed valve on the clutch release cover.
2. Place a clean shop cloth over the exhaust pipe and frame to protect it from accidental brake fluid spills.
3. Assemble the vacuum bleeder tool according to its manufacturer's instructions. Secure it to the bleed valve.
4. Clean all dirt and foreign matter from the top of the master cylinder.
5. Turn the handlebars to level the clutch master cylinder. Then, remove the screws, reservoir cover and diaphragm.
6. Fill the reservoir almost to the top with DOT 4 brake fluid and reinstall the diaphragm and cover. Leave the cover in place during this procedure to prevent the entry of dirt.

NOTE
Carefully monitor the fluid level in the reservoir. It will drop quite rapidly. Stop often and check the brake fluid level. Keep the level 3/8 in. (10 mm) from the top of the reservoir so air will not be drawn into the system. If this occurs, the procedure must be repeated.

7. Operate the pump several times to create a vacuum in the line, and open the bleed valve approximately a half turn. Fluid will be quickly drawn from the system and into the pump's reservoir. Maintain vacuum with the pump while the bleed valve is still open. Tighten the bleed valve well before the fluid in the master cylinder runs empty. To prevent air from being drawn through the master cylinder, frequently add fluid to maintain its level at or near the top of the reservoir.

8. Continue the bleeding process until the fluid drawn from the bleed valve is bubble-free. If bubbles are withdrawn with the fluid, more air is still trapped in the line. Repeat the bleeding procedure, making sure to refill the master cylinder often to prevent air from being drawn into the system.

9. When the fluid is free of bubbles, tighten the bleed valve. On 2006 models, tighten the bleed valve to 80-100 in.-lb. (9.0-11.3 N•m). On 2007-2009 models, tighten the bleed valve to 12-15 in.-lb. (1.4-1.7 N•m).

10. Remove the brake bleeder assembly. Reinstall the bleed valve dust cap.

NOTE
Dispose of the used fluid responsibly. Do not reuse the old fluid.

11. If necessary, add fluid to correct the level in the master cylinder reservoir. When topping off the clutch master cylinder, turn the handlebar until the reservoir is level; add fluid to the full level mark in the reservoir.

12. Reinstall the reservoir diaphragm and cover. Install the reservoir cover screws, and tighten them to 6-8 in.-lb. (0.7-0.9 N•m).

13. Test the feel of the clutch lever. It must be firm and offer the same resistance each time it's operated. If it feels spongy, it is likely that there is still air in the system and it must be bleed again. After bleeding the system, check for leaks and tighten all fittings and connections as necessary.

WARNING
Do not ride the motorcycle until the clutch lever is operating correctly with full hydraulic advantage.

14. Test ride the motorcycle slowly at first to make sure that the clutch is operating properly.

Without a Brake Bleeder

NOTE
Before bleeding the clutch, check that all hoses and lines are tight.

1. Remove the dust cap from the bleed valve on the clutch release cover.
2. Place a clean shop cloth over the exhaust pipe and frame to protect it from accidental brake fluid spills.
3. Connect a length of clear tubing to the bleed valve on the release cover. Place the other end of the tube into a clean container. Fill the container with enough fresh DOT 4 brake fluid to keep the end of the tube submerged. The tube must be long enough so that a loop can be made higher than the bleeder valve to prevent air from being drawn into the release cylinder during bleeding.
4. Clean all dirt and foreign matter from the top of the clutch master cylinder.
5. Remove the screws securing the master cylinder cover, and then remove the cover and the diaphragm.
6. Fill the reservoir almost to the top with DOT 4 brake fluid. Then, reinstall the diaphragm and cover. Leave the cover in place during this procedure to prevent the entry of dirt.

NOTE
During this procedure, it is important to check the fluid level in the master cylinder reservoir often. If the reservoir runs dry, more air will enter the system.

7. Slowly apply the clutch lever several times. Hold the lever in the applied position and open the bleed valve about a half turn. Allow the lever to travel to its limit. When the limit is reached, tighten the bleed valve and release the clutch lever. As the fluid enters the system, the fluid level will drop in the master cylinder reservoir. Maintain the fluid level at the top of the reservoir to prevent air from being drawn into the system.

8. Continue the bleeding process until the fluid emerging from the hose is completely free of air bubbles. If the fluid is being replaced, continue until the fluid emerging from the hose is clean.

NOTE
If bleeding is difficult, allowing the fluid to stabilize for a few hours. Repeat the bleeding procedure when the tiny bubbles in the system settle out.

9. Hold the lever in the applied position and tighten the bleed valve. On 2006 models, tighten the bleed valve to 80-100 in.-lb. (9.0-11.3 N•m). On 2007-2009 models, tighten the bleed valve to 12-15 in.-lb. (1.4-1.7 N•m). Remove the bleed tube and install the bleed valve dust cap.

NOTE
Dispose of the used fluid responsibly. Do not reuse the old fluid.

10. If necessary, add fluid to correct the level in the master cylinder reservoir. When topping off the front master cylinder, turn the handlebar until the reservoir is level; add fluid to the full level mark in the reservoir.

11. Reinstall the reservoir diaphragm and cover. Install the reservoir cover screws, and tighten them to 6-8 in.-lb. (0.7-0.9 N•m).

12. Test the feel of the clutch lever. It must be firm and offer the same resistance each time it's operated. If it feels spongy, it is likely that there is still air in the system and it must bleed it again. After bleeding the system, check for leaks and tighten all fittings and connections as necessary.

WARNING
Do not ride the motorcycle until the clutch is operating correctly with full hydraulic advantage.

13. Test ride the motorcycle slowly at first to make sure that the clutch is operating properly.

CLUTCH AND PRIMARY DRIVE

Table 1 CLUTCH SPECIFICATIONS AND SPROCKET SIZES

Item	Specification
Clutch type	Wet, multi-plate disc
Clutch lever free play	1/16-1/8 in. (1.6-3.2 mm)
Clutch screw adjustment	loosen 1/2 turn after lightly seating
Clutch friction plate thickness	
Service limit	0.143 in. (3.63 mm)
Clutch plain plate warp	
Service limit	0.006 in. (0.15 mm)
Compensating sprocket	
2006 models	25 teeth
2007-2009 models	34 teeth
Clutch sprocket	
2006 models	36 teeth
2007-2008 models	46 teeth
2009 models	46 teeth
Rear wheel sprocket	
2006 models	70 teeth
2007-2008 models	66 teeth
2009 models	68 teeth
Transmission sprocket	32 teeth
Primary chain alignment (2006 models)	
Variance	0.030 in. (0.76 mm)
Clutch pushrod and release plate	
movement (Screamin' Eagle models)	0.065 in. (1.65 mm)

Table 2 SPROCKET ALIGNMENT SPACERS (2006 MODELS)

Spacer part No.	in.	mm
35850-84	0.010	0.25
35851-84	0.020	0.51
35852-84	0.030	0.76
24032-70	0.060	1.52
24033-70	0.090	2.29
24034-70	0.120	3.05
24035-70	0.150	3.81
24036-70	0.180	4.57
24037-70	0.210	5.33

Table 3 CLUTCH AND PRIMARY CHAINCASE TORQUE SPECIFICATIONS

Item	ft.-lb.	in.-lb.	N•m
Clutch nut	70-80	–	94.9-108.5
Clutch lever clamp bolt			
2006-2007 models except			
Screamin' Eagle	–	108-132	12.2-14.9
2008-2009 models and Screamin'			
Eagle	–	60-80	6.8-9.0
Clutch cover Torx screws (T27)	–	84-108	9.5-12.2
Clutch master cylinder			
(Screamin' Eagle models)			
Banjo bolt			
2006-2007 models	17-22	–	23.0-29.8
2008-2009 models	12.5-14.5	–	16.9-19.7
Reservoir cover screw	–	6-8	0.7-0.9
Clutch release cover (all			
models except Screamin' eagle)			
Bolts	–	84-108	9.5-12.2
Clutch cable fitting			
2006-2007 models	–	36-60	4.1-6.8
2008-2009 models	–	90-120	10.2-13.6

(continued)

Table 3 CLUTCH AND PRIMARY CHAINCASE TORQUE SPECIFICATIONS (continued)

Item	ft.-lb.	in.-lb.	N•m
Clutch release cover (Screamin' Eagle models)			
Long and short bolts	10-12	–	13.5-16.3
Clutch hose flare nut	–	80-115	9.0-13.0
Bleed valve			
2006 models	–	80-100	9.0-11.3
2007-2009 models	–	12-15	1.4-1.7
Compensating sprocket nut (2006 models)	see text		
Compensating sprocket bolt			
2007-2008 models	155-165	–	210.2-223.7
2009 models	see text		
Diaphragm spring retainer bolts	–	90-110	10.2-12.4
Jackshaft bolt (2006 models)	–	60-80	6.8-9.0
Center nut (2006 models)	21-24	–	28.5-32.5
Primary chain tensioner bolt			
2007 models	21-24	–	28.5-32.5
2008-2009 models	15-19	–	20.3-25.8
Primary chaincase cover bolts	–	108-120	12.2-13.6
Primary chaincase housing			
Housing-to engine bolts (2006 models)	15-19	–	20.3-25.8
Housing-to-transmission bolts (2006 models)	15-19	–	20.3-25.8
Sealing fasteners			
2007 models	25-27	–	33.9-36.6
2008-2009 models	26-28	–	35.3-38.0
Primary chaincase inspection cover (2006 models)	–	84-108	9.5-12.2
Transmission sprocket nut			
2006 models	60	–	81.4
2007-2009 models	100	–	135.6

CHAPTER SEVEN

FIVE SPEED TRANSMISSION (2006 MODELS)

This chapter covers procedures for the transmission, shift linkage and oil pan. All 2006 models are equipped with a five speed transmission, which is separate from the engine. The transmission shaft assemblies and the shift assemblies can be serviced with the transmission case mounted in the frame.

Specifications are in **Tables 1-3** at the end of this chapter.

SHIFT ASSEMBLY

The shift assembly (**Figure 1** or **Figure 2**) consists of the external shift linkage, internal shift cam and shift arm components. The internal components can be serviced with the transmission installed by removing the top cover.

If a shift problem is encountered, refer to the troubleshooting procedures in Chapter Two and eliminate all clutch and shift mechanism possibilities *before* considering transmission repairs.

Shift Linkage Adjustment

The shift linkage assembly connects the transmission shift rod lever to the foot-operated shift levers. The shift linkage does not require adjustment unless the shift linkage is replaced or the transmission gears do not engage properly.

CAUTION
The heel shift lever must never touch the footboard when shifting gears. To ensure proper gear engagement and avoid possible transmission damage, there must be a minimum clearance of 3/8 in. (9.5 mm) between the bottom of the heel shift lever and the top of the footboard. If the clearance is not as specified, reposition the heel shift lever as described in External Shift Mechanism (this chapter).

NOTE
Always disarm the optional TSM/TSSM security system prior to disconnecting the battery or pulling the Maxi-Fuse so the siren will not sound.

1. Disconnect the negative battery cable as described in Chapter Eleven.
2. Loosen the two shift linkage rod locknuts (A, **Figure 3**).
3. Remove the acorn nut (B, **Figure 3**) and washers securing the shift linkage rod to the inner shift lever.
4. Turn the shift linkage rod (C, **Figure 3**) as necessary to change the linkage adjustment.
5. Reconnect the shift linkage rod to the shift rod lever and tighten the locknuts to 80-120 in.-lb. (9-13.6 N•m).
6. Recheck the shifting. Readjust if necessary.
7. If proper shifting cannot be obtained by performing this adjustment, check the shift linkage for any interference problems. Then, check the shift linkage assembly for worn or damaged parts.

CHAPTER SEVEN

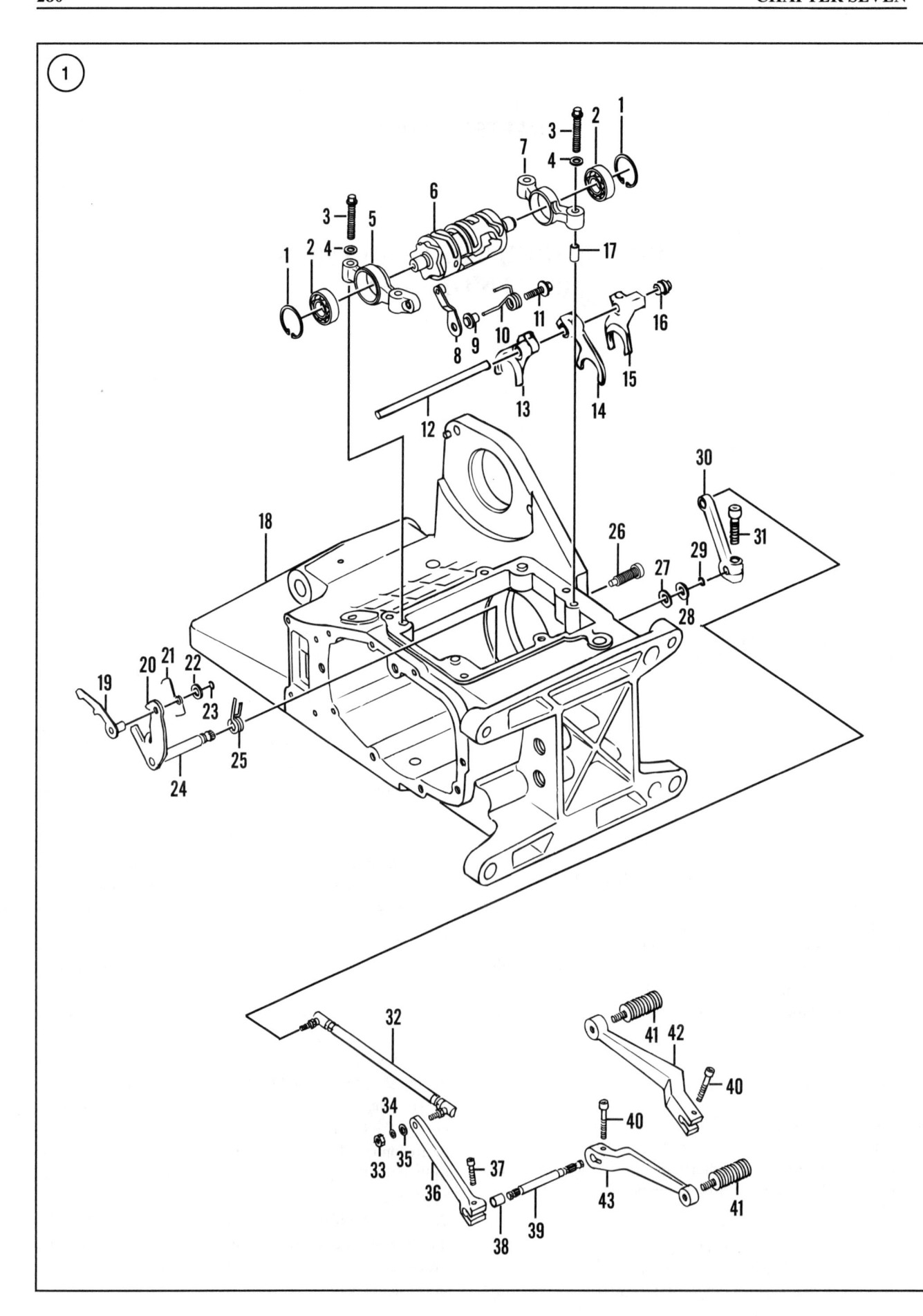

FIVE SPEED TRANSMISSION (2006 MODELS)

SHIFT ASSEMBLY (ALL MODELS EXCEPT SCREAMIN' EAGLE)

1. Snap ring
2. Bearing
3. Bolt
4. Washer
5. Support (right side)
6. Shift drum
7. Support (left side)
8. Cam follower
9. Sleeve
10. Spring
11. Bolt
12. Shift fork shaft
13. Shift fork No.3
14. Shift fork No. 2
15. Shift fork No. 1
16. Set screw
17. Locating dowel
18. Transmission case
19. Shift cam pawl
20. Shift cam pawl
21. Spring
22. Washer
23. Snap ring
24. Shift cam pawl shaft
25. Return spring
26. Adjusting screw
27. Oil seal
28. Washer
29. Snap ring
30. Shift rod lever (inner)
31. Bolt
32. Shift rod
33. Nut
34. Lockwasher
35. Washer
36. Shift lever (outer)
37. Bolt
38. Bushing
39. Shift lever shaft
40. Clamp bolt
41. Shift peg
42. Shift lever (toe)
43. Shift lever (heel)

EXTERNAL SHIFT MECHANISM

Removal/Installation

Refer to **Figure 1** and **Figure 2**.

NOTE
Always disarm the optional TSM/TSSM security system prior to disconnecting the battery or pulling the Maxi-Fuse so the siren will not sound.

1. Disconnect the negative battery cable as described in Chapter Eleven.
2. Remove the front left side footboard as described in Chapter Seventeen.
3. Make an alignment mark on the heel shift lever and on the shift lever shaft.
4. Remove the clamp bolt, and then remove the heel shift lever (**Figure 4**).
5. Make an alignment mark on the toe shift lever and on the shift lever shaft.
6. Remove the clamp bolt, and then remove the toe shift lever (**Figure 5**).
7. Remove the spacer (**Figure 6**) from the shift lever shaft.
8. On Screamin' Eagle models, remove the jiffy stand as described in Chapter Seventeen.
9. Remove the primary chaincase assembly as described in Chapter Five.
10. Remove the nut, washer and lockwasher securing the shift rod to the outer shift lever.
11. Remove the clamp bolt (A, **Figure 7**) securing the inner shift rod lever (B) to the transmission case.
12. Remove the outer shift rod lever (A, **Figure 8**), shift rod (B), inner shift lever and shift lever shaft as an assembly.
13. Install the external shift mechanism by reversing the removal steps. Tighten the shift rod lever clamp bolts to 18-22 ft.-lb. (24.4-29.8 N•m).

TRANSMISSION COVER

The transmission cover assembly can be serviced with the transmission installed in the frame.

Removal/Installation

NOTE
Always disarm the optional TSM/TSSM security system prior to disconnecting the battery or pulling the Maxi-Fuse so the siren will not sound.

1. Disconnect the negative battery cable as described in Chapter Eleven.
2. Remove the right side exhaust system as described in Chapter Four.

282

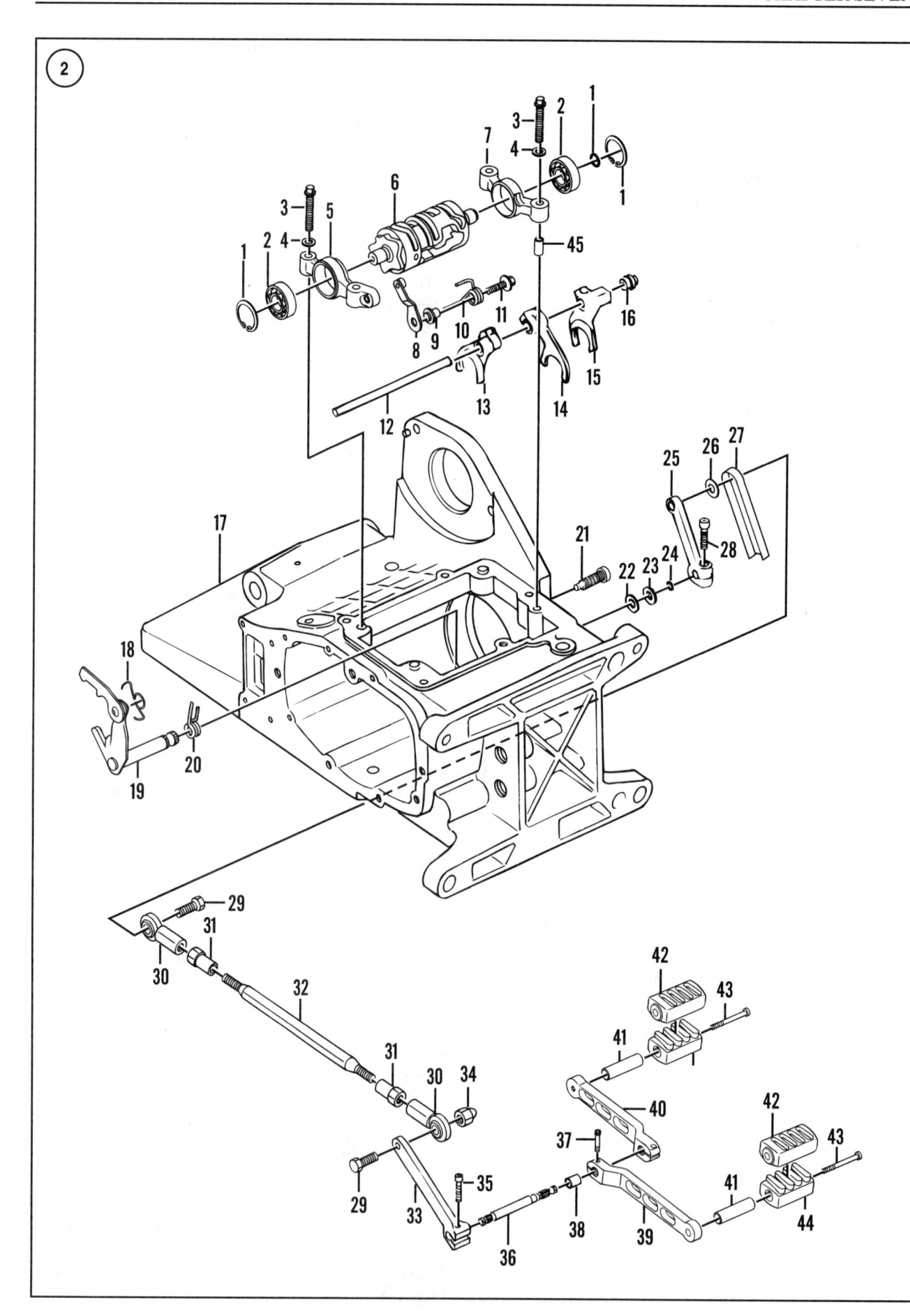

CHAPTER SEVEN

②

FIVE SPEED TRANSMISSION (2006 MODELS)

SHIFT ASSEMBLY (2006 SCREAMIN' EAGLE MODELS)

1. Snap ring
2. Bearing
3. Bolt
4. Washer
5. Support (right side)
6. Shift cam
7. Support (left side)
8. Cam follower
9. Sleeve
10. Spring
11. Bolt
12. Shift fork shaft
13. Shift fork No. 3
14. Shift fork No. 2
15. Shift fork No. 1
16. Set screw
17. Transmission case
18. Spring
19. Shift cam pawl shaft
20. Return spring
21. Adjusting screw
22. Oil seal
23. Washer
24. Snap ring
25. Shift rod lever (inner)
26. Spacer
27. Cover
28. Bolt
29. Bolt
30. Rod end
31. Nut
32. Shift rod
33. Shift rod lever (outer)
34. Acorn nut
35. Bolt
36. Shift lever shaft
37. Bolt
38. Spacer
39. Shift lever (toe)
40. Shift lever (heel)
41. Spacer
42. Shifter pedal peg
43. Bolt
44. Shifter pedal pad
45. Locating dowel

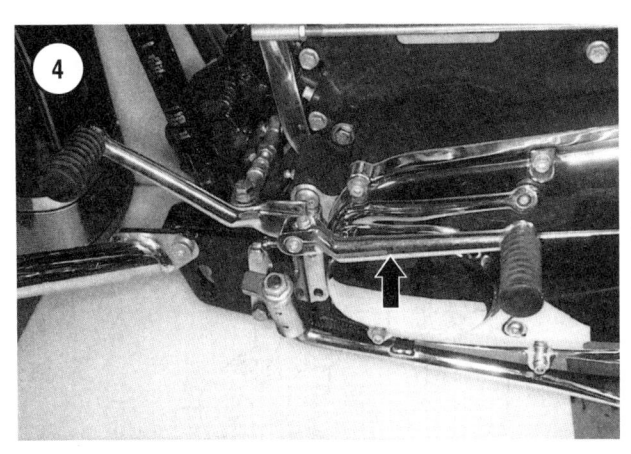

284 CHAPTER SEVEN

SHIFT CAM ASSEMBLY

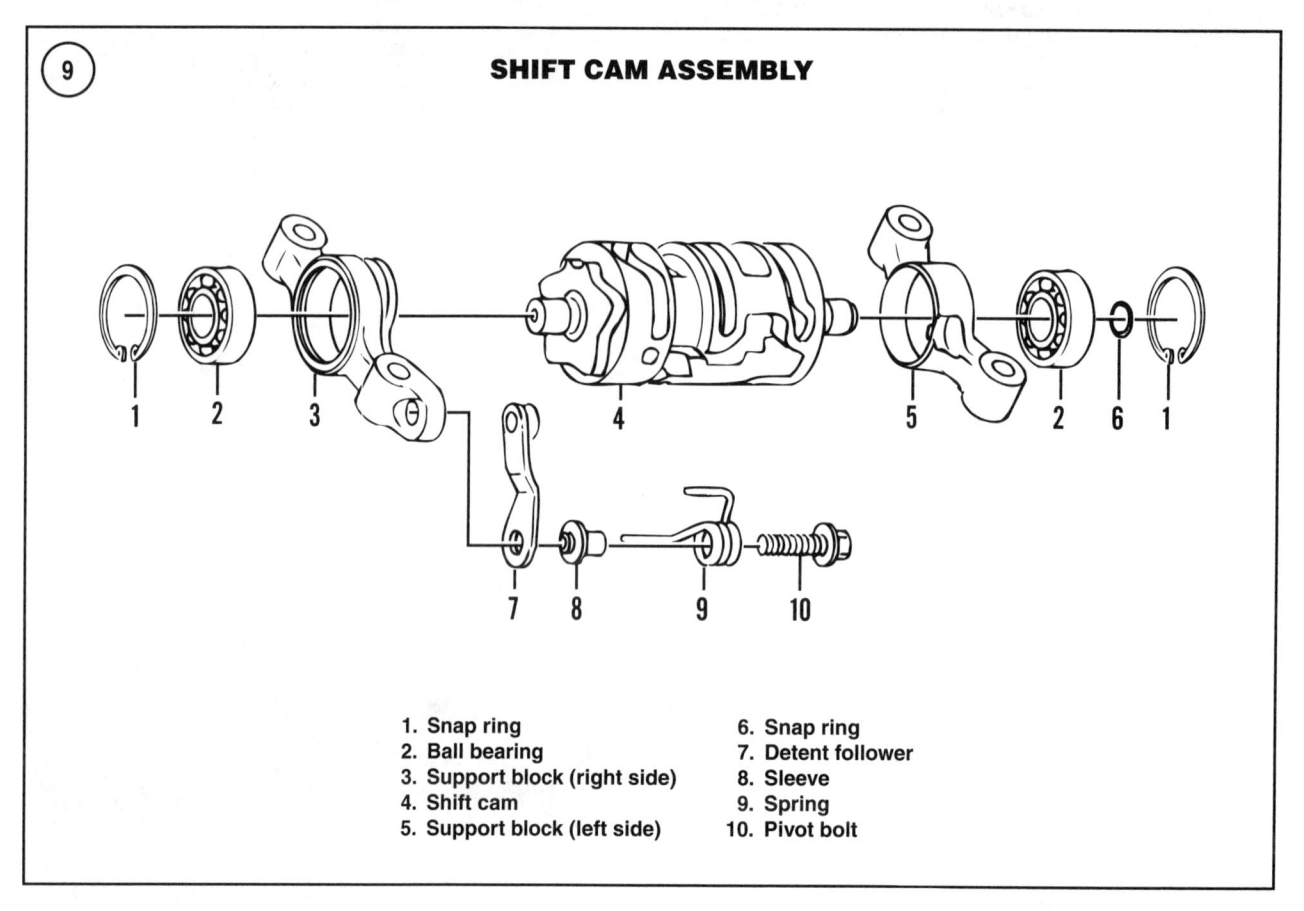

1. Snap ring
2. Ball bearing
3. Support block (right side)
4. Shift cam
5. Support block (left side)
6. Snap ring
7. Detent follower
8. Sleeve
9. Spring
10. Pivot bolt

3. Disconnect the wire from the neutral indicator switch (Chapter Eleven).
4. Disconnect the vent hose from the cover fitting.
5. Remove the bolts and washers securing the transmission cover to the transmission case. Remove the cover and the gasket.
6. Carefully remove the gasket residue from the transmission cover and transmission case mating surfaces.
7. Install a *new* gasket onto the transmission case.
8. Install the transmission cover, the bolts and the washers. Using a crossing pattern, tighten the transmission cover bolts to 84-132 in.-lb. (9.5-14.9 N•m).
9. Reconnect the vent hose to the fitting and install a *new* hose clamp.
10. Connect the wire to the neutral indicator switch (Chapter Eleven).
11. Connect the negative battery cable as described in Chapter Eleven.
12. Install the right side exhaust system as described in Chapter Four.

SHIFT CAM

The shift cam mounts on top of the transmission case, underneath the transmission top cover. The shift cam assembly can be serviced with the transmission installed in the frame.

Refer to **Figure 9**.

FIVE SPEED TRANSMISSION (2006 MODELS)

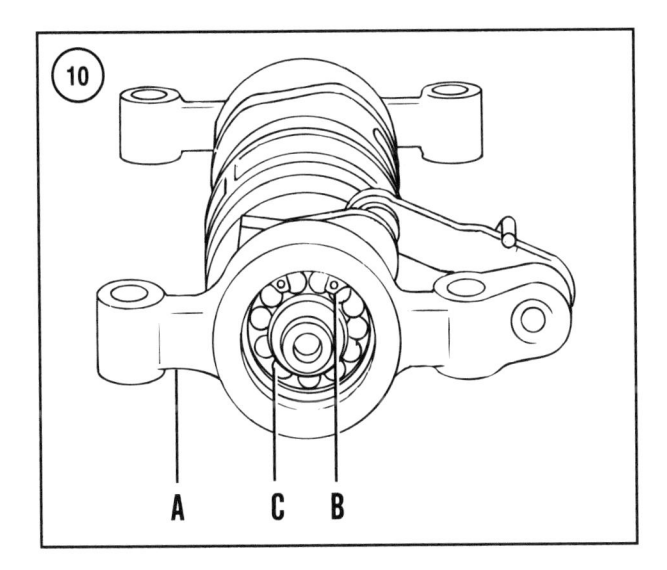

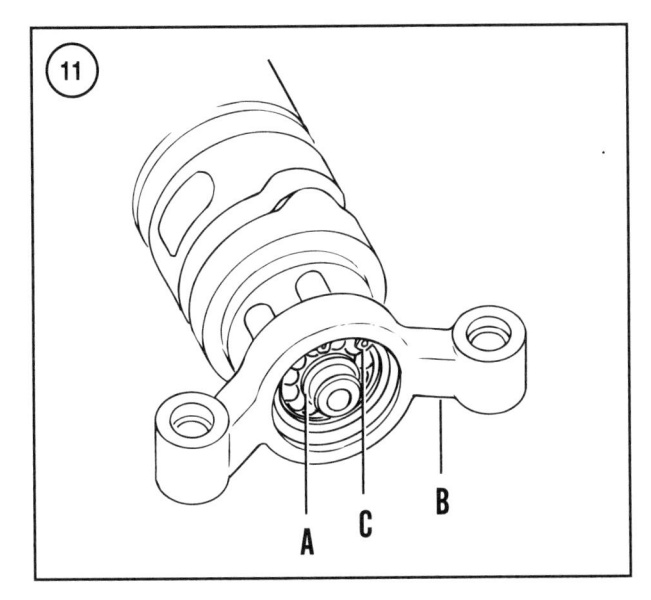

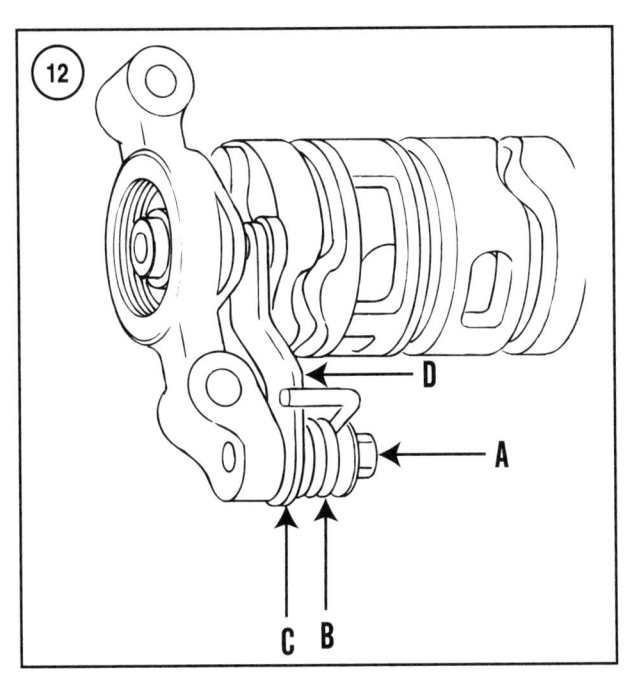

Removal

1. Remove the transmission top cover as described in this chapter.
2. Remove the shift cam support block mounting bolts and lockwashers.
3. Lift the shift cam pawl off the cam pins to free the assembly.
4. Carefully lift the shift cam assembly up and out of the transmission case.
5. Remove the four dowel pins from the transmission case.

Installation

1. Install the four dowel pins into the transmission case.
2. Lift the shift cam pawl up out of the way.
3. Carefully install the shift cam assembly into the transmission case. Align the shift fork pins with the shift cam slots.
4. Lower the shift cam pawl and engage it with the cam pins.
5. Install the shift cam support block mounting bolts and lockwashers. Using a crossing pattern, tighten the bolts to 84-108 in.-lb. (9.5-12.2 N•m).
6. Install the transmission top cover as described in this chapter.

Disassembly

1. On the right side, perform the following:
    a. Slide the right side support block (A, **Figure 10**) off the shift cam.
    b. Remove the snap ring (B, **Figure 10**) and withdraw the bearing (C) from the support block.
2. On the left side, perform the following:
    a. Remove the small snap ring (A, **Figure 11**) from the shift cam.
    b. Slide the left side support block (B, **Figure 11**) off the shift cam.
    c. Remove the large snap ring (C, **Figure 11**) and withdraw the bearing from the support block.
3. To remove the detent follower, unscrew the pivot bolt (A, **Figure 12**). Remove the spring (B, **Figure 12**), spring sleeve (C) and the detent follower (D).

Assembly

1. Coat all bearing and sliding surfaces with assembly oil.
2. To install the detent follower, perform the following:
    a. Slide the spring sleeve (C, **Figure 12**) into the spring (B).
    b. Insert the pivot bolt (A, **Figure 12**) through the spring and sleeve.
    c. Correctly position the detent follower onto the bolt and place the spring end over the detent follower.
    d. Install the assembly onto the right side support and insert the spring's other end into the receptacle in the right side support. Install the pivot bolt into place and tighten to 84-108 in.-lb. (9.5-12.2 N•m).

3. On the left side, perform the following:
   a. Position the bearing with the manufacturer's numbers facing out. Install the bearing into the support block.
   b. Position a *new* large snap ring (C, **Figure 11**) so the larger tab will be on the right side when looking at the end of the support block. Install the large snap ring.
   c. Make sure the large snap ring is correctly seated in the groove.
   d. Slide the left side support block (B, **Figure 11**) onto the shift cam.
   e. Install a *new* small snap ring (A, **Figure 11**) onto the shift cam.
   f. Make sure the small snap ring is correctly seated in the groove.
4. On the right side, perform the following:
   a. Position the bearing with the manufacturer's numbers facing out. Install the bearing into the support block.
   b. Position a *new* snap ring (B, **Figure 10**) with the beveled side facing out when looking at the end of the support block. Install the snap ring.
   c. Make sure the snap ring is correctly seated in the groove.
   d. Slide the right side support block (A, **Figure 10**) onto the shift cam.

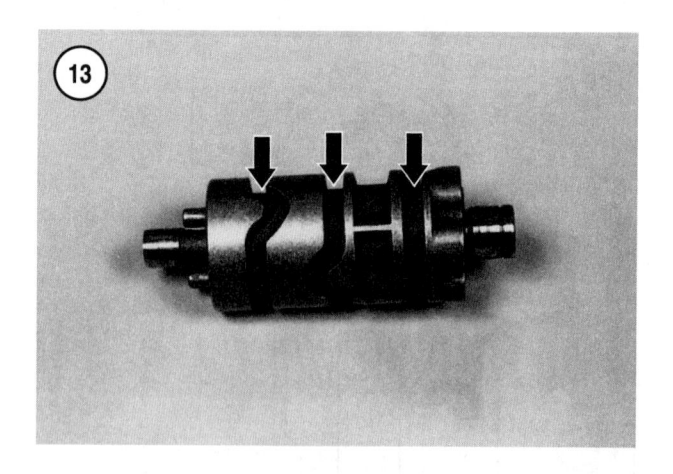

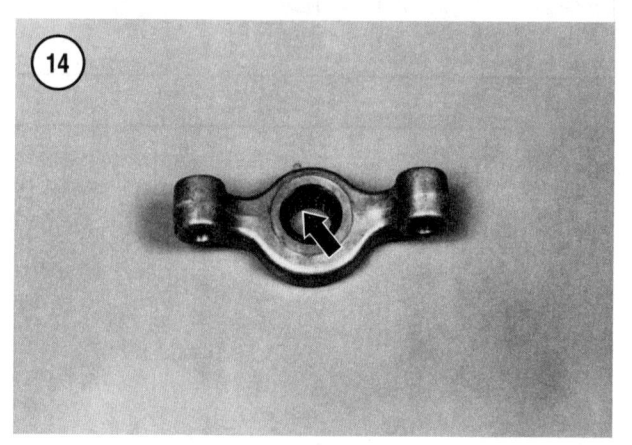

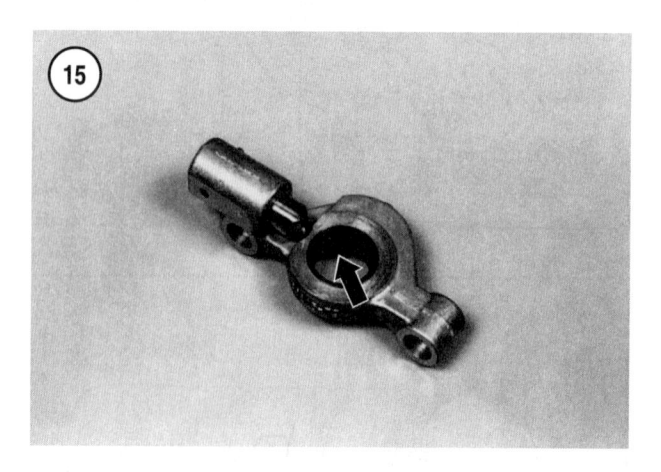

Inspection

1. Clean all parts except the support block bearings in solvent and dry thoroughly.
2. Check the shift cam grooves (**Figure 13**) for wear or roughness. Replace the shift cam if the groove profiles show excessive wear or damage.
3. Check the shift cam ends where the cam contacts the bearings. If the ends show wear or damage, replace the shift cam and both support block bearings as described in this section.
4. Check the support block bearings (**Figure 14** and **Figure 15**) for excessive wear, cracks, or other damage. If necessary, replace the bearings as described in this section.
5. Check the support blocks for wear, cracks or other damage. Replace the support blocks if necessary.

SHIFT ARM ASSEMBLY

Removal/Disassembly

Refer to **Figure 16**.
1. Make an alignment mark on the shift rod lever and the end of the shift arm shaft.
2. Remove the clamp bolt and remove the shift rod lever from the shift arm shaft.
3. Remove the snap ring and washer from the shift arm shaft.
4. Withdraw the shift arm shaft, sleeve and spring from the inside of the transmission case.
5. If the components require replacement, remove the snap ring and washer and remove the shift cam pawl and spring from the shift arm shaft.

Assembly/Installation

1. If disassembled, install the shift cam pawl and spring onto the shift arm shaft. Secure it with the washer and a *new* snap ring.
2. Install the shift arm shaft assembly into the transmission case.

FIVE SPEED TRANSMISSION (2006 MODELS)

16 **SHIFT ARM ASSEMBLY**

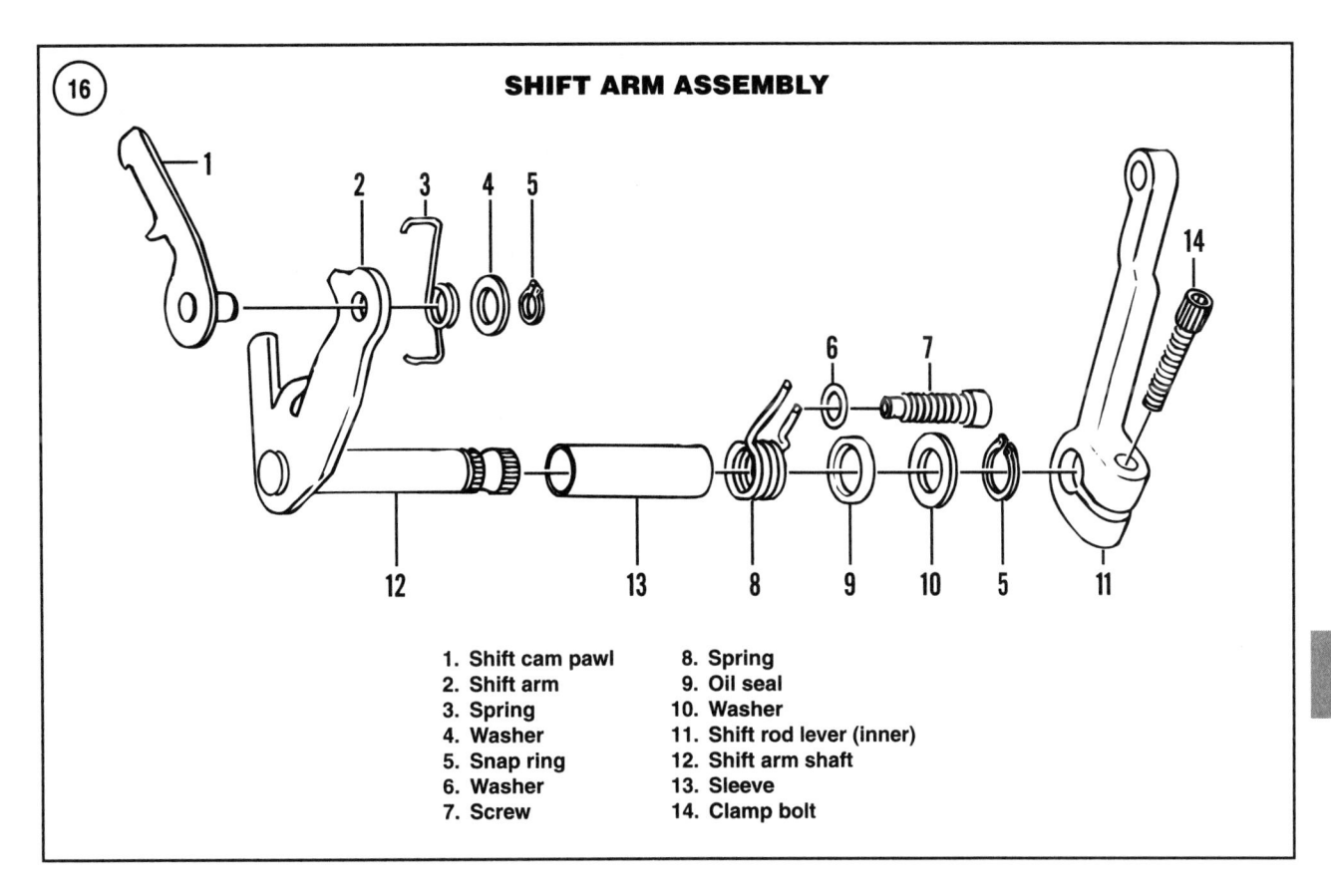

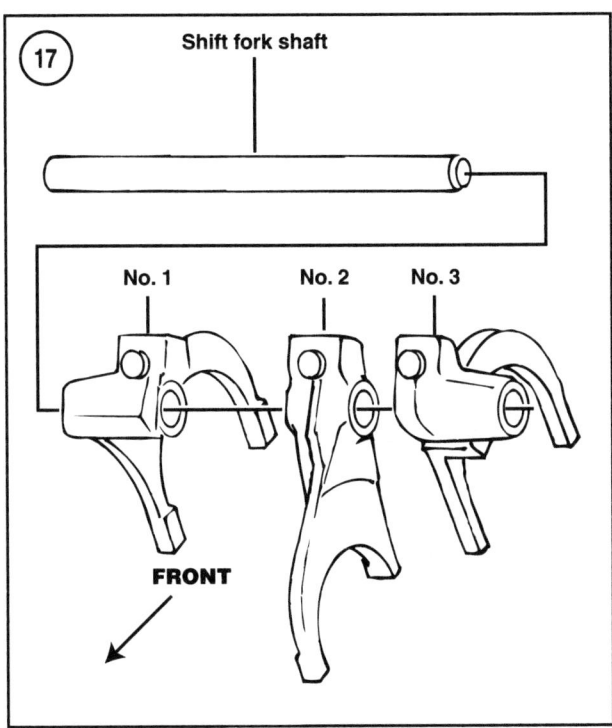

1. Shift cam pawl
2. Shift arm
3. Spring
4. Washer
5. Snap ring
6. Washer
7. Screw
8. Spring
9. Oil seal
10. Washer
11. Shift rod lever (inner)
12. Shift arm shaft
13. Sleeve
14. Clamp bolt

17 Shift fork shaft — No. 1, No. 2, No. 3 — FRONT

3. Align the spring with the screw.
4. Refer to the alignment marks made during removal and install the shift rod lever onto the shift arm shaft. Push it on until the bolt hole aligns with the shift arm shaft groove.
5. Install the shift rod lever clamp bolt and tighten to 18-22 ft.-lb. (24-30 N•m).

Inspection

1. Check the shift pawl for wear. Replace the pawl if damaged.
2. Check the springs for wear or damage. Assemble the shift cam pawl and spring on the shift arm pin. If the spring will not hold the pawl on the cam, replace it.
3. Check the shift arm shaft for wear or damage. Check the end splines for wear or damage.
4. Check the shift rod lever for wear or damage. Check the internal splines for wear or damage.

SHIFT FORKS

The shift forks can be serviced with the transmission installed in the frame by removing the transmission cover.
Refer to **Figure 1** and **Figure 2**.

Removal

1. Remove the shift cam as described in this chapter.
2. Remove the transmission side cover as described in this chapter.

CAUTION
*Use a waterproof felt-tip pen or scribe to mark the installed position of each shift fork as it sits in the transmission. All three shift forks (**Figure 17**) are unique and must be reinstalled in the correct position.*

3. Withdraw the shift fork shaft (A, **Figure 18**) from the transmission case. Then, remove the shift forks (**Figure 19**) from the transmission case.

Installation

Refer to **Figure 20** to identify the transmission gears.
1. Coat all bearing and sliding surfaces with assembly oil.
2. To install the shift forks and shift fork shaft (**Figure 17**), perform the following:
    a. Insert the No. 1 shift fork into the mainshaft first gear groove.
    b. Install the No. 2 shift fork into the countershaft third gear groove.
    c. Install the No. 3 shift fork into the mainshaft second gear groove.
3. Insert the shift fork shaft through the transmission case (A, **Figure 18**), through each of the three shift forks and into the transmission case.
4. Install the transmission side door as described in this chapter.
5. Check that the shift forks move smoothly when shifting the gears by hand.
6. Install the shift cam as described in this chapter.

Inspection

1. Inspect each shift fork (**Figure 21**) for excessive wear or damage. Replace worn or damaged shift forks as required.
2. Measure the thickness of each shift fork finger (A, **Figure 22**) where it contacts the sliding gear groove (**Figure 23**). Replace any shift fork with a finger thickness worn to the specification listed in **Table 2**.
3. Check each shift fork channel (B, **Figure 22**) for any arc-shaped wear or burn marks. Replace damaged shift forks.
4. Roll the shift fork shaft on a flat surface and check for bending. Replace the shaft if bent.
5. Install each shift fork on the shift fork shaft. The shift forks must slide smoothly on the shaft with no binding or roughness.

TRANSMISSION SIDE DOOR ASSEMBLY

This section describes the removal and installation of the transmission side-door assembly, which includes the side door, mainshaft and countershaft. The transmission side door assembly can be serviced with the transmission case installed in the frame.

Tools

The following tools are used during disassembly and assembly:
1. Mainshaft bearing race puller/installer tool (JIMS part No. 34902-84).
2. Transmission side door puller (JIMS part No. 2283).

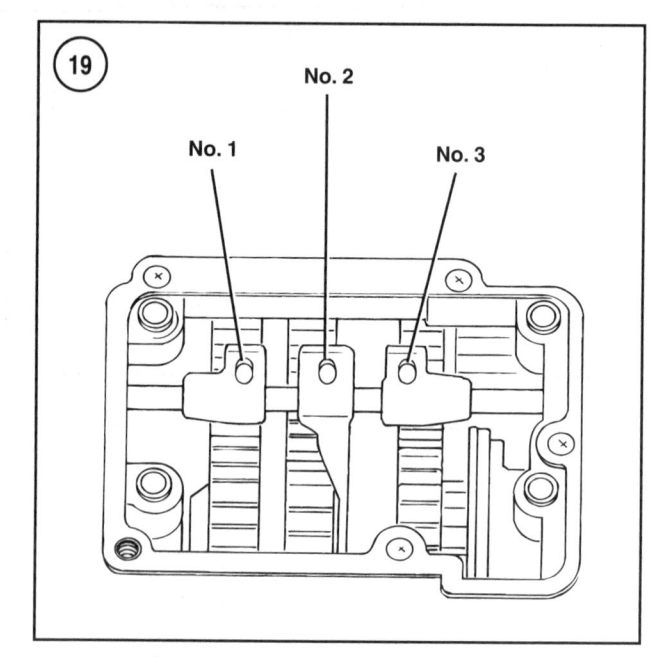

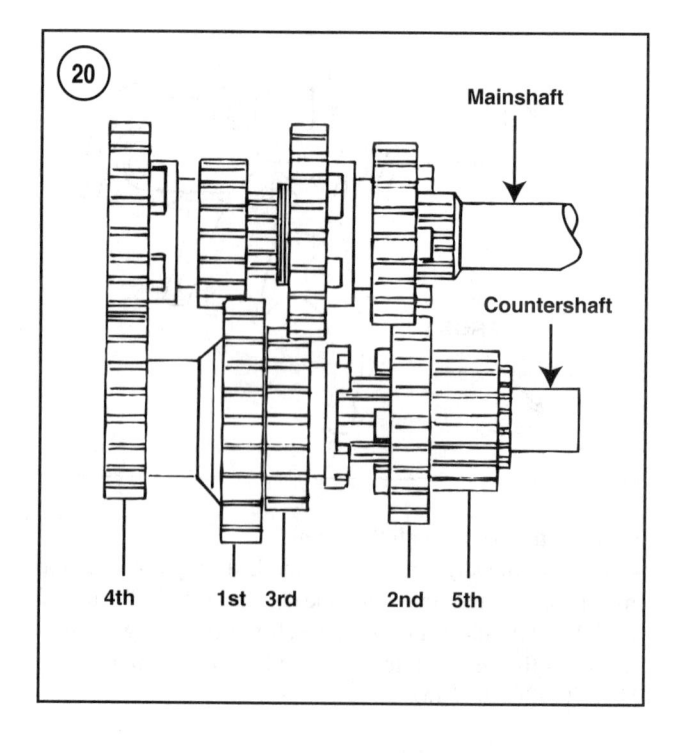

FIVE SPEED TRANSMISSION (2006 MODELS)

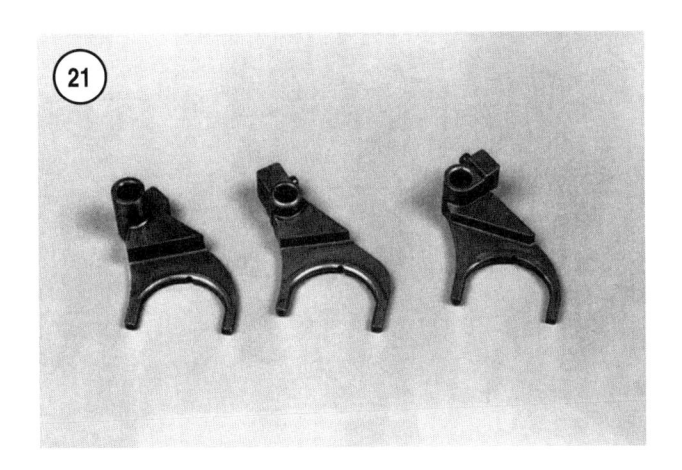

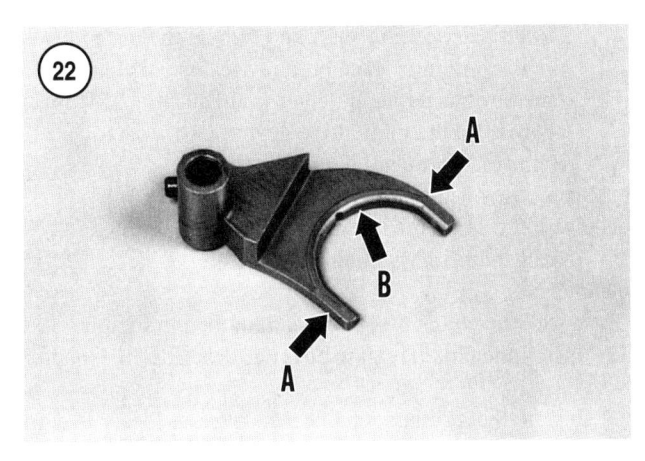

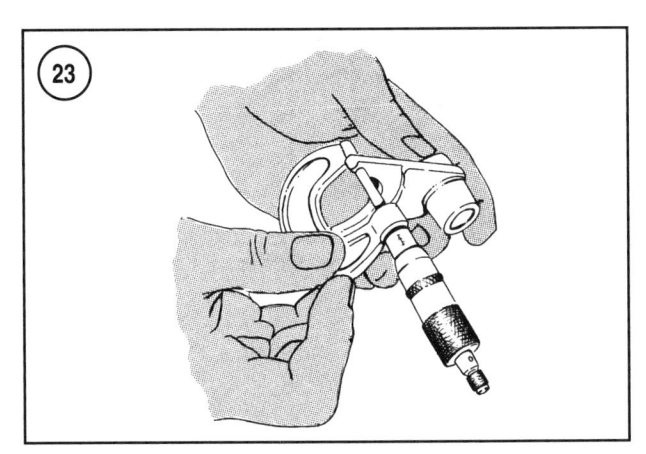

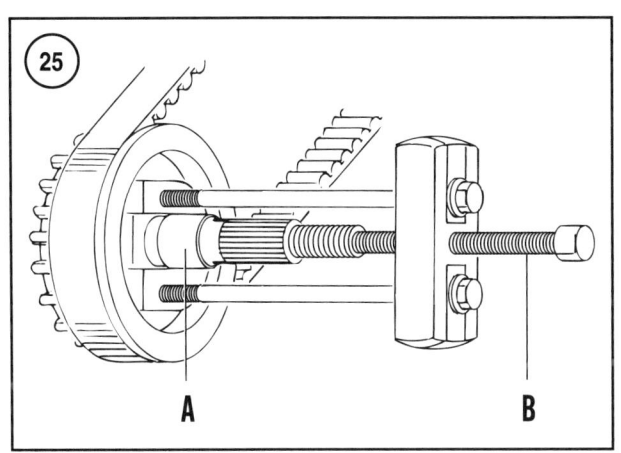

3. Transmission side door bearing remover and installer (JIMS part No. 1078).
4. Transmission shaft installers (JIMS part No. 2189).

Removal

Remove the transmission side door assembly as follows:
1. Remove the exhaust system as described in Chapter Four.
2. Drain the transmission oil as described in Chapter Three.
3. Remove the primary chaincase cover as described in Chapter Six.
4. Remove the clutch release cover as described in Chapter Six.
5. Remove the clutch assembly as described in Chapter Six.
6. Remove the primary chaincase housing as described in Chapter Six.
7. Remove the shift forks as described in this chapter.
8. Remove the bearing inner race (**Figure 24**) from the mainshaft, as follows:
   a. Attach the mainshaft bearing race puller and installation tool against the inner bearing race (A, **Figure 25**) following the manufacturer's instructions.
   b. Tighten the puller bolt (B, **Figure 25**) and withdraw the inner race from the mainshaft.
9. Remove the oil slinger assembly (B, **Figure 18**).
10. Turn the transmission by hand and shift the transmission into two different gears to keep the gears from turning.
11. If the transmission shaft assemblies are going to be removed from the side door, loosen, but do not remove, the countershaft and mainshaft locknuts.
12. If the main drive gear is going to be removed, remove the drive sprocket as described in *Drive Sprocket* (this chapter).
13. Remove the bolts securing the transmission side door to the transmission case.

CAUTION
When removing the transmission side door, do not tap against the transmission shafts from the opposite side. This will damage the side door bearings.

14. Tap against the transmission side door to loosen its seal against the transmission case.

15. Install the transmission side door puller tool onto the door following the manufacturer's instructions. Tighten the outside screws one-half turn at a time, alternating from side-to-side until the door releases from the transmission case. Remove the tool.

16. Slowly withdraw the transmission side door and the transmission shaft assemblies from the transmission case.

17. Remove the transmission side door gasket. Do not lose the locating pins.

18. If necessary, service the side door and transmission shaft assemblies as described in this chapter.

Installation

1. If the main drive gear was removed, install it as described in this chapter.
2. Remove all gasket residue from the side door and transmission case mating surfaces.
3. Install a *new* gasket onto the transmission case. If removed, install the locating pins.
4. Install the side door and transmission shaft assemblies into the transmission case. Make sure the side door fits flush against the transmission case.
5. Install the transmission side door bolts finger-tight. Tighten the 5/16 in. bolts to 13-16 ft.-lb. (17.6-21.7 N•m). Then, tighten the 1/4 in. bolts to 84-108 in.-lb. (9.5-12.2 N•m).
6. Turn the transmission by hand and shift the transmission into two different gears to keep the gears from turning.
7. Install the bearing inner race (**Figure 24**) onto the mainshaft as follows:
   a. The bearing inner race is 0.950-1.000 in. (24.13-25.40 mm) long. When installing a *new* race, measure it to confirm its length. Race length determines its installation position.
   b. Use the same tool set-up used for bearing inner race removal.
   c. Apply clean oil to the transmission shaft bearing surface, shaft threads and to the inner surface of the inner race.
   d. Position the bearing inner race with the chamfered end first going on first and slide it onto the mainshaft (**Figure 26**).
   e. Install the extension shaft onto the mainshaft.
   f. Place the pusher tube and the two flat washers and nut over the extension shaft.

CAUTION
Install the inner bearing race to the dimension listed. This aligns the race with the bearing outer race installed in the primary chaincase. Installation of the wrong race or installing it incorrectly will damage the bearing and race assembly.

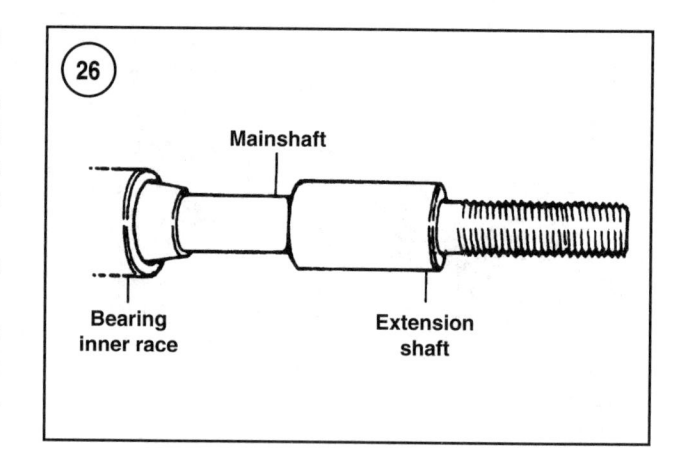

   g. Hold the extension shaft and tighten the nut to press the bearing inner race onto the mainshaft. Install the race so that its inside edge is 0.100 in. (2.54 mm.) away from the main drive gear.
   h. Remove the tools.
8. Install the oil slinger assembly (B, **Figure 18**).
9. Install the shift forks as described in this chapter.
10. Install the primary chaincase housing as described in Chapter Six.
11. Install the clutch assembly as described in Chapter Six.
12. Install the clutch release cover as described in Chapter Six.
13. Install the primary chaincase cover as described in Chapter Six.
14. Install the drain plug and refill the transmission oil as described in Chapter Three.
15. Install the exhaust system as described in Chapter Four.
16. Test-ride the motorcycle slowly and check for proper transmission operation.

TRANSMISSION SHAFTS

This section describes disassembly and assembly of the side door and each transmission shaft.

Transmission Disassembly

The transmission shaft assemblies (**Figure 27**) must be partially disassembled prior to removing both shafts from the side door. Do not try to remove the shafts with all of the gears in place.

The snap rings are very difficult to loosen and remove. A pair of heavy-duty snap ring pliers (H-D part No. J-5586), or an equivalent, is recommended for this procedure.

Store all of the transmission gears, snap rings, washers and split bearings in their order of removal.

1. Remove the transmission side door assembly as described in this chapter.
2. Protect the splines and threads on the mainshaft with tape or a plastic sleeve (**Figure 28**).
3. Remove the mainshaft second gear (**Figure 29**).

FIVE SPEED TRANSMISSION (2006 MODELS)

27 **TRANSMISSION SHAFTS**

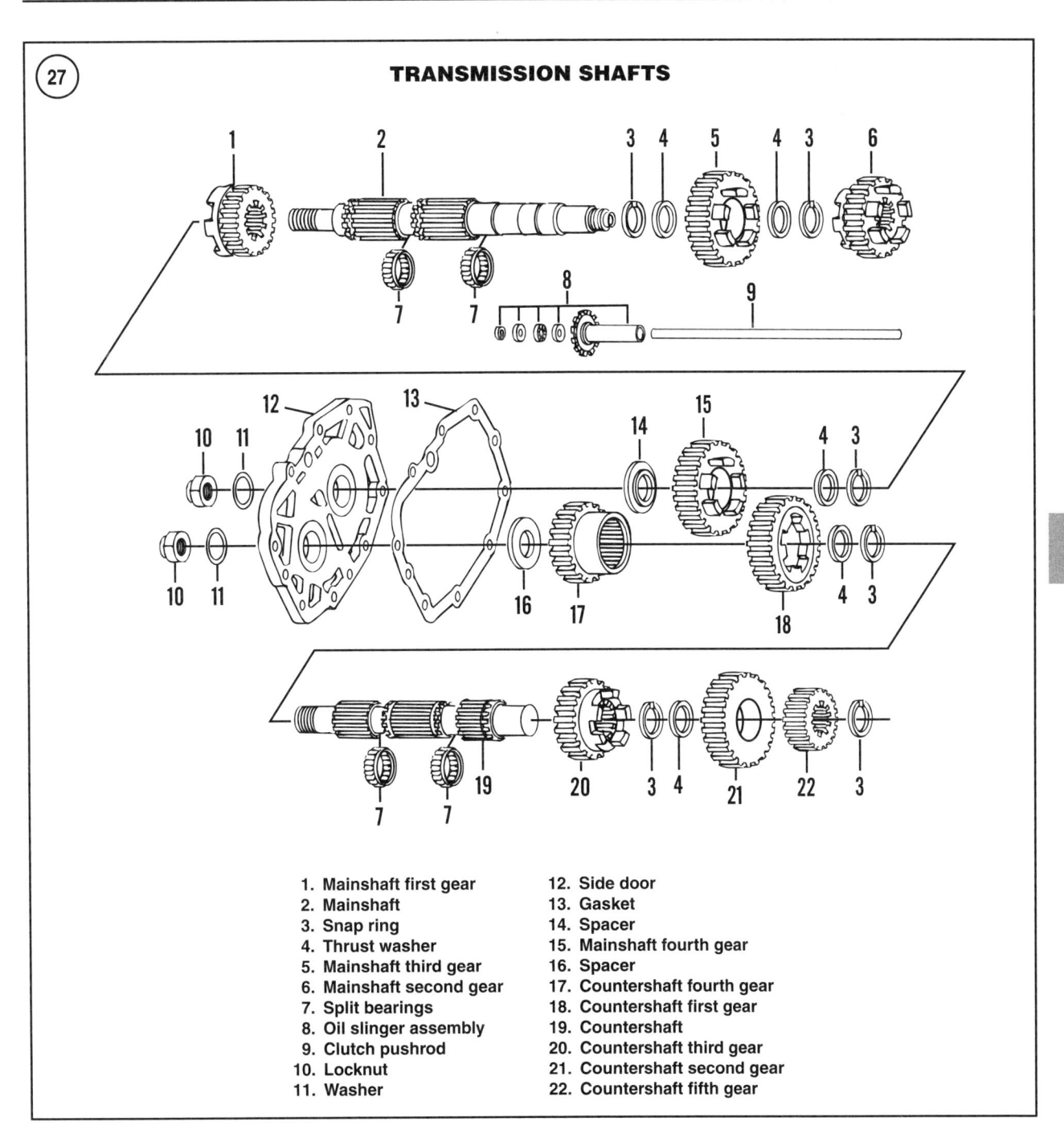

1. Mainshaft first gear
2. Mainshaft
3. Snap ring
4. Thrust washer
5. Mainshaft third gear
6. Mainshaft second gear
7. Split bearings
8. Oil slinger assembly
9. Clutch pushrod
10. Locknut
11. Washer
12. Side door
13. Gasket
14. Spacer
15. Mainshaft fourth gear
16. Spacer
17. Countershaft fourth gear
18. Countershaft first gear
19. Countershaft
20. Countershaft third gear
21. Countershaft second gear
22. Countershaft fifth gear

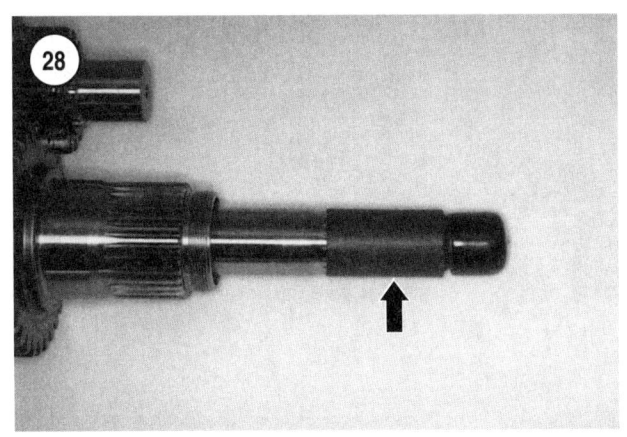

28

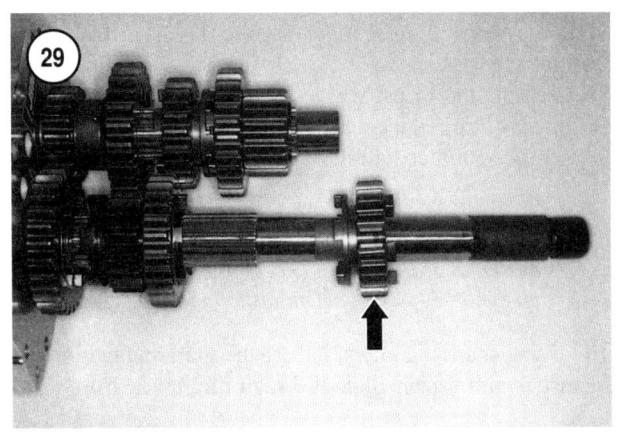

29

4. Remove the snap ring (**Figure 30**) from the countershaft.
5. Remove countershaft fifth gear (**Figure 31**).
6. Remove countershaft second gear (**Figure 32**).
7. Remove the split bearing (**Figure 33**) from the countershaft.
8. Slide off the thrust washer and remove the snap ring (**Figure 34**) from the countershaft.
9. Remove countershaft third gear (**Figure 35**).

NOTE
*The snap ring (**Figure 36**) must be released and moved in order to gain access to the snap ring on the other side of the mainshaft third gear.*

10. Using snap ring pliers, release the snap ring behind the mainshaft third gear. Slide the snap ring away from third gear.

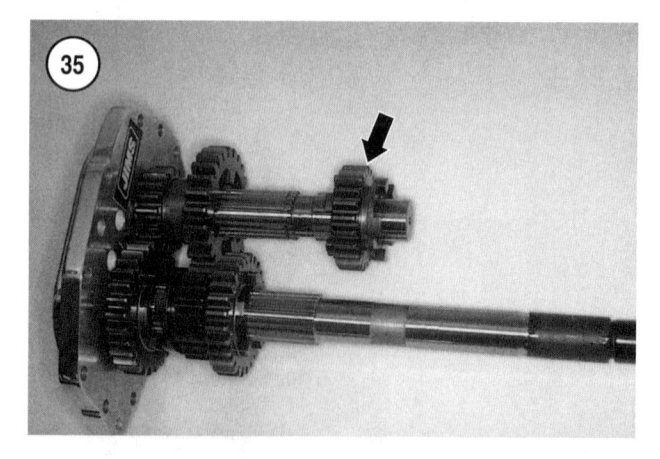

FIVE SPEED TRANSMISSION (2006 MODELS)

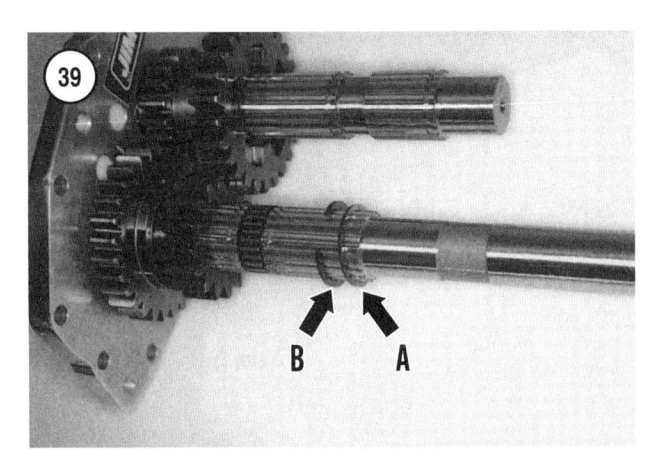

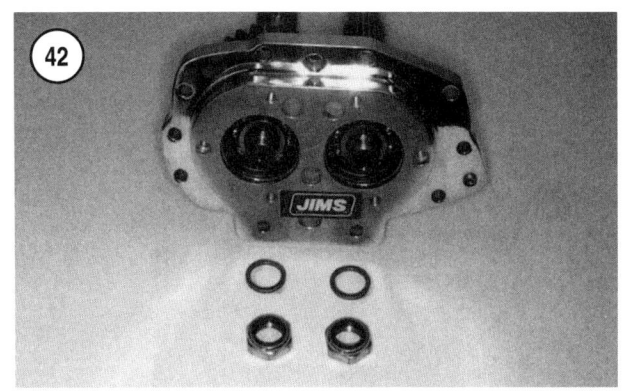

11. Slide third gear toward the side door and remove the snap ring (**Figure 37**) and thrust washer.
12. Remove mainshaft third gear (**Figure 38**).
13. Remove the thrust washer (A, **Figure 39**) and snap ring (B).
14. Remove the split bearing (**Figure 40**) from the mainshaft.
15. Place a brass or aluminum washer (**Figure 41**) between countershaft fourth gear and mainshaft fourth gear. This locks both transmission shafts from rotation.
16. Unscrew and remove the locknuts and washers (**Figure 42**) securing the shaft assemblies to the side door. Remove the brass or aluminum washer. New locknuts must be installed during assembly.
17. Press the countershaft out of its side door bearing as follows:
    a. Support countershaft first gear on a tube (A, **Figure 43**) in a press so that the countershaft can be pressed

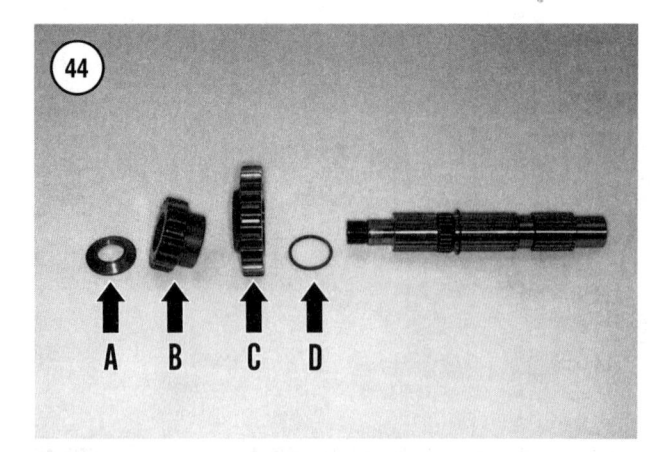

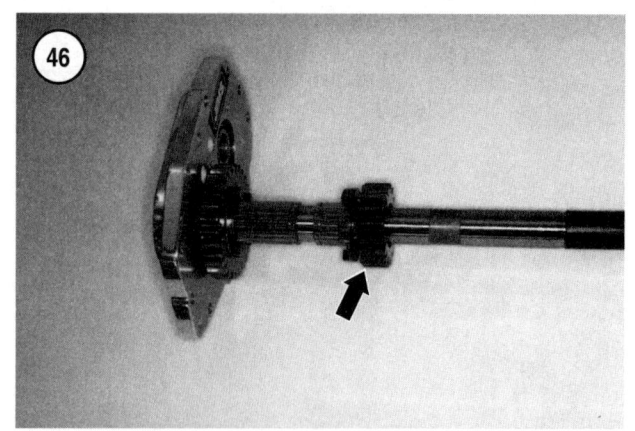

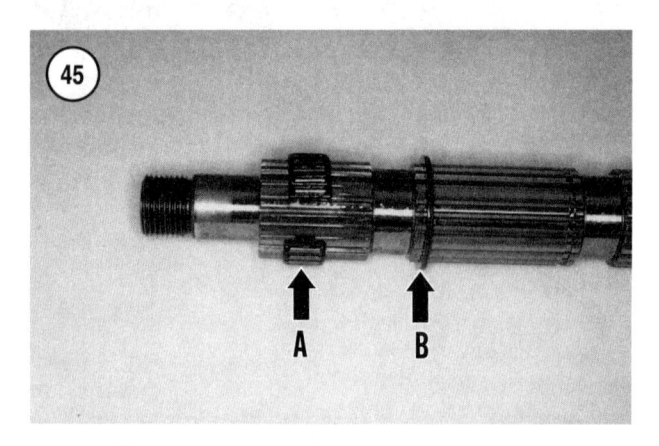

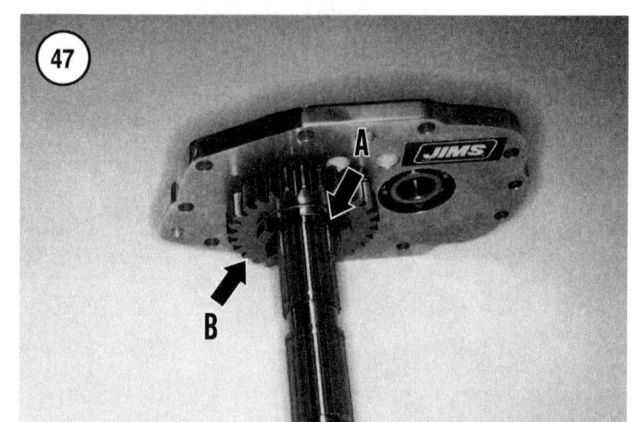

out without any interference. Center the countershaft under the press ram.

b. Place a mandrel (B, **Figure 43**) on top of the countershaft and press the countershaft out of the side door.

18. Remove the spacer (A, **Figure 44**), fourth gear (B) and its split bearing, first gear (C) and thrust washer (D) from the countershaft.
19. Remove the split bearing (A, **Figure 45**) from the countershaft.
20. If necessary, remove the snap ring (B, **Figure 45**) from the countershaft.
21. Remove first gear (**Figure 46**) from the mainshaft.
22. Remove the snap ring and thrust washer (A, **Figure 47**) from the mainshaft.
23. Press the mainshaft out of its side door bearing as follows:

a. Support the mainshaft fourth gear on a tube (A, **Figure 48**) in a press so that the mainshaft can be pressed out without any interference. Center the mainshaft under the press ram.

b. Place a mandrel (B, **Figure 48**) on top of the mainshaft and press the mainshaft out of the side door.

24. From the mainshaft, remove fourth gear (B, **Figure 47**) and the spacer.
25. Inspect all parts as described in this section.

Transmission Assembly

Refer to **Figure 27**.

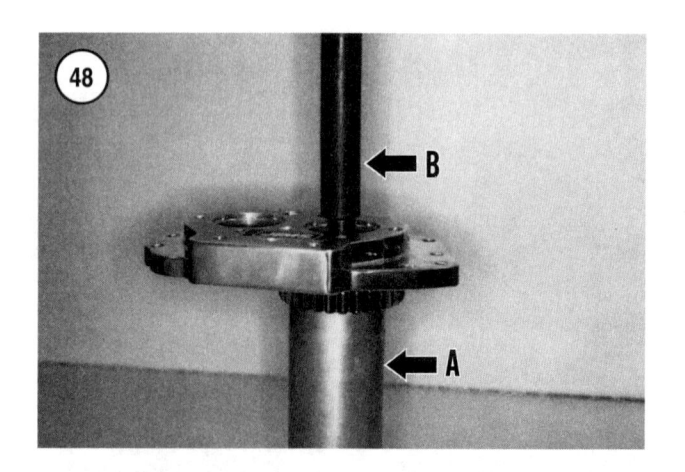

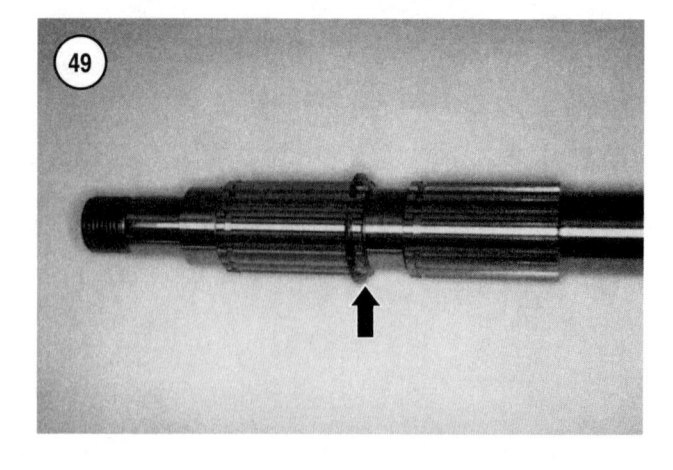

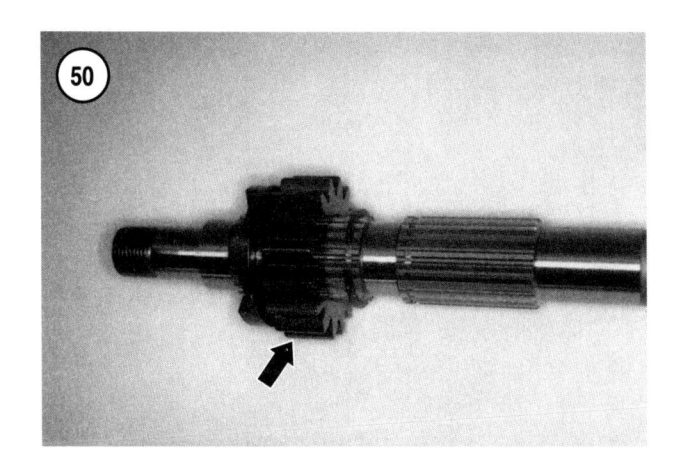

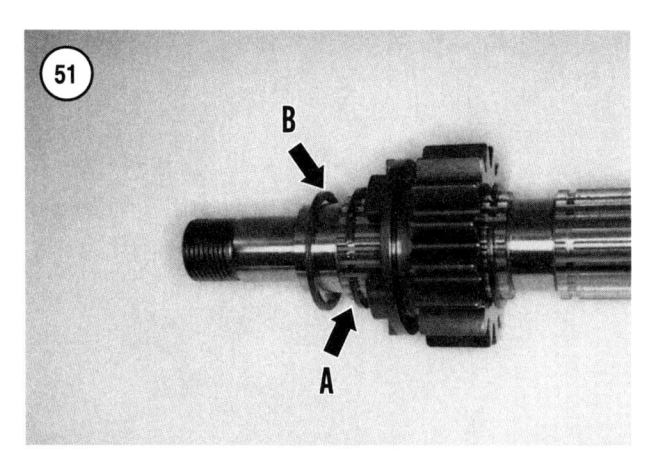

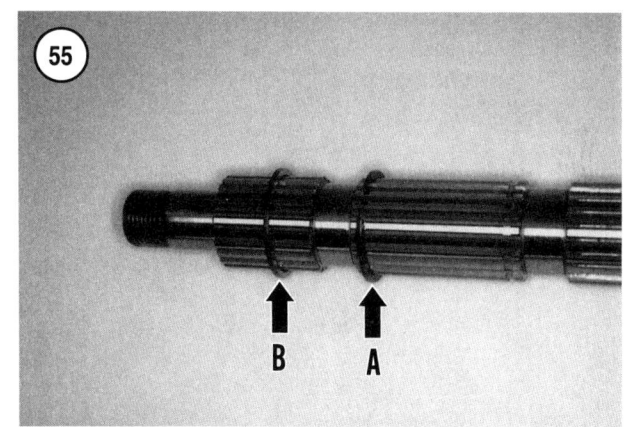

FIVE SPEED TRANSMISSION (2006 MODELS)

CAUTION
*Install a **new** snap ring at every location to ensure proper gear alignment and engagement. Never reinstall a snap ring that has been removed since it has become distorted and weakened and may fail. Make sure each **new** snap ring is correctly seated in its respective shaft groove.*

1. Apply a light coat of clean transmission oil to all mating gear surfaces and to all split bearing halves before assembly.
2. If removed, install the side door bearings as described in this chapter.
3. Install the following onto the mainshaft:
    a. Install a *new* snap ring (**Figure 49**).
    b. Position first gear with the shift dog side going on last, and then install first gear (**Figure 50**).
    c. Install a *new* snap ring (A, **Figure 51**) and the thrust washer (B).
    d. Install the split bearing (**Figure 52**).
    e. Position fourth gear with the shift dog side going on first, and then install fourth gear (**Figure 53**).
    f. Position the spacer with the beveled side (**Figure 54**) facing out, and then install the spacer.
4. Install the following onto the countershaft:
    a. Install a *new* snap ring (A, **Figure 55**).
    b. Install the thrust washer (B, **Figure 55**) and push it against the snap ring.

296　　　CHAPTER SEVEN

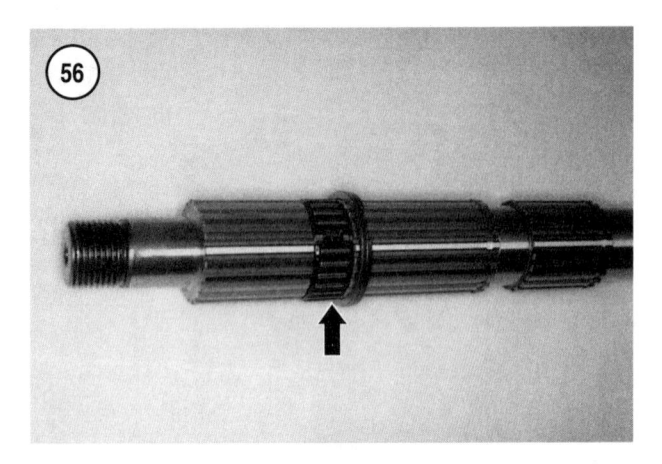

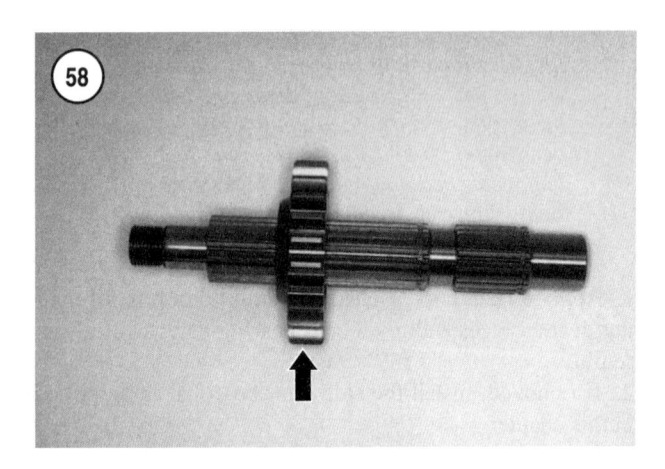

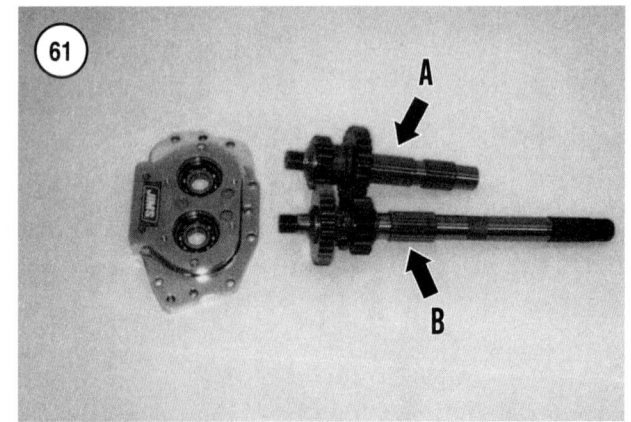

c. Install the split bearing (**Figure 56**).
d. Position first gear with the shoulder side (**Figure 57**) going on last, and then install first gear onto the split bearing (**Figure 58**).
e. Position fourth gear with the wide shoulder (**Figure 59**) going on first, and then install fourth gear.
f. Position the spacer with the beveled side (**Figure 60**) facing out and install the spacer.

5. Apply transmission oil to the inner race of both bearings and onto the shoulder of both shaft assemblies. Also apply transmission oil to the inner threads and ends of the tools used to install the shaft assemblies.

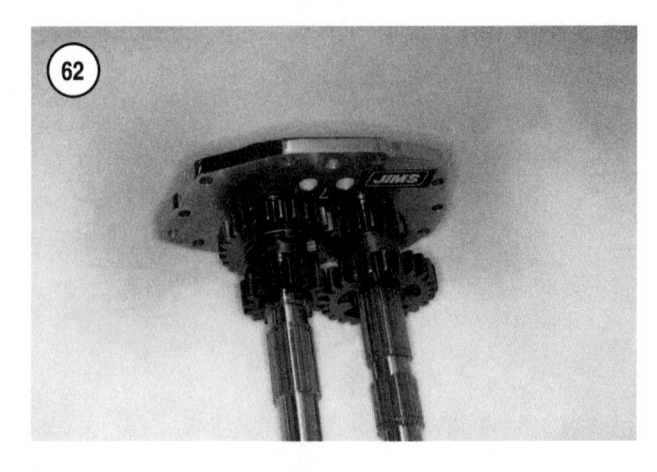

FIVE SPEED TRANSMISSION (2006 MODELS)

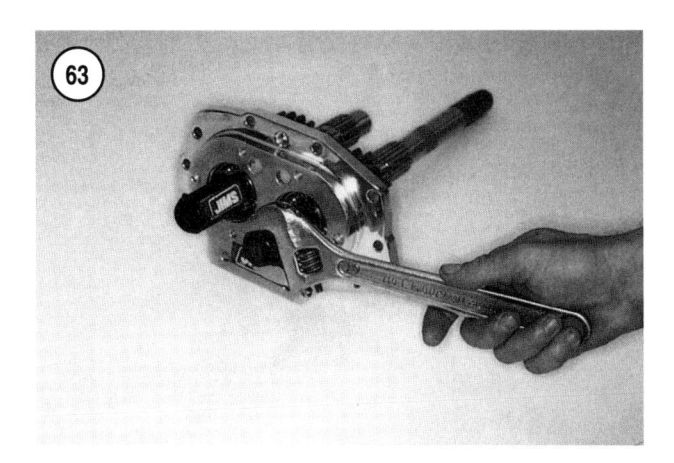

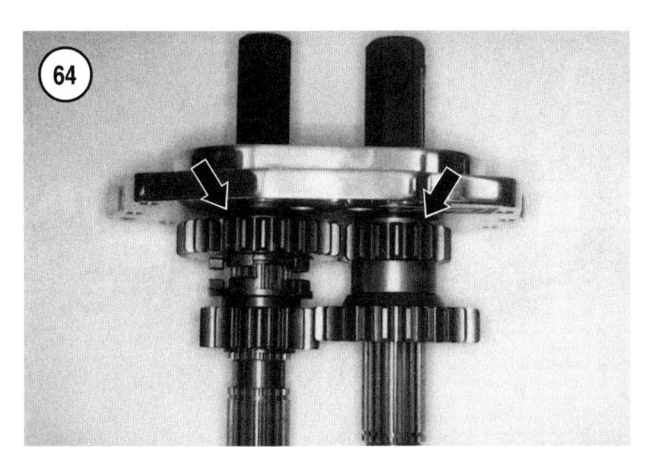

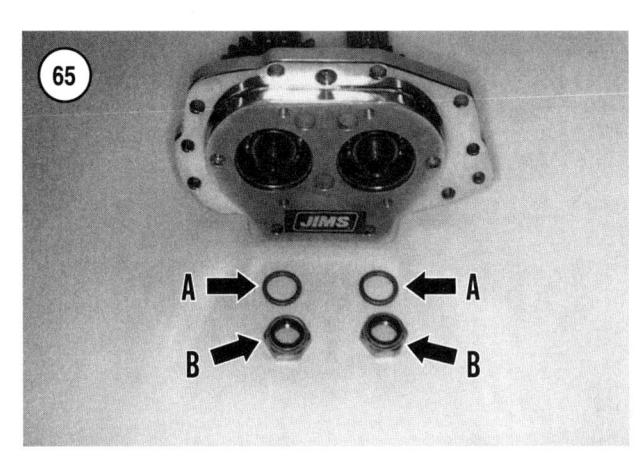

6. Position the countershaft (A, **Figure 61**) on the left side of the side door. Position the mainshaft (B, **Figure 61**) on the right side of the side door.
7. Mesh the two shaft assemblies together and start them into the side door bearings (**Figure 62**).
8. Attach the shaft installers (JIMS part No. 2189) onto the ends of both shafts.
9. Tighten the installation tools (**Figure 63**), alternating between both shafts, until both shaft shoulders (**Figure 64**) bottom on the inner race of the side door bearings.
10. Unscrew and remove the installation tools.

CAUTION
*Always install **new** locknuts. If an old locknut is reinstalled it may work loose, resulting in transmission damage.*

11. Install the spacers (A, **Figure 65**) and *new* locknuts (B).
12. Start the *new* locknuts by hand until the locking portion of the nut touches the end of the transmission shaft.
13. Place a brass or aluminum washer between countershaft fourth gear and mainshaft fourth gear. This will lock both transmission shafts.
14. Tighten the transmission shaft locknuts (**Figure 66**) to 45-55 ft.-lb. (61.0-74.6 N•m).
15. Install the following onto the mainshaft:
    a. Install the split bearing (**Figure 67**).
    b. Move the previously installed snap ring (A, **Figure 68**) out of the groove and toward first gear.

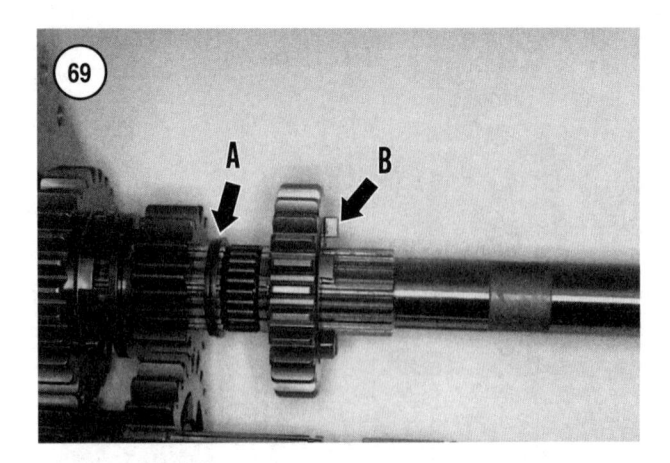

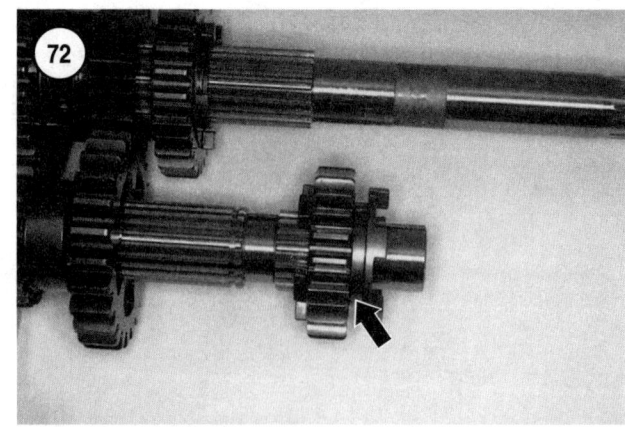

c. Install the thrust washer (B, **Figure 68**) and slide it against the snap ring (A, **Figure 69**).
d. Position third gear with the shift dogs side (B, **Figure 69**) going on last. Install third gear onto the split bearing (**Figure 70**).
e. Install the thrust washer (A, **Figure 71**) and snap ring (B). Make sure the snap ring is correctly seated in the mainshaft groove.
f. Move third gear away from first gear, and up against the thrust washer and snap ring.
g. Reposition the thrust washer and snap ring (**Figure 68**) behind third gear. Make sure the snap ring is correctly seated in the mainshaft groove.

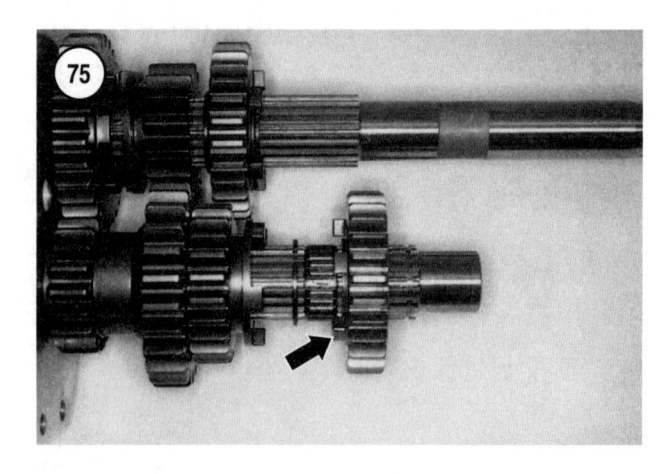

FIVE SPEED TRANSMISSION (2006 MODELS)

16. Install the following onto the countershaft:
    a. Position third gear with the shift fork groove (**Figure 72**) side going on last and install third gear.
    b. Install the snap ring (A, **Figure 73**) and thrust washer (B).
    c. Install the split bearing (**Figure 74**).
    d. Position second gear with the shift dog side (**Figure 75**) going on first. Install second gear onto the split bearing (**Figure 76**).
17. Onto the mainshaft, position second gear with the shift fork groove (**Figure 77**) side going on first and install the second gear (**Figure 78**).
18. Onto the countershaft, install fifth gear (**Figure 79**), and then install a *new* snap ring (**Figure 80**). Make sure the snap ring is correctly seated in the countershaft groove.
19. Refer to **Figure 81** for correct placement of all gears. Also, check that the gears mesh properly with their adjoining gears where applicable. This is the last chance prior to installing the shaft assemblies into the transmission case to make sure they are correctly assembled.

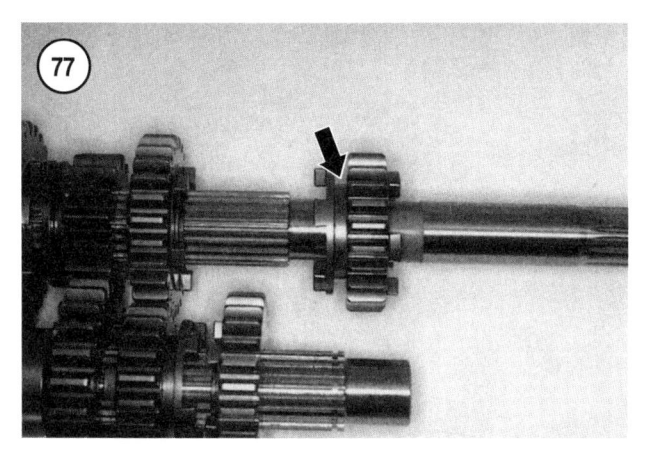

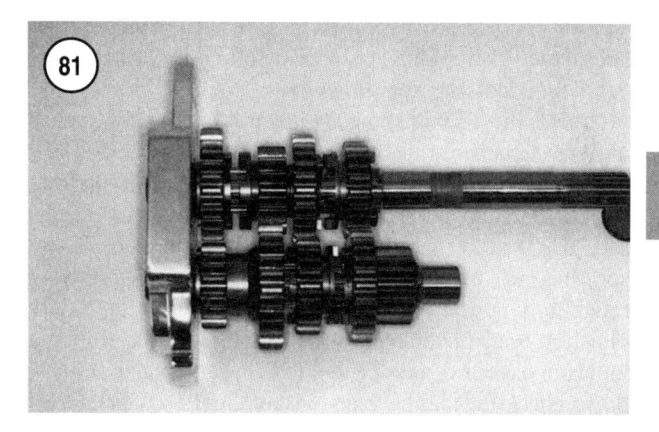

Transmission Inspection

Maintain the alignment of the transmission components when cleaning and inspecting the individual parts. To prevent intermixing parts, work on only one shaft at a time.

Refer to **Table 2** and inspect the service clearance and end play of the indicated gears and shafts. Replace parts that show excessive wear or damage as described in this section.

CAUTION
Do not clean the split bearings in solvent. It is difficult to remove all traces of solvent from the bearing plastic retainers. Flush the bearings clean with new transmission oil.

1. Clean and dry the shaft assembly.
2. Inspect the mainshaft and countershaft for:
   a. Worn or damages splines (A, **Figure 82**).
   b. Excessively worn or damaged bearing surfaces (B, **Figure 82**).
   c. Cracked or rounded-off snap ring grooves (C, **Figure 82**).
   d. Worn or damaged threads (D, **Figure 82**).
3. Check each gear for excessive wear, burrs, or pitting and for chipped or missing teeth. Check the inner splines (**Figure 83**) on sliding gears and the bore on stationary gears for excessive wear or damage.
4. Check the gear bushings (**Figure 84**) for wear, cracks or other damage.
5. To check stationary gears for wear, install them on their correct shaft and in the original operating position. If necessary, use the old snap rings to secure them in place. Then, spin the gear by hand. The gear should turn smoothly. A rough turning gear indicates heat damage–check for a dark bluish coloring or galling on the operating surfaces. Rocking indicates excessive wear, either to the gear or shaft or both.
6. To check the sliding gears, install them on their correct shaft and in their original operating position. The gear should slide back and forth without any binding or excessive play.
7. Check the shift fork groove (**Figure 85**) for wear or damage.

NOTE
*If there is excessive or uneven wear to the gear engagement dogs (**Figure 86**), check the shift forks carefully for bending and other damage. Refer to **Shift Forks** in this chapter.*

8. Check the dogs on the gears for excessive wear, rounding, cracks or other damage. When wear is noticeable, make sure it is consistent on each gear dog. If one dog is worn more than the others, the others will be overstressed during operation and will eventually crack and fail.
9. Check each gear dog slot for cracks, rounding and other damage.

NOTE
Replace defective gears along with their mating gears, though they may not show as much wear or damage.

10. Check engaging gears by installing the 2 gears on their respective shaft and in their original operating position. Mesh the gears together. Twist one gear against the other, and then check the dog engagement. Then, reverse the thrust load to check in the other operating position. Make sure the engagement in both directions is positive and without any slippage. Check that there is equal engagement across all of the engagement dogs.

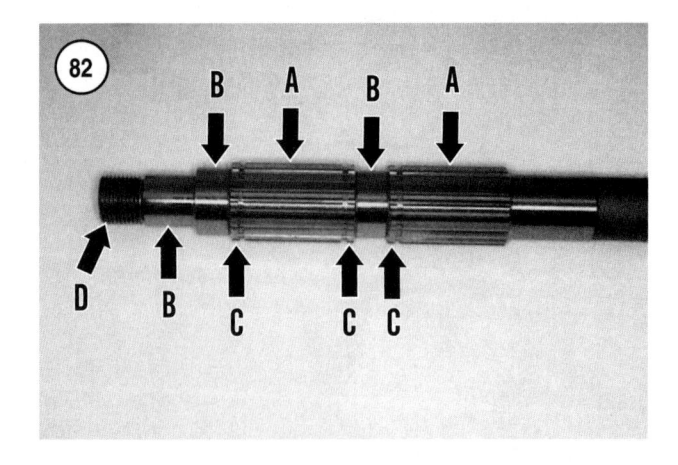

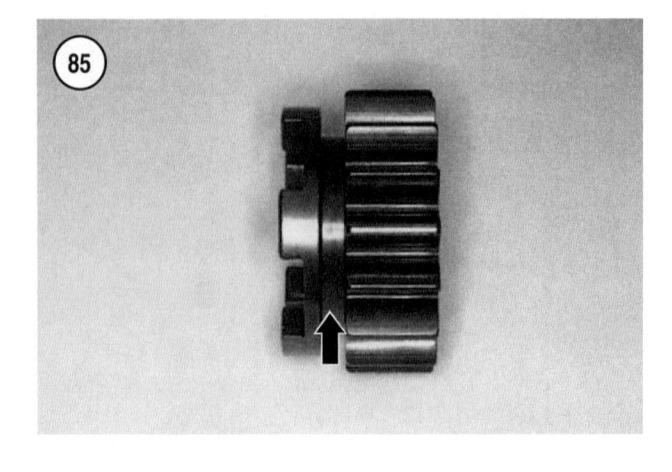

FIVE SPEED TRANSMISSION (2006 MODELS)

and installed using a transmission door bearing remover and installer (JIMS part No. 1078), or an equivalent. If this tool set is not available, a press is required.

1. Clean the side door and bearings in solvent and dry with compressed air.
2. Turn each bearing inner race (**Figure 90**) by hand. The bearings must turn smoothly. If replacement is necessary, replace the bearings as described in this section.
3. Remove both snap rings (**Figure 91**) from the outer surface of the side door.
4A. To remove the bearings with the removal tool, follow the tool manufacturer's instructions.
4B. Remove the bearings with a press as follows:
   a. Support the side door on the press bed with the outer surface facing up.
   b. Use a driver or socket and press the bearing out of the backside of the side door.
   c. Repeat the process to remove the opposite bearing.
5. Clean the side door again in solvent and dry thoroughly.
6. Inspect the bearing bores in the side cover for cracks or other damage. Replace the side door if damaged.

NOTE
Both side door bearings have the same part number.

7A. If the installation tool is used, follow the tool manufacturer's instructions and install the bearings.
7B. Install the bearings with a press as follows:
   a. Support the side door in a press with the backside facing up.
   b. Install bearings with their manufacturer's marks facing out.
   c. Use a driver that matches the bearing outer race. Press the bearing into the side door until it bottoms.
   d. Repeat the process to install the opposite bearing.
8. Position the beveled snap ring with the sharp side facing toward the bearing outer race and install both snap rings. Make sure the snap rings (**Figure 91**) are correctly seated in the side door groove.

MAIN DRIVE GEAR

The main drive gear (**Figure 92**) and bearing assembly are pressed into the transmission case. If the transmission case is installed in the frame, a transmission main drive gear tool set (JIMS part No. 35316-80), or an equivalent, is required to remove the main drive gear. If the transmission has been removed, use a press to remove and install the main drive gear.

Whenever the main drive gear is removed, the main drive gear bearing must be replaced at the same time.

Removal

1. Remove the transmission shaft assemblies from the transmission case as described in this chapter.
2. Remove the spacer from the main drive gear oil seal.
3. Remove the snap ring behind the bearing.

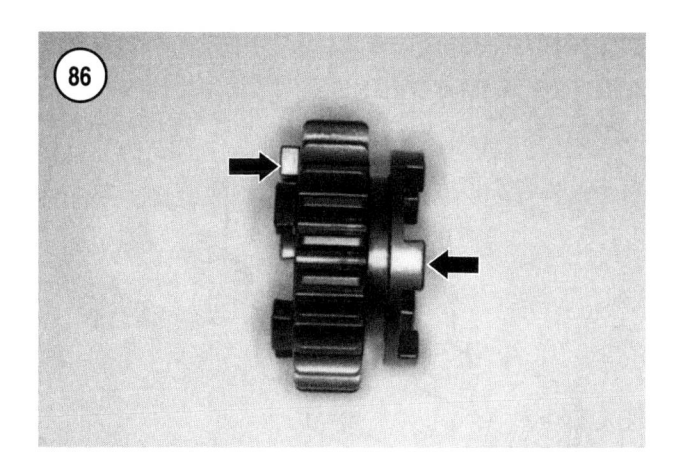

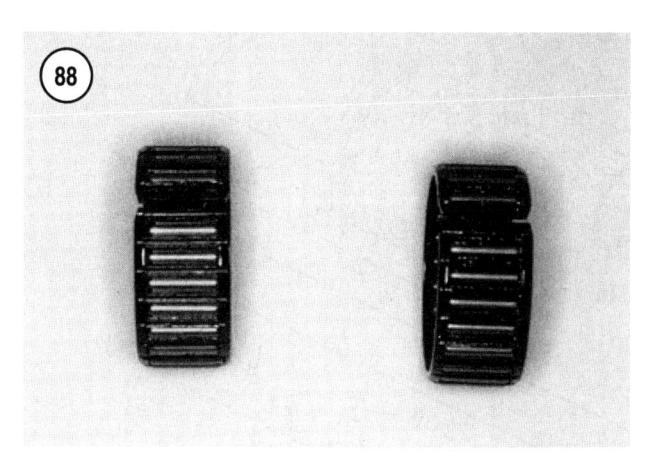

11. Check the spacers (**Figure 87**) for wear or damage.
12. Check the split bearings (**Figure 88**) for excessive wear or damage.
13. Replace all of the snap rings during re-assembly. In addition, check the thrust washers for burn marks, scoring or cracks. Replace as necessary.

SIDE DOOR BEARINGS

Inspection and Replacement

The side door bearings (**Figure 89**) are pressed into place and secured with a snap ring. They can be removed

CHAPTER SEVEN

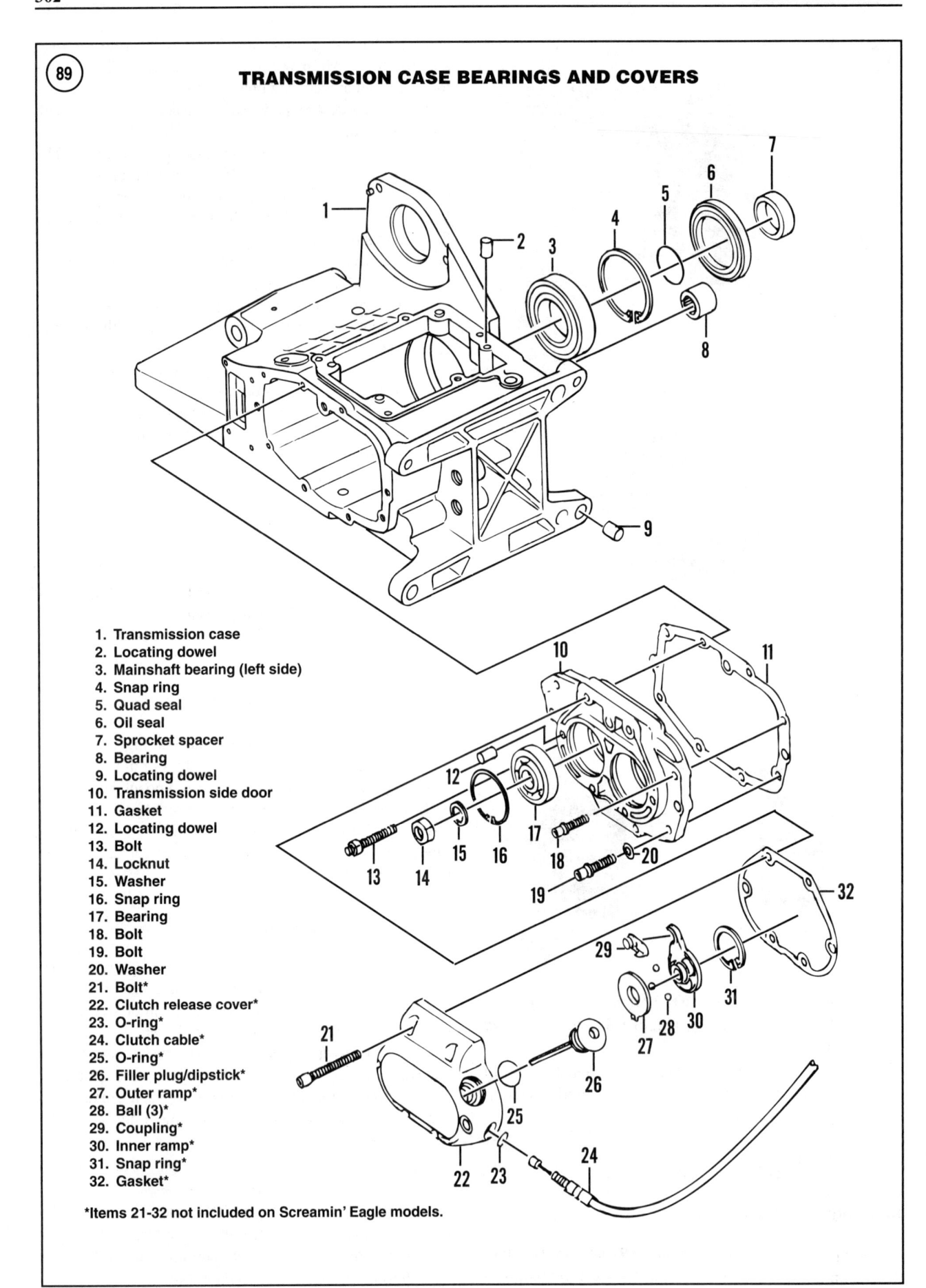

89 **TRANSMISSION CASE BEARINGS AND COVERS**

1. Transmission case
2. Locating dowel
3. Mainshaft bearing (left side)
4. Snap ring
5. Quad seal
6. Oil seal
7. Sprocket spacer
8. Bearing
9. Locating dowel
10. Transmission side door
11. Gasket
12. Locating dowel
13. Bolt
14. Locknut
15. Washer
16. Snap ring
17. Bearing
18. Bolt
19. Bolt
20. Washer
21. Bolt*
22. Clutch release cover*
23. O-ring*
24. Clutch cable*
25. O-ring*
26. Filler plug/dipstick*
27. Outer ramp*
28. Ball (3)*
29. Coupling*
30. Inner ramp*
31. Snap ring*
32. Gasket*

*Items 21-32 not included on Screamin' Eagle models.

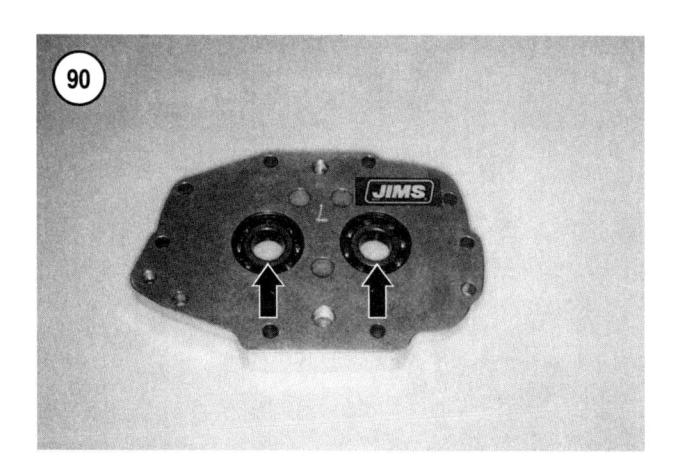

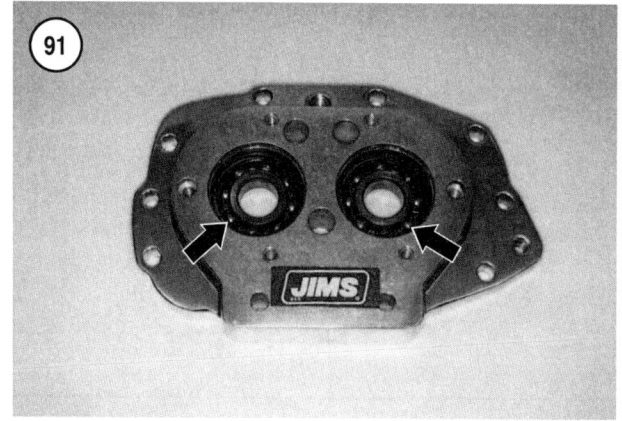

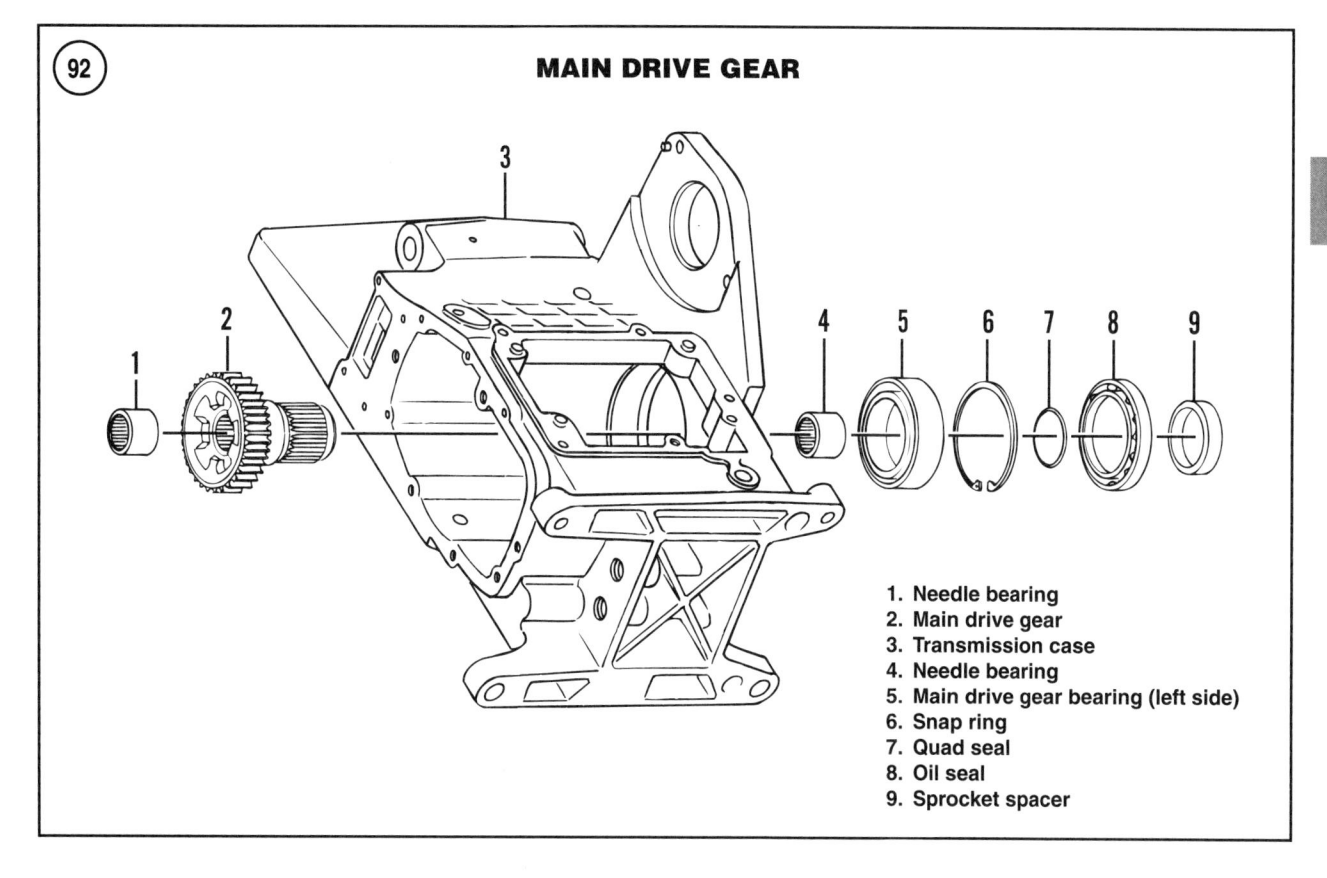

FIVE SPEED TRANSMISSION (2006 MODELS)

90

91

92 MAIN DRIVE GEAR

1. Needle bearing
2. Main drive gear
3. Transmission case
4. Needle bearing
5. Main drive gear bearing (left side)
6. Snap ring
7. Quad seal
8. Oil seal
9. Sprocket spacer

NOTE
If the main drive gear will not loosen from the bearing due to corrosion, remove the tools and heat the bearing with a heat gun.

4. Assemble the tool set onto the main drive gear following the tool manufacturer's instructions. Then, tighten the puller nut slowly to pull the main drive gear from the bearing in the transmission case.

5. Remove the main drive gear bearing from the transmission case as described in this section.

Installation

1. Replace the main drive gear bearing and oil seal as described in this section.

2. Install a *new* snap ring with the flat side facing the bearing.

3. Position the snap ring with the open end facing the rear of the transmission and within a 45° angle to horizontal (**Figure 93**). Make sure it is fully seated in the snap ring groove.

4. Install a *new* oil seal into the case so its closed side faces out.

5. Apply transmission oil to the bearing bore and to the outer surface of the main drive gear. Also apply oil to the nut and threaded shaft of the installer tool.

6. Insert the main drive gear into the main drive gear bearing as far as it will go. Hold it in place and assemble the tool onto the main drive gear and transmission case following the tool manufacturer's instructions.

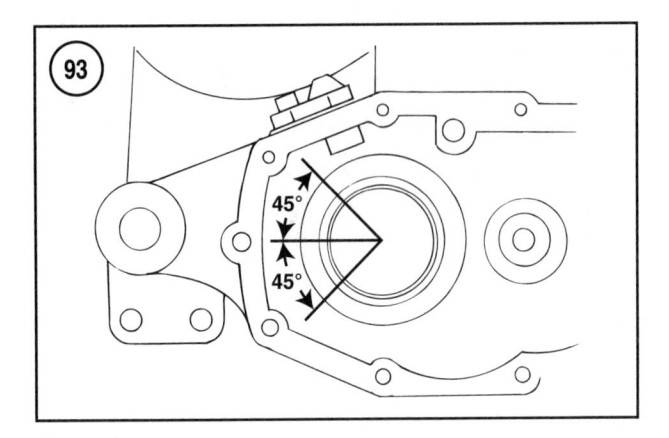

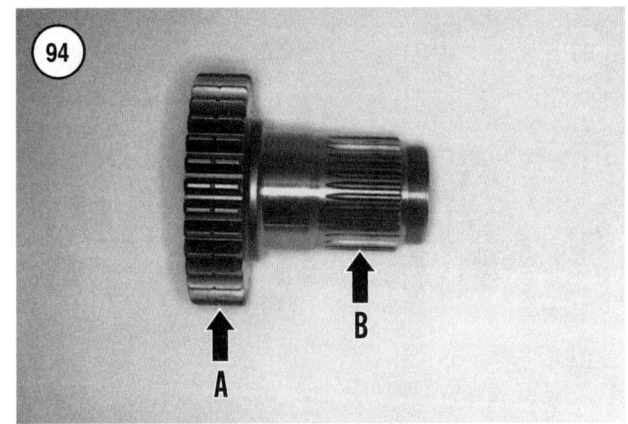

7. Slowly tighten the puller nut to pull the main drive gear into the bearing in the transmission case. Continue until the gear bottoms in the bearing's inner race.
8. Disassemble and remove the installation tool.
9. Install the spacer into the main drive gear oil seal.
10. Install the transmission shaft assemblies into the transmission case as described in this chapter.

Inspection

1. Clean the main drive gear in solvent and dry with compressed air, if available.
2. Check each gear tooth (A, **Figure 94**) for excessive wear, burrs, galling and pitting. Check for missing teeth.
3. Check the gear splines (B, **Figure 94**) for excessive wear, galling or other damage.
4. Inspect the two main drive gear needle bearings (**Figure 95** and **Figure 96**) for excessive wear or damage. Insert the mainshaft into the main drive gear to check bearing wear. If necessary, replace the bearings as described in this section.

Needle Bearing Replacement

Both main drive gear needle bearings must be installed to the correct depth within the main drive gear. The correct depth is obtained with a main drive gear bearing tool (JIMS part No. 37842-91), or an equivalent. This tool is also used to install the oil seal. If this tool is not available, a press is required.

If the tool is not available, measure the depth of both bearings before removing them.

Replace both main drive gear needle bearings as a set.

CAUTION
Never re-install a main drive gear needle bearing, as it is distorted during removal.

1. Remove the oil seal (**Figure 97**) from the clutch side of the main drive gear.
2. If the main drive hear bearing tool is not used, measure and record the depth of both bearings.
3. Support the main drive gear in a press and press out one needle bearing. Then, turn the gear over and press out the opposite bearing.
4. Clean the gear and its bearing bore in solvent and dry thoroughly.
5. Apply transmission oil to the bearing bore in the main drive gear and to the outer surface of both bearings.

NOTE
Install both needle bearings with the manufacturer's marks facing out.

6A. Install the bearings with the main drive gear bearing tool as follows:
   a. The tool has two different length ends. The tool's long side (A, **Figure 98**) is for the clutch side (**Figure 96**) of the main drive gear. The tool's short side (B,

FIVE SPEED TRANSMISSION (2006 MODELS)

6B. If the bearings are being installed without the installation tool, use a suitable mandrel and press in the bearing to the depth recorded prior to removal.

7. Install a *new* oil seal (**Figure 97**) into the clutch side of the main drive gear.

Main Drive Gear Bearing Replacement

The main drive gear bearing is pressed into the transmission case. If the transmission case is installed in the frame, a transmission main bearing remover set (JIMS part No. 1720), or an equivalent, is required to remove the main drive gear bearing. If the transmission has been removed, use a press to remove the main drive gear bearing.

Whenever the main drive gear is removed, the main drive gear bearing is damaged and must be replaced at the same time.

CAUTION
Failure to use the correct tools to install the bearing will cause premature failure of the bearing and related parts.

1. Remove the main drive gear from the transmission case as described in this section.
2. Assemble the removal tool set onto the main drive gear bearing following the tool manufacturer's instructions. Then, tighten the bolt and nut slowly to pull the main drive gear bearing from the transmission case.
3. Clean the bearing bore and dry with compressed air. Check the bore for nicks or burrs. Check the snap ring groove for damage.

NOTE
Install the bearing into the transmission case with the manufacturer's marks facing out.

4. Apply transmission oil to the bearing bore in the transmission case and to the outer surface of the bearing. Also apply oil to the nut and threaded shaft of the installer tool.
5. Install the bearing onto the installation tool and assemble the installation tool following the manufacturer's instructions.
6. Slowly tighten the puller nut to pull the bearing into the transmission case. Continue until the bearing bottoms in the case.
7. Disassemble and remove the installation tool.
8. Install the main drive gear into the transmission case as described in this section.

DRIVE SPROCKET

Removal/Installation

NOTE
It is not necessary to remove the mainshaft bearing race to remove the transmission drive sprocket.

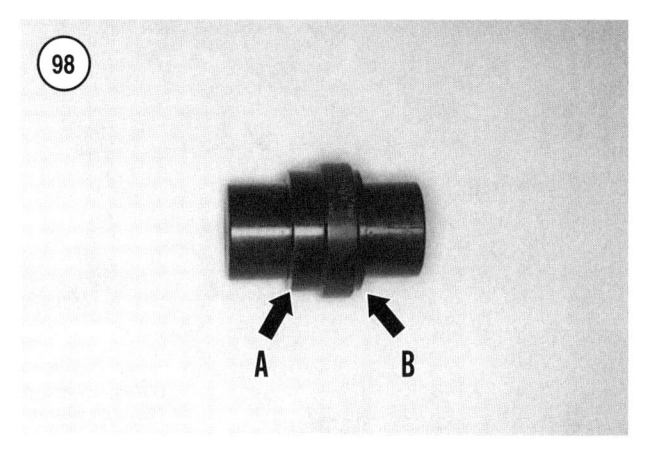

Figure 98) is for the transmission side (**Figure 95**) of the main drive gear.

b. Install the main drive gear in a press with the transmission end facing up. Align the *new* bearing with the main drive gear and place the installation tool, with the *short side facing down* (**Figure 99**), inserted into the bearing. Operate the press until the tool's shoulder bottoms against the main drive gear.

c. Turn the main drive gear over so that the inner end faces up. Align the *new* bearing with the main drive gear and place the installation tool, with the *long side facing down*, and inserted into the bearing. Operate the press until the tool's shoulder bottoms against the gear.

1. Remove the primary chaincase assembly as described in Chapter Six.
2. Perform the following to create sufficient slack in the drive belt:
    a. Remove the E-clip and loosen the rear axle nut.
    b. Support the motorcycle with the rear wheel off the ground.
    c. Turn each axle adjuster in equal amounts to loosen belt tension.
    d. Push the rear wheel forward to provide sufficient slack in the drive belt.
3. If necessary, install a transmission drive sprocket locker tool (JIMS part No. 2260), or an equivalent, (**Figure 100**) onto the transmission drive sprocket, following the tool manufacturer's instructions.
4. Remove the Allen bolts and the lock plate (**Figure 101**).
5A. Shift the transmission into gear.
6B. If the drive belt is still in place, have an assistant apply the rear brake.
7. Use a transmission mainshaft sprocket locknut socket (JIMS part No. 94660-37A). Install the inner collar (**Figure 102**) onto the mainshaft.

CAUTION
*The sprocket nut has left-hand threads. Turn the tool **clockwise** to loosen it.*

8. Install the wrench onto the nut (**Figure 103**), and then turn it *clockwise* and loosen the nut.
9. Remove the tools and the nut from the mainshaft.
0. Carefully remove the transmission drive sprocket from the mainshaft, being careful to not damage the bearing race.
10. Install by reversing the removal steps, while noting the following:
    a. Use the same tool set-up used during removal.
    b. Apply Loctite TB1360, or an equivalent, to the nut and Allen bolts prior to installation.
    c. Locate the nut with the flanged side facing the drive sprocket.
    d. Tighten the drive sprocket nut *counterclockwise* to 60 ft.-lb (81.4 N•m).

CAUTION
*When aligning the lockplate bolt holes, tighten the nut an additional 35-40°. **Do not exceed 45°**. The nut will be damaged.*

    e. Scribe a horizontal line on the sprocket nut and onto the sprocket. Tighten the nut an additional 35-40° until the lock plate holes are aligned. Do not exceed 45°.
    f. Install the lock plate and its Allen bolts, and then tighten the bolts to 84-108 in-lb. (9.5-12.2 N•m).

TRANSMISSION CASE

Only remove the transmission case (**Figure 104**) if it requires replacement, when performing extensive frame repair or if replacing the frame. All internal components can be removed with the case in the frame.

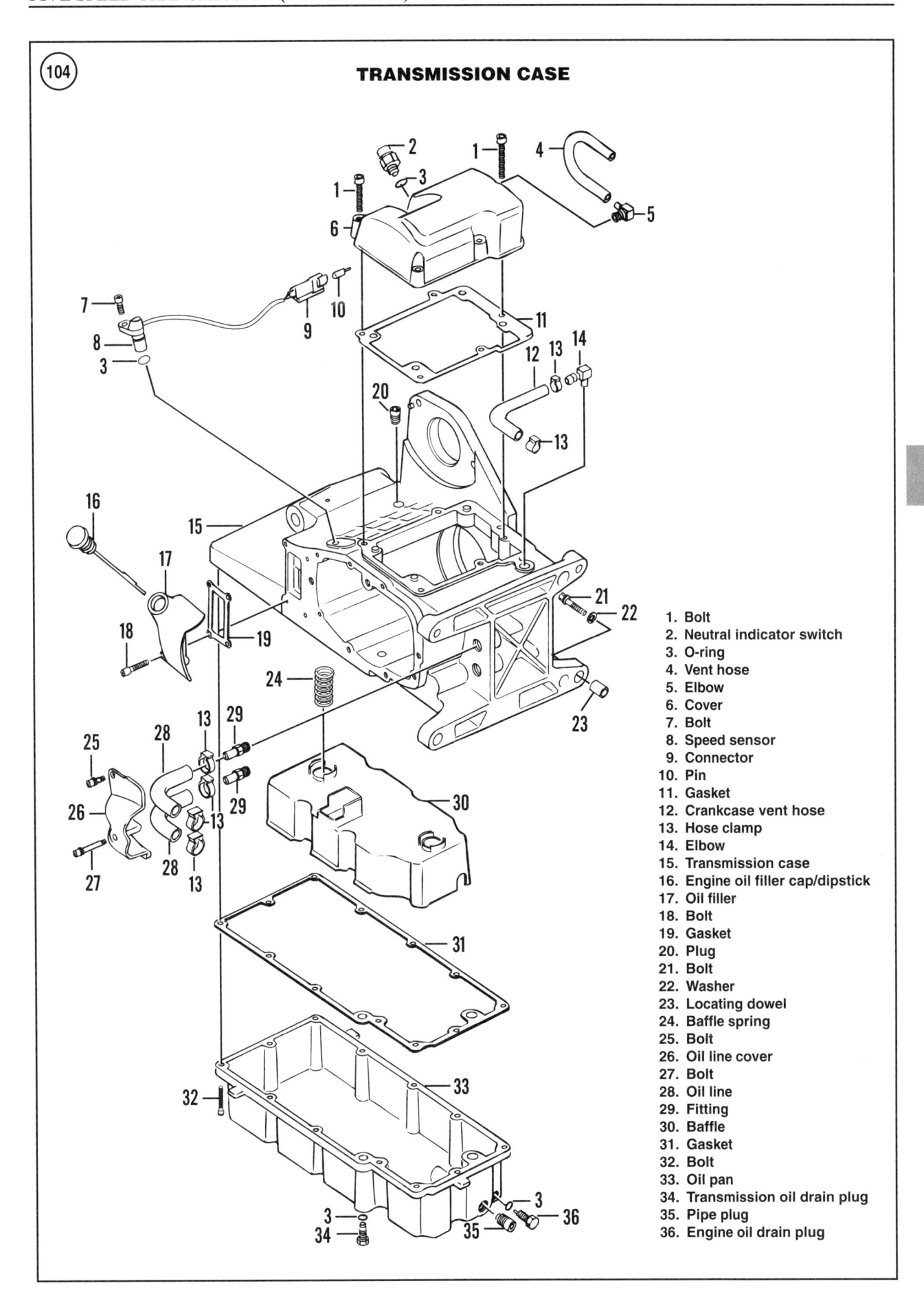

FIVE SPEED TRANSMISSION (2006 MODELS)

TRANSMISSION CASE

1. Bolt
2. Neutral indicator switch
3. O-ring
4. Vent hose
5. Elbow
6. Cover
7. Bolt
8. Speed sensor
9. Connector
10. Pin
11. Gasket
12. Crankcase vent hose
13. Hose clamp
14. Elbow
15. Transmission case
16. Engine oil filler cap/dipstick
17. Oil filler
18. Bolt
19. Gasket
20. Plug
21. Bolt
22. Washer
23. Locating dowel
24. Baffle spring
25. Bolt
26. Oil line cover
27. Bolt
28. Oil line
29. Fitting
30. Baffle
31. Gasket
32. Bolt
33. Oil pan
34. Transmission oil drain plug
35. Pipe plug
36. Engine oil drain plug

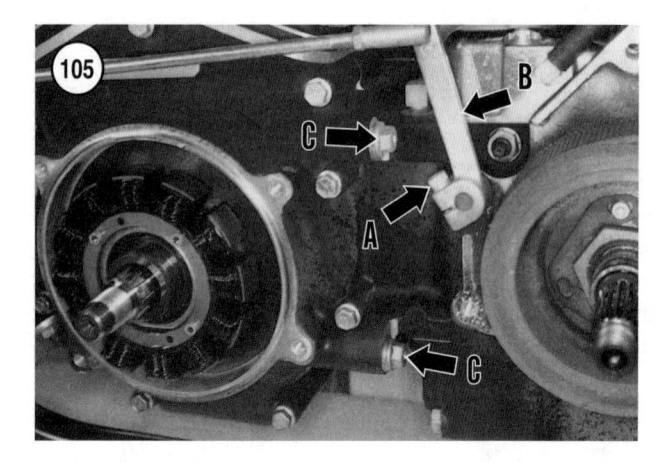

Removal/Installation

1. Drain the transmission oil and primary chaincase lubricant as described in Chapter Three.
2. Remove the exhaust system as described in Chapter Four.
3. Remove the primary chaincase cover as described in Chapter Six.
4. Remove the clutch assembly as described in Chapter Six.
5. Remove the transmission side cover (this chapter) and the clutch release mechanism (Chapter Six).
6. Remove the primary chaincase housing as described in Chapter Six.
7. Remove the transmission drive sprocket as described in this chapter.
8. Remove the transmission shaft assemblies as described in this chapter.
9. Remove the external shift linkage from the transmission as described in this chapter.
10. Make an alignment mark on the shift rod lever and the end of the shift shaft.
11 Remove the clamping bolt (A, **Figure 105**) securing the shift rod lever (B).
12. Use a Torx driver (T50) and back out the centering screw (A, **Figure 106**) until it clears the centering slot in the shift pawl assembly.
13. Remove the snap ring (B, **Figure 106**) and flat washer (C) from the shift shaft (D).
14. Remove the starter as described in Chapter Eleven.
15. Remove the rear wheel as described in Chapter Twelve.
16. Remove the oil pan and baffle from the bottom of the transmission case as described in this chapter.
17. Support the swing arm, and then remove the swing arm pivot bolt as described in Chapter Fourteen.
18. Remove the hose clamps and disconnect the two oil hoses connecting the transmission to the crankcase.
19. Place a jack under the crankcase to support the engine after the transmission case is removed.
20. Remove the four transmission case-to-engine mounting bolts (C, **Figure 105**). There are two bolts on each side. 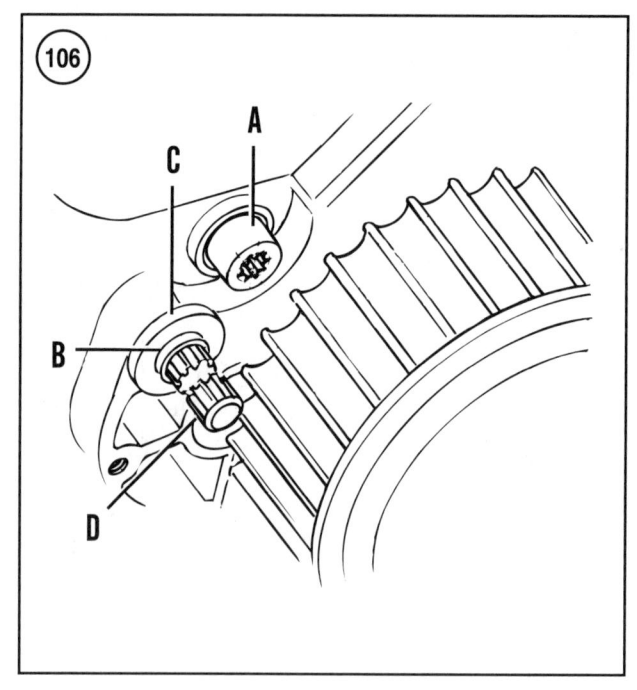
21. Move the transmission case to the rear to clear the two lower locating dowels.
22. Move the transmission toward the right side and remove the transmission case from the frame.
23. Install the transmission case by reversing the removal steps, while noting the following:
   a. Make sure the two locating dowels (**Figure 107**) are in place on the engine or transmission case.
   b. Using a crossing pattern, tighten the transmission mounting bolts evenly in two steps. Tighten the bolts to an initial torque of 15 ft.-lb. (20.3 N•m), and then tighten the bolts again to a final torque of 30-35 ft.-lb. (40.7-47.5 N•m).

OIL PAN

The oil pan mounts onto the bottom of the transmission case (**Figure 104**). It can be removed with the transmission mounted in the frame.

Removal

1. Drain the engine oil as described in Chapter Three.
2. Drain the transmission oil as described in Chapter Three.

CAUTION
The dipstick will be damaged if left in place during oil pan removal.

3. Remove the engine oil dipstick (**Figure 108**).
4. Remove the rear wheel as described in Chapter Twelve.

NOTE
Access the hidden bolts through the holes in the frame cross member.

FIVE SPEED TRANSMISSION (2006 MODELS)

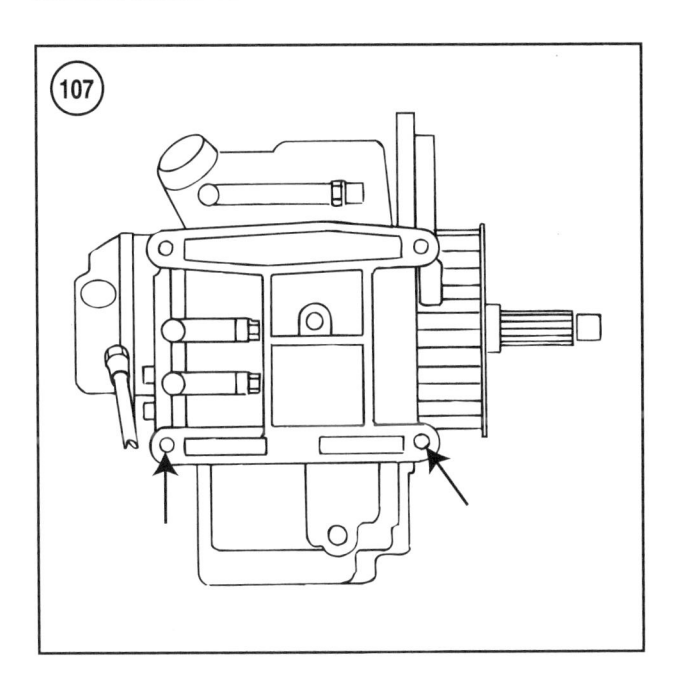

107

108

5. Remove the twelve Allen bolts securing the oil pan to the transmission case.
6. Lower and slide the oil pan toward the rear and remove it from the transmission case and the frame. Do not lose the baffle spring.
7. Remove the gasket.

Installation

1. Coat the oil pan gasket surface with a thin coat of Hylomar gasket sealer, or an equivalent.
2. Install a *new* gasket on the oil pan.
3. Install the baffle and baffle spring into the oil pan.
4. Partially install the oil pan onto the bottom of the transmission case. Use a long flat bladed screwdriver and compress the baffle spring as the oil pan moves into place.

Make sure the baffle spring is not cocked or distorted or it will hold the oil pan away from the transmission gasket surface.

5. Hold the oil pan in place and install the twelve Allen bolts. Using a crossing pattern, tighten the oil pan bolts to 84-132 in.-lb. (9.5-14.9 N•m).
6. If necessary, replace the engine oil filter as described in Chapter Three.
7. Refill the oil pan with *new* engine oil as described in Chapter Three.
8. Refill the transmission with *new* oil as described in Chapter Three.
9. Start the engine and check for leaks.

Inspection

1. Clean the oil tank, baffle and spring in solvent and dry thoroughly.
2. Remove all old gasket residue from the oil pan and transmission case mating surfaces.
3. Inspect the oil pan for cracks or damage. Replace if necessary.

Table 1 TRANSMISSION GENERAL SPECIFICATIONS

Transmission type	5-speed, constant mesh
Gear ratios	
First	3.21
Second	2.21
Third	1.57
Fourth	1.23
Fifth	1.00
Transmission overall ratios	
First	10.110
Second	6.958
Third	4.953
Fourth	3.862
Fifth	3.150
Transmission fluid capacity	
Oil change	20-24 U.S. oz. (591-710 ml)
Rebuild (dry)	24 U.S. oz. (710 ml)

Table 2 TRANSMISSION SERVICE SPECIFICATIONS

Item	in.	mm
Countershaft		
Runout	0.000-0.003	0.00-0.08
Endplay	None	
First gear		
Clearance	0.003-0.0019	0.008-0.048
End play	0.005-0.0039	0.127-0.099
Second gear		
Clearance	0.003-0.0019	0.008-0.048
End play	0.005-0.0440	0.127-1.118
Third gear		
Clearance	0.000-0.0080	0.000-0.203
Fourth gear		
Clearance	0.000-0.0080	0.000-0.203
End play	0.005-0.0390	0.127-0.991
Fifth gear		
Clearance	0.000-0.0080	0.000-0.203
End play	0.0040-0.0050	0.102-0.127
Mainshaft		
Runout	0.00-0.003	0.00-0.08
Endplay	None	
First gear		
Clearance	0.000-0.0080	0.000-0.203
Second gear		
Clearance	0.000-0.0800	0.000-2.032
Third gear		
Clearance	0.003-0.0019	0.008-0.048
End play	0.005-0.0420	0.127-1.067
Fourth gear		
Clearance	0.0003-0.0019	0.008-0.048
End play	0.005-0.0310	0.127-0.787
Main drive gear (fifth)		
Bearing fit in transmission case	0.0003-0.0017	0.0076-0.043
Fit in bearing		
Tight fit	0.0009	0.023
Loose fit	0.0001	0.0025
Fit on mainshaft	0.0001-0.0009	0.0025-0.023
End play	None	
Shift cam assembly		
Right edge of middle cam groove to right support block distance	1.992-2.002	50.60-50.85
Shift cam end play	0.001-0.004	0.025-0.10
Shift dog gears		
Clearance		
First-third	0.035-0.157	0.889-3.99
Second-fifth	0.035-0.139	0.889-3.53
Second-third	0.035-0.164	0.889-4.17
First-fourth	0.035-0.152	0.889-3.86
Shift forks		
Shift fork-to-cam groove end play	0.0017-0.0019	0.043-0.048
Shift fork-to-gear groove end play	0.0010-0.0110	0.025-0.0279
Shift fork finger thickness	0.165	4.19

Table 3 TRANSMISSION TORQUE SPECIFICATIONS

Item	ft.-lb.	in.-lb.	N•m
Bleed valve (Screamin' Eagle models)	–	80-100	9.0-11.3
Clutch cable fitting	–	36-60	4.1-6.8
Clutch fluid line flare nut (Screamin' Eagle models)	–	80-115	9.0-13.0
Clutch fluid reservoir banjo bolt (Screamin' Eagle models)	17-22	–	23.0-29.8
Clutch fluid reservoir cover screw (Screamin' Eagle models)	–	6-8	0.7-0.9

(continued)

FIVE SPEED TRANSMISSION (2006 MODELS)

Table 3 TRANSMISSION TORQUE SPECIFICATIONS (continued)

Item	ft.-lb.	in.-lb.	N•m
Clutch fluid filler cap/dipstick	–	25-75	2.8-8.5
Clutch release cover bolts			
All models except Screamin' Eagle	–	84-108	9.5-12.2
Screamin' Eagle models	10-12	–	13.6-16.3
Oil pan Allen bolts	–	84-132	9.5-14.9
Shift cam detent follower pivot bolt	–	84-108	9.5-12.2
Shift cam support block bolts	–	84-108	9.5-12.2
Shift rod lever clamp bolt	18-22	–	24.4-29.8
Shift rod locknuts	–	80-120	9.0-13.6
Swing arm pivot shaft nut	90-110	–	122.0-149.1
Top cover bolts	–	84-132	9.5-14.9
Transmission drain plug	14-21	–	19.0-28.5
Transmission drive sprocket			
Mounting nut*	60	–	81.3
Lock plate bolts	–	84-108	9.5-12.2
Transmission shaft locknuts			
(at side door)	45-55	–	61.0-74.6
Transmission side door			
1/4 in. bolts	–	84-108	9.5-12.2
5/16 in. bolts	13-16	–	17.6-21.7
Transmission-to-engine mounting bolts			
Initial torque	15	–	20.3
Final torque	30-35	–	40.7-47.5

*Tighten an additional 30°–not to exceed 45°.

CHAPTER EIGHT

SIX SPEED TRANSMISSION (2007-2009 MODELS)

This chapter covers procedures for the transmission, shift linkage and oil pan. All 2007-2009 models are equipped with a six-speed transmission, which is separate from the engine. The transmission shaft assemblies and the shift assemblies can be serviced with the transmission case mounted in the frame.

Refer to **Tables 1-4** at the end of this chapter for specifications.

SHIFT ASSEMBLY

The shift assembly (**Figure 1**) consists of the external shift linkage, internal shift cam and shift arm components.

If a shift problem is encountered, refer to the troubleshooting procedures in Chapter Two and eliminate all clutch and shift mechanism possibilities *before* considering transmission repairs. On all models except Screamin' Eagle, improper clutch adjustment (Chapter Three) is often a cause of poor shifting.

Shift Linkage Adjustment

The shift linkage assembly connects the transmission shift rod lever to the foot-operated shift levers. The shift linkage does not require adjustment unless the shift linkage is replaced or the transmission gears do not engage properly.

NOTE
Always disarm the optional TSSM/HFSM security system prior to disconnecting the battery or pulling the Maxi-Fuse so the siren will not sound.

1. Remove the Maxi-Fuse as described under *Fuses* in Chapter Eleven.

2. Loosen the two shift linkage rod locknuts (A, **Figure 2** and **Figure 3**).
3. Remove the acorn nut (B, **Figure 2**) and washers securing the shift linkage rod to the inner shift lever. Do not remove the rod from the shift lever.
4. Turn the shift linkage rod (C, **Figure 2**) as necessary to change the linkage adjustment.
5. Securely tighten the shift linkage rod to the shift rod lever.
6. Tighten the shift linkage rod locknuts to 80-120 in.-lb. (9.0-13.6 N•m).
7. Recheck the shifting. Readjust if necessary.
8. If proper shifting cannot be obtained by performing this adjustment, check the shift linkage for any interference problems. Then, check the shift linkage assembly for worn or damaged parts.
9. Once linkage is properly adjusted, reinstall the Maxi-Fuse as described in Chapter Eleven.

EXTERNAL SHIFT MECHANISM

Removal/Installation

Refer to **Figure 1**.

NOTE
Always disarm the optional TSSM/HFSM security system prior to disconnecting the battery or pulling the Maxi-Fuse so the siren will not sound.

1. Remove the Maxi-Fuse as described in *Fuses* (Chapter Eleven).
2. Remove the front left footboard as described in Chapter Seventeen.
3. Make an alignment mark on the heel shift lever and the end of the shift lever shaft.

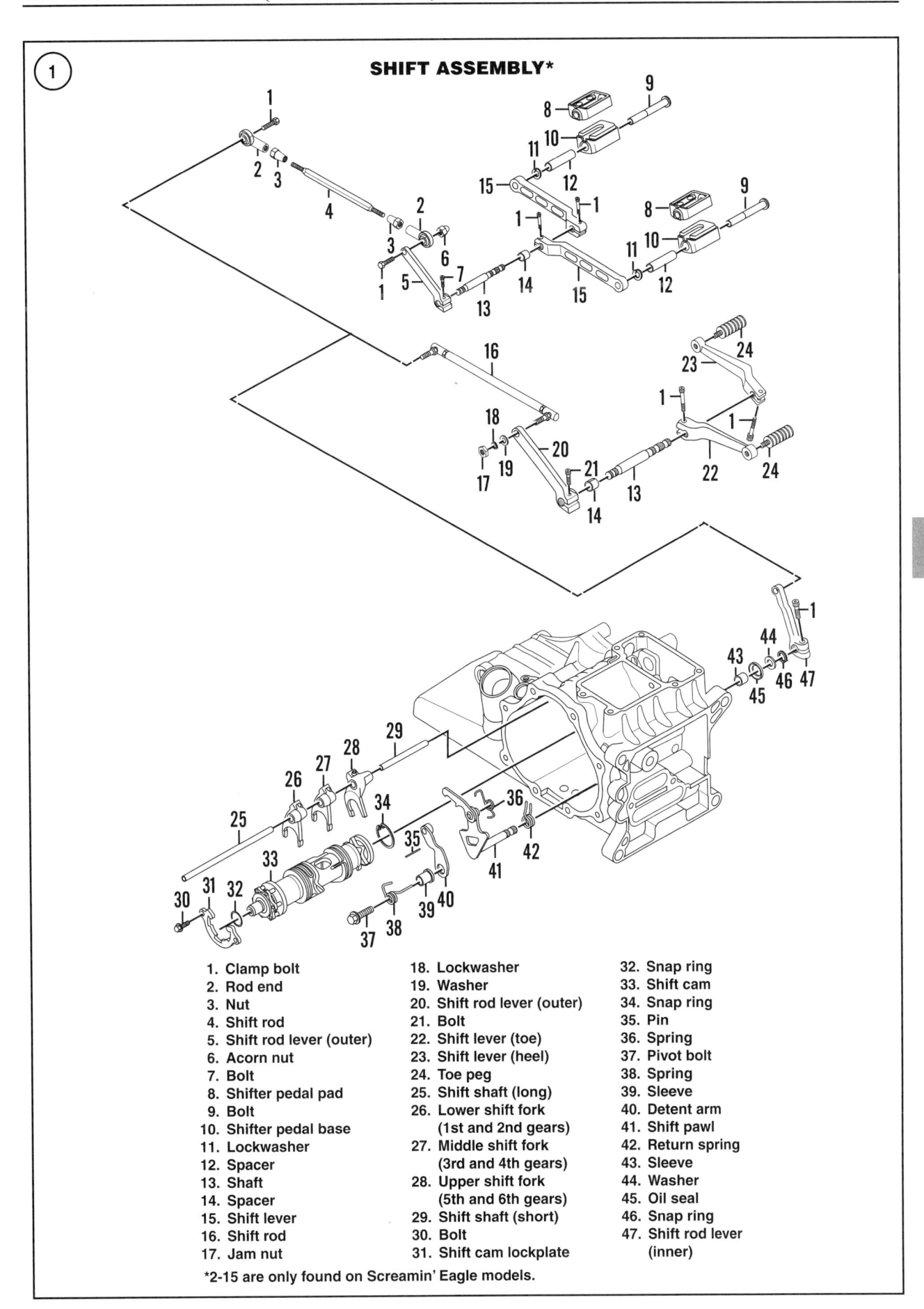

SIX SPEED TRANSMISSION (2007-2009 MODELS)

SHIFT ASSEMBLY*

1. Clamp bolt
2. Rod end
3. Nut
4. Shift rod
5. Shift rod lever (outer)
6. Acorn nut
7. Bolt
8. Shifter pedal pad
9. Bolt
10. Shifter pedal base
11. Lockwasher
12. Spacer
13. Shaft
14. Spacer
15. Shift lever
16. Shift rod
17. Jam nut
18. Lockwasher
19. Washer
20. Shift rod lever (outer)
21. Bolt
22. Shift lever (toe)
23. Shift lever (heel)
24. Toe peg
25. Shift shaft (long)
26. Lower shift fork (1st and 2nd gears)
27. Middle shift fork (3rd and 4th gears)
28. Upper shift fork (5th and 6th gears)
29. Shift shaft (short)
30. Bolt
31. Shift cam lockplate
32. Snap ring
33. Shift cam
34. Snap ring
35. Pin
36. Spring
37. Pivot bolt
38. Spring
39. Sleeve
40. Detent arm
41. Shift pawl
42. Return spring
43. Sleeve
44. Washer
45. Oil seal
46. Snap ring
47. Shift rod lever (inner)

*2-15 are only found on Screamin' Eagle models.

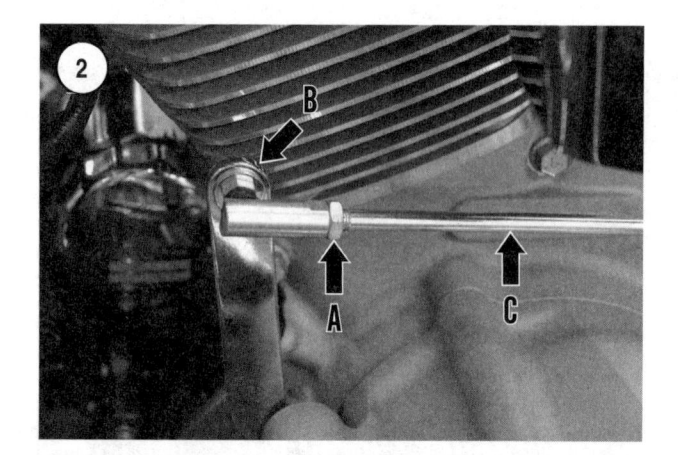

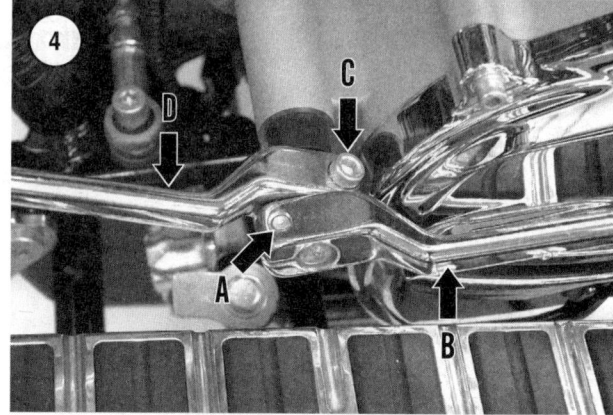

4. Remove the clamp bolt (A, **Figure 4**) and remove the heel shift lever (B).
5. Make an alignment mark on the toe shift lever and the end of the shift lever shaft.
6. Remove the clamp bolt (C, **Figure 4**) and remove the toe shift lever (D).
7. Remove the spacer (**Figure 5**) from the shift lever shaft.
8. On Screamin' Eagle models, remove the jiffy stand as described in Chapter Seventeen.
9. Remove the primary chaincase assembly as described in Chapter Six.
10. Remove the nut, washer and lockwasher securing the shift rod to the outer shift lever.
11. Remove the clamp bolt (A, **Figure 6**) securing the inner shift rod lever (B) to the transmission case.
12. Remove the outer shift rod lever (A, **Figure 7**), shift rod (B), inner shift lever and shift lever shaft as an assembly.
13. Install by reversing the removal steps. Tighten the shift rod lever clamp bolts to 18-22 ft.-lb. (24.4-29.8 N•m).

TRANSMISSION COVER

The transmission cover assembly can be serviced with the transmission installed in the frame.

SIX SPEED TRANSMISSION (2007-2009 MODELS)

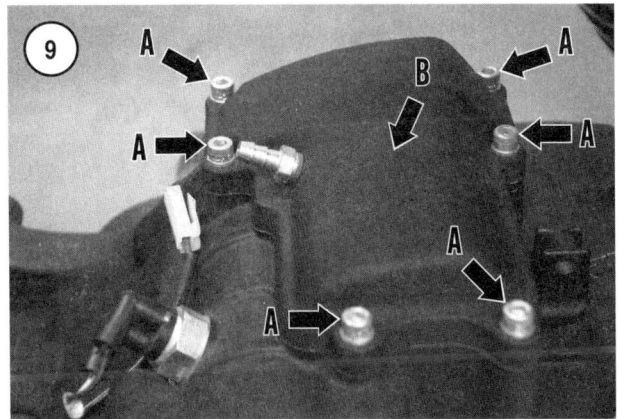

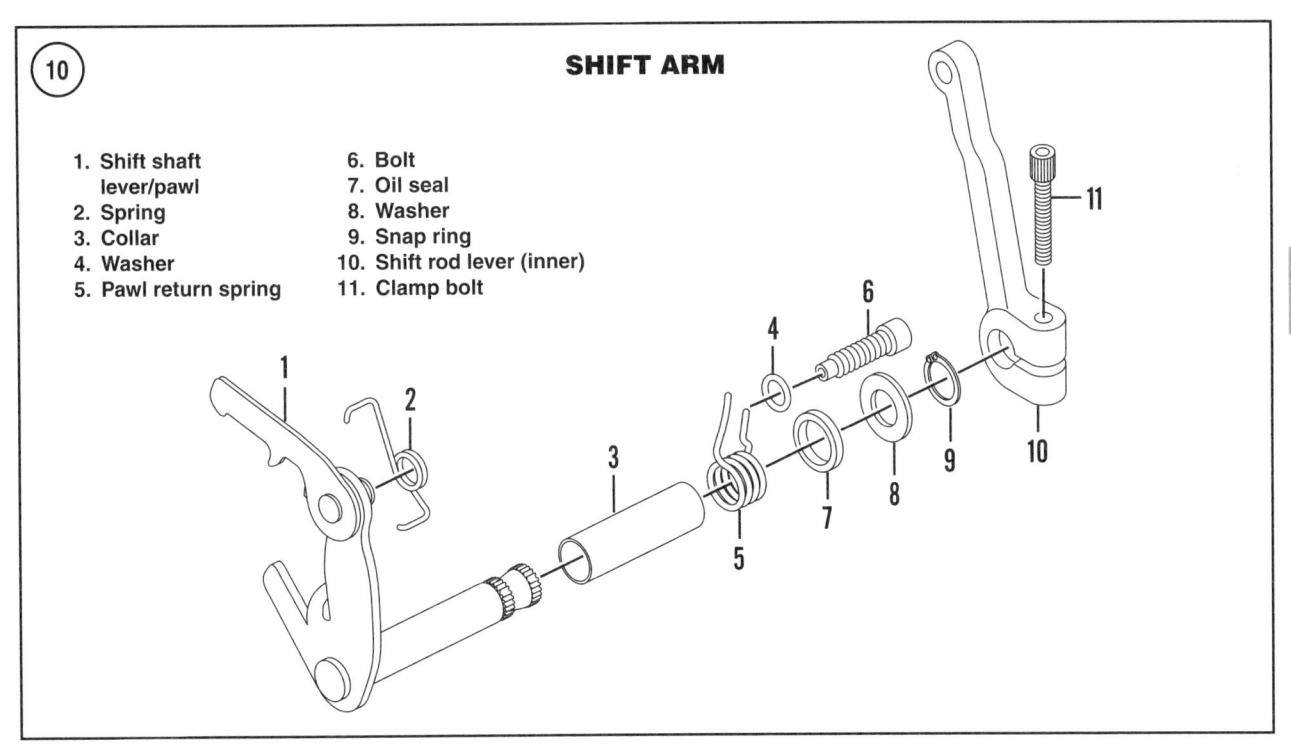

SHIFT ARM

1. Shift shaft lever/pawl
2. Spring
3. Collar
4. Washer
5. Pawl return spring
6. Bolt
7. Oil seal
8. Washer
9. Snap ring
10. Shift rod lever (inner)
11. Clamp bolt

Removal/Installation

NOTE
Always disarm the optional TSSM/HFSM security system prior to disconnecting the battery or pulling the Maxi-Fuse so the siren will not sound.

1. Remove the Maxi-Fuse as described in *Fuses* (Chapter Eleven).
2. Remove the right side exhaust system as described in Chapter Four.
3. Remove the clamp, and disconnect the vent hose (**Figure 8**) from the transmission cover fitting.
4. Remove the bolts (A, **Figure 9**) securing the transmission cover to the transmission case. Remove the cover (B, **Figure 9**) and the gasket.
5. Remove the gasket residue from the transmission cover and transmission case mating surfaces.
6. Install a *new* gasket onto the transmission case.
7. Install the transmission cover, the bolts and the washers. Using a crossing pattern, tighten the transmission cover bolts to 84-132 in.-lb. (9.5-14.9 N•m).
8. Reconnect the vent hose (**Figure 8**) to the fitting and install a *new* hose clamp.
9. Reinstall the Maxi-Fuse as described in *Fuses* (Chapter Eleven).
10. Install the right side exhaust system as described in Chapter Four.

SHIFT ARM ASSEMBLY

Removal

Refer to **Figure 10**.

1. Remove the transmission side door assembly as described in this chapter.

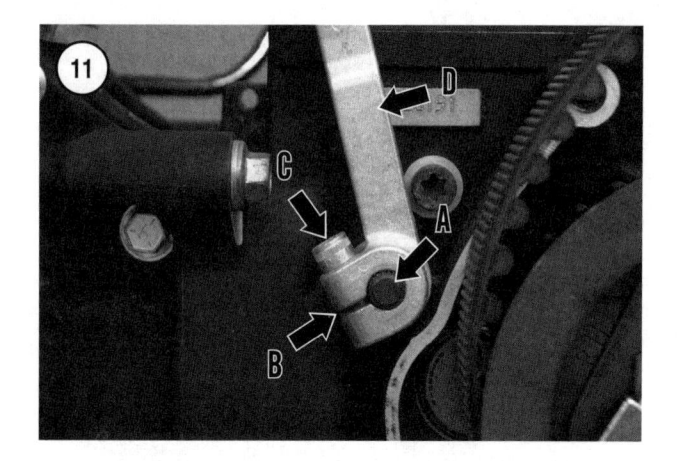

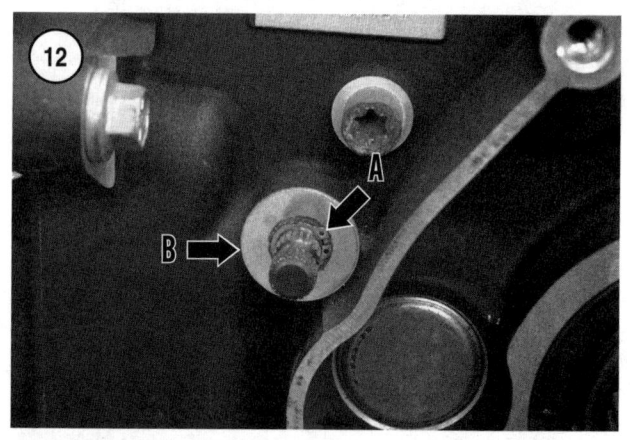

2. Make an alignment mark on the shift shaft (A, **Figure 11**) that relates to the split part (B) of the shift rod lever.
3. Remove the clamp bolt (C, **Figure 11**), and then remove the shift rod lever from the shift shaft.
4. Remove the snap ring (A, **Figure 12**) and washer (B) from the shift shaft.
5. Withdraw the shift shaft, sleeve and pawl return spring as an assembly (A, **Figure 13**) from the inside of the transmission case.
6. Remove the shift shaft oil seal from the transmission case. Discard the seal and snap ring.

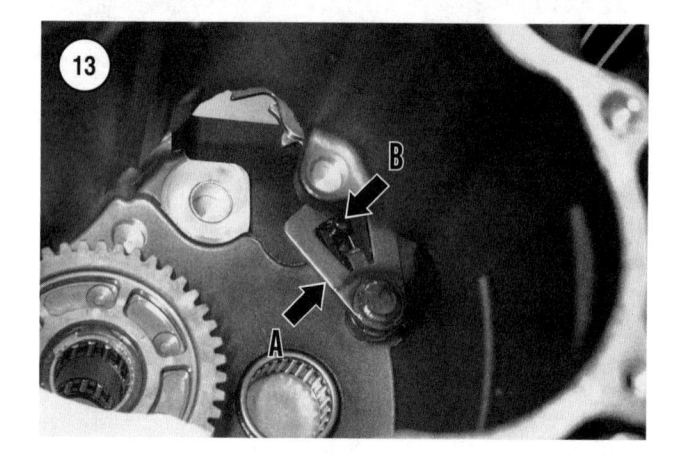

Installation

1. Check that the sleeve is still in place in the transmission case.
2. Make sure the arms of the shift shaft spring straddle (A, **Figure 14**) the tab on the shift shaft body.
3. If removed, install the shift pawl return spring.
4. Install the shift shaft assembly (A, **Figure 13**) into the transmission case so the arms of the shift shaft spring straddle the centering pin (B, **Figure 13**) in the case.
5. Carefully install a new oil seal over the shift shaft and into the transmission case. Make sure the shift shaft splines do not damage the seal.
6. Install the washer (B, **Figure 12**) and a *new* snap ring (A) onto the shaft. Make sure the snap ring is correctly seated in the shaft.
7. Refer to the indexing marks made during removal and install the inner shift rod lever onto the end of the shift shaft. Push the lever on until its clamp bolt hole aligns with the shift shaft groove.
8. Install the shift rod lever clamp bolt (C, **Figure 11**) and tighten the bolt to 18-22 ft.-lb. (24.4-29.8 N•m).
9. Install the transmission side door assembly as described in this chapter.

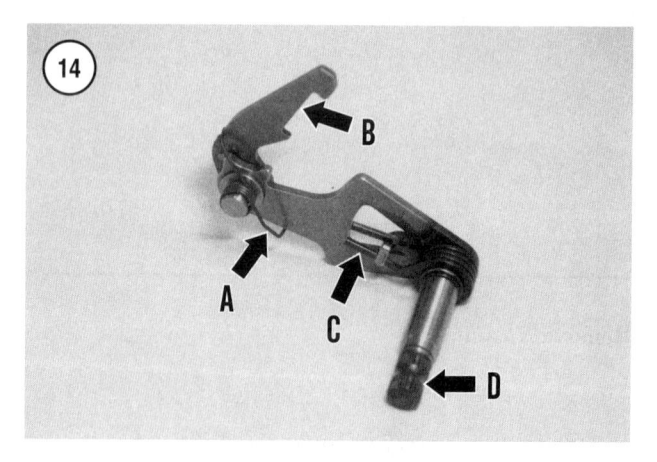

Inspection

Replace any part that is worn or damaged.
1. Check the shift pawl (B, **Figure 14**) for wear. Replace the shift shaft assembly if the pawl is damaged.

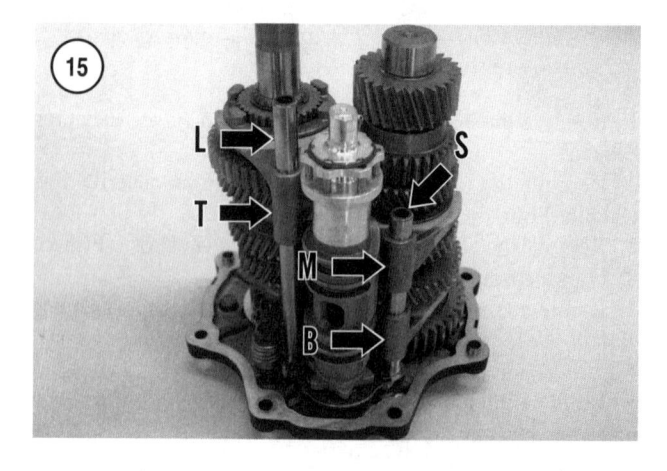

SIX SPEED TRANSMISSION (2007-2009 MODELS)

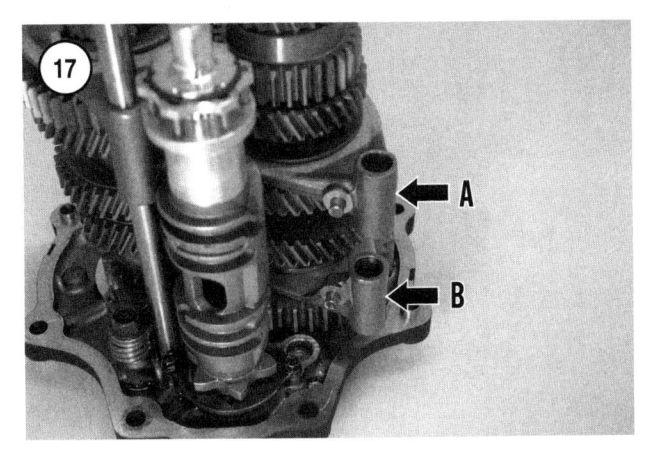

2. Check the shift shaft spring (A, **Figure 14**) and pawl return spring (C) for fatigue or damage.
3. Check the shift shaft for wear or damage. Make sure the end splines (D, **Figure 14**) are in good condition.
4. Check the inner shift rod lever (D, **Figure 11**) for wear or damage. Make sure the internal splines are in good condition.

SHIFT FORKS AND SHIFT CAM

The 6-speed shift fork shaft remover (JIMS part No. 985), a twist-type screw extractor, or an equivalent tool, is needed for this procedure.

Refer to **Figure 1**.

Removal

1. Remove the transmission side door assembly as described in this chapter.
2. If still installed, remove the clutch push rod from the mainshaft tunnel.

NOTE
Use a waterproof felt-tip pen or scribe and mark the installed position of each shift fork (T, M, B, Figure 15) as it sits in the transmission. Each shift fork is unique and must be reinstalled in the groove of a particular dog ring. Also mark the top of the long (L, Figure 15) or short (S) shift fork shafts so they can be reinstalled with the original orientation.

3. Carefully install the shift fork shaft remover (A, **Figure 16**) and remove the short shift fork shaft (B).
4. Remove the middle (3rd/4th gear) shift fork (A, **Figure 17**) and the bottom (1st/2nd gear) shift fork (B).
5. Carefully install the shift fork shaft remover (A, **Figure 18**), and remove the long shift fork shaft (B).
6. Remove the top (5th/6th gear) shift fork (**Figure 19**).
7. Remove the shift drum lock plate bolts (**Figure 20**), and remove the shift cam lock plate (**Figure 21**). Discard the bolts.

8. Use a flat-bladed screwdriver to gently push the detent arm (A, **Figure 22**) away from the shift cam.
9. Pull straight up and withdraw the shift cam (B, **Figure 22**) and bearing from the bore in transmission door.
10. If necessary, remove the detent arm assembly (A, **Figure 23**) by performing the following:
    a. Before removal, note how the lower arm of the detent spring engages the boss (B, **Figure 23**) in the side door. The assembly must be reinstalled so this arm engages the correct boss.
    b. Remove the detent arm pivot bolt (C, **Figure 23**) and remove the detent arm (D). Note how the upper arm of the detent spring passes through the hole in the detent arm.
    c. Remove the sleeve and the detent spring. Discard the pivot bolt.
11. Inspect all parts as described in this section.

Installation

NOTE
Refer to the marks made during removal and install each shift fork in the correct location.

1. Coat all bearing and sliding surfaces with transmission oil.
2. If removed, install the detent arm assembly (A, **Figure 23**) by performing the following:
    a. Assemble the detent arm with a *new* pivot bolt (C, **Figure 23**). Make sure the detent spring's upper arm engages the hole in the detent arm.
    b. Lower the assembly into the side door so the spring's lower arm engages the boss (B, **Figure 23**) noted during removal.
    c. Install the detent arm pivot bolt (C, **Figure 23**), and then tighten the bolt to 120-150 in.-lb. (13.6-17.0 N•m).
3. Move the detent arm out of the way, and hold it in this position.
4. Lower the shift cam (A, **Figure 24**) so it's bearing engages the bore (B) in transmission side door. Carefully push straight down on the shift cam (B, **Figure 22**) until

SIX SPEED TRANSMISSION (2007-2009 MODELS)

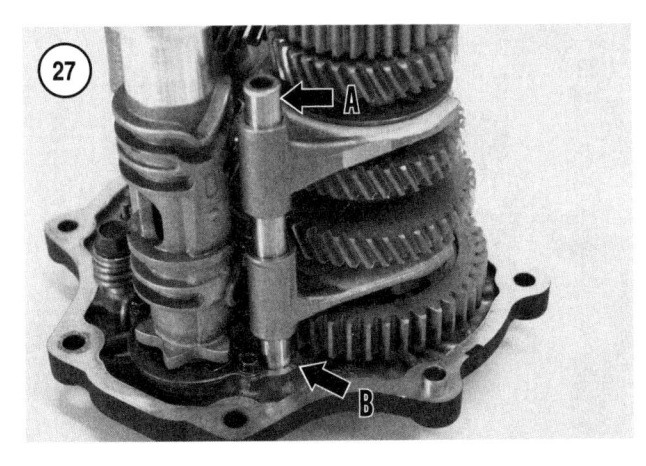

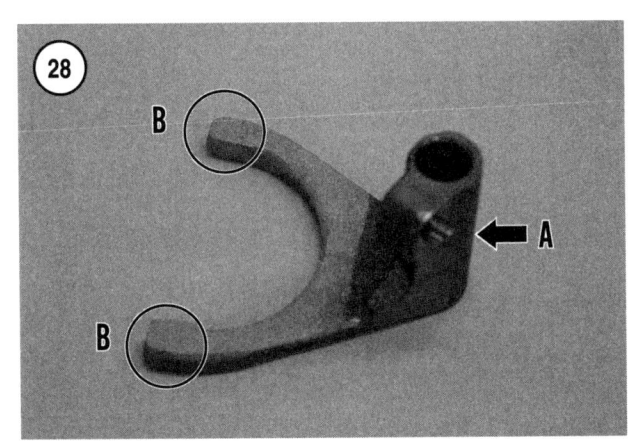

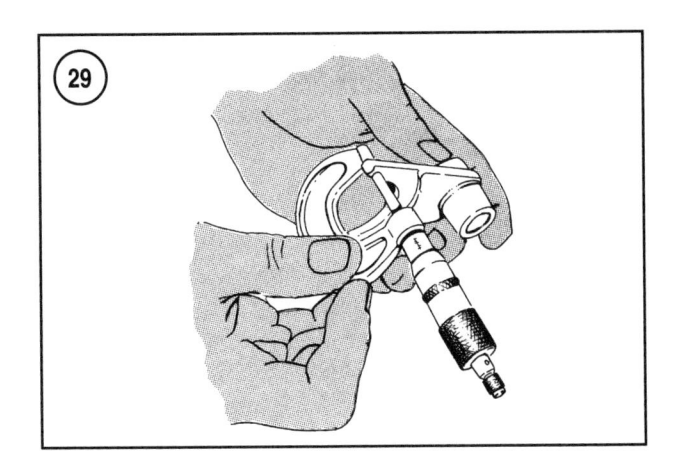

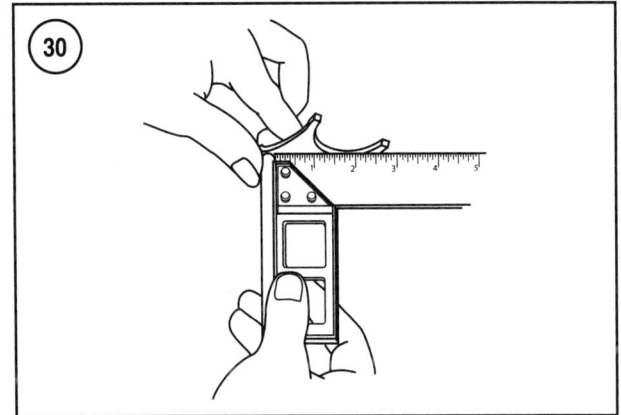

the bearing bottoms. Once the shift cam is correctly installed, release the detent arm onto the shift cam.

5. Install the shift cam lock plate (**Figure 21**) and install *new* lock plate bolts. Tighten the shift cam lock plate bolts (**Figure 20**) to 57-63 in.-lb. (6.4-7.1 N•m).

6. Install the top (5th/6th gear) shift fork (**Figure 19**) into the slot of the dog ring atop mainshaft 5th gear.

7. Move the shift fork into alignment with the shift-fork-shaft receptacle in the side door. Position the long shift fork shaft with the marked end facing up, and install it (**Figure 25**) through the shift fork and into the shaft receptacle in the side door (**Figure 26**). Tap the shaft in until it bottoms in the receptacle.

8. Install the bottom (1st/2nd gear) shift fork (B, **Figure 17**) into slot of the dog ring between countershaft 1st and 2nd gear.

9. Install the middle (3rd/4th gear) shift fork (A, **Figure 17**) into slot of the dog ring between countershaft 3rd and 4th gear.

10. Move the shift forks so the receptacles align with the shift-fork-shaft boss in the side door. Position the short shift fork shaft with the marked end facing up, and install it (A, **Figure 27**) through both shift forks and into the shaft receptacle (B) in the side door. Tap the shaft in until it bottoms in the receptacle.

11. The clutch pushrod will be installed in the mainshaft channel once the transmission side door assembly is installed in the transmission case.

Inspection

Replace any part that is worn, damaged or out of specification.

1. Inspect each shift fork (A, **Figure 28**) for excessive wear or damage. Replace worn or damaged shift forks as required.

2. Measure the thickness (**Figure 29**) of each shift fork finger (B, **Figure 28**) where it contacts the dog ring groove. Replace the shift fork if any finger is worn to the service limit (**Table 3**).

3. Inspect the shift forks for any arc-shaped wear or burn marks.

4. Place each shift fork and shaft along the side of a square (**Figure 30**) and check for bending.

5. Roll each shift fork shaft on a flat surface and check for bending.
6. Install each shift fork onto its shift shaft and slide it back and forth (**Figure 31**). Each shift fork must slide smoothly with no binding or tight spots.
7. Check the ramps (A, **Figure 32**) and the pins (B) on the shift cam for wear or damage.
8. Inspect the shift cam grooves (C, **Figure 32**) for wear or roughness.
9. Check that the bearing (D, **Figure 32**) is tight on the end of shift cam. Turn the bearing by hand. It must rotate freely with no binding. The bearing cannot be replaced separately.
10. Make sure the roller (A, **Figure 33**) on the detent arm turns freely.
11. Inspect the sleeve (B, **Figure 33**) for wear or roughness.
12. Inspect the detent spring (C, **Figure 33**) for cracks or other signs of fatigue.

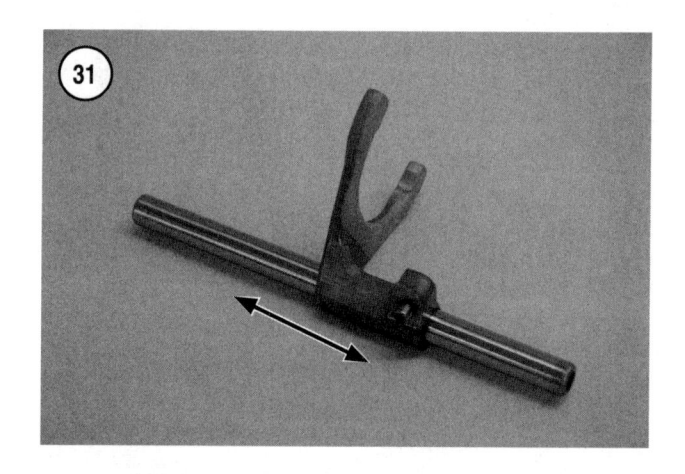

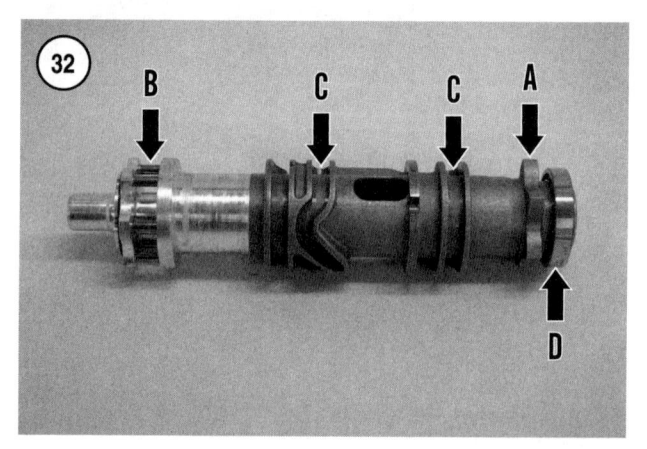

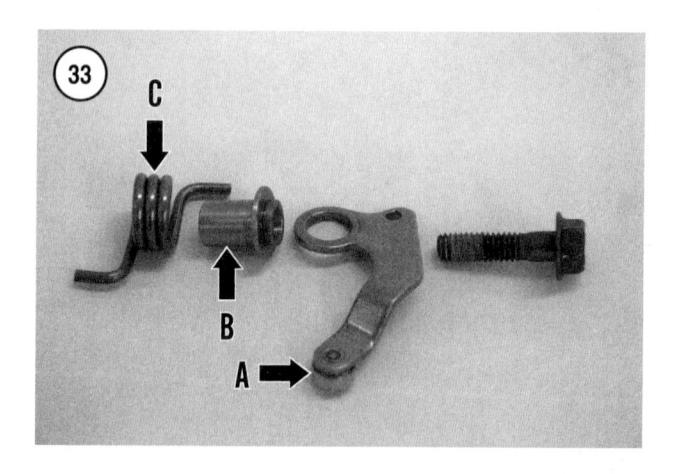

TRANSMISSION SIDE DOOR ASSEMBLY

Refer to **Figure 34**.

The transmission side door assembly includes the side door, mainshaft, countershaft, shift forks and shift cam. The transmission side door assembly can be serviced with the transmission case installed in the frame.

The following tools are used during side door assembly removal/installation or disassembly/assembly:
1. The mainshaft bearing race puller and installation tool (JIMS part No. 34902-84 or H-D part No. HD-34902-C).
2. The transmission main drive gear installer (JIMS part No. 981).
3. The transmission side door puller tool (JIMS part No. 984).
4. The transmission mainshaft pulley locknut socket (JIMS part No. 989).

Removal

1. Remove the exhaust system as described in Chapter Four.
2. Drain the transmission oil and the primary chaincase oil as described in Chapter Three.
3. Remove the transmission filler plug/dipstick (**Figure 35**). If left in place it will interfere with the removal of the transmission side door assembly.
4. Remove the primary chaincase housing and the clutch release cover as described in Chapter Six.
5. On all models except Screamin' Eagles, remove the oil slinger (**Figure 36**) from the mainshaft.
6. Withdraw the clutch pushrod (**Figure 37**).
7. Remove the bearing inner race (A, **Figure 38**) from the mainshaft as follows:
   a. Attach the mainshaft bearing race puller and installation tool (A, **Figure 39**) against the inner bearing race (B) following the tool manufacturer's instructions.
   b. Tighten the puller center bolt and withdraw the inner race (B, **Figure 39**) from the mainshaft (C).
   c. Remove the tool and the inner race.
   d. Tape the clutch splines (B, **Figure 38**) on the mainshaft so they will not damage the needle bearings in the main drive gear.
8. Remove the transmission cover as described in this chapter.
9. Lift the shift pawl (**Figure 40**) from the shift cam pins, and set it onto the transmission cover gasket surface.
10. If the transmission shaft assemblies will be removed from the side door, perform the following:
    a. Turn the transmission by hand and shift the transmission into 6th gear to keep the shafts from turning.
    b. Loosen, but do not remove, the countershaft (A, **Figure 41**) and mainshaft (B) locknuts.

SIX SPEED TRANSMISSION (2007-2009 MODELS)

TRANSMISSION CASE BEARINGS AND COVERS

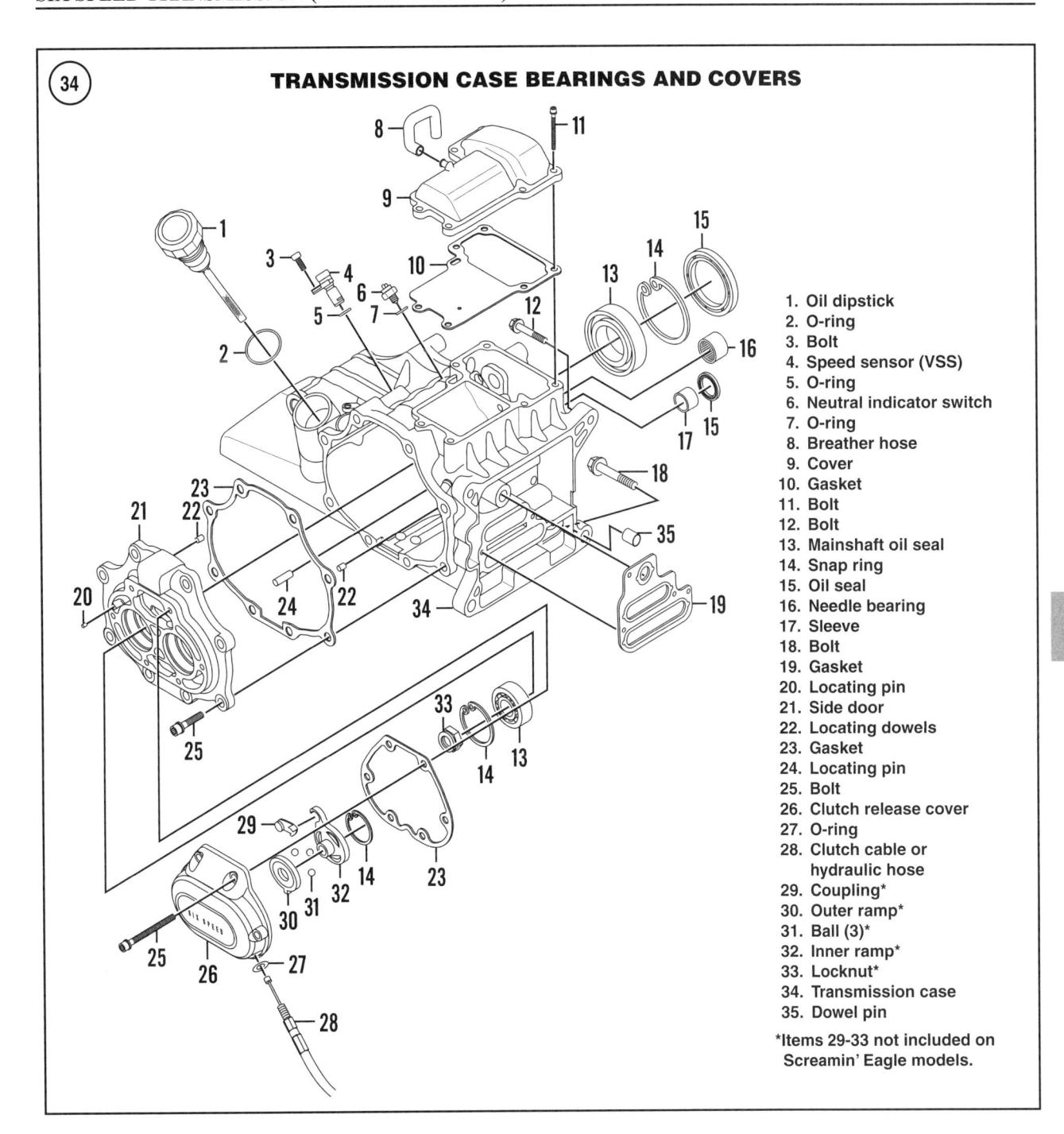

1. Oil dipstick
2. O-ring
3. Bolt
4. Speed sensor (VSS)
5. O-ring
6. Neutral indicator switch
7. O-ring
8. Breather hose
9. Cover
10. Gasket
11. Bolt
12. Bolt
13. Mainshaft oil seal
14. Snap ring
15. Oil seal
16. Needle bearing
17. Sleeve
18. Bolt
19. Gasket
20. Locating pin
21. Side door
22. Locating dowels
23. Gasket
24. Locating pin
25. Bolt
26. Clutch release cover
27. O-ring
28. Clutch cable or hydraulic hose
29. Coupling*
30. Outer ramp*
31. Ball (3)*
32. Inner ramp*
33. Locknut*
34. Transmission case
35. Dowel pin

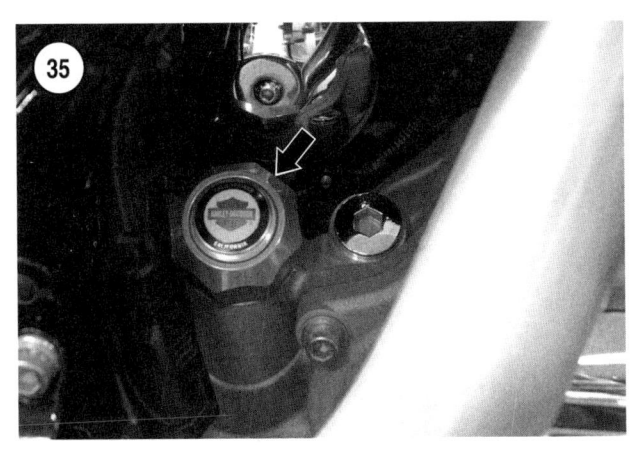

*Items 29-33 not included on Screamin' Eagle models.

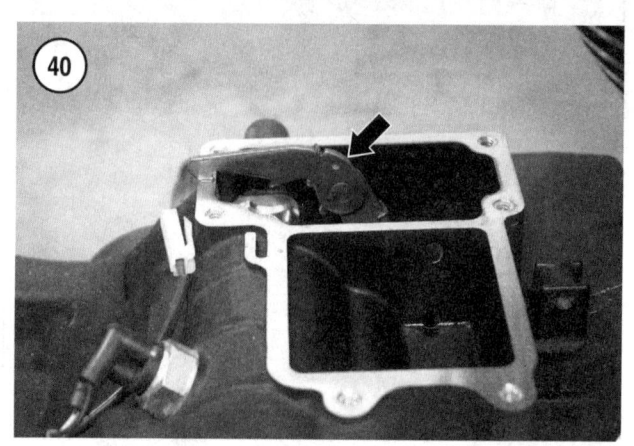

11. If the main drive gear is going to be removed, remove the transmission drive sprocket as described in this chapter.

NOTE
*There are two different length side door bolts. The two longer bolts (C, **Figure 41**) are located in the bottom two holes of the side door.*

12. Using a crossing pattern, evenly loosen the side door bolts, and then remove the bolts.

CAUTION
*When removing the transmission side door (D, **Figure 41**), do not tap against the mainshaft from the opposite side. This will damage the side door bearings.*

13A. Install the transmission side door puller (**Figure 42**) onto the side door following the tool manufacturer's instructions. Tighten the outside screws one-half turn at a time, alternating from side-to-side until the side door releases from the transmission case. Remove the tool.

13B. If the remover tool is not available, use a soft-face mallet, and carefully tap against the transmission side door to loosen its seal against the transmission case. If necessary, insert a large, flat-bladed screwdriver into the pry points (**Figure 43**) and work the door loose (**Figure 44**).

14. Slowly withdraw the transmission side door assembly and the transmission shafts (**Figure 45**) from the trans-

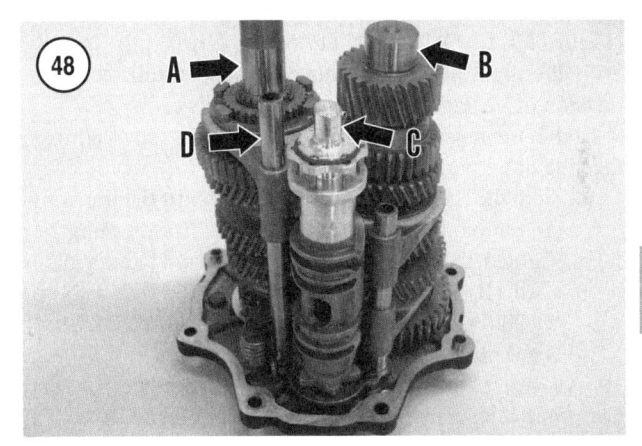

SIX SPEED TRANSMISSION (2007-2009 MODELS)

mission case, and then remove it. Do not lose the locating dowels behind the side door.

15. Remove and discard the transmission side door gasket.
16. If necessary, service the side door and transmission assembly as described in *Transmission Shafts* (this chapter).

Installation

1. If the main drive gear was removed, install it as described in this chapter.
2. Remove all gasket residue from mating surfaces of the side door and transmission case.
3. If removed install the dowels, and then install a *new* side-door gasket onto the transmission case.
4. Wrap the clutch splines (B, **Figure 38**) on the mainshaft with tape to protect the main drive gear needle bearings and oil seal during installation.
5. Apply clean transmission oil to the following:
   a. The main drive gear small oil seal (A, **Figure 46**), the outer needle bearing (B) and the inner needle bearing (A, **Figure 47**).
   b. The countershaft needle bearings (B, **Figure 47**).
   c. The journals on the mainshaft (A, **Figure 48**), countershaft (B), and the shift cam (C).
   d. The end of the long shift fork shaft (D, **Figure 48**).
6. Slowly and carefully slide the side door assembly into the transmission case (**Figure 45**) so the mainshaft passes through the main drive gear needle bearings (A, **Figure**

47), and the countershaft seats in its needle bearing (B). Also, make sure the shift cam seats in its transmission case receptacle (A, **Figure 49**) and that the long shift fork shaft sits in its receptacle (B). Check all of these items if the side door does not seat directly against the transmission case.

NOTE
*There are two different length side door bolts. The two longer bolts (C, **Figure 41**) are located in the bottom two holes of the side door.*

7. Install the two longer side door bolts and captive washers and finger-tighten the bolts. Install the remaining six shorter bolts and finger-tighten the bolts. Tighten the transmission side door bolts evenly in the sequence shown (**Figure 50**) to 13-18 ft.-lb. (17.6-24.4 N•m).
8. If the main drive gear was removed, install the transmission drive sprocket as described in this chapter.
9. If the transmission shaft assemblies were removed from the side door, perform the following:
    a. Turn the transmission by hand and shift the transmission into 6th gear to keep the gears from turning.
    b. Tighten the countershaft (A, **Figure 41**) and mainshaft (B) locknuts to 45-55 ft.-lb. (61.0-74.6 N•m) on 2007-2008 models or to 55-65 ft.-lb. (74.6-88.1 N•m) on 2009 models.
10. Move the shift pawl forward and lower the free end down onto engagement with the shift cam pins.
11. Install the transmission cover as described in this chapter.
12. Install the mainshaft bearing inner race (A, **Figure 38**) onto the mainshaft by performing the following:
    a. Assemble the mainshaft bearing race puller and installation tool according to the tool manufacturer's instructions.
    b. Apply clean oil to the mainshaft shaft bearing surface, shaft threads and to the inner surface of the inner race.
    c. Position the bearing inner race with the chamfered end goes on first. Slide the bearing inner race onto the mainshaft until it stops prior to being pressed on.
    d. Thread the extension shaft (A, **Figure 51**) onto the mainshaft.
    e. Place the pusher tube (B, **Figure 51**) over the extension shaft, add the two flat washers (C). Thread on the nut (D, **Figure 51**) and hand tighten securely against the flat washers.

CAUTION
Install the inner bearing race to the dimension listed. This aligns the race with the bearing outer race installed in the primary chaincase. Installing the wrong race or installing it incorrectly will damage the bearing and race assembly.

    f. Secure the extension shaft (A, **Figure 51**) and tighten the nut (D) to press the bearing inner race onto the mainshaft. Install the race so that it's inside edge is 0.100-0.125 in. (2.540-3.180 mm) away from the main drive gear.
    g. Remove the tools.
13. Install the clutch pushrod (**Figure 37**) into the mainshaft.
14. On all models except Screamin' Eagle, install the oil slinger assembly (**Figure 36**) into the mainshaft.
15. Install the primary chaincase housing, primary drive and clutch release cover as described in Chapter Six.
16. Install the drain plugs, and add oil to the transmission and to the primary chaincase described in Chapter Three.

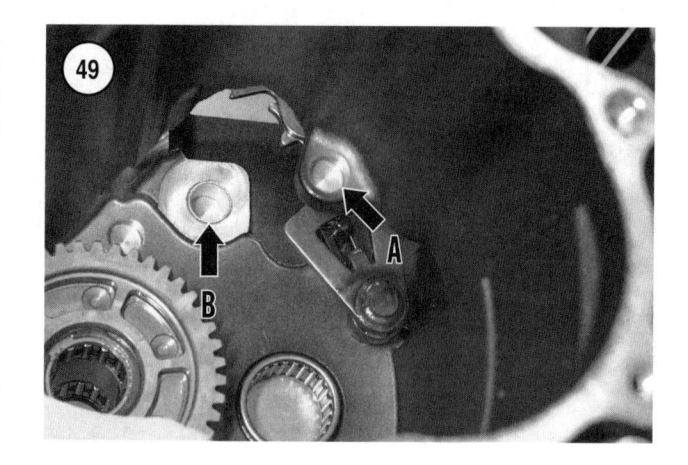

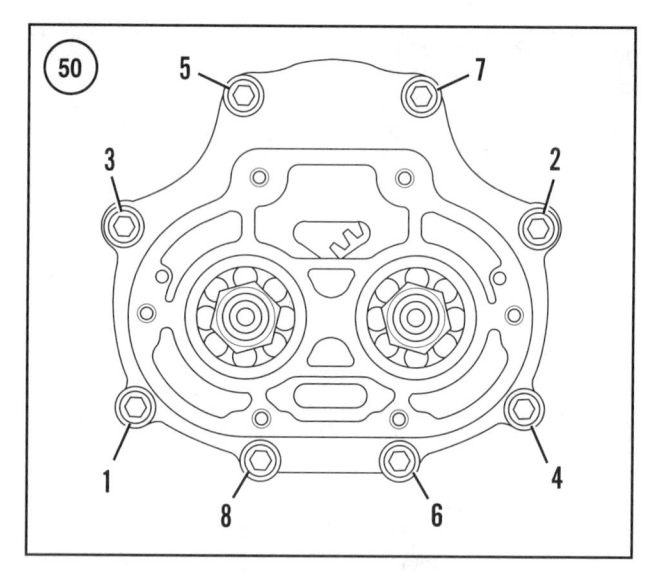

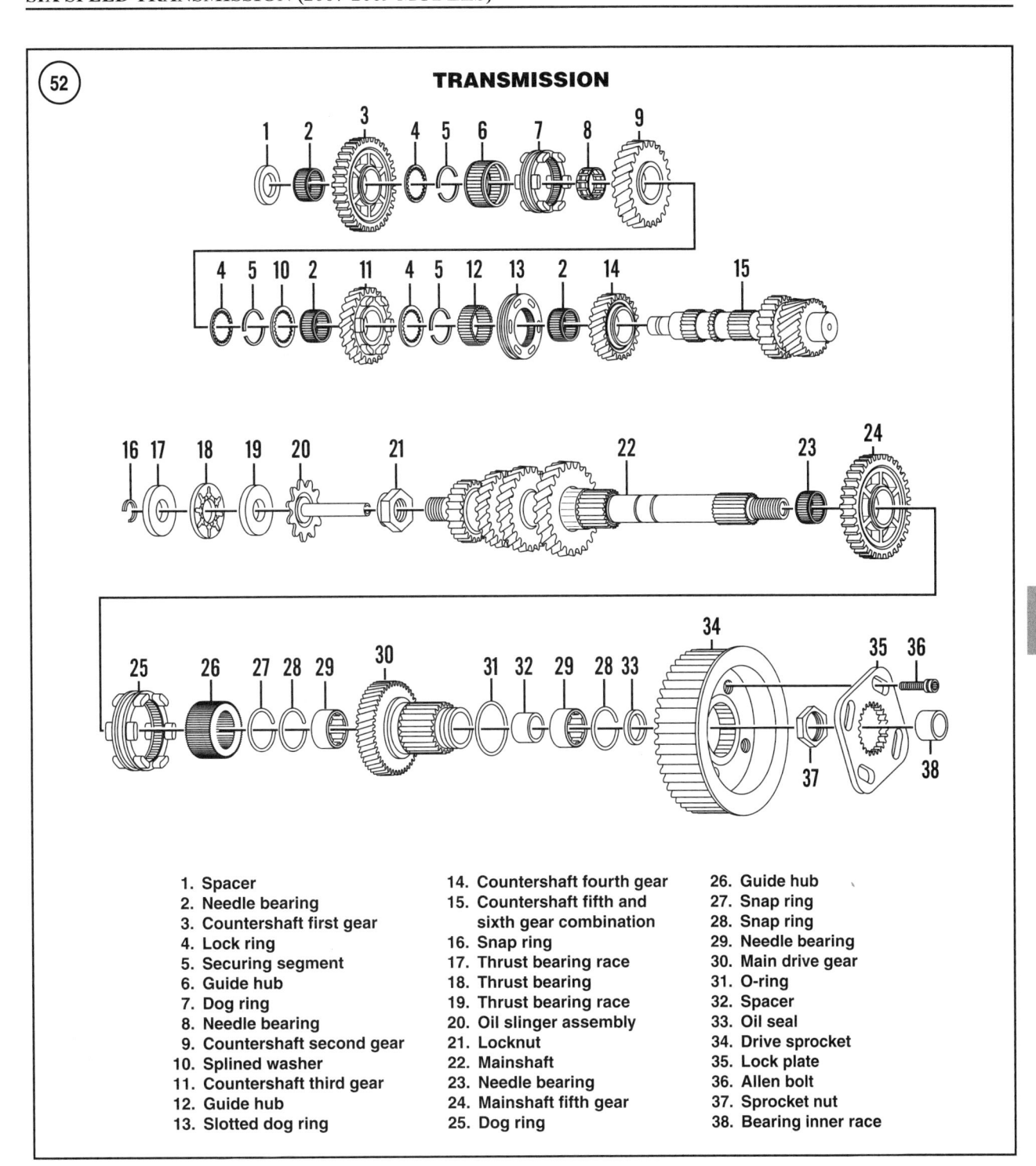

SIX SPEED TRANSMISSION (2007-2009 MODELS)

52 **TRANSMISSION**

1. Spacer
2. Needle bearing
3. Countershaft first gear
4. Lock ring
5. Securing segment
6. Guide hub
7. Dog ring
8. Needle bearing
9. Countershaft second gear
10. Splined washer
11. Countershaft third gear
12. Guide hub
13. Slotted dog ring
14. Countershaft fourth gear
15. Countershaft fifth and sixth gear combination
16. Snap ring
17. Thrust bearing race
18. Thrust bearing
19. Thrust bearing race
20. Oil slinger assembly
21. Locknut
22. Mainshaft
23. Needle bearing
24. Mainshaft fifth gear
25. Dog ring
26. Guide hub
27. Snap ring
28. Snap ring
29. Needle bearing
30. Main drive gear
31. O-ring
32. Spacer
33. Oil seal
34. Drive sprocket
35. Lock plate
36. Allen bolt
37. Sprocket nut
38. Bearing inner race

17. Install the transmission filler plug/dipstick (**Figure 35**).
18. Install the exhaust system as described in Chapter Four.
19. Test-ride the motorcycle slowly and check for proper transmission operation.

TRANSMISSION SHAFTS

The snap rings are very difficult to loosen and remove even with high quality snap ring pliers. It is recommended that heavy-duty retaining ring pliers (H-D part No. J-5586), or an equivalent, be used.

Store all of the transmission gears, snap rings, washers and split bearings in their order of removal.

Refer to **Figure 52**.

Mainshaft Disassembly

First, second, third and forth gears are an integral part of the mainshaft assembly and cannot be replaced separately. If any one of these is damaged, the mainshaft must be replaced.

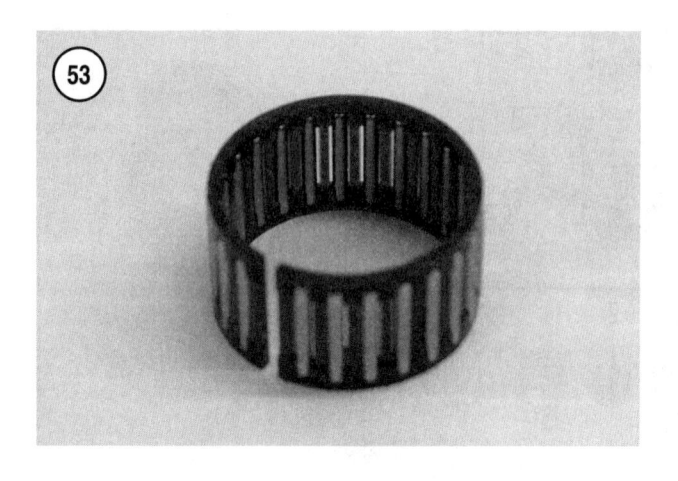

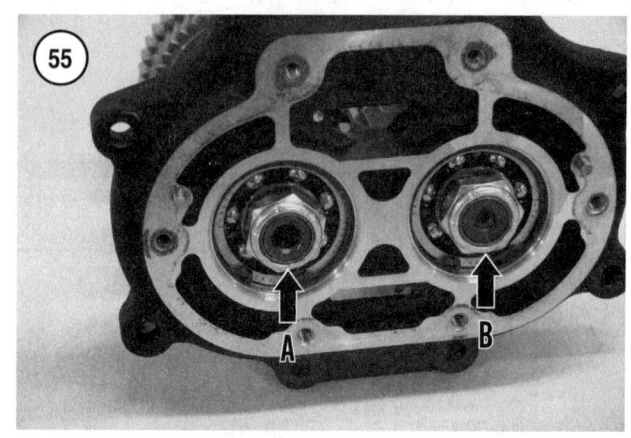

NOTE
*The mainshaft needle bearings are split bearings (**Figure 53**) and must be partially opened during removal. Doing so weakens the plastic cage securing the needles. Discard all removed needle bearings and always install new bearings during assembly.*

1. Remove the transmission side door assembly, the shift forks and the shift cam as described in this chapter.
2. If still in place, remove the dowels (**Figure 54**) from the inboard side of the side door.
3. Remove the locknut (A, **Figure 55**) from the right end of the mainshaft. If the countershaft will also be serviced, remove the locknut (B, **Figure 55**) from the countershaft.
4. Remove the snap ring (**Figure 56**) from the left end of the mainshaft.
5. Slide the dog ring (A, **Figure 57**) and its guide hub (B) from the mainshaft.
6. Remove fifth gear (A, **Figure 58**) from the mainshaft.
7. Remove fifth gear needle bearing (**Figure 59**).
8. Place the transmission assembly on the hydraulic press with the side door (A, **Figure 60**) facing up. Make sure the side door lies flat on the press bed.

CAUTION
Do not apply pressure on the bearing inner race as the bearing and/or side door will be damaged.

9. Place an appropriate size mandrel or socket (B, **Figure 60**) onto the end of the mainshaft.
10. Secure the lower end of the mainshaft assembly, and slowly press the assembly out of the side door bearing. Carefully guide the mainshaft gears past the countershaft gears.
11. If the countershaft also requires service, remove it as described in *Countershaft Disassembly* (this section).

NOTE
Replace the side door bearing whenever the shaft(s) is removed.

12. Replace the side door bearing as described in this chatper.
13. Inspect all parts (**Figure 61**) as described in this section.

SIX SPEED TRANSMISSION (2007-2009 MODELS)

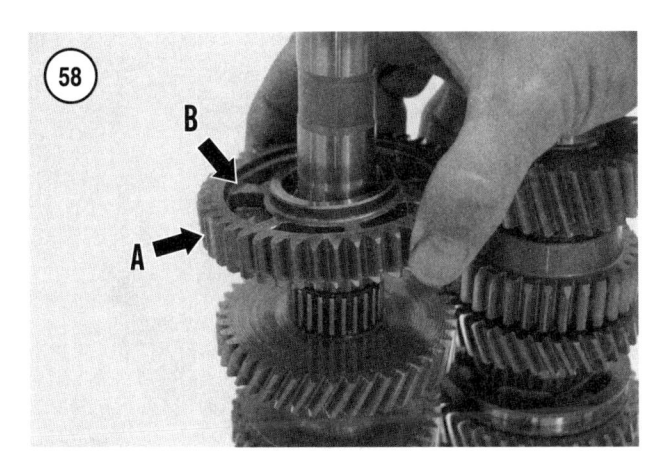

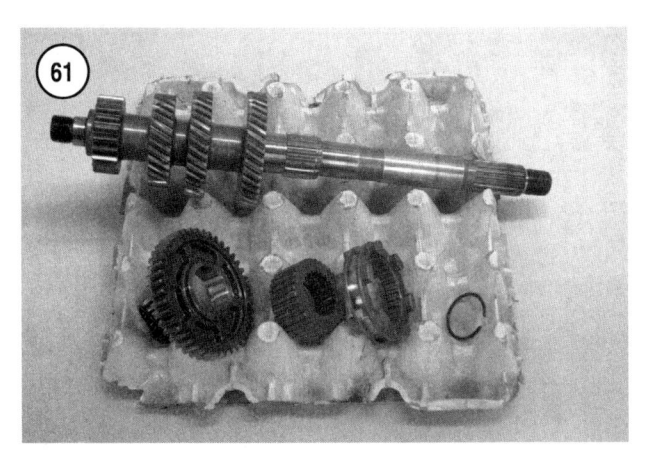

Mainshaft Assembly

CAUTION
*Install a new snap ring to ensure proper gear alignment and engagement. Never reinstall a snap ring that has been removed since it has become distorted and weakened and may fail. Make sure the **new** snap ring is correctly seated in its respective shaft groove.*

1. If the countershaft was serviced, install it into the side door as described in *Countershaft Assembly* (this section).
2. Apply a light coat of clean transmission oil to the side door bearing inner race and to the mainshaft bearing surface.
3. Place the mainshaft on the press plate supported by fourth gear.
4. Place the side door and countershaft assembly next to the mainshaft, and align both transmission shaft assemblies.
5. Position the countershaft so it clears the press bed. Have an assistant secure both shaft assemblies in this position.

CAUTION
*The countershaft dog ring (A, **Figure 62**) must be fully engaged with countershaft third gear (B). Failure to do so will push the shafts out of alignment and cause damage to the bearings and gears on both shafts. Do **not** press the side door onto the mainshaft while this dog ring engages countershaft fourth gear.*

6. Have the assistant lift the countershaft dog ring (A, **Figure 62**) up so it is fully engaged with countershaft third gear (B) during the mainshaft assembly procedure.
7. Place an appropriate size mandrel or socket (**Figure 63**) onto the side door bearing inner race. The outer diameter of the mandrel or socket must only rest on the inner race of the side door bearing.
8. Slowly press the side door bearing onto the mainshaft until the bearing inner race contacts mainshaft first gear. The gear must contact the bearing inner race to ensure correct alignment between both shaft assemblies.
9. Release ram pressure, and remove the side door assembly from the press bed.

10. Slowly rotate both shaft assemblies within the side door (**Figure 64**) to ensure the gears are aligned correctly. Do not spin too hard as the locknuts are not in place.

11. Install a *new* needle bearing (**Figure 59**) onto the mainshaft. Make sure it is seated correctly on the shaft.

12. Position mainshaft fifth gear (A, **Figure 58**) with the dog ring slot side (B) going on last and install the fifth gear.

13. Position the guide hub (**Figure 65**) with the counter bored end going on first (facing fifth gear with the flat side facing out), and then install the guide hub.

14. Install the dog ring (A, **Figure 57**) onto fifth gear and make sure it is correctly seated.

15. Install a *new* snap ring (A, **Figure 56**). Make sure it is seated correctly in the mainshaft groove.

16. Refer to **Figure 66** to ensure the correct placement of the gears. Also check that the gears mesh properly with an adjoining gear where applicable. This is the last opportunity to check the shaft assemblies before they are installed into the transmission case.

CAUTION
The transmission shaft assembly must be installed in the transmission case prior to tightening the locknuts to achieve for correct alignment. The side door bearings can be damaged if the locknuts are tightened while the assembly is on the bench.

17. If removed, install the dowels (**Figure 54**) into the inboard side of the transmission door.

18. Use the dog rings to lock the two shafts together, and temporarily install the side door and transmission assembly into the transmission case.

19. Thread a *new* locknut on the mainshaft (A, **Figure 55**) and the countershaft (B).

20. Tighten each locknut (**Figure 67**) to 45-55 ft.-lb. (61.0-74.6 N•m) on 2007-2008 models or to 55-65 ft.-lb. (74.6-88.1 N•m) on 2009 models.

21. Remove the side door assembly, and install the shift forks and the shift cam as described in this chapter.

22. Install the transmission side door assembly as described in this chapter.

SIX SPEED TRANSMISSION (2007-2009 MODELS)

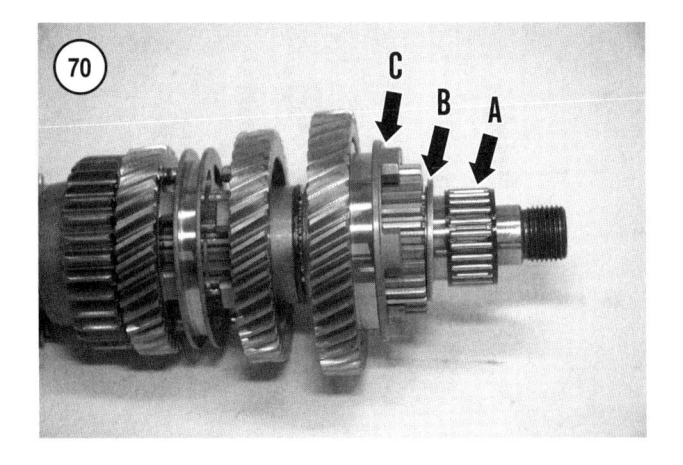

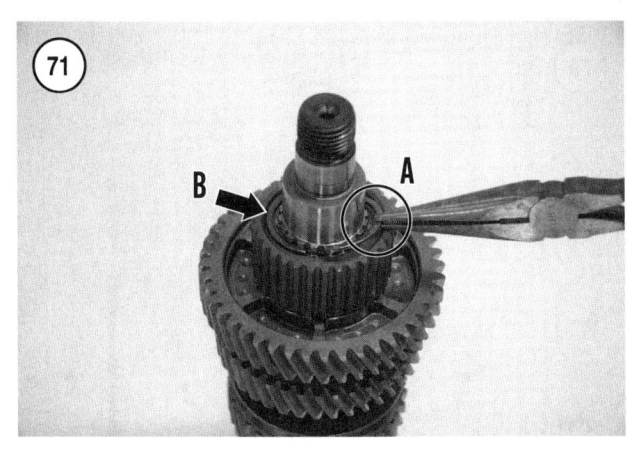

Countershaft Disassembly

Fifth and sixth gear are an integral part of the countershaft assembly and cannot be replaced separately. If either of these gears is damaged, the countershaft must be replaced.

NOTE
The countershaft needle bearings are split bearings (Figure 53) and must be partially opened during removal. Doing so weakens the plastic cage securing the needles. Discard all removed needle bearings and always install new bearings during assembly.

1. Remove the transmission side door assembly, shift forks and shift cam as described in this chapter.
2. Press the mainshaft from the side door as described in *Mainshaft Disassembly* (this section).
3. Remove the locknut (B, **Figure 55**) from the right side of the countershaft.
4. Place the transmission assembly in the hydraulic press with the side door (A, **Figure 68**) facing up. Make sure the side door lies flat on the press bed.

CAUTION
Do not apply pressure to the bearing inner race as the bearing and/or side door will be damaged.

5. Place an appropriate size mandrel or socket (B, **Figure 68**) onto the end of the countershaft.
6. Secure the lower end of the countershaft assembly, and slowly press the countershaft out of the side door bearing.
7. Remove the side door and countershaft assembly from the press bed.
8. Remove the spacer (A, **Figure 69**) and first gear (B) from the side door end of the countershaft.
9. Remove the needle bearing (A, **Figure 70**), the lock ring (B), and the dog ring (C).
10. Remove both securing segments (A, **Figure 71**) from the guide hub counter bore (B).
11. Remove the guide hub (A, **Figure 72**).
12. Remove second gear (A, **Figure 73**) and its needle bearing (**Figure 74**) from the shaft.

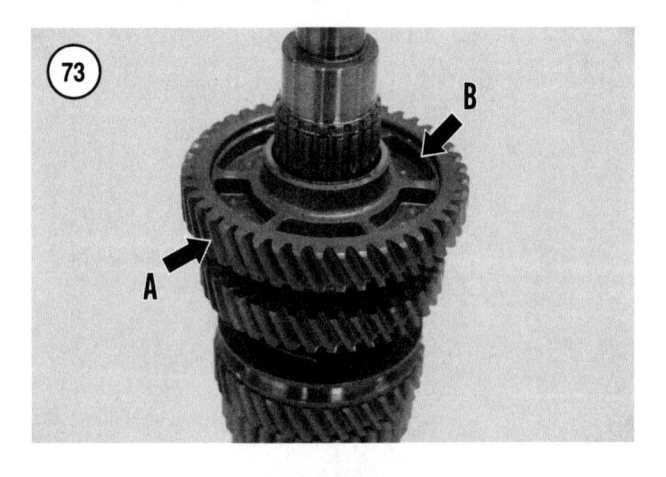

13. Remove the lock ring (**Figure 75**), both securing segments (**Figure 76**) and the splined washer (**Figure 77**) from the shaft.
14. Remove third gear (A, **Figure 78**) and its needle bearing (**Figure 79**) from the countershaft.
15. Remove the lock ring (**Figure 80**).
16. Remove both securing segments (**Figure 81**) and the slotted dog ring (**Figure 82**) from the shaft.
17. Remove the guide hub (A, **Figure 83**) and fourth gear (B).
18. Remove fourth gear needle bearing (**Figure 84**).
19. Replace the side door bearings as described in this chapter.
20. Inspect all parts (**Figure 85**) as described in this section.

SIX SPEED TRANSMISSION (2007-2009 MODELS) 331

Countershaft Assembly

1. Apply a light coat of clean transmission oil to all sliding surfaces and needle bearings.
2. Install a *new* needle bearing (**Figure 84**). Make sure it is seated correctly on the shaft.
3. Position countershaft fourth gear with the shift dogs (C, **Figure 83**) facing up, and then install countershaft fourth gear (B).
4. Install the guide hub (A, **Figure 83**) and the slotted dog ring (**Figure 82**).
5. Install both securing segments (**Figure 81**) so their straight sides face the guide hub. Each segment must be completely seated in the shaft groove.

NOTE
When installing lock rings next to securing segments, make sure the shouldered side of the lock ring faces and surrounds the securing segments. The parts are properly installed when the securing segments are nested within the lock ring.

6. Position the lock ring (**Figure 80**) so its shouldered side faces and surrounds the securing segments. Install the lock ring.
7. Install a *new* needle bearing (**Figure 79**). Make sure it is seated correctly on the shaft.

8. Position countershaft third gear with the shouldered side (B, **Figure 78**) faces out, and install the third gear (A).
9. Install the spline washer (**Figure 77**).
10. Seat both securing segments (**Figure 76**) in the shaft groove so their straight sides face the splined washer.
11. Position the lock ring (**Figure 75**) so it's shouldered side faces and surrounds the securing segments. Install the lock ring.
12. Install a *new* needle bearing (**Figure 74**). Make sure it is seated correctly on the shaft.
13. Position second gear so its engagement slots (B, **Figure 73**) face out, and then install second gear (A).
14. Position the guide hub with the recessed side (B, **Figure 72**) facing out. Install the guide hub (A, **Figure 72**).
15. Seat both securing segments (**Figure 71**) in the guide hub so their straight sides face the hub.
16. Install the dog ring (**Figure 86**) onto the guide hub.
17. Position the lock ring (B, **Figure 70**) so it's shouldered side faces and surrounds the securing segments. Install the lock ring.
18. Install a *new* needle bearing (A, **Figure 70**). Make sure it is seated correctly on the shaft.
19. Position countershaft first gear so its engagement slots face the dog ring, and then install countershaft first gear (B, **Figure 69**).
20. Install the spacer (A, **Figure 69**).
21. Refer to **Figure 87** to ensure all gears are in the correct location.

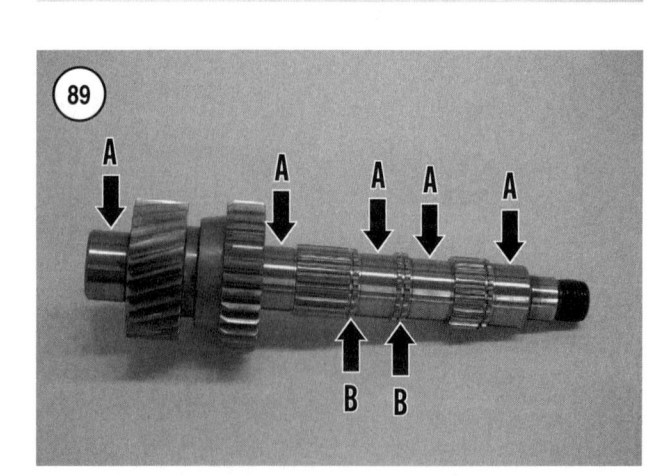

Transmission Inspection

Maintain the alignment of the transmission components when cleaning and inspecting the individual parts in the following section. To prevent mixing parts, work on only one shaft at a time.

Refer to **Table 2** when inspecting the service clearance and end play of the indicated gears and shafts. Replace parts that are worn, damaged or out of specification.

1. Clean and dry the shaft assemblies.
2. Inspect the mainshaft (**Figure 88**) and countershaft (**Figure 89**) for:
   a. Worn or damaged splines (A, **Figure 88**).

SIX SPEED TRANSMISSION (2007-2009 MODELS)

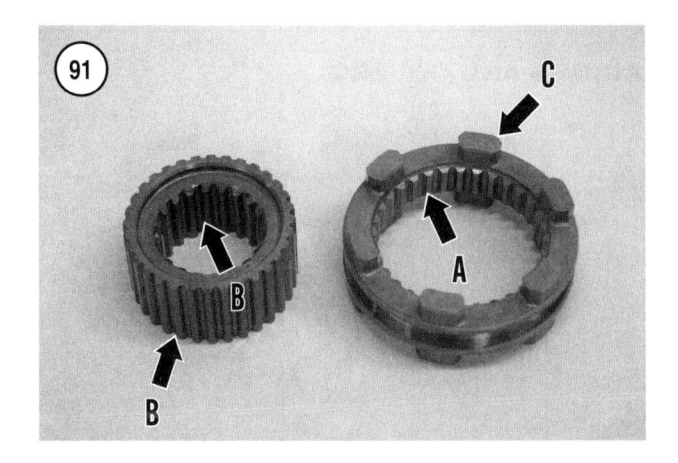

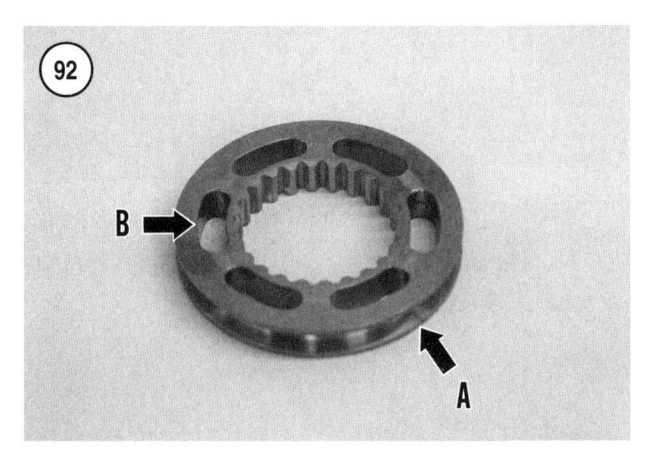

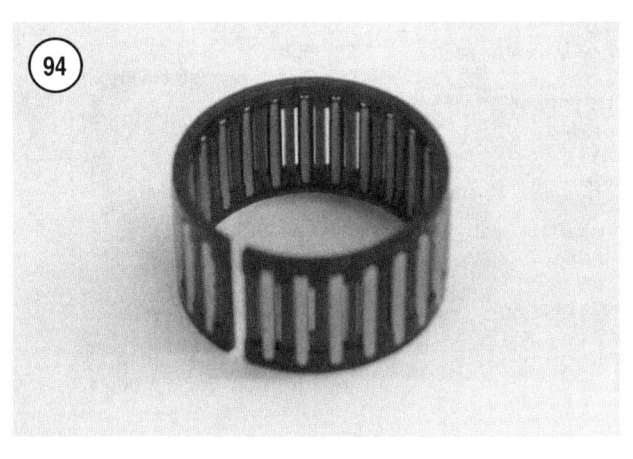

b. Excessively worn or damaged bearing surfaces (A, **Figure 89**).
c. Cracked or rounded-off securing segment grooves (B, **Figure 89**).
d. Worn or damaged threads (B, **Figure 88**).

3. Check each gear for excessive wear, burrs, pitting, or chipped or missing teeth (A, **Figure 90**).
4. Check the gear bearing surface (B, **Figure 90**) for wear, cracks or other damage.
5. To check gears for wear, install them on their correct shaft and in the original operating position. If necessary, use the old snap rings to secure them in place. Then, spin the gear by hand. The gear should turn smoothly. A rough turning gear indicates heat damage–check for a dark bluish coloring or galling on the operating surfaces. Rocking indicates excessive wear, either to the gear or shaft or both.
6. Check for excessive wear or damage on the inner splines of the dog rings (A, **Figure 91**) and on the inner and outer splines of the guide hubs (B).
7. To check the dog rings and guide hubs, install them onto their correct shaft and in their original operating position. They should slide back and fourth without any binding or excessive play.
8. Check the shift fork groove on each dog ring (A, **Figure 92**) for wear or damage.

NOTE
*If there is excessive or uneven wear to the gear engagement dogs, check the shift forks carefully for bending and other damage. Refer to **Shift Assembly** in this chapter.*

9. Check the dogs on the gears (**Figure 93**) and dog rings (C, **Figure 91**) for excessive wear, rounding, cracks or other damage. When wear is noticeable, make sure it is consistent on each gear dog. If one dog is worn more than the others, the others will be overstressed during operation and will eventually crack and fail.
10. Check each engagement slot in the gears (C, **Figure 90**) and slotted dog ring (B, **Figure 92**) for cracks, rounding and other damage.

NOTE
Replace defective gears along with their mating gears, though they may not show as much wear or damage.

11. Check engaging gears by installing the two gears on their respective shaft and in their original operating position. Mesh the gears together. Twist one gear against the other, and then check the dog engagement. Then, reverse the thrust load to check in the other operating position. Make sure the engagement in both directions is positive and without any slippage. Check that there is equal engagement across all of the engagement dogs.
12. Check the split bearings (**Figure 94**) for excessive wear or damage. Replace all of the split bearings during re-assembly.

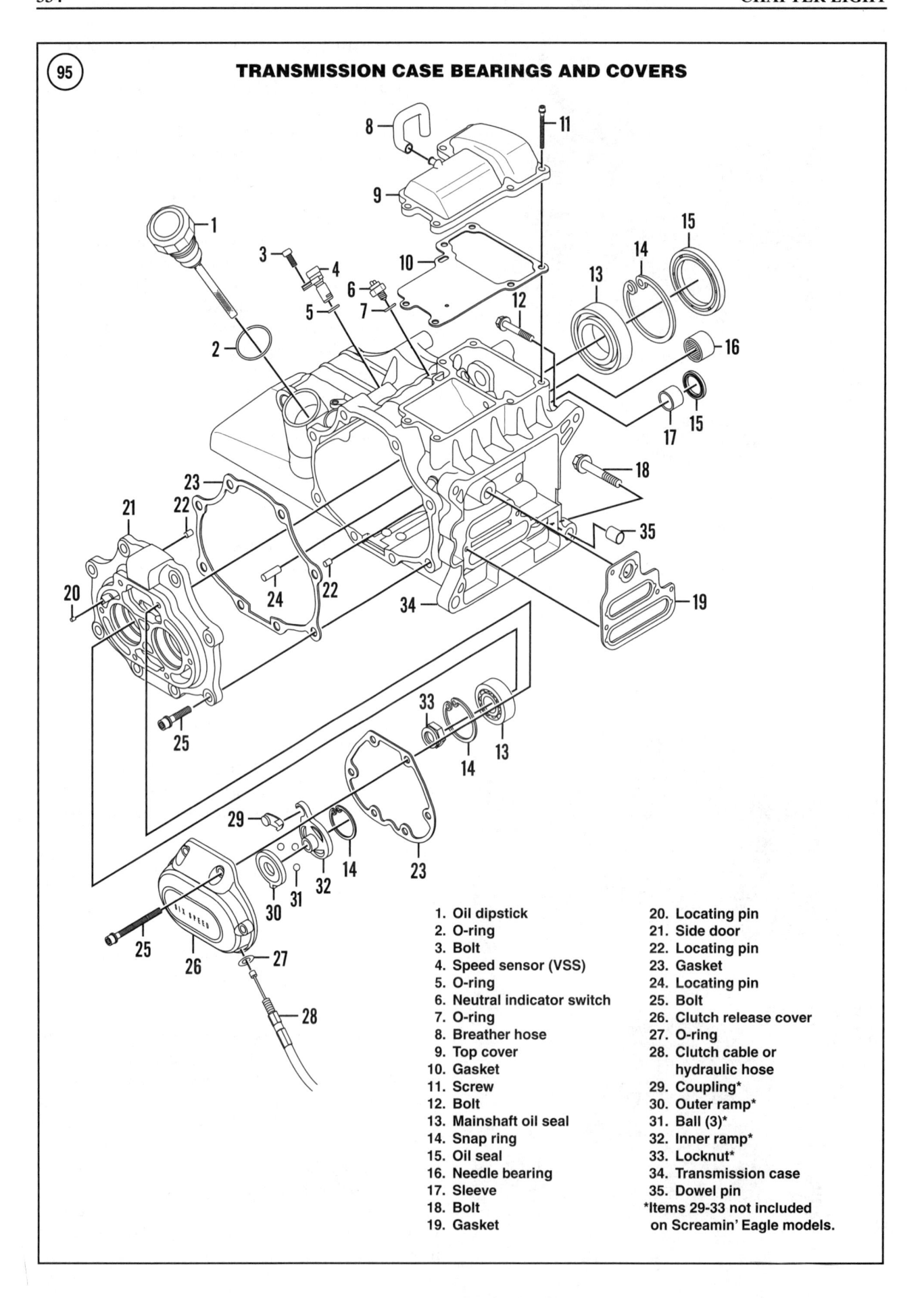

TRANSMISSION CASE BEARINGS AND COVERS

1. Oil dipstick
2. O-ring
3. Bolt
4. Speed sensor (VSS)
5. O-ring
6. Neutral indicator switch
7. O-ring
8. Breather hose
9. Top cover
10. Gasket
11. Screw
12. Bolt
13. Mainshaft oil seal
14. Snap ring
15. Oil seal
16. Needle bearing
17. Sleeve
18. Bolt
19. Gasket
20. Locating pin
21. Side door
22. Locating pin
23. Gasket
24. Locating pin
25. Bolt
26. Clutch release cover
27. O-ring
28. Clutch cable or hydraulic hose
29. Coupling*
30. Outer ramp*
31. Ball (3)*
32. Inner ramp*
33. Locknut*
34. Transmission case
35. Dowel pin

*Items 29-33 not included on Screamin' Eagle models.

SIX SPEED TRANSMISSION (2007-2009 MODELS)

13. Replace all of the snap rings during re-assembly. In addition, check the washers for burn marks, scoring or cracks. Replace the washers as necessary.
14. Check the spacers for wear or damage.
15. Check the securing segments for cracks, wear or other damage.

SIDE DOOR BEARINGS

Replacement

The side door bearings (**Figure 95**) are pressed into place and secured with a snap ring. They can be removed and installed using the transmission door bearing remover and installer (JIMS part No. 1078). If the tool set is not available, a press is required.

Replace the side door bearings whenever the transmission shafts have been removed.

1. Clean the side door and bearings in solvent, and dry them with compressed air.
2. Remove each snap ring (**Figure 96**) from the outer surface of the side door.
3A. If the tool set is used, follow the tool manufacturer's instructions and remove the bearings.
3B. If a press is used, perform the following:
   a. Support the side door on the press bed with its inner surface facing up.
   b. Use a driver or socket that matches the diameter of the bearing inner races, and press the bearing out of the side-door bore (**Figure 97**).
   c. Repeat the process to remove the opposite bearing.
4. Clean the side door again in solvent and dry thoroughly.
5. Inspect the bearing bores in the side cover for cracks or other damage. Replace the side door if damaged.

NOTE
Both side door bearings have the same part number.

6A. If the tool set is used, follow the tool manufacturer's instructions and install the bearings.
6B. If a press is used, perform the following:
   a. Support the side door in a press with its outer surface acing up.
   b. Center the bearing in the bore so the side with the manufacturer's marks faces up.
   c. Using a driver that presses against the bearing outer race, press the bearing (**Figure 98**) into the bore until it bottoms.
   d. Repeat the process to install the opposite bearing.
7. Install *new* snap rings so the side with the sharp edge faces the bearing outer race. Make sure the snap rings (**Figure 99**) are correctly seated in the side door groove.

MAIN DRIVE GEAR

The main drive gear assembly (**Figure 100**) is pressed into the transmission case. Whenever the main drive gear

100) MAIN DRIVE GEAR

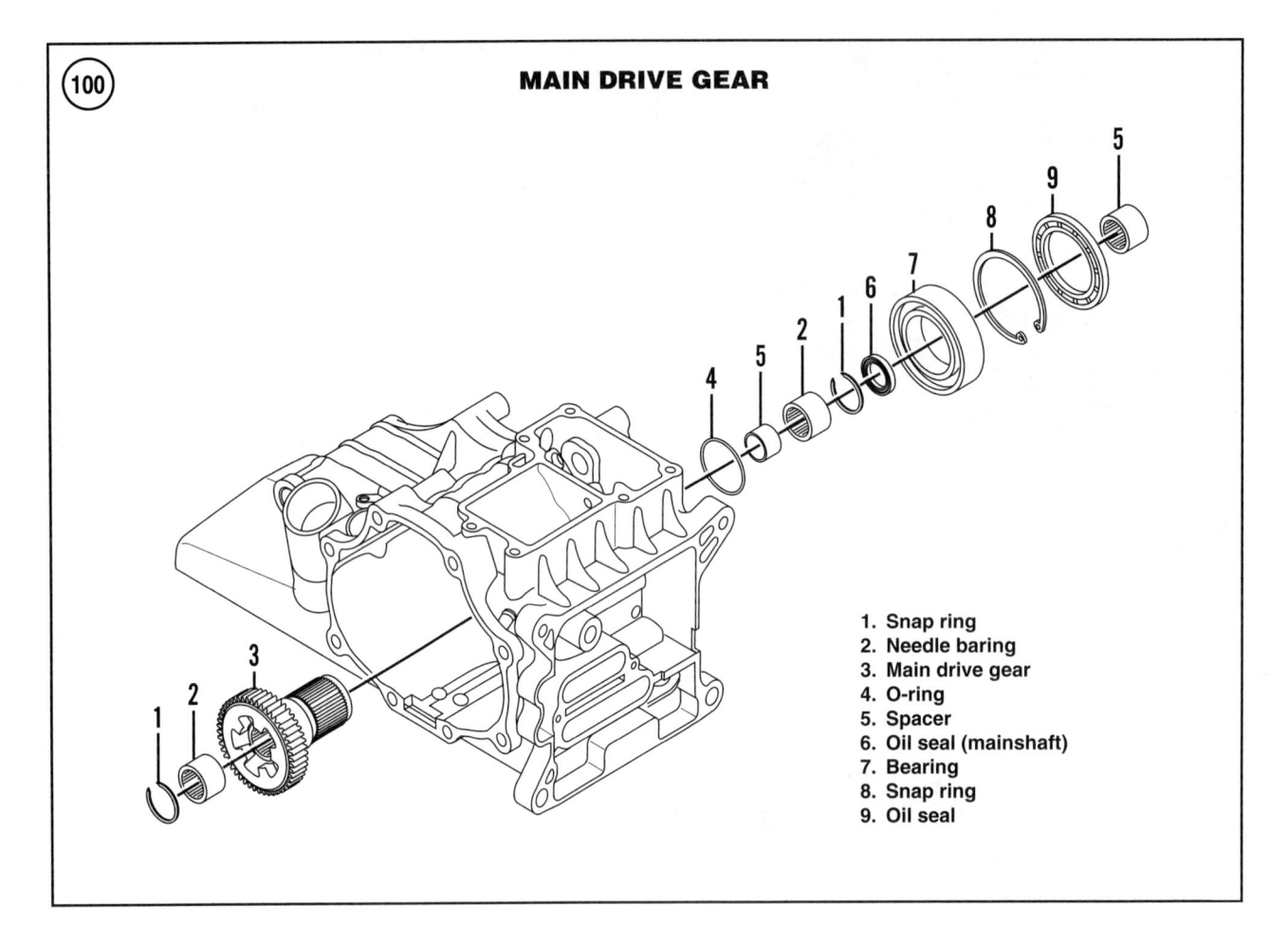

1. Snap ring
2. Needle baring
3. Main drive gear
4. O-ring
5. Spacer
6. Oil seal (mainshaft)
7. Bearing
8. Snap ring
9. Oil seal

is removed, the main drive bearing is damaged and must be replaced at the same time.

Tools

If the transmission case is installed in the frame, the following tools are used to remove and install the main drive gear and the main drive bearing:
1. The main drive gear/bearing remover and installer (JIMS part No. 987 or H-D part No. HD-35316-C).
2. The transmission main drive gear seal installer (JIMS part No. 972 or H-D part No. HD-47856) is required to install the large oil seal.
3. The transmission main drive gear installer (JIMS part No. 981).

If the transmission case has been removed, use a press to remove and install the main drive gear and main drive bearing.

Removal

1. Remove the transmission side door assembly and the transmission drive sprocket as described in this chapter.
2. Remove large oil seal (A, **Figure 101**) from the main drive gear.
3. Remove the snap ring from the main drive bearing behind the large seal.

NOTE
If the main drive gear will not release from the bearing due to corrosion, remove the tools and heat the bearing with a heat gun.

4. Assemble the tool set onto the main drive gear following the tool manufacturer's instructions. Tighten the puller nut slowly to pull the main drive gear from the main drive bearing in the transmission case.
5. Remove the main drive bearing from the transmission case as described in this section.

NOTE
The main drive bearing inner race may remain on the main drive gear. If the main drive gear will be reinstalled, the inner race must be removed.

6. Remove the bearing inner race from the main drive gear by performing the following:
   a. Install the transmission main drive gear wedge attachment (H-D part No HD-95637-46B) or a bearing puller (A, **Figure 102**) beneath the inner race.
   b. Support the tool in a hydraulic press (B, **Figure 102**), and press the main drive gear (C) from the inner race.
   c. Be prepared to catch the main drive gear as it is released from the bearing.

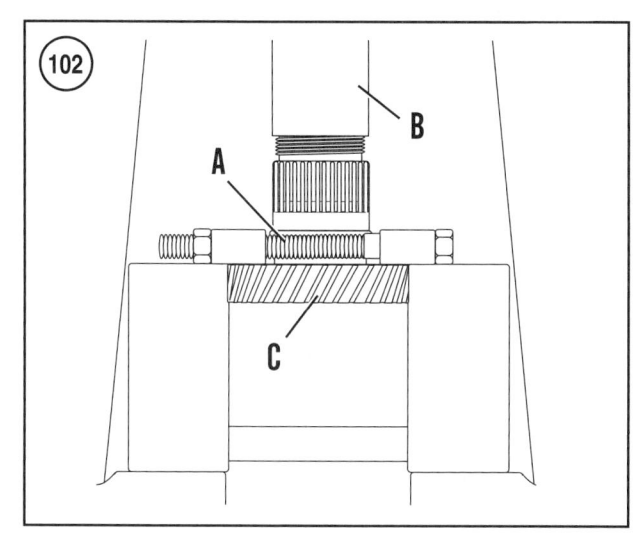

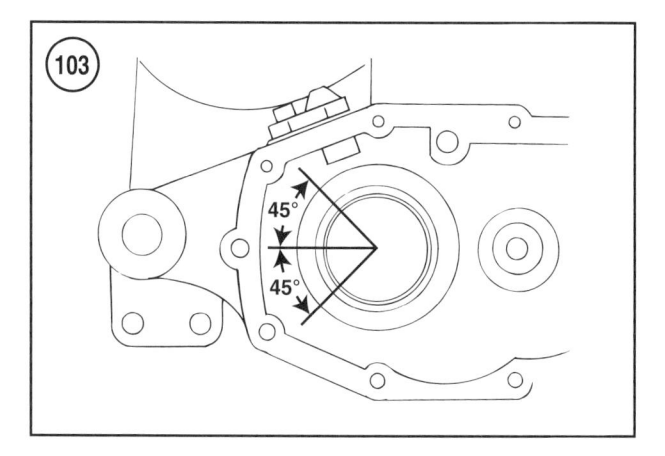

SIX SPEED TRANSMISSION (2007-2009 MODELS)

5. Apply transmission oil to the main drive bearing inner race and to the outer surface of the main drive gear. Also apply oil to the nut and threaded shaft of the installer tool.

6. Insert the main drive gear into the main drive gear bearing as far as it will go. Hold it in place and assemble the tool onto the main drive gear and transmission case following the tool manufacturer's instructions.

7. Slowly tighten the puller nut to pull the main drive gear into the bearing in the transmission case. Continue until the gear bottoms in the bearing inner race.

8. Disassemble and remove the installation tool.

9A. If the transmission main drive gear seal installer (H-D part No. HD-47856) is available; install the large oil seal per the tool manufacturer's instructions.

9B. If the seal installer is not available, perform the following:

    a. Lubricate the lips of a *new* main-drive-gear large oil seal with clean transmission oil.

    b. Position the seal in the bearing bore so its closed side faces out.

    c. Using a mandrel that matches the diameter of the seal, drive the seal into the bore until the seal is flush with the outer edge of the transmission case (A, **Figure 101**).

10. Install the transmission side door assembly and the transmission drive sprocket as described in this chapter.

NOTE
If a new small oil seal was not installed into the main drive gear during needle bearing installation or if the small oil seal is damaged, it can be replaced now. The transmission main drive gear bearing and seal installer tool (JIMS part No. 972 or H-D part No. HD-47933) is needed for this procedure.

11. If necessary, install the small oil seal by performing the following:

    a. Install the protector sleeve over the mainshaft.

    b. Lubricate the sleeve and the small oil seal with clean transmission oil.

    c. Fit the oil seal over the protector sleeve so the seal's closed side faces out.

    d. Slide the seal driver onto the protector, and manually press the seal into the main drive gear. The seal is properly seated when the tool bottoms against the main drive gear.

Installation

1. Install a new main drive bearing as described in this section.

2. Install a *new* snap ring so its flat side faces the bearing.

3. Position the snap ring with the open end facing the rear of the transmission and within a 45° angle to horizontal (**Figure 103**). Make sure it is fully seated in the snap ring groove.

4. Lubricate a new O-ring with engine oil, and install it into the groove on the main drive gear.

Inspection

CAUTION
Do no allow solvent to enter the inside of the main drive gear. The solvent will wash contaminants behind the needles in the bearings. If this occurs, the needle bearing must be replaced.

1. Clean the main drive gear in solvent, and dry with compressed air, if available.

2. Check each gear tooth (A, **Figure 104**) for excessive wear, burrs, galling and pitting. Check for missing teeth.
3. Check the gear splines (B, **Figure 104**) for excessive wear, galling or other damage.
4. Inspect the two main drive gear needle bearings (**Figure 105** and **Figure 106**) for excessive wear or damage. Insert the mainshaft into the main drive gear to check bearing wear. If necessary, replace the bearings as described in this section.

Needle Bearing Replacement

Both main drive gear needle bearings must be installed to the correct depth within the main drive gear. The correct depth is obtained with a main drive gear bearing and seal installer tool (JIMS part No. 986 or H-D part No HD-47933). This tool (**Figure 107**) is also used to install the small oil seal.

If the seal installer is not available, measure the depth of both bearings before removing them.

Replace both main drive gear needle bearings as a set.

CAUTION
Never reuse a main drive gear needle bearing, as it is distorted during removal.

1. Remove O-ring (**Figure 108**) from the main drive gear. Discard the O-ring.
2. Remove the small oil seal (**Figure 109**) from the clutch side of the main drive gear.
3. Remove the retaining ring from each end of the main drive gear bore. Discard the rings.
4. If the seal installer is not available, measure and record the depth of both bearings.
5. Use a blind bearing puller to remove the needle bearings and spacer.
6. Clean the main drive gear and its bearing bore in solvent. Dry it thoroughly.
7. Apply transmission oil to the bearing bore in the main drive gear and to the outer surface of both bearings.

NOTE
Install each needle bearing with the manufacturer's marks facing out.

8. Set the main drive gear (A, **Figure 110**) in the press so its clutch side faces up. Center the main drive gear bore under the press ram.
9. Set a *new* needle bearing into the clutch side of the drive gear bore. Insert the 0.400-in. (10.16 mm) step of the seal installer (B, **Figure 110**) into the bearing.
10. Press the bearing into the bore until the tool lightly contacts the main drive gear.
11. Raise the press ram. Install a *new* retaining ring so the ring's flat side faces the bearing.
12. Insert a new small oil seal into the drive gear bore. The side with the manufacturer's marks must face out.

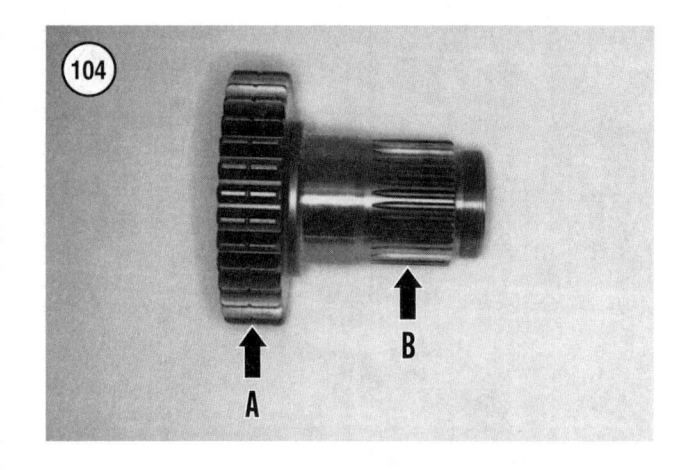

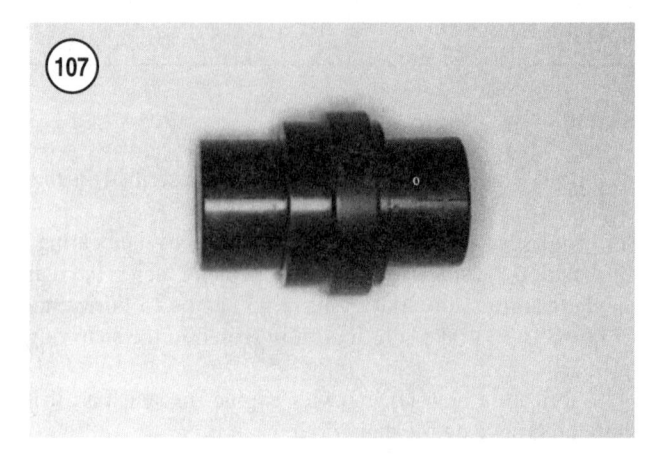

SIX SPEED TRANSMISSION (2007-2009 MODELS)

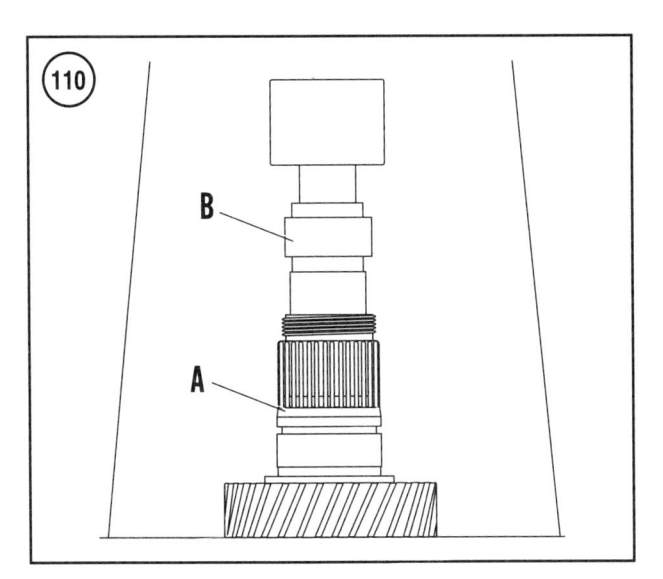

13. Insert the 0.090-in. (2.29 mm) end of the seal installer into the oil seal, and press the seal into the bore until the tool lightly contact the main drive gear.

14. Turn the main drive gear (A, **Figure 111**) over so it transmission side faces up, install the spacer, and center the bore under the press ram.

15. Start a *new* needle bearing into the bore.

16. Insert the tool's 0.188-in. (4.78 mm) step into the needle bearing, and press the bearing into the bore until the tool (B, **Figure 111**) lightly contacts the main drive gear.

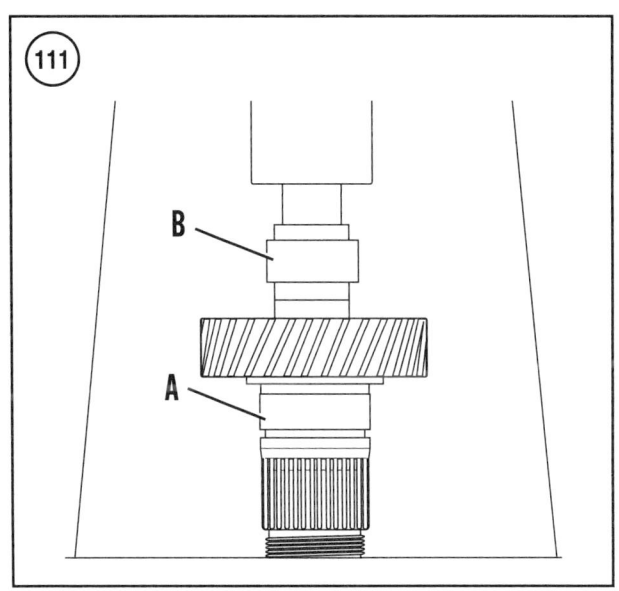

17. Install a *new* retaining ring into the main drive gear. Make sure the ring is completely seated in its groove.

18. Install a *new* small oil seal (B, **Figure 101**) into the clutch side of the main drive gear.

19. Install a *new* O-ring into the main drive gear.

20. Install the main drive gear as described in this section.

Main Drive Bearing Replacement

The main drive bearing (**Figure 100**) is pressed into the transmission case. Whenever the main drive gear is removed, the main drive bearing is damaged and must be replaced at the same time.

CAUTION
Failure to use the correct tools can cause premature bearing failure.

The transmission main drive gear/bearing remover and installer (H-D part No. HD-35316-C) and the transmission main drive gear bearing installer (JIMS part No. 987) are used to remove and install the main drive bearing if the transmission case is installed in the frame.

If the transmission has been removed, a press can be used to remove the main drive bearing.

1. Remove the main drive gear from the transmission case as described in this section.

2. Assemble the tool set onto the main drive bearing following the tool manufacturer's instructions. Tighten the bolt and nut slowly to pull the main drive gear bearing from the transmission case.

3. Clean the bearing bore and dry with compressed air. Check the bore for nicks or burrs and check the snap ring groove for damage.

NOTE
Install the bearing into the transmission case with the manufacturer's marks facing out.

4. Apply transmission oil to the bearing bore in the transmission case and to the outer surface of the bearing. Also apply oil to the nut and threaded shaft of the installer tool.
5. Install the bearing onto the installation tool and assemble the installation tool following the tool manufacturer's instructions.
6. Slowly tighten the puller nut to pull the bearing into the transmission case. Continue until the bearing bottoms in the case.
7. Disassemble and remove the installation tool.

TRANSMISSION DRIVE SPROCKET

Removal/Installation

The transmission drive sprocket locker tool (JIMS part No. 2260 or H-D part No. HD-46282) and the mainshaft pulley locknut socket (JIMS part No. 989 or H-D part No. HD-47910 and part No. HD-94660-2) are used to remove the transmission drive sprocket.

NOTE
It is not necessary to remove the mainshaft bearing inner race when removing the transmission drive sprocket.

1. Remove the primary chaincase assembly as described in Chapter Six.
2. If necessary, remove the belt guard and debris deflector.
3. Perform the following to create sufficient slack in the drive belt.
    a. Remove the E-clip (A, **Figure 112**) and loosen the rear axle nut (B).
    b. Support the motorcycle with the rear wheel off the ground.
    c. Turn each axle adjuster (C, **Figure 112** and **Figure 113**) in equal amounts.
    d. Push the rear wheel forward to provide sufficient slack in the drive belt.
4. Remove the two Allen bolts (A, **Figure 114**) and the lock plate (B).
5. Install a sprocket locker tool (A, **Figure 115**) onto the transmission drive sprocket, following the tool manufacturer's instructions.
6. Install the tool inner collar (B, **Figure 115**) onto the mainshaft.
7. Install the pulley nut socket (**Figure 116**), and then loosen the pulley nut.
8. Remove the tools and the sprocket nut (C, **Figure 115**) from the mainshaft.
9. Carefully slide the transmission drive sprocket (**Figure 117**) from the mainshaft so the bearing inner race (D, **Figure 115**) is not damaged.
10. Fit the drive belt onto the pulley, and slide the transmission drive pulley onto the mainshaft.
11. Finger-tighten the pulley nut onto the main drive gear.
    a. If installing a new sprocket nut, apply a very light coat of clean engine oil onto the inboard side of the

SIX SPEED TRANSMISSION (2007-2009 MODELS)

12. Install the tool inner collar (B, **Figure 115**) and the drive sprocket nut (**Figure 116**).

13A. On 2007 models, tighten the drive sprocket mounting nut to 100 ft.-lb. (135.6 N•m).

13B. On 2008-2009 models tighten the drive sprocket mounting nut to 35 ft.-lb. (47.5 N•m).

14. On all models, perform the following:

CAUTION
*Once the nut has been re-tightened to 35 ft.-lb. (47.5 N•m), the final tightening of the nut must not exceed 45°, which is 1/8th of a turn. If further tightening is needed, watch the scribe lines so total nut movement does not exceed 45° (**Figure 118**).*

a. Loosen the nut, and then retighten it to 35 ft.-lb. (47.5 N•m).
b. Scribe a horizontal line onto the sprocket nut and onto the sprocket as shown in **Figure 118**).

CAUTION
Do not tighten the nut more than an additional 45° to align the lockplate bolt holes. The nut will be damaged.

c. Tighten the nut an additional 35-40° until the lockplate holes align with the holes on the drive sprocket.

15. Remove the tools.

16. Install the lockplate (B, **Figure 114**) over the nut, aligning two of the opposite holes with the threaded holes in the sprocket nut. Remove and refit the lockplate until two opposite holes align. If hole alignment cannot be achieved; tighten the nut additionally as needed. However, the total movement of the nut must not exceed maximum of 45°.

NOTE
New lockplate bolts have threadlock pre-applied to the threads and can be reused up to three times. They must be replaced after the fourth use.

NOTE
Apply Loctite High Strength Threadlocker 271 (red) if reusing the old bolts. Do not apply threadlock when using new bolts.

17. Install and tighten the lockplate bolts (A, **Figure 114**) to 84-108 in.-lb. (9.5-12.2 N•m) on 2007-2008 models or to 84-132 in.-lb. (9.5-14.9 N•m) on 2009 models.

18. Adjust the belt deflection as described in Chapter Three.

TRANSMISSION CASE

Only remove the transmission case (**Figure 119** and **Figure 120**) if it requires replacement, when performing extensive frame repair or if replacing the frame. All internal components can be removed with the case in the frame.

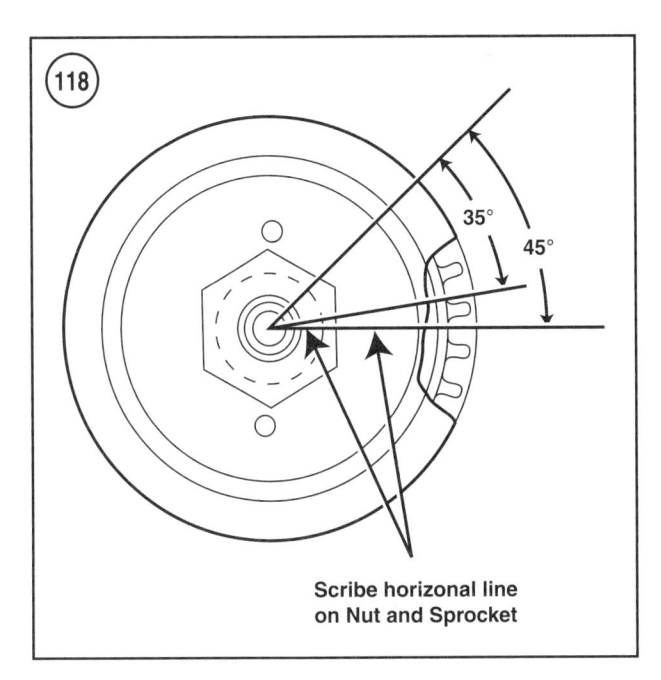

new nut. Do not allow any oil to contact the patch of threadlock on the pulley nut threads.

b. If reinstalling the old nut, apply Loctite High Strength Threadlocker 271 (red) to the nut threads. Also apply a very light coat of clean engine oil onto the inboard face of the locknut and to the surface of the sprocket where the nut makes contact.

CHAPTER EIGHT

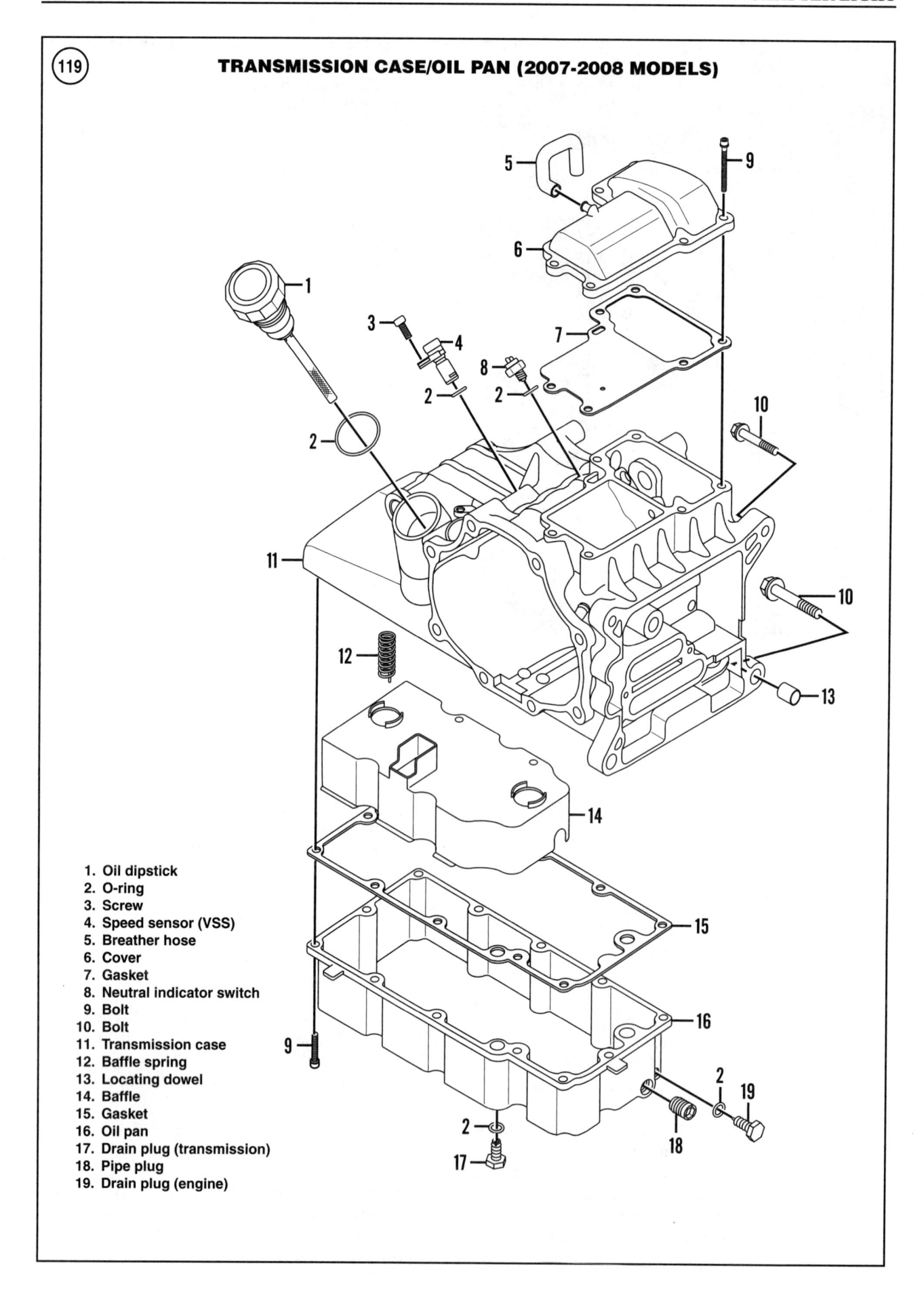

TRANSMISSION CASE/OIL PAN (2007-2008 MODELS)

1. Oil dipstick
2. O-ring
3. Screw
4. Speed sensor (VSS)
5. Breather hose
6. Cover
7. Gasket
8. Neutral indicator switch
9. Bolt
10. Bolt
11. Transmission case
12. Baffle spring
13. Locating dowel
14. Baffle
15. Gasket
16. Oil pan
17. Drain plug (transmission)
18. Pipe plug
19. Drain plug (engine)

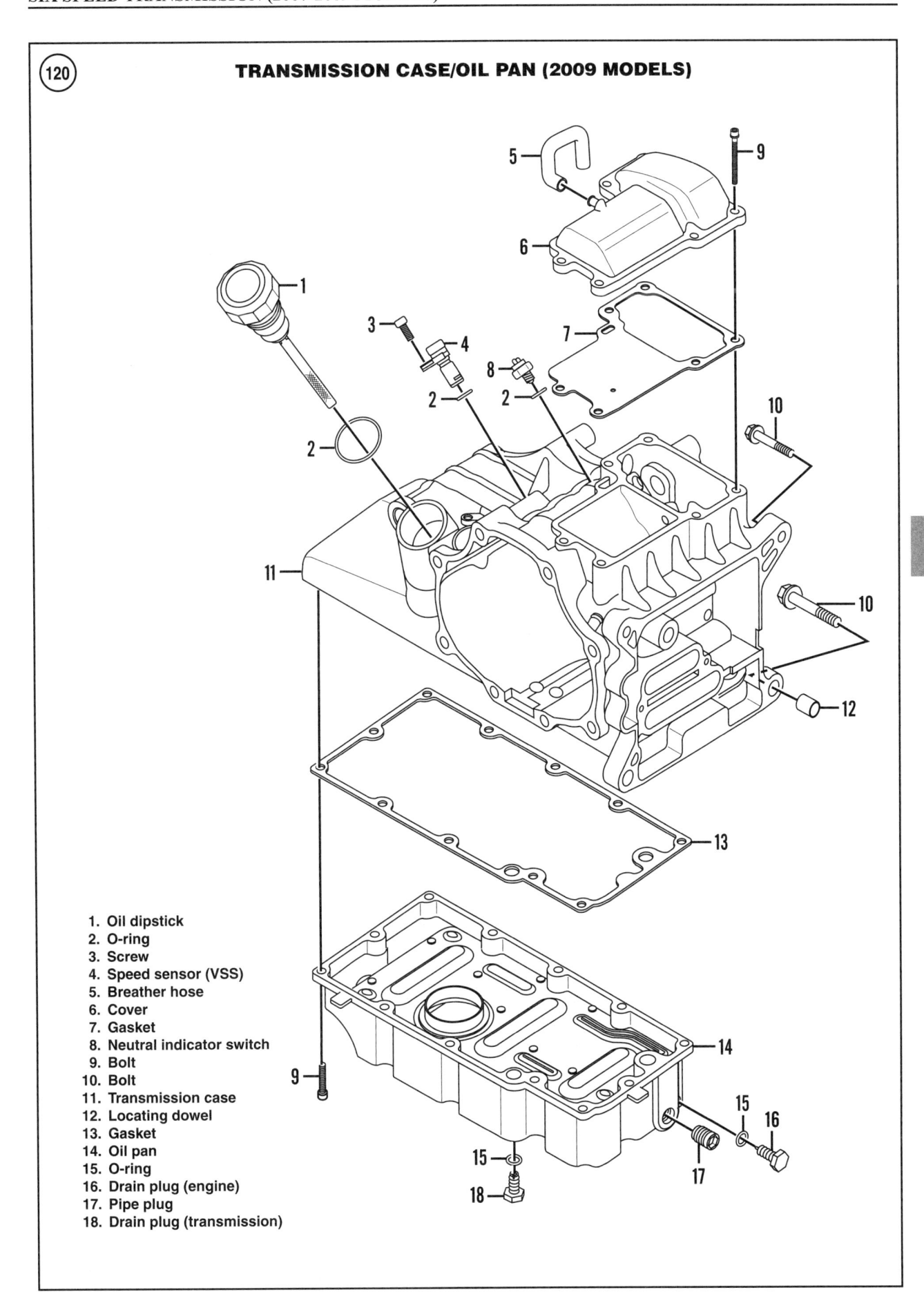

SIX SPEED TRANSMISSION (2007-2009 MODELS)

TRANSMISSION CASE/OIL PAN (2009 MODELS)

120

1. Oil dipstick
2. O-ring
3. Screw
4. Speed sensor (VSS)
5. Breather hose
6. Cover
7. Gasket
8. Neutral indicator switch
9. Bolt
10. Bolt
11. Transmission case
12. Locating dowel
13. Gasket
14. Oil pan
15. O-ring
16. Drain plug (engine)
17. Pipe plug
18. Drain plug (transmission)

Removal/Installation

NOTE
Always disarm the TSSM/HFSM security system before disconnecting the battery or pulling the Maxi-Fuse so the alarm will not sound.

1. Remove the Maxi-Fuse as described in Chapter Eleven.
2. Drain the transmission oil and primary chaincase lubricant as described in Chapter Three.
3. Remove the exhaust system as described in Chapter Four.
4. Remove the starter as described in Chapter Eleven.
5. Remove the neutral switch as described in Chapter Eleven.
6. Disconnect the electrical connector from the vehicle speed sensor (VSS), located on top of the transmission case under the starter.
7. Disconnect the ground post from the top of the transmission case.
8. Remove the main power cable from the clip on the T-stud at the front of the battery tray, Move it toward the left side of the motorcycle.
9. Remove the primary chaincase cover as described in Chapter Six.
10. Remove the clutch assembly as described in Chapter Six.
11. Remove the clutch release cover and the clutch release mechanism (Chapter Six).
12. Remove the primary chaincase housing as described in Chapter Six.
13. Remove the transmission drive sprocket as described in this chapter.
14. Remove the side door and transmission shaft assemblies as described in this chapter, if necessary.
15. Remove the external shift linkage from the transmission as described in this chapter.
16. Make an alignment mark on the shift rod lever and the end of the shift shaft.
17. Remove the clamping bolt (A, **Figure 121**) securing the shift rod lever (B).
18. Use a Torx driver (T50) and back out the centering screw (A, **Figure 122**) until it clears the centering slot in the shift pawl assembly.
19. Remove the snap ring (B, **Figure 122**) and flat washer (C) from the shift shaft (D).
20. Remove the rear wheel as described in Chapter Twelve.
21. Remove the engine oil dipstick (**Figure 123**).
22. Remove the oil pan and baffle (2007-2008 models only) from the bottom of the transmission case as described in this chapter.
23. Support the swing arm. Then, remove the swing arm pivot bolt as described in Chapter Fourteen.
24. Place a jack under the crankcase to support the engine after the transmission case is removed.

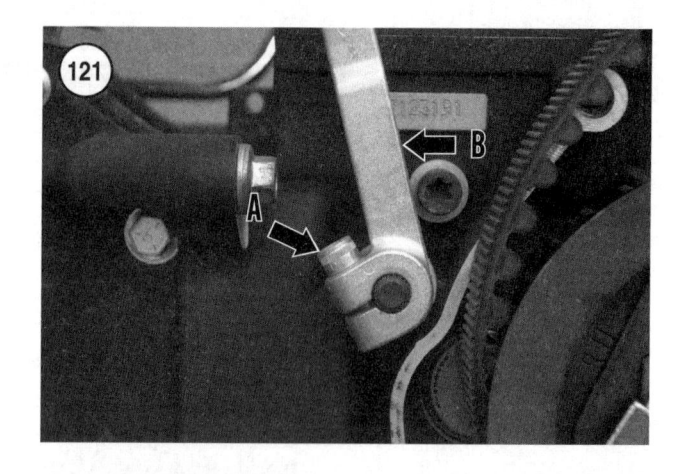

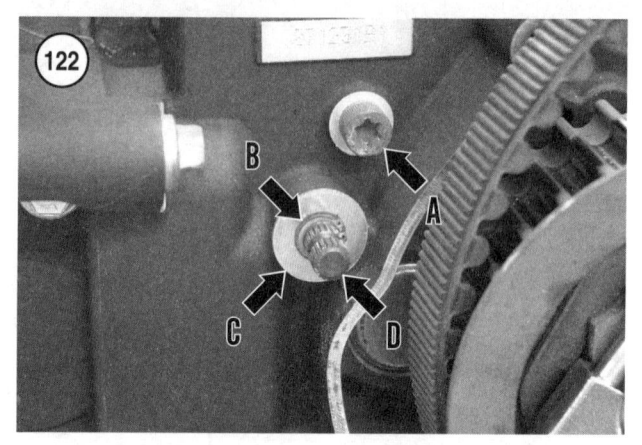

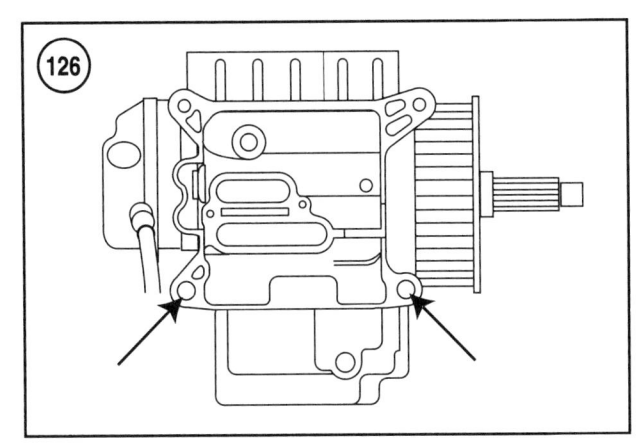

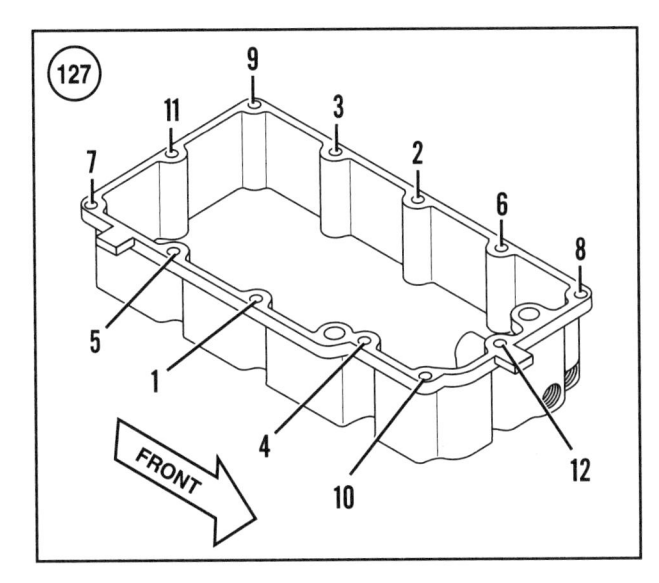

SIX SPEED TRANSMISSION (2007-2009 MODELS)

a. Make sure the two locating dowels (**Figure 126**) are in place on the engine or transmission case.
b. Install the shorter (1/2 in.) transmission mounting bolts at the lower locations and the longer (9/16 in.) bolts at the upper locations.
c. On all models, use a crossing pattern to tighten the transmission-to-engine mounting bolts. Tighten the bolts evenly, in two steps, to the specification listed in **Table 4**.
d. Tighten the oil pan bolts in the sequence shown in **Figure 127** to 84-132 in.-lb. (9.5-14.9 N•m).
e. Install the ground post on top of the transmission.

OIL PAN

The oil pan (**Figure 119** and **Figure 120**) mounts onto the bottom of the transmission case. It can be removed with the transmission mounted in the frame.

Removal

1. Drain the engine oil as described in Chapter Three.
2. Drain the transmission oil as described in Chapter Three.

CAUTION
The dipstick will be damaged if left in place during oil pan removal.

3. Remove the engine oil dipstick (**Figure 123**).
4. Remove the left side muffler, crossover pipe and crossover pipe clamp bracket from the transmission as described in Chapter Four.

NOTE
Access hidden bolts through the holes in the frame cross member.

5. Use 3/16 inch ball hex socket driver, and remove the twelve bolts securing the oil pan to the transmission case.
6. Lower and slide the oil pan toward the rear and remove it from the transmission case and the frame. On 2007-2008 models, do not lose both baffle springs.
7. Remove the gasket.

Installation

1. Thoroughly clean the gasket surface of the oil pan.
2. Coat the oil pan gasket surface with a thin coat of Hylomar gasket sealer, or an equivalent. Allow the sealer to dry until tacky.
3. Install a *new* oil pan gasket on the oil pan.
4. Install the baffle and both baffle springs into the oil pan.
5A. On 2007-2008 models, partially install the oil pan onto the bottom of the transmission case. Use a long, flat-bladed screwdriver and compress the baffle springs as the oil pan moves into place. Make sure the baffle springs are not

25. Remove the short (1/2 in.) upper (**Figure 124**) and the long (9/16 in.) lower (**Figure 125**) bolts and washers on each side securing the engine to the transmission.
26. Move the transmission case to the rear to clear the two lower locating dowels, and rest it on the frame cross member.
27. Move the transmission toward the left side and remove the transmission case from the frame.
28. Install the transmission case by reversing the removal steps, while noting the following:

cocked or distorted or it will hold the oil pan away from the transmission gasket surface.

5B. On 2009 models, install the oil pan onto the bottom of the transmission case.

6. Hold the oil pan in place, install the twelve bolts and tighten them just 2 full turns.

7. Check that the oil pan is still positioned correctly. Tighten the oil pan bolts in the sequence shown in **Figure 127** to 84-132 in.-lb. (9.5-14.9 N•m).

8. Install the left side muffler, crossover pipe and crossover pipe clamp bracket from the transmission as described in Chapter Four.

9. If necessary, replace the engine oil filter as described in Chapter Three.

10 Refill the engine with *new* engine oil as described in Chapter Three and install the dipstick.

11. Refill the transmission with *new* oil as described in Chapter Three.

12. Start the engine and check for leaks.

Inspection

1. On 2007-2008 models, separate the baffle from the oil pan. Clean the oil pan, baffle and springs in solvent and dry thoroughly.

2. Remove all old gasket residue from the oil pan and transmission case mating surfaces.

3. Inspect the oil pan for cracks or damage. Replace if necessary.

4. On 2007-2008 models, check the baffle springs for weakness or damage, and replace both springs as a set if necessary.

Table 1 TRANSMISSION GENERAL SPECIFICATIONS

Transmission type	6-speed, constant mesh
Gear ratios	
First	3.34
Second	2.31
Third	1.72
Fourth	1.39
Fifth	1.18
Sixth	1.00
Transmission fluid capacity	32 U.S. oz. (946.4 ml)

Table 2 TRANSMISSION SERVICE SPECIFICATIONS

Item	in.	mm
Countershaft		
Runout	0.000-0.003	0.00-0.08
Endplay	None	
First gear		
Clearance	0.0004-0.0015	0.010-0.038
End play	0.002-0.0023	0.05-0.08
Second gear		
Clearance		
2007 models	0.0001-0.0012	0.003-0.030
2008-2009 models	0.0005-0.0012	0.013-0.030
End play	0.002-0.40	0.05-1.02
Third gear		
Clearance	0.0004-0.0015	0.010-0.038
End play	0.002-0.042	0.05-1.07
Fourth gear		
Clearance	0.0004-0.0015	0.010-0.038
End play	0.001-0.028	0.03-0.71
Mainshaft		
Runout	0.00-0.003	0.00-0.08
Endplay	None	
Fifth gear		
Clearance	0.0004-0.0015	0.010-0.038
End play	0.002-0.026	0.05-0.66

(continued)

SIX SPEED TRANSMISSION (2007-2009 MODELS)

Table 2 TRANSMISSION SERVICE SPECIFICATIONS (continued)

Item	in.	mm
Main drive gear (sixth)		
Bearing fit in transmission case	0.0003-0.0017	0.008-0.043
Fit in bearing (press-fit)		
2007 models	None	None
2008-2009 models	0.001-0.003	0.025-0.076
Fit on mainshaft (2007 models)	0.0009-0.0022	0.002-0.056
End play	None	
Shift dog service limit		
First	0.015-0.112	0.381-2.845
Second	0.021-0.136	0.533-3.454
Third	0.014-0.118	0.356-2.997
Fourth	0.033-0.115	0.838-2.921
Fifth	0.016-0.115	0.406-2.921
Sixth	0.026-0.123	0.660-3.124
Shift forks		
Shift fork-to-cam groove end play	0.004-0.012	0.102-0.305
Shift fork-to-gear groove end play	0.004-0.013	0.102-0.330
Shift fork service limit		
First and second gear shift fork	0.258	6.55
Third and fourth gear shift fork	0.198	5.03
Fifth and sixth gear shift fork	0.258	6.55
Mainshaft bearing race-to-main drive gear clearance	0.100-0.125	2.54-3.18

Table 3 SIDE DOOR BEARINGS SPECIFICATIONS

Item	2007 models in. (mm)	2008-2009 models in. (mm)
Fit in side door	0.001-0.0014 (0.025-0.0356)	0.001-0.0014 (0.025-0.0356)
Fit on countershaft		
Tight fit	0.0007 (0.018)	0.0007 (0.018)
Loose fit	0.001 (0.025)	0.001 (0.025)
Fit on mainshaft		
Tight fit	0.0007 (0.018)	0.0007 (0.018)
Loose fit	0.001 (0.025)	0.001 (0.025)

Table 4 TRANSMISSION TORQUE SPECIFICATIONS

Item	ft.-lb.	in.-lb.	N•m
Transmission shaft locknuts (at side door)			
2007-2008 models	45-55	–	61.0-74.6
2009 models	55-65	–	74.6-88.1
Oil pan bolts	–	84-132	9.5-14.9
Shift cam detent arm pivot bolt	–	120-150	13.6-17.0
Shift cam lock plate bolt	–	57-63	6.4-7.1
Shift rod locknuts	–	80-120	9.0-13.6
Shift rod lever clamp bolt	18-22	–	24.4-29.8
Top cover bolts	–	84-132	9.5-14.9
Transmission side door bolts	13-18	–	17.6-24.4
Transmission drain plug	14-21	–	19.0-28.5
Transmission mounting bolts			
2007-2008 models			
Initial torque	15	–	20.3
Final torque	30-35	–	40.7-47.5
2009 models			
Initial torque	15	–	20.3
Final torque	34-39	–	46.1-52.9
Transmission drive sprocket			
Mounting nut	see text		
Lock plate bolts			
2006-2008	–	84-108	9.5-12.2
2009	–	84-132	9.5-14.9
Vehicle speed sensor screw	–	84-108	9.5-12.2

CHAPTER NINE

AIR/FUEL AND EMISSION CONTROL SYSTEMS (CARBURETED MODELS)

This chapter covers the carburetor and emission control systems. Maintenance items are covered in Chapter Three. Refer to *Safety* in Chapter One.

Specifications are in **Table 1** and **Table 2** at the end of the chapter.

WARNING
Gasoline is carcinogenic and flammable. Handle gasoline carefully. Wear nitrile gloves to avoid skin contact. If gasoline does contact skin, immediately and thoroughly wash the area with soap and warm water.

AIR FILTER AND BACKPLATE

Refer to **Figure 1**. Air filter service is covered in Chapter Three.

Removal

NOTE
Always disarm the TSSM/HFSM security system prior to disconnecting the battery or pulling the Maxi-Fuse so the siren will not sound.

1. Disconnect the negative battery cable as described in Chapter Eleven.
2. Remove the air filter cover screw (A, **Figure 2**), and then remove the cover (B).
3. Remove the Torx screws and bracket (A, **Figure 3**) from the air filter element (B).
4. Gently pull the air filter element away from the backplate and disconnect the two breather hoses (A, **Figure 4**) from the breather hollow bolts on the backplate. Remove the air filter element (B, **Figure 4**).
5. Unscrew and remove the breather hollow bolts (A, **Figure 5**) securing the backplate (B) to the cylinder heads.
6A. On California models, pull the backplate partially away from the cylinder heads and the carburetor, and disconnect the clean air inlet hose (**Figure 6**). Remove the backplate.
6B. On all other models, pull the backplate (B, **Figure 5**) away from the cylinder heads and remove it.
7. Remove the carburetor gasket from the air filter and from the backplate.

Installation

1. Apply a small amount of gasket sealer to a *new* carburetor gasket to hold it in place and attach it to the backside of the backplate.
2. Move the backplate into position toward the cylinder heads.
3. On California models, move the backplate part way into position. Connect the clean air inlet hose (**Figure 6**) to the fitting on the backside of the backplate.
4. Position the backplate (B, **Figure 5**) against the carburetor and cylinder heads. Make sure the Torx bolt holes in

AIR/FUEL AND EMISSION CONTROL SYSTEMS (CARBURETED MODELS)

① AIR FILTER AND BACKPLATE

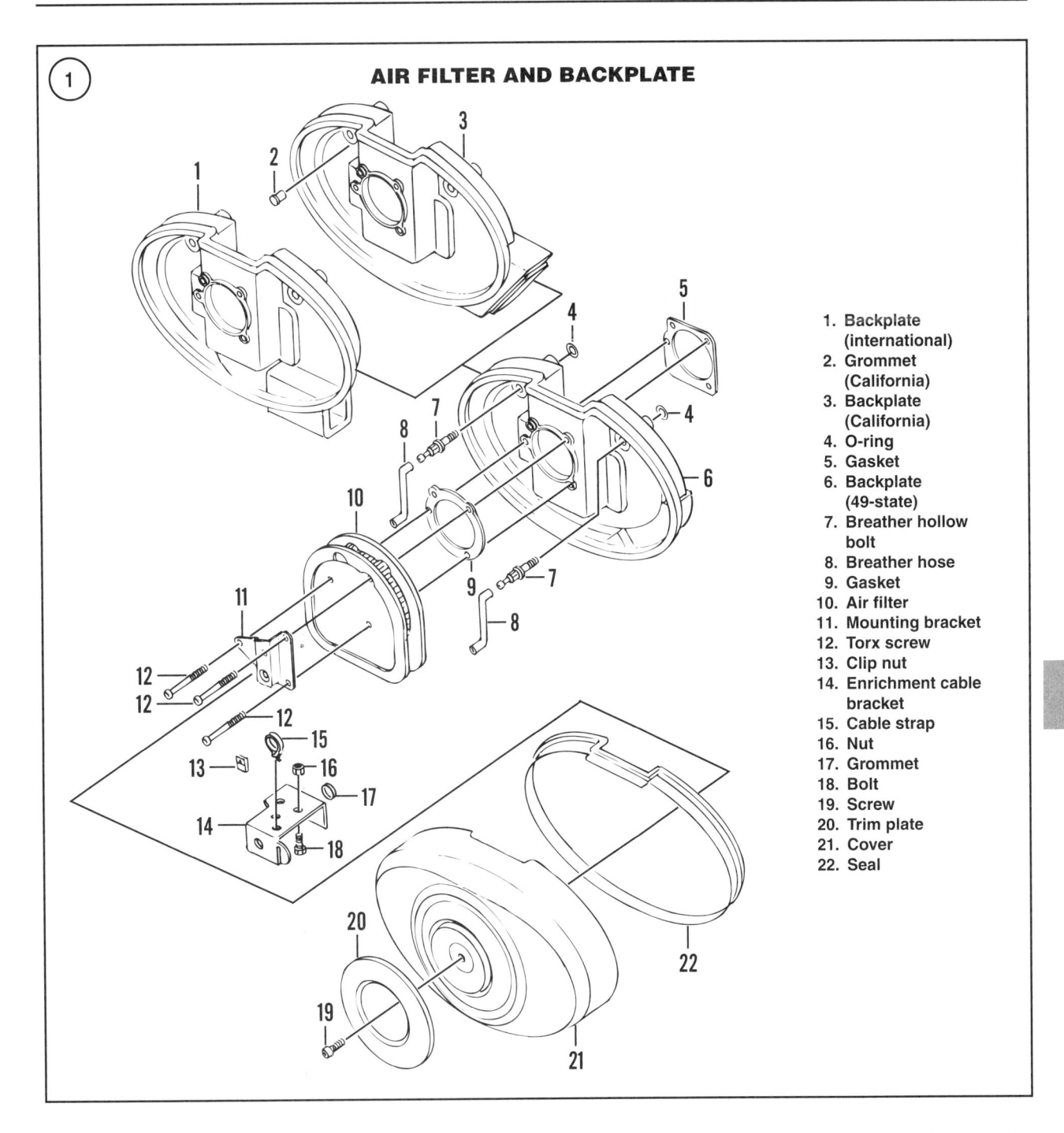

1. Backplate (international)
2. Grommet (California)
3. Backplate (California)
4. O-ring
5. Gasket
6. Backplate (49-state)
7. Breather hollow bolt
8. Breather hose
9. Gasket
10. Air filter
11. Mounting bracket
12. Torx screw
13. Clip nut
14. Enrichment cable bracket
15. Cable strap
16. Nut
17. Grommet
18. Bolt
19. Screw
20. Trim plate
21. Cover
22. Seal

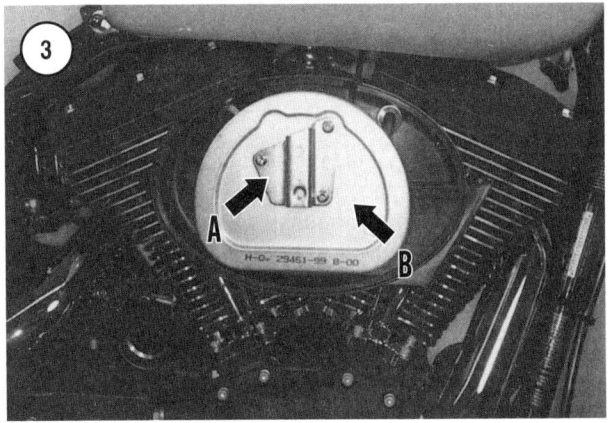

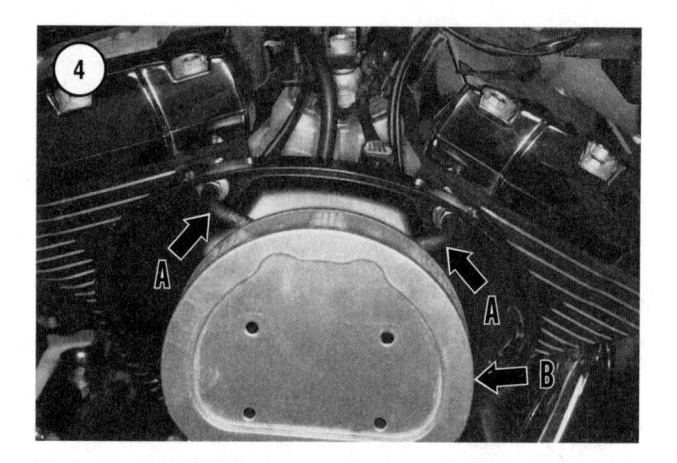

the gasket and backplate are aligned with the carburetor. Reposition the gasket if necessary.

5. Install the breather hollow bolts (A, **Figure 5**) securing the backplate to the cylinder heads and tighten the bolts to 124-142 in.-lb. (14-16 N•m).
6. If removed, install a *new* gasket (**Figure 7**) onto the air filter element.
7. Position the element (B, **Figure 4**) with the flat side facing down and attach the breather hoses (A) to the backside of the element.
8. Move the element (B, **Figure 3**) into position and install the mounting bracket (A) and the Torx screws. Tighten the Torx screws to 40-60 in.-lb. (4.5-6.8 N•m).
9. Inspect the seal ring (**Figure 8**) on the air filter cover for hardness or deterioration. Replace if necessary.
10. Apply a drop of ThreeBond TB1342 (blue), or an equivalent threadlock, to the cover screw prior to installation.
11. Install the air filter cover (B, **Figure 2**) and the screw (A). Tighten the screw to 35-60 in.-lb. (4.0-6.8 N•m).
12. Connect the negative battery cable as described in Chapter Eleven.

Inspection

1. Inspect the backplate (**Figure 9**) for damage.
2. On California models, make sure the trap door (**Figure 10**) swings freely.
3. Make sure the breather hollow bolts and breather hoses (**Figure 11**) are clear. Clean out if necessary.

CARBURETOR

Operation

An understanding of the function of each of the carburetor components and their relation to one another is a valuable aid for pinpointing a source of carburetor trouble.

The carburetor's purpose is to supply and atomize fuel and mix it in the correct proportions with air that is drawn in through the air intake. At the primary throttle opening (idle), a small amount of fuel is siphoned through the pilot jet by the incoming air. As the throttle is opened further, the air stream begins to siphon fuel through the main jet and

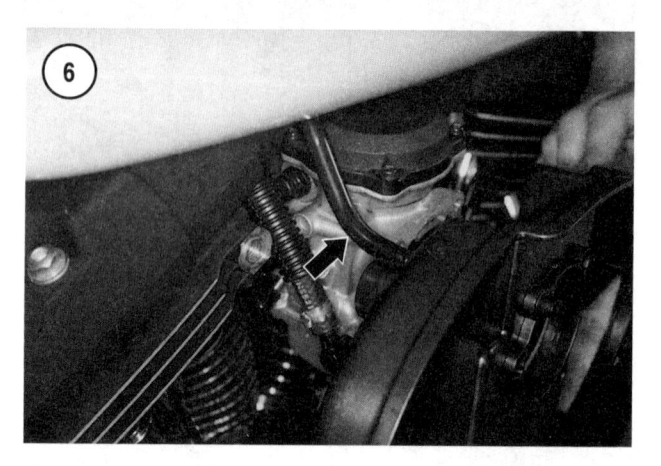

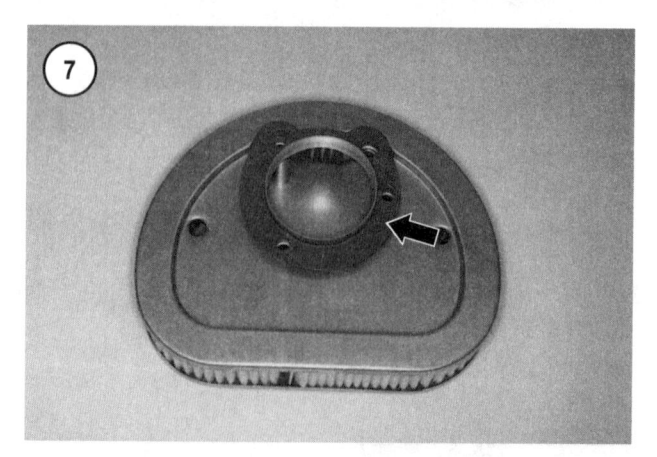

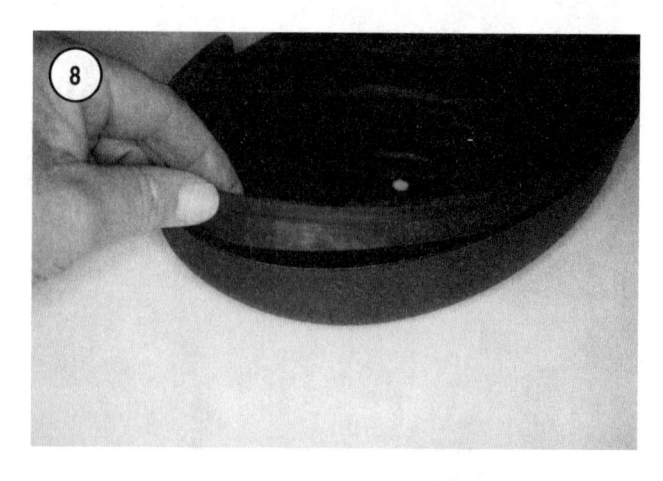

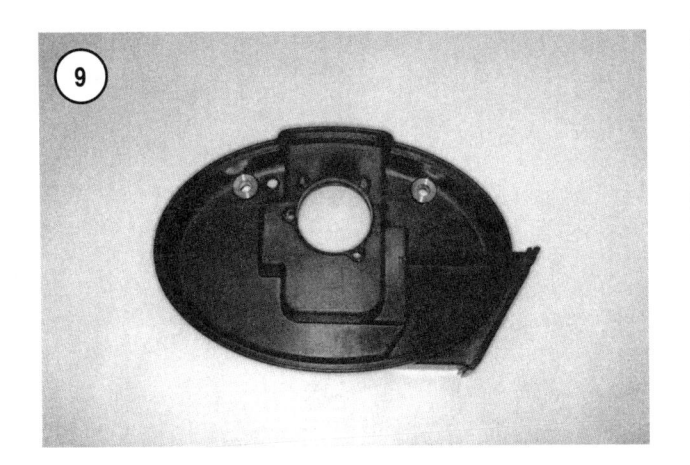

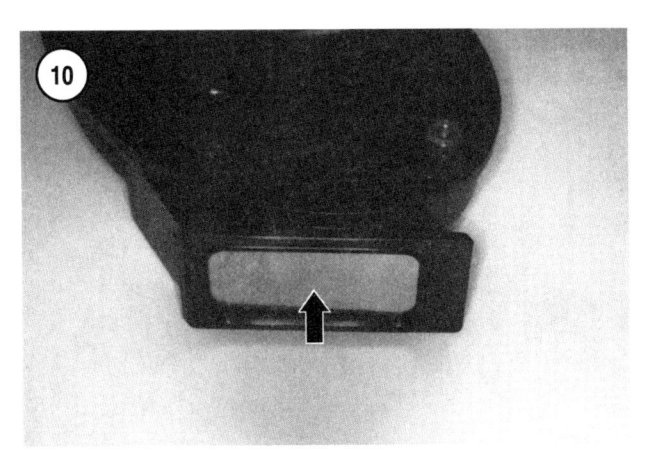

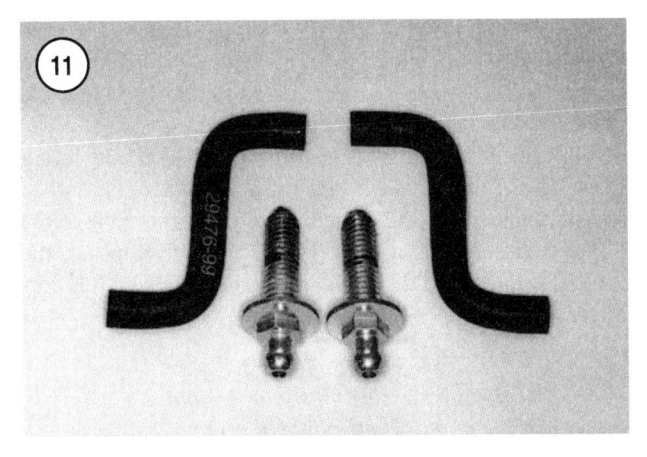

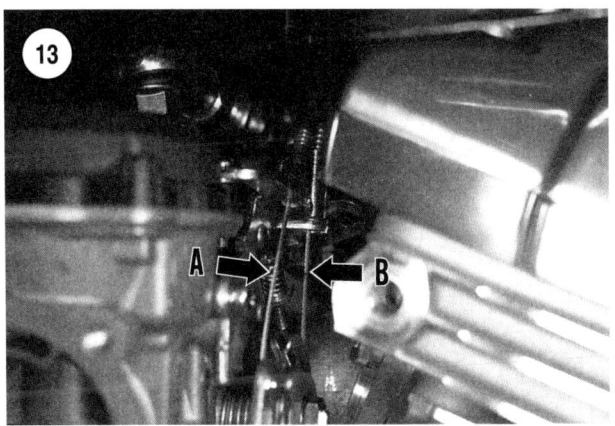

AIR/FUEL AND EMISSION CONTROL SYSTEMS (CARBURETED MODELS)

needle jet. The tapered needle increases the effective flow capacity of the needle jet as it is lifted, in that it occupies progressively less of the area of the jet. At full throttle the carburetor venturi is fully open and the needle is lifted far enough to permit the main jet to flow at full capacity.

The choke circuit is a starting enrichment valve system in which the choke knob on the left side of the engine next to the horn opens an enrichment valve; rather than closing a butterfly in the venturi area as on some carburetors. In the open position, the slow jet discharges a stream of fuel into the carburetor venturi to enrich the mixture when the engine is cold.

The accelerator pump circuit reduces engine hesitation by injecting a fine spray of fuel into the carburetor intake passage during sudden acceleration.

Removal

NOTE
Always disarm the TSSM/HFSM security system prior to disconnecting the battery or pulling the Maxi-Fuse so the siren will not sound.

1. Disconnect the negative battery cable as described in Chapter Eleven.
2. Remove the air filter and backplate as described in this chapter.
3. Remove the fuel tank as described in this chapter.
4. Loosen the locknut (A, **Figure 12**, typical) and disconnect the starting enrichment valve cable from the mounting bracket (B). Move the end of the cable out of the mounting bracket slot.
5. There are two different throttle cables. Label the two cables at the carburetor before disconnecting them. One is the throttle control cable and the other is the idle control cable. They are identified as follows:
   a. Throttle control cable: A, **Figure 13**.
   b. Idle control cable: B, **Figure 13**.
6. On cruise control models, remove the E-clip from the groove at the end of the cruise control housing. Remove the cruise control cable housing from the cable guide in the

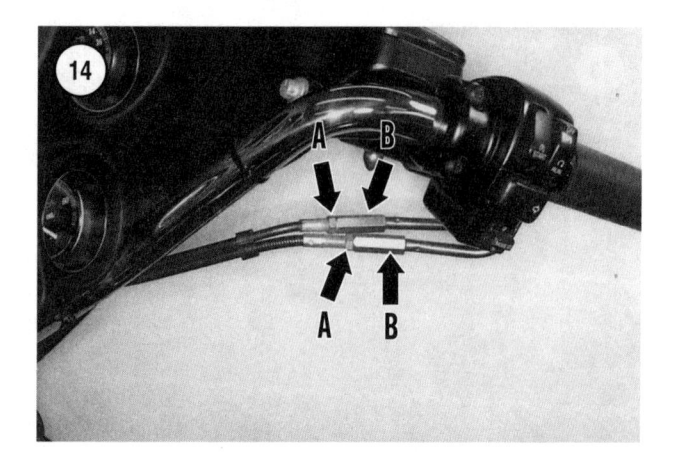

throttle cable bracket. Push the plastic cable end fitting to the outboard side and release it from the wheel pin.

7. At the handlebar, loosen both control cable adjuster locknuts (A, **Figure 14**). Then, turn the cable adjusters (B, **Figure 14**) *clockwise* as far as possible to increase cable slack.
8. Disconnect the fuel supply hose (A, **Figure 15**) from the carburetor fitting (B).
9. Twist, and then pull the carburetor off the seal ring and intake manifold.
10. Disconnect the vacuum hose from the carburetor fitting.
11. Disconnect the throttle control cable (A, **Figure 16**) and the idle control cable (B) from the carburetor cable guides (C) and the throttle wheel (D).
12. Drain the gasoline from the carburetor assembly.
13. Inspect the carburetor seal ring (**Figure 17**) on the intake manifold for wear, hardness, cracks or other damage. Replace if necessary.
14. If necessary, service the intake manifold as described in this chapter.
15. Insert a clean, lint-free shop cloth into the intake manifold opening.

Installation

1. Remove the shop cloth inside the intake manifold opening.
2. If removed, seat the seal ring onto the intake manifold. Make sure it is correctly seated to avoid a vacuum leak.
3. Route the starting enrichment valve cable between the cylinders and toward its mounting bracket on the left side.
4. Connect the idle cable to the carburetor as follows:
    a. The idle cable has the small spring (A, **Figure 18**) on the end of the cable.
    b. Insert the idle cable sheath into the rear cable guide (B, **Figure 18**) on the carburetor bracket.
    c. Attach the end of the idle cable (C, **Figure 18**) to the throttle wheel.
5. Connect the throttle cable to the carburetor as follows:
    a. Insert the throttle cable sheath into the front cable guide on the carburetor bracket.
    b. Attach the end of the throttle cable to the throttle wheel.

6. Operate the throttle grip a few times, making sure the throttle wheel operates smoothly with no binding. Also check that both cable ends are seated squarely in the cable guides and in the throttle wheel.
7. On cruise control models, slide the plastic end fitting over the cap of the wheel pin. Push on end fitting until it snaps in place. Slip the cable housing into the cable guide in the throttle cable bracket. Install a *new* E-clip into the groove at the end of the cable housing. Make sure it is correctly seated.

CAUTION
The carburetor must fit squarely onto the intake manifold. If misaligned, it may damage the intake manifold seal ring, resulting in a vacuum leak.

8. Align the carburetor (**Figure 19**) squarely with the intake manifold. Then, push it into the manifold until it bottoms. Position the carburetor so that it sits vertical and square with the manifold.
9. Connect the vacuum hose onto the carburetor fitting. Make sure it is seated correctly.
10. Slide a *new* hose clamp (A, **Figure 15**) over the fuel supply hose, and then connect the fuel hose to the hose fitting (B) on the carburetor.
11. Position the starting enrichment valve cable into the mounting bracket slot (B, **Figure 12**), and then tighten the locknut (A) securely.

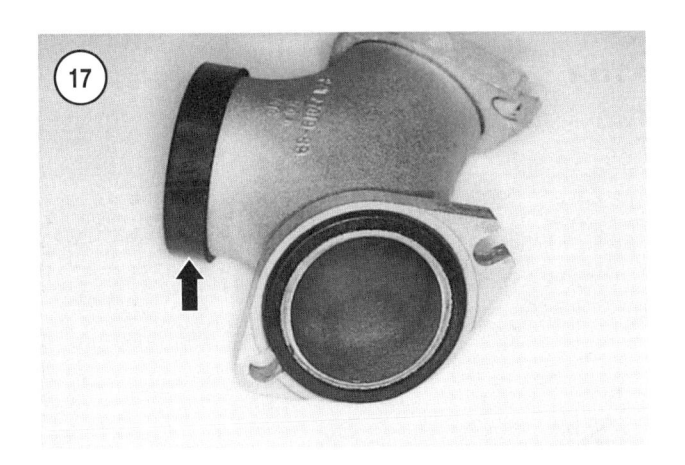

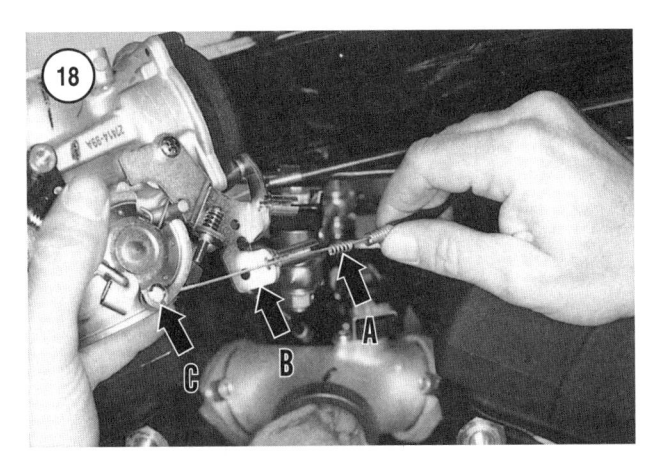

AIR/FUEL AND EMISSION CONTROL SYSTEMS (CARBURETED MODELS)

12. Before installing the fuel tank, recheck the idle and throttle cable operation. Open and release the throttle grip. Make sure the carburetor throttle valve opens and closes smoothly. Check that both cables are routed properly. Adjust the throttle cables as described in Chapter Three.
13. Install the air filter and backplate as described in this chapter.
14. Install the fuel tank as described in this chapter.
15. Connect the negative battery cable as described in Chapter Eleven.
16. Start the engine and allow it to idle. Check for fuel leaks.
17. With the engine idling in neutral, turn the handlebar from side to side. The idle speed must remain the same. If the idle speed increases while turning the handlebars, the cables are installed incorrectly or damaged. Remove the fuel tank and inspect the cables. Readjust or replace if necessary.

Disassembly

Refer to **Figure 20**.

1. Unscrew and remove the starting enrichment valve and cable (**Figure 21**).
2. Remove the screw (A, **Figure 22**) and washer on the side and the top screw (A, **Figure 23**) securing the throttle cable bracket to the carburetor. Remove the bracket (B, **Figure 23**). 
3. Remove the collar (**Figure 24**) from the cover.
4. Remove the remaining cover screws (**Figure 25**). Remove the cover and spring (A, **Figure 26**).
5. Remove the vacuum piston (B, **Figure 26**) from the carburetor housing. Do not damage the jet needle extending out of the bottom of the vacuum piston.
6. Remove the float bowl as follows:
   a. Remove the screws (**Figure 27**) securing the float bowl to the carburetor.
   b. Slowly remove the float bowl body and withdraw the pump rod (**Figure 28**) from the boot on the bowl.
   c. Disconnect the pump rod from the lever assembly (**Figure 29**) on the carburetor.

CAUTION
*One of the float pin pedestals has an interference fit that holds the float pin in place. An arrow, (**Figure 30**) cast into the carburetor, points to this pedestal. To remove the float pin, tap it out from the interference side in the direction of the arrow. If the float pin is removed in the direction opposite of the arrow, the opposite pedestal may break off. If this occurs the carburetor must be replaced.*

7. Carefully tap the float pin (**Figure 31**) out of the pedestals and remove it.
8. Remove the float (**Figure 32**) and needle valve assembly.
9. Unscrew and remove the pilot jet (**Figure 33**).
10. Unscrew and remove the main jet (**Figure 34**).
11. Unscrew and remove the main jet holder (**Figure 35**).
12. Remove the needle jet (A, **Figure 36**) from the needle jet bore in the carburetor.

Assembly

NOTE
The needle jet has two different size ends and must be installed correctly.

1. Position the needle jet with the long end (**Figure 37**) going in first and install it.

354

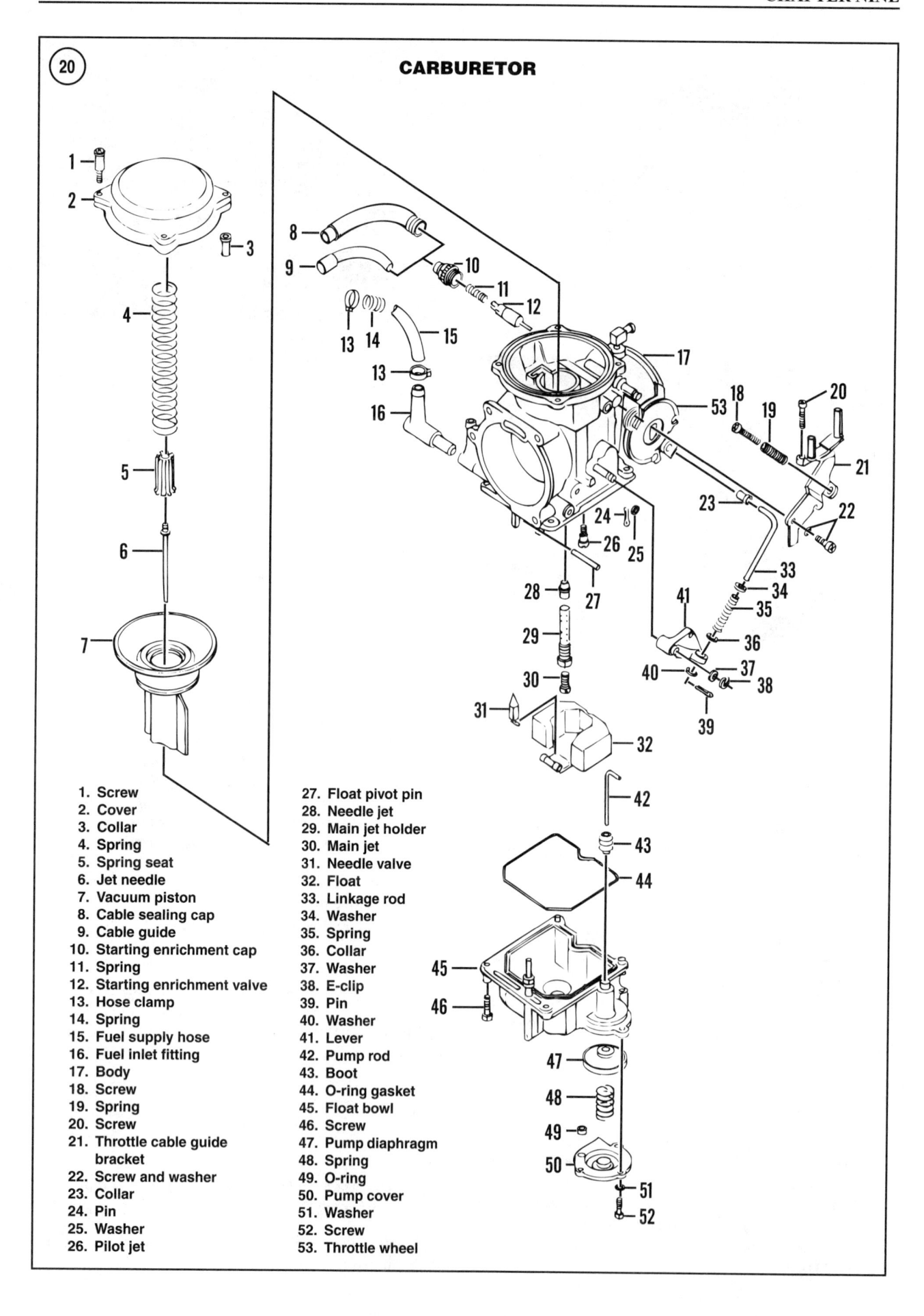

CHAPTER NINE

CARBURETOR

(20)

1. Screw
2. Cover
3. Collar
4. Spring
5. Spring seat
6. Jet needle
7. Vacuum piston
8. Cable sealing cap
9. Cable guide
10. Starting enrichment cap
11. Spring
12. Starting enrichment valve
13. Hose clamp
14. Spring
15. Fuel supply hose
16. Fuel inlet fitting
17. Body
18. Screw
19. Spring
20. Screw
21. Throttle cable guide bracket
22. Screw and washer
23. Collar
24. Pin
25. Washer
26. Pilot jet
27. Float pivot pin
28. Needle jet
29. Main jet holder
30. Main jet
31. Needle valve
32. Float
33. Linkage rod
34. Washer
35. Spring
36. Collar
37. Washer
38. E-clip
39. Pin
40. Washer
41. Lever
42. Pump rod
43. Boot
44. O-ring gasket
45. Float bowl
46. Screw
47. Pump diaphragm
48. Spring
49. O-ring
50. Pump cover
51. Washer
52. Screw
53. Throttle wheel

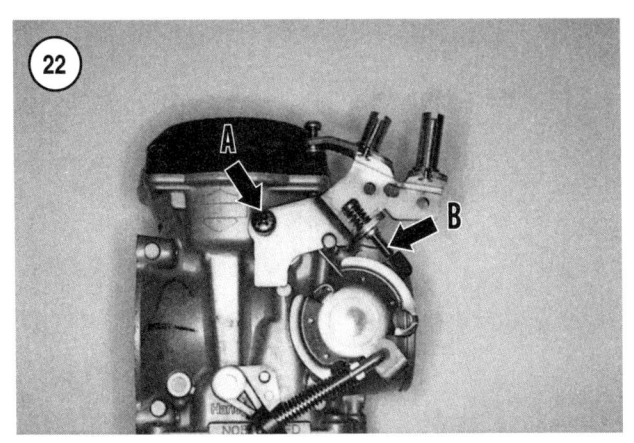

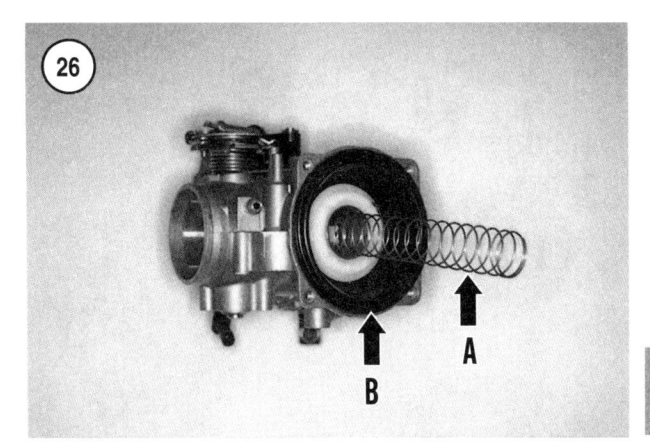

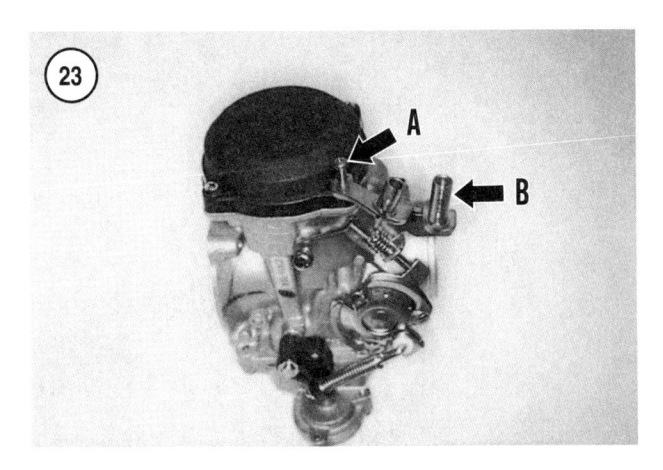

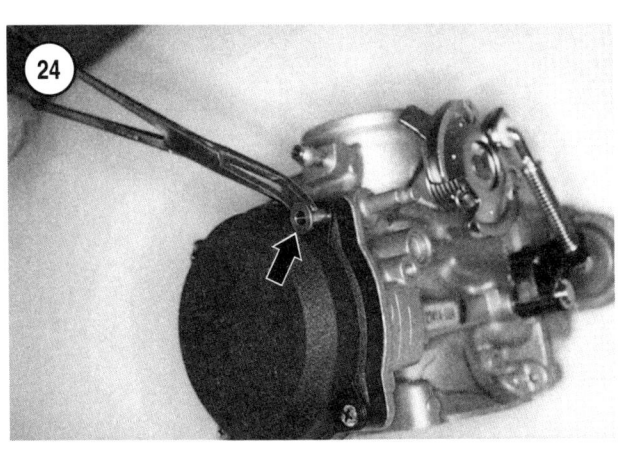

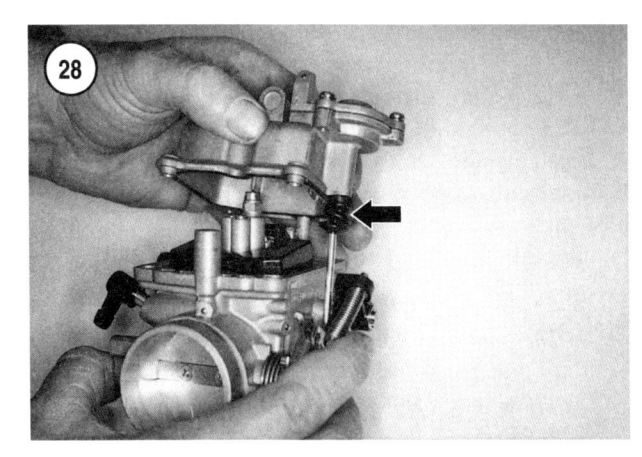

AIR/FUEL AND EMISSION CONTROL SYSTEMS (CARBURETED MODELS) 355

CHAPTER NINE

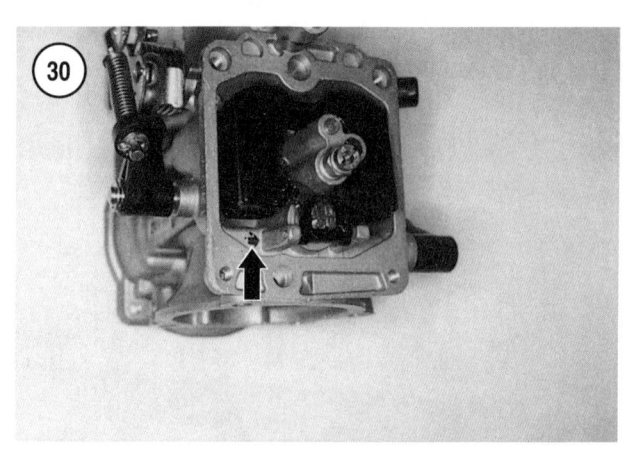

2. Install the main jet holder (**Figure 35**) into the main jet passage. Make sure it passes through the opening (**Figure 38**) in the venturi, and tighten securely.
3. Install the main jet (**Figure 34**) and tighten securely.
4. Install the pilot jet (**Figure 33**) and tighten securely.
5. Install the needle valve (**Figure 39**) onto the float and position the float onto the carburetor so that the valve drops into its seat.

CAUTION
The pedestals that support the float pin are fragile. In the next step, support the pedestal on the arrow side while tapping the float pin into place.

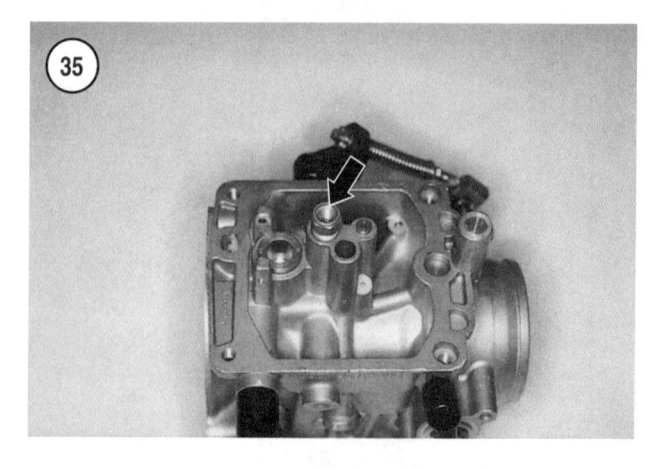

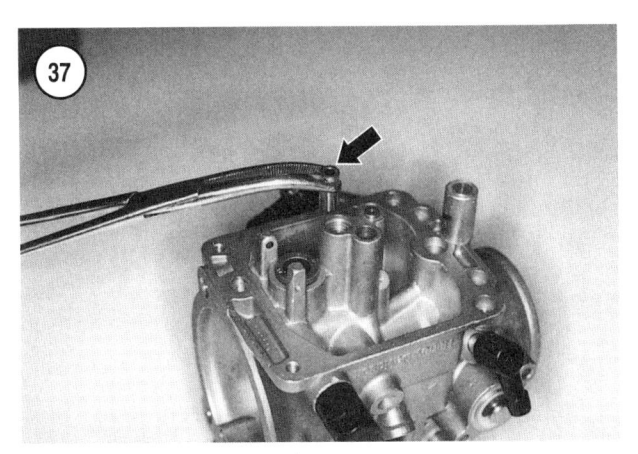

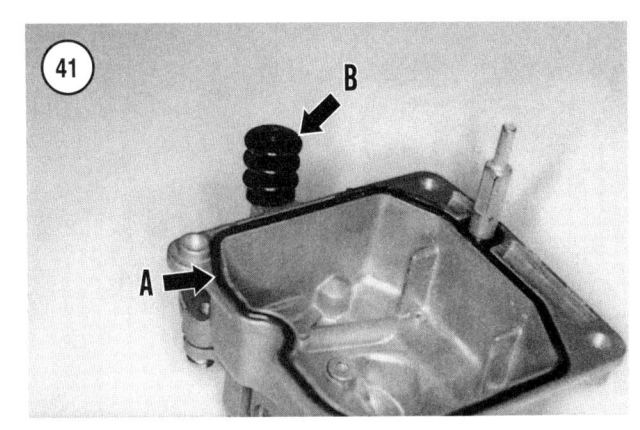

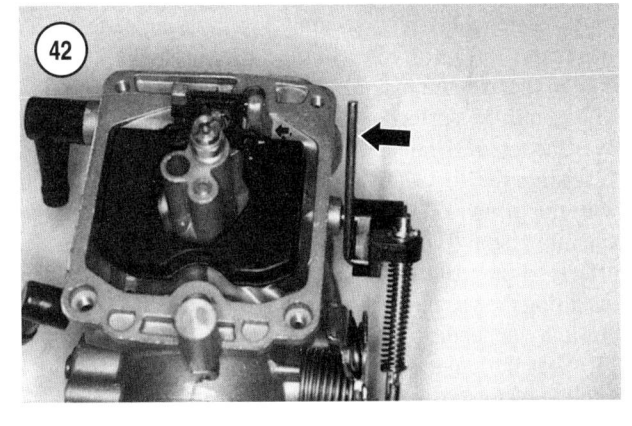

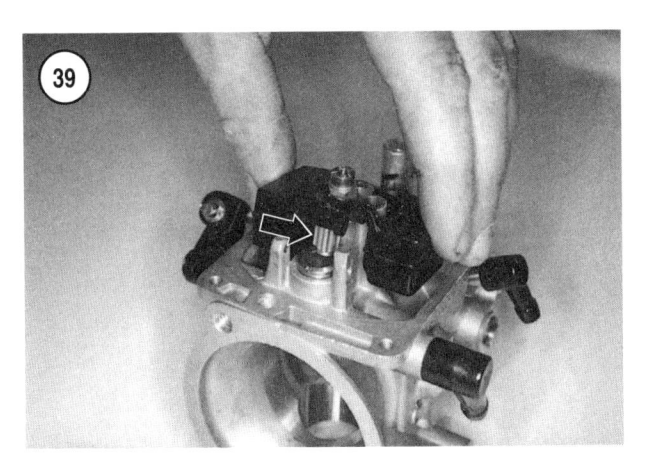

AIR/FUEL AND EMISSION CONTROL SYSTEMS (CARBURETED MODELS)

6. Align the float pin with the two pedestals.
7. Install the float pin (A, **Figure 40**) from the side opposite the arrow (B). Support the pedestal and tap the float pin into place in the pedestal.
8. Check the float level and adjust, if necessary, as described in this chapter.
9. Install the float bowl as follows:
   a. Make sure the float bowl O-ring seal (A, **Figure 41**) and accelerator pump rod boot (B) are in place.
   b. Connect the pump rod (**Figure 42**) onto the lever assembly on the carburetor.
   c. Slowly install the float bowl body and insert the accelerator pump rod through the boot (**Figure 28**) on the float bowl. Engage the rod with the diaphragm while installing the float bowl.

358

CHAPTER NINE

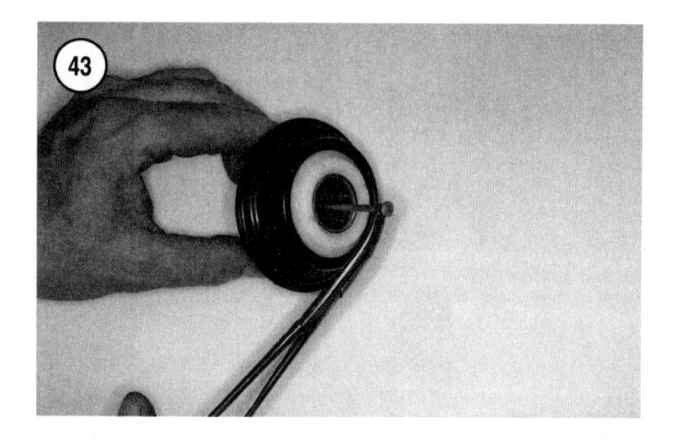

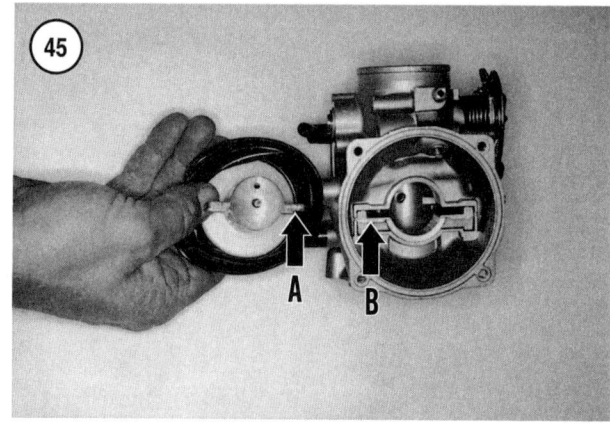

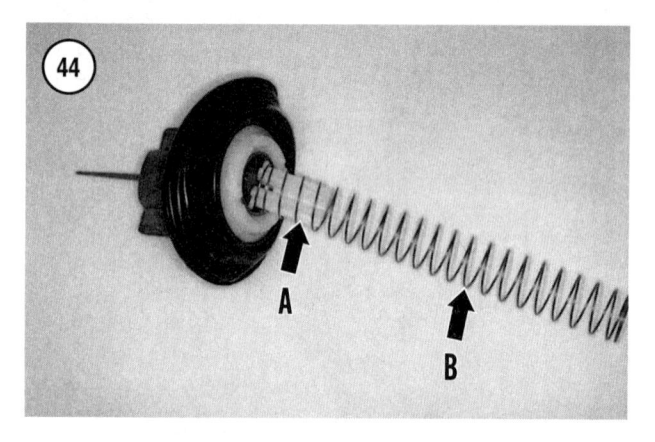

d. Install the float bowl and screws (**Figure 27**) and tighten the screws securely in a crossing pattern.

10. Insert the jet needle (**Figure 43**) through the center hole in the vacuum piston.
11. Install the spring seat (A, **Figure 44**) and spring (B) over the top of the needle to secure it in place.
12. Align the slides (A, **Figure 45**) on the vacuum piston with the grooves (B) in the carburetor bore and install the vacuum piston (B, **Figure 26**). The slides on the piston are offset, so the piston can only be installed one way. When installing the vacuum piston, make sure the jet needle drops through the needle jet.
13. Seat the outer edge of the vacuum piston diaphragm into the piston chamber groove (**Figure 46**).
14. Align the free end of the spring with the carburetor top and install the top onto the carburetor.
15. Hold the carburetor top in place and lift the vacuum piston with a finger (**Figure 47**). The piston must move smoothly. If the piston movement is rough or sluggish, the spring is installed incorrectly. Remove the carburetor top and reinstall the spring.
16. Install the three cover screws (**Figure 25**) finger-tight.
17. Install the collar (**Figure 24**) into the cover.
18. Install the throttle cable bracket (B, **Figure 23**) onto the carburetor so that the end of the idle speed screw (B, **Figure 22**) engages the top of the throttle cam stop. Hold the bracket in place and install the side mounting screw (A, **Figure 22**) and washer. Finger-tighten the screw.
19. Align the throttle cable bracket and install the remaining cover screw. Tighten the four cover screws securely.

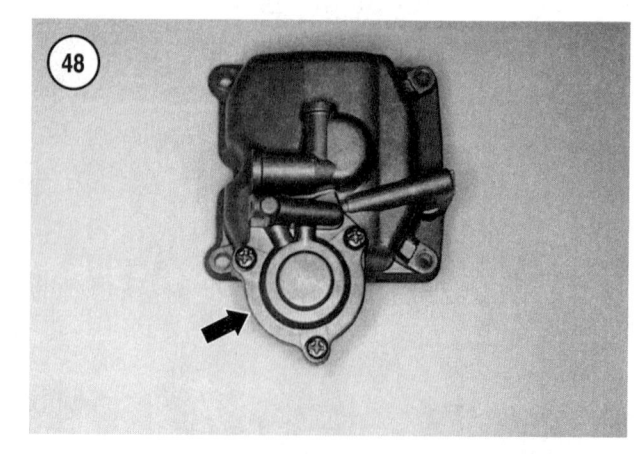

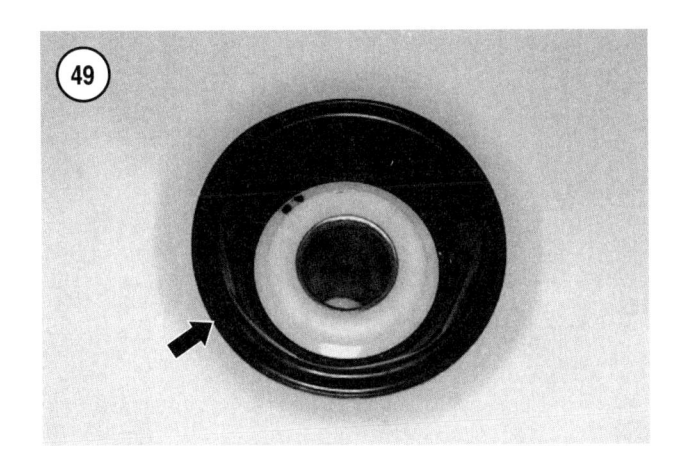

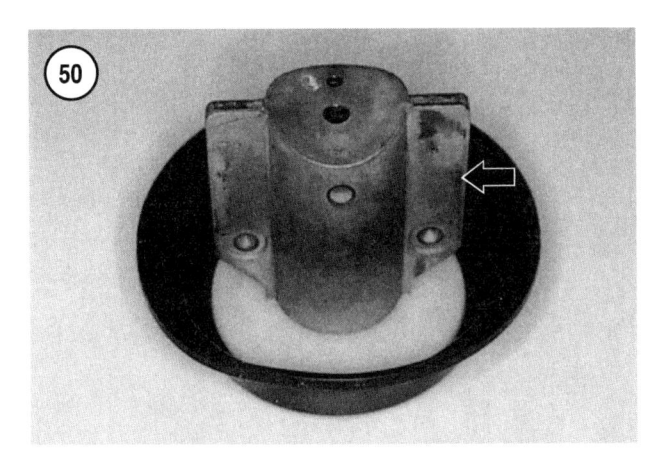

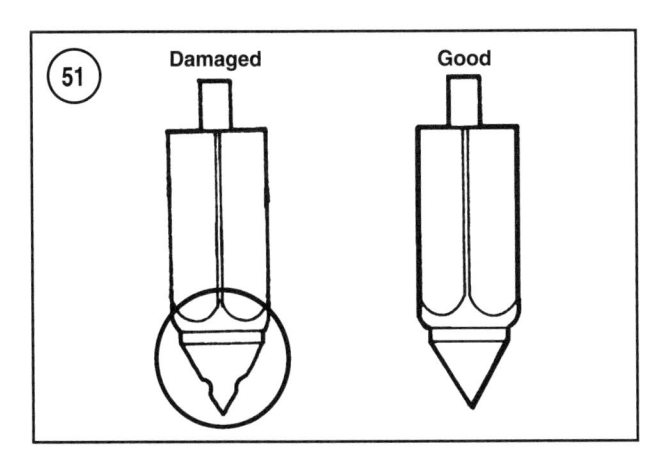

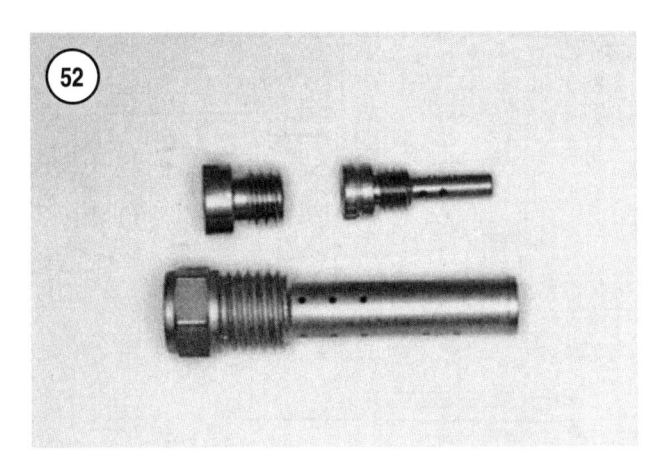

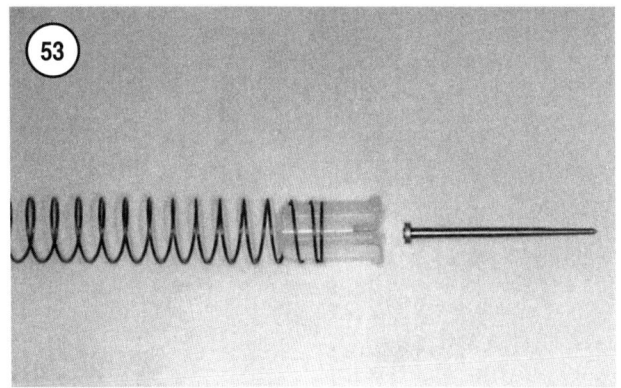

AIR/FUEL AND EMISSION CONTROL SYSTEMS (CARBURETED MODELS)

20. Tighten the side bracket mounting screws securely.
21. Install the starting enrichment cable and valve (**Figure 21**) into the carburetor body and tighten the nut securely.

Cleaning and Inspection

CAUTION
Do not clean the jet orifices or seats with wire or drill bits. These items can scratch the surface and damage the carburetor.

1. Clean all parts in mild petroleum-based cleaning solution. Then, clean them again in hot, soapy water and rinse with cold water. Thoroughly dry all parts with low-pressure compressed air.
2. Allow the carburetor to dry thoroughly before assembly. Blow dry with compressed air if necessary. Blow out the jets with compressed air.
3. Inspect the float bowl O-ring gasket (A, **Figure 41**) for hardness or deterioration.
4. Inspect the accelerator pump boot (B, **Figure 41**) for hardness, cracks or tears. Replace the boot if it is starting to deteriorate.
5. Make sure the accelerator pump cover (**Figure 48**) screws are tight.
6. Inspect the vacuum piston diaphragm (**Figure 49**) for cracks or deterioration. Check the vacuum piston sides (**Figure 50**) for excessive wear. Install the vacuum piston into the carburetor body and move it up and down in the bore. The vacuum piston should move smoothly with no binding or excessive play. If there is excessive play, the vacuum piston slide and/or carburetor body must be replaced.
7. Inspect the needle valve (**Figure 51**) tapered end for steps, uneven wear or other damage.
8. Inspect the needle valve seat (B, **Figure 36**) for steps, uneven wear or other damage. Insert the needle valve and slowly move it back and forth and check for smooth operation. If either part is worn or damaged, replace both parts as a pair for maximum performance.
9. Inspect the main jet holder, pilot jet and main jet (**Figure 52**). Make sure all holes are open and none of the parts are either worn or damaged.
10. Inspect the jet needle, spring and spring seat (**Figure 53**) for deterioration or damage.

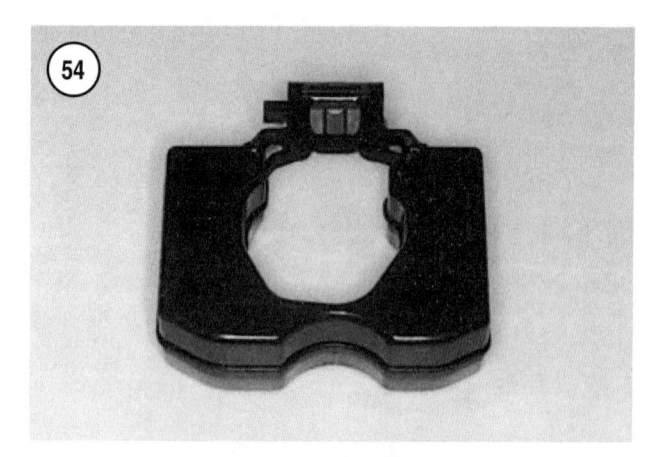

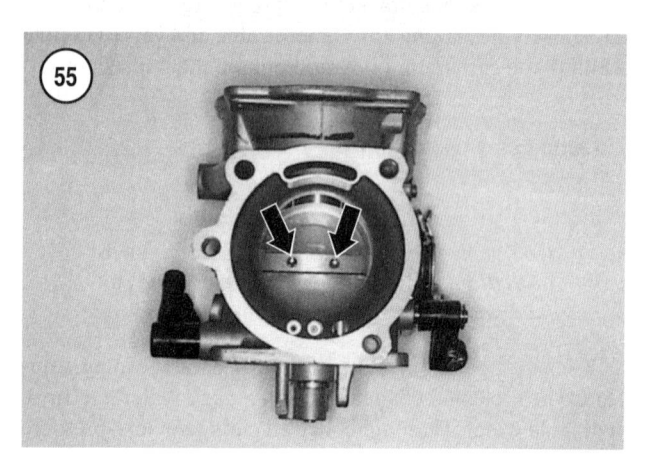

11. Inspect the jet needle tapered end for steps, uneven wear or other damage.
12. Inspect the float (**Figure 54**) for deterioration or damage. If the float is suspected of leaking, place it in a container of water and push it down. If the float sinks or if bubbles appear (indicating a leak), the float must be replaced.
13. Make sure the throttle plate screws (**Figure 55**) are tight. Tighten if necessary.
14. Move the throttle wheel (**Figure 56**) back and forth from stop to stop and check for free movement. The throttle lever should move smoothly and return under spring tension.
15. Check the throttle wheel return spring (**Figure 57**) for free movement. Make sure it rotates the throttle wheel back to the stop position with no hesitation.
16. Make sure all openings in the carburetor housing are clear. Clean out if they are plugged in any way, and apply compressed air to all openings.
17. Inspect the carburetor body for internal or external damage. If damaged, replace the carburetor assembly, as the body cannot be replaced separately.
18. Check the top cover for cracks or damage.
19. Check the starting enrichment valve and cable as follows:
   a. Check the end of the valve (**Figure 58**) for damage.
   b. Check the entire length of the cable for bends, chaffing or other damage.
   c. Check the knob, nut and lock washer for damage. Move the knob and check for ease of movement.

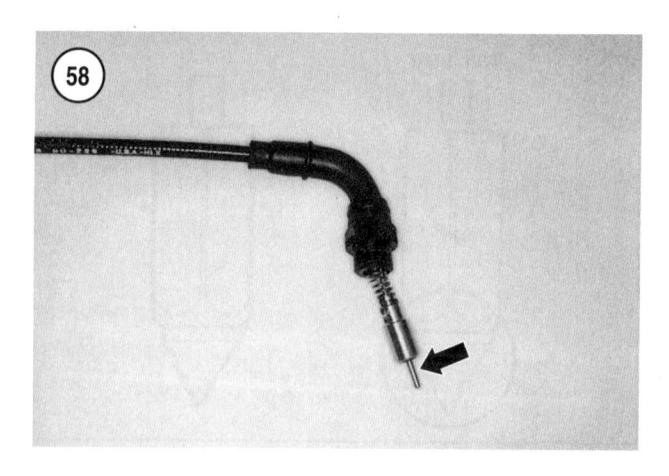

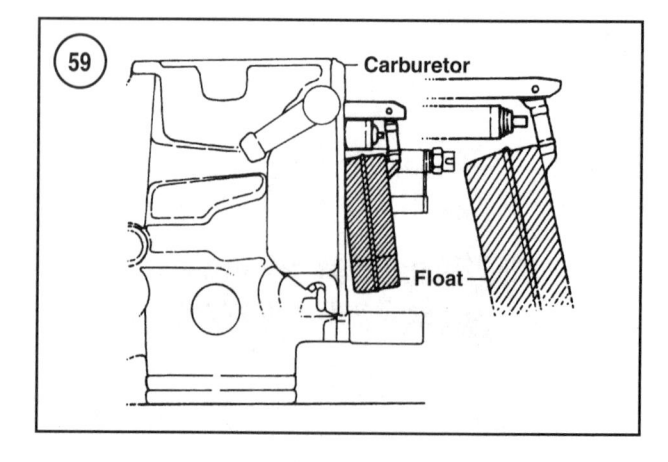

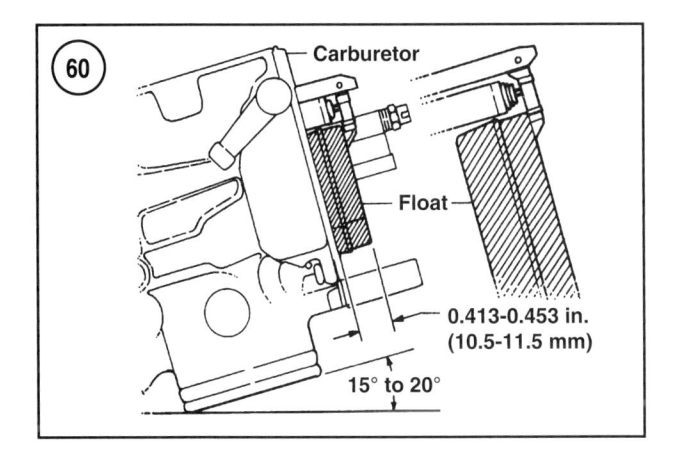

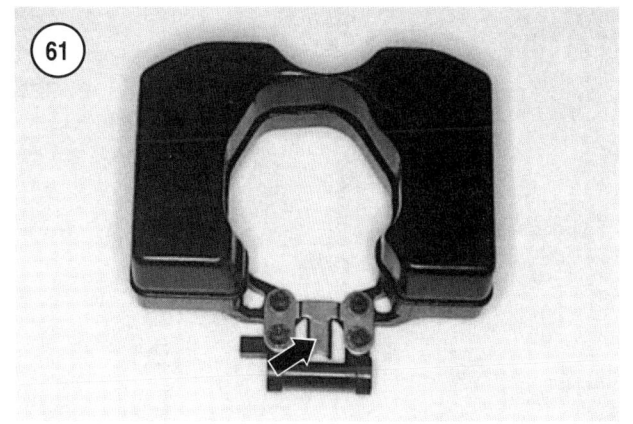

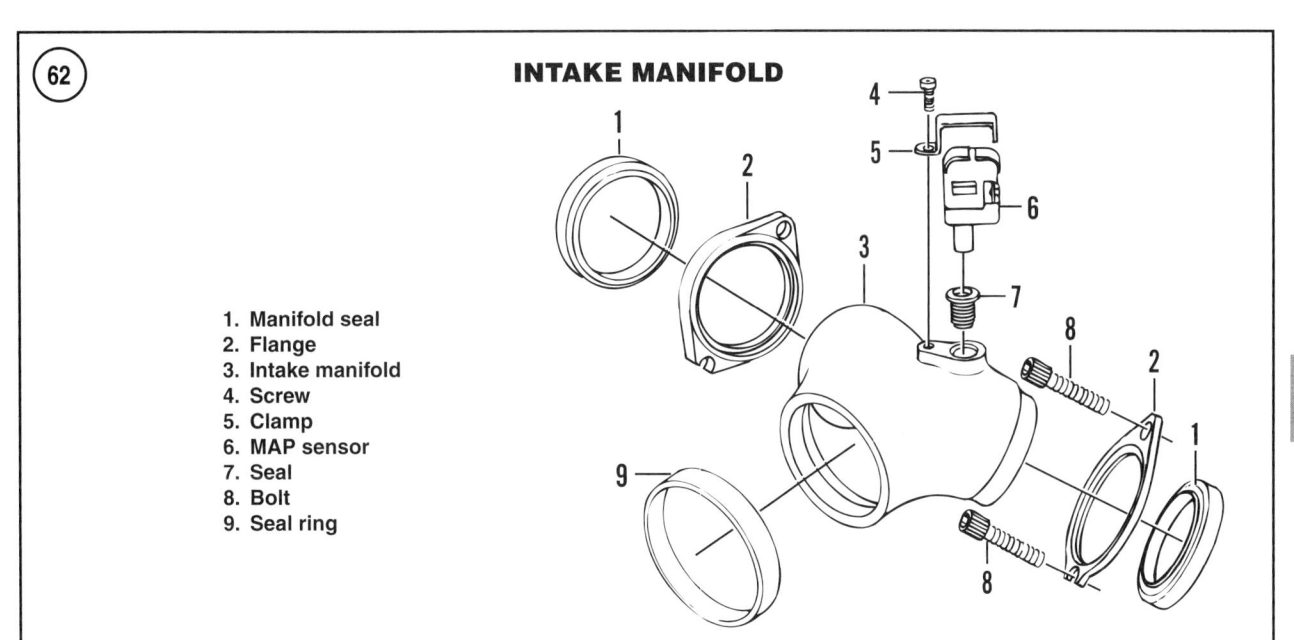

AIR/FUEL AND EMISSION CONTROL SYSTEMS (CARBURETED MODELS)

⑥⓪ Carburetor / Float / 0.413-0.453 in. (10.5-11.5 mm) / 15° to 20°

⑥①

⑥② INTAKE MANIFOLD

1. Manifold seal
2. Flange
3. Intake manifold
4. Screw
5. Clamp
6. MAP sensor
7. Seal
8. Bolt
9. Seal ring

Float Adjustment

The carburetor must be removed and partially disassembled for this adjustment.

1. Remove the carburetor as described in this section.
2. Remove the float bowl as described in this section.
3. Place the intake manifold side of the carburetor on a clean flat surface as shown in **Figure 59**. This is the base position.

NOTE
If the carburetor is tilted less than 15° or more than 20°, the float measurement will be incorrect.

4. Tilt the carburetor upward 15-20° as shown in **Figure 60**. At this position, the float will come to rest without compressing the pin return spring.
5. Measure from the carburetor flange surface to the top of the float as shown in **Figure 60**. When measuring float level, do not compress the float. The correct float level measurement is 0.413-0.453 in. (10.5-11.5 mm).
6. If the float level is incorrect, remove the float pin and float as described in this section.
7. Slowly bend the float tang (**Figure 61**) with a screwdriver and adjust to the correct position.
8. Reinstall the float and the float pin as described in this section. Recheck the float level.
9. Repeat the adjustment procedure until the float level is correct.
10. Install the float bowl and carburetor as described in this section.

INTAKE MANIFOLD

Removal/Installation

Refer to **Figure 62**.

1. Remove the carburetor as described in this chapter.

NOTE
The front and rear intake manifold flanges are different. If the flanges are not marked, label them with an F and R so they will be reinstalled in the correct location.

2. Disconnect the electrical connector from the MAP sensor (A, **Figure 63**), located on top of the intake manifold.

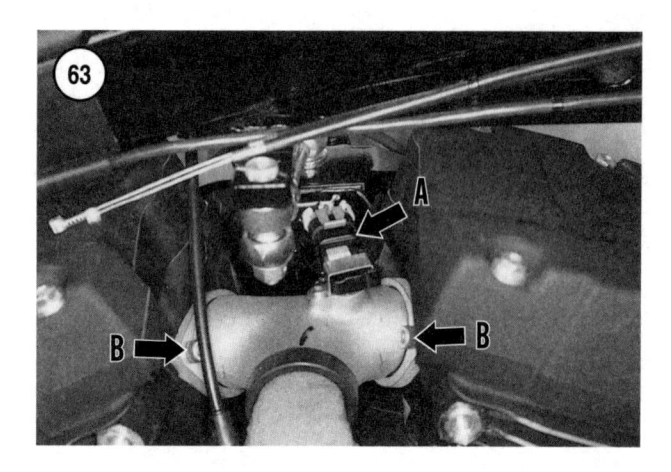

NOTE
Figure 63 shows only two of the Allen bolts. Remove all four bolts.

3. Remove the four Allen bolts (B, **Figure 63**) securing the intake manifold to the cylinder heads.
4. Remove the intake manifold flanges (A, **Figure 64**), manifold seals (B) and sealing ring (C).
5. Inspect the intake manifold as described in this section.
6. Install the flanges (A, **Figure 64**) and manifold seals (B) onto the intake manifold.
7. Install the intake manifold onto the cylinder head intake ports.
8. Check that the front and rear seals seat squarely against the cylinder head mating surfaces.
9. Install all four Allen bolts. Finger-tighten the bolts at this time.
10. Temporarily install the carburetor (**Figure 65**) into the intake manifold.

CAUTION
Do not attempt to align the intake manifold after tightening the bolts. This will damage the manifold seals. If necessary, loosen the bolts, and align the manifold.

11. Check that the intake manifold seats squarely against the cylinder heads. Then, check that the carburetor seats squarely in the intake manifold. Remove the carburetor.

NOTE
*It is difficult to access the two inboard Allen bolts with an Allen wrench and torque wrench to tighten them to a specific torque value. Tighten the outboard Allen bolts to the torque value specified in **Table 2**, and then tighten the inboard Allen bolts to the same approximate tightness.*

12. Tighten the intake manifold Allen bolts to 96-144 in.-lb. (10.8-16.3 N•m).
13. If the MAP sensor was removed, reinstall it as follows:
   a. Install a *new* seal in the manifold receptacle.

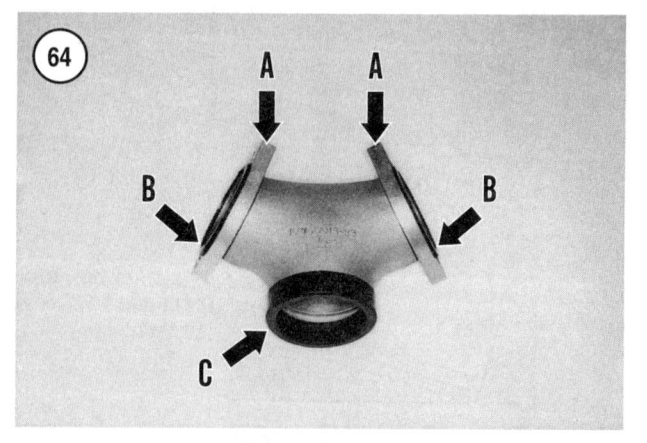

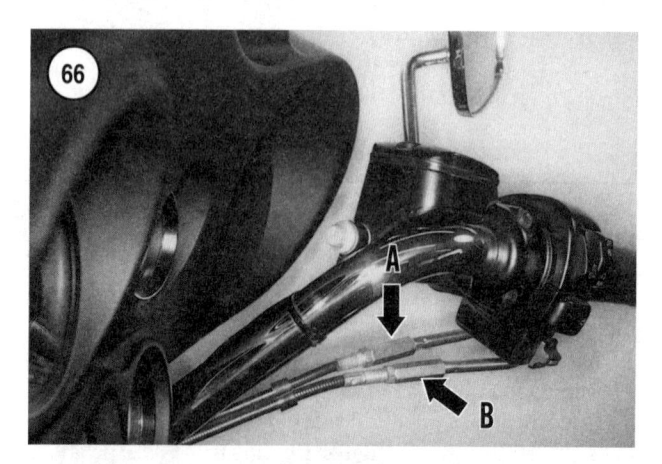

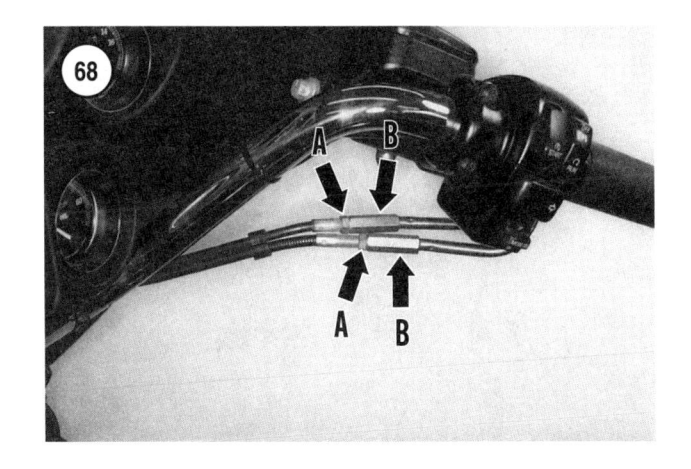

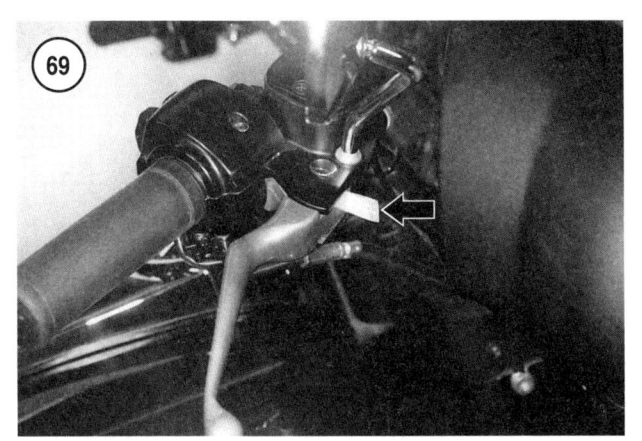

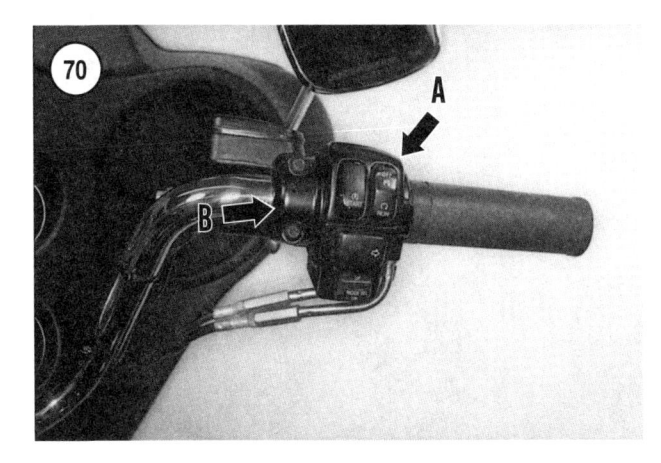

AIR/FUEL AND EMISSION CONTROL SYSTEMS (CARBURETED MODELS)

b. Install the MAP sensor and push it in until it bottoms in the receptacle.
c. Install the clamp over the sensor, and then install the mounting screw to secure the clamp in place.
d. Tighten the MAP sensor screw to 20-35 in.-lb. (2.3-4.0 N•m).

14. Connect the electrical connector onto the MAP sensor (A, **Figure 63**).
15. Install the carburetor as described in this chapter.

Inspection

1. Check the intake manifold seals (B, **Figure 64**) for wear, deterioration or other damage. Replace the seals as a set if necessary.
2. Check the intake manifold seal ring (C, **Figure 64**) for cracks, flat spots or other damage. Replace if necessary.
3. If necessary, remove the self-tapping screw and clamp. Then, remove the MAP sensor. Inspect the sensor seal in the manifold port for hardness. Replace as necessary.

THROTTLE AND IDLE CABLES (2006-2007 NON-CRUISE CONTROL MODELS)

There are two different throttle cables. At the throttle grip, the front cable (A, **Figure 66**) is the throttle control cable and the rear cable (B) is the idle control cable. At the carburetor the outboard cable (A, **Figure 67**) is the throttle control cable and the inboard cable (B) is the idle control cable.

Removal

1. Remove the fuel tank as described in this chapter.
2. Remove the air filter and backplate as described in this chapter.
3. Make a drawing or take a picture of the cable routing from the carburetor through the frame to the right side handlebar.
4. At the right side handlebar, loosen both control cable adjuster locknuts (A, **Figure 68**). Then, turn the cable adjusters (B, **Figure 68**) *clockwise* as far as possible to increase cable slack.

CAUTION
Failure to install the spacer will result in damage to the rubber boot and plunger on the front brake switch.

5. Insert a 5/32 in. (4 mm) thick spacer (**Figure 69**) between the brake lever and lever bracket. Make sure the spacer stays in place during the removal procedure.
6. Remove the upper and lower Torx screws (T25) securing the right side switch assembly (A, **Figure 70**) together.
7. Remove the front master cylinder (B, **Figure 70**) as described in Chapter Fifteen.
8. Remove the brass ferrules (**Figure 71**) from the notches on the inboard side of the throttle grip. Remove the ferrules from the cable end fittings.

9. Remove the friction shoe from the end of the tension adjusting screw.
10. Remove the throttle grip from the handlebar.

NOTE
Use a rocking motion while pulling on the control cable housings. If necessary, place a drop of engine oil on the retaining rings to ease removal.

11. Pull the crimped inserts at the end of the throttle and idle control cable housings from the switch lower housing.
12. Partially remove the carburetor (this chapter) to provide access to the cables. Disconnect the throttle control cable and idle control cable from the carburetor cable guides and throttle wheel.
13. On cruise control models, disconnect the two single electrical connectors (**Figure 72**) on the throttle cable.
14. On all FLHT and FLHX series models, withdraw the throttle and idle cables from the inner fairing rubber grommet. Move the idle and throttle cables forward and out of the way.
15. Remove all clips and tie-wraps securing the throttle and idle control cables from the frame backbone and ignition coil bracket.
16. Disconnect the cables from the J-clamp on the right side of the frame backbone.
17. If necessary, remove the bolts, washer, P-clamp and locknut securing the cables to the right side of the steering head.
18. Remove the cables from the frame.
19. Clean the throttle grip assembly and dry thoroughly. Check the throttle slots for cracks or other damage. Replace the throttle if necessary.
20. The friction adjust screw is secured to the lower switch housing with a circlip. If necessary, remove the friction spring, circlip, spring and friction adjust screw. Check these parts for wear or damage. Replace damaged parts and reverse to install. Make sure the circlip seats in the friction screw groove completely.
21. Clean the throttle area on the handlebar with solvent.

Installation

WARNING
Do not ride the motorcycle until the throttle cables are properly adjusted. Improper cable routing and adjustment can cause the throttle to stick open. This could cause loss of control. Recheck the adjustment before riding the bike.

1. On all FLHT and FLHX series models, insert the throttle and idle cables through the inner fairing rubber grommet.
2. Apply a light coat of graphite to the housing inside surfaces and to the handlebar.
3. On the lower housing, push the larger diameter, silver crimped insert on the throttle cable into the larger hole in front of the tension adjust screw. Push it in until it snaps into place.
4. Push the smaller diameter, gold crimped insert on the throttle cable into the smaller hole in the rear of the tension adjusting screw in the switch lower housing. Push it in until it snaps into place.
5. Position the friction shoe with the concave side facing up and install it so that the pin hole is over the point of the adjuster screw.
6. Install the throttle grip onto the handlebar. Push it on until it stops, and then pull it back about 1/8 in. (3.2 mm). Rotate it until the ferrule notches are at the top.
7. Place the lower switch housing below the throttle grip. Install the brass ferrules onto the cables so the end fittings seat in the ferrule recess. Seat the ferrules in their respective notches on the throttle control grip. Make sure the cables are captured in the molded grooves in the grip.

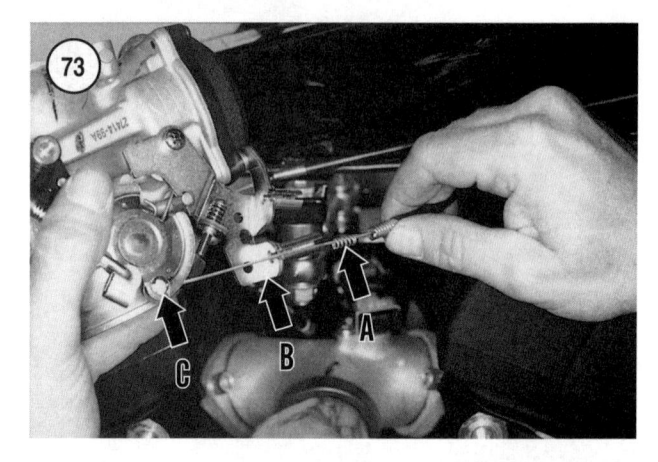

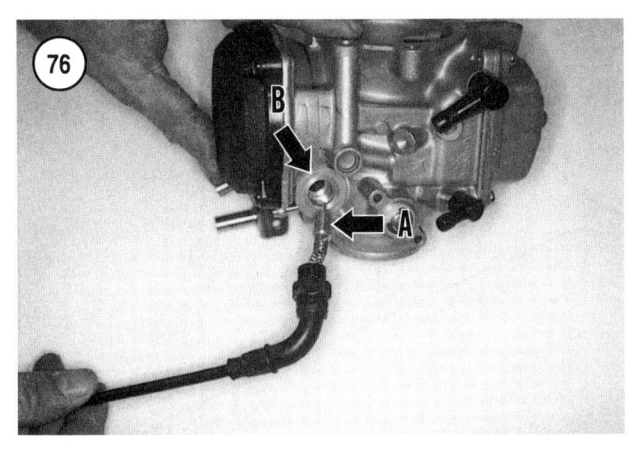

AIR/FUEL AND EMISSION CONTROL SYSTEMS (CARBURETED MODELS)

8. Assemble upper and lower switch housing. Install the switch assembly (A, **Figure 70**) and the throttle grip assembly. Install and finger-tighten the lower switch housing screws.
9. If not in place, insert the 5/32 in. (4 mm) thick spacer between the brake lever and lever bracket. Make sure the spacer stays in place during installation of the master cylinder and switch housing.
10. Install the front master cylinder (B, **Figure 70**) onto the handlebar as described in Chapter Fifteen.
11. Tighten the switch housing screws securely. Tighten the front screw first so any gap between the housing halves sits at the front of the switch.
12. Remove the spacer from the front master cylinder.
13. Operate the throttle grip and make sure both cables move in and out correctly.
14. Correctly route the cables from the handlebar to the carburetor along the same path noted their during removal. Secure the cables with the original clamps and tie-wraps.
15. On cruise control models, connect the two single electrical connectors (**Figure 72**) onto idle cable.
16. Connect the idle cable to the carburetor as follows:
    a. The idle cable has the small spring (A, **Figure 73**) on the end of the cable.
    b. Insert the idle cable sheath into the rear cable guide on the carburetor bracket (B, **Figure 73**).
    c. Attach the end of the idle cable into the throttle wheel (C, **Figure 73**).
17. Connect the throttle cable to the carburetor as follows:
    a. Insert the throttle cable sheath into the front cable guide on the carburetor bracket.
    b. Attach the end of the throttle cable into the throttle wheel.
18. At the throttle grip, tighten the cables to keep the cable ends from being disconnected from throttle wheel.
19. Operate the throttle grip a few times, making sure the throttle barrel operates smoothly with no binding. Also check that both cable ends are seated squarely in their cable guides and in the throttle barrel.
20. Adjust the throttle and idle cables as described in Chapter Three.
21. If removed, reinstall the carburetor as described in this chapter.
22. Install the air filter and backplate as described in this chapter.
23. Install the fuel tank as described in this chapter.
24. Start the engine and allow it to idle in neutral. Then turn the handlebar from side to side. Do not operate the throttle. If the engine speed increases when turning the handlebar assembly, the throttle cables are routed incorrectly or damaged. Recheck cable routing and adjustment.

STARTING ENRICHMENT VALVE (CHOKE) CABLE REPLACEMENT

1. Remove the air filter and backplate as described in this chapter.
2. Note the routing of the enrichment cable from its mounting bracket to the carburetor.
3. Loosen the locknut (A, **Figure 74**) and disconnect the starting enrichment valve cable from the mounting bracket (B). Move the end of the cable out of the mounting bracket slot.
4. Partially remove the carburetor, as described in this chapter, until the starting enrichment valve cable can be disconnected from the backside of the carburetor.
5. Unscrew and remove the starting enrichment valve and cable (**Figure 75**) from the carburetor. Then, remove the cable from the frame.
6. Install by reversing the removal steps while noting the following:
    a. Align the starting enrichment valve needle (A, **Figure 76**) with the needle passage (B) in the carburetor body and install the starting enrichment valve. Tighten the valve securely.
    b. Position the starting enrichment valve cable into the mounting bracket slot (B, **Figure 76**), and then tighten the locknut (A) securely.
    c. Adjust the cable as described in Chapter Three.

FUEL TANK CONSOLE

Removal/Installation

Refer to **Figures 77-79**.

CHAPTER NINE

FUEL TANK CONSOLE (FLHT AND FLHX MODELS)

1. Nut
2. Console door
3. Lock
4. Key
5. Fuel filler cap
6. Bolt
7. Gasket
8. Screw
9. Rubber boot
10. Clip
11. Hinge pin
12. Trim insert
13. Console
14. Screw
15. Staked nut
16. Trim
17. Clip nut

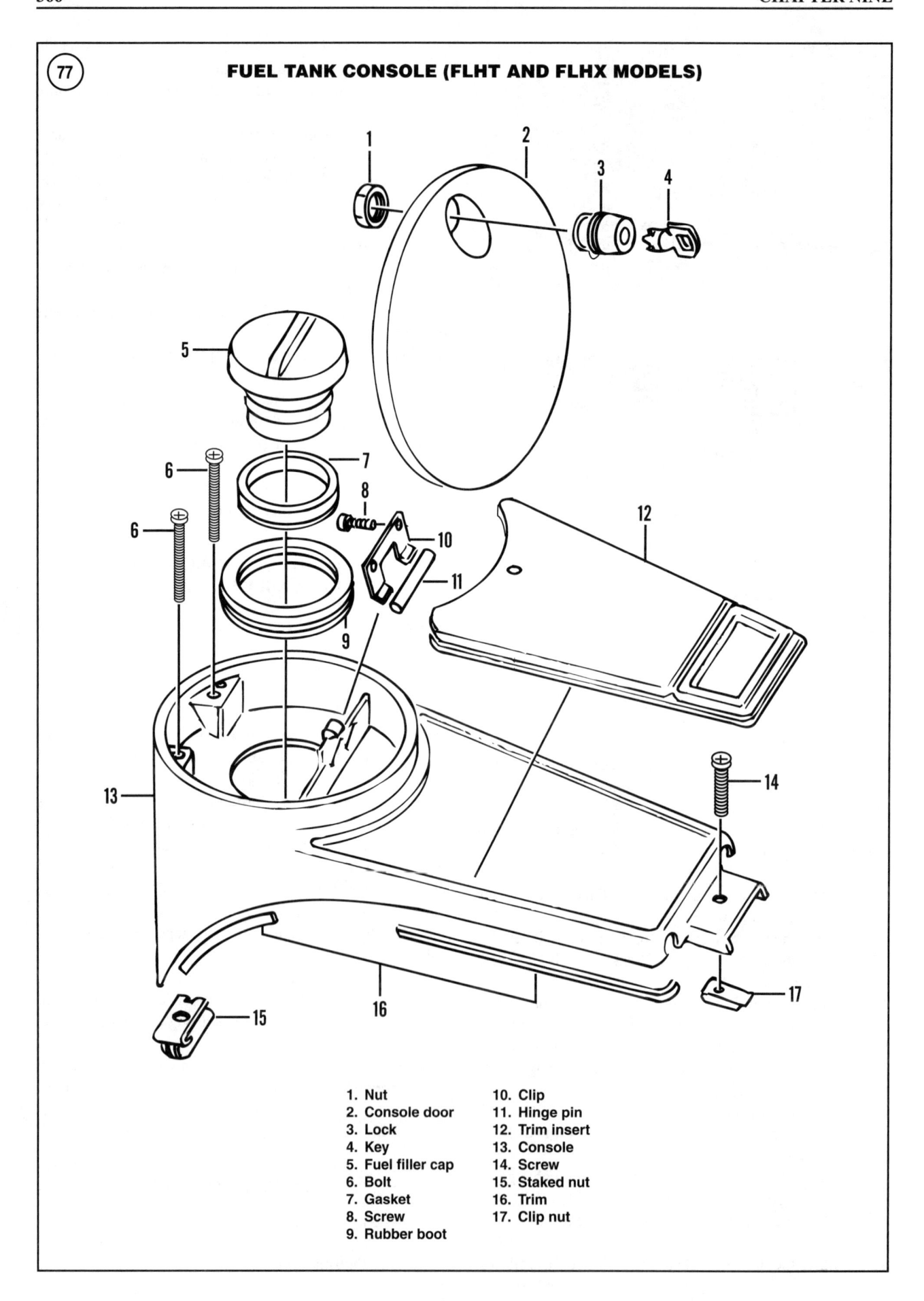

AIR/FUEL AND EMISSION CONTROL SYSTEMS (CARBURETED MODELS)

(78) FUEL TANK CONSOLE (FLHRS MODELS)

1. Rubber boot
2. Odometer reset switch
3. Speedometer
4. Gasket
5. Console
6. Bezel
7. Acorn nut
8. Name plate
9. Key
10. Trim insert
11. Trim gasket
12. Threaded stud
13. Fuel gauge
14. Gasket
15. Lower clamp
16. Connector
17. Screw
18. Indicator lamp housing
19. Clip
20. Mounting bracket
21. Fuel tank mounting bolt
22. Ignition switch

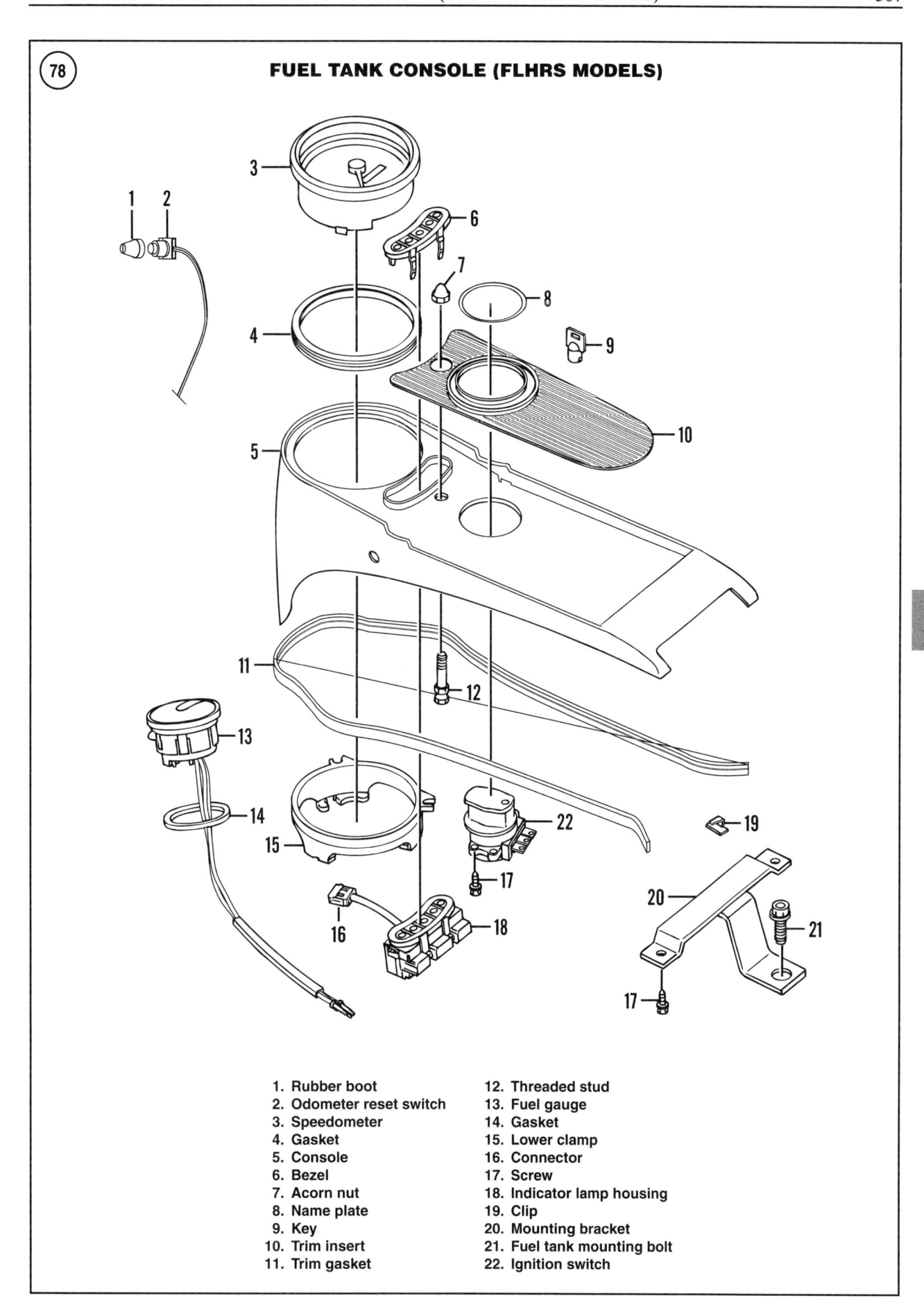

368 CHAPTER NINE

⑦⁹ FUEL TANK CONSOLE (FLHR MODELS)

1. Speedometer
2. Gasket
3. Console
4. Rubber boot
5. Odometer reset switch
6. Threaded stud
7. Lower clamp
8. Fuel level gauge
9. Gasket
10. Indicator lamp housing
11. Screw
12. Ignition switch
13. Clip nut
14. Trim
15. Washer
16. Screw
17. Name plate
18. Key
19. Bezel
20. Acorn nut

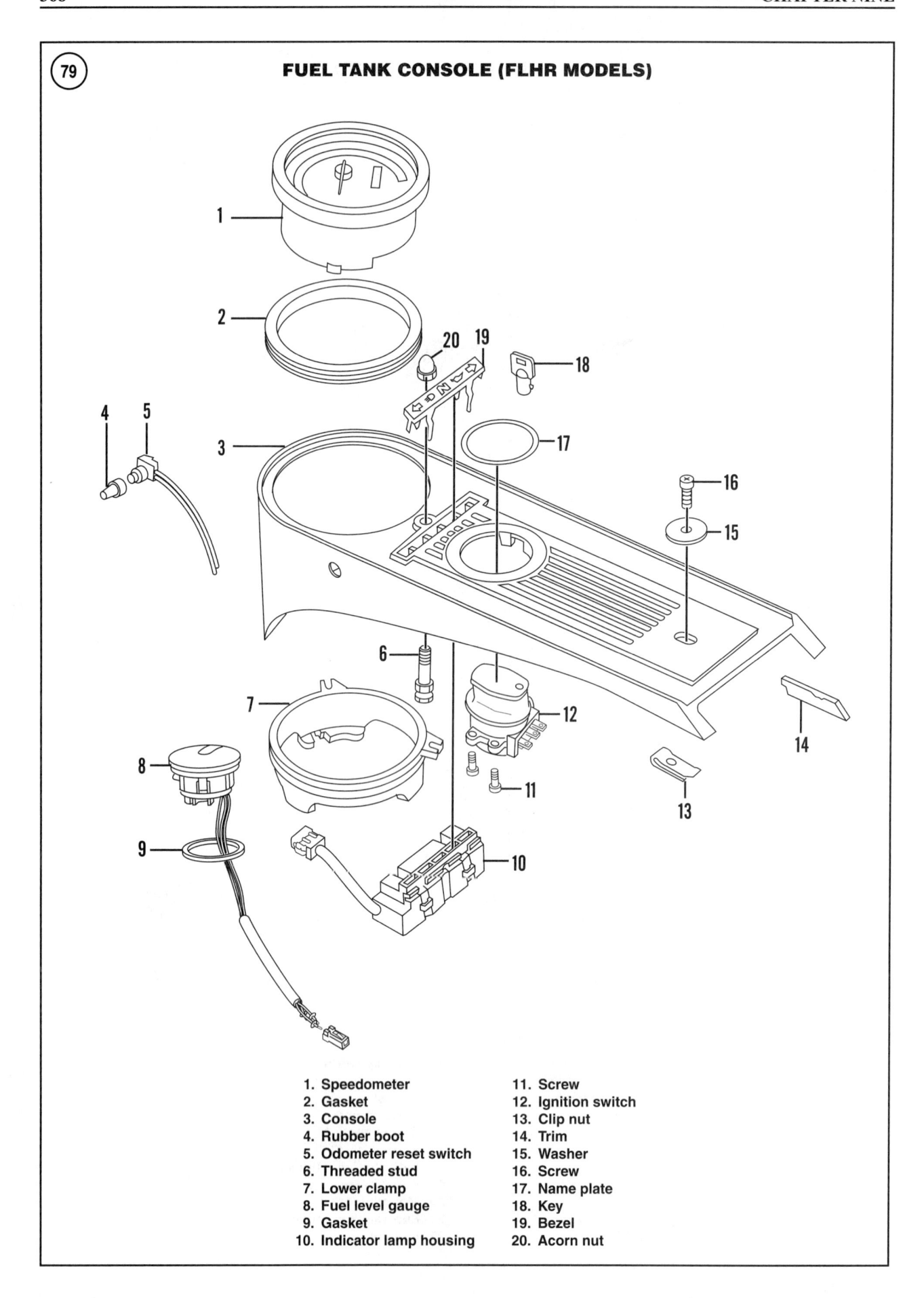

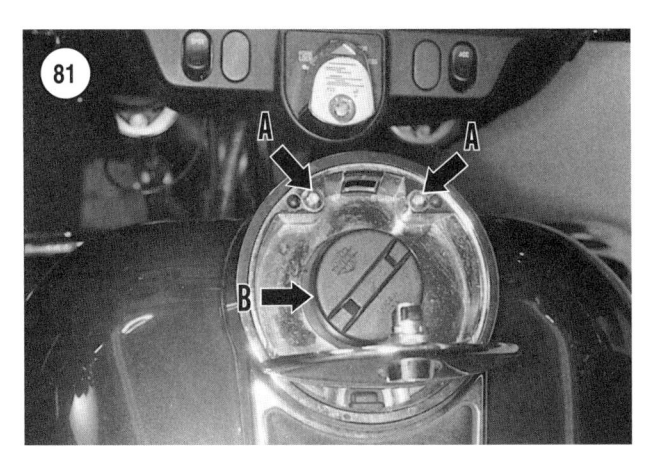

AIR/FUEL AND EMISSION CONTROL SYSTEMS (CARBURETED MODELS)

4. Carefully remove the console and lay it upside down on some shop cloths or towels.
5. On FLHT and FLHX series models, reinstall the fuel filler cap (B, **Figure 81**) and tighten securely.
6. Install by reversing the removal steps, while noting the following:
   a. Carefully route the electrical cables and fuel vapor hose between the console and fuel tank so they will not get pinched.
   b. On FLHR series models, reposition the fuel level sender wires to the main harness on the left side frame rail and install a *new* cable strap.

FUEL TANK

Removal/Installation

Refer to **Figure 82** and **Figure 83**.
The fuel hoses are secured to the fuel tank with a non-reusable clamp. Purchase *new* ones before servicing the fuel tank.
1. Disconnect the negative battery cable as described in Chapter Eleven.
2. Remove the fuel tank console as described in this chapter.
3. Turn the fuel valve (A, **Figure 84**, typical) to the OFF position.
4. Remove the hose clamp and disconnect the fuel hose (B, **Figure 84**) from the fuel valve.

NOTE
A crossover tube connects the two fuel tank compartments. Drain both sides of the tank before removing the tank in the following steps.

5. Drain the fuel tank as follows:

NOTE
A vacuum-operated fuel valve is installed on all models. A hand-operated vacuum pump is required to drain the fuel tank.

   a. Connect the drain hose to the fuel valve and secure it with a hose clamp. Insert the end of the drain hose into a gas can.
   b. Unscrew the fuel filler cap.
   c. Disconnect the vacuum hose from the fuel valve.
   d. Connect a hand-operated vacuum pump (**Figure 85**) to the fuel valve vacuum hose fitting.
   e. Turn the fuel valve to the RES position.

CAUTION
Do not apply excess vacuum or the fuel valve diaphragm will be damaged.

   f. Gently operate the vacuum pump handle and apply up to a *maximum* of 25 in. (635 mm) Hg of vacuum. Once the vacuum is applied the fuel will start to flow into the gas can. Maintain vacuum until the tank is drained.

NOTE
Always disarm the TSSM/HFSM security system prior to disconnecting the battery or pulling the Maxi-Fuse so the siren will not sound.

1. Disconnect the negative battery cable as described in Chapter Eleven.
2. Remove the seat as described in Chapter Seventeen.
3A. On FLHT and FLHX series models, perform the following:
   a. Remove the screw (**Figure 80**) securing the console to the fuel tank.
   b. Open the console door.
   c. Remove the two front Allen bolts (A, **Figure 81**) securing the console to the fuel tank mounting brackets.
   d. Unscrew the fuel filler cap (B, **Figure 81**).
3B. On FLHR series models, perform the following:
   a. Cut the cable strap securing the fuel level sender wires to the main harness on the left side frame rail.
   b. At the rear of the fuel tank, disconnect the 4-pin Multi-lock electrical connector (No. 141) from the main harness.
   c. Remove the front acorn nut and the rear screw and washer securing the console to the fuel tank.
   d. Lift the console partially up off the fuel tank. Bend back the flexible clamp and release the main harness from the console. Disconnect the speedometer, ignition switch and the indicator lamp housing electrical connector from the main harness.

CHAPTER NINE

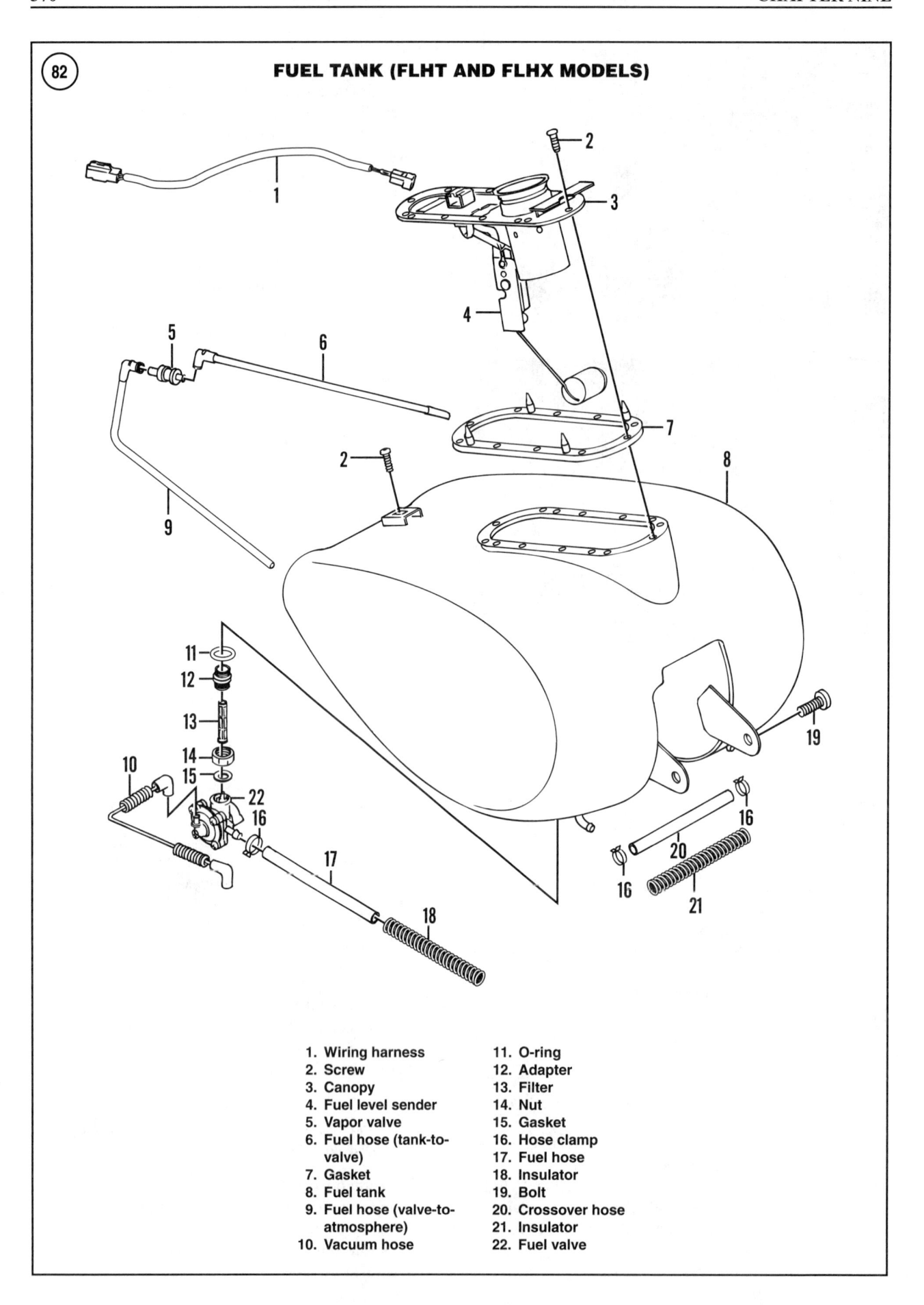

82 FUEL TANK (FLHT AND FLHX MODELS)

1. Wiring harness
2. Screw
3. Canopy
4. Fuel level sender
5. Vapor valve
6. Fuel hose (tank-to-valve)
7. Gasket
8. Fuel tank
9. Fuel hose (valve-to-atmosphere)
10. Vacuum hose
11. O-ring
12. Adapter
13. Filter
14. Nut
15. Gasket
16. Hose clamp
17. Fuel hose
18. Insulator
19. Bolt
20. Crossover hose
21. Insulator
22. Fuel valve

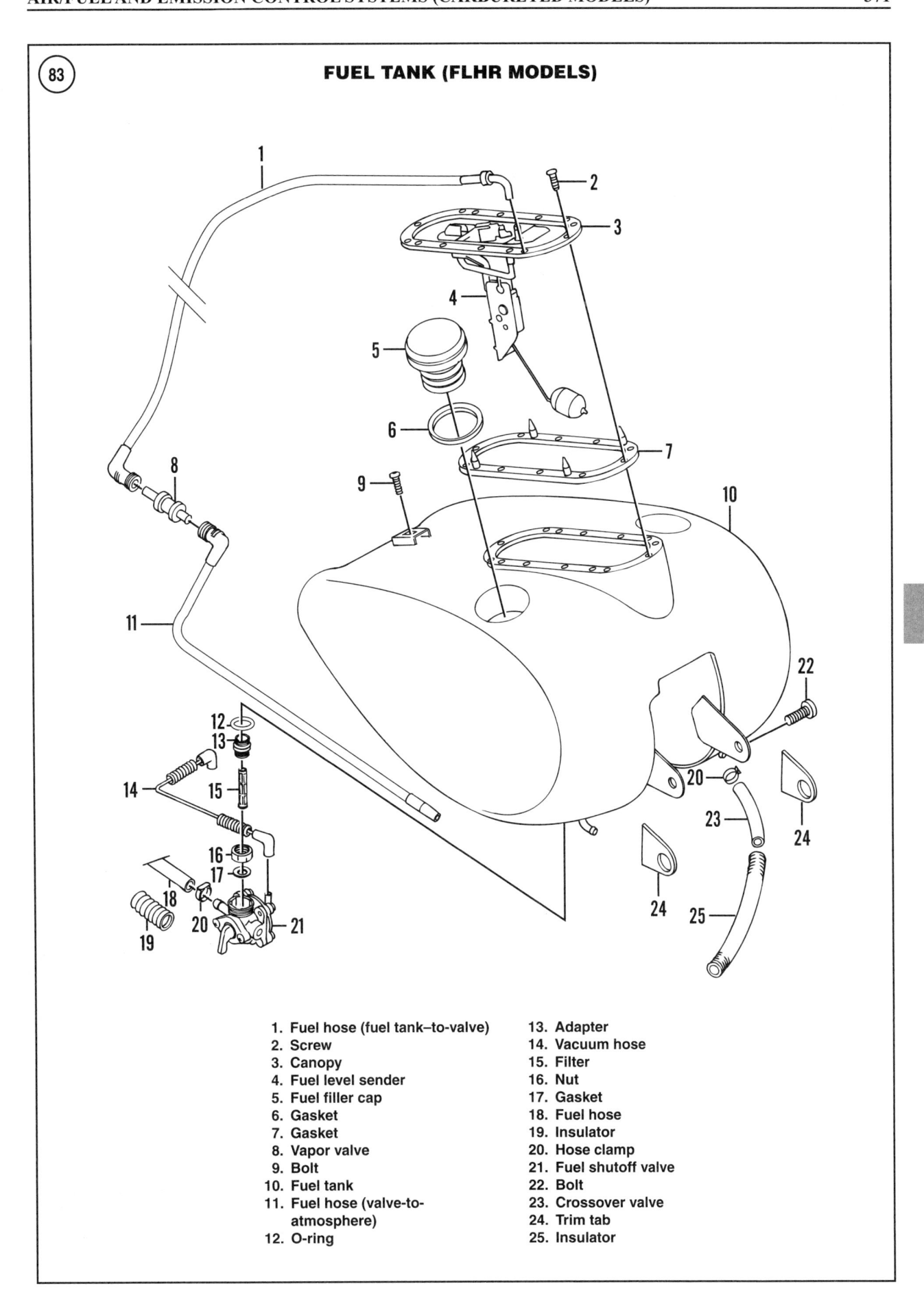

AIR/FUEL AND EMISSION CONTROL SYSTEMS (CARBURETED MODELS)

FUEL TANK (FLHR MODELS)

1. Fuel hose (fuel tank–to–valve)
2. Screw
3. Canopy
4. Fuel level sender
5. Fuel filler cap
6. Gasket
7. Gasket
8. Vapor valve
9. Bolt
10. Fuel tank
11. Fuel hose (valve-to-atmosphere)
12. O-ring
13. Adapter
14. Vacuum hose
15. Filter
16. Nut
17. Gasket
18. Fuel hose
19. Insulator
20. Hose clamp
21. Fuel shutoff valve
22. Bolt
23. Crossover valve
24. Trim tab
25. Insulator

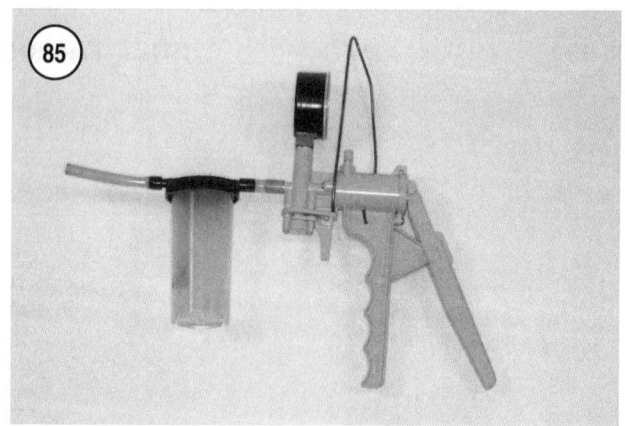

g. When fuel stops flowing through the hose, turn the fuel valve off and release the vacuum. Disconnect the vacuum pump and drain hose.
6. Disconnect the vent hose from the fuel tank.
7. Place a shop cloth directly under one the cross over fittings.
8. Apply a clamping tool (A, **Figure 86**) to the crossover hose to cut off fuel flow.
9. Carefully cut and remove the hose clamp (B, **Figure 86**).
10. Disconnect the crossover hose from one of the fittings on the fuel tank and immediately plug the tank opening.
11. At the front of the fuel tank, remove the Torx bolt (T40) and washer (**Figure 87**) on each side securing the fuel tank to the frame.
12. At the rear of the fuel tank, remove the bolt and washer (**Figure 88**) securing the fuel tank to the frame.
13. Lift off and remove the fuel tank.
14. Drain any remaining fuel left in the tank into a gas can.
15. Install the fuel filler cap.
16. Installation is the reverse of removal, while noting the following:
   a. Tighten the front and rear fuel tank mounting bolts to 15-20 ft.-lb. (20.3-27.1 N•m).
   b. Reconnect the fuel hose to the fuel valve and secure it with a *new* hose clamps.
   c. Reconnect the crossover hose to the tank fitting and release the clamping tool. Secure the hose with *new* clamps.
   d. Refill the tank and check for leaks.

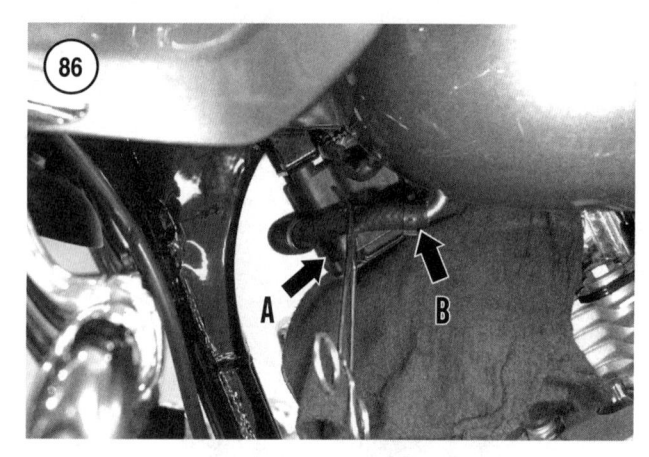

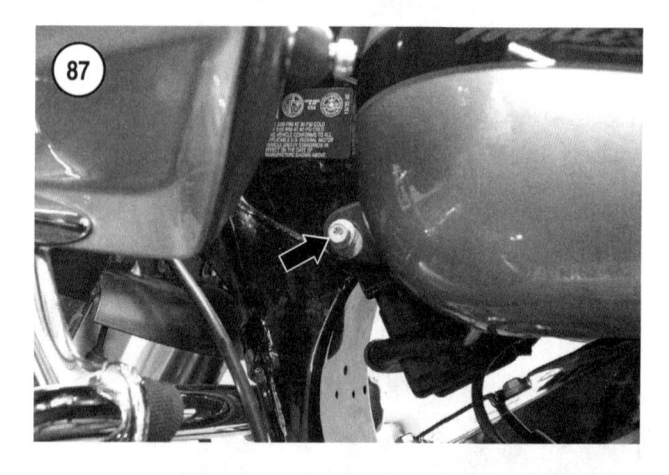

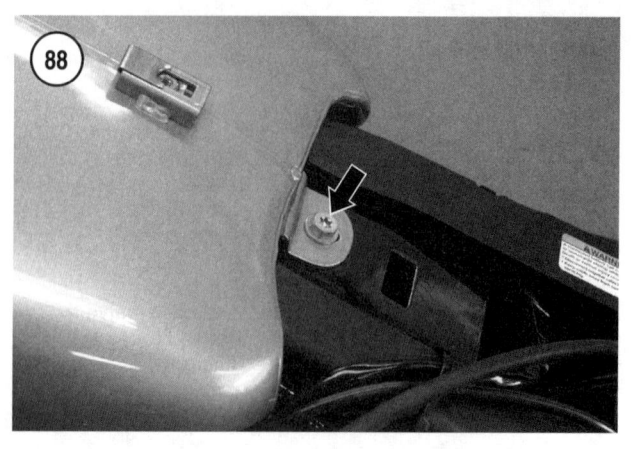

Inspection

1. Inspect the fuel cross over hose (A, **Figure 89**) hose for cracks or deterioration. Replace as necessary.
2. Check the front mounting tabs (B, **Figure 89**) and the rear mounting tab (**Figure 90**) for cracks or fractures.
3. Check the fuel tank console mounting clip nut (**Figure 91**) for damage.
4. Check the canopy (**Figure 92**) mounting screws for tightness; tighten if necessary.
5. Inspect all of the fuel and vent hoses for cracks, deterioration or damage. Replace damaged hoses with the same

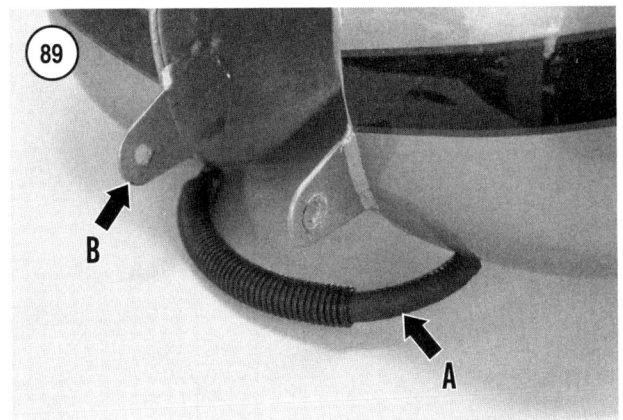

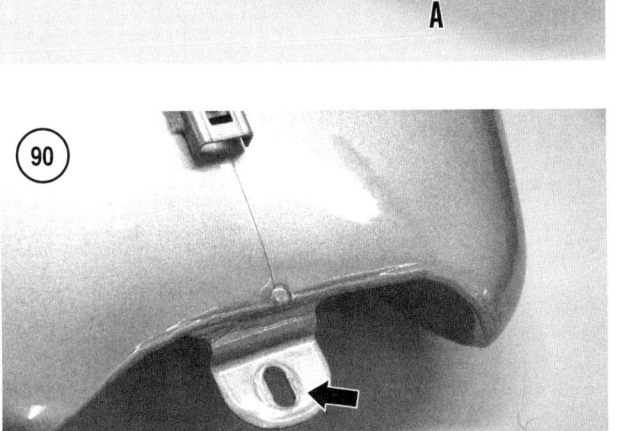

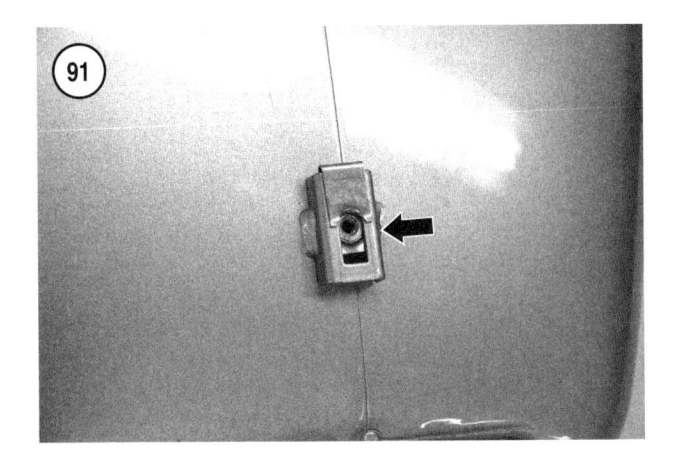

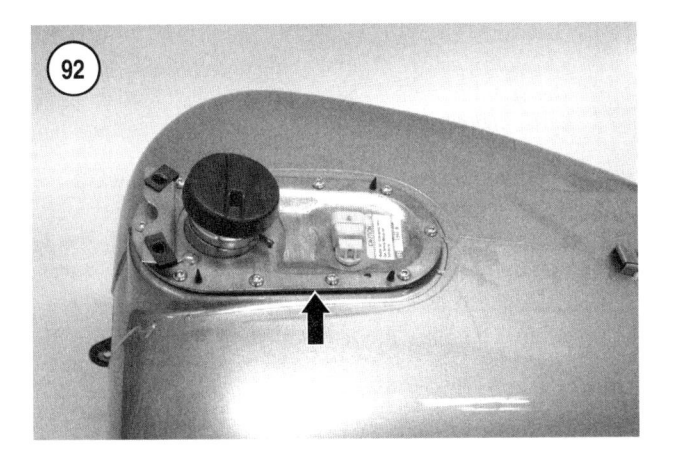

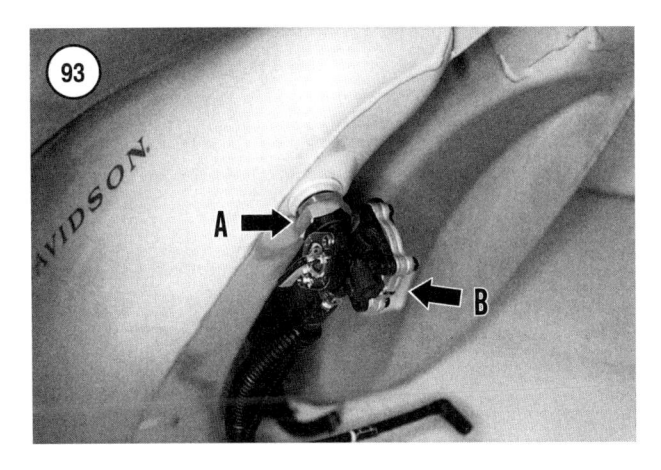

AIR/FUEL AND EMISSION CONTROL SYSTEMS (CARBURETED MODELS)

type and size materials. The fuel line must be flexible and strong enough to withstand engine heat and vibration.
6. Check the fuel line insulator for damage.
7. Remove the fuel filler cap and inspect the tank for rust or contamination. If there is a rust buildup inside the tank, clean and flush the tank.
8. Inspect the fuel tank for leaks.

FUEL SHUTOFF VALVE

A three-way vacuum-operated fuel shutoff valve is mounted to the left side of the fuel tank. A replaceable fuel filter is mounted to the top of the fuel shutoff valve.

To troubleshoot this valve, refer to *Vacuum Operated Fuel Shutoff Valve Testing* in Chapter Two.

Removal

NOTE
Always disarm the TSSM/HFSM security system prior to disconnecting the battery or pulling the Maxi-Fuse so the siren will not sound.

1. Disconnect the negative battery cable as described in Chapter Eleven.
2. Turn the fuel shutoff valve off.
3. Drain the fuel tank as described in *Fuel Tank Removal/Installation* (this chapter).

NOTE
The fuel shutoff valve can be removed with the fuel tank in place. Figure 93 is shown with the fuel tank removed to better illustrate the step.

4. Loosen the fuel valve fitting (A, **Figure 93**) and remove the fuel shutoff valve (B) from the fuel tank. Drain any residual gasoline that may still be in the tank after the valve is removed.

Installation

1. Install a *new* filter gasket onto the fuel shutoff valve.

94 **EVAPORATIVE EMISSION CONTROL SYSTEM (2006 CALIFORNIA MODELS)**

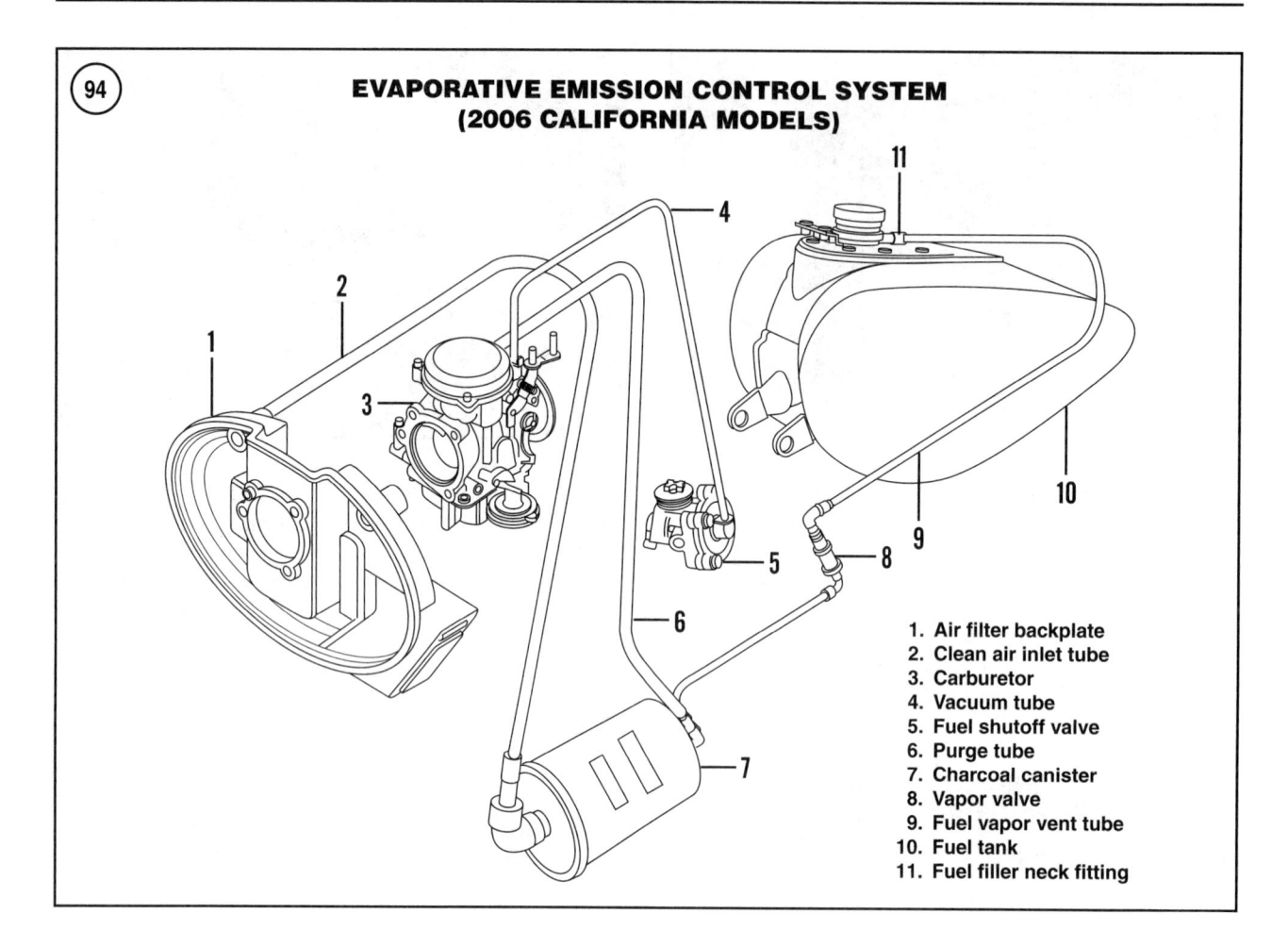

1. Air filter backplate
2. Clean air inlet tube
3. Carburetor
4. Vacuum tube
5. Fuel shutoff valve
6. Purge tube
7. Charcoal canister
8. Vapor valve
9. Fuel vapor vent tube
10. Fuel tank
11. Fuel filler neck fitting

2. Clean the adapter threads.

3. With the hex side facing down, turn the hex jam nut two full turns *counterclockwise* into the adapter.

WARNING
Do not thread the fuel valve into the jam nut more than two full turns as the jam nut may bottom out on the valve and cause a fuel leak.

4. Insert the fuel filter into the fuel tank. Secure the hex jam nut to keep it from turning, and turn the fuel valve two full turns *clockwise* into the jam nut.

5. Install the insulator tube over the fuel hose.

6. Reconnect the fuel hose to the fuel shutoff valve and secure it with a *new* hose clamp.

7. Refill the fuel tank and check for leaks.

Cleaning and Inspection

1. Inspect the filter mounted on top of the fuel valve. Remove and clean the filter of all contamination. Replace the filter if damaged.

2. Inspect the fuel tank adapter for fuel leaks. If necessary, remove the adapter as follows:

   a. Unscrew the adapter from the fuel tank, remove the O-ring and discard it.

   b. Install a *new* O-ring and apply a light coat of engine oil to the new O-ring.

   d. Install the adapter onto the fuel tank. Install the adapter and tighten to 22-25 ft.-lb. (29.8-33.9 N•m).

FUEL LEVEL SENDER (CANOPY)

Removal/Installation

1. Remove the fuel tank console as described in this chapter.

2. Remove the ten Torx screws (T20) securing the canopy unit (**Figure 92**) to the top of the fuel tank. Discard the screws as they cannot be reused.

CAUTION
Do not bend the float arm during removal of the sending unit. If bent, the gauge will give inaccurate readings.

3. Tilt the canopy and the fuel sending unit toward the right side at a 45° angle to the top of the fuel tank.

4. Carefully withdraw the sending unit from the left side of the fuel tank.

5. Remove the gasket from the fuel tank and discard it.

6. Install by reversing the removal steps, while noting the following:

   a. Install a *new* gasket between the canopy and fuel tank.

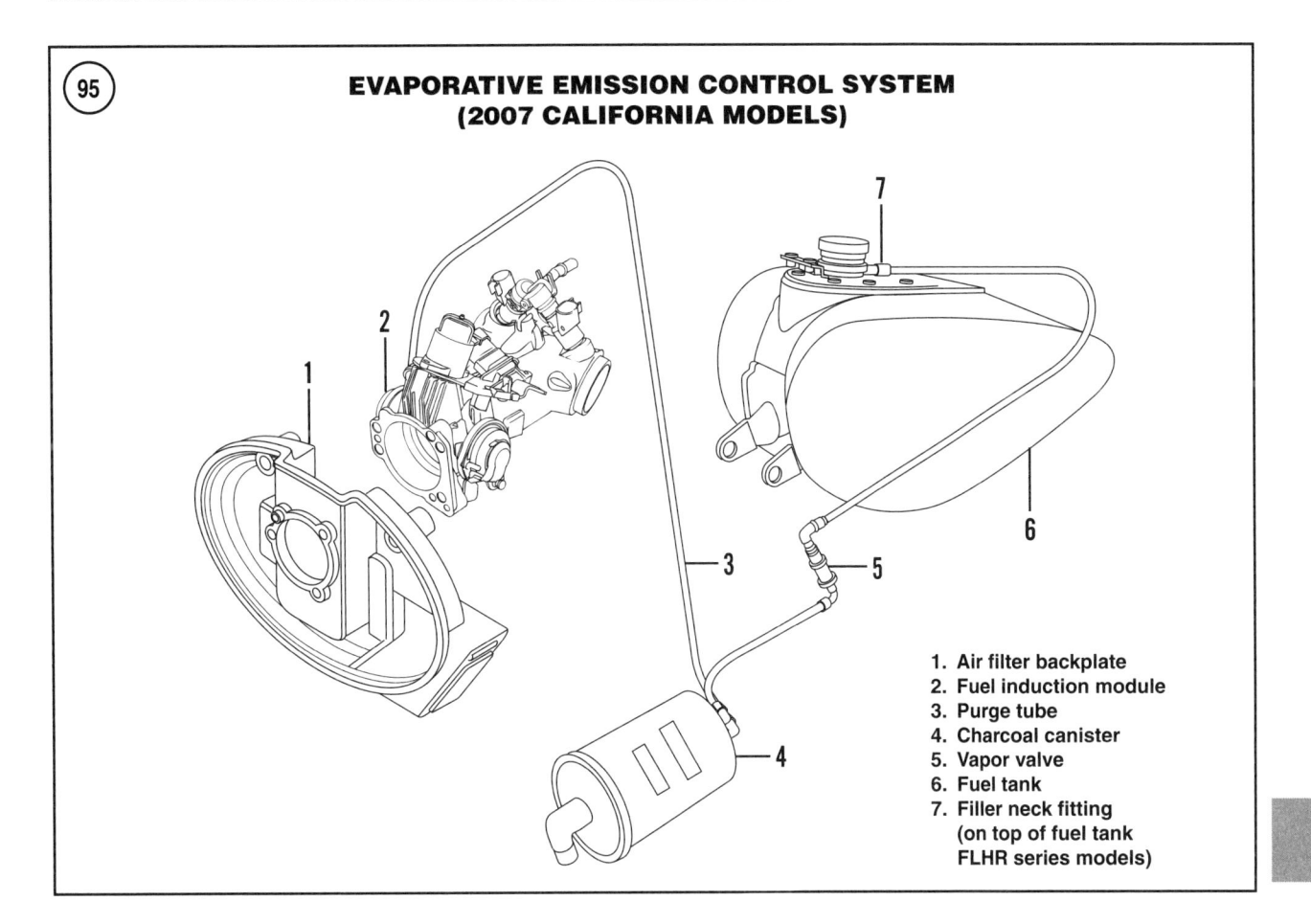

AIR/FUEL AND EMISSION CONTROL SYSTEMS (CARBURETED MODELS)

95

EVAPORATIVE EMISSION CONTROL SYSTEM (2007 CALIFORNIA MODELS)

1. Air filter backplate
2. Fuel induction module
3. Purge tube
4. Charcoal canister
5. Vapor valve
6. Fuel tank
7. Filler neck fitting (on top of fuel tank FLHR series models)

WARNING
Do not reuse the old Torx screws as this could cause a fuel leak.

b. Install all *new* Torx screws (T20) equipped with the integral sealing device.
c. Using a crossing pattern, tighten the Torx screws (T20) to 18-24 in.-lb. (2-2.7 N•m).

EVAPORATIVE EMISSION CONTROL SYSTEM (CARBURETED AND FUEL-INJECTED MODELS)

WARNING
Make sure hoses are routed so they cannot contact any hot engine or exhaust component. These hoses may contain flammable vapor.

The evaporative emission control system prevents gasoline vapors from escaping into the atmosphere.

When the engine is not running, the system directs the fuel vapor from the fuel tank through the vapor valve and into the charcoal canister.

When the engine is running, these vapors are drawn through a purge hose and into the carburetor, where they burn in the combustion chambers. The vapor valve also prevents gasoline vapors escaping from the charcoal canister if the motorcycle falls onto its side.

Non-California models are equipped with a vapor valve, or a vapor vent tube, but no charcoal canister or purge control valve. The lower end of the vent tube is routed to the atmosphere.

Refer to **Figure 94** and **Figure 95** for 2006 carbureted and 2007 fuel-injected models.

Refer to **Figure 96** and **Figure 97** for 2008-2009 fuel-injected models.

Inspection (All Models)

Before removing the hoses from any of the parts, mark the hose and the fitting with a piece of masking tape to identify where the hose goes. Consider taking photographs of hose routing and location to aid installation.
1. Check all emission control lines and hoses to make sure they are correctly routed and connected.
2. Make sure there are no kinks in the lines or hoses. Also inspect the hose and lines for excessive wear or for melting on lines that are routed near engine hot spots.
3. Check the physical condition of all lines and hoses in the system. Check for cuts, tears or loose connections. These lines and hoses are subjected to various temperature and operating conditions and eventually become brittle and crack. Replace damaged lines and hoses.
4. Check all components in the emission control system for damage, such as broken fittings or broken nipples on the component.

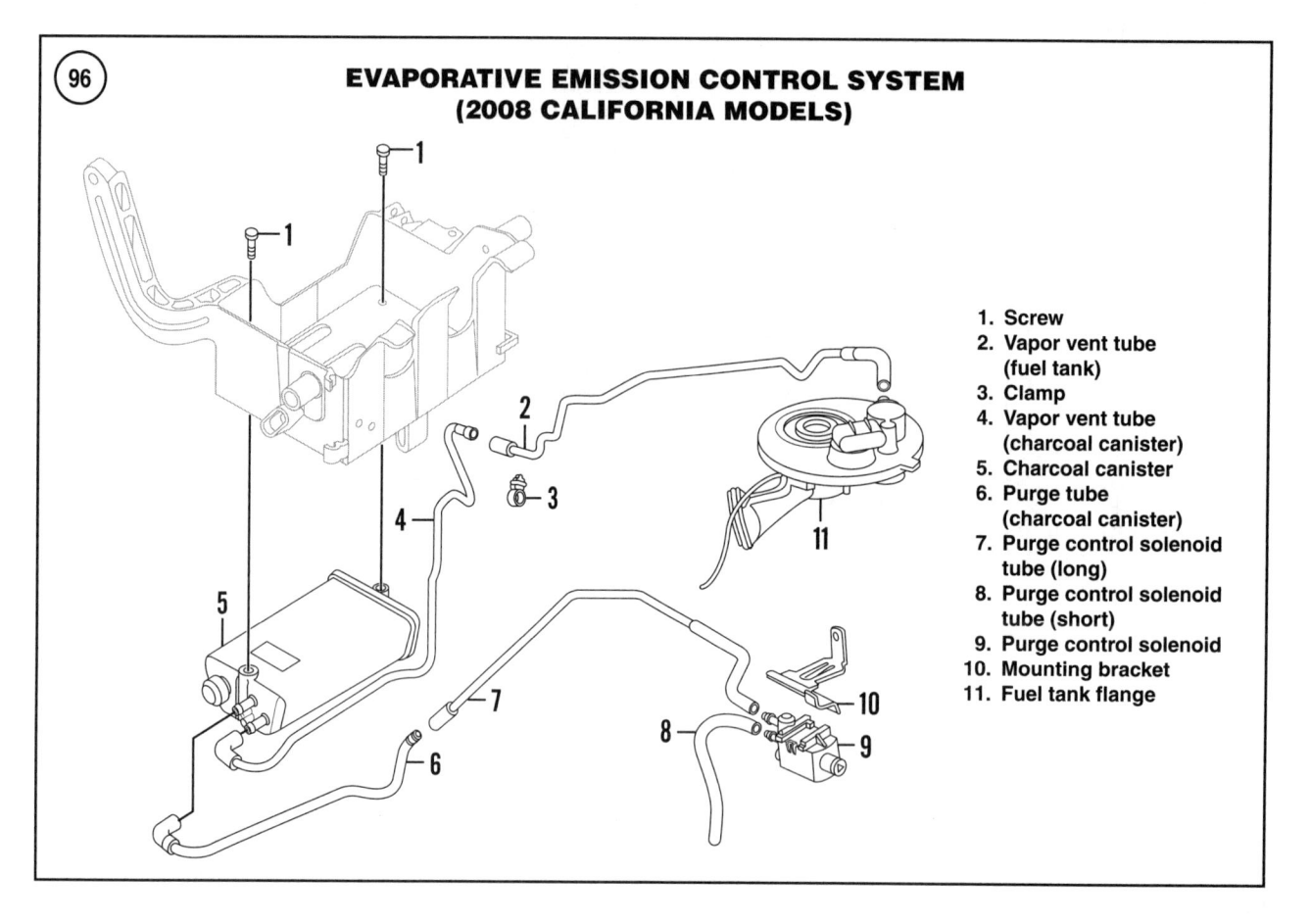

EVAPORATIVE EMISSION CONTROL SYSTEM (2008 CALIFORNIA MODELS)

1. Screw
2. Vapor vent tube (fuel tank)
3. Clamp
4. Vapor vent tube (charcoal canister)
5. Charcoal canister
6. Purge tube (charcoal canister)
7. Purge control solenoid tube (long)
8. Purge control solenoid tube (short)
9. Purge control solenoid
10. Mounting bracket
11. Fuel tank flange

Vapor Valve Removal/Installation
2006-2007 Models

The vapor valve is connected in the vent hose between the fuel tank and charcoal canister.

1. Remove the seat, the left side saddlebag and the left frame side cover as described in Chapter Seventeen.
2. Label the hoses at the vapor valve, and then disconnect them.
3. Note that one end of the vapor valve is longer than the other end. The longer end must face up.
4. Cut and remove the cable strap securing the vapor valve to the mounting bracket.
5. Remove the 135° elbow from the top fitting.
6A. On California models, raise the vapor valve slightly and pull the vent tube from the bottom fitting.
6B. On all other models, pull the vapor valve with bottom vent tube attached. Remove the vent tube from the valve.
7. Remove and replace the vapor valve.
8. Install the vapor valve with the longer end facing up and secure with a new cable strap.
9. Install the vapor valve and secure both hoses. The vent hose must be in a vertical position.

Charcoal Canister Removal/Installation
2006-2007 California Models

1. Remove the Maxi-Fuse as described in *Fuses* (Chapter Eleven).
2. Remove the rear fender as described in Chapter Seventeen.
3. Remove the battery from the battery box as described in Chapter Eleven.
4. Within the battery box, remove the retaining pin from the battery box.
5A. On carbureted models, pull the clean air tube from the fitting on the right side of the charcoal canister, located between the battery box and the right side frame member.
5B. On fuel-injected models, pull the 90° elbow from the fitting (no hose attached to this fitting).
6. On the left side, disconnect both tubes from the charcoal canister.
7. On the right side, use the rubber mallet handle and tap the charcoal canister toward the left side of the frame to release the charcoal canister from the battery box grooves.
8. Remove the charcoal canister from the right side of the frame.
9. Install the charcoal canister by reversing the removal steps while noting the following:
   a. Slide the canister into the battery box mounting grooves until it clicks.
   b. Attach the hoses to the correct fittings as noted during removal. On the left side, the purge tube runs to CARB and the vent tube runs to TANK. On the right side, clean air tube runs to the backplate on carbureted models.

AIR/FUEL AND EMISSION CONTROL SYSTEMS (CARBURETED MODELS)

EVAPORATIVE EMISSION CONTROL SYSTEM (2009 CALIFORNIA MODELS)

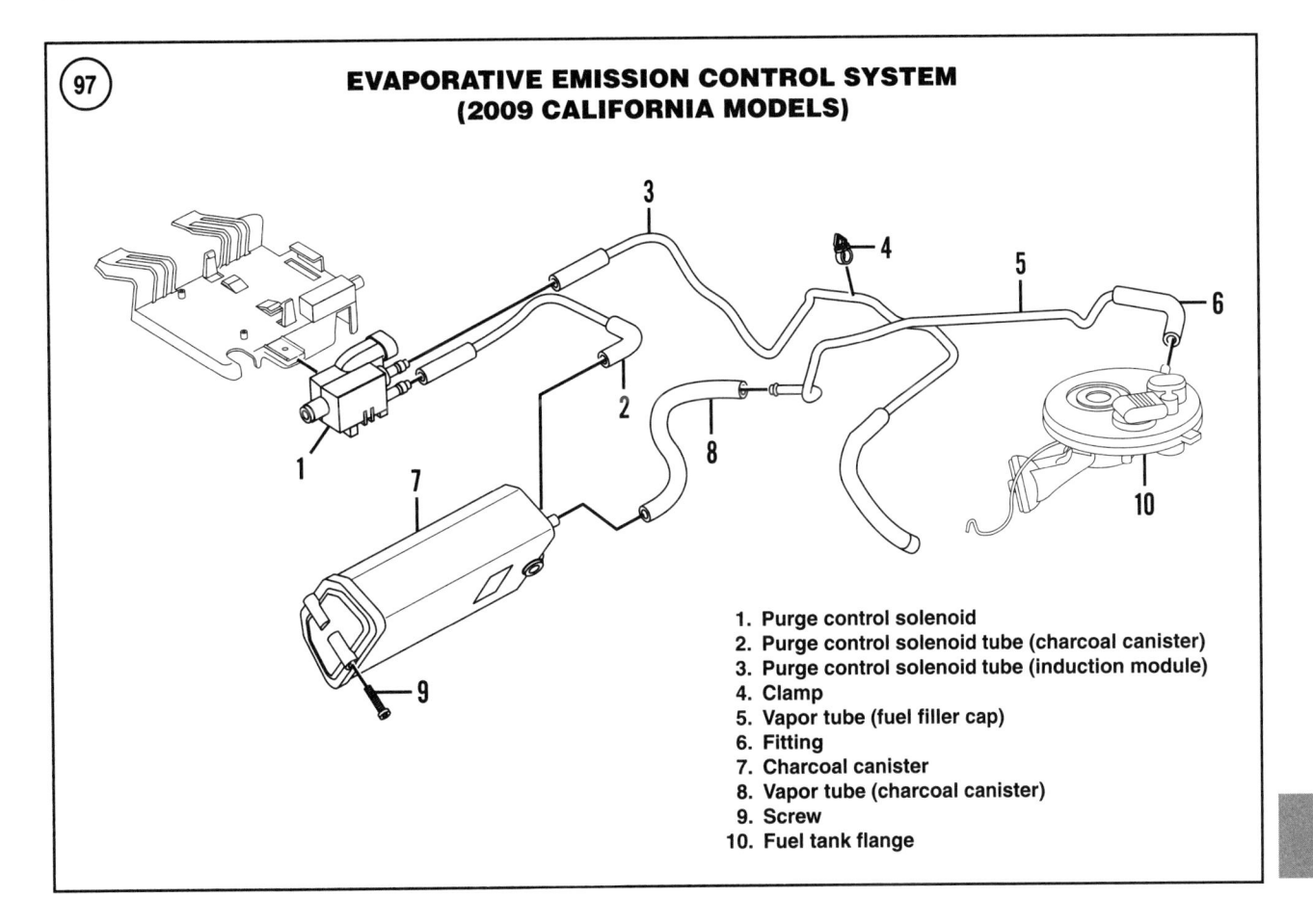

1. Purge control solenoid
2. Purge control solenoid tube (charcoal canister)
3. Purge control solenoid tube (induction module)
4. Clamp
5. Vapor tube (fuel filler cap)
6. Fitting
7. Charcoal canister
8. Vapor tube (charcoal canister)
9. Screw
10. Fuel tank flange

Vapor Vent Tube Removal/Installation

2008 models

The vapor valve is an integral part of the fuel tank top plate and cannot be replaced separately. If defective, replace the fuel tank top plate as described in Chapter Ten
1. Remove the Maxi-Fuse as described in *Fuses* (Chapter Eleven).
2. Remove the fuel tank console as described in this chapter.
3. Disconnect the vapor vent tube from the vapor valve on the fuel tank top plate.
4A. On California models, perform the following:
   a. Remove the charcoal canister as described in this section.
   b. Raise the battery tray sufficiently to release the vapor vent tube from the battery tray lower channel.
   c. Carefully pull the vapor vent tube out through the opening on the right side and remove the vent tube.
4B. On all other models, perform the following:
   a. Disconnect the vapor vent tube from the fuel tank top plate.
   b. Carefully pull the vapor vent tube rearward along the inside of the upper frame tube, and downward along the middle frame down tube. Then, remove the vent tube. The free end (vented to the atmosphere) is routed to the outboard side of the frame weldment and out through the bottom of it along the swing arm bracket.

5. Install the vapor vent tube by reversing the removal steps. Make sure the tube is not pinched or kinked and that there is no contact with the exhaust system.

2009 models

1. Remove the seat as described in Chapter Seventeen.
2. Remove the fuel tank as described in this chapter.
3. Disconnect the vapor vent tube from the vapor valve on the fuel tank top plate.
4. Disconnect the vapor vent tube from the charcoal canister and remove the vent tube.
5. Install the purge tube by reversing the removal steps. Make sure the tube is not pinched or kinked and that there is no contact with the exhaust system.

Purge Tubes Removal/Installation 2008 Models

Long

1. Remove the fuel tank as described in this chapter.
2. Disconnect the long purge tube from the purge control solenoid top fitting.
3. Release the long purge tube from the clips on the bottom of the frame cross member.
4. Remove the charcoal canister as described in this section. The long purge tube is disconnected at this time.

5. Raise the battery tray and release the long purge tube from the bottom channel.
6. Remove the long purge tube from the right side.
7. Install the purge tube by reversing the removal steps. Make sure the tube is not pinched or kinked and that there is no contact with the exhaust system.

Short

1. Remove the fuel tank as described in this chapter.
2. Disconnect the short purge tube from the purge control solenoid bottom fitting.
3. Disconnect the short purge tube from fuel-injection induction module.
4. Install the purge tube by reversing the removal steps. Make sure the tube is not pinched or kinked and that there is no contact with the exhaust system.

Purge Control Solenoid-to-Induction Module Tube Removal/Installation
2009 California Models

1. Remove the seat as described in Chapter Seventeen.
2. Remove the fuel tank as described in this chapter.
3. Disconnect the tube from upper fitting on the purge control solenoid. Remove the tube from under the frame cross member.
4. Remove the clip and disconnect the purge tube from the induction module. Then, remove the purge tube.
5. Install the purge control solenoid-to-induction module tube by reversing the removal steps. Make sure the tube is not pinched or kinked and that there is no contact with the exhaust system.

Purge Control Solenoid-to-Charcoal Canister Tube Removal/Installation
2009 California Models

1. Remove the seat as described in Chapter Seventeen.
2. Remove the fuel tank as described in this chapter.
3. Disconnect the curved section of the tube from lower fitting on the purge control solenoid.
4. Disconnect the tube from lower fitting on the charcoal canister and remove the tube.
5. Install the purge control solenoid-to-charcoal canister tube by reversing the removal steps. Make sure the tube is not pinched or kinked and that there is no contact with the exhaust system.

Purge Control Solenoid Removal/Installation
2008-2009 California Models

1. Remove the fuel tank as described in this chapter.
2. Disconnect the 2-pin electrical connector from the purge control solenoid.
3. Disconnect the purge control solenoid-to-charcoal cannister tube from the purge control solenoid top fitting.
4. Disconnect the purge control solenoid-to-induction module tube from the purge control solenoid bottom fitting.
5. Insert a small, flat-bladed screwdriver between the purge control solenoid and the mounting bracket. Rotate the screwdriver slightly, depress the middle locking finger, and remove the purge control solenoid.
6. Install the purge control solenoid by reversing the removal steps, while noting the following:
   a. Make sure the purge control solenoid locks into place on the mounting bracket. Bend down the middle locking finger of the mounting bracket to insure a better lock if necessary.
   b. Make sure the tubes are not pinched or kinked and that there is no contact with the exhaust system.

Charcoal Canister Removal/Installation
2008 California models

1. Remove the Maxi-Fuse as described in *Fuses* (Chapter Eleven).
2. Remove both saddlebags and frame side covers as described in Chapter Seventeen.
3. Remove the battery as described in Chapter Eleven.
4. Remove the spring clip securing the TSM/TSSM module to the frame cross member and move the module out of the way. Do not disconnect the electrical connector.
5. On models equipped with ABS, remove the right side electrical caddy as described in Chapter Eleven.
6. Remove the Allen bolt securing the left side caddy to the battery tray.
7. Remove the Allen bolt and lifting strap, and release the battery tray middle finger from the frame cross member.
8. Pull up on the battery tray and release the left side caddy from the battery tray slot.
9. Disconnect the vapor valve-to-charcoal canister tube from the front fitting (TANK) on the charcoal canister.
10. Disconnect the canister-to-purge control solenoid tube from the rear fitting (PURGE) on the charcoal canister.
11. Remove the two Torx screws (T25) and flat washers securing the charcoal canister to the bottom of the battery tray.
12. Raise the battery tray and slide the charcoal canister out through the right side.
13. Install the charcoal canister by reversing the removal steps, while noting the following:
   a. Install the tubes onto the correct fitting on the canister.
   b. Make sure the tubes are captured in the channel in the bottom of the battery tray. Also, make sure the tubes are positioned outboard of the tab at front of the left side of caddy to prevent contact with the drive belt.
   c. Tighten the Torx screws (T25) to 10-16 in.-lb. (1.1-1.8 N•m).
   d. Tighten the electrical caddy Allen bolts to 72-96 in.-lb. (8.1-10.8 N•m).

AIR/FUEL AND EMISSION CONTROL SYSTEMS (CARBURETED MODELS)

2009 California models

1. Remove the Maxi-Fuse as described under *Fuses* in Chapter Eleven.
2. Remove the seat as described in Chapter Seventeen.
3. Remove both saddlebags and frame side covers as described in Chapter Seventeen.
4. Remove the battery as described in Chapter Eleven.
5. Remove the two screws securing the battery hold down bracket and remove it.
6. Remove the strap securing the main wiring harness to the frame next to the left side of the electrical caddy.
7. Remove the two screws securing the electrical caddy to the frame.
8. On the left side, disconnect the following tubes from the canister:
    a. Vapor vent tube from the fitting marked TANK.
    b. Purge control tube from the fitting marked PURGE.
9. Remove the nut securing the three ground terminals to the left side ground stud.
10. Remove the nut securing the two ground terminals to the right side ground stud.
11. Remove the two Torx screws securing the charcoal canister to the frame cross-member.
12. Move the right end of the canister down and into the battery tray. Then, pass it under the wiring harness and remove the canister from the frame.
13. Install the charcoal canister by reversing the removal steps, while noting the following:
    a. Install the tubes onto their correct fittings on the canister.
    b. Tighten the canister mounting Torx screws to 10-16 in.-lb. (1.1-1.7 N•m).
    c. Tighten the two electrical caddy mounting screws to 72-96 in.-lb. (8.1-10.8 N•m).
    d. Tighten the battery hold down bracket screws to 32-40 in.-lb. (3.6-4.5 N•m).

Table 1 FUEL SYSTEM SPECIFICATIONS

Item	Specification
Carburetor	
Main jet	
Domestic	190
California	195
HDI	195
Pilot jet	45
Float level	0.413-0.453 in. (10.49-11.51 mm)
Idle speed	950-1050 rpm
Fuel tank	
Capacity	5.0 gal (18.93 L)
Reserve	0.9 gal (3.41 L)

Table 2 FUEL SYSTEM TORQUE SPECIFICATIONS

Item	ft.-lb.	in.-lb.	N•m
Air filter backplate			
Breather hollow bolts	–	124-142	14.6-16.0
Mounting bracket Torx screws	–	40-60	4.5-6.8
Cover screw	–	35-60	4.0-6.8
Electrical caddy Allen bolts	–	72-96	8.1-10.8
Fuel tank bolt (front and rear)	15-20	–	20.3-27.1
Fuel shutoff valve adapter	22-25	–	29.8-33.9
Fuel level sender Torx screws	–	18-24	2.0-2.7
Intake manifold Allen bolts	–	96-144	10.8-16.3
Charcoal canister			
Mounting screws (caddly)	–	72-96	8.1-10.9
Torx screws	–	10-16	1.1-1.8
Battery hold down bracket screws (2009 models)	–	32-40	3.6-4.5
MAP sensor clamp screw	–	20-35	2.3-4.0

CHAPTER TEN

AIR/FUEL AND EMISSION CONTROL SYSTEMS (FUEL-INJECTED MODELS)

This chapter covers the fuel injection system. Refer to Chapter Nine for the emission control systems on all California models. Air filter maintenance is covered in Chapter Three. Refer to *Safety* in Chapter One.

Specifications are located in **Table 1** and **Table 2** at the end of the chapter.

WARNING
Gasoline is carcinogenic and flammable. Handle gasoline carefully. Wear nitrile gloves to avoid skin contact. If gasoline does contact skin, immediately and thoroughly wash the area with soap and warm water.

AIR FILTER AND BACKPLATE (ALL MODELS EXCEPT 2007 FLHRSE3 AND 2009 FLTRSE3)

Refer to **Figure 1** and **Figure 2**.

Removal

1. Support the motorcycle on level ground with a swing arm stand.
2. Remove the air filter cover Allen screw (A, **Figure 3**) and remove the cover (B).
3. Remove the Torx screws (**Figure 4**) and bracket from the air filter element.
4. Gently pull the air filter element away from the backplate and disconnect the two breather hoses (A, **Figure 5**) from the hollow bolts on the backplate. Remove the air filter element (B, **Figure 5**).
5. Pull each breather hose (**Figure 6**) from the fitting on the hollow bolts.
6. Use a deep socket and remove the two breather hollow bolts (A, **Figure 7**) securing the backplate (B) to the cylinder heads.
7A. On California models, pull the backplate (B, **Figure 7**) partially away from the cylinder heads. Disconnect the clean air inlet hose (**Figure 8**) from the fitting on the backplate, and then remove the backplate and gasket.
7B. On 2007-2009 HDI models, pull the backplate partially away from the cylinder heads. Disconnect the active intake solenoid 2-pin electrical connector from the inboard side of the backplate. Remove the backplate.
7C. On all other models, pull the backplate (B, **Figure 7**) partially away from the cylinder heads, and remove the backplate and gasket (A, **Figure 9**). Remove the O-rings (B, **Figure 9**) from the breather bolt bosses in the backplate. Discard the O-rings.
8. Remove and discard the air filter gasket (**Figure 10**).

Installation

1. Apply a small amount of gasket sealer to a *new* backplate gasket to hold it in place and fit it onto the backplate (**Figure 10**).
2A. On California models, connect the clean air inlet hose (**Figure 8**) to the fitting on the inboard side of the backplate.
2B. On 2007-2009 HDI models, move the backplate part way into position, connect the active intake solenoid 2-pin electrical connector onto the inboard side of the backplate.

AIR/FUEL AND EMISSION CONTROL SYSTEMS (FUEL-INJECTED MODELS)

① AIR FILTER AND BACKPLATE (2006-2007 MODELS)

1. Torx screw
2. Mounting bracket
3. Air filter
4. Breather hose
5. Breather hollow bolt
6. Gasket
7. O-ring
8. Gasket
9. Backplate (domestic)
10. Screw
11. Trim plate
12. Cover (except Screamin' Eagle)
13. Rubber seal
14. Backplate (HDI)
15. Trim plate
16. Torx screw
17. Screw
18. Cover (2007 Screamin' Eagle)
19. Rubber seal

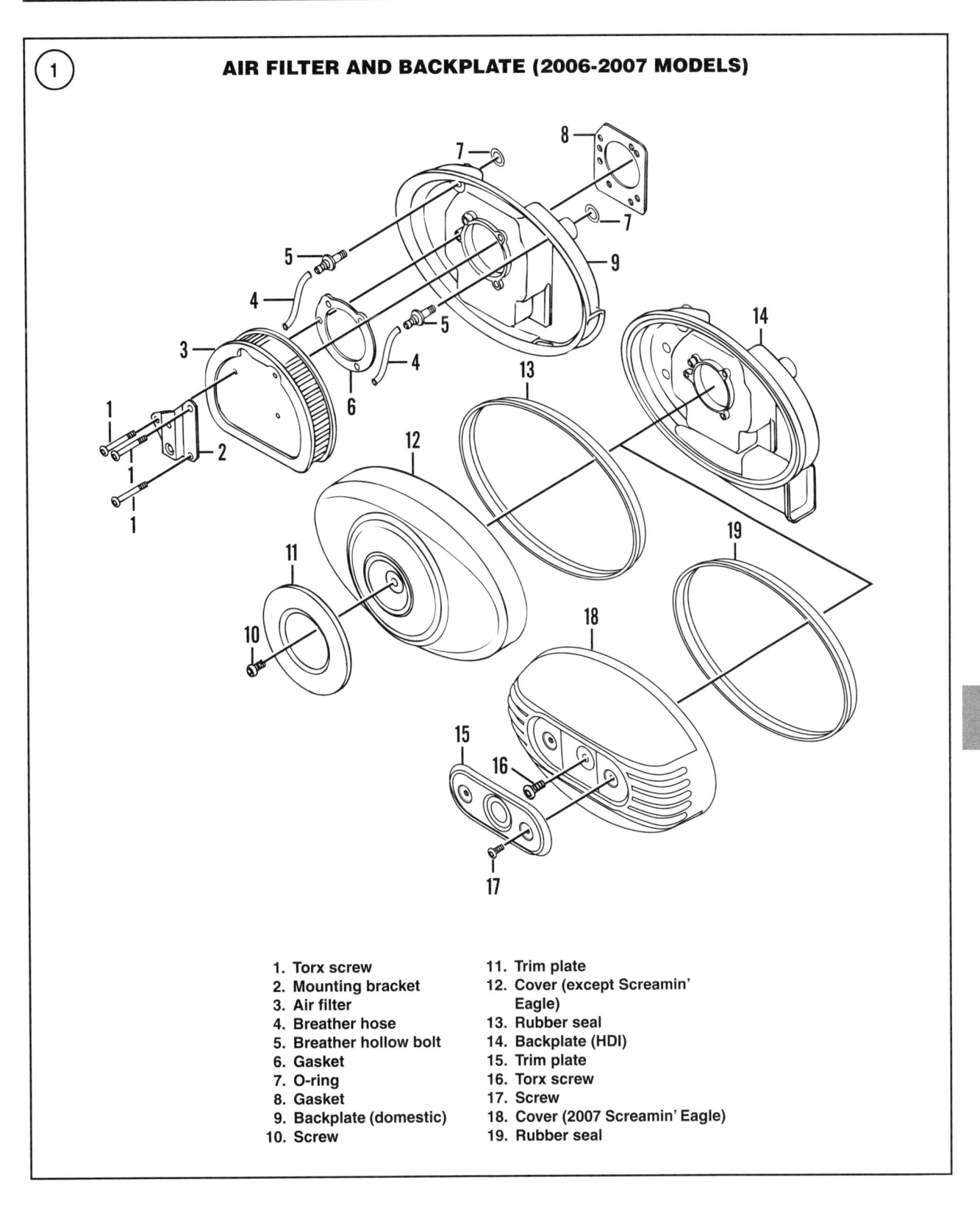

Make sure the connector is secured to the rear of the backplate.

3. Install *new* O-rings (B, **Figure 9**) into the inboard side of the breather bolt bosses in the backplate.

4. Position the backplate (B, **Figure 7**) against the fuel injection module. Reposition the gasket as necessary to align the bolt holes with those of the induction module.

5. Install the breather hollow bolts (A, **Figure 7**) securing the backplate. Tighten the bolts to 22-24 ft.-lb. (29.8-32.5 N•m).

6. Install the breather hoses (**Figure 6**) onto the breather hollow bolt fittings.

7. Apply a couple dabs of gasket sealer to a *new* air filter gasket. Fit the gasket onto air filter element.

382

CHAPTER TEN

② AIR FILTER AND BACKPLATE (2008-2009 MODELS AND 2007-2009 SCREAMIN' EAGLE EXCEPT 2007 FLHRSE3 AND 2009 FLTRSE3 MODELS)

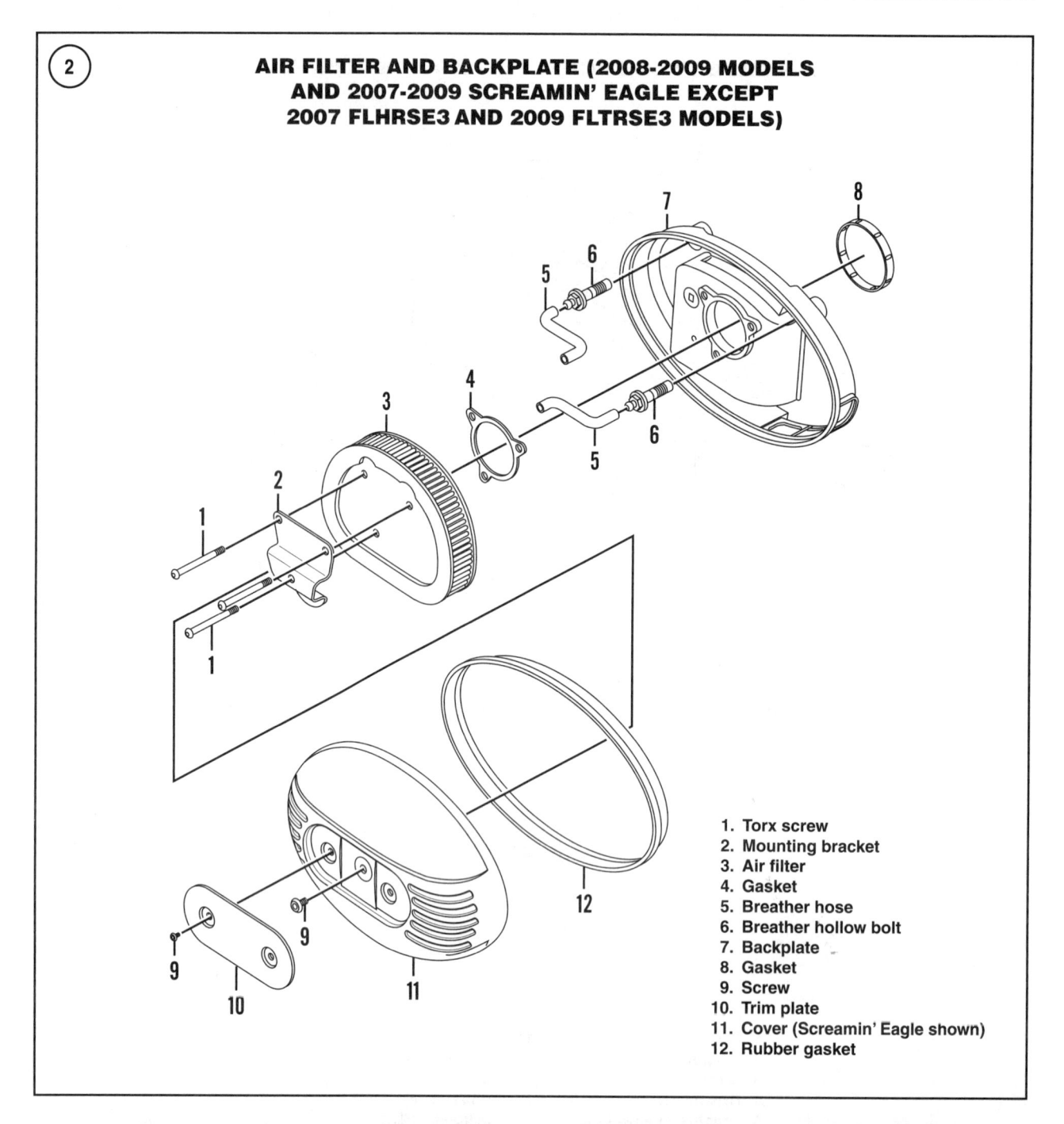

1. Torx screw
2. Mounting bracket
3. Air filter
4. Gasket
5. Breather hose
6. Breather hollow bolt
7. Backplate
8. Gasket
9. Screw
10. Trim plate
11. Cover (Screamin' Eagle shown)
12. Rubber gasket

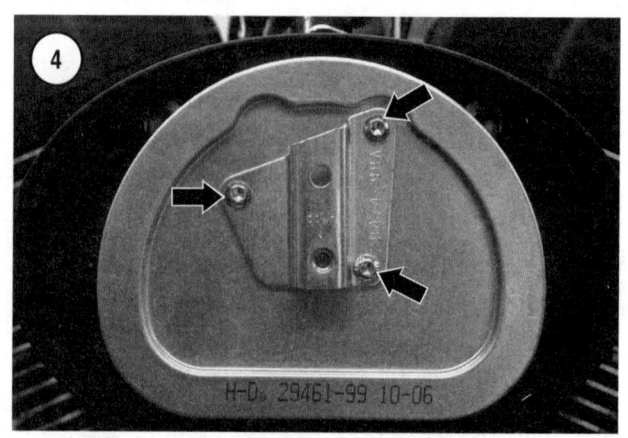

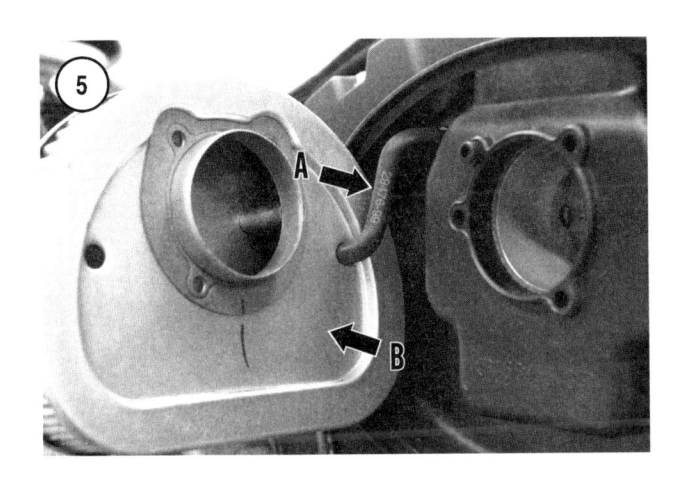

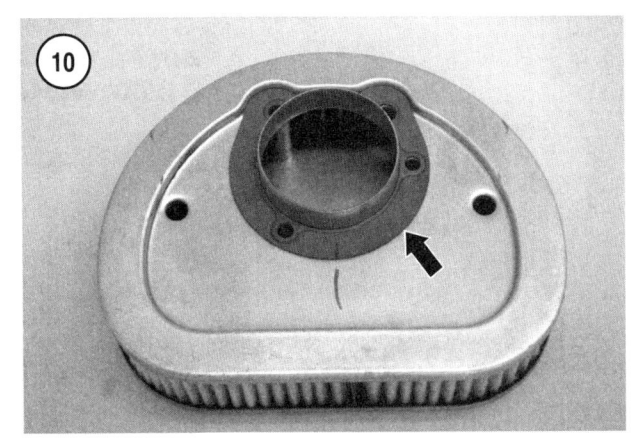

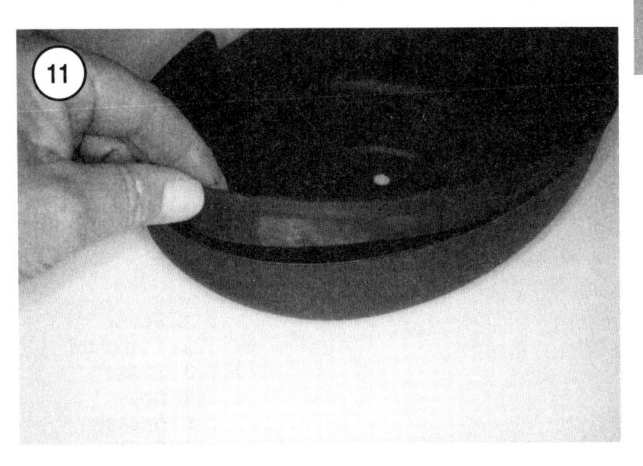

AIR/FUEL AND EMISSION CONTROL SYSTEMS (FUEL-INJECTED MODELS)

8. Position the element (B, **Figure 5**) with the flat side facing down and insert the breather hoses (A) to the backside of the element.

9. Set the element into position, and then install the mounting bracket and the Torx screws (**Figure 4**). Tighten the Torx screws (T27) to 40-60 in.-lb. (4.5-6.8 N•m).

10. Apply a drop of Loctite Threadlocker 243 (blue), or an equivalent threadlock, to the cover screw prior to installation.

11. Inspect the seal ring (**Figure 11**) on the air filter cover for hardness or deterioration. Replace if necessary.

12. Install the air filter cover (B, **Figure 3**) and the screw (A). Tighten the cover screw to 36-60 in.-lb. (4.1-6.8 N•m).

AIR FILTER AND BACKPLATE (2007 FLHRSE3 MODELS)

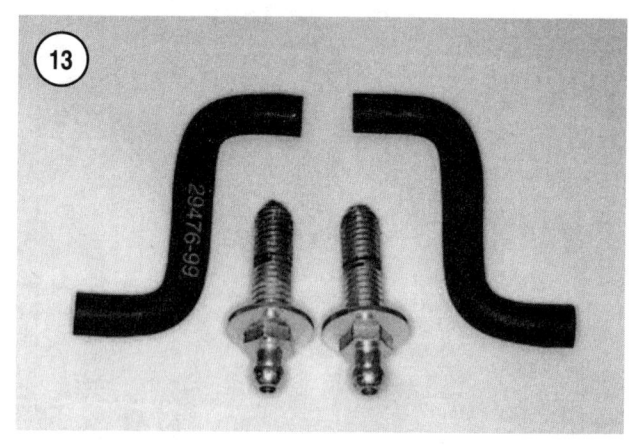

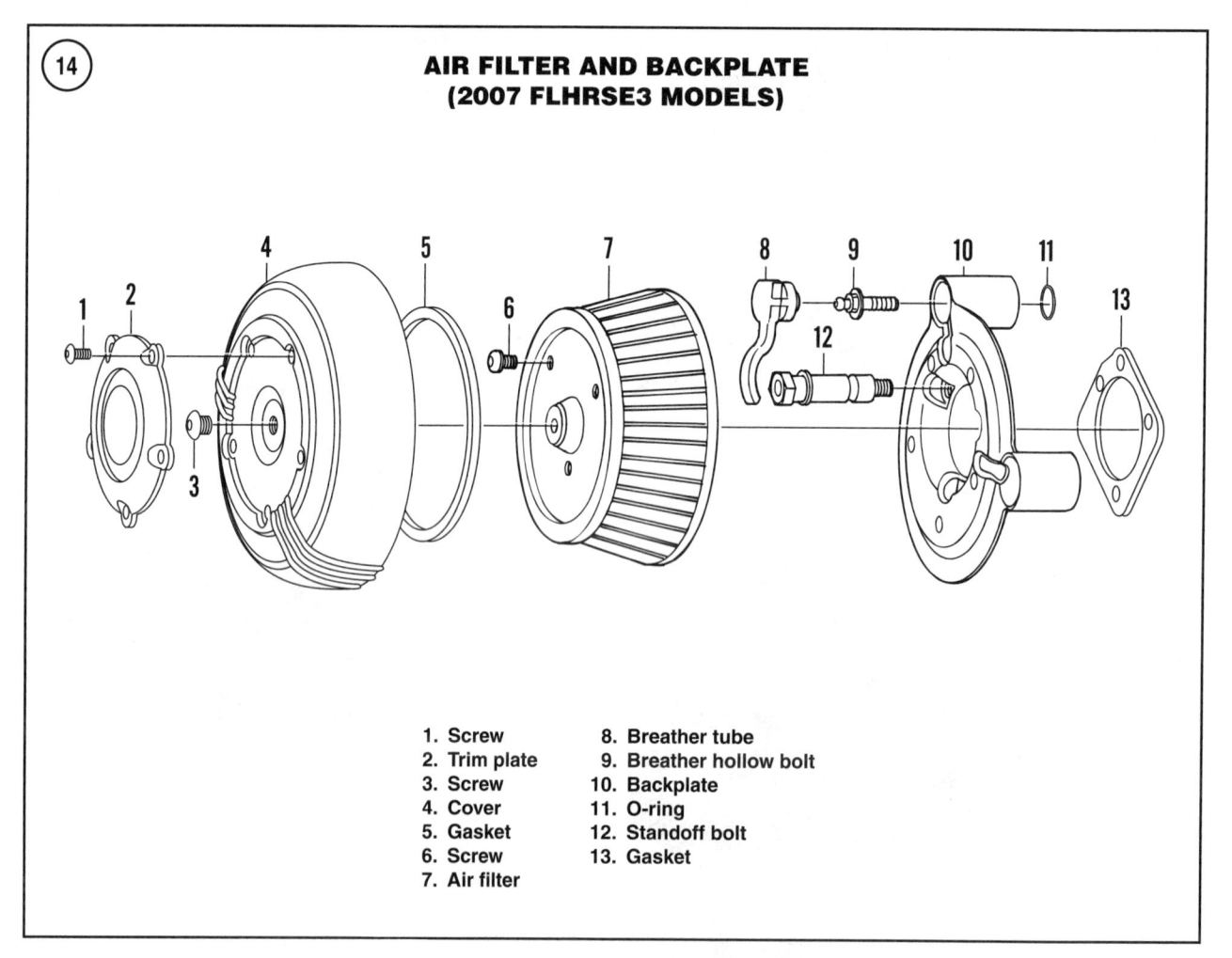

1. Screw
2. Trim plate
3. Screw
4. Cover
5. Gasket
6. Screw
7. Air filter
8. Breather tube
9. Breather hollow bolt
10. Backplate
11. O-ring
12. Standoff bolt
13. Gasket

Inspection

1. Inspect the backplate (**Figure 12**) for damage.
2. Make sure the breather hollow bolts and breather hoses (**Figure 13**) are clear. Clean out if necessary.

AIR FILTER AND BACKPLATE (2007 FLHRSE3 AND 2009 FLTRSE3 DOMESTIC MODELS)

Refer to **Figure 14** and **Figure 15**.

Removal

1. Support the motorcycle on level ground with a swing arm stand.
2. Remove the screws securing the trim plate, and then remove the trim plate.
3. Remove the air filter cover Torx screw, and then remove the cover.
4. Remove the three screws and the air filter element.
5. Carefully pull the breather tubes (A, **Figure 16**, typical) from the backplate.

AIR/FUEL AND EMISSION CONTROL SYSTEMS (FUEL-INJECTED MODELS)

AIR FILTER AND BACKPLATE (2009 FLTRSE3 MODELS)

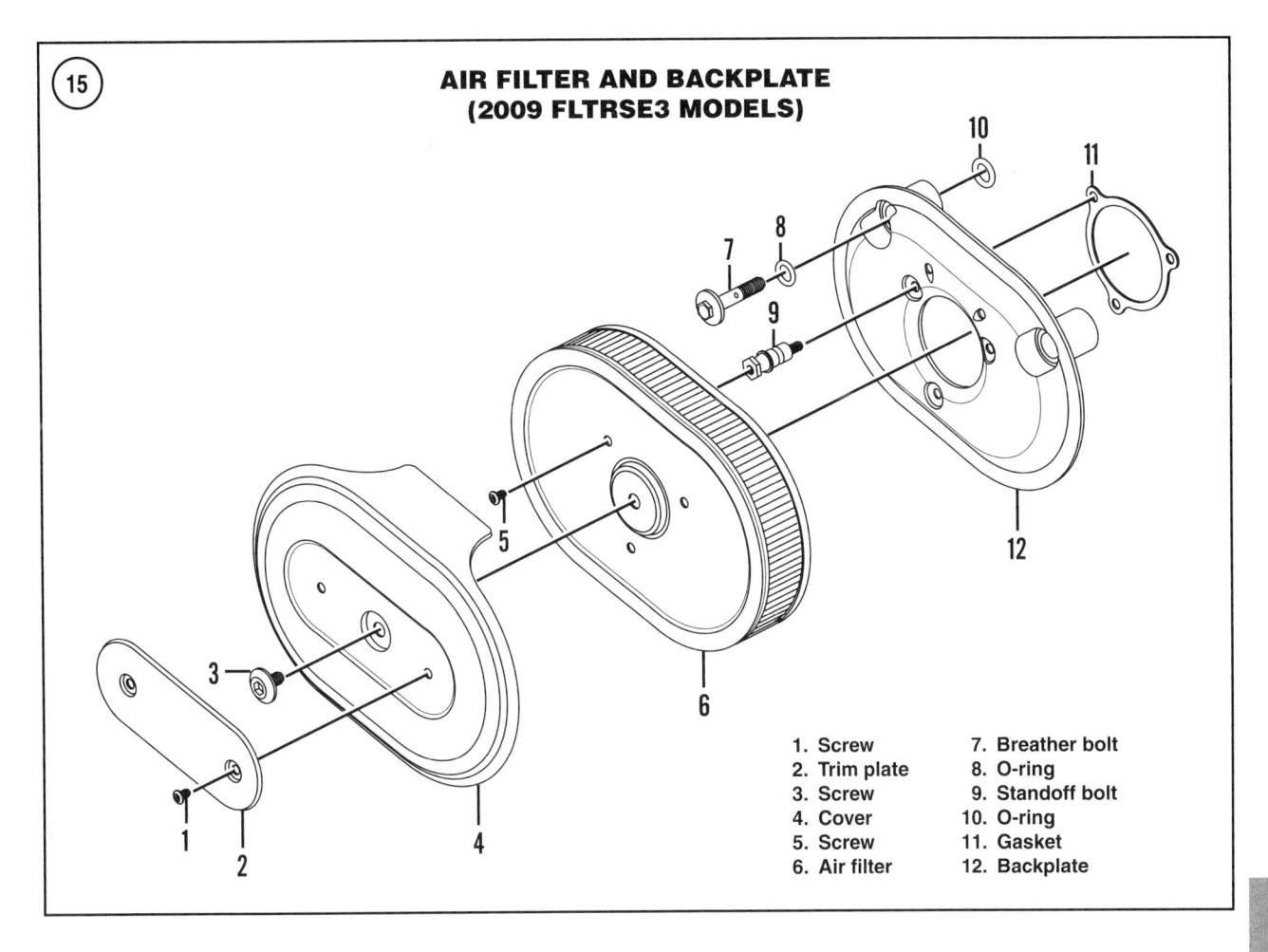

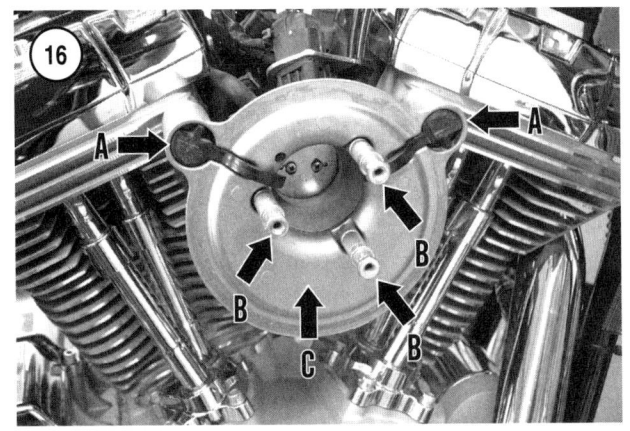

1. Screw
2. Trim plate
3. Screw
4. Cover
5. Screw
6. Air filter
7. Breather bolt
8. O-ring
9. Standoff bolt
10. O-ring
11. Gasket
12. Backplate

6. Remove the breather bolts located under the breather tubes.
7. Remove the standoff bolts (B, **Figure 16**, typical), and remove the backplate (C) and gasket.
8. Remove the O-rings from the breather bolt bosses in the backplate. Discard the O-rings.
9. Remove and discard the air filter gasket.

Installation

1. Apply a couple dabs of gasket sealer to a *new* backplate gasket and fit it onto the backplate.
2. Install *new* O-rings into the inboard side of the breather bolt bosses in the backplate.
3. Position the backplate (C, **Figure 16**) against the fuel injection induction module. Reposition the gasket as necessary to align its bolts holes with those of the induction module.
4. Install the breather hollow bolts securing the backplate, and tighten to 22-24 ft.-lb. (29.8-32.5 N•m).
5. Install the standoff bolts (B, **Figure 16**, typical), and tighten to 55-60 in.-lb. (6.3-6.8 N•m).
6. Install the breather tubes (A, **Figure 16**, typical) over the breather hollow bolts and onto the backplate. Push them until they are seated.
7. Install air filter cover and tighten the screw securely.
8. Install the trim plate and tighten the screws securely.

DEPRESSURIZING THE FUEL SYSTEM

WARNING
The fuel system is under pressure at all times, even when the engine is not operating. The system must be depressurized prior to loosening fittings or disconnecting any fuel lines within the fuel injection system. Gasoline will spurt out unless the system is depressurized.

1. Remove the left frame side cover as described in Chapter Seventeen.

NOTE
*The location of some fuses varies during model years. Check the diagram on the cover (**Figure 17**) of the fuse/relay panel to determine the precise location of the fuel pump fuse on a particular model.*

2. Lift the cover from the fuse/relay panel, and pull the fuel pump fuse from the panel.
3. Start the engine. Let it idle until it runs out of gasoline.
4. After the engine has stopped, operate the starter for three seconds to eliminate any residual gasoline in the fuel lines.
5. After all service procedures have been completed, install the fuel pump fuse.
6. Install the left frame side cover as described in Chapter Seventeen.

FUEL TANK

WARNING
Some fuel may spill from the fuel tank hose during this procedure. Because gasoline is extremely flammable and explosive, perform this procedure away from all open flames, including appliance pilot lights and sparks. Do not smoke or allow anyone to smoke in the work area, as an explosion and fire may occur. Always work in a well-ventilated area. Wipe up any spills immediately.

WARNING
Make sure to route the fuel tank vapor hoses so that they cannot contact any hot engine or exhaust component. These hoses contain flammable vapors. If a hose melts from contacting a hot part, leaking vapors may ignite, causing a fire.

Draining

The crossover fuel hose is secured to the fuel tank with non-reusable clamps. If the same type of clamps are going to be reinstalled, purchase *new* ones before servicing the fuel tank.

1. Depressurize the fuel system as described in this chapter.
2. Make a drain hose from 5/16 inch (7.9 mm) I.D. hose and plug one end of it. Make it long enough to go from the fuel tank crossover hose fitting to a gas can.
3. Place a shop cloth directly under one the crossover hose fittings.
4. Secure a clamping tool (A, **Figure 18**) on line to cut off fuel flow.
5. Carefully cut and remove the hose clamp (B, **Figure 18**).
6. Disconnect the crossover hose from one of the fittings on the fuel tank. Immediately connect the drain hose to the fuel tank fitting.
7. Remove the fuel filler cap.
8. Place the plugged end of the drain hose into the gas can and remove the plug. Drain the fuel from that side of the fuel tank.
9. Disconnect the drain hose and reinstall the plug into one end of it. Reconnect the crossover hose to the fitting.
10. Repeat the process for the other side of the fuel tank.
11. Plug the fuel tank crossover fittings to prevent any residual fuel from draining.

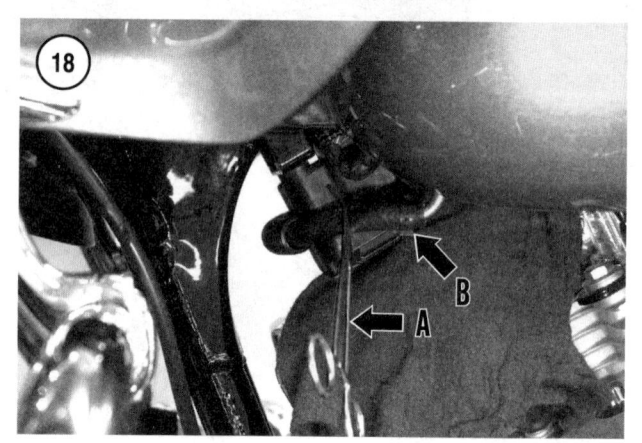

Removal/Installation

Refer to **Figures 19-25**.

The crossover fuel hose is secured to the fuel tank with non-reusable clamps. If the same type of clamps are going to be reinstalled, purchase *new* ones before servicing the fuel tank.

NOTE
Always disarm the TSSM/HFSM security system prior to disconnecting the battery or pulling the Maxi-Fuse so the siren will not sound.

1. Depressurize the fuel system as described in this chapter.

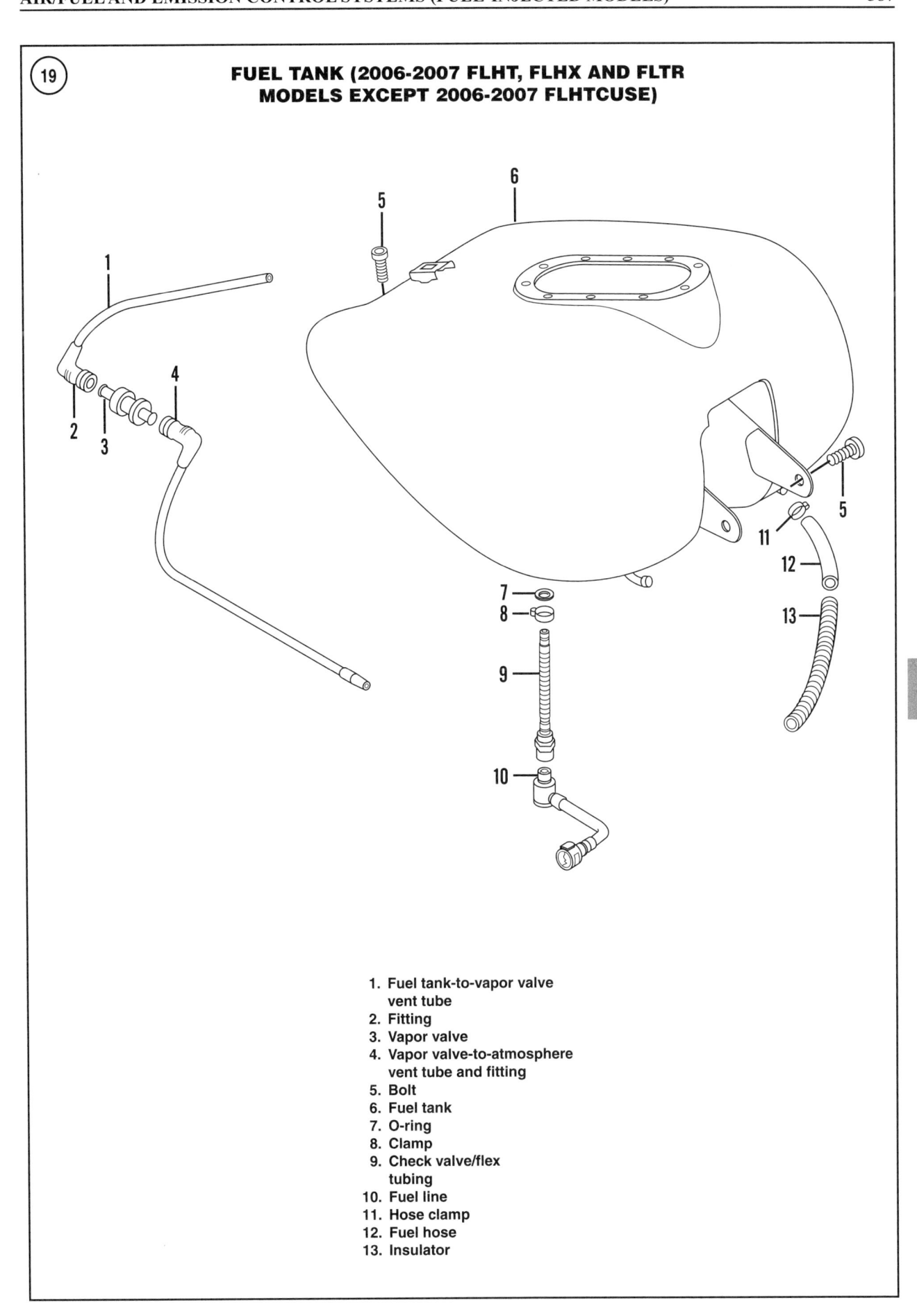

AIR/FUEL AND EMISSION CONTROL SYSTEMS (FUEL-INJECTED MODELS)

(19) FUEL TANK (2006-2007 FLHT, FLHX AND FLTR MODELS EXCEPT 2006-2007 FLHTCUSE)

1. Fuel tank-to-vapor valve vent tube
2. Fitting
3. Vapor valve
4. Vapor valve-to-atmosphere vent tube and fitting
5. Bolt
6. Fuel tank
7. O-ring
8. Clamp
9. Check valve/flex tubing
10. Fuel line
11. Hose clamp
12. Fuel hose
13. Insulator

FUEL TANK (2006-2007 FLHTCUSE MODELS)

1. Fuel hose (vapor valve-to-atmosphere)
2. Vapor valve
3. Fuel hose (fuel tank-to-valve)
4. Bolt
5. Fuel tank
6. O-ring
7. Hose clamp
8. Check valve
9. Fuel line
10. Bolt
11. Hose clamp
12. Crossover hose
13. Insulator
14. Trim tab

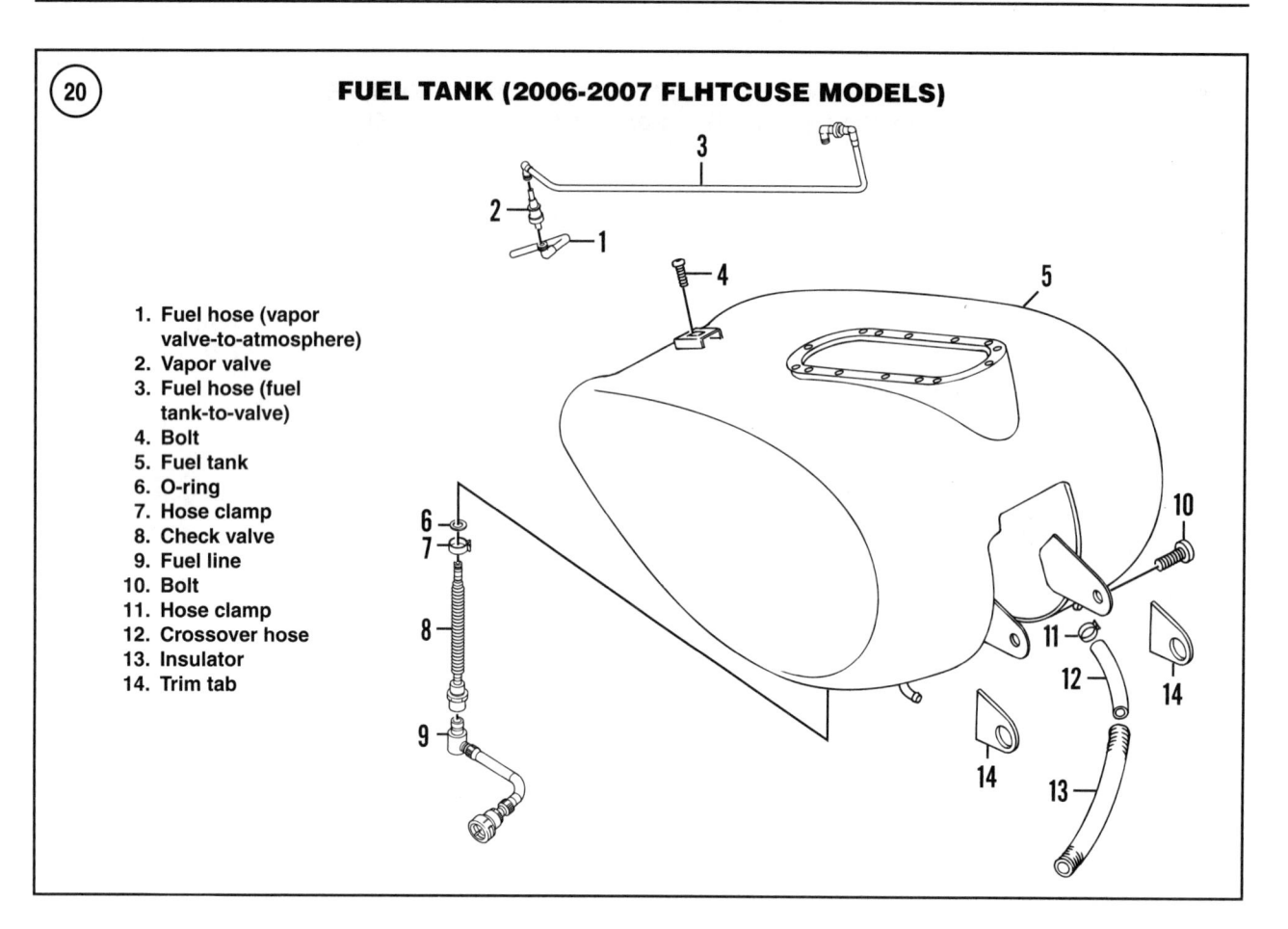

FUEL TANK (2008-2009 FLHT, FLHX AND FLTR MODELS, 2008-2009 FLHTCUSE AND 2009 FLTRSE MODELS)

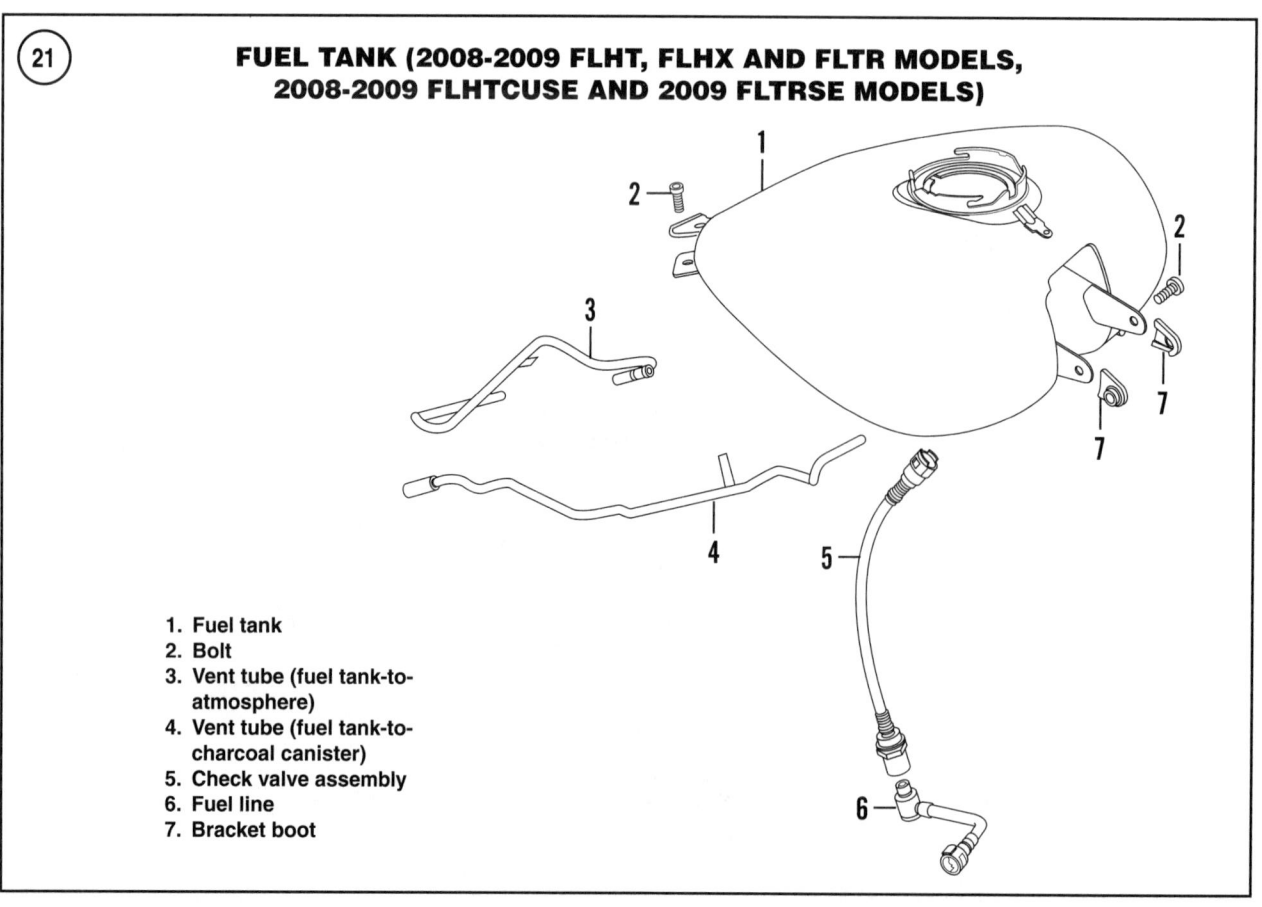

1. Fuel tank
2. Bolt
3. Vent tube (fuel tank-to-atmosphere)
4. Vent tube (fuel tank-to-charcoal canister)
5. Check valve assembly
6. Fuel line
7. Bracket boot

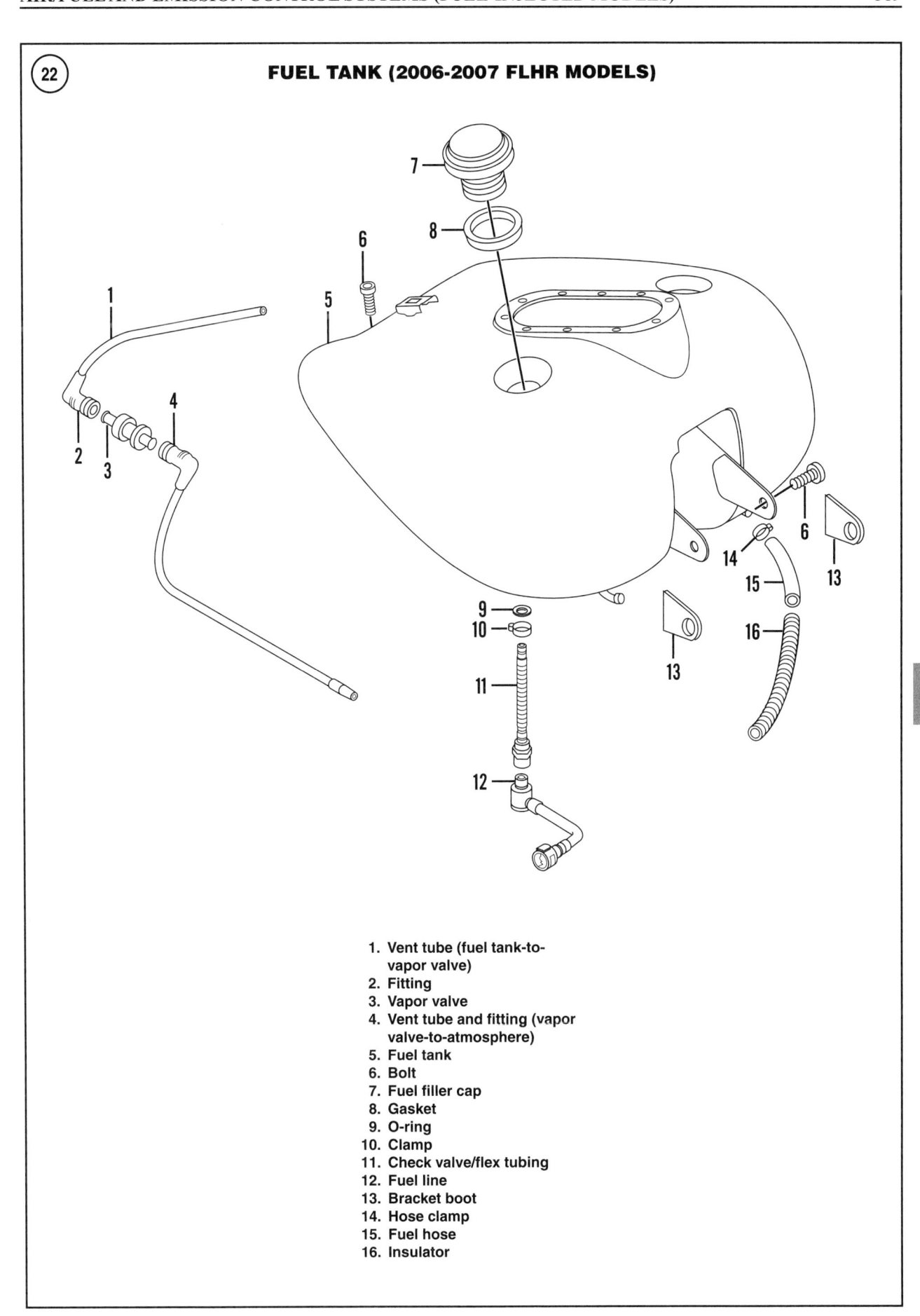

AIR/FUEL AND EMISSION CONTROL SYSTEMS (FUEL-INJECTED MODELS)

FUEL TANK (2006-2007 FLHR MODELS)

1. Vent tube (fuel tank-to-vapor valve)
2. Fitting
3. Vapor valve
4. Vent tube and fitting (vapor valve-to-atmosphere)
5. Fuel tank
6. Bolt
7. Fuel filler cap
8. Gasket
9. O-ring
10. Clamp
11. Check valve/flex tubing
12. Fuel line
13. Bracket boot
14. Hose clamp
15. Fuel hose
16. Insulator

CHAPTER TEN

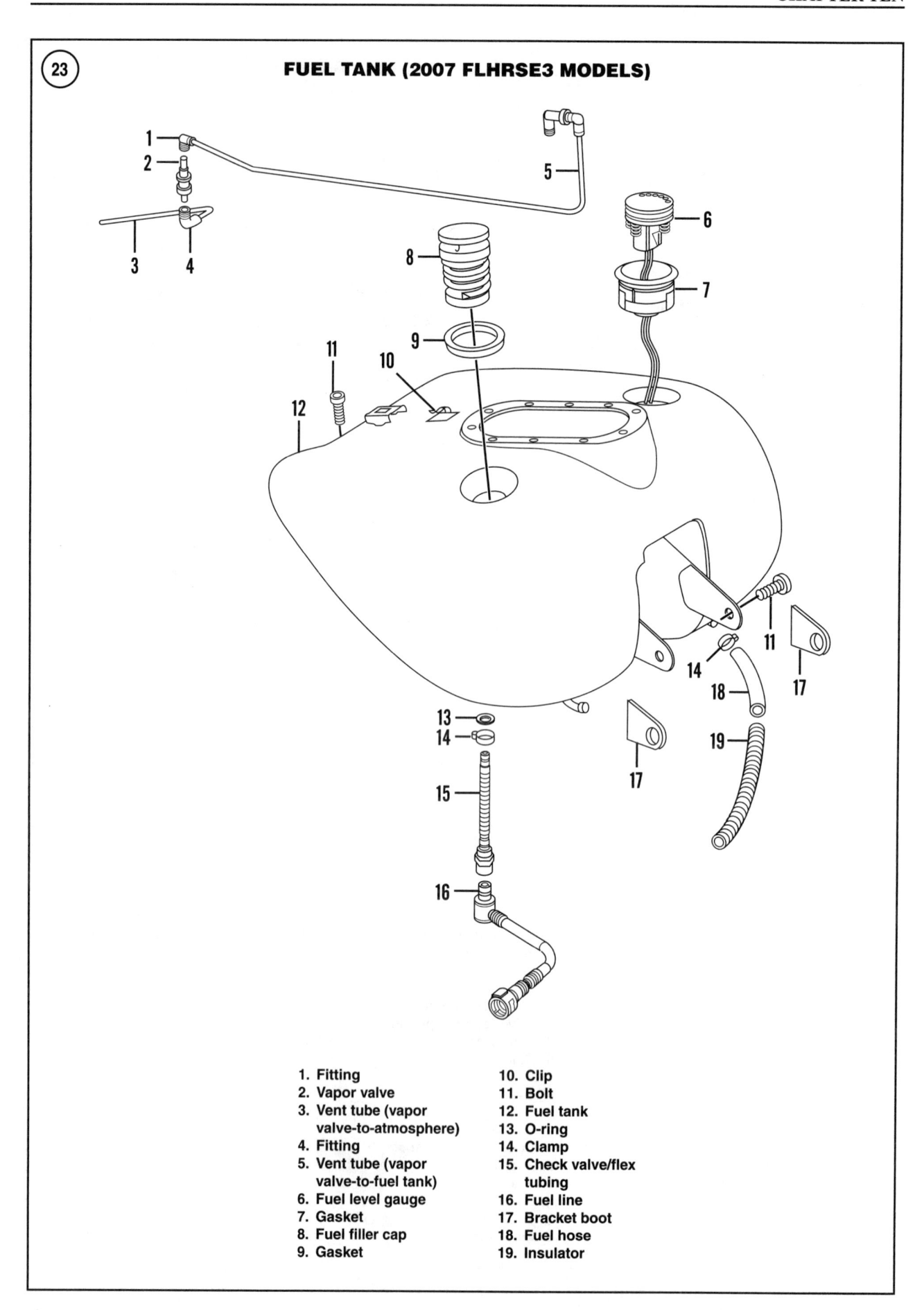

FUEL TANK (2007 FLHRSE3 MODELS)

1. Fitting
2. Vapor valve
3. Vent tube (vapor valve-to-atmosphere)
4. Fitting
5. Vent tube (vapor valve-to-fuel tank)
6. Fuel level gauge
7. Gasket
8. Fuel filler cap
9. Gasket
10. Clip
11. Bolt
12. Fuel tank
13. O-ring
14. Clamp
15. Check valve/flex tubing
16. Fuel line
17. Bracket boot
18. Fuel hose
19. Insulator

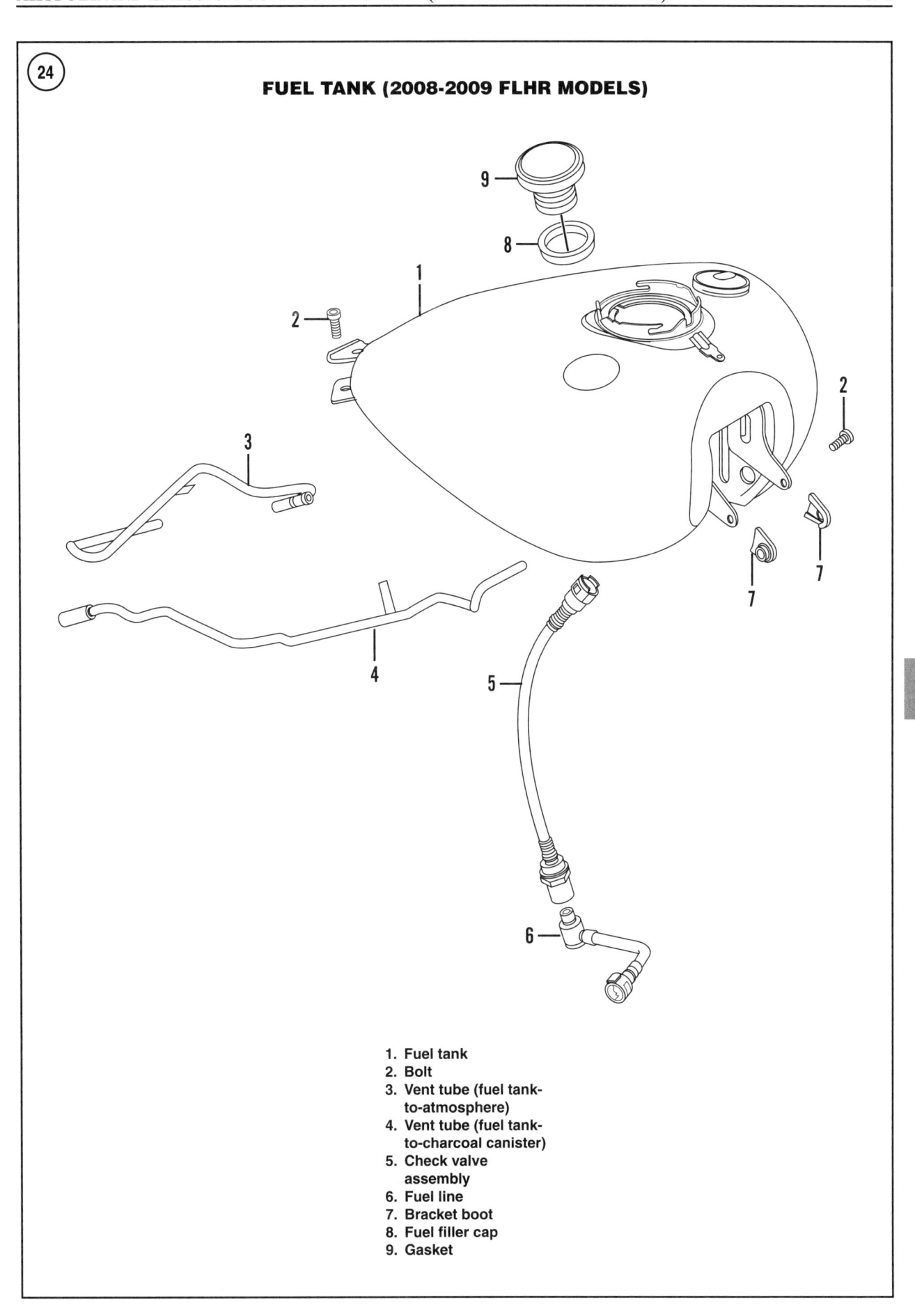

AIR/FUEL AND EMISSION CONTROL SYSTEMS (FUEL-INJECTED MODELS)

㉔

FUEL TANK (2008-2009 FLHR MODELS)

1. Fuel tank
2. Bolt
3. Vent tube (fuel tank-to-atmosphere)
4. Vent tube (fuel tank-to-charcoal canister)
5. Check valve assembly
6. Fuel line
7. Bracket boot
8. Fuel filler cap
9. Gasket

FUEL TANK (2008 FLHRSE4 MODELS)

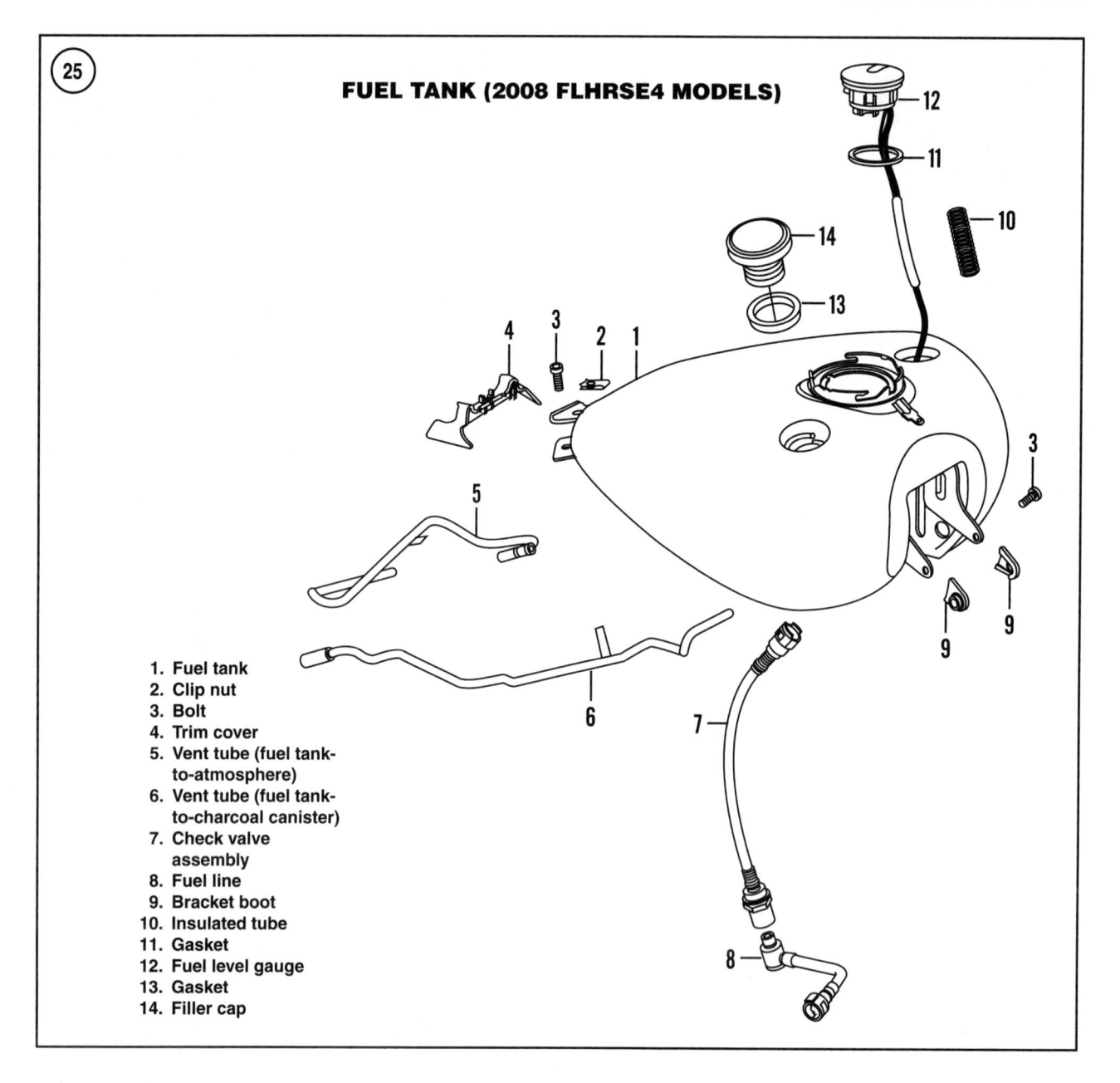

1. Fuel tank
2. Clip nut
3. Bolt
4. Trim cover
5. Vent tube (fuel tank-to-atmosphere)
6. Vent tube (fuel tank-to-charcoal canister)
7. Check valve assembly
8. Fuel line
9. Bracket boot
10. Insulated tube
11. Gasket
12. Fuel level gauge
13. Gasket
14. Filler cap

2. Disconnect the negative battery cable as described in Chapter Eleven.
3. Remove the seat as described in Chapter Seventeen.
4. Remove the fuel tank console as described in this chapter.
5. Drain the fuel tank as described in this section.
6. Disconnect the vent hose from the fuel tank.
7. On models so equipped, on the bottom left side of the fuel tank, gently pull the convoluted tubing down. Carefully pull down and disconnect the electrical connector for the fuel gauge.
8. Disconnect the fuel pump electrical connector (A, **Figure 26**, typical) and vapor vent hose (B) from the fuel tank canopy.

WARNING
A small amount of fuel will drain out of the fuel tank when the fuel line is disconnected from the base of the tank. Place several shop cloths under the fuel line fittings to catch any spilled fuel prior to disconnecting them. Discard the shop cloths in a suitable safe manner.

WARNING
Do not twist the plastic fuel line fitting as it may crack.

9. On the left side, pull up the chrome sleeve on the fuel line quick-connect fitting (A, **Figure 27**) and disconnect the fuel supply line (B) from the fuel tank.
10. On models so equipped, remove the lower fairing cap on each side as described in Chapter Seventeen.
11. At the front of the fuel tank, remove the bolt (**Figure 28**) on each side securing the fuel tank to the frame. Do not misplace the trim tabs, on models so equipped.

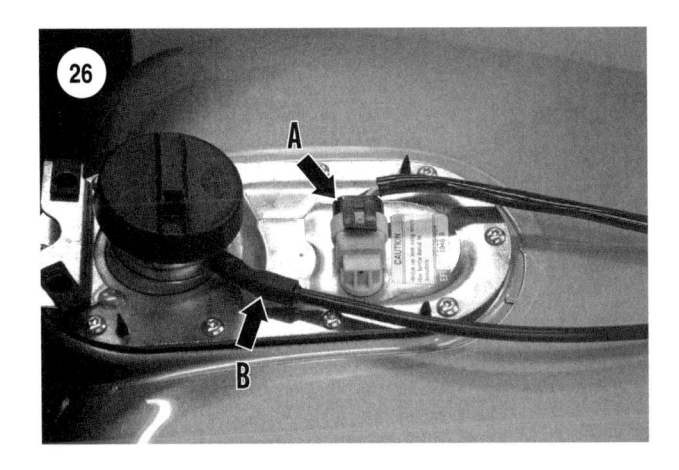

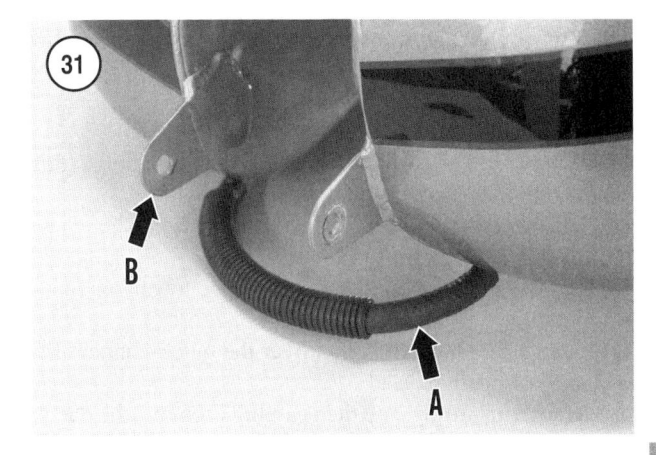

AIR/FUEL AND EMISSION CONTROL SYSTEMS (FUEL-INJECTED MODELS)

12. At the rear of the fuel tank, remove the bolt and flat washer (**Figure 29**) securing the fuel tank to the frame. On FLHX and FLHRS models, the rear bolt was already removed during console removal.
13. Lift off and remove the fuel tank.
14. Drain any remaining fuel into a gas can.
15. Installation is the reverse of removal. Note the following:
    a. Tighten the front bolts and rear bolt to 15-20 ft.-lb. (20-27 N•m).
    b. Install a *new* hose clamp and secure it with the pincer tool (JIMS part No. 1171) as shown in **Figure 30**. Remove the hemostat (A, **Figure 18**).
    c. Reconnect the fuel line quick-connect fitting (B, **Figure 27**) onto the fuel tank until it clicks into the locked position. Pull down on the fuel line to make sure it is secured to the fitting.
    d. Refill the tank and check for leaks.

Inspection

1. Inspect the fuel tank quick-connect fitting for leaks. Replace the fitting as necessary.
2. Inspect the fuel crossover hose (A, **Figure 31**) hose for cracks or deterioration and replace as necessary.
3. Check the front mounting tabs (B, **Figure 31**) and the rear mounting tab (**Figure 32**) for cracks or fractures.

4. Check the fuel tank console mounting clip nut (**Figure 33**) for damage.
5. Check the top plate (**Figure 34**) mounting screws tightness; tighten if necessary.
6. Check the fuel line insulator for damage.
7. Remove the filler cap and inspect the tank for rust or contamination. If there is a rust buildup inside the tank, clean and flush the tank.
8. Inspect the fuel tank for leaks.

FUEL SUPPLY CHECK VALVE

Removal/Installation

The check valve is mounted in the quick-connect fitting. The valve keeps fuel from draining from the tank when the external line is disconnected.

Refer to **Figure 35**.

1. Remove the fuel tank as described in this chapter.
2. Remove the fuel pump/level sender assembly (this chapter).
3. Place several towels or blanket on the work bench to protect the fuel tank finish.
4. Turn the fuel tank upside down on the towels or blanket.
5. Install a 7/8 in. deep socket over the quick-connect fitting and onto its hex head.
6. Remove the fitting, and then carefully remove the check valve and fuel line from the fuel tank.
7. Remove and discard the O-ring from the fitting.
8. Lubricate a *new* O-ring with a light coat of clean engine oil, and install the O-ring onto the fitting.
9. Insert the fuel line into the fuel tank opening. Manually thread the quick-connect fitting into the tank until it is snug. Tighten the quick-connect fitting to 18 ft.-lb. (24.4 N•m).
10. Install fuel pump/level sender assembly as described in this chapter.
11. Install the fuel tank as described in this chapter.

FUEL PUMP/LEVEL SENDER ASSEMBLY (2006-2007 MODELS)

The fuel hoses in this assembly are secured to their fittings with non-reusable hose clamps. These hose clamps must be removed with cutting pliers and discarded. Do *not* re-use a hose clamp that has been removed.

New clamps must be crimped into place with the hose clamp pincer tool (JIMS part No. 1171), or an equivalent.

Assembly Removal

Refer to **Figures 36-38**.

NOTE
Always disarm the TSSM/HFSM security system prior to disconnecting the battery or pulling the Maxi-Fuse so the siren will not sound.

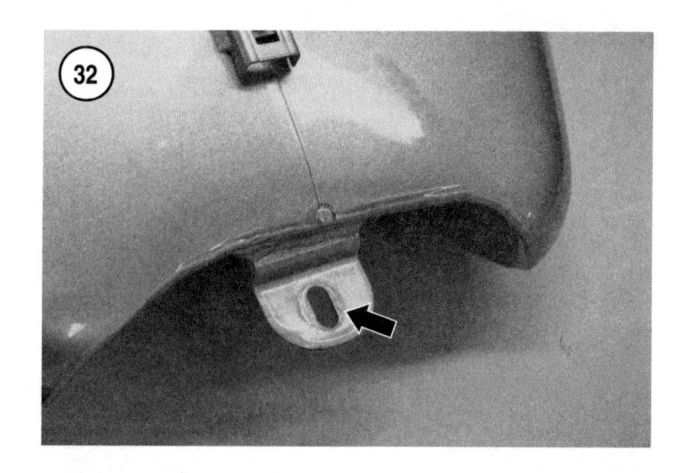

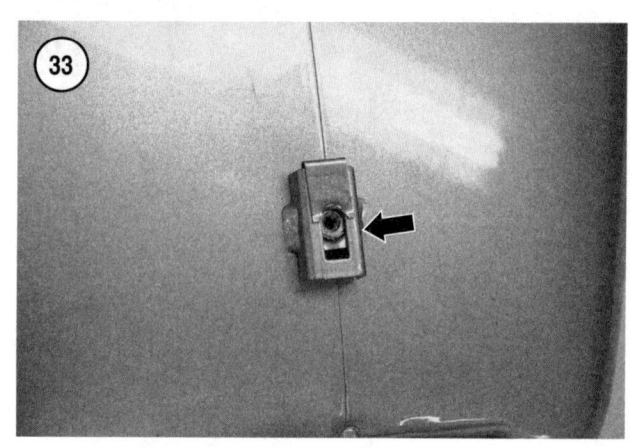

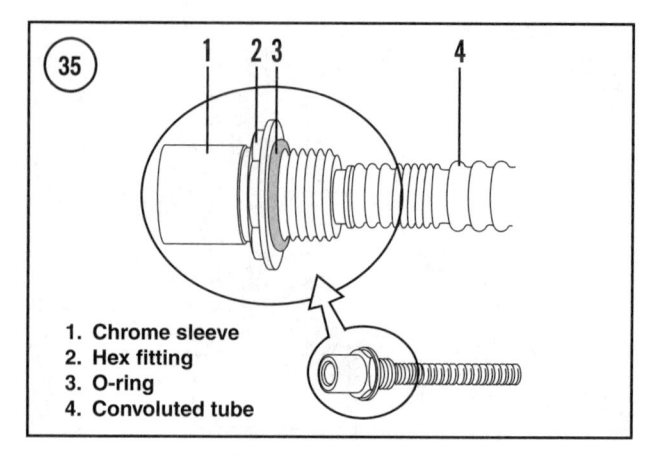

35
1. Chrome sleeve
2. Hex fitting
3. O-ring
4. Convoluted tube

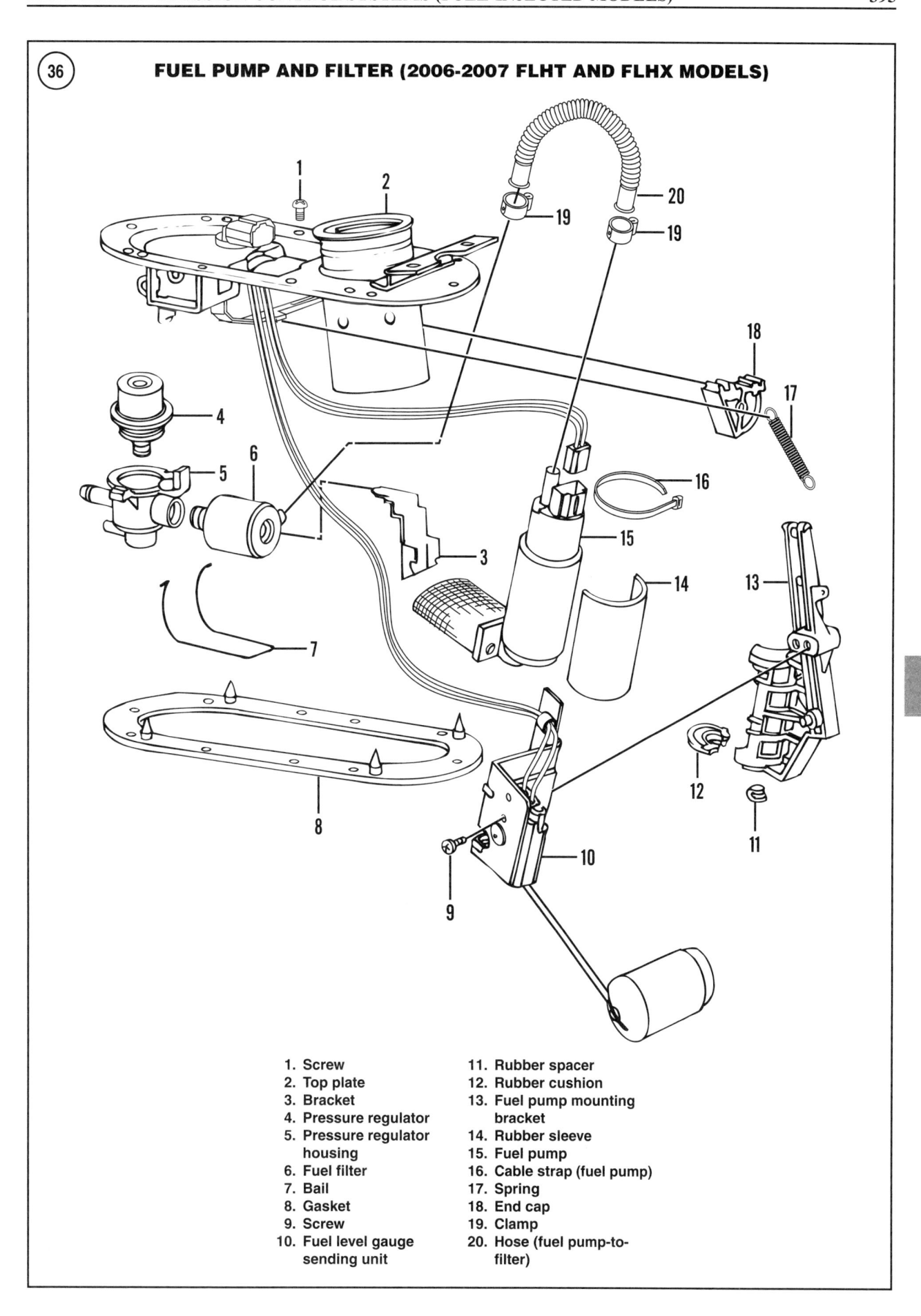

AIR/FUEL AND EMISSION CONTROL SYSTEMS (FUEL-INJECTED MODELS)

㊱ FUEL PUMP AND FILTER (2006-2007 FLHT AND FLHX MODELS)

1. Screw
2. Top plate
3. Bracket
4. Pressure regulator
5. Pressure regulator housing
6. Fuel filter
7. Bail
8. Gasket
9. Screw
10. Fuel level gauge sending unit
11. Rubber spacer
12. Rubber cushion
13. Fuel pump mounting bracket
14. Rubber sleeve
15. Fuel pump
16. Cable strap (fuel pump)
17. Spring
18. End cap
19. Clamp
20. Hose (fuel pump-to-filter)

396

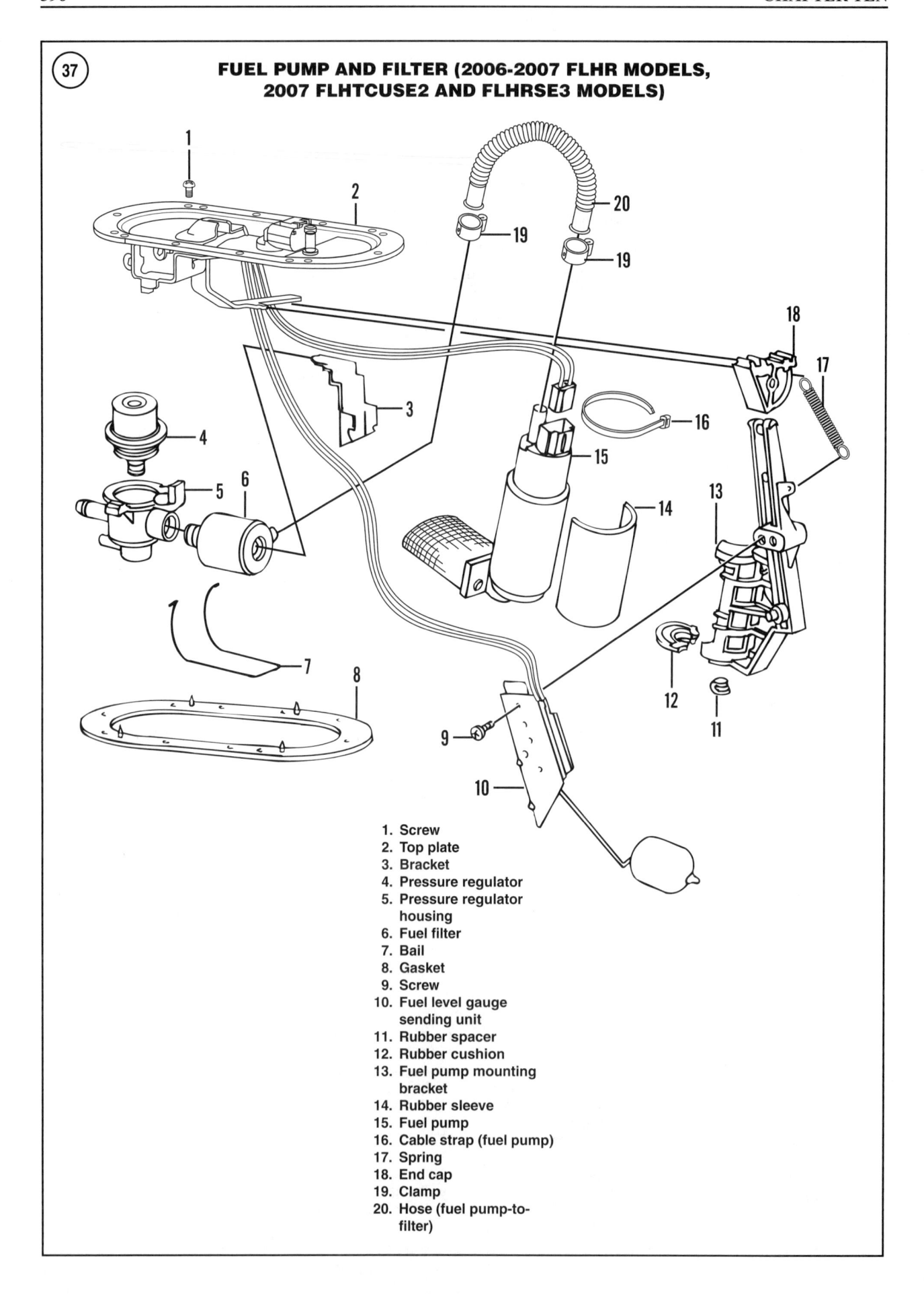

CHAPTER TEN

FUEL PUMP AND FILTER (2006-2007 FLHR MODELS, 2007 FLHTCUSE2 AND FLHRSE3 MODELS)

1. Screw
2. Top plate
3. Bracket
4. Pressure regulator
5. Pressure regulator housing
6. Fuel filter
7. Bail
8. Gasket
9. Screw
10. Fuel level gauge sending unit
11. Rubber spacer
12. Rubber cushion
13. Fuel pump mounting bracket
14. Rubber sleeve
15. Fuel pump
16. Cable strap (fuel pump)
17. Spring
18. End cap
19. Clamp
20. Hose (fuel pump-to-filter)

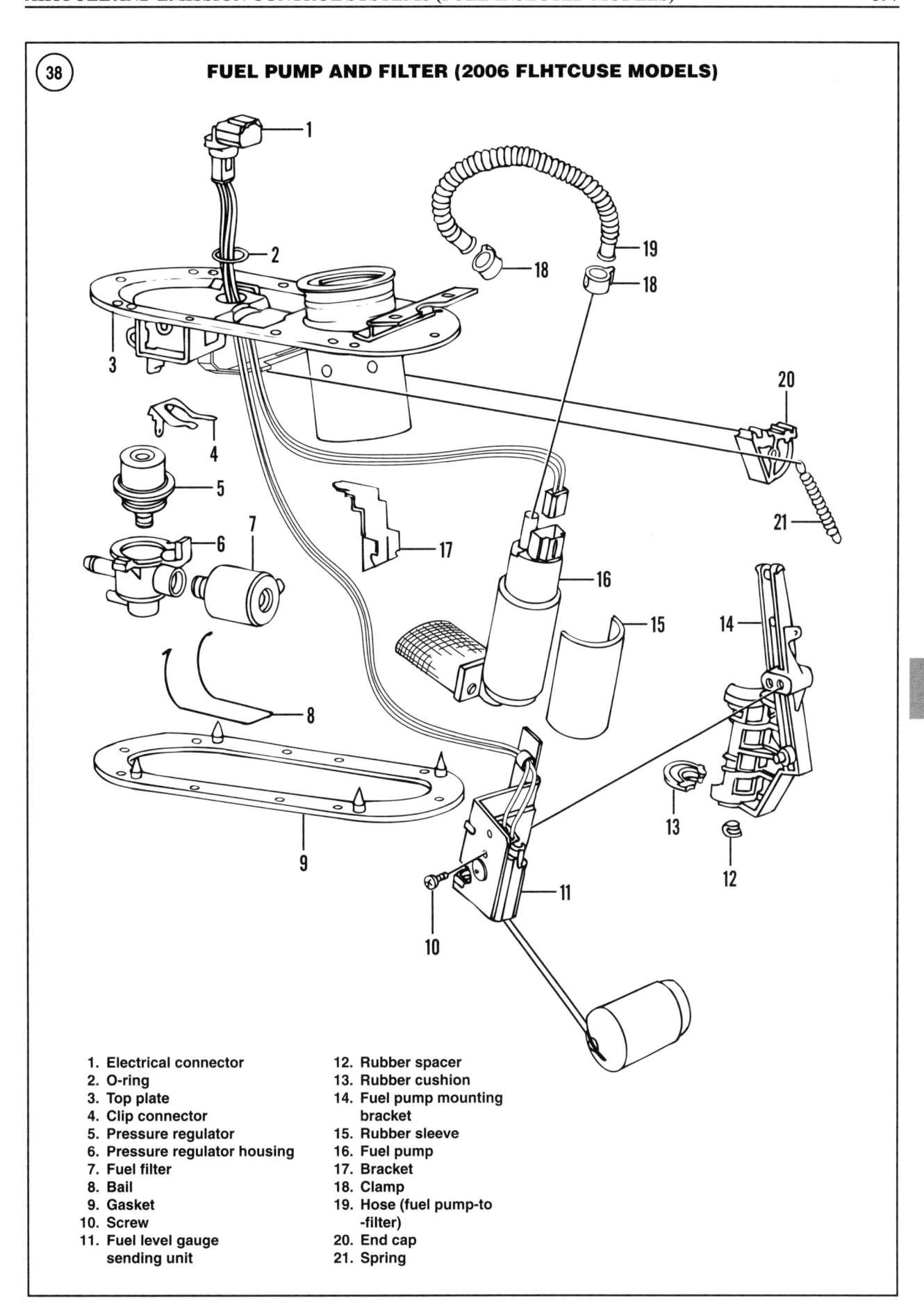

AIR/FUEL AND EMISSION CONTROL SYSTEMS (FUEL-INJECTED MODELS)

FUEL PUMP AND FILTER (2006 FLHTCUSE MODELS)

1. Electrical connector
2. O-ring
3. Top plate
4. Clip connector
5. Pressure regulator
6. Pressure regulator housing
7. Fuel filter
8. Bail
9. Gasket
10. Screw
11. Fuel level gauge sending unit
12. Rubber spacer
13. Rubber cushion
14. Fuel pump mounting bracket
15. Rubber sleeve
16. Fuel pump
17. Bracket
18. Clamp
19. Hose (fuel pump-to-filter)
20. End cap
21. Spring

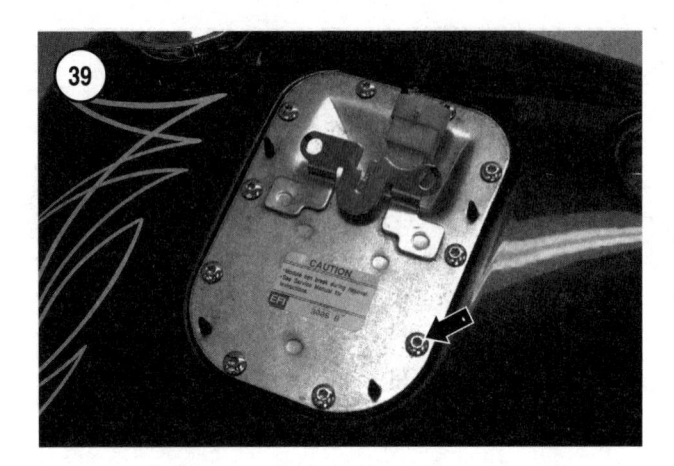

1. Depressurize the fuel system as described in this chapter.
2. Disconnect the negative battery cable as described in Chapter Eleven.
3. Remove the seat as described in Chapter Seventeen.
4. Remove the fuel tank console as described in this chapter.
5. Drain the fuel tank as described in this chapter.
6. Remove and discard the top plate screws (**Figure 39**).
7. Partially lift the top plate away from the fuel tank to access the fuel hose.

CAUTION
Do not cut the fuel supply hose while cutting the hose clamp free.

8. Tie a string to the output hose, and use side-cutting pliers to carefully cut the hose clamp (**Figure 40**). Then, disconnect the output hose from the fitting (**Figure 41**) on the pressure regulator housing.

NOTE
The fuel pump sits in the left side of the tank; the fuel level sender sits in the right side.

9. Reach into the tank, and press the fuel pump housing until it disengages from the end cap.
10. Pull the fuel pump from the tank until the fuel level sender is accessible.
11. Pull the tab towards the fuel tank top, and release the fuel level sender from the mounting tabs.
12. Remove the top plate, fuel pump and fuel level sender from the fuel tank. Exercise caution to not damage the float arm.
13. Remove and discard the top plate gasket.

Assembly Installation

1. Install a *new* gasket beneath the top plate.
2. Fit the fuel level sender onto its mounting tabs. Press the sender down until it is seated in the tabs.

NOTE
The fuel pump sits on the left side of the tank, the fuel level sender on the right.

3. Insert the fuel pump into the tank until its rubber damper sits on the bottom of the tank.
4. Slip a *new* clamp onto the output hose, and connect the hose onto the fitting (**Figure 41**) on the pressure regulator housing. Use the hose clamp pliers to crimp the hose clamp in place.
5. Rotate the top plate until the end cap aligns with the fuel pump housing, and press the plate down until the end cap engages the fuel pump housing.
6. Set the top plate and gasket into position on the tank. The spring loaded end cap returns the fuel pump to the original position once the top plate is seated on the fuel tank. Install and finger-tighten *new* top plate screws (**Figure 39**).
7. Using a crossing pattern, tighten the top plate screws to 18-24 in.-lb. (2.0-2.7 N•m).
8. Install the fuel tank console as described in this chapter.
9. Reinstall the fuel pump fuse, and connect the negative battery cable.
10. Add fuel to the tank, and check for leaks.
11. Perform the fuel pressure test as described in this chapter.

Fuel Filter
Removal/Installation

1. Remove the fuel pump/level sender assembly as described in this section.

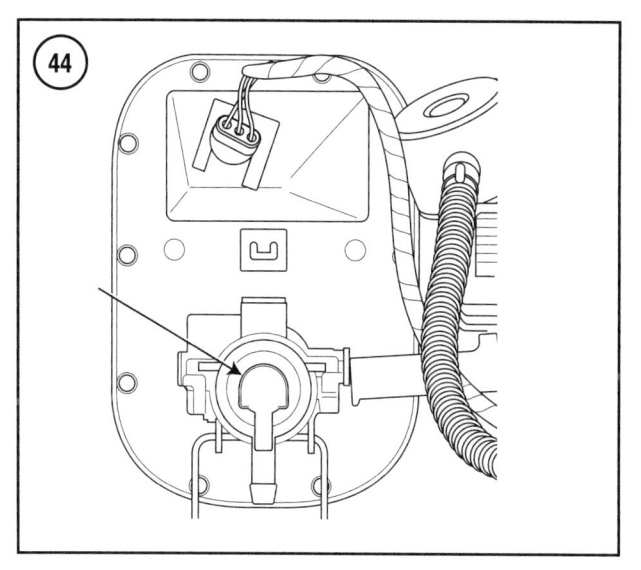

AIR/FUEL AND EMISSION CONTROL SYSTEMS (FUEL-INJECTED MODELS)

2. Depress the external latch, and disconnect the electrical connector from the fuel pump.
3. Use side-cutting pliers to cut the hose clamp. Disconnect fuel pump hose from the fuel pump output port.
4. Release the return spring from the fuel pump housing.
5A. If the fuel pump will be replaced, use a small, flat-bladed screwdriver (A, **Figure 43**) and crack the plastic webbing on top of the end cap. Remove the end cap from the top plate arm.
5B. If the fuel pump will be reinstalled, use the tip of needlenose pliers to depress the pin (B, **Figure 43**), and slide the end cap off top plate arm.
6. Discard the fuel pump and housing assembly if faulty.

Fuel Pump Installation

1. If removed, slide the end cap onto the top plate arm. Pull on the end cap to make sure it is locked by the pin on the top plate arm.
2. Hook the other end of the spring onto the fuel pump housing.
3. Install a *new* clamp onto the free end of the fuel pump hose, and connect it to the fuel pump output port. Use the hose clamp pliers to crimp the clamp in place, however, avoid cracking the output port.
4. Install the electrical connector onto the fuel pump, and push it on until it clicks into the locked position. Pull straight up on the connector to make sure the latch is locked in place.
5. Install the fuel pump/level sender assembly as described in this section.

Fuel Pressure Regulator Removal/Installation

1. Remove the fuel pump/level sender assembly as described in this section.
2. Remove the fuel filter assembly (this section).
3. Slide the pressure regulator housing (**Figure 44**) forward, and release its arms from the top plate.

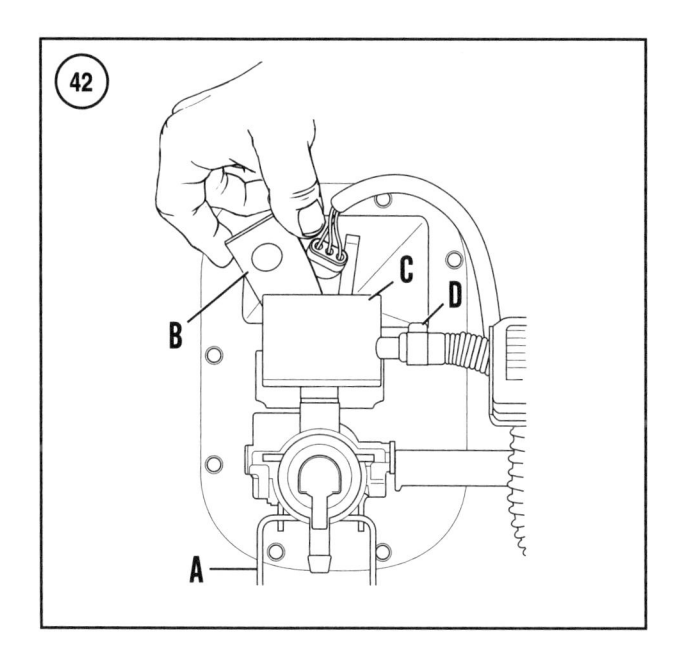

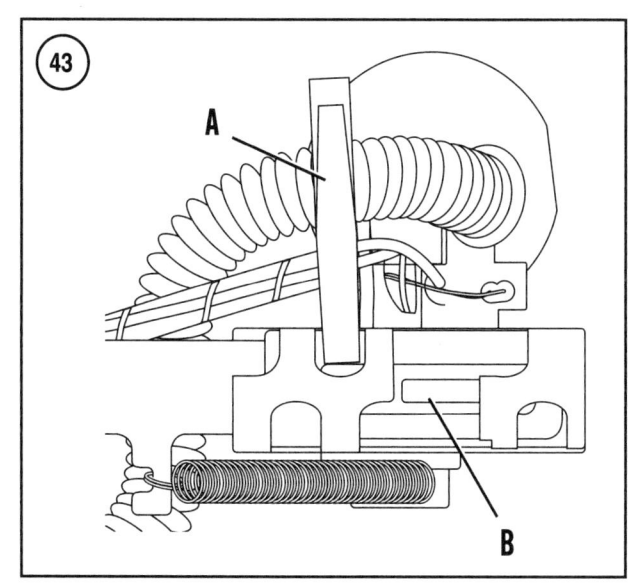

2. Release the wire bail (A, **Figure 42**) from the bail bracket (B) and pivot the bail out of the way.
3. Remove the bail bracket (B, **Figure 42**) from the slot in the top plate.
4. Pull the fuel filter (C, **Figure 42**) from the pressure regulator housing.
5. Use side-cutting pliers to carefully cut the hose clamp (D, **Figure 42**). Then, remove the fuel pump hose from the filter input fitting. Do not damage the hose.
6. Discard the fuel filter.
7. Installation is the reverse of removal. Use a *new* hose clamp to secure the fuel pump hose to the filter input fitting. Crimp the hose clamp with the hose clamp pliers.

Fuel Pump Removal

1. Remove the fuel pump/level sender assembly as described in this section.

4. Using a rocking motion, pull the pressure regulator from the housing.
5. Remove and discard the large and small O-rings from the regulator.
6. Apply a light coat of clean engine oil to the *new* O-rings, and install them onto the regulator.
7. Carefully press the fuel pressure regulator into the housing until it bottoms.
8. Slide the pressure regulator housing into place on the top plate.
9. Install the fuel filter assembly as described in this section.
10. Install the fuel pump/level sender assembly as described in this section.

Fuel Level Sender
Removal/Installation

1. Remove the fuel pump/level sender assembly as described in this section.
2. Disconnect the connector from the fuel pump.
3. Push the lock tab toward the fuel level sender connector, and pull the connector from the top plate.
4. Remove the fuel level sender and its wiring harness.
5. Installation is the reverse of removal.

FUEL PUMP AND FUEL FILTER (2008-2009 MODELS)

Refer to **Figure 45**.

Fuel Tank Top Plate

Removal

1. Depressurize the fuel system as described in this chapter.
2. Remove the seat as described in Chapter Seventeen.
3. Drain the fuel tank as described in this chapter. Do not remove the fuel tank as it needs to be secured while using the tools to loosen the cam ring.
4. Remove the fuel filler cap, on models so equipped.

CAUTION
Do not try to loosen the cam ring without the correct tool. The tabs on the cam ring are fragile and will break off if pried or tapped on. Using the incorrect tool may also damage the fuel tank finish.

5. Install the cam ring tool (JIMS part No. 954 or H-D part No. HD-48646) onto the top plate cam ring. Align the tool notches with the four projecting tabs on the cam ring.
6. Use a 1/2 inch drive ratchet and slowly rotate the cam ring *counterclockwise* until it is free from the engagement slots in the fuel tank collar. Push down on the tool and drive ratchet to prevent the tool from slipping.
7. Carefully, remove the tools and completely remove the cam ring from the fuel tank.
8. Partially remove the top plate until the electrical connector is accessible.
9. Insert a small, flat-bladed screwdriver between the latch and top plate. Depress either side of the electrical connector and disconnect the harness and connector from the top plate.
10. At the upper surface of the top plate, insert a small, flat-bladed screwdriver through the small window and depress the tang on the ground wire. Pull the wire terminal from the slot.
11. Depress the tabs on the fuel line quick-connect fittings and disconnect both fuel hoses from the fuel filter.
12. Remove the top plate assembly.

Installation

1. Inspect the seal ring at the bottom of the top plate for cuts, tears of deterioration; replace as necessary. If installing a *new* seal ring, position the seal ring with the nubs facing the ring groove walls. Press it in until it bottoms.
2. Install the fuel hoses to the correct fuel filter fittings. The small diameter hose goes from the fuel pump to the fuel filter housing, the large diameter hose goes from the fuel supply valve to the pressure regulator housing. Press the fuel hoses on until they click and lock in place.
3. Install the electrical connector onto the top plate and push it on until it clicks into the locked position. Gently pull straight down on the connector to make sure the latch is locked in place.

NOTE
If the terminal does not lock in place, use a small Xacto knife blade to slightly bend the tang away from the terminal body.

4. Route the ground wire along the inboard side of the vapor valve and install the spade terminal into the slot in the top plate. Gently pull straight down on the wire to make sure the terminal is locked in place.
5. Position the top plate with the index tab pointing forward and install the top plate into the index slot in the fuel tank collar. Push it down until it bottoms.
6. Position the cam ring with the *TOP* mark facing up and install it onto the top plate. Locate the cam ring tabs into the engagement slots in the fuel tank collar.
7. On models so equipped, remove the fuel filler cap.
8. Install the cam ring tool onto the top plate cam ring. Align the tool notches with the four projecting tabs on the cam ring.
9. Use a 1/2 inch drive ratchet and slowly rotate the cam ring *clockwise* until it is locked into the engagement slots in the fuel tank collar. Push down on the tool and drive ratchet with both hands to prevent the tool from slipping.
10. On models so equipped, install the fuel filler cap.
11. Install the seat as described in Chapter Seventeen.

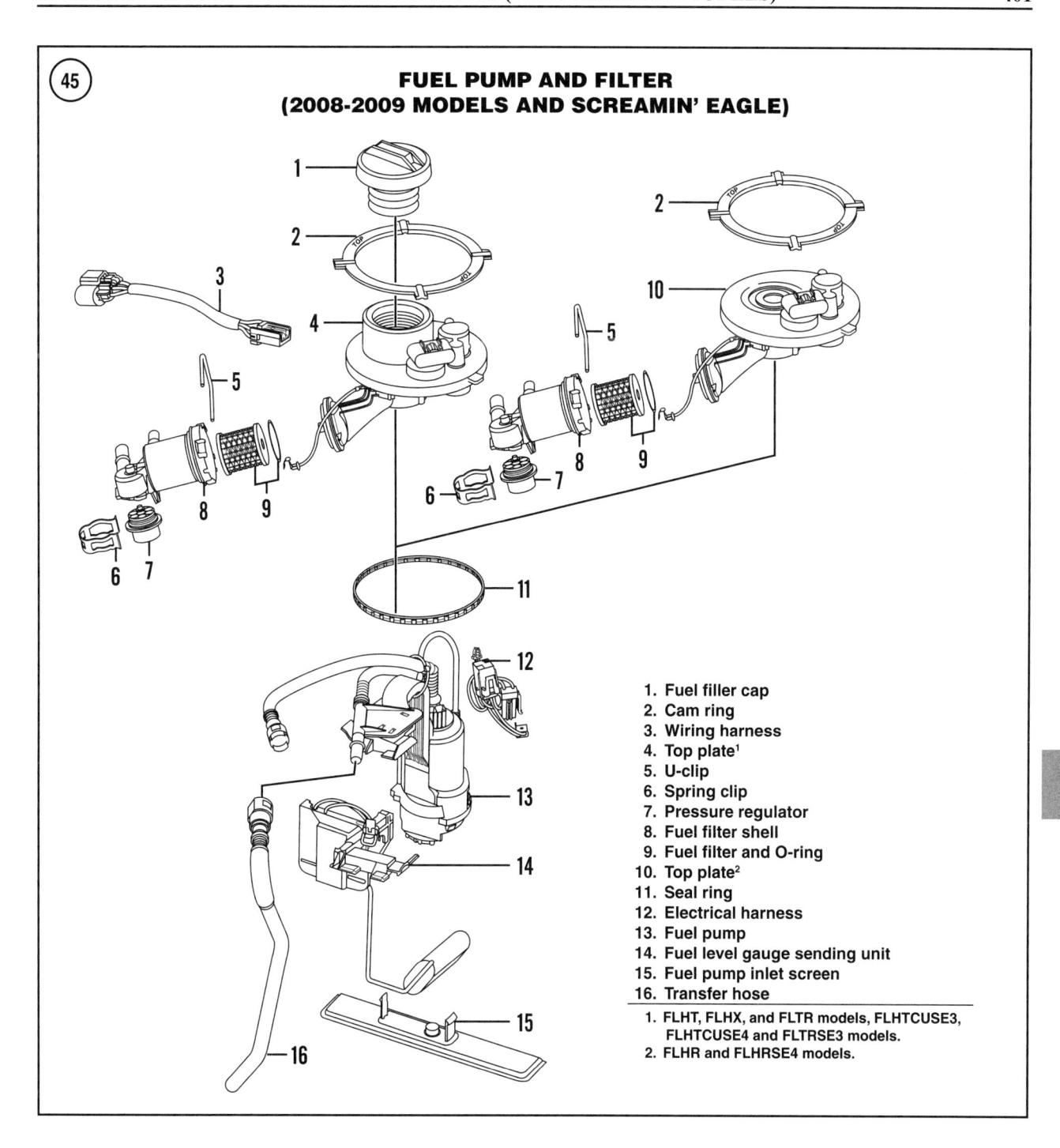

AIR/FUEL AND EMISSION CONTROL SYSTEMS (FUEL-INJECTED MODELS)

**(45) FUEL PUMP AND FILTER
(2008-2009 MODELS AND SCREAMIN' EAGLE)**

1. Fuel filler cap
2. Cam ring
3. Wiring harness
4. Top plate[1]
5. U-clip
6. Spring clip
7. Pressure regulator
8. Fuel filter shell
9. Fuel filter and O-ring
10. Top plate[2]
11. Seal ring
12. Electrical harness
13. Fuel pump
14. Fuel level gauge sending unit
15. Fuel pump inlet screen
16. Transfer hose

1. FLHT, FLHX, and FLTR models, FLHTCUSE3, FLHTCUSE4 and FLTRSE3 models.
2. FLHR and FLHRSE4 models.

Fuel Filter

Removal/installation

1. Remove the top plate as described in this section.
2. Insert a small, flat-bladed screwdriver through the small window and depress the tang on the ground wire. Pull the wire terminal from the slot.
3. Carefully raise the locking arm and pull the U-clip from the holes in the fuel filter shell.
4. Remove fuel filter shell from top plate.
5. Withdraw the fuel filter from the filter shell and remove the O-ring from the shell.
6. Install a *new* fuel filter into the shell.
7. Install a *new* O-ring into the counter bore at the top of the fuel filter. Make sure it is correctly seated.
8. Position the fuel filter shell so the slot in the shell engages the top cap index pin, and install the fuel filter shell.
9. Push the U-clip through the holes on the locking arm of the fuel filter shell until the ends exit the holes on the opposite side. Retract the U-clip until contact is made with the step in the locking arm of the filter shell.

NOTE
If the terminal does not lock in place, use a small Xacto knife blade to slightly bend the tang away from the terminal body.

10. Route the ground wire around the index pin side of the end cap and install the terminal into the slot in the fuel filter shell. Gently pull on the wire to make sure the terminal is locked in place.

11. Install the top plate as described in this section.

Fuel Pump

Removal

1. Remove the top plate as described in this section.
2. Remove the fuel level sender as described in this section.
3. Pull up on transfer tube bracket and release the two tabs at the bottom from the slots at the top of the fuel pump bracket.
4. Depress the collar on each side of the transfer hose and disconnect the hose from the fuel pump bracket.
5. Reach down into the fuel tank, and pull up on the rear finger. Slide the fuel pump bracket forward and free the four ears on the bracket from the catches at top of the fuel tank tunnel.
6. On the left side of the fuel tank, rotate the fuel pump 90° *clockwise* so the transfer hose is facing toward the rear. Carefully withdraw the fuel pump from the fuel tank.
7. To remove the fuel filter, depress the fingers on the fuel filter and release it from the base of the fuel pump.

Installation

1. If removed, install the fuel filter onto the base of the fuel pump. Press it on until it clicks into place.
2. Position the fuel pump with the transfer hose pointing toward the rear and insert the pump into the fuel tank.
3. Rotate the fuel pump 90° *counterclockwise* and check that the fuel pump inlet screen is laying flat on the bottom of the fuel tank. Make sure the screen ends are not folded under.
4. Check that the wiring harness is still captured in the folded clip at the front of the fuel pump bracket.
5. Reach down into the fuel tank, and make sure the finger on the fuel pump bracket is pointing toward the rear. Push the fuel pump toward the rear and engage the four ears on the bracket onto the catches at top of the fuel tank tunnel.
6. Connect the transfer hose onto the fuel pump bracket. Install the two tabs on the bottom of the transfer hose into the slots on the fuel pump bracket. Check that the transfer hose is captured in the weld clip on the right side of the tunnel and the free end contacts the bottom of the fuel tank.
7. Install the fuel level sender as described in this section.
8. Install the top plate as described in this section.

Fuel Pump and Fuel Level Sender Electrical Harness Replacement

WARNING
Use only OEM Teflon-coated wiring if the harness requires replacement. Standard wiring insulation materials will deteriorate when exposed to gasoline.

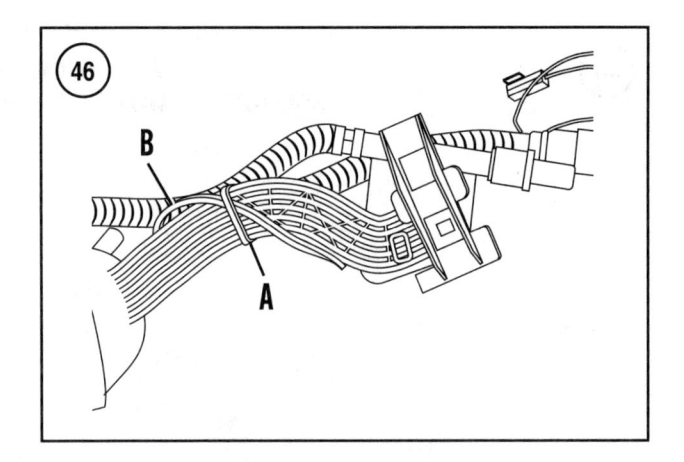

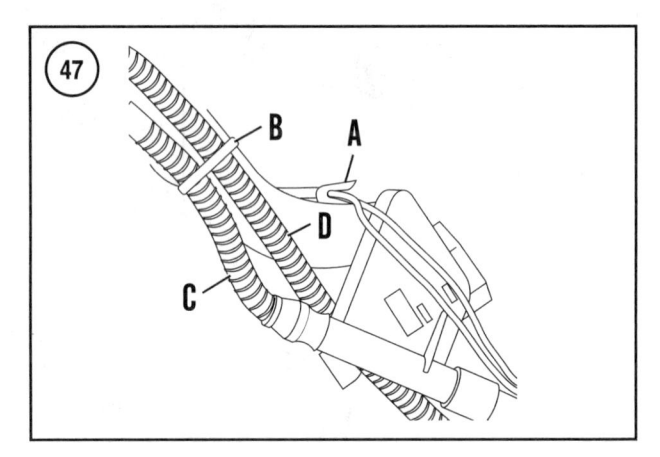

1. Remove the fuel pump as described in this section.
2. Carefully cut the cable strap (A, **Figure 46**) and separate the harness (B) from the fuel pump bracket.
3. Release the electrical connector from the fuel pump molded clip (A, **Figure 47**), and disconnect the electrical connector from the fuel pump. Remove the harness.
4. Connect the electrical connector onto the fuel pump. Make sure the connector snaps into place.
5. Route the harness toward the rear and then toward the front under the arm of the fuel pump bracket.
6. Install a *new* cable strap (B, **Figure 47**) at the elbow, securing the fuel pump hose (C) and the transfer hose (D) at the top of the arm and the harness at the bottom of the bracket.
7. Route the harness through the fuel pump molded clip (A, **Figure 47**).
8. Install the fuel pump as described in this section.

Fuel Pressure Regulator
Removal/Installation

1. Remove the top plate as described in this section.
2. Insert a small, flat-bladed screwdriver through the small window and depress the tang on the ground wire. Pull the wire terminal from the slot on the fuel filter shell.
3. Free one side of the spring clip first, and then the other. Then, remove the spring clip from the fuel pressure regulator.
4. Remove the fuel pressure regulator assembly from the fuel filter shell.

AIR/FUEL AND EMISSION CONTROL SYSTEMS (FUEL-INJECTED MODELS)

Fuel Level Sender
Removal/Installation

1. Remove the top plate as described in this section.
2. Disconnect the 2-pin electrical connector from the harness.
3. Look down into the fuel tank at the left side of the top tunnel. Note the orientation of the front and rear fingers on top of the fuel level sensor.
4. Reach into the fuel tank and pull up on the front finger while sliding the fuel level sensor toward the rear. Move the senor back until the four ears on the bracket are free from the fuel tank tunnel mounts.
5. Carefully withdraw the fuel level sensor from the left side of the fuel tank.
6. Position the fuel level sensor with the front finger facing toward the front of the fuel tank.
7. Install the fuel level sensor into the left side of the fuel tank.
8. Move the fuel level sensor toward the rear and engage the four ears of the bracket onto the fuel tank tunnel mounts. Push it forward until it locks into place.
9. Connect the 2-pin electrical connector onto the harness.
10. Install the top plate as described in this section.

FUEL PRESSURE TEST (ALL MODELS)

WARNING
This procedure is performed adjacent to a hot exhaust system while handling gasoline-related test equipment. Have an approved fire extinguished rated for gasoline fires (Class B) available.

1. The following tools, or their equivalents, are required for this test:
   a. Fuel pressure gauge (H-D part No. HD-41182).
   b. Two fuel pressure gauge adapters (H-D part No. HD-44061).
2. Depressurize the fuel system as described in this chapter.
3. Lift the chrome sleeve (A, **Figure 48**) on the quick-connect fitting, and disconnect the fuel line (B) from the fuel tank fitting.
4. Install the pressure gauge adapters as follows:
   a. Pull in the knurled sleeve on the female end of the first fuel pressure gauge adapter.
   b. Insert male end of second adapter into the first adapter, and push down on knurled sleeve until locked. Gently tug on the adapters to make sure they are locked in place and will not come loose.
   c. Pull in the knurled sleeve on the second fuel pressure gauge adapter. Insert the male end of fuel supply line (A, **Figure 49**) into the second adapter, and then pull down on the knurled sleeve until locked place. Gently tug on the fuel supply fitting to make sure it is locked in place and will not come loose.

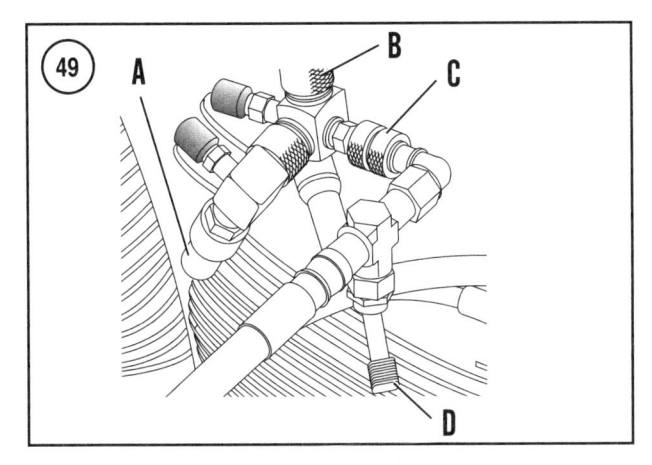

5. Remove the regulator seat, large O-ring, screen and small O-ring from the regulator body.
6. Inspect all O-rings, regulator seat and screen for hardness and deterioration. Replace the fuel pressure regulator if any parts require replacement as they are not available separately.
7. Install the small O-ring onto the top of the pressure port bore.
8. Position the screen so the sleeve faces the small O-ring, and install the screen.
9. Install the regulator seat and evenly press the screen correctly into place. Remove the regulator seat.
10. Install the large O-ring at the top of the screen.
11. Install the regulator seat and make sure it seats correctly.
12. Install the fuel pressure regulator onto the fuel filter shell.
13. Install the spring clip so the indented sides engage the top of the center rib of the fuel pressure regulator. The rounded side must engage the bottom tabs of the fuel filter shell.

NOTE
If the terminal does not lock in place, use a small Xacto knife blade to slightly bend the tang away from the terminal body.

14. Route the ground wire around the index pin side of the end cap and install the terminal into the slot in the fuel filter shell. Gently pull on the wire to make sure the terminal is locked in place.
15. Install the top plate as described in this section.

FUEL TANK CONSOLE (2006-2007 FLHT AND FLHX MODELS)

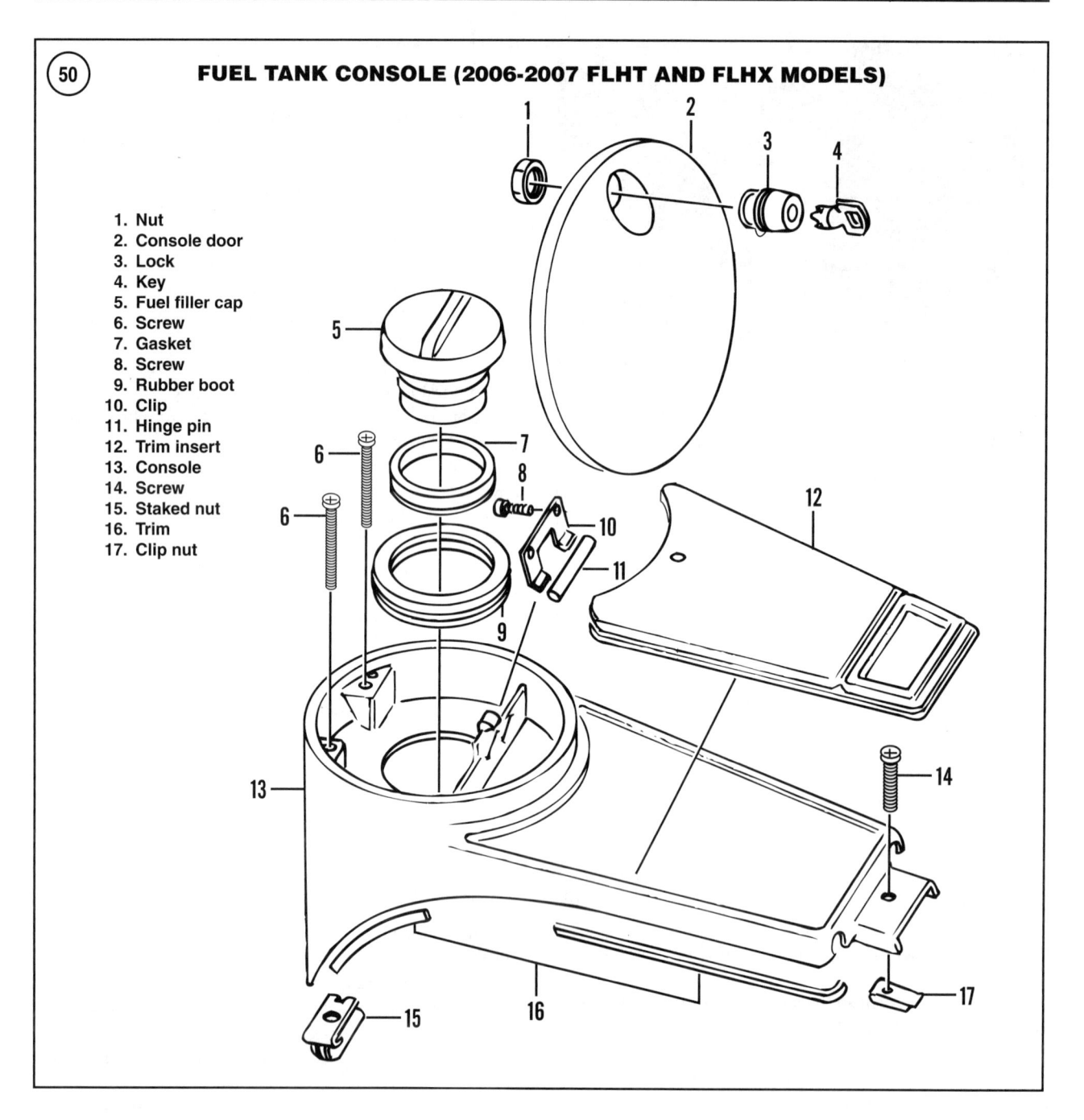

1. Nut
2. Console door
3. Lock
4. Key
5. Fuel filler cap
6. Screw
7. Gasket
8. Screw
9. Rubber boot
10. Clip
11. Hinge pin
12. Trim insert
13. Console
14. Screw
15. Staked nut
16. Trim
17. Clip nut

d. Pull up on the fuel tank quick-connect chrome sleeve (B, **Figure 49**), insert the male end of the first fuel pressure gauge adapter. Pull down on the chrome sleeve until locked. Gently tug on the adapter to make sure it is locked in place and will not come loose.

5. Make sure the fuel valve and the air bleed petcock on the fuel pressure gauge are in the *closed* position.

6. Remove the protective cap from the Schrader valve on the fuel pressure gauge adapter closest to the fuel tank. Connect the fuel pressure gauge (C, **Figure 49**) to this Schrader valve.

7. Gently tug on the fuel pressure gauge to make sure it is locked in place and will not come loose.

8. Install the fuel pump fuse.

WARNING
The exhaust system warms up rapidly, protect yourself accordingly.

9. Start the engine to pressurize the fuel system. Allow the engine to idle.

10. Slowly open the fuel valve (D, **Figure 49**) and allow fuel to flow to the pressure gauge.

11. Position the clear air bleed tube into a suitable container and open and close the air bleed petcock to purge the air from the fuel gauge and hose. Repeat this several times until only bubble-free fuel flows from the bleed tube into the container. Close the petcock.

12. Increase engine above idle, and then decrease engine speed several times. Note the gauge readings. The fuel

AIR/FUEL AND EMISSION CONTROL SYSTEMS (FUEL-INJECTED MODELS)

51 **FUEL TANK CONSOLE (2008-2009 FLHT, FLHX, FLTR AND FLHTCUSE MODELS, AND 2009 FLTRSE3 MODELS)**

1. Pod console and insert[1]
2. Cap and O-ring[2]
3. Pod console[2]
4. Electrical harness[2]
5. Speed nut
6. Bolt
7. Mounting bracket
8. Clip (adhesive backed)
9. Screw
10. Clip (vent hose)
11. Rubber molding
12. Trim cover
13. Console
14. Bumper
15. Boot
16. Gasket
17. Fuel filler cap
18. Insert
19. Screw
20. Hinge clip
21. Hex nut
22. Door
23. Lock
24. Key

1. FLTRSE3 models
2. FLHTCUSE models (2008-2009)

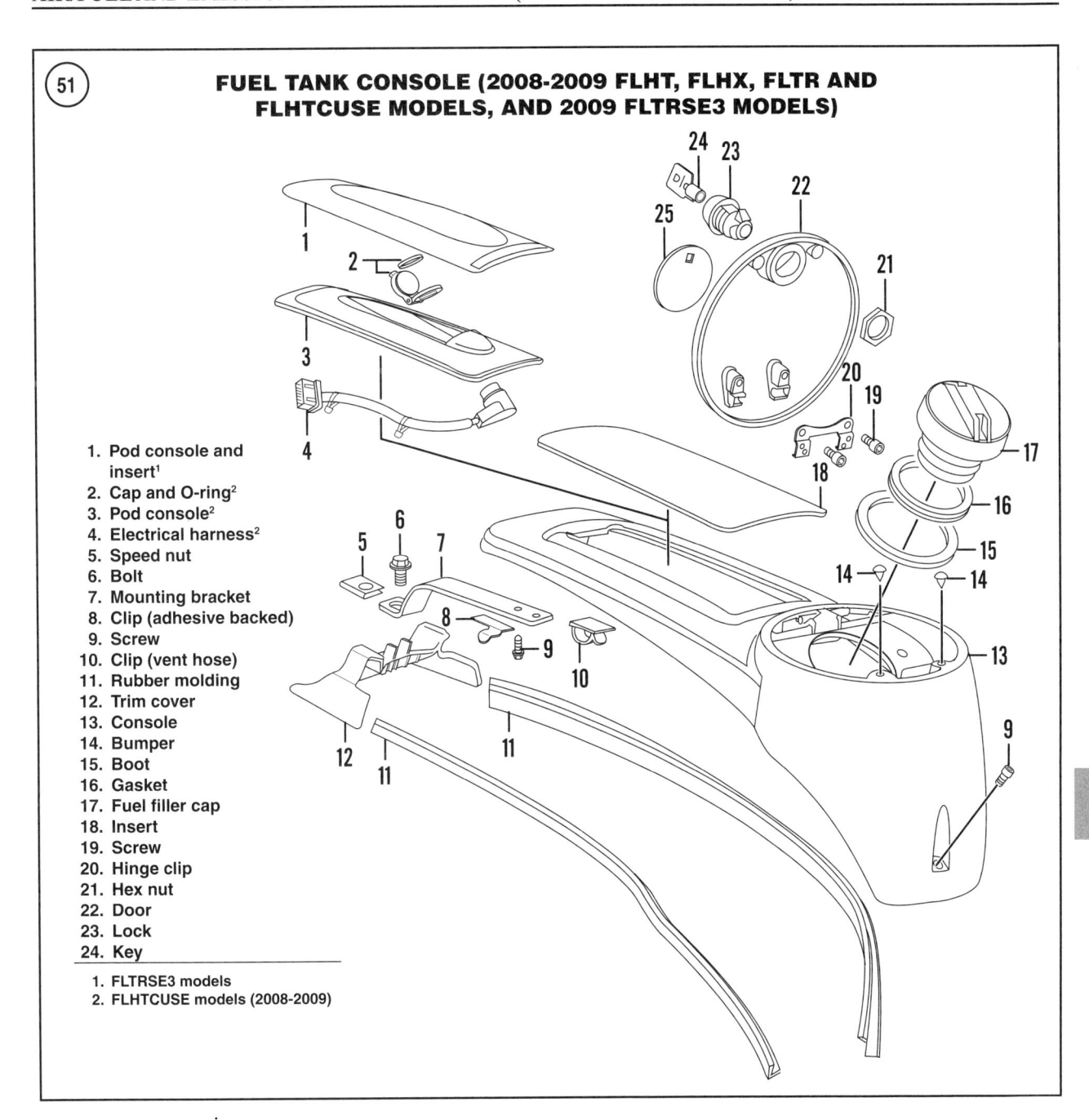

pressure should remain constant as specified in **Table 2** at all engine speeds. Repeat several times.

13. Turn the engine off.
14. Open the bleed valve petcock to relieve all fuel pressure and purge fuel from the pressure gauge.
15. Place a shop cloth beneath the Schrader valve to catch any remaining fuel, and disconnect the fuel pressure gauge from the Schrader valve. Dispose of the shop cloth in a suitable manner.
16. Install the protective cap onto the Schrader valve, and tighten it securely.
17. Disconnect the fuel pressure adapters from the fuel supply line and from the quick-connect fitting on the tank.
18. Pull up the chrome sleeve of quick-connect fitting, and insert fuel supply line onto tank fitting. Gently pull down on the fuel supply line to make sure it is locked in place and will not come loose.

FUEL TANK CONSOLE

Removal/Installation

Refer to **Figures 50-57**.

NOTE
Always disarm the TSSM/HFSM security system prior to disconnecting the battery or pulling the Maxi-Fuse so the siren will not sound.

1. Disconnect the negative battery cable as described in Chapter Eleven.

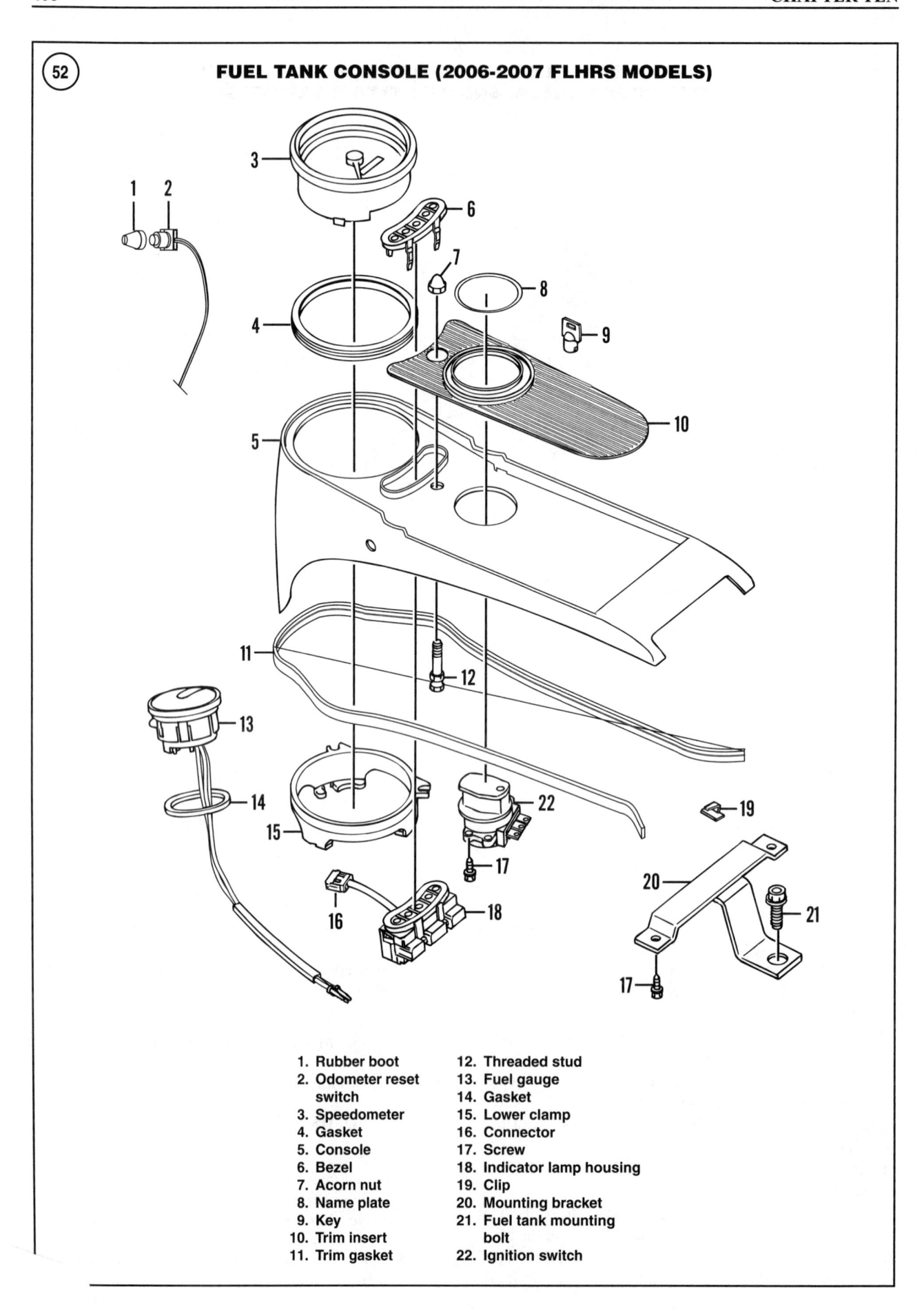

FUEL TANK CONSOLE (2006-2007 FLHRS MODELS)

1. Rubber boot
2. Odometer reset switch
3. Speedometer
4. Gasket
5. Console
6. Bezel
7. Acorn nut
8. Name plate
9. Key
10. Trim insert
11. Trim gasket
12. Threaded stud
13. Fuel gauge
14. Gasket
15. Lower clamp
16. Connector
17. Screw
18. Indicator lamp housing
19. Clip
20. Mounting bracket
21. Fuel tank mounting bolt
22. Ignition switch

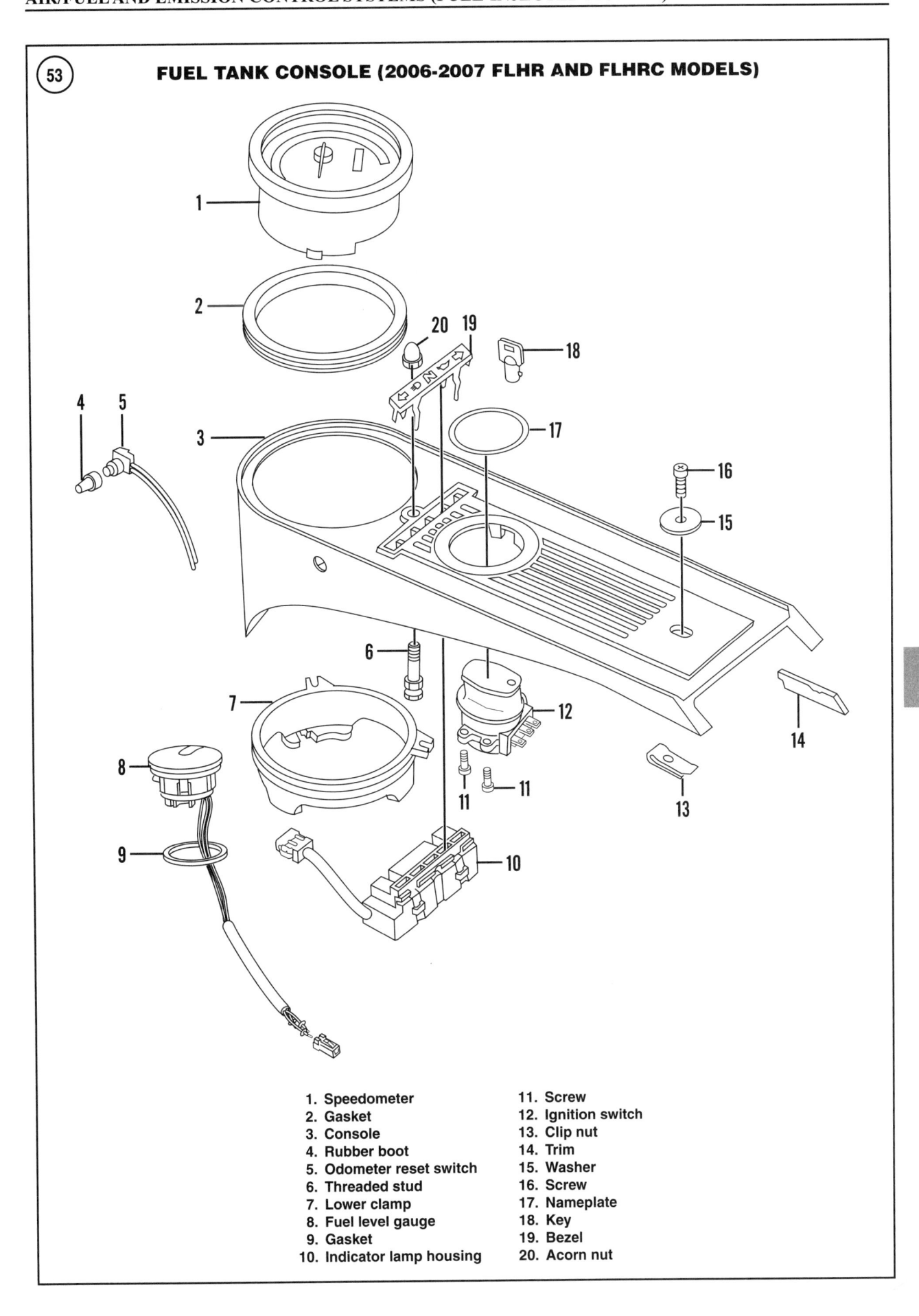

AIR/FUEL AND EMISSION CONTROL SYSTEMS (FUEL-INJECTED MODELS)

FUEL TANK CONSOLE (2006-2007 FLHR AND FLHRC MODELS)

1. Speedometer
2. Gasket
3. Console
4. Rubber boot
5. Odometer reset switch
6. Threaded stud
7. Lower clamp
8. Fuel level gauge
9. Gasket
10. Indicator lamp housing
11. Screw
12. Ignition switch
13. Clip nut
14. Trim
15. Washer
16. Screw
17. Nameplate
18. Key
19. Bezel
20. Acorn nut

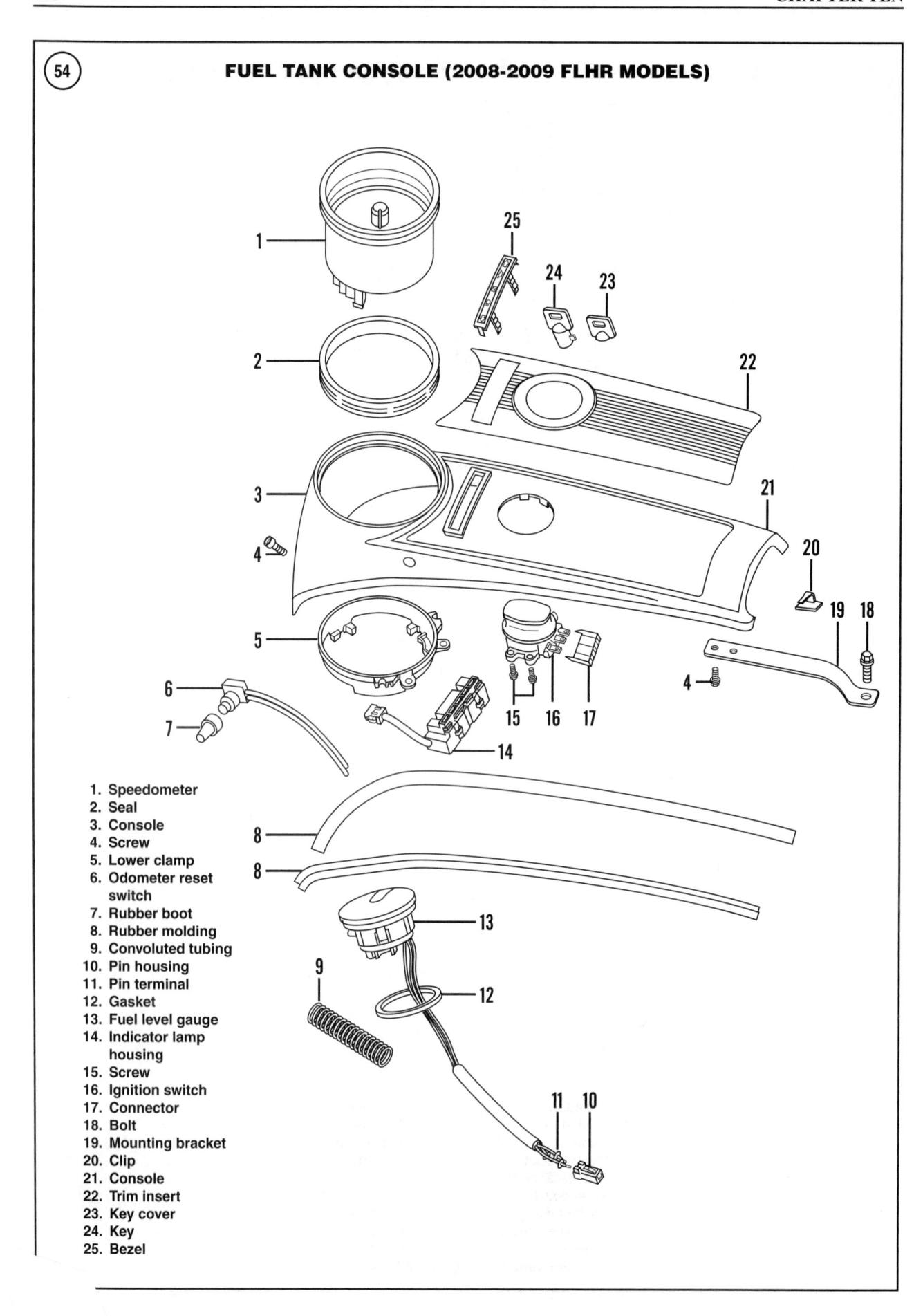

FUEL TANK CONSOLE (2008-2009 FLHR MODELS)

㊹

1. Speedometer
2. Seal
3. Console
4. Screw
5. Lower clamp
6. Odometer reset switch
7. Rubber boot
8. Rubber molding
9. Convoluted tubing
10. Pin housing
11. Pin terminal
12. Gasket
13. Fuel level gauge
14. Indicator lamp housing
15. Screw
16. Ignition switch
17. Connector
18. Bolt
19. Mounting bracket
20. Clip
21. Console
22. Trim insert
23. Key cover
24. Key
25. Bezel

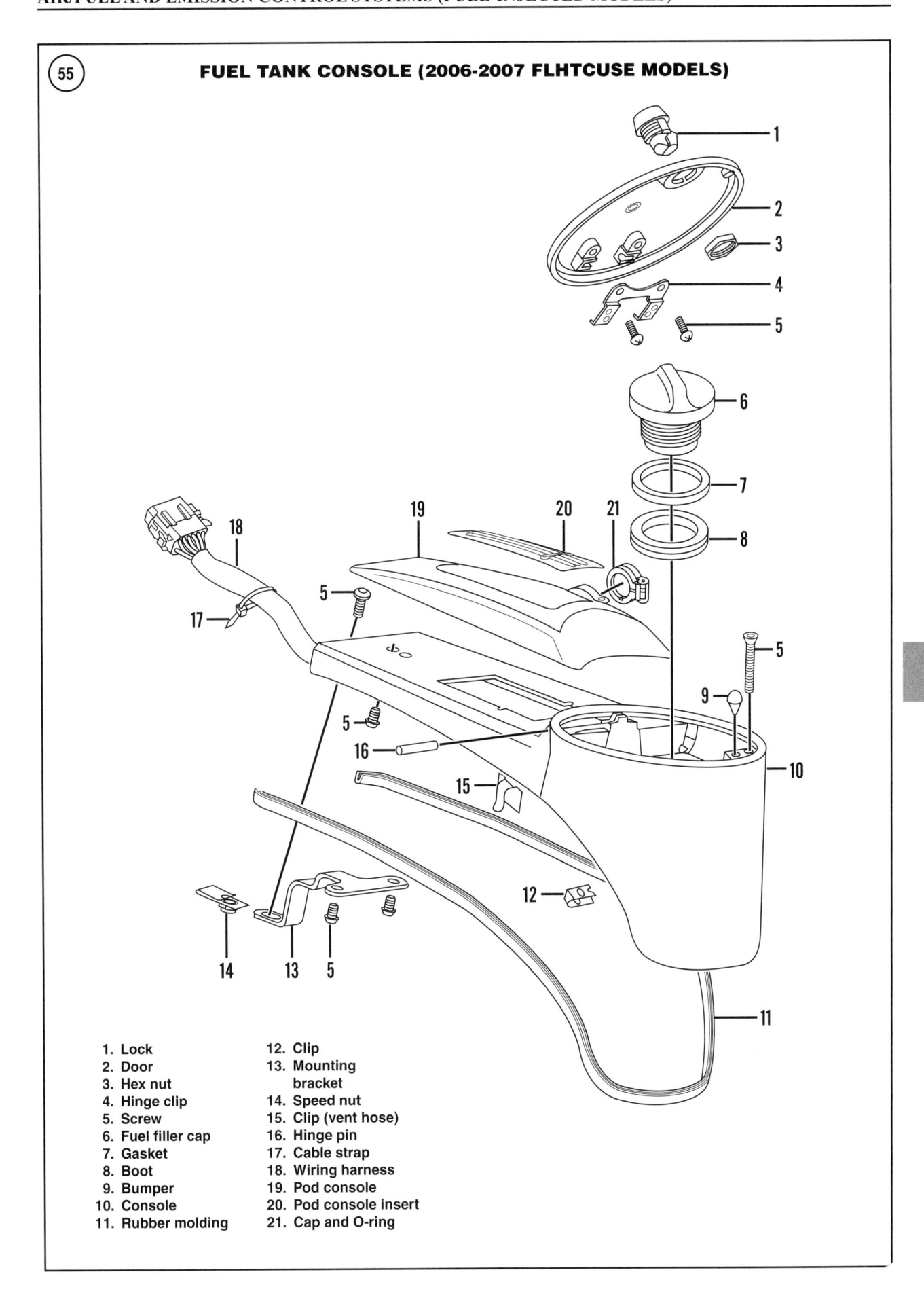

AIR/FUEL AND EMISSION CONTROL SYSTEMS (FUEL-INJECTED MODELS)

⑤⑤ FUEL TANK CONSOLE (2006-2007 FLHTCUSE MODELS)

1. Lock
2. Door
3. Hex nut
4. Hinge clip
5. Screw
6. Fuel filler cap
7. Gasket
8. Boot
9. Bumper
10. Console
11. Rubber molding
12. Clip
13. Mounting bracket
14. Speed nut
15. Clip (vent hose)
16. Hinge pin
17. Cable strap
18. Wiring harness
19. Pod console
20. Pod console insert
21. Cap and O-ring

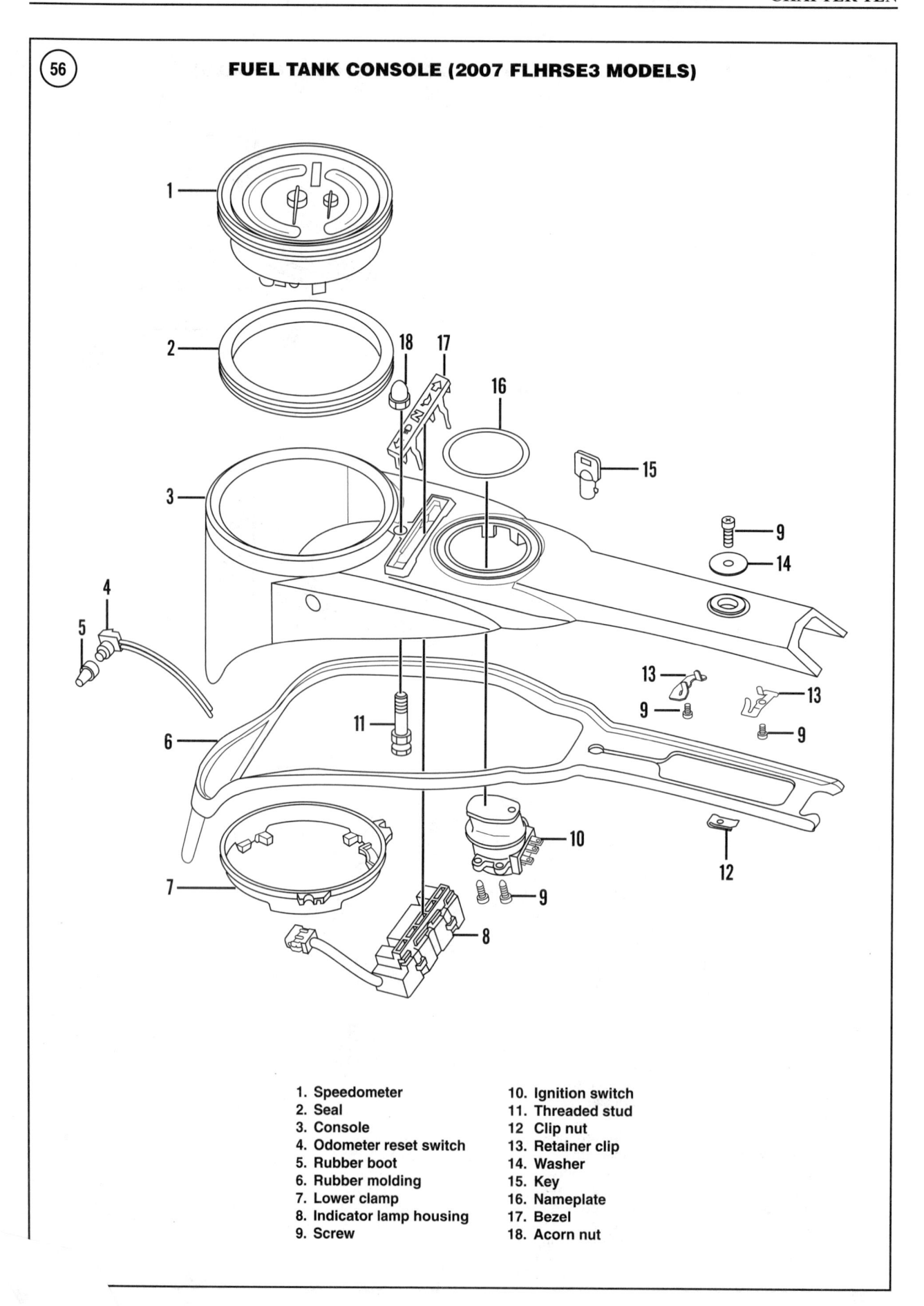

FUEL TANK CONSOLE (2007 FLHRSE3 MODELS)

1. Speedometer
2. Seal
3. Console
4. Odometer reset switch
5. Rubber boot
6. Rubber molding
7. Lower clamp
8. Indicator lamp housing
9. Screw
10. Ignition switch
11. Threaded stud
12. Clip nut
13. Retainer clip
14. Washer
15. Key
16. Nameplate
17. Bezel
18. Acorn nut

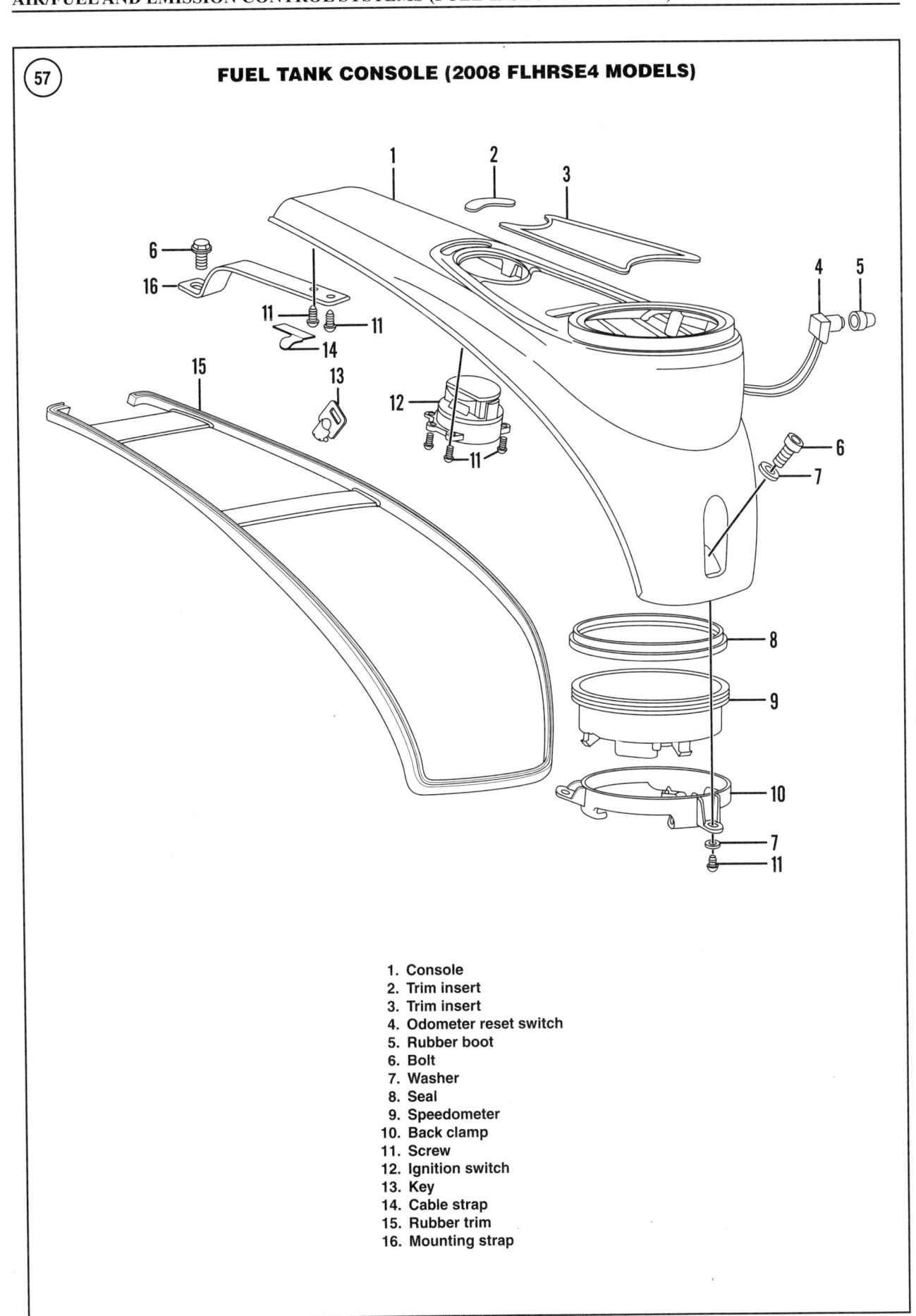

AIR/FUEL AND EMISSION CONTROL SYSTEMS (FUEL-INJECTED MODELS)

⑤⑦ FUEL TANK CONSOLE (2008 FLHRSE4 MODELS)

1. Console
2. Trim insert
3. Trim insert
4. Odometer reset switch
5. Rubber boot
6. Bolt
7. Washer
8. Seal
9. Speedometer
10. Back clamp
11. Screw
12. Ignition switch
13. Key
14. Cable strap
15. Rubber trim
16. Mounting strap

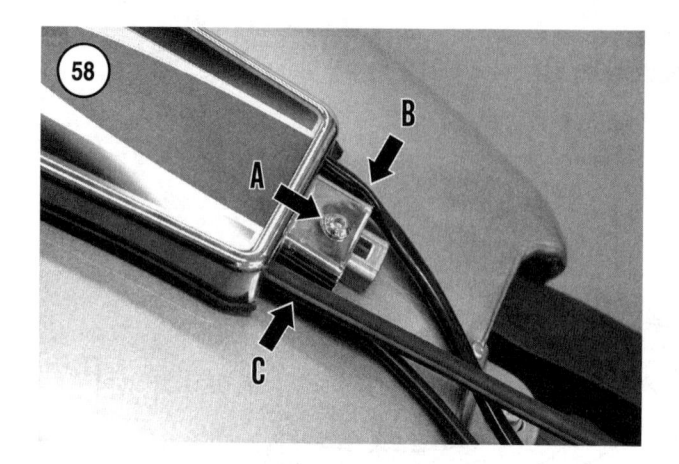

2. Remove the seat as described in Chapter Seventeen.
3. Make a drawing or take a photo of the wiring harness, fuel vapor tube and overflow hose routing under the rear of the console prior to removal. These items must be reinstalled in the correct location to avoid damage.
4. On FLHR models, perform the following:
   a. Cut the cable strap securing the fuel level sender wires to the main harness on the left side frame rail.
   b. At the rear of the fuel tank, disconnect the fuel level sensor electrical connector from the main harness.
   c. Remove the front acorn nut, on models so equipped, and the rear screw and washer securing the console to the fuel tank.
   d. On 2008-2009 models, remove the screw securing the front of the console to the fuel tank.
   e. Lift the console partially up off the fuel tank and disconnect the electrical connector from the ignition switch and the indicator lamp housing, on models so equipped.
5. On FLHT, FLTR and FLHX models, perform the following:
   a. Remove the screw (A, **Figure 58**) securing the rear of the console to the fuel tank.
   b. On 2006-2007 models, open the console door and remove the two front Allen bolts (A, **Figure 59**) securing the console to the fuel tank mounting brackets.
   c. On 2008-2009 models, remove the screw securing the front of the console to the fuel tank.
   d. Unscrew the fuel filler cap (B, **Figure 59**).
   e. Lift the console part way off the fuel tank and disconnect the electrical connector from the ignition switch, on models so equipped.
6. Carefully remove the console and lay it upside down on shop cloths or towels spread on the workbench.
7. On FLHT, FLTR and FLHX models, disconnect the overflow hose (**Figure 60**) from the lower fitting. Reinstall the fuel filler cap (B, **Figure 59**).
8. On FLHT, FLTR and FLHX models, check the tightness of the clip mounting screws (A, **Figure 61**) and the hinge pin (B).
9. Install by reversing the removal steps, while noting the following:
   a. Make sure the trim pieces or the rubber boot is in place prior to installation.

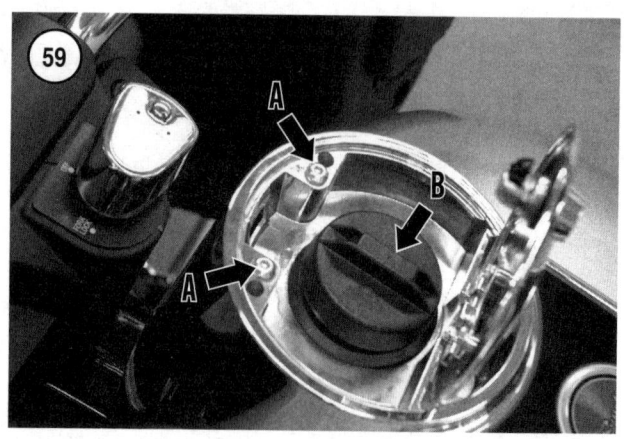

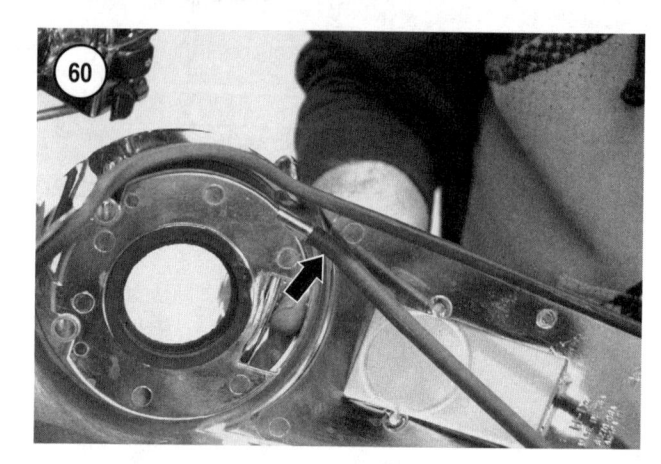

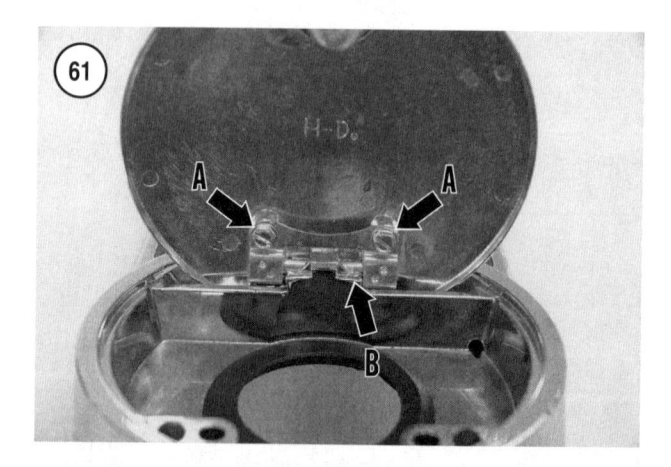

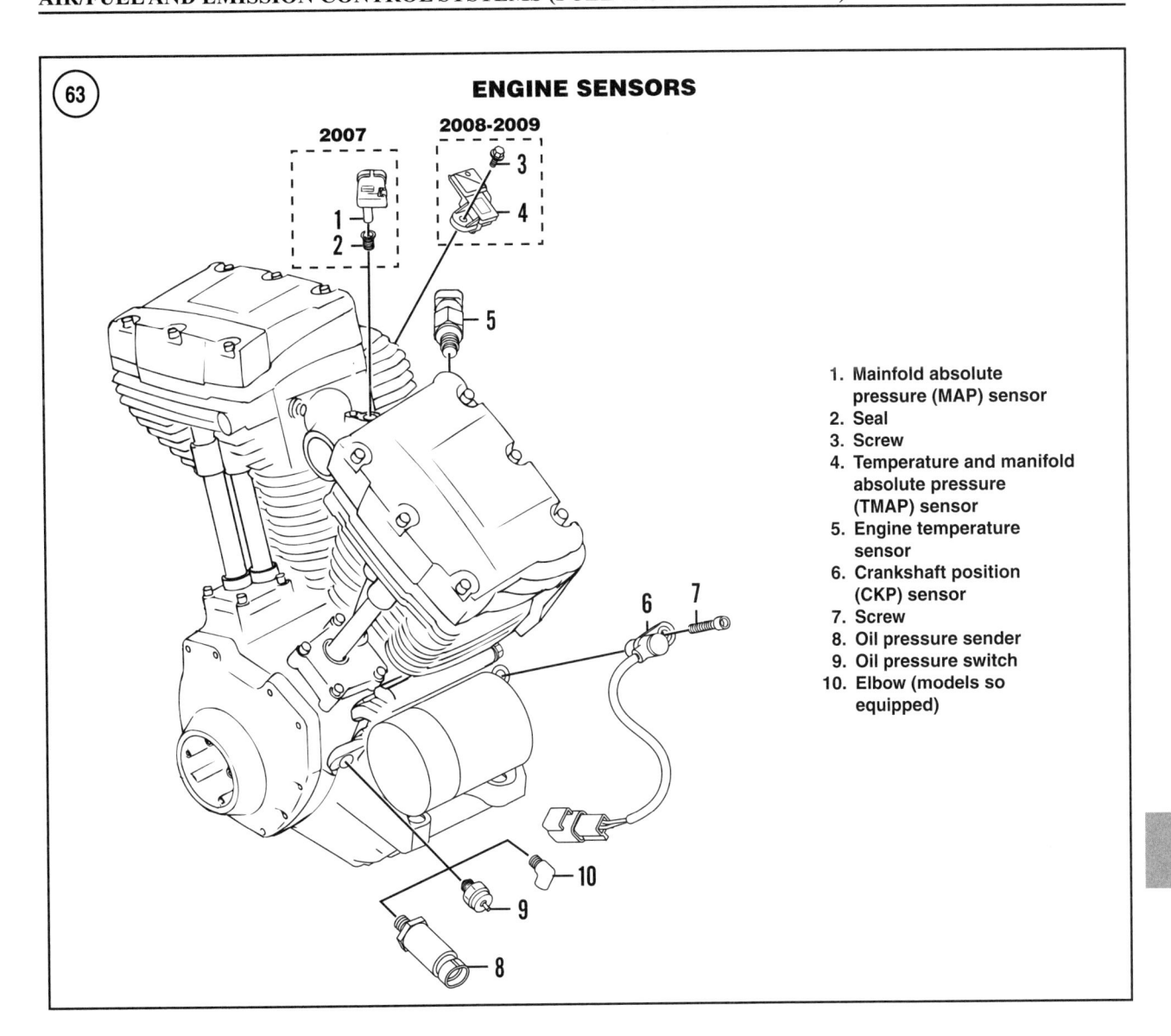

AIR/FUEL AND EMISSION CONTROL SYSTEMS (FUEL-INJECTED MODELS) 413

ENGINE SENSORS

1. Mainfold absolute pressure (MAP) sensor
2. Seal
3. Screw
4. Temperature and manifold absolute pressure (TMAP) sensor
5. Engine temperature sensor
6. Crankshaft position (CKP) sensor
7. Screw
8. Oil pressure sender
9. Oil pressure switch
10. Elbow (models so equipped)

b. Correctly and carefully route the electrical cables (B, **Figure 58**) and hoses (C) between the console and fuel tank so they will not get pinched or damaged, on models so equipped.

ELECTRONIC FUEL INJECTION (EFI)

This section describes the components and the operation of the electronic, sequential-port fuel injection (EFI) system. Fuel injection eliminates an inefficient cold start enrichment device, yet it provides accurate idle-speed control. It also improves torque characteristics while increasing fuel economy and reducing exhaust emissions. The fuel injection system constantly adjusts the air/fuel ratio and ignition timing to match the load conditions. Engine performance can be modified by simply changing the operating parameters of the electronic control module (ECM).

Complete service of the system requires a H-D digital technician, a breakout box and a number of other special tools. However, basic troubleshooting diagnosis is no different on a fuel-injected motorcycle than on a carbureted one. If the check engine light comes on or if there is a drivability problem, troubleshoot the system as described in *Electronic Diagnostic System* (Chapter Two). Make sure all related electrical connections are clean and secure. A high or erratic idle speed may indicate a vacuum leak. If the basic tests fail to reveal the cause of a problem, refer service to a dealership. Incorrectly-performed diagnostic procedures can result in damage to the fuel injection system.

Electronic Control Module (ECM) and Sensors

The electronic control module, or ECM (**Figure 62**), mounted under the right frame side cover, determines the optimum fuel injection and ignition timing based on input from six or seven sensors.

Make sure the ECM is securely mounted on the rubber isolators to prevent damage from vibration. Do not tamper with the ECM; it is sealed to prevent moisture contamination.

The engine-mounted sensors are shown in **Figure 63**. Additional sensors and their locations (**Figure 64** and **Figure 65**) and functions are as follows:

1. 2006-2007 models:
   a. The throttle position (TP) sensor, located on the front of the induction module and attached directly to the throttle shaft, indicates throttle angle. The ECM indicates the air volume entering the engine based on the throttle angle.
   b. The intake air temperature (IAT) sensor is located inside the induction module (rear cylinder's intake runner). The ECM determines the air density and adjusts the injector opening time based on input from this sensor.
   c. The manifold absolute pressure sensor (MAP) is located on top of the induction module. The MAP monitors intake manifold pressure (vacuum) and sends this information to the ECM.
   d. Idle air control (IAC) sensor is located on top of the induction module. The ECM controls the engine speed by moving the IAC to open or close the passage around the throttle plate.
2. 2008-2009 models:
   a. The temperature and manifold absolute pressure sensor (TMAP) is located on top of the induction module. One portion of the TMAP measures temperature of the air entering the induction manifold and the remaining portion measures air pressure within the induction module.
   b. The throttle grip sensor (TGS) is mounted on the right side of the handlebar. It is a Hall-effect sensor that operates the TCA in the induction module.
   c. The throttle control actuator (TCA) is mounted on the induction module. The TCA receives inputs from the TGS, throttle position sensors and the ECM. The TCA controls the throttle plates within the induction module.
3. All models and years:
   a. The crankshaft position (CKP) sensor, located on the forward position of the left crankcase, is an inductive type sensor. The ECM determines the engine speed by how fast the machined teeth on the flywheel pass by the sensor.
   b. The engine temperature (ET) sensor, is located on the front cylinder head. The ECM adjusts the injector opening time based on input from this sensor.
   c. The bank angle sensor (BAS), located within the turn signal module (TSM) or the turn signal security module (TSSM), interrupts the ignition and shuts off the engine if the motorcycle's lean angle is greater than 45° from vertical for more than one second.
   d. Vehicle speed sensor (VSS) is located on top of the crankcase behind the transmission cover. The VSS monitors gear tooth movement on the top gear and sends data to the ECM.
   e. Oxygen (O_2) sensors (2007-2009 domestic models) are screwed into the front and rear exhaust header. The O_2 sensors monitor the oxygen content of the exhaust system, and adjust the air/fuel mixture to maintain the desired 14.7:1 air/fuel mixture.

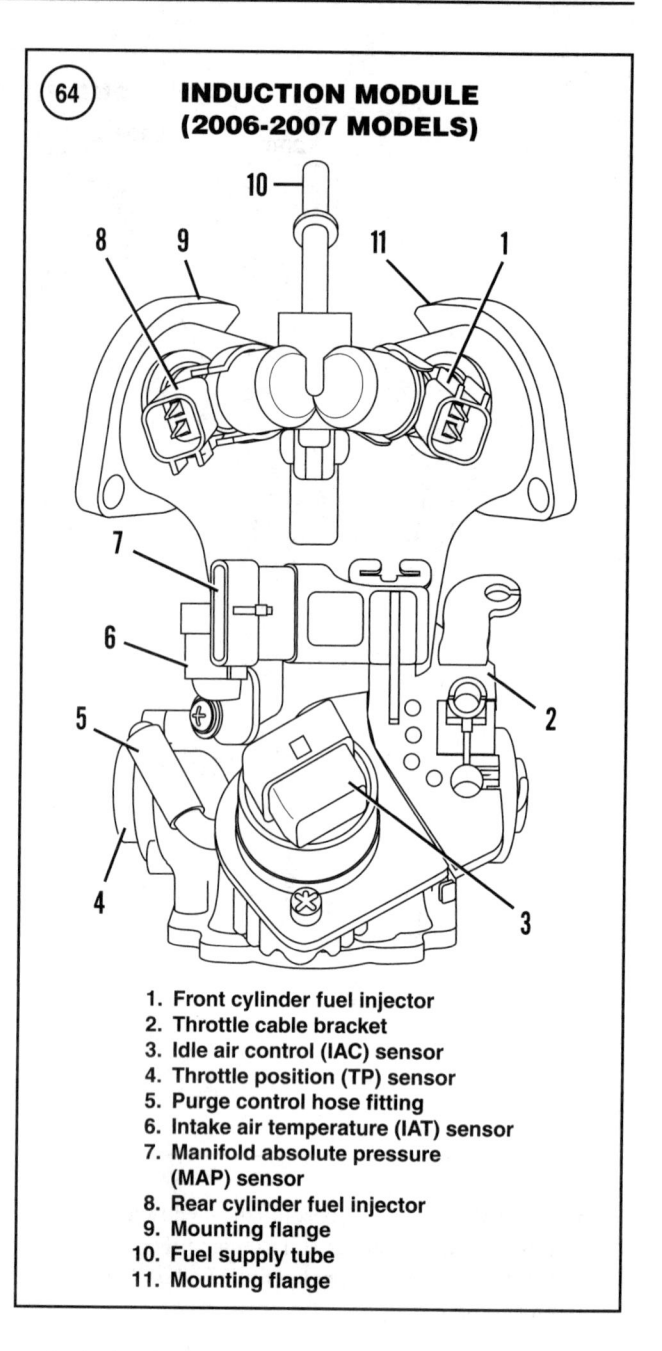

64 INDUCTION MODULE (2006-2007 MODELS)

1. Front cylinder fuel injector
2. Throttle cable bracket
3. Idle air control (IAC) sensor
4. Throttle position (TP) sensor
5. Purge control hose fitting
6. Intake air temperature (IAT) sensor
7. Manifold absolute pressure (MAP) sensor
8. Rear cylinder fuel injector
9. Mounting flange
10. Fuel supply tube
11. Mounting flange

   f. Active intake solenoid (HDI models only) is located in the air filter backplate. The solenoid opens a valve in the backplate to allow additional air to enter the engine and change the air/fuel mixture at speeds greater than 43 mph (70 kph) when the throttle opening is greater than 50%.
   g. Active exhaust system (HDI models only) is attached to the base of the battery case and operates a valve in the rear cylinder's exhaust pipe. The valve's position automatically adjusts, enhancing engine performance.

Heat Management System (2007-2009 Models)

The optional heat management system reduces engine temperature for rider comfort. The system turns off the rear

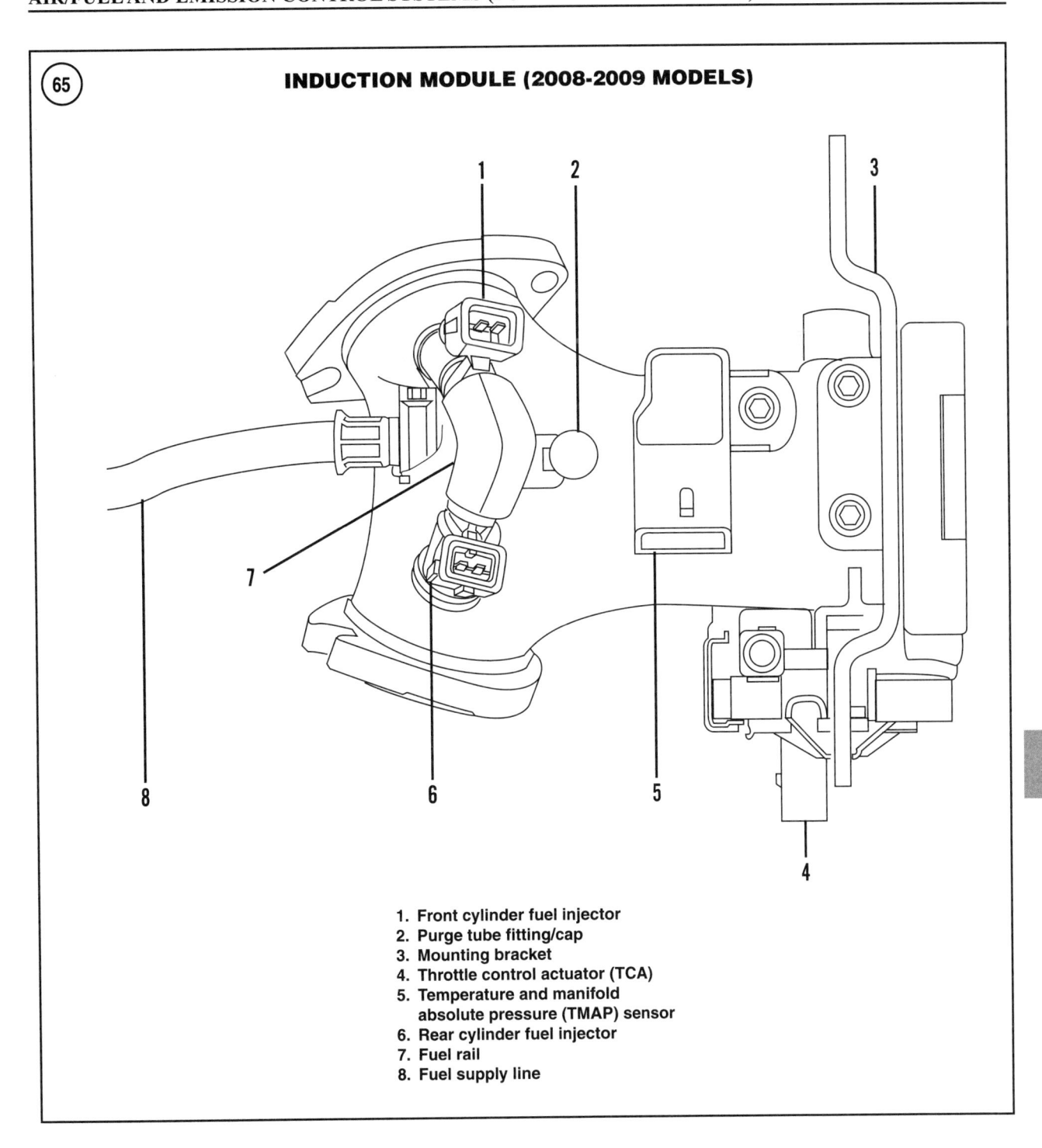

AIR/FUEL AND EMISSION CONTROL SYSTEMS (FUEL-INJECTED MODELS) 415

65 **INDUCTION MODULE (2008-2009 MODELS)**

1. Front cylinder fuel injector
2. Purge tube fitting/cap
3. Mounting bracket
4. Throttle control actuator (TCA)
5. Temperature and manifold absolute pressure (TMAP) sensor
6. Rear cylinder fuel injector
7. Fuel rail
8. Fuel supply line

cylinder fuel injector whenever the following four conditions are present; high engine temperature, engine is running at idle speed, motorcycle is not moving and when the clutch lever is pulled in or the transmission is in neutral.

Idle speed is maintained even though the rear cylinder is no longer firing, but it acts like an air pump to help cool the engine. This cooling continues until one of the previously mentioned conditions is no longer evident at which time the fuel injector is activated and the rear cylinder fires normally.

During the cooling mode, the idle cadence is different and there is a unique exhaust odor. Both of these are normal and they not to be construed as an idle problem.

Fuel Supply System

Fuel pump and filters

The fuel pump and filter assembly is located inside the fuel tank. This assembly is part of the removable top plate that is attached to the top of the fuel tank. The top plate allows for easy removal and installation of the attached components without having to work within the fuel tank cavity. To provide maximum filtration prior to the fuel reaching the fuel injectors there is an inlet screen on the fuel pump and then a secondary fuel filter canister located downstream from the fuel pump.

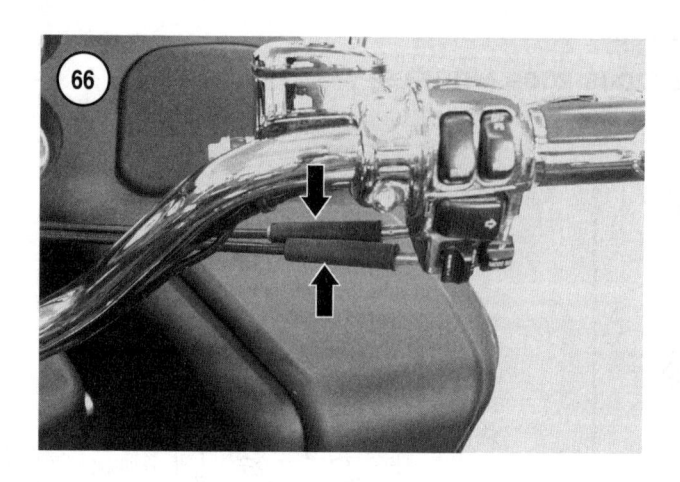

Fuel lines

One fuel line is equipped with a quick-connect fitting at the base of the fuel tank. The supply fuel line is pressurized at 58 psi (400 kPa) and is controlled by the pressure regulator.

A check valve is located on both the supply and return lines where they attach to the fuel tank.

Fuel injectors

The solenoid-actuated constant-stroke pintle-type fuel injectors consist of a solenoid plunger, needle valve and housing. The fuel injector's opening is fixed and fuel pressure is constant. The fuel injectors are part of the fuel rail assembly.

The ECM controls the time the injectors open and close.

Fuel pump and filters

The fuel pump and filter assembly is an integral unit that is located within the fuel tank.

This assembly can easily be removed from the top of the fuel tank and serviced on the workbench.

Induction module

The induction module consists of two fuel injectors, throttle position sensor (TPS), intake air temperature (IAT) sensor, manifold absolute pressure (MAP) sensor, idle air control (IAC) sensor, fuel rail, fuel supply tube and purge tube fitting (California models).

THROTTLE AND IDLE CABLES NON-CRUISE CONTROL MODELS (2006 AND 2007 MODELS)

There are two different throttle cables. At the throttle grip, the front cable is the throttle control cable and the rear cable is the idle control cable. At the induction control module the idle control cable is located at the top of the throttle wheel and the throttle control cable is located at the bottom.

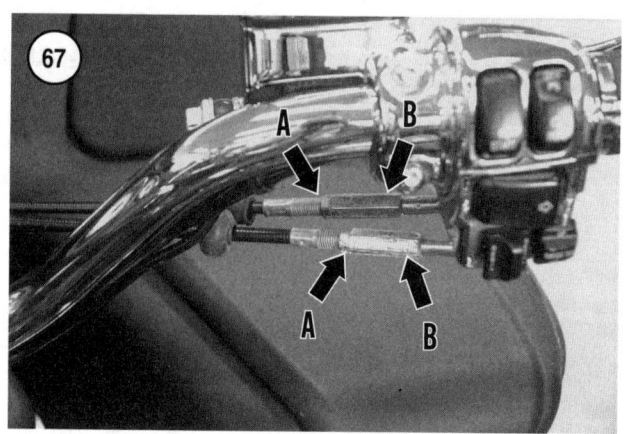

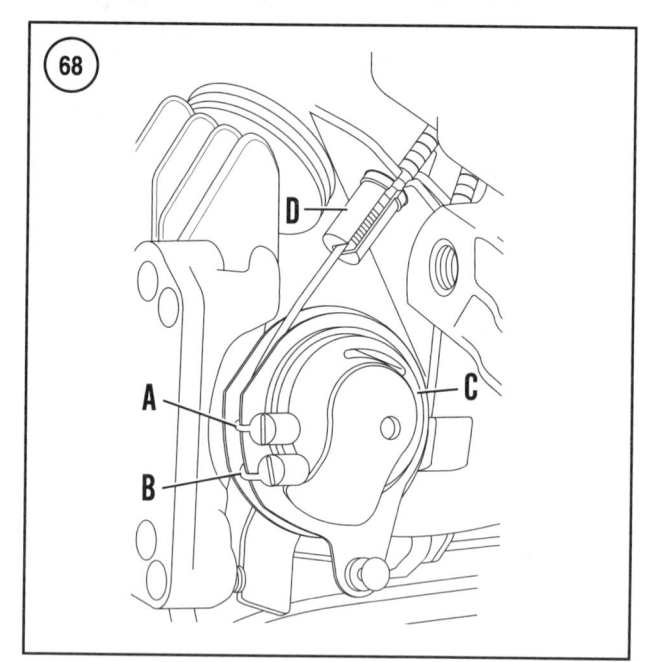

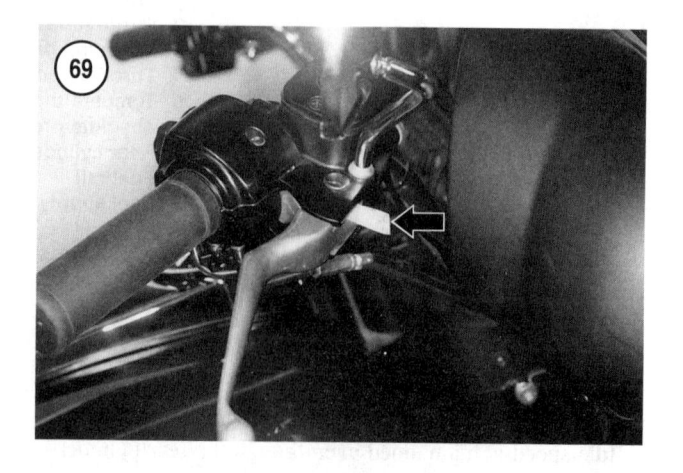

WARNING
Do not ride the motorcycle unless the throttle control cables are properly adjusted. Improper cable routing and adjustment can cause the throttle to stick open. This could cause loss of control. Recheck the cable adjustment before riding the bike.

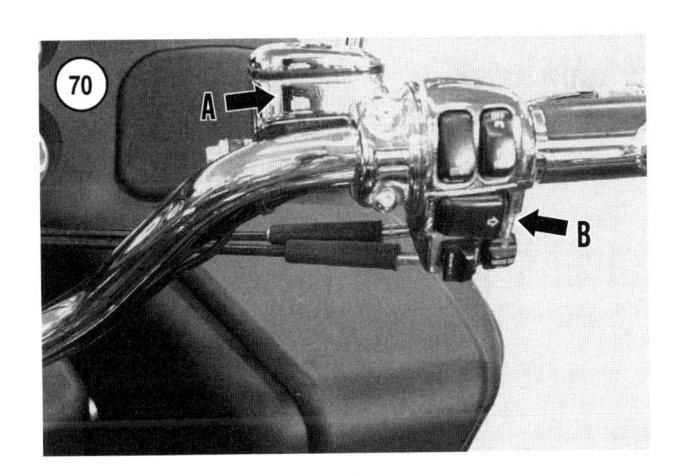

AIR/FUEL AND EMISSION CONTROL SYSTEMS (FUEL-INJECTED MODELS)

THROTTLE CABLES

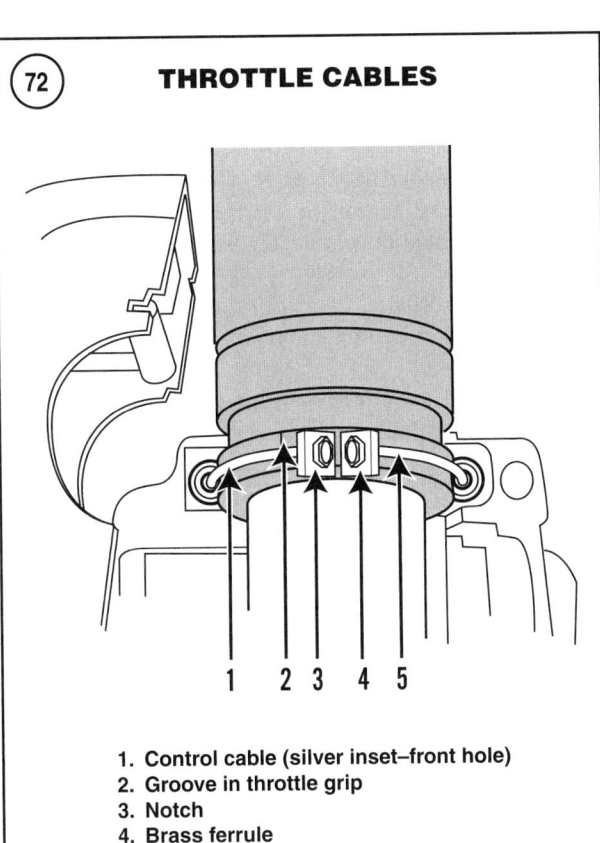

1. Control cable (silver inset–front hole)
2. Groove in throttle grip
3. Notch
4. Brass ferrule
5. Idle cable (gold inset–rear hole)

NOTE
The 2008-2009 models are not equipped with throttle or cruise control cables as the system is controlled electronically by the ECM.

Removal

1. Remove the fuel tank as described in this chapter.
2. Remove the air filter and backplate as described in this chapter.
3. Make a drawing or take a picture of the control cable routing from the induction module through the frame to the right side handlebar. Note any clamps or other devices securing the cables.
4. Slide the boots (**Figure 66**) off the cable adjusters.
5. At the handlebar, loosen both control cable adjuster locknuts (A, **Figure 67**). Then, turn the cable adjusters (B, **Figure 67**) *clockwise* as far as possible to increase cable slack.
6. At the induction module, use needlenose pliers and disconnect the idle control cable (A, **Figure 68**) and the throttle control cable (B) from the throttle wheel (C).
7. Release the cables from the integral cable guides (D, **Figure 68**) on the induction module.

CAUTION
Failure to install the spacer will result in damage to the rubber boot and plunger on the front brake switch.

8. Insert a 5/32 in. (4 mm) thick spacer (**Figure 69**) between the brake lever and lever bracket. Make sure the spacer stays in place during the removal procedure.
9. Remove the front master cylinder (A, **Figure 70**) as described in Chapter Fifteen.
10. Remove the upper and lower Torx screws (T25) securing the right side switch assembly (B, **Figure 70**) together.
11. Separate the switch halves (**Figure 71**) and note the location of both throttle control cables within the throttle grip as shown in **Figure 72**.
12. Remove the brass ferrules (**Figure 73**) from the notches on the inboard side of the throttle grip. Remove the ferrules from the cable end fittings.

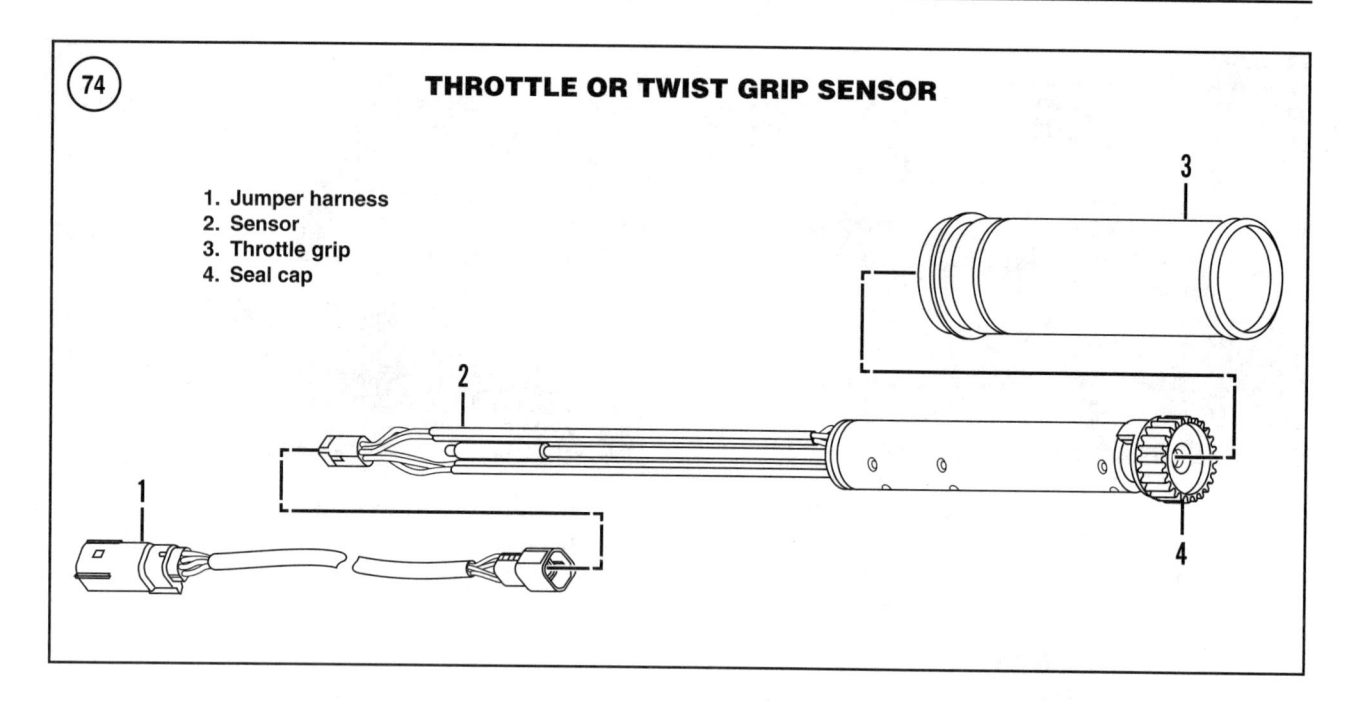

THROTTLE OR TWIST GRIP SENSOR

1. Jumper harness
2. Sensor
3. Throttle grip
4. Seal cap

NOTE
The friction shoe is a loose fit and may fall out or move if the switch lower housing is turned upside down or is shaken.

13. Remove the friction shoe from the end of the tension adjusting screw.
14. Remove the throttle grip from the handlebar.

NOTE
Use a rocking motion while pulling on the control cable housings. If necessary, place a drop of engine oil on the housings retaining rings to ease removal.

15. Pull the crimped inserts at the end of the throttle and idle control cable housings from the switch lower housing.
16. On all FLHT and FLHX series models, withdraw the throttle and idle cables from the inner fairing rubber grommet. Move the idle and throttle cables forward and out of the way.
17. Remove all clips and ties securing the throttle and idle control cables onto the frame backbone and ignition coil bracket.
18. Disconnect the cables from the J-clamp on the right side of the frame backbone.
19. If necessary, remove the bolts, washer, P-clamp and locknut securing the cables to the right side of the steering head.
20. Remove the cables from the frame.
21. Clean the throttle grip assembly and dry thoroughly. Check the throttle slots for cracks or other damage. Replace the throttle if necessary.
22. The friction adjust screw is secured to the lower switch housing with a snap ring. If necessary, remove the friction spring, snap ring, spring and friction adjust screw. Check these parts for wear or damage. Replace any damaged parts and reverse removal to install the screw. Make sure the snap ring seats in the friction screw groove completely.
23. Clean the throttle area on the handlebar with solvent.

Installation

1. Apply a light coat of graphite to the housing inside surfaces and to the handlebar.
2. Push the larger diameter silver insert on the throttle cable into the larger hole in front of the tension adjust screw in the switch lower housing. Push it in until it snaps into place.
3. Push the smaller diameter gold insert on the throttle cable into the smaller hole in the rear of the tension adjust screw in the switch lower housing. Push it in until it snaps into place.
4. Position the friction shoe with the concave side facing up and install it so that the pin hole is over the point of the adjuster screw.
5. Install the throttle grip onto the handlebar. Push it on until it stops, and pull it back about 1/8 in. (3.2 mm). Rotate it until the ferrule notches are at the top.
6. Place the switch lower housing below the throttle grip. Install the brass ferrules onto the cables so the end fittings seat in the ferrule recess. Seat ferrules (**Figure 73**) in their respective notches on the throttle control grip. Check that the cables are captured in the molded grooves in the grip.
7. Assemble the upper and lower switch housings (**Figure 71**) and the throttle grip. Install the lower switch housing screws and finger-tighten.
8. If not in place, insert the 5/32 in. (4 mm) thick spacer (**Figure 69**) between the brake lever and lever bracket. Make sure the spacer stays in place during the installation procedure.
9. Install the front master cylinder (A, **Figure 70**) as described in Chapter Fifteen.

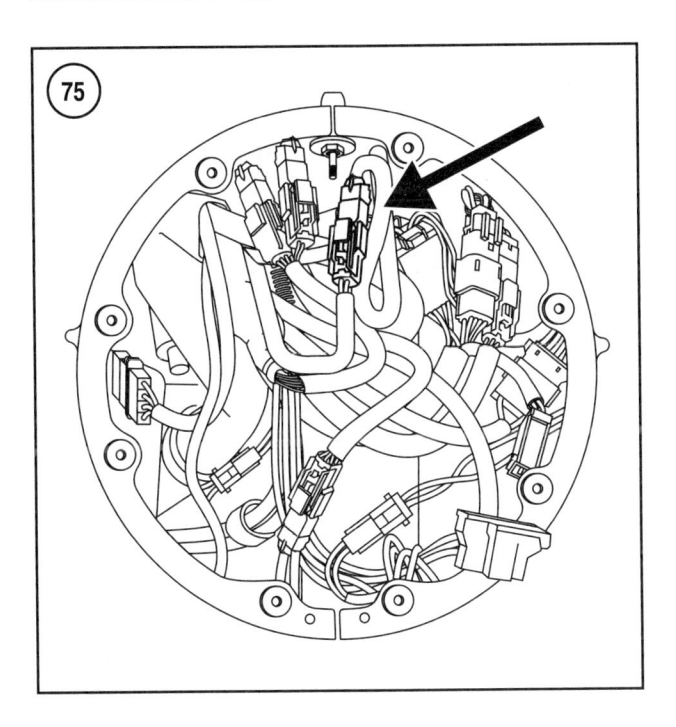

AIR/FUEL AND EMISSION CONTROL SYSTEMS (FUEL-INJECTED MODELS)

75

10. Tighten the switch housing screws securely; do not overtighten.
11. Remove the spacer from between the front master cylinder and the brake lever.
12. Operate the throttle and make sure both cables move in and out properly.
13. Correctly route the cables from the handlebar to the induction module. Secure the cables with the clamps and tie-wraps that were noted during removal.
14. At the induction module, perform the following:
    a. Install the idle cable (A, **Figure 68**) ball end over the top of the throttle wheel (C) and install the cable ball end into the upper hole in the throttle wheel. Make sure it is properly seated.
    b. Install the throttle control cable (B, **Figure 68**) ball end under the bottom of the throttle wheel (C) and install the cable ball end into the lower hole in the throttle wheel. Make sure it is properly seated.
    c. Install the cables into the integral cable guides (D, **Figure 68**) in the induction module.
15. At the throttle grip, tighten the cables to keep the ball ends from being disconnected from throttle wheel.
16. Operate the throttle grip a few times, making sure the throttle wheel operates smoothly with no binding. Also check that both cable ends are seated squarely in their cable bracket guides and in the throttle wheel.
17. Adjust the throttle and idle control cables as described in Chapter Three.
18. Install the backplate and air filter as described in this chapter.
19. Install the fuel tank as described in this chapter.
20. Start the engine and allow it to idle in neutral. Then turn the handlebar from side to side. Do not operate the throttle. If the engine speed increases when turning the handlebar assembly, the throttle cables are routed incorrectly or damaged. Recheck cable routing and adjustment.

CRUISE CONTROL MODELS (2006 AND 2007 MODELS)

Refer to Chapter Sixteen for throttle, idle and stepper control cable service procedures.

NOTE
The 2008-2009 models are not equipped with throttle or cruise control cables as the system is controlled electronically by the ECM.

THROTTLE CONTROL ACTUATOR (TCA) (2008-2009 MODELS)

The Throttle Control Actuator is an internal component of the induction module. If the TCA is defective, the entire induction module must be replaced as described in this chapter.

THROTTLE OR TWIST GRIP SENSOR (TGS) (2008-2009 MODELS)

Refer to **Figure 74**.

Removal

NOTE
Always disarm the TSSM/HFSM security system prior to disconnecting the battery or pulling the Maxi-Fuse so the siren will not sound.

1. Disconnect the negative battery cable as described in Chapter Eleven.
2. Remove the left side saddlebag and frame side cover as described in Chapter Seventeen.
3. Remove the front brake master cylinder as described in Chapter Fifteen.
4. Remove the right side switch assembly as described in Chapter Eleven.
5. Tug slightly on the throttle grip to release the index pins in the throttle grip from the seal cap receptacle of the twist grip sensor. Remove the throttle grip from the handlebar.
6. Remove the two wiring harness clips from the holes in the handlebar, on models so equipped.
7A. On FLHR and FLHRC models, perform the following:
    a. Remove the headlight and nacelle as described in Chapter Eleven.
    b. Disconnect black 6-pin twist grip sensor jumper wire connector (**Figure 75**).
    c. Withdraw the jumper wire and connector through the opening in the headlight case.
    d. Remove the jumper wire from the t-stud on the fork stem lock plate on the right side.
7B. On FLHX, FLHT, FLHTC and FLHTCU models, perform the following:

10

a. Remove the upper front fairing and windshield as described in Chapter Seventeen.
b. Disconnect black 6-pin twist grip sensor jumper wire connector.
c. Withdraw the jumper wire and connector through the opening in the fairing.
d. Remove the jumper wire from the t-stud on the inboard top right side fairing support brace.

7C. On FLTR models, perform the following:
a. Remove the upper front fairing and windshield (**Figure 76**) as described in Chapter Seventeen.
b. Disconnect black 6-pin twist grip sensor jumper wire connector (**Figure 77**).
c. Withdraw the jumper wire and connector through the opening in the headlight case.

CAUTION
Do not pull too hard on the twist grip sensor or the external latch on the pin housing will break. If broken, the twist grip sensor will not reconnect positively and the twist grip sensor must be replaced.

8. Gently withdraw the twist grip sensor part way out of the handlebar sufficiently to gain access to the sensor connector. Straighten the conduit on the connector end of the jumper harness. Feed it though the slot at the front of the handlebar while pulling. If the harness sticks inside the handlebar, carefully pull on the connector end and retract the conduit slightly. Gently work the conduit back and forth until the connector is past the handlebar opening.

CAUTION
Do not pry the connector, or twist it with the screwdriver; the external latch on the pin housing will break. If broken, the twist grip sensor harness will not reconnect positively and the twist grip sensor jumper harness must be replaced.

9. Carefully insert a small, flat-bladed screwdriver (A, **Figure 78**) between the pin and socket housing. When the bottom edge of the latch is disengaged, pull the pin housing from the socket housing (B, **Figure 78**).
10. Remove the twist grip sensor (**Figure 79**).

Installation

1. If missing, purchase a *new* seal cap and O-ring.
2. Make sure the seal cap is in place in the end of the twist grip sensor, and verify that the seal cap is engaged on the index pins at the end of the sensor.
3. Install the new seal cap, engaging the legs into the slots in the end of the twist grip sensor. Install one leg first, and depress the second leg with a small, flat-bladed screwdriver (A, **Figure 80**). Push down on the seal cap (B, **Figure 80**) until it bottoms.
4. Connect the jumper harness to the twist grip sensor.

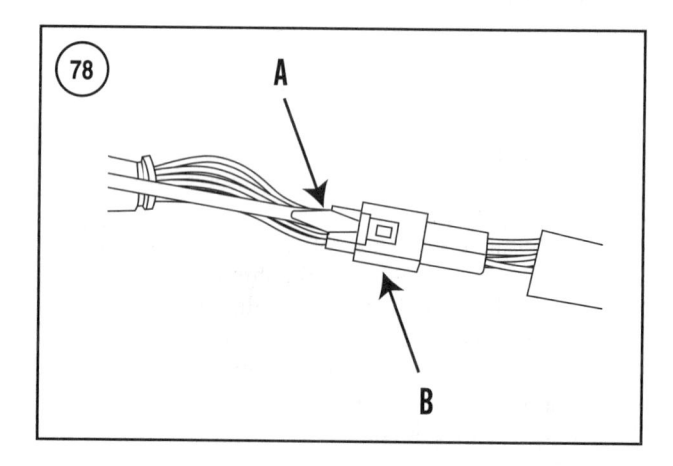

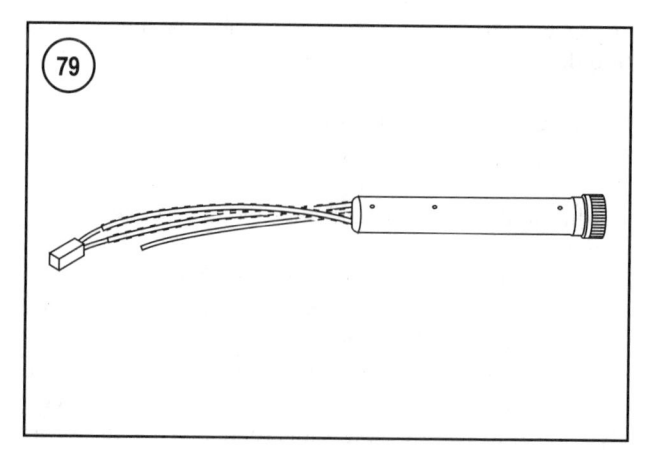

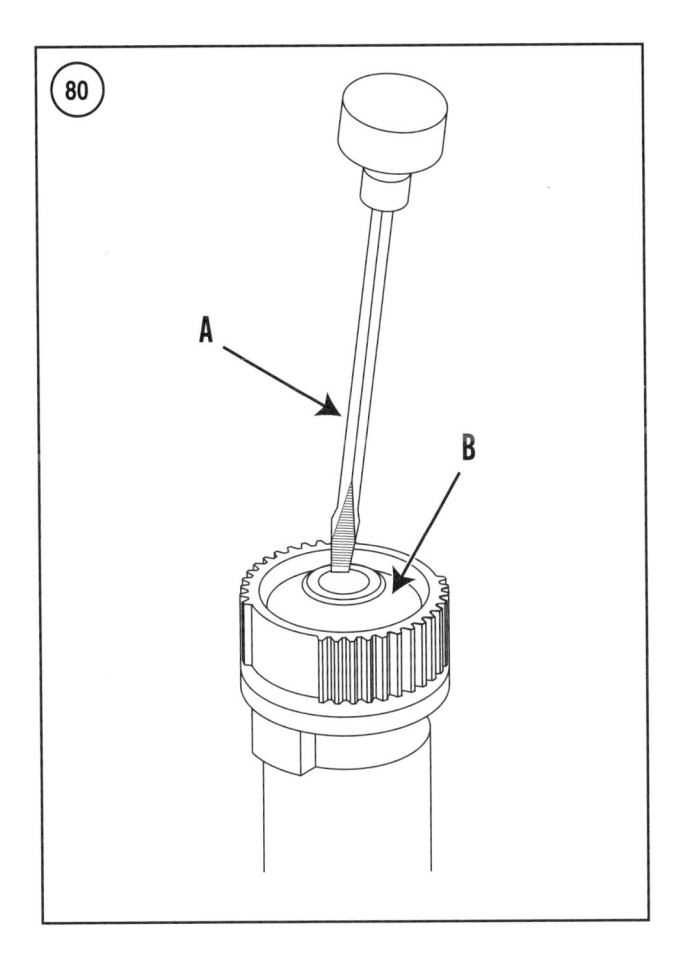

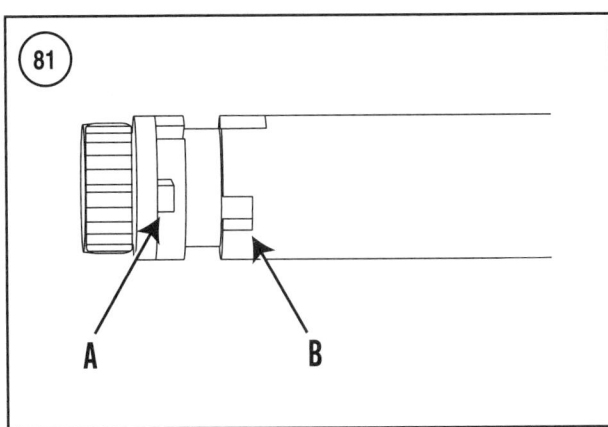

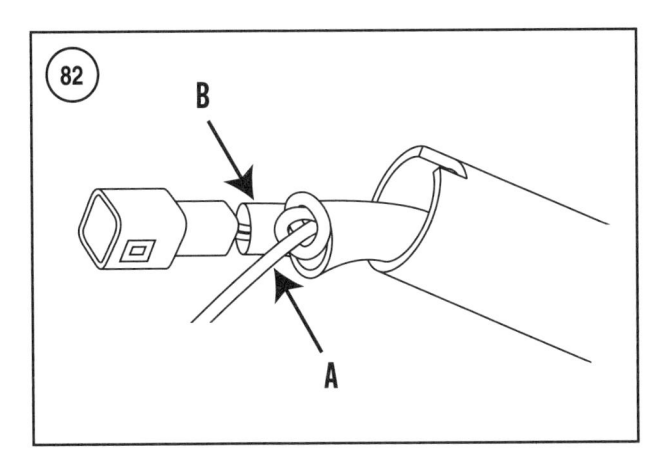

AIR/FUEL AND EMISSION CONTROL SYSTEMS (FUEL-INJECTED MODELS)

5. Slowly pull on the jumper harness Molex connector and draw the twist grip sensor into the handlebar.

6. Carefully twist the twist grip sensor and align the grips' index tabs (A, **Figure 81**) with the slots (B) in the handlebar. Ensure that the small index tab is aligned with the small slot in the handlebar.

7. Slowly pull the twist grip sensor into the handlebar until it bottoms. The twist grip sensor is now secure to the handlebar and will not slide out.

8. Install the throttle grip onto the handlebar and onto the twist grip sensor, engaging the index pins.

9. Install the right side switch assembly as described in Chapter Eleven.

10. Install the front brake master cylinder as described in Chapter Fifteen.

11A. On FLHR and FLHRC models, perform the following:
   a. Connect black 6-pin twist grip sensor jumper wire connector (**Figure 75**) onto the t-stud on the fork stem lock plate.
   b. Install the headlight and nacelle as described in Chapter Eleven.

11B. On FLHX, FLHT, FLHTC and FLHTCU models, perform the following:
   a. Connect black 6-pin twist grip sensor jumper wire connector onto the t-stud on the inboard top right side fairing support brace.
   b. Install the upper fairing and windshield as described in Chapter Seventeen.

11C. On FLTR models, perform the following:
   a. Connect black 6-pin twist grip sensor jumper wire connector (**Figure 77**).
   b. Install the upper fairing and windshield (**Figure 76**) as described in Chapter Seventeen.

12. Install the two wiring harness clips into the holes in the handlebar, on models so equipped.

13. Install the left side saddlebag and frame side cover as described in Chapter Seventeen.

14. Connect the negative battery cable as described in Chapter Eleven.

TWIST GRIP SENSOR JUMPER WIRE (2008-2009 MODELS)

Removal/Installation

1. Remove the twist grip sensor as described in this chapter.

2. Use a length of fish wire long enough to span the entire length between the openings of the handlebar with an additional 24 inches (610 mm) left over.

3. Securely attach the fish wire to the jumper wire conduit inboard of the twist grip connector (**Figure 82**). Tie the wire onto the conduit to prevent it from bunching up within the handlebar when being pulled.

4. Secure the loose end of the fish wire to the frame to prevent it from working its way completely through the handlebar.

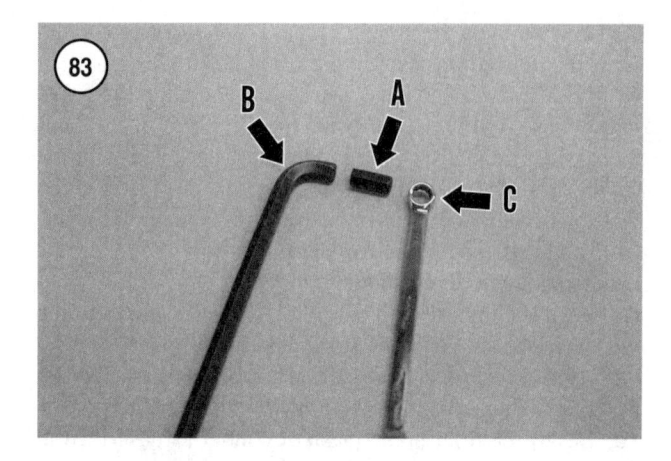

5. At the handlebar center opening, gently pull the jumper wire harness though the center slot in the handlebar. If the harness binds within the handlebar, gently pull on the fish wire at the other end of the handlebar to free it. Try again and pull the jumper wire harness out of the center opening slot of the handlebar with the fish wire.
6. Untie the fish wire from the old jumper wire.
7. Securely attach the fish wire to the *new* jumper wire conduit inboard of the twist grip connector. Tie the fish wire onto the conduit to prevent it from bunching up within the handlebar when being pulled.
8. Guide the electrical connector and conduit through the slot in the handlebar. Keep the harness straight and feed it into the handlebar slot while pulling on the fish wire.
9. At the twist grip end of the handlebar, gently pull the jumper wire harness though the center slot in the handlebar. If the harness binds within the handlebar, gently pull on the fish wire at the other end of the handlebar to free it. Try again and pull the jumper wire harness toward the twist grip end of the handlebar with the fish wire.
10. Only pull the fish wire and jumper harness sufficiently to gain access to the twist grip electrical connector. Disconnect the fish wire from the harness and the frame.
11. Install the twist grip sensor as described in this chapter.

INDUCTION MODULE

The induction module is secured with Allen bolts that are difficult to reach and remove. Use the intake manifold wrench (K&L part No. 35-3975 or H-D part No. HD-47250). If this tool is not available, make a special tool as follows:
1. Cut a 9/16 in. (14 mm) long section (A, **Figure 83**) from a 1/4-in. Allen wrench.
2. Use the shortened wrench (B, **Figure 83**) when leverage is needed to break loose or tighten an Allen bolt.
3. Use the stub (A, **Figure 83**) and a 1/4-in. wrench (C, **Figure 83**) to remove or thread in an Allen bolt.

Removal

Refer to **Figures 84-87**.

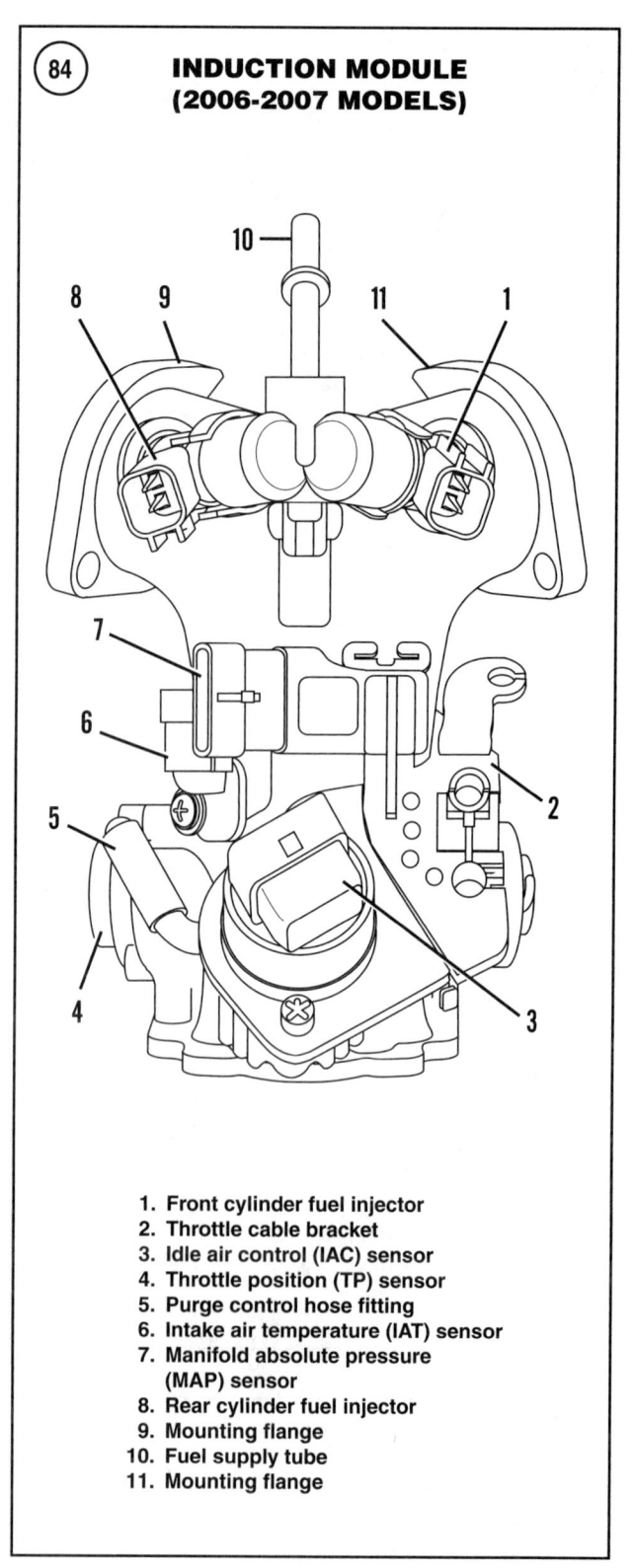

INDUCTION MODULE (2006-2007 MODELS)

1. Front cylinder fuel injector
2. Throttle cable bracket
3. Idle air control (IAC) sensor
4. Throttle position (TP) sensor
5. Purge control hose fitting
6. Intake air temperature (IAT) sensor
7. Manifold absolute pressure (MAP) sensor
8. Rear cylinder fuel injector
9. Mounting flange
10. Fuel supply tube
11. Mounting flange

This procedure illustrates the 2006-2007 model induction module. Where differences occur, they are identified.
1. Remove the fuel tank as described in this chapter.
2. Remove the air filter and backplate as described in this chapter.
3. Remove the horn assembly as described in Chapter Eleven.

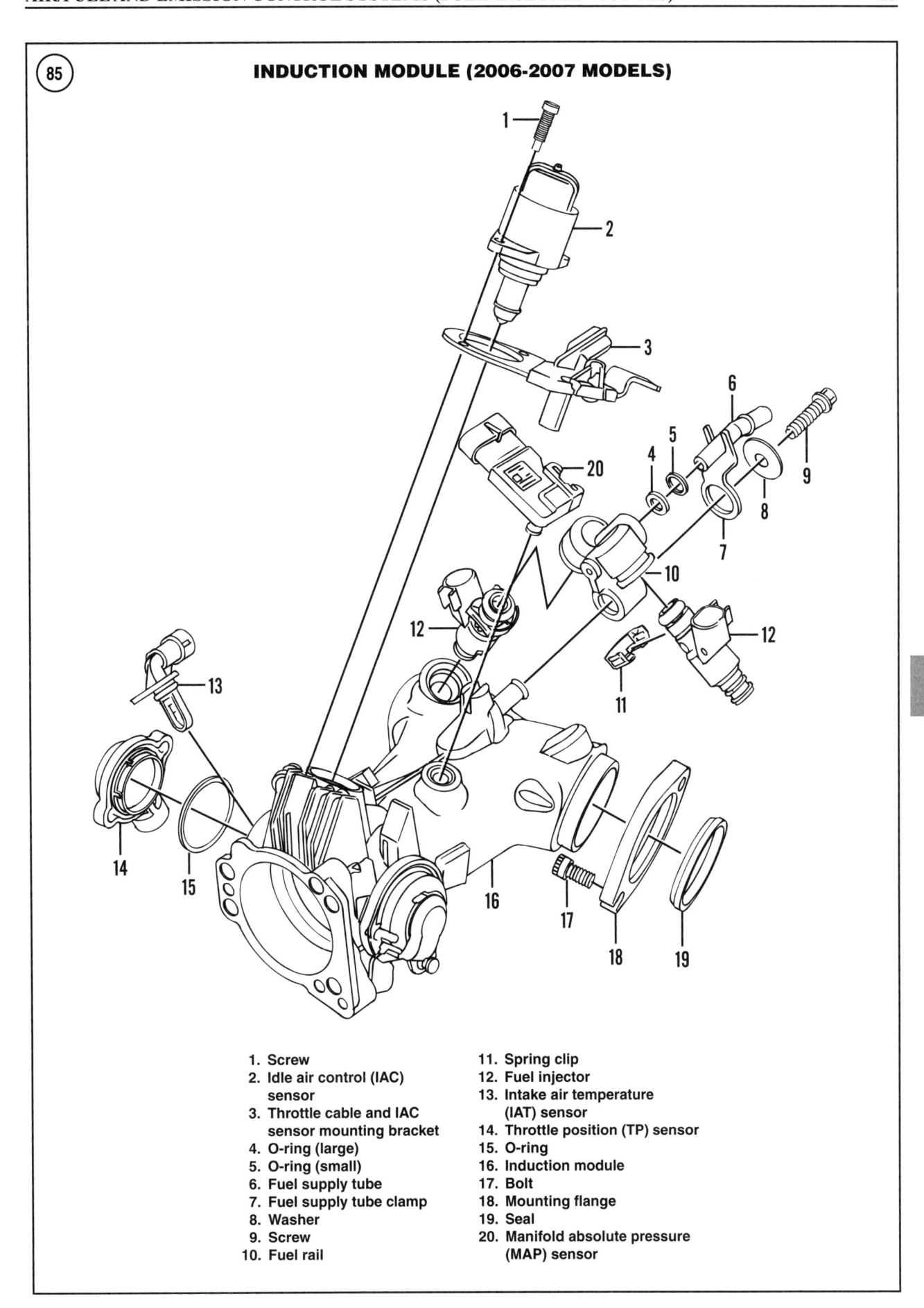

AIR/FUEL AND EMISSION CONTROL SYSTEMS (FUEL-INJECTED MODELS)

85 **INDUCTION MODULE (2006-2007 MODELS)**

1. Screw
2. Idle air control (IAC) sensor
3. Throttle cable and IAC sensor mounting bracket
4. O-ring (large)
5. O-ring (small)
6. Fuel supply tube
7. Fuel supply tube clamp
8. Washer
9. Screw
10. Fuel rail
11. Spring clip
12. Fuel injector
13. Intake air temperature (IAT) sensor
14. Throttle position (TP) sensor
15. O-ring
16. Induction module
17. Bolt
18. Mounting flange
19. Seal
20. Manifold absolute pressure (MAP) sensor

CHAPTER TEN

⑧⑥ INDUCTION MODULE (2008-2009 MODELS)

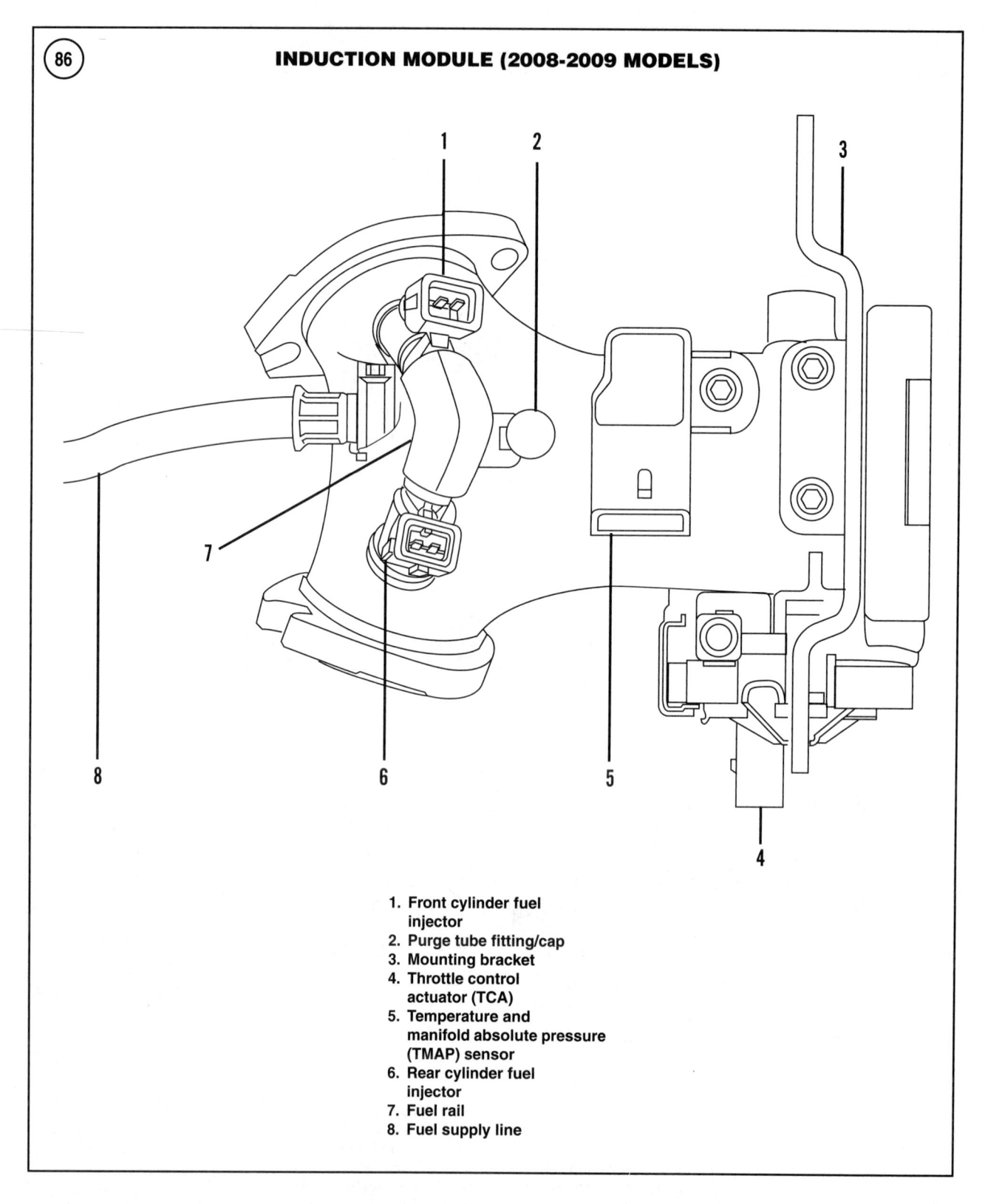

1. Front cylinder fuel injector
2. Purge tube fitting/cap
3. Mounting bracket
4. Throttle control actuator (TCA)
5. Temperature and manifold absolute pressure (TMAP) sensor
6. Rear cylinder fuel injector
7. Fuel rail
8. Fuel supply line

4. On California models, remove the purge hose (A, **Figure 88**) from the fitting on top of the induction module.
5. Disconnect the fuel supply line (**Figure 89**) from the induction module supply tube.
6. Disconnect the throttle- and idle-control cables from the induction module throttle wheel (**Figure 90**) as described in this chapter.

7. Carefully use a rocking motion and disconnect the electrical connector from each fuel injector (**Figure 91**).
8A. On 2006-2007 models, disconnect the electrical connector from the following:
   a. IAC (B, **Figure 88**).
   b. MAP sensor (C, **Figure 88**).
   c. TP sensor (**Figure 92**).

AIR/FUEL AND EMISSION CONTROL SYSTEMS (FUEL-INJECTED MODELS)

INDUCTION MODULE (2008-2009 MODELS)

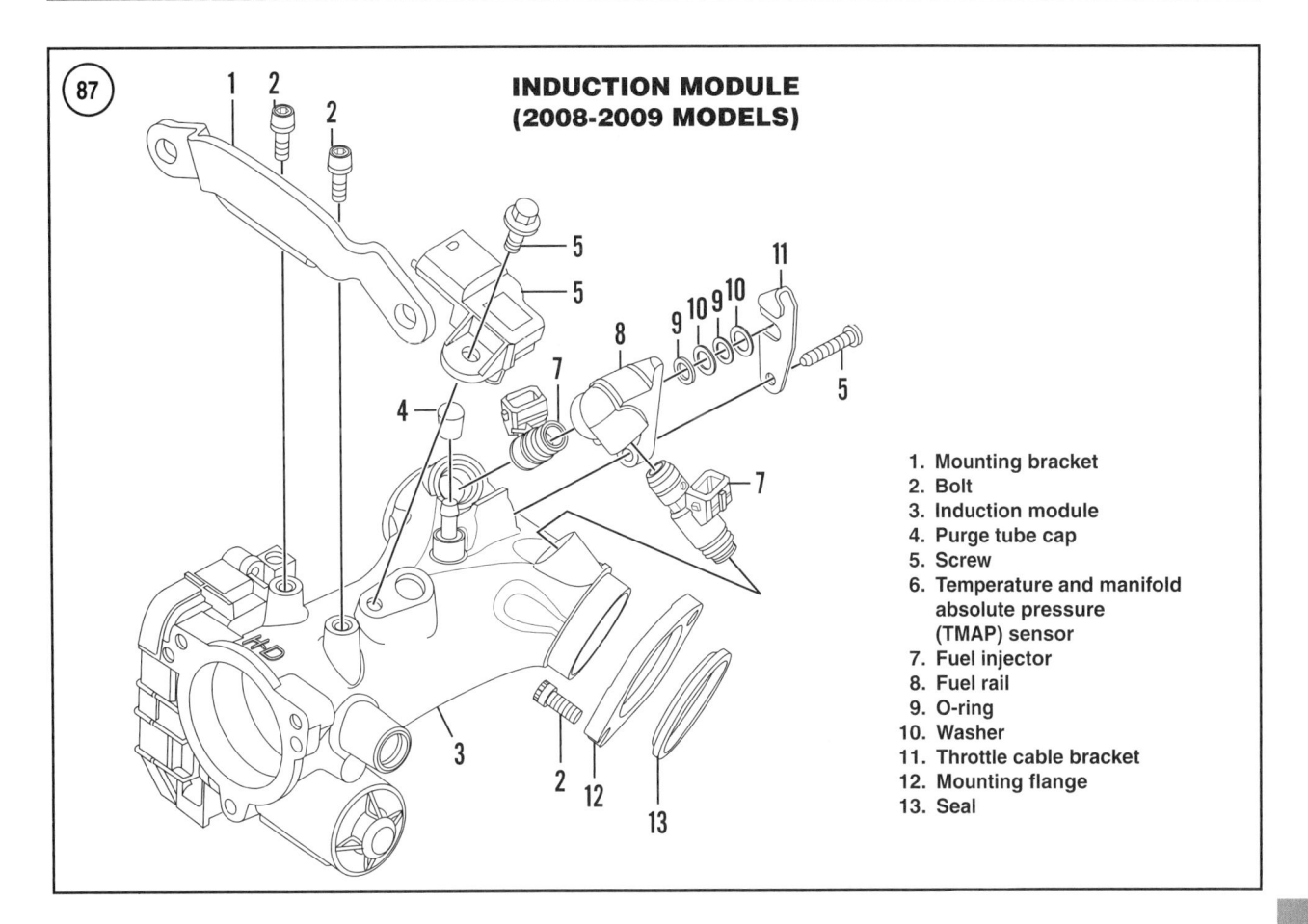

1. Mounting bracket
2. Bolt
3. Induction module
4. Purge tube cap
5. Screw
6. Temperature and manifold absolute pressure (TMAP) sensor
7. Fuel injector
8. Fuel rail
9. O-ring
10. Washer
11. Throttle cable bracket
12. Mounting flange
13. Seal

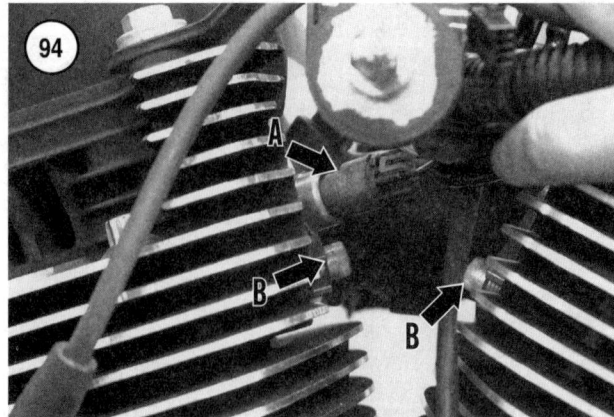

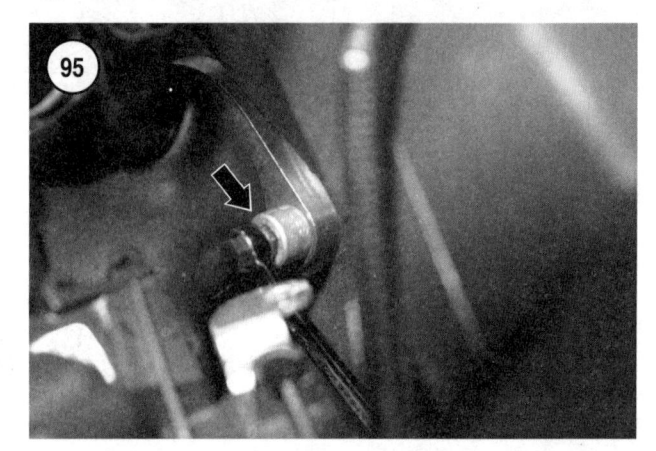

d. IAT sensor (**Figure 93**).

8B. On 2008-2009 models, disconnect the electrical connector from the following:

   a. TMAP sensor.
   b. TCA sensor.

9. Pull back the boot, and disconnect the connector from engine temperature (ET) sensor (A, **Figure 94**).

10. Working on the left side of the motorcycle, loosen the lower flange bolts (B, **Figure 94**) that secure the induction module flange to the front and rear cylinder heads. Leave these bolts loosely in place in the heads.

11. Working on the right side of the motorcycle, use the Allen wrench stub and 1/4 inch wrench (**Figure 95**) to remove the upper flange bolts (**Figure 96**).

NOTE
Each flange rotates on its induction module port.

12. Slide the induction module flanges off the lower flange bolts, and partially remove the induction module from the right side (A, **Figure 97**). Be careful not to damage the fuel line.

13. Press the button (**Figure 98**) on the fuel line (**Figure 99**), and disconnect the fuel supply line from the induction module supply tube.

14. Remove the mounting flanges (A, **Figure 100**), and discard the seals (B). Mark each flange so it can be reinstalled on the correct port.

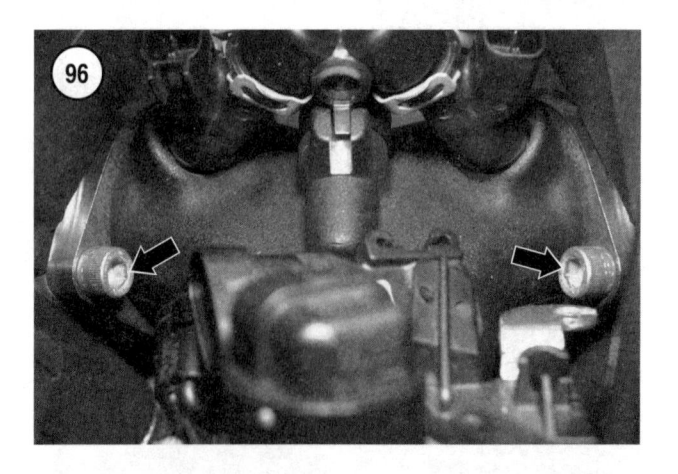

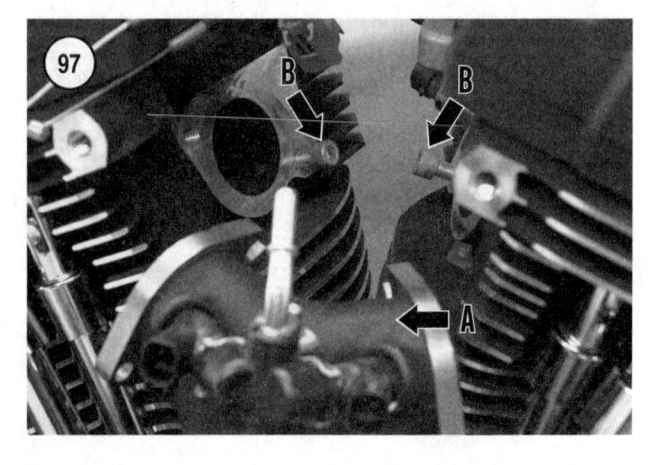

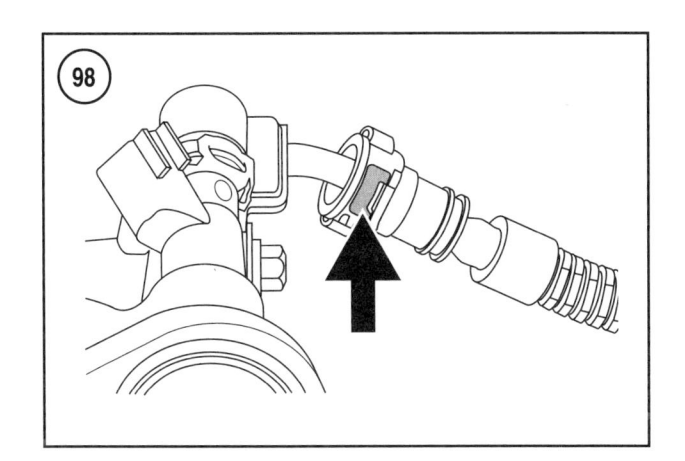

AIR/FUEL AND EMISSION CONTROL SYSTEMS (FUEL-INJECTED MODELS)

15. Inspect the induction module as described in this section.

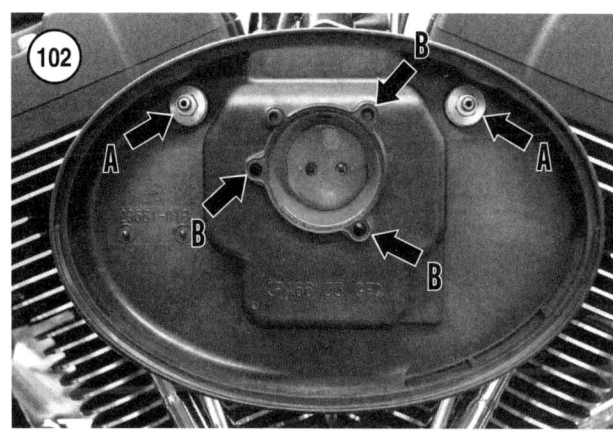

Installation

1. Refer to the marks made during removal, and install the flanges (**Figure 101**) onto the correct sides of the induction module. Make sure the seal counter bore of each flange faces outward, away from the induction module.
2. Install a *new* seal (B, **Figure 100**) into each flange so the beveled side faces into the flange.
3. Connect the fuel supply line (**Figure 99**) onto the induction module supply tube. Pull on the fuel line to ensure it is attached correctly.
4. On the right side, carefully position the induction module (A, **Figure 97**) between the cylinder head ports. Slide the flanges into place onto the lower flange bolts (B, **Figure 97**).
5. Align the mounting flanges with the cylinder head ports. Install and finger-tighten the two upper flange bolts (**Figure 96**).
6. To ensure correct alignment of the induction module to the cylinder heads, perform the following:
    a. Fit the air filter backplate into place against the cylinder heads. Install and finger-tighten the breather bolts (A, **Figure 102**).
    b. Install the air filter bracket Torx screws (B, **Figure 102**) to secure the backplate to the induction module. Finger-tighten the screws.
7. Working on the right side of the motorcycle, tighten the two upper flange bolts (**Figure 96**) until snug. Do not tighten to the final torque specification at this time. Use the same tool set-up used to loosen the Allen bolts.
8. Working on the left side of the motorcycle, tighten the two lower flange bolts (B, **Figure 94**) to 96-144 in.-lb. (10.8-16.3 N•m).
9. Remove the air filter backplate bracket screws (B, **Figure 102**), and then remove the backplate.
10. Working on the right side of the motorcycle, tighten the two upper flange bolts (**Figure 96**) bolts to 96-144 in.-lb. (10.8-16.3 N•m).
11. Carefully attach the electrical connector (**Figure 91**) onto each fuel injector. Push the connector on until it latches in place.

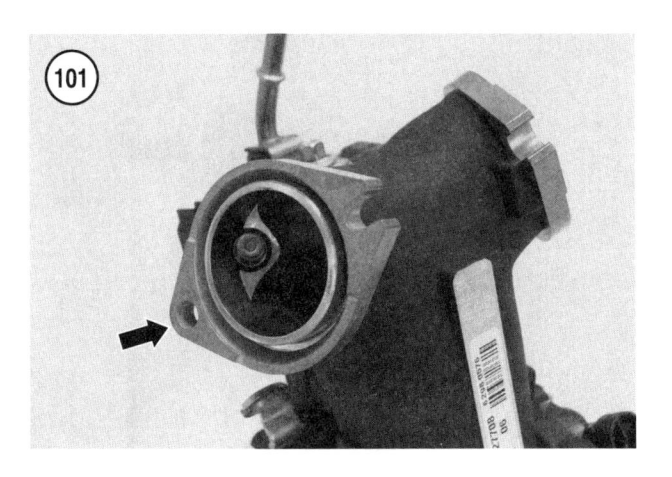

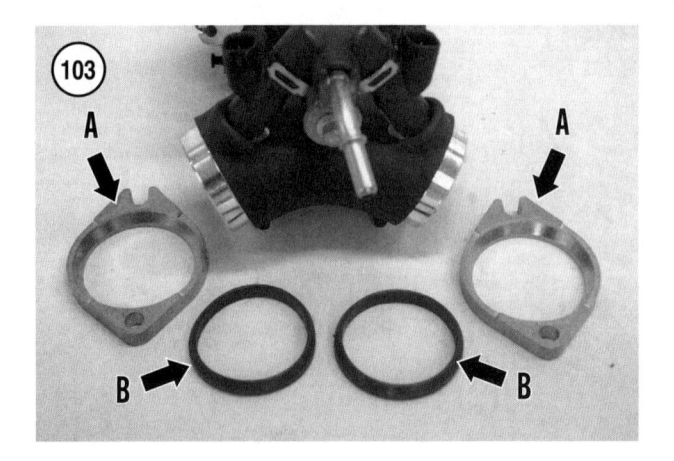

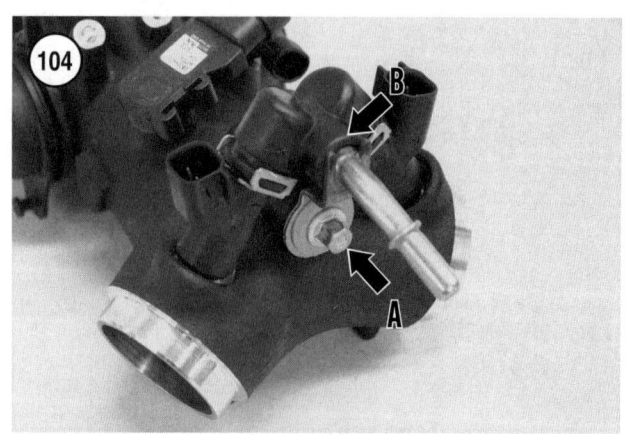

428

CHAPTER TEN

12A. On 2006-2007 models, connect the electrical connector onto the following:
   a. IAT sensor (A, **Figure 93**).
   b. TP sensor (**Figure 92**).
   c. MAP sensor (C, **Figure 88**).
   d. IAC (B, **Figure 88**).

12B. On 2008-2009 models, connect the electrical connector from the following:
   a. TMAP sensor.
   b. TCA sensor.

13. On California models, install the purge hose (A, **Figure 88**) onto the fitting on top of the induction module.

14. Connect the throttle- and idle-control cables to the throttle wheel (**Figure 90**) as described in this chapter. Adjust the cables as described in Chapter Three.

15. Install the fuel supply line (**Figure 89**) onto the induction module supply tube. Pull on the fuel line to ensure it is attached correctly.

16. Connect the engine temperature sensor connector to the sensor (A, **Figure 94**), and roll the boot back over the sensor.

17. Install the backplate and air filter as described in this chapter.

18. Install the fuel tank as described in this chapter.

19. Turn the ignition switch ON and OFF to reset the idle air control to its park position.

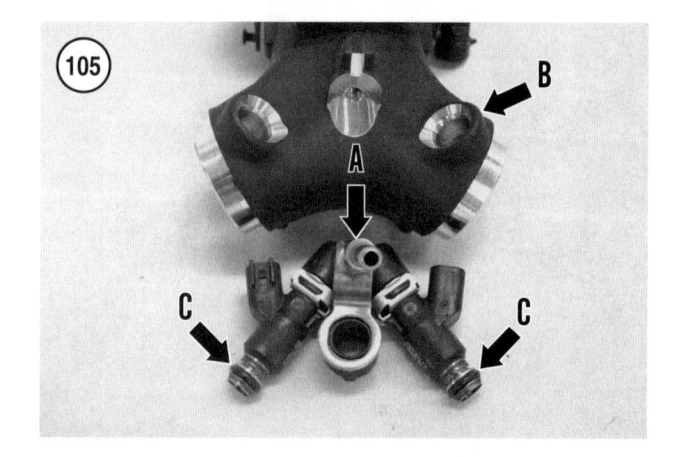

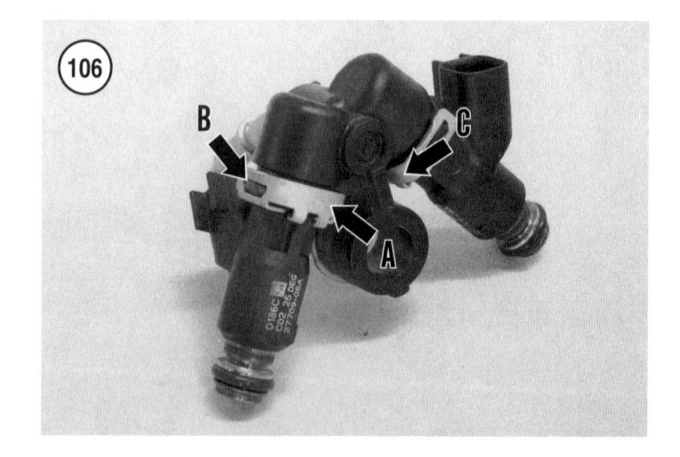

Inspection

1. Check the induction module for wear, deterioration or other damage.

2. Inspect each flange (A, **Figure 103**) and its seal (B) on the induction module.

FUEL INJECTORS

Removal

1. Remove the induction module as described in this chapter.

2. Remove the fuel supply tube bolt (A, **Figure 104**) and washer.

3. Gently rock the fuel injector and fuel rail assembly (B, **Figure 104**) back and forth while pulling up, and remove

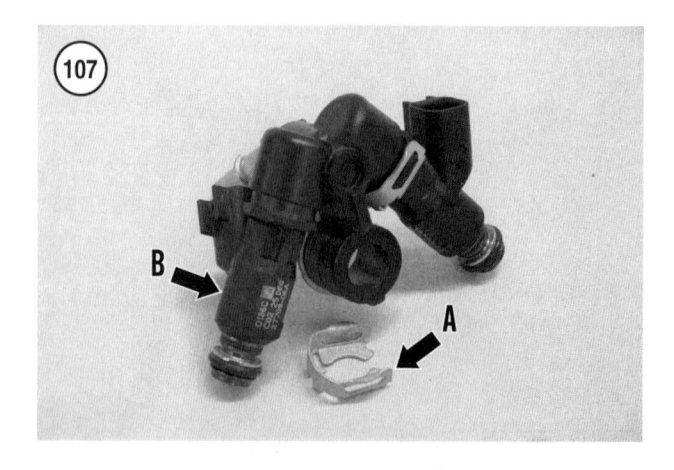

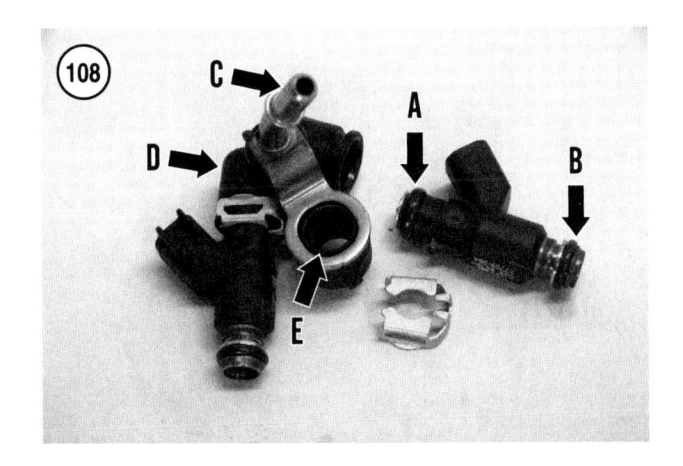

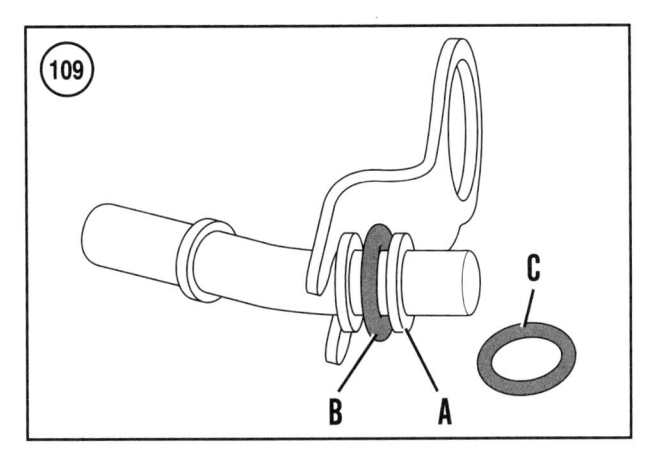

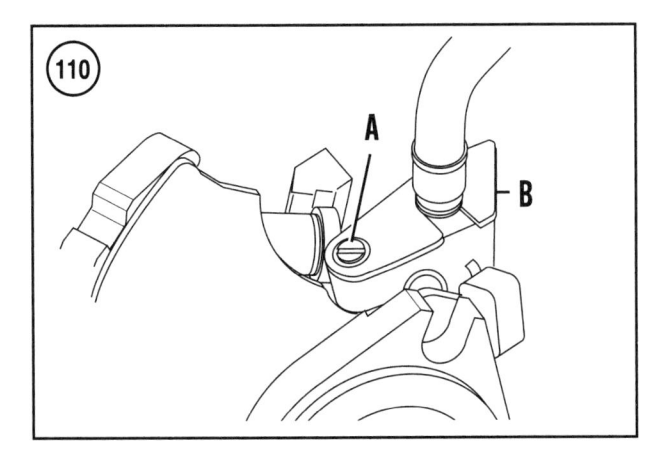

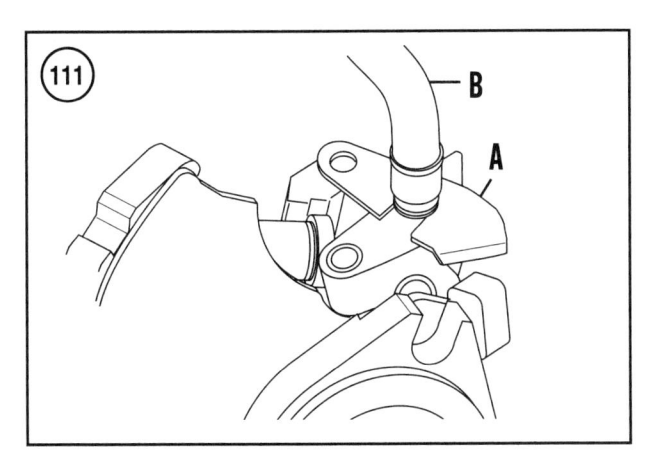

AIR/FUEL AND EMISSION CONTROL SYSTEMS (FUEL-INJECTED MODELS)

the assembly (A, **Figure 105**) from the induction module (B). Do not lose the bottom O-ring (C, **Figure 105**) on each fuel injector.

4. Rotate the fuel injector 90° so the closed end (A, **Figure 106**) of the spring clip is accessible. Note that the arms of the spring clip straddle the tab (B, **Figure 106**) on the injector.

5. Remove the spring clip (A, **Figure 107**), and pull the fuel injector (B) from the fuel rail. Gently rock the injector back and forth, if necessary.

6. Remove and discard the top (A, **Figure 108**) and bottom (B) O-rings.

7. Repeat the process to remove the remaining fuel injector.

8A. On 2006-2007 models, perform the following:
   a. If necessary, remove the fuel supply tube (C, **Figure 108**) from the fuel rail (D).
   b. Remove the sealing washer (A, **Figure 109**) and O-ring (B) from the fuel supply tube. Discard the washer and O-ring.
   c. Remove the second O-ring (C, **Figure 109**) from the fuel rail bore. Discard the O-ring.

8B. On 2008-2009 models, perform the following:
   a. Remove the Torx screw (A, **Figure 110**) securing the fuel supply tube clamp bracket (B) and fuel rail.
   b. Rotate the bracket (A, **Figure 111**) 90° *clockwise* and remove it from the fuel supply tube.
   c. Withdraw the fuel supply tube (B, **Figure 111**) from the fuel rail. Remove a washer, an O-ring, a washer and an O-ring from the end of the fuel supply tube. These items may remain within the fuel rail. These items must be removed to ensure correct fuel tube installation to avoid fuel leaks.

Installation

1. Apply a light coat of clean engine oil to all *new* O-rings.

2A. On 2006-2007 models, perform the following:
   a. Install a *new* O-ring (B, **Figure 109**) onto the fuel supply tube until it contacts the collar, and then install the sealing washer (A). Install the second O-ring (C) into the fuel rail bore.
   b. Insert the fuel supply tube into the fuel rail bore until the clamp seats in the round step of the fuel rail (E, **Figure 108**).

2B. On 2008-2009 models, perform the following:
   a. Insert the fuel supply tube into the fuel rail bore. Push it in until it bottoms. Rotate the fuel supply tube *clockwise* until the fuel tank quick-connect fitting is point upward. Now rotate the fuel supply tube and additional 90° so the fitting is pointing toward the TCA sensor on the induction module.
   b. Engage the fuel supply tube clamp bracket into the slot in the fuel supply hose fitting.
   c. Rotate the bracket (A, **Figure 111**) 90° *counterclockwise* until the flange of the bracket bottoms on the fuel rail.

d. Align the screw hole in the clamp bracket with the induction module, and then install the Torx screw (A, **Figure 110**). Tighten the screw to 66-82 in.-lb. (7.5-9.3 N•m).

3. Install the O-ring (A, **Figure 108**) with the thicker base and smaller ID onto the fuel rail end of the fuel injector. Install the remaining O-ring (B, **Figure 108**) onto the induction module and of the fuel injector.

4. Push the electrical connector side of each fuel injector (B, **Figure 107**) into the fuel rail until it bottoms.

5. Position the concave side of the spring clip (A, **Figure 107**) toward the fuel rail, and press the spring clip into the slot in the fuel injector. When properly installed, the spring clip engages the lip on each side of the fuel injector and the fingers on the back of the clip straddle the tab (B, **Figure 106**) on the fuel injector.

6. Rotate the fuel injectors so the closed side of the spring clip faces the fuel rail (C, **Figure 106**).

7. Position the fuel rail assembly onto the induction module so each injector (**Figure 112**) is started into its port.

8. Carefully install the fuel injectors into the induction module ports until the fuel rail tab (**Figure 113**) engages the slot at the top of the induction module.

9. On 2006-2007 models, install the fuel supply tube hex bolt and washer. Tighten the bolt to 90-110 in.-lb. (10.2-12.4 N•m).

10. Install the induction module assembly as described in this chapter.

Inspection

1. Inspect the fuel injectors for damage. Check for corrosion on the electrical connector pins; clean if necessary.
2. Inspect the fuel rail and fuel supply tube for damage.
3. Inspect the injector ports (**Figure 114**) in the induction module.
4. Replace any worn or damaged part.

INDUCTION MODULE SENSORS (2006-2007 MODELS)

Refer to **Figure 115**.

NOTE
Always disarm the TSSM/HFSM security system prior to disconnecting the battery or pulling the Maxi-Fuse so the siren will not sound.

Intake Air Temperature (IAT) Sensor Removal/Installation

1. Disconnect the negative battery cable as described in Chapter Eleven.
2. Remove the air filter and backplate as described in this chapter.
3. On California models, remove the purge hose (A, **Figure 116**) from the fitting on top of the induction module.
4. Disconnect the IAC connector (B, **Figure 116**) and the MAP sensor connector (C).
5. Disconnect the 2-pin connector (A, **Figure 117**) from the IAT sensor.
6. Remove the IAT sensor screw (B, **Figure 117**) and its captive washer, and then remove the sensor from the induction module and throttle shaft.
7. Remove and discard the IAT sensor O-ring.
8. Apply a light coat of clean engine oil to a *new* O-ring.
9. Install the *new* O-ring onto the sensor.
10. Install the sensor into the induction module and push it in until it bottoms. Turn the sensor until the electrical connector (A, **Figure 117**) faces the left side of the motorcycle.

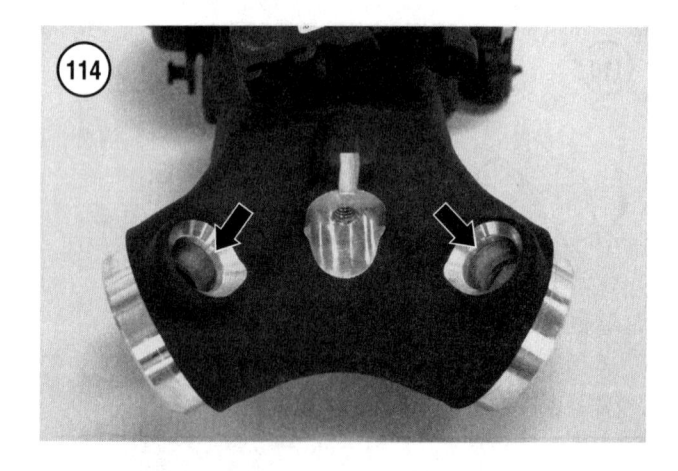

AIR/FUEL AND EMISSION CONTROL SYSTEMS (FUEL-INJECTED MODELS)

115 INDUCTION MODULE SENSORS (2006-2007 MODELS)

1. Screw
2. Idle air control (IAC) sensor
3. Throttle cable and IAC sensor mounting bracket
4. O-ring (large)
5. O-ring (small)
6. Fuel supply tube
7. Fuel supply tube clamp
8. Washer
9. Screw
10. Fuel rail
11. Spring clip
12. Fuel injector
13. Intake air temperature (IAT) sensor
14. Throttle position (TP) sensor
15. O-ring
16. Induction module
17. Bolt
18. Mounting flange
19. Seal
20. Manifold absolute pressure (MAP) sensor

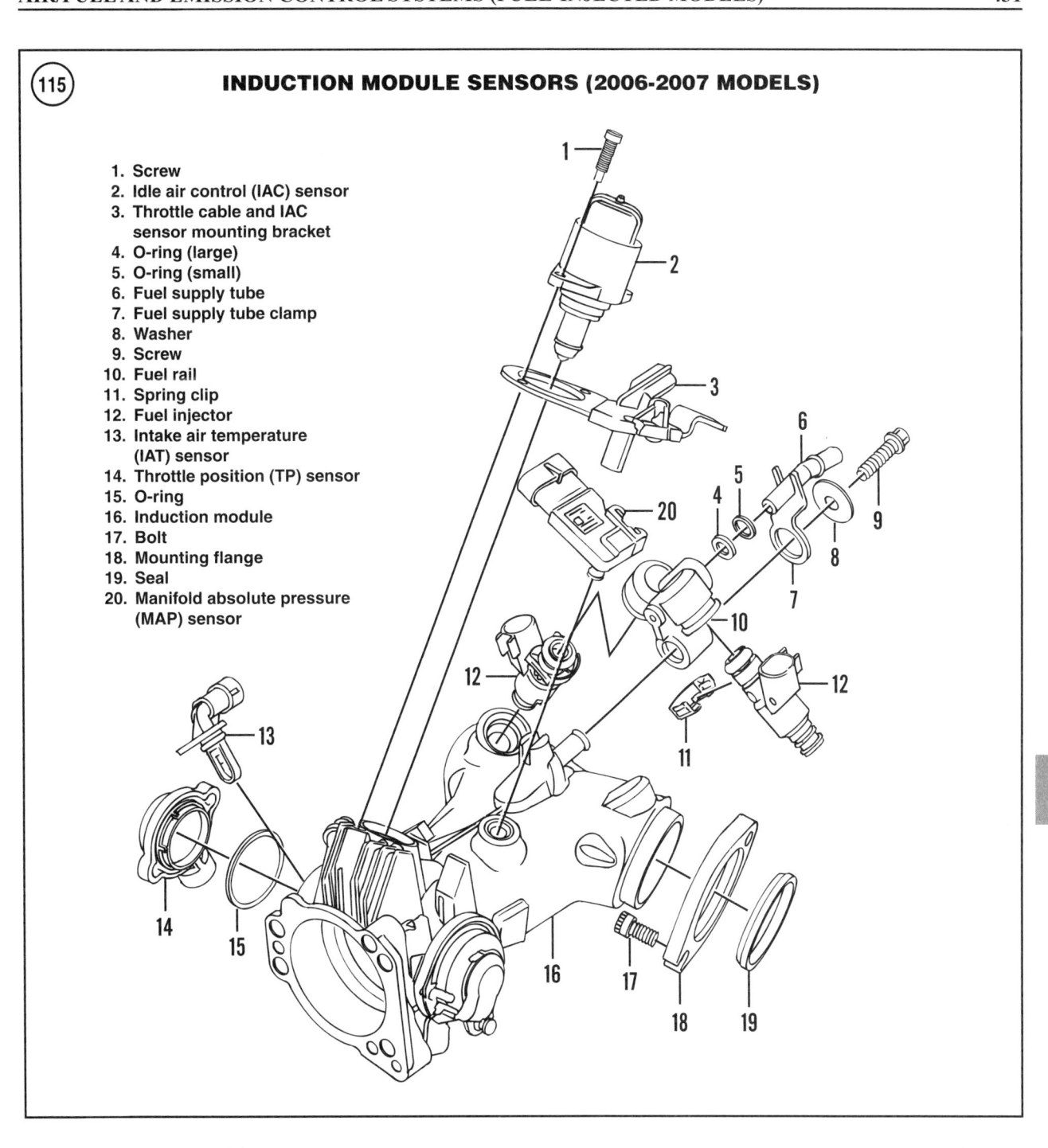

432

11. Install a *new* IAT sensor screw (B, **Figure 117**) and its captive washer. Tighten the screw to 15-20 in.-lb. (1.7-2.3 N•m).
12. Press the connector (A, **Figure 117**) onto the IAT sensor.
13. Reconnect the IAC connector (B, **Figure 116**) and the MAP sensor connector (C, **Figure 116**). On California models, reconnect the purge hose (A, **Figure 116**) to its fitting.
14 Install the backplate and air filter as described in this chapter.
15. Connect the negative battery cable as described in Chapter Eleven.

Throttle Position (TP) Sensor
Removal/Installation

1. Disconnect the negative battery cable as described in Chapter Eleven.
2. Remove the air filter and backplate as described in this chapter.
3. Disconnect the 3-pin connector (A, **Figure 118**) from the TP sensor.
4. Remove the TP sensor screws (B, **Figure 118**) and captive washers. Then, remove the sensor from the induction module. Discard the screws and captive washers.
5. Remove the O-ring from the sensor.
6. Apply a light coat of clean engine oil onto a *new* O-ring.
7. Install the *new* O-ring onto the sensor.
8. Slide the TP sensor onto the throttle shaft so the sensor's flat (A, **Figure 119**) engages the shaft, and the indexing pin (B) engages the hole on the induction module.
9. Install *new* TP sensor screws (B, **Figure 118**) and captive washers. Tighten the screws to 15-20 in.-lb. (1.7-2.3 N•m).
10. Operate the throttle several times to open and close the throttle plates. Make sure the sensor operates smoothly.
11. Install the connector (A, **Figure 118**) onto the TP sensor.
12 Install the backplate and air filter as described in this chapter.
13. Connect the negative battery cable as described in Chapter Eleven.

Idle Air Control (IAC) Sensor
Removal/Installation

1. Remove the induction module as described in this chapter.
2. Remove the throttle cable bracket screws (A, **Figure 120**), and lift the throttle cable bracket (B) from the IAC. Discard the screws.
3. Gently rock the IAC sensor (A, **Figure 121**) back and forth and pull it from the induction module.
4. Remove the O-ring (**Figure 122**) from the induction module bore. Discard the O-ring.

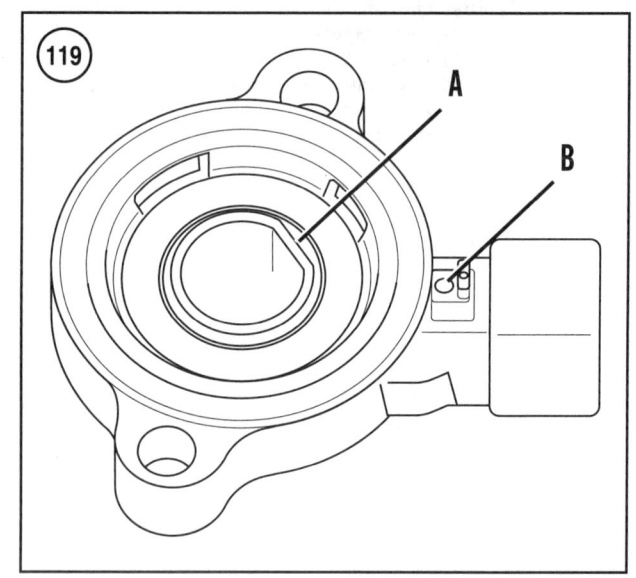

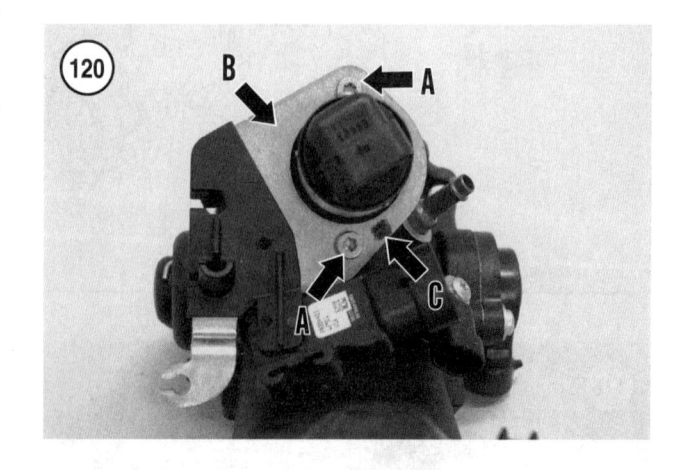

5. Apply a light coat of clean engine oil to a *new* O-ring, and install it into the induction module bore.
6. Position the IAC so its electrical connector faces the left side of the induction module. Press the IAC (A, **Figure 121**) into the induction module bore until the IAC bottoms.
7. Set the throttle cable bracket (B, **Figure 120**) over the IAC so the bracket's indexing pin (C) aligns with the indexing hole in the induction module.

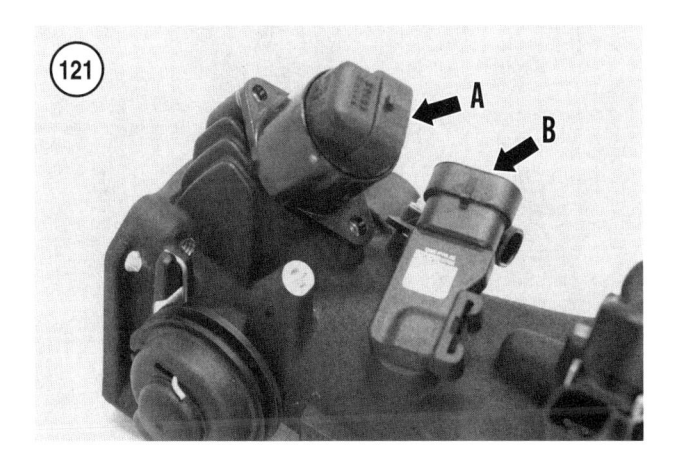

AIR/FUEL AND EMISSION CONTROL SYSTEMS (FUEL-INJECTED MODELS)

CAUTION
Do not try to remove the MAP sensor with the induction module installed on the engine as the sensor will be damaged.

1. Remove the induction module as described in this chapter.
2. Remove the throttle cable bracket screws (A, **Figure 120**), and lift the throttle cable bracket (B) from the idle air control. Discard the screws.
3. Gently rock the MAP sensor (B, **Figure 121**) back and forth while pulling up and remove it from the induction module.
4. Inspect the sensor seal for tears or deterioration; replace if necessary.
5. Position the sensor with the electrical connector facing opposite the throttle wheel. Install the MAP sensor and push it in until it bottoms.
6. Set the throttle cable bracket (B, **Figure 120**) over the IAC so the bracket's indexing pin (C) aligns with the indexing hole in the induction module.
7. Install *new* throttle cable bracket screws (A, **Figure 120**). Make sure the screws pass through the holes on the IAC and into the threads in the induction module.
8. Tighten the throttle cable bracket screws to 20-35 in.-lb. (2.3-4.0 N•m).
9. Install the induction module as described in this chapter.

Engine Temperature (ET) Sensor

The engine temperature (ET) sensor (**Figure 123**) is located below the induction module in the area between the two cylinders.

Refer to *Sensors* in Chapter Eleven for removal and installation procedures.

Bank Angle (BAS) Sensor

The Bank Angle Sensor (BAS) is an integral part of the TSM/TSSM/HFSM.

Refer to *Turn Signal and Security Modules* in Chapter Eleven.

8. Install new throttle cable bracket screws (A, **Figure 120**). Make sure the screws pass through the holes on the IAC and into the threads in the induction module.
9. Tighten the throttle cable bracket screws to 20-35 in.-lb. (2.3-4.0 N•m).
10. Install the induction module as described in this chapter.

Manifold Absolute Pressure (MAP) Sensor
Removal/Installation

The MAP sensor is located on top of the induction module.

Oxygen (O_2) Sensor (2007 Models)
Removal/Installation

The oxygen sensors are located on the inboard side of the front and rear exhaust pipe. An oxygen sensor socket (JIMS part No. 969 or H-D part No. HD-48262), or an equivalent, must be used to remove and install the sensors. Other sockets will damage the sensor.

1. Disconnect the negative battery cable as described in Chapter Eleven.
2. Follow the front O_2 sensor (**Figure 124**) wiring harness to the connector. Disconnect the halves of the 2-pin front oxygen sensor connector.

3. Follow the rear O_2 sensor (**Figure 125**) wiring harness to the connector. Disconnect the halves of the 2-pin rear oxygen sensor connector.
4. Release any cable ties securing the wire to the frame. Sketch how the wire is routed through the frame and also note the location of the cable ties.
5. Install the sensor socket onto the sensor (**Figure 126**) without damage to the electrical wires.
6. Loosen the sensor with the socket. After the sensor is loosened, unscrew the sensor by hand and remove it.

NOTE
Do not reinstall an oxygen sensor that has been dropped or damaged by other components. It may be damaged internally, and will not function correctly.

7. Apply a light coat of Loctite Anti-Seize to the threads prior to installation.
8. Carefully thread the sensor into the exhaust pipe by hand. Do not cross thread it.
9. Install the socket (**Figure 126**) onto the sensor without damaging the electrical wires.
10. Tighten the oxygen sensor to 29-44 ft.-lb. (39.3-59.7 N•m).
11. Route the electrical cable along the path sketched during removal.
12. Connect the oxygen sensor to the harness. Secure the cable to the frame at the locations noted during removal.
13. Connect the negative battery cable as described in Chapter Eleven.

INDUCTION MODULE SENSORS (2008-2009 MODELS)

NOTE
Always disarm the TSSM/HFSM security system prior to disconnecting the battery or pulling the Maxi-Fuse so the siren will not sound.

Manifold Absolute Pressure (TMAP) Sensor Removal/Installation

Refer to **Figure 127**.
1. Disconnect the negative battery cable as described in Chapter Eleven.
2. Remove the fuel tank as described in this chapter.
3. Remove the electrical connector from the TMAP sensor.
4. Remove the hex screw, and then remove the sensor from the induction module. Discard the hex screw.
5. Inspect the O-ring for tears or deterioration; replace if necessary.
6. Position the sensor with the electrical connector facing toward the TCA sensor. Align the screw hole with the induction module and carefully install the TMAP sensor. Push it in until it bottoms.
7. Install a *new* hex screw and tighten to 84-108 in.-lb. (9.5-12.2 N•m).   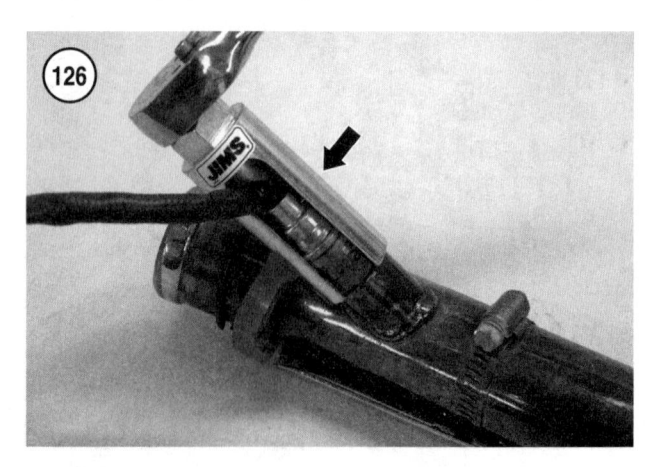
8. Install the fuel tank as described in this chapter.
9. Connect the negative battery cable as described in Chapter Eleven.

Engine Temperature (ET) Sensor Removal/Installation

Refer to *Sensors* in Chapter Eleven.

O_2 Sensor Removal/Installation

Refer to *Induction Module Sensors (2006-2007 Models)* in this chapter.

AIR/FUEL AND EMISSION CONTROL SYSTEMS (FUEL-INJECTED MODELS)

INDUCTION MODULE SENSORS (2008-2009 MODELS)

1. Mounting bracket
2. Bolt
3. Induction module
4. Purge tube cap
5. Screw
6. Temperature and manifold absolute pressure (TMAP) sensor
7. Fuel injector
8. Fuel rail
9. O-ring
10. Washer
11. Throttle cable bracket
12. Mounting flange
13. Seal

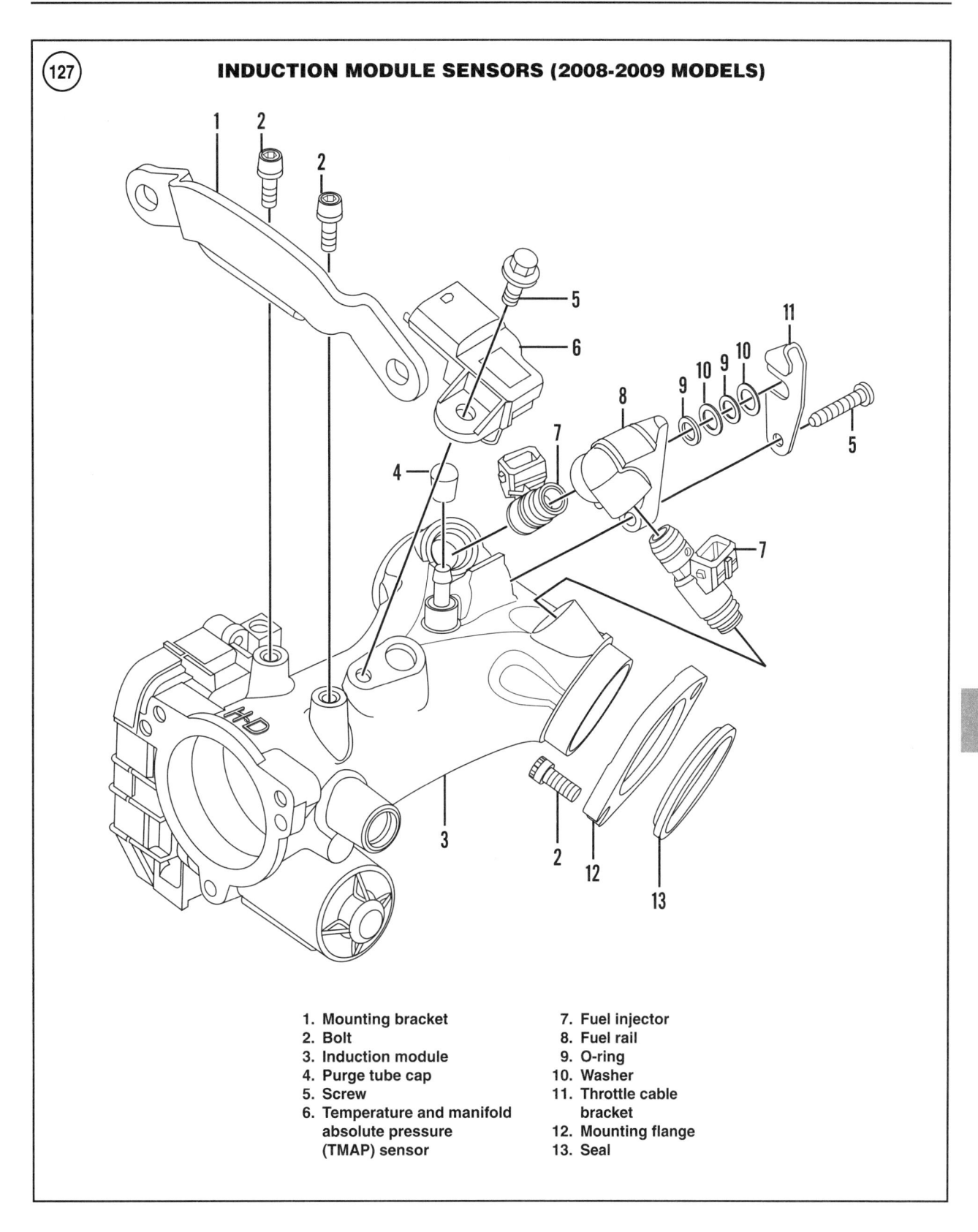

Throttle Control Actuator (TCA)

The throttle control actuator is an internal component of the induction module. If the TCA is defective, the entire induction module must be replaced as described in this chapter.

EVAPORATIVE EMISSION CONTROL SYSTEM (ALL CALIFORNIA MODELS)

Refer to Chapter Nine for evaporative emission control system components on all models and years.

Table 1 FUEL SYSTEM SPECIFICATIONS

Item	Specification
Idle speed	950-1050 rpm
Fuel pressure (2008-2009 models)	55-62 psi (379-427 kPa)
Fuel tank capacity	
2006-2007 models	5.0 gal. (18.93 L)
2008-2009 models	6.0 gal. (22.7 L)
Fuel tank reserve*	
2006-2007 models	0.9 gal. (3.4 L)
2008-2009 models	1.0 gal. (3.79 L)

*Low fuel warning light on.

Table 2 FUEL SYSTEM TORQUE SPECIFICATIONS

Item	ft.-lb.	in.-lb.	N•m
Air filter (2007 FLHRSE3 and 2009 FLTHRSE3 models)			
Breather hollow bolts	22-24	–	29.8-32.5
Filter element mounting screws	–	55-60	6.2-6.8
Standoff bolts	–	55-60	6.2-6.8
Air filter (all other models)			
Breather hollow bolts	22-24	–	29.8-32.5
Mounting bracket Torx screws	–	40-60	4.5-6.8
Cover screw	–	36-60	4.1-6.8
Engine temperature sensor (ET)	10-15	–	13.6-20.3
Fuel pump/level sender top plate screw			
2006-2007 models	–	18-24	2.0-2.7
Fuel supply tube			
2006-2007 models hex bolt	–	90-110	10.2-12.4
2008-2009 models Torx screws	–	66-82	7.5-9.3
Fuel tank check valve	18	–	24.4
Fuel tank front and rear mounting bolt	15-20	–	20.3-27.1
Fuel tank quick-connect fitting	18	–	24.4
Induction module mounting flange Allen bolts	–	96-144	10.8-16.3
Idle air control (IAC) sensor throttle cable bracket screws (2006-2007 models)	–	20-35	2.3-4.0
Intake air temperature sensor screw (2006-2007 models)	–	15-20	1.7-2.3
Oxygen sensor (2007-2009 models)	29-44	–	39.3-59.7
Manifold absolute pressure sensor			
2006-2007 models (MAP) throttle cable bracket screws	–	20-35	2.3-4.0
2008-2009 models (TMAP) hex screw	–	84-108	9.5-12.2
Throttle position sensor screws (2006-2007 models)	–	15-20	1.7-2.3

CHAPTER ELEVEN

ELECTRICAL SYSTEM

This chapter contains service and test procedures for electrical system components. Refer to Chapter Three for spark plugs service.

Specifications are located in **Tables 1-6** at the end of the chapter. Wiring diagrams are located on the CD inserted into the back cover of the manual.

ELECTRICAL COMPONENT REPLACEMENT

Most dealerships and parts suppliers will not accept the return of any electrical part. If the exact cause of an electrical system malfunction cannot be determined, have a dealership retest the specific system to verify test results. If a new electrical component is installed and the system still does not work, the unit, in all likelihood, cannot be returned for a refund.

Consider any test results carefully before replacing a component that tests only slight out of specification, especially when testing for resistance. A number of variables affect test results dramatically. These include the test meter's internal circuitry, ambient air temperature, and the condition under which the machine has been operated. All instructions and specifications have been check for accuracy. However, successful test results depend largely upon individual accuracy.

FUSES

All models are equipped with a series of fuses to protect the electrical system. The number of fuses varies depending on the model. Refer to **Table 3** for fuse specifications.

The fuse panel is located under the seat, behind the battery. If there is an electrical failure, first check for a blown fuse. A blown fuse has a break in the element.

Whenever a fuse blows, find the reason for the failure before replacing the fuse. Usually, the trouble is a short circuit in the wiring. This may be caused by worn-through insulation or a disconnected wire shorted to ground. Check the circuit that the fuse protects.

Spare fuses are included in the fuse block. When a spare fuse is used, replace it as soon as possible. Consider carrying additional spare fuses.

NOTE
Always disarm the optional security system (TSSM/HFSM) before disconnecting the battery or before pulling the Maxi-Fuse so the siren will not sound.

Fuse Replacement (2006-2007 Models)

Refer to **Figure 1**.
1. Remove the left side saddlebag and frame side cover as described in Chapter Seventeen.
2. Remove the Maxi-Fuse as described in this chapter.
3. Depress both latches (A, **Figure 2**) on the Maxi-Fuse holder, slide the holder (B) toward the rear and disengage the tongue from groove on the fuse holder.
4. Pull the fuse block (**Figure 3**) straight out and release it from the tabs on the frame mounting bracket.
5. Locate the blown fuse and install a *new* fuse with the *same* amperage. Fuse description and location is printed on the fuse block cover (**Figure 4**, typical).

6. Push the fuse block (**Figure 3**) straight in and onto the tabs on the frame mounting bracket. Push it in until it bottoms.
7. Slide the Maxi-Fuse holder (B, **Figure 2**) tongue onto the groove on the fuse holder until it is seated and both latches (A) lock in place.
8. Install the Maxi-Fuse as described in this chapter.
9. Install the left side saddlebag and frame side cover as described in Chapter Seventeen.

Fuse Replacement (2008-2009 Models)

1. Remove the left side saddlebag and frame side cover as described in Chapter Seventeen.
2. Remove the Maxi-Fuse as described in this chapter.
3. Push up on the tongue at bottom of fuse block cover and release it from the electrical caddy. Rotate the cover up and disengage it from the hinge.
4. Locate the blown fuse and install a *new* fuse with the *same* amperage. Fuse description and location is printed on the fuse block cover.
5. Engage hinge and rotate the cover down over the fuse block. Push up on the tongue at the bottom of the cover and engage it with the slot in the electrical caddy.
6. Install the Maxi-Fuse as described in this chapter.
7. Install the left side saddlebag and frame side cover as described in Chapter Seventeen.

EFI Fuse Block (2006-2007 Models)

Refer to **Figure 5**.
1. Remove the right side saddlebag and frame side cover as described in Chapter Seventeen.
2. Remove the Maxi-Fuse as described in this chapter.
3. Release and move the data link connector (**Figure 6**) from the mounting bracket.
4. Gently press on the white dot on the inboard side of the fuse block. Gently pull on the wiring harness, and release the tabs on the fuse block (**Figure 7**) from the slots in the mounting bracket. Remove the fuse block.
5. Locate the fuse, and install a new one with the *same* amperage rating. Fuse description and location is printed on the fuse block cover.
6. Install the Maxi-Fuse as described in this chapter.
7. Install the right side saddlebag and frame side cover as described in Chapter Seventeen.

MAXI-FUSE

NOTE
Always disarm the optional security system (TSSM/HFSM) before disconnecting the battery or before pulling the Maxi-Fuse so the siren will not sound.

① **FUSE AND RELAY PANEL (LEFT SIDE)**

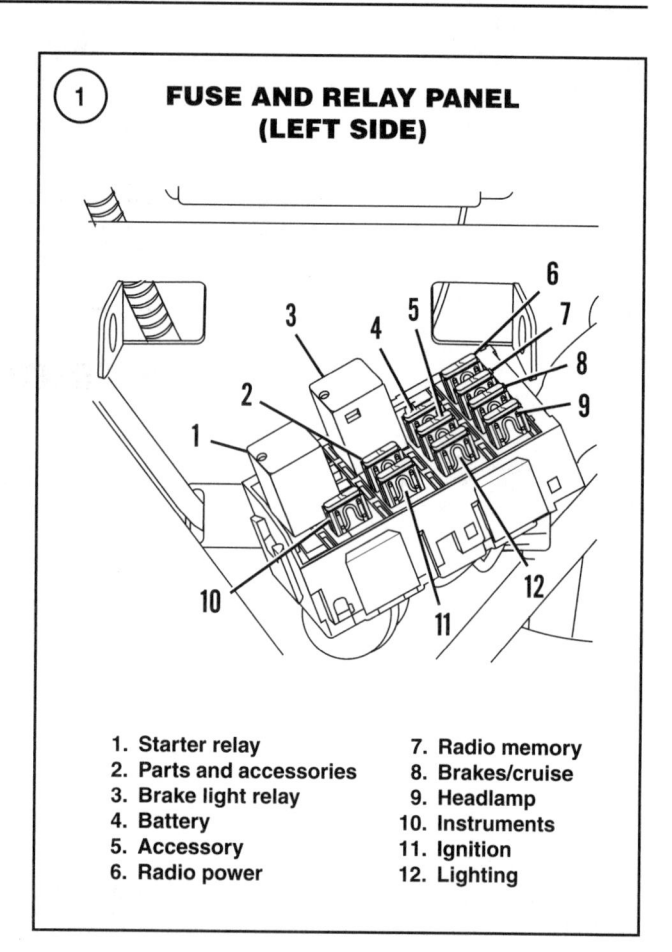

1. Starter relay
2. Parts and accessories
3. Brake light relay
4. Battery
5. Accessory
6. Radio power
7. Radio memory
8. Brakes/cruise
9. Headlamp
10. Instruments
11. Ignition
12. Lighting

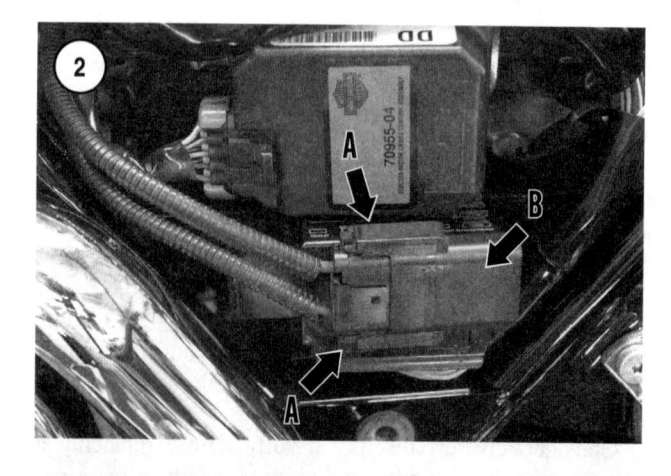

ELECTRICAL SYSTEM

FUSE PANEL (RIGHT SIDE)

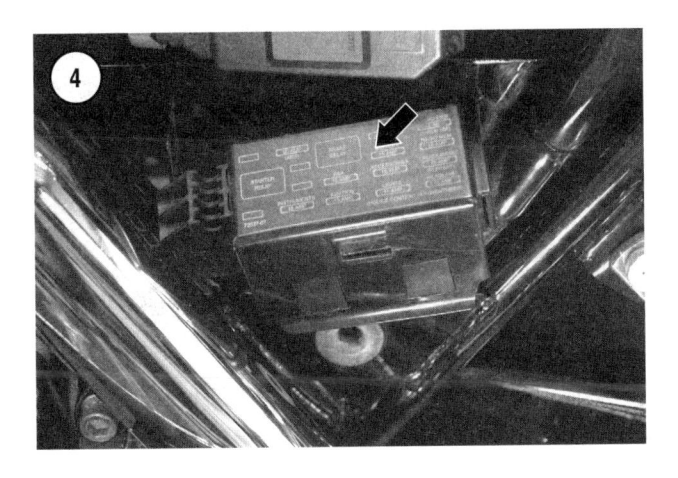

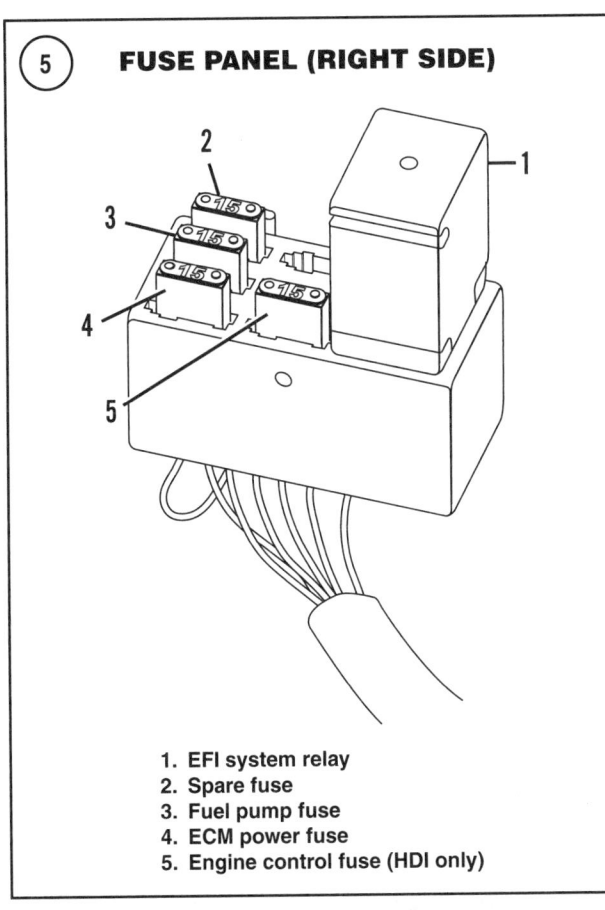

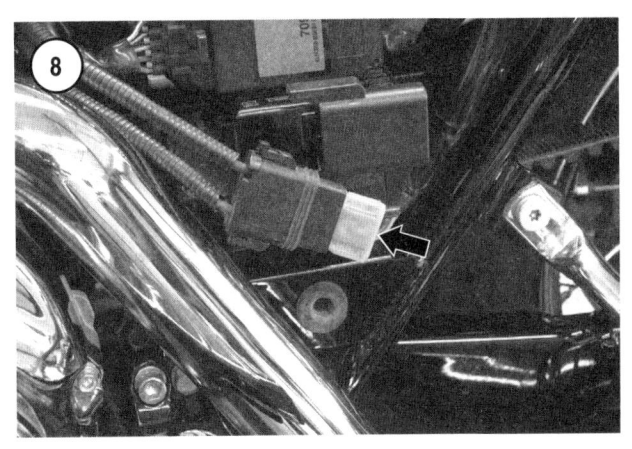

1. EFI system relay
2. Spare fuse
3. Fuel pump fuse
4. ECM power fuse
5. Engine control fuse (HDI only)

Removal/Installation (2006-2007 Models)

The 40-amp Maxi-Fuse functions as the electrical system main fuse.

1. Remove the seat, the left side saddlebag and the left frame side cover as described in Chapter Seventeen.
2. Depress both latches (A, **Figure 2**) on the Maxi-Fuse holder, slide the holder (B) toward the rear and disengage the tongue from groove on the fuse holder.
3. Press both latches together, and pull the cover from the fuse holder.
4. Pull the Maxi-Fuse (**Figure 8**) from the fuse holder.
5. Install the Maxi-Fuse into the holder and press it in until it bottoms. Install the cover onto the holder.
6. Install the holder tongue onto the groove on the fuse holder.
7. Install the left saddlebag, the left frame side cover and the seat as described in Chapter Seventeen.

Removal/Installation (2008-2009 Models)

The 40-amp Maxi-Fuse functions as the electrical system main fuse.

1. Remove the seat, the left side saddlebag and the left frame side cover as described in Chapter Seventeen.
2. Pull the Maxi-Fuse straight out from the fuse holder.

3. Install the Maxi-Fuse into the holder and press it in until it bottoms.
4. Install the left side saddlebag, the left frame side cover and the seat as described in Chapter Seventeen.

BATTERY

NOTE
Always disarm the optional security system (TSSM/HFSM) before disconnecting the battery or before pulling the Maxi-Fuse so the siren will not sound.

A sealed, maintenance-free battery is installed on all models. The battery electrolyte level cannot be serviced. When replacing the battery, use a sealed type; do not install a non-sealed battery as the electrolyte will leak out. Never attempt to remove the sealing caps from the top of the battery. The battery does not require periodic electrolyte inspection or refilling.

Disconnect the negative (ground) cable first, and then the positive cable, when removing the battery. This minimizes the chance of a tool shorting to ground when disconnecting the battery positive cable.

Refer to Chapter Two for charging system troubleshooting.

Negative Cable

Some of the component replacement procedures and test procedures require disconnecting the negative battery cable as a safety precaution.
1. Remove the seat as described in Chapter Seventeen.
2. On 2008-2009 models, partially remove the electrical caddy as described in this chapter.
3. Remove the bolt (**Figure 9**) securing the negative cable to the battery. Move the cable away from the battery to avoid making accidental contact with the battery post.
4. Connect the negative cable onto the battery, and then reinstall the bolt. Tighten the bolt to 60-96 in.-lb. (6.8-10.9 N•m).
5. On 2008-2009 models, install the electrical caddy as described in this chapter.
6. Install the seat as described in Chapter Seventeen.

Cable Service

To ensure good electrical contact between the battery and the electrical cables, the cables must be clean and free of corrosion.
1. If the electrical cable terminals are badly corroded, disconnect them from the motorcycle's electrical system.
2. Thoroughly clean each connector with a wire brush and a baking soda solution. Rinse thoroughly with clean water and wipe dry with a clean cloth.
3. After cleaning, apply a thin layer of dielectric grease to the battery terminals before reattaching the cables.

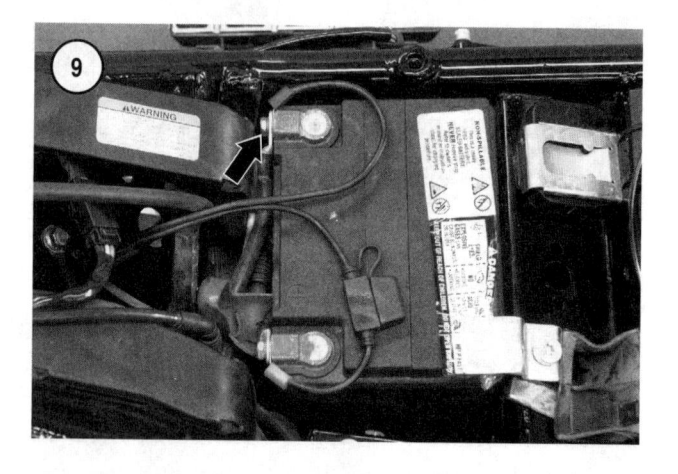

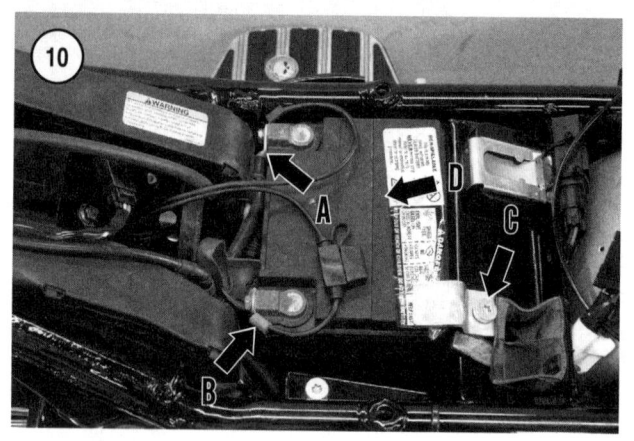

4. Reconnect the electrical cables to the motorcycle's electrical system if they were disconnected.
5. After connecting the electrical cables, apply a light coat of dielectric grease to the connectors to retard corrosion.

Removal/Installation

1. Turn the ignition switch off.
2. Remove the seat as described in Chapter Seventeen.
3A. On 2006-2007 models, perform the following:
   a. Disconnect the negative battery cable (A, **Figure 10**) from the battery.
   b. Remove the bolt and disconnect the positive battery cable (B, **Figure 10**) from the battery.
   c. Remove the bolt (C, **Figure 10**) securing the battery hold-down and remove the hold-down.
   d. Carefully lift the battery (D, **Figure 10**) up and out of the frame.
3B. On 2008-2009 models, perform the following:
   a. Release the HFSM antenna tongue from the groove on the front of the ECM top caddy. Move the HFSM antenna and wiring out of the way.
   b. Remove the bolt(s) securing the ECM top caddy to the frame.
   c. Carefully lift the ECM top caddy up from the battery and rotate the top caddy, ECM, and the ECM wiring harness toward the right and set it on the upper right frame tube.

ELECTRICAL SYSTEM 441

b. Install the bolt(s) securing the ECM top caddy to the frame. Tighten the bolt(s) to 15-20 ft.-lb. (20.3-27.1 N•m).
c. Install the HFSM antenna tongue onto the groove on the front of the ECM top caddy.

11. After connecting the electrical cables, apply a light coating of dielectric grease to the electrical terminals of the battery to retard corrosion and decomposition of the terminals.
12. Install the seat as described in Chapter Seventeen.

Inspection

WARNING
Electrolyte is extremely harmful to the eyes. Always wear safety glasses while working with a battery. If electrolyte gets into the eyes, call a physician immediately. Force the eyes open, and flood them with cool, clean water for approximately 15 minutes.

The battery electrolyte level cannot be serviced in a maintenance-free battery. *Never* attempt to remove the sealing bar cap from the top of the battery. The battery does not require periodic electrolyte inspection or water refilling. Refer to the label (A, **Figure 11**) on top of the battery.

Even though the battery is sealed, protect eyes, skin and clothing. The corrosive electrolyte may have spilled out and can cause severe chemical skin burns and permanent injury. The battery case may be cracked and leaking electrolyte. If electrolyte is spilled or splashed on clothing or skin, immediately neutralize it with a baking soda and water solution, and flush with an abundance of clean water.

1. Remove the battery as described in this section. Do not clean the battery while it is mounted in the frame.
2. Set the battery on a stack of newspapers or shop cloths to protect the surface of the workbench.
3. Check the entire battery case (**Figure 12**) for cracks or other damage. If the battery case is warped, discolored or has a raised top, the battery has been overcharged and overheated.
4. Check the battery terminal bolts, spacers and nuts (B, **Figure 11**) for corrosion or damage. Clean parts thoroughly with a baking soda and water solution. Replace corroded or damaged parts.
5. If the top of the battery is corroded, clean it with a stiff bristle brush using the baking soda and water solution.
6. Check the battery cable ends for corrosion and damage. If corrosion is minor, clean the battery cable ends with a stiff wire brush. Replace severely coroded or damaged cables.
7. Perform the open circuit voltage test (this section).
8. Inspect the battery case for contamination or damage. Clean it with a baking soda and water solution.
9. Install the battery as described in this section.

Open Circuit Voltage Test

1. Remove the battery as described in this section.
2. Connect a digital voltmeter between the battery negative and positive terminals. Note the following:

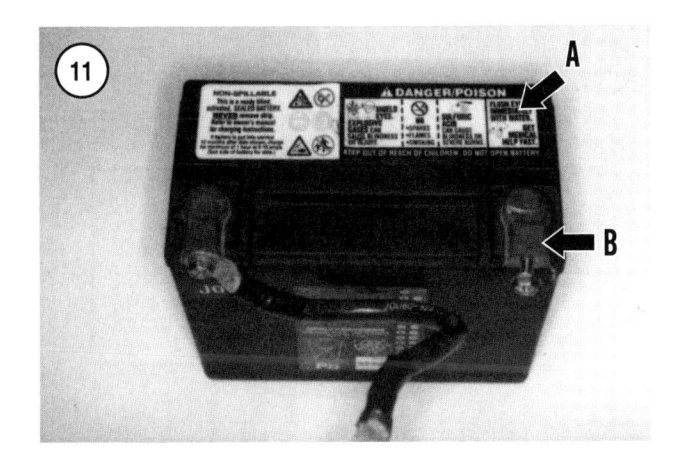

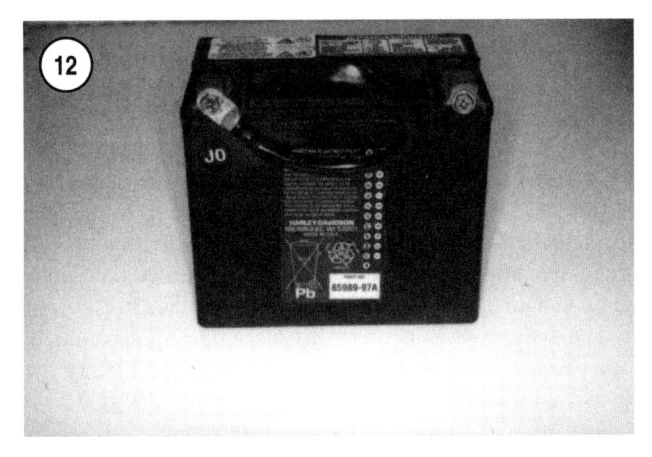

d. Disconnect the negative battery cable from the battery.
e. Remove the bolt and disconnect the battery positive cable from the battery.
f. Unfold the lifting strap. Grasp the lifting strap loop end and lift the battery up sufficiently until a firm grip is possible under the battery.
g. Remove the battery up and out of the frame.
h. Release the lifting strap.

4. Inspect the battery tray for corrosion or damage. Clean or replace it if necessary.
5. On 2008-2009 models, first run the lifting strap toward the rear and down the center of the battery tray. Then, run it up and over the frame cross member.
6. Position the battery with the cable terminals facing toward the front of the frame.
7. Reinstall the battery onto the battery tray in the frame.
8. Connect the positive cable (B, **Figure 10**) onto the battery. Tighten the terminal bolt to 60-96 in.-lb. (6.8-10.9 N•m).
9. Connect the negative cable (A, **Figure 10**) onto the battery. Tighten the terminal bolt to 60-96 in.-lb. (6.8-10.9 N•m).
10A. On 2006-2007 models, install battery hold-down and the bolt (C, **Figure 10**). Tighten the hold-down bolt to 15-20 ft.-lb. (20.3-27.1 N•m).
10B. On 2008-2009 models, perform the following:
   a. Correctly reposition the ECM top caddy onto the battery.

a. If the battery voltage is 12.7 volts (at 68° F [20° C]), or greater, the battery is fully charged. At 12.6 volts, it is 75% charged.
b. If the battery voltage is 12.0 to 12.5 volts (at 68° F [20° C]), or lower, the battery is undercharged and requires charging.

3. If the battery is undercharged, charge it as described in this section. Then, test the charging system as described in Chapter Two.

Load Test

A load test checks the battery's performance under full current load and is the best indication of battery condition.

A battery load tester is required for this procedure. When using a load tester, follow the manufacturer's instructions. **Figure 13** shows a typical load tester and battery arrangement.

1. Remove the battery from the motorcycle as described in this section.

NOTE
Let the battery stand for at least one hour if the battery has been recently charged before performing this test.

2. The battery must be fully charged before beginning this test. If necessary, charge the battery as described in this section.

WARNING
The battery load tester must be turned off prior to connecting or disconnecting the test cables to the battery. Otherwise, a spark could cause the battery to explode.

CAUTION
To prevent battery damage during load testing, do not load test a discharged battery. Performing a load test on a discharged battery can cause permanent battery damage. Do not load test the battery for more than 20 seconds.

3. Load test the battery as follows:
   a. Connect the load tester cables to the battery following the tester manufacturer's instructions.
   b. Load the battery at 50% of the cold cranking amperage (CCA) or 135 amperes.
   c. After 15 seconds, the voltage reading with the load still applied should be 9.6 volts or higher at 70° F (21° C). Now quickly remove the load and turn the tester OFF.

4. If the voltage reading is 9.6 volts or higher, the battery output capacity is good. If the reading is below 9.6 volts, the battery is defective.
5. With the tester OFF, disconnect the cables from the battery.
6. Install the battery as described in this section.

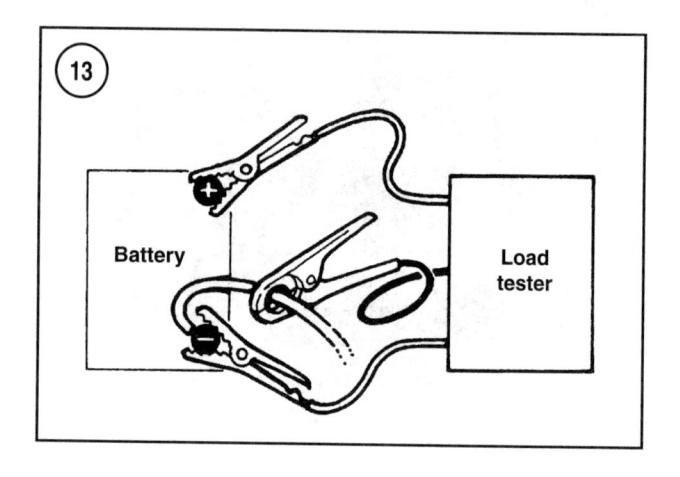

Charging

Refer to *Battery Initialization* (this section) if the battery is new.

To recharge a maintenance-free battery, a digital voltmeter and a charger with an adjustable amperage output are required. If this equipment is not available, have the battery charged by a repair shop with the proper equipment. Excessive voltage and amperage from an unregulated charger can damage the battery and shorten service life.

The battery should only self-discharge approximately one percent of its given capacity each day. If a battery not in use, without any loads connected, loses its charge within a week after charging, the battery is defective.

If the motorcycle is not used for long periods of time, an automatic battery charger with variable voltage and amperage outputs is recommended for optimum battery service life.

WARNING
During charging, highly explosive hydrogen gas is released from the battery. Only charge the battery in a well-ventilated area away from open flames, including pilot lights on appliances. Do not allow smoking in the area. Never check the charge of the battery by arcing across the terminals; the resulting spark can ignite the hydrogen gas.

CAUTION
Always disconnect the battery cables from the battery. If the cables are left connected during the charging procedure, the charger may damage the diodes within the voltage regulator/rectifier.

1. Remove the battery from the motorcycle as described in this section.
2. Set the battery on a stack of newspapers or shop cloths to protect the surface of the workbench.
3. Make sure the battery charger is turned off prior to attaching the charger leads to the battery.
4. Connect the positive charger lead to the positive battery terminal and the negative charger lead to the negative battery terminal.

ELECTRICAL SYSTEM

BATTERY TRAY (2006-2007 MODELS)

1. Bolt
2. Hold down bracket
3. Pad
4. Battery tray
5. Bolt
6. Cap (thread protector)
7. Cable clip
8. Boot (positive cable)
9. Battery negative cable (battery to ground)
10. Battery positive cable
11. Battery terminal cover
12. Cap (thread protector)

5. Set the charger at 12 volts. If the output of the charger is variable, select the low setting.

6. The charging time depends on the discharged condition of the battery. Refer to **Table 2** for the suggested charging time. Normally, a battery should be charged at 1/10th its given capacity.

CAUTION
If the battery emits an excessive amount of gas during the charging cycle, decrease the charge rate. If the battery becomes hotter than 110° F (43° C) during the charging cycle, turn the charger off and allow the battery to cool. Then continue with a reduced charging rate and continue to monitor the battery temperature.

7. Turn the charger on.
8. After the battery has been charged for the predetermined time, turn the charger off, disconnect the leads and measure the battery voltage. Refer to the following:
   a. If the battery voltage is 12.7 volts (at 68° F [20° C]), or greater, the battery is fully charged.
   b. If the battery voltage is 12.5 volts (at 68° F [20° C]), or lower, the battery is undercharged and requires additional charging time.
9. If the battery remains stable for one hour, the battery is charged.
10. Install the battery as described in this section.

Battery Initialization

A new battery must be *fully* charged to a specific gravity of 1.260-1.280 before installation. To bring the battery to a full charge, give it an initial charge. Using a new battery without an initial charge will cause permanent battery damage. The battery will never be able to hold more than an 80% charge. Charging a new battery after it has been used will not bring its charge to 100%. When purchasing a new battery, verify its charge status.

NOTE
Recycle the old battery. *When a new battery is purchased, turn in the old one for recycling. Most motorcycle dealerships will accept the old battery in trade for a new one. Never place an old battery in the household trash since it is illegal, in most states, to place any acid or lead (heavy metal) in landfills.*

BATTERY TRAY

Removal/Installation
(2006-2007 Models)

Refer to **Figure 14**.

1. Remove the battery from the motorcycle as described in this chapter.
2. Remove both frame side covers as described in Chapter Seventeen.
3. Remove the electrical bracket on the right side as described in this chapter.

NOTE
Do not disconnect the components from any wiring harness. Move them out of the way.

BATTERY TRAY (2008 MODELS)

1. Bolt
2. ECM top caddy
3. Bolt
4. Strap
5. Spacer
6. Battery tray
7. Battery negative cable (battery to ground)
8. Boot (battery positive)
9. Battery positive cable
10. Nut
11. Battery terminal cover

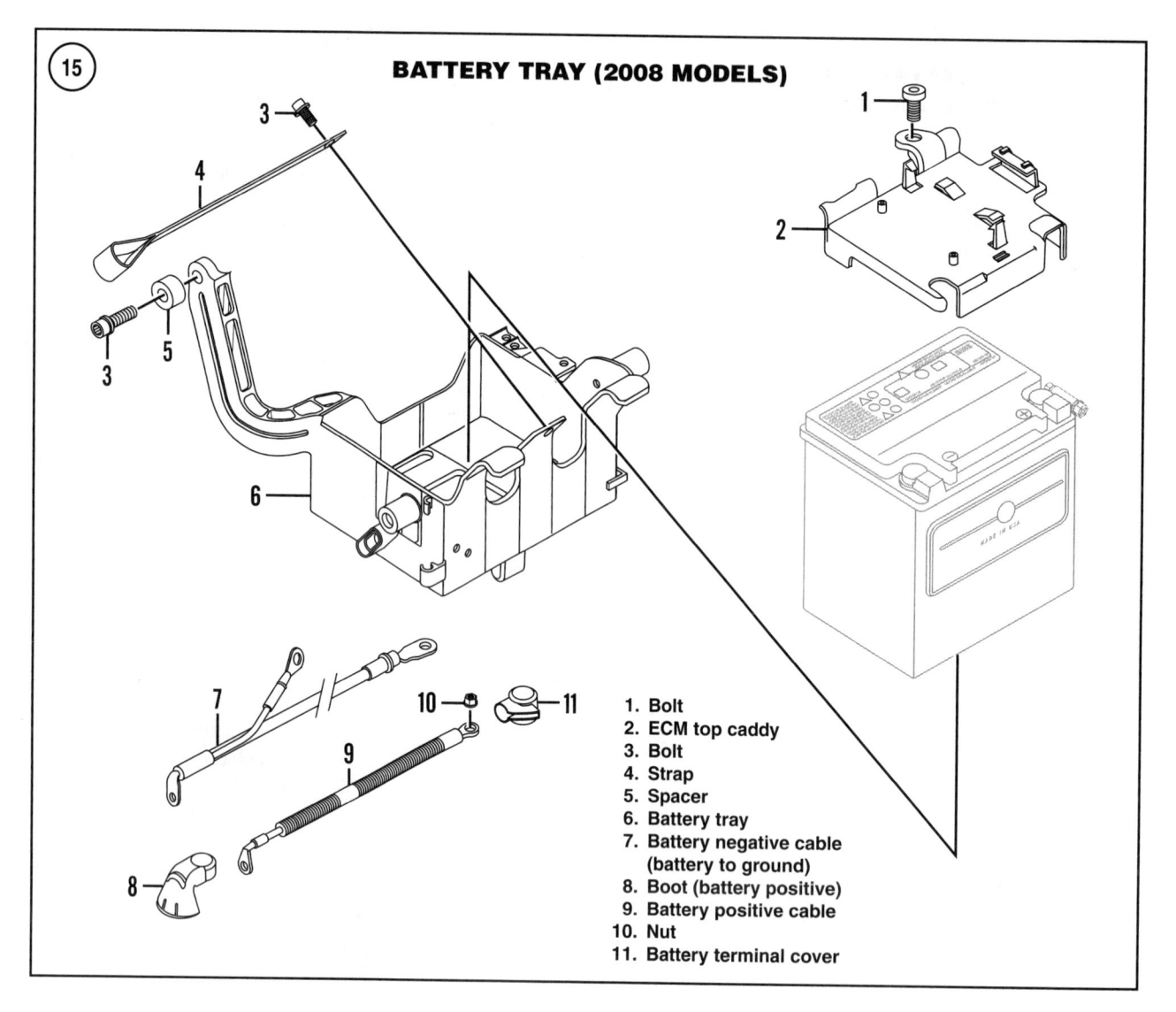

4. Remove the Maxi-Fuse holder and fuse block from the battery tray on the left side as described in this chapter.
5. On cruise control models, remove the cruise control module on the left side as described in Chapter Sixteen.
6. Remove the screws securing the battery tray, and then remove the tray.
7. Install by reversing the removal steps. Tighten the battery tray mounting screws securely. Tighten the remaining fasteners to the specification in **Table 5**.

Removal/Installation (2008 Models)

Refer to **Figure 15**.

1. Remove the battery from the motorcycle as described in this chapter.
2. Remove both frame side covers as described in Chapter Seventeen.
3. Remove both saddlebags as described in Chapter Seventeen.
4. On the left side, remove the screw and spacer securing the battery tray to the frame.
5. Remove the left side electrical caddy as described in this chapter, on models so equipped.
6. On FLHR and FLHRC models, pull the 4-pin Packard connector anchor pin from the hole in the left side of the battery tray.
7. Loosen the middle finger screw, and lifting strap securing the battery tray to the frame cross member.
8. Remove the right side caddy as described in this chapter, on models so equipped.
9. Remove the spring clip securing the Turn Signal Security Module and remove it from the opening on the right side frame cross member.
10. Place a towel over the rear fender to protect the finish.
11. On models with HFSM, withdraw the HFSM antenna and jumper harness out through the empty slot in the rubber boot below the frame cross member on the left side. Pull it back up and through the right side opening and lay the jumper harness across the rear fender.
12. Pull up on the left finger of the battery tray, and work the main power cable to the Maxi-Fuse holder from the inboard side to the outboard side of the tray.

ELECTRICAL SYSTEM

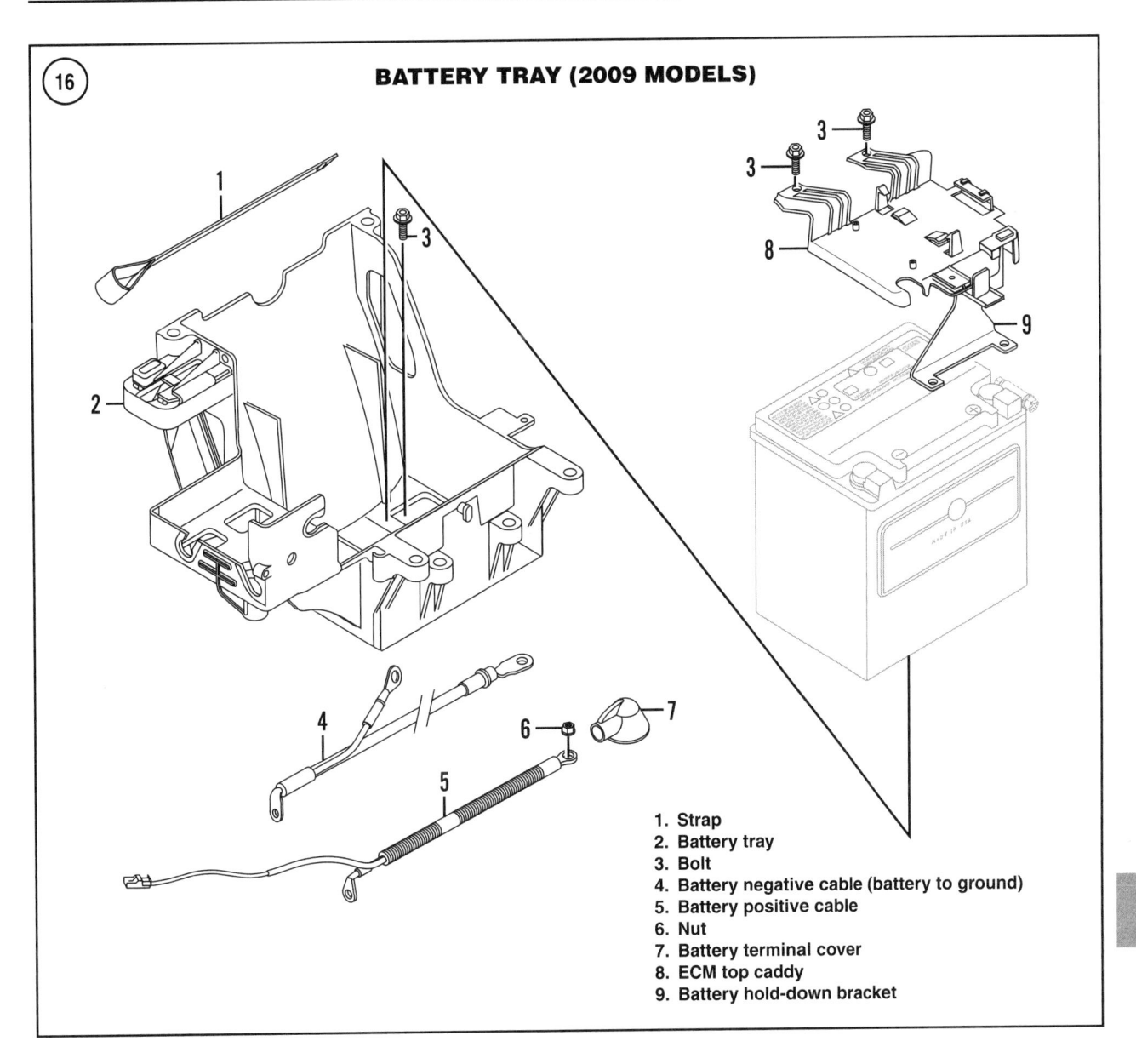

16 **BATTERY TRAY (2009 MODELS)**

1. Strap
2. Battery tray
3. Bolt
4. Battery negative cable (battery to ground)
5. Battery positive cable
6. Nut
7. Battery terminal cover
8. ECM top caddy
9. Battery hold-down bracket

13. Feed the battery positive cable forward under the frame cross member and toward the starter.
14. Remove the flange nut from the rear ground stud on the left side of the frame backbone. Remove the chassis ground ring terminal from the stud.
15. Pull battery ground cable and the chassis ground ring into the battery tray, forward under the frame cross-member, and toward the starter.
16. Pull the fuel overflow hose forward to the front frame down tube, and then up and out of the way, on models so equipped.
17. On ABS-equipped models, carefully rotate the ABS module outward and release the rear brake caliper hose(s) from the battery cable channels.
18. Remove the charcoal canister from the base of the battery tray as described in Chapter Nine, on models so equipped.
19. Check that all wiring and components are removed from the battery tray.

20. Slowly rotate the battery tray *counterclockwise* until the three fingers at the front of the tray are pointing up.
21. Move the battery tray toward the rear until the fingers are under the rear frame cross member.
22. Pull the battery tray out through the right side opening.
23. Inspect the battery tray for damage and/or corrosion. Thoroughly clean the tray and replace it if necessary.
24. Install by reversing the removal steps. Tighten the rear ground strap flange nut to 50-90 in.-lb. (5.7-10.2 N•m). Tighten all of the remaining screws securely.

Removal/Installation (2009 Models)

Refer to **Figure 16**.
1. Remove the battery from the motorcycle as described in this chapter.
2. Remove both frame side covers as described in Chapter Seventeen.

446   CHAPTER ELEVEN

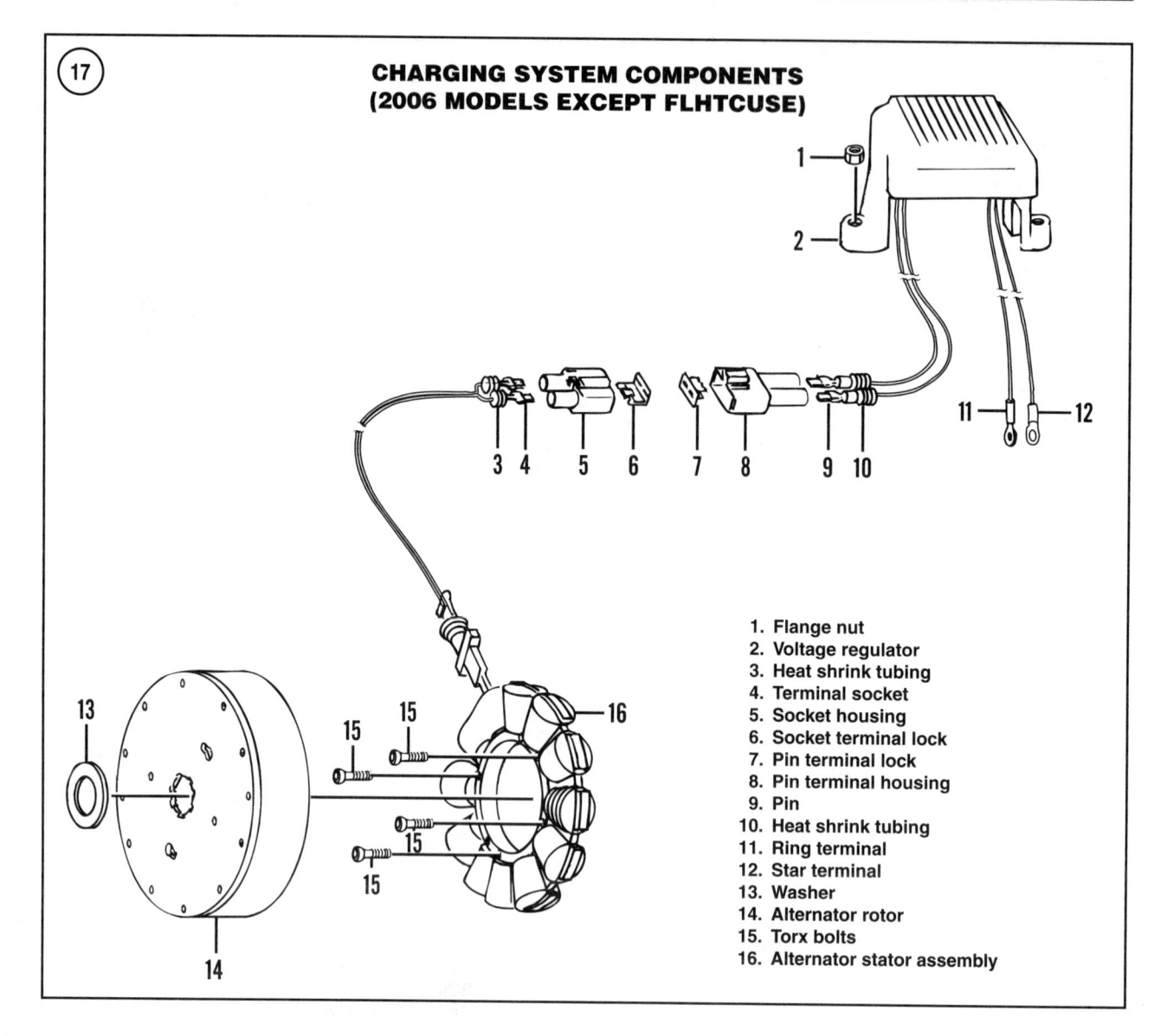

⑰ CHARGING SYSTEM COMPONENTS (2006 MODELS EXCEPT FLHTCUSE)

1. Flange nut
2. Voltage regulator
3. Heat shrink tubing
4. Terminal socket
5. Socket housing
6. Socket terminal lock
7. Pin terminal lock
8. Pin terminal housing
9. Pin
10. Heat shrink tubing
11. Ring terminal
12. Star terminal
13. Washer
14. Alternator rotor
15. Torx bolts
16. Alternator stator assembly

3. Remove both saddlebags as described in Chapter Seventeen.
4. Remove the rear wheel as described in Chapter Twelve.
5. Remove the left side electrical caddy as described in this chapter.
6. Disconnect the Tour-Pak electrical connectors if routed through side of battery tray, on models so equipped.
7. Remove the ignition coil as described in this chapter.
8. Remove the ABS module, on models so equipped.
9. Pull the Turn Signal Security Module away from the battery tray, do not disconnect it.
10. Remove the four bolts securing the battery tray to the frame.
11. Carefully pull the battery tray toward the rear and remove it through the frame.
12. Inspect the battery tray for damage and/or corrosion. Thoroughly clean the tray and replace it if necessary.
13. Install by reversing the removal steps. Tighten the four battery tray mounting bolts to 72-96 in.-lb. (8.1-10.9 N•m).

CHARGING SYSTEM

Refer to **Figures 17-19**.

The charging system consists of the battery, alternator and a voltage regulator/rectifier. Alternating current generated by the alternator is rectified to direct current. The voltage regulator maintains the voltage to the battery and provides power for additional electrical loads, such as the lights and ignition system, at a constant voltage regardless of variations in engine speed and load.

A malfunction in the charging system generally causes the battery to remain undercharged. To prevent damage to the alternator and the regulator/rectifier when testing and repairing the charging system, note the following precautions:

1. Always disarm the optional TSSM/HFSM security system before disconnecting the battery or Maxi-Fuse so the siren will not sound.
2. Always disconnect the negative battery cable, as described in this chapter, before removing a component from the charging system.

ELECTRICAL SYSTEM

⑱ CHARGING SYSTEM COMPONENTS (2007-2009 MODELS)

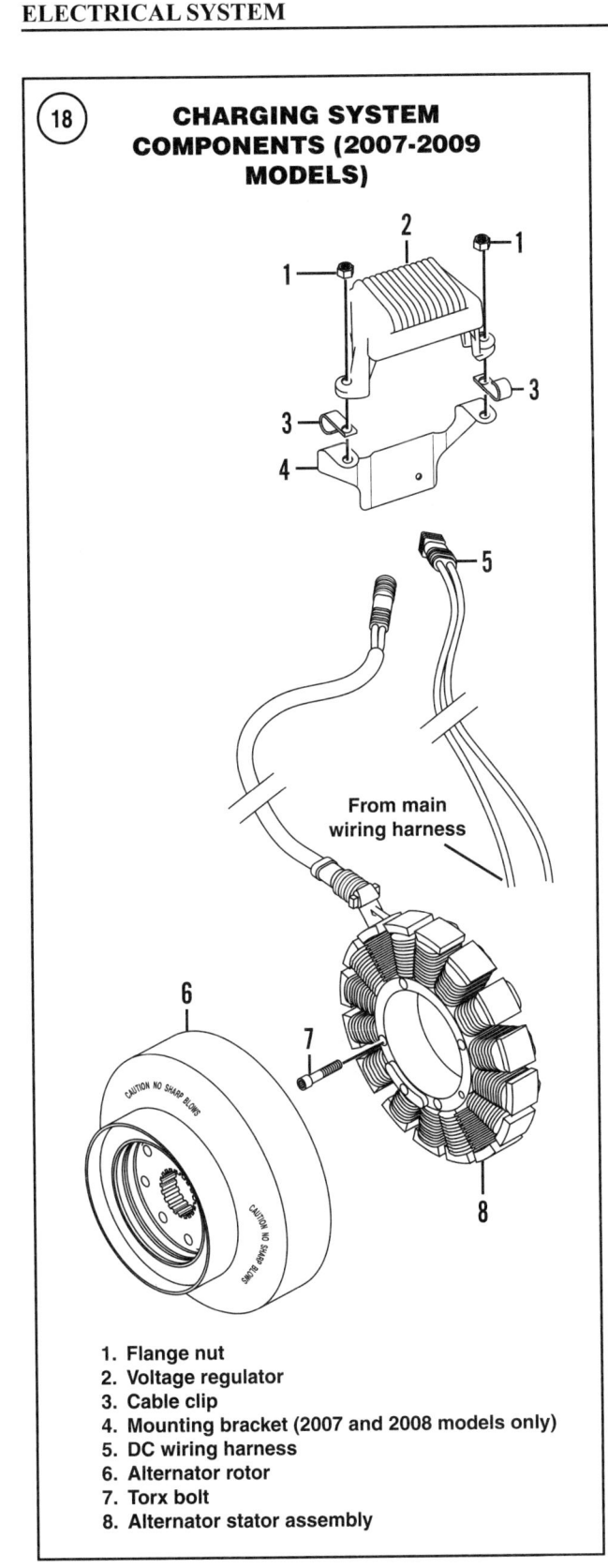

1. Flange nut
2. Voltage regulator
3. Cable clip
4. Mounting bracket (2007 and 2008 models only)
5. DC wiring harness
6. Alternator rotor
7. Torx bolt
8. Alternator stator assembly

⑲ CHARGING SYSTEM COMPONENTS (2006 FLHTCUSE MODELS)

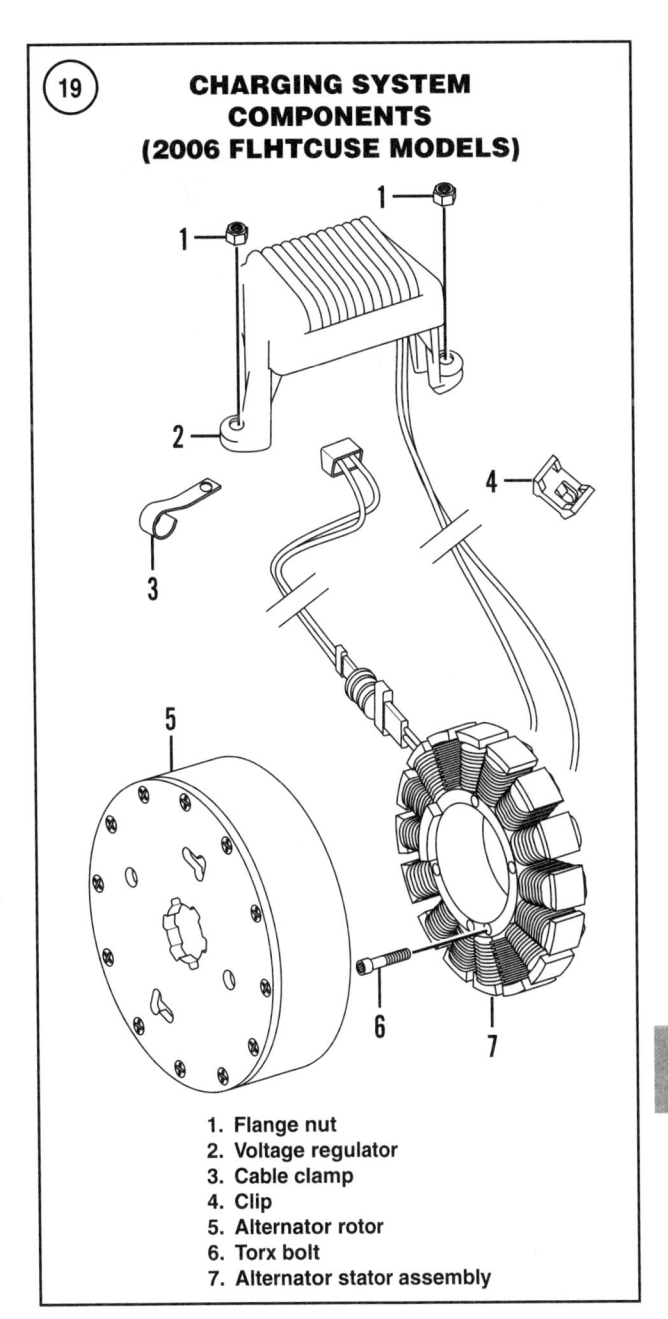

1. Flange nut
2. Voltage regulator
3. Cable clamp
4. Clip
5. Alternator rotor
6. Torx bolt
7. Alternator stator assembly

3. To charge the battery, remove it from the motorcycle and recharge as described in this chapter.
4. Inspect the battery case (**Figure 12**). Look for bulges or cracks in the case, leaking electrolyte or corrosion build-up.
5. Check the charging system wiring for signs of chafing, deterioration or other damage.
6. Check the wiring for corroded or loose connections. Clean, tighten or reconnect wiring as required. Replace any damaged parts.

Inspection

A malfunction in the charging system generally causes the battery to remain undercharged. Perform the following visual inspections to determine the cause of the problem. If the visual inspection proves satisfactory, test the charging system as described in Chapter Two.

1. Make sure the battery cables are properly connected to the battery terminals and that the negative cable is properly connected to the frame ground.
2. Inspect the terminals for loose or corroded connections. Tighten or clean them as required.

3. Inspect the battery case. Look for bulges or cracks in the case, leaking electrolyte or corrosion buildup.
4. Carefully check all connections at the alternator to make sure they are clean and tight.
5. Check the circuit wiring for corroded or loose connections. Clean, tighten or connect wiring as required.

ALTERNATOR

WARNING
*All models have a laminated high-output rotor that is equipped with **very strong** magnets. A rotor puller (H-D part No. HD-41771), or an equivalent, must be used for rotor removal and installation. During installation, the magnets will quickly pull the rotor into place, trapping fingers between the rotor (**Figure 20**) and the sharp edge of the crankcase.*

NOTE
Always disarm the optional security system (TSSM/HFSM) before disconnecting the battery or before pulling the Maxi-Fuse so the siren will not sound.

Rotor Removal/Installation
(2006 Models)

Refer to **Figure 17** and **Figure 19**.
1. Disconnect the negative battery cable as described in this chapter.
2. Remove the primary chaincase cover and housing as described in Chapter Six.
3. Remove the primary chain, clutch assembly, chain tensioner assembly and compensating sprocket components as an assembly (Chapter Six).
4. If still in place, remove the shaft extension and washer from the crankshaft.
5. Assemble the rotor puller (**Figure 21**) or use a generic bearing puller and two 5/16 in. × 3 in. coarse thread bolts.
6. Install the rotor puller over the crankshaft and against the rotor.

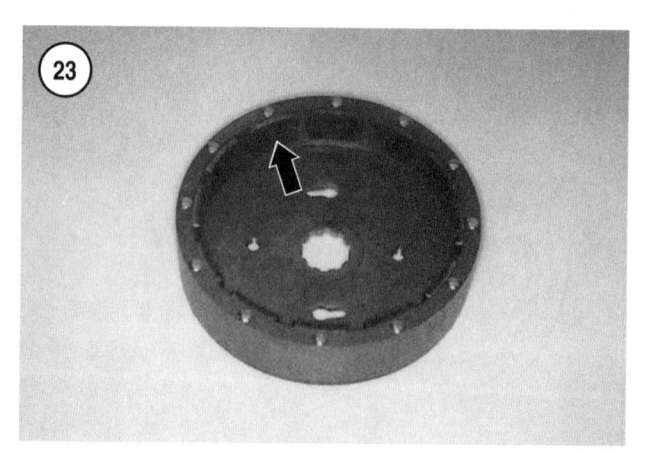

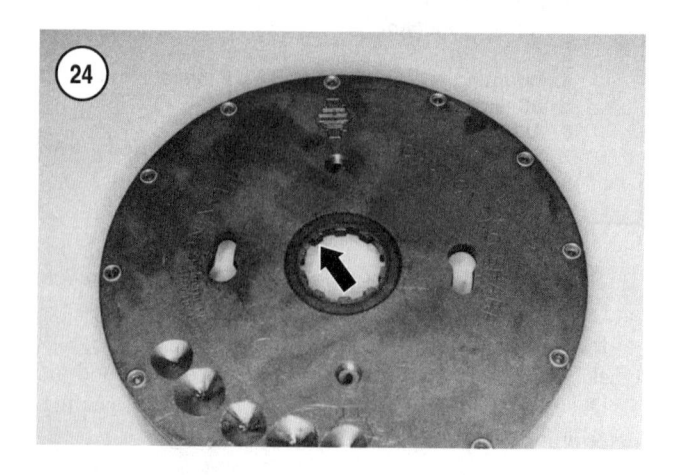

ELECTRICAL SYSTEM

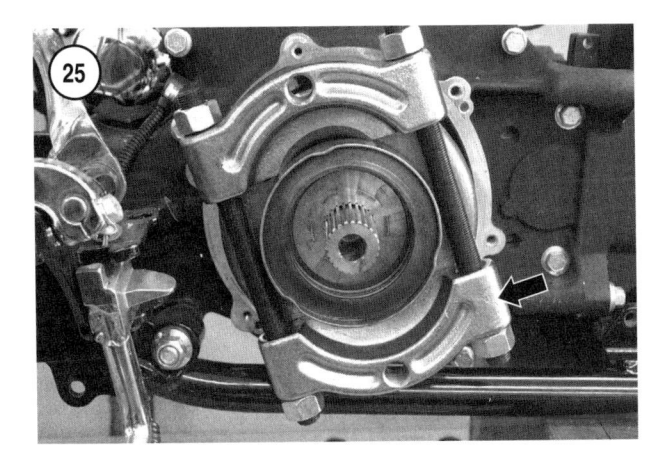

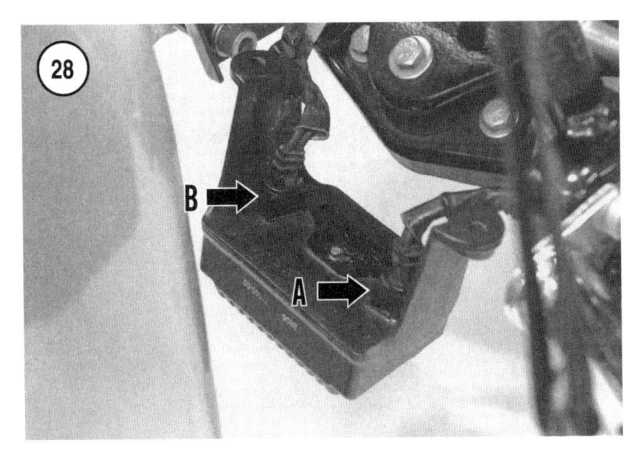

7. Secure the rotor puller to the rotor with the two bolts (A, **Figure 22**).
8. Slowly turn the center bolt (B, **Figure 22**) and withdraw the rotor from the stator coils.
9. Remove the rotor and puller. Separate the puller from the rotor.
10. Inspect the rotor magnets (**Figure 23**) for small bolts, washers or other metal debris that may have been picked up by the magnets. These small metal bits can cause severe damage to the alternator stator assembly.
11. Check the inner splines (**Figure 24**) for wear or damage. Replace the rotor if necessary.
12. Install by reversing the removal steps. Align the rotor splines with the crankshaft splines.

Rotor Removal/Installation (2007-2009 Models)

Refer to **Figure 18**.
1. Disconnect the negative battery cable as described in this chapter.
2. Remove the primary chaincase cover and housing as described in Chapter Six.
3. Remove the primary chain, clutch assembly, chain tensioner assembly and compensating sprocket components as an assembly (Chapter Six).
4. If still in place, remove the shaft extension and washer from the crankshaft.
5. Install a large bearing puller (**Figure 25**) or strap-type flywheel holder (**Figure 26**) onto the rotor.
6. Pull on the bearing puller or flywheel holder and remove the rotor from the crankshaft.
7. Separate the tool from the rotor.
8. Inspect the rotor magnets for small bolts, washers or other metal debris that may have been picked up by the magnets. These small metal bits can cause severe damage to the alternator stator assembly.
9. Check the inner splines for wear or damage. Replace the rotor if necessary.
10. Install by reversing the removal steps. Align the rotor splines with the crankshaft splines.

Stator Removal

NOTE
Some of the photographs in this procedure are shown with the engine removed to better illustrate the steps.

1. Remove the rotor as described in this section.
2. Remove the flange nuts (A, **Figure 27**) securing the voltage regulator to the mounting bracket or frame.
3. Lift the voltage regulator (B, **Figure 27**) off the studs, release the wiring harness from the cable clip on the left side of the voltage regulator, and lower the regulator.
4. Disconnect the round 3-pin stator connector (A, **Figure 28**) from the base of the voltage regulator.

5. Remove the four Torx screws (**Figure 29**) securing the stator assembly to the crankcase. New Torx screws must be used on installation.

6. Insert a small awl (A, **Figure 30**), or screwdriver, into the space between the grommet and the crankcase and carefully lift the capped rib (B) on the grommet away from the crankcase opening (C). Tilt the awl slightly and squirt isopropyl alcohol or glass cleaner into the opening. Repeat this at one or two additional locations around the opening.

7. Push on the capped rib (B, **Figure 30**) from the outside of the opening. Place needlenose pliers on the cable stop, and withdraw the grommet through the crankcase bore. Rock the grommet back and forth to ease removal if necessary. Be careful not to damage the grommet ribs if the stator is going to be reused.

8. Remove the stator assembly.

Inspection

1. Inspect the stator mounting surface on the crankcase for any oil residue that may have passed by a damaged oil seal. Clean off if necessary.

2. Inspect the stator wires (A, **Figure 31**) for fraying or damage.

3. Inspect the rubber grommet (B, **Figure 31**) for deterioration or hardness.

4. Check the stator electrical connector pins for corrosion, looseness or damage.

Stator Installation

1. Thoroughly clean the grommet with isopropyl alcohol so the ribs are free of oil residue and debris.

2. Apply a light coat of glass cleaner to the wiring harness grommet to help ease it into the crankcase boss receptacle.

NOTE
Figure 32 is shown with the engine removed to better illustrate the step.

3. Insert the electrical harness and grommet into the crankcase boss receptacle and carefully pull it through until the grommet is correctly seated (**Figure 32**).

CAUTION
New Torx screws (T27) must be installed. The threadlock originally applied to the Torx screws is sufficient for one time use only. If a used Torx screw is installed it can work loose and cause engine damage.

4. Move the stator into position on the crankcase and install four *new* Torx screws (**Figure 29**). Tighten the stator screws (T27) to 55-75 in.-lb. (6.2-8.5 N•m).

5. Insert the electrical harness under the front engine stabilizer link and then forward along the outboard side of the voltage regulator.

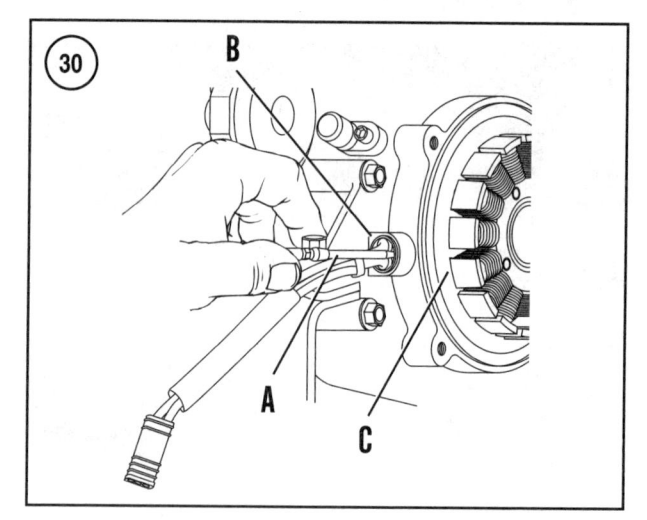

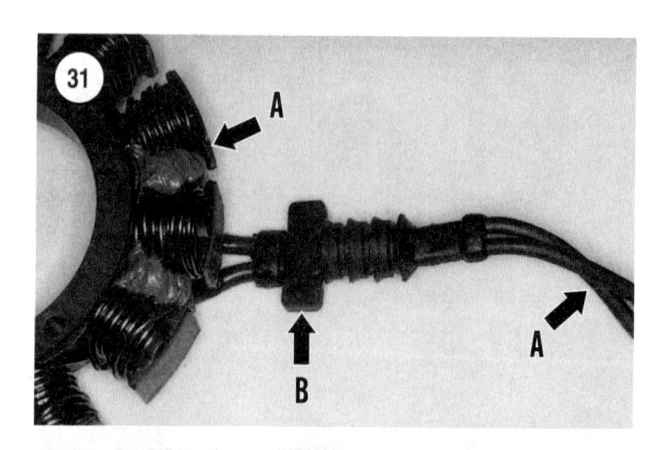

ELECTRICAL SYSTEM

33   **ENGINE SENSORS**   2007 models   2008-2009 models

1. Manifold abosolute pressure (MAP) sensor
2. Seal
3. Screw
4. Temperature manifold absolute pressure (TMAP) sensor
5. Engine temperature sensor
6. Crankshaft position (CKP) sensor
7. Screw
8. Oil pressure sender
9. Oil pressure switch
10. Elbow (models so equipped)

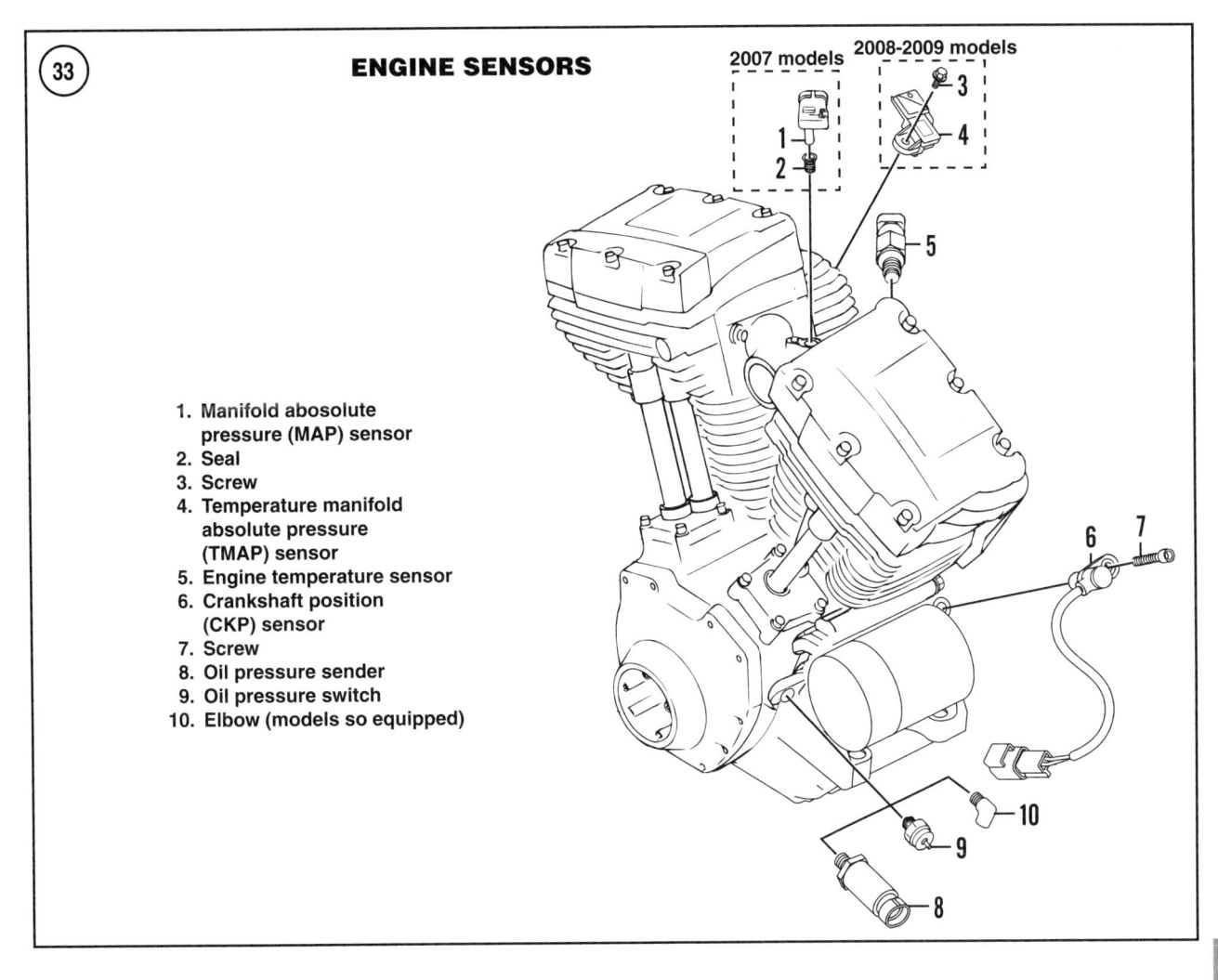

6. Secure the electrical harness in the cable clip under the left side of the voltage regulator. Remove all slack in the harness so it will not rub against the engine stabilizer link.
7. Connect the round 3-pin stator connector (A, **Figure 28**) onto the base of the voltage regulator. Push it on until it bottoms.
8. Move the voltage regulator (B, **Figure 27**) onto the mounting studs and install the flange nuts (A, **Figure 27**). Tighten the flange nuts to 70-100 in.-lb. (7.9-11.3 N•m).
9. Install the rotor as described in this section.

VOLTAGE REGULATOR

Removal/Installation

1. Disconnect the negative battery cable as described in this chapter.
2. Remove the flange nuts (A, **Figure 27**) securing the voltage regulator to the mounting bracket or frame.
3. Lift the voltage regulator (B, **Figure 27**) off the studs, release the wiring harness from the cable clip on the left side of the voltage regulator, and then turn it over.
4. Disconnect the round 3-pin stator connector (A, **Figure 28**) and the 2-pin square electrical connector (B) from the base of the voltage regulator.

5. Remove the voltage regulator from the frame.
6. Install by reversing the removal steps while noting the following:
   a. Install both electrical connectors onto the voltage regulator. Push them on until they click and lock into place.
   b. When installing the voltage regulator onto the lower frame member studs, move the electrical wires away from the studs. Make sure they are not pinched between frame member and the voltage regulator flange.
   c. Install the flange nuts (A, **Figure 27**) and tighten to 70-100 in.-lb. (7.9-11.3 N•m).

IGNITION SYSTEM

Operation

The ignition system consists of an ignition coil, two spark plugs, the ignition control module (ICM on carbureted models), electronic control module (ECM on fuel-injected models), crankshaft position (CKP) sensor, manifold absolute pressure (MAP or TMAP) sensor, intake air temperature (IAT) sensor, idle air control (IAC), engine temperature (ET) sensor and vehicles speed sensor (VSS). Refer to **Figure 33** for sensor locations on the engine. The remaining sensors are located on the intake manifold (carbureted models) or the induction module (fuel-injected models).

The ICM or ECM is located on the electrical bracket behind the right frame side cover (2006-2007 models) or on the electrical caddy (2008-2009 models). The ICM or ECM determines the spark advance for correct ignition timing based on signals from the IAT, ET, TP and O_2 sensors. The ignition system fires the spark plugs near top dead center for starting, and then varies the spark advance from 0° to 50° depending on engine speed, crankshaft position, and intake manifold pressure. It also regulates the low-voltage circuits between the battery and the ignition coil.

The ICM or ECM modules are not repairable and must be replaced if defective.

The crankshaft position (CKP) sensor is located in the front left side of the crankcase. The CKP sensor takes readings off the 30 teeth on the left side flywheel. There is a two-tooth wide gap in the rotor. This gap creates a reference point to determine engine speed so the ECM can regulate ignition timing. The gap can also be used as a reference point to establish TDC.

The MAP sensor is located on top of the intake manifold or induction module. This sensor monitors the intake manifold vacuum and sends this information to the ignition module (carbureted models) or electronic control module (EFI models). The module adjusts the ignition timing advance curve for maximum performance.

The bank angle sensor is an integral part of the turn signal/turn signal security module (TSM/TSSM/HFSM). The sensor consists of a small magnetic disc that rides within a V-shaped channel. If the motorcycle is tilted at a 45° angle for more than one second, the ignition system shuts off. Once the sensor is activated, the motorcycle must be uprighted and the ignition must be turned off, and then back on so the ignition system is operational and the engine can be restarted.

The ignition systems components are shown in **Figures 34-36**. When servicing the ignition system, refer to the wiring diagrams located on the CD inserted into the back cover of the manual. Refer to Chapter Two for trouble shooting procedures.

IGNITION COIL

NOTE
Always disarm the optional security system (TSSM/HFSM) before disconnecting the battery or before pulling the Maxi-Fuse so the siren will not sound.

Removal/Installation

2006-2008 models

1. Disconnect the negative battery cable as described in this chapter.

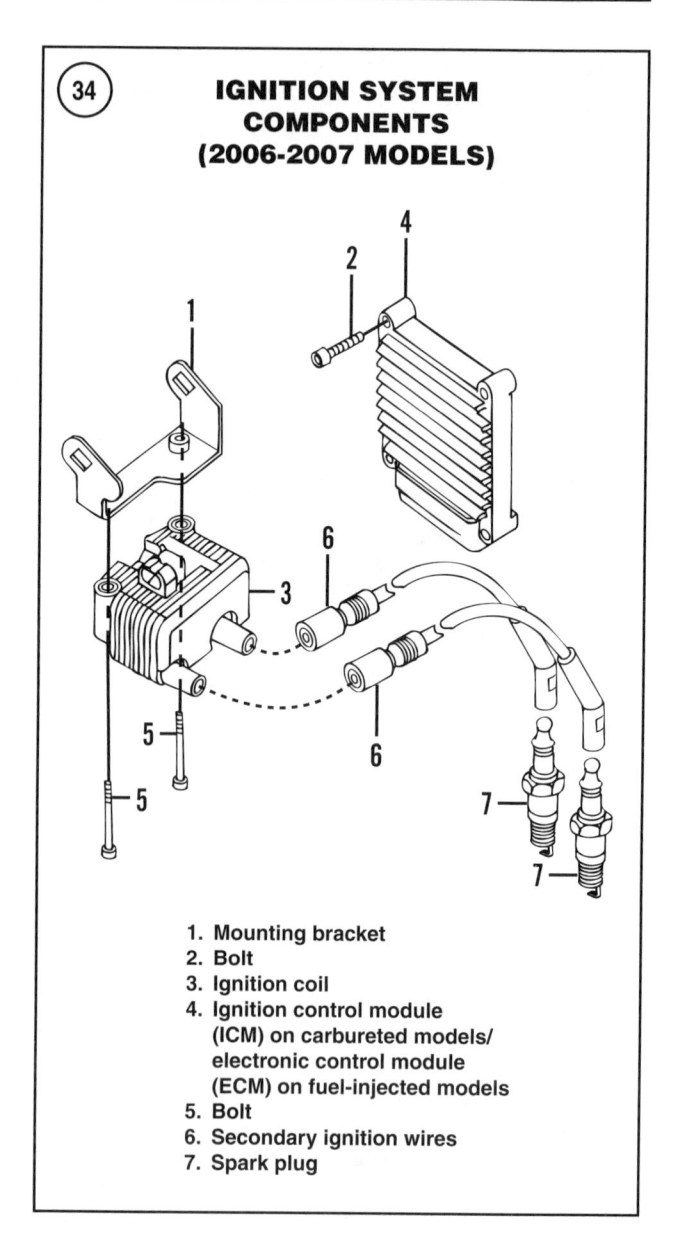

IGNITION SYSTEM COMPONENTS (2006-2007 MODELS)

1. Mounting bracket
2. Bolt
3. Ignition coil
4. Ignition control module (ICM) on carbureted models/ electronic control module (ECM) on fuel-injected models
5. Bolt
6. Secondary ignition wires
7. Spark plug

2. Remove the fuel tank as described in Chapter Nine or Chapter Ten.

NOTE
Label all wiring connectors prior to disconnecting them.

3. Disconnect the secondary cables (A, **Figure 37**) from both spark plugs.
4. Carefully remove the secondary leads from the clips (B, **Figure 37**) on the frame backbone.
5. Pull the sides of the ignition coil bracket (A, **Figure 38**) out to remove it from bosses (B) on the fuel tank mount.
6. Remove the ignition coil (C, **Figure 38**) and mount from the frame.
7. Remove the bolts securing the bracket to the ignition coil and separate the two parts, if necessary.
8. Install the ignition coil by reversing the removal steps. Tighten the coil-to-bracket bolts to 84-144 in.-lb. (9.5-16.3 N•m), if removed.

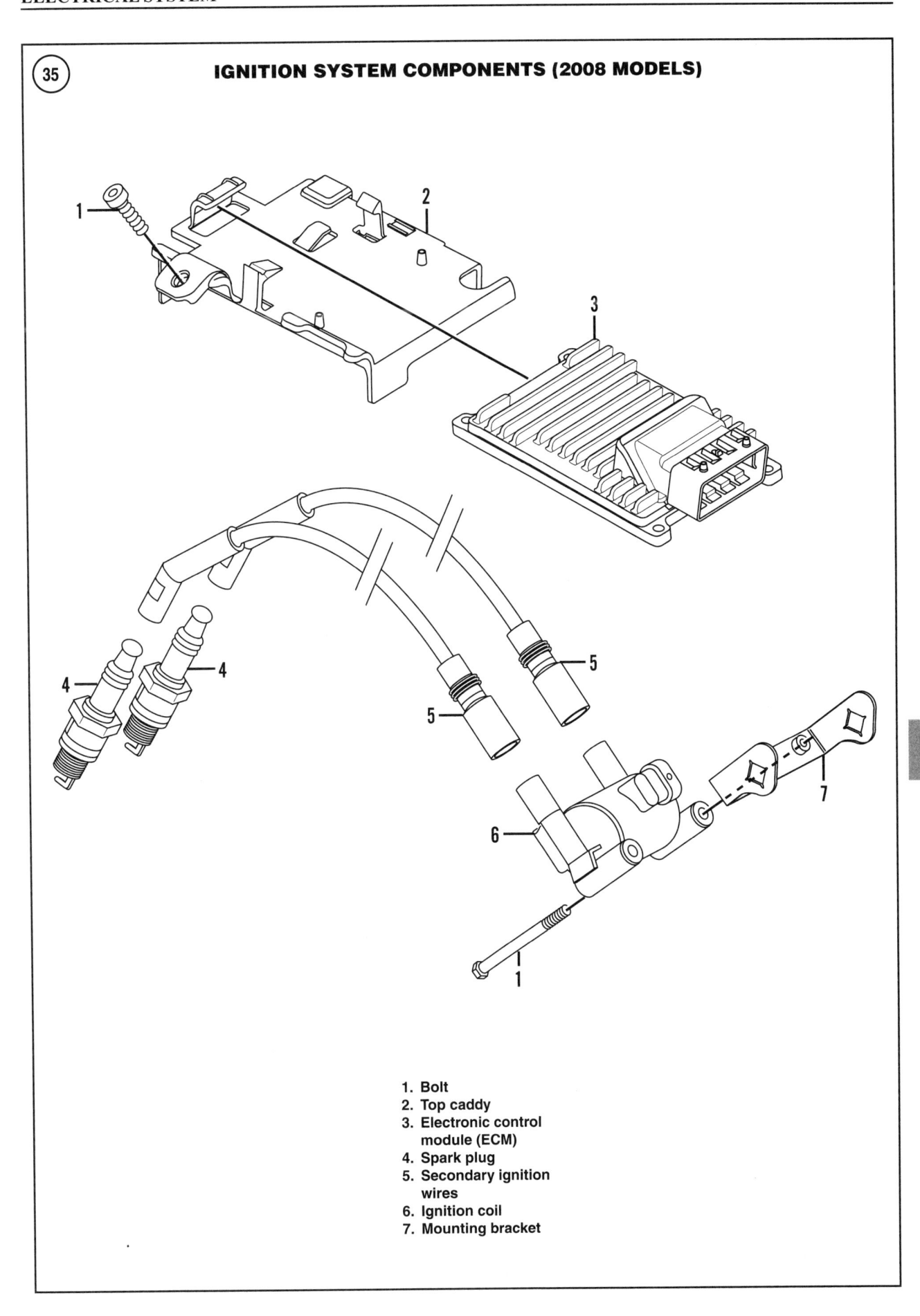

ELECTRICAL SYSTEM

IGNITION SYSTEM COMPONENTS (2008 MODELS)

㉟

1. Bolt
2. Top caddy
3. Electronic control module (ECM)
4. Spark plug
5. Secondary ignition wires
6. Ignition coil
7. Mounting bracket

454   CHAPTER ELEVEN

(36) IGNITION SYSTEM COMPONENTS (2009 MODELS)

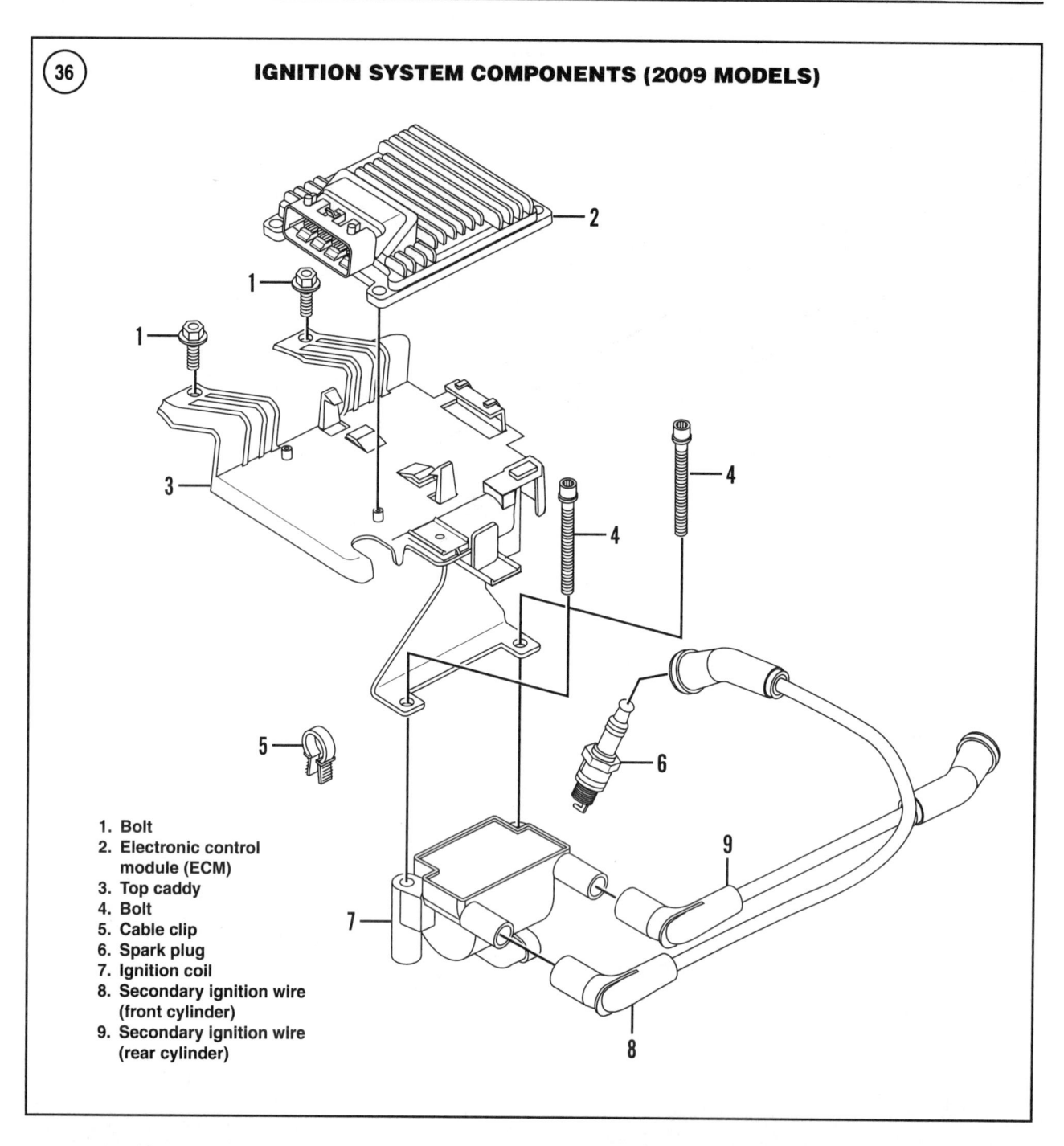

1. Bolt
2. Electronic control module (ECM)
3. Top caddy
4. Bolt
5. Cable clip
6. Spark plug
7. Ignition coil
8. Secondary ignition wire (front cylinder)
9. Secondary ignition wire (rear cylinder)

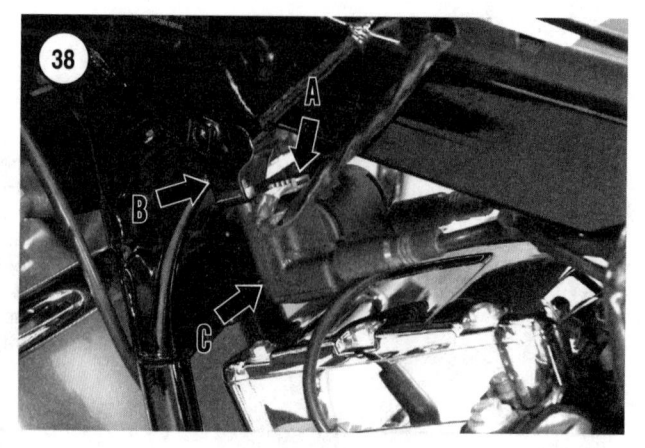

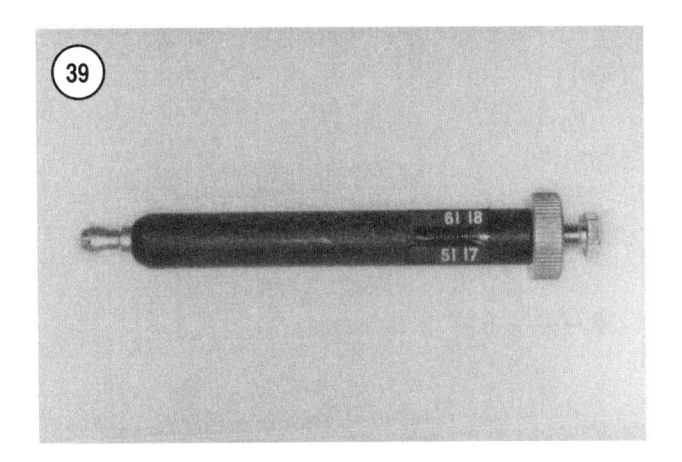

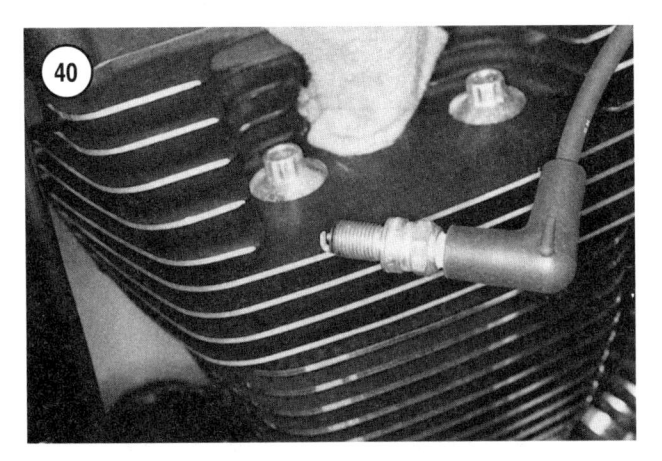

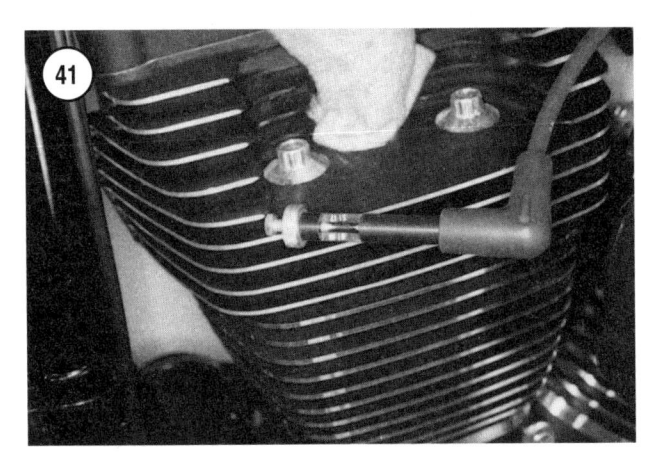

ELECTRICAL SYSTEM

7. Install the ignition coil by reversing the removal steps. Tighten the bolts to 32-40 in.-lb. (3.6-4.5 N•m).

Performance Test

1. Disconnect the plug wire and remove one of the spark plugs as described in Chapter Three.

NOTE
*A spark tester (**Figure 39**) is a useful tool for testing the ignition system spark output. This tool (Motion Pro part No. 08-0122), or its equivalent, is inserted in the spark plug cap and its base is grounded against the cylinder head. The tool's air gap is adjustable, and it allows the visual inspection of the spark while testing the intensity of the spark.*

2. Insert a clean shop cloth into the spark plug hole in the cylinder head to lessen the chance of gasoline vapors being emitted from the hole.

WARNING
The firing of the spark plug can ignite fuel that is ejected through the spark plug hole. Mount the spark plug, or tester, away from the spark plug hole. If the engine is flooded, do not perform this test.

3. Insert a new spark plug (**Figure 40**), or a spark tester (**Figure 41**), into the spark plug cap and touch the base of the plug or tester against the cylinder head to ground it. Position the spark plug or tester so the electrical contacts are visible.

WARNING
*If necessary, hold onto the spark plug wire with a pair of insulated pliers. Do **not** hold the spark plug, wire or connector or a serious electrical shock may result.*

4. Turn the engine over with the starter. A fat blue spark should be evident across the spark plug electrode or spark tester. If there is strong sunlight on the plug, or tester, shade it so the spark is more visible. Repeat test for the other cylinder.

5. If a fat blue spark occurs, the ignition coil is good. If not, perform a resistance test as described in this section.

Resistance Test

NOTE
*Refer to **Electrical Component Replacement** at the beginning of this chapter.*

1. Remove the ignition coil as described in this section.
2. Disconnect the secondary wires from the ignition coil.

2009 models

Refer to **Figure 36**.
1. Remove the battery as described in this chapter.
2. Remove the top electrical caddy as described in this chapter.
3. Disconnect the secondary wire from each spark plug.
4. Disconnect the electrical connector from the ignition coil.
5. Remove the two bolts securing the ignition coil and the battery hold-down bracket on the electrical caddy.
6. Loosen the ground terminal nut, do not remove it. Hold the ground terminals out of the way, and remove the ignition coil.

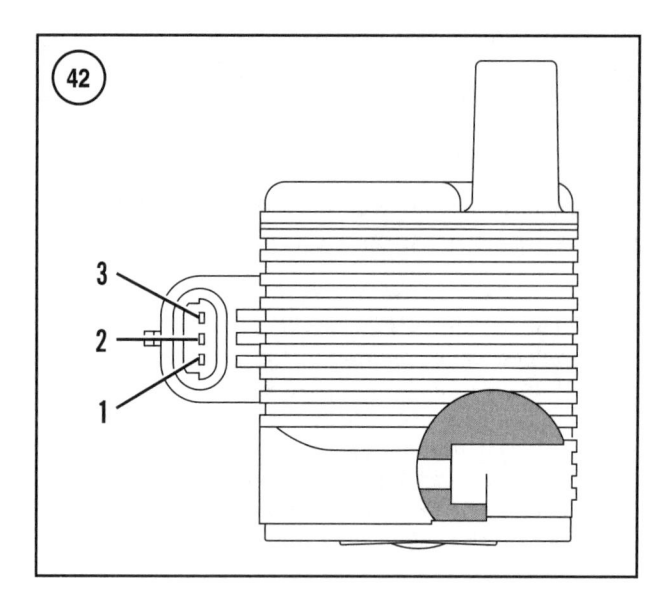

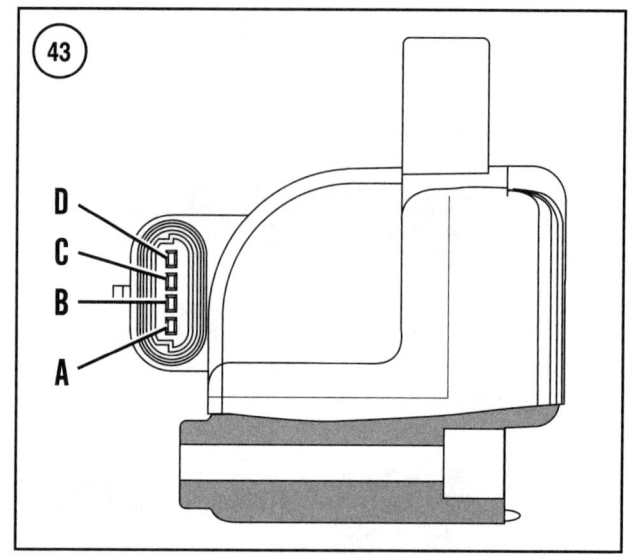

456

CHAPTER ELEVEN

42

43

44

3A. On carbureted models, measure the primary coil resistance between the terminals shown in **Figure 42**.
   a. Front coil: Terminal 2 and 3.
   b. Rear coil: Terminal 1 and 2.

3B. On fuel-injected models, measure the primary coil resistance between the terminals shown in **Figure 43**.
   a. Front coil: Terminal A and D.
   b. Rear coil: Terminal A and C.

4. Set the ohmmeter on its highest scale. Measure the resistance between the secondary terminals.

5. If the resistance values are less than specified in **Table 1**, there is most likely a short in the coil windings. Replace the coil (this section).

6. If the resistance values are more than specified, this may indicate corrosion or oxidation of the coil's terminals. Thoroughly clean the terminals, and spray with an aerosol electrical contact cleaner. Repeat the test and if the resistance value is still high, replace the coil (this section).

7. If the coil resistance does not meet (or come close to) either of these specifications, replace the coil. If the coil exhibits visible damage, replace it as described in this section.

8. Install the ignition coil as described in this section.

IGNITION CONTROL MODULE (ICM) (CARBURETED MODELS)

Removal/Installation

The ignition module is located behind the left frame side cover.

NOTE
Always disarm the optional security system (TSSM/HFSM) before disconnecting the battery or before pulling the Maxi-Fuse so the siren will not sound.

1. Disconnect the negative battery cable as described in this chapter.

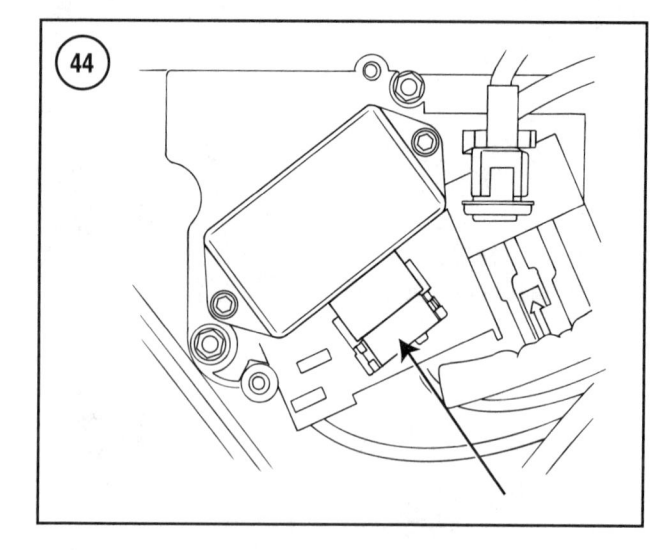

2. Remove the seat and the left side saddlebag as described in Chapter Seventeen.

3. Remove the left frame side cover as described in Chapter Seventeen.

4. Disconnect the 12-pin Deutsch connector from the ICM (**Figure 44**).

5. Remove the two Allen screws and remove the ignition module from the battery tray.

6. Install the ignition module by reversing the removal steps. Tighten the screws to 50-60 in.-lb. (5.7-6.8 N•m).

ELECTRONIC CONTROL MODULE (ECM) (FUEL-INJECTED MODELS)

Removal/Installation

NOTE
Always disarm the optional security system (TSSM/HFSM) before disconnecting the battery or before pulling the Maxi-Fuse so the siren will not sound.

ELECTRICAL SYSTEM

45

ECM

Electrical connector

46

D E C A

C E B

2006-2007 models

1. Disconnect the negative battery cable as described in this chapter.
2. Remove the seat and the right side saddlebag as described in Chapter Seventeen.
3. Remove the right frame side cover as described in Chapter Seventeen.
4. Depress external latch on the electrical connector. Use a rocking motion and disconnect the 36-pin connector from the ECM (**Figure 45**).

5. Remove the two Allen screws securing the ECM to the electrical bracket.
6. Install the ECM by reversing the removal steps. Tighten the screws to 50-60 in.-lb. (5.7-6.8 N•m).

2008-2009 models

Refer to **Figure 35** and **Figure 36**.

1. Disconnect the negative battery cable as described in this chapter.
2. Remove the seat as described in Chapter Seventeen.
3. Push the rear catch away, and carefully lift the ECM up and off the electrical caddy.

CAUTION
Do not force the socket housing with the latches partially engaged. Doing so will damage the connector.

4. Depress the button on the socket housing, and rotate the locking bar until it is seated in the rear most position. The locking bar index pin should now be engaged with the rear notch in the socket housing.
5. Gently pull the 73-pin Delphi connector from the ECM.
6. Install the ECM by reversing the removal steps. Ensure the ECM is correctly installed on the electrical caddy and that the rear catch is securely engaged.

ELECTRICAL BRACKET (2006-2007 MODELS)

Removal/Installation
(2006 Models)

NOTE
Always disarm the optional security system (TSSM/HFSM) before disconnecting the battery or before pulling the Maxi-Fuse so the siren will not sound.

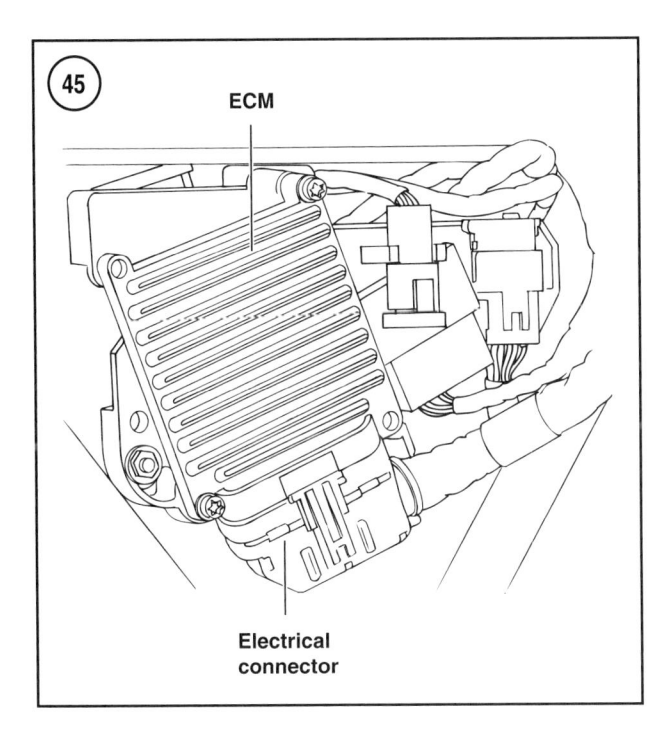

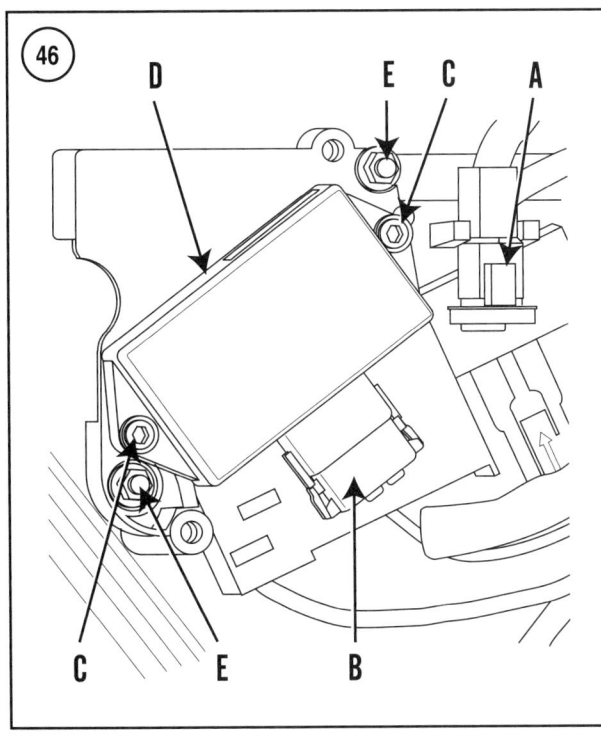

1. Disconnect the negative battery cable as described in this chapter.
2. Remove the right saddlebag and frame side cover as described in Chapter Seventeen.
3. Gently remove the data link terminal (A, **Figure 46**) from the clip on the electrical bracket and move it out of the way.
4. Disconnect the 12-pin Deutsch connector (B, **Figure 46**) from the ICM.
5. Remove the two Allen screws (C, **Figure 46**) securing the ignition control module (D), and then remove it from the electrical bracket.
6. Remove the two nuts (E, **Figure 46**) securing the electrical bracket to the frame studs.
7. Pull straight out and remove the bracket from the frame. Make sure there is nothing attached to the backside of the bracket.
8. Install by reversing the removal steps. Tighten the nuts and screws securely.

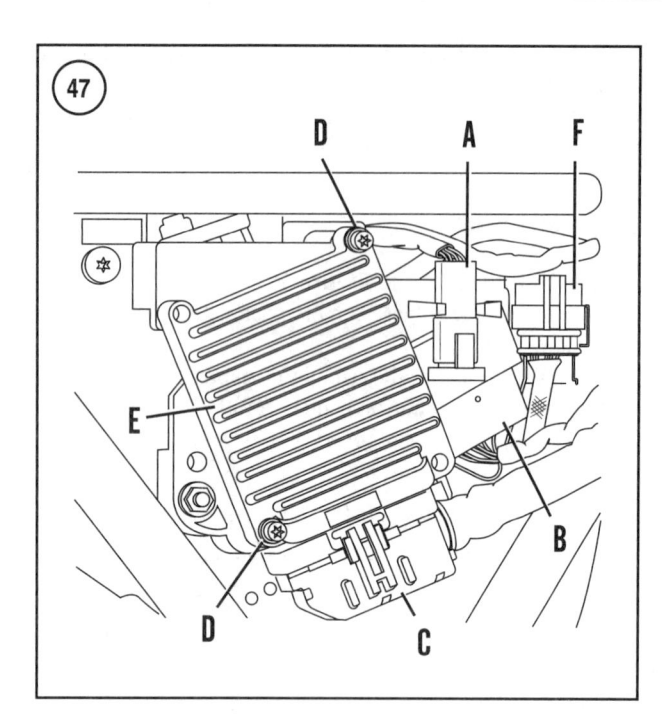

Removal/Installation (2007 Models)

1. Disconnect the negative battery cable as described in this chapter.
2. Remove the right saddlebag and frame side cover as described in Chapter Seventeen.
3. Gently remove the data link terminal (A, **Figure 47**) from the clip on the electrical bracket and move it out of the way.
4. Press on the white dot, located on the backside of the fuse block (B, **Figure 47**), and gently pull on the wiring harness and release the fuse block from the wiring harness.
5. Depress the external latch and using a rocking motion, disconnect the electrical connector (C, **Figure 47**) from the ECM.
6. Remove the two mounting screws (D, **Figure 47**) securing the ECM to the electrical bracket and remove the ECM (E).
7. On HDI models, gently remove the active exhaust connector (F, **Figure 47**) from the clip on the electrical bracket and move it out of the way.
8. Remove the two flange nuts securing the electrical bracket to the frame studs.
9. Pull straight out and partially remove the electrical bracket from the frame.
10. Turn the electrical bracket over, disconnect the 3-pin Delphi connector, and remove the security siren connector (A, **Figure 48**) on models without siren or the siren (B) from the electrical bracket.
11. Install by reversing the removal steps, while noting the following:
    a. Tighten the two flange nuts to 36-48 in.-lb. (4.1-5.4 N•m).
    b. Tighten the two mounting screws to 50-60 in.-lb. (5.7-6.8 N•m).

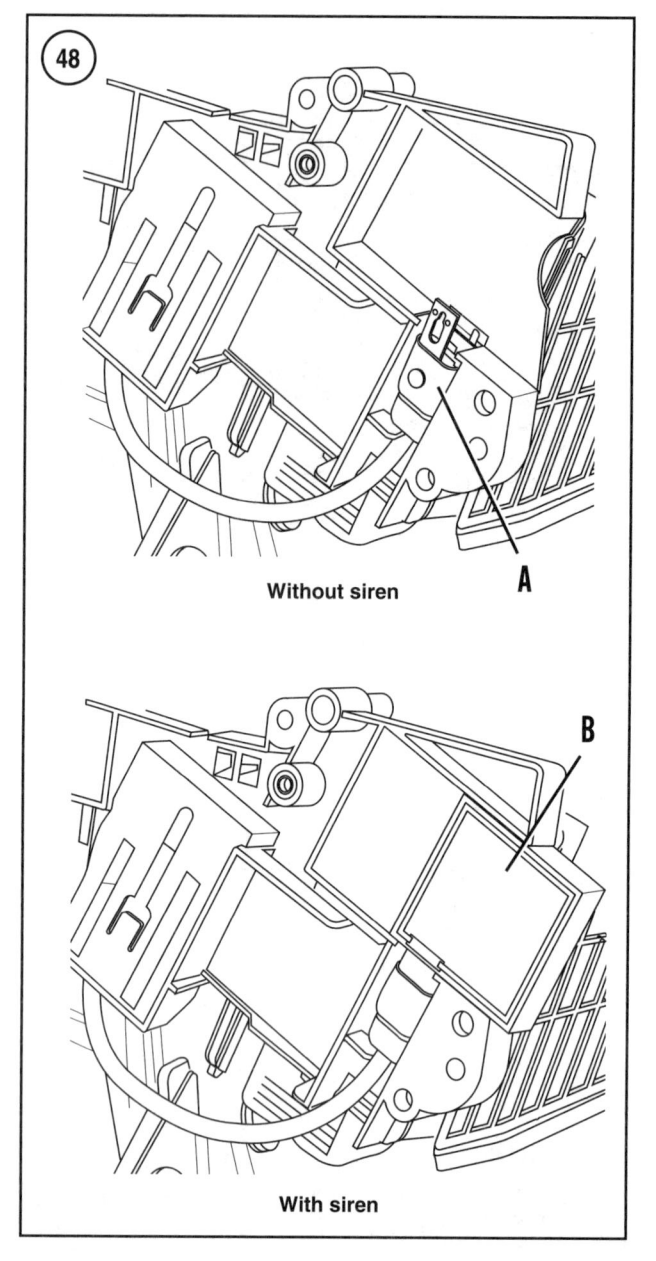

ELECTRICAL CADDIES (2008-2009 MODELS)

Top Electrical Caddy
Removal/Installation

Refer to **Figure 35** and **Figure 36**.
1. Disconnect the negative battery cable as described in this chapter.
2. Remove the seat as described in Chapter Seventeen.
3. Release the groove in the HFSM antenna from the tongue at the front of the caddy, on models so equipped. Move the connector and electrical harness out of the way.
4. Release catch and lift the ECM up and off the caddy. Move it out of the way.
5. Remove the bolt securing the top caddy to the frame cross member, and then remove the caddy from frame.
6. Install by reversing the removal steps. Tighten bolt to 15-20 ft.-lb. (20-27 N•m).

ELECTRICAL SYSTEM

Left Side Electrical Caddy Removal/Installation

2008 models

1. Remove the left saddlebag and frame side cover as described in Chapter Seventeen.
2. Remove the battery as described in this chapter.
3. Remove the front screw and release the caddy from the battery tray.
4. Remove the rear screw and release caddy from the frame weldment.
5. Disconnect the electric socket from the siren, on models so equipped.
6. Push the two remaining latches forward and pull the siren from the caddy compartment.
7. Carefully cut the front cable strap and release the main harness and main power cable (to Maxi-Fuse holder) from the inboard side of the caddy.
8. Carefully cut the rear cable strap and release the data link, diode pack (ABS models only), siren, rear fender lights and ignition switch jumper connector harness (FLHRS and FLHRC models) from inboard side of caddy.
9. Release tongue on data link connector from top groove on the caddy. Release the tongue on diode pack connector from bottom groove, on ABS models. Feed connectors and wire harness through small square opening toward the inboard side of the caddy.
10. Disconnect the siren electrical connector housing from lock pin housing on caddy socket, on models so equipped. Free the wiring harness from the hooks and feed the harness through small square opening toward the inboard side of the caddy.
11. On FLHRS and FLHRC models, pull the 4-pin Packard anchor or the ignition switch jumper harness connector from the hole in the left side of the battery tray.
12. Loosen the screw and lifting strap in the middle finger of the battery tray.
13. Pull up on the battery tray and pull out on caddy until the tab is free from the battery tray slot.
14. Pull straight up on the caddy and remove it from the frame weldment down tubes.
15. Remove the harness cover from the inboard side of caddy. Push up on the tongue at the bottom of cover and release the slot in the caddy. Then, rotate it up to disengage the hinge.
16. Push on the bottom of the fuse block and move it slightly inboard. Lift up on the top center ear of the caddy and push on top of the fuse block and remove it.
17. Depress the latches on the Maxi-Fuse holder and pull from the oblong hole in the caddy.
18. Remove the left side electrical caddy from the frame.
19. Install by reversing the removal steps while noting the following:
    a. Tighten caddy front and rear screws to 72-96 in.-lb. (8.1-10.8 N•m).
    b. Tighten the screw and lifting strap to 72-96 in.-lb. (8.1-10.8 N•m).

2009 models

1. Disconnect the Maxi-Fuse as described in this chapter.
2. Remove the seat as described in Chapter Seventeen.
3. Remove the left saddlebag and frame side cover as described in Chapter Seventeen.
4. Disconnect the rear fender tip harness connector and slide the connector body off of the mounting tab.
5. Carefully cut the cable strap securing the excess AM/FM antenna wire loop, on models so equipped.
6. Disconnect the siren and remove it from the caddy, on models so equipped.
7. Remove the data link connector, fuse block cover and ABS diode pack, on models so equipped.
8. Remove the two screws securing the caddy to the frame posts.
9. Carefully cut the front and rear cable straps securing the caddy to main wiring harness.
10. Remove the harness cover from the backside of the caddy.
11. Remove the wiring harness through the square opening in caddy.
12. On the backside of the caddy, squeeze the tabs at top and bottom of Maxi-Fuse holder, and pull it away from caddy.
13. On the backside of the caddy, pull the tabs securing the fuse block to the caddy and remove it.
14. Remove the left side electrical caddy from the frame.
15. Install by reversing the removal steps. Tighten the two screws to 72-96 in.-lb. (8.1-10.8 N•m).

Right Side Electrical Caddy Removal/Installation

2008-2009 models with ABS

1. Remove the right saddlebag and frame side cover as described in Chapter Seventeen.
2. Remove the three screws securing the ABS module onto the caddy.
3. Pull the 2-pin rear wheel sensor Amp (Tyco) connector anchor from the hole at the rear of the caddy.
4. Remove the front screw securing the caddy to the battery tray.
5. Remove the rear screw and release the battery tray support arms and the caddy from the frame weldment.
6. Pull the caddy toward the front and release the support arm lip from behind the frame weldment.
7. Hold onto the ABS module, pull the caddy toward the outside and release the caddy from the frame down tube saddles.
8. Install by reversing the removal steps while noting the following:
    a. Tighten the two screws to 72-96 in.-lb. (8.1-10.9 N•m).
    b. Tighten the three ABS module screws to 39-60 in.-lb. (4.4-6.8 N•m).

2008-2009 HDI models

1. Remove the right saddlebag and frame side cover as described in Chapter Seventeen.
2. Remove the cable clip from the slotted flange at front of active exhaust valve.
3. Push the cam toward the rear to relieve tension on the actuator cable. Release the cable ball end from slot in actuator.
4. Release actuator cable from the J-clamp on the swing arm bracket.
5. Pull anchored cable strap from the hole in the middle frame down tube adjacent to swing arm bracket, and release the main wiring harness.
6. Push the main wiring harness forward to allow clearance of actuator cable.
7. Disconnect the 5-pin connector from the actuator.
8. Remove the front screw securing the caddy to the battery tray.
9. Remove the rear screw and release the battery tray support arms and the caddy to the frame weldment.
10. Pull the caddy toward the front and release the support arm lip from behind the frame weldment.
11. Hold onto the ABS module, pull the caddy toward the outside and release the caddy from the frame down tube saddles, on models so equipped.
12. Remove the two screws and flat washers securing the actuator to the base of the caddy.
13. Install by reversing the removal steps while noting the following:
    a. Tighten the two screws to 72-96 in.-lb. (8.1-10.8 N•m).
    b. Tighten the two actuator screws and flat washers to 32-40 in.-lb. (3.6-4.5 N•m).
    c. Tighten the J-clamp to 39-60 in.-lb. (4.4-6.8 N•m).

SENSORS

MAP Sensor (Carbureted Models) Removal/Installation

NOTE
Always disarm the optional security system (TSSM/HFSM) before disconnecting the battery or before pulling the Maxi-Fuse so the siren will not sound.

1. Disconnect the negative battery cable as described in this chapter.
2. Remove the fuel tank as described in Chapter Nine.
3. Remove the carburetor as described in Chapter Nine. Place a lint-free shop cloth into the intake manifold opening (A, **Figure 49**) to prevent the entry of debris.
4. Remove the Torx screw and clip (B, **Figure 49**) securing the MAP sensor to the top of the intake manifold.
5. Pull the MAP sensor (C, **Figure 49**) straight up out of the seal in the intake manifold. 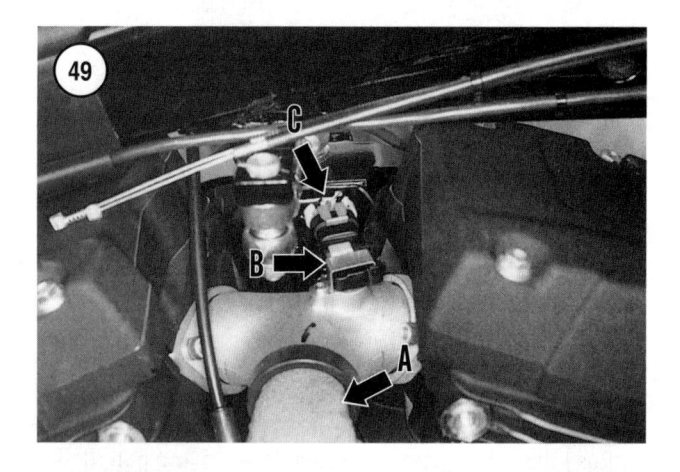 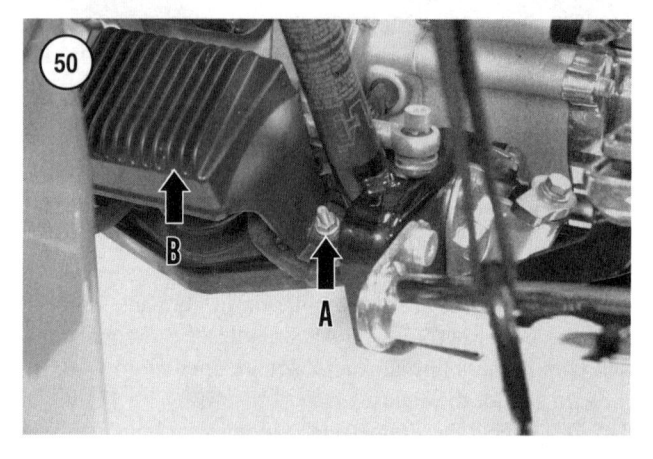
6. Disconnect the 3-pin Packard connector from the MAP sensor and remove the sensor.
7. Install the MAP sensor by reversing the removal steps while noting the following:
    a. If necessary, replace the seal in the intake manifold.
    b. Tighten the Torx screw to 25-35 in.-lb. (2.8-3.9 N•m).

Crankshaft Position Sensor (CKP) Sensor Removal/Installation

NOTE
Always disarm the optional security system (TSSM/HFSM) before disconnecting the battery or before pulling the Maxi-Fuse so the siren will not sound.

1. Disconnect the negative battery cable as described in this chapter.
2. Remove the flange nuts (A, **Figure 50**) securing the voltage regulator (B) to the mounting bracket or frame.
3. Move the voltage regulator off the studs and lower it.
4. On the front, left side of the motorcycle, remove the Allen screw (A, **Figure 51**) and withdraw the CKP sensor and O-ring from the crankcase. Discard the O-ring.
5. Follow the wiring harness (B, **Figure 51**) down under the frame lower cross member, and locate the 2-pin CKP connector.

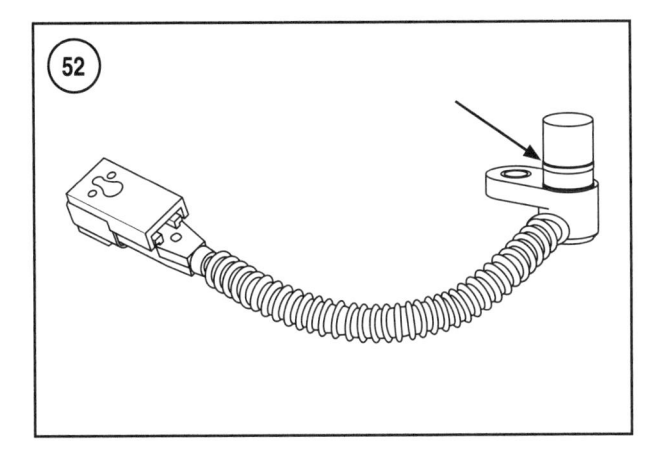

ELECTRICAL SYSTEM

6. Disengage the small end of slot on attachment clip from T-stud on the bracket.
7. Depress the button on socket terminal side and disconnect the electrical connector.
8. Note the path of the harness and tubing out behind the lower stabilizer link and through the frame.
9. Carefully pull the wiring harness and convoluted tube out from under the voltage regulator mounting area. The harness and tube must be routed along the same path noted during removal.
10. Install by reversing the removal steps while noting the following:
   a. Apply clean engine oil to a *new* O-ring (**Figure 52**) on the CKP sensor prior to installation.
   b. Install the sensor and tighten the Allen screw to 90-120 in.-lb. (10.2-13.6 N•m).

Engine Temperature (ET) Sensor
Removal/Installation

NOTE
Always disarm the optional security system (TSSM/HFSM) before disconnecting the battery or before pulling the Maxi-Fuse so the siren will not sound.

1. Disconnect the negative battery cable as described in this chapter. 
2. Remove the fuel tank as described in Chapter Nine or Chapter Ten.
3. Remove the horn assembly (A, **Figure 53**) as described in this chapter.
4. On the left rear side of the front cylinder head, pull the rubber boot (B, **Figure 53**) back off the ET sensor.
5. Disconnect the electrical connector from the ET sensor.
6. Use a 3/4 in. deep socket and loosen the sensor. When the socket turns easily, remove the socket and completely unscrew the sensor by hand.
7. Install a new sensor and start it by hand. Using the socket, tighten the ET sensor to 120-180 in.-lb. (13.6-20.3 N•m).
8. Install the electrical connector and push it on until it locks into place.
9 Pull the rubber boot back over the electrical connector.
10. Install the horn assembly (A, **Figure 53**) as described in this chapter.
11. Install the fuel tank as described in Chapter Nine or Chapter Ten.
12. Connect the negative battery cable as described in this chapter.

Bank Angle (BAS) Sensor

The bank angle sensor is an integral part of the Turn Signal Security Module.

Vehicle Speed Sensor (VSS)
Removal/Installation

2006 models

1. Disconnect the negative battery cable as described in this chapter.
2. Remove the seat and the right side saddlebag as described in Chapter Seventeen.
3. Remove the right frame side cover as described in Chapter Seventeen.
4. Remove the two flange nuts securing the electrical bracket to the battery tray.
5. Carefully pull the electrical bracket from the studs on the battery tray.

6. Disconnect the 3-pin VSS connector (**Figure 54**) on the backside of the electrical bracket.
7. Remove the terminals from the electrical connector pin housing. Refer to *Electrical Connectors* in this chapter. Remove the harness from the electrical bracket.
8. Carefully cut the wiring harness cable strap on the inboard of the rear passenger footboard screw. Release the harness from the frame down tube.
9. Remove the Allen screw securing the VSS onto the top right side of the transmission housing, and withdraw the sensor from the transmission case.
10. Install by reversing the removal steps while noting the following:
    a. Apply clean engine oil to a *new* O-ring on the VSS sensor prior to installation.
    b. Install the sensor and tighten the Allen screw to 84-132 in.-lb. (9.5-14.9 N•m).

2007-2009 models

1. Remove the starter as described in this chapter.
2. Disconnect the 3-pin VSS connector (**Figure 55**) on the top of the transmission case.
3. Remove the screw securing the VSS to the top right side of the transmission housing and withdraw the sensor from the transmission case.
4. Install by reversing the removal steps while noting the following:
    a. Apply clean engine oil to a *new* O-ring on the VSS sensor prior to installation.
    b. Install the sensor and tighten the Allen screw to 84-132 in.-lb. (9.5-14.9 N•m).

STARTING SYSTEM

When servicing the starting system, refer to the wiring diagrams located on the CD inserted into the back cover of the manual.

CAUTION
Do not operate the starter for more than five seconds at a time. Let it cool approximately 10 seconds before operating it again.

Troubleshooting

Refer to Chapter Two.

STARTER

Refer to **Figure 56** and **Figure 57**.

Removal

1. Remove the seat as described in Chapter Seventeen.
2. Remove the exhaust system as described in Chapter Four.
3. Remove the battery and battery tray as described in this chapter.
4. On 2006 models, remove the starter jackshaft as described in Chapter Six.
5. Remove the engine oil dipstick from the transmission.
6. Wipe the area around the oil filler cap with a clean rag. Unscrew the oil filler cap/dipstick out of the transmission case. Cover the fill spout to keep out debris.
7. Remove the cover screw and chrome cover, on models so equipped.
8. Remove the nut from the bracket tab and remove the exhaust pipe support bracket.
9. Slide back the rubber boot, and remove the terminal nut from the battery-terminal post, and disconnect the positive battery cable ring terminals from the post.
10. Disconnect the solenoid connector (A, **Figure 58**) from the starter.
11. Remove the starter mounting bolts (B, **Figure 58**) and washers.
12. From the right side of the motorcycle, pull the starter straight out of the crankcase and remove it. Do not lose the

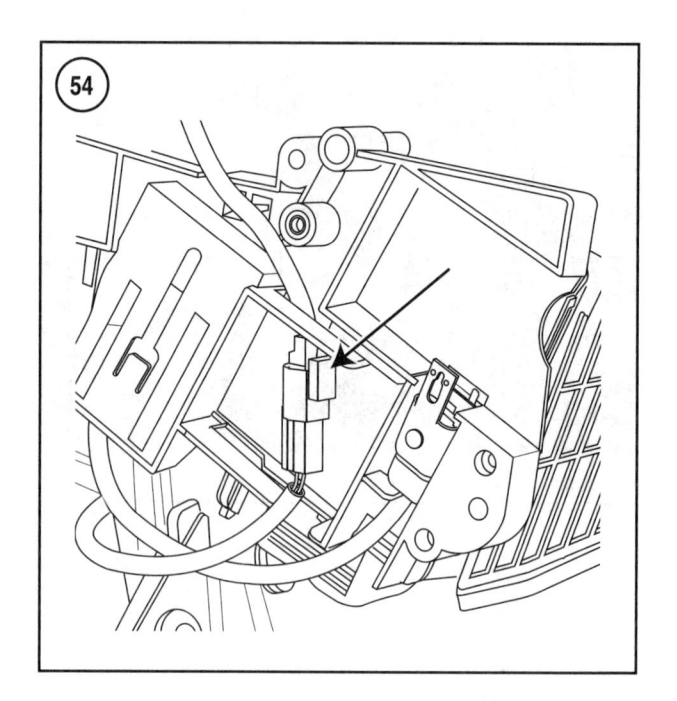

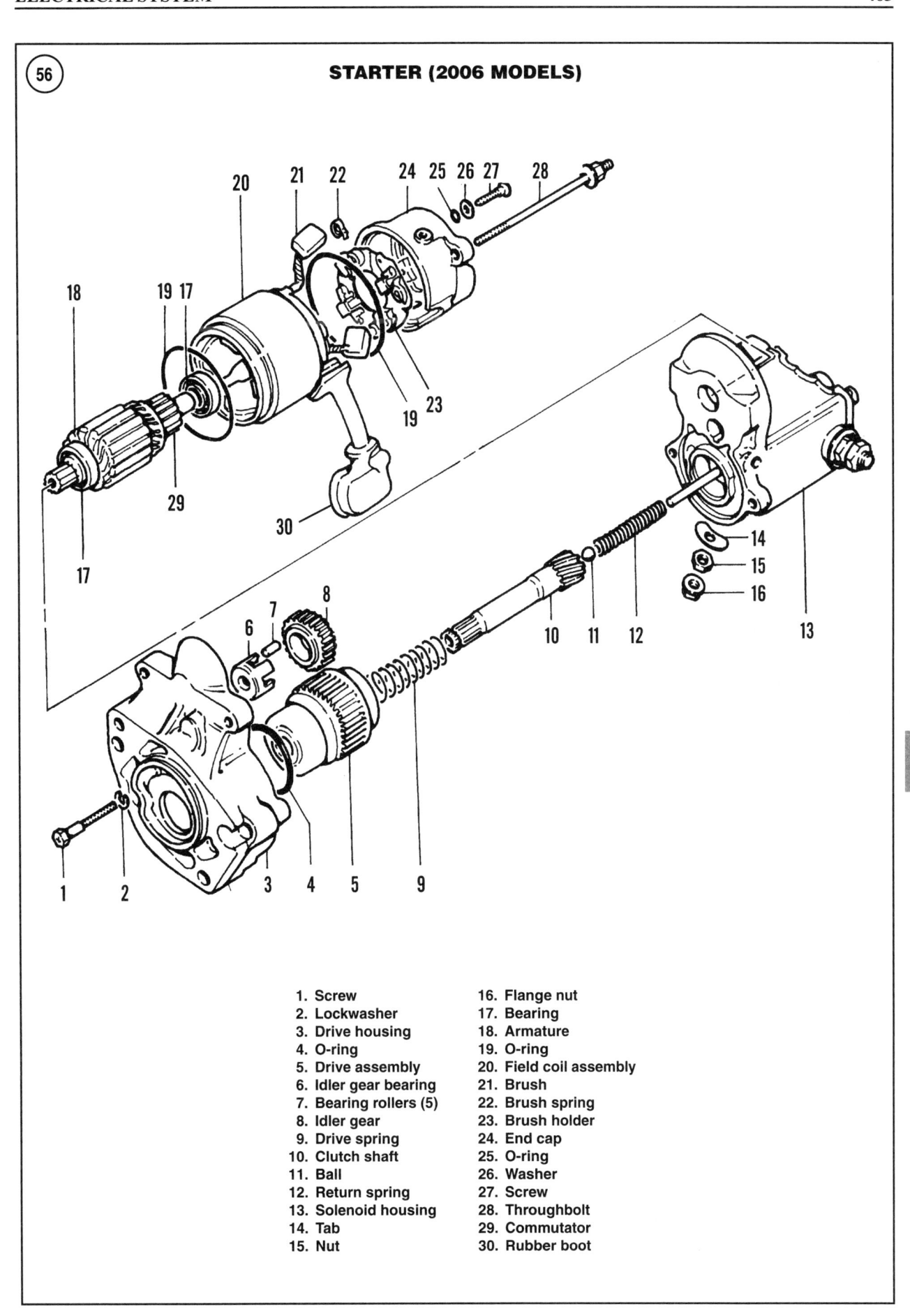

ELECTRICAL SYSTEM

⑤⑥ STARTER (2006 MODELS)

1. Screw
2. Lockwasher
3. Drive housing
4. O-ring
5. Drive assembly
6. Idler gear bearing
7. Bearing rollers (5)
8. Idler gear
9. Drive spring
10. Clutch shaft
11. Ball
12. Return spring
13. Solenoid housing
14. Tab
15. Nut
16. Flange nut
17. Bearing
18. Armature
19. O-ring
20. Field coil assembly
21. Brush
22. Brush spring
23. Brush holder
24. End cap
25. O-ring
26. Washer
27. Screw
28. Throughbolt
29. Commutator
30. Rubber boot

CHAPTER ELEVEN

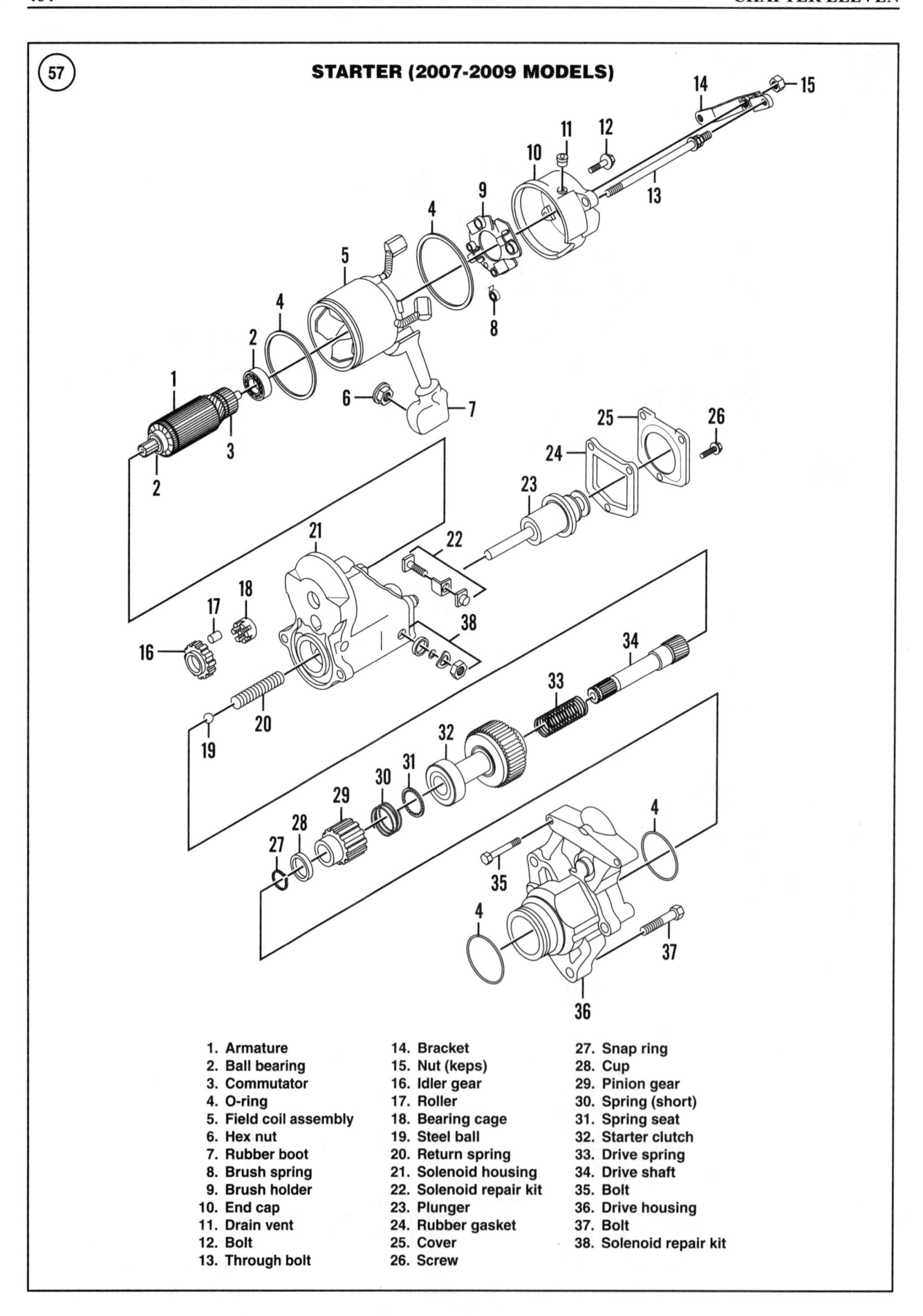

STARTER (2007-2009 MODELS)

1. Armature
2. Ball bearing
3. Commutator
4. O-ring
5. Field coil assembly
6. Hex nut
7. Rubber boot
8. Brush spring
9. Brush holder
10. End cap
11. Drain vent
12. Bolt
13. Through bolt
14. Bracket
15. Nut (keps)
16. Idler gear
17. Roller
18. Bearing cage
19. Steel ball
20. Return spring
21. Solenoid housing
22. Solenoid repair kit
23. Plunger
24. Rubber gasket
25. Cover
26. Screw
27. Snap ring
28. Cup
29. Pinion gear
30. Spring (short)
31. Spring seat
32. Starter clutch
33. Drive spring
34. Drive shaft
35. Bolt
36. Drive housing
37. Bolt
38. Solenoid repair kit

ELECTRICAL SYSTEM

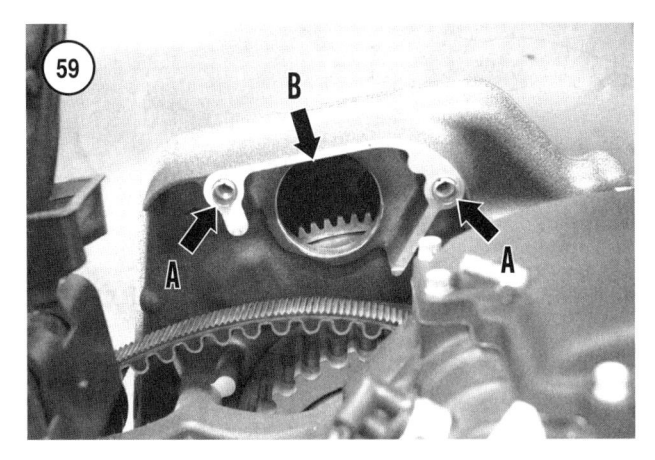

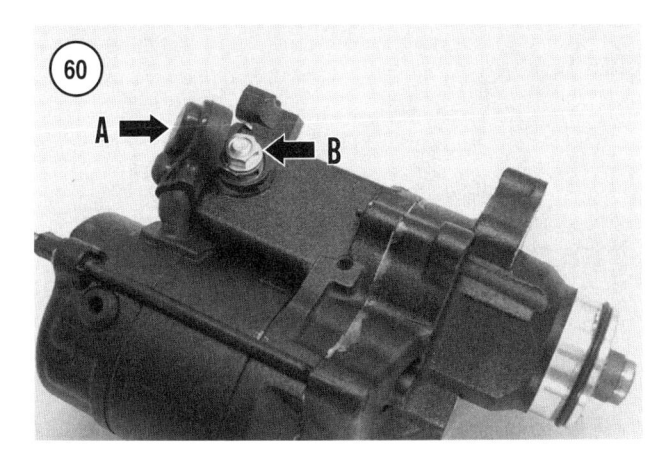

locating dowels (A, **Figure 59**). On 2006 models, the jackshaft inner coupling remains with the starter shaft.

13. Close off the primary chaincase opening (B, **Figure 59**) with a shop cloth to prevent the entry of debris.

14. If necessary, service the starter, drive housing or solenoid housing as described in this section.

Installation

1. Remove the shop cloth from the crankcase opening (B, **Figure 59**).
2. Press the locating dowels (A, **Figure 59**) into the crankcase, if removed.
3. Install the starter, and push it in until it bottoms.
4. Apply Loctite Threadlocker 243 (blue) to the bolt threads. Install the starter mounting bolts (B, **Figure 58**) and washers. On 2006-2007 models, tighten the starter mounting bolts to 13-20 ft.-lb. (17.6-27.1 N•m). On 2008-2009 models, tighten the mounting bolts to 25-27 ft.-lb. (33.9-36.6 N•m).
5. Connect the solenoid connector (A, **Figure 58**) to the starter.
6. Connect the positive battery cable onto the battery-terminal post, and install the terminal nut. Tighten the nut securely, and slide the rubber boot into position. On 2006 models, tighten the positive-terminal nut to 60-85 in.-lb. (6.8-9.6 N•m).
7. Install the exhaust pipe support bracket and nut onto the bracket tab, and tighten the nut securely.
8. Install the chrome cover and screw, on models so equipped. Tighten the screw securely.
9. Uncover the fill spout and screw the oil filler cap/dipstick into of the transmission case. Tighten the dipstick securely.
10. On 2006 models, install the starter jackshaft as described in Chapter Six.
11. Install the battery as described in this chapter. On 2008-2009 models, also install the battery tray (this chapter).
12. Install the exhaust system as described in Chapter Four.
13. Install the seat as described in Chapter Seventeen.

Disassembly

NOTE
*If only the solenoid assembly requires service, refer to **Solenoid Housing Disassembly/Inspection/Assembly** in this section.*

1. Clean all grease, dirt and carbon from the exterior of the starter assembly.
2. Where equipped, remove the nuts from the through bolts, and remove the cover bracket.
3. Pull back the rubber field coil boot (A, **Figure 60**) from the starter-terminal post on the solenoid housing.
4. Remove the nut (B, **Figure 60**) from the starter-terminal post, and disconnect the field coil wire from the post.
5. Remove the through bolts (**Figure 61**), and pull the field coil (A, **Figure 62**) from the solenoid housing (B).

6. Remove the end cap screws (A, **Figure 63**), washers and O-rings, and then remove the end cap (B) from the field coil assembly (C).
7. Pull the brush holder (A, **Figure 64**) away from the commutator, and remove the armature (B) from the field coil assembly.
8. Remove the two field coil brushes from the brush holder.
9. Clean all grease, dirt and carbon from the armature, field coil assembly and end cover.

CAUTION
Be extremely careful when selecting a solvent to clean the electrical components. Do not immerse any of the wire windings in solvent, because the insulation may be damaged. Wipe the windings with a cloth lightly moistened with solvent, and allow the solution to dry thoroughly.

10. To service the drive housing assembly, refer to *Drive Housing Disassembly/Inspection/Assembly* in this section.
11. To service the solenoid housing, refer to *Solenoid Housing Disassembly/Inspection/Assembly* in this section.

Assembly

1. If necessary, assemble the drive housing as described in this section.
2. If necessary, assemble the solenoid housing as described in this section.
3. Lubricate the armature bearings (A, **Figure 65**) with high-temperature grease.
4. Install a *new* O-ring (A, **Figure 66**) onto each end of the field coil housing.
5. At the brush holder (A, **Figure 67**), pull back each spring from its brush, and insert a paper clip (B) between the spring and brush holder to keep spring pressure off the brush.
6. Install armature into the housing so the commutator (A, **Figure 68**) goes through the brush holder.
7. Pull the paper clips (B, **Figure 68**) and release the field coil brush springs from the holder. Make sure each brush (**Figure 69**) presses against the commutator.

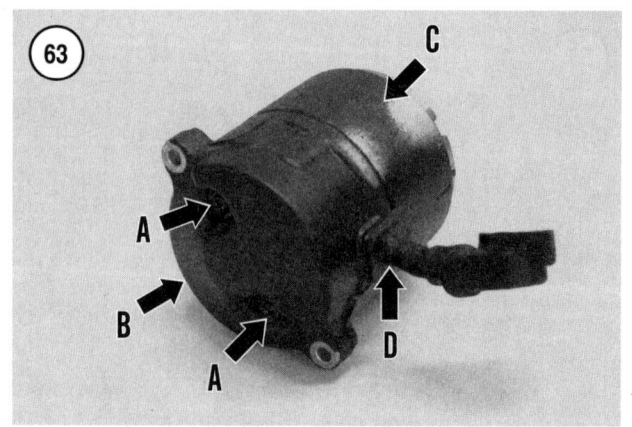

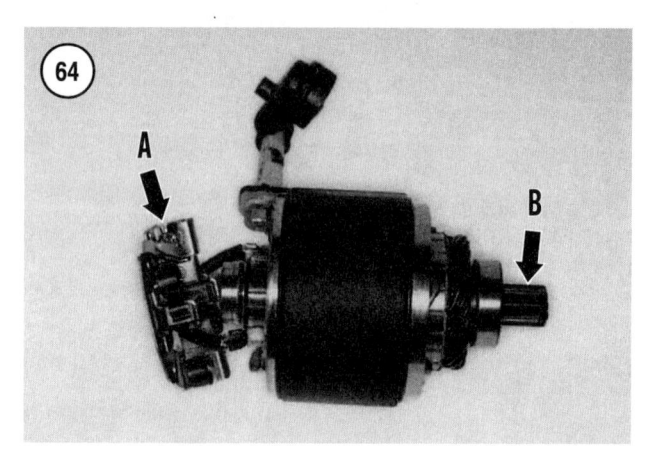

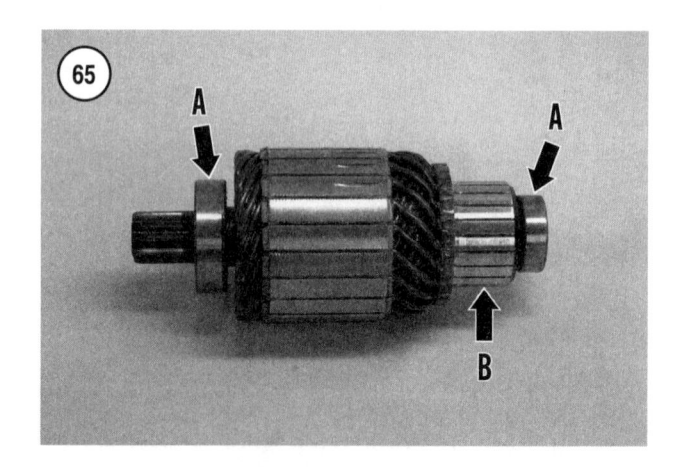

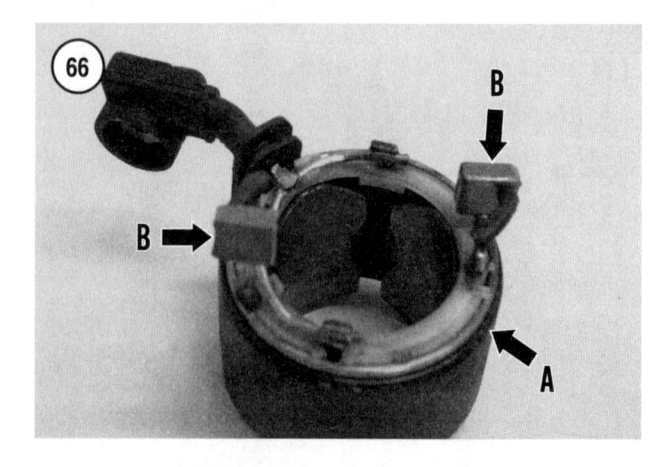

ELECTRICAL SYSTEM

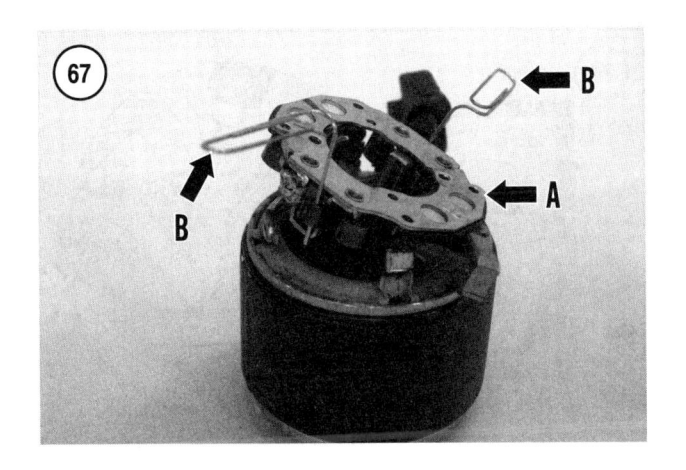

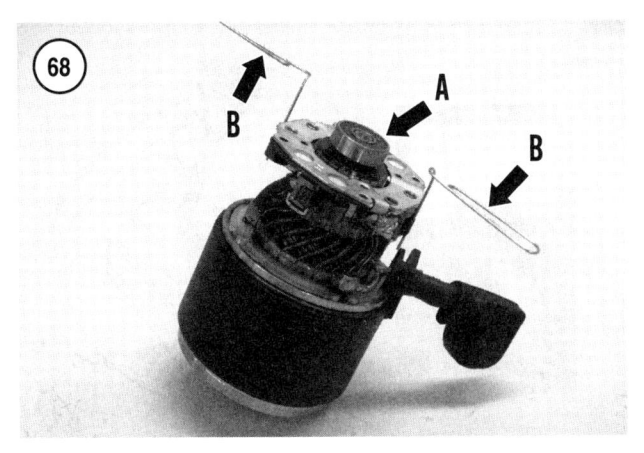

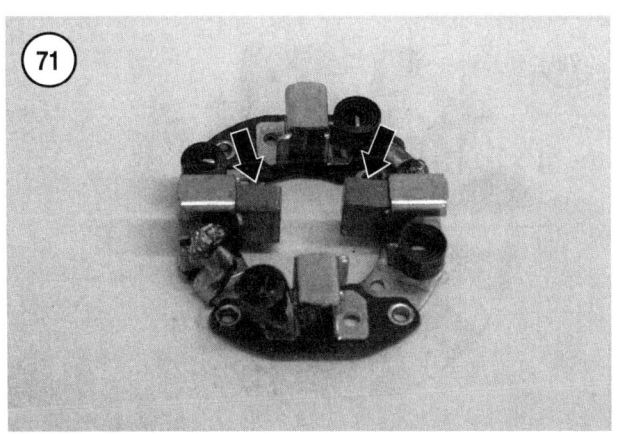

8. Install the end cap (B, **Figure 63**) onto the field coil housing so the cap's cutout engages the grommet (D) on the field coil wire.
9. Install the screws (A, **Figure 63**) into the end cap (B) and tighten securely. Keep the housing horizontal so the armature will not fall out of the housing.
10. Align the field coil assembly (A, **Figure 62**) with the solenoid housing (B) and assemble both housings.
11. Install the throughbolts (**Figure 61**). Tighten the throughbolts to 39-65 in.-lb. (4.4-7.3 N•m).
12. Connect the field coil wire to the positive starter-terminal post on the solenoid housing, and install the nut (B, **Figure 60**). Tighten the positive starter-terminal nut to 70-90 in.-lb. (7.9-10.2 N•m).
13. Install the rubber boot (A, **Figure 60**) over the starter-terminal post.

Inspection

NOTE
The field coil brushes (B, Figure 66) are soldered into position. To replace them, unsolder the brushes by heating their joints with a soldering gun, and pull them out with a pair of pliers. Position the new brushes and solder them in place with rosin core solder. Do not use acid core solder.

1. Measure the length of each brush with a caliper (**Figure 70**). If the brush length is less than specified in **Table 1**, replace all of the brushes as a set. Measure both the field coil brushes (B, **Figure 66**) and the brush holder brushes (**Figure 71**).
2. Inspect the commutator (B, **Figure 65**) on the armature. The mica should be below the surface of the copper commutator segments (**Figure 72**). If the commutator bars are worn to the same level as the mica insulation, have the commutator serviced by a dealership or electrical repair shop.
3. Inspect the commutator copper segments for discoloration. If the commutator segments are rough, discolored or worn, have the commutator serviced by a dealership or electrical repair shop.

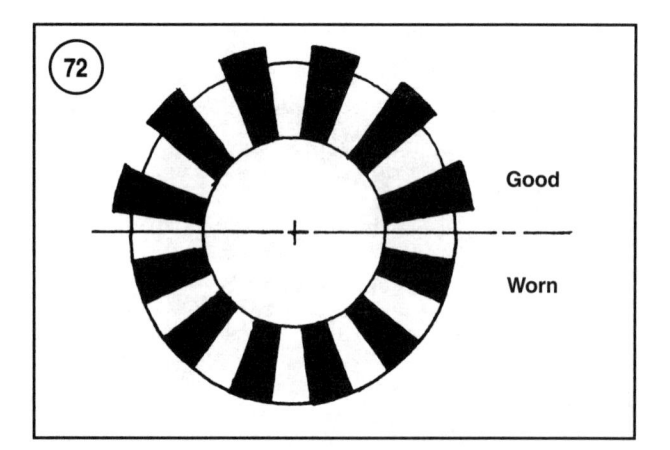

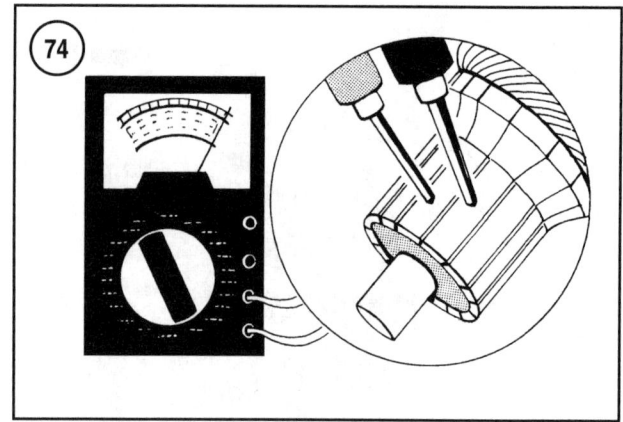

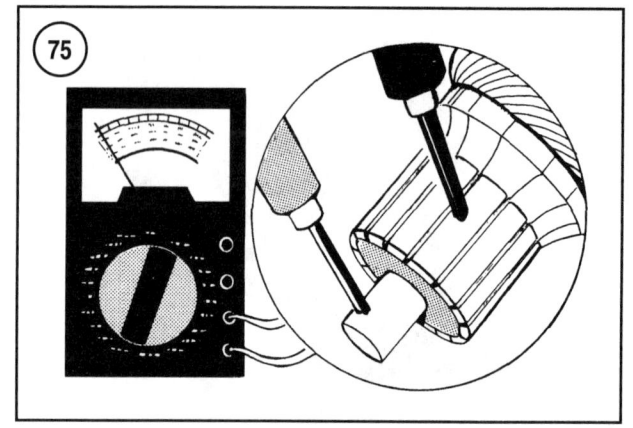

4. Measure the outer diameter of the commutator with a caliper (**Figure 73**). Replace the armature if it is less than the specification in **Table 1**.
5. Use an ohmmeter to perform the following tests.
   a. Check for continuity between each pair of commutator bars (**Figure 74**); there should be continuity between pairs of bars.
   b. Check for continuity between each commutator bar and the shaft (**Figure 75**). There should be no continuity.
   c. If the unit fails either test, replace the armature.
6. Use an ohmmeter to perform the following tests.
   a. Check for continuity between the field coil wire and each field coil brush (**Figure 76**); there should be continuity.
   b. Check for continuity between the field coil housing and each field coil brush (**Figure 77**); there should be no continuity.
   c. If the unit fails either test, replace the field coil assembly.
7. Use an ohmmeter to check for continuity between the brush holder plate and each positive (insulated) brush holder (**Figure 78**); there should be no continuity. If the unit fails this test, replace the brush holder plate.
8. Inspect the armature bearings as follows:
   a. Check the bearings (A, **Figure 65**) on the armature shaft. Replace worn or damaged bearings.
   b. Check the bearing bores in the end cover (**Figure 79**) and solenoid housing (C, **Figure 62**). Replace the cover or housing if the area is worn or cracked.

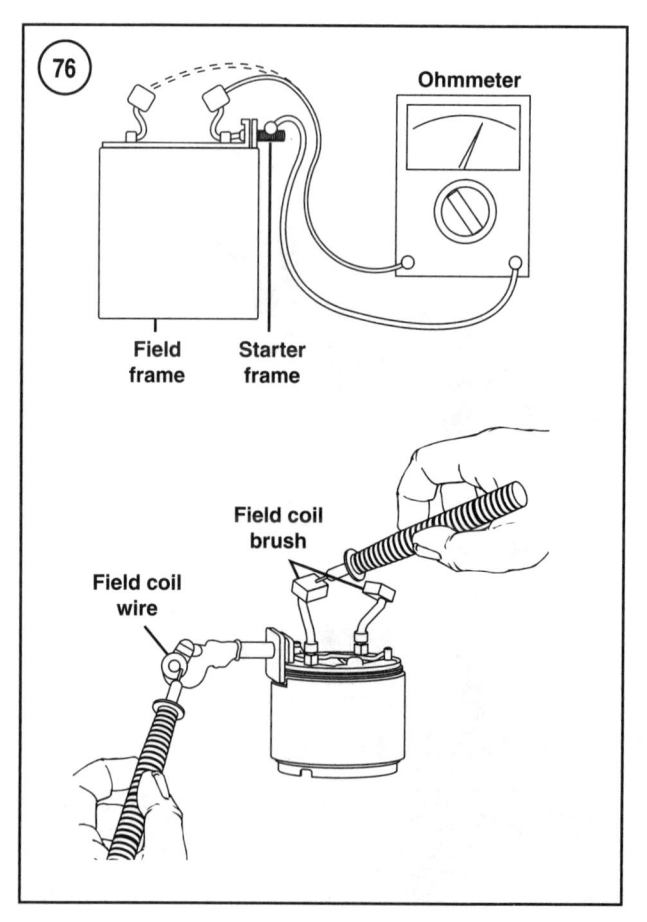

ELECTRICAL SYSTEM

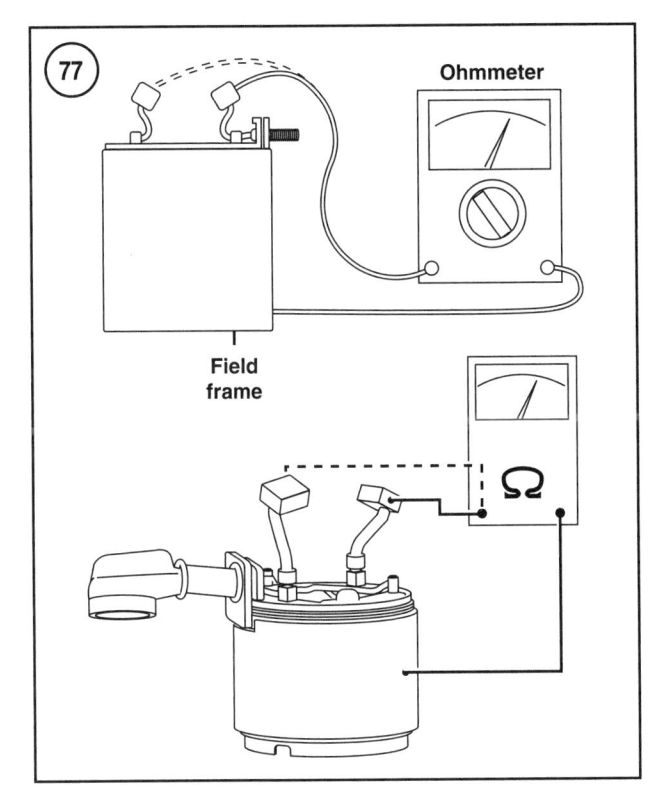

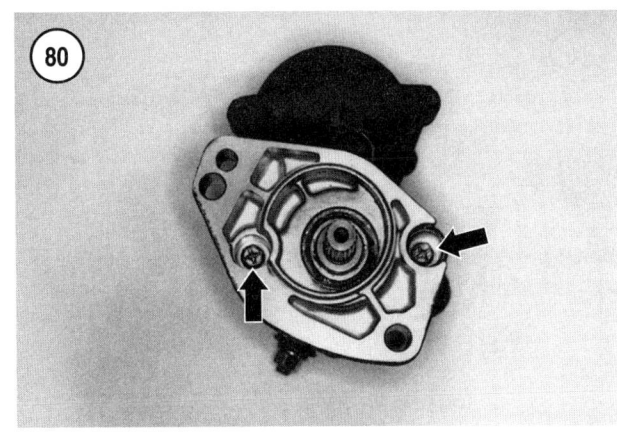

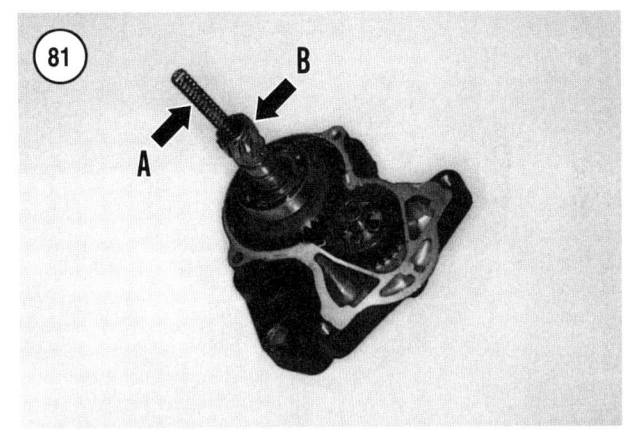

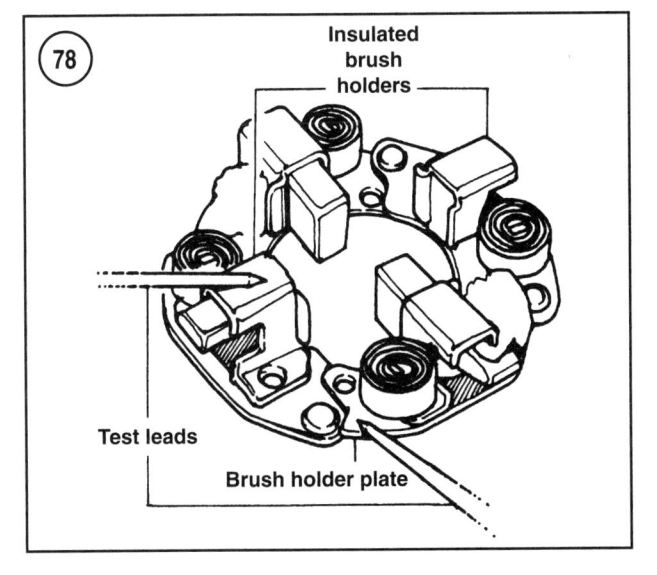

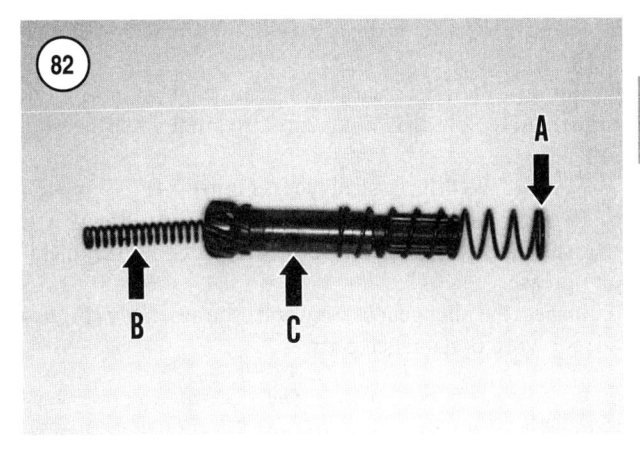

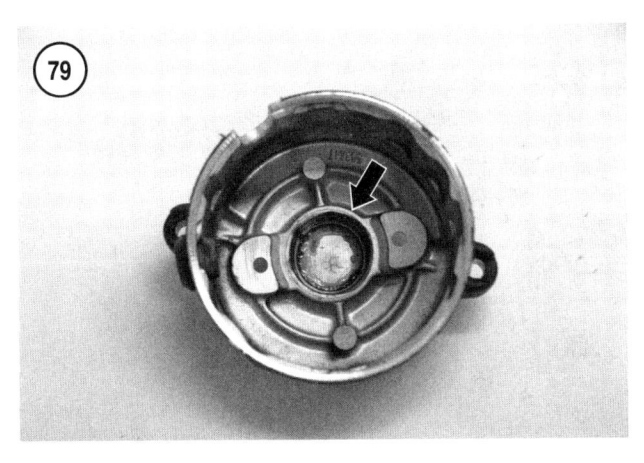

469

Drive Housing Disassembly/Inspection/Assembly (2006 Models)

1. Remove the field coil assembly as described in *Starter Disassembly* (this section).
2. Remove the two drive housing Phillips screws (**Figure 80**) and lockwashers.
3. Tap the drive housing, and remove it from the solenoid housing.
4. Remove the return spring (A, **Figure 81**), ball, clutch shaft (B) and drive spring (A, **Figure 82**) from the drive assembly.

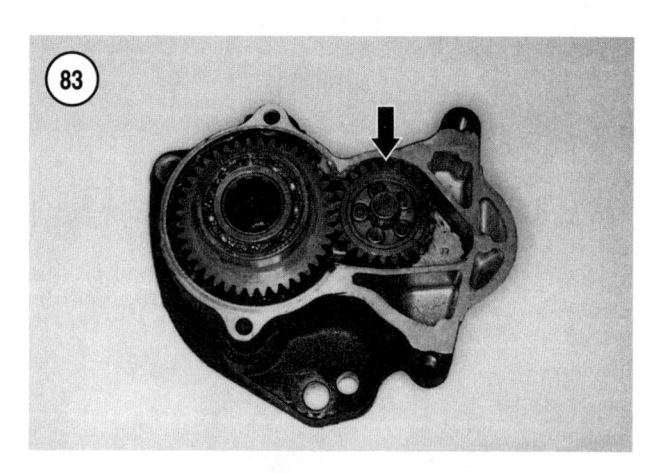

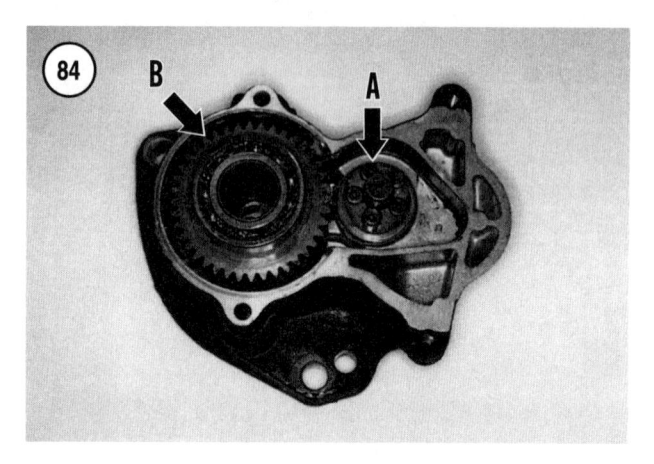

5. Remove the idler gear (**Figure 83**) from the drive housing.
6. Remove the idler gear bearing and cage assembly (A, **Figure 84**). Note that it contains five individual bearing rollers.
7. Remove the drive assembly (B, **Figure 84**).
8. Replace the drive housing O-ring (**Figure 85**) if it is worn or damaged. Lubricate the O-ring with high temperature grease.
9. Inspect the idler gear bearing and cage assembly (**Figure 86**) for worn or damaged parts.

CAUTION
*The drive assembly (**Figure 87**) is a sealed unit. Do not clean or soak it in any type of solvent.*

10. Inspect the drive assembly and its bearings (**Figure 87**) for worn or damaged parts. If the bearings are worn or damaged, replace the drive assembly and bearings as a set.
11. Lubricate the following components with high-temperature grease.
    a. Idler gear bearing and cage assembly (**Figure 86**).
    b. Drive housing O-ring (**Figure 85**) and shaft.
    c. Drive assembly (**Figure 87**).
    d. Clutch shaft, drive spring, return spring and ball.
12. Assemble the drive housing by reversing the disassembly steps. Note the following:

ELECTRICAL SYSTEM

a. Install the idler gear bearing and cage assembly so the open side of the cage (A, **Figure 84**) faces toward the solenoid housing.
b. Fit the drive housing onto the solenoid housing, and install the two drive housing Phillips screws (**Figure 80**) and lockwashers. Tighten them securely.
c. Install the field coil assembly as described in *Starter Assembly* (this section).

Drive Housing Disassembly/Inspection (2007-2009 Models)

1. Remove the field coil assembly as described in *Starter Disassembly* (this section).
2. Remove the two drive housing Phillips screws (**Figure 88**).
3. Tap the drive housing, and remove it from the solenoid housing.
4. Remove the idler gear (**Figure 89**) from the bearing cage, and then remove the bearing cage (**Figure 90**). Do not lose the five rollers in the cage.
5. Push the drive shaft, and remove the starter clutch assembly (A, **Figure 91**) from the housing.
6. If necessary, disassemble the starter clutch assembly by performing the following:
    a. Compress the assembly's internal springs, and remove the snap ring from the end of the drive shaft.
    b. Remove the cup and pinion gear (**Figure 92**).
    c. Remove the short spring and spring seat.
    d. Press the splined end of the drive shaft, and remove it from the starter clutch.
    e. Remove the return spring (B, **Figure 82**) from the drive shaft (C) bore or from the solenoid plunger shaft (**Figure 93**) in the solenoid housing.
    f. Remove the steel ball from the drive shaft bore.
    g. Remove the drive spring (A, **Figure 82**) from the drive shaft.
7. Inspect the idler gear bearing and cage assembly (A, **Figure 94**) for worn or damaged parts.
8. Inspect the springs for kinks or fatigue.
9. Check the idler gear (B, **Figure 94**), pinion gear (A, **Figure 95**) and starter clutch gear (B) for worn or damage teeth.

10. Inspect the bearings (C, **Figure 95**). They should rotate freely with no roughness.
11. Inspect the drive shaft (C, **Figure 82**) for worn or damaged splines or gear teeth.
12. Inspect the drive housing outer O-ring (B, **Figure 91**) and the O-ring in the housing bore. Replace as needed.

Drive Housing Assembly (2007-2009 Models)

1. Lubricate the starter drive shaft (C, **Figure 82**) with a high-temperature grease and install the return spring (B) into the shaft.
2. Lubricate the drive housing outer O-ring (B, **Figure 91**) and the O-ring in the housing bore with a high-temperature grease.
3. If disassembled, assemble the starter clutch assembly by performing the following:
    a. Slide the drive spring (A, **Figure 82**) onto the splined end of the drive shaft (C).
    b. Slide the splined end of the drive shaft into the gear end of the starter clutch bore.
    c. Select a deep socket that matches the outside diameter of the drive shaft. Insert the socket into the starter clutch bore, and stand the socket upright on the bench.
    d. Press the starter clutch down so the socket presses the drive shaft into the starter clutch bore until the splined end of the shaft emerges from the starter clutch bearing.
    e. Install the spring seat, short spring, pinion gear and cup onto the splined end of the drive shaft. The collar on the pinion gear and the concave side of the cup must face up away from the starter clutch.
    f. Continue to compress the assembly, and install a new snap ring onto the drive shaft. Make sure the ring is completely seated in the shaft groove. Release the tension on the starter clutch and check the snap ring. It must be completely seated within the concave part of the cup.
    g. Remove the socket from the starter clutch bore.
4. Lubricate the starter clutch bearing (A, **Figure 91**) with a high-temperature grease, and install the starter clutch into the drive housing (C). Make sure the clutch bearing is seated in the bearing bore.

STARTER SOLENOID (2006 MODELS)

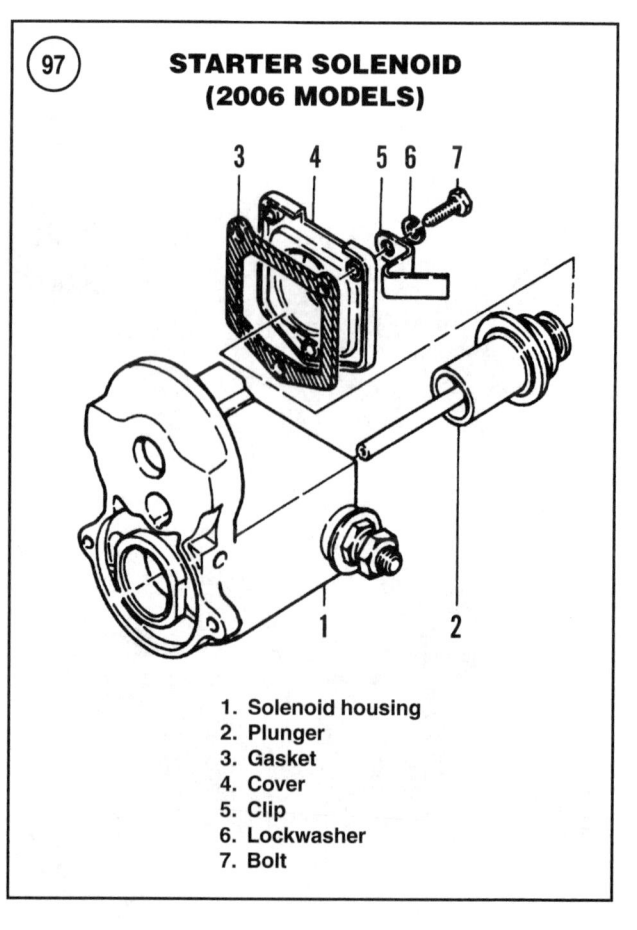

1. Solenoid housing
2. Plunger
3. Gasket
4. Cover
5. Clip
6. Lockwasher
7. Bolt

ELECTRICAL SYSTEM

SOLENOID ASSEMBLY (2007-2009 MODELS)

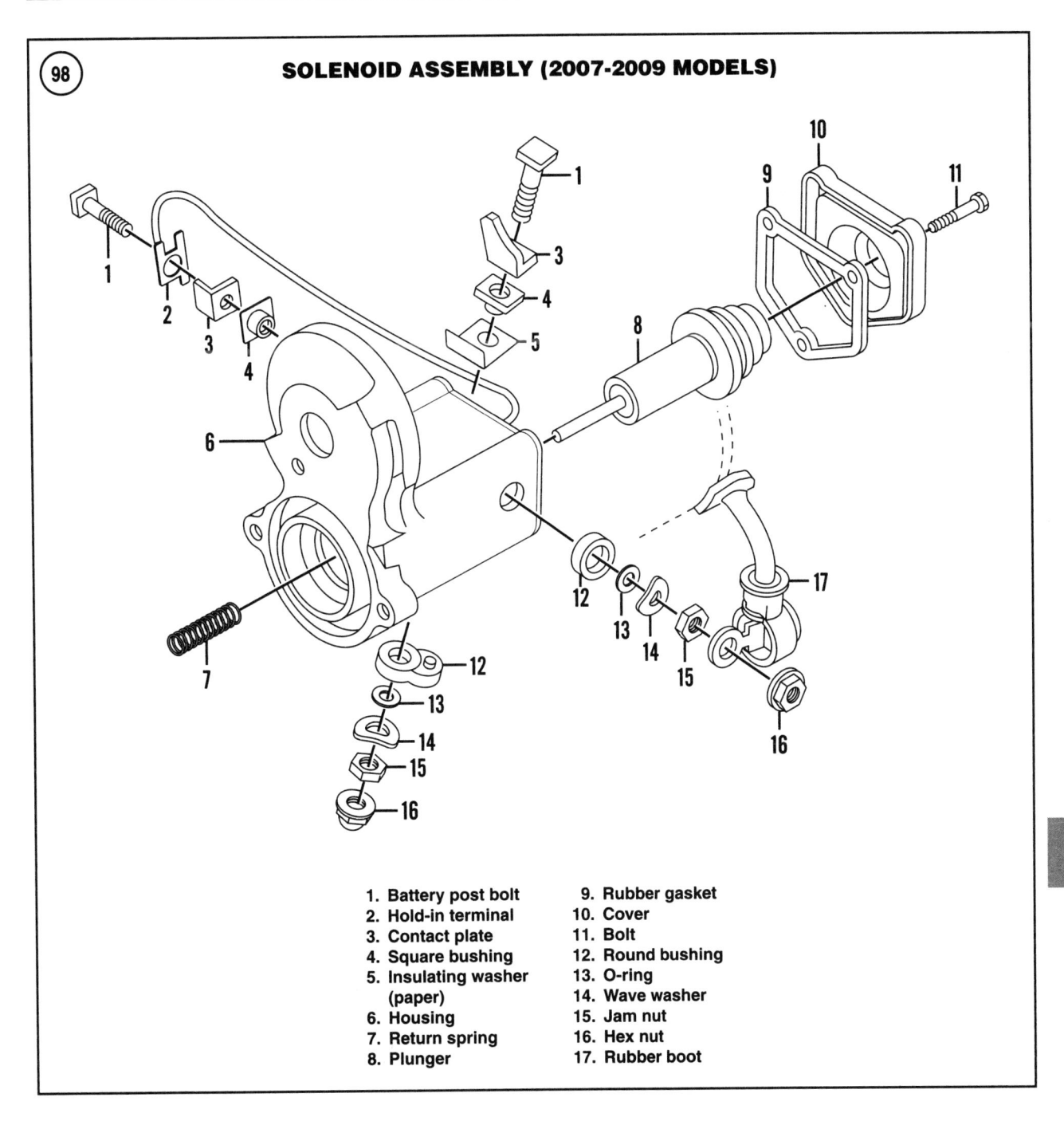

1. Battery post bolt
2. Hold-in terminal
3. Contact plate
4. Square bushing
5. Insulating washer (paper)
6. Housing
7. Return spring
8. Plunger
9. Rubber gasket
10. Cover
11. Bolt
12. Round bushing
13. O-ring
14. Wave washer
15. Jam nut
16. Hex nut
17. Rubber boot

5. Lubricate the bearing rollers and bearing cage with a high-temperature grease. Install the rollers into the cage (A, **Figure 94**), and then install the bearing cage (**Figure 90**) onto the shaft in the drive housing.
6. Lubricate the idler gear (**Figure 89**) with a high-temperature grease, and install it over the bearing cage.
7. Install the ball (**Figure 96**) into the drive shaft bore.
8. Apply a high-temperature grease to the solenoid plunger shaft, and slide the return spring (**Figure 93**) onto the shaft.
9. Fit the drive housing onto the solenoid housing so the return spring (**Figure 93**) will slide into the drive shaft bore within the starter clutch.
10. Install the two drive housing Phillips screws (**Figure 88**) and tighten securely.

11. Install the field coil assembly as described in *Starter Assembly* (this section).

Solenoid Housing Disassembly/Inspection/Assembly

Refer to **Figure 97** or **Figure 98**.

1. Remove the field coil assembly as described in *Starter Disassembly* (this section).
2. Remove the two drive housing Phillips screws (**Figure 88**).
3. Tap the drive housing, and remove it from the solenoid housing. If the return spring (**Figure 93**) remains with the solenoid plunger, do not lose the ball (**Figure 96**) in the starter clutch bore.

4A. On 2006 models, remove the bolts, washers and clip securing the end cover to the solenoid housing. Remove the end cover (**Figure 99**) and the gasket.

4B. On 2007-2009 models, remove the solenoid cover bolts (A, **Figure 100**), and remove the solenoid cover (B) and gasket.

5. Remove the plunger assembly (**Figure 101**) from the solenoid housing.

6. Inspect the rubber cap (A, **Figure 102**) for hardness or deterioration; replace if necessary.

7. Inspect the plunger (B, **Figure 102**) and shaft (C) for wear or damage; replace if necessary.

8. Inspect the solenoid housing (A, **Figure 103**) for wear, cracks or other damage.

9. Inspect each terminal post assembly on the solenoid housing. If any part is worn or damaged, install a new solenoid repair kit. Individual terminal parts are not available.

10. Assemble the solenoid housing by reversing the disassembly steps while noting the following:
   a. Lubricate the solenoid plunger with a high-temperature grease.
   b. Install a new gasket.
   c. Install the field coil assembly as described in *Starter Assembly* (this section).

Solenoid Contacts Removal/Installation

Refer to **Figure 98**.

NOTE
A solenoid contact repair kit is available from the manufacturer.

1. Purchase a solenoid contact repair kit prior to starting this procedure.

2. Perform *Solenoid Housing Disassembly* as described in this section.

3. Disassemble the field coil short post (B, **Figure 103**) as follows:
   a. Remove the hex nut, if still in place.
   b. Remove the jam nut, wave washer, round bushing and O-ring from the post.
   c. On the inside, remove the post bolt, hold-in terminal contact plate and square bushing.

4. Disassemble the battery long post (C, **Figure 103**) as follows:
   a. Remove the hex nut, if still in place.
   b. Remove the jam nut, wave washer, round bushing and O-ring from the post.
   c. On the inside, remove the post bolt, contact plate, square bushing and paper insulator washer.

5. Assemble the field coil short post (B, **Figure 103** as follows:
   a. Working inside the housing, insert the square bushing into the hole in the housing.
   b. Hold the inboard foot against the solenoid winding, and then align the contact plate hole with the square bushing.
   c. Move the hold-in terminal into position and insert the short post bolt through the hold-in terminal, contact plate, square bushing and solenoid housing. Hold the short post bolt in place.
   d. From the outside, install the round bushing, O-ring and wave washer onto the post bolt.
   e. Install the jam nut, but do not tighten it at this time.

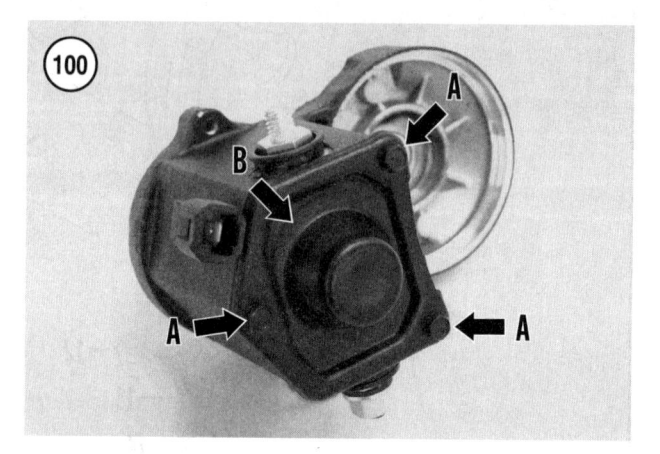

6. Assemble the battery long post (C, **Figure 103**) as follows:
   a. Working inside the housing, align the paper insulator washer with the hole in the housing.
   b. Insert the square bushing sleeve into the paper insulator.

ELECTRICAL SYSTEM

102

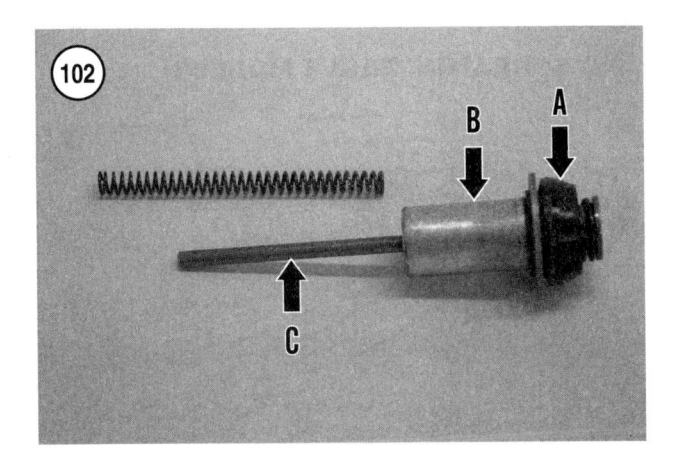

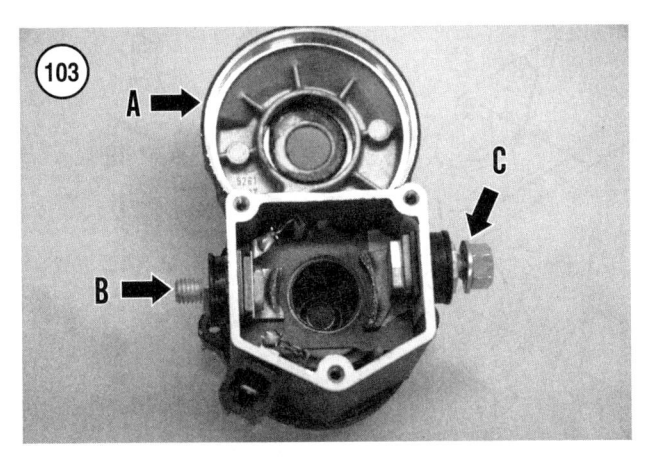

103

c. Hold the inboard foot against the solenoid winding, and then align the contact plate hole with the square bushing.

d. Insert the long post bolt through the contact plate, square bushing and solenoid housing. Hold the long post bolt in place.

e. From the outside, install the round bushing, O-ring and wave washer onto the post bolt. Make sure that the round bushing index pin enters the blind hole in the solenoid housing.

f. Install the jam nut, but do not tighten it at this time.

7. Complete the *Solenoid Housing Assembly* procedure as described in this section.

8. Alternately tighten the jam nuts to 65-80 in.-lb. (7.3-9.0 N•m). Ensure that the contact plates are still correctly aligned with the plunger. If necessary, loosen the jam nut(s), reposition the contact plates and retighten the jam nuts to specification.

LIGHTING SYSTEM

The lighting system consists of a headlight, passing lights, taillight/brake light combination, turn signals and Tour-Pak lighting.

Always use the correct wattage bulb. The use of a larger wattage bulb will give a dim light and a smaller wattage bulb will burn out prematurely. Refer to **Table 4** for bulb specifications.

Many of the following procedures refer to disconnecting a specific electrical connector located within the headlight or the front fairing assembly. Refer to *Electrical Connector Location and Identification* (this chapter).

HEADLIGHT

WARNING
If the headlight has just burned out or just been turned off, it will be hot. To avoid burned fingers, allow the bulb to cool prior to removal.

CAUTION
All models are equipped with a quartz-halogen bulb. Do not touch the bulb glass. Traces of body oil left on the bulb will drastically reduce its life. Clean all traces of oil from the bulb glass with a cloth moistened in alcohol or lacquer thinner.

Headlight Bulb Replacement (FLHT, FLHX and FLHR Models and Screamin' Eagle Except 2007-2008 FLHRSE Models)

Refer to **Figure 104** and **Figure 105**.

1. Place a shop cloth or towel on the front bumper to protect the finish.

2. Remove the screw (A, **Figure 106**) at the base of the trim bezel (B), and then remove the trim bezel from the headlight lens assembly. Do not lose the two springs on the trim bezel.

3. Remove the three screws securing the retaining ring (**Figure 107**) and remove the ring while holding the headlight lens assembly in place.

4. Pull the lens assembly (**Figure 108**) out of the front fairing, or headlight nacelle.

5. On models so equipped, squeeze the two external tabs to release the electrical connector from the lens assembly.

6. Pull *straight out* and disconnect the electrical connector from the bulb (**Figure 109**) and remove the headlight assembly.

7. Remove the rubber cover (**Figure 110**) from the back of the headlight lens. Check the rubber boot for tears or deterioration; replace if necessary.

8. Unhook the light bulb retaining clip (**Figure 111**) and pivot it out of the way.

9. Remove and discard the blown bulb (**Figure 112**).

10. Align the tangs on the new bulb with the notches in the headlight lens and install the bulb.

11. Securely hook the retaining clip over the bulb (**Figure 111**).

12. Install the rubber boot (**Figure 110**) and makes sure it is correctly seated against the bulb and the retainer.

13. Correctly align the electrical plug terminals with the bulb and connect it. Push it *straight on* until it bottoms on the bulb and the rubber cover (**Figure 109**).

14. Check headlight operation.

CHAPTER ELEVEN

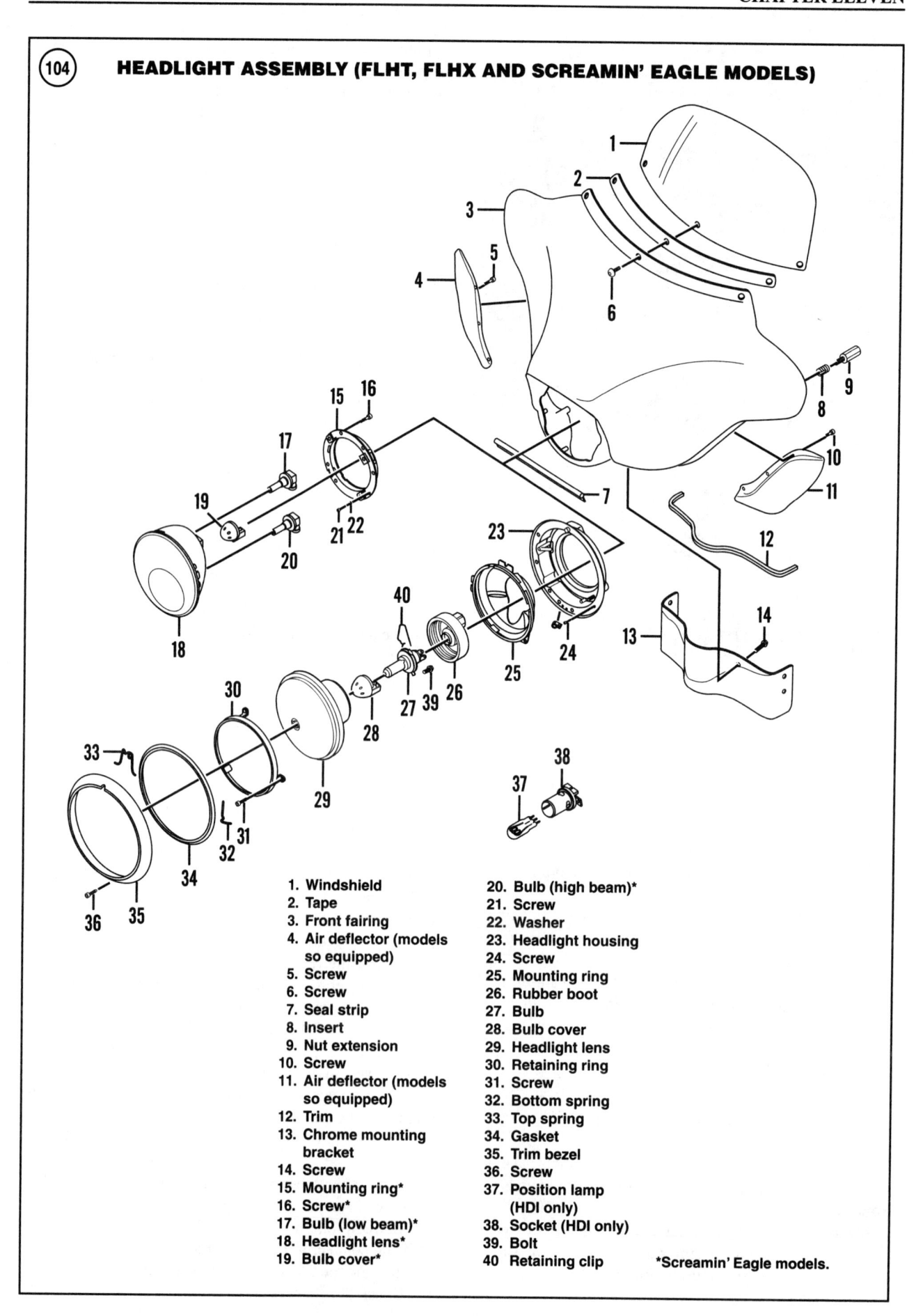

104 HEADLIGHT ASSEMBLY (FLHT, FLHX AND SCREAMIN' EAGLE MODELS)

1. Windshield
2. Tape
3. Front fairing
4. Air deflector (models so equipped)
5. Screw
6. Screw
7. Seal strip
8. Insert
9. Nut extension
10. Screw
11. Air deflector (models so equipped)
12. Trim
13. Chrome mounting bracket
14. Screw
15. Mounting ring*
16. Screw*
17. Bulb (low beam)*
18. Headlight lens*
19. Bulb cover*
20. Bulb (high beam)*
21. Screw
22. Washer
23. Headlight housing
24. Screw
25. Mounting ring
26. Rubber boot
27. Bulb
28. Bulb cover
29. Headlight lens
30. Retaining ring
31. Screw
32. Bottom spring
33. Top spring
34. Gasket
35. Trim bezel
36. Screw
37. Position lamp (HDI only)
38. Socket (HDI only)
39. Bolt
40. Retaining clip

*Screamin' Eagle models.

ELECTRICAL SYSTEM

HEADLIGHT AND NACELLE (FLHR MODELS)

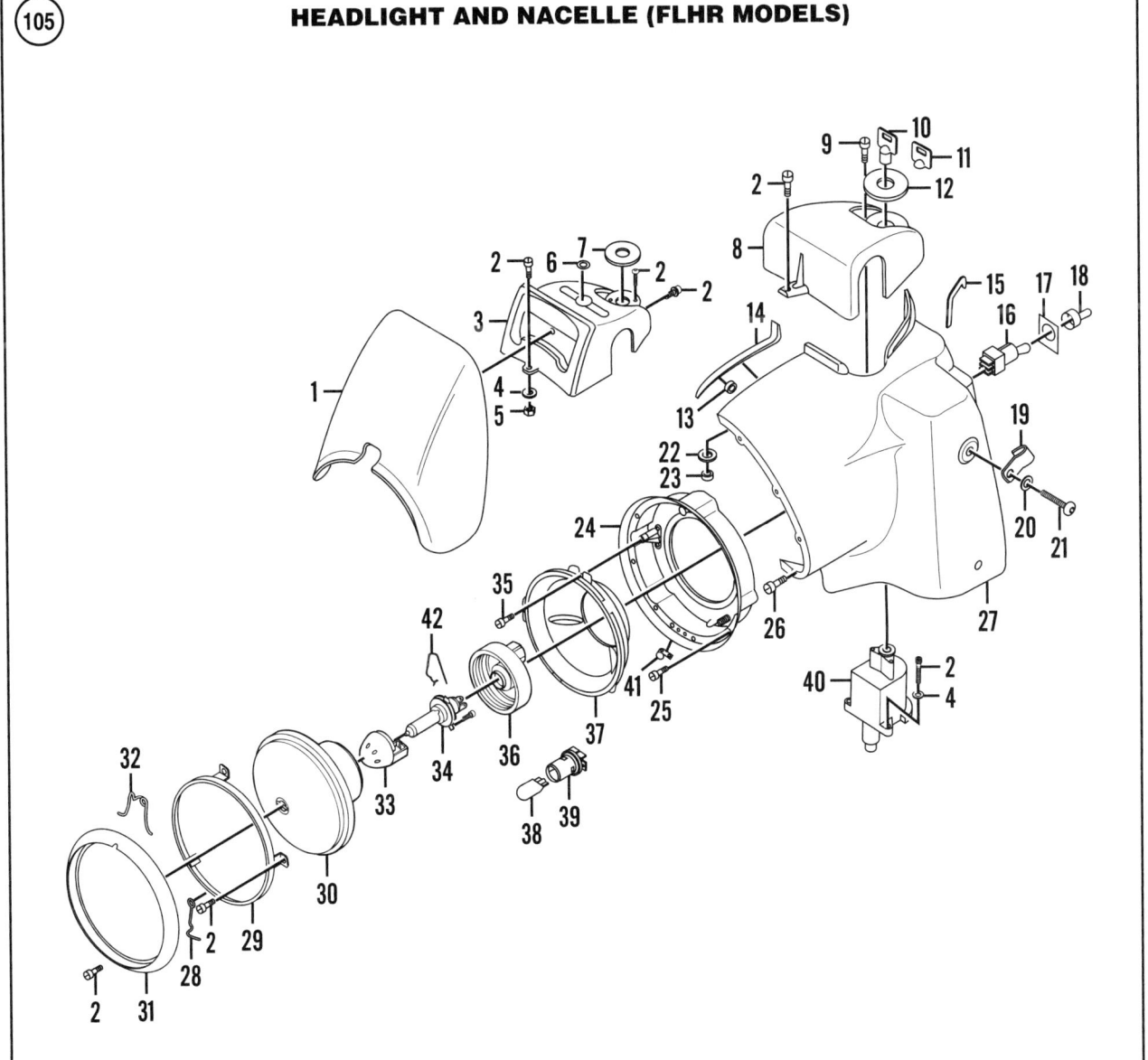

1. Deflector wing (models so equipped)
2. Screw
3. Handlebar cover (FLHRS and FLHRSI models only)
4. Washer
5. Nut with washer
6. Label
7. Trim plate (FLHR models except FLHRS and FLHRSI)
8. Handlebar cover (FLHR models except FLHRS and FLHRSI)
9. Screw
10. Key
11. Key cover
12. Trim plate (FLHR models except FLHRS and FLHRSI)
13. Speed nut
14. Trim
15. Trim
16. Switch
17. Label
18. Rubber boot
19. Clamp
20. Washer
21. Screw
22. Washer
23. Nut with washer
24. Headlight housing
25. Screw
26. Screw
27. Headlight nacelle (left side shown)
28. Bottom spring
29. Retaining ring
30. Headlight lens
31. Trim bezel
32. Top spring
33. Bulb cover
34. Bulb
35. Screw
36. Rubber boot
37. Mounting ring
38. Position lamp (HDI only)
39. Position lamp socket (HDI)
40. Ignition switch
41. Clamp
42. Retaining clip

478   CHAPTER ELEVEN

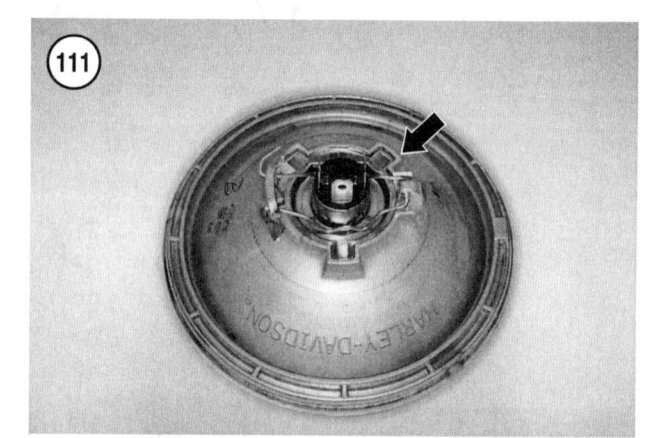

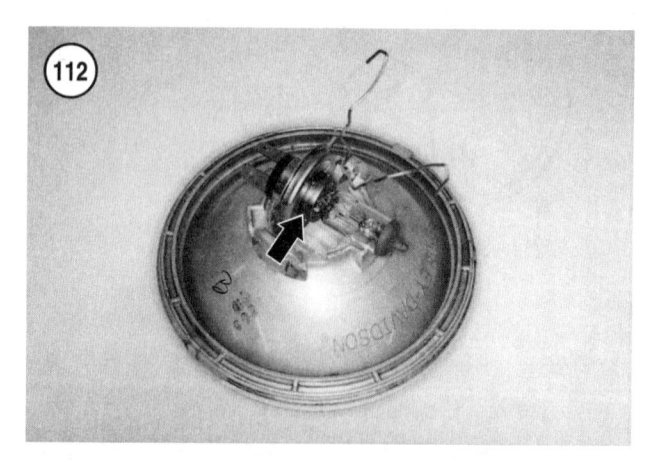

ELECTRICAL SYSTEM

(114) HEADLIGHT AND NACELLE (FLHRSE MODELS)

1. Handlebar cover (2008-2009 models)
2. Indicator light bezel (2008 models)
3. LED indicator light (2008 models)
4. Screw
5. Key
6. Key cover
7. Trim plate
8. Handlebar cover
9. Trim
10. Speed nut
11. Washer
12. Nut with washer
13. Trim
14. Switch
15. Label
16. Rubber boot
17. Headlight nacelle (left side shown)
18. Washer
19. Ignition switch
20. Headlight assembly
21. Cable strap
22. Bulb (low beam)
23. Mounting ring
24. Bulb cover
25. Headlight lens
26. Bulb (high beam)
27. Screw
28. Washer
29. Screw
30. Wiring harness (2008 models)
31. Screw
32. Trim bezel
33. Top spring
34. Screw
35. Retaining ring
36. Headlight lens*
37. Bulb cover*
38. Bulb*
39. Rubber boot*
40. Screw
41. Mounting ring
42. Headlight housing
43. Headlight assembly*
44. Position lamp*
45. Position lamp socket*
46. Terminal (2008 models)*
47. Jumper harness (2008 models)*
48. Terminal (2008 models)*
49. Retaining clip*
50. Clamp

*HDI models only.

15. Insert the lens assembly (**Figure 108**) into the headlight housing and seat it correctly.

16. Install the retaining ring (**Figure 107**) and the three screws. Tighten the screws securely.

17. Install the square portion of the top spring (**Figure 113**) into the slot in the trim bezel and snap the trim bezel into place. Install the screw and tighten securely.

18. Check headlight adjustment as described in this section.

Headlight Bulb Replacement (FLHRSE Models)

Refer to **Figure 114**.

1. Place a shop cloth or towel on the front bumper to protect the finish.
2. Remove the screw at the base of the trim bezel, and then remove the trim bezel from the headlight lens assembly. Do not lose the top spring on the trim bezel.
3. Support the headlight lens and remove the three Phillips screws (A, **Figure 115**).
4. Carefully pull straight out on the bottom of the ring (B, **Figure 115**). Lift the ring up and remove it from the headlight lens while holding the headlight lens assembly in place. Lay the lens assembly on cloths covering the front fender.
5. Pinch the two latches on the low beam electrical connector (A, **Figure 116**) and remove it from the bulb socket (B).
6. Grasp the low bulb socket (B, **Figure 116**) and turn it approximately 1/8 turn *counterclockwise*. Withdraw it from the headlight shell and discard the blown low beam bulb.
7. Pinch the two latches on the high beam electrical connector (C, **Figure 116**) and remove it from the bulb socket (D).
8. Grasp the bulb socket (D, **Figure 116**) and turn it approximately 1/8 turn *counterclockwise*. Withdraw it from the headlight shell and discard the blown high beam bulb.
9. Align the tangs on the new low beam bulb (green label) with the notches in the headlight lens and install the bulb (B, **Figure 116**). Turn it approximately 1/8 turn *clockwise*.
10. Align the tangs on the new high beam bulb (yellow label) with the notches in the headlight lens and install the bulb (D, **Figure 116**). Turn it approximately 1/8 turn *clockwise*.
11. Attach the connector to each bulb assembly. Push on each of the connectors until it clicks into place.
12. Check headlight function.
13. Move the headlight lens assembly into place, install the retaining ring and the three Phillips screws (A, **Figure 115**). Tighten the screws to 23-28 in.-lb. (2.6-3.2 N•m).
14. Make sure the rubber gasket is in place in the trim bezel and is held in place with the three small springs.
15. Make sure the top spring is in place at the top center location.
16. Position the trim bezel onto the top portion of the headlight case. Fit the square shaped section of the spring into the slot at the top of the back plate.
17. Carefully press the trim bezel down until it is positioned correctly with equal amounts of gasket visible between the headlight assembly and the trim bezel.
18. Install the screw at the base of the trim ring and tighten to 9-16 in.-lb. (1.0-1.8 N•m).
19. Check headlight adjustment as described in this section.

Headlight Bulb Replacement
(FLTR Models and 2009 FLTRSE3 Models)

Refer to **Figure 117** and **Figure 118**.
1. Remove the front fairing and windshield assembly as described in Chapter Seventeen. 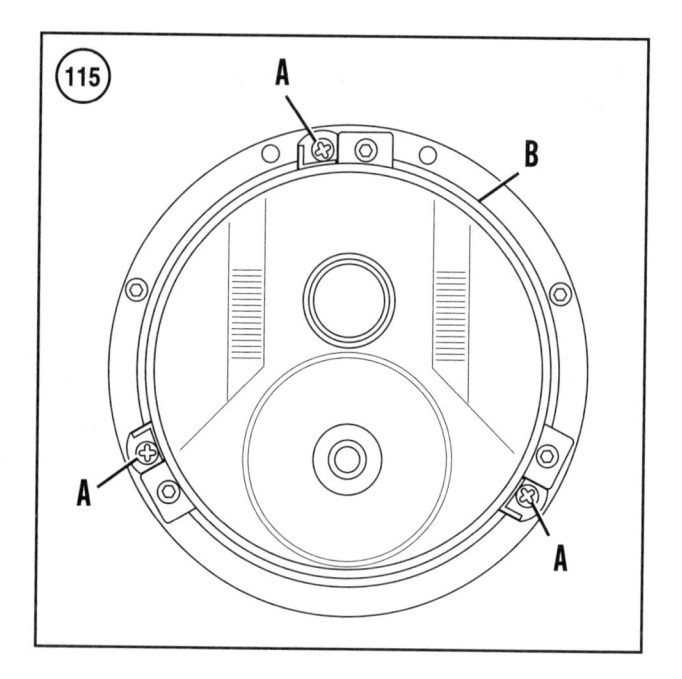 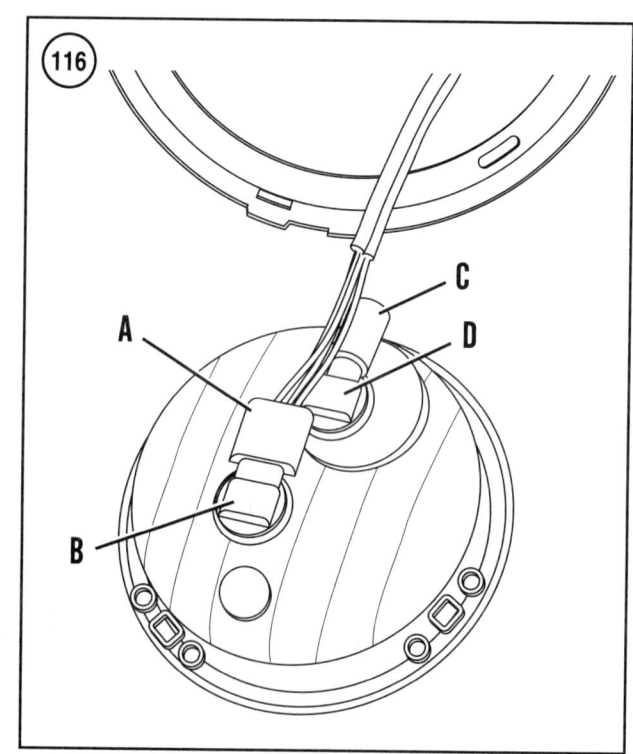
2. Place the front fairing on a workbench covered with several towels to protect the finish.
3. Remove the rubber boot (**Figure 119**) from the back of the lens assembly. Check the rubber boot for tears or deterioration; replace if necessary.
4. Rotate the bulb retainer (A, **Figure 120**) *counterclockwise* and remove it from the lens assembly.
5. Remove and discard the blown bulb (B, **Figure 120**).
6. Position the new bulb with the wider tab at the top. Insert this tab under the flange, and push the bottom of bulb flange so the lower two tabs side fit snugly in the slot of the bulb housing.

ELECTRICAL SYSTEM

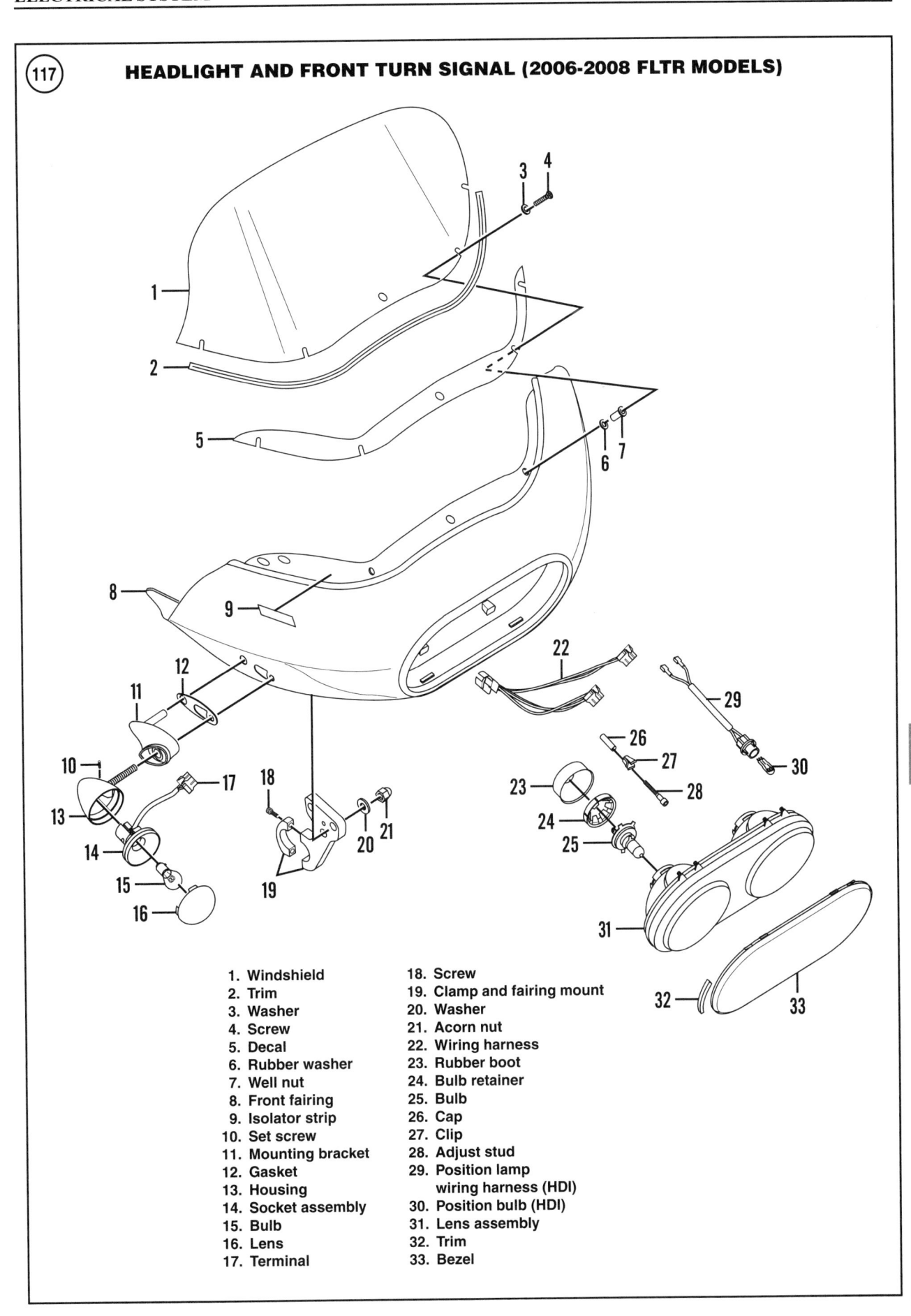

481

(117) HEADLIGHT AND FRONT TURN SIGNAL (2006-2008 FLTR MODELS)

1. Windshield
2. Trim
3. Washer
4. Screw
5. Decal
6. Rubber washer
7. Well nut
8. Front fairing
9. Isolator strip
10. Set screw
11. Mounting bracket
12. Gasket
13. Housing
14. Socket assembly
15. Bulb
16. Lens
17. Terminal
18. Screw
19. Clamp and fairing mount
20. Washer
21. Acorn nut
22. Wiring harness
23. Rubber boot
24. Bulb retainer
25. Bulb
26. Cap
27. Clip
28. Adjust stud
29. Position lamp wiring harness (HDI)
30. Position bulb (HDI)
31. Lens assembly
32. Trim
33. Bezel

11

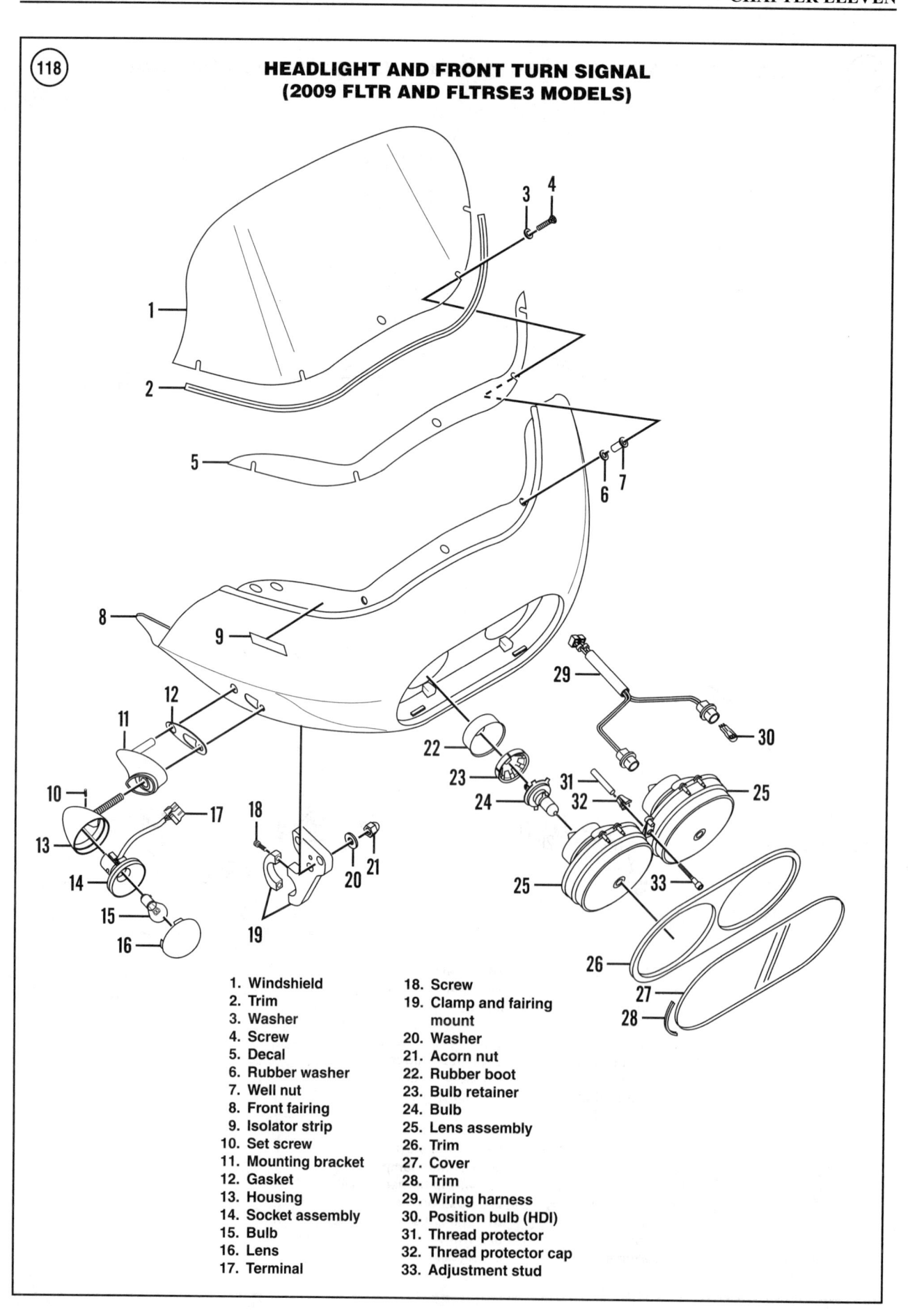

HEADLIGHT AND FRONT TURN SIGNAL (2009 FLTR AND FLTRSE3 MODELS)

1. Windshield
2. Trim
3. Washer
4. Screw
5. Decal
6. Rubber washer
7. Well nut
8. Front fairing
9. Isolator strip
10. Set screw
11. Mounting bracket
12. Gasket
13. Housing
14. Socket assembly
15. Bulb
16. Lens
17. Terminal
18. Screw
19. Clamp and fairing mount
20. Washer
21. Acorn nut
22. Rubber boot
23. Bulb retainer
24. Bulb
25. Lens assembly
26. Trim
27. Cover
28. Trim
29. Wiring harness
30. Position bulb (HDI)
31. Thread protector
32. Thread protector cap
33. Adjustment stud

ELECTRICAL SYSTEM

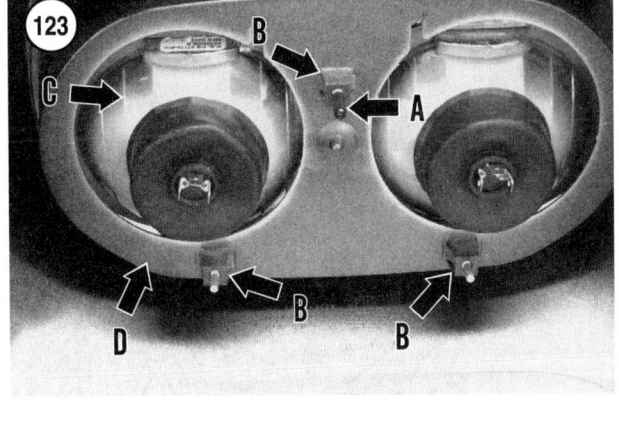

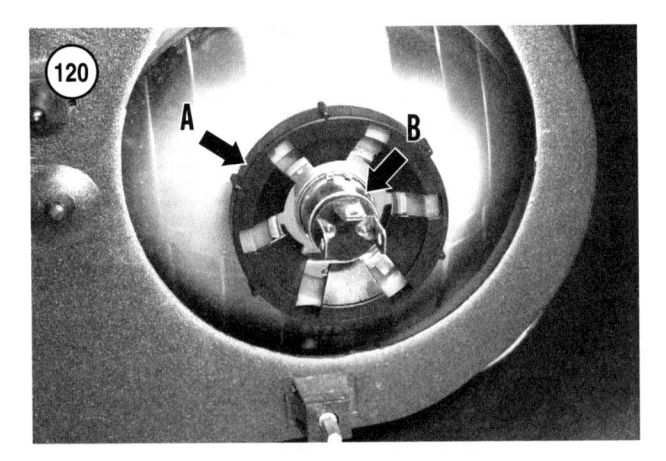

7. Place the bulb retainer (B, **Figure 120**) over the bulb, and carefully rotate it *clockwise* until it is secure in the lens assembly.
8. Install the rubber boot (**Figure 119**) and make sure it is correctly seated against the bulb and the retainer.
9. Repeat the process to replace the other bulb if necessary.
10. Install the front fairing and windshield assembly as described in Chapter Seventeen.
11. Check headlight operation.
12. Check headlight adjustment as described in this section.

Headlight Lens Removal/Installation (FLTR Models and 2009 FLTRSE3)

Refer to **Figure 117** and **Figure 118**.
1. Remove the front fairing and windshield assembly as described in Chapter Seventeen.
2. Place the front fairing on workbench covered with several towels to protect the finish.
3. On the inboard surface of the outer fairing, carefully depress the two upper tabs (**Figure 121**) of the lens cover with a flat-bladed screwdriver. Repeat for the two lower tabs and remove the lens cover (**Figure 122**) from the front side of the fairing.
4. Remove the plastic protective sleeve (A, **Figure 123**) from the top center hex adjuster stud.
5. Depress the mounting clips on all three hex adjuster studs (B, **Figure 123**) and carefully remove the lens assembly (C) from the front side of the front fairing (D). Do not damage the stud holes in the front fairing during lens removal.
6. Align the lens hex adjuster studs with the holes in the front fairing, and slowly push the lens assembly into the front fairing until the mounting clips engage the inboard side of the outer fairing. Ensure that all three studs are fully engaged with the outer fairing.
7. To avoid cutting or chafing headlight wiring, install the plastic protective sleeve (A, **Figure 123**) onto the top center hex adjuster stud.
8. Clean the outer surface of the lens assembly and the inner surface of the lens cover.

124

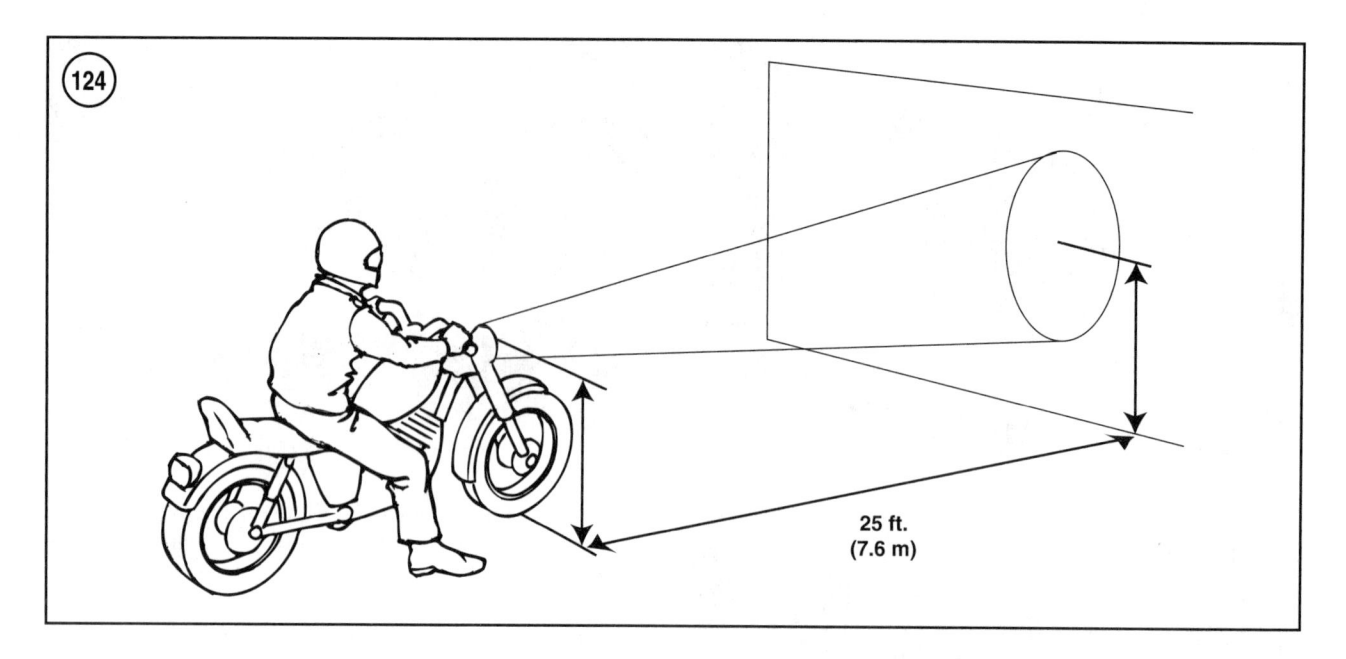

25 ft. (7.6 m)

9. Carefully snap the lens cover bottom two tabs into place in the inner fairing. Repeat for the upper two tabs and make sure the lens cover is securely held in place.
10. Install the front fairing and windshield assembly as described in Chapter Seventeen.

Headlight Adjustment (All Models)

1. Park the motorcycle on a level surface approximately 25 ft. (7.6 m) from the wall (**Figure 124**).
2. Check tire inflation pressure, readjust to the correct pressure if necessary as described in Chapter Three.
3. Draw a horizontal line on the wall at is same height above floor at the center of the headlight.
4. Have a helper the approximate weight of the principal rider sit on the seat.
5. Aim the headlight at the wall and turn on the headlight. Switch the headlight to the high beam.
6. Position the front wheel directly at straight ahead.
7. Check the headlight beam alignment. The broad, flat pattern of light (main beam of light) should be centered on the horizontal line (equal area of light above and below line).
8. Turn the key switch to the ignition position.
9. Now check the headlight beam lateral alignment. With the headlight beam pointed straight ahead (centered), there should be an equal area of light to the left and right of center.
10A. On FLTR models, if the beam is incorrect as described in this section, adjust the headlight as follows.

NOTE
Figure 125 is shown with the meter assembly removed. Do not remove the meter assembly for this procedure. The hex-adjusters are located on each side of the lower inner surface of the front fairing.

125

126

  a. Use a 4.5 mm socket on a flexible extension and adjust the hex-adjuster (**Figure 125**).
  b. Refer to **Table 5** for the correct rotation of the adjusters to achieve correct headlight aim.
10B. On all other models, if the beam is incorrect as described in this section, adjust the headlight as follows.
  a. Turn the top vertical adjuster (A, **Figure 126**) to adjust headlight vertically.

ELECTRICAL SYSTEM

127 PASSING LIGHTS/FRONT TURN SIGNALS (FLHR AND FLHT MODELS)

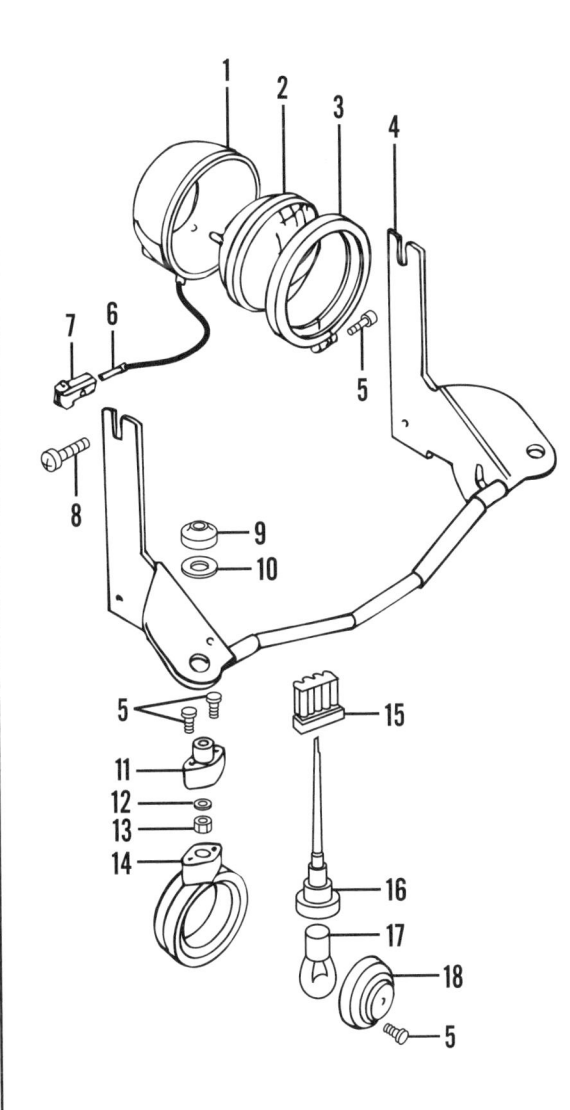

1. Passing light housing
2. Passing light lens/bulb assembly
3. Trim bezel
4. Mounting bracket
5. Screw
6. Wiring harness
7. Terminal housing
8. Bolt
9. Swivel block
10. Dished washer
11. Clamp block
12. Washer
13. Locknut
14. Turn signal housing
15. Socket connector
16. Bulb socket
17. Turn signal bulb
18. Turn signal lens

b. Turn the right side horizontal adjuster (B, **Figure 126**) to adjust headlight horizontally.

PASSING LIGHTS AND FRONT TURN SIGNALS

Passing Light and Front Turn Signal Bulb Replacement (FLHR and FLHT Models)

Refer to **Figure 127**.

1. To remove the passing light bulb, perform the following:
   a. Remove the screw (**Figure 128**) at the base of the trim bezel and remove the trim bezel from the passing light housing.
   b. Carefully pull the bulb/lens assembly partially out of the housing.
   c. Loosen the two screws securing the wiring harness (**Figure 129**) to the bulb/lens assembly and remove it.
   d. Connect the wiring harness to the *new* bulb/lens assembly and tighten the screws securely.
   e. Push the bulb/lens assembly into the housing and install the trim bezel.
   f. Tighten the screw securely.

2. To remove the front turn signal bulb, perform the following:

a. Remove the screws securing the lens (**Figure 130**).
b. Push in on the bulb, rotate it, and then remove the blown bulb (**Figure 131**).
c. Install a new bulb.
d. Install the lens and tighten the screws securely. Do not overtighten the screws as the lens may crack.

Passing Light and Front Turn Signal Bulb Replacement (FLHTCUSE Models)

Refer to **Figure 132**.

1. Remove the passing light bulb as follows:
   a. Loosen the clamping screw at the base of the trim bezel and remove the trim bezel from the passing light housing.
   b. Carefully pull the bulb reflector partially out of the housing.
   c. Disconnect the electrical connector from the bulb socket on the backside of the bulb reflector.
   d. Remove the bulb reflector from the housing.
   e. Remove the nesting ring from the bulb reflector.
   f. Secure the bulb reflector with one hand and rotate the bulb/socket assembly *counterclockwise* approximately 1/8 turn. Remove the bulb/socket assembly and discard it.
   g. Install a *new* bulb/socket assembly into the backside of the bulb reflector.
   h. Secure the bulb reflector with one hand and rotate the bulb/socket assembly *clockwise* approximately 1/8 turn to secure it.
   i. Position the nesting ring with the concave side facing out and install the nesting ring into the bulb reflector. Index the nesting ring slots into the bulb reflector tabs.
   j. Connect the electrical connector onto the bulb/socket assembly. Push it on until it clicks into place.
   k. Carefully install the bulb reflector into the housing and hold it in place.
   l. Install the trim bezel onto the passing light housing and rotate it so the clamping screw is located at the base of the housing. Tighten the clamping screw securely.
2. Remove the front turn signal bulb as follows:
   a. Locate the notch in the lens cap.
   b. Insert a coin into the notch and carefully twist the coin until the lens cap (A, **Figure 133**) comes off the housing.
   c. Push in on the bulb (B, **Figure 133**), rotate it and remove it.
   d. Install a new bulb.
   e. Push the lens cap into the housing until is snaps into place.

Passing Light Adjustment (All Models)

Refer to **Figure 134**.

1. Check the headlight aim and adjust if necessary as described in this chapter.

2. Park the motorcycle on a level surface approximately 25 ft. (7.6 m) from the wall.
3. Check tire inflation pressure. Readjust it if necessary, as described in Chapter Three.
4. Have a helper the approximate weight of the principal rider sit on the seat.
5. Draw a horizontal line on the wall the same height as the center of the headlight (**Figure 124**).
6. Aim the headlight at the wall. Switch the headlight to the HIGH beam. Point the front wheel straight ahead.
7. Check the headlight beam alignment. The broad, flat pattern of light (main beam of light) should be centered on the horizontal line with an equal area of light above and below line. Mark this location on the wall (A, **Figure 134**).
8. Turn off the headlight.
9. Measure the distance from the horizontal centerline of the headlight to the horizontal centerline of the left side passing light. Note the dimension.
10. Measure the distance from the vertical centerline of the headlight to the vertical centerline of the passing light. Note the dimension.
11. Repeat the vertical and horizontal measurement process for the right side passing light. Note both dimensions.
12. Refer to the dimensions recorded for the left and right passing light, and then mark these locations on the wall as shown in B and C, **Figure 134**.
13. Have the same helper sit on the seat and turn the headlight to HIGH beam. Verify that the headlight beam is still

ELECTRICAL SYSTEM

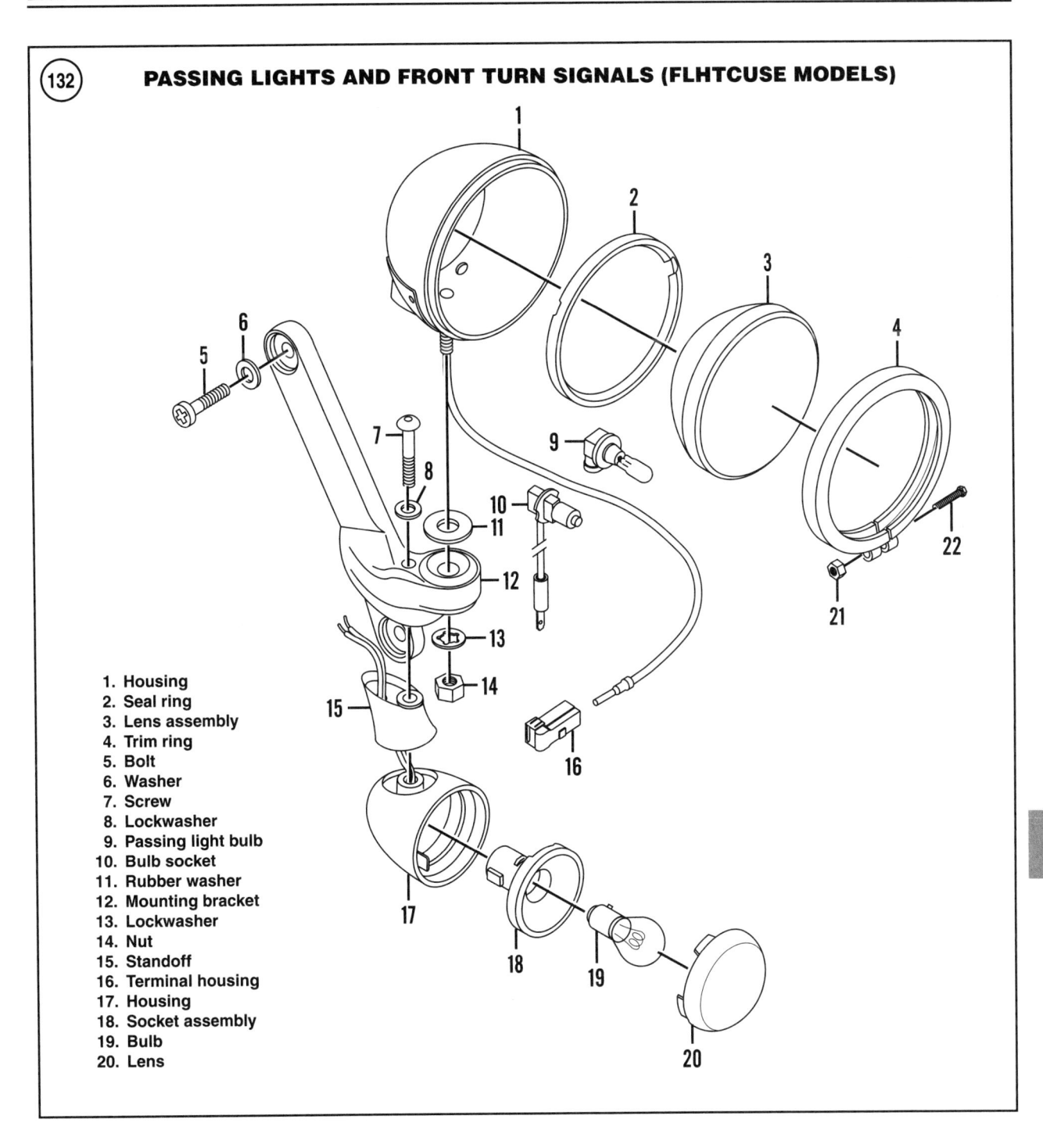

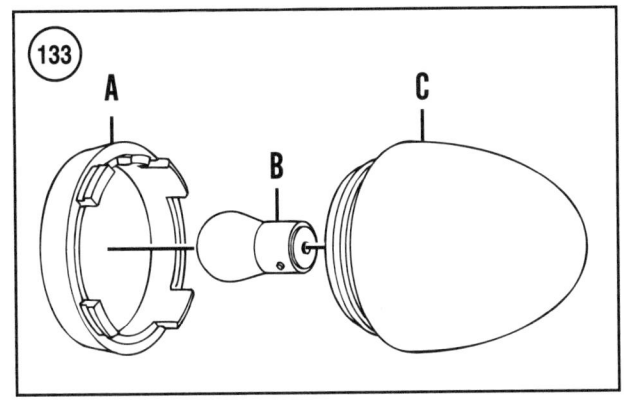

132 PASSING LIGHTS AND FRONT TURN SIGNALS (FLHTCUSE MODELS)

1. Housing
2. Seal ring
3. Lens assembly
4. Trim ring
5. Bolt
6. Washer
7. Screw
8. Lockwasher
9. Passing light bulb
10. Bulb socket
11. Rubber washer
12. Mounting bracket
13. Lockwasher
14. Nut
15. Standoff
16. Terminal housing
17. Housing
18. Socket assembly
19. Bulb
20. Lens

133

correctly aligned with the vertical and horizontal centerlines on the wall.

14. Turn the headlight to LOW beam.

15. Completely cover the headlight and the right side passing light so their beam is not visible on the wall.

16. Observe the location of the left side passing light on the wall. It should be within the area indicated in D, **Figure 134**. If the location is incorrect, adjust the passing light as described in this section.

17. Remove the cover from the right side passing light and place it over the left side passing light, so its beam is not visible on the wall.

488   CHAPTER ELEVEN

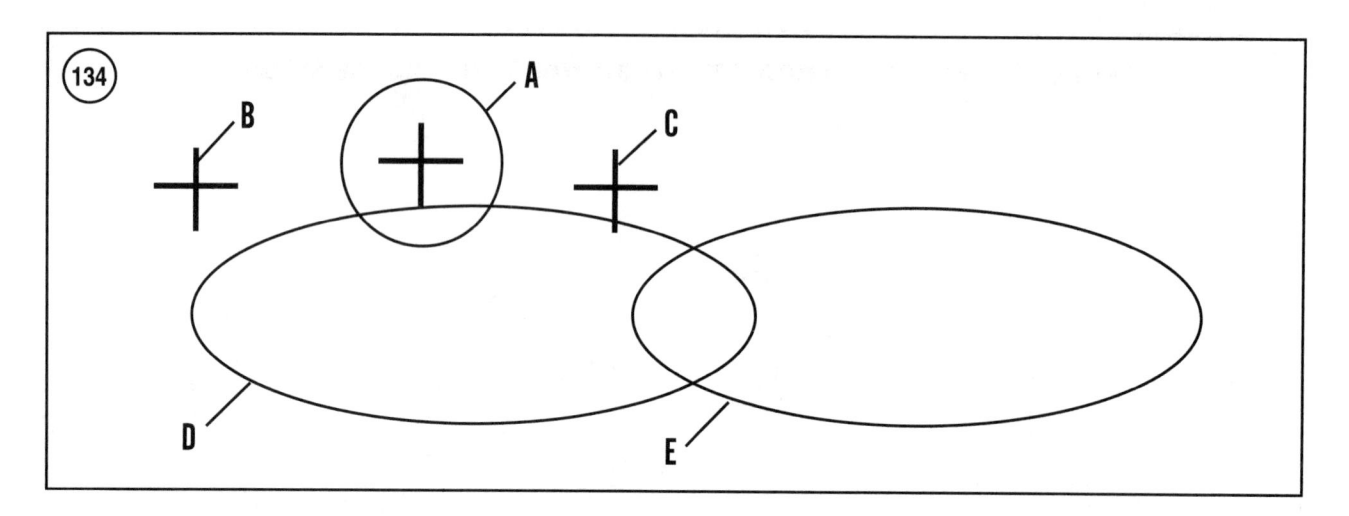

(134)

A, B, C, D, E

18. Leave the headlight still covered so its beam is not visible on the wall. Make sure it is still on LOW beam.
19. Observe the location of the right side passing light on the wall. It should be within the area indicated in E, **Figure 134**. If the location is incorrect, adjust the passing light as described in this section.
20A. On all models except FLHTCUSE, adjust the passing light as follows:
  a. Turn off the headlight and passing lights.
  b. Remove the two screws securing the turn signal light assembly to the mounting bracket, and lower the turn signal light assembly.
  c. Insert a flare nut socket (Snap-On part No. FRX181), or an equivalent, into the bottom of the turn signal mounting bracket and loosen the adjust nut.
  d. Move the housing in the desired direction to correct the aim.
  e. Tighten the adjust nut to 15-18 ft.-lb. (20.30-24.4 N•m).
  f. Tighten the turn signal mounting screws to 36-60 in.-lb. (4.1-6.8 N•m).
  g. Recheck alignment and repeat if necessary.
20B. On FLHTCUSE models adjust the passing light as follows:
  a. Loosen the nut securing the passing light to the mounting bracket.
  b. Move the housing in the desired direction to correct the aim.
  c. Tighten the nut to 15-18 ft.-lb. (20.3-24.4 N•m).

TURN SIGNALS

Front Turn Signal Bulb Replacement (FLHX Models and All Screamin' Eagle)

Refer to **Figure 135**.
1. Locate a notch in the lens and insert a coin into it. Carefully twist the coin until the lens (A, **Figure 133**) comes off the housing (C).
2. Push in on the bulb (B, **Figure 133**), rotate it and remove it from the socket.
3. Install a *new* bulb and rotate it until locked into place.

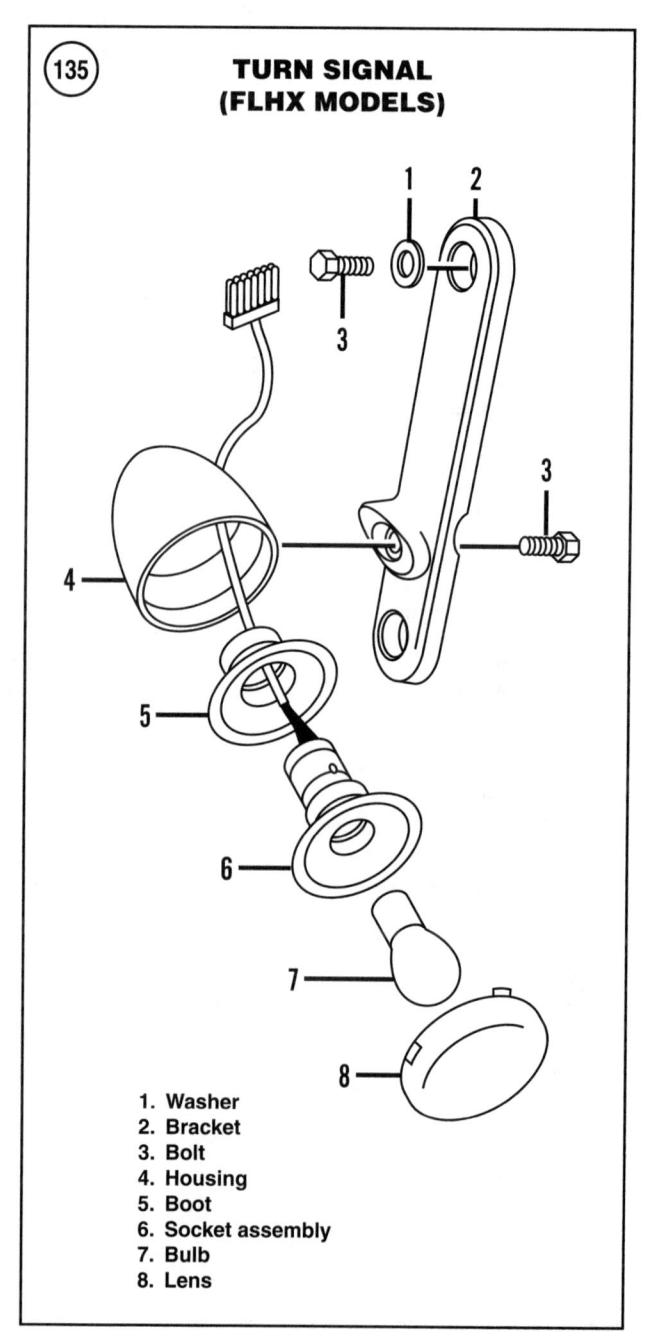

(135) TURN SIGNAL (FLHX MODELS)

1. Washer
2. Bracket
3. Bolt
4. Housing
5. Boot
6. Socket assembly
7. Bulb
8. Lens

ELECTRICAL SYSTEM 489

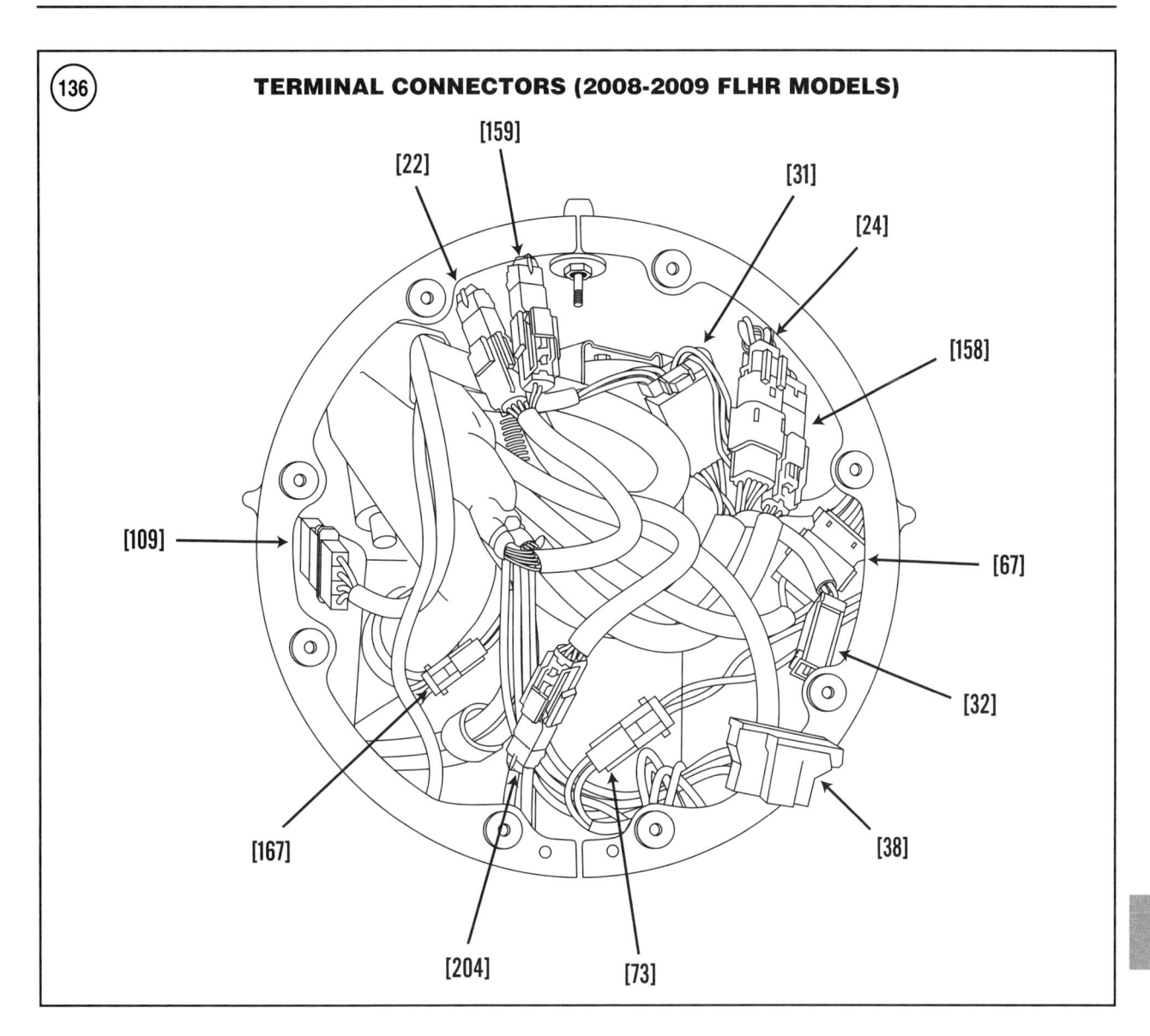

(136) TERMINAL CONNECTORS (2008-2009 FLHR MODELS)

[22], [159], [31], [24], [158], [109], [67], [32], [167], [204], [73], [38]

4. Push the lens into the housing until it snaps into place.

Front Turn Signal Removal/Installation (FLHT and FLHR Models)

Refer to **Figure 127**.
1. Support the motorcycle with the front wheel off the ground as described in *Motorcycle Stands* (Chapter Twelve).
2. Disconnect the negative battery cable as described in this chapter.
3A. On FLHR models, perform the following:
   a. Remove the headlight lens assembly as described in this chapter.
   b. Locate the 6-pin Multilock connector for the front turn signal located within the headlight housing (**Figure 136**). Depress the locking button and disconnect the connector.
3B. On FLHT models, perform the following:
   a. Remove the front fairing and windshield as described in Chapter Seventeen.
   b. Locate both 4-pin Multilock connectors for the front turn signals situated adjacent to the speakers in the inner fairing. Depress the locking button and disconnect the connectors.
4. Disconnect the appropriate terminals from within the socket housing. Refer to *Amp Multilock Connectors* (this chapter). Note the wire color location within the connector as they must be installed in the correct location.
5. Securely attach a piece of flexible fish wire to each wire terminal. Make each length of wire long enough to run from the connector, under the front fairing, through the wiring conduit, and to the front turn signal assembly. Apply liquid glass cleaner, or an equivalent, to the fish wire and wiring to assist in pulling the wires through the conduit.
6. Remove the two Allen bolts and remove the turn signal from the mounting bracket. Slowly lower the assembly from the mounting bracket.
7. Carefully pull one wire at a time out from the conduit and withdraw all three wires.
8. Withdraw the wires from the mounting bracket and standoff. Then, disconnect the fish wire.

FRONT TURN SIGNAL (FLHRS AND FLHRSE MODELS)

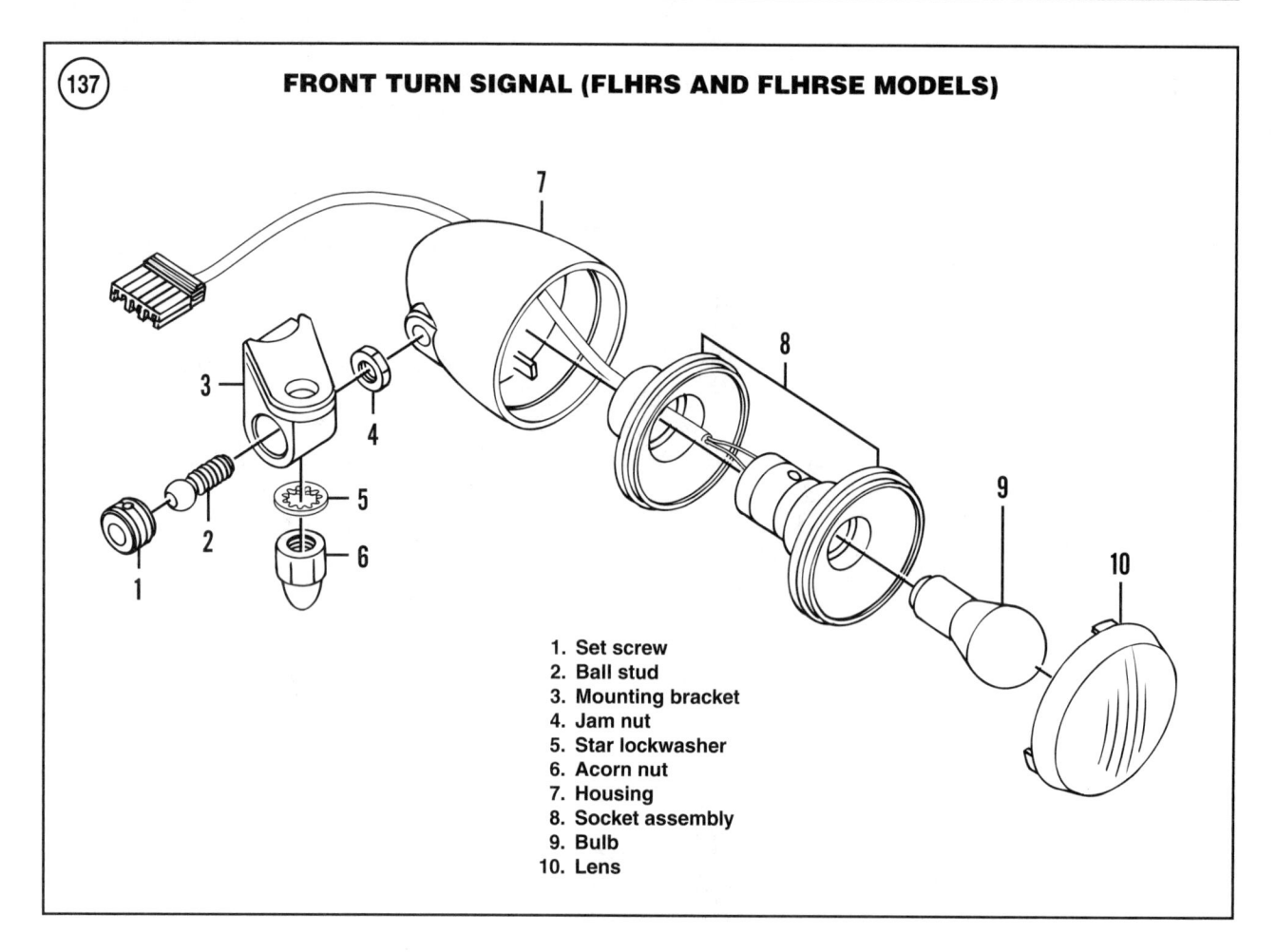

1. Set screw
2. Ball stud
3. Mounting bracket
4. Jam nut
5. Star lockwasher
6. Acorn nut
7. Housing
8. Socket assembly
9. Bulb
10. Lens

9. Strip 3/16 in. (4.8 mm) of insulation from the *new* wires. Crimp on *new* socket terminals.
10. Securely attach a piece of flexible fish wire to each new wire terminal.
11. Insert the wires into the standoff and mounting bracket.
12. Carefully pull one wire at a time into the conduit and remove the fish wire.
13A. On the right side of FLHT models, install the wires into the following terminal sockets:
    a. Socket 1: blue.
    b. Socket 2: brown.
    c. Socket 3: black.
13B. On the left side of FLHT models, install the wires into the following terminal sockets:
    a. Socket 1: blue.
    b. Socket 2: violet.
    c. Socket 3: black.
13C. On the right side of FLHR models, install the wires into the following terminal sockets:
    a. Socket 1: black.
    b. Socket 2: brown.
    c. Socket 3: blue.
13D. On the left side of FLHR models, install the wires into the following terminal sockets:
    a. Socket 1: blue.
    b. Socket 2: violet.
    c. Socket 3: black.
14. Install the turn signal assembly onto the mounting bracket. Make sure the wiring conduit is located within the slot at the back of the bracket and that it is not pinched.
15. Install the screws and lockwashers. Tighten the screws to 36-60 in.-lb. (4.1-6.8 N•m).
16. Connect the two 4-pin Multilock connectors for the front turn signals.
17. Connect the 6-pin Multilock connector for the front turn signal.
18. Connect the negative battery cable as described in this chapter.
19. Check operation of the turn signal(s) prior to installing the front fairing and windshield.
20. Install the front fairing and windshield as described in Chapter Seventeen or install the headlight as described in this chapter.

Front Turn Signal Removal/Installation (FLHRS and FLHRSE Models)

Refer to **Figure 137**.
1. Support the motorcycle with the front wheel off the ground as described in *Motorcycle Stands* (Chapter Twelve).
2. Disconnect the negative battery cable as described in this chapter.

ELECTRICAL SYSTEM

3. Remove the headlight lens and nacelle assembly as described in this chapter.
4. Locate the 6-pin Multilock connector for the front turn signal located within the headlight housing (**Figure 136**). Depress the locking button and disconnect the connector.
5. Disconnect the appropriate terminals from within the socket housing. Refer to *Amp Multilock Connectors* in this chapter. Note the wire color location within the connector as they must be installed in the correct location.
6. Cut the cable strap and release the wiring conduit from the lower handlebar clamp.
7. Remove the clips securing the conduit to the bottom of the handlebar.
8. Remove the acorn nut, star washer and mounting bracket from the stem of the mirror.
9. Remove the set screw from the bracket.
10. Use an Allen wrench and remove the ball stud from the housing.
11. Remove the jam nut from the ball stud.
12. Remove the ball stud from the turn signal light bracket.
13. Push the grommet at the end of the conduit into the light housing.
14. Insert a small screwdriver into the slot at the bottom of the lens and remove the lens.
15. Remove the bulb from the socket.
16. Insert the blade of a small screwdriver between the outer edge of the grommet and the inside of the housing. Gently pry and release the socket assembly.
17. Carefully pull the socket assembly, conduit and terminals out through the housing opening.
18. Remove the grommet from the housing, if necessary.
19. Insert the conduit and terminals through the interior of the housing opening.
20. Carefully pull until the socket is against the backside of the housing.
21. Install the socket tab with the slot in the housing. Carefully push on the socket until it is fully seated.
22. Install the bulb into the socket.
23. Install the lens onto the housing.
24. Install the ball stud through the mounting bracket and thread the jam nut all the way onto the ball stud.
25. Hold the housing in place on the mounting bracket and thread the ball stud onto the bracket. Finger-tighten the ball stud at this time.
26. Install a *new* set screw and finger-tighten it at this time.
27. Install the mirror onto the bracket, if removed.
28. Install a *new* star lockwasher and acorn nut. Finger-tighten the acorn nut.
29. Sit on the motorcycle in an upright position with the front wheel straight ahead. Properly adjust the mirror, and then tighten the acorn nut to 60-96 in.-lb. (6.8-10.8 N•m).
30. Correctly position the housing straight ahead and tighten the set screw to 50-70 in.-lb. (5.7-7.9 N•m).

NOTE
After the set screw is tightened, do not completely remove it for any adjustment. If necessary, only loosen the set screw 1/8 turn, adjust the housing and tighten to 50-70 in.-lb. (5.7-7.9 N•m).

31. Secure the housing and tighten the jam nut securely.
32. Feed the loose ends of the electrical conduit into the top of the headlight nacelle. Stay outboard of the lower handlebar clamp.
33A. On the right side, install the wires into the following terminal sockets:
   a. Socket 1: black.
   b. Socket 2: brown.
   c. Socket 3: blue.
33B. On the left side, install the wires into the following terminal sockets:
   a. Socket 1: blue.
   b. Socket 2: violet.
   c. Socket 3: black.
34. Connect the 6-pin Multilock connector (**Figure 136**).
35. Install the clips securing the conduit to the bottom of the handlebar.
36. Install a new cable strap securing the wiring conduit onto the lower handlebar clamp.
37. Install the headlight lens and nacelle assembly as described in this chapter.
38. Connect the negative battery cable as described in this chapter.

Front Turn Signal Removal/Installation (FLHX Models)

Refer to **Figure 135**.
1. Support the motorcycle with the front wheel off the ground as described in *Motorcycle Stands* (Chapter Twelve).
2. Remove the Maxi-Fuse as described in this chapter.
3. Remove the outer front fairing and windshield as described in Chapter Seventeen.
4. Locate the 4-pin Multilock connectors for both front turn signals situated adjacent to the speakers in the inner fairing. Depress the locking button and disconnect the connectors.
5. Remove the two Torx screws (T40) and washers securing the turn signal mounting bar to the upper and lower fork brackets.
6. Remove the electrical harness from the fame.
7. Position the turn signal mounting bar onto the upper and lower fork brackets.
8. Partially install the two Torx screws and washers into the mounting bar.
9. Correctly position the harness so it is routed forward through the relief at the front of the bracket, and then inboard using the relief in the upper outboard corner of the fork bracket skirt.
10. Alternately tighten the two Torx screws to 15-20 ft.-lb. (20.3-27.1 N•m).
11. Install the front fairing and windshield as described in Chapter Seventeen.

12. Reinstall the Maxi-Fuse as described in this chapter.

Front Turn Signal Removal/Installation (FLTR and FLTRSE3 Models)

Refer to **Figure 117** and **Figure 118**.
1. On the inboard side of the left fairing support, remove the rear acorn nut (**Figure 138**) and washer from the turn signal light bracket. Remove the front acorn nut and washer.
2. Carefully pull the front turn signal light assembly (**Figure 139**) from the fairing.
3. Disconnect the electrical connector (**Figure 140**) and remove the assembly.
4. Install the gasket (**Figure 141**) onto the turn signal mounting bracket.
5. Install by reversing the removal steps. Tighten the acorn nut to 96-120 in.-lb. (10.8-13.6 N•m).

Front Turn Signal Removal/Installation (FLHTCUSE Models)

Refer to **Figure 132**.
1. Support the motorcycle with the front wheel off the ground as described in *Motorcycle Stands* (Chapter Twelve).
2. Disconnect the negative battery cable as described in this chapter.
3. Remove the front outer fairing and windshield as described in Chapter Seventeen.
4. Locate both 4-pin Multilock connectors for the front turn signal (**Figure 137**) in the fairing. Depress the locking button and disconnect the connectors.

NOTE
The gray/black wire within the connector is for the passing lights and does not have to be disconnected.

5. Disconnect the appropriate terminals from within the socket housing. Refer to *Amp Multilock Connectors* in this chapter. Note the wire color location within the connector as they must be installed in the correct location.

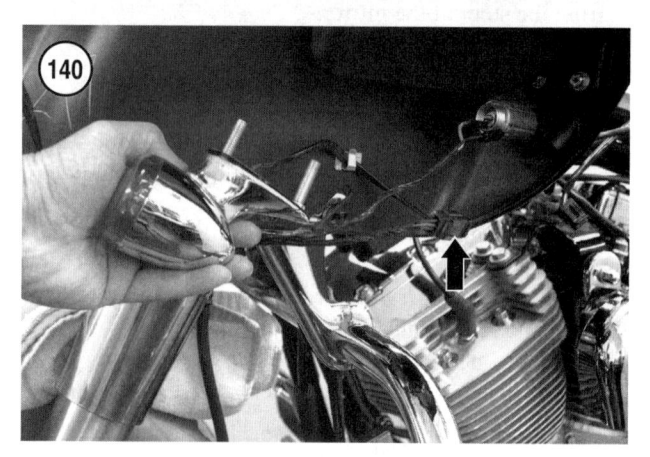

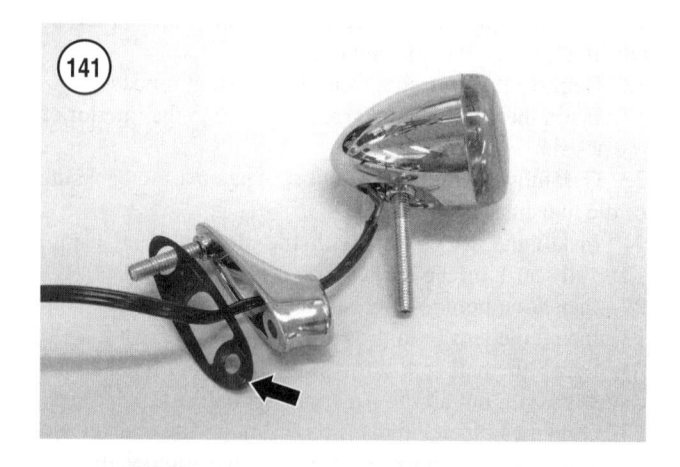

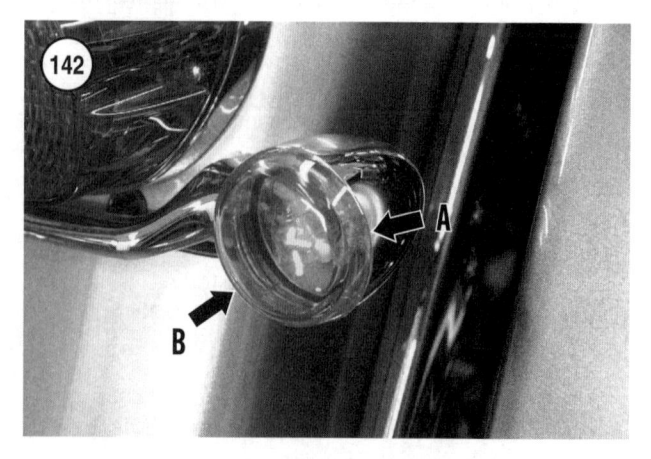

ELECTRICAL SYSTEM

6. Securely attach a piece of flexible fish wire to each wire terminal. Make each length of wire long enough to run from the connector, under the front fairing, through the wiring conduit, and to the front turn signal assembly. Apply liquid glass cleaner, or an equivalent, to the fish wire and wiring to assist in pulling the wires through the conduit.

7. Remove the screws and lockwashers securing the turn signal assembly to the mounting bracket and slowly lower the assembly from the mounting bracket.

8. Carefully pull one wire at a time out from the conduit and withdraw all three wires.

9. Withdraw the wires from the mounting bracket and standoff.

10. Insert the new wires into the standoff and mounting bracket.

11. Carefully pull one wire at a time into the conduit, and then remove the fish wire.

12. Install the turn signal assembly onto the mounting bracket and install the screws and lockwashers. Tighten the screws to 96-120 in.-lb. (10.8-13.6 N•m).

13. Strip 3/16 in. (4.8 mm) of insulation from the new wires. Crimp on *new* socket terminals.

14A. On the right side, install the wires into the following terminal sockets:
   a. Socket 1: blue.
   b. Socket 2: brown.
   c. Socket 3: black.

14B. On the left side, install the wires into the following terminal sockets:
   a. Socket 1: blue.
   b. Socket 2: violet.
   c. Socket 3: black.

15. Connect both 4-pin Multilock connectors for the front turn signals.

16. Connect the negative battery cable as described in this chapter.

17. Check operation of the turn signal(s) prior to installing the front fairing and windshield.

18. Install the front outer fairing and windshield as described in Chapter Seventeen.

Rear Turn Signal Bulb Replacement (All Models)

1. Locate a notch (A, **Figure 142**) in the lens and insert a coin into it. Carefully twist the coin until the lens (B, **Figure 142**) comes off the housing.

2. Push in on the bulb, rotate it and remove it from the socket.

3. Install a *new* bulb (**Figure 143**), push it in and rotate it until locked into place.

4. Push the lens into the housing until it snaps into place.

Rear Turn Signal Bracket Removal/Installation (All Models)

Refer to **Figure 144** and **Figure 145**.

143

144 REAR TURN SIGNAL (FLHT, FLHR AND FLHTCUSE MODELS)

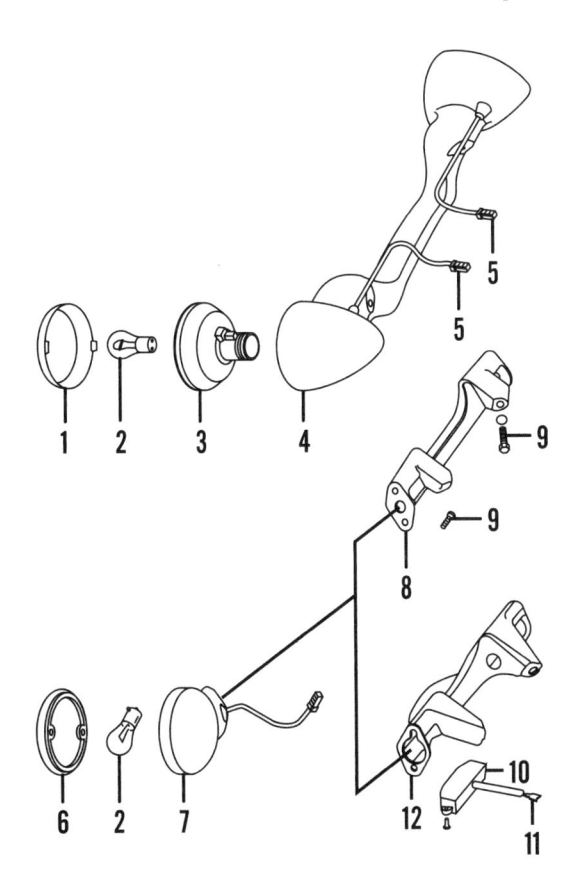

1. Lens
2. Bulb
3. Socket assembly
4. Light bar
5. Socket housing
6. Lens
7. Housing
8. Mounting bracket (non-HDI models)
9. Screw
10. Lamp assembly
11. Terminal
12. Mounting bracket (HDI models)

NOTE
Always disarm the optional security system (TSSM/HFSM) before disconnecting the battery or before pulling the Maxi-Fuse so the siren will not sound.

1. Support the motorcycle on a swing arm stand with the rear wheel off the ground.
2. Disconnect the negative battery cable as described in this chapter.
3. Remove both saddlebags as described in Chapter Seventeen.
4. Remove the screw (A, **Figure 146**) on each side securing the taillight lens (B) and remove the lens.
5. Disconnect the 4-pin taillight Multilock connector from the chrome base.
6. Use a pick or small, flat-bladed screwdriver and depress the release button on both 2-pin connectors. Disconnect the connectors (**Figure 147**) from the circuit board.
7. Carefully feed the connector and harness out through the opening on each side of the printed circuit board.
8. Reach under the rear fender and release the harness from the cable anchored on the T-stud.
9. Carefully pull the harness out of the rear fender opening and allow it to hang down below the turn signal bracket.
10. Insert a long-shank, ball-end socket (Snap-On part No. FABL5), or equivalent, through the channel in the bracket. Remove the screw on each side.
11. Remove the two flange bolts and remove the bracket assembly (C, **Figure 146**) from the rear fender.
12. Install by reversing the removal steps, while noting the following:
    a. Tighten the taillight lens screws to 20-24 in.-lb. (2.3-2.7 N•m).
    b. Apply one drop of Loctite Threadlocker No. 271 (red) to the flange bolts prior to installation.
    c. Tighten the flange bolts to 84-144 in.-lb. (9.5-16.3 N•m).

TAILLIGHT/BRAKE LIGHT

Taillight/Brake Light Bulb Replacement (FLHT, FLHR, FLHX and FLHTCUSE Models)

Refer to **Figure 148**.
1. Remove the screw (A, **Figure 146**) on each side securing the lens (B).
2. Pull the lens (A, **Figure 149**) off the base.
3. Rotate the bulb/socket assembly (B, **Figure 149**) 1/4 turn *counterclockwise* and pull it from the backside of the lens.
4. Gently the bulb (**Figure 150**) out of the socket assembly.
5. Install a new bulb into socket.
6. Rotate the bulb/socket assembly (B, **Figure 149**) 1/4 turn *clockwise* and push it back into the backside of the lens.
7. Inspect the gasket (C, **Figure 149**) for deterioration or damage; replace if necessary.

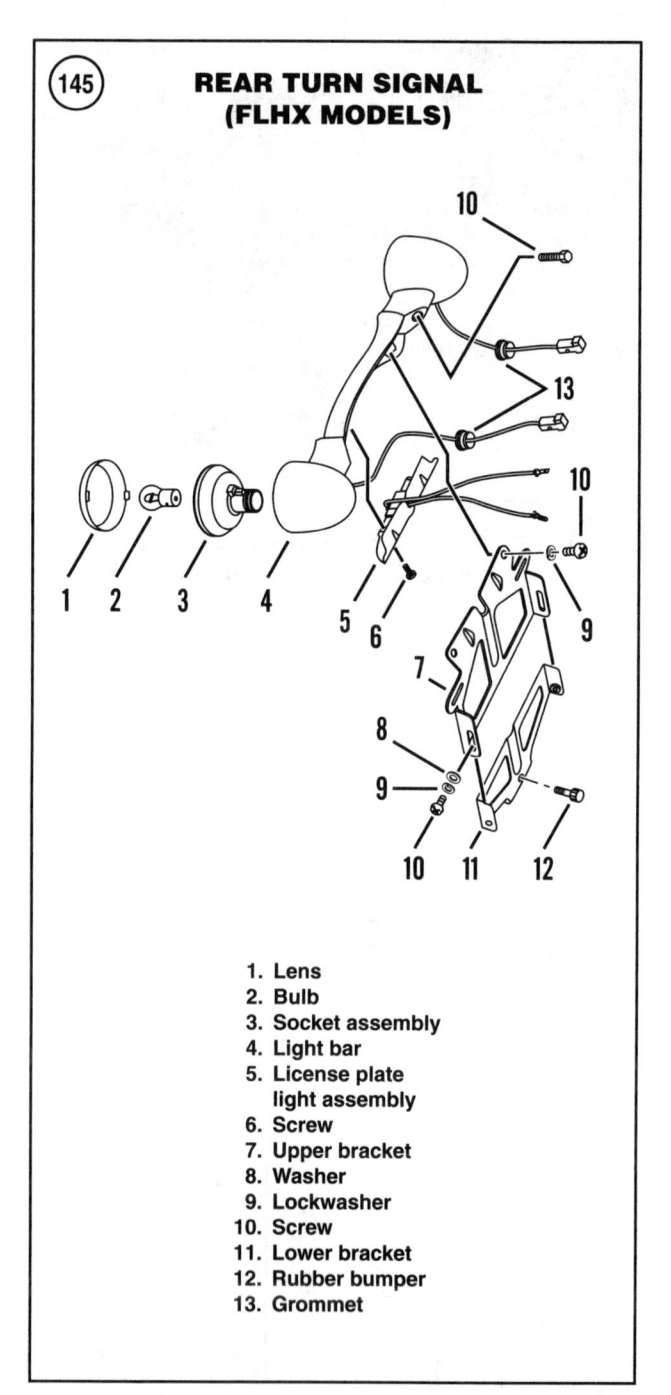

145 REAR TURN SIGNAL (FLHX MODELS)

1. Lens
2. Bulb
3. Socket assembly
4. Light bar
5. License plate light assembly
6. Screw
7. Upper bracket
8. Washer
9. Lockwasher
10. Screw
11. Lower bracket
12. Rubber bumper
13. Grommet

ELECTRICAL SYSTEM

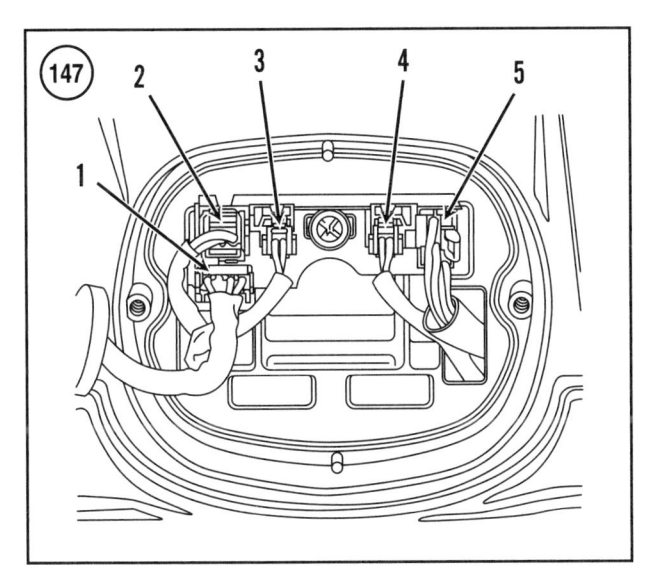

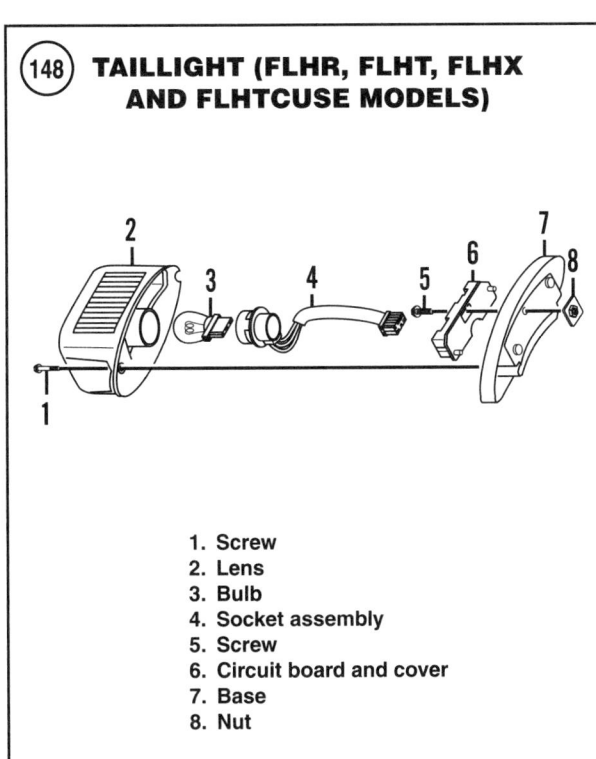

147

148 TAILLIGHT (FLHR, FLHT, FLHX AND FLHTCUSE MODELS)

1. Screw
2. Lens
3. Bulb
4. Socket assembly
5. Screw
6. Circuit board and cover
7. Base
8. Nut

149

150

8. Make sure the gasket is in place on the lens.
9. Install the lens and screws. Tighten the screws to 30-50 in.-lb. (3.4-5.7 N•m). Do not overtighten as the lens may crack.

Taillight/Brake Light Bulb Replacement (FLHRSE Models)

Refer to **Figure 151**.
1. Remove the screws securing the lens.
2. Remove the lens assembly from the mounting plate.
3. Rotate the bulb turn *counterclockwise* and remove it from the socket assembly.
4. Install a new bulb into the socket assembly.
5. Install the lens assembly onto the mounting plate.
6. Install the screws and tighten securely. Do not overtighten the screws as the lens may crack.

Taillight/Brake Light/Rear Turn Signal Replacement (2009 FLTRSE3 Models)

Refer to **Figure 152**.

NOTE
The taillight, brake light and turn signal base is an integral assembly. If any portion of the base is defective, replace the complete assembly.

1. Remove the saddlebag from the side being serviced as described in Chapter Seventeen.
2. Disconnect the 2-pin electrical connector from the base.
3. Remove the three screws securing the base to the rear fender fascia.
4. Pull straight back and remove the base from the rear fender fascia.
5. Install the base onto the posts on the rear fender fascia. Push it on until it bottoms.
6. Install the three screws securing the base to the rear fender fascia, and tighten securely. Do not overtighten the screws as the fascia posts may crack.
7. Connect the 4-pin electrical connector onto the base.
8. Install the saddlebag as described in Chapter Seventeen.
9. Repeat the procedure for the remaining side if necessary.

TAILLIGHT (FLHRSE MODELS)

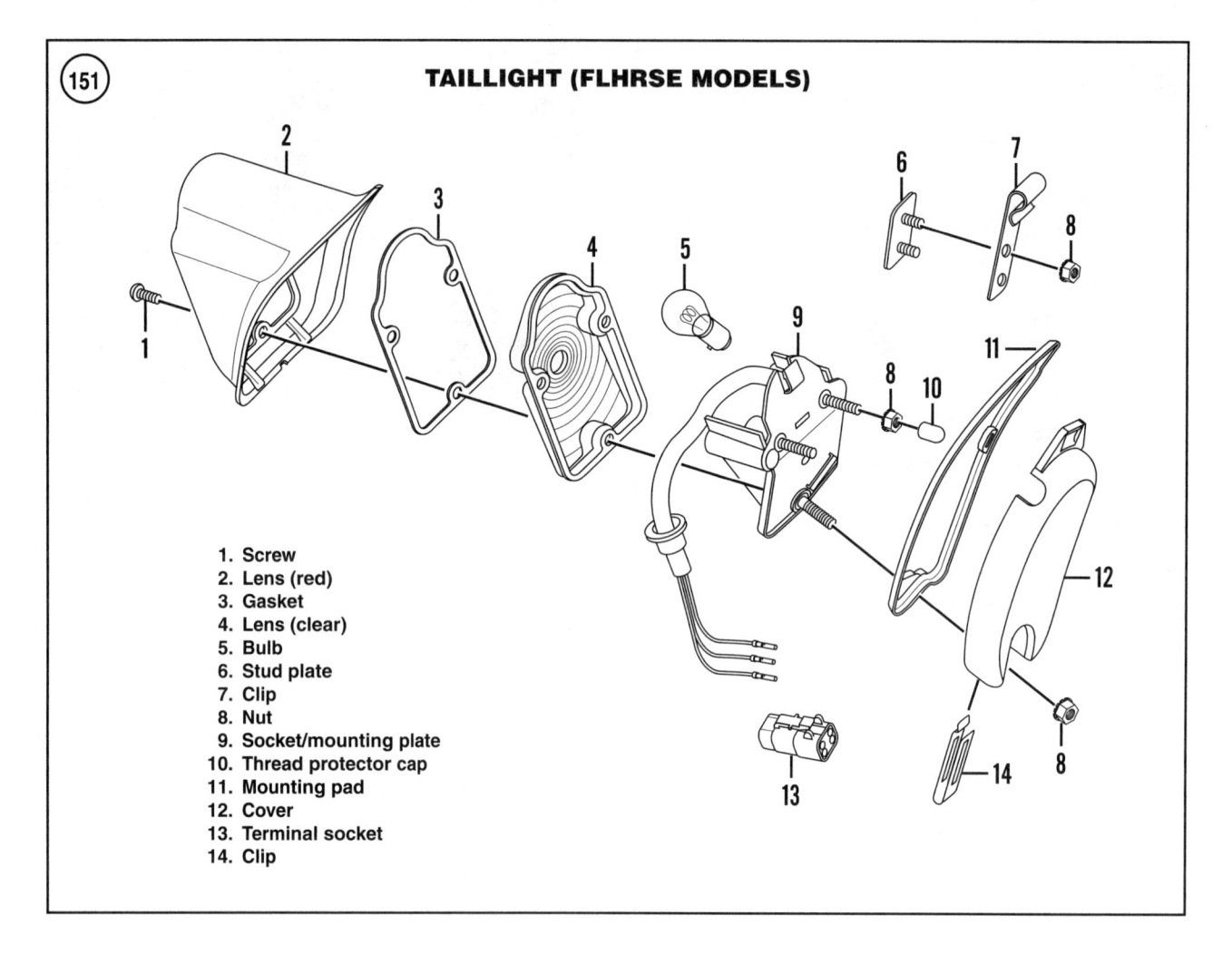

1. Screw
2. Lens (red)
3. Gasket
4. Lens (clear)
5. Bulb
6. Stud plate
7. Clip
8. Nut
9. Socket/mounting plate
10. Thread protector cap
11. Mounting pad
12. Cover
13. Terminal socket
14. Clip

Taillight/Brake Circuit Board/Chrome Base Removal/Installation (FLHT, FLHR and FLHTCUSE Models)

Refer to **Figure 148**.
1. Remove the screw (A, **Figure 146**) on each side securing the lens (B).
2. Pull the lens off the base and remove the bulb.
3. Disconnect the bulb connector.
4. Disconnect the rear fender tip light connector, on models so equipped.
5. Disconnect the rear fender light connector.
6. Use a pick or small, flat-bladed screwdriver and depress the release button on both 2-pin connectors. Disconnect the connectors (**Figure 147**) from the circuit board.
7. Remove the screw and captive washer securing the center of the printed circuit board and chrome base to the rear fender.
8. Use both thumbs and push the chrome base upward to free it from the rear fender, and remove it from the rear fender.
9. Carefully feed the wiring harness and terminal connectors out through the openings in the chrome base.
10. Remove the pin housing from the circuit board.
11. Install by reversing the removal steps. Tighten the screw and captive washer to 40-48 in.-lb. (4.5-5.4 N•m).

Taillight/Brake Light Removal/Installation (FLHRSE Series Models)

Refer to **Figure 151**.
1. Remove the taillight/brake light lens assembly as described in this section.
2. Remove the caps from the socket/mounting plate mounting studs under the rear fender.
3. Remove the three flange nuts securing the cover and mounting pad to the under side of the rear fender. Remove the cover and mounting pad.
4. Carefully remove the socket/mounting plate from the rear fender. Do not damage the rear fender finish.
5. Install by reversing the removal steps. Tighten the flange nuts to 40-48 in.-lb. (4.5-5.4 N•m).

FENDER TIP LIGHT

Front Fender Tip Light Removal/Installation

1. Insert the tip of a flat-bladed screwdriver into the slot at the top of the fender tip lens. Slowly rotate the screwdriver and unsnap the lens from the light base.
2. Secure the Keps nuts under the front fender to keep them from rotating.

ELECTRICAL SYSTEM

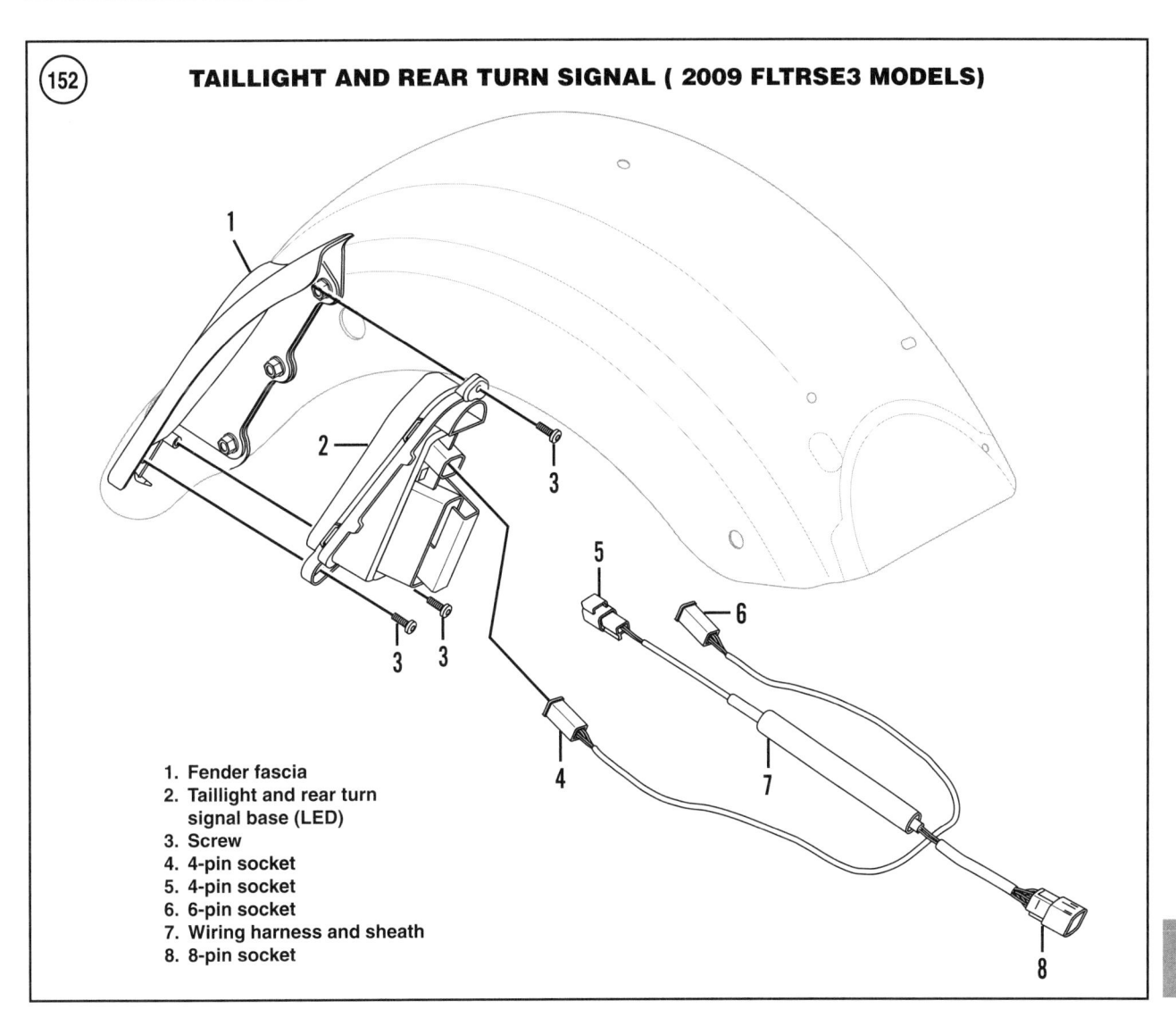

152 TAILLIGHT AND REAR TURN SIGNAL (2009 FLTRSE3 MODELS)

1. Fender fascia
2. Taillight and rear turn signal base (LED)
3. Screw
4. 4-pin socket
5. 4-pin socket
6. 6-pin socket
7. Wiring harness and sheath
8. 8-pin socket

3. Unscrew the two screws from the Keps nuts and partially remove the light base from the front fender.
4. Disconnect the light's 2-pin connector from the wiring harness.
5. Remove the light assembly from the front fender.
6. Install by reversing the removal steps. Tighten the two screws to 20-25 in.-lb. (2.3-2.8 N•m).

Rear Fender Tip Light Removal/Installation

1. Remove the two screws securing the light assembly to the rear fender.
2. Insert the tip of a flat blade screwdriver into the slot at the top of the fender tip lens. Slowly rotate the screwdriver and unsnap the lens from the light base.
3. Remove the two screws securing the base to the rear fender, and partially remove the light base from the rear fender.
4. Disconnect the fender tip light 2-pin connector from the wiring harness.
5. Feed the socket housing through opening in the chrome base and fender.

6. Release the wiring harness from the cable clip anchored on the T-stud and the fender clip.
7. Secure the Keps nuts under the rear fender to keep them from rotating.
8. Unscrew the two screws from the Keps nuts and partially remove the light base from the front fender.
9. Withdraw the wiring harness and connector out through the large hole in the rear fender.
10. Install by reversing these removal steps. Tighten the two screws to 20-25 in.-lb. (2.3-2.8 N•m).

REAR FASCIA LIGHT

Replacement (FLXH Models)

1. Remove the rear fascia as described in Chapter Seventeen.
2. On the left side, remove the bolt/flat washer and remove the passenger seat strap and saddlebag front mounting bracket from the frame tube chrome cover.
3. Remove the Phillips screw and the chrome cover from the frame.

4. Release the fascia light wires from the clip at the top of the radio antenna cable bracket.
5. Carefully cut the cable strap securing the rear fascia light wires and radio antenna cable to the slotted hole in the rear fender support.
6. Carefully cut the cable strap securing the rear fascia light wires and radio antenna cable to the shoulder on the upper frame tube, just in front of the air valve mounting bracket.

NOTE
The rear fascia light connector also serves as the Tour-Pak connector on FLHTC and FLHTCU models.

7. Disconnect the 3-pin rear fascia light connector from the harness at the inboard side of the upper frame tube.
8. Install by reversing the removal steps. Tighten the Phillips screws to 25-40 in.-lb. (2.8-4.5 N•m). Tighten the bolt securing the passenger seat strap and saddlebag to 60-96 in.-lb. (6.8-10.8 N•m).

LICENSE PLATE LIGHT

Bulb Replacement (FLHX Models)

Refer to **Figure 145**.
1. Remove the two Allen screws securing the lens assembly to the rear turn signal housing.
2. Lower the lens while being careful not to stress the wiring.
3. Remove the light bulb(s).
4, Apply a liberal amount of dielectric grease to the sockets and to the bulb contacts.
5. Install new bulb(s).
6. Carefully push the lens assembly back into the rear turn signal housing. Do not pinch the wiring.
7. Install the two Allen screws and tighten securely.

License Plate Light Assembly Removal/Installation (FLHX Models)

1. Remove the two Allen screws securing the lens assembly to the rear turn signal housing.
2. Lower the lens while being careful not to stress the wiring.
3. Remove the screws securing the taillight/brake light lens.
4. Pull the lens off the base and disconnect the 3-pin electrical connector (2, **Figure 147**).
5. Reach under the rear fender and release the harness from the cable anchored on the T-stud on the left side.
6. Disconnect the terminals from within the socket housing. Refer to *Amp Multilock Connectors* (this chapter). Note the wire color location within the connector as they must be installed in the correct location.
7. Carefully withdraw the wiring harness out through the hole in the rear fender.
8. Install by reversing the removal steps. Tighten the Allen screws securely.

TOUR-PAK

Side Marker Light Replacement (FLHTCU and FLHTCUSE Models)

1. Open the cover and keep it open.
2. Open the map pocket and remove the acorn nuts and washers securing the map pocket and molded liner. Remove the molded liner from the lower case.
3. Depress the external latch and remove the bulb socket.
4. Remove the bulb from the socket and install a new bulb.
5. Install the bulb socket into the receptacle and push it in until it bottoms.
6. Install the molded liner, and secure with the washers and acorn nuts. Tighten the nuts securely.

Wrap-Around Light Housing Removal/Installation (FLHTCU and FLHTCUSE Models)

Refer to **Figure 153**.
1. Open the cover and keep it open.
2. Open the map pocket and remove the acorn nuts and washers securing the map pocket and molded liner. Remove the molded liner from the lower case.
3. Depress the external latch and remove the bulb socket from both sides.
4. Disconnect the CB antenna cable connector on the right side.
5. Release the cable from the adhesive clip at the bottom of the Tour-Pak.
6. Remove the Keps nut, ring terminal and flat washer from the antenna loading coil stud.
7. Secure the hex head screw, and then remove the flange nut from the loading coil stud.
8. Secure the hex screw, and then remove the flange nut at the base of the Tour-Pak.
9. Remove the hex screw, with external tooth washer, and loading coil from the frame.
10. Remove the loading coil stud.
11. Remove the loading mast from the light housing.
12. On the left side, turn the knurled lock ring *counterclockwise*, and disconnect the radio antenna cable connector. Release the cable from the rear clip on the bottom of the Tour-Pak.
13. Remove the jam nut from the radio antenna cable connector at the back of the Tour-Pak. Remove the internal tooth lockwasher, ring terminal and large flat washer from the connector.
14. Install the jam nut back onto the connector. Thread a 1/2 in.-20 UNF nut onto the connector until contact is made with the jam nut. Turn the jam nut *counterclockwise* and remove the connector stud from the radio antenna mast. Remove the mast from the light housing.
15. Carefully remove the caulking from around the bulb housing.
16. Remove the four flange nuts and metal clips and remove the light housing from the Tour-Pak.

… **ELECTRICAL SYSTEM** 499

153 TOUR-PAK LIGHTS AND SPEAKERS (FLHT AND FLHTCUSE MODELS)

1. Fastener (velcro)
2. Acorn nut
3. Washer
4. Lockwasher
5. Lockwasher
6. Tour-Pak molded liner
7. Pouch
8. Trim decal
9. Cable strap
10. Pin housing (2-pin)
11. Wiring harness
12. Clip (antenna cable)
13. Pin housing (3-pin)
14. Bulb
15. Seal
16. Clip
17. Reflector
18. Lens (left side)
19. Nut
20. Bolt
21. Grommet
22. Nameplate
23. Bracket (rear switch control housing)
24. Screw
25. Switch terminals
26. Terminal
27. Nut
28. Bracket (rear headset tether)
29. Screw
30. Bolt
31. Washer
32. Crimp nut
33. Select knob
34. Housing (rear control switch)
35. Speaker box (left side shown)
36. Nut (well)
37. Speaker
38. Grill
39. Light housing

11

INSTRUMENTS (FLHT AND FLHX MODELS)

154

1. Speedometer (4 in.)
2. Gasket
3. Back clamp
4. Screw
5. 2 in. meters (voltmeter, oil pressure, ambient temperature, fuel level)
6. Back clamp
7. Nut
8. Rubber boot
9. Odometer reset switch
10. Indicator light bezel assembly (2007-2009 models)
11. Indicator light housing and harness (2007-2009 models)
12. Indicator light bezel assembly (2006 models)
13. Indicator light housing (2006 models)
14. Bulbs (2006 models)
15. Indicator light harness (2006 models)
16. Sensor (air temperature)
17. Tachometer (4 in.)
18. Back clamp

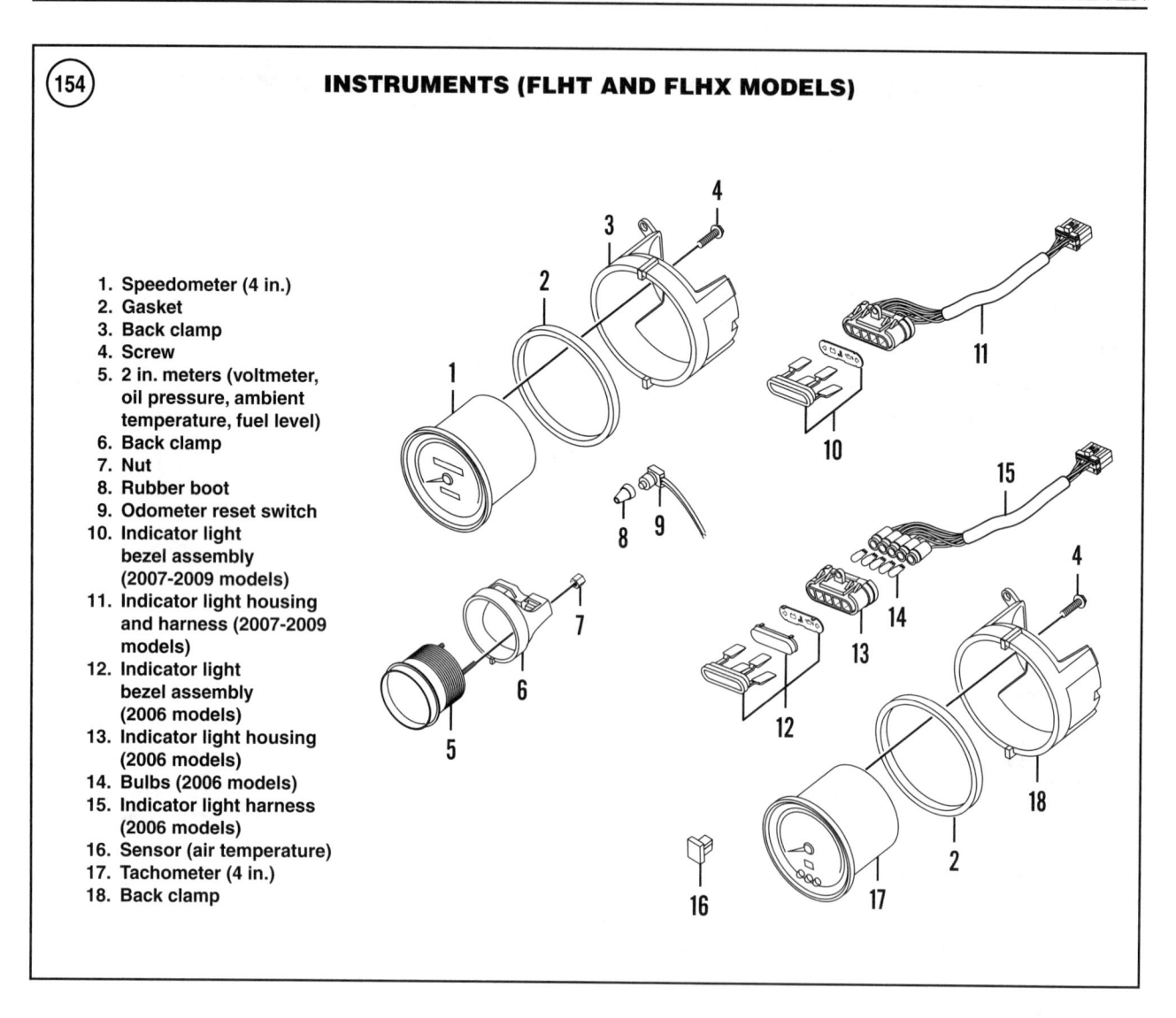

17. Install by reversing the removal steps. Tighten the flange nuts and acorn nuts securely.

INSTRUMENTS

NOTE
Speedometers that are housed in the fuel tank console are covered in Chapter Nine or Chapter Ten.

Removal/Installation (FLHT and FLHX Models)

Refer to **Figure 154** and **Figure 155**.

NOTE
Always disarm the optional security system (TSSM/HFSM) before disconnecting the battery or before pulling the Maxi-Fuse so the siren will not sound.

1. Remove the seat as described in Chapter Seventeen.

2. Disconnect the negative battery cable as described in this chapter.

3. Remove the outer front fairing as described in Chapter Seventeen.

4A. To remove the 2 inch (51 mm) diameter gauge, perform the following:
   a. Disconnect the electrical connector from the instrument to be removed.
   b. Remove the nuts securing the instrument to the mounting bracket.
   c. Remove gauge(s) from inner fairing.

4B. To remove the 4 inch (102 mm) diameter speedometer or tachometer, perform the following:
   a. Disconnect the 12-pin Packard connector from the backside of the speedometer or tachometer.
   b. Remove the two Phillips screws securing the instrument to the mounting bracket.
   c. Push the instrument toward the rear, out of the gasket, and remove it from the inner fairing.

5. Store the meters in a safe place.

6. If removed, install the gasket onto the speedometer and tachometer mounting brackets.

ELECTRICAL SYSTEM 501

(155) FAIRING CONNECTORS (2008-2009 FLHX AND FLHT MODELS)

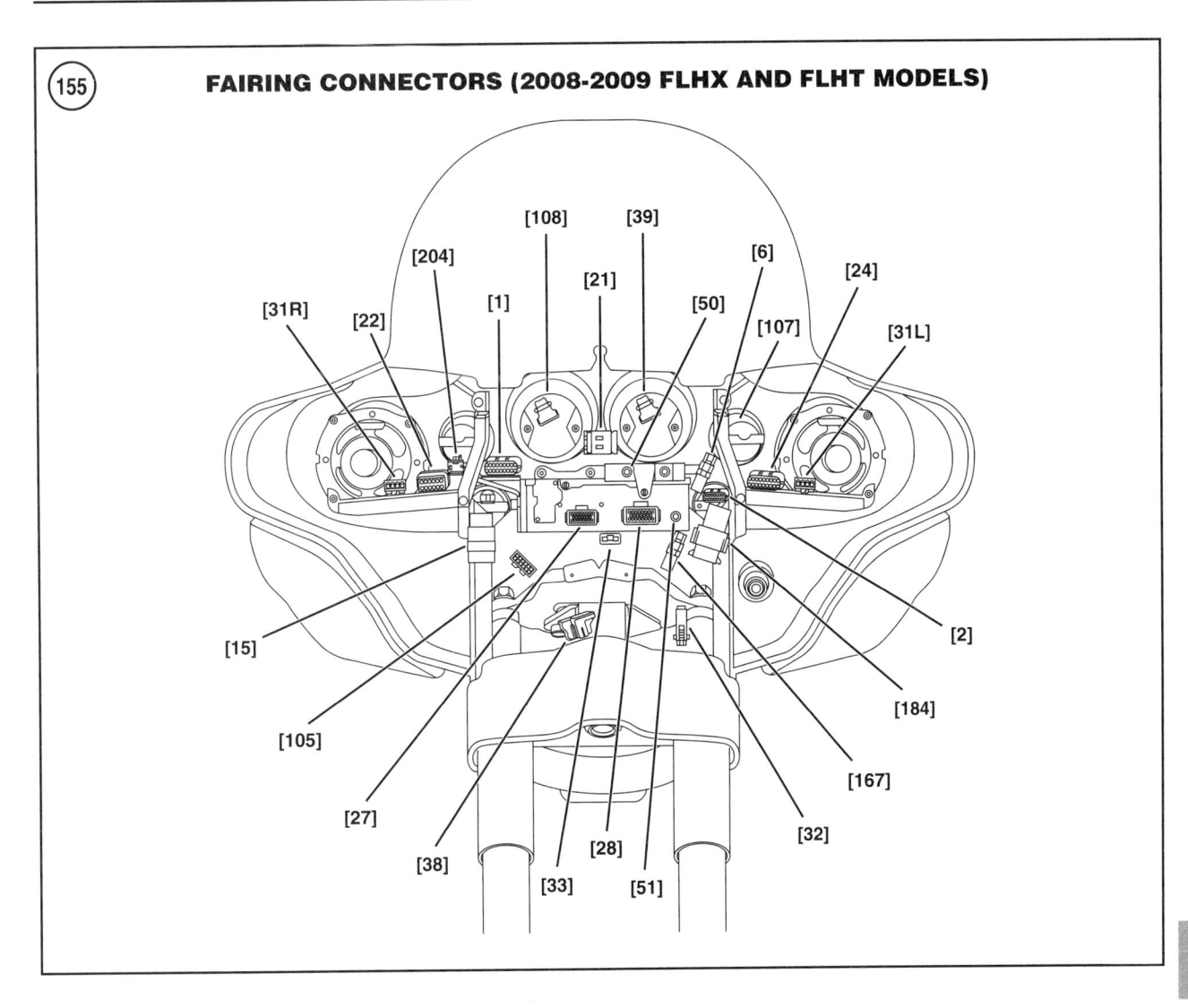

NOTE
If necessary, apply alcohol or glass cleaner to the gasket surfaces to ease installation of the meters.

7. Install by reversing the removal steps, while noting the following:
   a. Install the instruments into the mounting brackets. Press firmly until the instrument is correctly seated and secure with the screws or nuts. Tighten the screws or nuts to 10-20 in.-lb. (1.1-2.3 N•m).
   b. Connect the negative battery cable as described in this chapter.

Removal/Installation (FLTR Models)

Refer to **Figure 156**.
1. Place the motorcycle on level ground on the jiffy stand.
2. Remove the seat as described in Chapter Seventeen.

NOTE
Always disarm the optional TSSM/HFSM security system before disconnecting the battery or pulling the Maxi-Fuse so the siren will not sound.

3. Disconnect the negative battery lead as described in this chapter.
4. Remove the Torx screw (**Figure 157**) on each side securing the instrument bezel to the housing.
5. Pull up on the top of the instrument bezel (A, **Figure 158**) and detach it from the locking tabs (B) on the housing.
6. Slightly raise the bezel and remove the anchor on the ambient temperature sensor from the inboard ear of the speedometer bracket.
7. Disconnect the following electrical connectors from the interconnect harness as follows:
   a. The 12-pin Packard connector (A, **Figure 159**) from the speedometer.
   b. The 12-pin Packard connector (B, **Figure 159**) from the tachometer.
   c. The 10-pin Multilock connector (C, **Figure 159**) from the indicator lights.
8. Remove the bezel from the instrument housing.
9. Remove the two screws (**Figure 160**) securing the instrument(s) to the mounting bracket(s).

11

INSTRUMENTS (FLTR MODELS)

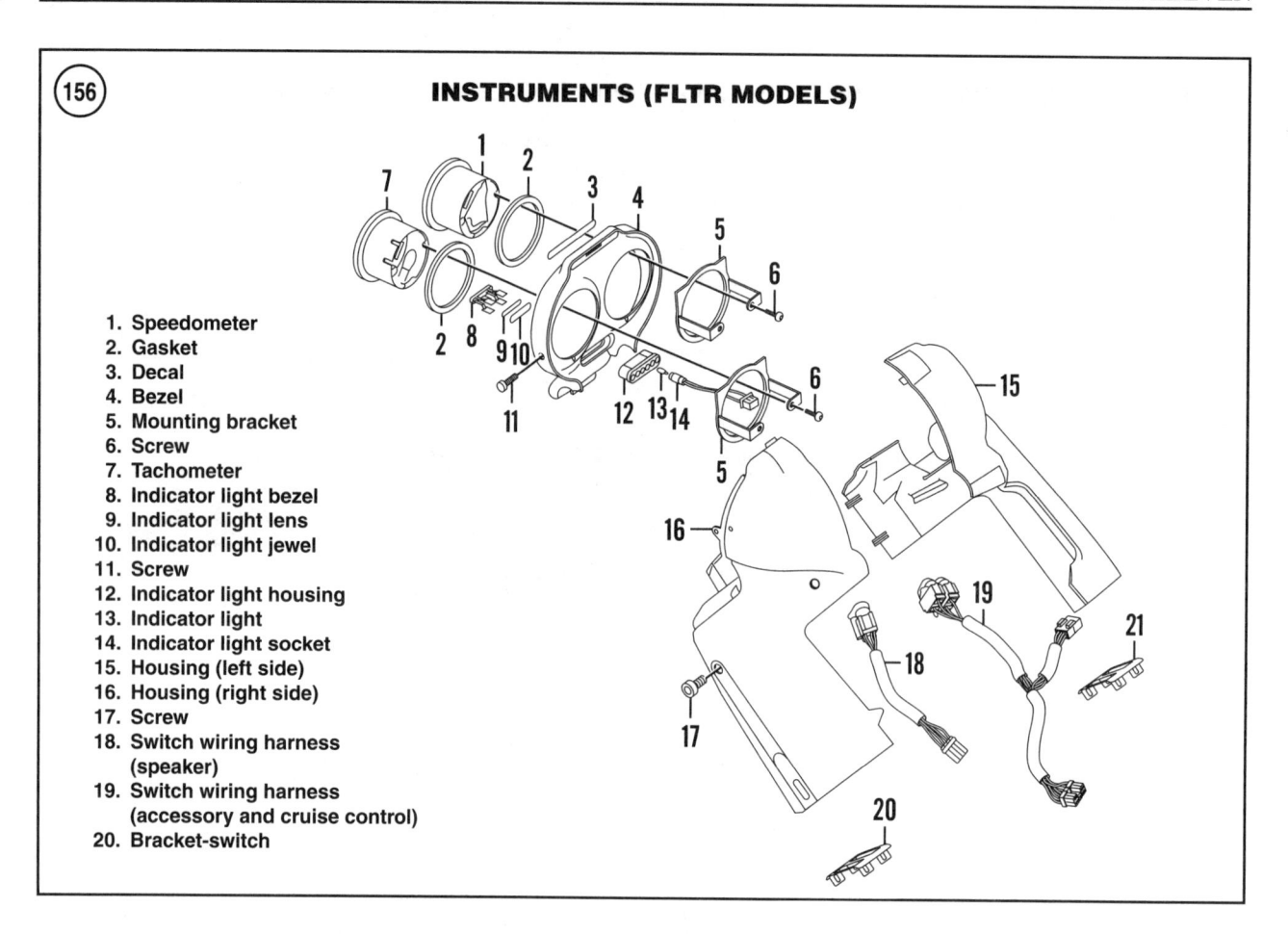

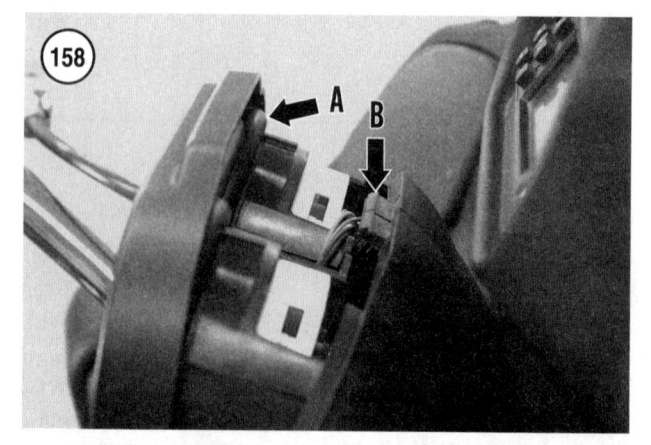

1. Speedometer
2. Gasket
3. Decal
4. Bezel
5. Mounting bracket
6. Screw
7. Tachometer
8. Indicator light bezel
9. Indicator light lens
10. Indicator light jewel
11. Screw
12. Indicator light housing
13. Indicator light
14. Indicator light socket
15. Housing (left side)
16. Housing (right side)
17. Screw
18. Switch wiring harness (speaker)
19. Switch wiring harness (accessory and cruise control)
20. Bracket-switch

10. Carefully separate the instrument bezel and housing halves and remove each one from the frame. Store the panels in a safe place.
11. Carefully push the speedometer and/or tachometer out through the gasket and the front of bezel.
12. Store the meters in a safe place.
13. If removed, install the gasket onto the speedometer and tachometer.

NOTE
If necessary, apply alcohol or glass cleaner to the gasket surfaces to ease installation of the meters.

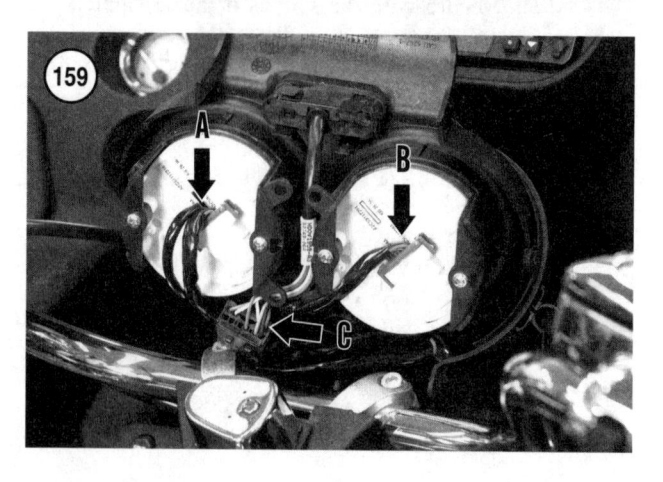

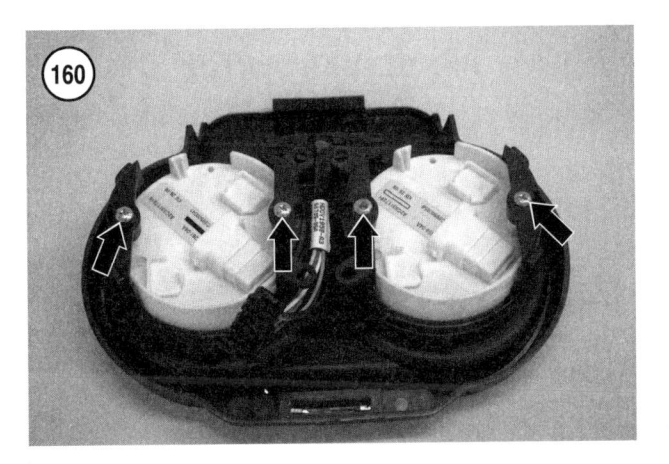

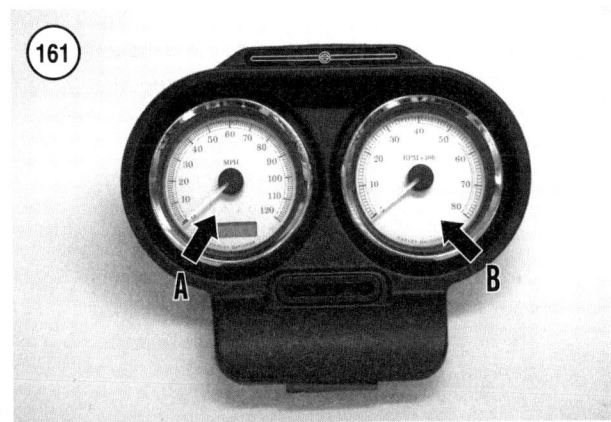

ELECTRICAL SYSTEM

162

SWITCH

Position / Switch	Red/Black	Red	Red/Gray
Off		•	
Acc.		•———	———•
Ignition	•———	———•———	———•

14. Install by reversing the removal steps, while noting the following:
   a. Install the instruments into the correct side of the mounting brackets. Install the speedometer (A, **Figure 161**) on the left side and the tachometer (B) on the right side.
   b. Press firmly until the instrument is correctly seated and secure it with the screws. Tighten the bracket screws to 10-20 in.-lb. (1.1-2.3 N•m).
   c. Tighten the Torx screws (T25) to 15-20 in.-lb. (1.7-2.3 N•m).

AUTOMATIC COMPRESSION RELEASE SOLENOID (2006-2009 SCREAMIN' EAGLE MODELS)

An ACR solenoid socket (H-D part No. HD-48498 for 2007-2008 models, or part No. HD-48498-A for 2009 models), or its equivalent, is needed for this procedure.

1. Remove the rocker arm support plate as described in *Rocker Arms, Pushrods and Valve Lifters* (Chapter Four).
2. Use the tool to remove the ACR solenoid from the cylinder head.
3. Installation is the reverse of removal. Note the following:

   a. Apply three dots of Loctite 246 Threadlocker to the bottom third of the threads on the ACR solenoid. Equally space the dots around the outer circumference of the threads.
   b. Tighten the ACR solenoid to 11-15 ft.-lb. (14.9-20.3 N•m).

SWITCHES

Testing

Test switches for continuity by using an ohmmeter or a self-powered test light at the switch connector while moving the switch to its various operating positions. Compare the results with the switch operating schematic included in the wiring diagrams (located on the CD inserted into the back cover of the manual).

For example, **Figure 162** shows the continuity diagram for a typical ignition switch. The horizontal lines on the diagram indicate which terminals should show continuity when the switch is in a given position. When the switch is set to ignition, there should be continuity between the red/black, red and red/gray terminals. An ohmmeter connected between these three terminals should indicate little or no resistance, or a test light should light. When the switch is off, there should be no continuity between the same terminals.

Replace a switch if it does not perform properly.

When testing the switches, note the following:

1. Check the battery as described in this chapter. Charge or replace the battery if necessary.

NOTE
Always disarm the optional security system (TSSM/HFSM) before disconnecting the battery or before pulling the Maxi-Fuse so the siren will not sound.

2. Disconnect the negative battery cable as described in this chapter.
3. Detach all connectors located between the switch and the electrical circuit.

CAUTION
Do not attempt to start the engine with the battery disconnected.

4. When separating a connector, pull on the connector housings and not the wires.
5. After locating a defective circuit, check the connectors to make sure they are all clean and properly mated. Check all wires going into a connector housing to make sure each wire is positioned properly and the wire end is not loose.
6. To reconnect a connector, push the housings together until they click or snap into place.

Handlebar Switches

Left handlebar switch description

The left side handlebar switch housing (**Figure 163**) is equipped with the following switches:
1. Headlight high/low beam.
2. Horn.
3. Left side turn signal.
4. Audio controls (on/off).
5. CB control.
6. Cruise control, on/off (models so equipped).
7. Clutch interlock switch (2007-2009 models).

Right handlebar switch description

The right side handlebar switch housing (**Figure 164**) is equipped with the following switches:
1. Engine stop/run.
2. Starter.
3. Right side turn signal.
4. Front brake light.
5. Mode select up/down (models so equipped).
6. Cruise control, set/resume (models so equipped).

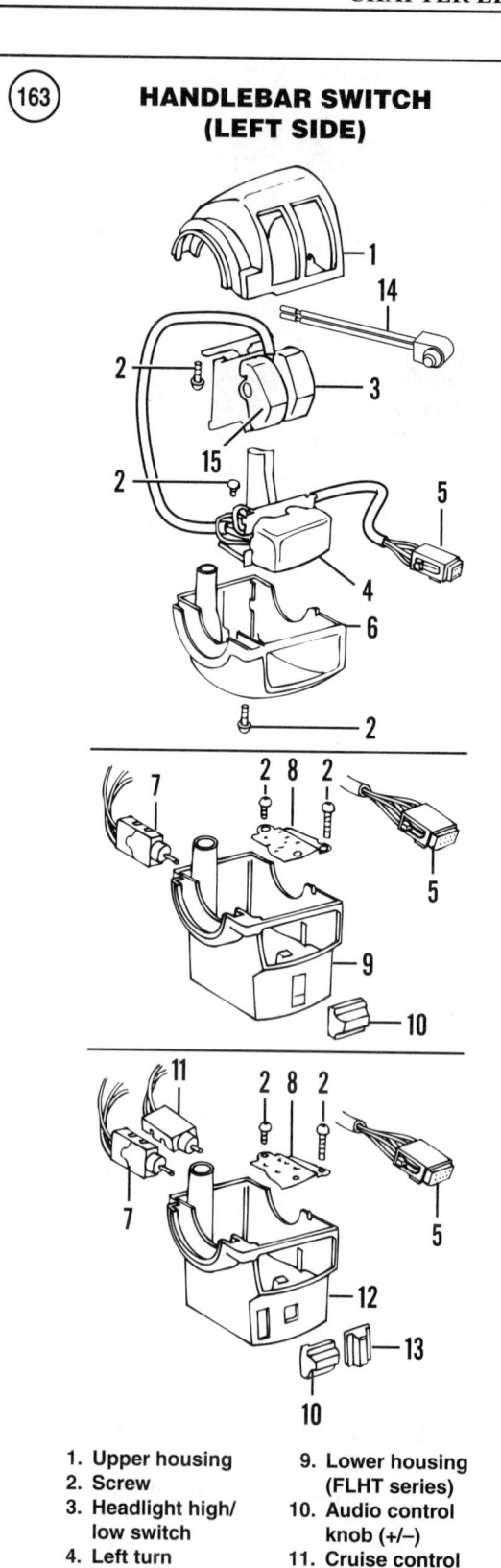

163 HANDLEBAR SWITCH (LEFT SIDE)

1. Upper housing
2. Screw
3. Headlight high/low switch
4. Left turn signal switch
5. Electrical connector
6. Lower housing (FLHR series)
7. Audio control switch (+/−)
8. Bracket
9. Lower housing (FLHT series)
10. Audio control knob (+/−)
11. Cruise control ON/OFF switch
12. Lower housing (FLTR series)
13. CB control knob
14. Clutch interlock switch (2007-2009 models)
15. Horn switch

ELECTRICAL SYSTEM

HANDLEBAR SWITCH (RIGHT SIDE)

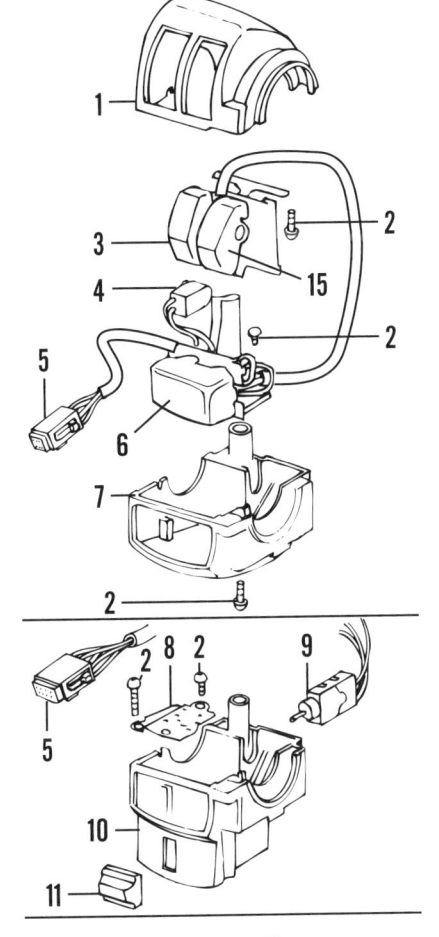

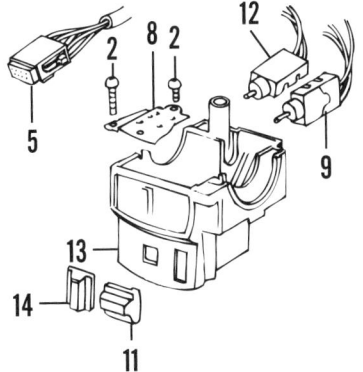

1. Upper housing
2. Screw
3. Engine starter switch
4. Front brake light switch
5. Electrical connector
6. Right turn signal switch
7. Lower housing (FLHR series)
8. Bracket
9. Mode select (up/down) switch
10. Lower housing (FLHT series)
11. Mode select (up/down) knob
12. Cruise control set/resume switch
13. Lower housing (FLTR series)
14. Cruise control set/resume knob
15. Engine run/stop switch

Handlebar switch replacement

1. Remove the screws securing the left side switch housing (**Figure 165**) to the handlebar. Then, carefully separate the switch housing (**Figure 166**) to access the defective switch.
2. Remove the screws securing the right side switch housing (**Figure 167**) to the handlebar. Then, carefully separate the switch housing (**Figure 166**) to access the defective switch.

NOTE
*To service the front brake light switch, refer to **Front Brake Light Switch Replacement** (this section).*

3A. On models without splices, remove the screw and bracket.
3B. On models with splices, remove the cable strap.
4. Pull the switch(es) out of the housing.
5. Cut the switch wire(s) from the defective switch(es).
6. Slip a piece of heat shrink tubing over each cut wire.
7. Solder the wire end(s) to the new switch. Then, shrink the tubing over the wire(s) by heating it.
8. Install the switch by reversing the removal steps, while noting the following:
   a. When clamping the switch housing onto the handlebar, check the wiring harness routing position to make sure it is not pinched between the housing and handlebar.
   b. On 2006-2007 models, refer to *Throttle and Idle Cable Replacement* in Chapter Nine or Chapter Ten, to install the right side switch housing.
   c. Tighten the housing screws securely.

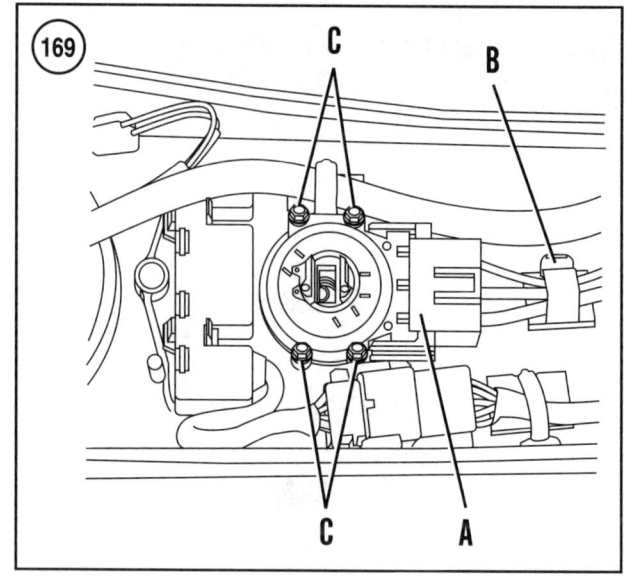

Front Brake Light Switch Replacement

The front brake light switch (**Figure 168**) is mounted in the right side switch lower housing.
1. Separate the right side switch housing as described in this section.
2. If still in place, remove the spacer between the switch and the switch housing.
3. While depressing the switch plunger, slowly rotate the switch upward, rocking it slightly, and remove it from the switch housing.
4. Cut the switch wires from the defective switch.
5. Slip a piece of heat shrink tubing over each cut wire.
6. Solder the wire ends to the new switch. Then, shrink the tubing over the wires.
7. Install the switch by reversing the removal steps while noting the following.
   a. When clamping the switch housing onto the handlebar, check the wiring harness routing position to make sure it is not pinched between the housing and handlebar.
   b. On 2006-2007 models, refer to *Throttle and Idle Cable Replacement* in Chapter Nine or Chapter Ten to install the right side switch housing.

IGNITION SWITCH (ALL MODELS EXCEPT FLHR AND SCREAMIN' EAGLE)

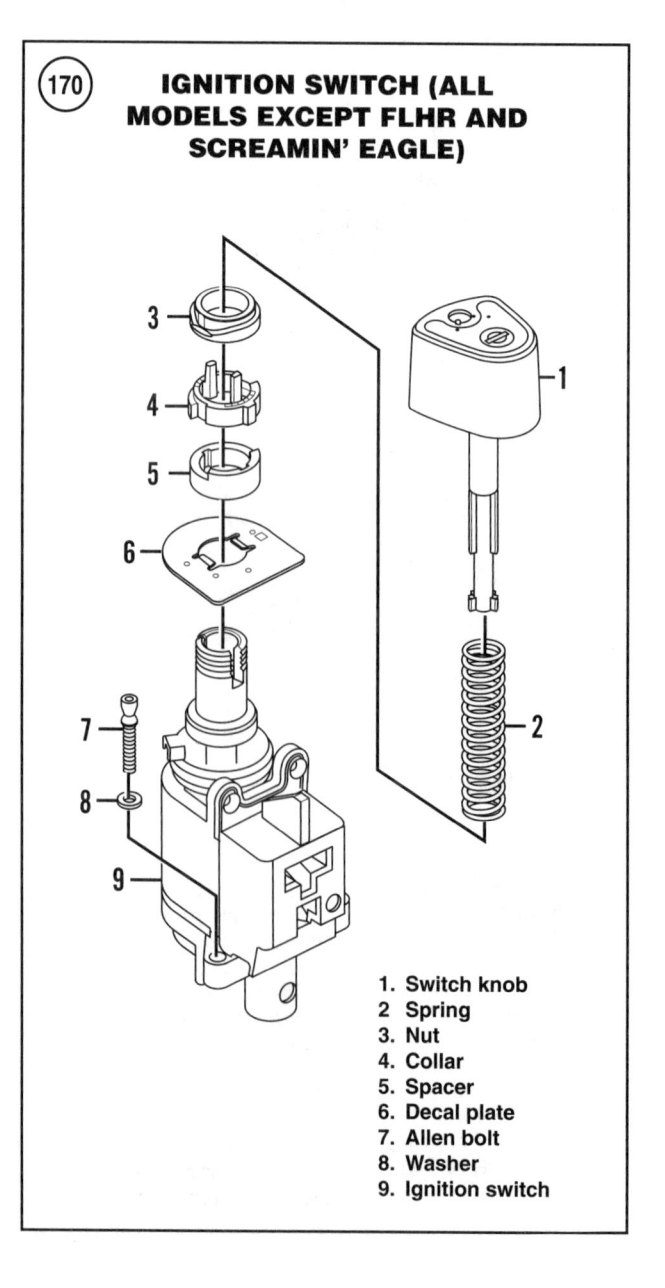

1. Switch knob
2. Spring
3. Nut
4. Collar
5. Spacer
6. Decal plate
7. Allen bolt
8. Washer
9. Ignition switch

ELECTRICAL SYSTEM

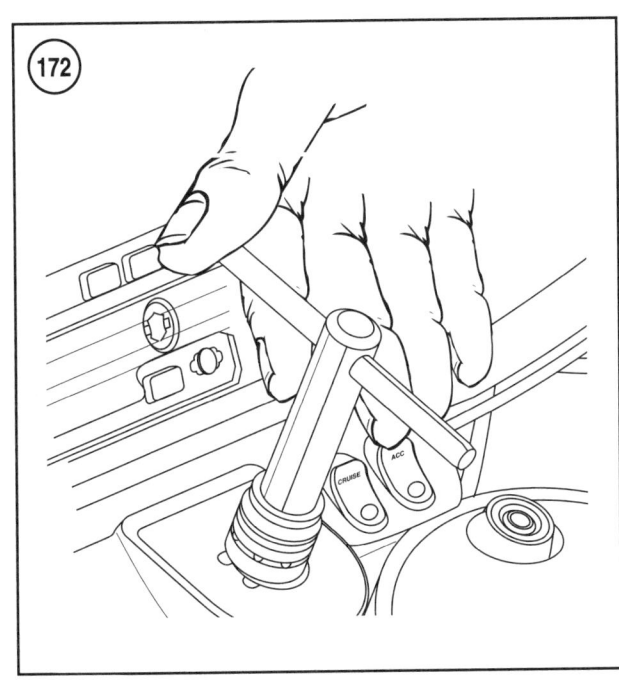

171

172

Ignition/Light Key Switch Removal/Installation (FLHR and Screamin' Eagle Models)

NOTE
Always disarm the optional TSSM/HFSM security system before disconnecting the battery or pulling the Maxi-Fuse so the siren will not sound.

1. Disconnect the negative battery cable as described in this chapter.
2. Remove the seat as described in Chapter Seventeen.
3. Lay several towels or a blanket on the frame and rear fender.
4. Partially remove the fuel tank console as follows:
    a. Remove the socket screw at the front of the fuel tank console.
    b. Remove the rear hex screw and release the rear of the fuel tank console bracket from the clip nut on the fuel tank bracket.

5. Turn the fuel tank console over onto towels and disconnect the 3-pin Packard connector (A, **Figure 169**) from the ignition switch.
6. Release the wiring harness from the clip (B, **Figure 169**).
7. Remove the four screws (C, **Figure 169**) securing the ignition switch to the bottom surface of the fuel tank console.
8. Remove the ignition switch.
9. Install by reversing the removal steps, while noting the following:
    a. Install the new ignition switch with the electrical connector terminal facing toward the rear of the fuel console.
    b. Tighten the four screws to 36-60 in.-lb. (4.1-6.8 N•m).

Ignition/Light Switch Removal/Installation (All Models Except FLHR and Screamin' Eagle)

Refer to **Figure 170**.

Removal

NOTE
Always disarm the optional TSSM/HFSM security system before disconnecting the battery or pulling the Maxi-Fuse so the siren will not sound.

1. Disconnect the negative battery cable as described in this chapter.
2. To remove the ignition switch knob, perform the following:
    a. Using the ignition key, turn the ignition switch to the unlock position. Keep the key installed in the knob.
    b. Turn the front wheel to the left fork stop. Turn the ignition switch to the fork lock position.
    c. Insert a small, flat-bladed screwdriver (A, **Figure 171**) under the left side of the switch knob and depress the release button. Keep it depressed.

NOTE
The spring will drop out of the underside of the knob as the knob is removed.

    d. Push the ignition key down, turn the ignition key 60° *counterclockwise* (B, **Figure 171**). Lift up and remove the switch knob.
3. To reposition switch after the switch knob has been removed, insert the ignition switch alignment tool (JIMS part No. 943 or H-D part No. HD-45962) into the switch housing until the bottom of the tool handle bottoms on the threaded post (**Figure 172**).
4. Turn the front wheel to the right fork stop.

11

5. Use a 7/8 in. open end wrench and loosen the ignition switch nut (**Figure 173**). Unscrew and remove the nut from the threaded post.
6. Remove the collar and spacer (**Figure 174**) from the threaded post.
7A. On FLHX and FLHT models, pull on the tabs and remove the decal plate (**Figure 175**) from the slots in the fairing cap.
7B. On FLTR models, pull on the tabs and remove the decal plate (**Figure 175**) from the slots in the instrument nacelle.
8A. On FLHX and FLHT models, perform the following:
 a. Remove the outer fairing as described in Chapter Seventeen.
 b. Insert a long shaft ball end socket (Snap-On part No. FABL6E), or an equivalent, through the oblong holes in the fairing brackets and remove the four Allen bolts. Release the radio, or storage box (on FLHT models), from the right and left radio support brackets and move it to one side.
 c. Carefully cut the straps securing the main harness to the lower right side corner of the radio, or storage box.
 d. Remove the fairing cap as described in Chapter Seventeen.
8B. On FLTR models, remove the headlight nacelle as described in this chapter.
9. On FLHX and FLHT models, perform the following:
 a. Remove the Torx screws (**Figure 176**) and washers securing the fairing cap on each side of the inner fairing.
 b. Carefully disengage the fairing cap (**Figure 177**) and pull it down. Disconnect the auxiliary switch electrical connectors (A, **Figure 178**) from the harness.
 c. Carefully remove the auxiliary switch wiring harness (B, **Figure 178**) from the ignition switch and remove the fairing cap from the inner fairing.
10. Disconnect the 3-pin ignition switch Packard connector at the front of the ignition as follows:
 a. Carefully insert the end of the ignition switch connector remover (H-D part No. HD-45961), or an equivalent, into the slot in the ignition switch housing until it bottoms.
 b. Hold onto the tool (A, **Figure 179**) and the wiring harness and pull on both parts at the same time, and release the socket housing (B) from the ignition switch.
11. Remove the handlebar upper clamp (Chapter Thirteen) and move the handlebar assembly out of the way.
12A. On non-HDI models, remove the two Allen screws (A, **Figure 180**) and flat washers securing the ignition switch to the upper fork bracket. Remove the ignition switch (B, **Figure 180**).
12B. On HDI models, remove the break-away screws as follows:

ELECTRICAL SYSTEM

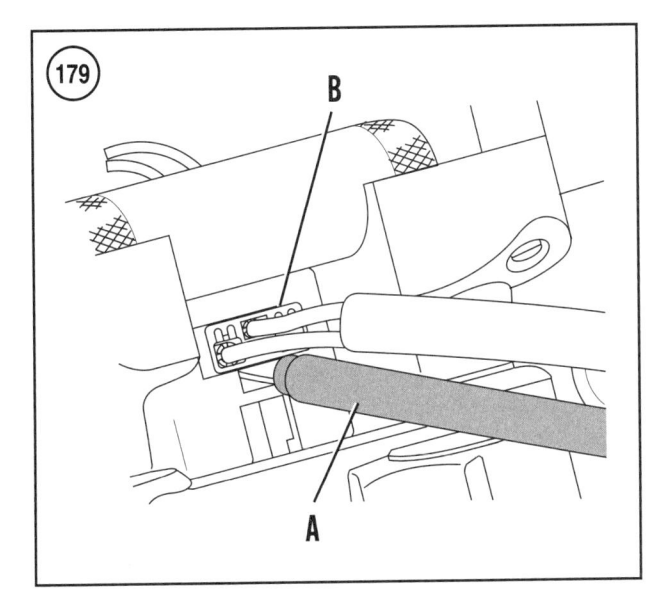

a. Make a pilot divot in the top of the screws (A, **Figure 180**) with a center punch and hammer. Make it deep enough to guide the drill bit in the next step.
b. Install a 1/8 inch left-handed drill bit into the drill and set the drill to *reverse direction*.
c. Center the drill bit in the divot. Turn the drill at low speed and spin out the break-away screw.
d. Repeat for the remaining screw.
e. Remove the ignition switch (B, **Figure 180**).

Installation

1. Insert the ignition switch into the upper fork bracket bore.
2A. On non-HDI models, install the two screws and flat washers securing the ignition switch. Tighten the screws to 36-60 in.-lb. (4.1-6.8 N•m).
2B. On HDI models, perform the following:
   a. Thoroughly clean the screw threads in the fork bracket.
   b. Install *new* screws and flat washers securing the ignition switch. Slowly tighten the screws until the heads snap off.
3. Install the handlebar as described in Chapter Thirteen.
4. Connect the 3-pin ignition switch Packard connector onto the front of the ignition switch.
5A. On FLHT and FLHX models, perform the following:
   a. Install a *new* strap securing the ignition switch main harness to the lower right side of the radio (or storage box).
   b. Install the fairing cap as described in Chapter Seventeen.
   c. Move the radio, or storage box on FLHT models, back into position.
   d. Install the four Allen screws securing the radio, or storage box on FLHT models, onto the right and left radio support brackets. Tighten the screws to 35-45 in.-lb. (4.0-5.1 N•m).
   e. Install the outer fairing as described in Chapter Seventeen.
5B. On FLTR models, install the headlight nacelle as described in this chapter.
6A. On FLHT and FLHX models, install the decal plate tabs (**Figure 175**) into the slots in the fairing cap.
6B. On FLTR models, install the decal plate tabs (**Figure 175**) into the slots in the instrument nacelle.
7. Position the spacer with the widest side facing forward and so the inside tabs align with the slots in the threaded post. Install the spacer (**Figure 174**) and push it down until it contacts the decal plate.
8. Position the collar so the outside tab is facing forward and the inside tabs align with the slots in the threaded post.

Install the collar (**Figure 174**) and push it down until it contacts the spacer.

9. Position the nut with the flange side going on first and thread the nut onto the threaded post.

10. Turn the front wheel to the right fork stop. Use a 7/8 in. open-end crowfoot and tighten the nut to 120-150 in.-lb. (14.1-16.9 N•m).

11. Install the spring into the bore on the underside of the knob.

12. Position the knob pointing toward the FORK LOCK position and install the knob onto the threaded post.

13. Hold the knob down, insert the knob shaft into the threaded post. Hold the known down, turn the knob *clockwise* to the UNLOCK position until a click is heard. This indicates that the knob and switch are properly engaged. Release the knob and rotate it through all four positions and verify proper operation.

14. Connect the negative battery cable as described in this chapter.

Oil Pressure Switch/Sender

Operation

The oil pressure switch, or sender, is located on the front right side of the crankcase.

A pressure-actuated, diaphragm-type oil pressure switch, or sender, is used. When the oil pressure is low or when oil is not circulating through a running engine, spring tension inside the switch, or sender, holds the switch contacts closed. This completes the signal light circuit and causes the oil pressure indicator lamp to light.

NOTE
The oil pressure indicator light may not come on when the ignition switch is turned off and then back on immediately. This is due to the oil pressure retained in the oil filter housing. Test the electrical part of the oil pressure switch as described in this section. If the oil pressure switch, indicator light and related wiring are in good condition, inspect the engine lubrication system as described in Chapter Two.

The oil pressure signal light should turn on when any of the following occurs:

1. The ignition switch is turned on prior to starting the engine.
2. The engine idle is below idle speed of 950-1050 rpm.
3. The engine is operating with low oil pressure.
4. Oil is not circulating through the running engine.

Testing/replacement

1A. On FLHR models including Screamin' Eagle, pull on the elbow connector and disconnect the electrical connector from the switch.

1B. On FLHT, FLHX and FLTR models, pull the external latch outward, use a rocking motion, and disconnect the 4-pin Delphi connector from the sender (**Figure 181**).

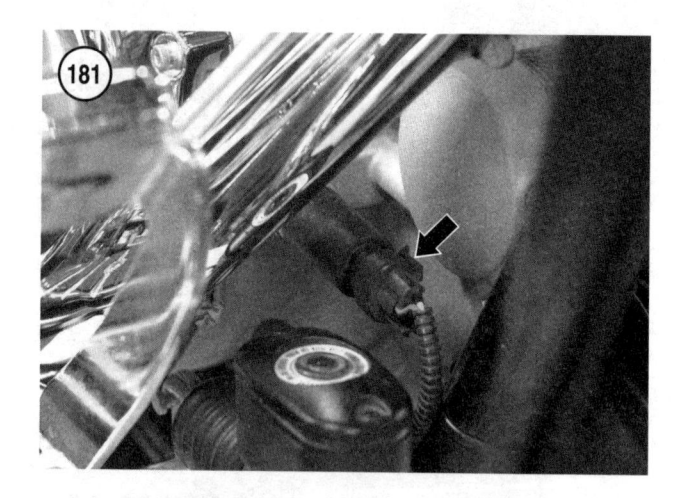

2. Turn the ignition switch on.

3A. On FLHR models with switch, ground the switch wire to the engine.

3B. On all models except FLHR with a switch, ground the brown/green terminal within the Delphi connector to the engine with a jumper wire.

4. The oil pressure indicator light on the instrument panel should light.

5. If the indicator lamp does not light, check for a defective indicator light and inspect all wiring between the switch or sender, and the indicator light.

6A. If the oil pressure warning light operates properly, attach the electrical connector to the pressure switch. Make sure the connection is tight and free from oil. On models with a switch, slide the rubber boot back into position.

6B. If the warning light remains on when the engine is running, shut the engine off. Check the engine lubrication system as described in Chapter Two.

7A. To replace the switch, perform the following:
   a. Use a 15/16 in. open-end crowfoot wrench and unscrew it from the engine.
   b. Apply Loctite pipe sealant with Teflon 565 to the switch threads prior to installation.
   c. Install the switch and tighten to 96-120 in.-lb. (10.8-13.6 N•m).
   d. Test the new switch as described in this section.

ELECTRICAL SYSTEM

183

7B. To replace the oil pressure sending unit, perform the following:
   a. Use a 1-1/16 in. open-end crowfoot wrench and unscrew it from the engine.
   b. Apply Loctite pipe sealant with Teflon 565 to the sender threads prior to installation.
   c. Install the sender and tighten to 96-120 in.-lb. (10.8-13.6 N•m).
   d. Test the new sender as described in this section.

Neutral Indicator Switch
Testing/Replacement

The neutral indicator switch is located on the rear left side of the transmission case. The neutral indicator light on the instrument panel should light when the ignition is on and the transmission is in neutral.

1. Disconnect the electrical connector (**Figure 182**) from the neutral indicator switch.
2. Turn the ignition switch to IGN.
3. Ground the neutral indicator switch wire to the transmission case.
4. If the neutral indicator lamp lights, the neutral switch is defective. Replace the neutral indicator switch and retest.
5. If the neutral indicator lamp does not light, check for a defective indicator light, faulty wiring or a loose or corroded connection.

NOTE
The electrical connector can be attached to either stud on the switch.

6A. If the neutral switch operates correctly, attach the electrical connector to the neutral switch. Make sure the connection is tight and free from oil.
6B. If the neutral switch is defective, replace the neutral indicator switch as described in this section.

NOTE
*On 2006-2007 models, if damaged, install a **new** type of neutral switch that is equipped with a heat-sealed butt splice connector.*

7. To replace the old switch, perform the following:
   a. Shift the transmission into neutral.
   b. Unscrew and remove the old switch and O-ring from the transmission cover.
   c. Apply clean transmission oil to the *new* O-ring seal.
   d. Install the new neutral switch and tighten to 120-180 in.-lb. (13.6-20.3 N•m).

Rear Brake Light Switch
Testing/Replacement

A hydraulic, normally-open rear brake light switch is used on all models. The rear brake light is attached to the rear brake caliper hose assembly. When the rear brake pedal is applied, hydraulic pressure closes the switch contacts, providing a ground path so the rear brake light comes on. If the rear brake light does not come on, perform the following.

NOTE
Removal of the exhaust system is not necessary, but it does provide additional work room.

1. If necessary, remove the exhaust system from the right side as described in Chapter Four.
2. Turn the ignition switch off.
3. Disconnect the electrical connector (A, **Figure 183**) from the switch.
4. Connect an ohmmeter between the switch terminals and check the following:
   a. Apply the rear brake pedal. There should be continuity.
   b. Release the rear brake pedal. There should be no continuity.
   c. If the switch fails either of these tests, replace the switch as described in the section.
5. Place a drip pan under the switch, as some brake fluid will drain out when the switch is removed.
6. Secure the brake line fitting (B, **Figure 183**) with a suitable size wrench to prevent it from rotating.
7. Unscrew the switch (C, **Figure 183**) from the fitting (B).
8. Apply Loctite pipe sealant with Teflon 565 to the switch threads prior to installation.
9. Install the *new* switch and tighten it to 12-15 ft.-lb. (16.3-20.3 N•m).
10. Reconnect the switch electrical connector.
11. Bleed the rear brake as described in Chapter Fifteen.
12. Check the rear brake light with the ignition switch turned on and the rear brake applied.
13. If removed, install the right side exhaust system as described in Chapter Four.

HORN

Testing

1. Remove the seat as described in Chapter Seventeen.

2. Partially remove the cover and horn (**Figure 184**) to access the backside of the horn.
3. Disconnect only the yellow/black electrical connector (A, **Figure 185**) from the backside of the horn.
4. Connect a voltmeter as follows:
   a. Positive test lead to the yellow/black electrical connector.
   b. Negative test lead to ground.
5. Turn the ignition switch to IGN.
6. Depress the horn button. If battery voltage is present the horn is faulty or is not grounded properly. If there is no battery voltage, either the horn switch or the horn wiring is faulty.
7. Replace the horn or horn switch as necessary.

Replacement

NOTE
Always disarm the optional TSSM/HFSM security system before disconnecting the battery or pulling the Maxi-Fuse so the siren will not sound.

1. Remove the seat as described in Chapter Seventeen.
2. Disconnect the negative battery cable as described in this chapter.
3. Remove the acorn nut (**Figure 184**) and washer securing the horn assembly to the frame's rubber mount stud.
4. Disconnect the elbow electrical terminals from the horn spade terminals (A and B, **Figure 185**). Open the J-clamp (C, **Figure 185**).
5. Remove the 10-mm flange nut (D, **Figure 185**) from the backside of the horn mounting bracket. Remove the horn from the cover.
6. Install the horn onto the chrome cover inserting the stud on the backside through the mounting bracket hole.
7. Apply several drops of Loctite Threadlocker No. 222 (purple) onto the horn stud.
8. Install the 10-mm flange nut (D, **Figure 185**) onto the horn stud and tighten to 80-100 in.-lb. (9.0-11.3 N•m).
9. Connect the elbow electrical terminals onto the horn spade terminals (A and B, **Figure 185**).
10. Capture the wiring harness into the J-clamp (C, **Figure 185**) and install the horn bracket onto the rubber mount.
11. Install the flat washer and acorn nut. Tighten the acorn nut to 80-120 in.-lb. (9.0-13.6 N•m).
12. Connect the negative battery cable as described in this chapter.
13. Check that the horn operates correctly.
14. Install the seat as described in Chapter Seventeen.

TURN SIGNAL SECURITY MODULE (TSM, TSSM AND HFSM)

This section describes the service procedures for the turn signal module (TSM), turn signal and security module (TSSM), and the hands-free security module (HFSM).

The turn signal module (TSM) is an electronic microprocessor that controls the turn signals and four-way hazard flasher. The turn signal module receives its information from the speedometer and turn signal switches. The bank angle sensor (BAS) is integrated into the module and provides motorcycle movement signals to the ECM.

The turn signal and security module (TSSM) performs the same function as the TSM. However, it also provides additional security and immobilization functions. When activated, the security system alternately flashes the left and right turn signals and sounds an optional siren on models so equipped.

The hands-free security module (HFSM) performs the same functions as a TSSM, and it includes a key fob for convenient arming and disarming of the security system. The HFSM is optional on 2007-2009 models.

NOTE
The security system is activated, and the optional siren sounds, whenever the ignition circuit is tampered with, if the vehicle is moved, or whenever the battery or ground connection is broken. Always disarm the security system before servicing the motorcycle, before disconnecting the negative battery cable or before pulling the Maxi-Fuse.

Removal/Installation

2006-2008 models

NOTE
Always disarm the optional TSSM/HFSM security system before disconnecting the battery or pulling the Maxi-Fuse so the siren will not sound.

1. Remove the seat as described in Chapter Seventeen.
2. Turn the ignition switch off.
3. Disconnect the negative battery cable as described in this chapter.
4. Depress the tab (A, **Figure 186**) at the front of the spring clip.
5. Release the clip legs from the holes in the frame cross member at the rear of the battery tray.

ELECTRICAL SYSTEM

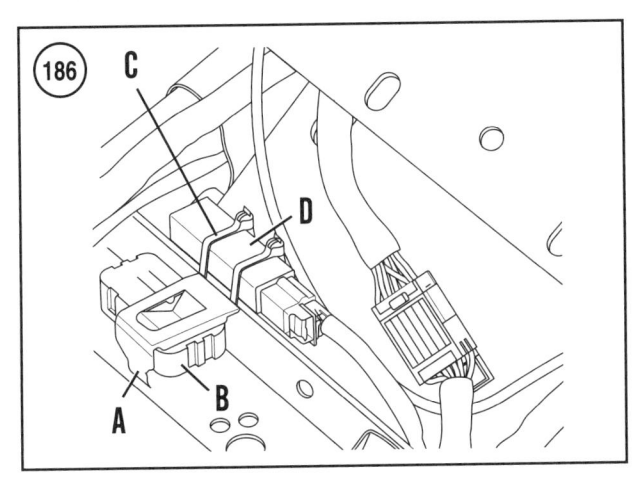

6. Carefully pull the TSSM (B, **Figure 186**) from the battery tray.
7. Disconnect the 12-pin Deutsch connector from the module and remove the module.
8. On 2007-2009 models so equipped, disconnect the 4-pin HFSM antenna jumper harness connector.
9. Install the module by reversing the removal steps. Note the following:
    a. Make sure the electrical connector is free of moisture.
    b. Make sure the turn signal and flasher systems work properly.

2009 models

NOTE
Always disarm the optional TSSM/HFSM security system before disconnecting the battery or pulling the Maxi-Fuse so the siren will not sound.

1. Remove the seat as described in Chapter Seventeen.
2. Remove the left side saddlebag and frame side cover as described in Chapter Seventeen.
3. With the security fob in the general area of the motorcycle, turn the ignition switch to IGN.
4. On models so equipped, release the rear wheel ABS sensor connector.

5. Carefully pull out on the bottom of the TSSM module and release it from the battery tray.
6. Remove the module from the upper retainer and disconnect the module connector and the HFSM antenna jumper harness connector, on models so equipped.
7. Remove the module from the battery tray.
8. Install the module by reversing the removal steps. Note the following:
    a. Make sure the electrical connector is free of moisture.
    b. Make sure the turn signal and flasher systems work properly.

Turn Signal Operation

Automatic cancellation

NOTE
The turn signal security module will not cancel the signal before the turn is actually completed.

1. When the turn signal switch is depressed, then released, the system begins a 20 count. As long as the motorcycle is moving above 7 MPH (11 KPH) the turn signals will always cancel after the 20 bulb flashes, providing the system does not receive any additional input.
2. If the motorcycle's speed drops to 7 MPH (11 KPH) or less, including stopping, the turn signals will continue to flash. The counting will continue when the motorcycle reaches 8 MPH (13 KPH) and will automatically cancel when the count total equals 20 bulb flashes.
3. The turn signals will cancel within two seconds after the turn of 45° or more is completed.

Manual cancellation

1. After the turn signal switch is depressed, and then released, the system begins a 20 count. To cancel the turn signal from flashing, depress the turn signal switch a second time.
2. If the turn direction is to be changed, depress the opposite turn signal switch. The primary signal is cancelled and the opposite turn signal will flash.

Four-way flashing

1. Turn the ignition switch to IGN. On models so equipped, disarm the security system. Press the right and left turn signal switches at the same time. All four turn signals will flash.
2. On models with the security system, the system can be armed so all four signals flash for up to two hours. Turn the ignition switch off and arm the security system. Press both the right and left turn signal switches at the same time.
3. To cancel the four-way flashing, disarm the security system, on models so equipped, and press both the right and left turn signal switches at the same time.

CHAPTER ELEVEN

Bank angle sensor (BAS)

The bank angle sensor automatically shuts off the engine if the motorcycle tilts more than 45° for longer than one second. The shutoff occurs even at a very slow speed. The sensor is an integral part of the TSM/TSSM/HFSM unit.

To restart the motorcycle, return the motorcycle to vertical. Turn the ignition switch off, and back to IGN. Then, restart the engine.

Security System Operation

If a theft attempt is detected when the TSSM/HFSM is armed, the system immobilizes the starting and ignition systems. It also alternately flashes the right and left turn signals and sounds the siren, if so equipped. The following conditions activate the armed security system.

1. If the system detects tampering with the ignition system or detects vehicle movement, it issues the first warning: the turn signals flash three times and the optional siren chirps once. If the motorcycle is not returned to its original position within four seconds, the system issues a second warning. If the tampering continues, the system goes into full alarm: the turn signals alternately flash and the optional siren sounds for 30 seconds. If the motorcycle is not returned to its original position after a ten second pause, the system repeats full alarm. It repeats this cycle (30-seconds on/10-seconds off) for ten times or for a total of five minutes.
2. If the system detects a battery or ground disconnect, the optional siren sounds but the turn signals do not flash.

> *NOTE*
> *Always disarm the optional TSSM/HFSM before disconnecting the battery or the siren will sound. If the TSSM is in auto-alarming mode, disarm the system with two clicks of the key fob, and disconnect the battery or remove the TSSM fuse before the 30-second arming period expires.*

HFSM Antenna (2007-2009 Models)
Removal/Installation

> *NOTE*
> *The 2006 models are not equipped with the HFSM system.*

1. Remove the seat as described in Chapter Seventeen.
2. Turn the ignition switch off.
3. Disconnect the negative battery cable as described in this chapter.
4. Cut the straps (C, **Figure 186**) securing the antenna to the battery tray.
5. Release the HFSM pins from the frame cross-member.
6. Disconnect the 2-pin HFSM antenna connector from the jumper harness and remove the antenna (D, **Figure 186**).

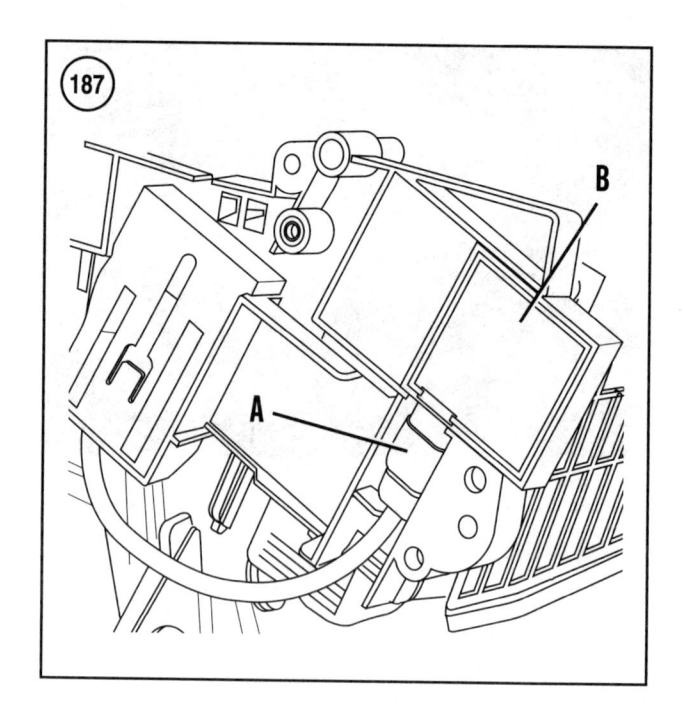

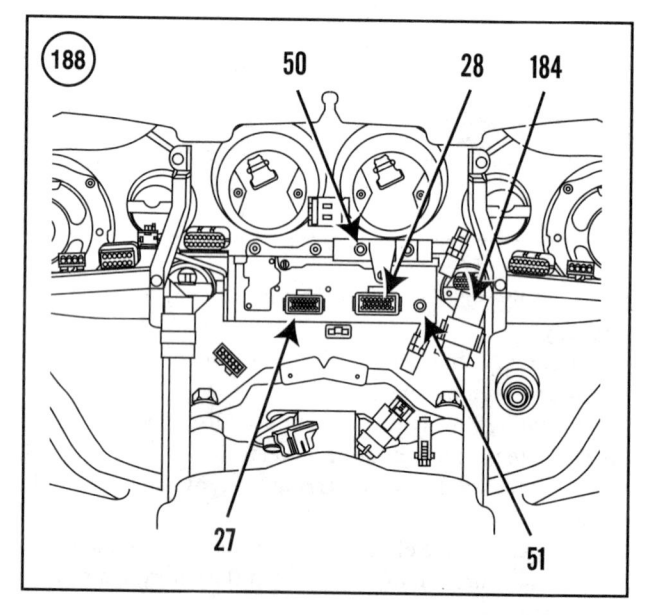

7. Install the module by reversing the removal steps. Make sure the electrical connector is free of moisture.

SECURITY SIREN (OPTIONAL ON 2007-2009 MODELS)

Removal/Installation

> *NOTE*
> *Always disarm the optional TSSM/HFSM security system before disconnecting the battery or pulling the Maxi-Fuse so the siren will not sound.*

1. Remove the right side saddlebag and frame side cover as described in Chapter Seventeen.

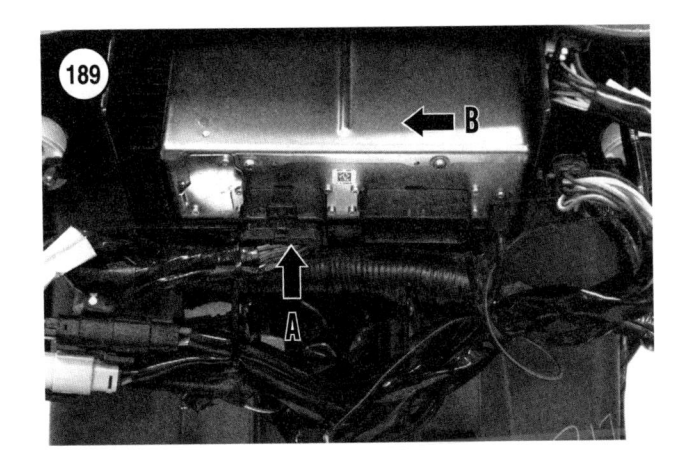

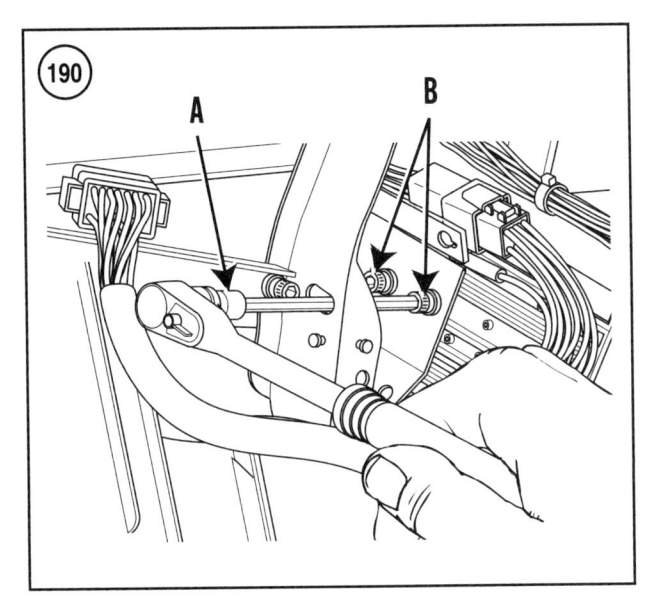

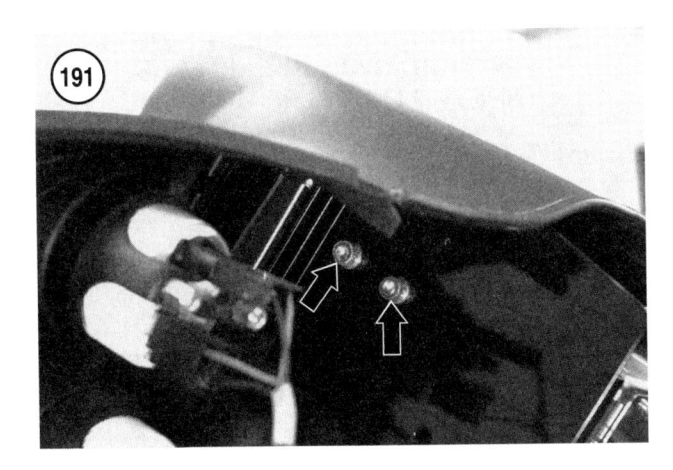

ELECTRICAL SYSTEM

189

190

191

2. Disconnect the negative battery cable as described in this chapter.

3. Remove the flange nuts, or screws, securing the electrical bracket to the frame studs.

4. Pull straight out and partially remove the electrical bracket or caddy from the frame.

5. Turn the electrical bracket or caddy over, disconnect the 3-pin Delphi connector (A, **Figure 187**), and remove the siren (B) from the bracket or caddy, on models so equipped.

6. Install by reversing the removal steps. Tighten the two flange nuts or screws to the specification listed in **Table 5**.

RADIO (STORAGE BOX)

Removal/Installation

Refer to **Figure 188** for radio connector locations.

NOTE
Always disarm the optional TSSM/HFSM security system before disconnecting the battery or pulling the Maxi-Fuse so the siren will not sound.

1. Disconnect the negative battery cable as described in this chapter.

2. Remove the outer front fairing as described in Chapter Seventeen.

3A. On FLHX, FLHTC and FLTR models, disconnect the following electrical connectors:
   a. The 23-pin connector (A, **Figure 189**) from the backside of the radio.
   b. The radio antenna cable connector from the backside of the radio.

3B. On FHLTCU models, disconnect the following electrical connectors:
   a. The 23-pin connector from the backside of the radio.
   b. The radio antenna cable connector from the backside of the radio.
   c. The 35-pin connector from the backside of the radio.
   d. The CB antenna cable connector from the backside of the radio.
   e. The 12-pin CB module connector from the backside of the radio.

4. On FHLTCU models, remove the screw and release the CB module flange from the radio.

5. Use a long-shank, ball-end socket (Snap-On part No. FABL6E) (A, **Figure 190**), or an equivalent tool, and remove the four screws (B) securing the radio or storage box to the right and left side support brackets.

6. Carefully pull the radio or storage box (B, **Figure 189**) forward and remove it from the inner fairing.

7. Install by reversing the removal steps. Tighten the screws (B, **Figure 190** and **Figure 191**) to 35-45 in.-lb. (4.0-5.1 N•m).

RADIO ANTENNA

Removal/Installation

1. Remove the fuel tank as described in Chapter Nine or Chapter Ten.

2. Remove the left frame side cover and saddlebag as described in Chapter Seventeen.

3. Remove the outer front fairing as described in Chapter Seventeen, on models so equipped.

4A. On FLTR and FLHX models, perform the following:
   a. Carefully cut the cable strap (A, **Figure 192**) and disconnect the antenna cable (B) from the connector.
   b. Remove the two Torx screws (C, **Figure 192**) securing the bracket, and remove the bracket and antenna mast assembly.

4B. On FLHT models, perform the following:
   a. Open the Tour-Pak cover and leave it open.
   b. Disconnect the antenna cable from the antenna base.
   c. Remove the screw, nut and washers securing the antenna base to the Tour-Pak bottom.
   d. Remove the reinforcement plate from the inside the Tour-Pak and remove the antenna base, gasket and antenna from the exterior of the Tour-Pak bottom.

5. Install by reversing the removal steps. Tighten the fasteners securely.

FRONT FAIRING SPEAKERS

Removal/Installation

NOTE
Always disarm the optional TSSM/HFSM security system before disconnecting the battery or pulling the Maxi-Fuse so the siren will not sound.

1. Disconnect the negative battery cable as described in this chapter.
2. Remove the outer front fairing as described in Chapter Seventeen.
3. Carefully, pull straight out and disconnect the socket terminals (A, **Figure 193**) from the speaker spade terminals.
4. Remove the three screws (B, **Figure 193**) securing the speaker to the speaker adapter. Note the location of the screws as they are different lengths.
5. Carefully withdraw the speaker (C, **Figure 193**) from the adapter and remove it.
6. Position the speaker with the spade terminals toward the bottom of the adapter, and install the speaker onto the adapter.
7. Thread the two top long screws securing the speaker and adapter to inner fairing.

NOTE
The lower inboard screw hole is not used.

8. Thread the lower short screw into the lower outboard hole, while positioning the washer between the adapter and support plate.
9. Tighten the single lower outboard screw to 22-28 in.-lb. (2.5-3.2 N•m).
10. Tighten the two upper screws to 35-50 in.-lb. (4.0-5.7 N•m).
11. Connect the socket terminals onto the speaker spade terminals. Push the connectors on until they bottom.
12. Install the outer front fairing as described in Chapter Seventeen.
13. Connect the negative battery cable as described in this chapter.

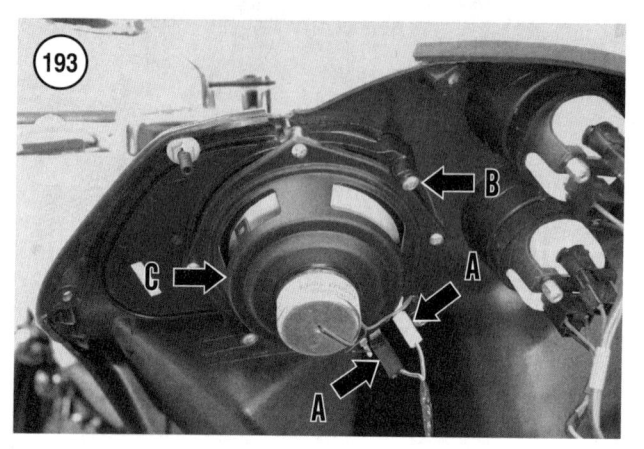

FRONT HEADSET RECEPTACLE (2008-2009 FLHTCUSE MODELS)

Removal/Installation

Refer to **Figure 194**.

NOTE
Always disarm the optional TSSM/HFSM security system before disconnecting the battery or pulling the Maxi-Fuse so the siren will not sound.

1. Remove the Maxi-Fuse as described in this chapter.
2. Remove the seat as described in Chapter Seventeen.
3. Remove the left saddlebag and frame side cover as described in Chapter Seventeen.
4. At the front and rear saddlebag rail, carefully cut the two cable straps securing the headset receptacle wiring conduit and audio harness to the inboard side of the left upper frame rail.
5. Release the 12-pin radio-to-headset harness connector from the attachment clip at the hole in the frame cross member at the rear of the battery. Disconnect the connector halves.

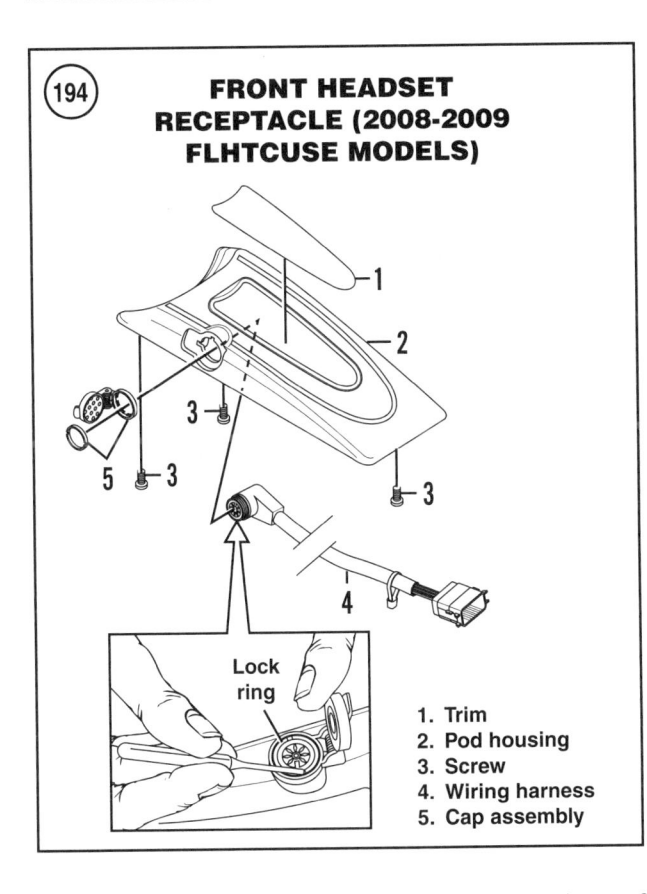

ELECTRICAL SYSTEM

FRONT HEADSET RECEPTACLE (2008-2009 FLHTCUSE MODELS)

1. Trim
2. Pod housing
3. Screw
4. Wiring harness
5. Cap assembly

Lock ring

6. Place several towels or blanket over the forward part of the rear fender.
7. Remove the Allen screw securing the console at the rear to the fuel tank.
8. Remove the console and place it on the rear fender.
9. Release the fuel door on the console, and remove the fuel filler cap.
10. Bend back the clips securing the wiring harness to the front headset receptacle.
11. Turn the fuel tank console over onto the blanket. Install the fuel filler cap.
12. Raise the headset receptacle cap. Place a small punch in either notch of lock ring and rotate it *counterclockwise* until loose.
13. Remove the lock ring and cap from headset receptacle.
14. Remove headset receptacle from console receptacle.
15. Install by reversing the removal steps. Tighten the fuel tank console Allen screw to 25-30 in.-lb. (2.8-3.4 N•m).

REAR PASSENGER SWITCHES

Removal/Installation

NOTE
Always disarm the optional TSSM/HFSM security system before disconnecting the battery or pulling the Maxi-Fuse so the siren will not sound.

1. Disconnect the negative battery cable as described in this chapter.
2. Open the cover on the Tour-Pak and leave it open.
3. Remove the four screws securing the speaker grill and remove it from the lower case.
4. Withdraw the speaker from the lower case, and carefully pull straight out and disconnect the socket terminals from the speaker spade terminals.
5. Remove the trim ring and carefully pull on wire harness. Withdraw the 6-pin rear speaker/passenger control connector from the speaker box. Disconnect the electrical connector.
6. Withdraw the socket portion of the electrical connector back into the speaker box and pull out through speaker opening.
7. Remove the two screws and release the switch bracket from inside of speaker box.
8. Carefully pull the switch housing assembly, wiring harness, speaker terminals and socket housing from speaker box through the hole on the outboard side.
9. Carefully pull the keycap from the switch shaft, and remove switch from housing.
10. Note the wire colors and terminal locations in switch housing. Remove all four terminals from the housing.
11. Pull one wire at a time and withdraw all four wires from the wiring harness.
12. Repeat the procedure to remove the remaining switch.
13. Install by reversing these removal steps. Tighten the screws securely.

REAR SPEAKERS

Removal/Installation

NOTE
Always disarm the optional TSSM/HFSM security system before disconnecting the battery or pulling the Maxi-Fuse so the siren will not sound.

1. Disconnect the negative battery cable as described in this chapter.
2. Open the cover on the Tour-Pak and leave it open.
3. Remove the four screws securing the speaker grill and remove it from the lower case.
4. Withdraw the speaker from the lower case, and carefully, pull straight out and disconnect the socket terminals from the speaker spade terminals.
5. Install by reversing the removal steps. Tighten the screws securely.

CB MODULE (FLHTCU MODELS)

Removal/Installation

NOTE
Always disarm the optional TSSM/HFSM security system before disconnecting the battery or pulling the Maxi-Fuse so the siren will not sound.

195 FUSE AND RELAY PANEL (LEFT SIDE)

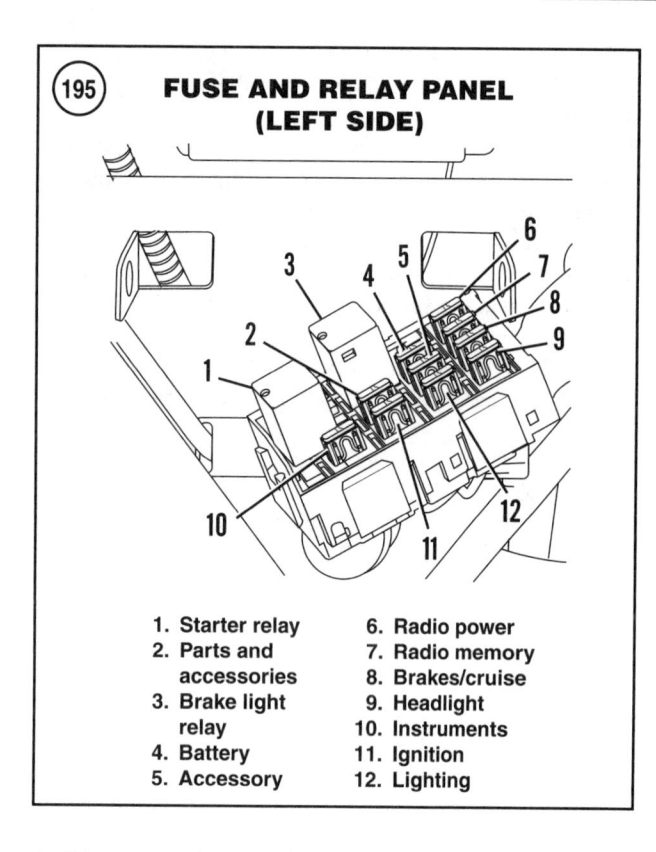

1. Starter relay
2. Parts and accessories
3. Brake light relay
4. Battery
5. Accessory
6. Radio power
7. Radio memory
8. Brakes/cruise
9. Headlight
10. Instruments
11. Ignition
12. Lighting

1. Disconnect the negative battery cable as described in this chapter.
2. Remove the outer front fairing as described in Chapter Seventeen.
3. Disconnect the following electrical connectors:
    a. The CB antenna cable connector from the backside of the radio.
    b. The 12-pin CB module connector from the backside of the radio.
4. Remove the screw(s) and release the CB module flange from the radio. Then, remove the CB module.
5. Install by reversing the removal steps. Tighten the screw(s) to 35-45 in.-lb. (4.0-5.1 N•m).

RELAYS

Starter and Brake Light Relay Replacement

Refer to **Figure 195**.

NOTE
Always disarm the optional TSSM/HFSM security system before disconnecting the battery or pulling the Maxi-Fuse so the siren will not sound.

1. Remove the left saddlebag and frame side cover as described in Chapter Seventeen.
2. Depress both latches (A, **Figure 196**) on the Maxi-Fuse holder, slide the holder (B) toward the rear and disengage the tongue from groove on the fuse holder.
3. Pull the fuse block (**Figure 197**) straight out and release it from the tabs on the frame mounting bracket.

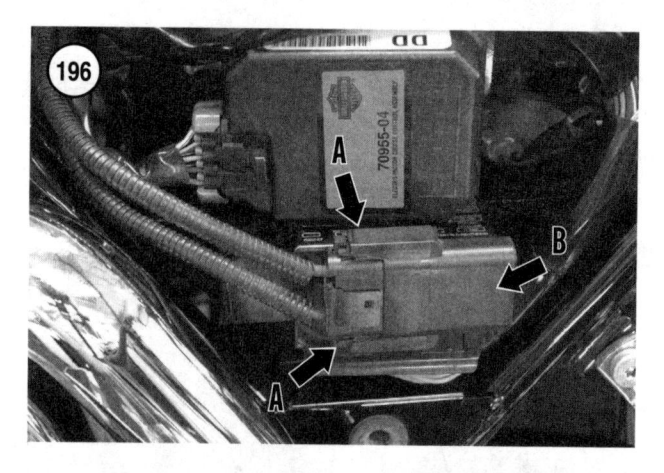

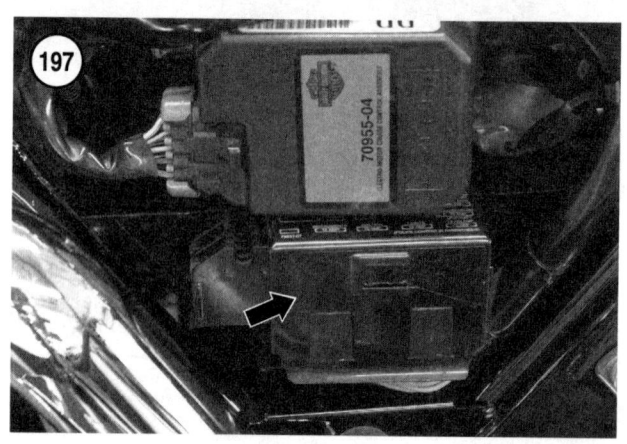

NOTE
*Relay description and location is printed on the fuse block cover (**Figure 198**, typical).*

4. Locate the defective relay, and install a new one with the same part number.
5. Install the Maxi-Fuse as described in this chapter.
6. Install the left saddlebag and the frame side cover as described in Chapter Seventeen.

EFI System Relay Replacement (2007 Models)

Refer to **Figure 199**.

ELECTRICAL SYSTEM

199 FUSE PANEL (RIGHT SIDE)

1. EFI system relay
2. Spare fuse
3. Fuel pump fuse
4. ECM power fuse
5. Engine control fuse (HDI only)

200

201

202

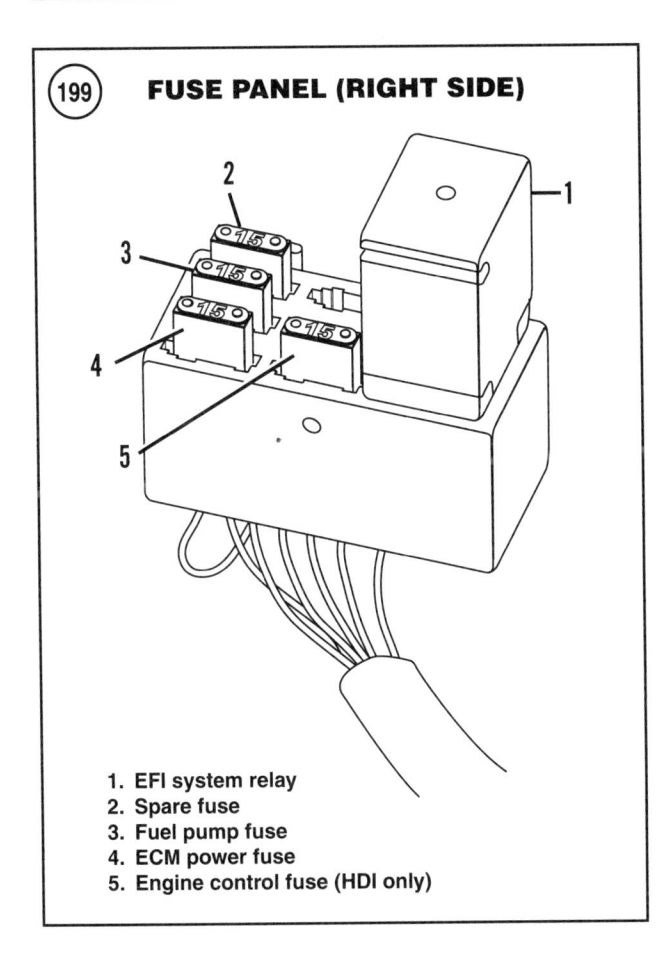

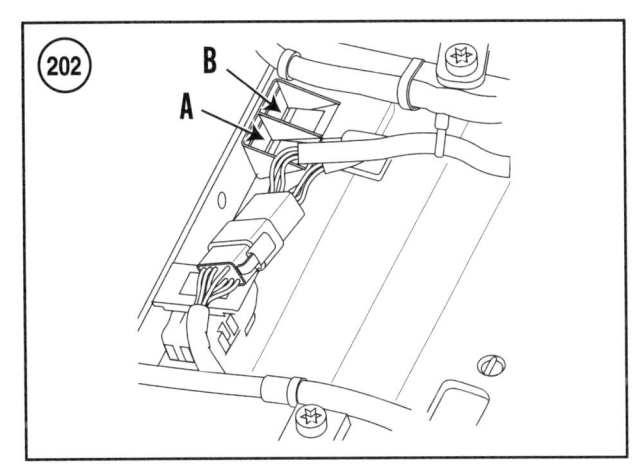

1. Remove the right saddlebag and frame side cover as described in Chapter Seventeen.
2. Remove the Maxi-Fuse as described in this chapter.
3. Release and move the data link connector (**Figure 200**) from the mounting bracket.
4. Gently press on the white dot on the inboard side of the fuse block. Gently pull on the wiring harness, and release the tabs on the fuse block (**Figure 201**) from the slots in the mounting bracket and remove it.

NOTE
*Relay description and location is printed on the fuse block cover (**Figure 198**, typical).*

5. Locate the blown relay, and install a new one with the same part number.
6. Install the Maxi-Fuse as described in this chapter.
7. Install the right frame side cover and saddlebag and as described in Chapter Seventeen.

EFI System Relay Replacement (2008-2009 Models)

1. Remove the right saddlebag and frame side cover as described in Chapter Seventeen.
2. Remove the Maxi-Fuse as described in this chapter.
3. Push up on the tongue at bottom of fuse block cover and release it from the electrical caddy, and then rotate it up and disengage the hinge.
4. Locate the relay, and install a new one with the *same* part number.
5. Install the Maxi-Fuse as described in this chapter.
6. Install the right frame side cover and saddlebag as described in Chapter Seventeen.

Starter and Ignition Switch Relay Replacement (2006 FLHT, FLHX and FLTR Models)

FLHT and FLHX models

1. Remove the seat as described in Chapter Seventeen.
2. Remove the Maxi-Fuse as described in this chapter.
3. Place a finger on the rubber molding and secure it in place.

203 TERMINAL CONNECTORS (2006-2007 FLHT, FLHX AND FLHTCUSE MODELS)

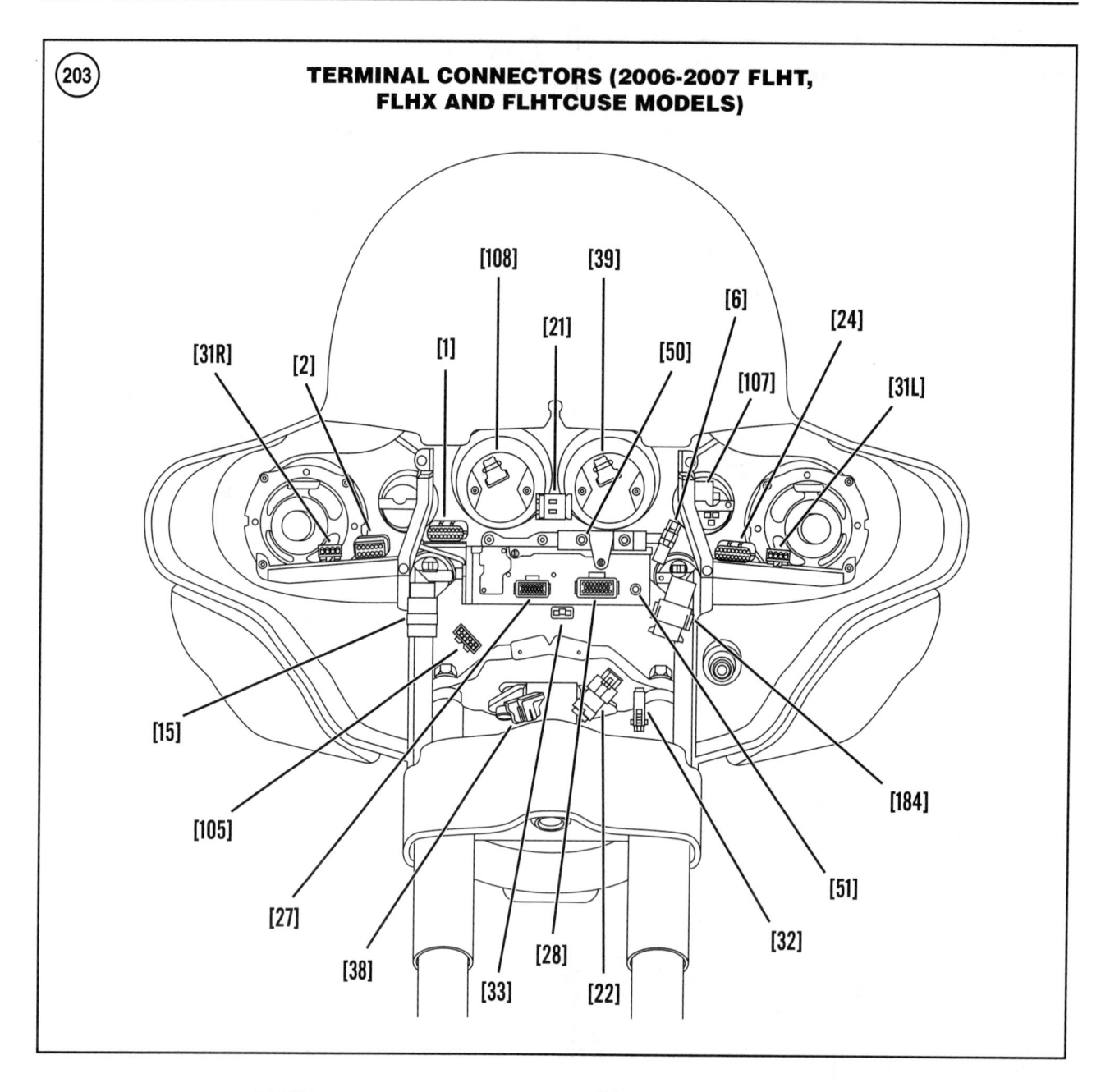

NOTE
Since the position of the relays may be reversed, check for a identification tag for possible identification. Also, the starter relay is unique with a heavy gauge green wire.

4A. Use needlenose pliers and pull on the tab of the starter relay (A, **Figure 202**). Pull the relay part way up, disconnect the 5-pin connector from the starter relay, and remove the relay.
4B. Use needlenose pliers and pull on the tab of the ignition switch relay (B, **Figure 202**). Pull the relay part way up, disconnect the 4-pin connector from the ignition switch relay, and remove the relay.
5. Install a new relay with the same part number.
6. Install the Maxi-Fuse as described in this chapter.
7. Install the seat as described in Chapter Seventeen.

FLTR models

Refer to **Figure 195**.
1. Remove the left frame side cover and saddlebag as described in Chapter Seventeen.
2. Remove the Maxi-Fuse as described in this chapter.
3. Depress both latches (A, **Figure 196**) on the Maxi-Fuse holder, slide the holder (B) toward the rear and disengage the tongue from groove on the fuse holder.
4. Pull the fuse block (**Figure 197**) straight out and release it from the tabs on the frame mounting bracket.

NOTE
*Relay description and location is printed on the fuse block cover (**Figure 198**, typical).*

5. Locate the defective relay, and install a new one with the same part number.

ELECTRICAL SYSTEM 521

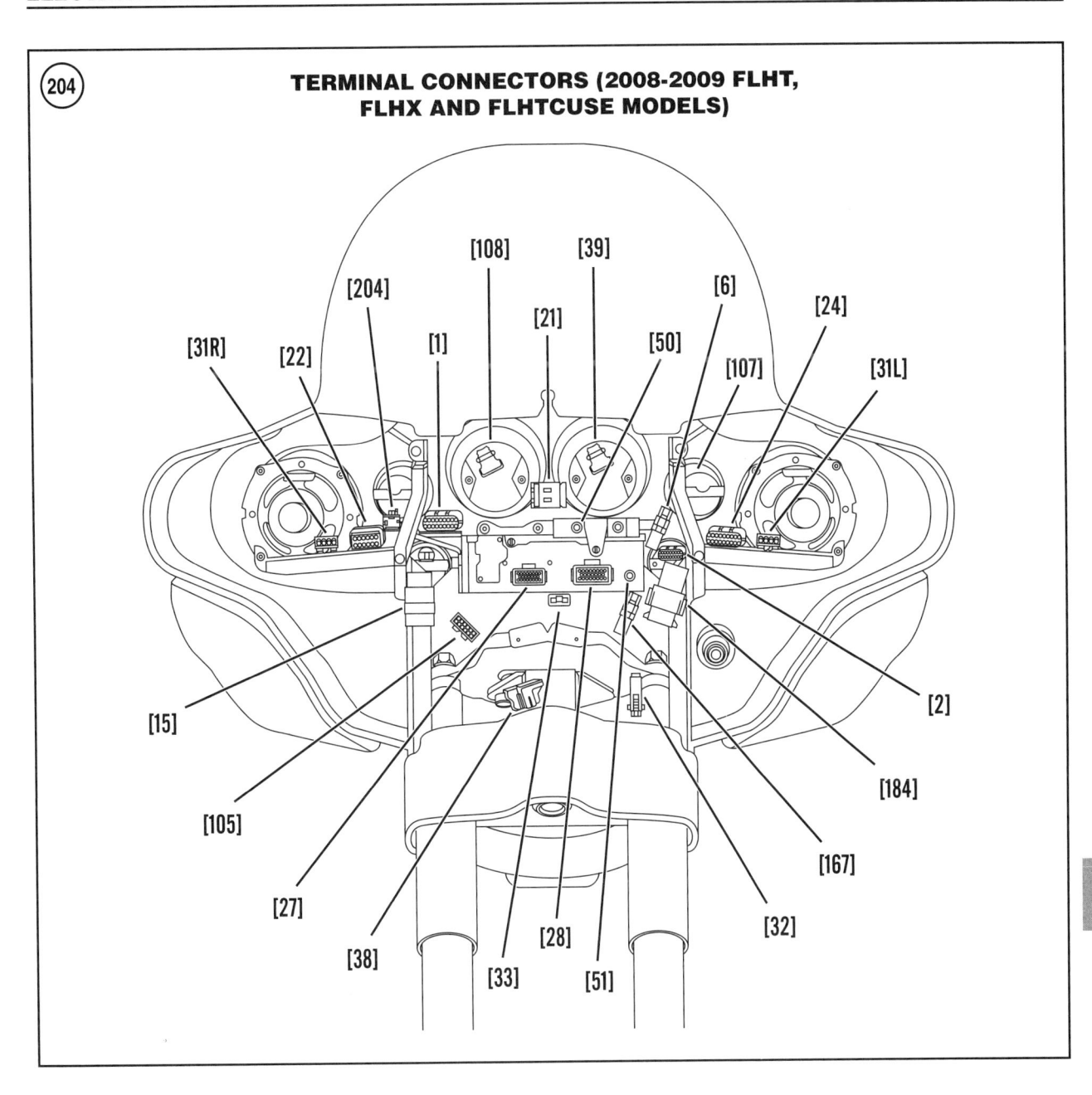

(204) **TERMINAL CONNECTORS (2008-2009 FLHT, FLHX AND FLHTCUSE MODELS)**

6. Install the Maxi-Fuse as described in this chapter.
7. Install the left frame side cover and saddlebag as described in Chapter Seventeen.

ELECTRICAL CONNECTOR LOCATION AND IDENTIFICATION

Refer to **Figures 203-208**.

The majority of the electrical connectors are located either within the headlight case and/or within the front inner fairing assembly. These illustrations will assist in locating most of the specific connectors and parts referred to in the text. The electrical connector terminal number for a specific part can be determined from the wiring diagrams located on the CD inserted into the back cover of the manual.

The manufacturer provides limited information on electrical connector locations for the Screamin' Eagle models.

Some of the connector terminal locations are similar to those on non-Screamin' Eagle models and may be found within the standard model illustrations.

ELECTRICAL CONNECTOR SERVICE

Different types of electrical connectors are used throughout the electrical system.

The following procedures describe the disassembly of the connectors so individual wires can be replaced.

NOTE
On models with an optional security system, disarm the system before disconnecting the battery cable or pulling the Maxi-Fuse so the siren will not sound.

205 **TERMINAL CONNECTORS (2006-2007 FLHR AND 2007 FLHRSE MODELS)**

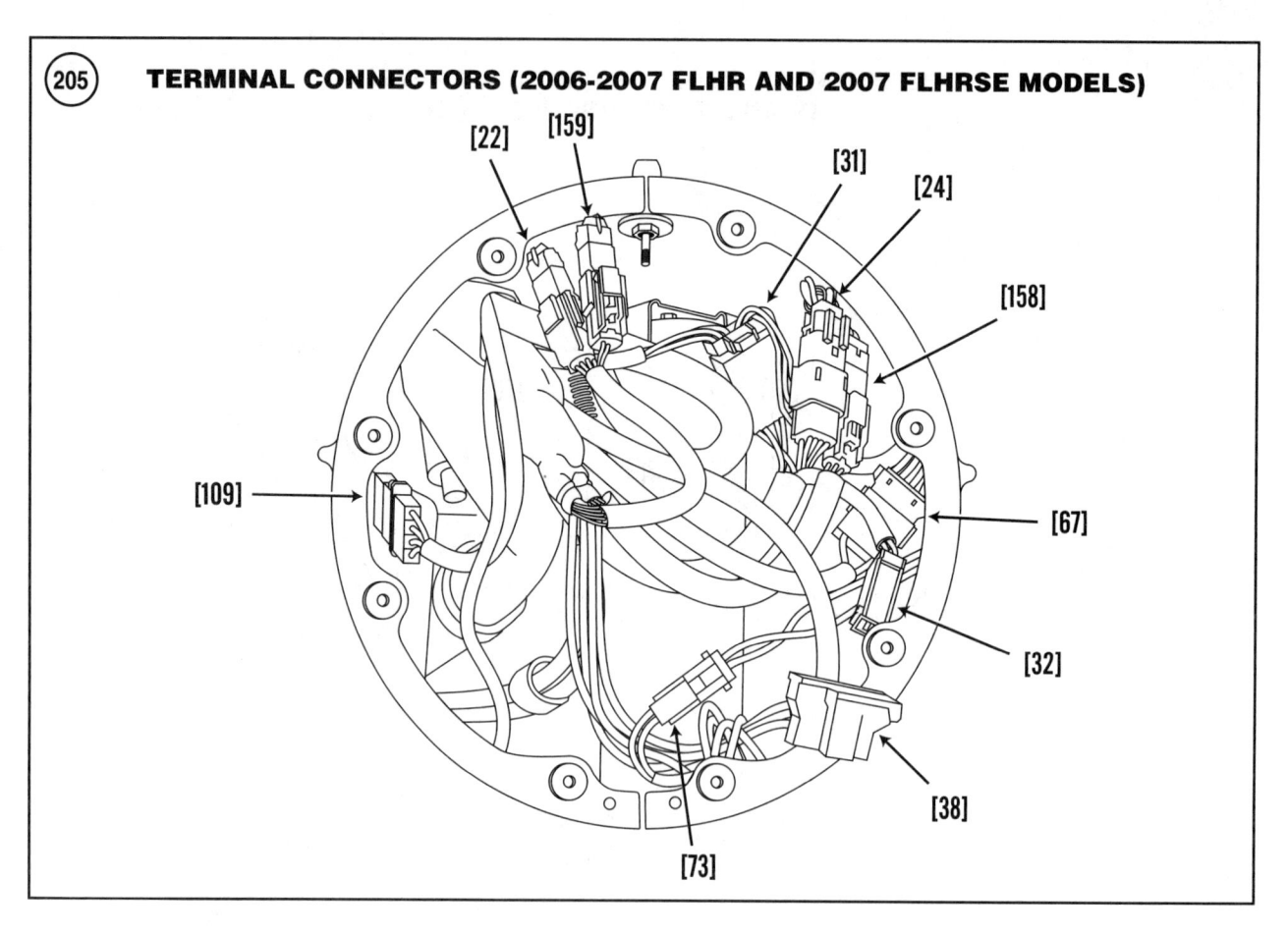

[22] [159] [31] [24] [158] [109] [67] [32] [73] [38]

206 **TERMINAL CONNECTORS (2008 FLHRSE AND 2008-2009 FLHR MODELS)**

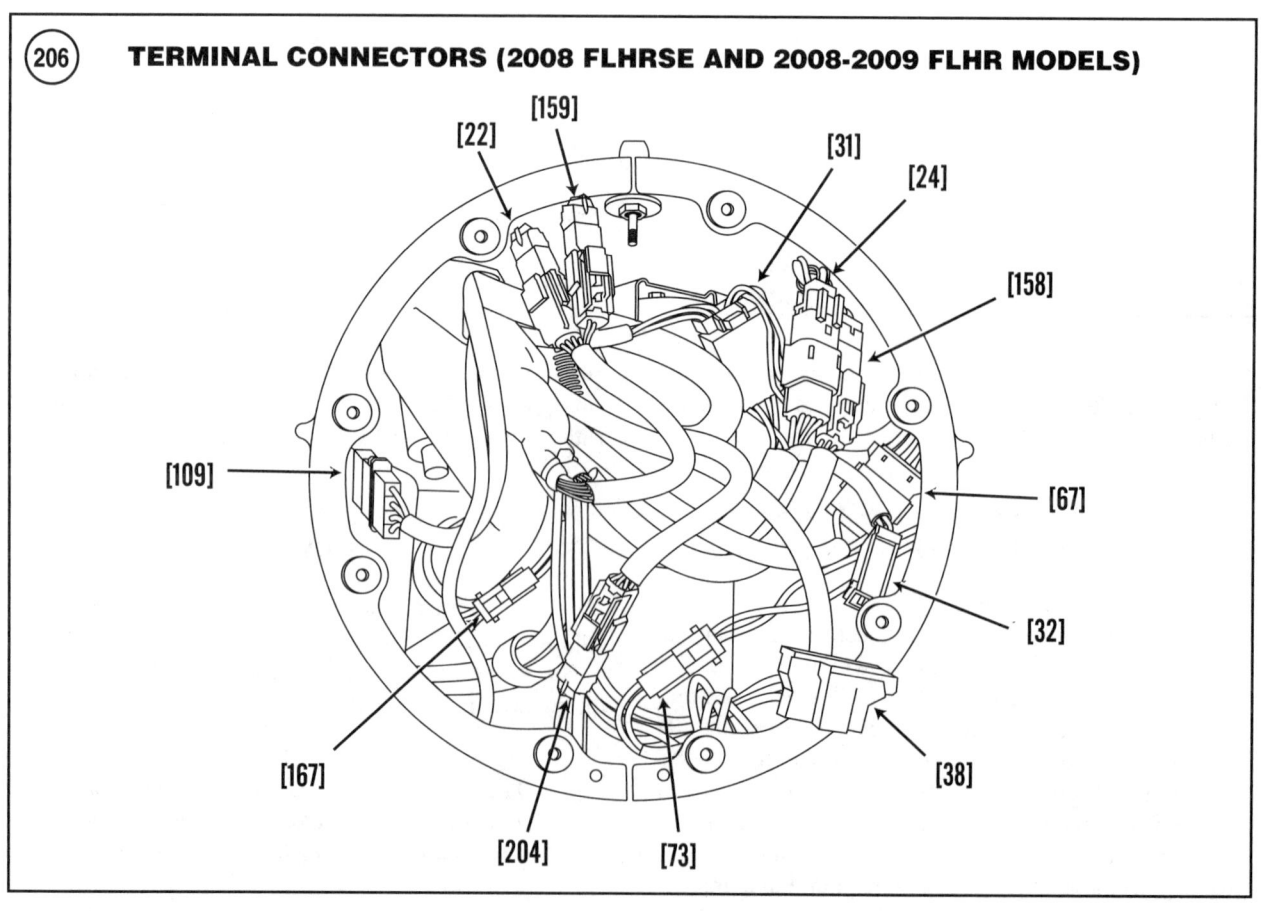

[22] [159] [31] [24] [158] [109] [67] [32] [167] [204] [73] [38]

ELECTRICAL SYSTEM

207

TERMINAL CONNECTORS (FLTR MODELS)

- [21]
- [39]
- [105A/B]
- [105C/D]
- [10B]
- [107]

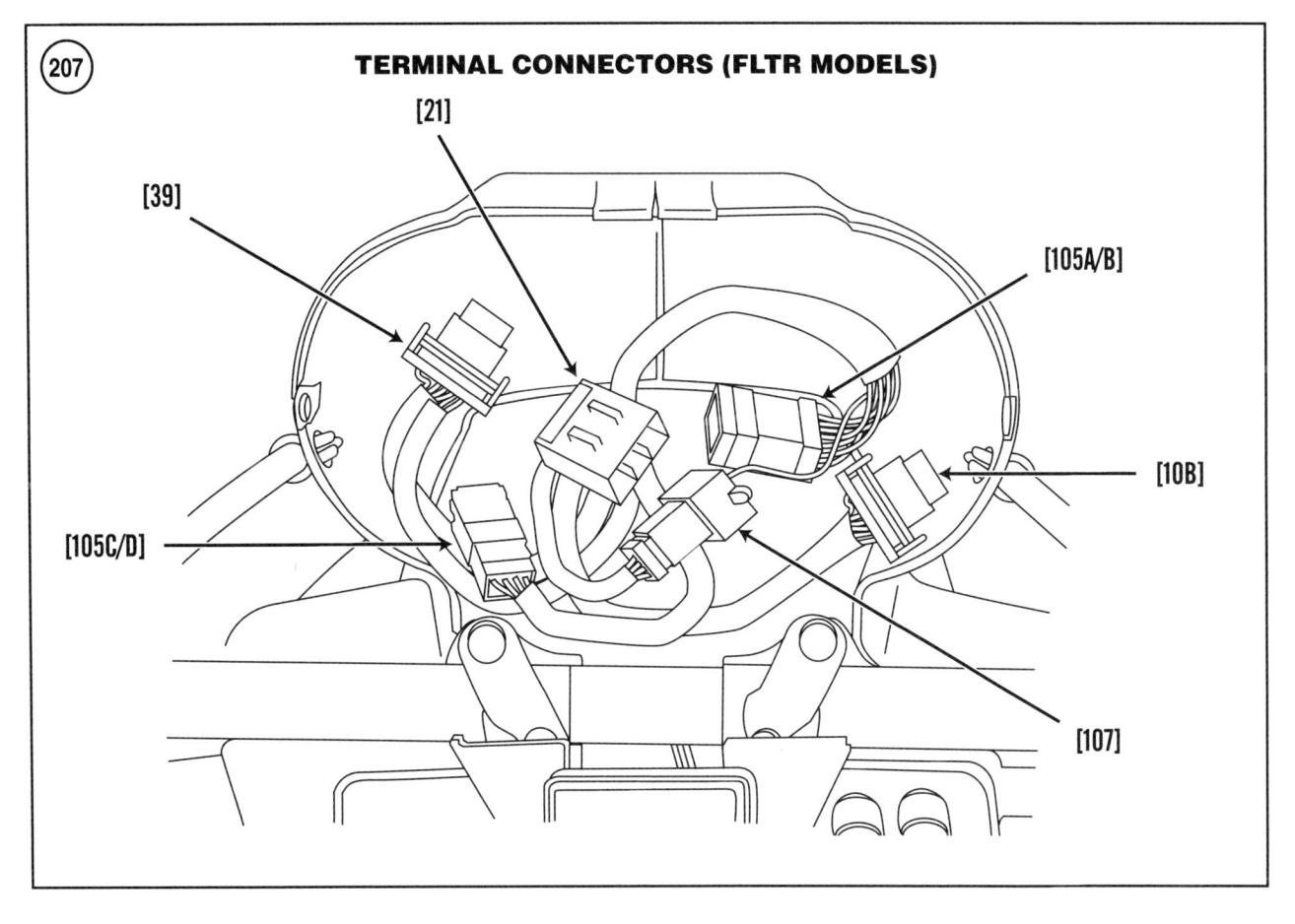

208

TERMINAL CONNECTORS (FLTR MODELS)

- [1]
- [27]
- [51]
- [24]
- [156]
- [22]
- [2]
- [31R]
- [15]
- [38]
- [31L]
- Radio ground

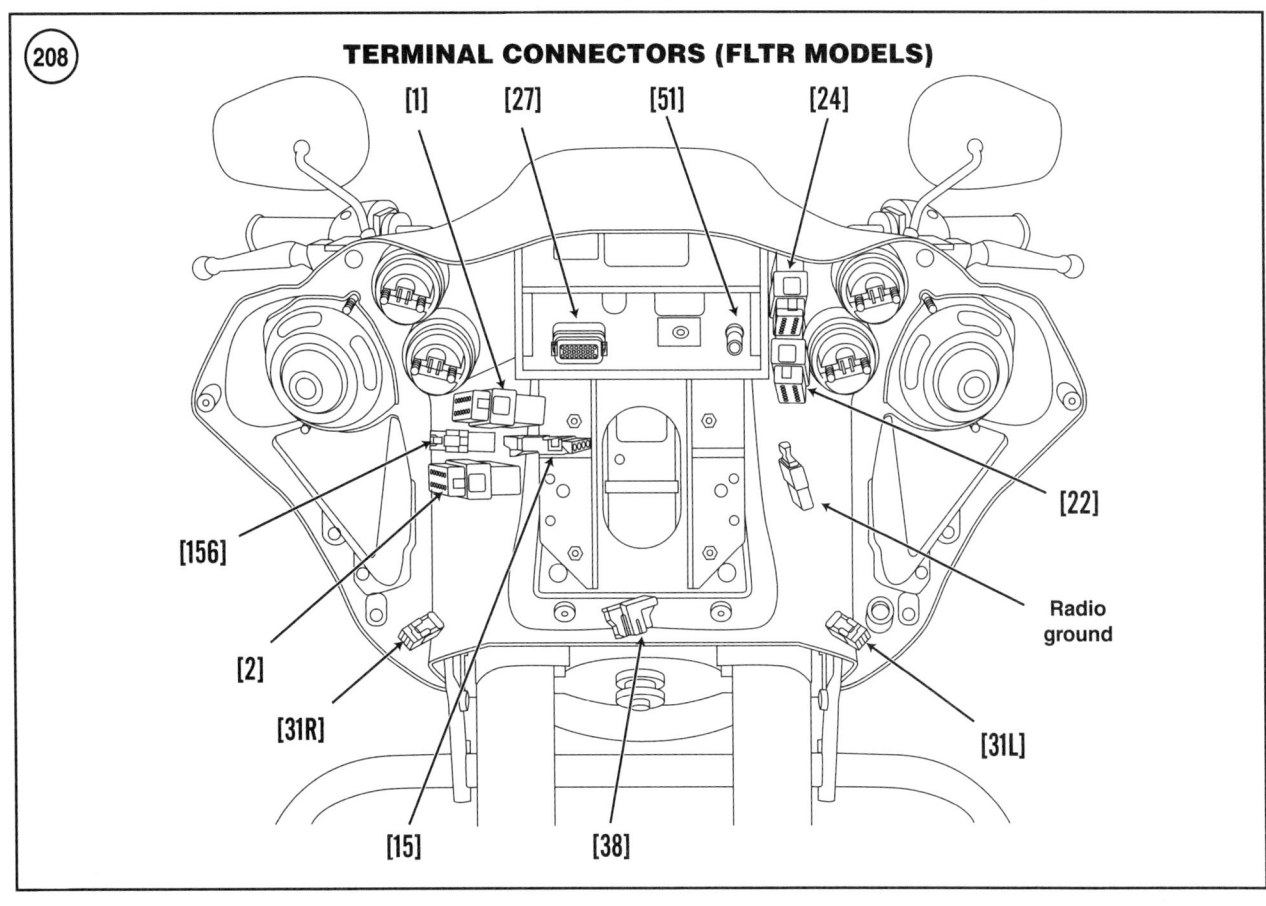

DEUTSCH CONNECTORS (2-PIN, 3-PIN AND 4-PIN)

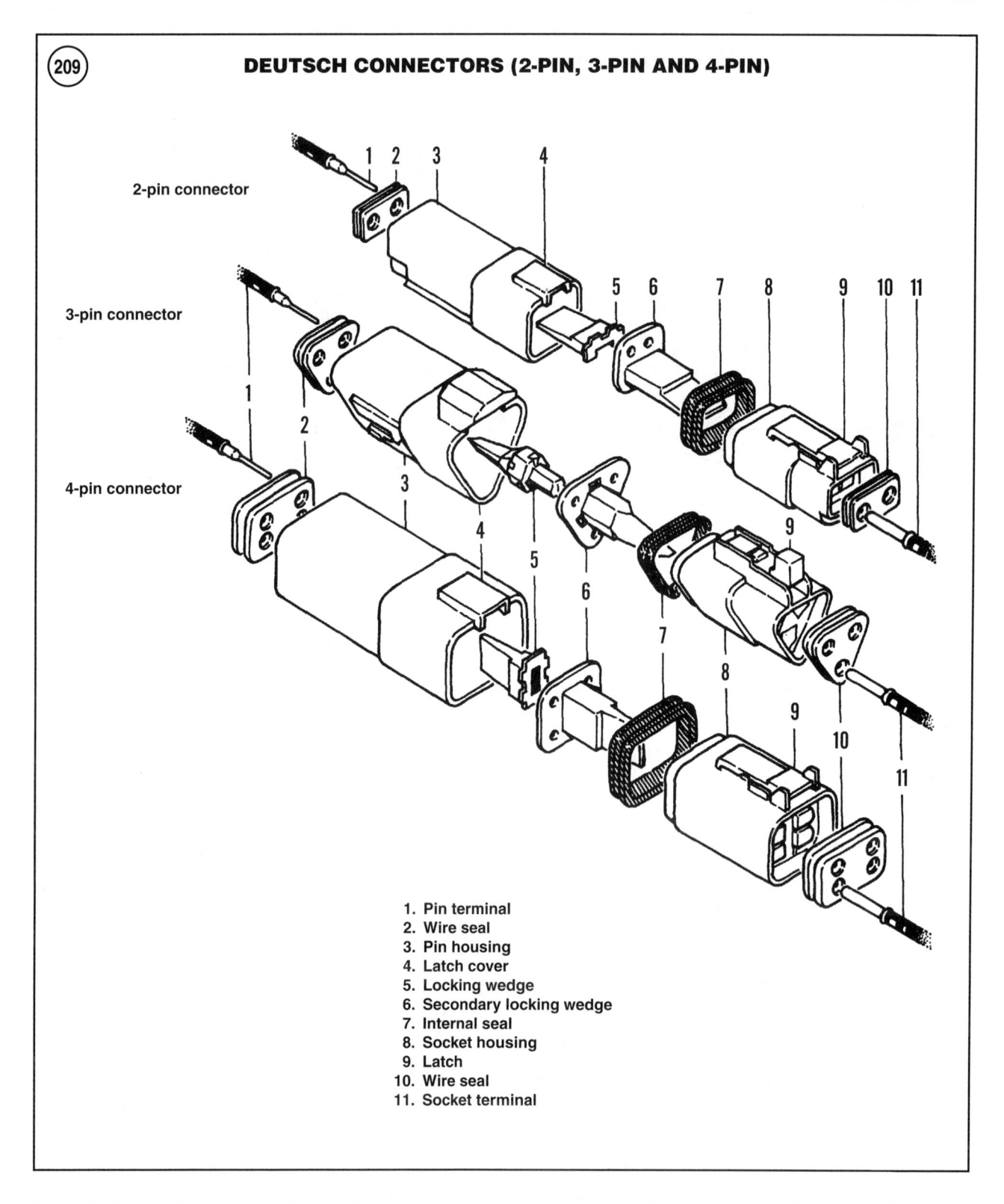

1. Pin terminal
2. Wire seal
3. Pin housing
4. Latch cover
5. Locking wedge
6. Secondary locking wedge
7. Internal seal
8. Socket housing
9. Latch
10. Wire seal
11. Socket terminal

Deutsch Electrical Connectors Socket Terminal Removal/Installation

Refer to **Figure 209** and **Figure 210**.

This procedure shows how to remove and install the socket terminals. This procedure is shown on a 12-pin Deutsch connector, which also applies to 2-, 3-, 4- and 6-pin Deutsch connectors.

1. Remove the Maxi-Fuse as described in this chapter.
2. Disconnect the connector housing.
3. Remove the secondary locking wedge as follows:
    a. Locate the secondary locking wedge in **Figure 209** or **Figure 210**.
    b. Insert a wide-bladed screwdriver between the socket housing and the secondary locking wedge. Turn the screwdriver 90° to force the wedge up (**Figure 211**).

ELECTRICAL SYSTEM

DEUTSCH CONNECTOR (12-PIN)

1. Pin terminal
2. Wire seal
3. Pin housing
4. Latch cover
5. Alignment grooves
6. Locking wedge
7. Secondary locking wedge
8. Internal seal
9. Alignment tabs
10. External latch
11. Socket housing
12. Wire seal
13. Seal pin
14. Socket terminal

Secondary locking wedge

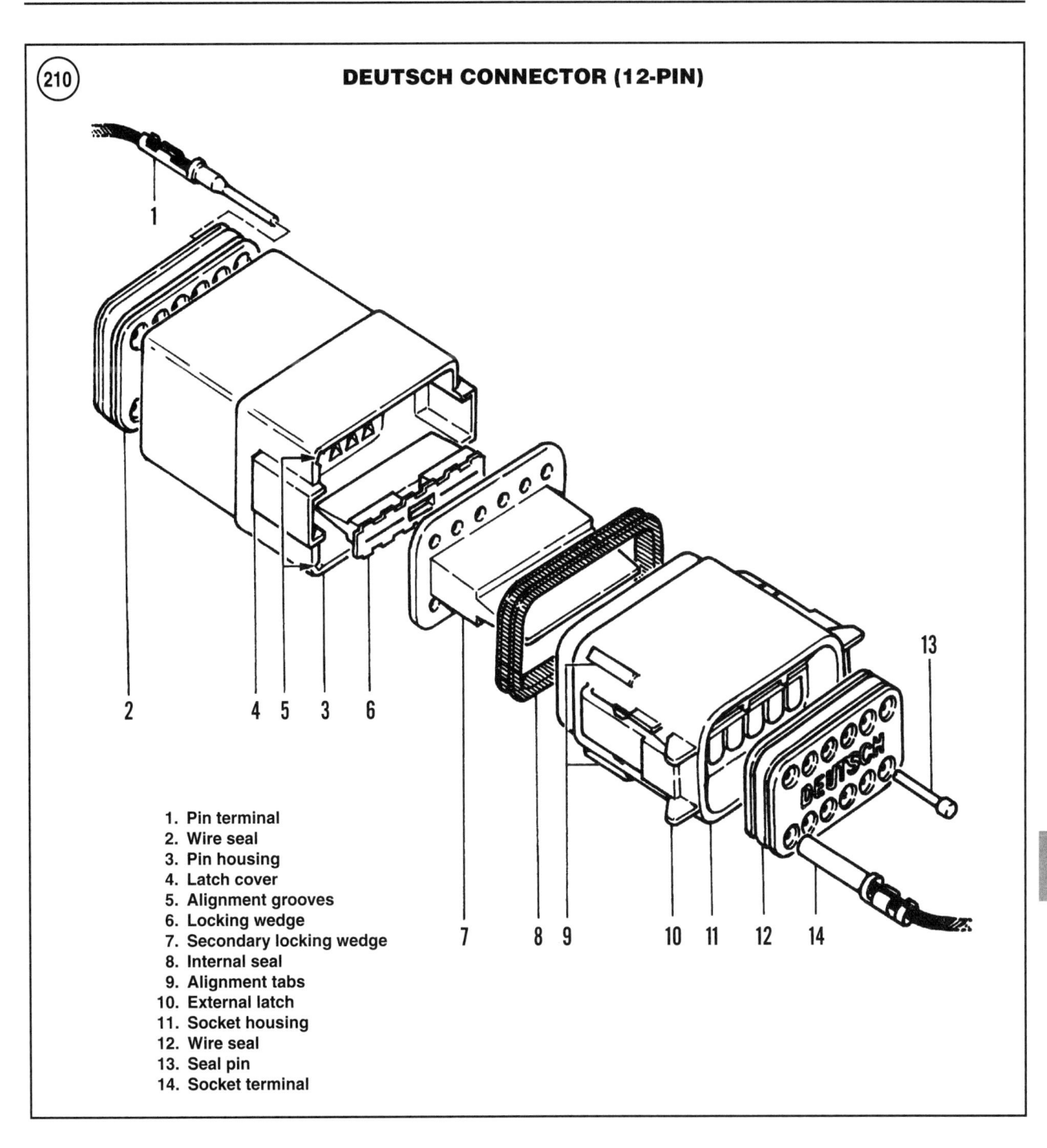

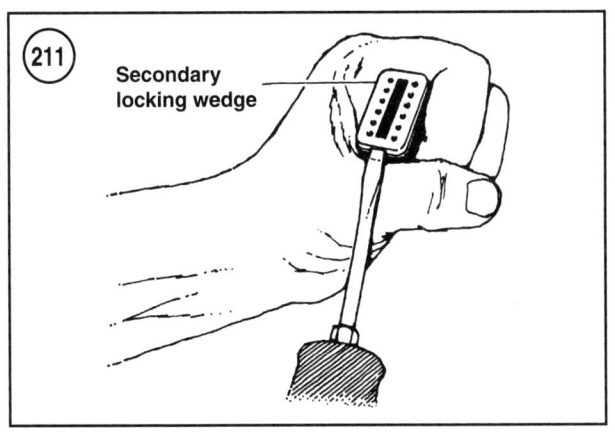

c. Remove the locking wedge.

4. Lightly press the terminal latches inside the socket housing and remove the socket terminal through the holes in the wire seal.

5. Repeat the process for each remaining socket terminal.

6. If necessary, remove the wire seal.

7. Install the wire seal into the socket housing, if it was removed.

8. Hold onto the socket housing and insert each socket terminal through the hole in the wire seal so it enters the correct chamber. Continue until the socket terminal locks into place. Then, lightly tug on the wire to make sure it is locked into place.

9. Set the internal seal onto the socket housing if it was removed.

NOTE
With the exception of the 3-pin Deutsch connector, all of the secondary locking wedges are symmetrical. When assembling the 3-pin connector, install the connector so the arrow on the secondary locking wedge points toward the external latch as shown in **Figure 212**.

NOTE
If the secondary locking wedge does not slide into position easily, one or more of the socket terminals are not installed correctly. Correct the problem at this time.

10. Install the secondary locking wedge into the socket housing as shown in **Figure 209** or **Figure 210**. Press the secondary locking wedge down until it locks into place.
11. Install the Maxi-Fuse as described in this chapter.

Deutsch Electrical Connectors Pin Terminal Removal/Installation

2, 3, 4, 6 and 12- pin

Refer to **Figure 209** or **Figure 210**.

This procedure shows how to remove and install the pin terminals. This procedure is shown on a 12-pin Deutsch connector, which also applies to all Deutsch connectors (2-, 3-, 4- and 6-pin).
1. Remove the Maxi-Fuse as described in this chapter.
2. Disconnect the connector housing.
3. Use needlenose pliers to remove the locking wedge.
4. Lightly press the terminal latches inside the pin housing, and remove the pin terminal(s) through the holes in the wire seal.
5. Repeat the process for each remaining pin terminal.
6. If necessary, remove the wire seal.
7. Install the wire seal into the pin housing, if it was removed.
8. Hold onto the pin housing and insert the pin terminals through the holes in the wire seal so they enter the correct chamber. Continue until the pin terminal locks into place. Lightly tug on the wire to make sure it is locked into place.
9. Set the internal seal onto the socket housing if it was removed.

NOTE
With the exception of the 3-pin Deutsch connector, all of the locking wedges are symmetrical. When assembling the three-pin connector, install the connector so the arrow on the locking wedge is pointing toward the external latch as shown in **Figure 212**.

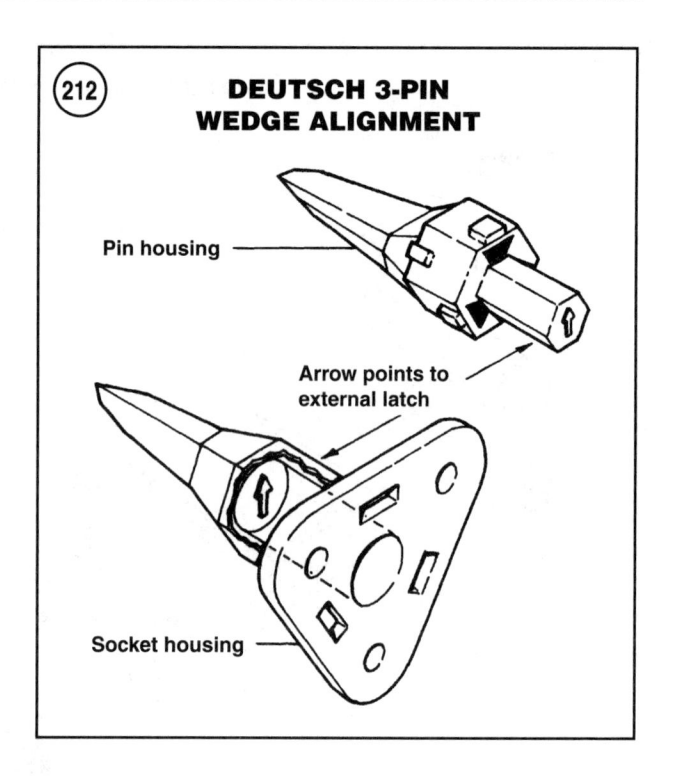

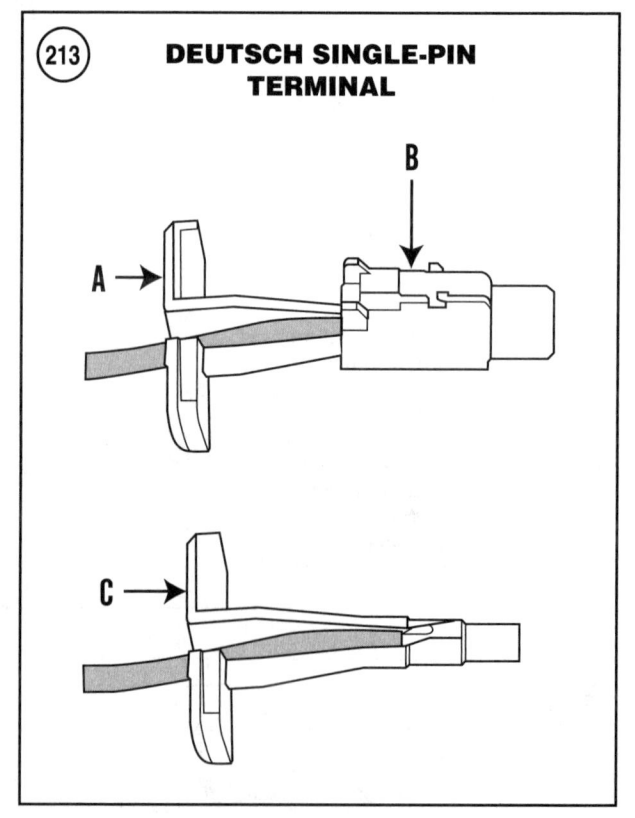

212 DEUTSCH 3-PIN WEDGE ALIGNMENT

Pin housing
Arrow points to external latch
Socket housing

213 DEUTSCH SINGLE-PIN TERMINAL

NOTE
If the locking wedge does not slide into position easily, one or more of the pin terminals are not installed correctly. Correct the problem at this time.

10. Install the locking wedge into the pin housing as shown in **Figure 209** or **Figure 210**. Press the locking wedge

ELECTRICAL SYSTEM

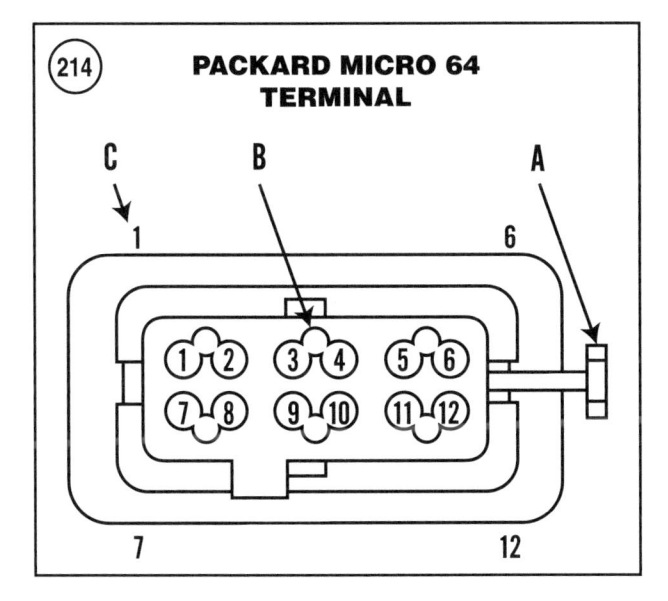

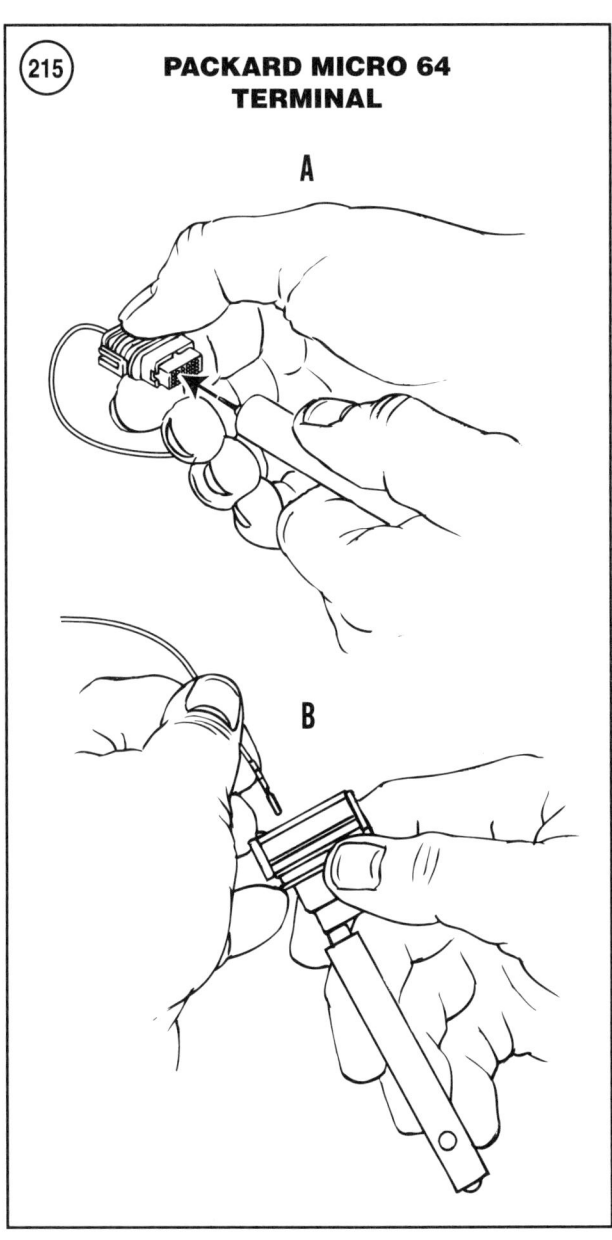

214 PACKARD MICRO 64 TERMINAL

215 PACKARD MICRO 64 TERMINAL

down until it locks into place. When properly installed, the wedge fits into the pin housing center groove.

11. Install the Maxi-Fuse as described in this chapter.

Single pin connector removal/installation

1. Remove the Maxi-Fuse as described in this chapter.
2. Disconnect the connector housing.
3. Pull the wire seal from back of the housing, and slide it down voltage regulator cable.
4. Insert the terminal pick tool (Deutsch part No. 114008) into the cable until the tapered end of the tool (A, **Figure 213**) is in the wire end of the housing (B).
5. Push pick tool into wire end of housing until it bottoms.
6. Gently tug on housing, and pull wire (C, **Figure 213**) from terminal.
7. Remove tool from electrical cable.
8. Insert the wire into the terminal until it *clicks* and is locked into place. Slightly pull on the wire to ensure it is locked into place.
9. Install the Maxi-Fuse as described in this chapter.

Packard Electrical Connectors

Micro 64 removal/installation

1. Remove the Maxi-Fuse as described in this chapter.
2. Bend back the external latches slightly and separate the connector.
3. Locate the head of the secondary lock (A, **Figure 214**).
4. Insert the tip of a narrow, flat-bladeded screwdriver between the center ear of the lock and the housing. Pry out the lock and remove it.

NOTE
Connector terminals are numbered 1-6 in one row and 7-12 in the remaining row. The numbers 1, 6, 7 and 12 are stamped on the connector to identify the row numbers.

5. Locate the pin hole (B, **Figure 214**) between terminals on the mating end of the connector. Refer to C, **Figure 214** for terminal number locations.
6. Push the adjacent terminal all the way into the connector housing. Insert the Packard Terminal Remover (H-D part No. HD-45928) into the hole (A, **Figure 215**). Press on it until it bottoms.
7. With the tool in place, gently pull on the wires (B, **Figure 215**) and pull one or both terminals from wire end of connector. Remove the tool.
8. To install the terminal, insert wire and terminal into the correct location on the wire end of the connector. Push on the terminal until it bottoms. Slightly pull on the wire and wiggle it a little to ensure it is locked into place.
9. The special tool releases two terminals at the same time. Repeat the removal and installation process for the adjacent terminal even if it was not removed.

216 PACKARD 100W CONNECTOR

217

218 PACKARD METRI-PACK TERMINALS/PULL TO SEAT

IAT sensor connector
2-pin

ET sensor connector
2-pin

TP sensor connector
3-pin

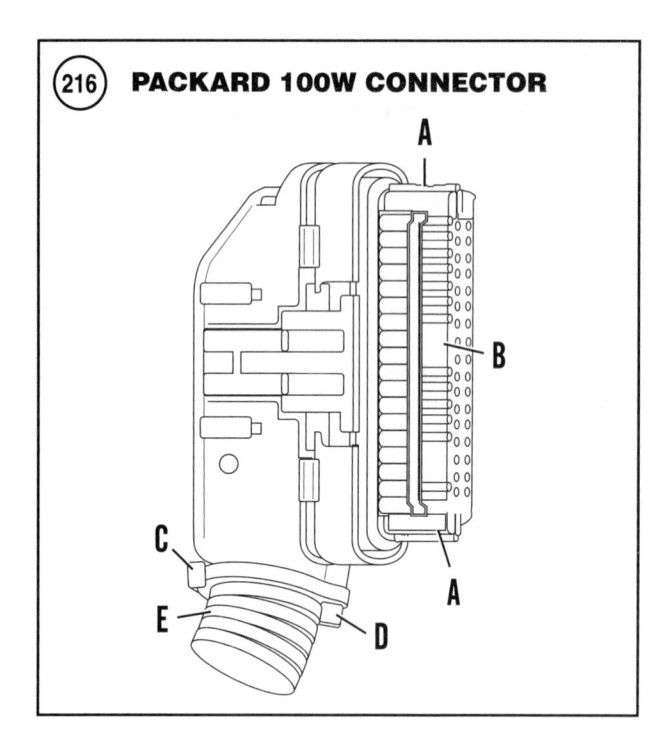

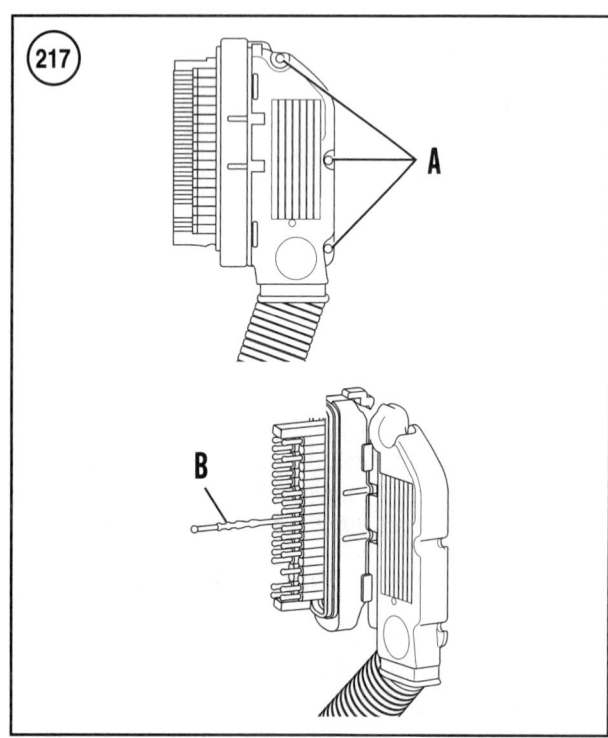

IAC valve connector
4-pin

10. Position the head of the secondary lock (A, **Figure 214**) facing the mating end of the connector. Press in on the secondary lock until it is flush with the connector housing.
11. Push the connector halves together until the latches lock together.
12. Install the Maxi-Fuse as described in this chapter.

100W ECM connector removal/installation

1. Remove the Maxi-Duse as described in this chapter.

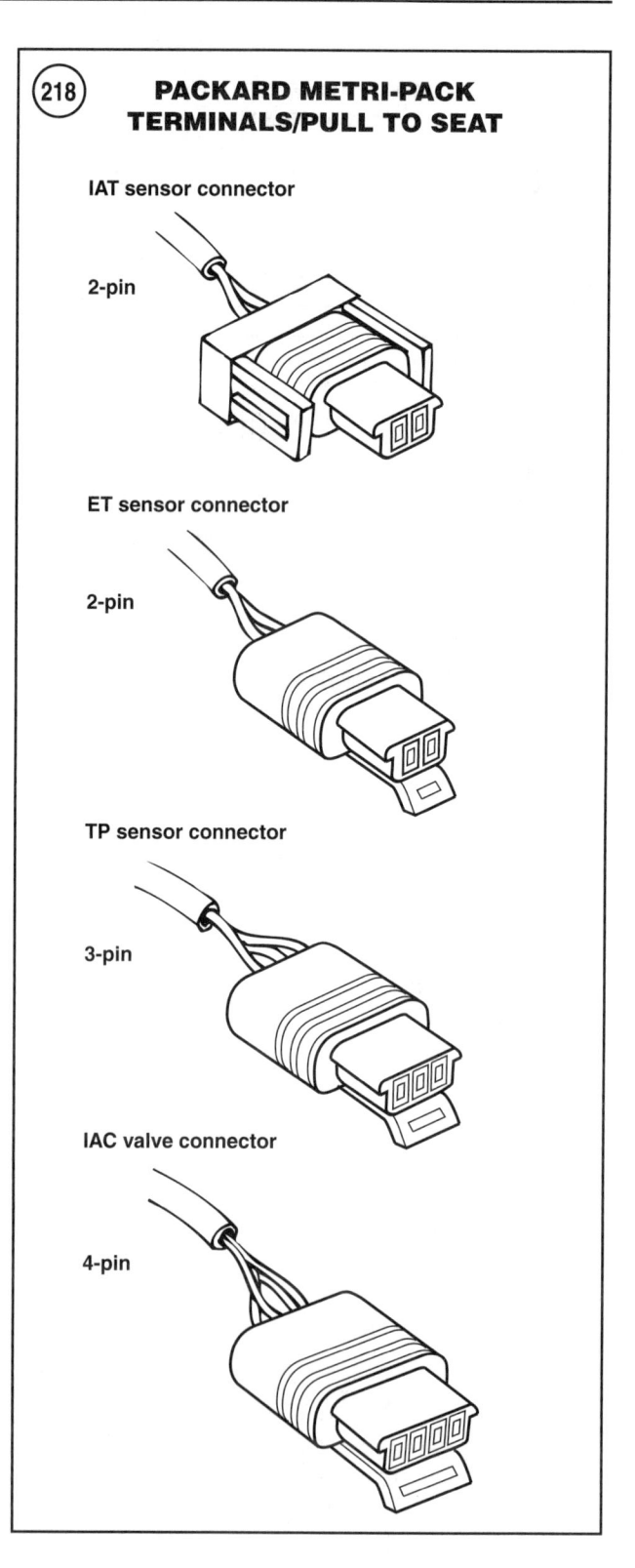

2. Disconnect the connector housing from the ECM (this chapter).
3. Press the latch (A, **Figure 216**) on each end of the connector, and remove the secondary lock (B).
4. Clip the cable strap (C, **Figure 216**), and release the strain relief collar (D) from the conduit (E).
5. Insert a thin blade, like an X-Acto knife, into the housing seam, and pry the housing halves apart at A, **Figure 27**

ELECTRICAL SYSTEM

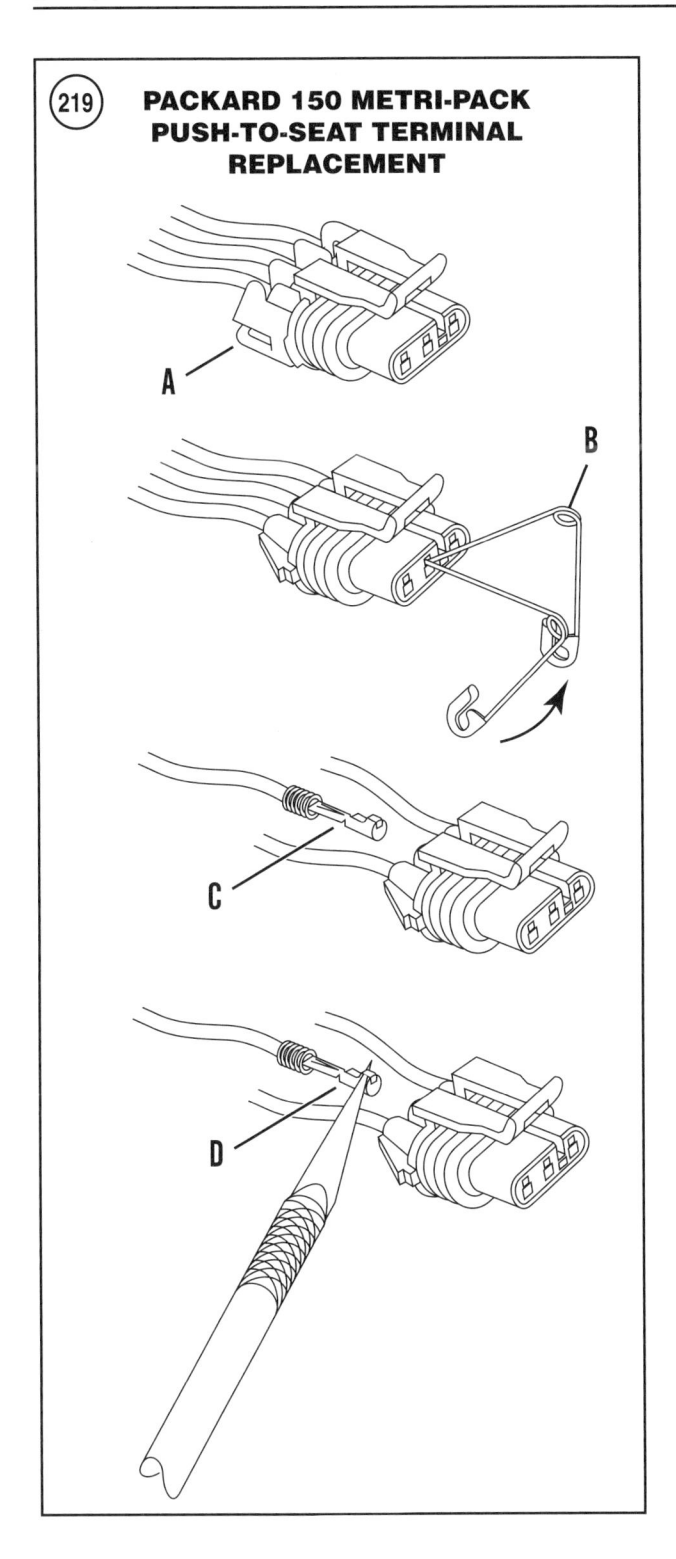

219 PACKARD 150 METRI-PACK PUSH-TO-SEAT TERMINAL REPLACEMENT

220 PACKARD 150 METRI-PACK PULL-TO-SEAT TERMINAL REPLACEMENT

until the pins release. Pivot the housing halves away from one another.

6. Push the relevant wire, and remove the socket (B, **Figure 217**) from the housing.

7. Insert the new wire into the relevant chamber of the housing, and carefully pull the wire until the socket is seated in the housing chamber.

8. Carefully close the housing halves together so no wires are pinched. Press the halves together until the pins lock (A, **Figure 216**).

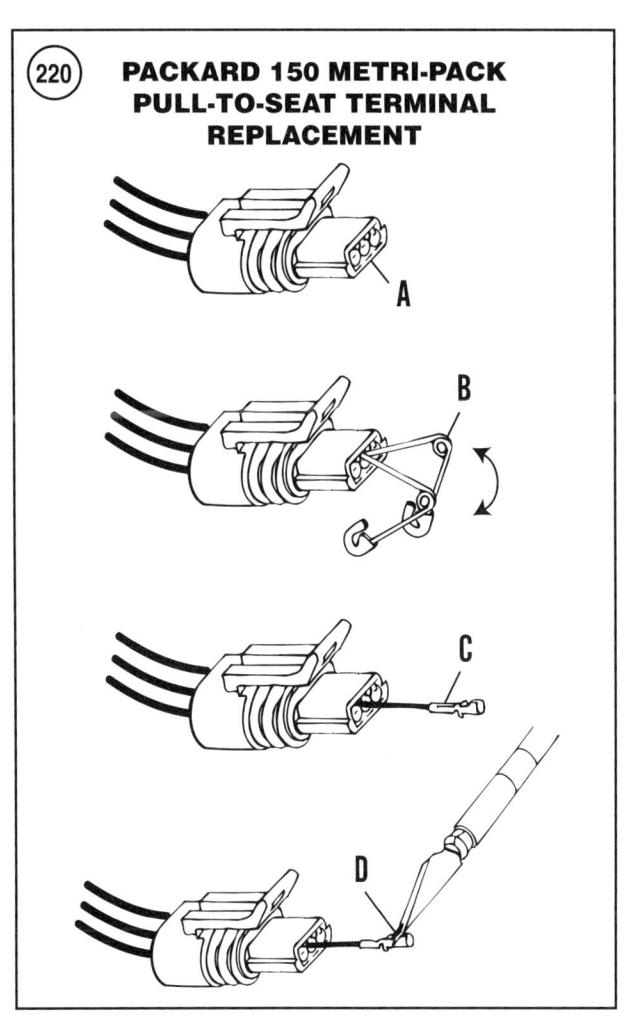

9. Install a new cable strap (C, **Figure 216**) so the strap seats in the groove of the strain relief collar (D). Make sure the collar secures the conduit (E, **Figure 216**) in place.

10. Install the secondary lock (B, **Figure 216**) over the terminals, and lock it in place.

11. Install the Maxi-Fuse as described in this chapter.

150 Metri-pack connector removal/installation

This procedure shows how to remove and install the electrical terminals from the Packard 150 Metri-pack connectors shown in **Figure 218**.

1. Remove the Maxi-Fuse as described in this chapter.

2. Bend back the external latch(es) slightly and separate the connector.

3. On push-to-seat connectors, remove the wire lock (A, **Figure 219**) from the connector housing.

4. Look into the mating end of the connector, on the external latch side, and locate the locking tang (A, **Figure 220**) in the middle chamber. On locking ear connectors, the tang is on the side opposite the ear.

5A. On pull-to-seat connectors, insert the point of a one-inch safety pin (B, **Figure 220**) about 1/8 in. into the middle chamber. Pivot the end of the safety pin up toward the terminal body until a click is heard.

5B. On push-to-seat connectors, insert the pin (B, **Figure 219**) into the small opening in the housing until a click is heard.

6. Repeat this process several times. The click is the tang returning to the locked position as it slips from the point of the safety pin. Continue to pick at the tang until the clicking stops and the safety pin seems to slide in at a slightly greater depth indicating the tang has been depressed. Remove the safety pin.

7A. On pull-to-seat connectors, push the wire end of the lead and remove the terminal and wire (C, **Figure 220**) from the connector. If additional slack is necessary, pull back on the harness conduit, and remove the wire seal at the back of the connector.

7B. On push-to-seat connectors, pull the wire, and remove the terminal (C, **Figure 219**) from the housing.

8. To install the terminal and wire back into the connector, use a thin flat blade of an X-Acto knife to carefully bend the tang away from the terminal (D, **Figure 220** or D, **Figure 219**).

9. Carefully pull or push the lead and terminal into the connector until a click is heard indicating the terminal is seated correctly within the connector. Gently push or pull on the lead to ensure the terminal is correctly seated.

10. If necessary, install the wire seal and push the harness conduit back into position on the backside of the connector.

11. Push the socket halves together until the latch(es) are locked together.

12. Install the Maxi-Fuse as described in this chapter.

280 Metri-pack connector removal/installation

1. Release the lock, and pull the connector halves apart.
2. Pry the rubber seal from the end of the connector housing, and slide the seal down the wires (A, **Figure 221**).
3. At the wire end of the housing, insert a safety pin (B, **Figure 221**) between the top of the terminal and in the chamber wall. Push the safety pin into the chamber until the terminal is seen moving slightly, which indicated the tang has bee depressed.
4. Remove the safety pin. Push the wire into the housing until the terminal emerges from the chamber (C, **Figure 221**), and remove the terminal and its wire.
5. To install the terminal and wire back into the connector, use a thin flat blade of an X-Acto knife to carefully bend the tang away from the terminal (D, **Figure 221**).
6. Carefully pull the wire into the housing until a click is heard indicating the terminal is correctly seated within the chamber.
7. Seat the rubber seal (E, **Figure 221**) into the end of the housing.

480 Metri-pack connector removal/installation

1. Use a small-bladed screwdriver to press the button on the lock (1, **Figure 222**), and separate the connector halves.

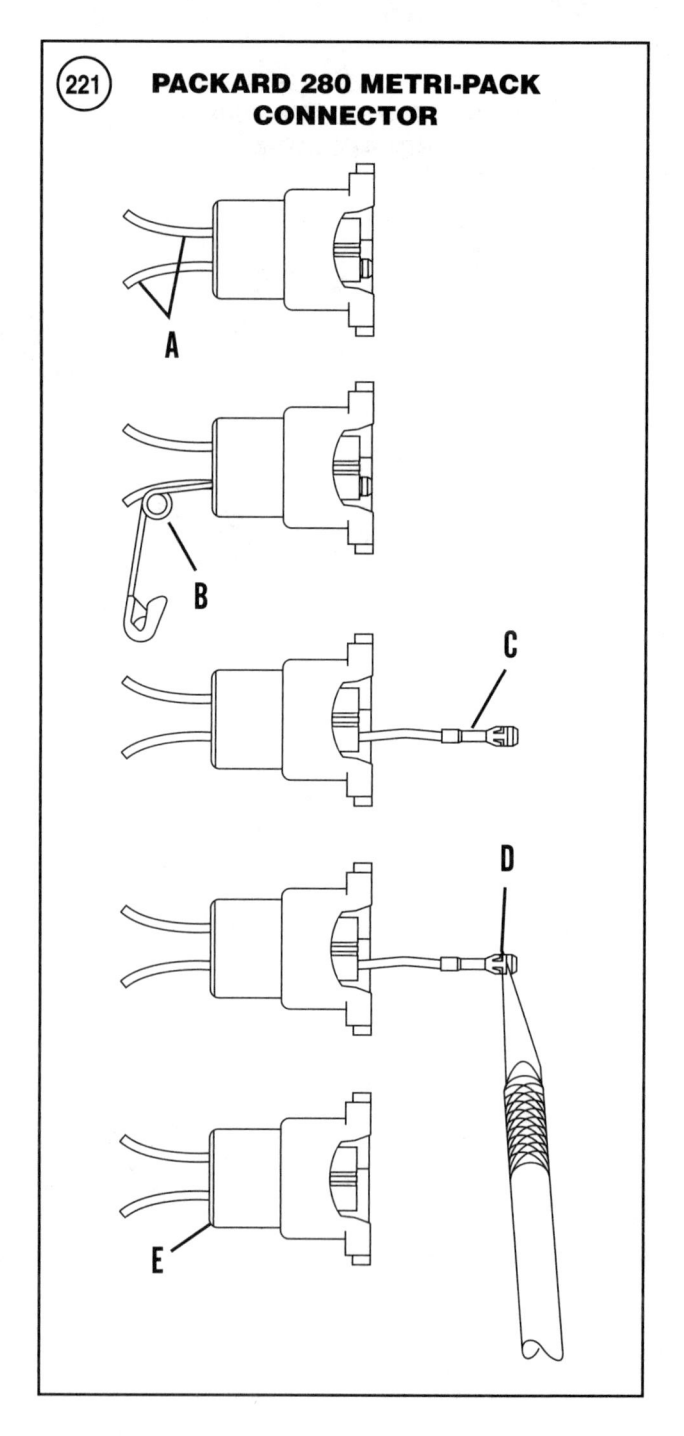

221 PACKARD 280 METRI-PACK CONNECTOR

2. Slightly pry the latch up and release one side of the secondary lock (B, **Figure 222**). Repeat on the other side of the housing, and open the secondary lock (C, **Figure 222**).
3. Examine the mating end of the housing chamber(s). Note that the tang on each terminal sits against the side of the chamber with a square-shaped opening. Insert a large pin into the chamber so the pin (D, **Figure 222**) sits between the tang and the chamber wall.
4. Press the pin toward the terminal to compress the tang.
5. Remove the pin, and pull the wire until the terminal emerges from the housing.
6. Use a thin blade, like an X-Acto knife, to bend the tang away from the terminal.

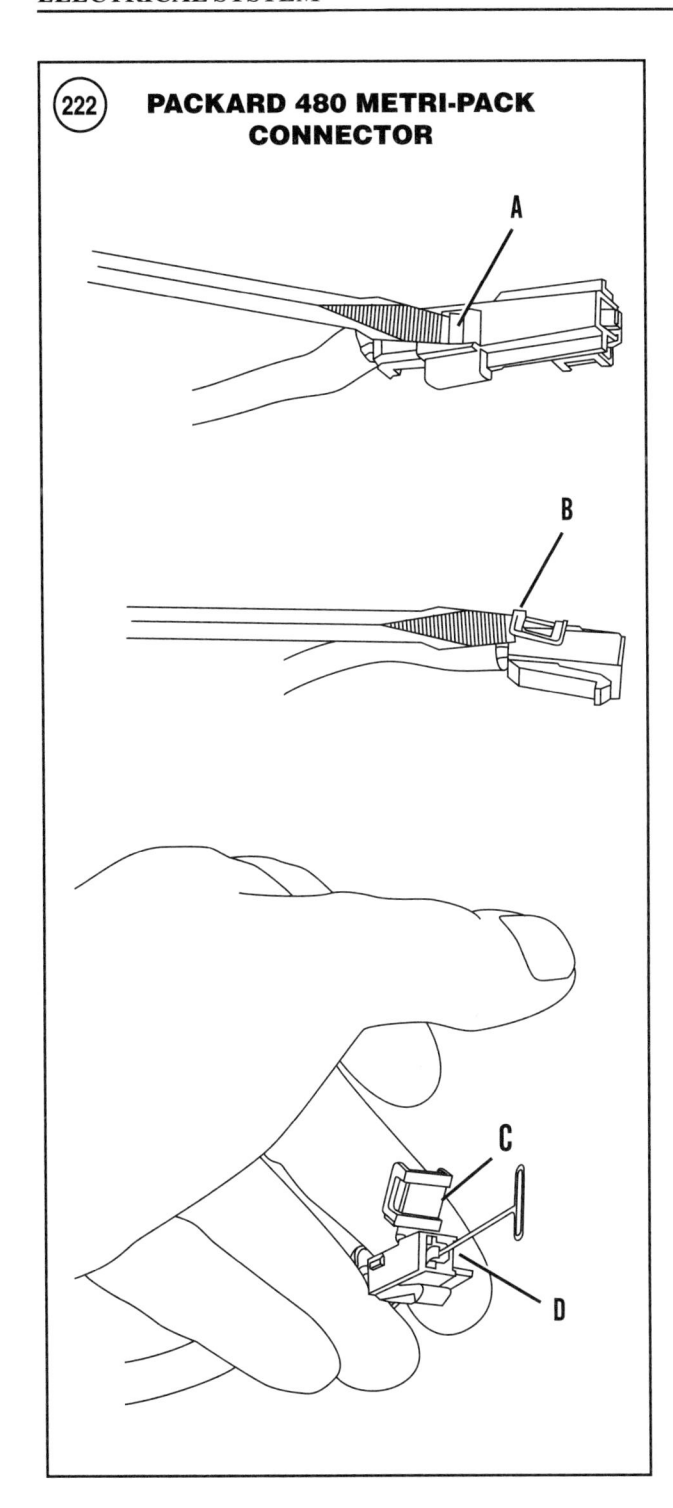

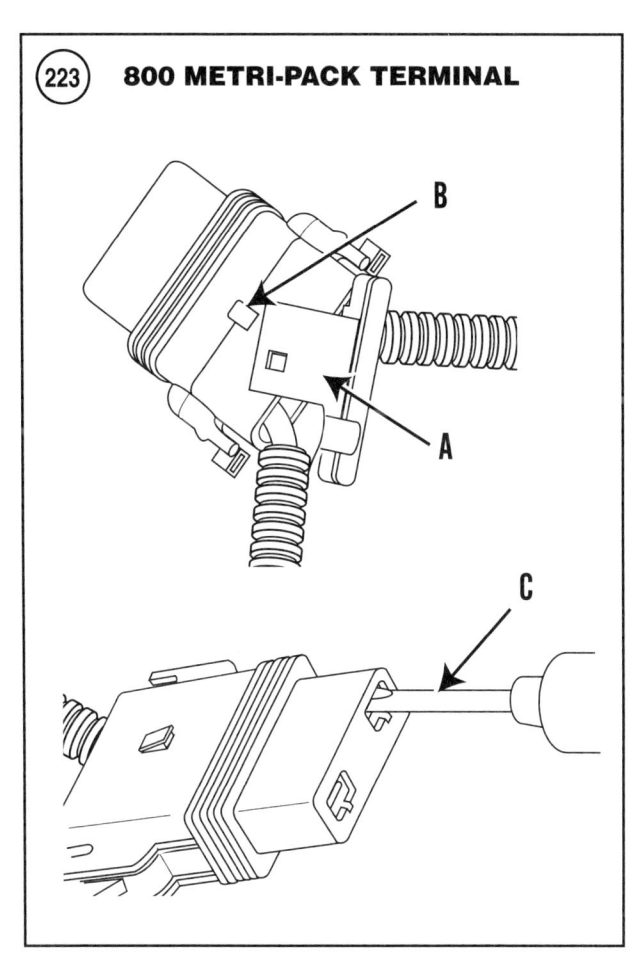

ELECTRICAL SYSTEM

222 PACKARD 480 METRI-PACK CONNECTOR

223 800 METRI-PACK TERMINAL

4. Rotate the secondary lock outward on the hinge to expose the terminals in the chambers of the housing connector. The terminal is locked in place by the rib in the chamber wall.
5. At the mating end of the connector, insert a pin or small pick (Snap-On part No. TT600-3) into the small opening on the chamber wall until it bottoms.
6. Pivot the end of the pick toward the terminal and depress the locking tang.
7. Remove the pin or pick and gently pull on the wiring and pull the terminal from the wire end of the connector. Repeat this step if the terminal is still locked in place.
8. Install the Maxi-Fuse as described in this chapter.

800 Metri-pack connectors removal/installation (2006-2007 models)

1. Remove the Maxi-Fuse as described in this chapter.
2. Gently pull the socket housing and disengage the slots on the secondary lock (A, **Figure 223**) from the tabs (B) on the socket housing. Remove the secondary lock from the cable.
3. Carefully insert the blade of a small screwdriver (C, **Figure 223**) into the opening until it stops. Pivot the screwdriver toward the terminal body and hold it in this position.

7. Insert the terminal into the chamber until it clicks into place. Make sure the tang faces the chamber side with the square-shaped opening.

630 Metri-pack connector removal/installation

1. Remove the Maxi-Fuse as described in this chapter.
2. Bend back the external latch slightly and separate the socket halves.
3. Bend back the latch slightly and free one side of the secondary lock. Repeat for the latch on the remaining side.

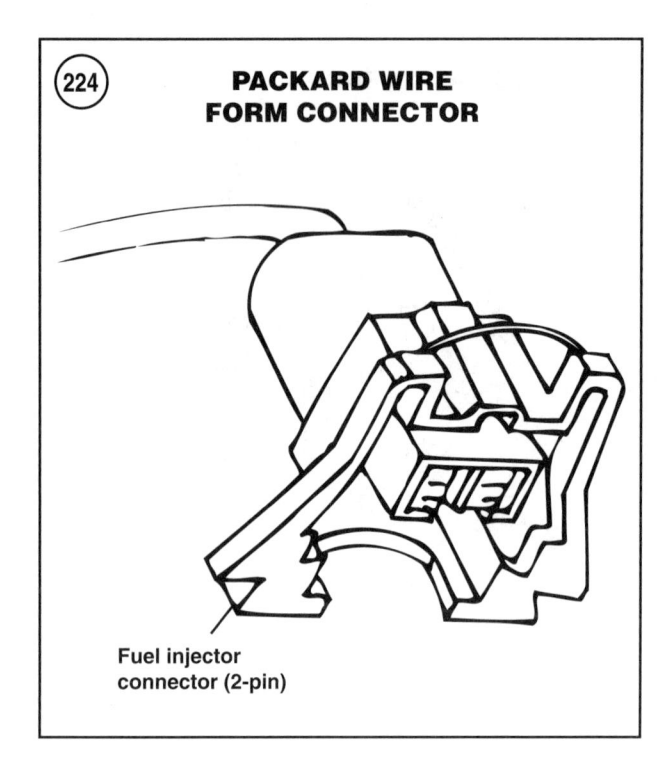

224 PACKARD WIRE FORM CONNECTOR

Fuel injector connector (2-pin)

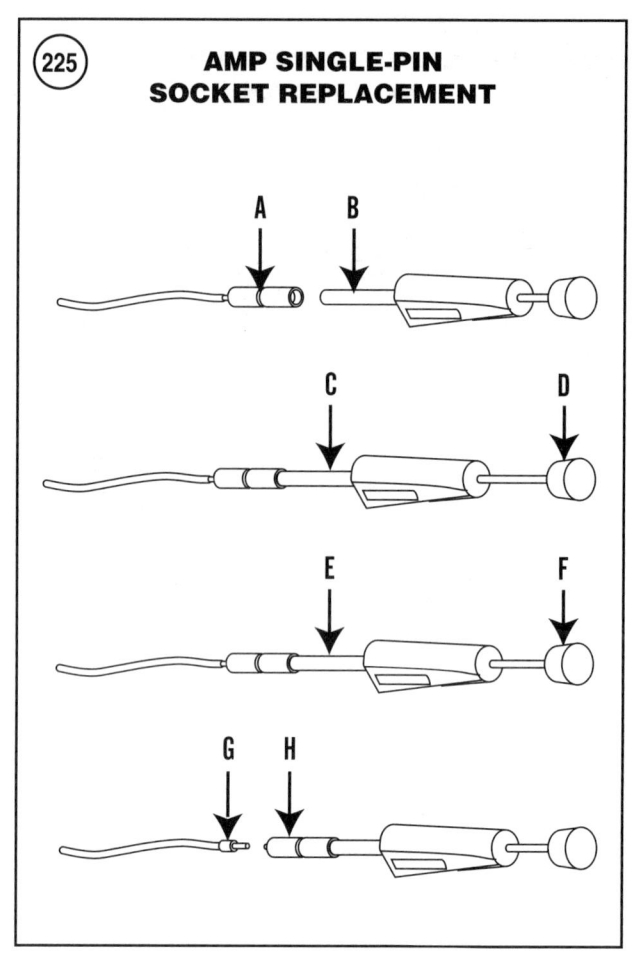

225 AMP SINGLE-PIN SOCKET REPLACEMENT

A B C D E F G H

4. Carefully pull the wire and withdraw the socket from the wire cable end of the housing.
5. Repeat this process to remove remaining socket terminal, if necessary.
6. Use a flat-bladed screwdriver and carefully bend the tang away from terminal body.
7. Insert socket and wire lead into wire end of socket housing until it *clicks* into place. Gently pull on the wire to ensure the terminal is correctly seated.
8. Push rubber seal back into place on the wire end of socket terminal, if necessary.
9. Repeat this process to install remaining socket terminal, if necessary.
10. Install the secondary lock (A, **Figure 223**) onto the cable and then push it onto the wire end of the socket housing until the slots engage the tabs (B) on the sides of the socket housing.
11. Install the Maxi-Fuse as described in this chapter.

Wire form type removal/installation

This procedure shows how to remove and install the electrical terminals from the pull-to-seat wire form type latch as shown in **Figure 224**.

1. Remove the Maxi-Fuse as described in this chapter.
2. Depress the wire form and separate the connector.
3. Hold the connector so the wire form is facing down.
4. Look into the mating end of the connector, and locate the plastic rib that separates the wire terminals. The terminal is on each side of the rib with the tang at the rear.
5. Use the thin, flat blade of an X-Acto knife to depress the tang. Tilt the blade at an angle and place the tip at the inboard edge of the terminal. Push down slightly until the spring tension is relieved and a click is heard. Repeat this process several times. The click represents the tang returning to the locked position as it slips from the point of the knife blade. Continue to push down until the clicking stops, indicating the tang has been depressed.
6. Remove the knife blade, push the wire end of the lead and remove the lead from the connector. If additional slack is necessary, pull back on the harness conduit and remove the wire seal at the back of the connector.
7. To install the terminal and wire back into the connector, use the thin, flat blade of an X-Acto knife to carefully bend the tang away from the terminal.
8. Carefully pull the lead and terminal into the connector until a click is heard indicating the terminal is seated correctly within the connector. Gently push and pull on the lead to ensure the terminal is correctly seated.
9. If necessary, install the wire seal and push the harness conduit back into position on the backside of the connector.
10. Push the socket halves together until the latch(es) are locked together.

Amp Single Connectors (2008-2009 Models)

Socket removal/installation

1. Grasp the lead on the wire end of the socket housing (A, **Figure 225**) and push the terminal forward toward the mat-

ELECTRICAL SYSTEM

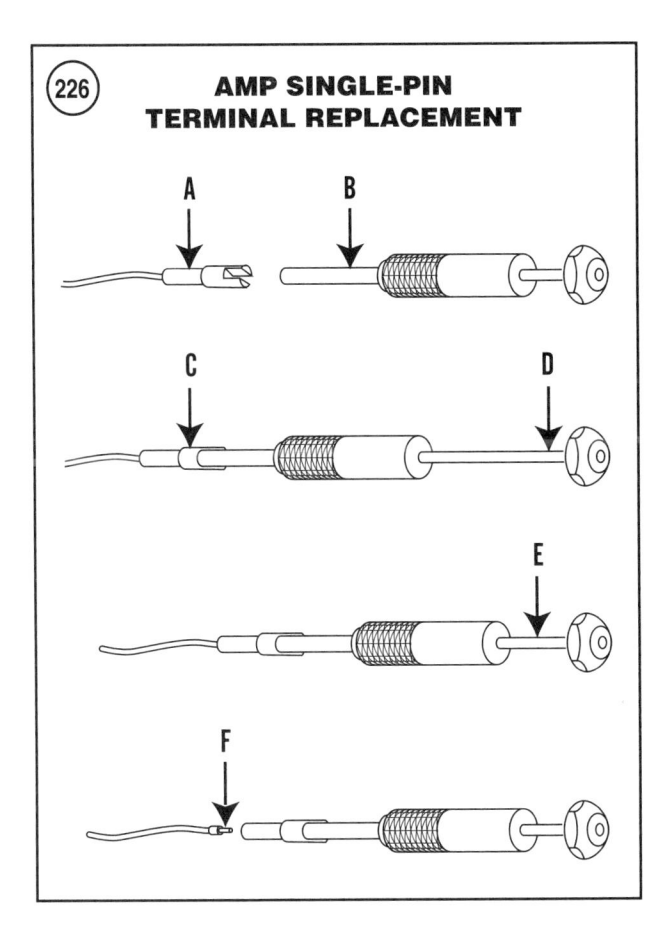

226 AMP SINGLE-PIN TERMINAL REPLACEMENT

A B C D E F

ing end of the connector until it bottoms. This disengages the locking tang from the connector groove.

2. Install the barrel (B, **Figure 225**) of the socket terminal tool (H-D part No. HD-39621-27) over the socket housing.

3. Lightly rotate the tool and push it in until it bottoms (C, **Figure 225**) in the socket housing allowing the plunger (D) to back out of the handle.

4. Secure the socket housing and keep the tool firmly depressed into the socket housing (E, **Figure 225**).

5. Depress the plunger (F, **Figure 225**) and the terminal (G) will eject out of the wire end of the connector (H).

6. Insert the lead and wire terminal into the flat lip side of the socket housing.

7. Push the lead into the socket housing until it a *click* is heard. Gently pull on the lead to ensure the terminal is correctly seated.

Pin terminal removal/installation

1. Grasp the lead on the wire end of the pin housing and push the terminal forward toward the mating end of the connector until it stops unlocking the tang from the groove in the connector.

2. Install the barrel (A, **Figure 226**) of the socket terminal tool (H-D part No. HD-39621-27) over the pin (B).

3. Lightly rotate the tool and push it in until it bottoms (C, **Figure 226**) in the pin housing allowing the plunger (D) to back out of the handle.

4. Secure the pin housing and keep the tool firmly depressed.

5. Depress the plunger (E, **Figure 226**) and the pin (F) will eject out of the wire end of the connector.

6. Insert the pin into the pin housing until a *click* is heard. Gently pull on the lead to ensure the pin is correctly seated.

Amp Multilock Connectors (2006-2007 Models)

2-, 3-, 4-, 6- and 10-pin connector terminals removal/installation

Refer to **Figure 227**.

1. Remove the Maxi-Fuse as described in this chapter.
2. Press the button on the socket on the terminal side and pull the connector apart.
3. Slightly bend the latch back and free one side of the secondary lock. Repeat for the other side of the secondary lock.
4. Open the secondary lock (A, **Figure 228**) around the hinge to access the terminals within the connector.

NOTE
Do not pull too hard on the wire until the tang is released or the terminal will be difficult to remove.

5. Insert a pin or a pick tool (B, **Figure 228**) into the flat edge of the terminal cavity until it stops. Pivot the pick tool away (C, **Figure 228**) from the terminal and gently pull on the wire to pull the terminal (D) from the terminal chamber. Note the wire location number on the connector (**Figure 229**).

NOTE
The release button used to separate the connectors is at the top of the connector.

6. A tang in each chamber engages the terminal slot to lock the terminal into position. The tangs (**Figure 228**) are located as follows:
   a. Pin housing side: the tangs are located at the bottom of each chamber. The pin terminal slot, on the side opposite the crimp, must face downward.
   b. Socket housing side: the tangs are located at the top of each chamber. The socket terminal slot, on the same side as the crimp, must face upward.

7. On the secondary lock side of the connector, push the wire and terminal into the correct location until it snaps into place. Gently pull on the lead to ensure the terminal is correctly seated.

8. Rotate the hinged secondary lock down and inward until the tabs are fully engaged with the latches on both sides of the connector. Pull upward to make sure the tabs are locked in place.

9. Insert the socket housing into the pin housing and push it in until it locks into place.

10. Install the Maxi-Fuse as described in this chapter.

CHAPTER ELEVEN

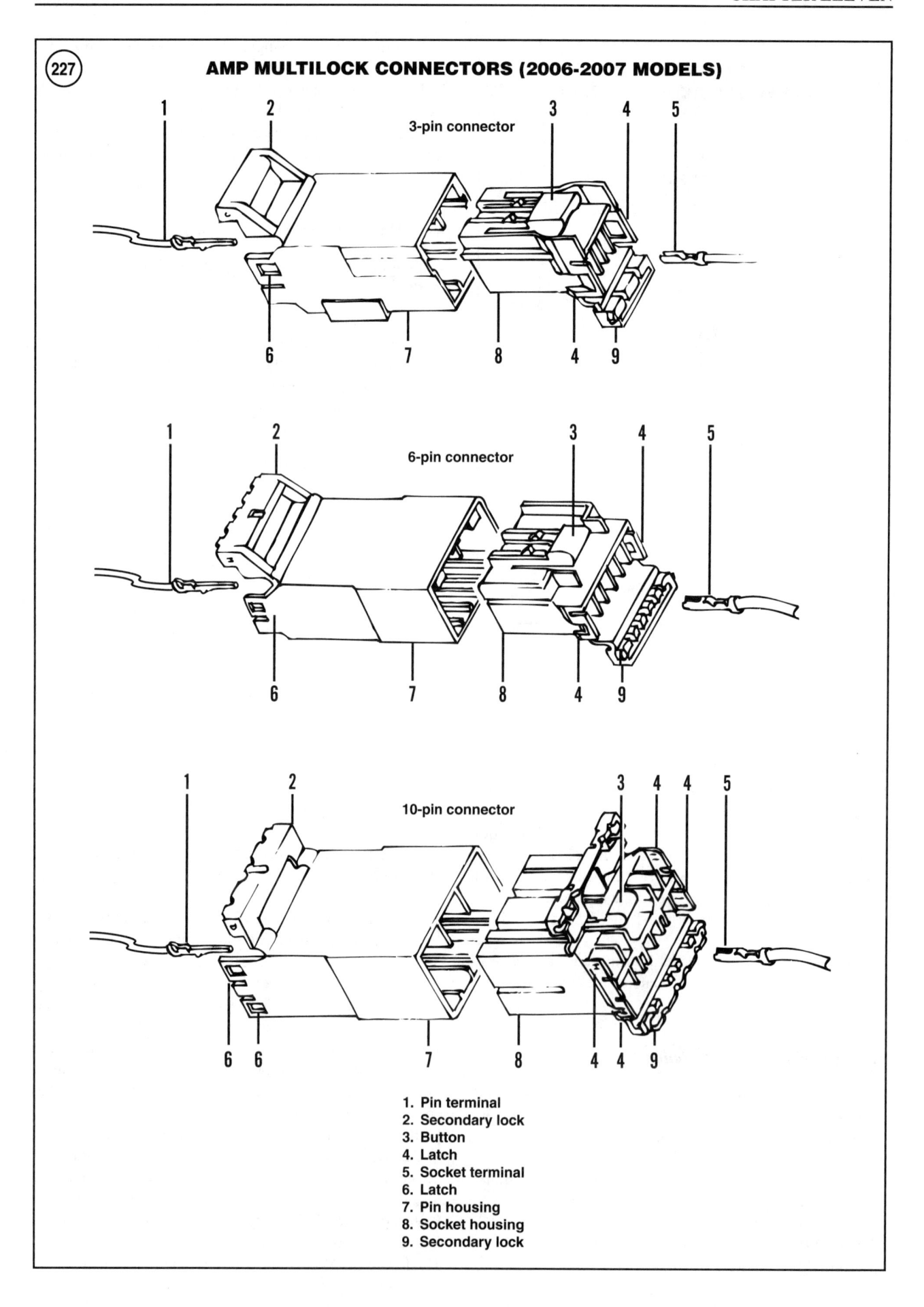

227 AMP MULTILOCK CONNECTORS (2006-2007 MODELS)

3-pin connector

6-pin connector

10-pin connector

1. Pin terminal
2. Secondary lock
3. Button
4. Latch
5. Socket terminal
6. Latch
7. Pin housing
8. Socket housing
9. Secondary lock

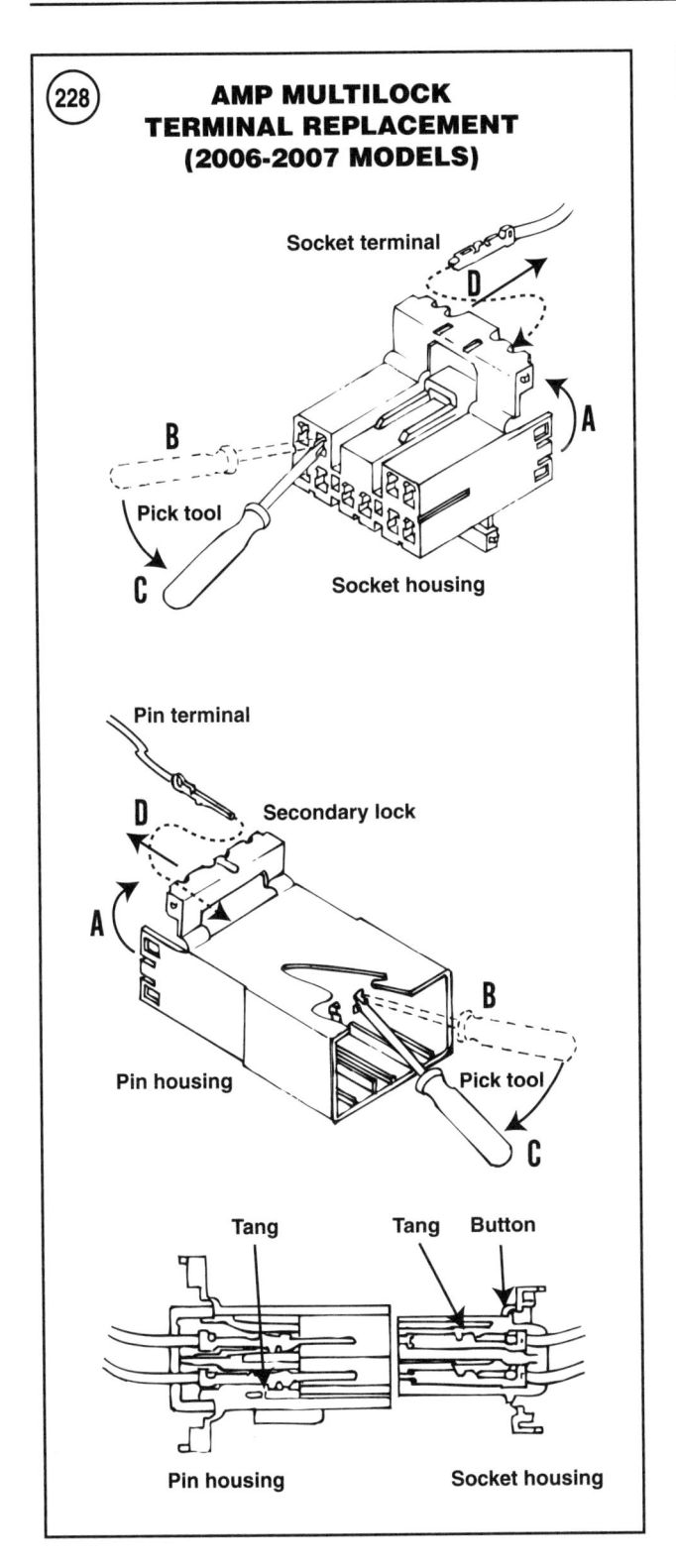

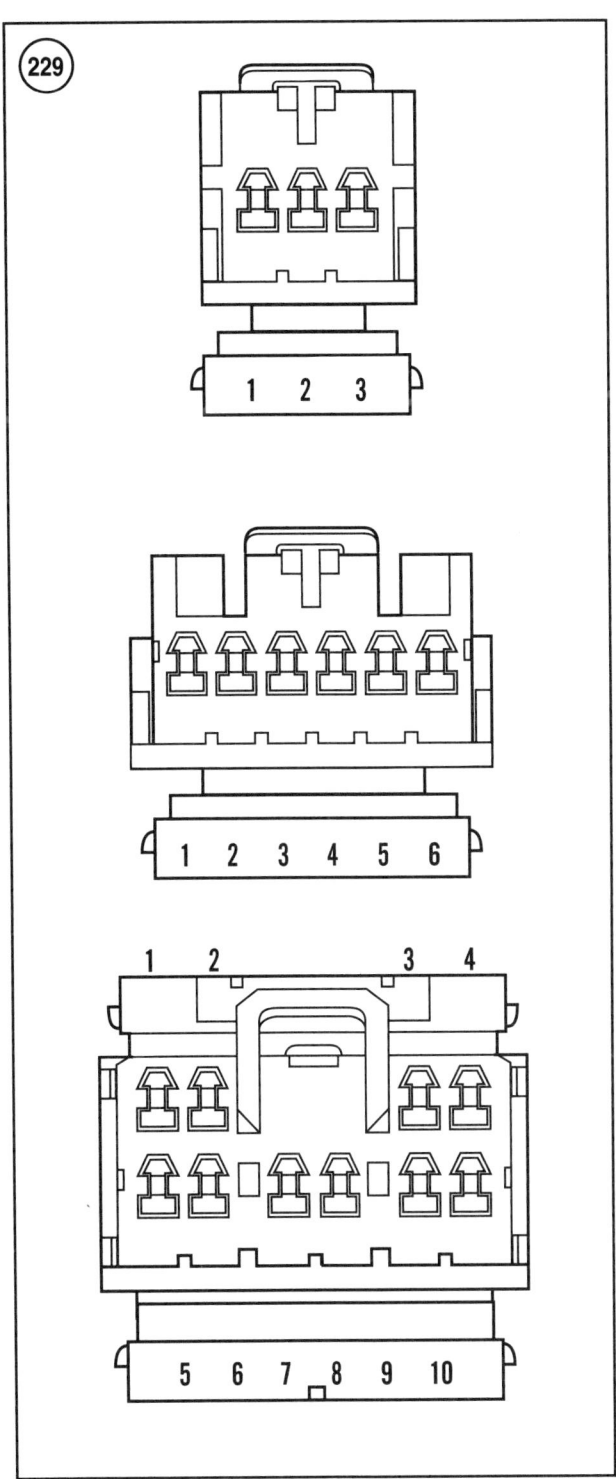

ELECTRICAL SYSTEM

228 AMP MULTILOCK TERMINAL REPLACEMENT (2006-2007 MODELS)

229

Amp Multilock Connectors (2008-2009 Models)

3-, 6- and 10-pin connector and pin terminals removal/installation

Refer to **Figure 230**.

1. Remove the Maxi-Fuse as described in this chapter.
2. Slide the connector attachment clip T-stud to the large end of the opening.
3. Press the release button on the socket on the terminal side and pull the connector apart.
4. Slightly bend the latch (1, **Figure 230**) back and free one side of the secondary lock (2). Repeat for the other side of the secondary lock.
5. Look into the terminal side of the connector that is opposite the secondary lock and note the location of each connector and cavity.
6. Insert a pin or a pick tool into the terminal cavity until it stops.

NOTE
Use the connector release button to determine the up and down side of the connector. The release button is on the top of the connector.

7. Press the tang in the housing to release a terminal. A click is heard when the tang is released:
   a. Press down on the tang (7, **Figure 230**) in the housing to release a pin.
   b. Lift up on the socket tang (8, **Figure 230**) to release the socket.

NOTE
Do not pull too hard on the wire. If the tang is bent downward, the terminal will be difficult to remove. If necessary, repeat the process and release the tang.

8. Gently pull on the wire to pull the wire and terminal (5, **Figure 230**) from the terminal chamber. Note the wire location number on the connector (**Figure 229**).
9. Hold the pin terminal so the catch faces (7, **Figure 230**) the tang in the chamber:
   a. On the pin side of the connector, the tangs sit on the bottom of the housing. Install a pin sit it catch faces down.
   b. On the socket side of the connector, the tangs sit at the top of the housing. Install a socket so its catch faces up.
10. Inset the terminal into the secondary lock side of the housing, and push the wire and terminal into the correct location until it snaps into place. Gently pull on the lead to ensure the terminal is correctly seated.
11. Rotate the hinged secondary lock inward until the tabs are fully engaged with the latches on both sides of the connector. Pull upward to make sure the tabs are locked in place.
12. Insert the socket housing into the pin housing and push it in until it locks into place.
13. Install the Maxi-Fuse as described in this chapter.

Delphi Electrical Connectors
Removal/Installation

1. Remove the Maxi-Fuse as described in this chapter.
2. Bend back the external latches (**Figure 231**) and separate the socket halves.
3. Free one side of the wire lock (A, **Figure 232**) from the ear on the wire end of the socket housing. Release the wire lock on the other side.
4. Release the wires from the channels in the wire lock, and remove them from the socket housing.
5. Remove the terminal lock (B, **Figure 232**) from the socket housing.
6. Use a thin blade (unsharpened end of an X-Acto knife), and gently pry the tang outward away from the terminal (C, **Figure 232**).

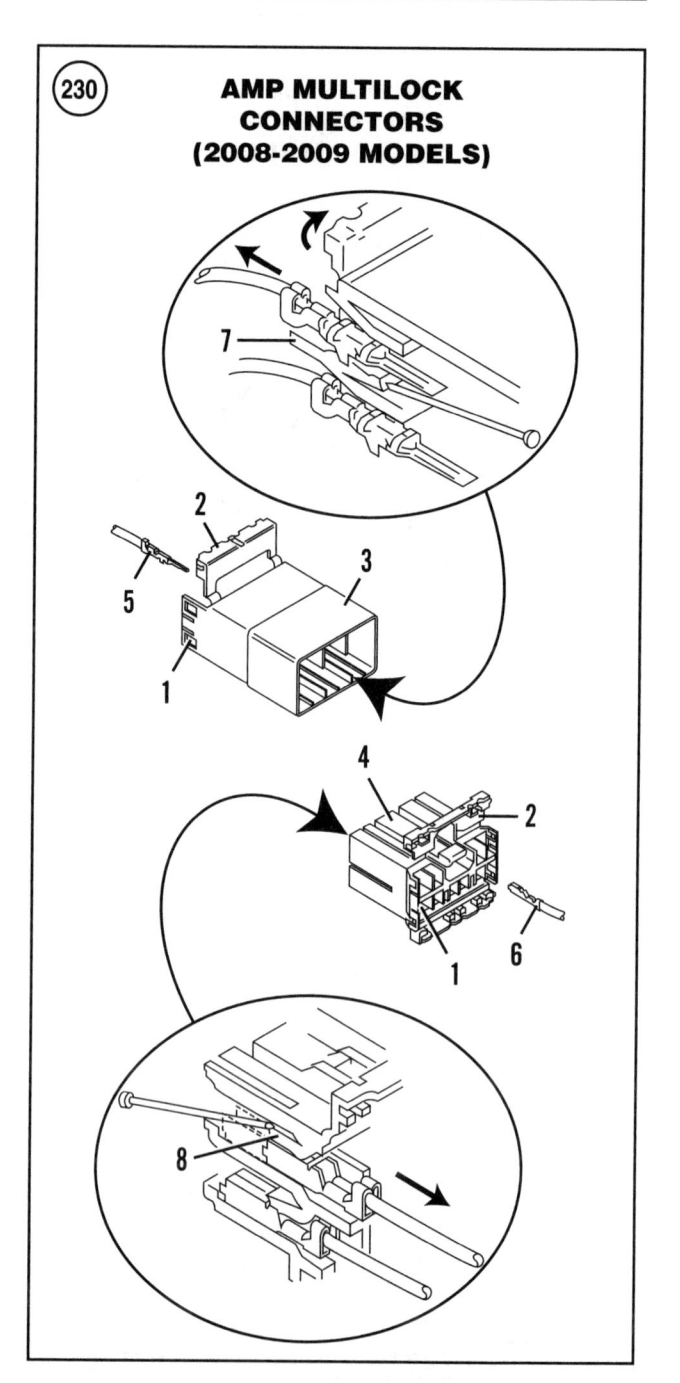

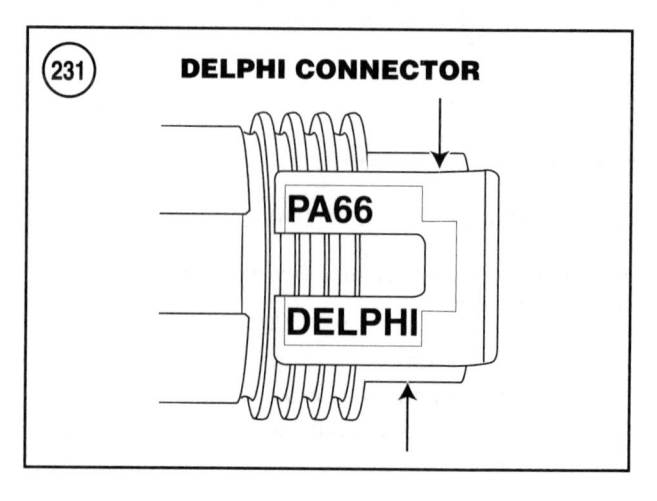

ELECTRICAL SYSTEM

232 DELPHI CONNECTOR TERMINAL REPLACEMENT

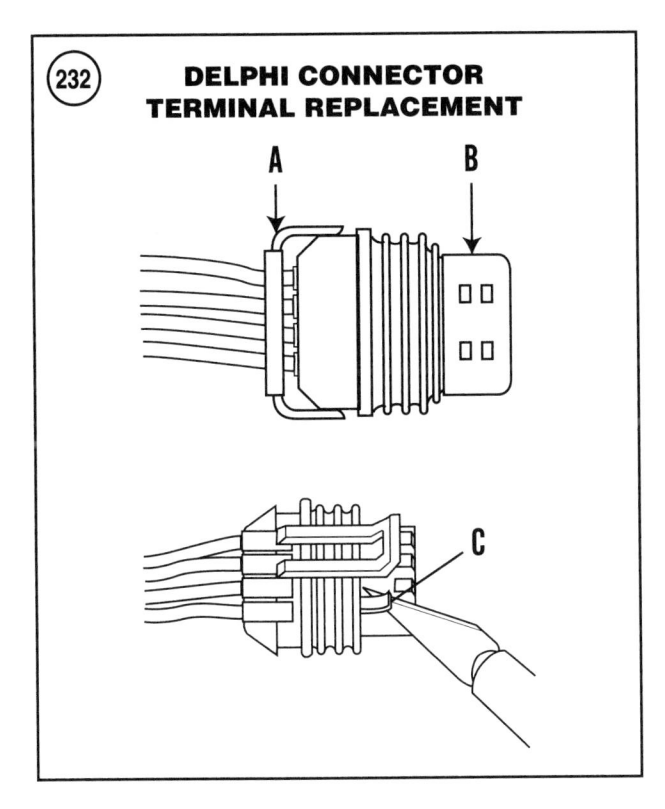

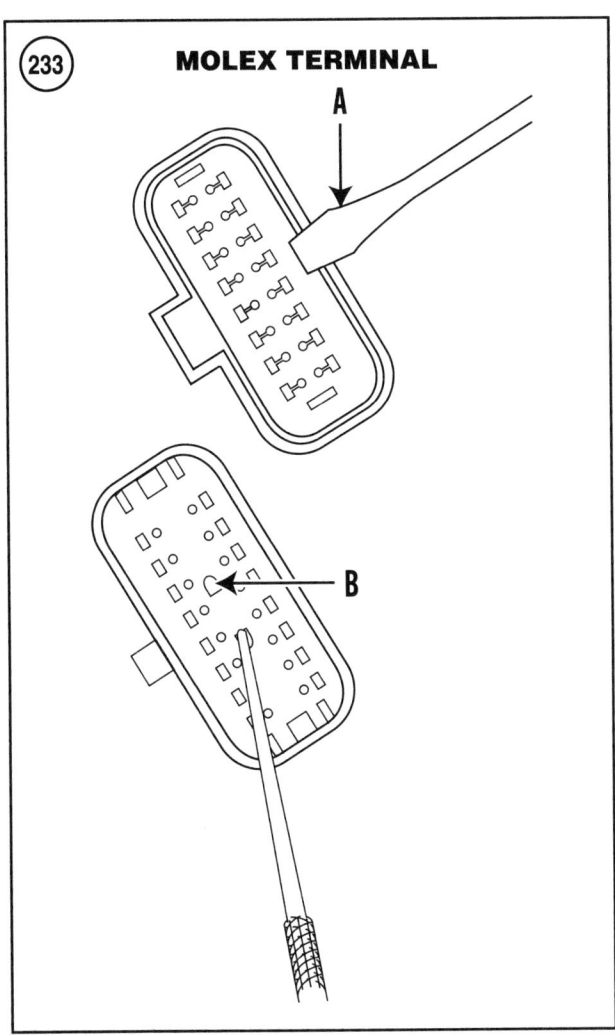

233 MOLEX TERMINAL

7. Carefully pull the wire to back the terminal out of the connector, and remove it. Do not pull the wire until the terminal is released or it will be difficult to remove it.

8. Gently push the tang on the socket housing inward toward the chamber.

9. Position the terminal so its open side faces the tang, insert the terminal into the wire end of the housing, and seat the terminal in its chamber. Gently pull the wire to ensure the terminal is correctly seated.

10. Install the terminal lock (B, **Figure 232**) onto the socket housing.

11. Install the wire lock (A, **Figure 232**) onto each side of the socket housing. Make sure they are correctly seated.

12. Push the connector halves together until the external latches engage (**Figure 231**).

13. Install the Maxi-Fuse as described in this chapter.

Molex Electrical Connector
Removal/Installation

1. Remove the Maxi-Fuse as described in this chapter.
2. Pull the secondary lock approximately 3/16 in (4.8 mm) away from the terminals until it stops by performing the following. Do not remove the secondary lock.
   a. On the socket housing, insert a flat-bladed screwdriver into the pry slot (A, **Figure 233**) and pry the secondary lock from the terminals.
   b. On the pin housing, use a hooked pick or needle nose pliers and loosen the secondary lock (B, **Figure 233**).
3. Insert the Molex Electrical Connector Terminal Remover (H-D part No. HD-48114) into the desired terminal pin hole. Push it in until the tool bottoms.
4. Gently pull on the wire lead and remove it from the housing cavity.
5. Insert the wire into the correct terminal chamber.
6. Orient the terminal so the tang opposite the crimp engages the slot in the terminal cavity. Push the terminal into the cavity until it bottoms. Gently pull on the wire lead to ensure the terminal is correctly seated.
7. Push the secondary lock into the socket housing, and lock the terminals into the housing.
8. Install the socket housing into the terminal.

AUTOFUSE ELECTRICAL CONNECTORS

The Autofuse electrical connector terminals are located in the ignition switch and on some fuse blocks. Use a terminal pick (JIMS Receptacle Extractor part No. 1764 or Snap-On part No. GA500A) for this procedure.

1. Insert the smallest pair of the terminal picks (**Figure 234**) into the mating chamber on the end of the socket housing. Simultaneously depress the tangs on each side of the terminal housing.
2. Gently pull on the wire and remove the terminal from the socket housing.

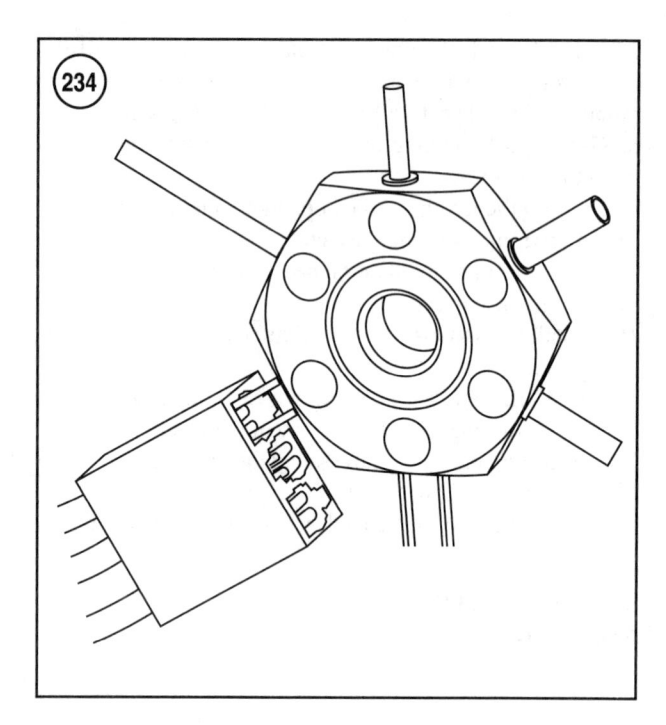

3. Crimp *new* terminals onto the end of the wires, if necessary.
4. Use a thin blade (unsharpened end of an X-Acto knife), and gently pry the tang outward away from the terminal body.
5. Position the open side of the terminal with the rib facing down.
6. Insert the terminal into the wire side of the chamber and carefully push it until it locks in place. Pull gently on the wire to make sure it is locked in place.

SEALED BUTT CONNECTORS

Replacing some switches requires sealed butt connectors to connect the switch wiring to the existing wiring. Stagger the position of the connectors so they are not side-by-side.

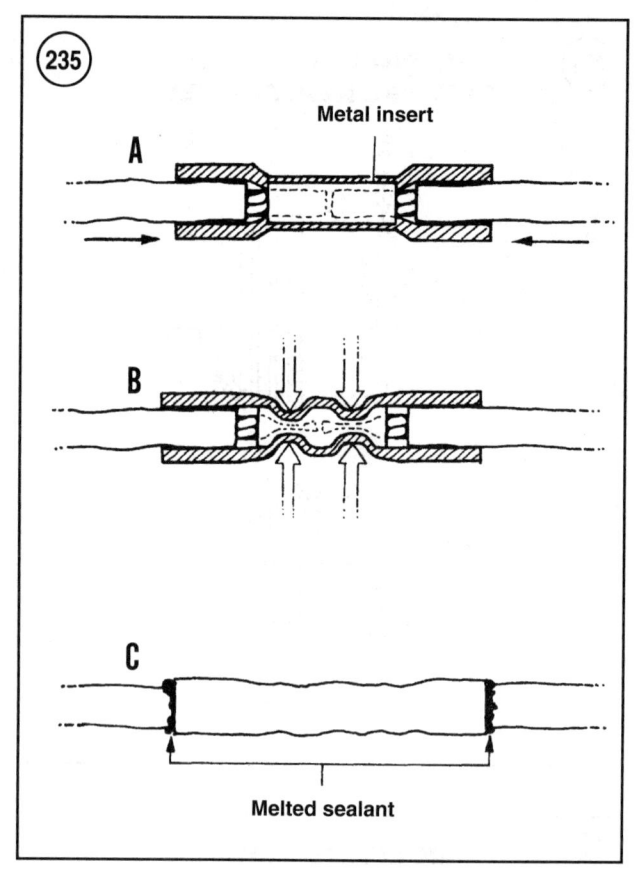

1. Insert the stripped wire into the connector (A, **Figure 235**).
2. Crimp the connector/wire ends (B, **Figure 235**).
3. Heat the connector and allow it to cool (C, **Figure 235**).

WIRING DIAGRAMS

Color wiring diagrams for all models are located on the CD inserted into the back cover of this manual.

Table 1 ELECTRICAL SYSTEM SPECIFICATIONS

Item	Specification
ACR solenoid compression test	
ACR-connector connected	130-170 psi (896-1172 kPa)
ACR-connector disconnected	200-220 psi (1379-1517 kPa)
Alternator	
AC voltage output	
2006-2007 models	30-40 VAC @ 2000 rpm
2008-2009 models	32-46 VAC @ 2000 rpm
Stator coil resistance	0.1-0.3 ohm
Voltage regulator	
Voltage output @ 3600 rpm	14.4-14.6 @ 75° F (24° C)
Amps @ 3600 rpm	50 amps

(continued)

ELECTRICAL SYSTEM

Table 1 ELECTRICAL SYSTEM SPECIFICATIONS (continued)

Item	Specification
Battery capacity	12 volts, 28 amp hour
Ignition coil resistance	
Primary resistance	
Carbureted models	0.5-0.7 ohms
EFI models	0.3-0.5 ohms
Secondary resistance	
2006 models	5500-7500 ohms
2007-2009 models	2500-3500 ohms
Spark plug cable resistance	5000-11,666 ohms
Spark plug	
Size	12 mm
Gap	0.038-0.043 in. (0.97-1.09 mm)
Type	H-D No. 6R12
Starter	
Minimum free speed	3000 rpm @ 11.5 volts
Maximum free current	90 amp @ 11.5 volts
Cranking current	200 amp maximum @ 68° F (20° C)
Brush length (minimum)	0.433 in. (11.0 mm)
Commutator diameter (minimum)	1.141 in. (28.981 mm)

Table 2 BATTERY CHARGING RATES/TIMES (APPROXIMATE)

Voltage	% of charge	3 amp charger	6 amp charger	10 amp charger	20 amp charger
12.8	100%	–	–	–	–
12.6	75%	1.75 hours	50 minutes	30 minutes	15 minutes
12.3	50%	3.5 hours	1.75 hours	1 hour	30 minutes
12.0	25%	5 hours	2.5 hours	1.5 hours	45 minutes
11.8	0%	6 hours and 40 minutes	3 hours and 20 minutes	2 hours	1 hour

Table 3 FUSE SPECIFICATIONS (AMPERES)

Item	Specification	Color
Maxi-fuse	40	Orange
Instruments	15	blue
Ignition	15	blue
Lighting	15	blue
Headlight	15	blue
Brakes/cruise	15	blue
Radio memory	15	blue
Radio power/siren	15	blue
Accessory	15	blue
Battery	15	blue
Parts and accessories	15	blue
ABS (2008-2009 models)	30	–
Fuel-injected models		
Fuel pump	15	blue
ECM power	15	blue
Security fuse (EFI models)	15	
Engine control	15	blue
Active exhaust/intake (HDI)	15	blue

Table 4 BULB SPECIFICATIONS

Item	Current draw amperage	Quantity
Headlight (high beam/low beam)	4.85	1
Position light (HDI)	0.32	1
Taillight	0.59	1
Stop light	2.10	1
Front turn signal/running lights	2.25/0.59	2
	(continued)	

Table 4 BULB SPECIFICATIONS (continued)

Item	Current draw amperage	Quantity
Front turn signal (HDI)	1.75	2
Rear turn signal	2.25	2
Rear turn signal (HDI)	1.75	2
Auxiliary lights	2.1	2
License plate lights (FLHX models)		
Domestic	0.35	1
HDI	0.37	1
Fender tip lights		
Front	0.30	1
Rear	LED	1
Tour-Pak side lights	0.14	–
Gauge lights (FLHT, FLTR and FLHX models)		
Voltmeter	0.24	1
Oil pressure indicator	0.24	1
Air temperature gauge	0.24	1
Fuel level gauge	0.24	1
Fuel level gauge (FLHR and FLHRC models)	0.24	1

TABLE 5 HEADLIGHT AIM ADJUSTMENTS (FLTR MODELS)

Hex adjuster	Rotation	Beam movement
Left bulb	Clockwise	To the right
Right bulb	Counterclockwise	To the right
Left bulb	Clockwise	To the left
Right bulb	Counterclockwise	To the left
Left and right bulb equally	Clockwise	Upward
Left and right bulb equally	Counterclockwise	Downward

Table 6 ELECTRICAL SYSTEM TORQUE SPECIFICATIONS

Item	ft.-lb.	in.-lb.	N•m
Alternator stator Torx screws	–	55-75	6.2-8.5
Automatic compression release (ACR) solenoid (Screamin' Eagle models)	11-15	–	14.9-20.3
Battery			
Terminal nut (2006 models)	–	60-85	6.8-9.6
Terminal nut (2007-2009 models)	–	60-96	6.8-10.9
Hold-down bolt	15-20	–	20.3-27.1
Tray ground strap flange nut (2008 models)	–	50-90	5.7-10.2
Tray mounting screws (2009 models)	–	72-96	8.1-10.9
CB module (FLHTCU models)			
Mounting screw(s)	–	35-45	4.0-5.1
Cruise control module			
Mounting flange nuts	–	60-96	6.8-10.8
Electrical caddy (2008-2009 models)			
Top caddy mounting bolt (ECM)	15-20	–	20.3-27.1
Left side			
Mounting screws (front and rear)	–	72-96	8.1-10.8
Lifting strap	–	72-96	8.1-10.8
Electrical caddy (2008-2009 models) with ABS			
Two screws	–	72-96	8.1-10.8
Three ABS module screws	–	39-60	4.4-6.8
Electrical caddy (HDI models)			
Two screws	–	72-96	8.1-10.8
Two actuator screws	–	32-40	3.6-4.5
J-clamp	–	39-60	4.4-6.8
Electrical bracket (2006-2007 models)			
Flange nuts	–	36-48	4.1-5.4
Allen mounting screws (ECM)	–	50-60	5.7-6.8

(continued)

Table 6 ELECTRICAL SYSTEM TORQUE SPECIFICATIONS (continued)

Item	ft.-lb.	in.-lb.	N•m
Fender tip light assembly screw (front and rear)			
Mounting screw	–	20-25	2.3-2.8
Front turn signals			
FLHT and FLHR models			
Mounting screws	–	36-60	4.1-6.8
FLHRS and FLHRSE models			
Acorn nut	–	60-96	6.8-10.8
Set screw	–	50-70	5.7-7.9
FLHTCUSE models			
Mounting screws	–	96-120	10.8-13.6
FLHX models			
Torx screws	15-20	–	20.3-27.1
FLTR and FLTRSE3 models			
Acorn nut	–	96-120	10.8-13.6
Fuel tank console rear Allen screw (2008-2009 FLHTCUSE models)	–	25-30	2.8-3.4
Headlight (2007-2008 FLHRSE models)			
Lens assembly Phillips screws	–	23-28	2.6-3.2
Trim ring	–	9-16	1.0-1.8
Headset–front receptacle (2008-2009 FLHTCUSE models)			
Console mounting Allen screw	–	36-60	4.1-6.8
Horn			
Stud mounting flange nut	–	80-100	9.0-11.3
Mounting acorn nut	–	80-120	9.0-13.6
Ignition coil-to-bracket mounting bolts			
2006-2008 models	–	84-144	9.5-16.3
2009 models	–	32-40	3.6-4.5
Ignition control module (carbureted models)			
Mounting screws	–	50-60	5.7-6.8
Ignition switch			
Mounting screws			
All FLHR and Screamin' Eagle models and all other non-HDI models (except FLHR and Screamin' Eagle)	–	36-60	4.1-6.8
FLTR models radio support bracket Allen screws	–	35-45	4.0-5.1
Mounting nut (7/8 in.)	–	120-150	13.6-16.9
Instruments			
FLHT and FLHX models			
Screw or nut	–	10-20	1.1-2.3
FLTR models			
Bracket screw	–	10-20	1.1-2.3
Torx mounting screws	–	15-20	1.7-2.3
Instrument console mounting screw			
Front and rear	–	30-40	3.4-4.5
License plate bracket fasteners	–	30-50	3.4-5.7
License plate support	–	60-90	6.8-10.2
Neutral indicator switch	–	120-180	13.6-20.3
Oil pressure			
Switch	–	96-120	10.8-13.6
Sender	–	96-120	10.8-13.6
Passing light			
All models except FLHTCUSE			
Adjust nut	15-18	–	20.3-24.4
Turn signal mounting screws	–	36-60	4.1-6.8
FLHTCUSE models mounting nut	15-18	–	20.3-24.4
Radio/storage box mounting screws	–	35-45	4.0-5.1
Rear fascia light assembly (FLXH models)			
Phillips screw	–	25-40	2.8-4.5
Passenger seat strap bolt	–	60-96	6.8-10.8
Rear brake light switch	12-15	–	16.3-20.3

(continued)

Table 6 ELECTRICAL SYSTEM TORQUE SPECIFICATIONS (continued)

Item	ft.-lb.	in.-lb.	N•m
Rear turn signal bracket (all models)			
Taillight lens screw	–	30-50	3.4-5.7
Flange bolt	–	84-144	9.5-16.3
Sensors			
Crankshaft position (CKP)			
Allen screw	–	90-120	10.2-13.6
Engine temperature (ET)	–	120-180	13.6-20.3
Manifold absolute pressure (MAP)			
Torx screw	–	25-35	2.8-4.0
Vehicle speed (VSS)			
Allen screw	–	84-132	9.5-14.9
Speakers–front fairing			
Single lower outboard screw	–	22-28	2.5-3.2
Two upper screws	–	35-50	4.0-5.7
Starter			
Field coil starter terminal post nut	–	70-80	7.9-9.0
Mounting bolts			
2006-2007 models	13-20	–	17.6-27.1
2008-2009 models	25-27	–	33.9-36.6
Positive terminal nut	–	70-90	7.9-10.2
Solenoid contact jam nut (short and long post)	–	65-80	7.3-9.0
Through bolt	–	39-65	4.4-7.3
Stator screw	–	55-75	6.2-8.5
Tail/brake light assembly			
FLHT, FLHR and FLHTCUSE models			
Lens screws	–	20-24	2.3-2.7
Circuit board/chrome base			
screw/captive washer	–	40-48	4.5-5.4
FLHRSE series models flange nut	–	40-48	4.5-5.4
Tail/brake light-to-fender fasteners	–	60-90	6.8-10.2
Turn signals			
Front turn signal screws			
FLHT, FLHTC and FLHTCU models	–	36-60	4.1-6.8
FLHX models	15-20	–	20.3-27.1
FLHR, FLHRC, FLHRS and FLHRSE models	–	50-70	5.7-7.9
FLTR, FLTRSE3 and FLHTCUSE models	–	96-120	10.8-13.6
Rear turn signal screws	–	96-120	10.8-13.6
Rear turn signal bracket flange bolts	–	84-144	9.5-16.3
Turn signal housing set screw	–	50-70	5.7-7.9
Voltage regulator flange nut	–	70-100	7.9-11.3

CHAPTER TWELVE

WHEELS, HUBS AND TIRES

This chapter includes procedures for repair of the front and rear wheels, and hubs and tire service. Refer to Chapter Three for maintenance procedures.

Specifications are in **Tables 1-4** at the end of the chapter.

MOTORCYCLE STANDS

Many procedures in this chapter require that the front or rear wheel be lifted off the ground. A motorcycle front end stand (**Figure 1**), or suitable size jack is required. Before purchasing or using a stand, check with the manufacturer to make sure the stand will work with the specific model being worked on. If any adjustments or accessories are required to the motorcycle and/or stand, perform the necessary adjustments or install the correct parts before lifting the motorcycle. When using the stand, have an assistant standing by to help. Some means to tie down one end of the motorcycle may also be required. After lifting on a stand, make sure the motorcycle is properly supported before walking away from it.

FRONT WHEEL

Removal

CAUTION
On ABS-equipped models, keep the ABS sensor and the ABS encoder wheel bearings away from any magnetic fields or they will be damaged.

1. Support the motorcycle with the front wheel off the ground. Refer to *Motorcycle Stands* in this chapter.
2. On ABS-equipped models, push in on lip at the rear of clip (A, **Figure 2**) and release it. Rotate the ABS tab (B, **Figure 2**) toward the rear until the clip is perpendicular to the bracket. Remove the clip and move the cable out of the way.
3. On FLHTCUSE models, loosen the set screw and remove the cover from the axle nut.
4. On the right side, insert a drift or screwdriver through the front axle hole (**Figure 3**) to prevent it from rotating.
5. On the left side, loosen the axle nut (**Figure 4**).
6. On the left side, remove the axle nut (**Figure 4**), lockwasher (on models so equipped) and flat washer.
7. On the right side, loosen the nuts (A, **Figure 5**) on the fork slider cap.

NOTE
Place a plastic or wooden spacer between the brake pads in place of the disc. Then, if the brake lever is inadvertently applied, the pistons will not be forced out of the calipers. If this occurs on 2006-2007 models, disassemble the caliper to reseat the pistons.

8. Remove the caliper mounting bolts (**Figure 6**), and then remove both calipers as described in Chapter Fifteen. On ABS models, do not lose the clip located under the mounting bolts on the left side caliper.
9. Prior to removing the front axle, note the location of the short right side spacer and long left side spacer. The spacers are not interchangeable and must be reinstalled on the correct side during installation.
10. Use a screwdriver or drift and withdraw the front axle (B, **Figure 5**) from the forks sliders and front wheel. Remove the tool from the axle.

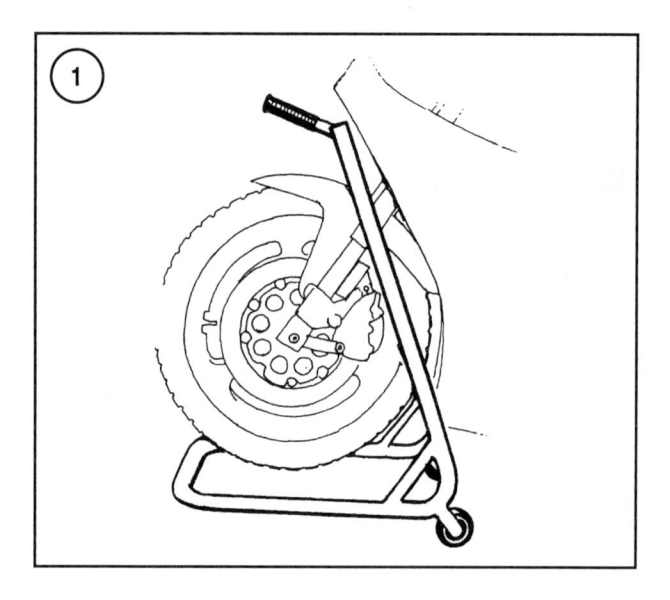

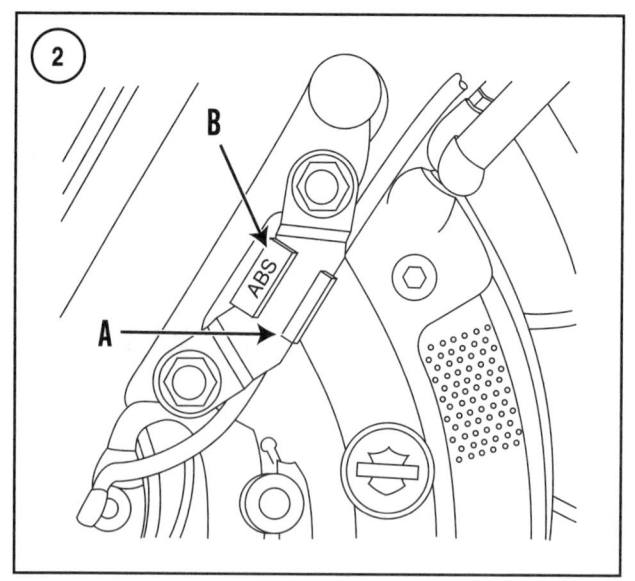

CAUTION
Never pull the ABS cable taut or use the cable to supoprt the suspension components as the cable will be damaged.

11A. On ABS-equipped models, perform the following:
   a. Slowly pull the wheel away from the fork sliders. Remove the ABS sensor from the hub and remove the wheel.
   b. Remove the spacer from the right side of the wheel.
11B. On all other models, perform the following:
   a. Pull the wheel away from the fork sliders and remove it.
   b. Identify the spacers before removing them.
   c. Remove the short right side spacer and the long left side spacer from the wheel.

CAUTION
Do not set the wheel down on the brake disc surface, as it may be damaged.

12. Inspect the front wheel assembly as described in this section.

Installation

1. Clean the axle in solvent and dry thoroughly. Make sure the axle bearing surfaces on both fork sliders and the axle are free of burrs and nicks.
2. Apply an antiseize lubricant to the axle shaft prior to installation.
3. If the oil seals or bearings were replaced, confirm the front axle spacer alignment is correct as described in *Front Hub* (this chapter).

NOTE
Position the axle spacer(s) with the groove facing outboard away from the wheel.

4A. On ABS-equipped models, perform the following:
   a. Install the spacer on the right side of the wheel.  
   b. Move the ABS sensor into position adjacent to the left fork leg.
   c. Install the wheel between the fork tubes and correctly position the ABS sensor onto the hub.
   d. Install the axle from the right side.
   e. Rotate the ABS sensor *counterclockwise* until the index pin (**Figure 7**) makes contact with the left fork slider.
4B. On all other models, perform the following:

WHEELS, HUBS AND TIRES 545

a. Install the short right side spacer (**Figure 8**) and the long left side spacer (**Figure 9**) into the correct side of the wheel.
b. Install the wheel between the fork tubes.
c. Check that axle spacers are still located correctly.
d. Install the axle from the right side.

5. Install the flat washer, lockwasher (on models so equipped) and axle nut (**Figure 4**). Finger-tighten the axle nut. Check that axle spacer(s), or ABS sensor, are installed correctly.
6. Insert a drift or screwdriver into the hole (**Figure 3**) in the end of the front axle to keep it from rotating.  
7. Tighten the front axle nut (**Figure 4**) as follows:
    a. 2006-2007 models: 50-55 ft.-lb. (67.8-74.6 N•m).
    b. 2008-2009 models: 60-65 ft.-lb. (81.3-88.1 N•m).
8. Remove the tool from the front axle.
9. Insert a 7/16 in. drill bit into the hole in the front axle. Pull the fork leg up against the drill bit and hold it there. Tighten the nuts (A, **Figure 5**) on the fork slider cap to 132-180 in.-lb. (14.9-20.3 N•m).
10. Remove the drill bit from the hole in the front axle.
11. On FLHTCUSE models, install the cover on the axle nut. Apply a small mount of medium-strength threadlock on the set screw and tighten to 60-84 in.-lb. (6.8-9.5 N•m).
12. Install the front brake calipers as described in Chapter Fifteen. On ABS models, make sure the cable clip is located under the mounting bolts on the left side caliper.
13. Secure the wheel sensor cable as follows:
    a. Move the cable into position in the bracket.
    b. Rotate the ABS tab (B, **Figure 2**) toward the front until the clip is inline with the bracket. Press on the tab until the tab lip is engaged.
    c. Push in on lip at the rear of clip (A, **Figure 2**) and lock it in place.
14. With the front wheel off the ground, rotate it several times and apply the front brake to seat the brake pads against the discs.
15. Remove the stand and lower the front wheel onto the ground.

Inspection

Replace any worn or damaged parts as described in this section.

1. Turn each bearing inner race by hand. The bearing must turn smoothly. Some axial play (end play) is normal, but radial play (side play) as shown in **Figure 10** must be negligible. If one bearing is damaged, replace both bearings as a set. Refer to *Front and Rear Hubs* in this chapter.
2. Clean the axle and axle spacers in solvent to remove all grease and dirt. Make sure the axle contact surfaces are clean and free of dirt and old grease.
3. Check the axle runout with a set of V-blocks and dial indicator (**Figure 11**).
4. Check the spacers for wear, burrs and damage. Replace as necessary.
5. Check the brake disc bolts (**Figure 12**) for tightness. To service the brake disc, refer to Chapter Fifteen.
6. Check wheel runout as described in this chapter.

REAR WHEEL

Removal

CAUTION
On ABS-equipped models, keep the ABS sensor and the ABS encoder wheel bearings away from any magnetic field or they will be damaged.

1. Remove both saddlebags as described in Chapter Seventeen.
2. Remove both mufflers as described in Chapter Four.
3. Support the motorcycle with the rear wheel off the ground on an appropriate jack or stand.
4. Remove the left side lower saddlebag support rail as described in Chapter Seventeen, on models equipped with low profile shock absorbers.
5. On ABS-equipped models, carefully cut the strap securing the wheel sensor cable to the rear caliper brake hose.

NOTE
Place a plastic or wooden spacer between the brake pads in place of the disc. Then, if the brake pedal is inadvertently depressed, the pistons will not be forced out of the caliper. If this occurs, disassemble the caliper to reseat the pistons.

6. On 2008-2009 models, remove the rear caliper assembly from the caliper mounting bracket as described in Chapter Fifteen, and tie it up to the frame with a bungee cord or wire.
7. Remove the large E-clip (A, **Figure 13**) from the rear axle nut and axle.
8. Loosen and remove the axle nut (B, **Figure 13**) and adjuster cam (C).
9. Using a soft-faced mallet, gently tap the rear axle toward the left side.

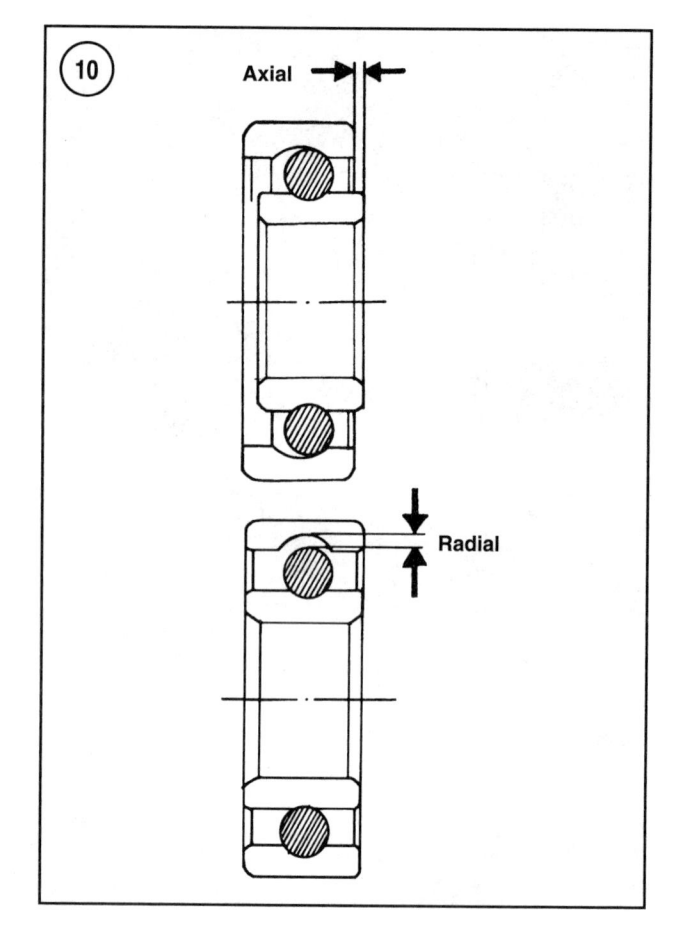

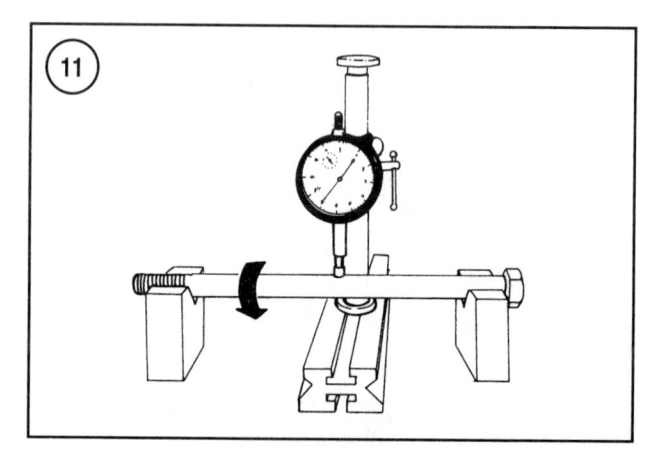

WHEELS, HUBS AND TIRES

NOTE
The rear wheel is heavy and can be difficult to remove. Check the tire-to-ground clearance before removing the rear axle. If necessary, have an assistant help in the removal.

10. From the left side, withdraw the rear axle (**Figure 14**) while holding onto the rear wheel.

CAUTION
Never pull the ABS cable taut or use the cable to support the suspension components as the cable will be damaged.

NOTE
On 2008-2009 models so equipped, secure the compensator bowl to the driven sprocket to prevent it from falling off.

11A. On ABS-equipped models, perform the following:
   a. Slowly lower the wheel to the ground. Remove the ABS sensor and cable from the left side of the hub.
   b. Remove the spacer from the right side of the wheel.

11B. On all other models, perform the following:
   a. Slowly lower the rear wheel to the ground.
   b. Remove the right side (**Figure 15**) and left side (**Figure 16**) spacers from the wheel hub.

12. Disengage the drive belt from the driven sprocket and remove the rear wheel.

NOTE
Place a plastic or wooden spacer between the brake pads in place of the disc. Then, if the brake pedal is inadvertently depressed, the pistons will not be forced out of the caliper. If this occurs, disassemble the caliper to reseat the pistons.

13A. On 2006-2007 models, remove the rear brake caliper from the swing arm and tie it up to the frame with a bungee cord or wire.

13B. On 2008-2009 models, remove the rear caliper mounting bracket from the swing arm weldment.

CAUTION
Do not set the wheel down on the brake disc surface, as it may be damaged.

14. Inspect the rear wheel as described in this section.

Installation

1. Clean the axle in solvent and dry thoroughly. Make sure the bearing surfaces on the axle are free from burrs and nicks.
2. Apply an antiseize lubricant to the axle shaft prior to installation.
3. On 2008-2009 models, install the rear caliper mounting bracket onto the swing arm weldment.
4. Position the rear wheel between the swing arm sides and place the drive belt on the driven sprocket.

5A. On ABS-equipped models, perform the following:
   a. Install the spacer onto the right side of the wheel.
   b. Install the ABS sensor and cable onto the left side of the hub.
5B. On all other models, install the right side (**Figure 15**) and left side (**Figure 16**) spacers onto the wheel hub.
6. Remove the spacer block from between the brake pads.

CAUTION
On 2006-2007 models, when installing the rear wheel, carefully insert the brake disc between the brake pads in the caliper assembly. Do not force the brake disc as it can damage the leading edge of both brake pads.

7. On 2006-2007 models, move the rear brake caliper into position on the swing arm.
8. On 2008-2009 models so equipped, install the compensator bowl onto the driven sprocket, if removed.
9. Lift the rear wheel and install the rear axle from the right side. Install the axle through the swing arm, the rear brake caliper mounting bracket and the other side of the swing arm.
10. After the rear axle is installed, check to make sure both axle spacer(s), or the spacer and the ABS sensor are still in place.
11. On ABS-equipped models, rotate the ABS sensor until the index pin (A, **Figure 17**) makes contact with the caliper bracket notch (B).
12. On 2008-2009 models, install the rear caliper assembly onto the caliper mounting bracket as described in Chapter Fifteen.
13. On ABS-equipped models, secure the wheel sensor cable to the rear caliper brake hose with a tie warp.
14. Install the adjuster cam (C, **Figure 13**) and axle nut (B).
15. Check drive belt deflection and alignment as described in Chapter Three.
16. Tighten the rear axle nut as follows:
   a. On 2006-2007 models: 95-105 ft.-lb. (128.8-142.4 N•m).
   b. On 2008-2009 models: 95-105 ft.-lb. (128.8-142.4 N•m). Loosen the nut one full turn, and then re-tighten to 95-105 ft.-lb. (128.8-142.4 N•m).
17. Install a *new* E-clip (A, **Figure 13**) and make sure it is correctly seated in the axle groove.
18. Install the left side lower saddlebag support rail as described in Chapter Seventeen, on models equipped with low profile shock absorbers.
19. Install both mufflers as described in Chapter Four.
20. Rotate the wheel several times to make sure it rotates freely. Then, apply the rear brake pedal several times to seat the pads against the disc.
21. Remove the jack and lower the rear wheel to the ground.
22. Install the saddlebags as described in Chapter Seventeen.

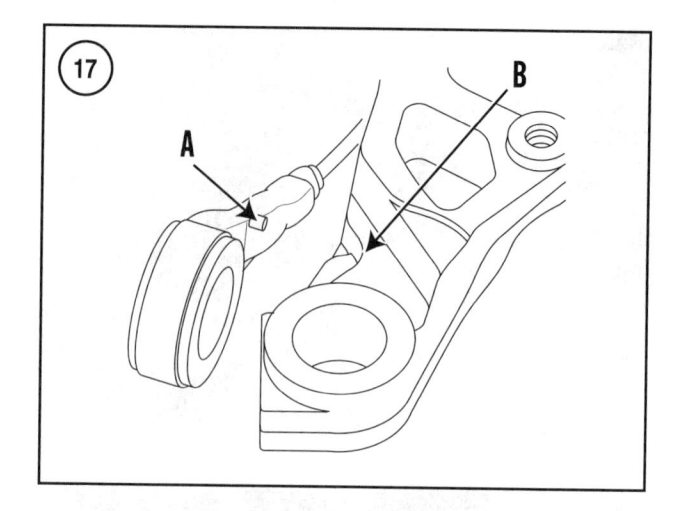

Inspection

Replace any worn or damaged parts as described in this section.

1. Turn each bearing inner race by hand. The bearing must turn smoothly. Some axial play (end play) is normal, but radial play (side play), as shown in **Figure 10**, must be negligible. If one bearing is damaged, replace both bearings as a set. Refer to *Front and Rear Hubs* in this chapter.
2. Clean the axle and axle spacers in solvent to remove all grease and dirt. Make sure the axle contact surfaces are free of dirt and old grease.
3. Check the axle runout with a set of V-blocks and a dial indicator (**Figure 11**).
4. Check the spacers for wear, burrs and damage. Replace as necessary.
5. Check the brake disc bolts (**Figure 12**) for tightness. To service the brake disc, refer to Chapter Twelve.
6. Check the driven sprocket bolts (**Figure 18**) for tightness as decribed in this chapter.
7. Check wheel runout as described in this chapter.

FRONT AND REAR HUBS

Sealed ball bearings are installed on each side of the hub. Do not remove the bearing assemblies unless they require replacement. On models with ABS, install the en-

WHEELS, HUBS AND TIRES

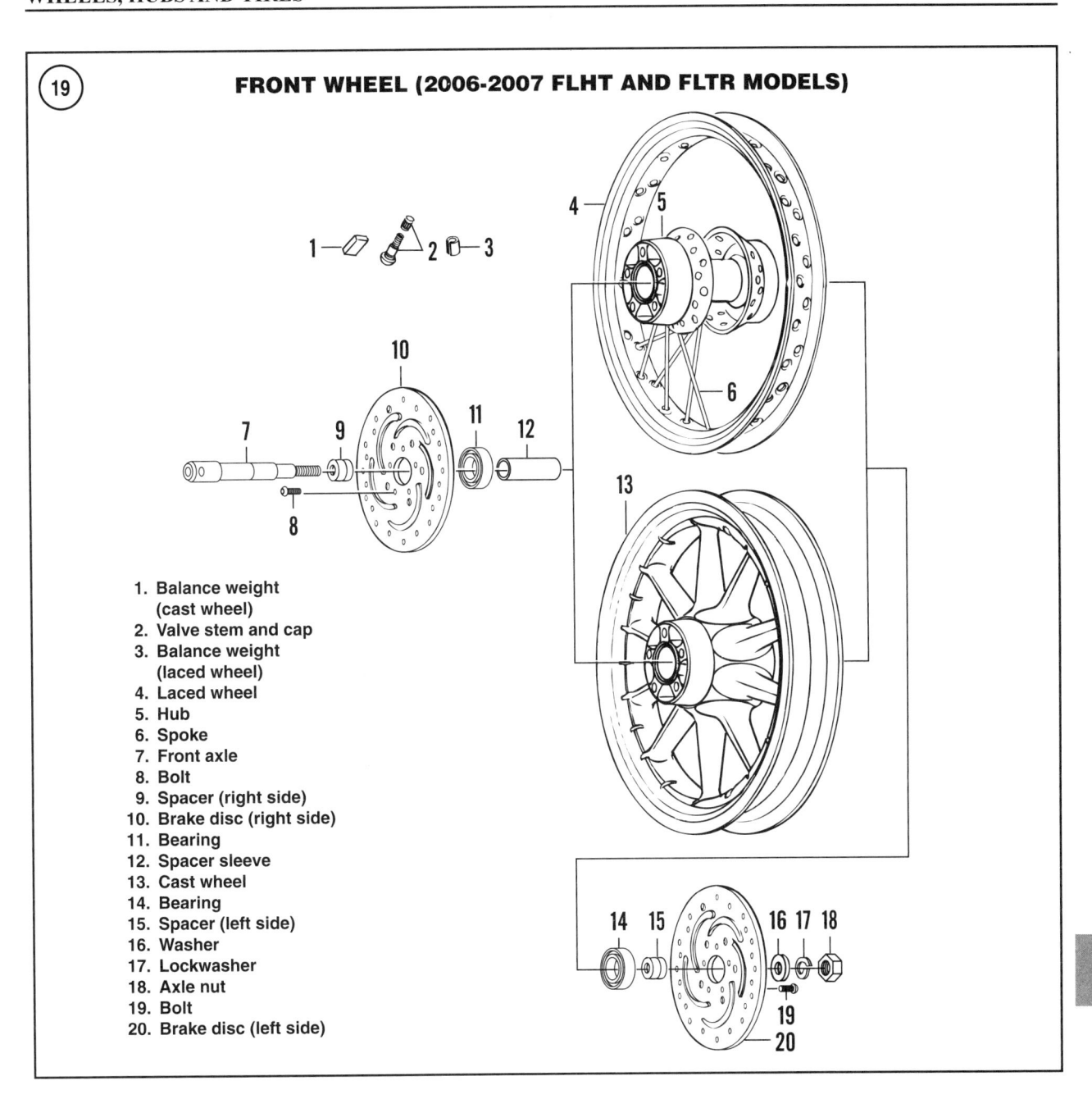

19 **FRONT WHEEL (2006-2007 FLHT AND FLTR MODELS)**

1. Balance weight (cast wheel)
2. Valve stem and cap
3. Balance weight (laced wheel)
4. Laced wheel
5. Hub
6. Spoke
7. Front axle
8. Bolt
9. Spacer (right side)
10. Brake disc (right side)
11. Bearing
12. Spacer sleeve
13. Cast wheel
14. Bearing
15. Spacer (left side)
16. Washer
17. Lockwasher
18. Axle nut
19. Bolt
20. Brake disc (left side)

coder bearing onto the correct side of the hubs. At the front wheel, install it on the left side. At the rear wheel, install the encoder bearing on the right side.

Preliminary Inspection

Inspect each wheel bearing prior to removing it from the wheel hub.

CAUTION
Do not remove the wheel bearings for inspection purposes as they will be damaged during the removal process. Remove wheel bearings only if they are to be replaced.

1. Remove the front or rear wheel as described in this chapter.

2. If still in place, remove the axle spacers from the hub.
3. If necessary, remove the bolts securing the disc, and then remove the disc as described in Chapter Fifteen.
4. Turn each bearing by hand. The bearings must turn smoothly with no roughness.
5. Inspect the play of the inner race of each wheel bearing. Check for excessive axial play and radial play (**Figure 10**). Replace the bearing if it has an excess amount of free play.

Disassembly

This procedure applies to both the front and rear wheel and hub assemblies. Where differences occur between the different hubs they are identified. Refer to **Figures 19-27** for the front wheel/hubs and **Figures 28-36** for the rear wheel/hub assemblies.

CHAPTER TWELVE

FRONT WHEEL (2006-2007 FLHX AND FLHR MODELS)

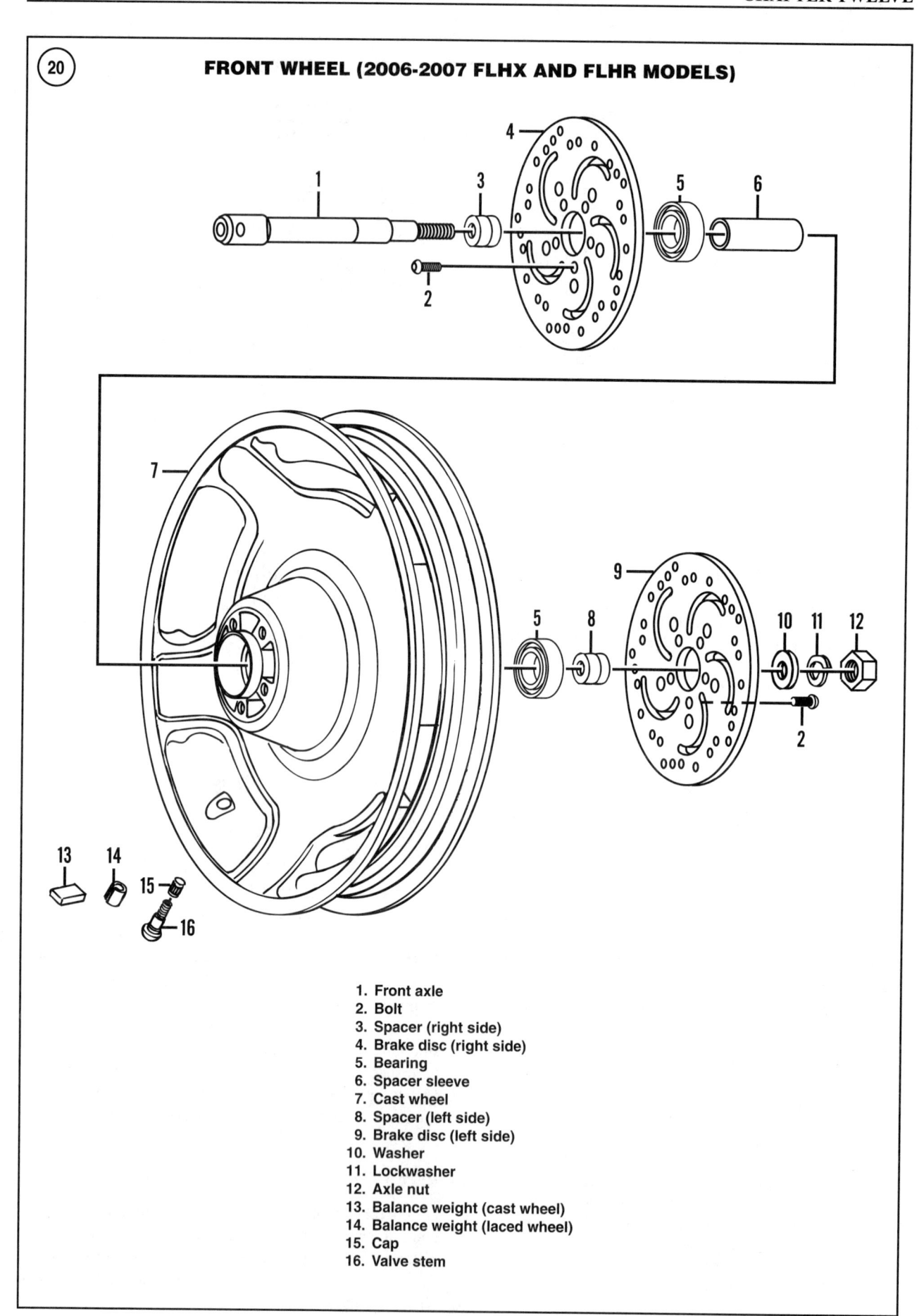

1. Front axle
2. Bolt
3. Spacer (right side)
4. Brake disc (right side)
5. Bearing
6. Spacer sleeve
7. Cast wheel
8. Spacer (left side)
9. Brake disc (left side)
10. Washer
11. Lockwasher
12. Axle nut
13. Balance weight (cast wheel)
14. Balance weight (laced wheel)
15. Cap
16. Valve stem

WHEELS, HUBS AND TIRES

551

㉑ FRONT WHEEL (ALL 2008 MODELS EXCEPT FLHX)

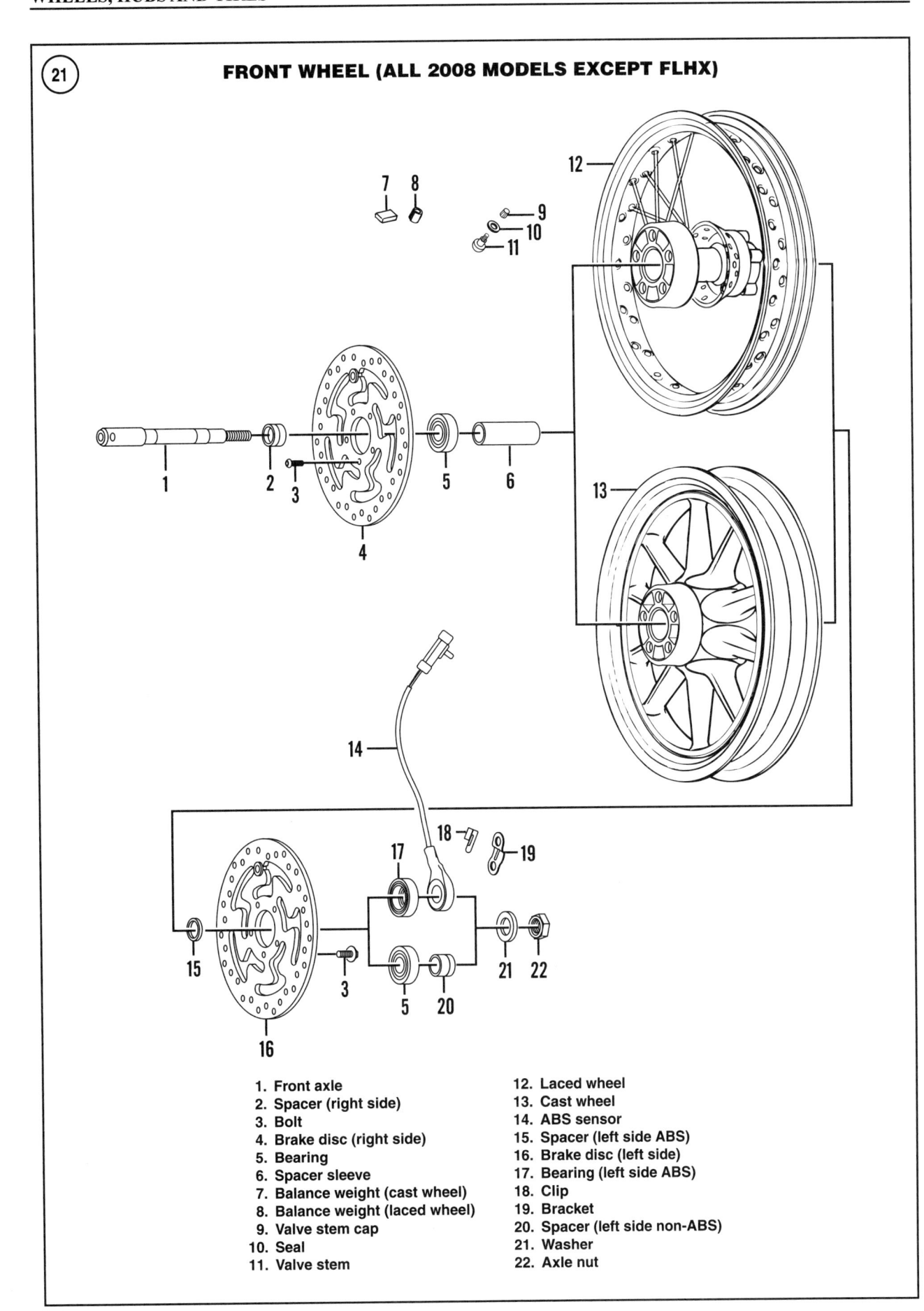

1. Front axle
2. Spacer (right side)
3. Bolt
4. Brake disc (right side)
5. Bearing
6. Spacer sleeve
7. Balance weight (cast wheel)
8. Balance weight (laced wheel)
9. Valve stem cap
10. Seal
11. Valve stem
12. Laced wheel
13. Cast wheel
14. ABS sensor
15. Spacer (left side ABS)
16. Brake disc (left side)
17. Bearing (left side ABS)
18. Clip
19. Bracket
20. Spacer (left side non-ABS)
21. Washer
22. Axle nut

12

FRONT WHEEL (2008 FLHX MODELS)

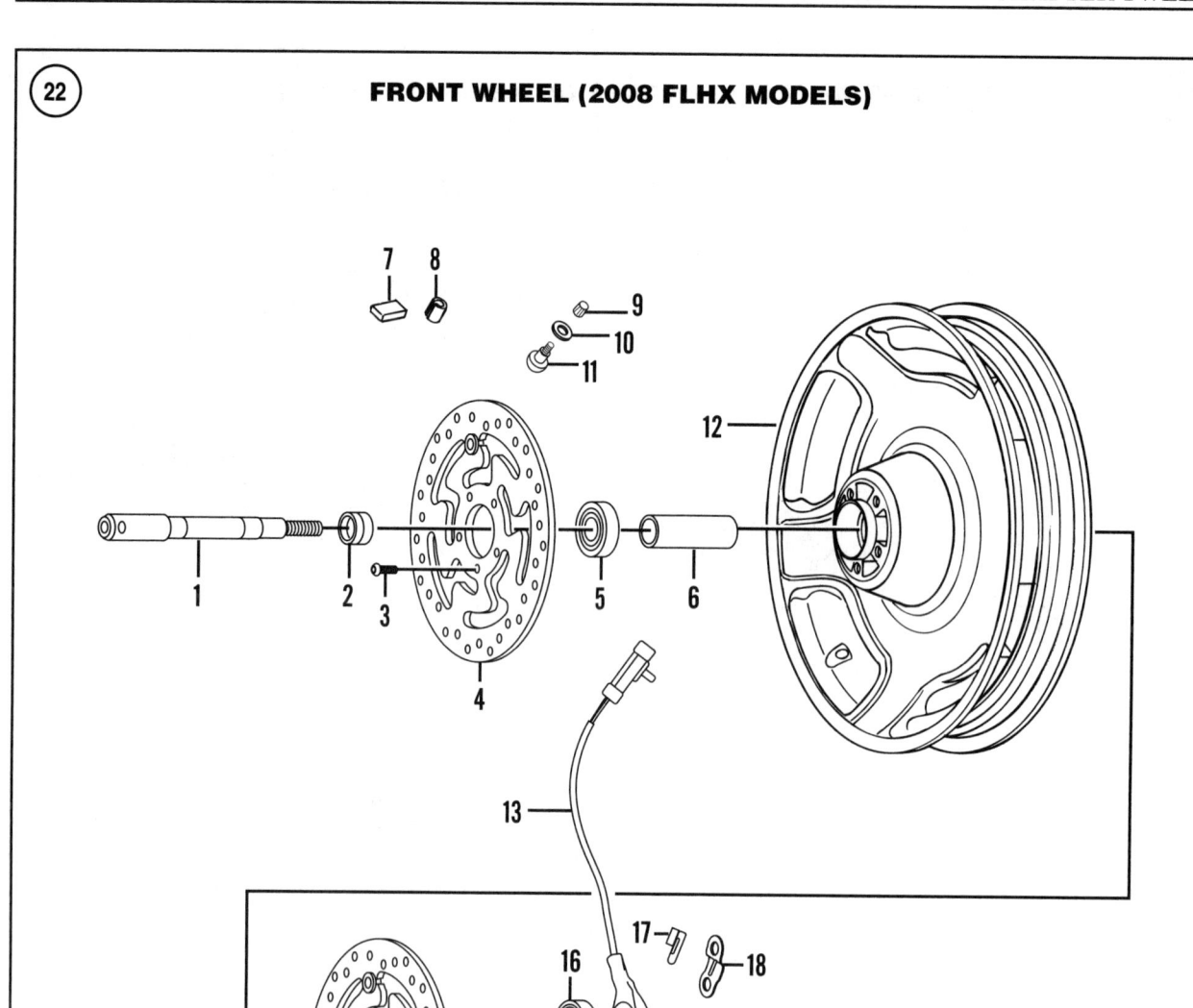

1. Front axle
2. Spacer (right side)
3. Bolt
4. Brake disc (right side)
5. Bearing
6. Spacer sleeve
7. Balance weight (cast wheel)
8. Balance weight (laced wheel)
9. Valve stem cap
10. Seal
11. Valve stem
12. Cast wheel
13. ABS sensor
14. Spacer (left side ABS)
15. Brake disc (left side)
16. Bearing (left side ABS)
17. Clip
18. Bracket
19. Spacer (left side non-ABS)
20. Washer
21. Axle nut

WHEELS, HUBS AND TIRES

㉓ FRONT WHEEL (2009 FLHT, FLHX AND FLHR MODELS)

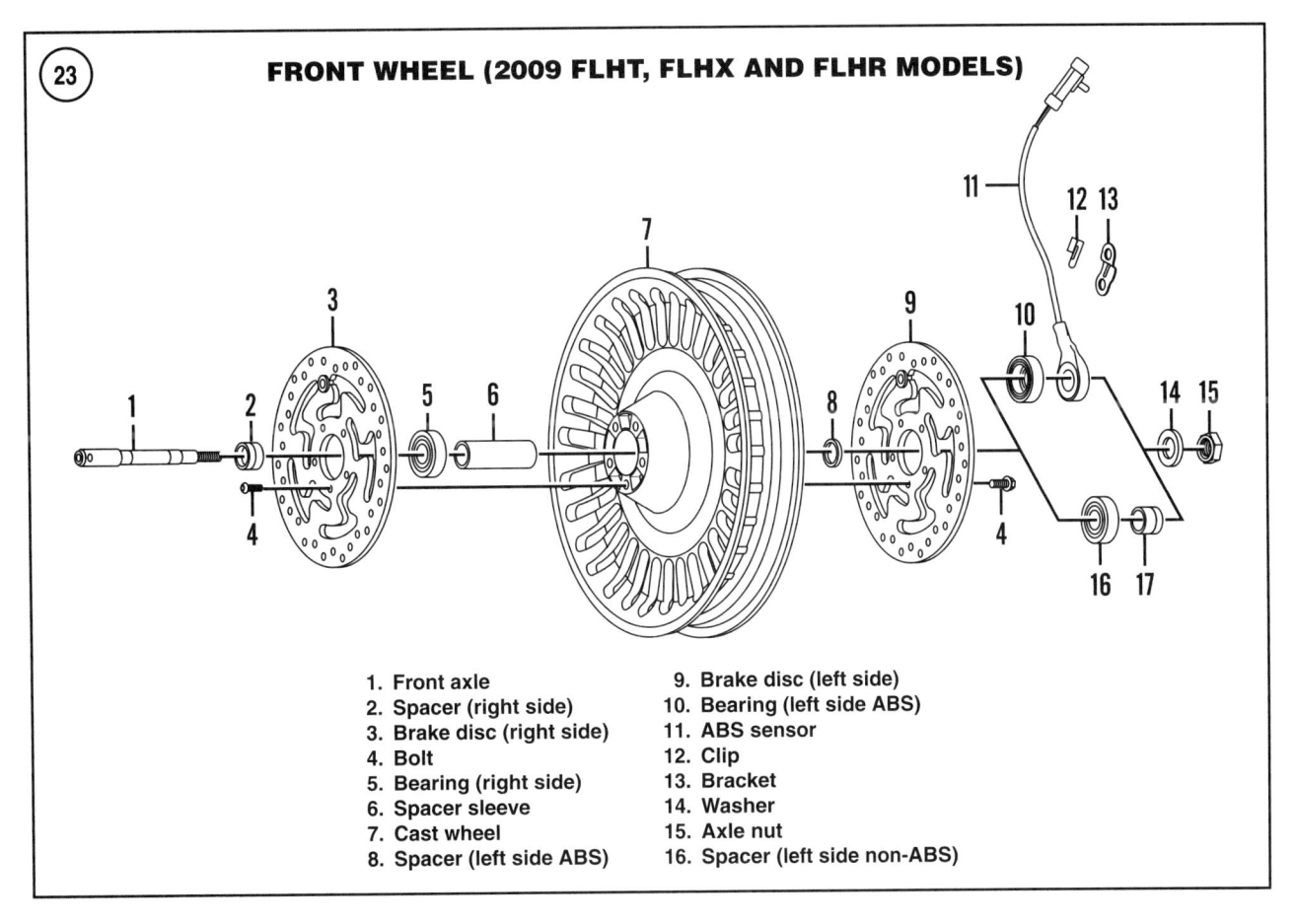

1. Front axle
2. Spacer (right side)
3. Brake disc (right side)
4. Bolt
5. Bearing (right side)
6. Spacer sleeve
7. Cast wheel
8. Spacer (left side ABS)
9. Brake disc (left side)
10. Bearing (left side ABS)
11. ABS sensor
12. Clip
13. Bracket
14. Washer
15. Axle nut
16. Spacer (left side non-ABS)

㉔ FRONT WHEEL (2006 FLHTCUSE MODELS)

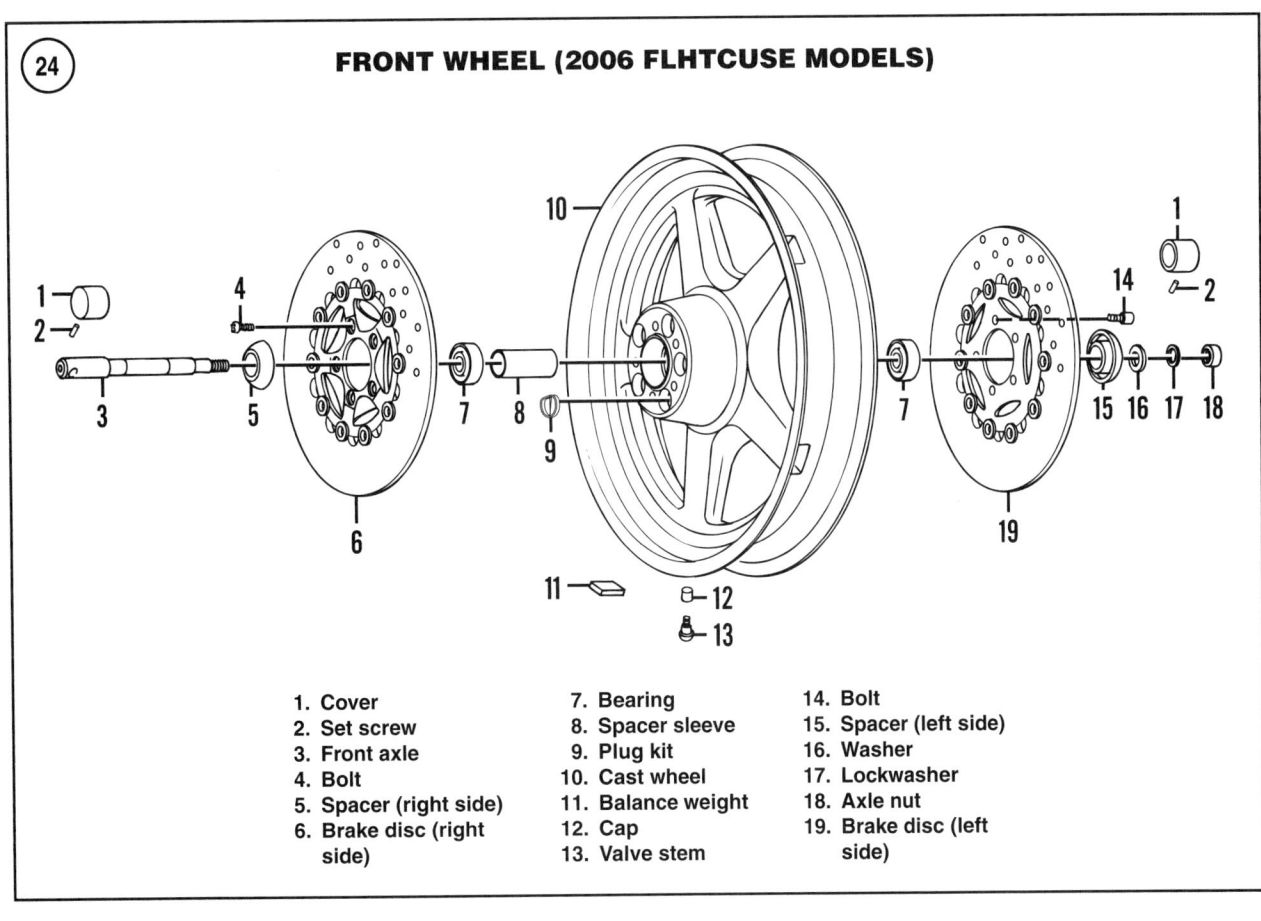

1. Cover
2. Set screw
3. Front axle
4. Bolt
5. Spacer (right side)
6. Brake disc (right side)
7. Bearing
8. Spacer sleeve
9. Plug kit
10. Cast wheel
11. Balance weight
12. Cap
13. Valve stem
14. Bolt
15. Spacer (left side)
16. Washer
17. Lockwasher
18. Axle nut
19. Brake disc (left side)

FRONT WHEEL (2007-2008 FLHTCUSE MODELS)

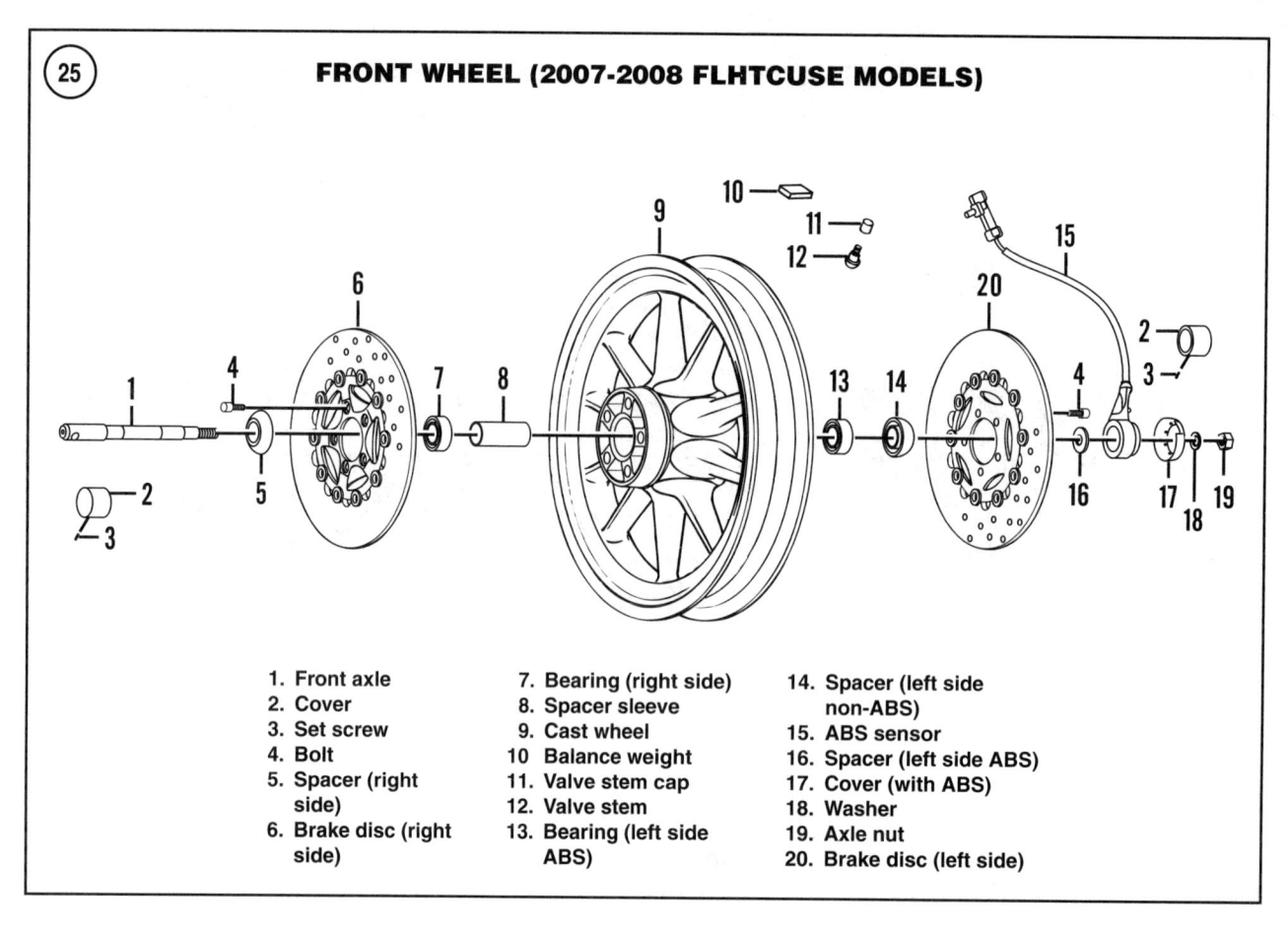

1. Front axle
2. Cover
3. Set screw
4. Bolt
5. Spacer (right side)
6. Brake disc (right side)
7. Bearing (right side)
8. Spacer sleeve
9. Cast wheel
10. Balance weight
11. Valve stem cap
12. Valve stem
13. Bearing (left side ABS)
14. Spacer (left side non-ABS)
15. ABS sensor
16. Spacer (left side ABS)
17. Cover (with ABS)
18. Washer
19. Axle nut
20. Brake disc (left side)

FRONT WHEEL (2007-2008 FLHRSE MODELS)

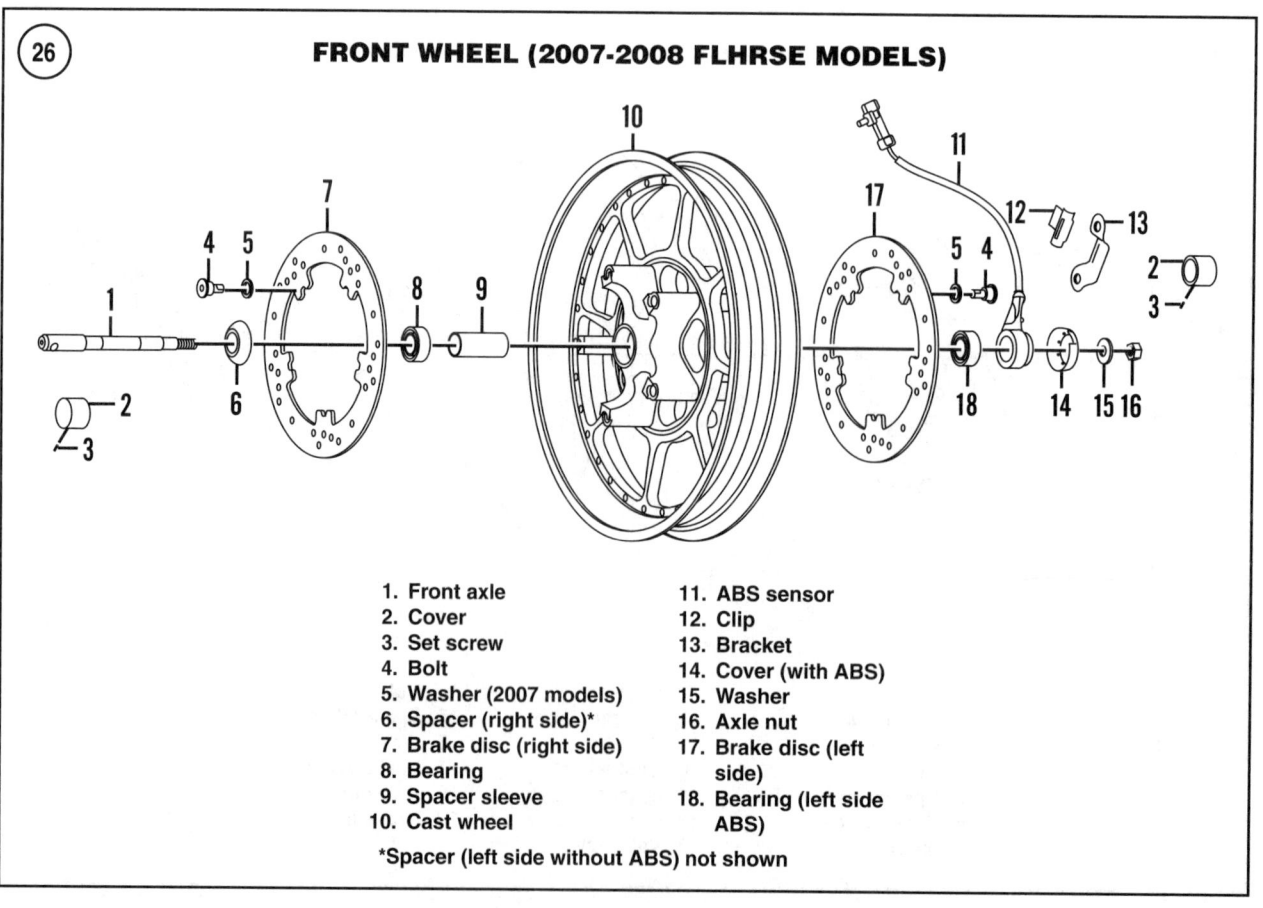

1. Front axle
2. Cover
3. Set screw
4. Bolt
5. Washer (2007 models)
6. Spacer (right side)*
7. Brake disc (right side)
8. Bearing
9. Spacer sleeve
10. Cast wheel
11. ABS sensor
12. Clip
13. Bracket
14. Cover (with ABS)
15. Washer
16. Axle nut
17. Brake disc (left side)
18. Bearing (left side ABS)

*Spacer (left side without ABS) not shown

WHEELS, HUBS AND TIRES

FRONT WHEEL (2009 FLHTCUSE MODELS)

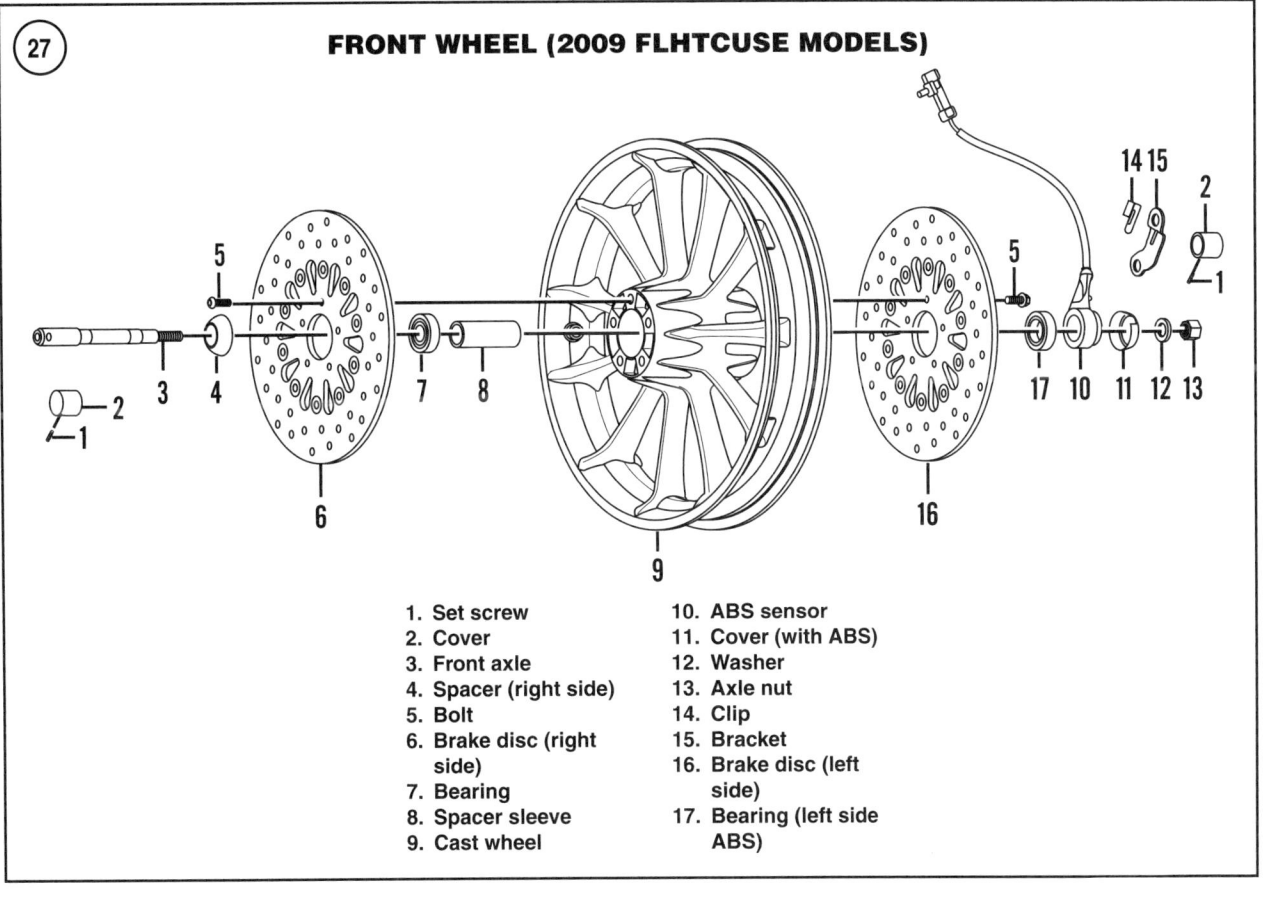

1. Set screw
2. Cover
3. Front axle
4. Spacer (right side)
5. Bolt
6. Brake disc (right side)
7. Bearing
8. Spacer sleeve
9. Cast wheel
10. ABS sensor
11. Cover (with ABS)
12. Washer
13. Axle nut
14. Clip
15. Bracket
16. Brake disc (left side)
17. Bearing (left side ABS)

REAR WHEEL (2006-2007 FLHT AND FLTR MODELS)

1. Balance weight (cast wheel)
2. Valve stem and cap
3. Balance weight (laced wheel)
4. Laced wheel
5. E-clip
6. Axle nut
7. Adjuster cam
8. Spacer (right side)
9. Brake disc
10. Screw
11. Bearing
12. Spacer sleeve
13. Driven sprocket
14. Bolt
15. Spacer (left side)
16. Cast wheel
17. Rear axle

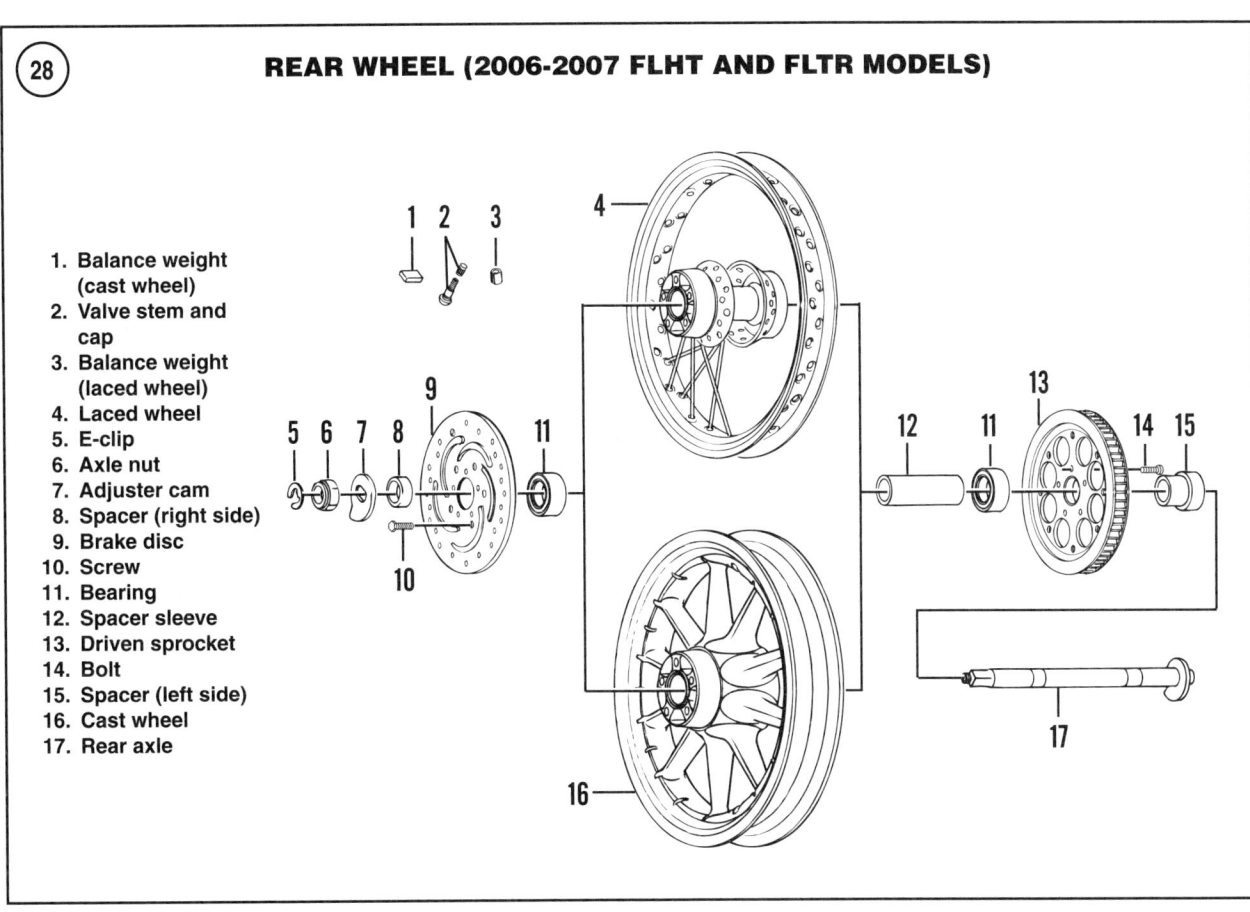

556

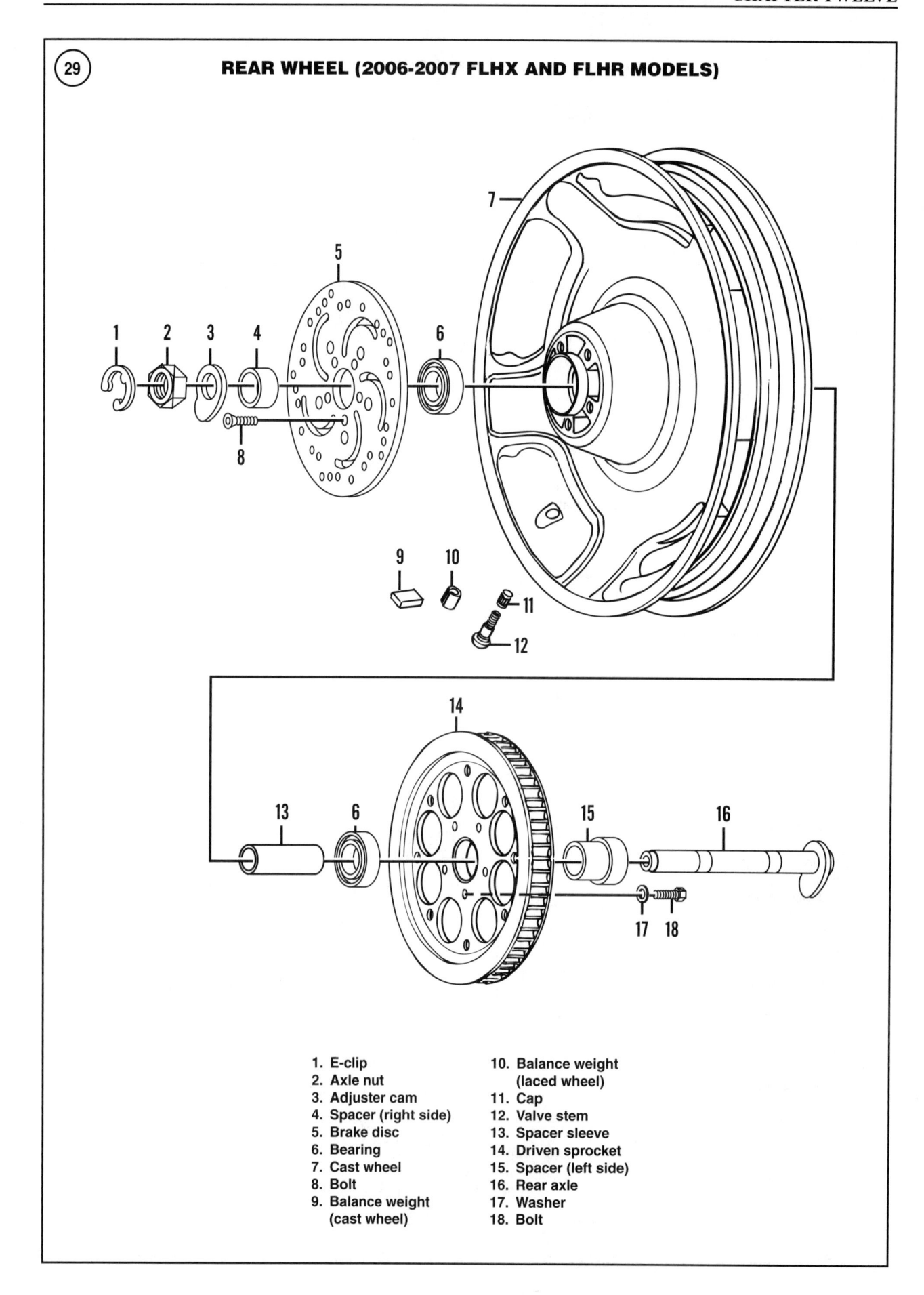

CHAPTER TWELVE

REAR WHEEL (2006-2007 FLHX AND FLHR MODELS)

1. E-clip
2. Axle nut
3. Adjuster cam
4. Spacer (right side)
5. Brake disc
6. Bearing
7. Cast wheel
8. Bolt
9. Balance weight (cast wheel)
10. Balance weight (laced wheel)
11. Cap
12. Valve stem
13. Spacer sleeve
14. Driven sprocket
15. Spacer (left side)
16. Rear axle
17. Washer
18. Bolt

WHEELS, HUBS AND TIRES

REAR WHEEL (ALL 2008 MODELS EXCEPT FLHX AND FLHTCUSE)

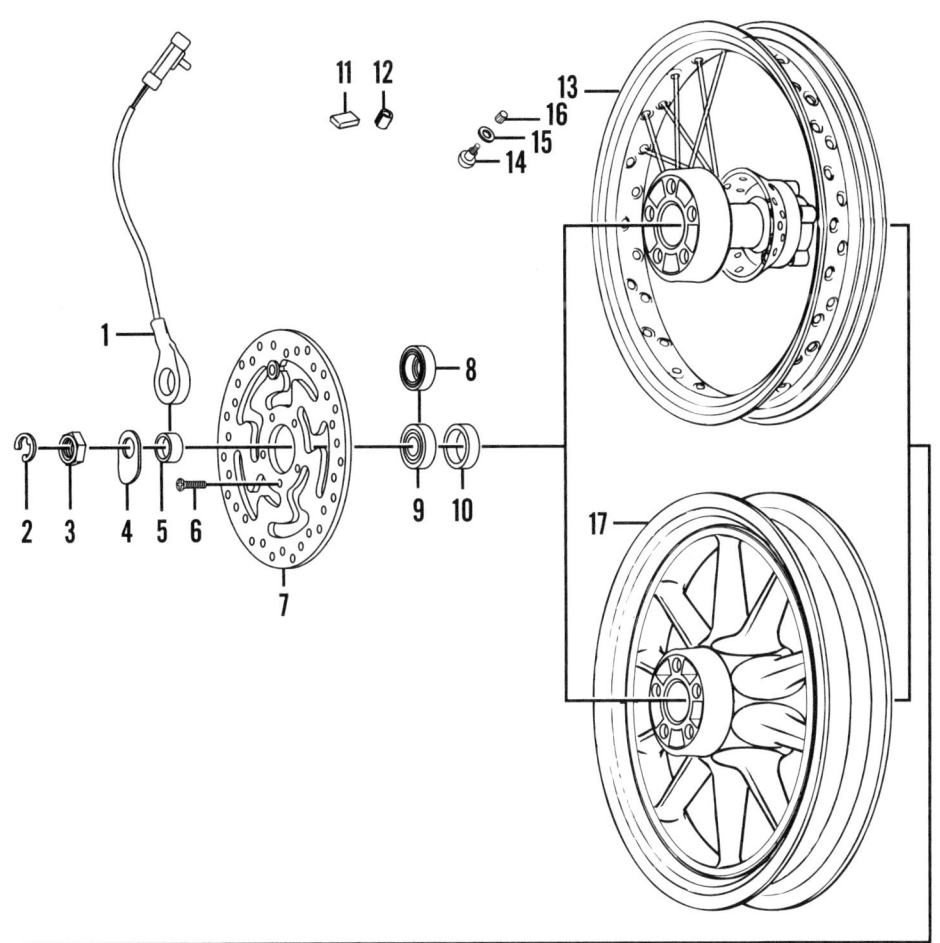

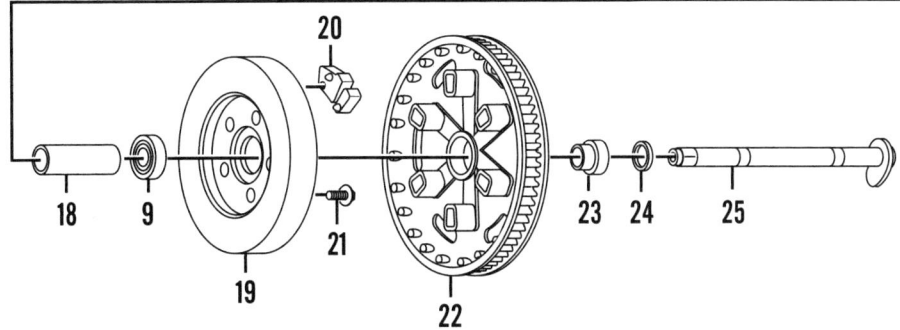

1. ABS sensor
2. E-clip
3. Axle nut
4. Adjuster cam
5. Spacer (right side non-ABS)
6. Bolt
7. Brake disc
8. Wheel bearing (ABS)
9. Wheel bearing (non-ABS)
10. Spacer (right side)
11. Balance weight (cast wheel)
12. Balance weight (laced wheel)
13. Wheel (laced)
14. Valve stem
15. Seal
16. Valve stem cap
17. Wheel (cast)
18. Spacer sleeve
19. Compensator bowl
20. Rubber isolator
21. Screw
22. Driven sprocket
23. Spacer (left side)
24. Washer
25. Rear axle

CHAPTER TWELVE

31 **REAR WHEEL (2008-2009 FLHX MODELS)**

1. ABS sensor
2. E-clip
3. Axle nut
4. Adjuster cam
5. Spacer (right side non-ABS)
6. Bolt
7. Brake disc
8. Wheel bearing (ABS)
9. Wheel bearing (non-ABS)
10. Spacer
11. Wheel (cast)
12. Balance weight (cast wheel)
13. Balance weight (laced wheel)
14. Valve stem
15. Seal
16. Valve stem cap
17. Spacer sleeve
18. Wheel bearing
19. Compensator bowl
20. Rubber isolator
21. Screw
22. Driven sprocket
23. Spacer (left side)
24. Washer
25. Rear axle

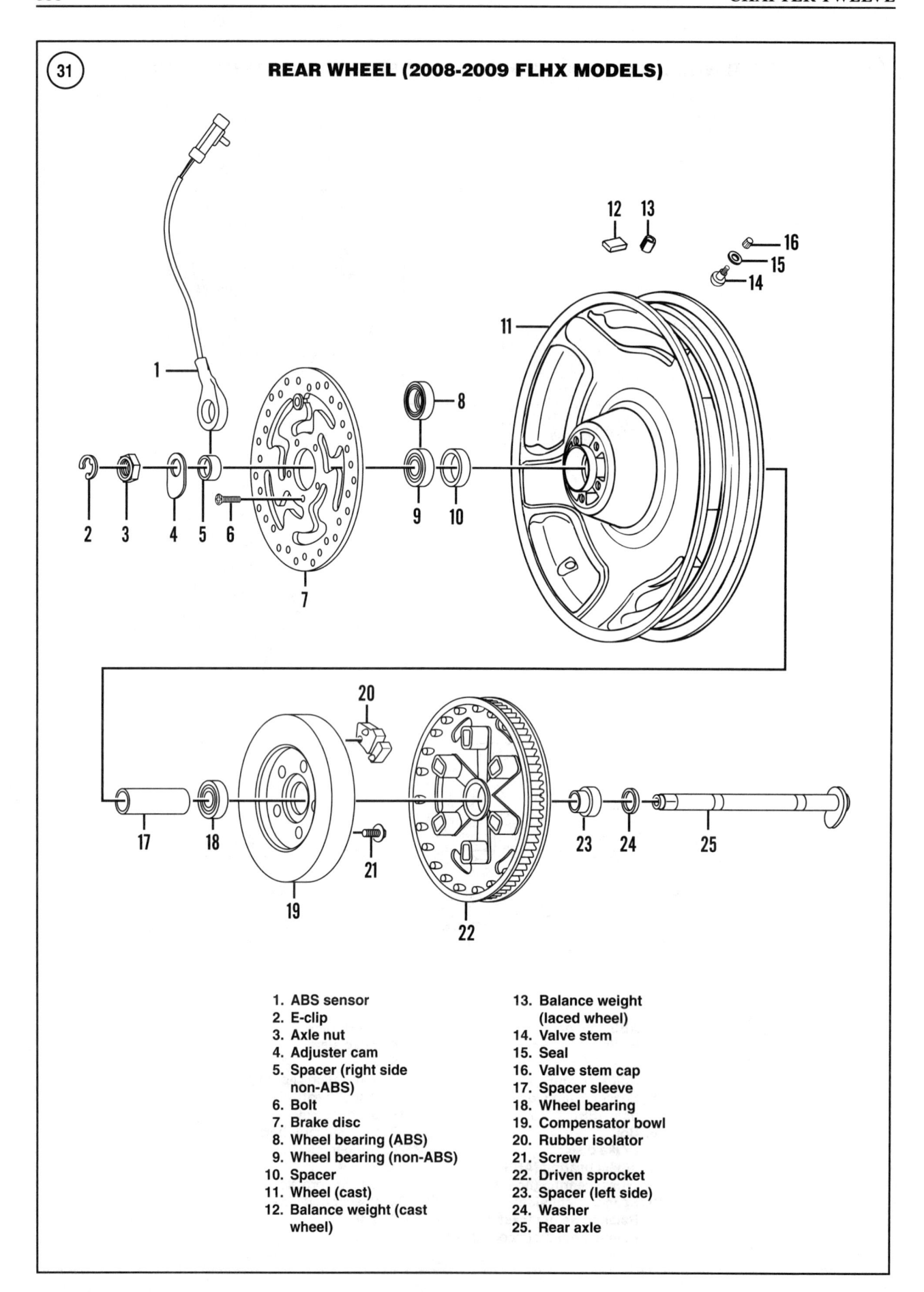

WHEELS, HUBS AND TIRES

(32) REAR WHEEL (ALL 2009 MODELS EXCEPT FLHX AND FLHTCUSE)

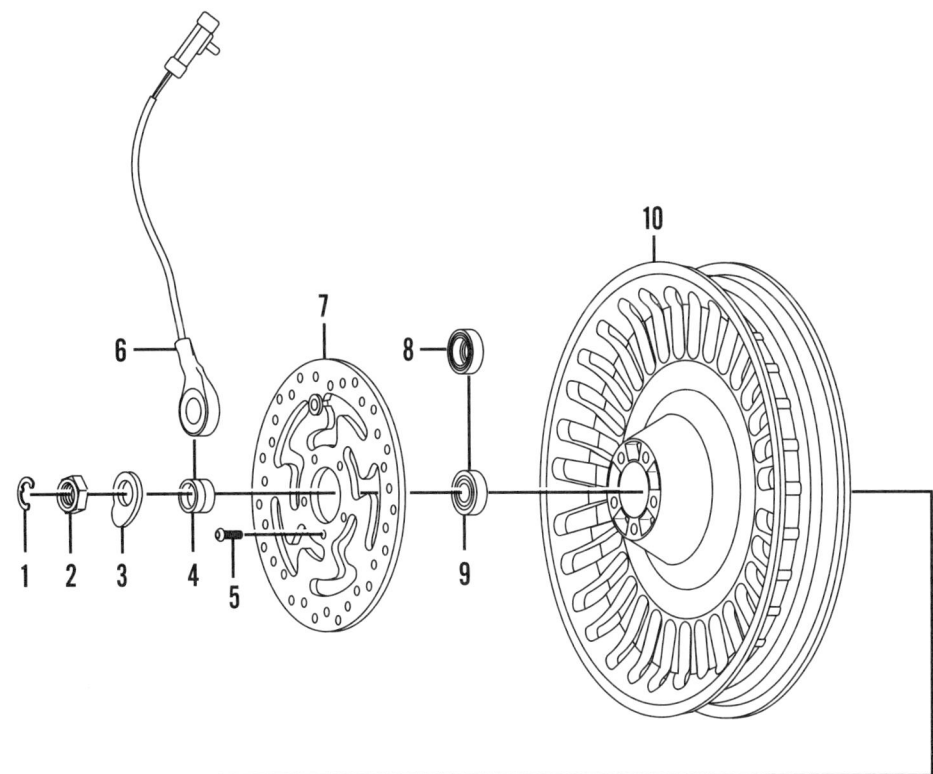

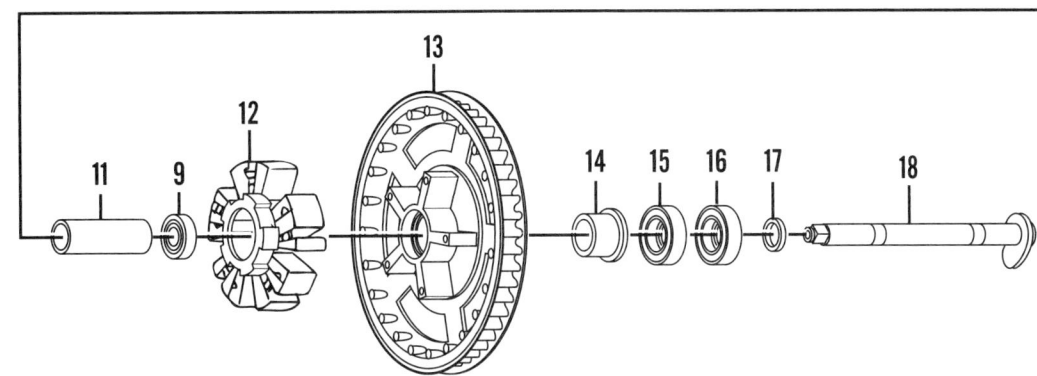

1. E-clip
2. Axle nut
3. Adjuster cam
4. Spacer (right side non-ABS)
5. Bolt
6. ABS sensor
7. Brake disc
8. Wheel bearing (ABS)
9. Wheel bearing (non-ABS)
10. Wheel (cast)
11. Spacer sleeve
12. Rubber isolator
13. Driven sprocket
14. Spacer (left side)
15. Wheel bearing
16. Wheel bearing
17. Spacer (left side)
18. Rear axle

33 REAR WHEEL (2006 FLHTCUSE MODELS)

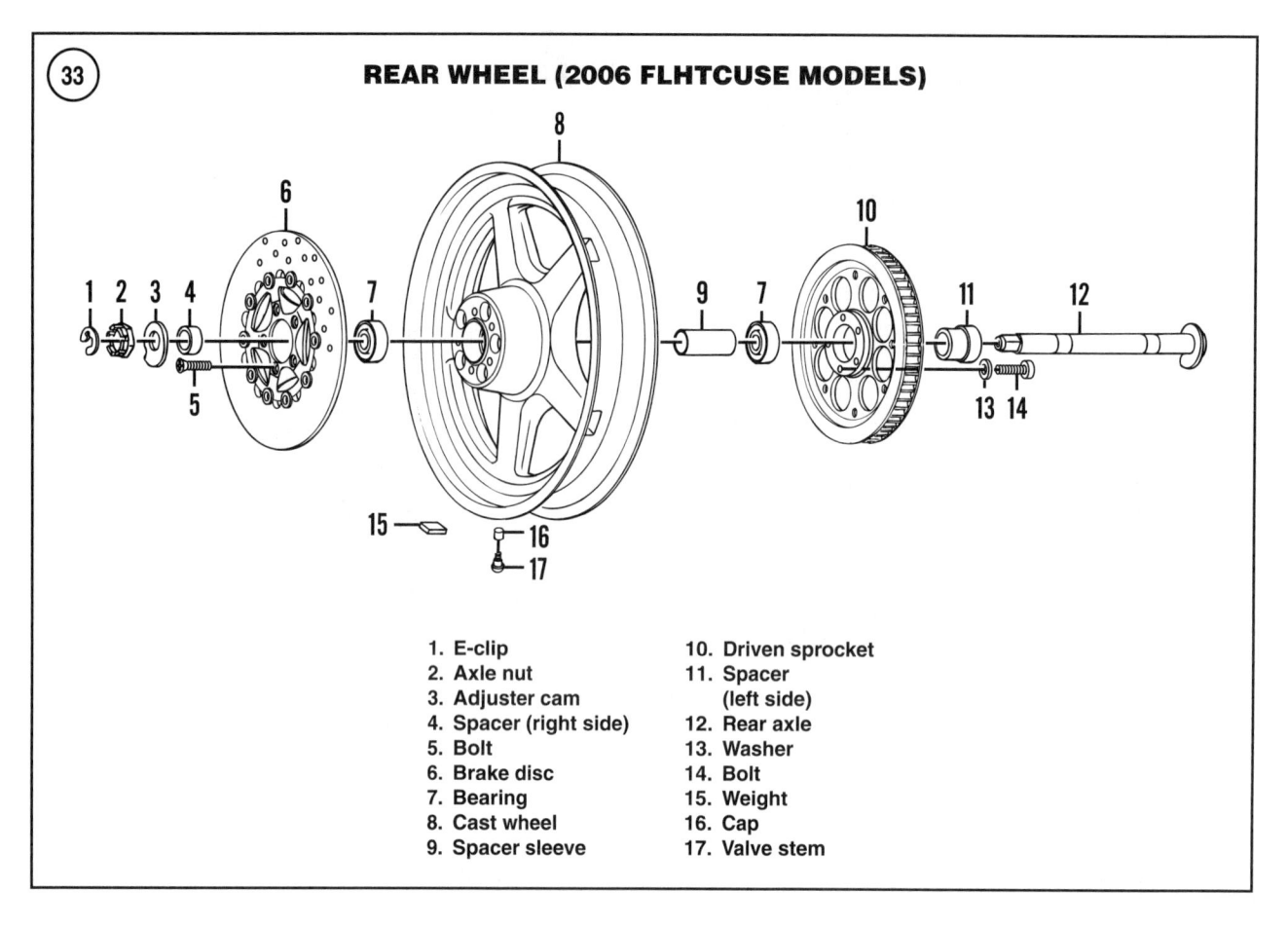

1. E-clip
2. Axle nut
3. Adjuster cam
4. Spacer (right side)
5. Bolt
6. Brake disc
7. Bearing
8. Cast wheel
9. Spacer sleeve
10. Driven sprocket
11. Spacer (left side)
12. Rear axle
13. Washer
14. Bolt
15. Weight
16. Cap
17. Valve stem

34 REAR WHEEL (2007 FLHRSE MODELS)

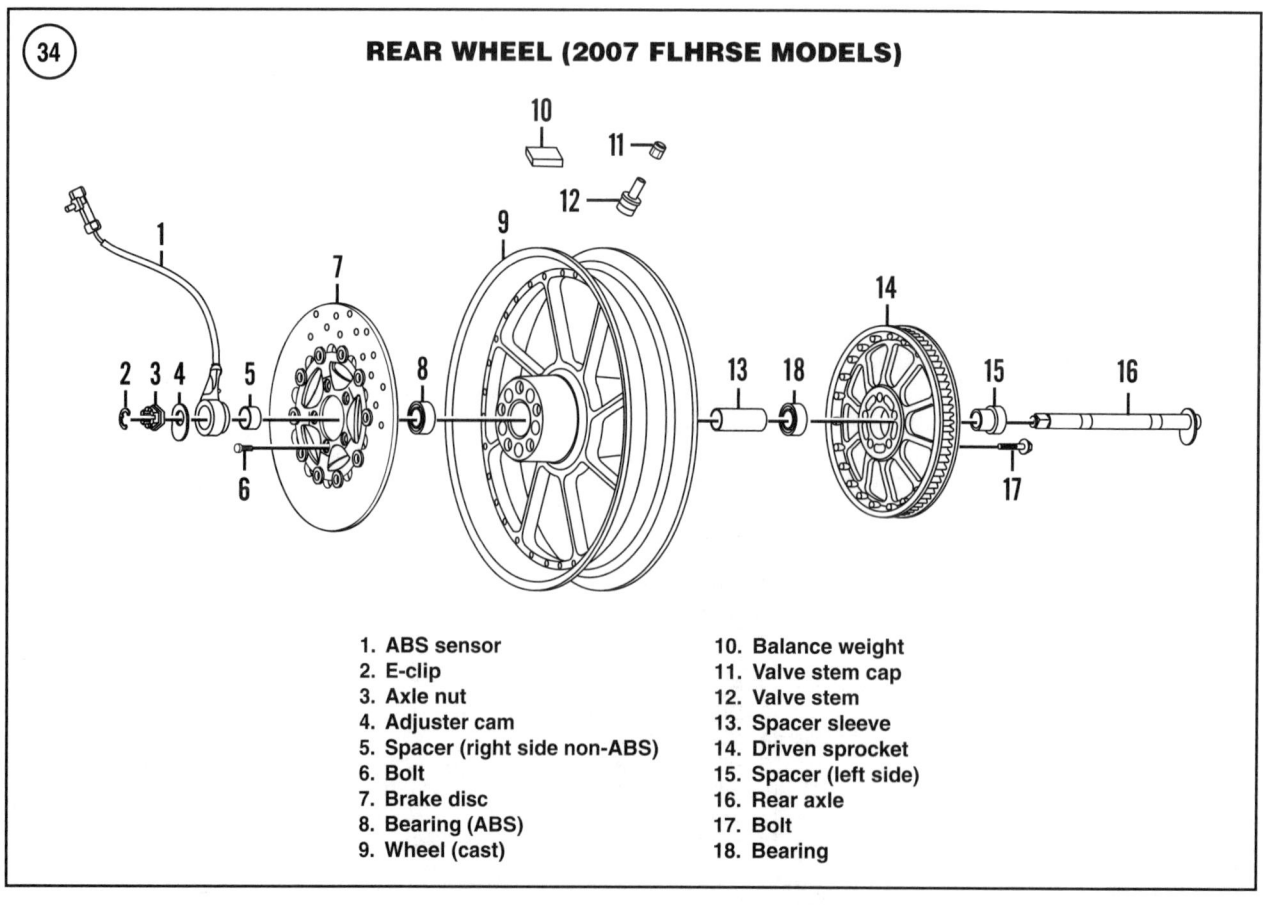

1. ABS sensor
2. E-clip
3. Axle nut
4. Adjuster cam
5. Spacer (right side non-ABS)
6. Bolt
7. Brake disc
8. Bearing (ABS)
9. Wheel (cast)
10. Balance weight
11. Valve stem cap
12. Valve stem
13. Spacer sleeve
14. Driven sprocket
15. Spacer (left side)
16. Rear axle
17. Bolt
18. Bearing

WHEELS, HUBS AND TIRES

③ REAR WHEEL (2007-2008 FLHTCUSE MODELS)

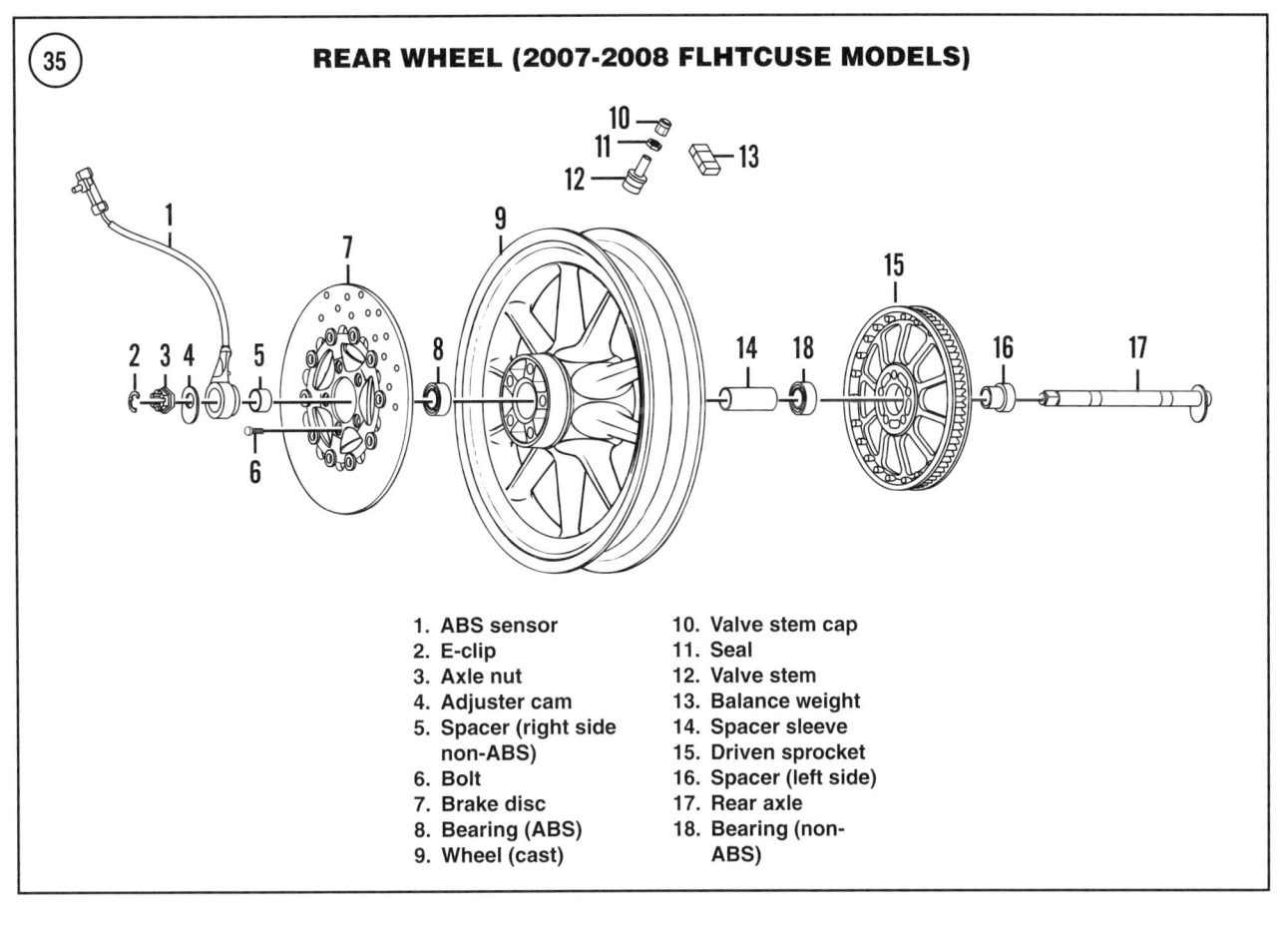

1. ABS sensor
2. E-clip
3. Axle nut
4. Adjuster cam
5. Spacer (right side non-ABS)
6. Bolt
7. Brake disc
8. Bearing (ABS)
9. Wheel (cast)
10. Valve stem cap
11. Seal
12. Valve stem
13. Balance weight
14. Spacer sleeve
15. Driven sprocket
16. Spacer (left side)
17. Rear axle
18. Bearing (non-ABS)

③ REAR WHEEL (2009 FLHTCUSE MODELS)

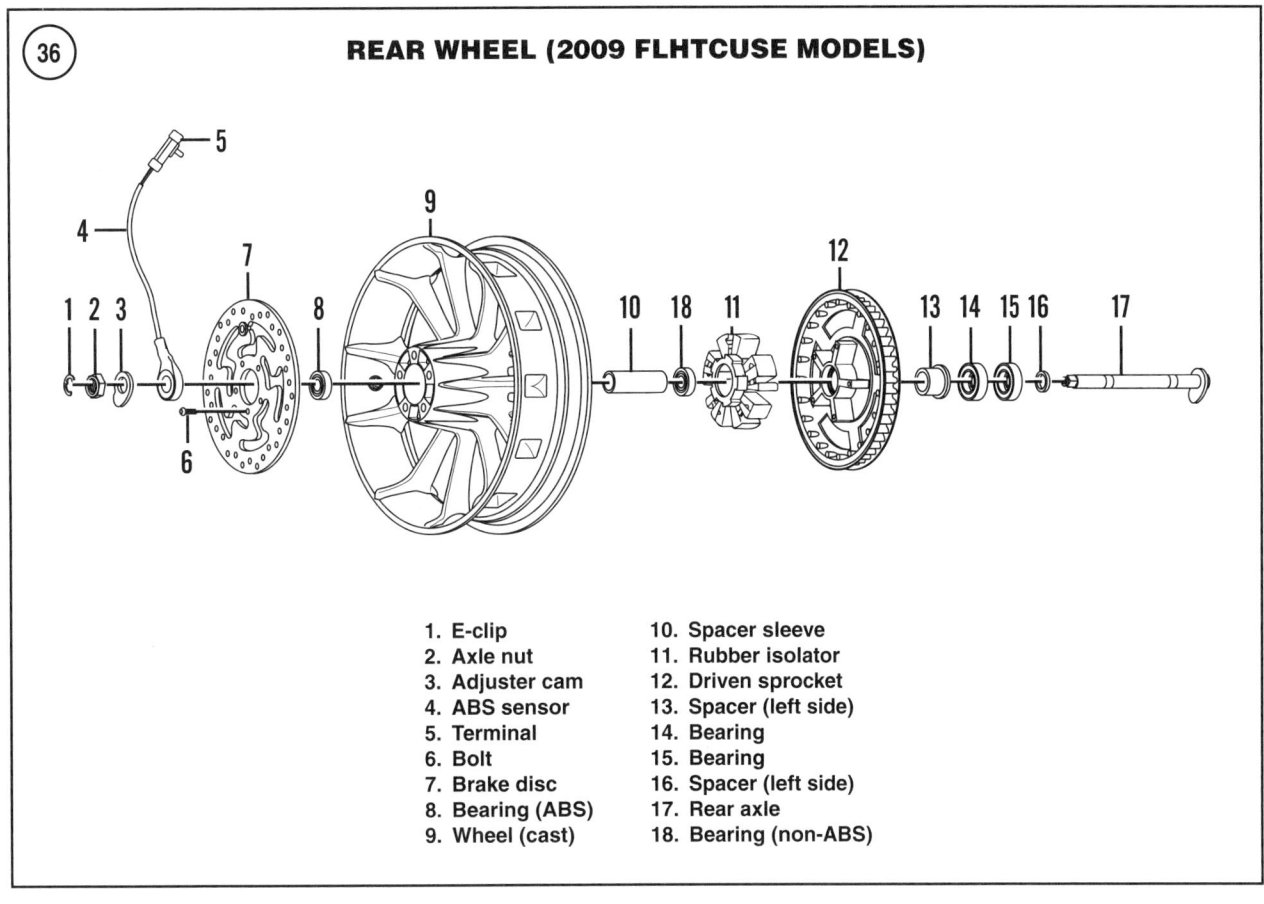

1. E-clip
2. Axle nut
3. Adjuster cam
4. ABS sensor
5. Terminal
6. Bolt
7. Brake disc
8. Bearing (ABS)
9. Wheel (cast)
10. Spacer sleeve
11. Rubber isolator
12. Driven sprocket
13. Spacer (left side)
14. Bearing
15. Bearing
16. Spacer (left side)
17. Rear axle
18. Bearing (non-ABS)

1A. Remove the front wheel as described in this chapter.
1B. Remove the rear wheel as described in this chapter.
2. If still in place, remove the axle spacer(s) from each side of the hub.
3. If necessary, remove the bolts securing the brake disc and remove the disc.
4. Before proceeding further, inspect the wheel bearings as described in this section. If they must be replaced, proceed as follows.
5A. To remove the bearings without the bearing removal set, perform the following:
   a. To remove the right- and left-hand bearings and spacer sleeve, insert a soft aluminum or brass drift into one side of the hub.
   b. Push the spacer sleeve over to one side and place the drift on the inner race of the lower bearing.
   c. Tap the bearing out of the hub with a hammer, working around the perimeter of the inner race (**Figure 37**). Remove the bearing and spacer sleeve.
   d. Repeat the process to remove the bearing on the other side.

WARNING
Be sure to wear safety glasses while using the wheel bearing remover set.

5B. To remove the bearings with a bearing removal set (Motion Pro part No. 08-0410), perform the following:
   a. Select the correct size of adapter and insert it into the bearing.
   b. Turn the wheel over and insert the remover shaft into the backside of the adapter. Tap the wedge and force it into the slit in the adapter (**Figure 38**). This will force the adapter out against the bearing inner race.
   c. Tap on the end of the wedge bar (**Figure 39**) with a hammer and drive the bearing out of the hub. Remove the bearing and the spacer sleeve.
   d. Repeat the process to remove the bearing on the other side.
6. Clean the inside and the outside of the hub with solvent. Dry with compressed air.

Assembly

CAUTION
*The removal process will generally damage the bearings. Replace the wheel bearings in pairs along with the one located within the driven sprocket drum. **Never** reinstall the bearings after they have been removed. Always install **new** bearings.*

1. Blow any debris out of the hub prior to installing the new bearings.
2. Apply a light coat of wheel bearing grease to the bearing seating areas of the hub. This will make bearing installation easier.

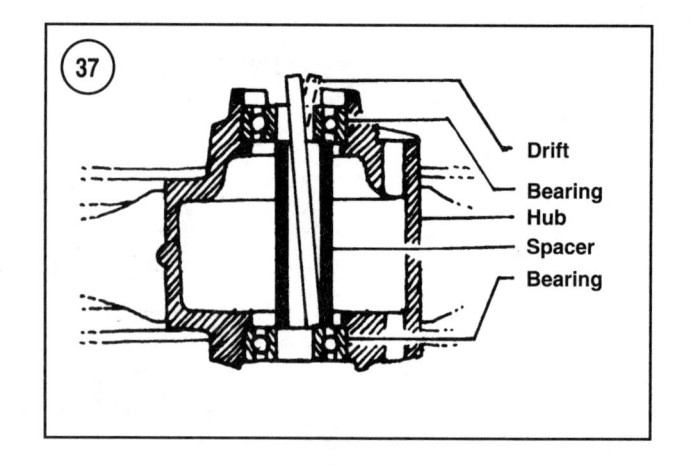

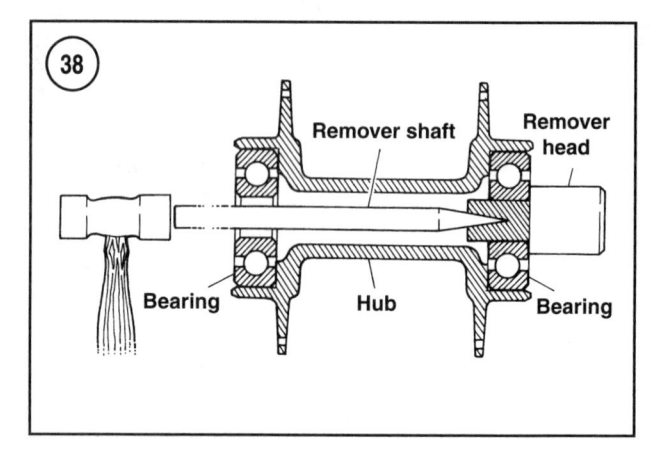

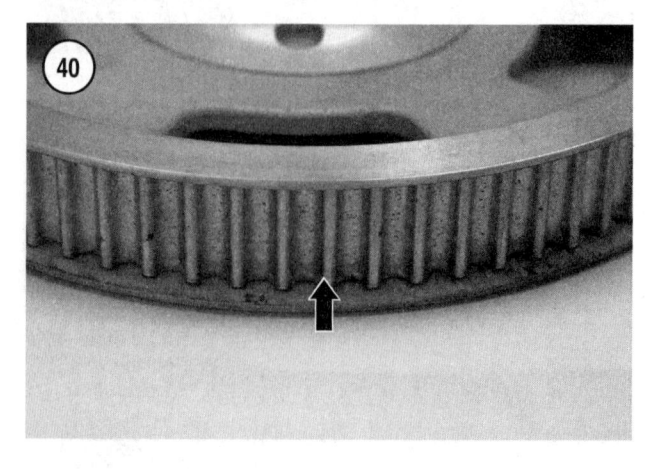

WHEELS, HUBS AND TIRES

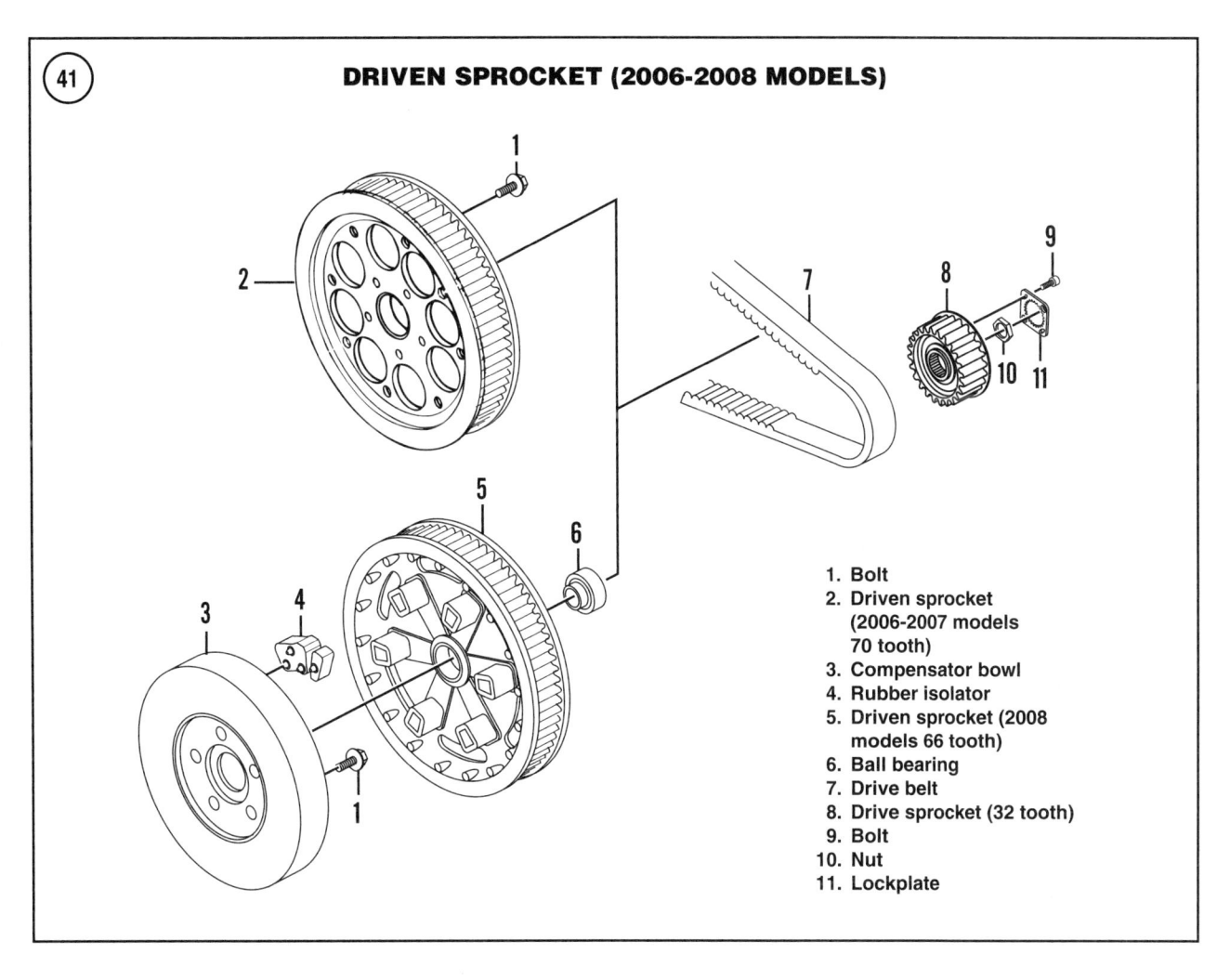

(41) DRIVEN SPROCKET (2006-2008 MODELS)

1. Bolt
2. Driven sprocket (2006-2007 models 70 tooth)
3. Compensator bowl
4. Rubber isolator
5. Driven sprocket (2008 models 66 tooth)
6. Ball bearing
7. Drive belt
8. Drive sprocket (32 tooth)
9. Bolt
10. Nut
11. Lockplate

3. Select a driver with an outside diameter slightly smaller than the bearing's outside diameter.

CAUTION
Install non-sealed bearings with the single sealed side facing outward. Do not tap on the inner race or the bearing might be damaged. Tap on the outer race only and make sure the bearings seat squarely into place. Be sure that the bearings are completely seated.

4. Position the right side bearing into place, and then tap the bearing into the hub bore until it bottoms. Be sure that the bearing is completely seated.

CAUTION
Do not set the wheel down on the brake disc surface, as it may be damaged.

5. Turn the wheel over (right side up) on the workbench and install the spacer collar.
6. Use the same tool set-up and drive in the left side bearing.
7. If the brake disc was removed, install it as described in Chapter Fifteen.
8A. Install the front wheel as described in this chapter.
8B. Install the rear wheel as described in this chapter.

DRIVEN SPROCKET ASSEMBLY

Preliminary Inspection

Inspect the sprocket teeth (**Figure 40**). If the teeth are visibly worn, replace the drive belt along with both the drive and driven sprockets.

Removal/Installation 2006-2007 Models

Refer to **Figure 41**.

1. Remove the rear wheel as described in this chapter.
2. Remove the bolts and washers securing the driven sprocket to the rear hub and remove the sprocket.
3. Install the sprocket onto the rear hub.
4. Install the sprocket bolts and washers and tighten to 55-65 ft.-lb. (74.6-88.1 N•m).
5. Install the rear wheel as described in this chapter.

Removal/Disassembly/Assembly

Refer to **Figure 41**.

DRIVEN SPROCKET (2009 MODELS)

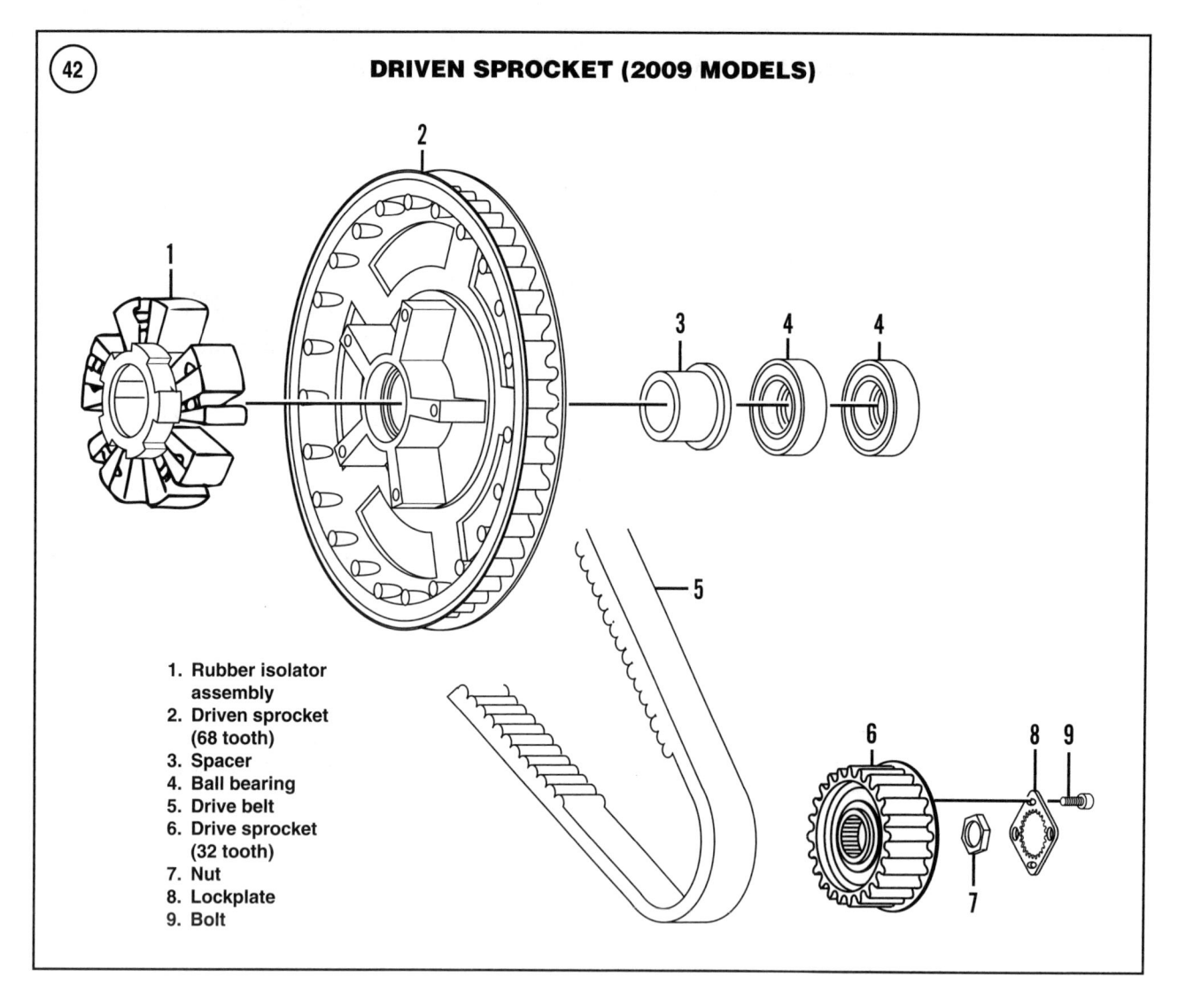

1. Rubber isolator assembly
2. Driven sprocket (68 tooth)
3. Spacer
4. Ball bearing
5. Drive belt
6. Drive sprocket (32 tooth)
7. Nut
8. Lockplate
9. Bolt

2008 models

1. Remove the rear wheel as described in this chapter.
2. Pull straight up and remove the driven sprocket from the rear hub and the compensator bowl. If the driven sprocket is difficult to remove from the hub, tap on the backside of the sprocket (from the opposite side of the wheel through the wheel spokes) with the wooden handle of a hammer.
3. Pull the individual rubber isolators straight up and out of the compensator bowl.
4. Remove the five hex bolts and captive washers, securing the compensator bowl to the rear hub, if necessary.
5. Inspect the components as described in this section.
6. If the compensating bowl was removed, perform the following:
   a. Position the compensator bowl with the concave side facing up.
   b. Align the bolt holes and install the five bolts and captive washers. Using a crossing pattern, tighten the bolts to 55-65 ft.-lb. (74.6-88.1 N•m).
7. Lubricate each rubber isolator with a 50:50 mixture of isopropyl alcohol and water. Lubricate their contact area within the compensator bowl.

8. Align the rubber isolators with the raised ribs in the compensator bowl, and install all five isolators. Push the isolators down until they bottom and the strap engages in each rib. Make sure that each one is flush against the ribs side walls.
9. Align the driven sprocket bosses with the grooves of the compensator bowl isolators and install the driven sprocket.
10. Push down evenly around the driven sprocket perimeter and press it down until it bottoms against the rear hub.
11. Install the rear wheel as described in this chapter.

Removal/Assembly

Refer to **Figure 42**.

2009 models

1. Remove the rear wheel as described in this chapter.
2. Pull straight up and remove the driven sprocket from the rear hub and the compensator bowl. If the driven sprocket is difficult to remove from the hub, tap on the backside of

WHEELS, HUBS AND TIRES

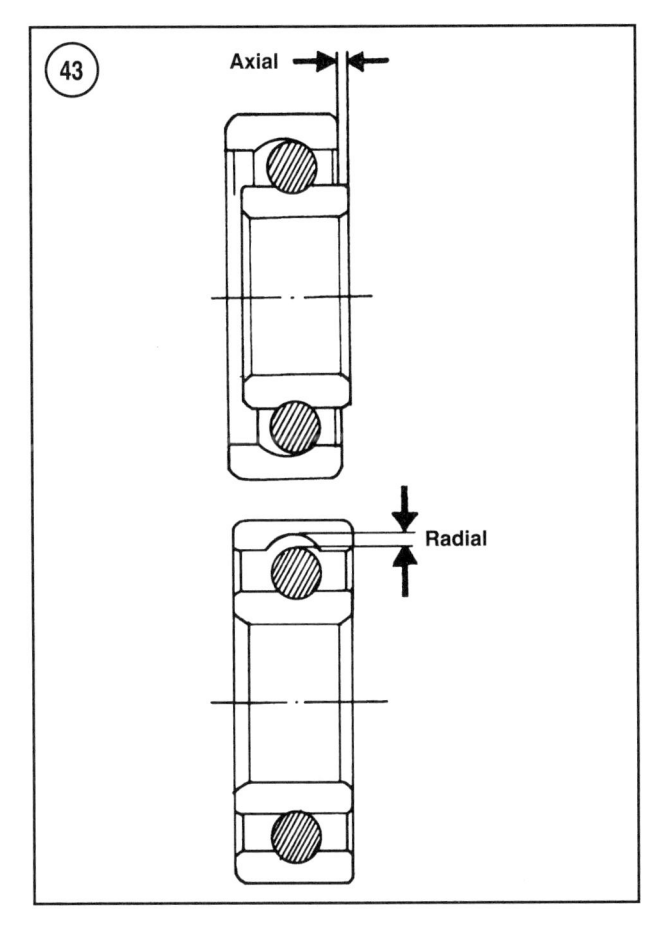

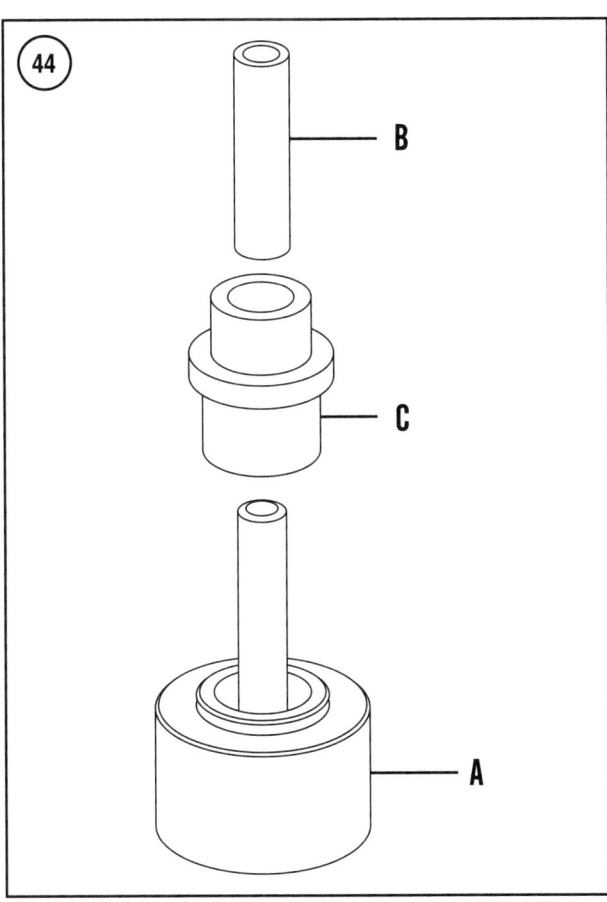

the sprocket (from the opposite side of the wheel through the wheel spokes) with the wooden handle of a hammer.

3. Pull the rubber isolator assembly straight up and out of the compensator bowl on the rear hub.
4. Inspect the components as described in this section.
5. Lubricate the rubber isolator assembly with a 50:50 mixture of isopropyl alcohol and water. Lubricate their contact area within the compensator bowl.
6. Align the rubber isolator assembly with the raised ribs in the wheel hub, and install the assembly. Push the isolator assembly down until it bottoms and the strap engages in each rib. Make sure it is flush against the ribs side walls.
7. Align the driven sprocket bosses with the grooves of the compensator isolators and install the driven sprocket.
8. Push down evenly around the driven sprocket perimeter and press it down until it bottoms against the rear hub.

Inspection (All Years)

1. On 2008-2009 models, inspect the rubber isolators, or rubber isolator assembly, for signs of cracking or deterioration. On 2008-2009 models, replace all isolators even if only one is damaged.
2. On 2008-2009 models, inspect the raised webs in the driven sprocket. Check for cracks or wear. If any damage is visible, replace the driven sprocket.
3. Inspect the driven sprocket for cracks or damage; replace it if necessary.
4. Inspect the driven sprocket teeth (**Figure 40**). If the teeth are visibly worn, replace the drive and driven sprockets and drive belt as a set.

NOTE
The bearing on the 2008-2009 models has a split race and cannot be rotated by hand to determine if it is bad. Even a good bearing will feel rough when spun by hand.

5. On 2006-2007 models, turn driven sprocket bearings inner race by hand. The bearing must turn smoothly with no roughness. Some axial play (side to side) is normal, but radial play (up and down), as shown in **Figure 43**, must be negligible.

CAUTION
The bearing outer seal is very important as the hubs are not equipped with oil seals.

6. Carefully check the bearing outer seal for buckling or other damage that would allow dirt to enter the bearing.

Bearing Replacement (2008-2009 Models)

Remove and install the bearing with the rear wheel compensator bearing remover/installer (H-D part No. HD-48921) tool set (**Figure 44**), or an equivalent, and a hydraulic press.

1. Remove the driven sprocket as described in this section.
2. Remove the isolators or isolator assembly from the driven sprocket, as described in this section.
3. Position the tool base (A, **Figure 44**) on the hydraulic press bed supports with the long portion of the pin facing down.
4. Install the sleeve (B, **Figure 44**) onto the short portion of the pin (C).
5. Position the inboard side of the sprocket facing up and slide the sprocket over the sleeve (B, **Figure 44**) until it rests on the tool base (A).
6. Slide the small outer diameter of the driver (C, **Figure 44**) over the sleeve (B) until it contacts the spacer within the hub.
7. Center the driven sprocket and driver (C, **Figure 44**) directly under the press ram.
8. Slowly apply ram pressure and drive the bearings and spacer out of the hub of the driven sprocket.
9. Remove the driven sprocket and tools from the press bed. Discard the bearings.
10. Thoroughly clean the driven sprocket bearing bore and check it for nicks or gouges. Thoroughly dry the bearing bore.
11. Position the tool base (A, **Figure 44**) on the hydraulic press bed supports with the long portion of the pin facing down.
12. Install the sleeve (B, **Figure 44**) onto the short portion of the pin (C).
13. Position the outboard side of the sprocket facing up and slide the sprocket over the sleeve (B, **Figure 44**) until it rests on the tool base (A).
14. Position the *new* bearing with the sealed side facing up and center it in the bearing bore.
15. Center the driver (C, **Figure 44**) with the large outer diameter on the bearing. Make sure it contacts the outer race around the entire perimeter.
16. Center the driven sprocket and driver (C, **Figure 44**) directly under the press ram.
17. Slowly apply ram pressure and drive the bearing into the hub until the driver makes contact with the driven sprocket hub. Relieve ram pressure.
18. Repeat the procdure and install the remaining *new* bearing.
19. Install the isolators or isolator assembly, as described in this section.
20. Install the driven sprocket as described in this section.

DRIVE SPROCKET

The drive sprocket is covered in *Transmission Drive Sprocket* (Chapter Seven or Chapter Eight).

DRIVE BELT

CAUTION
When handling a new or used drive belt, never wrap the belt in a loop that is smaller than 5 in. (130 mm) in diameter, or bend it sharply in any direction. This will weaken or break the belt fibers and cause premature belt failure.

Removal/Installation

1. Remove the rear wheel as described in this chapter.
2. Remove the swing arm as described in Chapter Fourteen.
3. Remove the compensating sprocket, clutch shell and chain tensioner as described in Chapter Six.
4. Remove the primary chaincase housing as described in Chapter Six.

NOTE
If the existing drive belt is going to be reinstalled, it must be installed so it travels in the same direction. Before removing the belt, draw an arrow on the top surface of the belt facing forward.

5. Remove the drive belt (**Figure 45**) from the drive sprocket.
6. Installation is the reverse of removal. Adjust the drive belt deflection as described in Chapter Three.

WHEELS, HUBS AND TIRES

DRIVE BELT INSPECTION (47)

1. Internal tooth cracks
2. Missing teeth
3. Fuzzy edge core
4. Stone damage
5. External tooth cracks
6. Chipping
7. Hook wear

Inspection

Do not apply any type of lubricant to the drive belt. Inspect the drive belt and teeth (**Figure 46**) for severe wear, damage or oil contamination.

Refer to **Figure 47** for various types of drive belt wear or damage. Replace the drive belt if worn or damaged.

LACED WHEEL SERVICE

The laced or wire wheel assembly consists of a rim, spokes, nipples and hub (containing the wheel bearings, spacer sleeve and seals).

Loose or improperly tightened spokes can cause hub damage. Periodically inspect the wheel assembly for loose, broken or missing spokes, rim damage and runout. Wheel bearing service is described in this chapter.

Component Condition

Wheels are subjected to a significant amount of punishment. Inspect the wheels regularly for lateral (side-to-side) and radial (up and down) runout, even spoke tension, and visible damage. When a wheel has a noticeable wobble, it is out of true. Loose spokes usually cause this, but it can be caused by impact damage.

Truing a wheel corrects the radial and lateral runout to bring the wheel back into specification. The condition of the individual wheel components will affect the ability to successfully true the wheel. Note the following:

1. Do not attempt to true a wheel with bent or damaged spokes. Doing so places an excessive amount of tension on the spoke and rim. The spoke may break and/or pull through the hole in the rim. Inspect spokes carefully and replace any that are damaged.
2. When truing a wheel, the nipple should turn freely on the spoke. It is common for the spoke threads to become corroded and make turning the nipple difficult. Spray a penetrating liquid onto the nipple and allow sufficient time for it to penetrate. Use a spoke wrench and work the nipple in both directions and apply additional penetrating liquid. If the spoke wrench rounds off the nipple, remove the tire from the rim and cut the spoke(s) out of the wheel.
3. Minor rim damage can be corrected by truing; however, trying to correct excessive runout caused by impact damage will damage the hub and rim due to over-tightened spokes. Inspect the rims for cracks, flat spots or dents. Check the spoke holes for cracks or enlargement.

Wheel Truing Preliminaries

Before checking runout and truing the wheel, note the following:

1. Make sure the wheel bearings are in good condition.
2. A small amount of runout is acceptable, do not attempt to true the wheel to a perfect zero reading. Refer to **Table 2** for runout specifications.

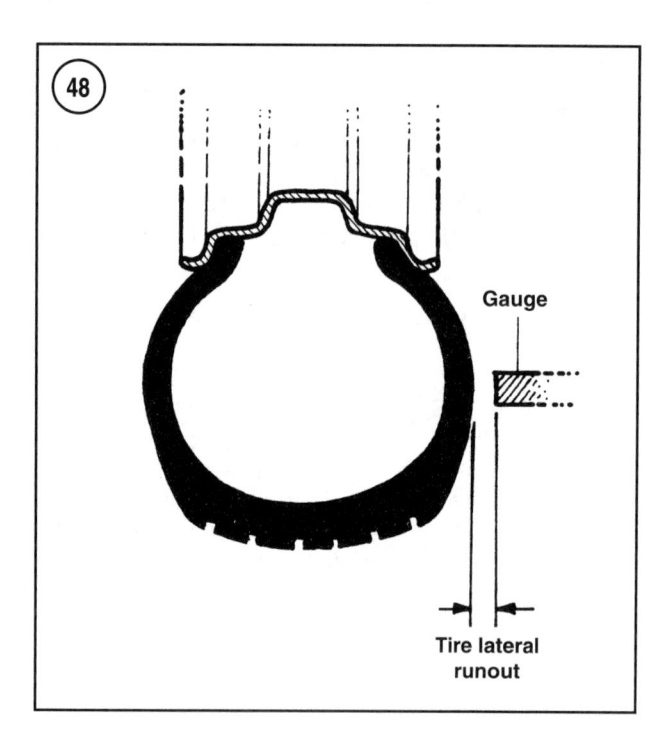

48

Gauge

Tire lateral runout

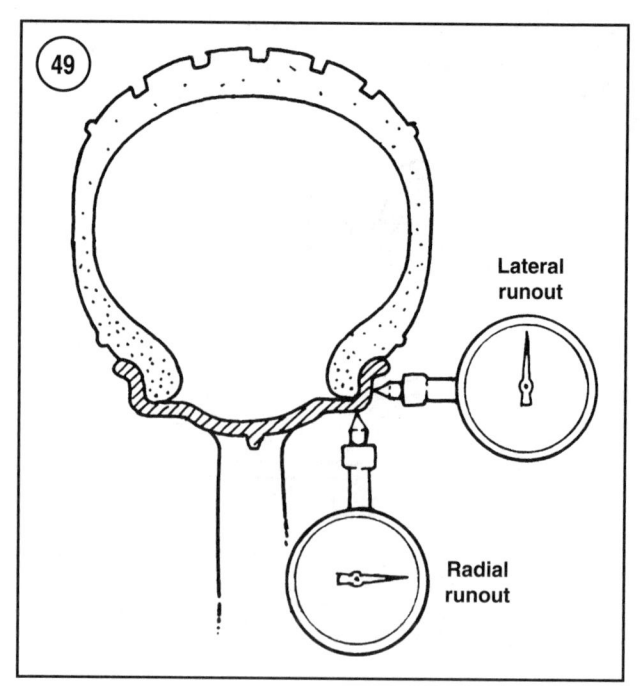

49

Lateral runout

Radial runout

50

Pointer

Lateral runout

Radial runout

3. Perform a quick runout check with the wheel on the motorcycle by placing a pointer against the fork or swing arm and slowly rotating the wheel (**Figure 48**).
4. Perform major wheel truing with the tire removed and the wheel mounted in a wheel truing stand.
5. Use a spoke nipple wrench of the correct size. Using the wrong type of tool or one that is the incorrect size will round off the spoke nipples, making further adjustment difficult. Quality wrenches grip the nipple on four corners to prevent damage. Tighten spokes to minimum of 55 in.-lb. (6.2 N•m).

Wheel Truing Procedure

1. Set the wheel in a truing stand.
2A. When using a dial indicator, check rim runout as follows:
   a. Measure the radial runout with a dial indicator positioned as shown in **Figure 49**. If radial runout exceeds the service limit specified in **Table 2**, replace the rim.
   b. Measure the lateral runout with a dial indicator positioned as shown in **Figure 49**. If lateral runout exceeds the service limit specified in **Table 2**, replace the rim.
2B. If a dial indicator is not available, check rim runout as follows:
   a. Position a pointer facing toward the rim as shown in **Figure 50**. Spin the wheel slowly and check the lateral runout.
   b. Adjust the position of the pointer and check the radial runout.
3. If lateral runout is out of specification, the rim needs to be moved relative to the centerline of the wheel. To move the rim to the left, for example, tighten the spoke(s) on the left of the rim and loosen the opposite spoke(s) on the right. Refer to **Figure 51**.

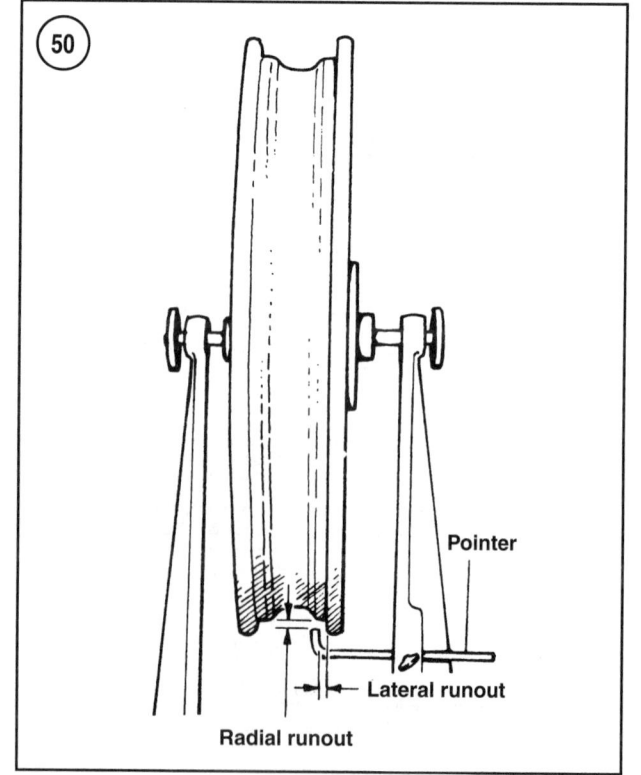

NOTE
The number of spokes to loosen and tighten will depend on the amount of runout. As a minimum, always adjust two or three spokes in the vicinity of the rim runout. If runout affects a greater area along the rim, adjust a greater number of spokes.

WHEELS, HUBS AND TIRES

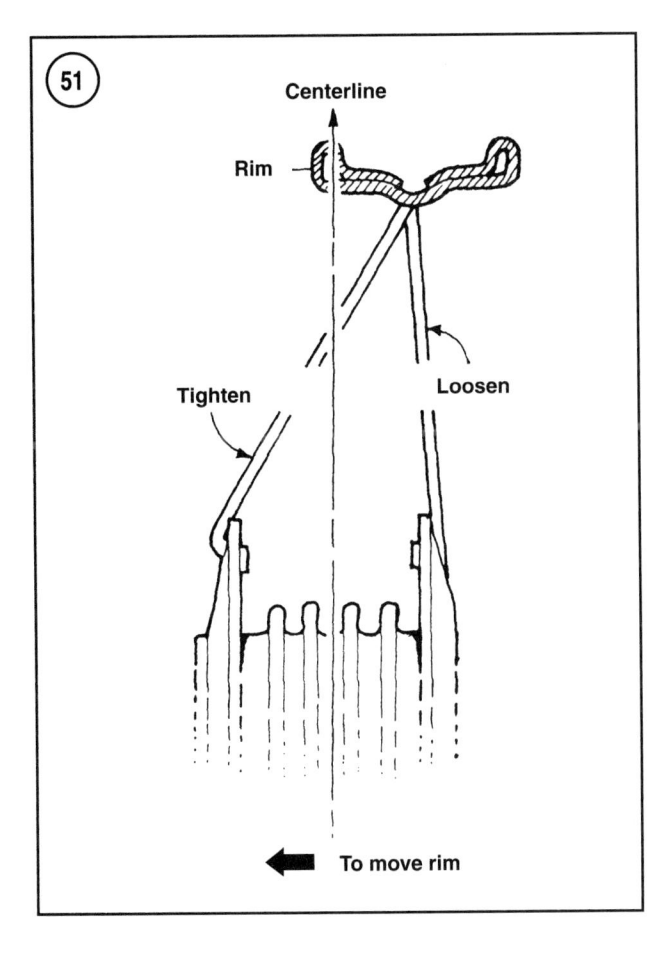

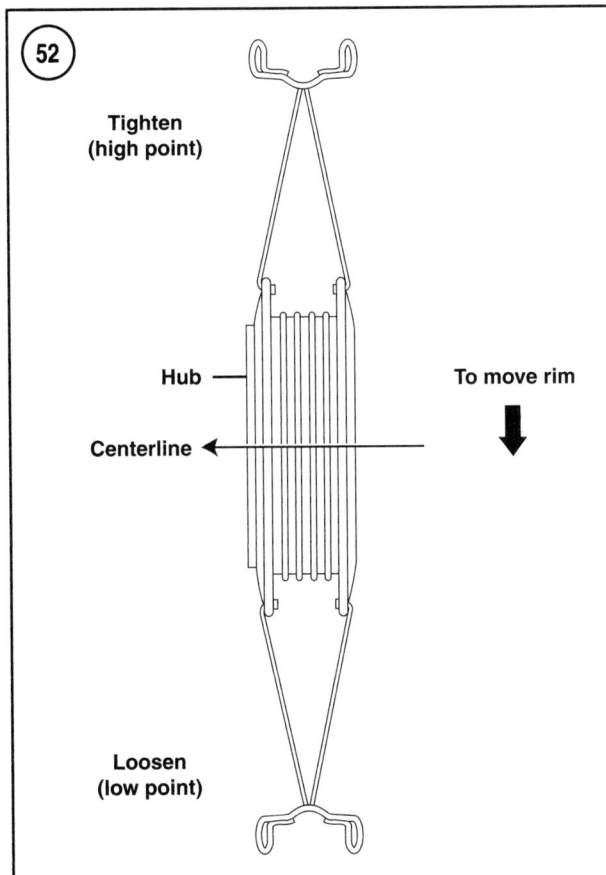

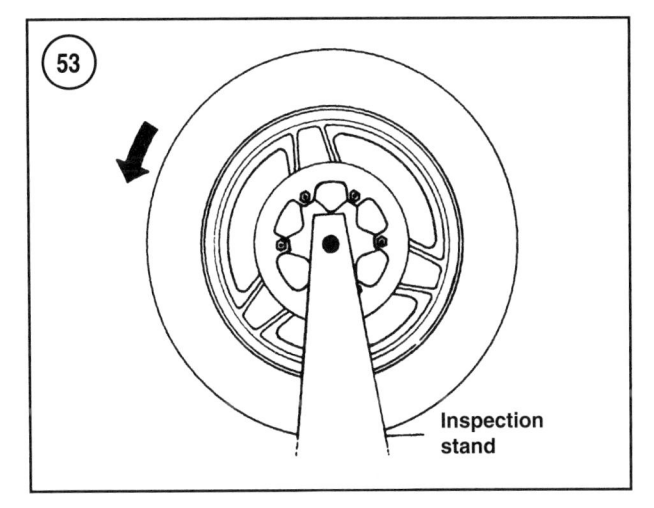

51
Centerline
Rim
Tighten
Loosen
To move rim

52
Tighten (high point)
Hub
To move rim
Centerline
Loosen (low point)

53
Inspection stand

4. If radial runout is excessive, the hub is not centered within the rim. The rim needs to move relative the centerline of the hub. Draw the high point of the rim toward the centerline of the hub by tightening the spokes in the area of the high point and by loosening spokes on the low side. Tighten and loosen the spokes in equal amounts to prevent distortion. Refer to **Figure 52**.

5. Rotate the wheel and check runout. Continue adjusting the spokes until runout is within the specification listed in **Table 2**. Be patient and thorough, adjusting the position of the rim a little at a time.

6. After truing the wheel, seat each spoke in the hub by tapping it with a flat nose punch and hammer. Recheck the spoke tension and wheel runout. Readjust if necessary.

7. Check the ends of the spokes on the tube side of the rim. Grind off any spoke that protrudes from the nipple so it will not puncture the tube.

WHEEL BALANCE

An unbalanced wheel is unsafe. Depending on the degree of unbalance and the speed of the motorcycle, a rider may experience anything from a mild vibration to a violent shimmy that may result in loss of control.

Before balancing a wheel, thoroughly clean the wheel assembly. Make sure the wheel bearings are in good condition and properly lubricated. The wheel must rotate freely. Also make sure the balance mark on the tire aligns with the valve stem. If not, break the tire loose from the rim and align it before balancing the wheel. Refer to *Tire Changing* in this chapter.

NOTE
Balance the wheels with the brake disc and driven sprocket assembly attached. These components rotate with the wheel and affect the balance.

1. Remove the wheel as described in this chapter.
2. Make sure the valve stem and the valve cap are tight.
3. Mount the wheel on a stand such as the one shown in **Figure 53** so it can rotate freely.

4. Check the wheel runout as described in this chapter. Do not try to balance a wheel with excessive runout.
5. Remove any balance weights mounted on the wheel.
6. Give the wheel a spin and let it coast to a stop. Mark the tire at the highest point (12 o'clock). This is the wheel's lightest point.
7. Spin the wheel several more times. If the wheel keeps coming to rest at the same point, it is out of balance. If the wheel stops at different points each time, the wheel is balanced.

NOTE
Adhesive test weights are available from motorcycle dealerships. These are adhesive-backed weights that can be cut to the desired length and attached directly to the rim.

8. Loosely attach a balance weight (or tape a test weight) at the upper or light side (12 o'clock) of the wheel.
9. Rotate the wheel 1/4 turn (3 o'clock). Release the wheel and observe the following:
    a. If the wheel does not rotate (if it stays at the 3 o'clock position), the correct balance weight was installed. The wheel is balanced.
    b. If the wheel rotates and the weighted portion goes up, replace the weight with the next heavier size.
    c. If the wheel rotates and the weighted portion goes down, replace the weight with the next lighter size.
    d. Repeat this process until the wheel remains at rest after being rotated 1/4 turn. Then, rotate the wheel another 1/4 turn, another 1/4 turn, and another to see if the wheel is correctly balanced.
10. Remove the test weight and install the correct weight.
    a. On laced wheels, firmly crimp the balance weight (**Figure 54**) onto the spoke(s) with a pair of pliers.
    b. On alloy wheels, crimp the balance weight (**Figure 55**) onto the rim.

TIRE CHANGING (LACED WHEELS)

The laced or wire wheels can easily be damaged during tire removal. Special care must be taken with tire irons to avoid scratches and gouges to the outer rim surface. Insert rim protectors or scraps of leather between the tire iron and the rim.

Removal

CAUTION
Support the wheel on two blocks of wood, so the brake disc does not contact the floor.

1. Remove the wheel as described in this chapter.
2. If the tire will be reinstalled, place a balance mark on the tire opposite the valve stem location (**Figure 56**) so the tire can be reinstalled in the same position for easier balancing.
3. Remove the valve core to deflate the tire.

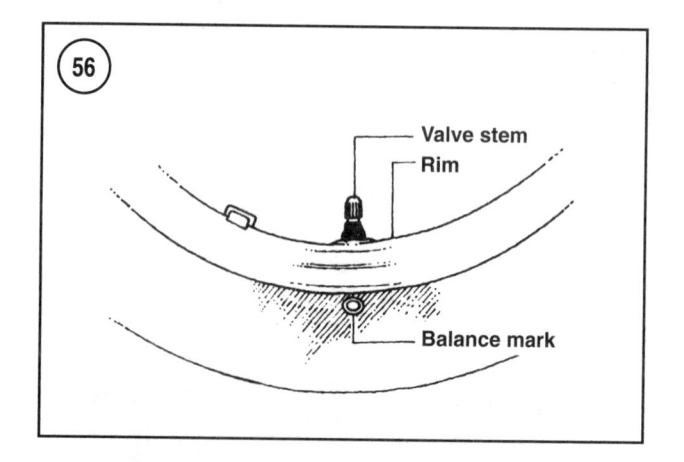

WHEELS, HUBS AND TIRES

4. Press the entire bead on both sides of the tire away from the rim and into the center of the rim.
5. Lubricate both beads with soapy water.

NOTE
Use rim protectors between the tire irons and the rim to protect the rim from damage. Also, use only quality tire irons without sharp edges. If necessary, file the ends of the tire irons to remove rough edges.

6. Insert the tire iron under the upper bead next to the valve stem (**Figure 57**). Press the lower bead into the center of the rim and pry the upper bead over the rim with the tire iron.
7. Insert a second tire iron next to the first to hold the bead over the rim (**Figure 58**). Work around the tire, prying the bead over the rim with the first tool. Be careful not to pinch the inner tube with the tire irons.
8. When the upper bead is off the rim, remove the nut from the valve stem. Remove the valve from the hole in the rim and remove the tube from the tire (**Figure 59**).
9. Stand the wheel upright. Force the second bead into the center of the rim. Insert the tire iron between the second bead and the side of the rim that the first bead was pried over. Pry the second bead off the rim (**Figure 60**), and continue working around the wheel with two tire irons until the tires is free of the rim.
10. Inspect the rim as described in this chapter.

Installation

NOTE
Before installing the tire, place it in the sun or in a hot, closed car. The heat will soften the rubber and ease installation.

1. Install a *new* rubber rim band. Align the hole in the band with the valve hole in the rim.
2. Liberally sprinkle the inside of the tire with talcum powder to reduce chafing between the tire and tube.
3. Most tires have directional arrows on the sidewall. Install the tire so the arrow points in the direction of forward rotation.
4. If the tire was removed, lubricate the lower bead of the tire with soapy water and place the tire against the rim. Align the valve stem balance mark (**Figure 56**) with the valve stem hole in the rim.
5. Using your hand, push as much of the lower bead past the upper rim surface as possible. Work around the tire in both directions (**Figure 61**).
6. Install the valve core into the valve stem in the inner tube.
7. Put the tube into the tire and insert the valve stem through the hole in the rim. Inflate the tube just enough to round it out. Too much air will make tire installation difficult; too little air increases the chance of pinching the tube with the tire irons.

8. Lubricate the upper tire bead and rim with soapy water.
9. Press the upper bead into the rim opposite the valve stem. Pry the bead into the rim on both sides of this initial point with your hands and work around the rim to the valve stem. If the tire pulls up on one side, either uses a tire iron or a knee to hold the tire in place. The last few inches are usually the toughest and also the place where most tubes are pinched. If possible, continue to push the tire into the rim with your hands. Re-lubricate the bead if necessary. If the tire bead pulls out from under the rim, use both of your knees to hold the tire in place. If necessary, use a tire iron and rim protector for the last few inches (**Figure 62**).

CAUTION
*Make sure the valve stem is not cocked in the rim (**Figure 63**).*

10. Wiggle the valve stem to make sure the tube is not trapped under the bead. Set the valve squarely in its hole.

WARNING
*Seat the tire on the rim by inflating the tire to approximately 10% above the recommended inflation pressure listed in **Table 3**. Do not exceed 10%. Never stand directly over a tire while inflating it. The tire could burst and cause severe injury.*

11. Check the bead on both sides of the tire for an even fit around the rim, and then re-lubricate both sides of the tire. Inflate the tube to seat the tire on the rim. Check to see that both beads are fully seated and the tire rim lines (**Figure 64**) are the same distance from the rim all the way around the tire. If the beads will not seat, release the air from the tire. Lubricate the rim and beads with soapy water, and re-inflate the tube.
12. Bleed the tire pressure down to the recommended pressure listed in **Table 3**. Install the valve stem nut, and tighten it against the rim. Then, install the valve stem cap.
13. Balance the wheel as described in this chapter.

Inspection

1. Remove and inspect the rubber rim band. Replace the band if it is deteriorated or broken.
2. Clean the inner and outer rim surfaces of all dirt, rust, corrosion and rubber residue.
3. Inspect the valve stem hole in the rim. Remove any dirt or corrosion from the hole.
4. Inspect the rim profiles for any cracks or other damage.
5. If the tube will be reused, reinstall the valve core, inflate the tube and check it for any leaks.
6. While the tube is inflated, clean it with water.
7. When reusing the tire, carefully check it inside and outside for damage. Replace the tire if there is any damage.
8. Make sure the spoke ends do not protrude from the nipples into the center of the rim. If necessary, grind off the end of the spokes.

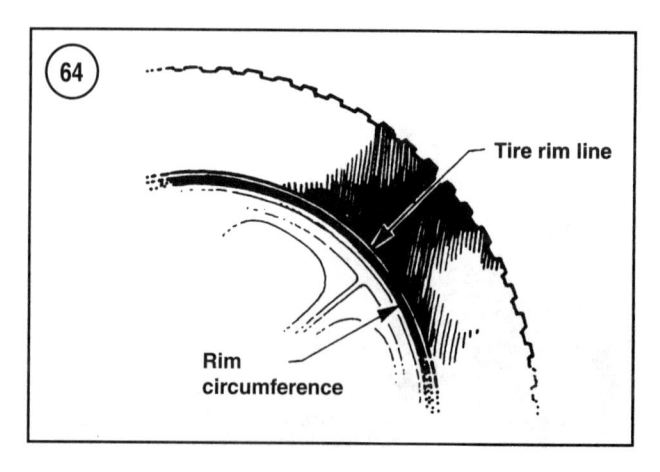

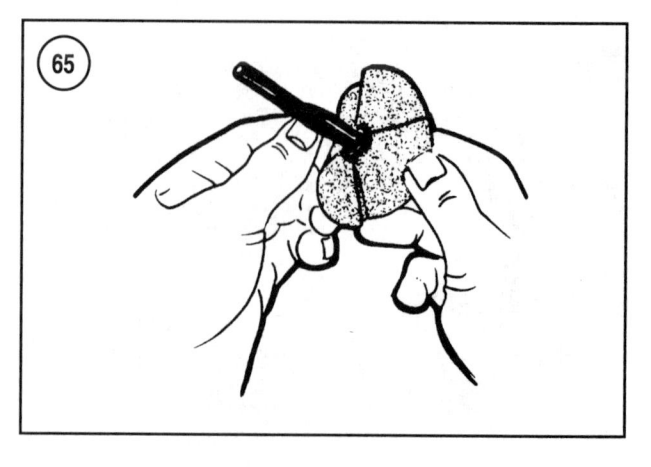

WHEELS, HUBS AND TIRES

If the tire is punctured, remove it from the rim to inspect the inside of the tire and apply a combination plug/patch from inside the tire (**Figure 65**). A plug applied from the outside of the tire should only be used as a temporary roadside repair.

Follow the repair kit manufacturer's instructions as to applicable repairs and any speed limitations. Replace a patched or plugged tire as soon as possible.

Removal

The alloy or cast wheels can easily be damaged during tire removal. Special care must be taken with tire irons to avoid scratching and gouging the outer rim surface. Protect the rim by using rim protectors or scraps of leather between the tire iron and the rim. The stock alloy wheels are designed for use with tubeless tires.

When removing a tubeless tire, be careful not to damage the tire beads, inner liner of the tire or the wheel rim flange. Use tire levers or flat-handled tire irons with rounded ends.

NOTE
While removing a tire, support the wheel on two blocks of wood, so the brake disc does not contact the floor.

1. Place a balance mark opposite the valve stem (**Figure 56**) on the tire sidewall so the tire can be reinstalled in the same position for easier balancing.
2. Remove the valve core to deflate the tire.

CAUTION
*Removal of tubeless tires from their rims can be very difficult because of the exceptionally tight bead/rim sealing surface. Breaking the bead seal may require the use of a bead breaker (**Figure 66**). Do not scratch the inside of the rim or damage the tire bead.*

3. Press the entire bead on both sides of the tire into the center of the rim.
4. Lubricate the beads with soapy water.

NOTE
Use rim protectors or insert scraps of leather between the tire irons and the rim to protect the rim from damage.

5. Insert the tire iron under the bead next to the valve stem (**Figure 67**). Force the bead on the opposite side of the tire into the center of the rim and pry the bead over the rim with the tire iron.
6. Insert a second tire iron next to the first to hold the bead over the rim (**Figure 68**). Then, work around the tire with the first tool prying the bead over the rim.
7. Set the wheel on its edge. Insert a tire tool between the second bead and the same side of the rim that the first bead was pried over (**Figure 69**). Force the bead on the opposite side from the tool into the center of the rim. Pry the second

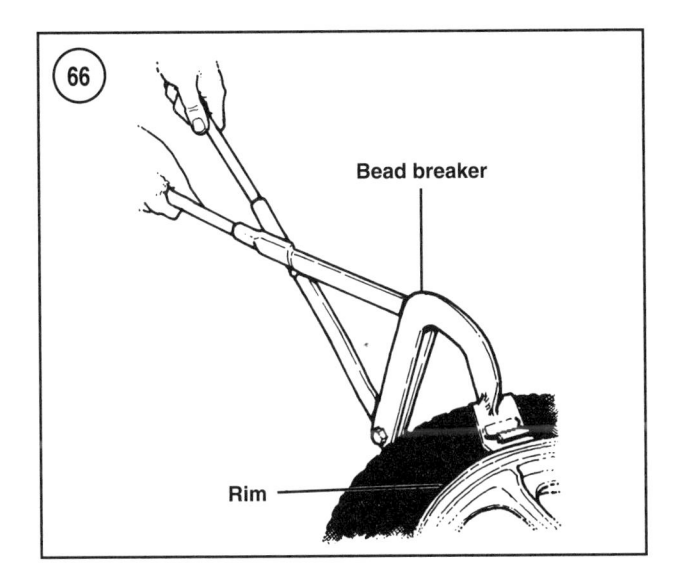

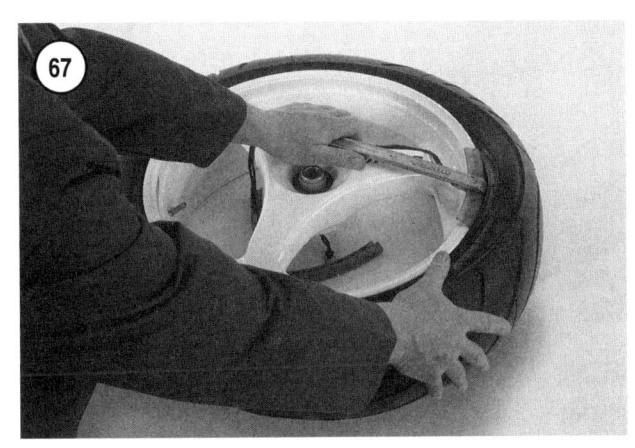

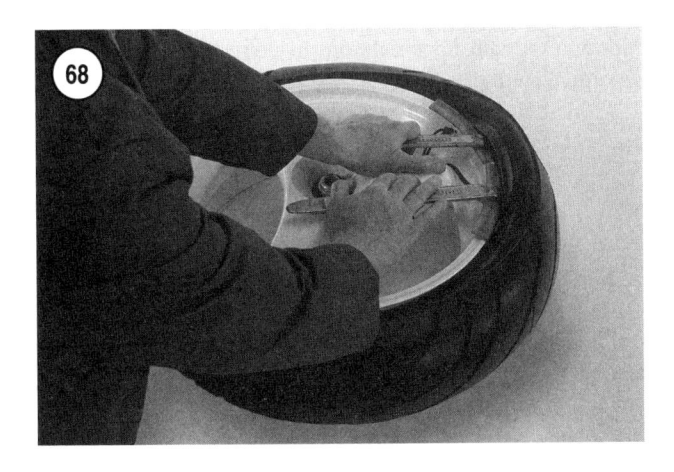

TIRE CHANGING (ALLOY WHEELS)

WARNING
Do not install an inner tube inside a tubeless tire. The tube will cause an abnormal heat buildup in the tire.

Tubeless tires have the word TUBELESS molded in the tire sidewall and the rims have TUBELESS cast or stamped into them.

bead off the rim, and continue working around the wheel with two tire irons until the tire is free of the rim.

8. Inspect the valve stem seal. Because rubber deteriorates with age, it is advisable to replace the valve stem when replacing a tire.

Installation

1. Carefully inspect the tire for any damage, especially inside.
2. A new tire may have balancing rubbers inside. These are not patches and should not be disturbed.
3. Manufacturers place a colored spot near the bead, indicating a lighter point on the tire. Install the tires so this balance mark (either the manufacturer's or the one made during removal) sits opposite the valve stem (**Figure 56**).
4. Most tires have directional arrows on the sidewall that indicate the direction of rotation. Install the tire so the arrow points in the direction of forward rotation.
5. Lubricate both beads of the tire with soapy water.
6. Place the backside of the tire into the center of the rim. The lower bead should go into the center of the rim and the upper bead outside. Work around the tire in both directions (**Figure 70**).
7. Starting at the side opposite the valve stem, press the upper bead into the rim (**Figure 71**). Pry the bead into the rim on both sides of the initial point with a tire tool, working around the rim to the valve (**Figure 72**).
8. Check the bead on both sides of the tire for an even fit around the rim.
9. Place an inflatable band around the circumference of the tire. Slowly inflate the band until the tire beads are pressed against the rim. Inflate the tire enough to seat it against the rim. Deflate and remove the band.

WARNING
Never exceed 40 psi (279 kPa) inflation pressure as the tire could burst causing severe injury. Never stand directly over the tire while inflating it.

10. After inflating the tire, check to see that the beads are fully seated and the tire rim lines are the same distance from the rim all the way around the tire (**Figure 64**). If the beards will not seat, deflate the tire, re-lubricate the rim and beads with soapy water, and then re-inflate the tire.
11. Inflate the tire to the required pressure. Refer to tire inflation pressure specifications listed in **Table 3**. Screw on the valve stem cap.
12. Balance the wheel assembly as described in this chapter.

TIRE REPAIRS

NOTE
Changing or patching a tire on the road is very difficult. A can of pressurized tire inflator and sealer may inflate the tire and seal the hole, although this is only a temporary fix.

WARNING
Do not install an inner tube inside a tubeless tire. The tube will cause an abnormal heat buildup in the tire.

Tubeless tires have the TUBELESS molded into the sidewall and the rims have SUITABLE FOR TUBELESS TIRES or equivalent stamped or cast on them.

If the tire is punctured, it must be removed from the rim to inspect the inside of the tire and to apply a combination plug/patch from inside the tire (**Figure 65**). Never attempt

WHEELS, HUBS AND TIRES

to repair a tubeless motorcycle tire using a plug or cord patch applied from outside the tire.

After repairing a tubeless tire, do not exceed 50 mph (80 km/h) for the first 24 hours.

As soon as possible, replace the patched tire with a new one.

Repair

Do not rely on a plug or cord patch applied from outside the tire. Use a combination plug/patch applied from inside the tire (**Figure 65**).

1. Remove the tire from the wheel rim as described in this chapter.
2. Inspect the rim inner flange. Smooth any scratches on the sealing surface with emery cloth. If a scratch is deeper than 0.020 in. (0.5 mm), replace the wheel.
3. Inspect the tire inside and out. Replace a tire if any of the following is found:
    a. A puncture larger than 1/8 in. (3 mm) diameter.
    b. A punctured or damaged side wall.
    c. More than 2 punctures in the tire.
4. Apply the plug/patch following the manufacturer's instructions included with the patch kit.
5. As soon as possible, replace the patched tire with a new one.

Table 1 LACED WHEEL OFFSET

Model/Wheel size	Offset in. (mm)
2006-2007 models	
Steel laced	
Front 16 in.	1.555-1.575 (39.50-40.01)
Rear 16 in.	1.472-1.492 (37.39-37.90)
Chrome aluminum profile laced	
Front 16 in.	1.270-1.290 (32.26-32.77)
Rear 16 in.	1.190-1.210 (30.23-30.73)
2008 models	
Steel laced	
Front and rear 17 in.	0.615-0.645 (15.62-16.38)
Front and rear 19 in.	1.135-1.165 (28.83-29.59)
Front and rear 21 in.	1.525-1.555 (38.74-39.50)
Chrome aluminum profile laced	
Front and rear 17 in.	0.385-0.415 (9.78-10.54)
Front and rear 19 in.	0.885-0.915 (22.48-23.24)
Front and rear 21 in.	1.555-1.585 (39.50-40.26)
2009 models	
Steel laced	
Front 16 in. × 3 in.	1.551-1.571 (39.40-39.90)
Rear 16 in. × 5 in.	1.098-1.118 (27.89-28.40)
Chrome aluminum profile laced	
Front 16 in. × 3 in.	1.267-1.287 (32.18-32.69)
Front 17 in. × 3 in.	1.267-1.287 (32.18-32.69)
Rear 16 in. × 5 in.	0.831-0.850 (20.11-21.59)

Table 2 WHEEL RUNOUT (MAXIMUM)

Item	in.	mm
Laced and cast wheels (front and rear)		
Lateral	0.40	10.2
Radial	0.30	7.6

Table 3 TIRE INFLATION PRESSURE (COLD)*

	PSI	kPa
Front wheels		
Rider only	36	248
Rider and one passenger	36	248
Rear wheels		
Rider only	36	248
Rider and passenger	40	276

*Tire pressure for original equipment tires. Aftermarket tires may require different inflation pressures.

Table 4 WHEEL TORQUE SPECIFICATIONS

Item	ft.-lb.	in.-lb.	N•m
Brake disc bolts			
Front wheel	16-24	–	21.7-32.5
Rear wheel	30-45	–	40.7-61.0
Driven sprocket bolts			
2006-2007 models	55-65	–	74.6-88.1
2008-2009 models			
(compensator bowl bolts)	55-65	–	74.6-88.1
Front axle nut			
2006-2007 models	50-55	–	67.8-74.6
2007-2009 models	60-65	–	81.3-88.1
Front axle cover set screw			
FLHTCUSE models	–	60-84	6.8-9.5
Front axle slider cap nuts	–	132-180	14.9-20.3
Rear axle nut			
2006-2007 models	95-105	–	128.8-142.4
2008-2009 models	refer to text		
Spoke nipples (all models)			
minimum	–	55	6.2

CHAPTER THIRTEEN

FRONT SUSPENSION AND STEERING

This chapter covers the handlebar, steering head and front fork.

Refer to **Table 1** and **Table 2** at the end of the chapter for specifications.

HANDLEBAR (ALL MODELS EXCEPT SCREAMIN' EAGLE)

Removal/Installation

Refer to **Figure 1**.
1. Disconnect the negative battery cable as described in Chapter Eleven.
2A. On FLHT and FLHX models, refer to Chapter Seventeen and perform the following:
   a. Remove the outer fairing.
   b. Partially remove the inner fairing (A, **Figure 2**) until the handlebar forward mounting bolts (B) are accessible. It is not necessary to completely remove the inner fairing.
2B. On all FLHR models, remove the headlight nacelle as described in Chapter Eleven.
2C. On all FLTR models, remove the instrument nacelle and housing (A, **Figure 3**) as described in Chapter Eleven.
3. Support the motorcycle with the front wheel off the ground as described in *Motorcycle Stands* (Chapter Twelve).

NOTE
Cover the fuel tank with a heavy cloth or plastic tarp to protect it from accidental scratches or dents when removing the handlebar.

NOTE
Before removing the handlebar, make a drawing of the clutch and throttle cable routing from the handlebar and through the frame. This information will prove helpful when reinstalling the handlebar and connecting the cables.

4. On the right side of the handlebar, perform the following:
   a. Unscrew and remove the mirror (A, **Figure 4**).
   b. Remove the screws securing the master cylinder (B, **Figure 4**). Do not disconnect the hydraulic brake line.
   c. Secure the master cylinder to the frame with a bungee cord or wire. Make sure the reservoir remains upright.
   d. Remove the screws joining the right side switch (C, **Figure 4**) halves and separate the housing. Remove the switch assembly from the handlebar.
   e. On 2006-2007 models, slide the throttle housing assembly (D, **Figure 4**) off the handlebar.

f. On 2008-2009 models, disconnect the twist grip sensor wire as described in Chapter Eleven.

5. On the left side of the handlebar, perform the following:
   a. Unscrew and remove the mirror (A, **Figure 5**).
   b. Remove the screws joining the left side switch (B, **Figure 5**) halves and separate the housing. Remove the switch assembly from the handlebar.
   c. Remove the clutch lever clamp mounting bolts (C, **Figure 5**) and washers and separate the clamp halves. Remove the lever assembly from the handlebar.

6. On 2008-2009 FLHR and FLHRC models, perform the following:
   a. Carefully remove the decorative trim plate from the handlebar clamp shroud.
   b. Remove the three screws securing the handlebar cover, and then remove the cover.

7. Disconnect or remove any wiring harness clamps at the handlebar.

8. Remove the two handlebar front clamp bolts (B, **Figure 3**), and then the rear clamp bolts (C). Remove the holder(s) and the handlebar.

9. Install the handlebar by reversing the removal steps, while noting the following:
   a. Check the knurled rings on the handlebar for galling and bits of aluminum. Clean the knurled section with a wire brush.
   b. Check the handlebar for cracks, bends or other damage. Replace the handlebar if necessary. Do not attempt to repair it.
   c. Thoroughly clean the clamp halves of all residue.
   d. After installing the handlebar, reposition it while sitting on the motorcycle.
   e. Tighten the handlebar clamp bolts to 16-20 ft.-lb. (21.7-27.1 N•m).
   f. Adjust both mirrors.
   g. On 2006-2007 models, adjust the throttle and idle cables as described in Chapter Three.

Lower Clamp Rubber Bushing Replacement

1. Turn the front fork fully to the right and loosen the bolt securing the left side lower clamp.
2. Turn the front fork fully to the left and loosen the bolt securing the right side lower clamp.
3. Remove the handlebar assembly as described in this section.
4. On the right side, perform the following:
   a. Secure the lower clamp to prevent rotation and remove the bolt.
   b. Remove the flat washer and upper cup washer from the top of the upper fork bridge.
   c. Remove the upper bushing from the upper fork bridge and discard it.
   d. Remove the large, flat washer and cup washer from the bottom of the upper fork bridge.
   e. Remove the spacer from lower bushing and discard the bushing.

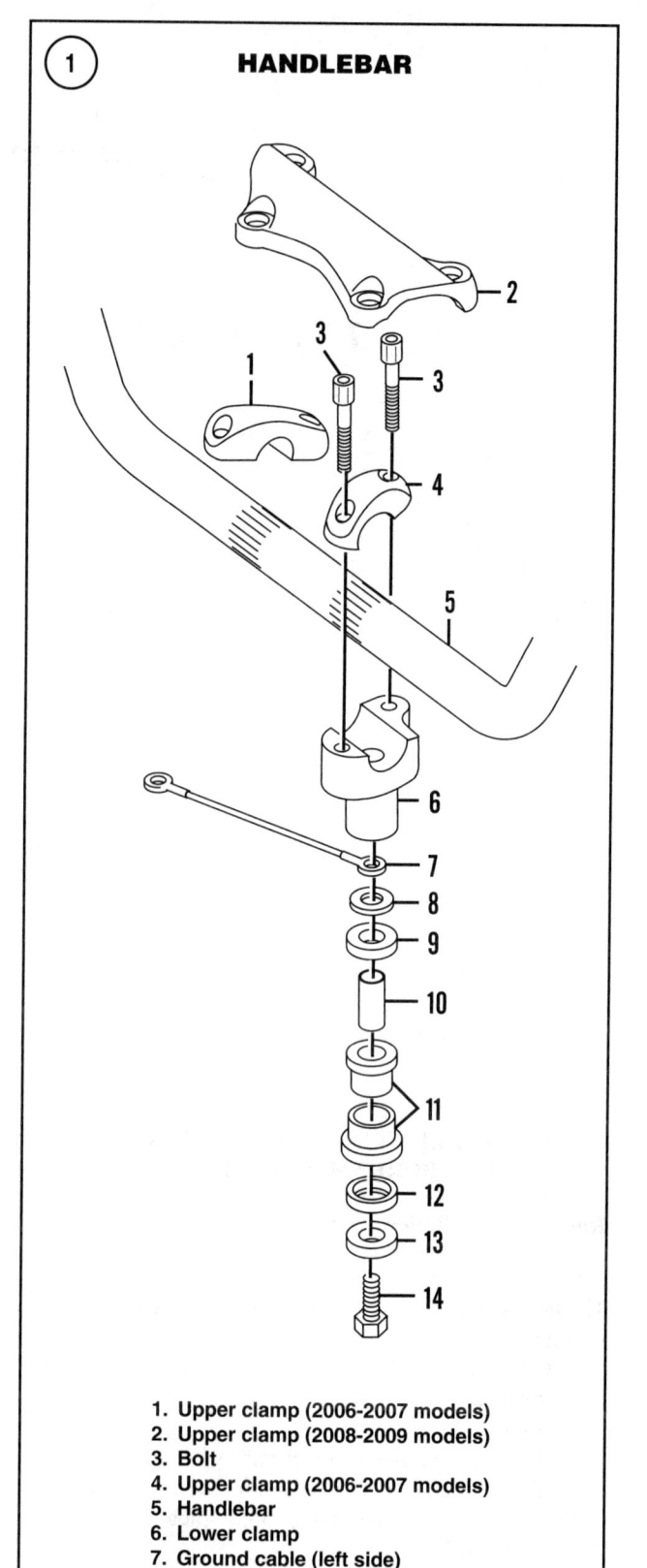

① HANDLEBAR

1. Upper clamp (2006-2007 models)
2. Upper clamp (2008-2009 models)
3. Bolt
4. Upper clamp (2006-2007 models)
5. Handlebar
6. Lower clamp
7. Ground cable (left side)
8. Washer (right side)
9. Cup washer
10. Spacer
11. Rubber bushings
12. Cup washer
13. Washer (right side only)
14. Bolt

FRONT SUSPENSION AND STEERING

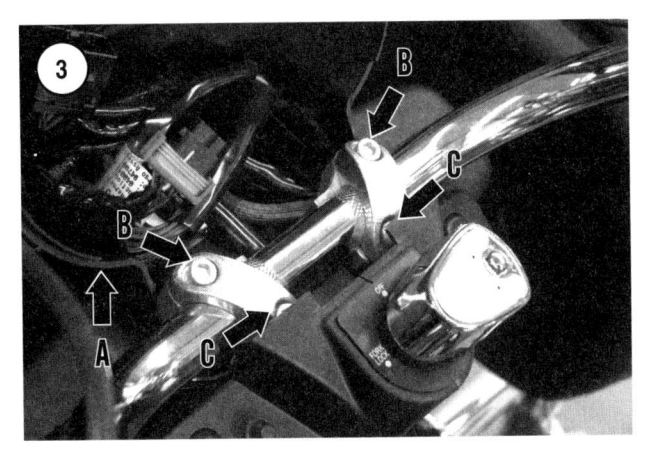

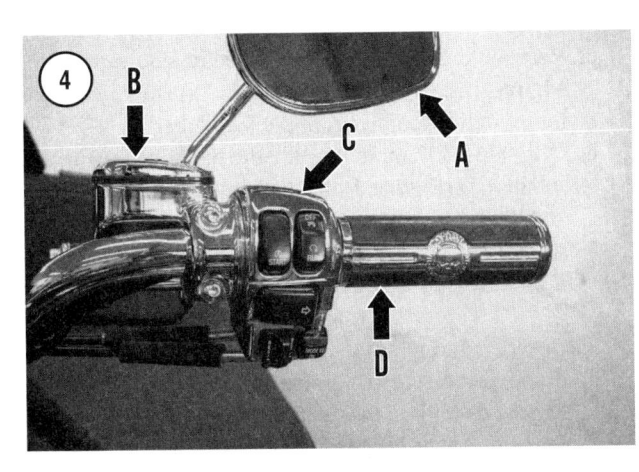

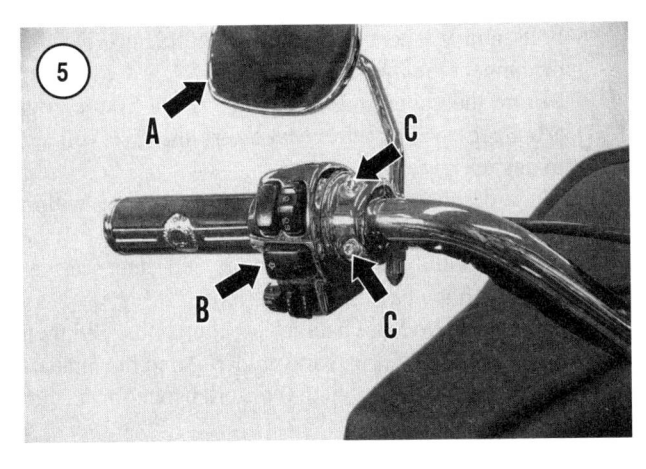

5. On the left side, perform the following:
   a. Secure the lower clamp to prevent rotation and remove the bolt.
   b. Remove the ground cable and upper cup washer from the top of the upper fork bridge.
   c. Remove the upper bushing from the upper fork bridge and discard it.
   d. Remove the cup washer from the bottom of the upper fork bridge.
   e. Remove the spacer from lower bushing and discard the bushing.
6. Install the *new* bushings onto the spacers until they are flush with the bottom of the spacer.
7. On the right side, perform the following:
   a. Insert the bushing spacer assembly into the bottom surface of the upper fork bridge. Fit the collar of the bushing over the lip of the boss.
   b. Install the large flat washer onto the bolt.
   c. Position the cup washer with the concave side going on last and install it onto the bolt.
   d. Insert the bolt into the bushing. Index the concave side of the cup washer over the collar of the bushing. Push the bolt up until it bottoms.
   e. Install the upper bushing onto the bolt and into the bore of the upper fork bridge. Fit the collar of the bushing over the lip of the boss.
   f. Position the cup washer with the concave side going on first and install the cup washer over the bolt and onto the bushing. Push the cup washer down until it bottoms.
   g. Install the flat washer onto the bolt.
   h. Apply medium-strength (blue) threadlock to the bolt threads.
   i. Install the lower clamp onto the bolt and secure it to prevent rotation.
   j. Finger-tighten the bolt.
8. On the left side, perform the following:
   a. Insert the bushing spacer assembly into the bottom surface of the upper fork bridge. Fit the collar of the bushing over the lip of the boss.
   b. Position the cup washer with the concave side going on last and install it onto the bolt.
   c. Insert the bolt into the bushing. Index the concave side of the cup washer over the collar of the bushing. Push the bolt up until it bottoms.
   d. Install the upper bushing onto the bolt and into the bore of the upper fork bridge. Fit the collar of the bushing over the lip of the boss.
   e. Position the cup washer with the concave side going on first and install the cup washer over the bolt and onto the bushing. Push the cup washer down until it bottoms.
   f. Install the ground strap onto the bolt.
   g. Apply medium-strength (blue) threadlock to the bolt threads.
   h. Install the lower clamp onto the bolt and secure it to prevent rotation.
   i. Finger-tighten the bolt.

9. Install the handlebar assembly as described in this section.
10. Turn the front fork fully to the right and tighten the left side bolt to 30-40 ft.-lb. (40.7-54.2 N•m).
11. Turn the front fork fully to the left and tighten the right side bolt to 30-40 ft.-lb. (40.7-54.2 N•m).

HANDLEBAR (SCREAMIN' EAGLE MODELS)

The electrical cables relating to the right and left hand handlebar switches and the throttle control twist grip are routed within the handlebar tubing. Extra care must be taken during the removal and installation to avoid scraping off any wiring insulation.

The connector terminal numbers are shown in the wiring diagrams located on the CD inserted into the back cover of the manual.

Removal/Installation (FLHTCUSE Models)

Refer to **Figure 1**.
1. Disconnect the negative battery cable as described in Chapter Eleven.
2. Support the motorcycle with the front wheel off the ground as described in *Motorcycle Stands* (Chapter Twelve).

CAUTION
Cover the fuel tank to protect it when removing the handlebar.

3. Remove the seat as described in Chapter Seventeen.
4. Remove the outer front fairing and fairing cap as described in Chapter Seventeen.
5. Label and identify the connectors and their wire colors to assist in reconnecting.
6A. On 2006 models, disconnect the following electrical connectors:
   a. Right-side handlebar switch 12-pin connector.
   b. Left-side handlebar switch 12-pin and 3-pin connectors.
   c. Handgrip heater power 2-pin connector.
   d. Handgrip heater 3-pin interconnect connector.
   e. AM/FM/WB receiver 28-pin or 35-pin connector.
   f. XM receiver module 12-pin connector.
   g. CB transceiver module 12-pin connector.
   h. XM antenna 2-pin connector.
   i. Garage door opener transmitter 3-pin connector.
6B. On 2007-2009 models, disconnect the following electrical connectors:
   a. Right-side handlebar switch 12-pin connector.
   b. Left-side handlebar switch 16-pin and 3-pin connectors.
   c. Handgrip heater power 3-pin connector.
   d. Handgrip heater 3-pin interconnect connector.
   e. Twist grip sensor connector (2008-2009 models).

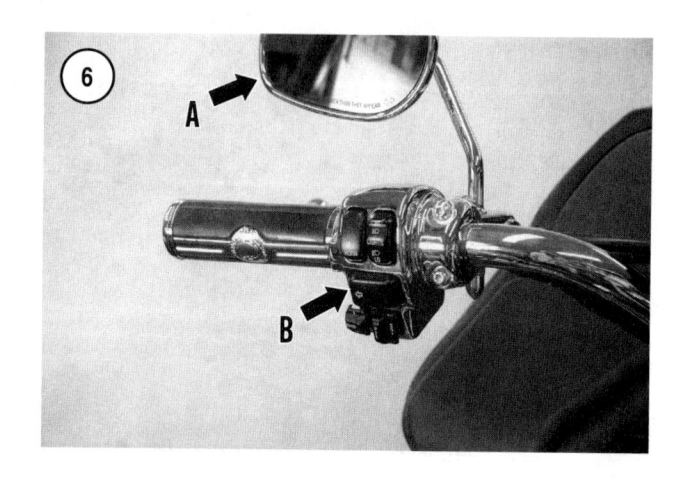

7. Remove the radio and storage box as described in Chapter Eleven.
8A. On 2007 models, disconnect the throttle cables and remove the throttle grip as described in Chapter Ten.
8B. On 2008-2009 models, remove the twist grip throttle control as described in Chapter Ten.
9. On the right side of the handlebar, perform the following:
   a. Unscrew and remove the mirror (A, **Figure 4**).
   b. Remove the brake master cylinder clamp mounting bolts and washers, and then separate the clamp. Do not disconnect the hydraulic brake line.
   c. Secure the master cylinder to the frame with a bungee cord or wire. Make sure the reservoir remains upright.
   d. Remove the screws joining the right side switch (C, **Figure 4**) halves and separate the housing. Remove the switch assembly from the handlebar.
   e. On 2006-2007 models, slide the throttle housing assembly (D, **Figure 4**) off the handlebar.
   f. On 2008-2009 models, disconnect the twist grip sensor wire as described in Chapter Eleven.
10. On the left side of the handlebar, perform the following:
   a. Unscrew and remove the mirror (A, **Figure 6**).
   b. Remove the screws joining the left side switch (B, **Figure 6**) halves and separate the housing. Remove the switch assembly from the handlebar.
   c. Remove the clutch master cylinder clamp mounting bolts and washers and separate the clamp. Do not disconnect the hydraulic brake line.
   d. Secure the clutch master cylinder to the frame with a bungee cord or wire. Make sure the reservoir remains upright.
11. Make a drawing of the electrical cable routing within the inner fairing and where it exits the inner fairing.
12. Carefully withdraw the connectors and electrical cables out through the back side of the inner fairing.
13. Remove the two front handlebar clamp bolts, and then the rear clamp bolts. Remove the holder(s) and the handlebar. Take handlebar assembly to the work bench for further disassembly if necessary.

FRONT SUSPENSION AND STEERING 581

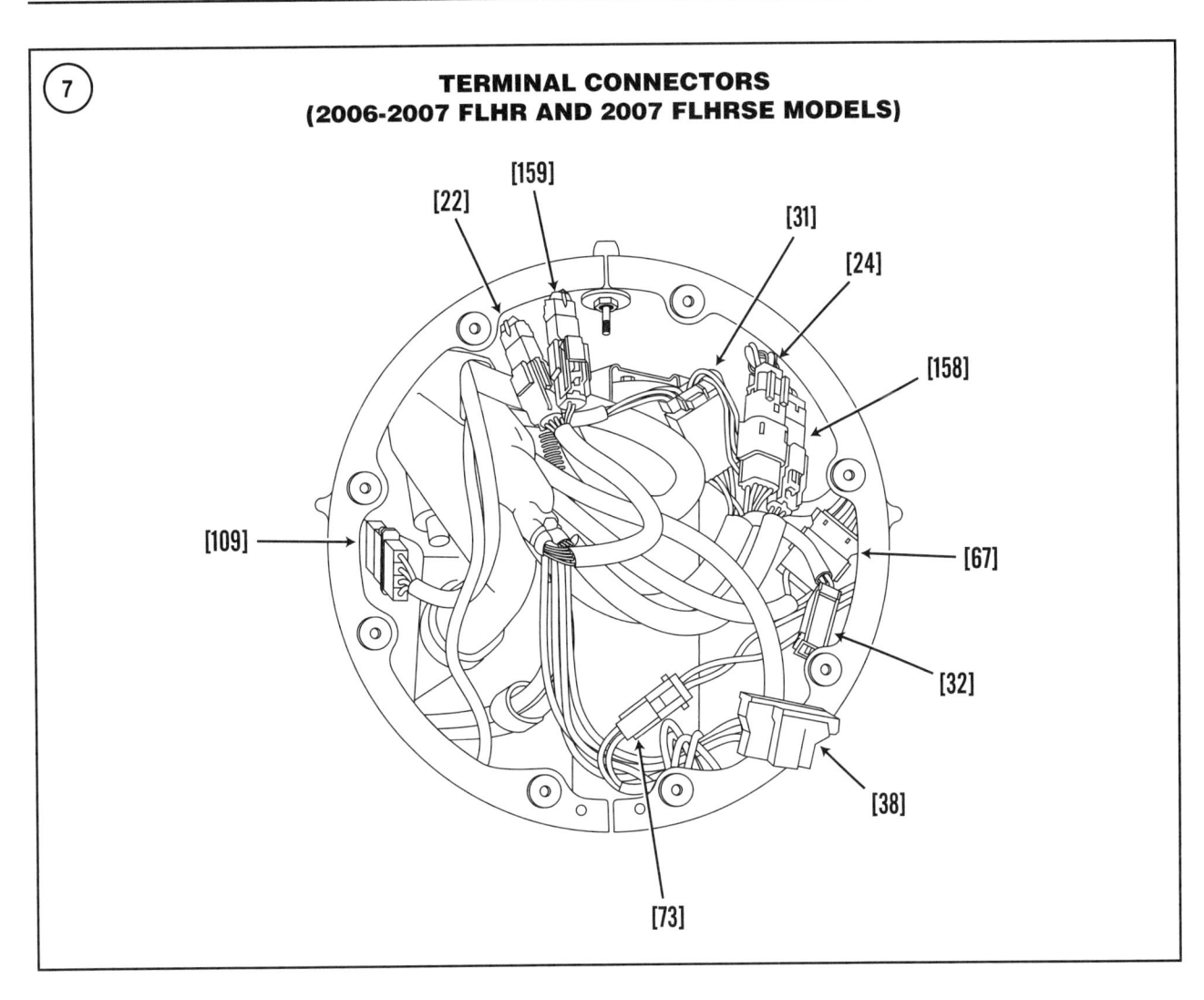

⑦ **TERMINAL CONNECTORS
(2006-2007 FLHR AND 2007 FLHRSE MODELS)**

[159] [22] [31] [24] [158] [109] [67] [32] [38] [73]

14. Install the handlebar by reversing the removal steps, while noting the following:
   a. Check the knurled rings on the handlebar for galling and bits of aluminum. Clean the knurled section with a wire brush.
   b. Check the handlebar for cracks, bends or other damage. Replace the handlebar if necessary. Do not attempt to repair it.
   c. Thoroughly clean the clamp halves of all residue.
   d. After installing the handlebar, reposition it while sitting on the motorcycle.
   e. Tighten the handlebar clamp bolts to 16-20 ft.-lb. (21.7-27.1 N•m).
   f. Adjust both mirrors.
   g. On 2006-2007 models, adjust the throttle and idle cables as described in Chapter Three.

**Removal/Installation
(FLHRSE and FLTRSE Models)**

Refer to **Figure 1**.
1. Disconnect the negative battery cable as described in Chapter Eleven.

2. Support the motorcycle with the front wheel off the ground as described in *Motorcycle Stands* (Chapter Twelve).

*CAUTION
Cover the fuel tank to protect it when removing the handlebar.*

3. Remove the seat as described in Chapter Seventeen.
4A. On FLHRSE models, remove the headlight assembly from the mounting ring as described in Chapter Eleven.
4B. On FLTRSE models, remove the instrument nacelle as described in Chapter Eleven.
5. Label and identify the connectors and their wire colors to assist in reconnecting.
6A. On FLHRSE models, refer to **Figure 7** and the appropriate wiring diagram (located on the CD inserted into the back cover of the manual) to help identify, locate and then disconnect the following electrical connectors:
   a. Right-side cruise control connector.
   b. Right-side turn signal connector.
   c. Turn signal Multi-lock connector.
   d. Left-side turn signal connector.
   e. Left-side cruise control connector.
   f. Throttle control 6-pin connector (not shown).

13

6B. On FLTRSE models, disconnect the following electrical connectors:
   a. Left-side turn signal connector.
   b. Right side switch control connector.
   c. Throttle control 6-pin connector (not shown).
7. Attach a length of heavy-duty fish wire to all of the disconnected electrical connector terminals. Wrap the connectors and wire with electrical tape to assist in withdrawing the connectors and wiring from the headlight nacelle.
8A. On 2007 models, disconnect the throttle cables and remove the throttle grip as described in Chapter Ten.
8B. On 2008-2009 models, remove the twist grip throttle control as described in Chapter Ten.
9. Loosen, but do not remove the handlebar cover retaining nut and large washer inside the nacelle.
10. Loosen, but do not remove the four acorn nuts and separate the headlight nacelle halves.
11. Remove the handlebar cover from the handlebar.
12. On the right side of the handlebar, perform the following:
   a. Unscrew and remove the mirror (A, **Figure 4**).
   b. Remove the brake master cylinder clamp mounting bolts and washers and separate the clamp. Do not disconnect the hydraulic brake line.
   c. Secure the master cylinder to the frame with a bungee cord or wire. Make sure the reservoir remains upright.
   d. Remove the screws joining the right side switch (C, **Figure 4**) halves and separate the housing. Remove the switch assembly from the handlebar.
   e. On 2007 models, slide the throttle housing assembly (D, **Figure 4**) off the handlebar.
   f. On 2008-2009 models, disconnect the twist grip sensor wire as described in Chapter Eleven.
13. On the left side of the handlebar, perform the following:
   a. Unscrew and remove the mirror (A, **Figure 6**).
   b. Remove the screws joining the left side switch (B, **Figure 6**) halves and separate the housing. Remove the switch assembly from the handlebar.
   c. Remove the clutch master cylinder clamp mounting bolts and washers and separate the clamp. Do not disconnect the hydraulic brake line.
   d. Secure the clutch master cylinder to the frame with a bungee cord or wire. Make sure the reservoir remains upright.
14. Carefully withdraw the connectors, electrical cables and fish wire out through the back side of the headlight nacelle.
15. Remove the electrical tape and fish wire from the electrical cables. Leave the fish wire running through the headlight nacelle as it will be used to pull the connectors and electrical cables back through the nacelle.
16. Remove the two front handlebar clamp bolts, and then the rear clamp bolts. Remove the holder(s) and the handlebar. Take handlebar assembly to the workbench for further disassembly if necessary.
17. Install the handlebar by reversing the removal steps, while noting the following:
   a. Check the knurled rings on the handlebar for galling and bits of aluminum. Clean the knurled section with a wire brush.
   b. Check the handlebar for cracks, bends or other damage. Replace the handlebar if necessary. Do not attempt to repair it.
   c. Thoroughly clean the clamp halves of all residue.
   d. After installing the handlebar, reposition the handlebar while sitting on the motorcycle.
   e. Tighten the handlebar clamp bolts to 16-20 ft.-lb. (21.7-27.1 N•m).
   f. Adjust both mirrors.
   g. On 2007 models, adjust the throttle as described in Chapter Three.

Handlebar Disassembly (All Models)

CAUTION
The electrical cables for the handlebar switches and the throttle control twist grip are routed within the handlebar tube. Take extra care during the removal and installation to avoid scraping off any wiring insulation.

1. Remove the handlebar assembly as described in this section.
2. Note their locations, and carefully cut and remove all cable straps on the wiring.
3. Separate the heated handgrip interconnect harness connector, on models so equipped.
4. Make a drawing and write down the exact wire color and its respective chamber number within the Molex and/or Deutsch connector. The wires *must* be installed into the correct chamber location for the switch or component to operate correctly.
5. Separate the wiring terminals from the Molex connectors as described in Chapter Eleven. Remove the wiring terminals from the following:
   a. Left-hand switch connector.
   b. Right-hand switch connector.
   c. Throttle twist grip sensor connector (2008-2009 models).
6. Separate the wiring terminals from the Multi-lock connectors as described in Chapter Eleven. Remove the wiring terminals from the turn signal Multi-lock connector.
7. Separate the wiring terminals from the Deutsch connectors as described in Chapter Eleven. Remove the wiring terminals from the following:
   a. Heated handgrip power connector.
   b. Interconnect harness connector.
8. Slide the boot off of the left-hand switch wiring and terminal. Save the boot as it will be reused.
9. Separate the wiring harness from the left and the right side of the handlebar.

FRONT SUSPENSION AND STEERING

10. Attach a 3 ft. (91.4 cm) length of fish wire to the end of each set of separated wiring harness and secure the fish wire in place. Bundle the harness together and wrap with several layers of electrical tape to prevent damage to the terminals as the wiring is pulled through the handlebar. Do not make the bundle too fat or it will be difficult to withdraw the wiring harness through the handle bar.
11. Remove the screws and disassemble the right and left side handlebar switch assemblies.
12. On 2008-2009 models, remove the throttle twist grip assembly from the right side as described in Chapter Ten.
13. Gently remove the left-side hand grip from the handlebar.
14. Apply glass cleaner to the bundles of wiring to ease the removal of the wiring assemblies from the handlebar.

CAUTION
The electrical wire(s) must be replaced if any insulation is scraped off during removal and installation.

NOTE
Do not pull the loose end of the fish wire out of the handlebar as it will be used to pull the new wiring harness back through.

15. Slowly and carefully, guide the right side wiring harness assembly through the center opening in the handlebar to the outer end being careful to avoid scraping off any insulation.
16. Repeat to remove the left side wiring harness.
17. Remove the electrical tape and detach the fish wire from the wiring harness.
18. Repair or replace any defective switch or wiring sockets as described in Chapter Eleven, if necessary.

Handlebar Assembly (All Models)

1. Make sure the rubber grommets are in place on the oval holes near the end of the handlebar.
2. Attach the end of the fish wire to the end of one of the sets of wiring harness and secure it in the same manner used during removal.
3. Apply liquid glass cleaner to the bundle of wiring to ease the installation of the wiring harness assemblies into the handlebar.

CAUTION
If there is any resistance in pulling the wiring harness assembly back into the handlebar, stop and solve the problem immediately. Do not damage any portion of the assembly.

4. Slowly pull on the fish wire and feed the wiring harness assembly into the outer end of the handlebar.
5. Continue to pull until the wiring harness is pulled into the correct location. Remove the electrical tape and detach fish wire.
6. Repeat the process to install the remaining wiring harness assembly.
7. On 2008-2009 models, install the throttle twist grip assembly as described in Chapter Ten.
8. Assemble the right and left side handlebar switch assemblies and tighten the screws.
9. Slide the boot onto the left-hand switch wiring and terminal.
10. Refer to the drawings and notes made in *Handlebar Disassembly*. The wires *must* be installed into the correct chamber location in the Molex and/or Deutsch connector for the switch or component to operate correctly.
11. Assemble the wiring connectors into the Deutsch terminals as described in Chapter Eleven. Install the wiring terminals into the following:
    a. Heated handgrip power connector.
    b. Interconnect harness connector.
12. Assemble the wiring terminals into the Multi-lock connectors as described in Chapter Eleven. Install the wiring terminals into the turn signal Multi-lock connector.
13. Assemble the wiring connectors into the Molex terminals as described in Chapter Eleven. Install the wiring terminals into the following:
    a. Left-hand switch connector.
    b. Right-hand switch connector.
    c. Throttle twist grip sensor connector (2008-2009 models).
14. Connect the heated handgrip power connector and the interconnect harness connector.
15. Install new cable straps in the original locations.
16. Install the handlebar assembly as described in this section.

FRONT FORK

Front Fork Service

To simplify fork service and to prevent the mixing of parts, remove, service and install the fork legs individually.

Removal (No Service)

1A. On all FLHT and FLHX models, remove the outer front fairing (Chapter Seventeen). On FLHTC models, also remove the storage box (Chapter Eleven).
1B. On all FLHR models, remove the headlight nacelle as described in Chapter Eleven.
1C. On all FLTR models, remove the instrument nacelle as described in Chapter Eleven.
2. On all models except FLTR, remove the passing light assembly as described in Chapter Eleven.
3. Support the motorcycle with the front wheel off the ground as described in *Motorcycle Stands* (Chapter Twelve).
4. Remove the front wheel as described in Chapter Twelve.
5. Remove the front fender as described in Chapter Seventeen.

6. Remove the screws securing the chrome mounting bracket (**Figure 8**) and remove the bracket, on models so equipped.
7. If both fork legs are going to be removed, mark them with an R (right side) and L (left side) so the legs will be reinstalled on the correct side.
8. Loosen the fork cap bolt (**Figure 9**) from top of the fork tube, but do not remove it yet.
9. Loosen the lower fork bridge pinch bolt (**Figure 10**) at the lower fork bridge, but do not remove it yet.
10. Spray a little glass cleaner all around the fork tube above the fork stop.
11. Slide the fork tube up against the upper fork bracket.
12. Secure the fork leg and remove the fork cap bolt (**Figure 9**).
13. Slide the fork leg down and remove the rubber stop (**Figure 11**) from the fork tube.
14. Continue to slide the fork tube out of the lower fork bracket. It may be necessary to rotate the fork tube slightly while pulling it down and out. Remove the fork leg and keep it vertical.
15. Tighten the fork cap bolt (**Figure 9**) securely to avoid the loss of fork oil.
16. Take the fork leg to the workbench for service. If the fork is not going to be serviced, wrap it in a large towel or blanket to protect the surface from damage.
17. Repeat the procedure to remove the remaining fork leg.

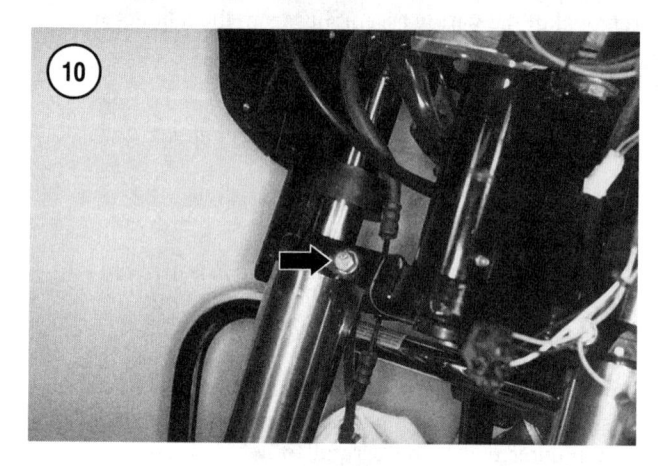

Installation (Not Serviced)

1. Hold the fork leg vertical and remove the fork cap bolt (**Figure 9**).
2. Install the fork tube through the lower fork bracket and install the rubber fork stop (**Figure 11**).
3. Continue to push the fork tube up through the lower fork bracket until it bottoms against the upper fork bracket.
4. Install the fork cap bolt (**Figure 9**) onto top of the fork tube and tighten it securely.
5. Tighten the lower fork bridge pinch bolt (**Figure 12**) to 30-35 ft.-lb. (40.7-47.5 N•m).
6. Tighten the fork cap bolt (**Figure 9**) to 50-60 ft.-lb. (67.8-81.3 N•m).
7. Install the chrome mounting bracket, on models so equipped. Install the screws and tighten securely.
8. Install the front fender as described in Chapter Seventeen.
9. Install the front wheel as described in Chapter Twelve.
10. On all models except FLTR, install the passing light assembly as described in Chapter Eleven.
11A. On all FLHT and FLHX models, install the outer front fairing (Chapter Seventeen). On FLHTC models, also install the storage box (Chapter Eleven).
11B. On all FLHR models, install the headlight nacelle as described in Chapter Eleven.
11C. On all FLTR models, install the instrument nacelle as described in Chapter Eleven.

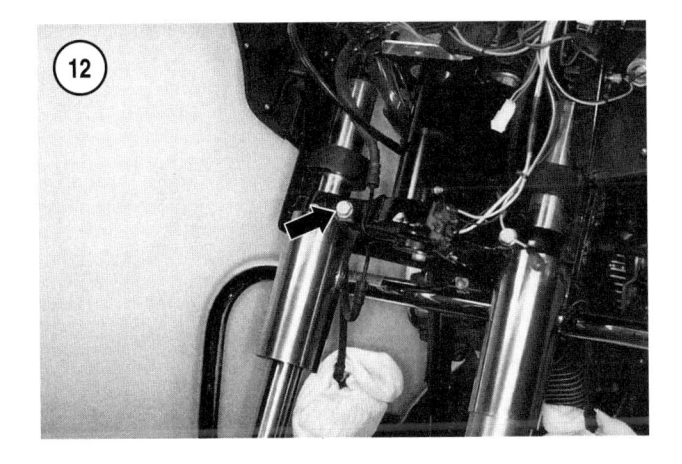

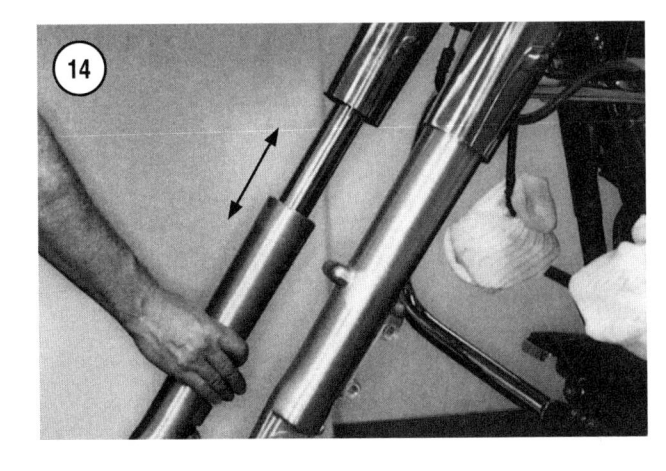

FRONT SUSPENSION AND STEERING

2. On all models except FLTR, remove the passing light assembly as described in Chapter Eleven.

3. Support the motorcycle with the front wheel off the ground as described in *Motorcycle Stands* (Chapter Twelve).

4. Remove the front wheel (A, **Figure 13**) as described in Chapter Twelve.

5. Remove the front fender as described in Chapter Seventeen.

6. Remove the screws securing the chrome mounting bracket (**Figure 8**) and remove the bracket, on model so equipped.

7. If both fork tube legs are going to be removed, mark them with an R (right side) and L (left side) so the legs will be reinstalled on the correct side.

8. Remove the fork cap bolt (**Figure 9**) from top of the fork tube.

9. Loosen the pinch bolt (**Figure 10**) at the lower fork bridge.

10. Slide the fork leg part way down and securely retighten the pinch bolt (**Figure 12**).

11. Place a drain pan under the fork slider to catch the fork oil.

12. Remove the drain bolt (B, **Figure 13**) and washer, and then drain the fork oil. Pump the slider several times to expel most of the fork oil. Reinstall the drain bolt and washer and tighten.

13. Use an 8-mm Allen wrench and impact driver and loosen the damper rod bolt at the base of the slider. Do not remove.

14. Remove the stopper ring from the fork slider.

15. Lower the fork slider on the fork tube.

NOTE
It may be necessary to slightly heat the area on the slider around the oil seal prior to removal. Use a rag soaked in hot water; do not apply a flame directly to the fork slider.

16. There is an interference fit between the bushing in the fork slider and the bushing on the fork tube. In order to remove the fork tube from the slider, pull hard on the fork tube using quick in-and-out strokes (**Figure 14**). This will withdraw the bushing and the oil seal from the slider.

17. Remove the slider from the fork tube. If still in place, remove the oil lock piece from the damper rod if it is still in place.

18. Loosen the pinch bolt (**Figure 12**). Slide the fork tube out of the lower fork bracket and remove the rubber stop (**Figure 11**) from the fork tube. It may be necessary to rotate the fork tube slightly while pulling it down and out. Remove the fork leg and take it to the workbench for service.

19. Repeat the procedure to remove the remaining fork leg.

20. Disassemble the fork leg as described in this section.

12. Apply the front brake and pump the front forks several times to seat the forks and front wheel.

Removal (For Service)

1A. On all FLHT and FLHX models, remove the outer front fairing (Chapter Seventeen). On FLHTC models, also remove the storage box (Chapter Eleven).

1B. On all FLHR models, remove the headlight nacelle as described in Chapter Eleven.

1C. On all FLTR models, remove the instrument nacelle as described in Chapter Eleven.

FRONT FORK

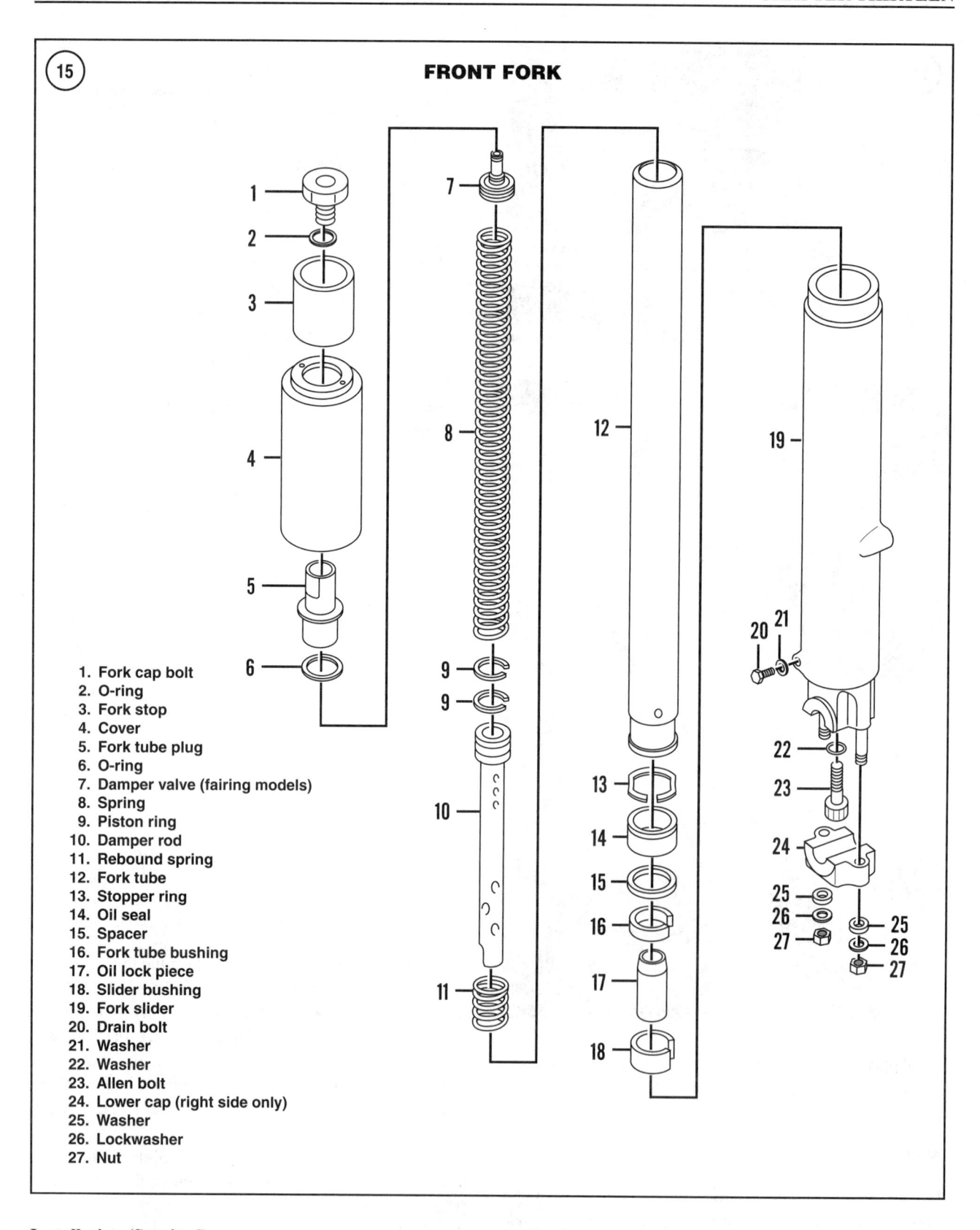

15

1. Fork cap bolt
2. O-ring
3. Fork stop
4. Cover
5. Fork tube plug
6. O-ring
7. Damper valve (fairing models)
8. Spring
9. Piston ring
10. Damper rod
11. Rebound spring
12. Fork tube
13. Stopper ring
14. Oil seal
15. Spacer
16. Fork tube bushing
17. Oil lock piece
18. Slider bushing
19. Fork slider
20. Drain bolt
21. Washer
22. Washer
23. Allen bolt
24. Lower cap (right side only)
25. Washer
26. Lockwasher
27. Nut

Installation (Serviced)

1. Assemble the fork and refill the fork oil as described in this section.

2. Install the fork tube through the lower fork bracket and install the rubber fork stop (**Figure 11**).

3. Continue to push the fork tube up through the lower fork bracket until it bottoms against the upper fork bracket.

4. Tighten the lower fork bridge pinch bolt (**Figure 10**) to 30-35 ft.-lb. (40.7-47.5 N•m).

5. Tighten the fork tube plug to 22-58 ft.-lb. (29.8-78.6 N•m).

FRONT SUSPENSION AND STEERING

11C. On all FLTR models, install the instrument nacelle as described in Chapter Eleven.

12. Apply the front brake and pump the front forks several times to seat the forks and front wheel.

Fork Tube
Disassembly

Refer to **Figure 15**.

NOTE
A fork holding tool is required to disassemble and assemble this fork assembly. The fork spring cannot be compressed sufficiently by hand to loosen and remove the fork tube plug.

1. Separate the fork tube from the slider as described in this section.
2. To protect the fork tube, place a steel washer (A, **Figure 16**) over the fork damper rod and up against the base of the fork tube.
3. Tighten the bolt (B, **Figure 16**) so it seated below the steel washer. Do not over tighten as the damper rod will be damaged. Make sure the tool is indexed properly against the steel washer.
4. Install the holding tool's upper bolt into the hole in the fork tube plug following the manufacturer's instructions. Make sure the tool (A, **Figure 17**) is indexed properly in the hole in the fork tube plug.

WARNING
Be careful when removing the fork tube plug as the spring is under pressure. Protect eyes and face accordingly.

5. Hold onto the fork tube and loosen the fork tube plug (B, **Figure 17**). Slowly loosen the tool while unscrewing the fork tube plug.
6. When the fork tube plug is completely unscrewed from the fork tube, remove the tool from the fork leg.
7. Remove the fork tube plug and fork spring and drain out any residual fork oil. Dispose of the fork oil properly.
8A. On non-fairing equipped models, turn the fork tube upside down, remove the damper rod and rebound spring.
8B. On fairing equipped models, turn the fork tube upside down, remove the damper valve, damper rod and rebound spring.

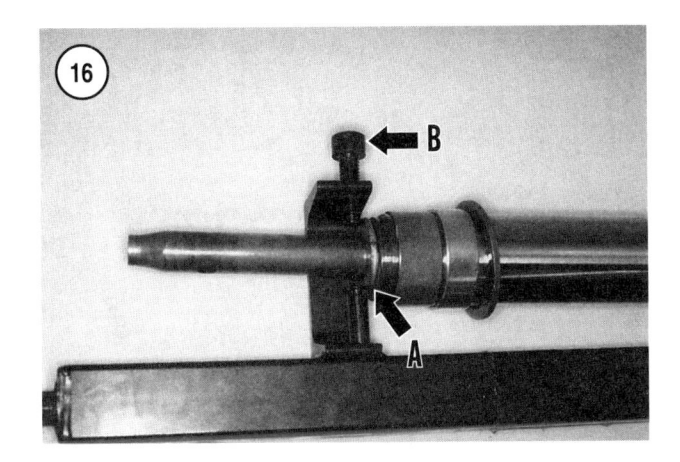

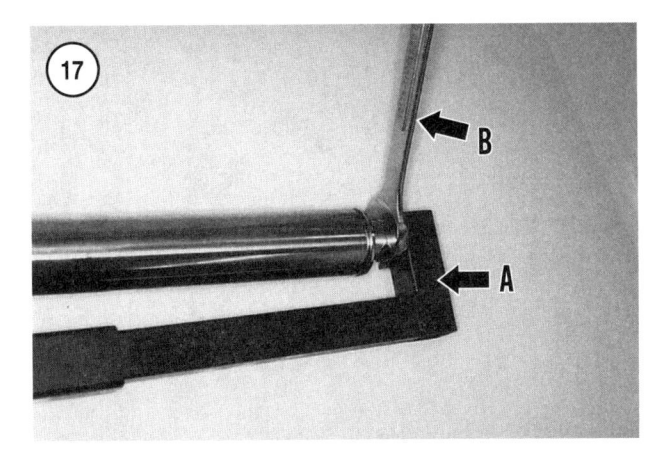

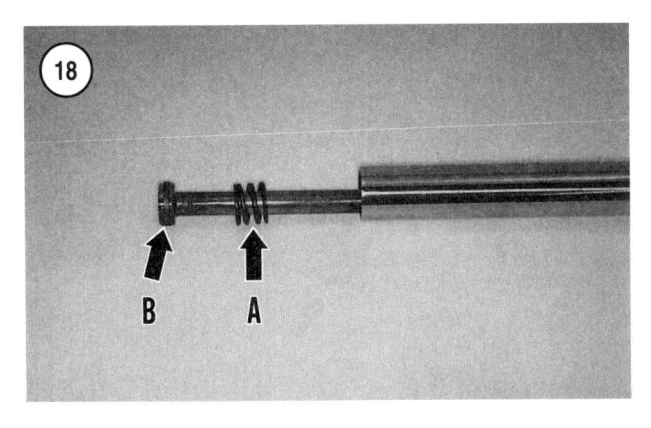

6. Install the fork cap bolt (**Figure 9**) onto top of the fork tube and tighten to 50-60 ft.-lb. (67.8-81.3 N•m).
7. Install the front fender as described in Chapter Seventeen.
8. Install the front wheel (A, **Figure 13**) as described in Chapter Twelve.
9. Make sure the drain bolt (B, **Figure 13**) is tightened securely.
10. On all models except FLTR, install the passing light assembly as described in Chapter Eleven.
11A. On all FLHT and FLHX models, install the outer front fairing (Chapter Seventeen). On FLHTC models, also install the storage box (Chapter Eleven).
11B. On all FLHR models, install the headlight nacelle as described in Chapter Eleven.

Fork Tube and Slider
Assembly

1. Coat all parts with H-D Type E, or an equivalent, fork oil before assembly.
2. Install the rebound spring (A, **Figure 18**) onto the damper rod and slide the damper rod (B) into the fork tube until it extends out the end of the fork tube.
3. Install the oil lock piece (**Figure 19**) onto the end of the damper rod.

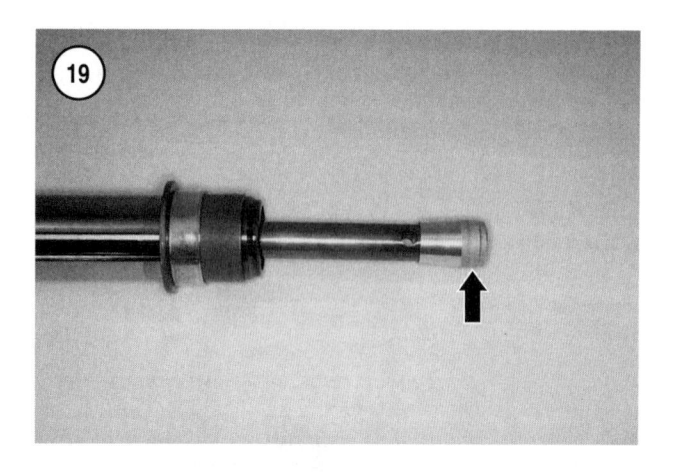

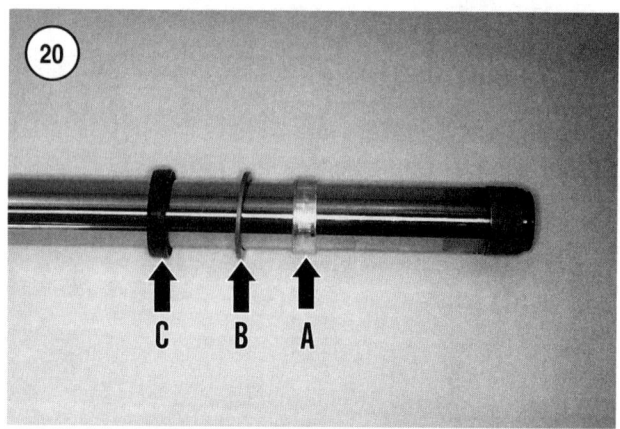

4. Slide the fork slider bushing (A, **Figure 20**) and oil seal spacer (B) down into the fork tube. Position the oil seal (C, **Figure 20**) with the letters facing up and slide it down the fork tube.

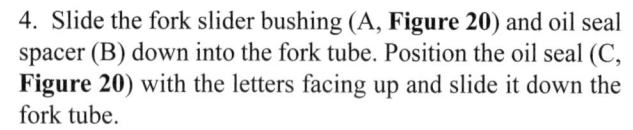

CAUTION
To protect the oil seal lips, place a thin plastic bag on top of the fork tube. Before installing the seal in the following steps, lightly coat the bag and the seal lips with fork oil.

5. Push the fork tube (A, **Figure 21**) and damper rod into the fork slider (B). Insert a Phillips screwdriver through the opening in the bottom of the fork tube and guide the damper rod end into the receptacle in the base of the slider. Remove the screwdriver.

6. Slide the oil seal (**Figure 22**) down into the fork tube receptacle.

NOTE
*A fork seal driver (A, **Figure 23**) is required to install the fork tube bushing and seal into the fork tube. A number of different aftermarket fork seal drivers (JIMS part No. 2046) are available. Another method is to use a piece of pipe or metal collar with correct dimensions to slide over the fork tube and seat against the seal. When selecting or fabricating a driver tool, it must have sufficient weight to drive the bushing and oil seal into the fork tube.*

7. Slide the fork seal driver down the fork tube and seat it against the oil seal (B, **Figure 23**).

8. Operate the fork seal driver, or an equivalent, and drive the fork slider bushing and new seal into the fork tube. Continue to operate the driver until the stopper ring groove in the tube is visible above the fork seal. Remove the fork seal driver tool.

9. Install the stopper ring (**Figure 24**) into the slider groove. Make sure the retaining ring seats in the groove (**Figure 25**).

10. Temporarily install the spring into the fork tube and onto the top of the damper rod.

11. Place several shop rags on the floor.

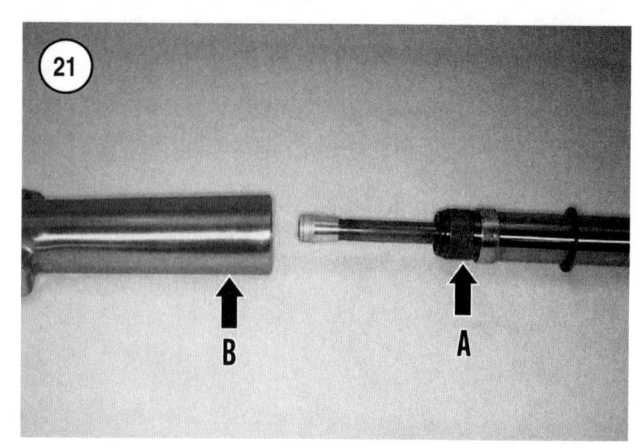

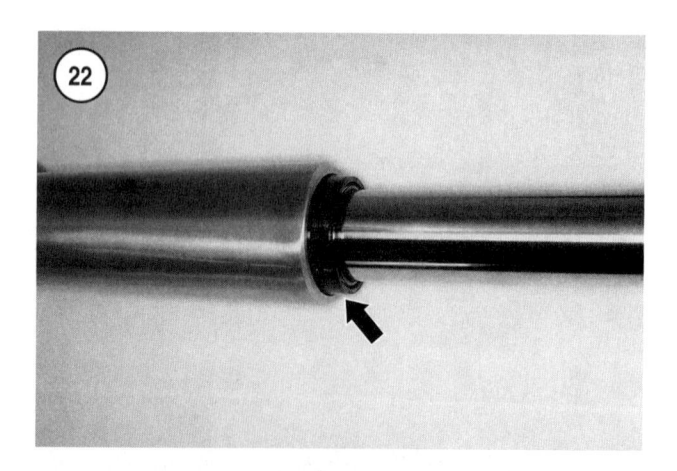

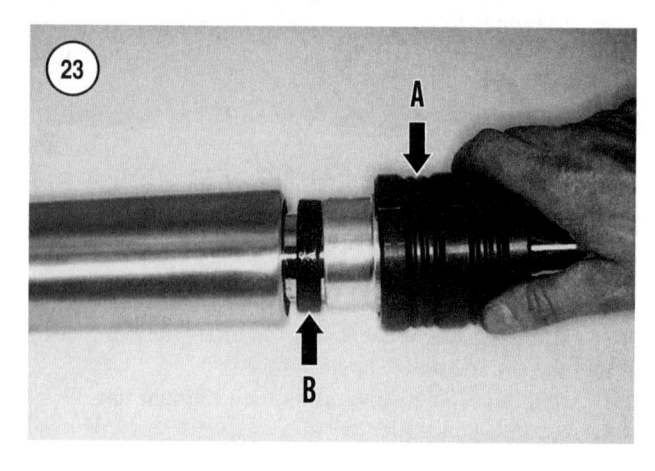

FRONT SUSPENSION AND STEERING

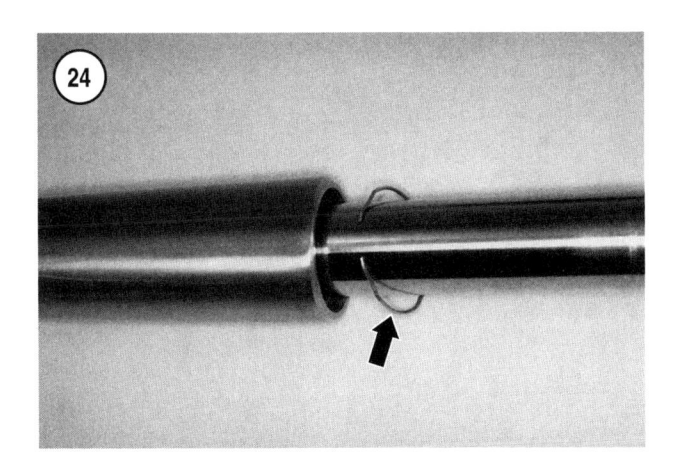

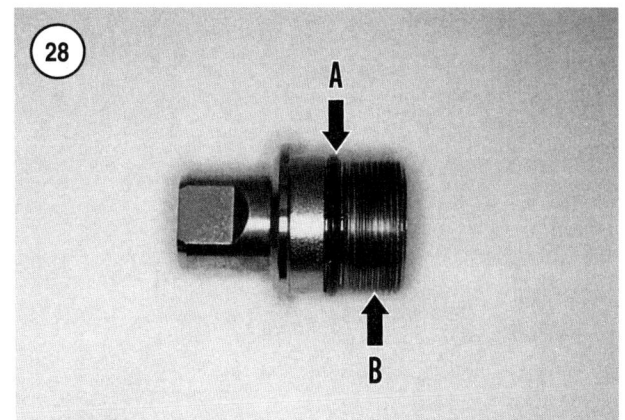

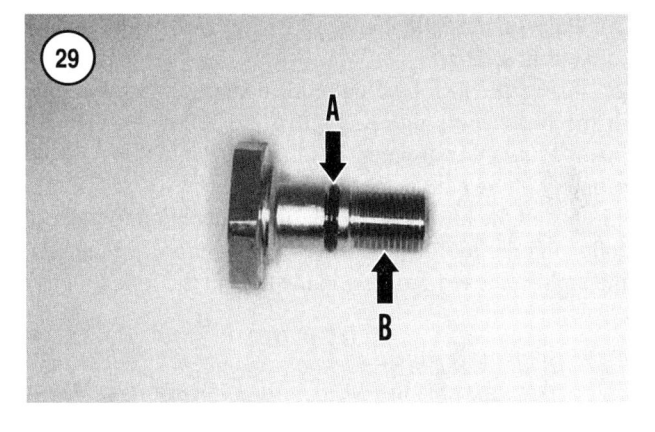

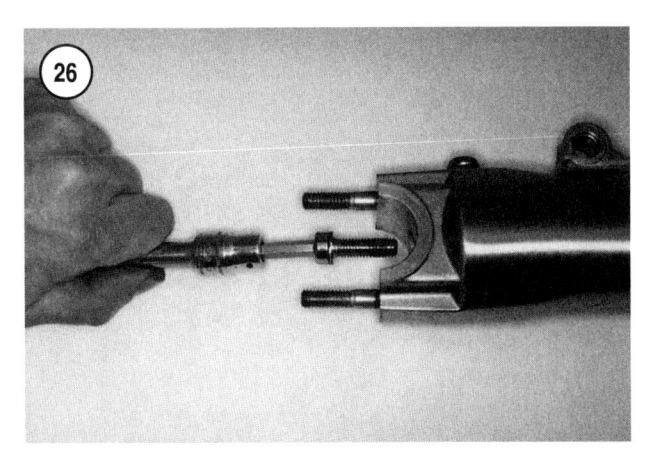

12. Hold the spring in place and turn the fork assembly upside down and place it vertically on the shop cloths.
13. Install a *new* washer on the Allen bolt.
14. Apply a medium-strength threadlock to the damper rod Allen bolt threads prior to installation. Insert the Allen bolt (**Figure 26**) through the lower end of the slider and thread it into the damper rod. Tighten the Allen bolt to 11-18 ft.-lb. (14.9-24.4 N•m).
15. Hold onto the spring and invert the fork assembly. Remove the fork spring.
16. Fill the fork oil and adjust the oil level. Refer to *Fork Oil Filling and Adjustment* in this section.

NOTE
Keep the fork assembly upright to avoid the loss of fork oil.

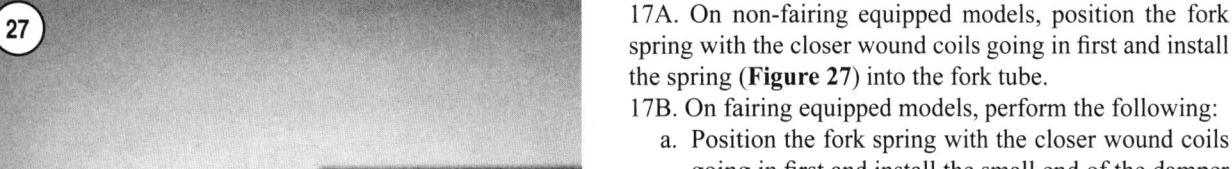

17A. On non-fairing equipped models, position the fork spring with the closer wound coils going in first and install the spring (**Figure 27**) into the fork tube.
17B. On fairing equipped models, perform the following:
   a. Position the fork spring with the closer wound coils going in first and install the small end of the damper valve onto the lower end of the fork spring.
   b. Install the fork spring and damper valve assembly into the fork tube and onto the top of the damper rod.
18. Install a *new* O-ring (A, **Figure 28**) onto the fork tube plug (B).
19. Install a *new* O-ring (A, **Figure 29**) onto on the fork cap bolt (B).

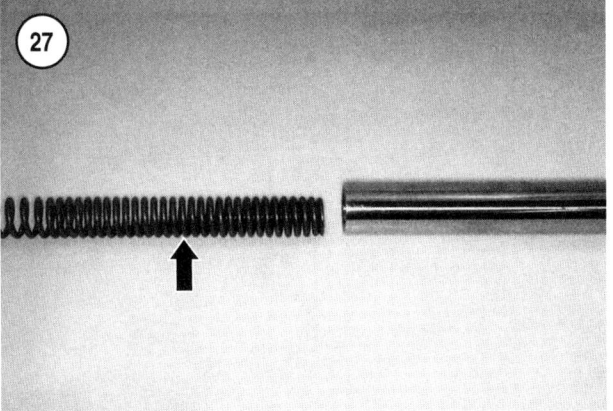

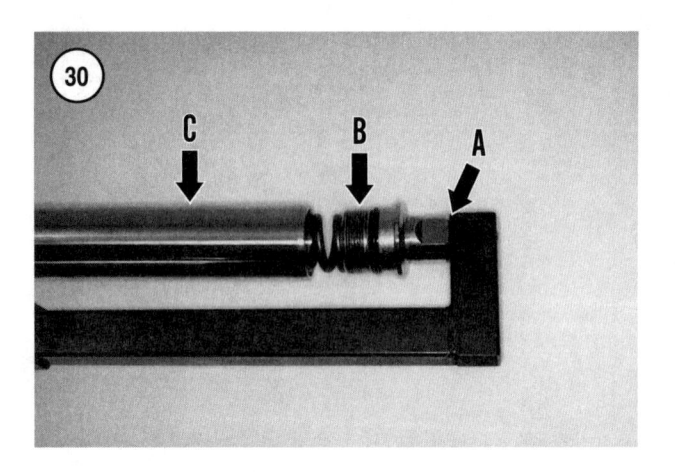

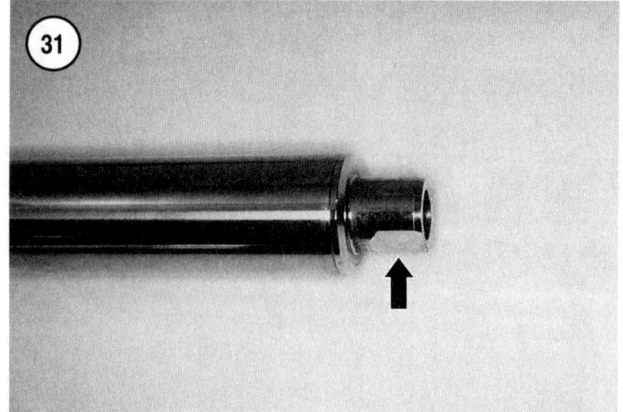

20. Position the fork tube plug (B, **Figure 28**) onto the top of the fork spring.
21. Install the fork holding tool's upper bolt into the hole in the fork tube plug (A, **Figure 30**) following the tool manufacturer's instructions. Make sure the tool is indexed properly in the hole in the fork tube plug.
22. Install the lower end of the fork assembly into the tool following the tool manufacturer's instructions. Make sure the tool is indexed properly in the hole in the fork slider.

CAUTION
While tightening the tool, do not force the fork tube plug into the threaded portion of the fork tube. Doing so will damage the threads on either or both parts.

23. Hold onto the fork tube plug and slowly tighten the tool while guiding the fork tube plug (B, **Figure 30**) into the top of the fork tube (C).
24. Place wrench on the fork tube plug (B, **Figure 17**) and screw the fork tube plug into the fork tube while tightening the tool. Once the fork tube plug has started to thread sufficiently into the fork tube, loosen the tool and remove it from the fork assembly.
25. Place the slider in a vise with soft jaws and tighten the fork tube plug (**Figure 31**) securely. It will be tightened to the final torque specification (**Table 2**) after the fork has been installed as decribed in this section.

Inspection

1. Thoroughly clean all parts in solvent and dry them. Check the fork tube for signs of wear or scratches.
2. Check the fork tube for bending, nicks, rust or other damage. Place the fork tube on a set of V-blocks and check runout with a dial indicator (**Figure 32**). If these tools are not available, roll the fork tube on a large plate glass or other flat surface.
3. Check the internal threads (**Figure 33**) in the top of the fork tube for stripping, cross-threading or sealer residue. Use a tap to true up the threads and to remove sealer deposits.
4. Check the external threads on the fork tube plug (B, **Figure 28**) for stripping, cross-threading or sealer residue.

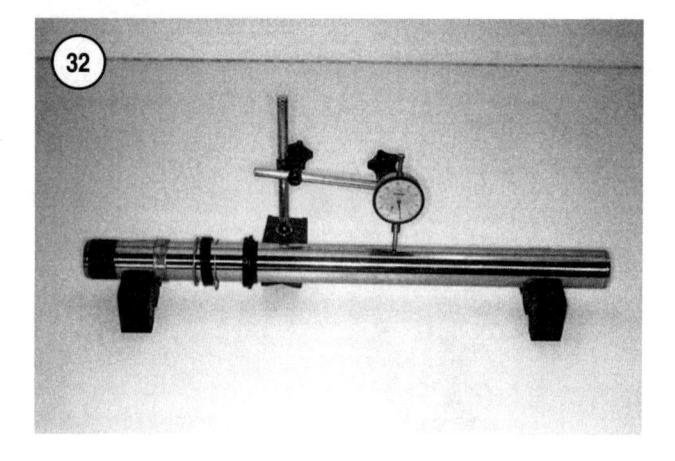

FRONT SUSPENSION AND STEERING

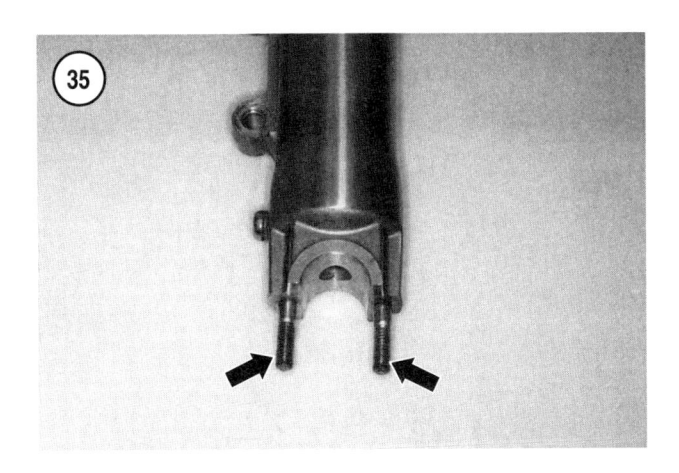

Use a die to true up the threads and to remove sealer deposits.

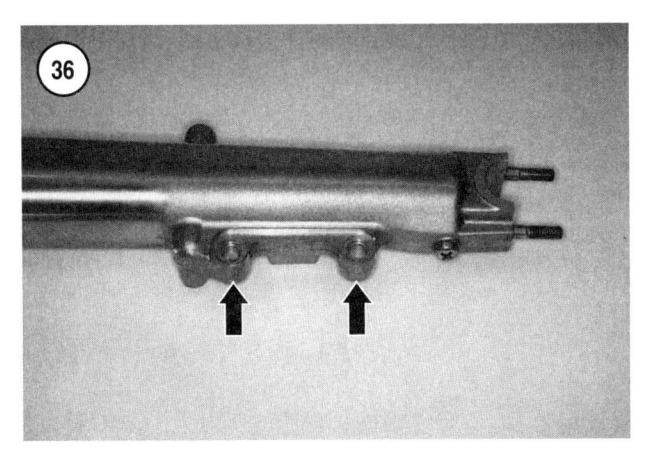

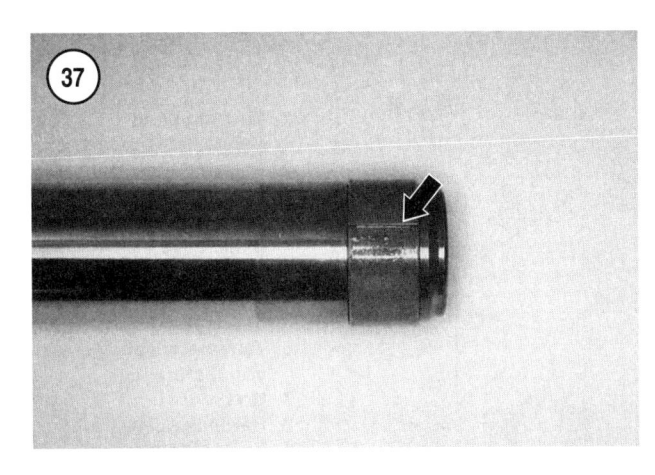

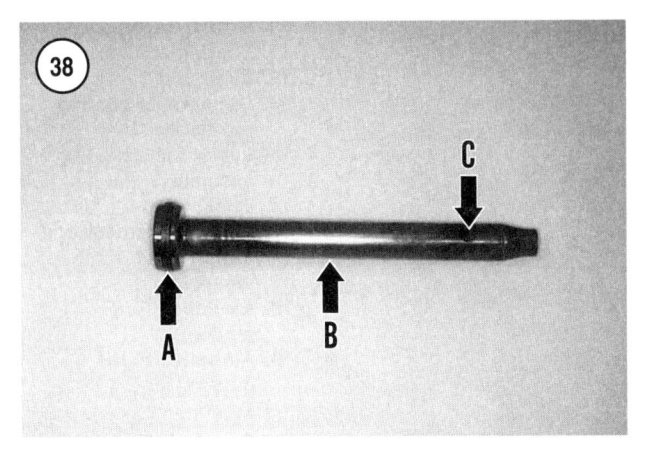

5. Check the external threads on the fork cap bolt (B, **Figure 29**) for stripping, cross-threading or sealer residue. Use a die to true up the threads and to remove sealer deposits.

6. Check the slider for dents or other exterior damage. Check the retaining ring groove (**Figure 34**) in the top of the slider for cracks or other damage.

7. Check the threaded studs (**Figure 35**) at the base of the right side slider for damage. Repair if necessary.

8. Check the front caliper mounting bosses (**Figure 36**) for cracks or damage.

9. Check the slider and fork tube bushings for excessive wear, cracks or damage.

10. Remove the fork tube bushing as follows:
    a. Expand the bushing slit (**Figure 37**) with a screwdriver and then slide the bushing off the fork tube.
    b. Coat the new bushing with new fork oil.
    c. Install the new bushing by expanding the slit slightly with a screwdriver.
    d. Seat the new bushing into the fork tube groove.

11. Check the damper rod piston ring(s) (A, **Figure 38**) for excessive wear, cracks or other damage. If necessary, replace both rings as a set.

12. Check the damper rod (B, **Figure 38**) for straightness with a set of V-blocks and a dial indicator (**Figure 39**) or by rolling it on a piece of plate glass. Specifications for runout are not available. If the damper rod is not straight, replace it.

13. Make sure the oil passage hole in the damper rod (C, **Figure 38**) is open. If clogged, flush with solvent and dry with compressed air.

14. Check the internal threads in the bottom of the damper rod for stripping, cross-threading or sealer residue. Use a tap to true up the threads and to remove sealer deposits.

15. Check the damper rod rebound spring and the fork spring for wear or damage. Service limit specifications for spring free length are not available from the manufacturer. If necessary, replace both springs as a set.

16. Replace the oil seal whenever it is removed. Always replace both oil seals as a set.

592 CHAPTER THIRTEEN

40

Oil level

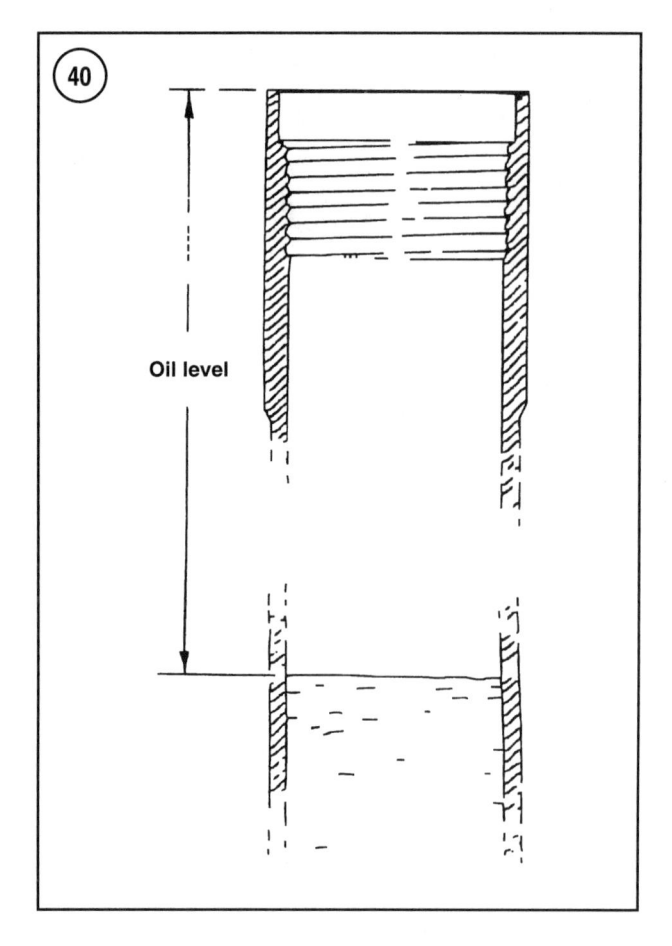

41

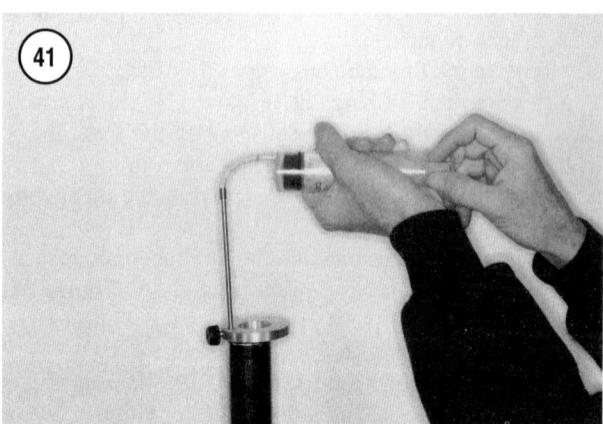

42

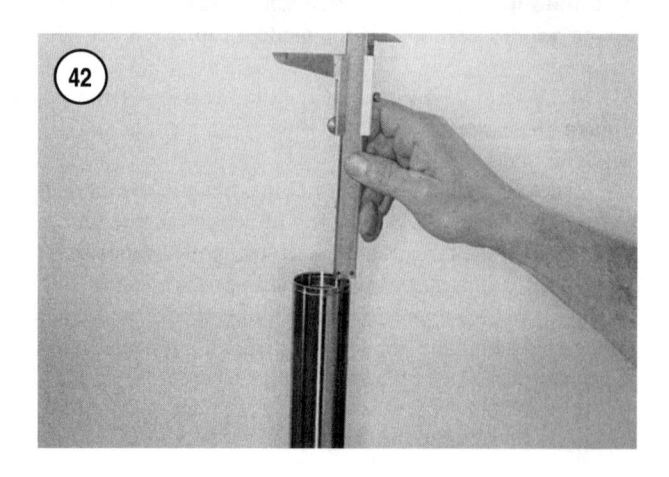

43 STEERING STEM

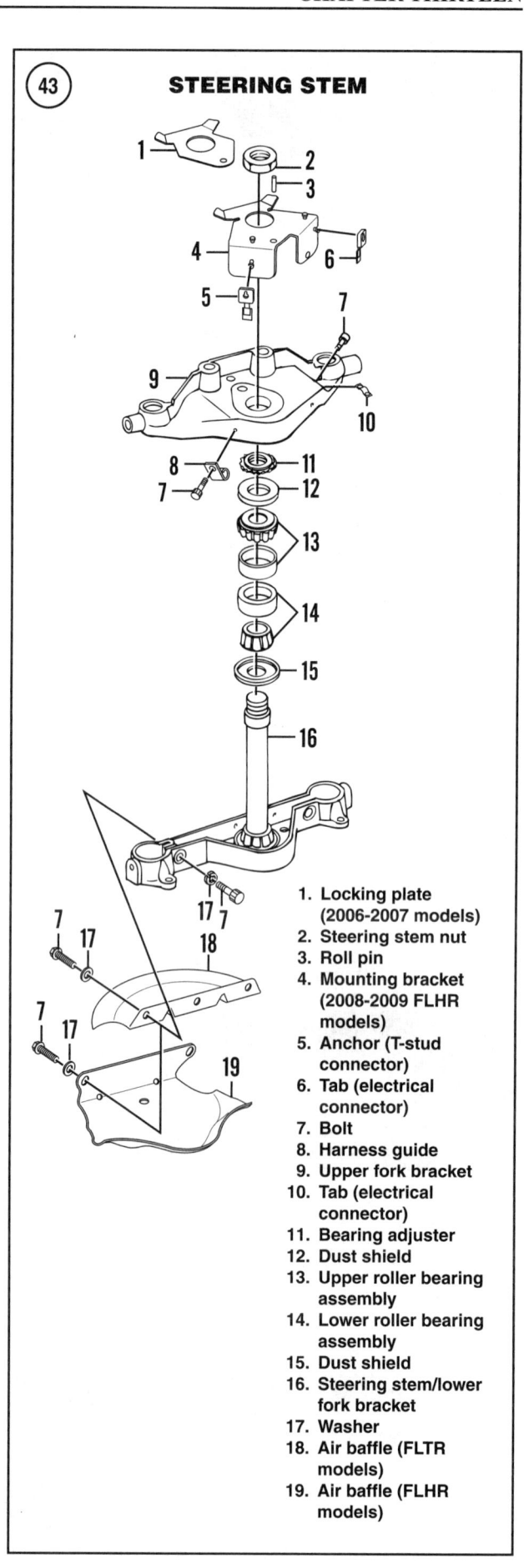

1. Locking plate (2006-2007 models)
2. Steering stem nut
3. Roll pin
4. Mounting bracket (2008-2009 FLHR models)
5. Anchor (T-stud connector)
6. Tab (electrical connector)
7. Bolt
8. Harness guide
9. Upper fork bracket
10. Tab (electrical connector)
11. Bearing adjuster
12. Dust shield
13. Upper roller bearing assembly
14. Lower roller bearing assembly
15. Dust shield
16. Steering stem/lower fork bracket
17. Washer
18. Air baffle (FLTR models)
19. Air baffle (FLHR models)

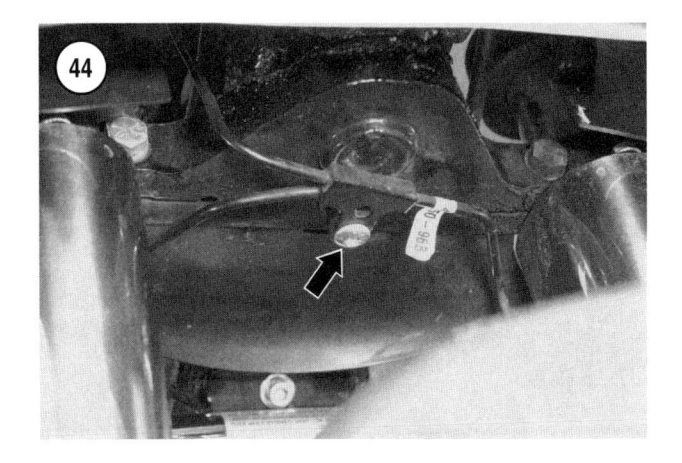

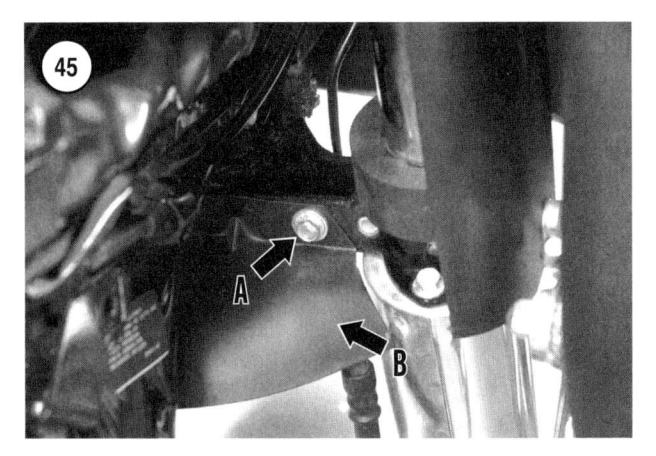

FRONT SUSPENSION AND STEERING

compression and rebound travel strokes. Stop when the fork tube has bottomed.

5. Set the fork assembly in a vertical position for approximately 5 minutes to allow any suspended air bubbles to surface and dissipate.

6. Set the oil level (**Figure 40**) as follows:
    a. Make sure the fork tube is bottomed against the slider and placed in a vertical position.
    b. Use a fork oil level gauge (**Figure 41**), or a caliper **Figure 42**, and set the oil level to the specification in **Table 1**.

NOTE
If no oil is drawn out when setting the oil level, not enough oil is in the fork tube. Add more oil and reset the level.

   c. If used, remove the fork oil level gauge.

7. Repeat the process for the remaining fork leg. Set the oil to exactly the same level in both fork legs.

8. Keep the fork leg vertical and perform Steps 17-25 of *Fork Tube And Slider Assembly* (this section).

STEERING HEAD AND STEM

Removal

Refer to **Figure 43**.

1A. On all FLHT and FLHX models, remove the front fairing assembly as described in Chapter Seventeen.

1B. On all FLHR models, remove the headlight nacelle as described in Chapter Eleven.

1C. On all FLTR models, remove the instrument nacelle as described in Chapter Eleven.

2. On all models except FLTR, remove the passing light assembly as described in Chapter Eleven.

3. Support the motorcycle with the front wheel off the ground as described in *Motorcycle Stands* (Chapter Twelve).

4. Remove the front wheel as described in Chapter Twelve.

5. Remove the front fender as described in Chapter Seventeen.

6. Remove both front fork legs as described in this chapter.

7. Remove the handlebar as described in this chapter.

8. Remove the bolt (**Figure 44**) securing the front brake line assembly to the bottom of the lower fork bracket. Do not disconnect any brake line connections.

9. On FLTR and FLHR models, remove the screw (A, **Figure 45**) and washer on each side securing the air dam (B) to the backside of the lower fork bracket and remove it.

10. On fairing equipped models, remove the interconnect harness ground socket terminal from the spade terminal on the upper fork bridge.

11. Move all electrical harnesses away from the area.

12. Pry the tabs on the locking plate away from the steering stem nut.

13. Loosen and remove the steering stem hex nut (**Figure 46**).

Fork Oil Filling and Adjustment

This section describes filling the fork with oil, setting the oil level and completing fork assembly.

1. Perform Steps 1-15 of *Fork Tube And Slider Assembly* (this section).

2. Secure the fork leg upright in a vise with soft jaws and fully compress the fork leg, or an equivalent.

3. Fill the fork leg with approximately 11 oz. (319 ml) of H-D Type E fork oil.

4. Hold the slider with one hand and slowly move the fork tube up and down. Repeat until the fork tube moves smoothly with the same amount of tension throughout the

14A. On 2006 and 2007 models, remove the lock plate (A, **Figure 47**).
14B. On 2008-2009 models, remove the roll pin and the lock plate.
15. Remove the upper fork bracket. (B, **Figure 47**).

NOTE
Hold or secure the steering stem as it may fall down after removing the bearing adjuster.

16. Remove the bearing adjuster (**Figure 48**) and dust shield (**Figure 49**).
17. Use a rubber mallet and tap the steering stem/lower fork bracket to free it from the upper bearing cone.
18. Slide the steering stem/lower fork bracket down and out (**Figure 50**) of the steering head.
19. Remove the upper bearing.
20. Remove the lower bearing and dust shield (**Figure 51**) from the lower fork bracket as described in this chapter, if necessary.
21. Inspect the steering stem and bearing assembly as described in this section.

Installation

1. Make sure to seat both steering head bearing races in the frame.
2. Wipe the bearing races with a clean lint-free cloth. Then lubricate each race with bearing grease.
3. Pack the upper and lower bearings with a quality bearing grease.
4. If removed, install a *new* lower dust shield on the steering stem and press it down until seated.

NOTE
Before installing the steering stem, make sure the threads on the stem are clean. Any dirt, grease or other residue on the threads affects the steering stem adjustment.

5. If removed, install the lower bearing onto the steering stem. Press the bearing into place with both thumbs until it bottoms against the dust seal.
6. Install the upper bearing (**Figure 52**) and seat it into to the upper race.
7. Insert the steering stem up (**Figure 50**) into the frame steering head through the upper bearing and hold it firmly in place.
8. Install the upper dust shield (**Figure 49**) and seat it in the upper race.
9. Install the bearing adjuster (**Figure 48**) and tighten to remove all bearing play within the steering head.
10. Install the upper fork bracket (B, **Figure 47**) over the steering stem.
11A. On 2006 and 2007 models, install the lock plate (A, **Figure 47**).
11B. On 2008-2009 models, install the roll pin and the lock plate.

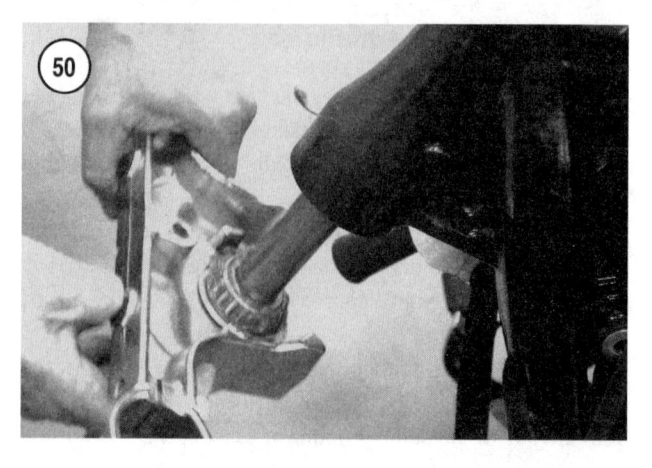

FRONT SUSPENSION AND STEERING

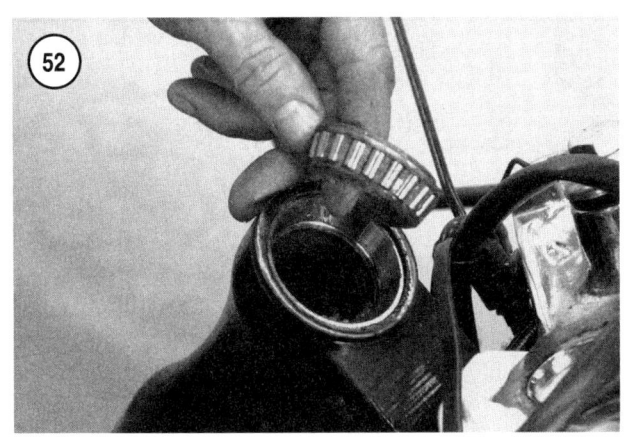

12. Install the steering stem hex nut (**Figure 46**). Hand-tight the nut at this time.
13. Install the front fork legs as described in this chapter.

CAUTION
Do not overtighten the steering stem nut or damage will occur to the bearings and races. Final adjustment of the fork stem will take place after the front wheel is installed.

14. Tighten the steering stem hex nut until the steering stem can be turned from side to side with no noticeable axial or lateral play. When the steering play feels correct, tighten the steering stem hex nut to 60-80 ft.-lb. (81.3-108.5 N•m).
15. Bend the tabs on the locking plate up against the flats on the steering stem nut.
16. On fairing-equipped models, install the interconnect harness ground socket connector onto the spade terminal on the upper fork bridge.
17. On FLTR and FLHR models, install the air dam (B, **Figure 45**) onto the backside of the lower fork bracket. Install the screws (A, **Figure 45**) and washer on each side. Tighten the screws to 120-144 in.-lb. (13.6-16.3 N•m).
18. Move the front brake line assembly onto the bottom of the lower fork bracket. Install the bolt (**Figure 44**) and tighten securely.
19. Install the handlebar as described in this chapter.
20. Install both front fork legs as described in this chapter.
21. Install the front fender as described in Chapter Seventeen.
22. Install the front wheel as described in Chapter Twelve.
23. On all models except FLTR, install the passing light assembly as described in Chapter Eleven.
24A. On all FLHT and FLHX models, install the front fairing assembly as described in Chapter Seventeen.
24B. On all FLHR models, install the headlight nacelle as described in Chapter Eleven.
24C. On all FLTR models, install the instrument nacelle as described in Chapter Eleven.
25. Adjust the steering play as described in *Steering Play Inspection and Adjustment* (this chapter).

Inspection

The bearing outer races are pressed into the steering head. Do not remove them unless they are going to be replaced as described in this chapter.
1. Wipe the bearing races with a solvent-soaked rag, and then dry with compressed air or a lint-free cloth. Check the races in the steering head (**Figure 53** and **Figure 54**) for pitting, scratches, galling or excessive wear. If any of these conditions exist, replace the races as described in this chapter. If the races are okay, wipe each race with grease.
2. Clean the bearings in solvent to remove all of the old grease. Blow the bearing dry with compressed air, making sure not to allow the air jet to spin the bearing. Do not

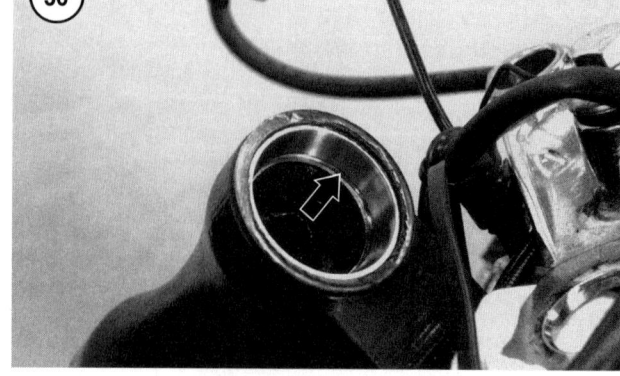

remove the lower bearing from the fork stem unless it is to be replaced. Clean the bearing while installed on the steering stem.

3. After the bearings are dry, hold the inner race with one hand and turn the outer race with the other hand. Turn the bearing slowly, the bearing must turn smoothly with no roughness. Visually check the bearing (**Figure 55**) for pitting, scratches or visible damage. If the bearings are worn, check the dust covers for wear or damage or for improper bearing lubrication. Replace the bearing if necessary. If a bearing is going to be reused, pack it with grease and wrap it with wax paper or some other type of lint-free material until it is reinstalled. Do not store the bearings for any length of time without lubricating them to prevent rust.

4. Check the steering stem for cracks or damage. Check the threads at the top of the stem for damage. Check the steering stem nut for damage. Thread it onto the steering stem; make sure the nut threads on easily with no roughness.

5. Replace all worn or damaged parts. Replace bearing races as described in this chapter.

6. If necessary, replace the lower steering stem bearing and the dust shield as described in this chapter.

7. Check for broken welds on the frame around the steering head. If any are found, have them repaired.

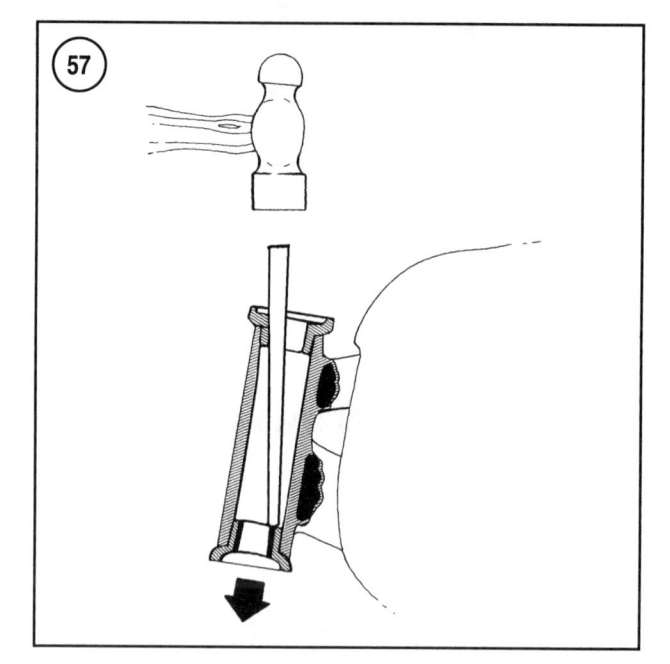

STEERING HEAD BEARING RACE REPLACEMENT

The upper and lower bearing outer races are pressed into the frame. Do not remove the bearing races unless replacement is necessary. If removed, replace both the outer race along with the bearing at the same time. Never reinstall an outer race that has been removed as it is no longer true and will damage the bearing if reused.

Steering Head Bearing Replacement

1. Remove the steering stem as described in this chapter.
2. To remove a race (**Figure 56**), insert an aluminum or brass rod into the steering head and carefully tap the race out from the inside (**Figure 57**). Tap all around the race so that neither the race nor the steering head is bent.
3. Clean the steering head with solvent and dry thoroughly.
4A. Install the bearing races with a steering head bearing race installer (JIMS part No. 1725), or an equivalent, by following the manufacturer's instructions.
4B. If the installer tool (**Figure 58**) is not available, install the bearing races as follows:

FRONT SUSPENSION AND STEERING

Figure 59

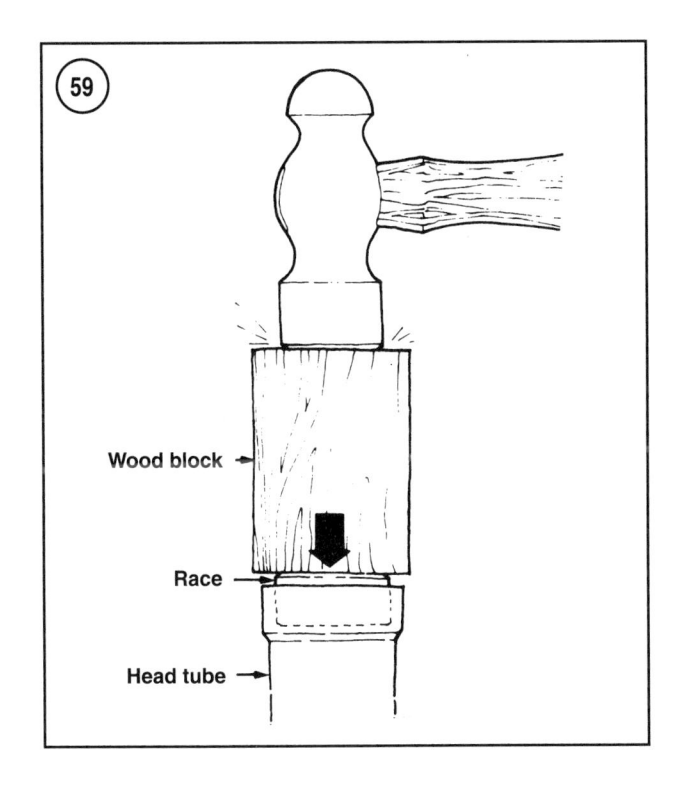

Wood block
Race
Head tube

Figure 60

Figure 61
Stem nut
Steering stem
Chisel
Dust seal and bottom race

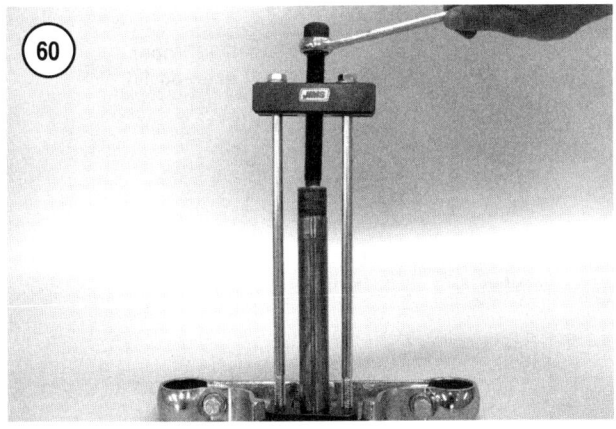

a. Place the new bearing races in the freezer for one hour. This will slightly reduce the outer diameter.
b. Clean the race thoroughly before installing it.
c. Position the bearing with the bevel side facing out.
d. Align the *new* outer race with the frame steering head and tap it slowly and squarely in place. Make sure not to contact the bearing race surfaces. Drive the race into the steering head tube until it bottoms out on the bore shoulder. Refer to **Figure 59**.
e. Repeat the process to install the lower race into the steering head tube.

5. Apply bearing grease to the face of each race.

Fork Stem Lower Bearing Replacement

Do not remove the steering stem lower bearing and lower seal unless they are going to be replaced. The lower bearing can be difficult to remove. If the lower bearing cannot be removed as described in this procedure, take the steering stem to a dealership and have them remove it and reinstall a new part.

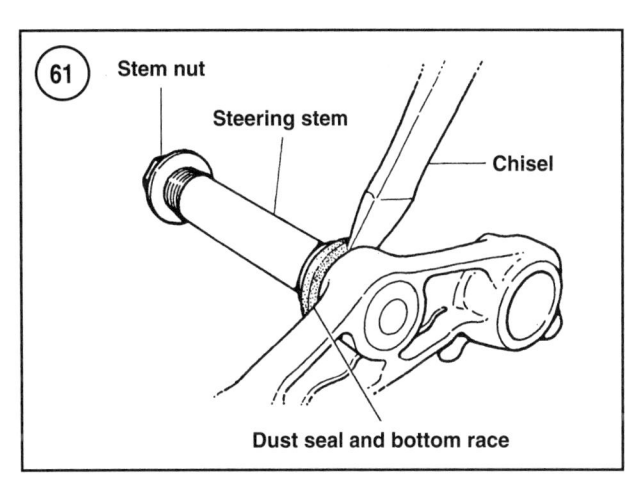

Never reinstall a lower bearing that has been removed as it is no longer true and will damage the rest of the bearing assembly if reused.

1A. Remove the lower bearing with fork stem bearing remover tool (JIMS part No. 1414) following the tool manufacturer's instructions.

1B. If the remover tool (**Figure 60**) is not available, remove the bearing as follows:
  a. Install the steering stem nut onto the top of the steering stem to protect the threads.
  b. Loosen the lower bearing from the shoulder at the base of the steering stem with a screwdriver or chisel as shown in **Figure 61**. Withdraw the lower bearing and grease seal from the steering stem.

2. Clean the steering stem with solvent and dry thoroughly.
3. Position the *new* lower dust seal with the flange side facing up, and install it onto the steering stem.
4. Slide the *new* lower bearing onto the steering stem until it stops on the raised shoulder.
5. Align the lower bearing with the machined shoulder on the steering stem. Press the bearing down with both thumbs until it bottoms on the dust seal.

STEERING PLAY INSPECTION AND ADJUSTMENT

If aftermarket components have been installed, they could affect this adjustment.

Swing Pattern

1. Use a centrally-located floor jack under the frame to support the motorcycle with both the front and rear wheels off the ground the same distance. If necessary, place a wooden block(s) under the rear wheel until the motorcycle is level.
2. Turn the front wheel full left and let it go.
3. The front wheel should swing right, left, then right and stop. The wheel does not need to stop in the center or

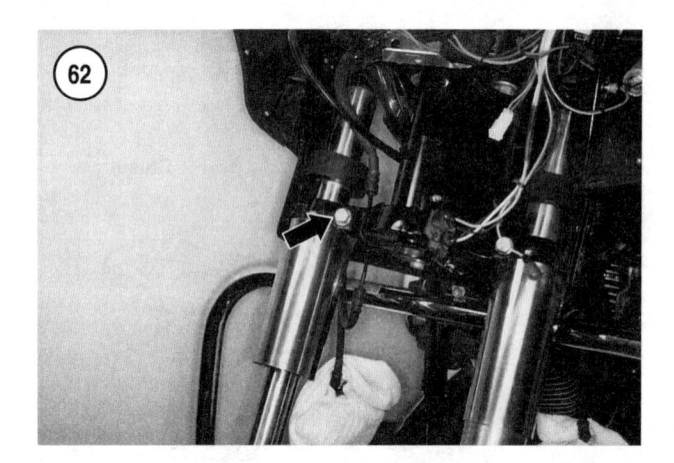

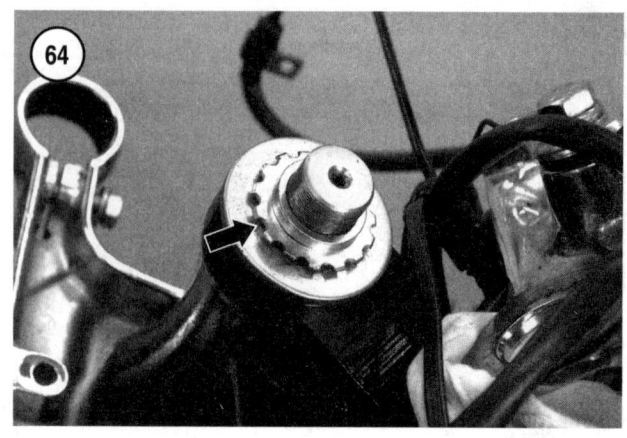

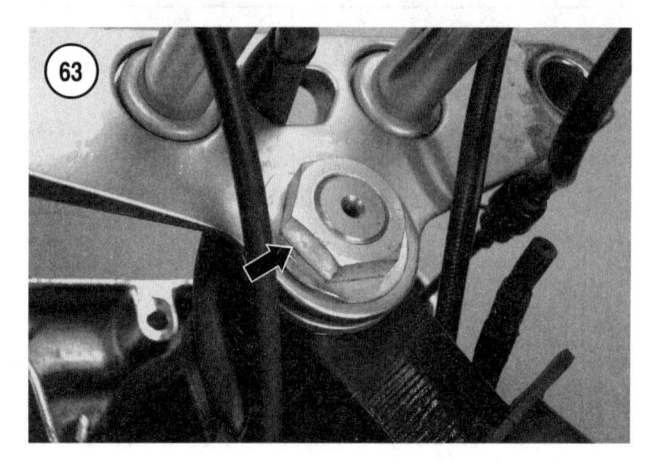

straight ahead position, but it must make at least a partial third swing to the right.

4. If the swing pattern is too short or too long, adjust the movement as described in this section.

Adjustment

1A. On all FLHT and FLHX models, remove the front fairing assembly as described in Chapter Seventeen.

1B. On all FLHR models, remove the headlight nacelle as described in Chapter Eleven.

1C. On all FLTR models, remove the instrument nacelle as described in Chapter Eleven.

2. Working at the base of the steering stem, loosen the lower fork bridge pinch bolt (**Figure 62**) on the fork legs.

3. To prevent any binding, slide the rubber fork stop up several inches on the both fork tubes.

4. Pry the tabs on the locking plate away from the steering stem hex nut.

5. Loosen and remove the steering stem hex nut (**Figure 63**).

NOTE
*Turning the bearing adjuster (**Figure 64**) one notch will make a noticeable difference in the swing pattern.*

6. Make an adjustment tool from 1/4 inch drill rod that is 16 inches long as shown in **Figure 65**.

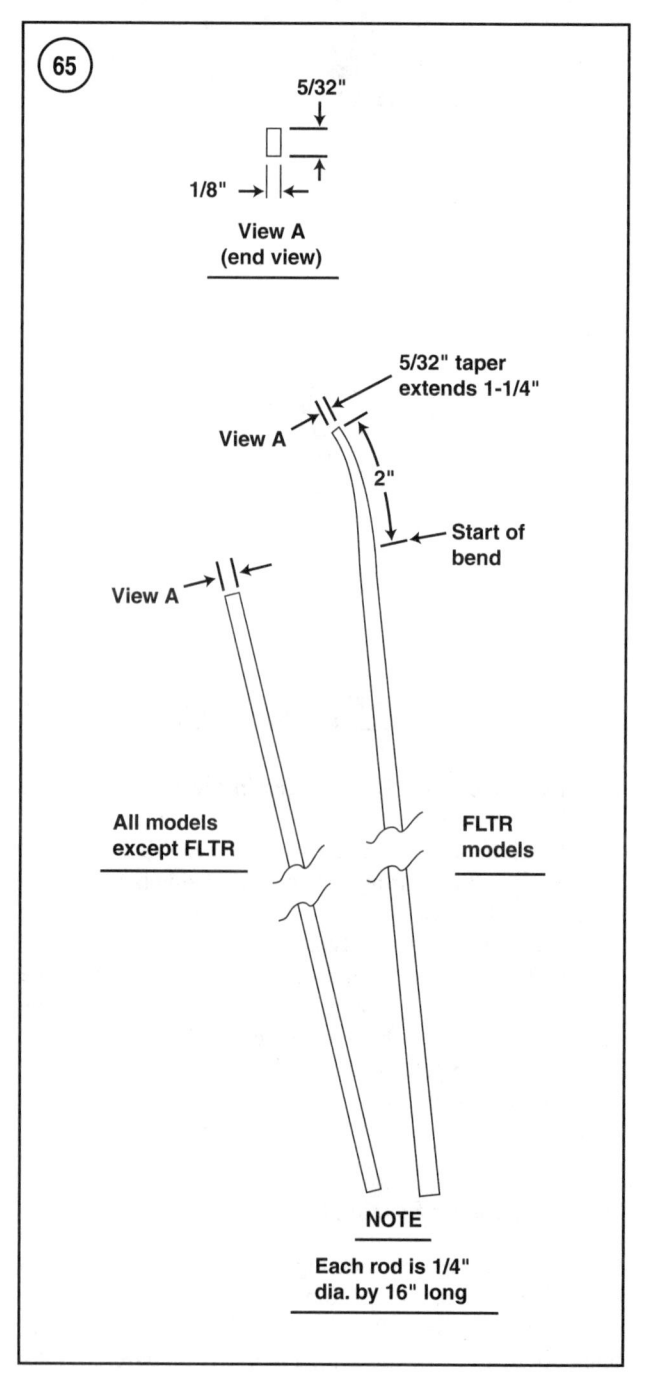

FRONT SUSPENSION AND STEERING

7. Working under the upper fork bracket, loosen the steering stem bearing adjuster with the drill rod tool.

8. To decrease the number of swings, stand on the *right side* of the motorcycle and insert the adjustment tool into the notches of the bearing adjuster. Push forward and rotate the adjuster *counterclockwise*.

9. To increase the number of swings, stand on the *left side* of the motorcycle and insert the adjustment tool into the notches of the bearing adjuster. Push forward and rotate the adjuster (**Figure 64**) *clockwise*.

10. Tighten the steering stem hex nut (**Figure 63**) to 60-80 ft.-lb. (81.3-108.5 N•m).

11. Recheck the swing pattern as previously described, and if necessary, repeat the adjustment procedure.

12. Tighten the lower fork bridge pinch bolt on both fork legs to 30-35 ft.-lb. (40.7-47.5 N•m).

13. Slide the rubber fork stop back down into position.

14A. On all FLHT and FLHX models, install the front fairing assembly as described in Chapter Seventeen.

14B. On all FLHR models, install the headlight nacelle as described in Chapter Eleven.

14C. On all FLTR models, install the instrument nacelle as described in Chapter Eleven.

15. Lower the motorcycle to the ground.

Table 1 FORK OIL CAPACITY AND OIL LEVEL SPECIFICATIONS

Model	Capacity – each fork leg U.S. oz. (cc)	Oil level height* in. (mm)
2006-2008 models (including Screamin' Eagle)		
FLHT, FLHX and FLTR models	10.8 (319)	5.59 (142)
FLHR models	11.1 (328)	5.24 (133)
2009 models (including Screamin' Eagle)		
FLHT, FLHX and FLTR models	10.7 (316)	4.92 (125)
FLHR models	11.0 (325)	5.92 (134)

*Measured from the top of the fork tube with the fork spring removed and the fork leg fully compressed.

Table 2 FRONT SUSPENSION TORQUE SPECIFICATIONS

Item	ft.-lb.	in.-lb.	N•m
Front axle nut			
2006-2007 models	50-55	–	67.8-74.6
2007-2009 models	60-65	–	81.3-88.1
Front axle cover set screw			
FLHTCUSE models	–	60-84	6.8-9.5
Front-slider axle-clamp nut	11-15	–	14.9-20.3
Front fender acorn nut	15-21	–	20.3-28.5
Front fender nut	15-21	–	20.3-28.5
Front fender screws			
FXSTD/I models	15-21	–	20.3-28.5
FXSTS/I models	20-25	–	27.1-33.9
Front fork			
Cap bolt	50-60	–	67.8-81.3
Tube plug	22-58	–	29.8-78.6
Damper rod Allen bolt	11-18	–	14.9-24.4
Handlebar			
Clamp bolts	16-20	–	21.7-27.1
Lower clamp rubber			
bushing bolt	30-40	–	40.7-54.2
Lower fork bridge pinch bolt	30-35	–	40.7-47.5
Steering stem			
Hex nut	60-80	–	81.3-108.5
Air dam screws			
(FLTR and FLHR models)	–	120-144	13.6-16.3

CHAPTER FOURTEEN

REAR SUSPENSION

This chapter covers repair and replacement procedures for the rear suspension components. **Tables 1-3** are located at the end of this chapter.

WARNING
*All rear suspension fasteners must be replaced with the exact same type of part. Do not use a substitute design of fastener, as it may affect the performance of the rear suspension or fail, leading to loss of control of the motorcycle. Refer to the torque specifications in **Table 1**.*

SHOCK AIR PRESSURE ADJUSTMENT

WARNING
Use caution when releasing the air from the rear shock absorber air valve. Moisture combined with oil may spurt out when the air pressure is released. Protect your eyes accordingly.

CAUTION
The air chambers within the rear shock are very small and will fill rapidly. Do not use compressed air. Only use only a small hand-held or foot-operated small air pump.

1. Place the motorcycle on the jiffy stand.
2. Remove the left side saddlebag as described in Chapter Seventeen.
3. Remove the air valve cap (**Figure 1**).
4. Use a no-loss air gauge to check air pressure. Refer to the recommended air pressure listed in **Table 2** and **Table 3**.
5. Increase or decrease air pressure to achieve the desired ride and control with a small, hand-held air pump.
6. Install the air valve cap and the saddlebag.

AIR PRESSURE LOSS INSPECTION

If there is a gradual loss of air pressure in the system, inspect the hoses, fittings and air valve assembly.
1. Check that the valve stem core is tightened securely.
2. Adjust the shock absorbers to the correct air pressure and wait overnight.
3. In the morning recheck the air pressure.
4A. If air pressure is okay, the system is holding the correct amount of air.
4B. If there is a loss of 5-10 psi (35-69 kPa), check the system as described in this section.
5. Remove the saddlebag(s) as described in Chapter Seventeen.
6. Adjust the shock absorbers to the correct air pressure.
7. Inspect the air line fittings (**Figure 2**) at the shock absorbers. Spray or brush a light film of soapy water onto the compression fittings on both shock absorbers and the air inlet tee-fitting. If air bubbles appear, perform the following:

REAR SUSPENSION

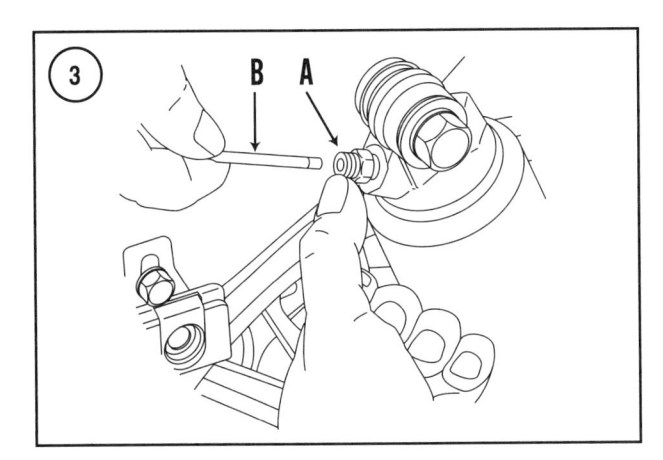

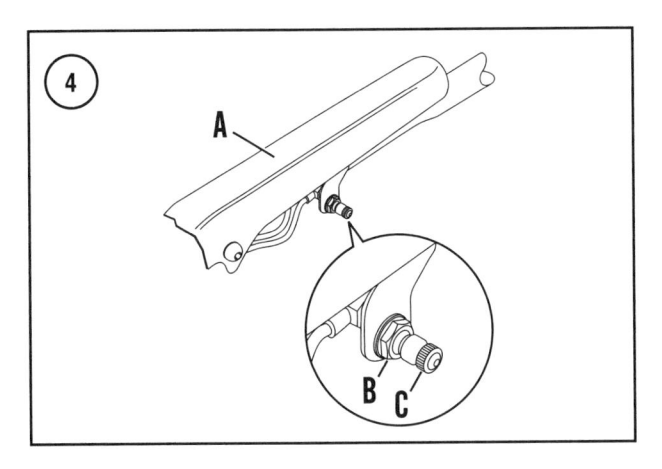

a. Cover the rear brake assembly and wheel prior to releasing the compressed air from the rear air valve. If necessary, wipe off any oil reside that may have been ejected from the air valve.
b. Remove the air valve cap (**Figure 1**). Use a no-loss air gauge and add 3-5 psi (21-35 kPa) to purge the air lines of any oil.
c. Slowly depress the air valve to evacuate the air from both shock absorbers.
d. Use a thumb to depress the collar (A, **Figure 3**) on the fitting, and then carefully pull the air hose (B) from the fitting.
e. Inspect the end of the air hose for burrs or damage. If damaged, cut off the damaged area and reinsert the air hose into the collar. Gently pull on the hose to ensure it is secure in the fitting.

8. Pressurize the system and recheck for air leaks. If there is still an air leak, perform the following to replace the fittings:
a. Remove the air hose from the fitting, and remove the fitting from the shock absorber.
b. Install a *new* fitting. Apply pipe sealant with Teflon to the fitting's threads and install the fitting into the shock absorber. Tighten the fitting securely.
c. Install the air line(s) into the new fitting(s). Gently pull on the hose to ensure it is secure in the fitting.

9. Pressurize the system as described in *Shock Air Pressure Adjustment* (this chapter). Spray or brush a light film of soapy water onto the compression fitting(s) on both shock absorber(s) and check for air bubbles. If bubbles appear, repeat the process until the leak is repaired.

10. Inspect the air lines at the air valve assembly. Spray or brush a light film of soapy water onto the fittings at the air valve assembly fittings. If air bubbles appear, perform the following:
a. Remove the frame side cover (A, **Figure 4**).
b. Remove the hex fitting (B, **Figure 4**) securing the air valve assembly to the frame bracket.
c. Carefully remove the air valve assembly from the frame bracket.
d. Depress the collars on the outlet tee (C, **Figure 4**) and remove both air tubes from the air valve assembly. Discard the air valve assembly.
e. Install the air tubes into the *new* air valve assembly and install the air valve assembly into the frame bracket.
f. Install the air valve hex fitting (B, **Figure 4**) and tighten to 40-50 in.-lb. (4.5-5.7 N•m).
g. Pressurize the system as described in *Shock Air Pressure Adjustment* (this chapter).

SHOCK ABSORBERS

All models are equipped with an air-adjustable suspension. The amount of air pressure in the rear shock absorbers can be varied to suit personal comfort. The lower the air pressure, the softer the ride and the higher the air pressure, the firmer the ride. Refer to **Table 2** and **Table 3** for the recommended air pressure for the rear shock absorbers.

REAR SHOCK ABSORBERS AND AIR LINES

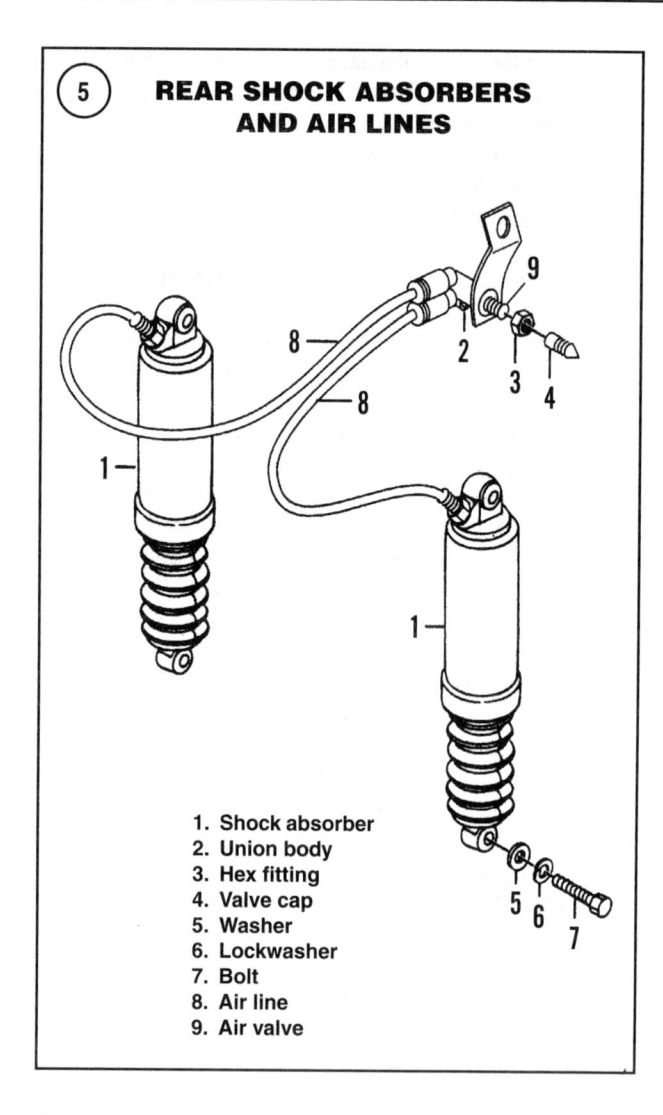

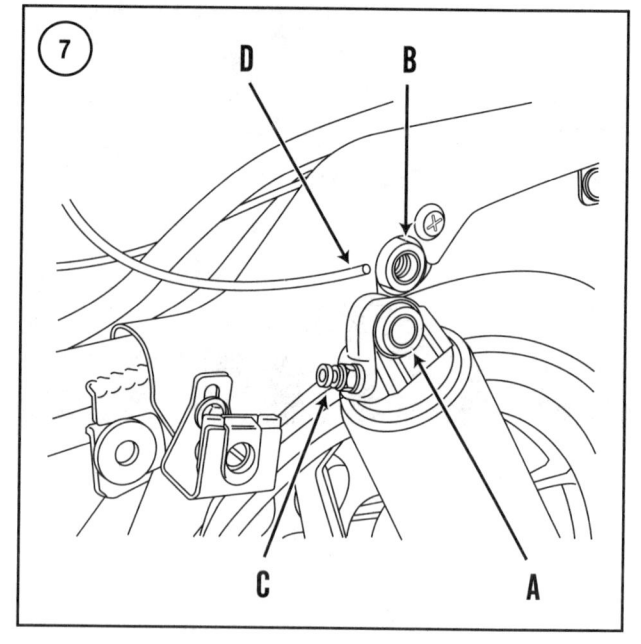

1. Shock absorber
2. Union body
3. Hex fitting
4. Valve cap
5. Washer
6. Lockwasher
7. Bolt
8. Air line
9. Air valve

Removal/Installation

Refer to **Figure 5**.

When servicing the rear shocks, remove one shock at a time. If it is necessary to remove both shocks, support the motorcycle on a suitable floor jack, with the rear wheel off the ground.

1. Support the motorcycle with the rear wheel off the ground. Refer to *Motorcycle Stands* in Chapter Twelve, if necessary.
2. Place wooden blocks under the rear wheel to place the rear wheel in a neutral position with no strain on the shock absorber mounting hardware.
3. Remove the saddlebag(s) as described in Chapter Seventeen.

WARNING
Use caution when releasing the air from the rear shock absorber air valve. Moisture combined with oil may spurt out when the air pressure is released. Protect your eyes accordingly.

4. Cover the rear brake assembly and wheel prior to releasing the compressed air from the rear air valve. If necessary, wipe off any oil reside that may have been ejected from the air valve.
5. Remove the air valve cap (**Figure 1**). Use a no-loss air gauge and add 3-5 psi (21-35 kPa) to purge the air lines of any oil.
6. Slowly depress the air valve to evacuate the air from both shock absorbers.
7. Use a thumb, and depress the collar (A, **Figure 3**) on the fitting and carefully pull the air hose (B) from the fitting.
8. Loosen both the upper (A, **Figure 6**) and lower (B) mounting bolts securing the shock absorber to the frame and to the swing arm.
9. Remove the lower bolt (B, **Figure 6**), lockwasher and washer securing the shock absorber to the swing arm.
10. Remove the upper bolt (A, **Figure 6**), lockwasher and washer securing the shock absorber to the frame.
11. Remove the shock absorber (C, **Figure 6**) from the motorcycle and store it in an *upright position* to avoid the loss of oil. Any loss of oil requires replacement of the shock absorber as oil cannot be added to the unit.
12. Repeat the procedure to remove the other shock absorber, if necessary.

REAR SUSPENSION

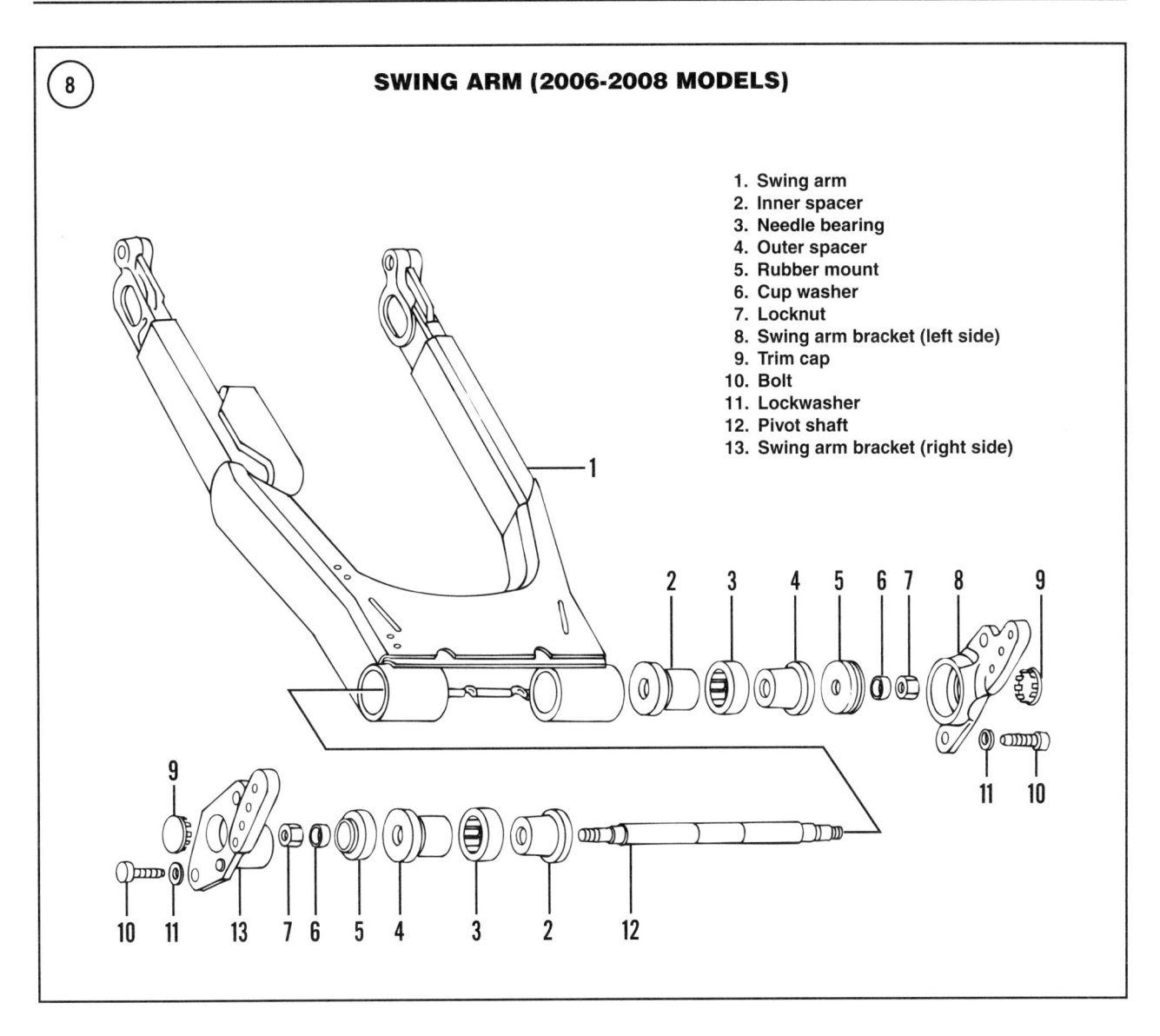

SWING ARM (2006-2008 MODELS)

1. Swing arm
2. Inner spacer
3. Needle bearing
4. Outer spacer
5. Rubber mount
6. Cup washer
7. Locknut
8. Swing arm bracket (left side)
9. Trim cap
10. Bolt
11. Lockwasher
12. Pivot shaft
13. Swing arm bracket (right side)

13. Inspect the shock absorber as described in this section.
14. Install the shock absorber (A, **Figure 7**) into position on the frame boss (B).
15. Apply a few drops of Loctite 243 (blue) threadlock, or an equivalent, to the shock mounting bolt threads.
16. Install the washers, the lockwashers and bolts. Tighten the bolts to 35-40 ft.-lb. (47.5-54.2 N•m).
17. Use a thumb to depress the collar (C, **Figure 7**) on the fitting. Insert the air hose (D, **Figure 7**) into the fitting until it bottoms, and release the fitting. Gently pull on the hose to ensure it is secure in the fitting.
18. Adjust the shock absorber air pressure as described in this chapter.
19. Install the saddlebag(s) as described in Chapter Seventeen.
20. Remove the wood block under the rear tire, and lower the motorcycle.
21. Test ride the motorcycle slowly at first to make the rear suspension is working properly.

Inspection

There are no shock replacement parts available for these models. If any part, other than the mounting hardware, is damaged, replace the shock assembly.

1. Remove the shock absorber as described in this section. Keep the shock absorber in an *upright position* to avoid the loss of oil.
2. Inspect the upper shock bushing and lower shock bushing for wear and deterioration.
3. Inspect the shock absorber. If the rubber boot portion is cracked or deteriorated, replace the shock absorber.

REAR SWING ARM

Refer to **Figure 8** and **Figure 9**.

Bearing Play Inspection

The swing arm needle bearings wear over time and require replacement. Worn or damaged needle bearings can

SWING ARM (2009 MODELS)

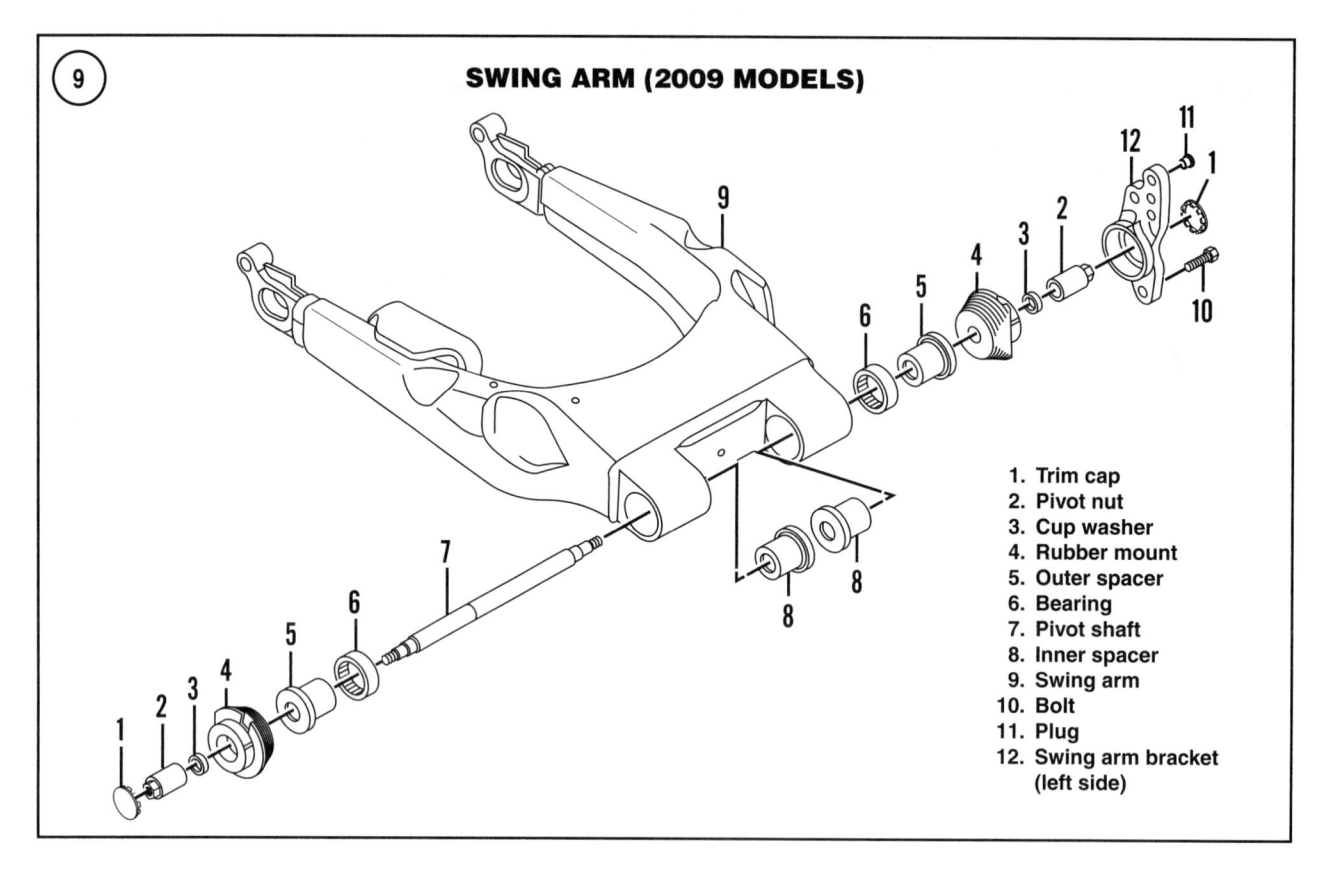

1. Trim cap
2. Pivot nut
3. Cup washer
4. Rubber mount
5. Outer spacer
6. Bearing
7. Pivot shaft
8. Inner spacer
9. Swing arm
10. Bolt
11. Plug
12. Swing arm bracket (left side)

produce erratic and dangerous handling. Common symptoms are wheel hop, pulling to one side during acceleration and pulling to the other side during braking.

1. Remove the rear wheel (A, **Figure 10**) as described in Chapter Twelve.
2. Remove the bolt, lockwasher and washer securing both shock absorbers (B, **Figure 10**) to the swing arm. Move them up away from the swing arm.
3. Make sure both nuts on the swing arm pivot shaft are tight.
4. Have an assistant hold the motorcycle securely.
5. Grasp the back of the swing arm and try to move it from side to side. Any play between the swing arm and the frame, or swing arm and transmission may suggest worn or damaged needle bearings. If there is any play, remove the swing arm and inspect the needle bearing assemblies.
6. Install all components removed.

Removal

1. Remove both saddlebags as described in Chapter Seventeen.
2. Remove both passenger footboards as described in Chapter Seventeen.
3. Remove the exhaust system as described in Chapter Four.
4. Remove the bolts securing the drive belt guard and remove the guard.
5. Place wooden blocks or a floor jack under the transmission and engine assembly to support it after the swing arm pivot shaft is removed.

6. Remove the rear wheel (A, **Figure 10**) as described in Chapter Twelve.
7. Remove the rear caliper bracket from the anchor weldment on swing arm.
8. Loosen the bolt securing both shock absorbers (B, **Figure 10**) to the swing arm. Do not remove the bolt at this time.
9. Remove the trim cap (A, **Figure 11**) from the bracket.
10. Remove the bolts (B, **Figure 11**), and lockwashers (2006-2008 models) securing the bracket on the left side. Remove the bracket (C, **Figure 11**) from the frame.
11A. On models without ABS, unhook the rear brake caliper hose from the clips on the right side of the swing arm.
11B. On models with ABS, unhook the rear brake caliper hose and the ABS rear wheel sensor from the clips on the right side of the swing arm.
12. Remove the chrome trim cap from the right side frame bracket. On 2006-2008 models, do not loosen or remove the bolts securing the bracket.
13. On the left side, secure the nut (A, **Figure 12**) within the rubber mount (B) with a socket to keep it from rotating during removal.
14. On the right side, loosen and remove the nut or pivot nut securing the pivot shaft. On 2006-2008 models, remove the cup washer.
15. Support the swing arm on a box.
16. Use a suitable size drift and tap on the right side the pivot shaft with a drift. Drive the pivot shaft assembly part way out through the left side.
17A. On 2006-2008 models, remove the pivot shaft assembly (C, **Figure 12**) consisting of the pivot shaft, locknut,

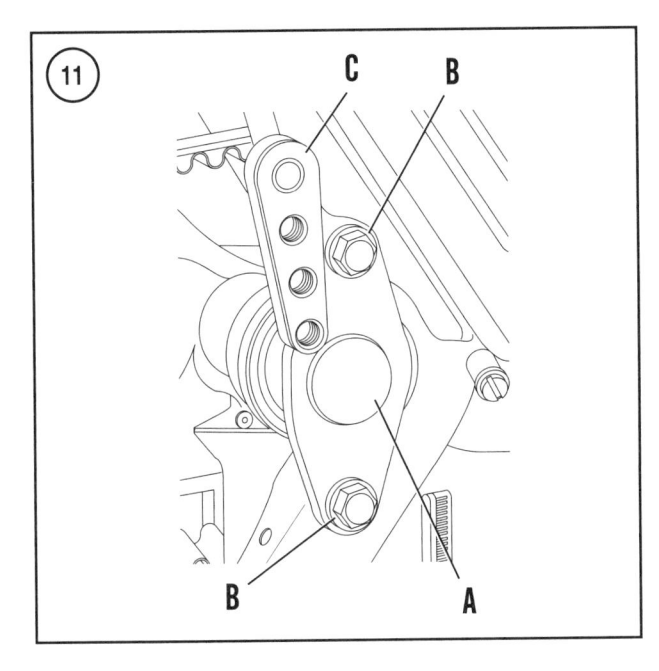

REAR SUSPENSION

605

cup washer, rubber mount and outer spacer, from the frame and transmission case.

17B. On 2009 models, remove the pivot shaft assembly (C, **Figure 12**) consisting of the pivot shaft, pivot nut, cup washer, rubber mount and outer spacer, from the frame and transmission case.

18. Remove the bolt, lockwasher and washer securing both shock absorbers (B, **Figure 10**) to the swing arm. Move them up away from the swing arm.

19. Slowly pull back and withdraw the swing arm from the transmission case and swing arm brackets.

20. Remove the outer spacer from the right side of the swing arm pivot point.

21. Remove the rubber mount from behind the right side swing arm bracket, or frame mount on 2009 models.

22. Inspect the swing arm as described in this section.

Installation

1. On the right side, position the slot (D, **Figure 12**) in the rubber mount between the twelve and one o'clock position, and install it into the backside of the swing arm bracket. Make sure the index tab on the inboard side of the bracket engages the slot in the rubber mount. Reposition the components, if necessary, to achieve this alignment.

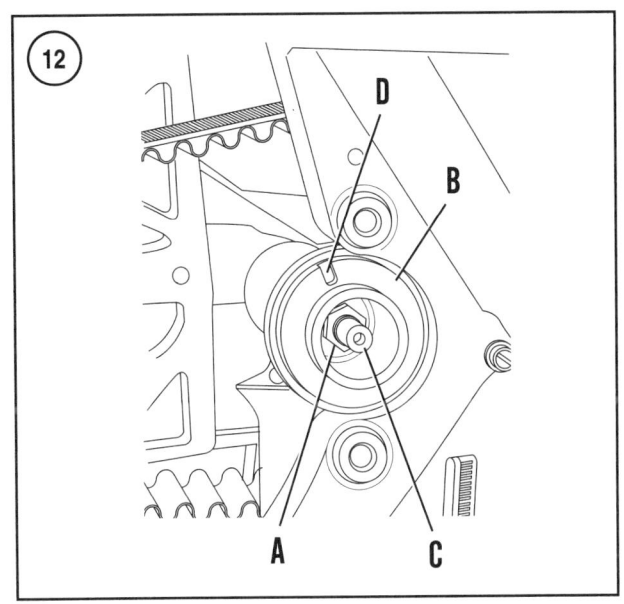

2. Install the outer spacer into the right side of the swing arm pivot point.

3. Position the drive belt on the inboard side of the swing arm and position the swing arm onto the pivot area of the transmission case and support it in this position. If necessary, use soft faced mallet and tap the swing arm into position.

4. Move the shock absorbers into position on the swing arm and loosely install the bolt, lockwasher and washer securing both shock absorbers (B, **Figure 10**) to the swing arm. Do not tighten at this time.

5. Coat the pivot shaft with Loctite antiseize, or an appropriate type of grease. Do not get any grease on the exposed threads.

6A. On 2006-2008 models, perform the following:
   a. Install the pivot shaft assembly (C, **Figure 12**) consisting of pivot shaft, locknut, cup washer, rubber mount and outer spacer, through the left side of the frame, the transmission and the swing arm. Guide the pivot shaft through the holes in the right side rubber mount and the frame.
   b. On the right side, position the cup washer with the concave side going on first and install it onto the pivot shaft.
   c. On the left side, rotate the rubber mount to position the slot in the rubber mount between the eleven and twelve o'clock position. Make sure the index tab on the inboard side of the bracket engages the slot in the rubber mount. Reposition the components, if necessary, to achieve this alignment.
   d. On the left side, install the swing arm bracket. Apply a few drops of Loctite 243 (blue) threadlock, or an equivalent, to the mounting bolts. Install the bolts and lockwashers. Tighten the swing arm bracket bolts to 34-42 ft.-lb. (46.1-56.9 N•m).

6B. On 2009 models, perform the following:

a. Install the pivot shaft assembly through the left side of the frame, transmission and the swing arm.
b. Install the outer spacer onto pivot shaft.
c. Position the rubber mount with the flat side going on first and install onto the pivot shaft.
d. On the left side, position the cup washer with the concave side going on first and install it onto the pivot shaft.
e. On the left side, rotate the rubber mount to position the slot in the rubber mount between the eleven and twelve o'clock position. Make sure the index tab on the inboard side of the bracket engages the slot in the rubber mount. Reposition the components, if necessary, to achieve this alignment.
f. On the left side, install the swing arm bracket. Apply a few drops of Loctite 243 (blue) threadlock, or an equivalent, to the mounting bolts. Install the swing arm bracket bolts and tighten to 55-65 ft.-lb. (74.6-88.1 N•m).

7. Apply a few drops of Loctite 243 (blue) threadlock, or an equivalent, to the threads on the locknuts, or pivot nuts.
8. Tighten the left side locknut, or pivot nut, to the following:
    a. 2006-2008 models locknut: approximately 40-45 ft.-lb. (54-61 N•m).
    b. 2009 models pivot nut: approximately 55-65 ft.-lb. (74.6-89.6 N•m).
9. Secure the left side locknut, or pivot nut, and tighten the right side locknut, or pivot nut, to the following:
    a. 2006-2008 models locknut: approximately 40-45 ft.-lb. (54-61 N•m).
    b. 2009 models pivot nut: approximately 55-65 ft.-lb. (74.6-89.5 N•m).
10. If necessary, repeat the process and tighten the left side locknut, or pivot nut, to the following.
    a. 2006-2008 models locknut: approximately 40-45 ft.-lb. (54-61 N•m).
    b. 2009 models pivot nut: approximately 55-65 ft.-lb. (74.6-89.5 N•m).
11. Remove the lower bolts, washers and lockwashers securing the rear shock absorbers to the swing arm.
12. Slowly raise and lower the swing arm to verify ease of movement without binding. If binding occurs, repeat the tightening procedure and correct the problem.
13. Install the chrome trim caps onto both frame brackets.
14. Move the shock absorbers into position and install the bolt, lockwasher and washer securing both shock absorbers (B, **Figure 10**) to the swing arm. Tighten the bolts to 35-40 ft.-lb. (47.5-54.2 N•m).
15A. On models without ABS, hook the rear brake caliper hose onto the clips on the right side of the swing arm.
15B. On models with ABS, hook the rear brake caliper hose and the ABS rear wheel sensor onto the clips on the right side of the swing arm.
16. Install the rear caliper bracket onto the anchor weldment on swing arm.
17. Install the rear wheel (A, **Figure 10**) as described in Chapter Twelve.

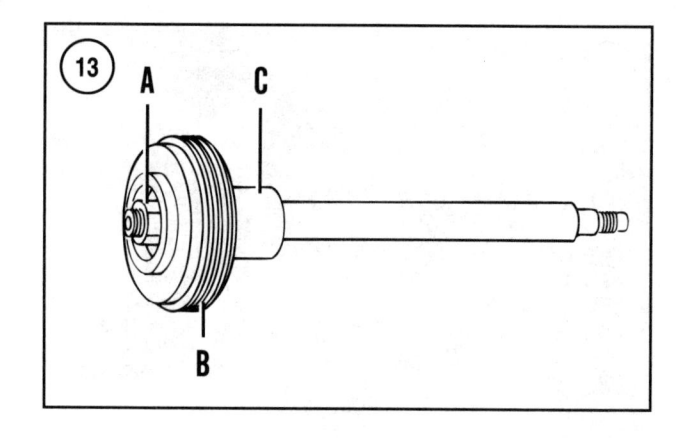

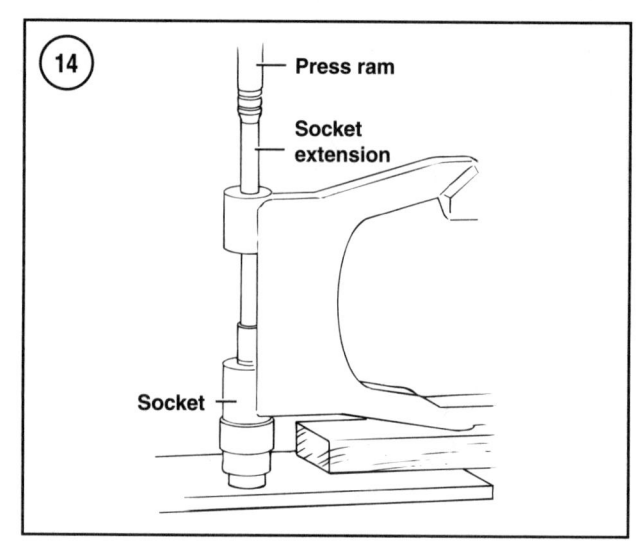

18. Remove the wooden blocks or floor jack from under the transmission and engine assembly.
19. Install the drive belt guard and tighten the bolts securely.
20. Install the exhaust system as described in Chapter Four.
21. Install both passenger footboards as described in Chapter Seventeen.
22. Install both saddlebags as described in Chapter Seventeen.

Inspection

1. Clean the exterior of the swing arm in solvent and thoroughly dry with compressed air.
2. Inspect the welded sections on the swing arm for cracks or fractures.
3. Inspect the right and left side rubber mounts on the pivot shaft. If replacement of the left side mount is necessary, hold onto the pivot shaft to keep it from rotating. Remove the locknut (A, **Figure 13**), rubber mount (B) and outer spacer (C) from the pivot shaft. Replace the rubber mounts as a pair if either one is starting to deteriorate or harden.
4. Inspect the pivot shaft for surface cracks, deep scoring, wear or heat distortion. Replace it if necessary.
5. Turn the needle bearings with a finger. The bearing should turn smoothly with no signs of roughness or dam-

REAR SUSPENSION

needle bearing and inner spacer out of the left side pivot bore and into the receiving socket.

6. Release ram pressure and remove the tools from the swing arm.
7. Turn the swing arm over, and repeat the process to remove the remaining needle bearing and inner spacer.
8. Clean the swing arm bearing bores with solvent and dry with compressed air.
9. Install the inner spacer into the *new* needle bearing (**Figure 15**) as follows:
   a. Place the bearing on a smooth, flat press plate.
   b. Position the spacer with the collar facing up and start the spacer into the needle bearing.
   c. Center the assembly under the press ram and apply pressure. Press the spacer into the bearing until it bottoms on the press plate.
   d. Repeat this process for the remaining spacer and bearing.

NOTE
There are two bearing installers in the swing arm bearing installer set (H-D part No. HD-45327). The longer installer is used on the left side (drive side) and the shorter installer is used on the right side (brake side).

10. Place the swing arm on the press bed so the right side faces up (**Figure 16**). Place a wooden block on the press bed first to protect the swing arm finish.
11. Make sure the pivot areas are square with the press bed.
12. Position the *new* needle bearing assembly wit the spacer side facing out.
13. Place the *new* needle bearing assembly over the right side bearing bore. Place the shorter *Brake Side* installer onto the bearing assembly.
14. Make sure the pivot areas are square with the press bed.
15. Hold the swing arm so it vertical and square. Then, slowly apply ram pressure on the installer, and drive the needle bearing assembly into the right side pivot bore. Press the bearing assembly into the swing arm until the shoulder of the installer tool makes contact with the swing arm.
16. Release the pressure and remove the installer from the swing arm.

CAUTION
*The longer drive side installer shoulder **must not** make contact with the swing arm on the left side. Only press the needle bearing assembly into the pivot bore until the bearing bottoms. Do not press it in until the installer shoulder contacts the swing arm as the swing arm will be damaged.*

17. Turn the swing arm over and repeat the process to install the remaining needle bearing assembly into the left side of the swing arm. Use the longer *Drive Side* installer to install the left side bearing assembly. Press the bearing assembly into the swing arm until the bearing bottoms.

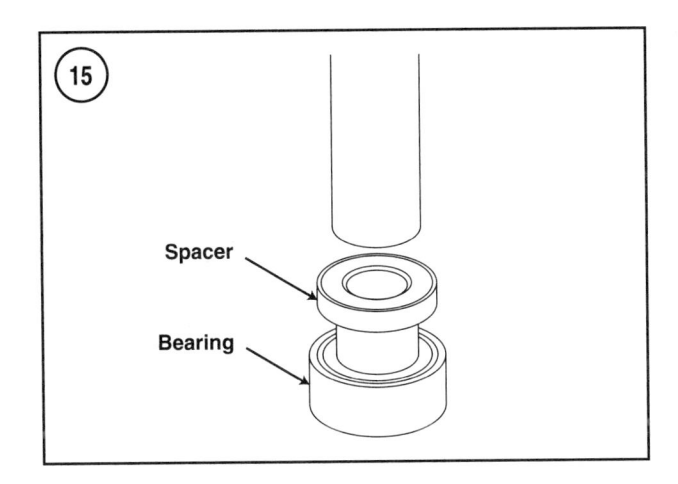

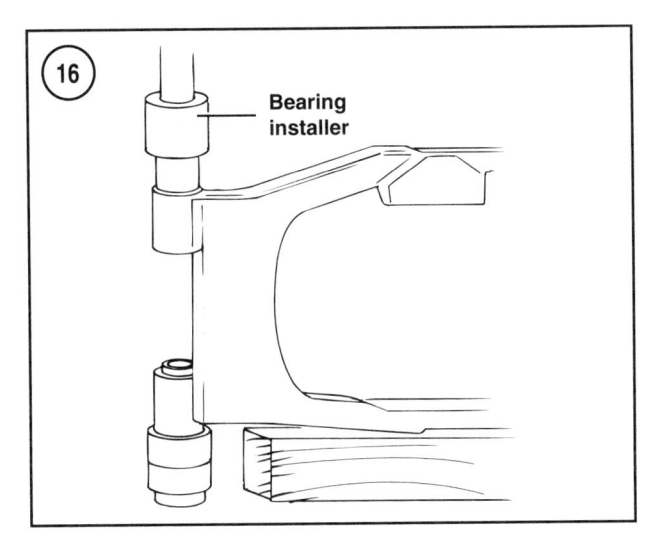

age. If necessary, replace the needle bearings as described in this section. Replace the needle bearings as a pair if either is damaged.

Needle bearing and Inner Spacer Replacement

Remove and install the needle bearings only if the bearing must be replaced. Never install a needle bearing that has been removed. Both the needle bearings and inner spacer must be replaced as a set.

A hydraulic press and several tools are required for bearing and inner race replacement.

1. Place the swing arm on the press bed with the left side facing down (**Figure 14**). Place a wooden block on the press bed to protect the swing arm finish.
2. Place a socket with an inner diameter larger than the needle bearing under the left side pivot point.
3. Select a long socket extension with another socket attached that matches the outer diameter of the needle bearing. Insert this tool setup down through the right side of the pivot point and place it on the left side needle bearing.
4. Make sure the swing arm pivot areas are square with the press bed.
5. Hold the swing arm vertical and square. Then, slowly apply ram pressure on the long extension and drive the

Table 1 REAR SUSPENSION TORQUE SPECIFICATIONS

Item	ft.-lb.	in.-lb.	N•m
Shock absorber			
Air valve hex fitting	–	40-50	4.5-5.7
Mounting bolts	35-40	–	47.5-54.2
Swing arm (2006-2008 models)			
Bracket bolt	34-42	–	46.1-56.9
Left side pivot shaft locknut	40-45	–	54.2-61.0
Right side pivot shaft locknut	40-45	–	54.2-61.0
Swing arm (2009 models)			
Left side swing arm bracket bolt	55-65	–	74.6-88.1
Left side pivot shaft pivot nut	55-65	–	74.6-88.1
Right side pivot shaft pivot nut	55-65	–	74.6-88.1

Table 2 FLHT, FLHR and FLTR MODELS REAR SUSPENSION AIR PRESSURE*

Load	Total weight	Pressure
Solo rider	up to 150 lb. (0-68 kg)	0 psi (0 kPa)
Solo rider	150-200 lb. (68-91 kg)	0-10 psi (0-69 kPa)
Solo rider	200-250 lb. (91-113 kg)	5-15 psi (35-103 kPa)
Passenger	up to 150 lb. (0-68 kg)	10-15 psi (69-103 kPa)
Passenger	up to 200 lb. (0-91 kg)	20-25 psi (138-172 kPa)

*Includes Screamin' Eagle models.

Table 3 FLHX MODELS REAR SUSPENSION AIR PRESSURE

Load	Total weight	Pressure
Solo rider	up to 160 lb. (0-73 kg)	0-5 psi (0-35 kPa)
Solo rider	over 200 lb. (over 91 kg)	5-10 psi (35-69 kPa)
Passenger	up to 150 lb. (0-68 kg)	20-30 psi (128-207 kPa)
Passenger	up to 200 lb. (over 68 kg)	25-35 psi (172-241 kPa)

CHAPTER FIFTEEN

BRAKES

This chapter covers the brake system. Specifications are located in **Table 1** and **Table 2** at the end of this chapter.

BRAKE SERVICE

WARNING
Do not ride the motorcycle without a properly functioning brake system. After any brake system service/repair, verify proper brake operation.

WARNING
Do not intermix DOT 4 with DOT 5 brake fluids, as they are not compatible. DOT 5 is silicone-based and the mistaken use of silicone brake fluid in these models can cause brake failure.

WARNING
*When working on the brake system, do **not** inhale brake dust. It may contain asbestos. Do **not** use compressed air to blow off brake dust. Use an aerosol brake parts cleaner. Wear a face mask and wash thoroughly after completing the work.*

The brake system transmits hydraulic pressure from the master cylinders to the brake calipers. This pressure is transmitted from the caliper(s) to the brake pads, which grip both sides of the brake disc(s) and slow the motorcycle. As the pads wear, the pistons move out of the caliper bores to automatically compensate for wear. As this occurs, the fluid level in the master cylinder reservoir goes down. Compensate for this by occasionally adding fluid. Check the fluid levels at the intervals noted in Chapter Three.

Consider the following when servicing the brake system:

1. The hydraulic components rarely require disassembly. Make sure disassembly is necessary.
2. Use the correct DOT 4 brake fluid. Make sure the brake fluid is in good condition. Small quantities of brake fluid stored in the original container will absorb moisture from the air in the container. Brake system performance depends on a supply of clean brake fluid and a clean service environment. Any debris entering the system can damage components.
3. Do not intermix brake fluid types and try to use the same brand of fluid if possible. Dispose of used or contaminated brake fluid properly.
4. Keep the reservoir covers in place to prevent the entry of moisture and debris contamination.
5. Do not allow brake fluid to contact plastic, painted or plated parts. It will damage the surface. When adding brake fluid, punch a small hole into the edge of the container's seal to help control the fluid flow. Cover all that may be contaminated by spilled fluid.
6. Clean up any spilled brake fluid with soapy water and rinse thoroughly.
7. If the hydraulic system, excluding the reservoir cover, has been opened, bleed the system to remove air from the system. Refer to *Brake Bleeding* in this chapter.
8. Clean parts with an aerosol brake parts cleaner or isopropyl alcohol. Never use petroleum-based solvents on internal brake system components. They will cause seals to swell and distort.

9. During overhaul, replace O-rings and seals. Never reuse these components.

10. The manufacturer does not provide wear limit specifications for the caliper and master cylinder assemblies. When inspecting these components, consult a dealer for advice. Brake pad and disc thickness specifications are provided.

FRONT BRAKE PAD REPLACEMENT

There is no recommended mileage interval for changing the brake pads. Pad wear depends greatly on riding habits and conditions. Frequently check the brake pads for wear. Increase the inspection interval when the wear indicator reaches the edge of the brake disc. After removal, measure the thickness of each brake pad with a caliper or ruler and compare to the dimensions in **Table 1**.

Always replace both pads in the caliper at the same time to maintain an even brake pressure on the discs. Also, replace both brake pads in *both calipers* at the same time. Do not disconnect the hydraulic brake hose from the brake caliper for brake pad replacement. Disconnect the hose only if the caliper assembly is going to be removed.

CAUTION
Check the pads more frequently when the lining approaches the pad metal backing plate. If pad wear happens to be uneven for some reason, the backing plate may come in contact with the disc and cause damage.

2006-2007 Models

1. Read the information in *Brake Service* (this chapter).
2. Support the motorcycle with the rear wheel off the ground as described in *Motorcycle Stands* (Chapter Twelve).
3. Block the front wheel so the motorcycle will not roll in either direction while the rear wheel is off ground.
4. Place a spacer between the brake lever and the throttle grip and secure it in place. If the brake lever is inadvertently squeezed, this will prevent the pistons from being forced out of the cylinders.
5. To prevent the reservoir from overflowing while repositioning the pistons in the caliper, perform the following:
   a. Move the front wheel so the front master cylinder is level.
   b. Clean all dirt and debris from the top of the master cylinder.
   c. Remove the screws securing the cover (**Figure 1**), and then remove the cover and diaphragm.
   d. Use a shop syringe and remove about 50% of the brake fluid from the reservoir. This will prevent the master cylinder from overflowing when the pistons are compressed for reinstallation. Do *not* drain more than 50% of the brake fluid or air will enter the system. Discard the brake fluid properly.
6. Loosen the pad pin bolts (**Figure 2**).

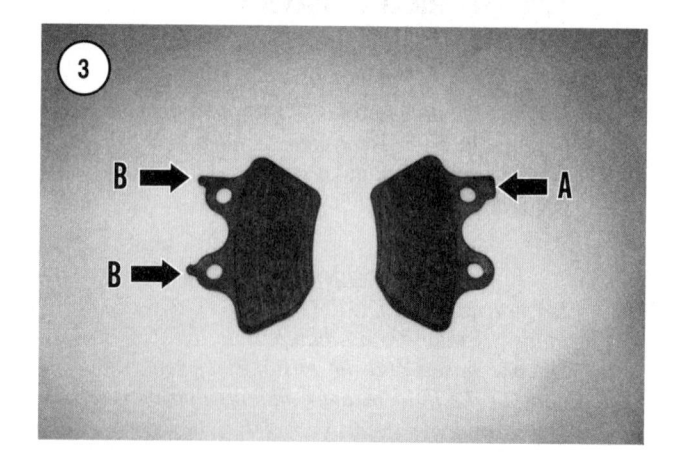

CAUTION
The brake disc is thin in order to dissipate heat, so it may bend easily. When pushing against the disc to compress the pistons, support the disc adjacent to the caliper to prevent damage to the disc.

7. Hold the caliper body from the outside and push it toward the brake disc. This will push the outer pistons into the caliper bores to make room for the new brake pads. Constantly check the reservoir to make sure brake fluid does not overflow. Remove fluid, if necessary, before it overflows. Install the diaphragm and cover. Tighten the screws finger-tight.
8. Remove the pad pin bolts (**Figure 2**).

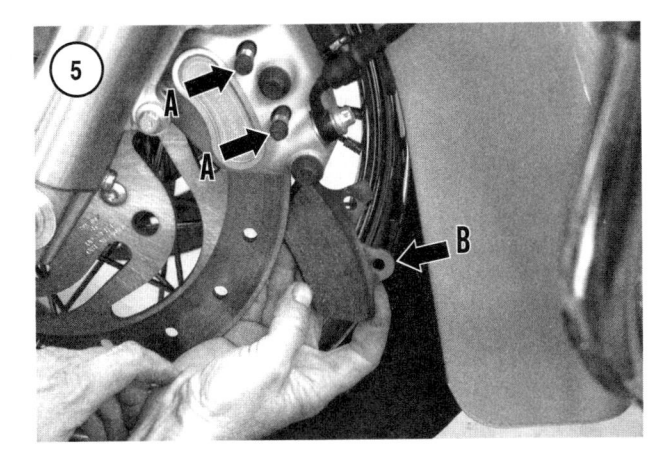

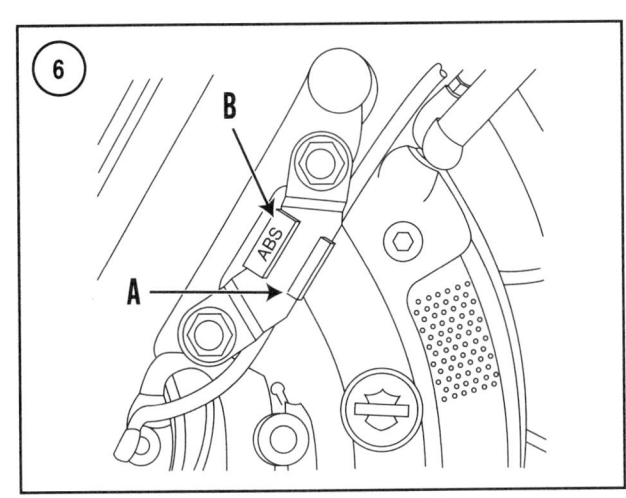

BRAKES

WARNING
When purchasing new pads, make sure the friction compound of the new pad is compatible with the disc material. Remove any roughness from the backs of the new pads with a fine-cut file. Then, thoroughly clean them off.

NOTE
*The pads are not symmetrical. The pad with one tab (A, **Figure 3**) must be installed on the inboard of the left side caliper, and on the outboard side of the right side caliper. The pad with two tabs (B, **Figure 3**) must be installed on the outboard side of the left caliper and on the inboard side of the right side caliper.*

14. Install the outboard pad (**Figure 4**) into the caliper.
15. Install the pad pin bolts (A, **Figure 5**) sufficiently to hold the outboard pad in position.
16. Install the inboard pad (B, **Figure 5**) into the caliper.
17. Hold the pads in place against the anti-rattle spring and push the pad pin bolts through the inboard pads.
18. Thread the pad pin bolts into the caliper body and tighten to 180-200 in.-lb. (20.3-22.6 N•m).
19. Repeat the procedure to replace the brake pads in the other caliper assembly.
20. Remove the spacer from the front brake lever.
21. Make sure there is sufficient brake fluid in the master cylinder reservoir. Top off if necessary with DOT 4 brake fluid.
22. Pump the front brake lever several times to reposition the brake pads against the brake disc.
23. Refill the master cylinder reservoir, if necessary, to maintain the correct fluid level as indicated on the side of the reservoir. Install the diaphragm and the top cover (**Figure 1**). Tighten the cover screws to 6-8 in.-lb. (0.7-0.9 N•m).

2008-2009 Models

CAUTION
On ABS-equipped models, keep the ABS sensors away from all magnetic fields or they will be damaged.

1. Read *Brake Service* information (this chapter).
2. Support the motorcycle on level ground on a swing arm stand.
3. Block the front wheel so the motorcycle will not roll in either direction while the rear wheel is off ground.
4A. On right side caliper only of ABS models, perform the following:
   a. Carefully cut the two cable straps securing the front fender tip lamp wires and wheel speed sensor wires to the right-side brake caliper hose.
   b. Push in on lip at the rear of clip (A, **Figure 6**) and release it. Rotate the ABS tab (B, **Figure 6**) toward the rear until the clip is perpendicular to the bracket. Remove the clip and move the cable out of the way.

9. Remove the inboard and outboard brake pads from the caliper.
10. Check the brake pads for wear or damage. Measure the thickness of the brake pad friction material. Replace the brake pads if they are worn to the service limit listed in **Table 1**.
11. Carefully remove any rust or corrosion from the disc.
12. Thoroughly clean the pad pin bolts of any corrosion or road dirt.
13. Check the friction surface of the new pads for any debris or manufacturing residue. If necessary, clean off with an aerosol brake cleaner.

4B. On all other models so equipped, carefully cut the two cable straps securing the front fender tip lamp wires to the left-side brake caliper hose.

5. Place a spacer between the brake lever and the throttle grip and secure it in place. If the brake lever is inadvertently squeezed, this will prevent the pistons from being partially forced out of the cylinders.

6. To prevent the reservoir from overflowing while repositioning the pistons in the caliper, perform the following:
   a. Clean all dirt and debris from the top of the master cylinder.
   b. Remove the screws securing the cover (**Figure 7**), and then remove the cover and diaphragm (**Figure 8**).
   c. Use a shop syringe and remove about 50% of the brake fluid from the reservoir to prevent overflow. Do *not* drain more than 50% of the brake fluid or air will enter the system. Discard the brake fluid properly.

7. Remove the cover (A, **Figure 9**) from the caliper.

8. Use needlenose pliers and remove the clip (**Figure 10**) from the pad pin and discard it.

9. Loosen the pad pin (**Figure 11**) in the caliper; do not remove it at this time.

10. Remove the bolts (B, **Figure 9**) securing the caliper to the fork slider and remove the caliper. On ABS models, do not lose the clip located under the mounting bolts on the right side caliper.

11. Insert a large screwdriver or tire iron between the brake pads and carefully pry the pads and pistons back into the caliper to make room for the new brake pads.

12. Remove the pad pin and discard it.

13. Remove the inboard and outboard brake pads from the caliper.

14. Carefully remove any rust or corrosion from the disc.

15. Check the friction surface of the new pads for debris or manufacturing residue. If necessary, clean them off with an aerosol brake cleaner.

WARNING
When purchasing new pads, make sure the friction compound of the new pad is compatible with the disc material. Remove roughness from the backs of the new pads with a fine-cut file and thoroughly clean them off.

16. Make sure the spring pad is still located properly within the caliper body. Refer to *Front Brake Caliper (2008-2009 models)* in this chapter.

17. Reinstall the caliper onto the fork slider and install the bolts (B, **Figure 9**). Tighten the caliper bolts to 28-38 ft.-lb. (38.0-51.5 N•m).

18. Correctly position the inboard brake pad with the pad pin tab going in last. Insert the inboard brake pad (**Figure 12**) up and into the caliper until it seats within the caliper.

19. Correctly position the outboard brake pad with the pad pin tab going in last. Insert the outboard brake pad (**Figure 13**) up and into the caliper until it seats within the caliper.

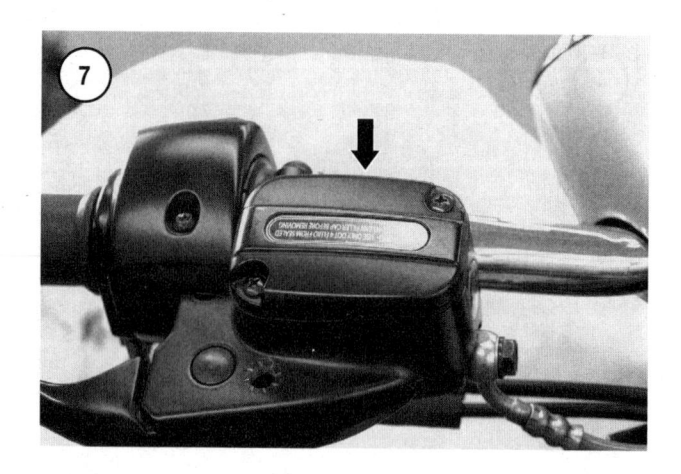

BRAKES

NOTE
Figure 14 *shown with the caliper removed from the brake disc to better illustrate the step.*

20. Make sure both brake pads are correctly seated within the caliper as shown in **Figure 14**.
21. Insert a *new* pad pin bolt (**Figure 11**) through the caliper and both brake pads. Install the pad pin into the caliper body and tighten it to 75-102 in.-lb. (8.5-11.5 N•m).
22. Install a *new* clip (**Figure 10**) onto the pad pin and push it down until it is correctly seated in the caliper.
23. Correctly position the screen with the two-pronged side going on first into the lower portion of the caliper and snap the upper end into position. Make sure the screen (A, **Figure 9**) is secured on the caliper.
24A. On the right side caliper only of ABS models, perform the following:
   a. Rotate the ABS tab until the clip is perpendicular to the bracket and install the cable.
   b. Rotate the ABS tab (B, **Figure 6**) toward the front until the clip is in-line with the bracket, and apply pressure to the tab lip until it is engaged. Gently tug on the cable to make sure the clip is properly installed.
   c. Install the first *new* clamp 2.5 in. (63.5 mm) above the bottom of the brake hose crimp capturing the front wheel sensor cable and brake hose.
   d. Install the second *new* clamp 2.5 in. (63.5 mm) below the top of the brake hose crimp capturing the front wheel sensor cable and brake hose. On models so equipped, also secure the front fender tip lamp wires within this clamp.
24B. On all other models so equipped, position the front fender tip lamp wires onto the left-side brake caliper hose. Secure the wires with two *new* cable straps.
25. Remove the spacer from the front brake lever.
26. Make sure there is sufficient brake fluid in the master cylinder reservoir. Top it off if with DOT 4 brake fluid if necessary. Temporarily install the cover and tighten the screws.
27. Remove the swing arm stand.
28. Pump the front brake lever several times to reposition the brake pads against the brake disc.
29. Refill the master cylinder reservoir, if necessary, to maintain the correct fluid level as indicated on the side of the reservoir. Install the diaphragm (**Figure 8**) and the top cover (**Figure 7**). Tighten the screws to 6-8 in.-lb. (0.7-0.9 N•m).
30. If necessary, bleed the front brakes as described in this chapter.

FRONT BRAKE CALIPER (2006-2007 MODELS)

Refer to *Brake Service* in this chapter.

Removal/Installation

1. Support the motorcycle on level ground on a swing arm stand.

FRONT BRAKE CALIPER (2006-2007 MODELS)

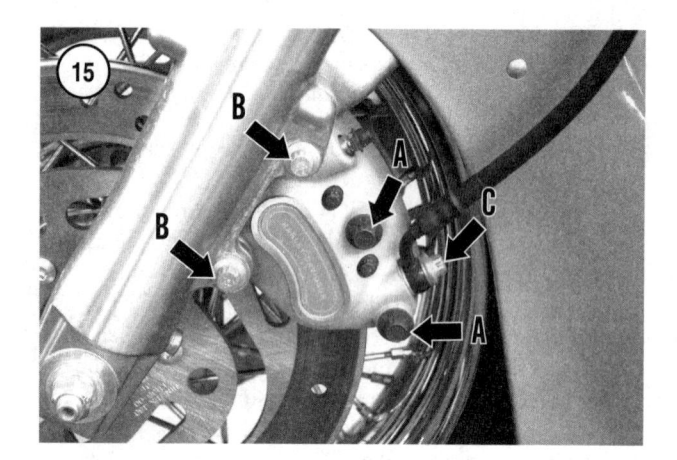

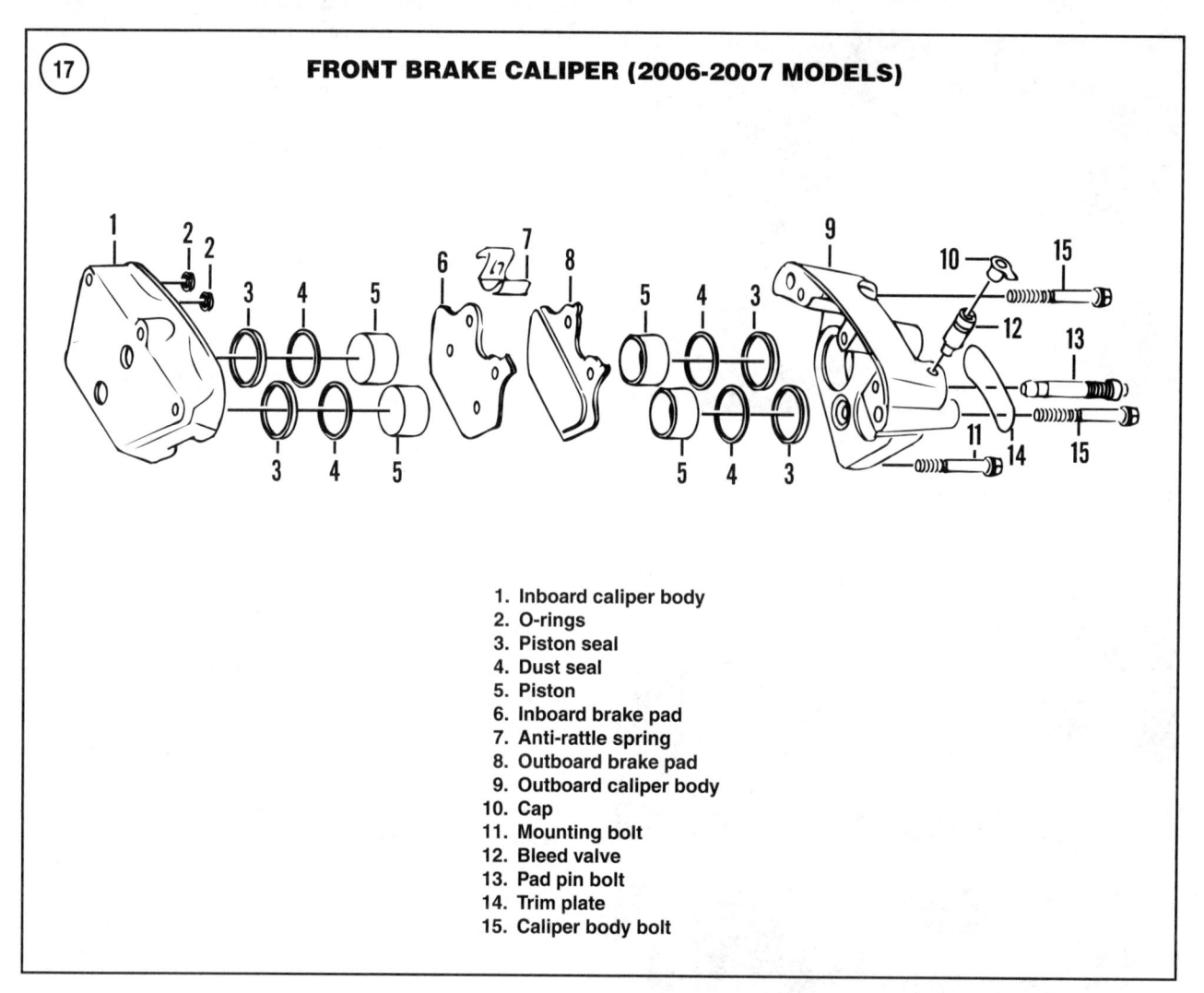

1. Inboard caliper body
2. O-rings
3. Piston seal
4. Dust seal
5. Piston
6. Inboard brake pad
7. Anti-rattle spring
8. Outboard brake pad
9. Outboard caliper body
10. Cap
11. Mounting bolt
12. Bleed valve
13. Pad pin bolt
14. Trim plate
15. Caliper body bolt

2. Block the front wheel so the motorcycle will not roll in either direction.
3. If the caliper assembly is going to be disassembled for service, perform the following:
 a. Loosen the two caliper body assembly bolts (A, **Figure 15**).
 b. Remove the caliper mounting bolts (B, **Figure 15**), and then remove the caliper from the brake disc and front fork.
 c. Remove the brake pads as described in this chapter.
 d. Insert a piece of wood (**Figure 16**) in place of the brake pads.
 e. Slowly apply the brake lever to push the pistons part way out of the caliper assembly for ease of removal during caliper service.
 f. Remove the piece of wood.
4. Remove the banjo bolt and sealing washers (C, **Figure 15**) attaching the brake hose to the caliper assembly.

BRAKES

Tighten the caliper mounting bolts to 28-38 ft.-lb. (38-51.5 N•m).

c. Apply clean DOT 4 brake fluid to the rubber portions of *new* sealing washers prior to installation.
d. Install the *new* sealing washers against each side of the hose fitting.
e. Install the banjo bolt (C, **Figure 15**). Tighten the banjo bolt to 17-22 ft.-lb. (23.1-29.8 N•m).
f. Bleed the brakes as described in *Bleeding the System* (this chapter).

Disassembly

Refer to **Figure 17**.

1. Remove the brake pads as described in this chapter.
2. Remove the caliper as described in this section.
3. Remove the two caliper body assembly bolts (**Figure 18**) loosened during removal (this section).
4. Separate the caliper body halves. Remove the O-ring seals (**Figure 19**) and discard them. *New* O-ring seals must be installed every time the caliper is disassembled.
5. Remove the anti-rattle spring from the outboard caliper body.

NOTE
If the pistons or caliper bores are corroded or very dirty, a small amount of compressed air may be necessary to completely remove the pistons from the body bores.

6. Place a piece of soft wood or a folded shop cloth over the end of the pistons and the caliper body. Turn the assembly over and place it on the workbench with the pistons facing down.

WARNING
Compressed air will force the pistons out of the caliper bodies under considerable force. Do no block the piston by hand as injury will occur.

7. Apply air pressure in short bursts to the hydraulic fluid passageway to force out the pistons. Repeat this for the other caliper body half. Use a service station air hose if compressed air is not available.

CAUTION
Do not use a sharp tool to remove the dust and piston seals from the caliper cylinders. Do not damage the cylinder surface.

8. Use a piece of wood or a plastic scraper to carefully push the dust seal and the piston seal (**Figure 20**) in toward the caliper cylinder and out of their grooves. Remove the dust and piston seals from all four cylinders.
9. If necessary, unscrew and remove the bleed valve (**Figure 21**).
10. Inspect the caliper assembly as described in this section.

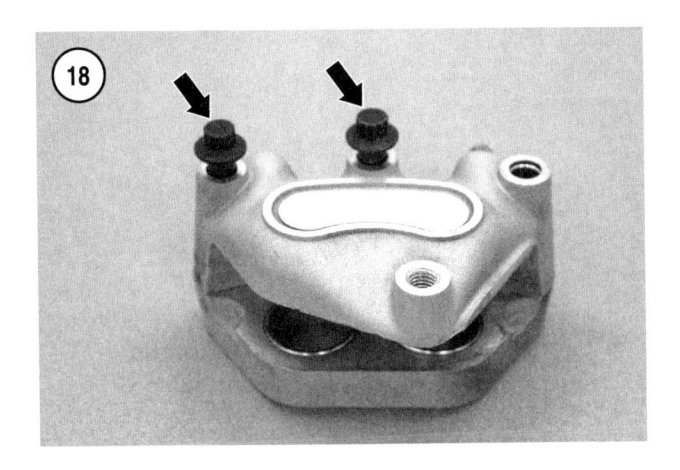

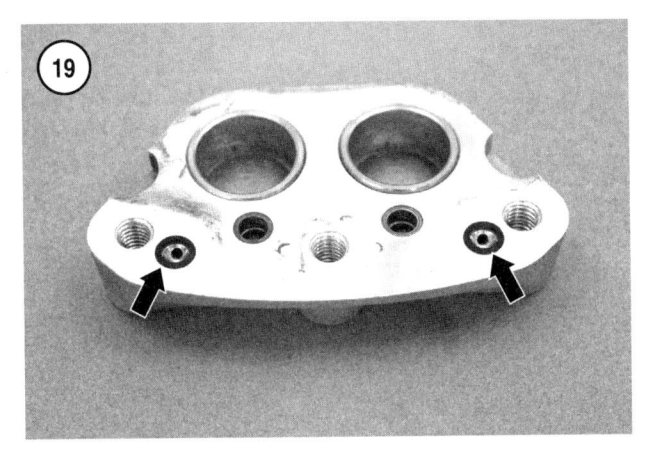

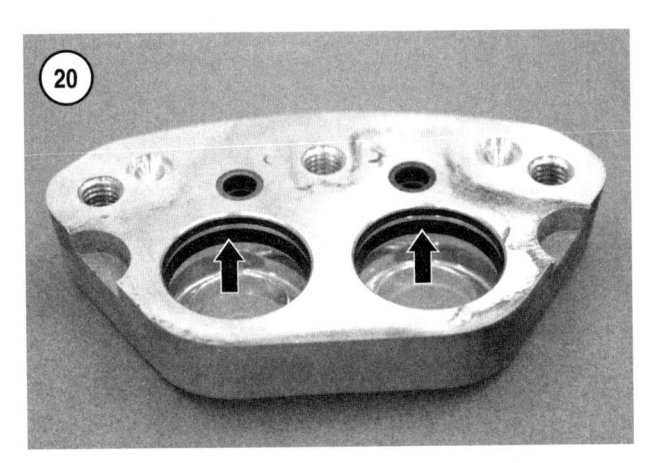

5. Place the loose end of the brake hose in a plastic bag to prevent the entry of debris and to contain any residual brake fluid leaking out.
6. If necessary, disassemble and service the caliper assembly as described in this section. If the front caliper is not going to be serviced, place it in a plastic bag to keep it clean.
7. Install by reversing the removal steps. Note the following:
   a. Install the caliper assembly onto the disc, being careful not to damage the leading edge of the brake pads.
   b. Install the caliper mounting bolts (B, **Figure 15**) securing the brake caliper assembly to the front fork.

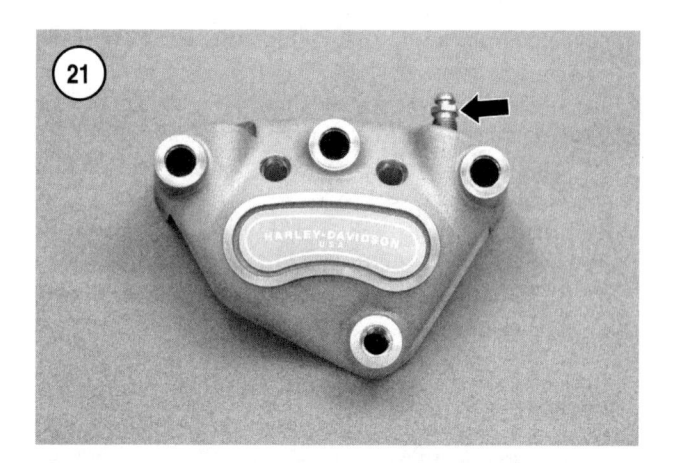

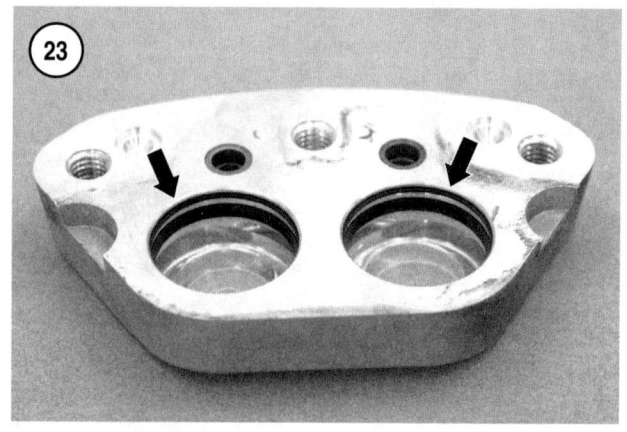

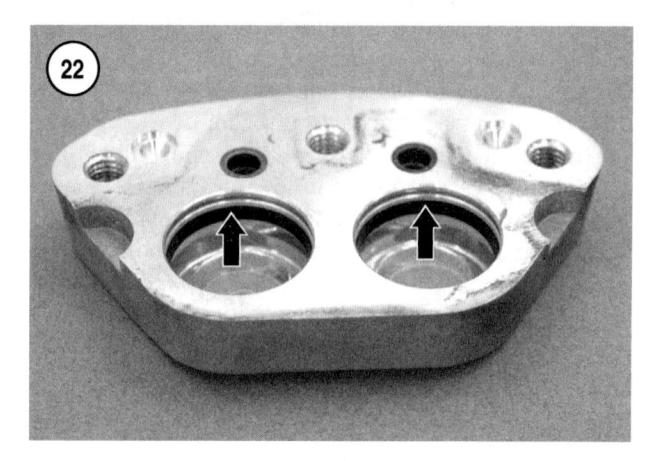

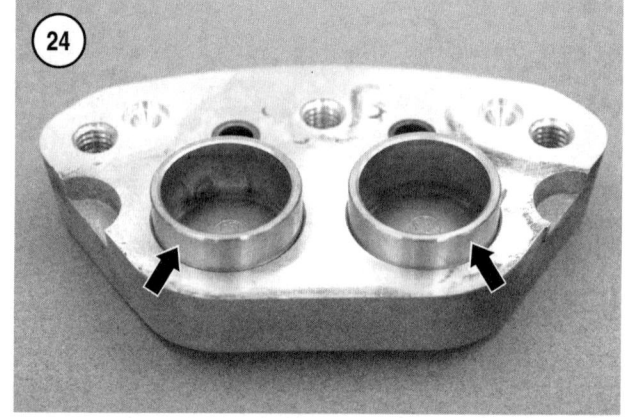

Assembly

WARNING
Do not use DOT 4 brake fluid for lubrication. If used, it will result in increased brake lever resistance.

WARNING
Never reuse old dust seals or piston seals. Very minor damage or age deterioration can make the seals ineffective.

1. Apply a light coat of G.E. Versilube #GE322L silicone grease to the following parts:
    a. Inside diameter surfaces of both piston and dust seals.
    b. Caliper bores.
    c. Outside surfaces of pistons.
    d. Closed end of pistons.
2. All remaining surfaces must remain dry.
3. Carefully install the *new* piston seals (**Figure 22**) into the lower grooves. Make sure the seals are properly seated in their respective grooves in all four cylinders.
4. Carefully install the *new* dust seals (**Figure 23**) into the upper grooves. Make sure all seals are properly seated in their respective grooves (**Figure 20**) in all four cylinders.

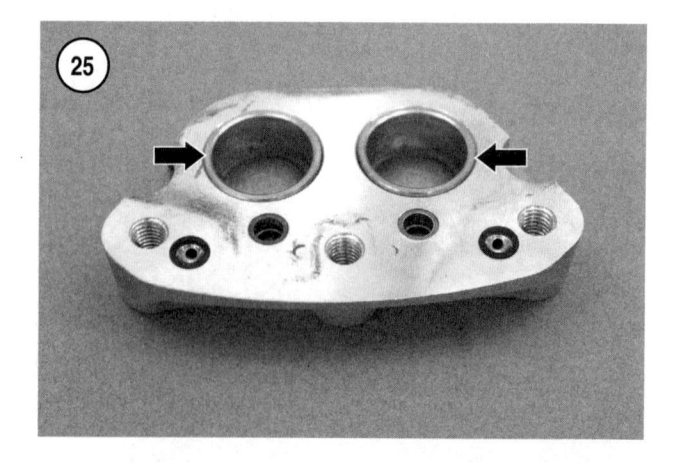

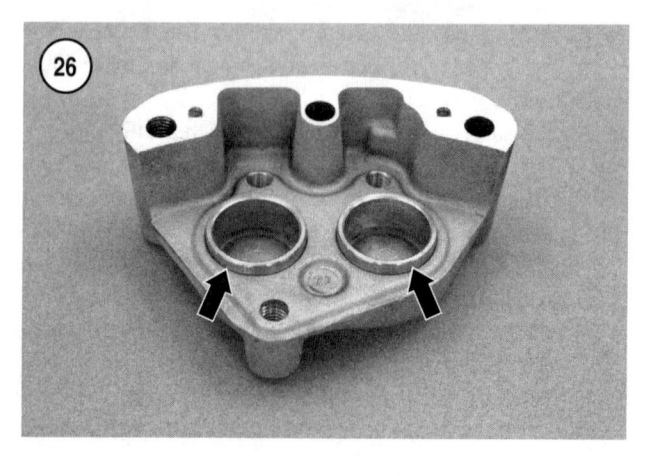

BRAKES

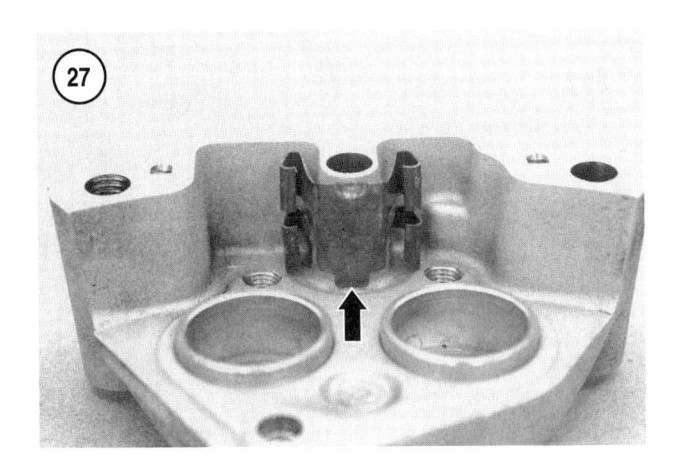

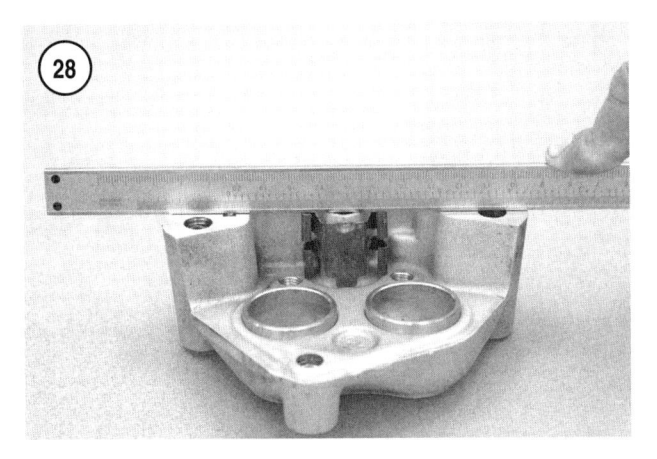

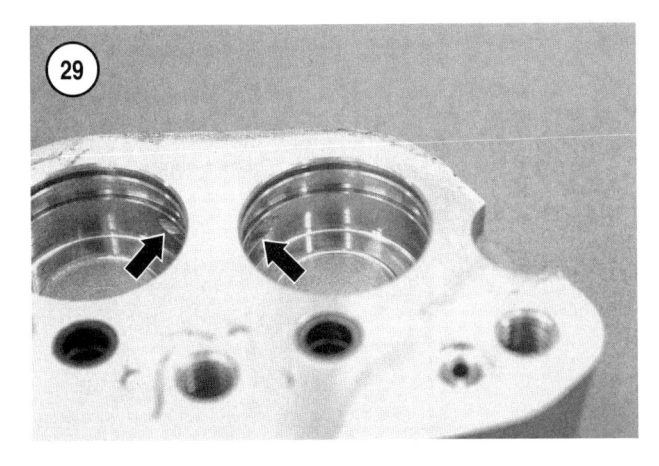

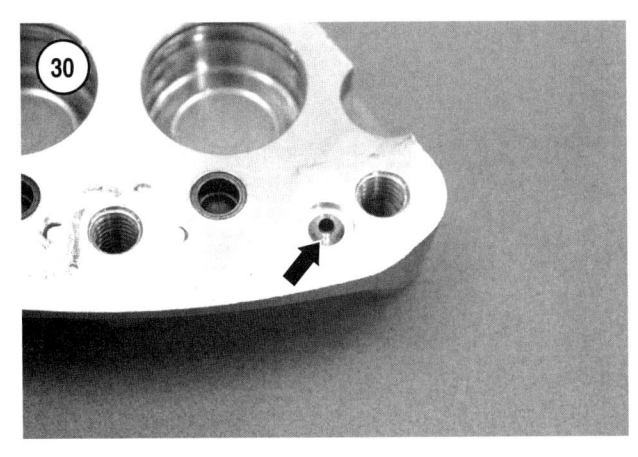

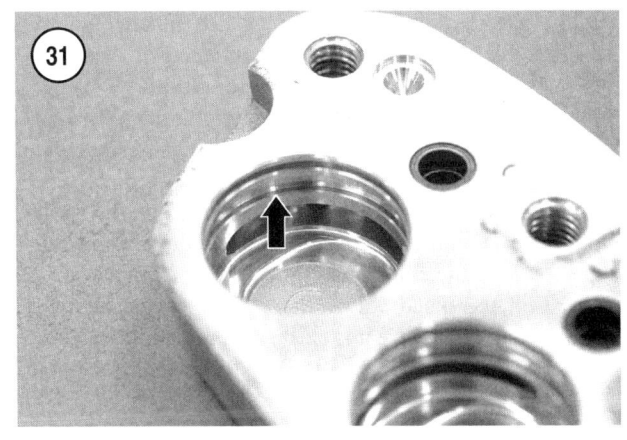

5. Position the pistons with the open end facing out and install the pistons (**Figure 24**) into the caliper cylinders. Push the pistons in until they all bottom (**Figure 25**).
6. Repeat the process for the other caliper body half (**Figure 26**). Make sure all pistons are installed correctly.
7. Install the anti-rattle spring into the outboard caliper body. Make sure the locating foot is located as shown in **Figure 27**. The upper edge of the spring must be flush with the caliper mating surface (**Figure 28**) or the caliper bodies cannot be assembled correctly.
8. Install the *new* O-rings (**Figure 19**) into the inboard caliper body.
9. Install the outboard caliper body onto the inboard body. Make sure the O-ring seals are still in place during the assembly of the caliper bodies.
10. Install the two caliper body assembly bolts (**Figure 18**), and tighten securely. Do not tighten them to final specification at this time.
11. If the bleed valve (**Figure 21**) was removed, install it and tighten it to 80-100 in.-lb. (9.0-11.3 N•m).
12. Install the brake pads as described in this chapter.
13. Install the caliper as described in this section.
14. Tighten the two caliper body assembly bolts (**Figure 18**) to 28-38 ft.-lb (38.0-51.5 N•m).
15. Bleed the brakes as described in this chapter.

Inspection

1. Clean both caliper body halves and pistons in clean DOT 4 brake fluid, or denatured alcohol. Dry them with compressed air.
2. Make sure the fluid passageways (**Figure 29**) in the piston bores are clear. Apply compressed air to the openings to make sure they are clear. Clean them out, if necessary, with clean brake fluid.
3. Make sure both fluid passageways (**Figure 30**) in both caliper bodies are clear. Apply compressed air to the openings to make sure they are clear. Clean them out, if necessary, with clean brake fluid.
4. Inspect the piston and dust seal grooves (**Figure 31**) in both caliper bodies for damage. If they are damaged or corroded, replace the caliper assembly.

5. Inspect the threaded banjo bolt hole (**Figure 32**) in the outboard caliper body. If it is worn or damaged, clean it out with a thread tap or replace the caliper assembly.
6. Inspect the banjo bolt passageway (**Figure 33**). Apply compressed air to the opening and make sure it is clear. Clean it out, if necessary, with clean brake fluid.
7. Inspect the threaded bleed valve hole in the caliper body. If it is worn or damaged, clean it out with a thread tap or replace the caliper assembly.
8. Inspect the bleed valve. Apply compressed air to the opening and make sure it is clear. Clean it out, if necessary, with clean brake fluid. Install the bleed valve and tighten it to 80-100 in.-lb. (9.0-11.3 N•m).
9. Inspect both caliper bodies (**Figure 34**) for damage. Check the inboard caliper mounting bolt hole threads (**Figure 35**) for wear or damage. Clean the threads with an appropriately sized tap or replace the caliper assembly.
10. Inspect the cylinder walls and pistons (**Figure 36**) for scratches, scoring or other damage.
11. Check the anti-rattle spring (**Figure 37**) for cracks or other damage.

FRONT BRAKE CALIPER (2008-2009 MODELS)

Refer *Brake Service* in this chapter.

CAUTION
On ABS-equipped models, keep the ABS sensors away from all magnetic fields or they will be damaged.

Removal/Installation

Refer to **Figure 38**.
1. Support the motorcycle on level ground on a swing arm stand.
2. Block the front wheel so the motorcycle will not roll in either direction while the rear wheel is off ground.
3A. On models equipped with ABS, perform the following:
   a. Carefully cut the two cable straps securing the front fender tip lamp wires and wheel speed sensor wires to the left-side brake caliper hose.
   b. Push in on lip at the rear of clip (A, **Figure 39**) and release it. Rotate the ABS tab (B, **Figure 39**) toward the rear until the clip is perpendicular to the bracket. Remove the clip and move the cable out of the way.
3B. On all other models so equipped, carefully cut the two cable straps securing the front fender tip lamp wires to the left-side brake caliper hose.
4. Remove the banjo bleed bolt and sealing washers attaching the brake hose to the caliper assembly.
5. Place the loose end of the brake hose in a plastic bag to prevent the entry of debris and to contain any residual brake fluid leaking out.
6. Remove the bolts securing the caliper to the fork slider, and then remove the caliper from the brake disc. On ABS

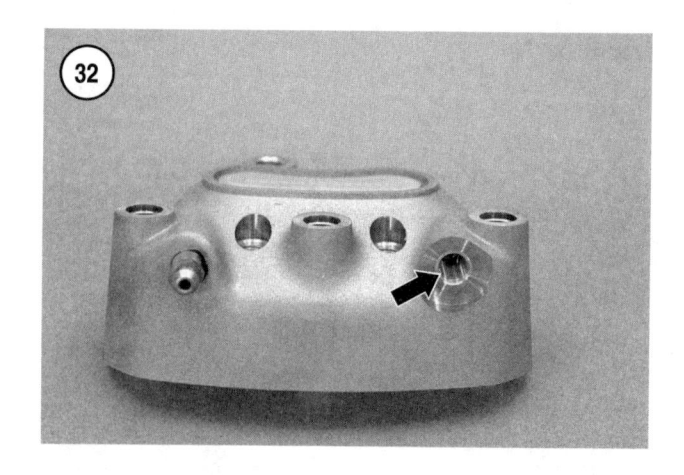

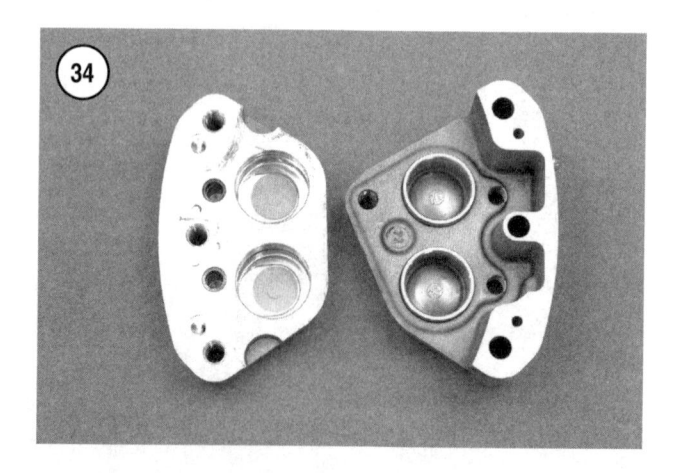

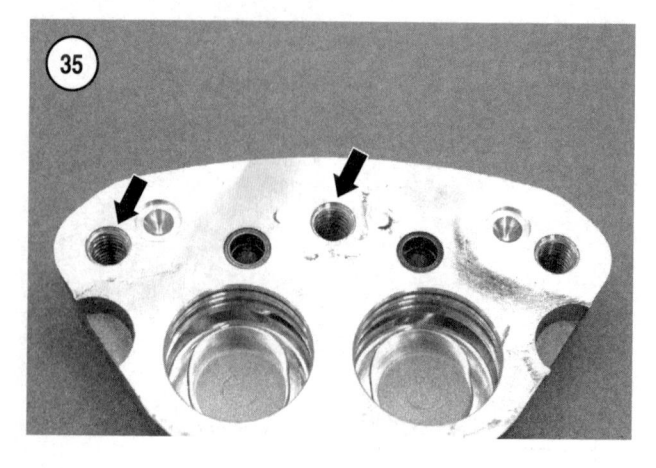

BRAKES

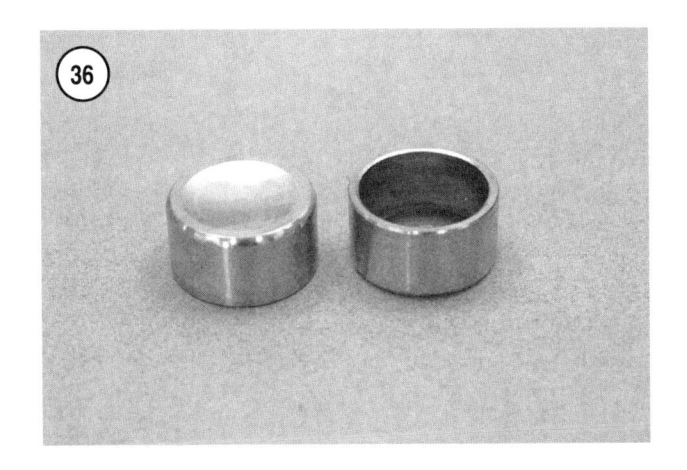

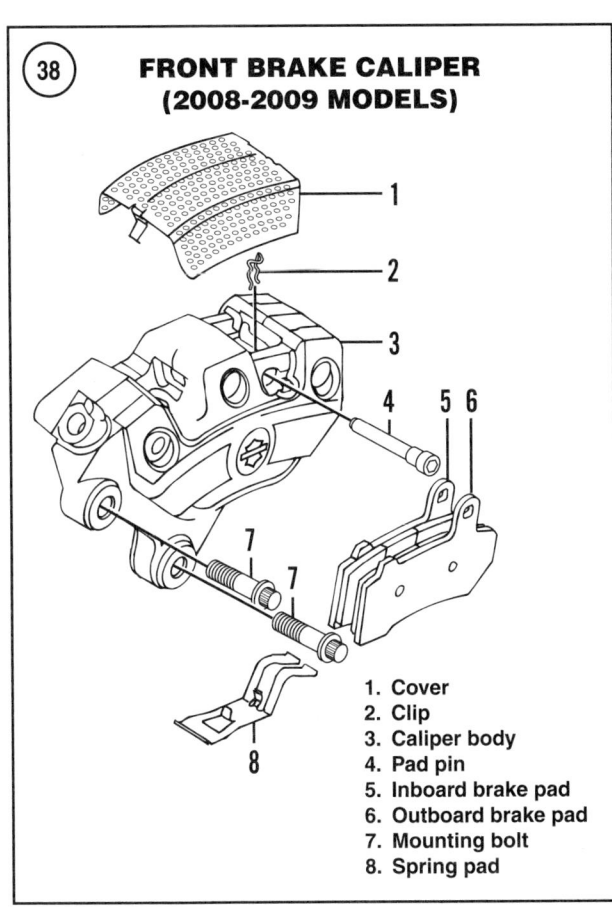

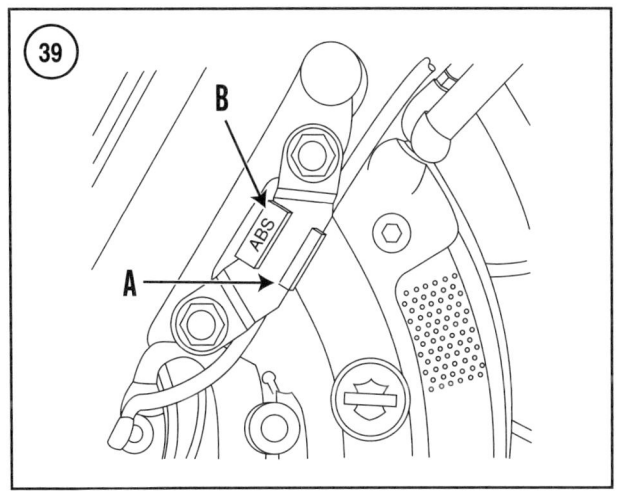

619

models, do not lose the clip located under the mounting bolts on the right side caliper. If the front caliper is going to be left off the motorcycle for an extended period of time, place it in a plastic bag to keep it clean.

7. Install the caliper assembly onto the disc, being careful not to damage the leading edge of the brake pads.

8. Install the front brake caliper mounting bolts and tighten the bolts to 28-38 ft.-lb (38.0-51.5 N•m).

9A. On models equipped with ABS, perform the following:

   a. Rotate the ABS tab until the clip is perpendicular to the bracket and install the cable.

   b. Rotate the ABS tab (B, **Figure 39**) toward the front until the clip is in-line with the bracket, and apply pressure to the tab lip until it is engaged. Gently tug on the cable to make sure the clip is properly installed.

   c. Install the first *new* clamp 2.5 in. (63.5 mm) above the bottom of the brake hose crimp capturing the front wheel sensor cable and brake hose.

   d. Install the second *new* clamp 2.5 in. (63.5 mm) below the top of the brake hose crimp capturing the front wheel sensor cable and brake hose. On models so equipped, also secure the front fender tip lamp wires within this clamp.

9B. On all other models so equipped, position the front fender tip lamp wires onto the left-side brake caliper hose. Secure the wires with two *new* cable straps.

10. Apply clean DOT 4 brake fluid to *new* copper sealing washers prior to installation.

11. Install the *new* sealing washers on each side of the hose fitting.

12. Install the banjo bleed bolt and tighten to 17-19 ft.-lb. (23.1-25.8 N•m).

13. Bleed the brakes as described in this chapter.

Disassembly

The Brembo caliper assembly cannot be disassembled for service. The only replacement parts available are shown in **Figure 38**.

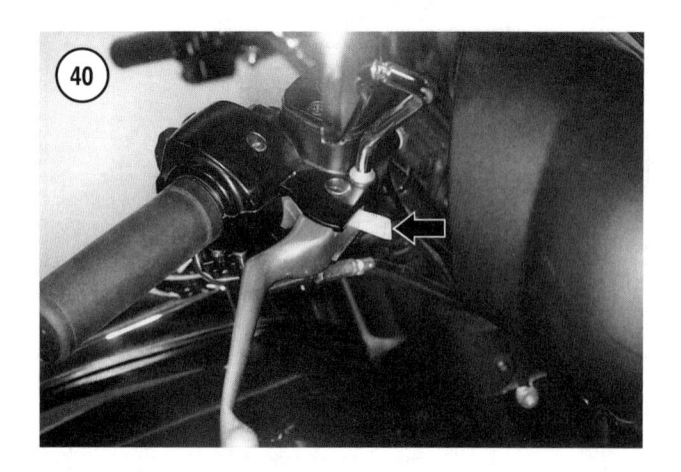

FRONT MASTER CYLINDER
(2006-2007 MODELS)

Refer to *Brake Service* in this chapter.

Removal

1. Support the motorcycle on level ground on a swing arm stand.
2. Block the front wheel so the motorcycle will not roll in either direction while the rear wheel is off ground.

CAUTION
Failure to install the spacer will result in damage to the rubber boot and plunger on the front brake switch within the right side switch assembly.

3. Insert a 5/32 in. (4 mm) thick spacer (**Figure 40**) between the brake lever and lever bracket. Make sure the spacer stays in place during the removal procedure.
4. Clean debris off the top of the master cylinder.
5. Remove the screws securing the cover, and then remove the cover (A, **Figure 41**) and diaphragm.
6. Use a shop syringe to draw all of the brake fluid out of the master cylinder reservoir.
7. Temporarily reinstall the diaphragm and the cover. Install the cover screws and finger-tighten them.
8. Remove the mirror (B, **Figure 41**) from the master cylinder.
9. Remove the banjo bolt and sealing washers (C, **Figure 41**) securing the brake hose to the master cylinder.
10. Remove the screw securing the right side switch halves together. Separate and remove the switch housing (D, **Figure 41**) from the handlebar.
11. Place the loose end of the brake hose in a reclosable plastic bag to prevent the entry of moisture and debris. Tie the loose end of the hose to the handlebar.
12. Remove the Torx bolts and washers securing the clamp (E, **Figure 41**) and master cylinder to the handlebar.
13. Remove the clamp and the master cylinder assembly from the handlebar.
14. Drain any residual brake fluid from the master cylinder and dispose of it properly.

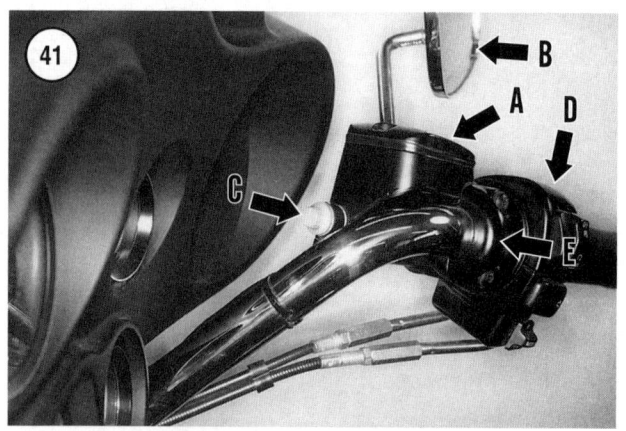

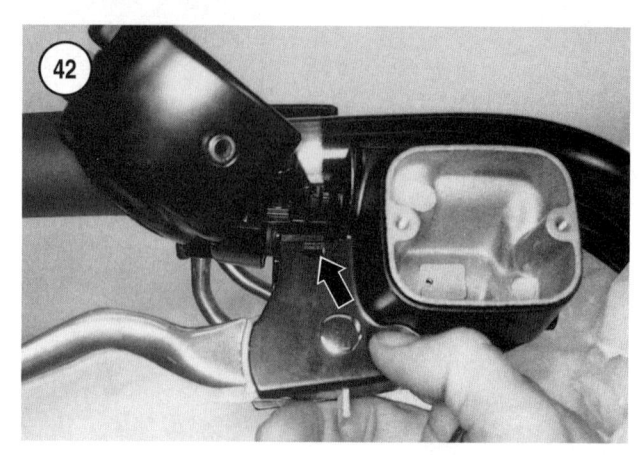

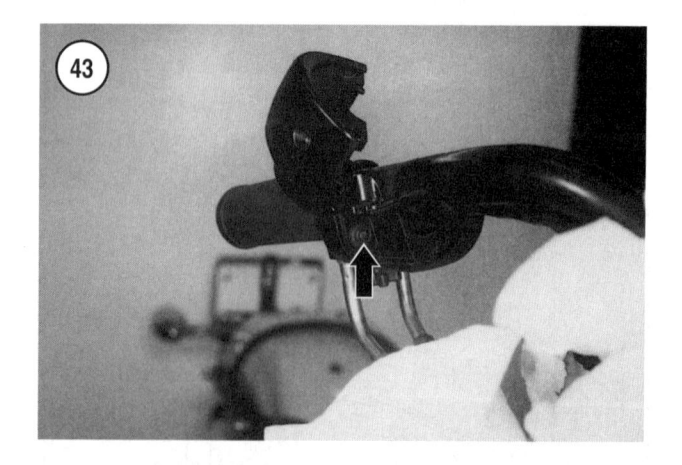

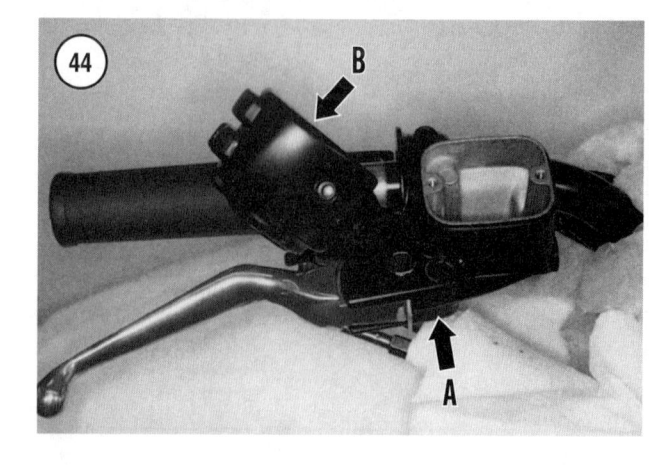

BRAKES

⑭ FRONT MASTER CYLINDER (2006-2007 MODELS)

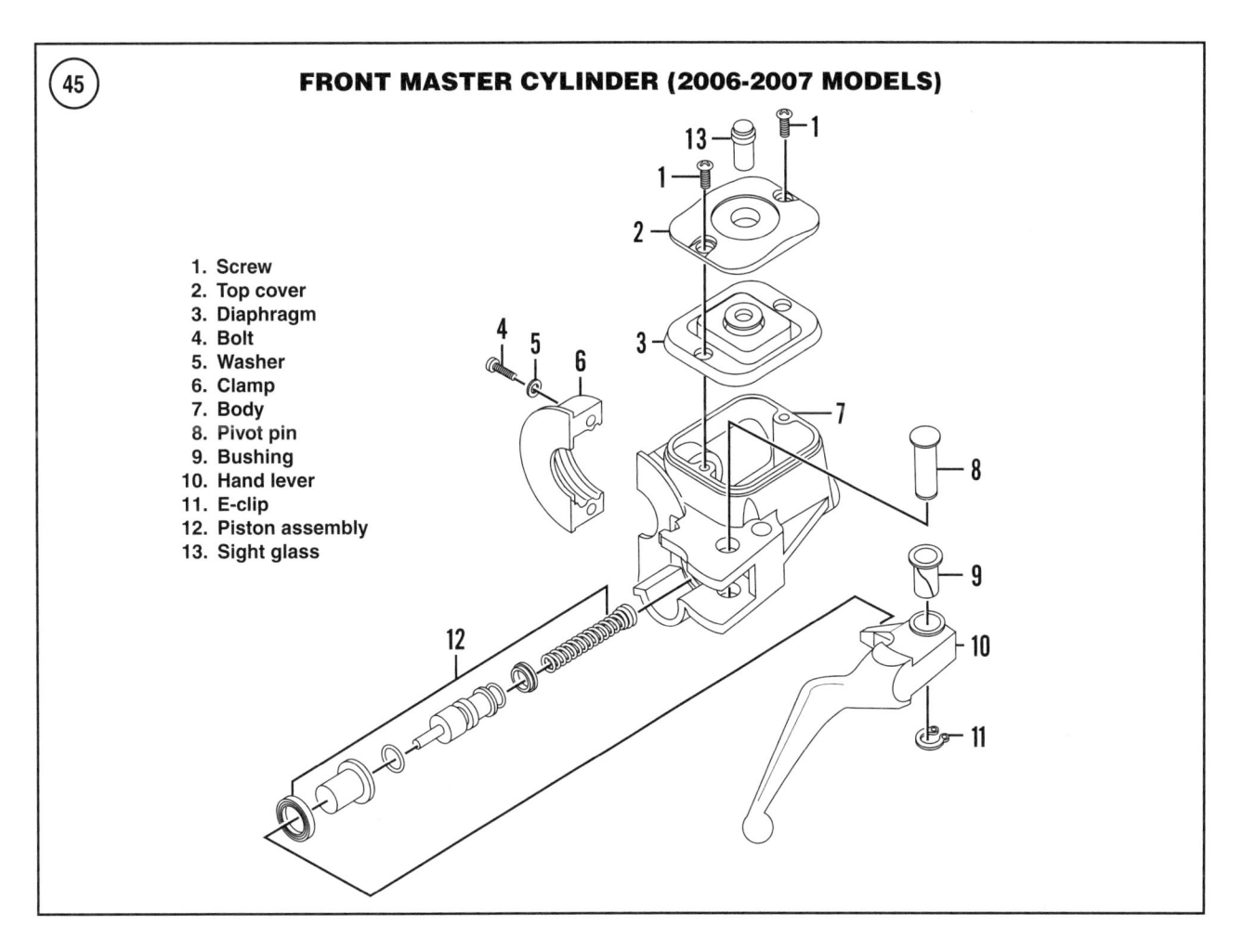

1. Screw
2. Top cover
3. Diaphragm
4. Bolt
5. Washer
6. Clamp
7. Body
8. Pivot pin
9. Bushing
10. Hand lever
11. E-clip
12. Piston assembly
13. Sight glass

15. If the master cylinder assembly is not going to be serviced, attach the clamp to the master cylinder and reinstall the Torx bolts. Place the assembly in a plastic bag to protect it.

Installation

1. Insert the 5/32 in. (4 mm) thick spacer between the brake lever and lever bracket (**Figure 40**), if not already in place. Make sure the spacer stays in place during the installation procedure.
2. Position the front master cylinder onto the handlebar. Align the master cylinder notch (**Figure 42**) with the locating tab on the lower portion of the right side switch.

CAUTION
*Do not damage the front brake light switch and rubber boot (**Figure 43**, typical) when installing the master cylinder.*

3. Push the master cylinder all the way onto the handlebar (A, **Figure 44**). Hold it in this position and install the upper portion of the switch (B, **Figure 44**). Install the switch's screw and tighten securely.
4. Position the clamp (E, **Figure 41**) and install the Torx bolts and washers. Tighten the upper, and then the lower clamp bolt to 60-80 in.-lb. (6.8-9 N•m).

5. Apply clean DOT 4 brake fluid to the rubber portions of *new* sealing washers prior to installation.
6. Install the *new* sealing washers on each side of the hose fitting.
7. Install the banjo bolt (C, **Figure 41**) and sealing washers securing the brake hose to the master cylinder. Tighten the banjo bolt to 17-22 ft.-lb. (23.1-29.8 N•m).
8. Remove the spacer (**Figure 40**) from the brake lever.
9. Temporarily install the diaphragm and top cover (**Figure 41**) onto the reservoir, if not in place. Install the screws and finger-tighten them at this time.
10. Install the mirror (B, **Figure 41**) onto the master cylinder and adjust to rider preference.
11. Refill the master cylinder reservoir and bleed the front brake system as described in this chapter.
12. Install the diaphragm and cover. Install the cover screws and tighten to 6-8 in.-lb. (0.7-0.9 N•m).

Disassembly

Refer to **Figure 45**.

1. Remove the master cylinder assembly as described in this section.
2. Store the master cylinder components in a divided container, such as a restaurant-size egg carton, to help maintain their correct alignment positions.

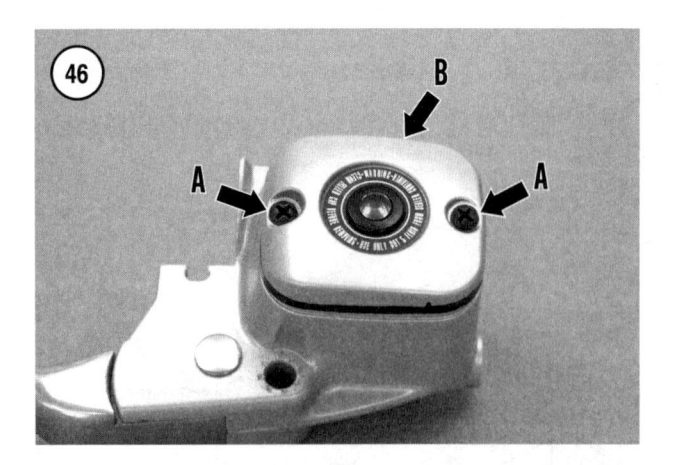

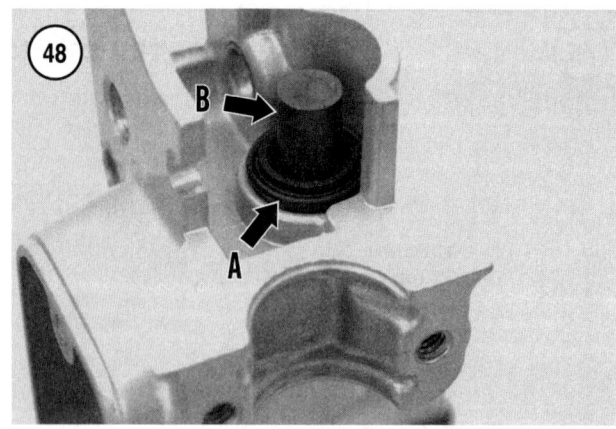

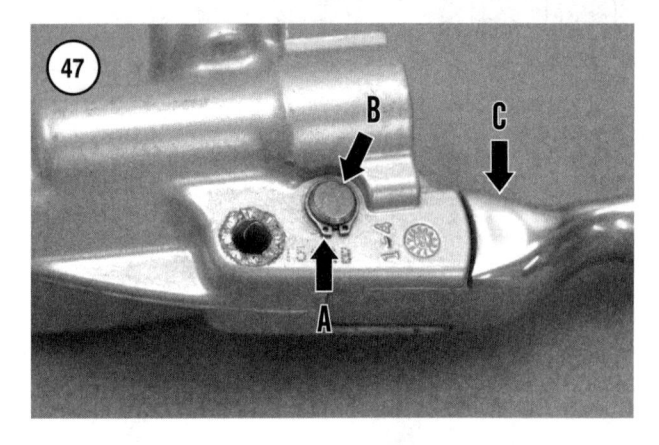

3. Remove the screws (A, **Figure 46**) securing the top cover (B) if they are still in place. Remove the top cover and the diaphragm from the master cylinder.
4. Remove the snap ring (A, **Figure 47**) and the pivot pin (B) securing the hand lever to the master cylinder. Remove the hand lever (C, **Figure 47**).
5. Remove the retainer (A, **Figure 48**) and the rubber boot (B) from the area where the hand lever actuates the piston assembly.
6. Remove the piston assembly (**Figure 49**) and the spring.
7. Inspect all parts as described in this section.

Assembly

WARNING
When installing a new piston assembly, apply the lubricant provided with the original equipment service parts kit. Coat all existing parts with a light coat of G.E. Versilube #GE322L silicone grease prior to installation.

CAUTION
The cover and diaphragm must be assembled as described. If the sight glass is not installed correctly through the cover and diaphragm neck, brake fluid will leak past these components.

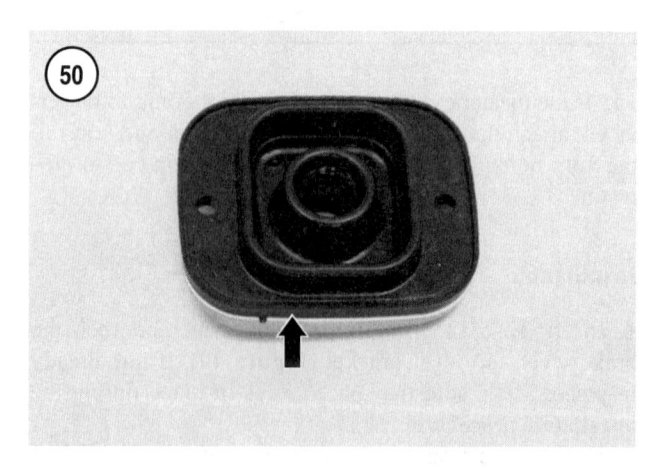

BRAKES

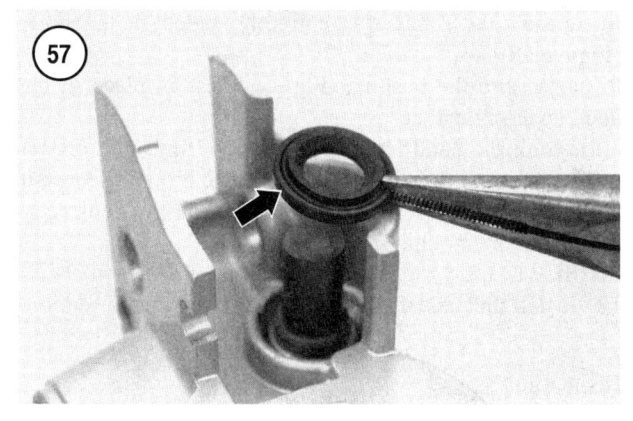

1. If the cover and the diaphragm were disassembled, assemble them as follows:
    a. Insert the neck of the diaphragm into the cover. Press it in until it seats correctly and the outer edges are aligned with the cover (**Figure 50**).
    b. Push the sight glass (**Figure 51**) straight down through the cover and the neck of the diaphragm until it snaps into place (**Figure 52**). The sight glass must lock these two parts together to avoid a brake fluid leak.
2. Coat the inside of the cylinder bore with the provided lubricant, or with G.E. Versilube #GE322L silicone grease.
3. Install a bolt into the banjo bolt threaded hole and mount the master cylinder in a vise (**Figure 53**).
4. Position the spring with retainer end facing out and install the spring into piston assembly (**Figure 54**).

CAUTION
When installing the piston assembly, do not allow the cup to turn inside out as it will be damaged and allow brake fluid leaks within the cylinder bore.

5. Install the spring and piston assembly into the cylinder. Push them in until they bottom in the cylinder (**Figure 49**).
6. Install the rubber boot (**Figure 55**) onto the piston assembly.
7. Push down on the piston and rubber boot until the rubber boot seats (**Figure 56**).
8. Position the retainer with the large side (**Figure 57**) going on first and install the retainer onto the rubber boot.

624

CHAPTER FIFTEEN

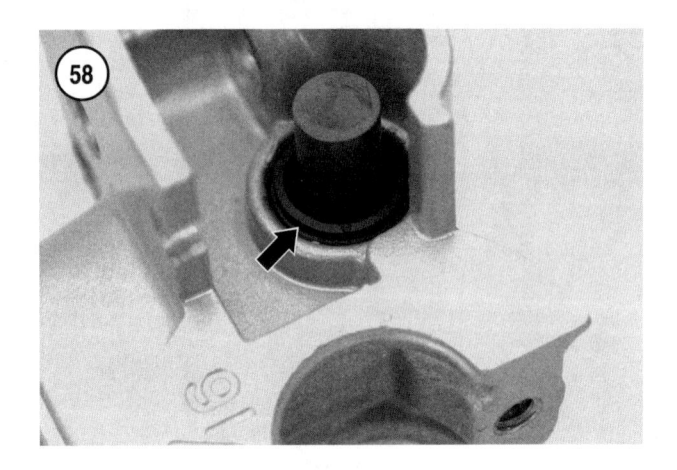

Make sure the retainer is correctly seated in the body (**Figure 58**).
9. Make sure the bushing (**Figure 59**) is in place in the hand lever pivot area.
10. Install the hand lever (C, **Figure 47**) into the master cylinder. Install the pivot pin (B, **Figure 47**) and secure it with the snap ring (A). Make sure the snap ring is correctly seated in the pivot pin groove.
11. Slowly apply the lever to make sure it pivots freely.
12. Install the master cylinder as described in this section.

Inspection

Replace worn or damage parts as described in this section. It is recommended that the OEM service parts kit be installed every time the master cylinder is disassembled.
1. Clean all parts in denatured alcohol or clean DOT 4 brake fluid. Inspect the master cylinder bore surface for signs of wear and damage. If it is less than perfect, replace the master cylinder assembly. The body cannot be replaced separately.
2. Inspect the piston cup (A, **Figure 60**), and the O-ring (B) for wear, and damage.
3. Make sure the fluid passage (**Figure 61**) in the bottom of the master cylinder body is clear. Clean it out if necessary.
4. Inspect the piston contact surface (**Figure 62**) in the bore for signs of wear and damage.
5. Check the end of the piston (C, **Figure 60**) for wear caused by the hand lever.
6. Check the hand lever pivot lugs (A, **Figure 63**) in the master cylinder body for cracks or elongation.
7. Inspect the threaded mirror hole (B, **Figure 63**) in the master cylinder body. If it is worn or damaged, clean it out with a thread tap or replace the master cylinder assembly.
8. Inspect the hand lever pivot hole and bushing (A, **Figure 64**) and the pivot pin (B) for wear, cracks or elongation.
9. Inspect the rubber boot and retainer (**Figure 65**) for deterioration, wear or damage.
10. Inspect the threaded banjo bolt hole (C, **Figure 63**). If it is worn or damaged, clean it out with a thread tap or replace the master cylinder assembly.

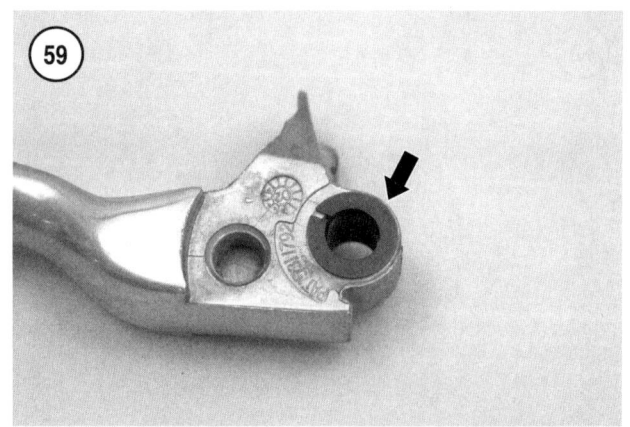

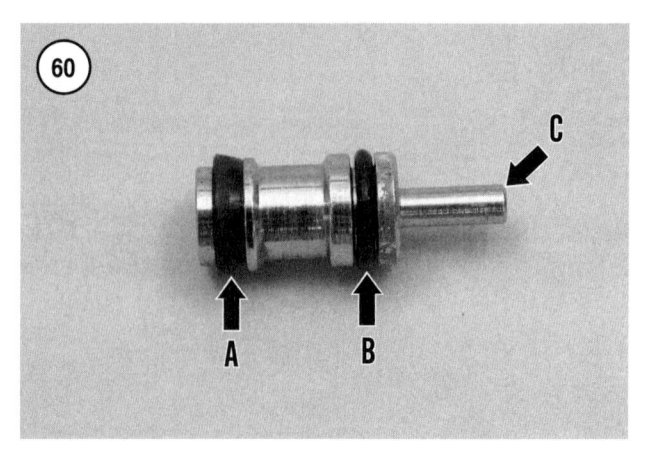

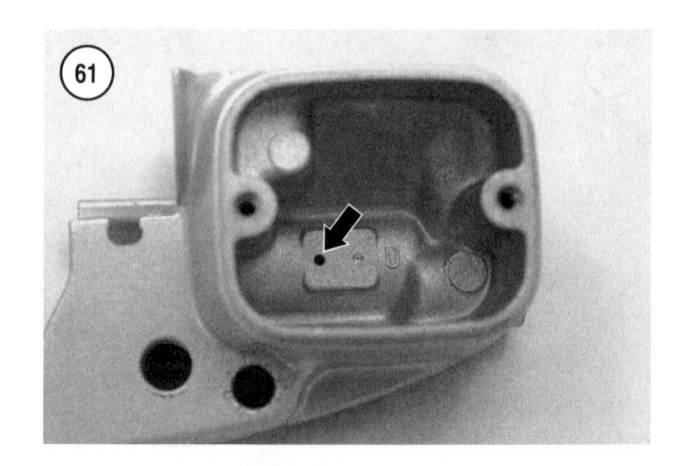

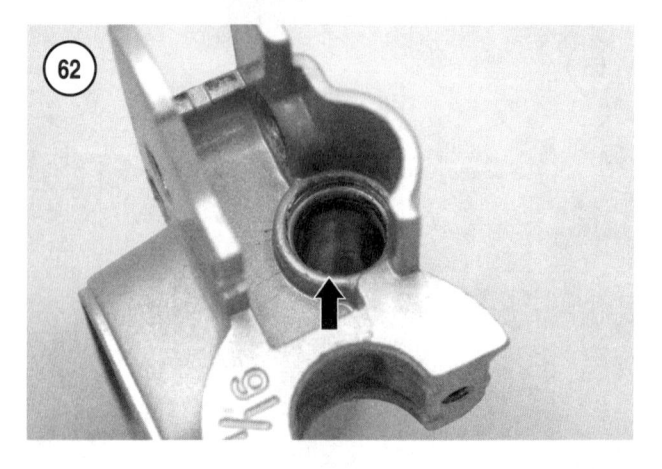

BRAKES

FRONT MASTER CYLINDER (2008-2009 MODELS)

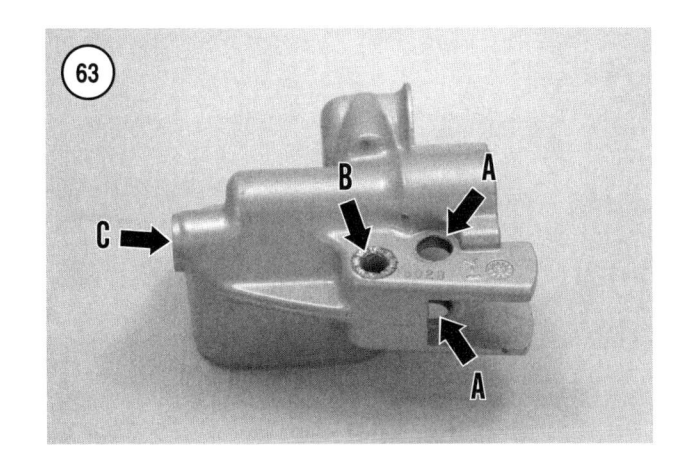

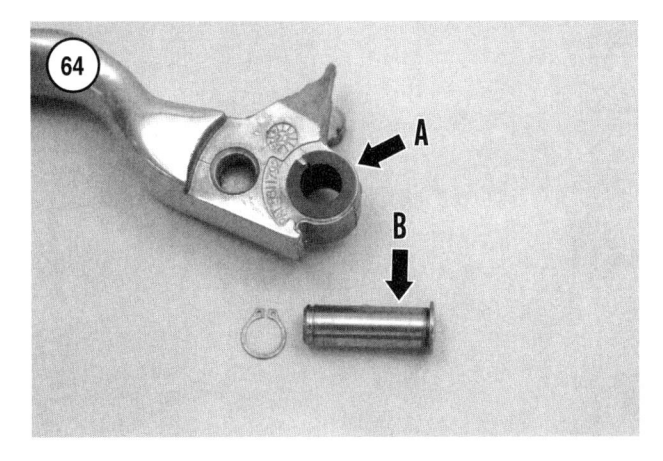

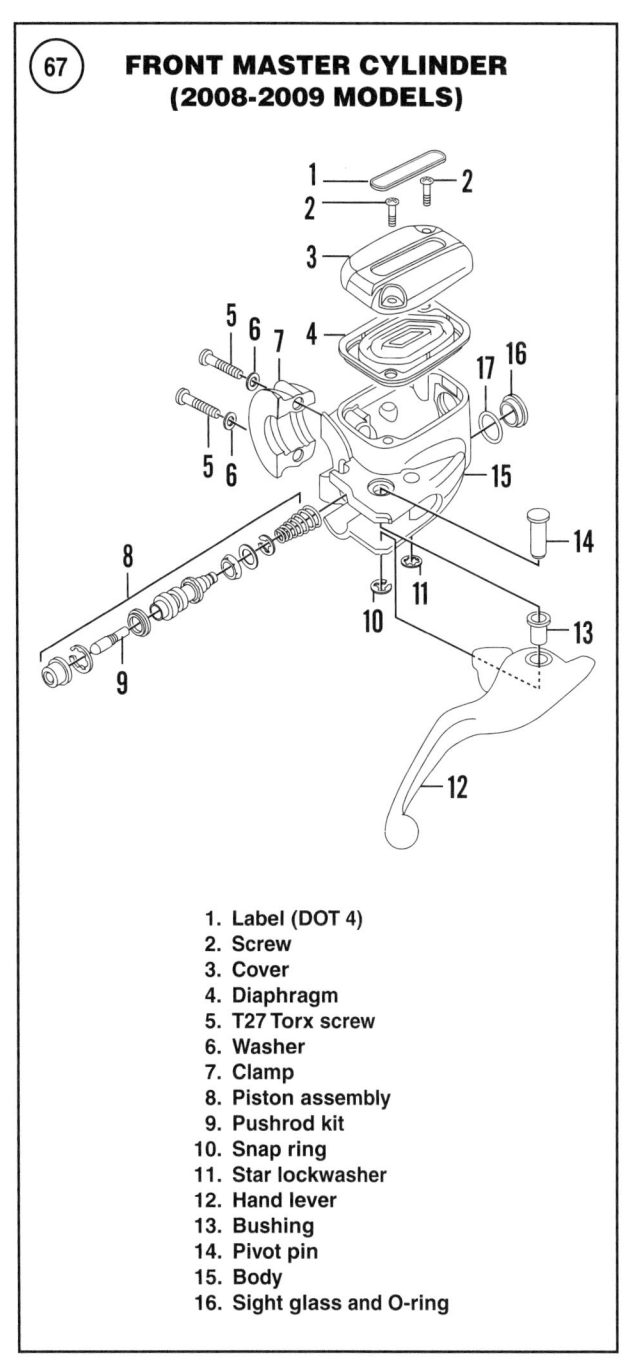

1. Label (DOT 4)
2. Screw
3. Cover
4. Diaphragm
5. T27 Torx screw
6. Washer
7. Clamp
8. Piston assembly
9. Pushrod kit
10. Snap ring
11. Star lockwasher
12. Hand lever
13. Bushing
14. Pivot pin
15. Body
16. Sight glass and O-ring

11. Check the top cover and diaphragm (**Figure 66**) for deterioration, damage or deterioration. Replace if necessary.

FRONT MASTER CYLINDER (2008-2009 MODELS)

Removal

Refer to *Brake Service* and **Figure 67**.

1. Support the motorcycle on level ground on a swing arm stand.
2. Block the front wheel so the motorcycle will not roll in either direction while the rear wheel is off ground.
3. Remove the mirror from the master cylinder.

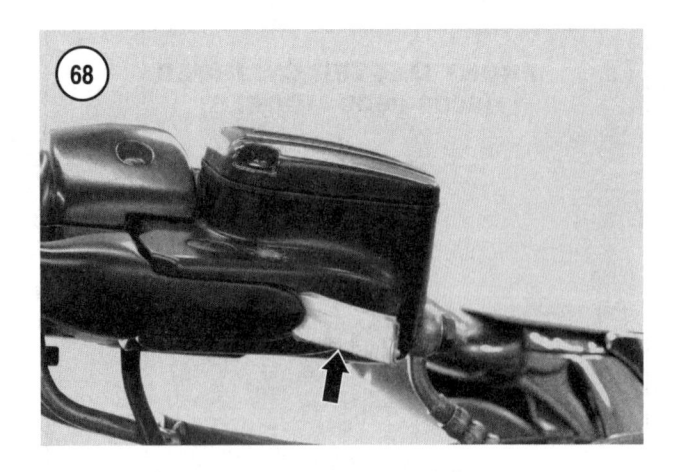

4. Clean all debris off the top of the master cylinder.

CAUTION
*Failure to install the spacer (**Figure 68**) will result in damage to the rubber boot and plunger on the front brake switch within the right side switch assembly.*

5. Insert a 5/32 in. (4 mm) thick spacer (**Figure 68**) between the brake lever and lever bracket. Make sure the spacer stays in place during the removal procedure.
6. Remove the screws securing the cover and remove the cover (**Figure 69**) and diaphragm (**Figure 70**).
7. Use a shop syringe to draw all of the brake fluid out of the master cylinder reservoir.
8. Temporarily reinstall the diaphragm and the cover. Install the cover screws and finger-tighten them.
9. Remove the banjo bolt (**Figure 71**) and sealing washers securing the brake hose to the master cylinder. Discard the sealing washers.
10. Place the loose end of the brake hose in a reclosable plastic bag to prevent the entry of moisture and debris. Tie the loose end of the hose to the handlebar.
11. Remove the Torx bolts (A, **Figure 72**) and washers securing the clamp and master cylinder to the handlebar.
12. Remove the clamp (B, **Figure 72**) and the master cylinder assembly (C) from the handlebar.
13. Drain any residual brake fluid from the master cylinder and dispose of it properly.
14. If the master cylinder assembly is not going to be serviced, attach the clamp to the master cylinder and reinstall the Torx bolts. Place the assembly in a plastic bag to protect it.

Installation

1. Insert the 5/32 in. (4 mm) thick spacer between the brake lever and lever bracket (**Figure 73**), if not in place. Make sure the spacer stays in place during the installation procedure.

CAUTION
Do not damage the front brake light switch and rubber boot when installing the master cylinder.

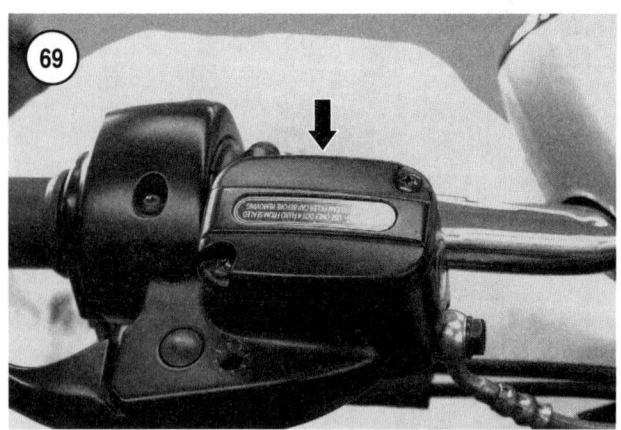

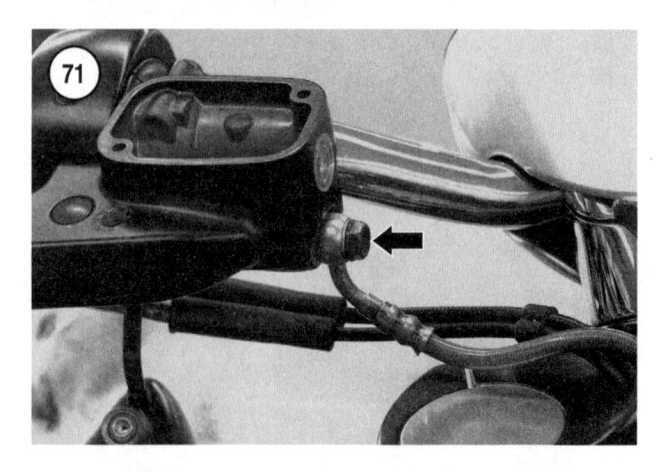

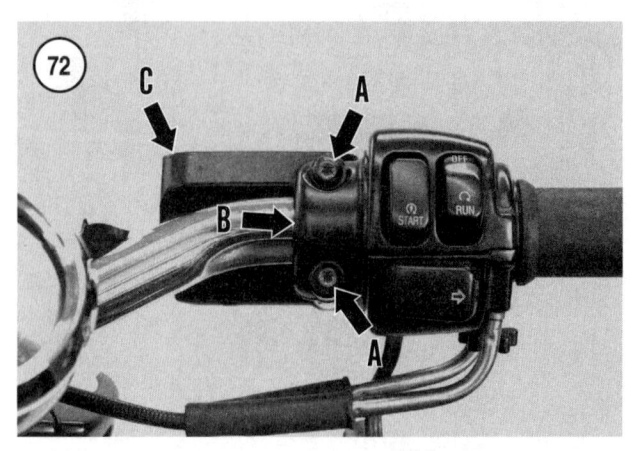

BRAKES

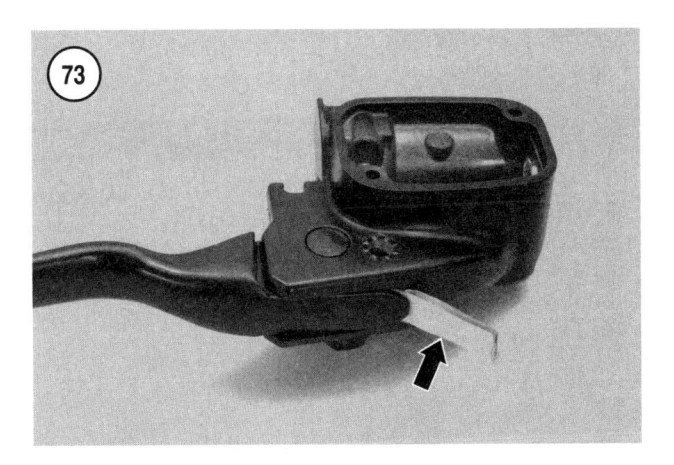

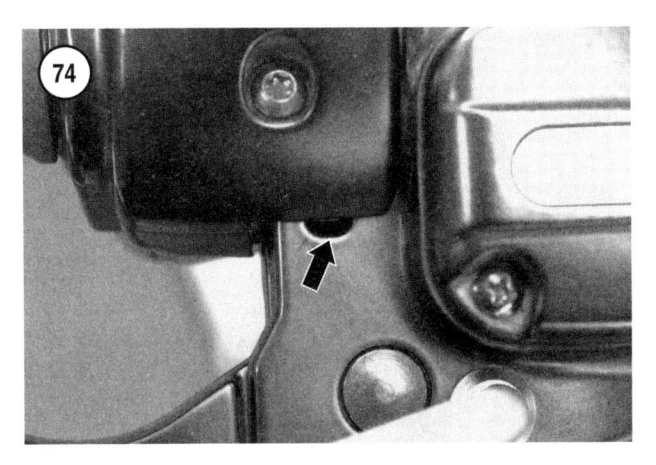

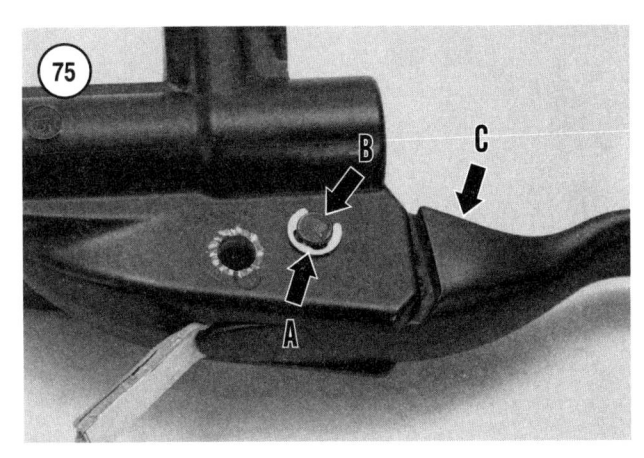

2. Position the front master cylinder (C, **Figure 72**) onto the handlebar. Align the master cylinder notch (**Figure 74**) with the locating tab on the lower portion of the right side switch.
3. Position the clamp (B, **Figure 72**) and install the Torx bolts (A) and washers. Tighten the upper, and then the lower clamp bolt to 71-80 in.-lb (8-9 N•m).
4. Apply clean DOT 4 brake fluid to *new* copper sealing washers prior to installation.
5. Install *new* sealing washers on each side of the hose fitting.
6. Install the banjo bolt (**Figure 71**) securing the brake hose to the master cylinder. Tighten the banjo bolt to the specification in **Table 2**.
7. Remove the spacer (**Figure 68**) from the brake lever.
8. Temporarily install the diaphragm (**Figure 70**) and top cover (**Figure 69**) onto the reservoir, if not in place. Install the screws and finger-tighten them at this time.
9. Install the mirror onto the master cylinder and adjust to rider preference.
10. Refill the master cylinder reservoir and bleed the front brake system as described in this chapter.
11. Install the diaphragm and cover. Install the cover screws and tighten to 6-8 in.-lb. (0.7-0.9 N•m).

Disassembly

1. Remove the master cylinder assembly as described in this section.
2. Store the master cylinder components in a divided container, such as a restaurant-size egg carton, to help maintain their correct alignment positions.
3. Remove the top cover (**Figure 69**) and the diaphragm (**Figure 70**) from the master cylinder.
4. Remove the E-clip (A, **Figure 75**) and the pivot pin (B) securing the hand lever to the master cylinder. Remove the hand lever (C, **Figure 75**).
5. Remove the pushrod (A, **Figure 76**) and rubber boot (B) from the area where the hand lever actuates the piston assembly.
6. Push down on the piston assembly and remove the snap ring (**Figure 77**).

7. Remove the piston assembly and the spring (**Figure 78**).
8. Inspect all parts as described in this section.

Assembly

1. Coat the inside of the cylinder bore and piston seals with DOT 4 brake fluid, prior to the assembly of parts.
2. Install a bolt into the threaded banjo bolt hole and mount the master cylinder in a vise (**Figure 79**).
3. Position the piston assembly with the spring end going in first (**Figure 80**) and install the piston assembly (**Figure 81**).

CAUTION
When installing the piston assembly, do not allow the cup to turn inside out as it will be damaged and allow brake fluid leaks within the cylinder bore.

4. Push down on the piston assembly (**Figure 81**) and install the snap ring (**Figure 77**). Make sure the snap ring is seated correctly in the master cylinder groove (**Figure 82**).
5. Install the rubber boot (B, **Figure 76**) and pushrod (A). Make sure the rubber boot is seated correctly in the master cylinder groove.
6. Make sure the bushing is in place in the hand lever pivot area.
7. Install the hand lever (C, **Figure 75**) into the master cylinder. Install the pivot pin (B, **Figure 75**) and secure it

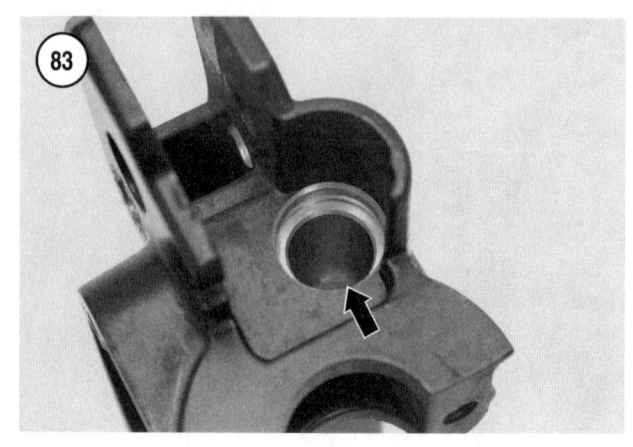

BRAKES

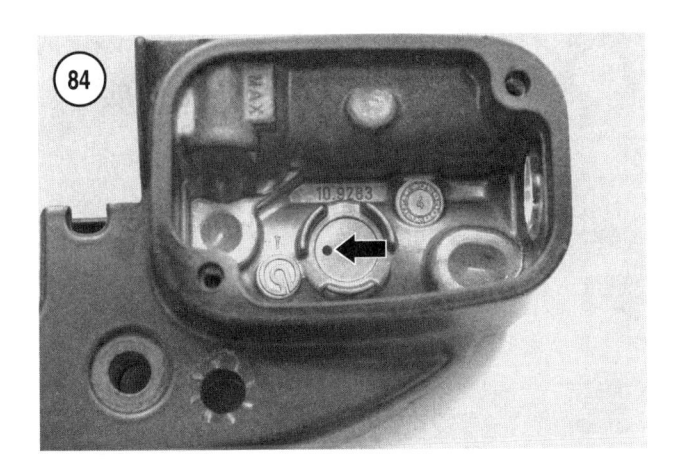

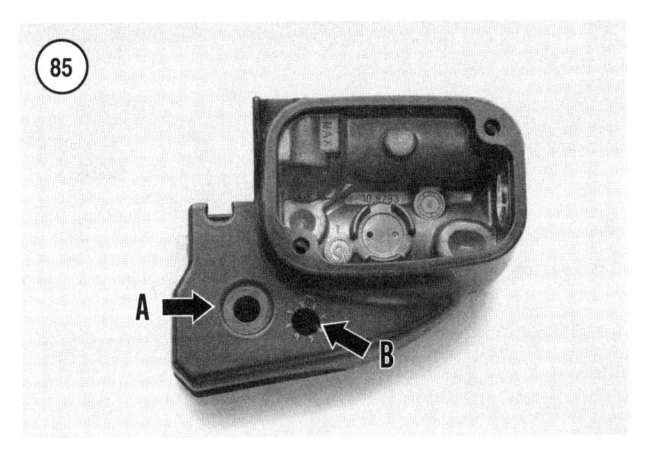

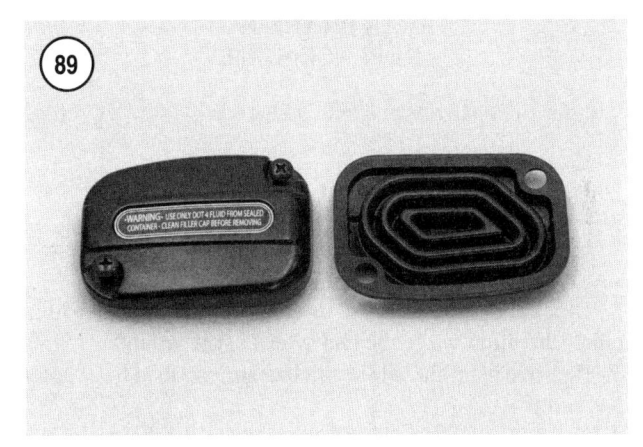

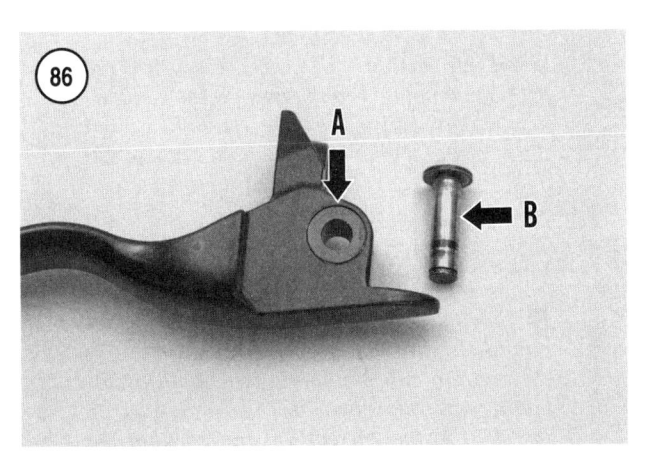

with the snap ring (A). Make sure the snap ring is correctly seated in the pivot pin groove.

8. Slowly apply the lever to make sure it pivots freely.
9. Install the master cylinder as described in this section.

Inspection

1. Clean all parts in denatured alcohol or clean DOT 4 brake fluid. Inspect the master cylinder bore surface (**Figure 83**) for signs of wear and damage. If it is less than perfect, replace the master cylinder assembly. The body cannot be replaced separately.
2. Make sure the fluid passage (**Figure 84**) in the bottom of the master cylinder body is clear. Clean it out if necessary.
3. Check the hand lever pivot lugs (A, **Figure 85**) in the master cylinder body for cracks or elongation.
4. Inspect the threaded mirror hole (B, **Figure 85**) in the master cylinder body. If it is worn or damaged, clean it out with a thread tap or replace the master cylinder assembly.
5. Inspect the hand lever pivot hole and bushing (A, **Figure 86**) and the pivot pin (B) for wear, cracks or elongation.
6. Inspect the threaded banjo bolt hole (**Figure 87**). If it is worn or damaged, clean it out with a thread tap or replace the master cylinder assembly.
7. Check the sight glass (**Figure 88**) for signs of brake fluid leaks; replace if necessary.
8. Check the top cover and diaphragm (**Figure 89**) for deterioration, damage or deterioration.

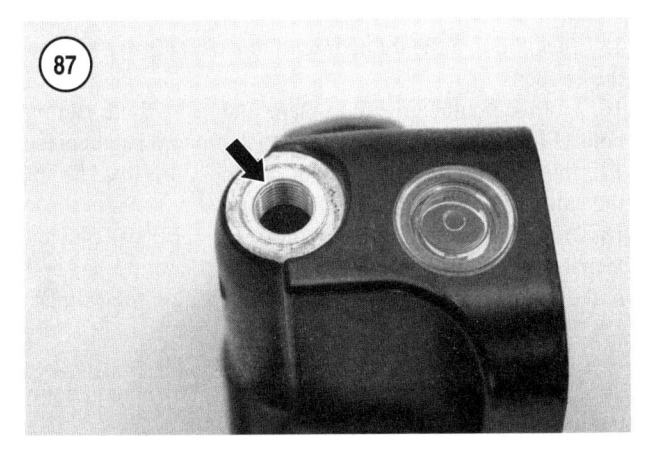

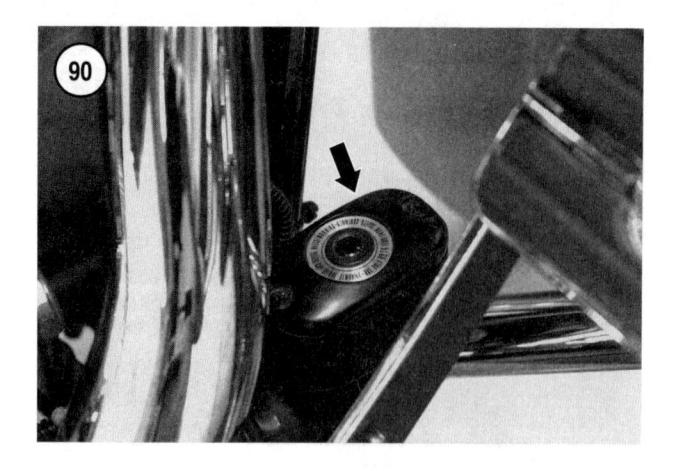

REAR BRAKE PAD REPLACEMENT

Refer to *Brake Service* in this chapter.

2006-2007 Models

1. Support the motorcycle on level ground on a swing arm stand.
2. Block the front wheel so the motorcycle will not roll in either direction while the rear wheel is off ground.
3. Remove the right side saddlebag as described in Chapter Seventeen.
4. Tie the end of the brake pedal up to the frame. If the brake pedal is inadvertently applied, this will prevent the piston from being forced out of the cylinder.
5. Clean all debris off the top of the rear master cylinder.
6. Remove the screws securing the cover and remove the cover (**Figure 90**) and diaphragm.
7. Use a shop syringe to remove about 50% of the brake fluid from the reservoir. This will prevent the master cylinder from overflowing when the pistons are compressed for reinstallation. Do *not* drain more than 50% of the brake fluid or air will enter the system. Discard the brake fluid.
8. Loosen the pad pin bolts (**Figure 91**).
9. Insert a stiff plastic or wooden wedge into the caliper between the brake disc and brake pads and carefully push the brake pads part way back into to caliper bores. This will make room for the new thicker brake pads. Constantly check the reservoir to make sure brake fluid does not overflow. Remove fluid, if necessary, before it overflows. Install the diaphragm and cover. Install the cover screws and finger-tighten them.
10. Remove the pad pin bolts, and then remove the inboard and outboard brake pads from the caliper.
11. Check the brake pads for wear or damage. Measure the thickness of the brake pad friction material. Replace the brake pads if they are worn to the service limit in **Table 1**.
12. Remove any rust or corrosion from the disc.
13. Clean the pad pins of any corrosion or debris.
14. Check the friction surface of the *new* pads for debris or manufacturing residue. If necessary, clean them off with an aerosol brake cleaner.

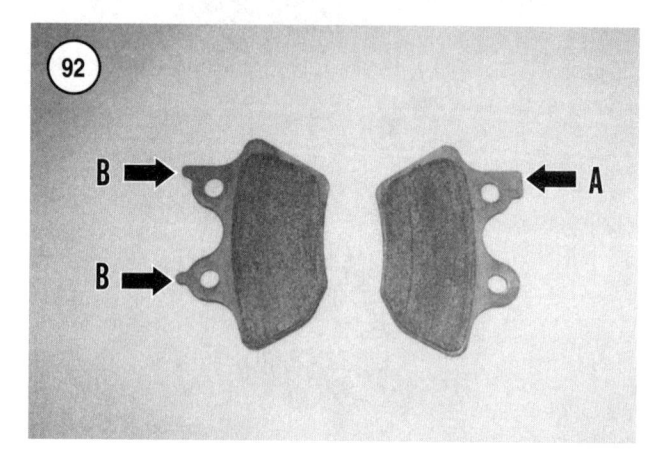

WARNING
When purchasing new pads, make sure the friction compound of the new pad is compatible with the disc. Remove roughness from the backs of the new pads with a fine-cut file and thoroughly clean with an aerosol brake cleaner.

NOTE
The pads are not symmetrical. The outboard pad (A, Figure 92) has one large tab next to the pad pin bolt mounting holes and the inboard pad (B) has two tabs. The pads must be installed in the correct locations within the caliper.

15. Install the outboard pad, with one tab (**Figure 93**) into the caliper.
16. Hold the outboard pad in place and install both pad pin bolts (**Figure 94**) part way to hold the outboard pad in place.
17. Install the inboard pad, with two tabs, (**Figure 95**) into the caliper.
18. Hold onto the brake pad, remove the upper pad pin, and then install a Phillips screwdriver through the caliper and both brake pads to correctly align both pads within the caliper.
19. Push the lower pad pin in, but do not tighten it at this time.
20. Remove the screwdriver and install the upper pad pin, but do not tighten it at this time.

BRAKES

21. Tighten both pad pin bolts to 180-200 in.-lb. (20.3-22.6 N•m).
22. Make sure there is sufficient brake fluid in the master cylinder reservoir. Top it off with DOT 4 brake fluid if necessary.
23. Untie the brake pedal from the frame and pump the rear brake pedal several times to reposition the brake pads against the brake disc.
24. Refill the master cylinder reservoir, if necessary, to maintain the correct fluid level as indicated on the side of the reservoir (Chapter Three). Install the diaphragm and the top cover (**Figure 90**). Tighten the cover screws to 6-8 in.-lb. (0.7-0.9 N•m).
25. Install the right side saddlebag as described in Chapter Seventeen.

2008-2009 Models

1. Support the motorcycle on level ground on a swing arm stand.
2. Block the front wheel so the motorcycle will not roll in either direction while the rear wheel is off ground.

NOTE
Muffler removal is not necessary, but it does provide additional work area.

3. Remove right side muffler as described in Chapter Four. 
4. Remove the right side saddlebag as described in Chapter Seventeen.
5. Tie the end of the brake pedal up to the frame. If the brake pedal is inadvertently applied, this will prevent the piston from being forced out of the cylinder.
6. Clean the top of the rear master cylinder of all debris.
7. Remove the screws securing the cover, and then remove the cover and diaphragm.
8. Use a shop syringe to remove about 50% of the brake fluid from the reservoir. This will prevent the master cylinder from overflowing when the pistons are compressed for reinstallation. Do *not* drain more than 50% of the brake fluid or air will enter the system. Discard the brake fluid.
9. On models equipped with ABS, carefully cut the cable strap securing the wheel speed sensor wires to the brake caliper hose.
10. Remove caliper mounting bolts and remove the caliper from the caliper bracket and disc.
11. Insert a stiff plastic or wooden wedge into the caliper between the brake pads and carefully push the brake pads partway back into to caliper bores. This will make room for the new, thicker brake pads. Constantly check the reservoir to make sure brake fluid does not overflow. Remove fluid, if necessary, before it overflows. Install the diaphragm and cover. Install the cover screws and finger-tighten them.
12. Remove the cover from the caliper.
13. Use needlenose pliers and remove the clip from the pad pin bolt. Discard the clip.
14. Loosen the pad pin bolt and withdraw it from the caliper. Discard the pad pin bolt.
15. Remove the inboard and outboard brake pads from the caliper.
16. Remove the pad pin spring if damaged or worn.
17. Check the brake pads for wear or damage. Measure the thickness of the brake pad friction material. Replace the brake pads if they are worn to the service limit in **Table 1**.
18. Remove any rust or corrosion from the disc.
19. Check the friction surface of the new pads for debris or manufacturing residue. If necessary, clean them off with an aerosol brake cleaner.
20. Make sure the spring pad is still located properly within the caliper body. If the spring was removed, seat the *new* pad spring on the flat in the caliper, so that the clips on the

spring engage the indentations in the caliper. Make sure the forked end of the spring is located on the pad pin side of the caliper.

21. Correctly position the *new* inboard brake pad so the pad pin tab aligns with the caliper pad pin hole. Insert the inboard brake pad into the caliper until it is correctly seated.

22. Correctly position the *new* outboard brake pad so the pad pin tab aligns with the caliper pad pin hole. Insert the inboard brake pad into the caliper until it is correctly seated.

23. Make sure both brake pads are correctly seated within the caliper with the square corner indexed into the pad slot in the caliper. Verify that the pad friction material faces the brake disc gap in the caliper.

24. Turn the caliper over and verify that the pad pin tabs are centered in the pad spring forks. Adjust the pads if necessary.

25. Insert a *new* pad pin bolt through the caliper and both brake pads. Install the pad pin bolt into the caliper body and finger-tighten the bolt.

26. Install the caliper onto the brake disc and caliper bracket.

27. Install the caliper mounting bolts and tighten to 43-48 ft.-lb. (58.3-65.1 N•m).

28. Tighten the pad pin bolt to 75-102 in.-lb. (8.5-11.5 N•m).

29. Position the *new* clip with the tab facing outward and install it onto the pad pin. Push it down until it is correctly seated.

30. Position the screen with the two-pronged side going on first into the lower portion of the caliper and snap the upper end into position. Make sure the screen is secured on the caliper.

31. Make sure there is sufficient brake fluid in the master cylinder reservoir. Top it off if with DOT 4 brake fluid if necessary.

32. Untie the brake pedal from the frame and pump the rear brake pedal several times to reposition the brake pads against the brake disc. Continue to pump the brake pedal as many times as it takes to refill the cylinders in the caliper and correctly position the brake pads against the disc.

33. Refill the master cylinder reservoir, if necessary, to maintain the correct fluid level as indicated on the side of the reservoir. Install the diaphragm and the top cover. Tighten the cover screws to 6-8 in.-lb. (0.7-0.9 N•m).

34. Install the right side saddlebag as described in Chapter Seventeen.

35. Install the right-side muffler as described in Chapter Four, if removed.

REAR BRAKE CALIPER (2006-2007 MODELS)

Removal/Installation

Refer to *Brake Service* in this chapter.

1. Support the motorcycle on level ground on a swing arm stand.
2. Block the front wheel so the motorcycle will not roll in either direction while the rear wheel is off ground.
3. Remove the right side saddlebag as described in Chapter Seventeen.
4. Remove the lower portion of the right rear shock absorber from the swing arm as described in Chapter Fourteen, if necessary. Pivot the shock absorber up out of the way and secure it with a bungee cord.
5. Tie the end of the brake pedal up to the frame. If the brake pedal is inadvertently applied, this will prevent the piston from being forced out of the cylinder.
6. If the caliper assembly is going to be disassembled for service, perform the following:
   a. Remove the brake pads as described in this chapter.

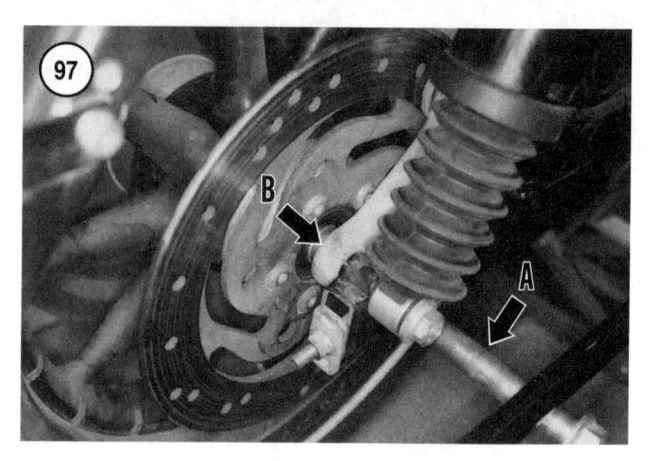

CAUTION
Do not allow the pistons to travel out far enough to come in contact with the brake disc. If this happens the pistons may scratch or gouge the disc during caliper removal.

   b. Slowly apply the brake lever to push the pistons part way out of caliper assembly for ease of removal during caliper service.
   c. Loosen the brake hose banjo bolt (A, **Figure 96**).
   d. Loosen the three body mounting bolts (B, **Figure 96**).

7. Remove the banjo bolt (A, **Figure 96**) and sealing washers attaching the brake hose to the caliper assembly.

BRAKES

REAR BRAKE CALIPER (2006-2007 MODELS)

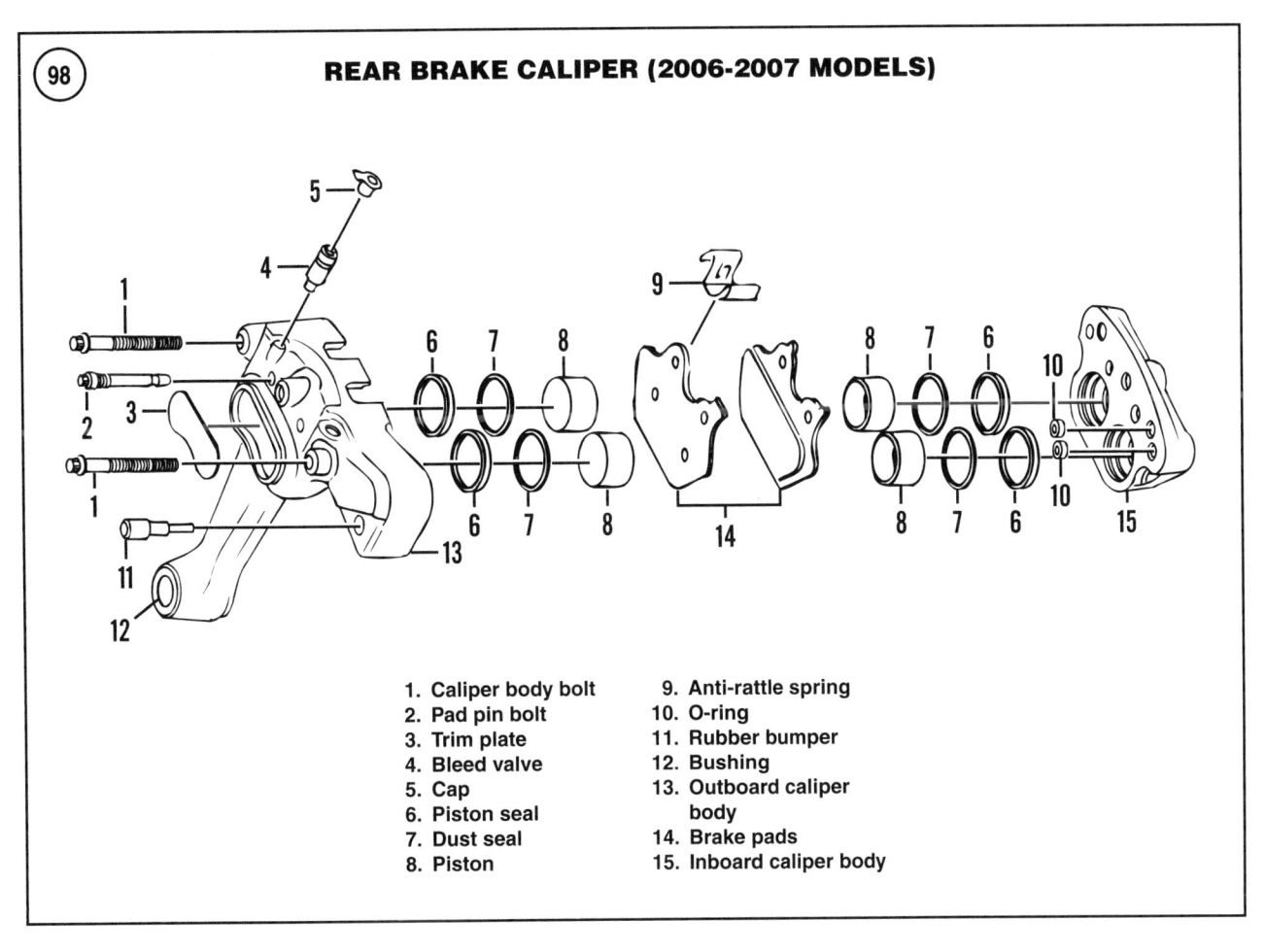

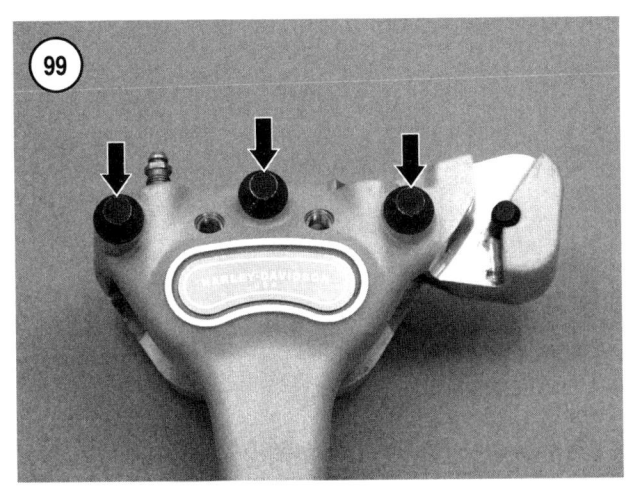

1. Caliper body bolt
2. Pad pin bolt
3. Trim plate
4. Bleed valve
5. Cap
6. Piston seal
7. Dust seal
8. Piston
9. Anti-rattle spring
10. O-ring
11. Rubber bumper
12. Bushing
13. Outboard caliper body
14. Brake pads
15. Inboard caliper body

8. Place the loose end of the brake hose in a plastic bag to prevent the entry of debris and contain any residual brake fluid leaking out.

9. Refer to Chapter Twelve and follow the rear wheel removal procedure until the rear axle is removed sufficiently (A, **Figure 97**) to allow removal of the rear caliper assembly as shown in B, **Figure 97**. After removal of the caliper assembly, push the rear axle back into place and install the nut on the other side.

10. If necessary, disassemble and service the caliper assembly as described in this section.

11. If the rear caliper is not going to be serviced, place it in a plastic bag to keep it clean.

12. Install by reversing the removal steps, while noting the following:
   a. Remove the rear axle just far enough to carefully install the caliper assembly onto the disc. Be careful not to damage the leading edge of the brake pads.
   b. Refer to Chapter Twelve and complete the installation of the rear axle.
   c. Apply clean DOT 4 brake fluid to the rubber portions of *new* sealing washers prior to installation.
   d. Install *new* sealing washers on each side of the hose fitting.
   e. Install the banjo bolt (A, **Figure 96**). Tighten the banjo bolt to 17-22 ft.-lb. (23.1-29.8 N•m).
   f. Tighten the three caliper body mounting bolts (B, **Figure 96**) to 28-38 ft.-lb. (38-51.5 N•m).
   g. Bleed the front brake system as described in this chapter.

Disassembly

Refer to **Figure 98**.

1. Remove the brake pads as described in this chapter.
2. Remove the front caliper as described in this section.
3. Remove the three caliper body bolts (**Figure 99**) loosened during the removal procedure.

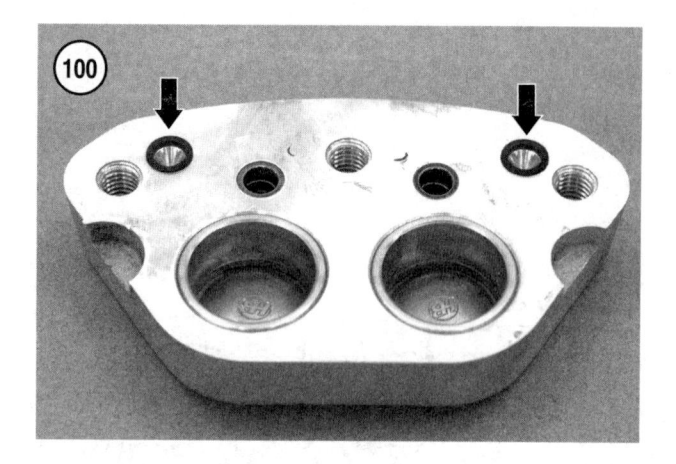

4. Separate the caliper body halves. Remove the O-ring seals (**Figure 100**) from the inboard caliper half and discard them. New O-ring seals must be installed every time the caliper is disassembled.

NOTE
If the pistons or caliper bores are corroded or very dirty, a small amount of compressed air may be necessary to completely remove the pistons from the body bores.

5. Place a piece of soft wood or folded shop cloth over the end of the pistons and the caliper body. Turn this assembly over with the pistons facing down over a workbench top.

WARNING
Compressed air will force the pistons out of the caliper bodies under considerable force. Do not block the piston by hand, as injury will result.

6. Apply air pressure in short bursts to the hydraulic fluid passageway and force out the pistons. Repeat for the other caliper body half. Use a service station air hose if compressed air is not available.

CAUTION
Do not use a sharp tool to remove the dust and piston seals from the caliper cylinders. Do not damage the cylinder surface.

7. Use a piece of wood or plastic scraper and carefully push the dust seal (A, **Figure 101**) and the piston seal (B) in toward the caliper cylinder and out of their grooves. Remove the dust and piston seals.
8. If necessary, unscrew and remove the bleed valve (**Figure 102**).
9. Inspect the caliper assembly as described in this section.

Assembly

WARNING
Do not use DOT 4 brake fluid for lubrication. If used, it will result in increased brake lever travel.

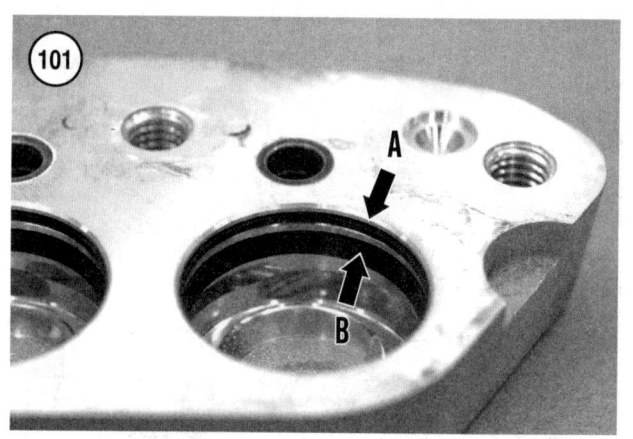

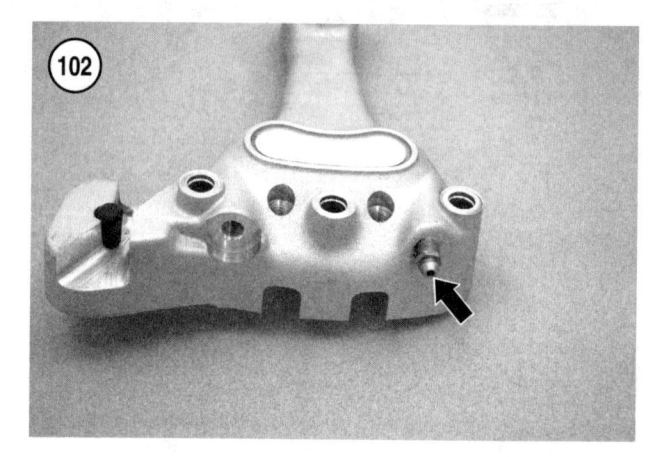

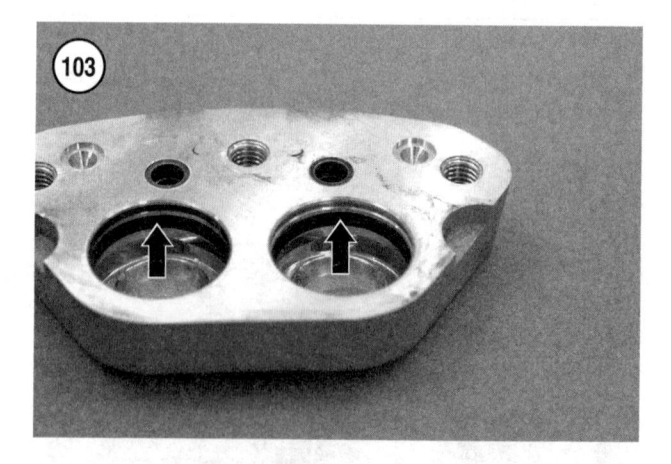

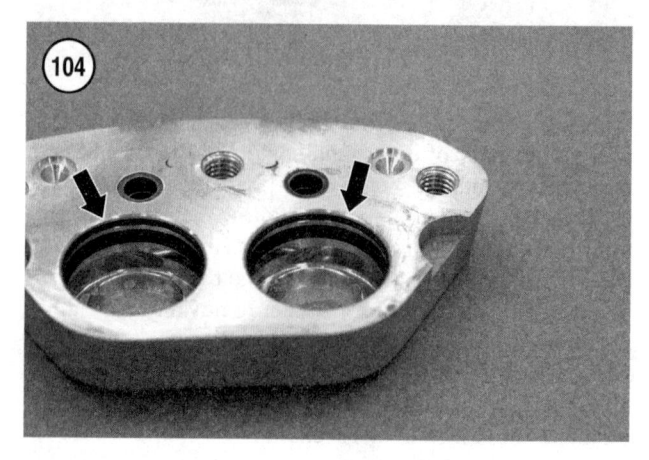

BRAKES

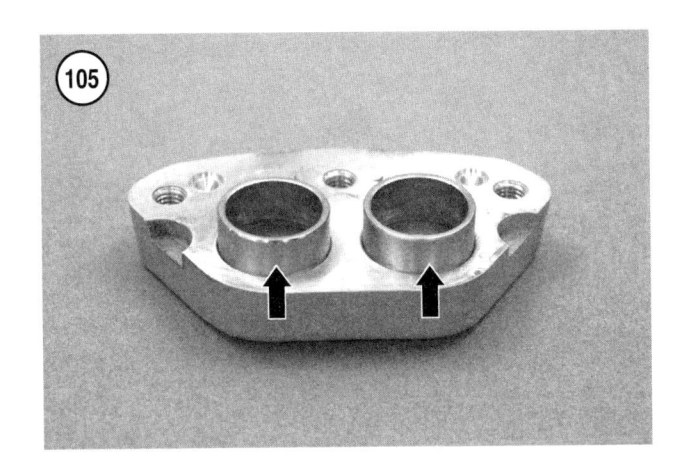

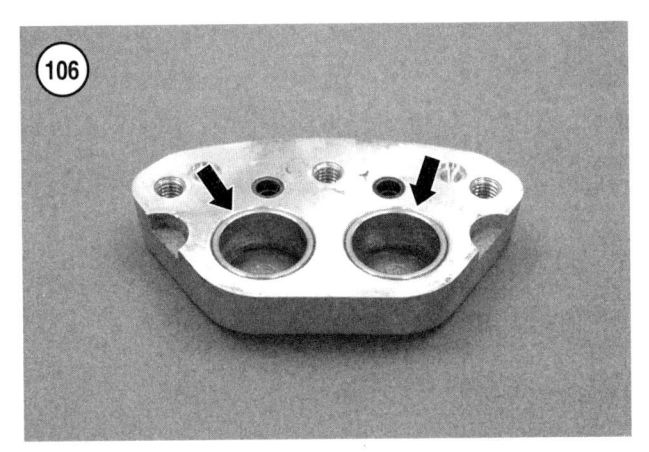

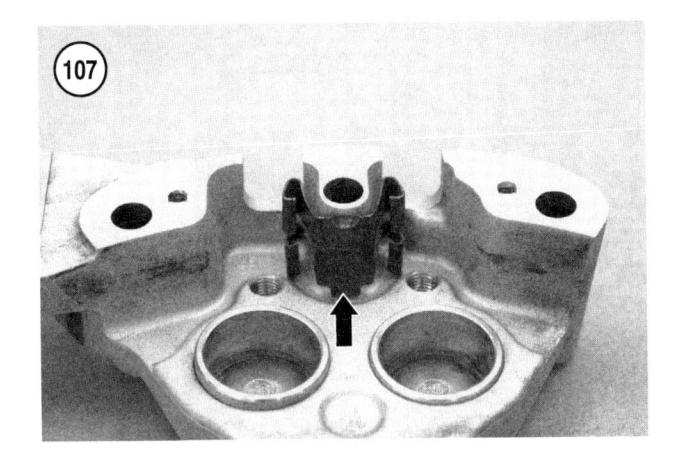

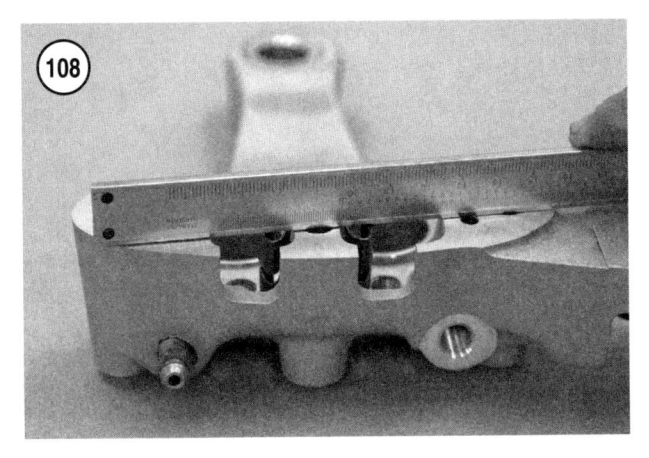

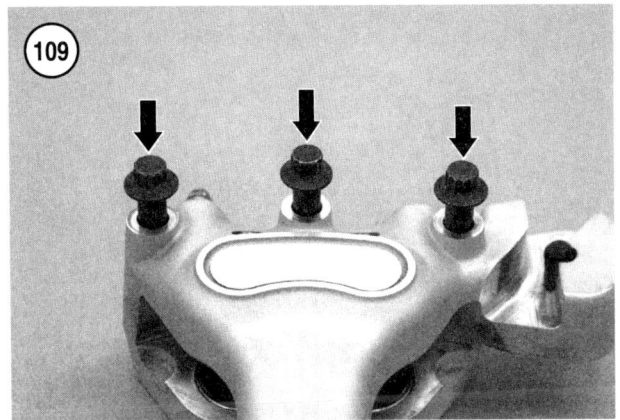

WARNING
Never reuse old dust seals or piston seals. Very minor damage or age deterioration can make the seals ineffective.

1. Apply a light coat of G.E. Versilube #GE322L silicone grease to the following parts:
   a. Inside diameter surfaces of both piston and dust seals.
   b. Caliper bores.
   c. Outside surfaces of pistons.
   d. Closed end of pistons.
2. All remaining surfaces must remain dry.
3. Carefully install *new* piston seals (**Figure 103**) into the lower grooves. Make sure the seals are properly seated in their respective grooves.
4. Carefully install *new* dust seals (**Figure 104**) into the upper grooves. Make sure the seals are properly seated in their respective grooves.
5. Repeat the process and install new piston seals and dust seals in the other caliper body.
6. Position the pistons with the open end facing out and install the pistons (**Figure 105**) into the caliper cylinders. Push the pistons in until they bottom (**Figure 106**).
7. Repeat the process to install the pistons in the other caliper body. Make sure all pistons are installed correctly.
8. Install the anti-rattle spring into the outboard caliper body. Make sure the location foot is located as shown in **Figure 107**. The upper edge of the spring must be flush with the caliper mating surface (**Figure 108**) or the caliper cannot be assembled correctly.
9. Install the *new* O-rings (**Figure 100**) into the inboard caliper body.
10. Install the outboard caliper half onto the inboard half. Make sure the O-rings are still in place and assemble the caliper.
11. Install the three caliper body bolts (**Figure 109**) and tighten securely. Do not tighten the bolts to the final torque specification yet.
12. Install a *new* rubber bumper (**Figure 110**) if it was removed.
13. Install the bleed valve (**Figure 102**) if it was removed, and tighten to 80-100 in.-lb. (9.0-11.3 N•m).

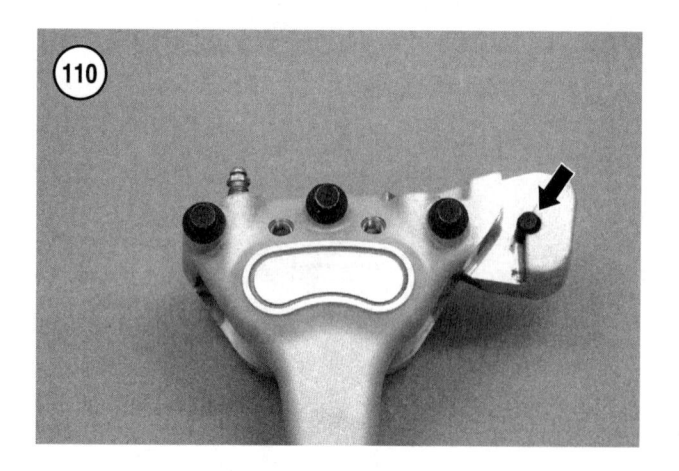

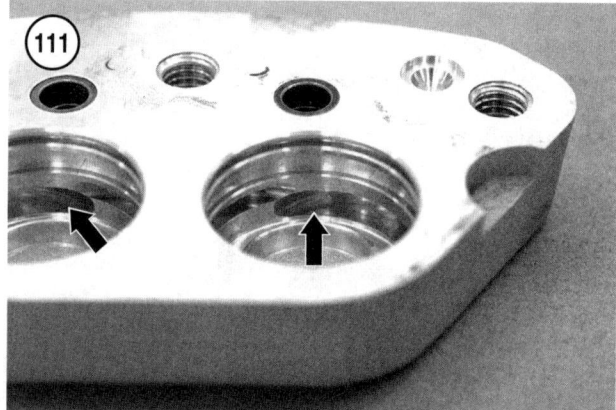

14. Install the caliper as described in this section.
15. Install the rear brake pads as described in this chapter.
16. Tighten the three caliper body mounting bolts to 28-38 ft.-lb. (38-51.5 N•m).
17. Bleed the front brake system as described in this chapter.

Inspection

1. Clean both caliper body halves and pistons in clean DOT 4 brake fluid or isopropyl alcohol and dry with compressed air.
2. Make sure the fluid passageways (**Figure 111**) in the piston bores are clear. Apply compressed air to the openings to make sure they are clear. Clean out if necessary with clean brake fluid.
3. Make sure the fluid passageways (**Figure 112**) in both caliper body halves are clear. Apply compressed air to the openings to make sure they are clear. Clean out, if necessary, with new brake fluid.
4. Inspect the piston and dust seal grooves (**Figure 113**) in both caliper halves for damage. If they are damaged or corroded, replace the caliper assembly.
5. Inspect the threaded banjo bolt hole (A, **Figure 114**) in the outboard caliper body. If it is worn or damaged, clean out with a thread tap or replace the caliper assembly.
6. Inspect the banjo bolt passageway (**Figure 115**). Apply compressed air to the opening and make sure it is clear. Clean out with new brake fluid. Install the banjo bolt and tighten to 17-22 ft.-lb. (23.1-29.8 N•m).
7. Inspect the threaded bleed valve hole in the outboard caliper body. If it is worn or damaged, clean out with a thread tap or replace the caliper assembly.
8. Inspect the bleed valve. Apply compressed air to the opening and make sure it is clear. Clean out if necessary with new brake fluid. Install the bleed valve and tighten to 80-100 in.-lb. (9.0-11.3 N•m).
9. Inspect both caliper bodies (**Figure 116**) for damage. Check the inboard caliper body mounting bolt hole threads (**Figure 117**) for wear or damage. Clean up with an appropriate size tap or replace the caliper assembly.
10. Inspect the cylinder walls and pistons (**Figure 118**) for scratches, scoring or other damage.

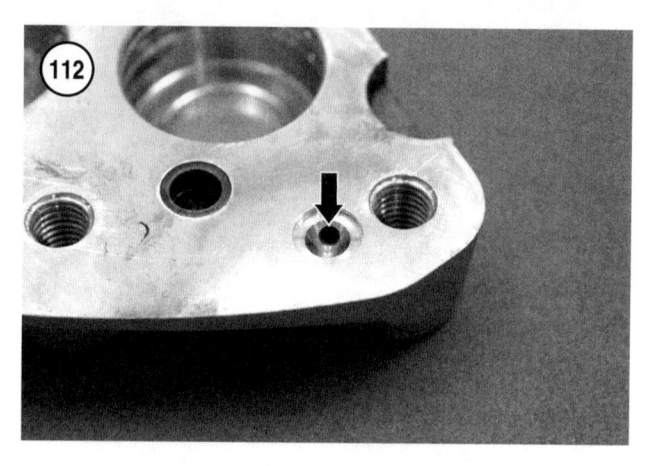

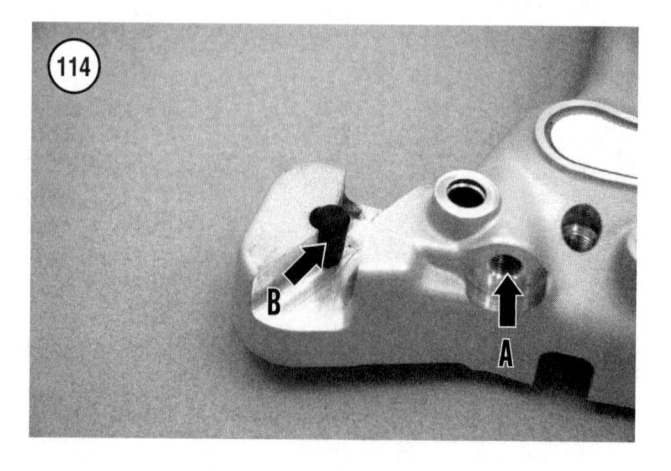

BRAKES

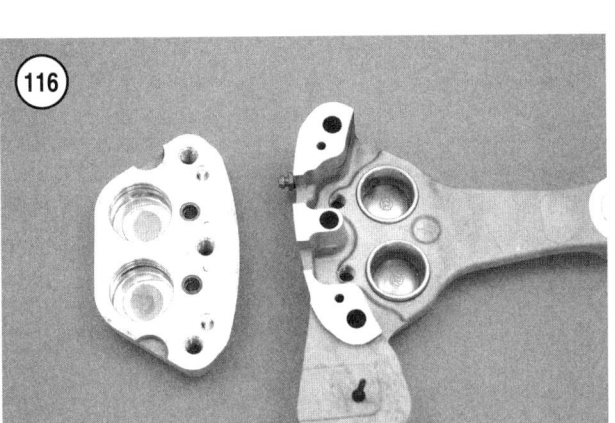

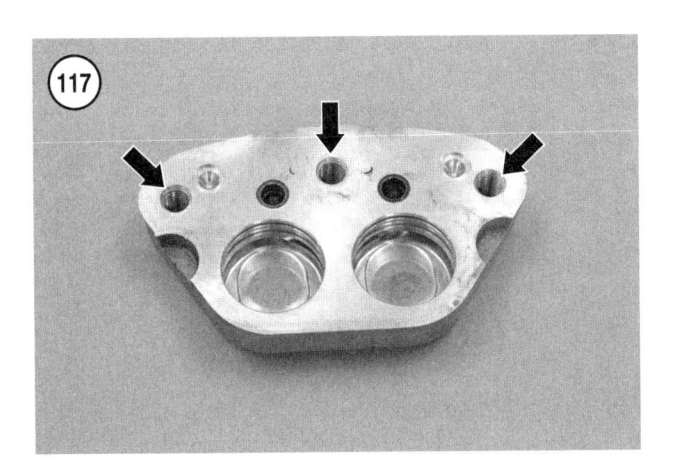

11. Check the anti-rattle spring (**Figure 119**) for wear or damage.

12. Check the rubber bumper (B, **Figure 114**) for damage or deterioration; replace as necessary.

REAR BRAKE CALIPER (2008-2009 MODELS)

CAUTION
On ABS-equipped models, keep the ABS sensors away from magnetic fields or they will be damaged.

Removal/Installation

Read *Brake Service* in this chapter.

1. Support the motorcycle on level ground on a swing arm stand.
2. Block the front wheel so the motorcycle will not roll in either direction while the rear wheel is off ground.
3. Remove the right side saddlebag as described in Chapter Seventeen.
4. Remove the muffler assembly as described in Chapter Four.
5. Remove the lower portion of the right rear shock absorber from the swing arm as described in Chapter Fourteen. Pivot the shock absorber up out of the way and secure it with a bungee cord.
6. On models equipped with ABS, carefully cut the cable strap securing the wheel speed sensor wires to the brake caliper hose.
7. Remove the banjo bolt and copper sealing washers attaching the brake hose to the caliper assembly. Discard the washers.
8. Place the loose end of the brake hose in a reclosable plastic bag to prevent the entry of debris and contain any residual brake fluid leaking out.
9. Remove the two bolts securing the caliper to the mounting bracket.
10. Slide the rear brake caliper forward and off the brake disc and mounting bracket.

11. Place it in a reclosable plastic bag to keep it clean.
12. Installation is the reverse of removal. Note the following:
    a. Install the caliper assembly onto the disc, being careful not to damage the leading edge of the brake pads.
    b. Slide the rear brake caliper onto the mounting bracket. Tighten the mounting bolts to 43-48 ft.-lb. (58.3-65 N•m).
    c. Apply clean DOT 4 brake fluid to *new* copper sealing washers prior to installation.
    d. Install the *new* sealing washers on each side of the hose fitting.
    e. Install the banjo bolt and tighten to 17-19 ft.-lb. (23.1-25.8 N•m).
    f. Bleed the brakes as described in this chapter.

Disassembly

The Brembo caliper assembly cannot be disassembled for service. The only replacement parts available are shown in **Figure 120**.

REAR MASTER CYLINDER AND REAR BRAKE PEDAL (ALL MODELS)

Read *Brake Service* in this chapter.

Removal

1. Support the motorcycle on level ground on a swing arm stand.
2. Block the front wheel so the motorcycle will not roll in either direction while the rear wheel is off ground.
3. Remove the exhaust system as described in Chapter Four.
4. Refer to Chapter Seventeen and perform the following:
    a. On models so equipped, remove the right side lower front fairing.
    b. Remove the right side saddlebag.
    c. Remove the right frame side cover.
    d. Remove the right side rider footboard.
5. At the rear brake caliper, perform the following:
    a. Insert a hose onto the end of the bleed valve (**Figure 121**). Insert the open end of the hose into a container.
    b. Open the bleed valve and operate the rear brake pedal to drain the brake fluid. Remove the hose and close the bleed valve after draining the master cylinder assembly. Discard the brake fluid properly.
6. Remove the screws securing the cover and remove the cover (A, **Figure 122**) and diaphragm.
7. Remove the banjo bolt and sealing washers (B, **Figure 122**) securing the brake hose to the front of the master cylinder cartridge body.
8. Remove and/or release any clips or ties securing the rear brake line to the chassis. Remove only enough to al-

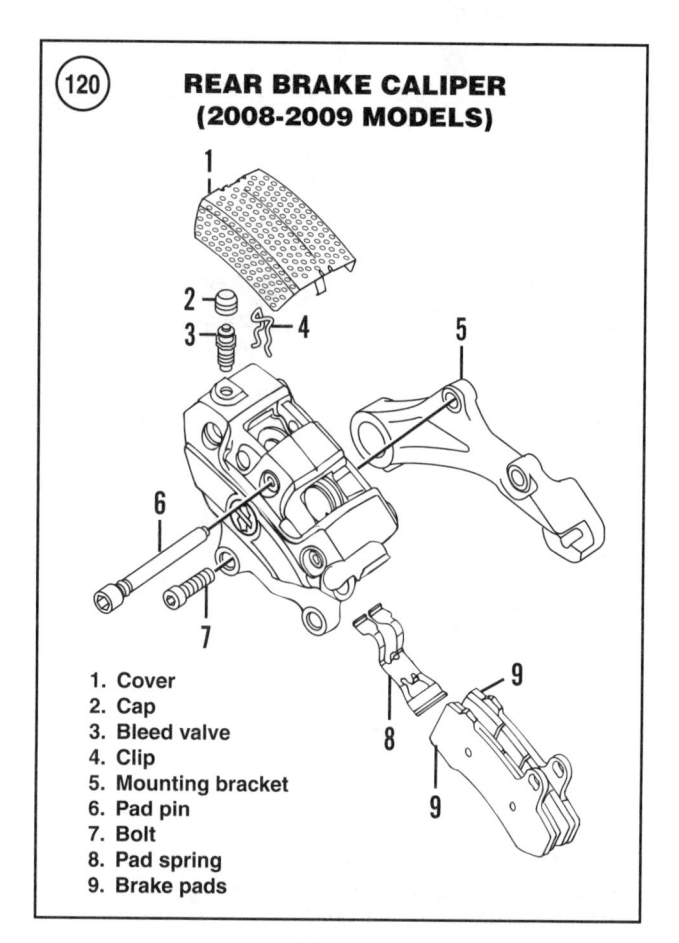

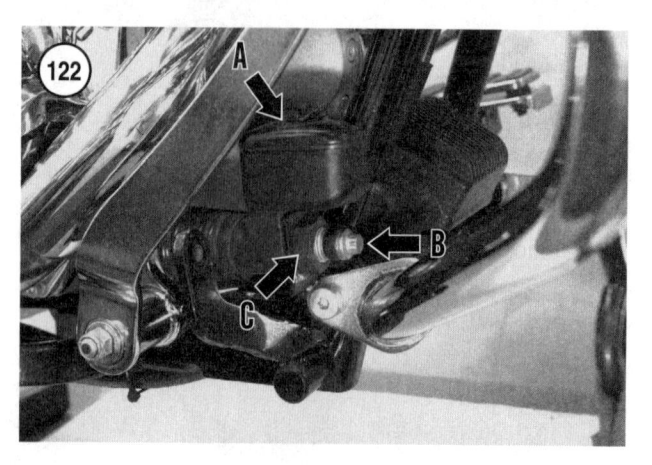

120 REAR BRAKE CALIPER (2008-2009 MODELS)

1. Cover
2. Cap
3. Bleed valve
4. Clip
5. Mounting bracket
6. Pad pin
7. Bolt
8. Pad spring
9. Brake pads

BRAKES

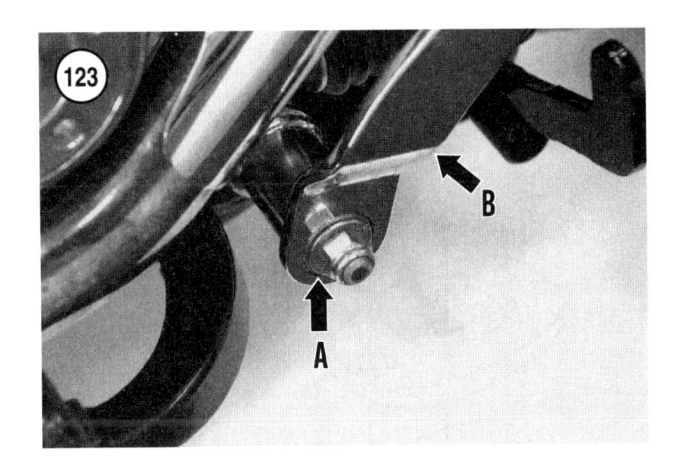

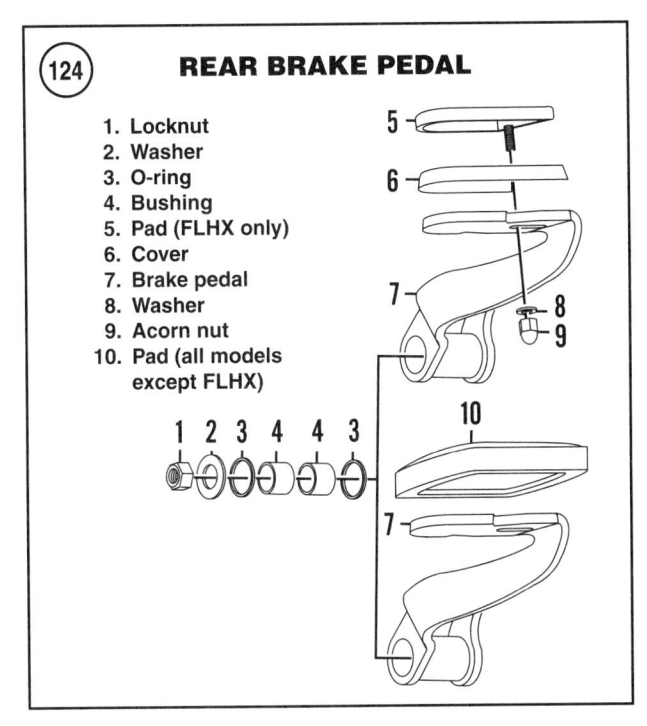

123

124 REAR BRAKE PEDAL

1. Locknut
2. Washer
3. O-ring
4. Bushing
5. Pad (FLHX only)
6. Cover
7. Brake pedal
8. Washer
9. Acorn nut
10. Pad (all models except FLHX)

low slack in the brake line to allow removal of the brake line from the front of the master cylinder fitting.

9. Disconnect the rear brake line from the front of the master cylinder. Place the loose end of the brake hose in a plastic bag to prevent the entry of debris and contain any residual brake fluid leaking out.

10A. On 2006-2007 models, use an 1-1/8 in. open-end wrench and remove the hex nut (C, **Figure 122**) securing the front of the master cylinder cartridge assembly to the frame boss. Pull the master cylinder free from the square hole in the frame boss.

10B. On 2008-2009 models, remove the bolts securing the master cylinder to the frame.

11. Remove the locknut and washer (A, **Figure 123**) securing the master cylinder and rear brake pedal assembly to the frame pivot post. Remove the assembly (B, **Figure 123**) from the frame. Remove the O-ring seals on each side of the pedal pivot bore.

12. If necessary, disconnect the rear brake pedal from the master cylinder as follows:

  a. Remove the cotter pin and washer from the clevis pin. Discard the cotter pin.
  b. Support the assembly in a vise. Use a brass drift and carefully tap out the clevis pin from both parts.

13. If necessary, inspect and service the master cylinder as described in this chapter. If the master cylinder is not going to be serviced, place it in a plastic bag to keep it clean.

Installation

1. If the brake pedal was disconnected from the master cylinder, perform the following:

  a. Reposition the rear brake pedal onto the rear master cylinder.
  b. Support the assembly in a vise and tap the clevis pin into both parts. Tap it in until it bottoms.
  c. Install the washer and a *new* cotter pin. Bend the ends of the pin over completely.

2. Install a *new* O-ring to each side of the brake pedal pivot bore.

3. Apply a light coat of wheel bearing grease to the brake pedal shaft and bore.

4. Install the master cylinder and rear brake pedal assembly (B, **Figure 123**) onto the frame pivot post.

5. Install the washer and a *new* locknut (A, **Figure 123**). Tighten the locknut to 15-20 ft.-lb. (20.3-27.1 N•m).

6. Carefully inset the master cylinder cartridge body into the square hole in the frame boss.

7A. On 2006-2007 models, apply Loctite Threadlocker (243 blue) to the hex nut threads prior to installation. Install the hex nut (C, **Figure 122**) and tighten to 30-40 ft.-lb. (40.7-54.2 N•m).

7B. On 2008-2009 models, install the bolts securing the master cylinder to the frame. Tighten bolts to 126-150 in.-lb. (14.2-17.0 N•m).

8. Connect the rear brake line from the front of the master cylinder cartridge body.

9. Install *new* sealing washers on each side of the hose fitting. Insert the banjo bolt through the washers and banjo fitting and thread into the cartridge body (B, **Figure 122**). Then, tighten the banjo bolt as follows:

  a. Non-ABS models: 12.5-14.5 ft.-lb. (17.0-19.7 N•m).
  b. ABS models: 13-15 ft.-lb. (17.6-20.3 N•m).

10. Secure the rear brake line to the chassis using new ties or clips.

11. Bleed the rear brake as described in this chapter.

12. Refer to Chapter Seventeen and perform the following:

  a. Install the right frame side cover.
  b. Install the right side rider footboard.
  c. Install the right side saddlebag.
  d. On models so equipped, install the right side lower front fairing.

13. Install the exhaust system as described in Chapter Four.

Rear Brake Pedal Inspection

Refer to **Figure 124**.

CHAPTER FIFTEEN

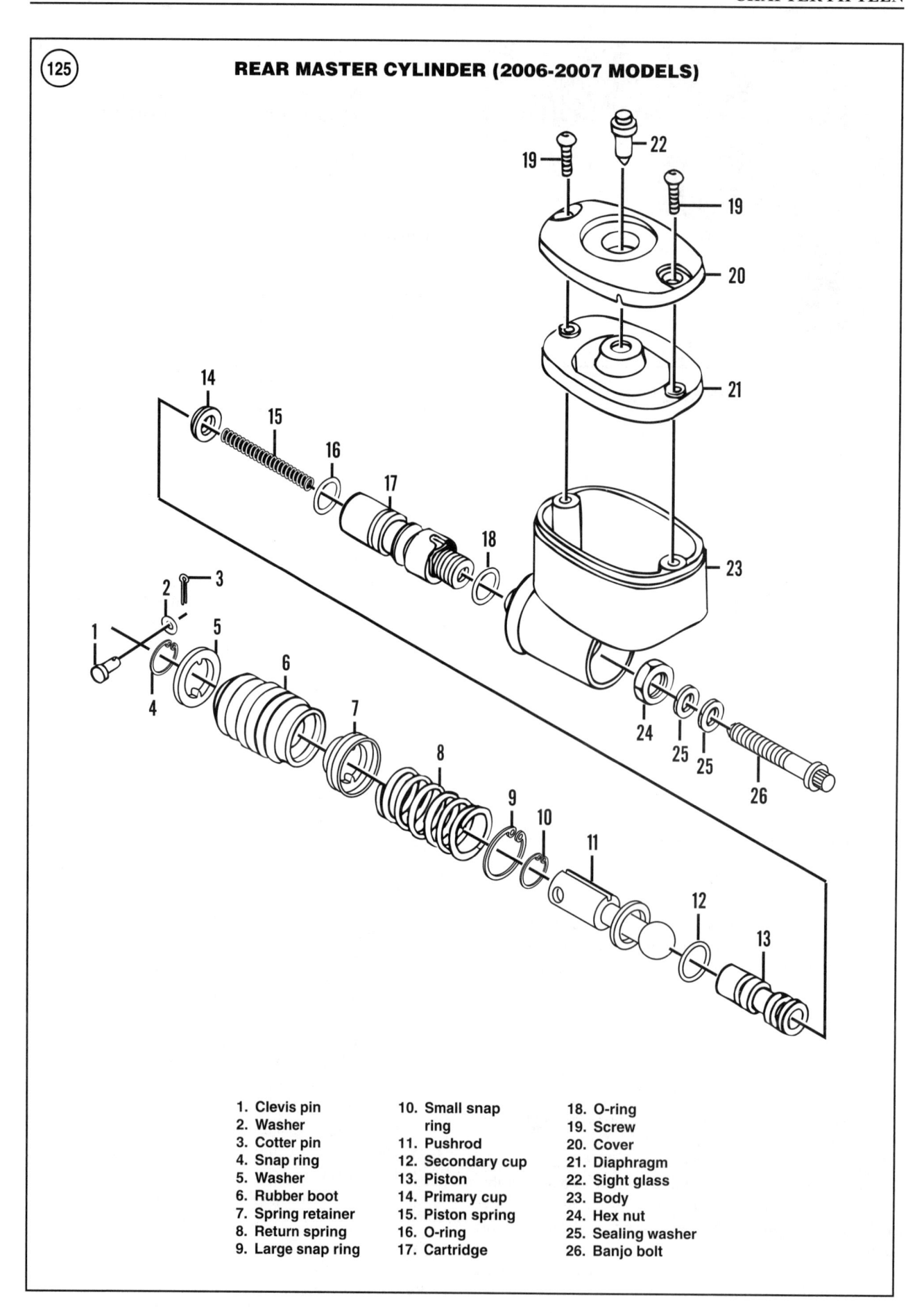

(125) REAR MASTER CYLINDER (2006-2007 MODELS)

1. Clevis pin
2. Washer
3. Cotter pin
4. Snap ring
5. Washer
6. Rubber boot
7. Spring retainer
8. Return spring
9. Large snap ring
10. Small snap ring
11. Pushrod
12. Secondary cup
13. Piston
14. Primary cup
15. Piston spring
16. O-ring
17. Cartridge
18. O-ring
19. Screw
20. Cover
21. Diaphragm
22. Sight glass
23. Body
24. Hex nut
25. Sealing washer
26. Banjo bolt

BRAKES

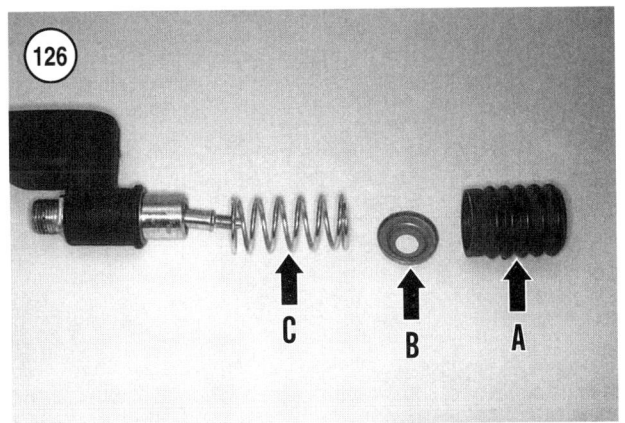

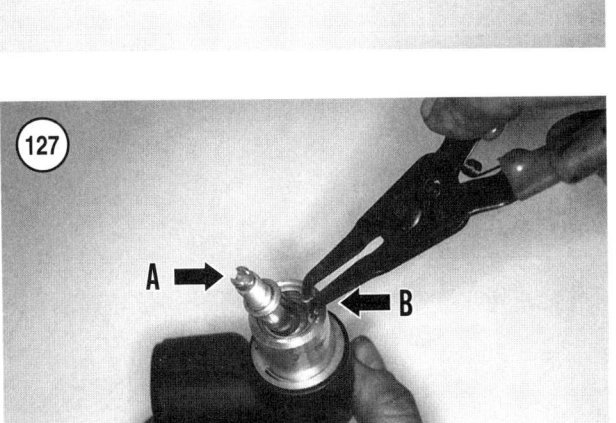

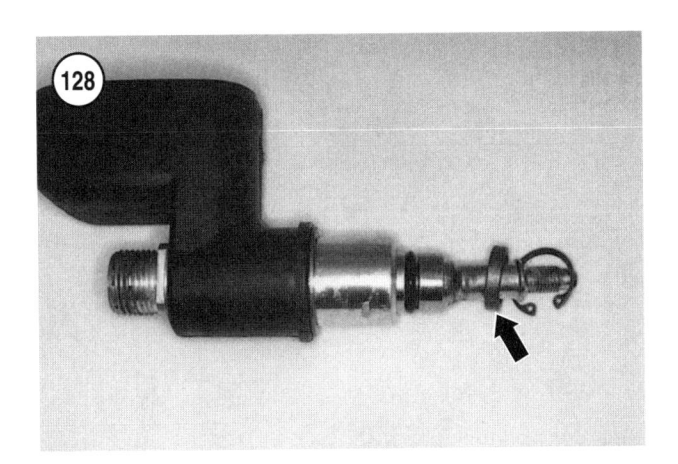

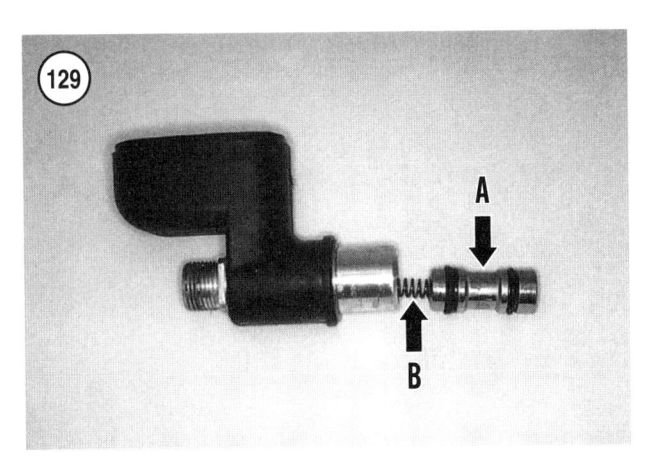

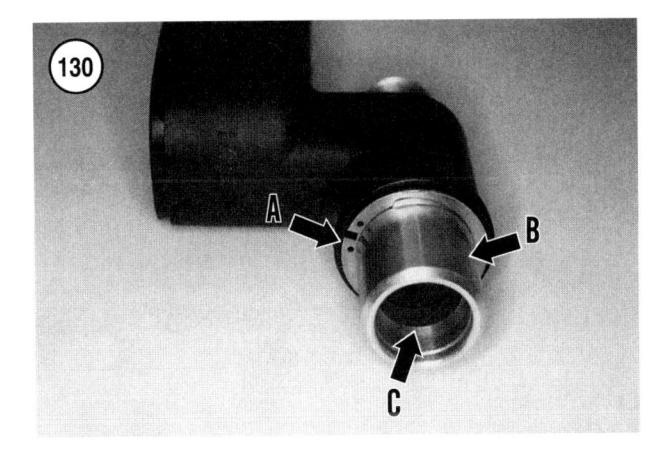

1. If still in place, remove the O-rings from both ends of the pivot bore.
2. Inspect the pivot bushings within the pivot bore for wear or damage.
3. Carefully press out the old bushings and install new bushings if necessary.
4. Install a *new* O-ring to each side of the brake pedal pivot bore.
5. Inspect the rear brake pedal for cracks or damage; replace as necessary.

REAR MASTER CYLINDER SERVICE (2006-2007 MODELS)

Read *Brake Service* in this chapter.

Disassembly

Refer to **Figure 125**.
1. Remove the rear master cylinder as described in this chapter.
2. Clean the exterior of the master cylinder housing with clean DOT 4 brake fluid or isopropyl alcohol and dry.
3. Store the master cylinder components in a divided container, such as a restaurant-size egg carton, to help maintain their correct alignment position.
4. If still installed, remove the master cylinder cover and diaphragm.
5. Remove the small snap ring from the pushrod.
6. Remove the washer, rubber boot (A, **Figure 126**), spring retainer (B) and return spring (C).
7. Depress the pushrod (A, **Figure 127**) and release the small snap ring (B) from the body.
8. Remove the pushrod (**Figure 128**).
9. Remove the piston assembly (A, **Figure 129**) and piston spring (B) from the cartridge.
10. Remove the large snap ring (A, **Figure 130**), push on the threaded end of the cartridge, and then withdraw the cartridge (B) from the body, if necessary.
11. Do not disassemble the cartridge as the internal components are not sold separately.

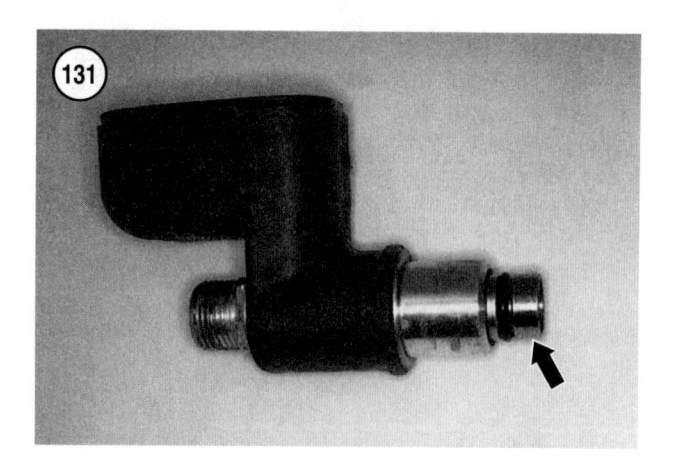

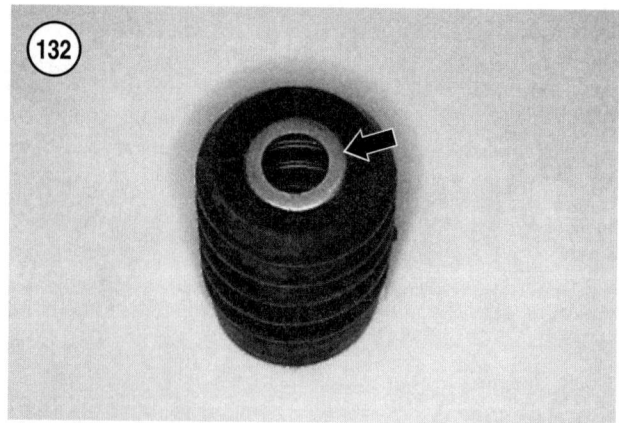

Assembly

1. Coat all parts with clean DOT 4 brake fluid.
2. Soak the primary cup, O-ring and piston assembly in clean DOT 4 brake fluid for at least 15 minutes to make them pliable. Coat the inside of the cartridge bore with clean brake fluid prior to the assembly of parts.
3. Position the cartridge with the threaded end going in first and install the cartridge (B, **Figure 130**) into the body, if removed. Push it in until it bottoms.
4. Install a *new* large snap ring (A, **Figure 130**) onto the cartridge and make sure it is correctly seated in the groove.

CAUTION
When installing the piston assembly, do not allow the primary cup to turn inside out as it will be damaged and allow brake fluid leaks within the cartridge cylinder bore.

5. Install the piston spring (B, **Figure 129**) into the piston (A).
6. Position the piston assembly with the primary cup (A, **Figure 129**) end going in first. Make sure the piston cup does not tear as it passes through the bore entrance.
7. Turn the reservoir on end on a shop cloth. Carefully push the piston assembly (**Figure 131**) into the cartridge with a screwdriver. Push the piston assembly in and then let it move out several times and check for ease of movement.
8. Position the pushrod onto the end of the piston (**Figure 128**) and push the piston and pushrod into the cartridge. Hold the pushrod in place (A, **Figure 127**) and install a *new* small snap ring (B). Make sure the small snap ring is correctly seated in the cartridge groove.
9. Install the return spring (C, **Figure 126**) and spring seat (B) onto the pushrod and cartridge.
10. Install the washer into the boot and push it all the way to the end of the boot (**Figure 132**).
11. Install the boot (**Figure 133**) and washer onto the pushrod and cartridge.
12. Install washer and *new* small snap ring onto the pushrod.
13. Install the diaphragm and reservoir cover (**Figure 134**). Install the cover screws and tighten to 6-8 in.-lb. (0.7-0.9 N•m).

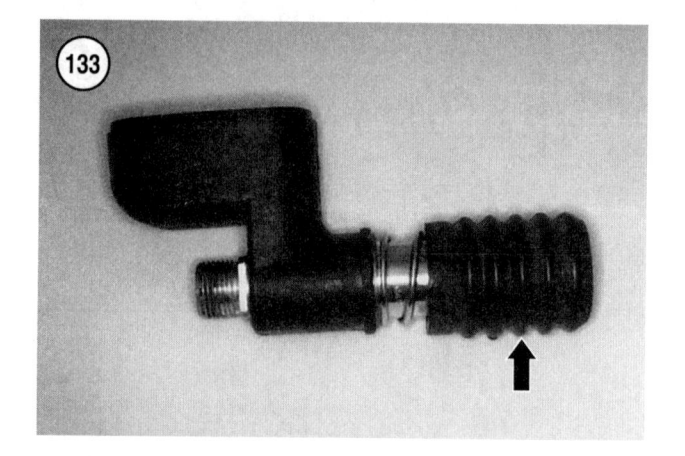

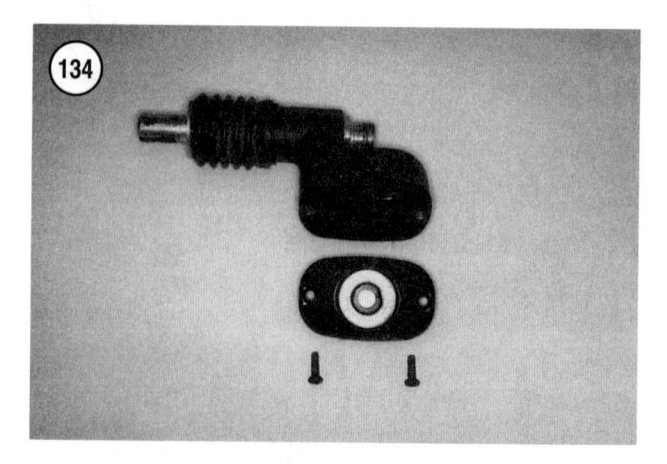

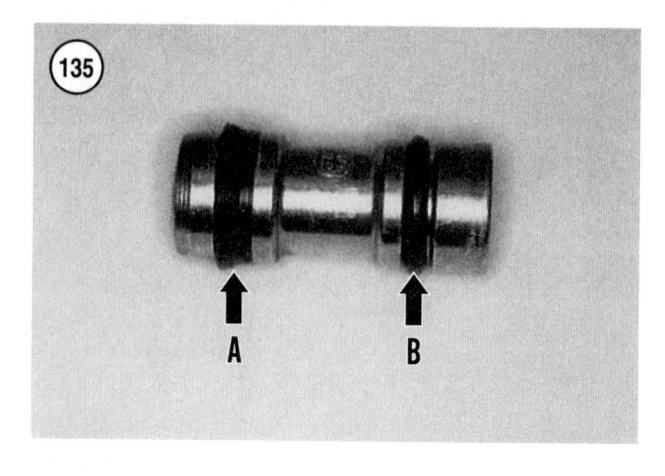

BRAKES

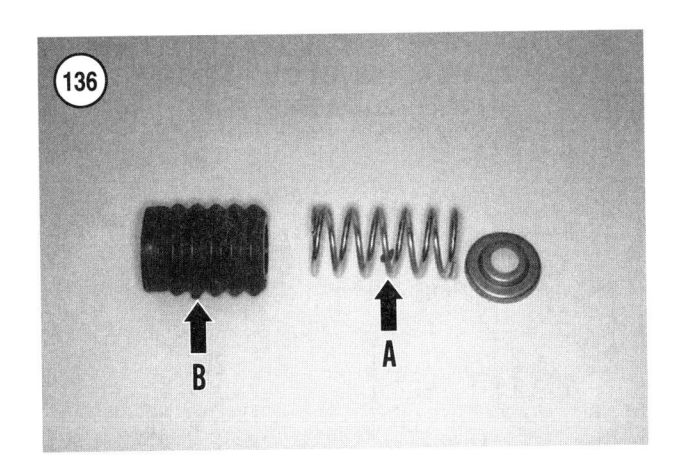

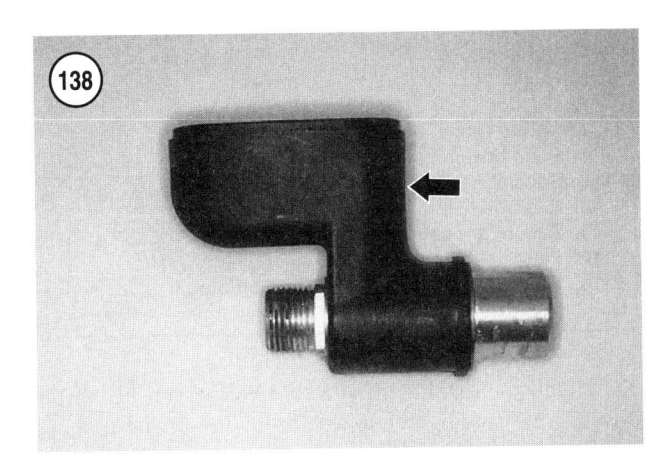

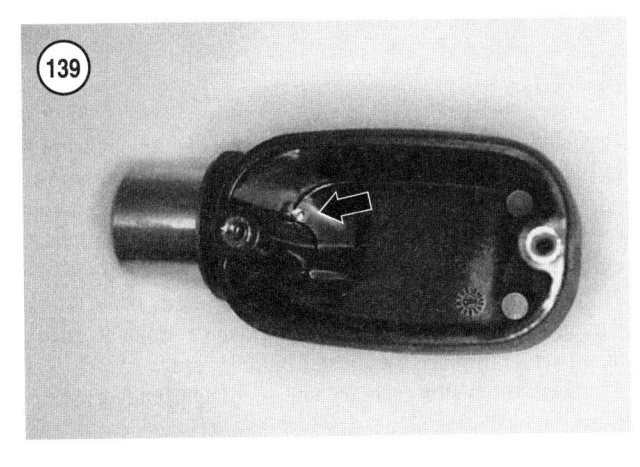

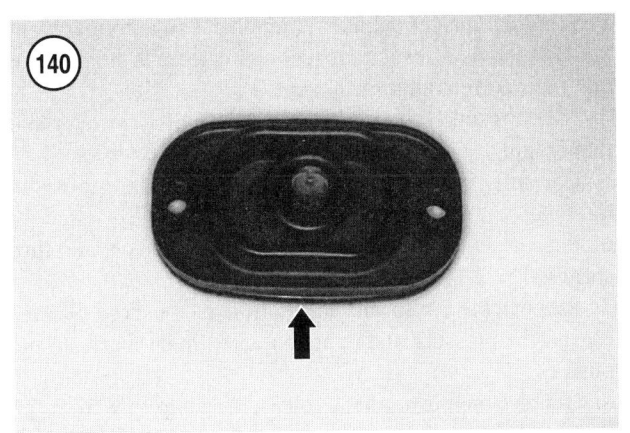

14. Install the rear master cylinder as described in this chapter.

Inspection

1. Clean all parts in clean DOT 4 brake fluid or isopropyl alcohol and dry with compressed air. Replace worn or damage parts as described in this section. It is recommended that a new cartridge rebuild kit assembly be installed every time the master cylinder is disassembled.
2. Inspect the cartridge bore surface (C, **Figure 130**) for signs of wear and damage. Do not hone the cartridge bore to clean or repair it. If less than perfect, replace the cartridge and/or the master cylinder reservoir.
3. Check the piston primary cup (A, **Figure 135**) and the O-ring (B) for deterioration or damage.
4. Check the return spring (A, **Figure 136**) for bending, unequally spaced coils or corrosion.
5. Inspect the boot (B, **Figure 136**) for tears or deterioration.
6. Check the pushrod, washer and snap ring (**Figure 137**) for bending, wear or damage.
7. Check the reservoir body (**Figure 138**) for corrosion or other damage. Make sure the opening (**Figure 139**) in the base is clear.
8. Check the reservoir cap and diaphragm (**Figure 140**) for damage.

REAR MASTER CYLINDER SERVICE (2008-2009 MODELS)

Read *Brake Service* in this chapter.

Disassembly

Refer to **Figure 141**.

1. Remove the rear master cylinder as described in this chapter.
2. Clean the exterior of the master cylinder housing with clean DOT 4 brake fluid or isopropyl alcohol and dry.

3. Store the master cylinder components in a divided container, such as a restaurant-size egg carton, to help maintain their correct alignment position.
4. If still installed, remove the master cylinder cover and diaphragm.
5. Carefully remove the rubber boot from the groove in the body.
6. Push down on the washer and compress the pedal return spring.
7. Remove the E-clip and washer from the pushrod. Slowly release the pressure and remove the return spring from the pushrod.
8. Depress the pushrod and release the snap ring from the body.
9. Remove the special washer, and slowly withdraw the pushrod. The pushrod is under pressure from the piston spring.
10. Remove the pushrod.
11. Withdraw the piston assembly and spring from the cartridge.

Assembly

1. Coat all parts with clean DOT 4 brake fluid.
2. Soak the primary cup, O-ring and piston assembly in clean DOT 4 brake fluid for at least 15 minutes to make them pliable. Coat the inside of the cartridge bore with clean brake fluid prior to the assembly of parts.
3. Position the piston spring with the larger coil end going in first and install it into the body.

CAUTION
When installing the piston assembly, do not allow the primary cup to turn inside out as it will be damaged and allow brake fluid leaks within the cartridge cylinder bore.

4. Position the piston with the spring end going in first and install it into the body.
5. Position the special washer with the inner collar facing away from the ball end of the pushrod, and install it onto the pushrod.
6. Position a *new* snap ring with the flat side facing the ball end of the pushrod, and install it onto the pushrod.
7. Install pushrod onto the end of the piston and push the piston and pushrod into the body and compress the piston spring. Push the piston assembly in and then let it move out several times and check for ease of movement. Hold the pushrod in place and install a *new* snap ring. Make sure the snap ring is correctly seated in the body groove.
8. Position the pedal return spring with the larger coil end going in first and install it into the body.
9. Install the washer and install a *new* E-clip onto the inboard groove of the pushrod. Make sure the E-clip is correctly seated in the pushrod groove.
10. Install the rubber boot and index the large end into the groove in the body. Index the small end into the outboard groove of the pushrod.

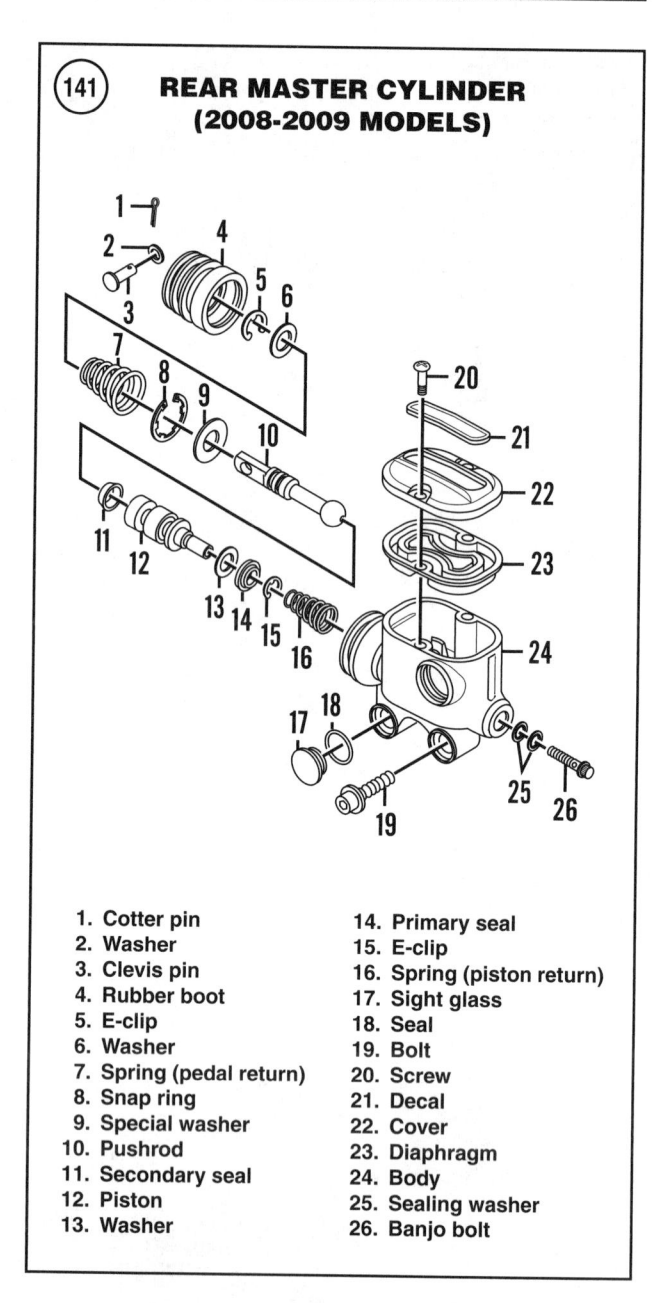

(141) REAR MASTER CYLINDER (2008-2009 MODELS)

1. Cotter pin
2. Washer
3. Clevis pin
4. Rubber boot
5. E-clip
6. Washer
7. Spring (pedal return)
8. Snap ring
9. Special washer
10. Pushrod
11. Secondary seal
12. Piston
13. Washer
14. Primary seal
15. E-clip
16. Spring (piston return)
17. Sight glass
18. Seal
19. Bolt
20. Screw
21. Decal
22. Cover
23. Diaphragm
24. Body
25. Sealing washer
26. Banjo bolt

11. Install the diaphragm and reservoir cover. Install the cover screws and tighten to 6-8 in.-lb. (0.7-0.9 N•m).
12. Install the rear master cylinder as described in this chapter.

Inspection

1. Clean all parts in clean DOT 4 brake fluid or isopropyl alcohol and dry with compressed air. Replace worn or damage parts as described in this section. It is recommended that a new rebuild kit be installed every time the master cylinder is disassembled.
2. Inspect the cylinder bore surface for signs of wear and damage. Do not hone the bore to clean or repair it. If less than perfect, replace the master cylinder assembly.
3. Check the piston primary and secondary cups for deterioration or damage.

BRAKES

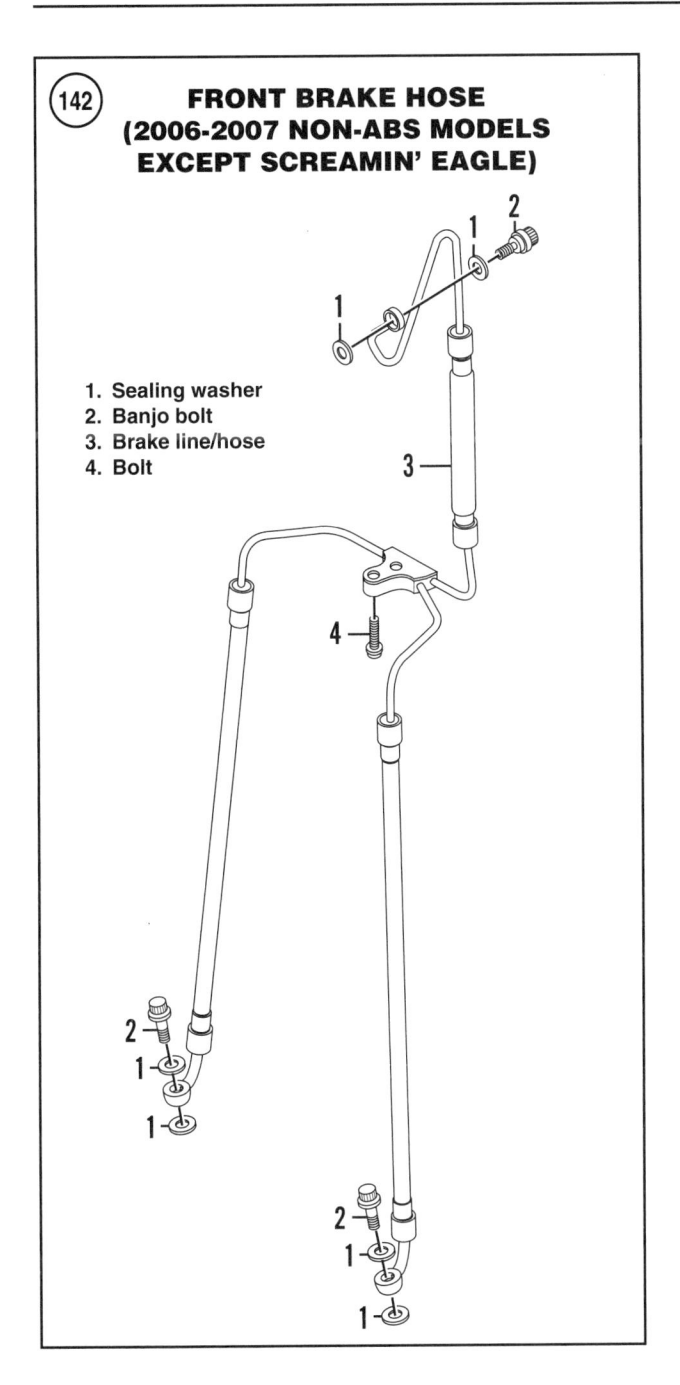

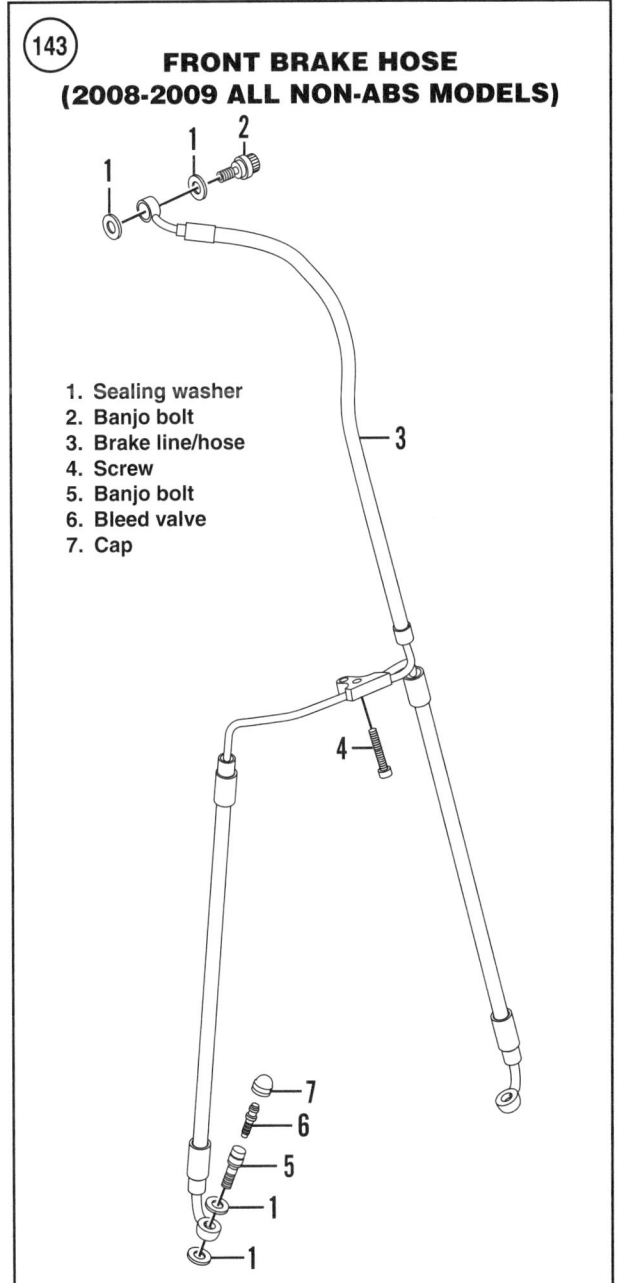

142 **FRONT BRAKE HOSE (2006-2007 NON-ABS MODELS EXCEPT SCREAMIN' EAGLE)**

1. Sealing washer
2. Banjo bolt
3. Brake line/hose
4. Bolt

143 **FRONT BRAKE HOSE (2008-2009 ALL NON-ABS MODELS)**

1. Sealing washer
2. Banjo bolt
3. Brake line/hose
4. Screw
5. Banjo bolt
6. Bleed valve
7. Cap

4. Check both springs for bending, unequally spaced coils or corrosion.
5. Inspect the rubber boot for tears or deterioration.
6. Check the pushrod, special washer and snap ring for bending, wear or damage.
7. Check the body for corrosion or other damage. Make sure the opening in the base is clear.
8. Check the reservoir cap and diaphragm for damage.

BRAKE HOSE AND LINE REPLACEMENT (NON-ABS MODELS)

A combination of metal brake pipes and flexible brake hoses connect the master cylinder to the brake calipers. Banjo fittings connect brake hoses to the master cylinder and brake calipers. At each connection, the banjo bolt is sealed with combination steel/rubber sealing washers. Replace the sealing washers every time a fitting is disassembled.

Replace the brake line assembly if the flexible portion is swelling, if cracking or other damage is visible, if the metal brake pipes leak or if there are dents or cracks. When replacing a new brake line assembly, make sure the length and angle of the steel pipe portions are correct. Install *new* banjo bolt sealing washers at the same time.

Read *Brake Service* in this chapter.

**Front Brake Hose
Removal/Installation**

Refer to **Figures 142-145**.

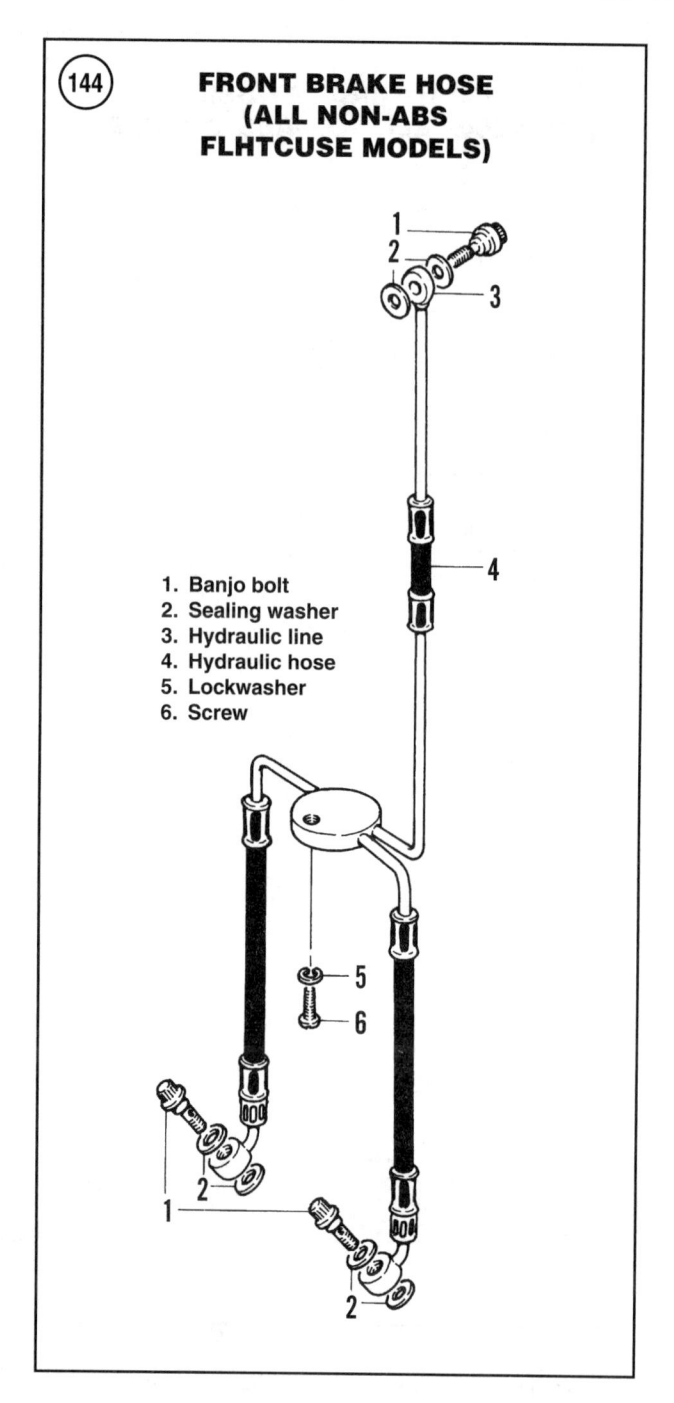

144 FRONT BRAKE HOSE (ALL NON-ABS FLHTCUSE MODELS)

1. Banjo bolt
2. Sealing washer
3. Hydraulic line
4. Hydraulic hose
5. Lockwasher
6. Screw

145 FRONT BRAKE HOSE (2007-2008 NON-ABS FLHRSE MODELS AND 2009 ABS FLTRSE MODELS

1. Sealing washer
2. Banjo bolt
3. Hydraulic line/hose
4. Bolt

1. Support the motorcycle on level ground on a swing arm stand.
2. Block the front wheel so the motorcycle will not roll in either direction while the rear wheel is off ground.
3. On models so equipped, refer to Chapter Seventeen and remove all necessary front fairing panels necessary to gain access to the front brake line where it attaches to the lower steering stem.
4. Drain the front brake systems as described in *Brake Fluid Draining* (this chapter).
5. Remove the fuel tank as described in Chapter Nine or Chapter Ten.
6. Before removing the brake line assembly, note the brake line routing from the master cylinder to the calipers.

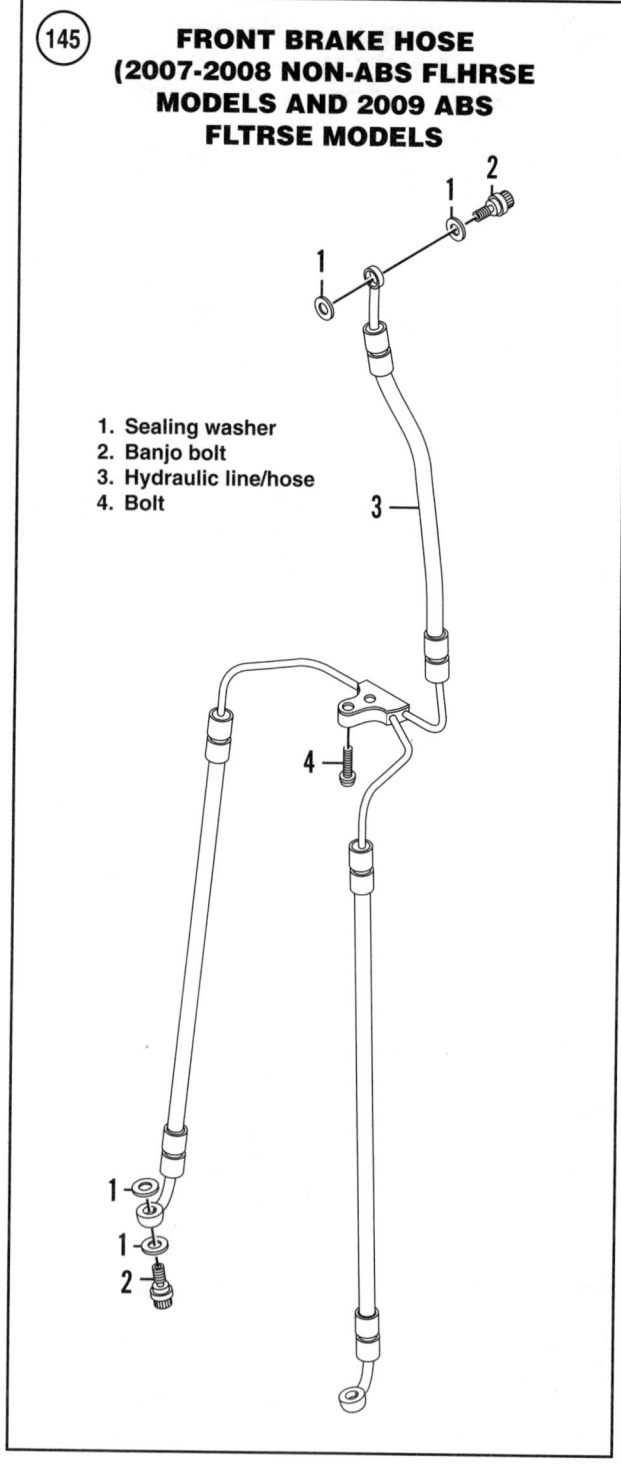

In addition, note the number and position of any metal hose clamps and/or plastic ties used to hold the brake lines in place. Install the brake hose assembly along its original path. The metal clamps can be reused.
7. Cut any plastic ties securing the brake line assembly and discard them.
8. Remove the bolt (**Figure 146**) securing the brake hose mounting plate to the lower steering stem. On models so equipped, do not lose the guide plate between the hose mounting plate and the steering stem.

BRAKES

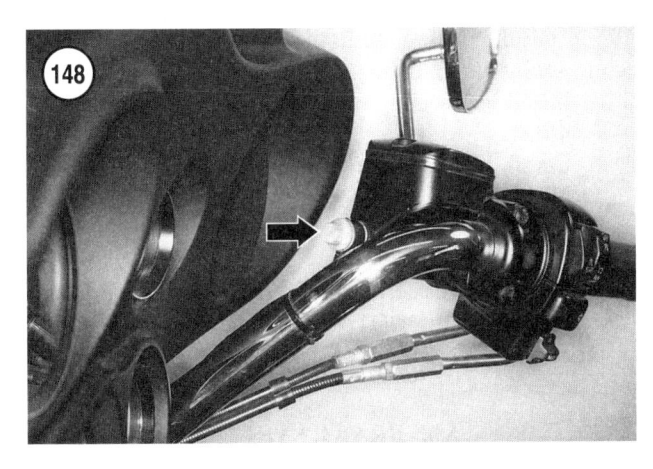

149 REAR BRAKE HOSE (ALL NON-ABS MODELS)

1. Sealing washer
2. Banjo bolt
3. Rear brake hose/brake line assembly
4. Hose clip
5. Hose clamp
6. Bolt
7. Bolt
8. Rear brake light switch

9. Remove the screw or nut securing the metal clamps around the brake line. Spread the clamp and remove it from the brake line.

10. Remove the banjo bolt (**Figure 147**) and washers securing the hose to each front brake caliper.

11. Remove the banjo bolt (**Figure 148**) and washers securing the hose to the front master cylinder.

12. Cover the ends of the brake hoses to prevent brake fluid from leaking onto the motorcycle.

13. Carefully remove the brake hose assembly from the frame.

14. If the existing brake hose assembly is going to be reinstalled, inspect it as follows:

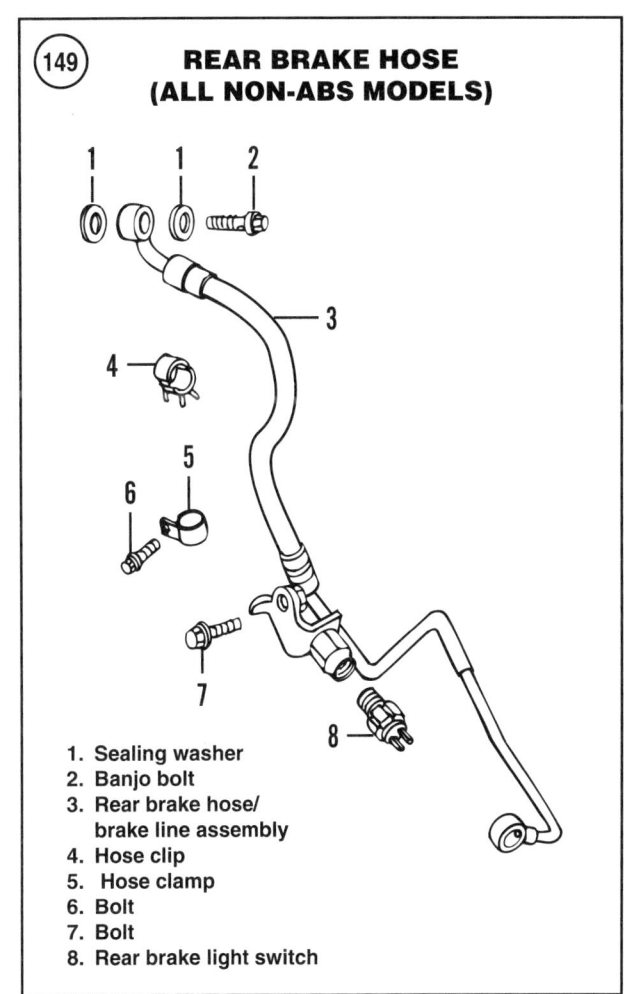

   a. Check the metal pipes where they enter and exit at the flexible hoses. Check the crimped clamp for looseness or damage.
   b. Check the flexible hose portions for swelling, cracks or other damage.
   c. If any wear or damage is found, replace the brake hose assembly.

15. Install the brake hose, washers and banjo bolts in the reverse order of removal while noting the following:

   a. Install *new* sealing washers on each side of the hose fitting.
   b. Carefully install the clips and guides to hold the brake hose in place.
   c. Tighten the banjo bolts to the specification listed in **Table 2**.
   d. Refill the front master cylinder with clean DOT 4 brake fluid. Bleed the front brake system as described in this chapter.

Rear Brake Hose Removal/Installation

Refer to **Figure 149**.

1. Support the motorcycle on level ground on a swing arm stand.

2. Block the front wheel so the motorcycle will not roll in either direction while the rear wheel is off ground.
3. Remove the right side frame side cover and the saddlebag as described in Chapter Seventeen.
4. Remove the right passenger footboard as described in Chapter Seventeen.
5. Remove the exhaust system as described in Chapter Four.
6. Drain the hydraulic brake fluid from the rear brake system as follows:
   a. Connect a hose to the rear caliper bleed valve. Refer to A, **Figure 150** (typical).
   b. Insert the loose end of the hose in a container to catch the brake fluid.
   c. Open the caliper bleed valve and operate the rear brake pedal to pump the fluid out of the master cylinder and brake line assembly. Continue until all of the fluid is removed.
   d. Close the bleed valve and disconnect the hose.
7. Before removing the brake line assembly, note the brake line routing from the master cylinder to the caliper. In addition, note the number and position of the metal hose clamps, plastic clips and plastic ties used to hold the brake line in place. Install the brake hose assembly along its original path. The metal clamp and plastic clips can be reused. However, new plastic ties must be installed.
8. Insert a small screwdriver into the gap at the side of the clip (**Figure 151**) and carefully rotate the screwdriver. Release the two clips on the lower frame tube T-studs.
9. At the rear brake light switch, cut and discard the plastic tie securing the rear brake light switch wires to the frame lower tube.
10. Remove the bolt and clamp securing the brake hose to the rear swing arm.
11. Open the two cable clips on the rear swing arm T-studs and release the brake hose from the clips.
12. Disconnect the electrical connector (A, **Figure 152**, typical) from the rear brake switch.
13. Remove the bolt (B, **Figure 152**) securing the brake light switch to the frame bracket.
14. Remove the banjo bolt (B, **Figure 150**) and washers securing the hose to the brake caliper.
15. Remove the banjo bolt (**Figure 153**) and washers securing the hose to the master cylinder.
16. Carefully move the rear brake line assembly forward and away from the rear swing arm bracket. Remove the brake hose from the motorcycle.
17. If the existing brake hose assembly is going to be reinstalled, inspect it as follows:
   a. Check the metal pipe where it enters and exits the flexible hose. Check the crimped clamp for looseness or damage.
   b. Check the flexible hose portion for swelling, cracks or other damage.
   c. If any wear or damage is found, replace the brake hose.
18. If necessary, remove the stoplight switch from the rear brake hose fitting. Reverse to install the switch. Tighten the switch to 12-15 ft.-lb. (16.3-20.3 N•m).
19. Install the brake hose in the reverse order of removal while noting the following:
   a. Install *new* sealing washers on each side of the hose fitting.
   b. Carefully install the clips and guides to hold the brake hose in place.
   c. Tighten the banjo bolts to the specification listed in **Table 2**.
   d. Refill the master cylinder with clean brake fluid clearly marked DOT 4. Bleed the rear brake system as described in this chapter.

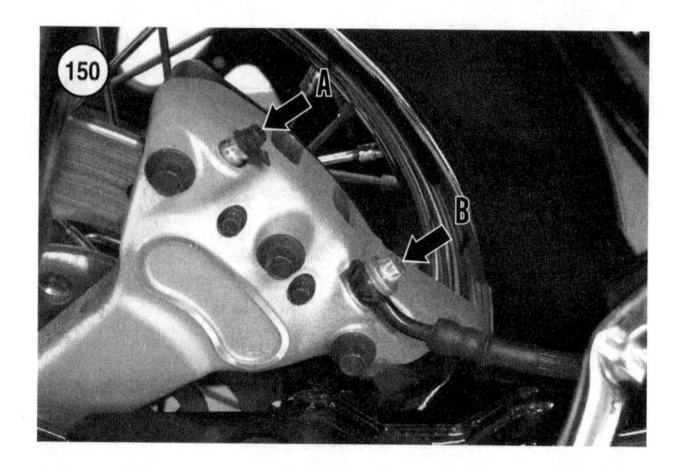

ABS BRAKE SYSTEM

The Anti-lock Brake System (ABS) is designed to prevent wheel lockup.

The ABS system consists of the ABS module assembly that controls the sensing and control functions of the system. The ABS module receives a signal from the ABS sensors located at each wheel, and they relay information regarding wheel rotation speed from the sensors to the ABS module.

The ABS module assembly consists of the hydraulic control unit (HCU) and the electronic control unit (ECU). On 2008 models, these two units are integral within the ABS module assembly and failure of either unit requires replacing the ABS module assembly. On 2009 models, they are separate components and can be replaced separately, if

BRAKES

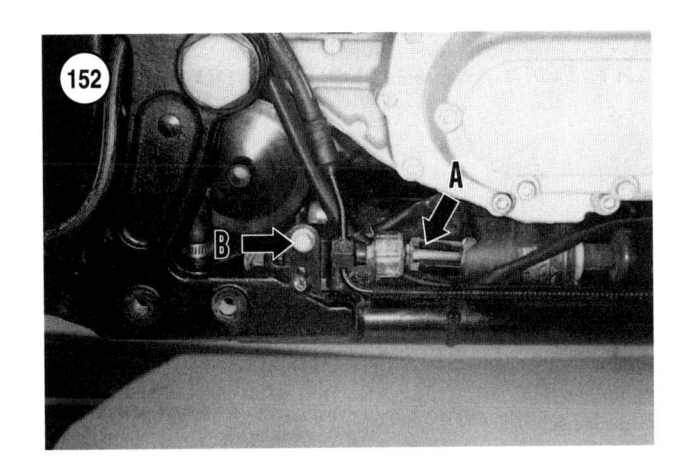

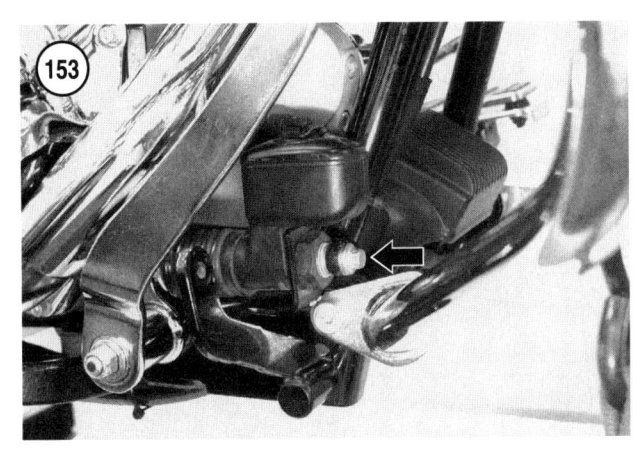

necessary. The hydraulic control unit (HCU) contains four solenoid valves (an apply valve and release valve for each wheel), two pumps, a pump motor and accumulators. The ABS module assembly is located on the right side in the battery caddy along with the battery. Also, there is an ABS diode pack attached to the fuse block under the left frame side cover.

The ABS module assembly interprets the signals from the wheel sensors (encoder wheel bearings located within each wheel hub) and sends this information to the various solenoid valves to prevent wheel lockup. When the master cylinder lever or pedal is applied, hydraulic pressure at the master cylinder is transmitted through the pressure modulator and then to the caliper assembly for braking action. During ABS braking there will be rapid pulsations felt in the brake lever and/or pedal. These pulsations are caused by the rapid changes in the positions of the individual solenoid valves within the module. This is normal.

Brake pressure is critical in an ABS system. The brake hoses are designed with specific characteristics. When replacing the brake hoses, or hose and metal brake line assembly, install only hoses specifically designed for use with the specific ABS system. Using a brake hose of an alternate design may the change the characteristics of the brake system.

If the ABS system malfunctions, the brakes will operate without ABS assist. If the ABS icon illuminates on the speedometer face, refer to *Electronic Diagnostic System* in Chapter Two for fault codes and troubleshooting information. If there is a fault within the system, the test procedures and repairs are addressed in the flow charts located on the CD inserted into the back cover of the manual.

The ABS indicator icon will illuminate after start up and will go off after the motorcycle reaches a speed greater than 10 mph (16 km/h). The icon will illuminate during a bulb check and will stay on when a malfunction has occurred within the system and a DTC has been set.

After more than one brake line has been removed, the system must be checked by a dealership with the H-D digital technician to make sure the system is properly connected. This must be done for safety concerns as well as maintaining any applicable warranty.

ABS WHEEL SPEED SENSORS

CAUTION
Keep the ABS sensor and the ABS encoder wheel bearings away from magnetic fields or they will be damaged.

Front Wheel

Removal

1A. On FLTR models, perform the following:
   a. Remove the outer front fairing as described in Chapter Seventeen.
   b. Turn the front wheel to the full left fork stop.
   c. Follow the speed sensor wire from the sensor, up the fork leg and to the left side of the front fairing bracket.
   d. Gently pull the sensor wire containing one black/blue wire and one black/violet wire until the black 2-pin connector is visible. Disconnect this electrical connector.

1B. On FLHR models, perform the following:
   a. Turn the front wheel to the full right fork stop.
   b. Follow the speed sensor wire from the sensor, up the fork leg and to the underside of the headlight nacelle on the left side of the steering head.
   c. Gently pull the sensor wire containing one black/blue wire and one black/violet wire until the black 2-pin connector is visible. Disconnect this electrical connector.
   d. Pull the connector housing and wire down through the opening in front of lower fork bracket.

1C. On FLHT and FLHX models, perform the following:
   a. Remove the outer front fairing as described in Chapter Seventeen.
   b. Turn the front wheel to the full right fork stop.
   c. Follow the speed sensor wire from the sensor, up the fork leg and to the underside of the front fairing cap on the left side of the steering head.
   d. Gently pull the sensor wire containing one black/blue wire and one black/violet wire until the black

CHAPTER FIFTEEN

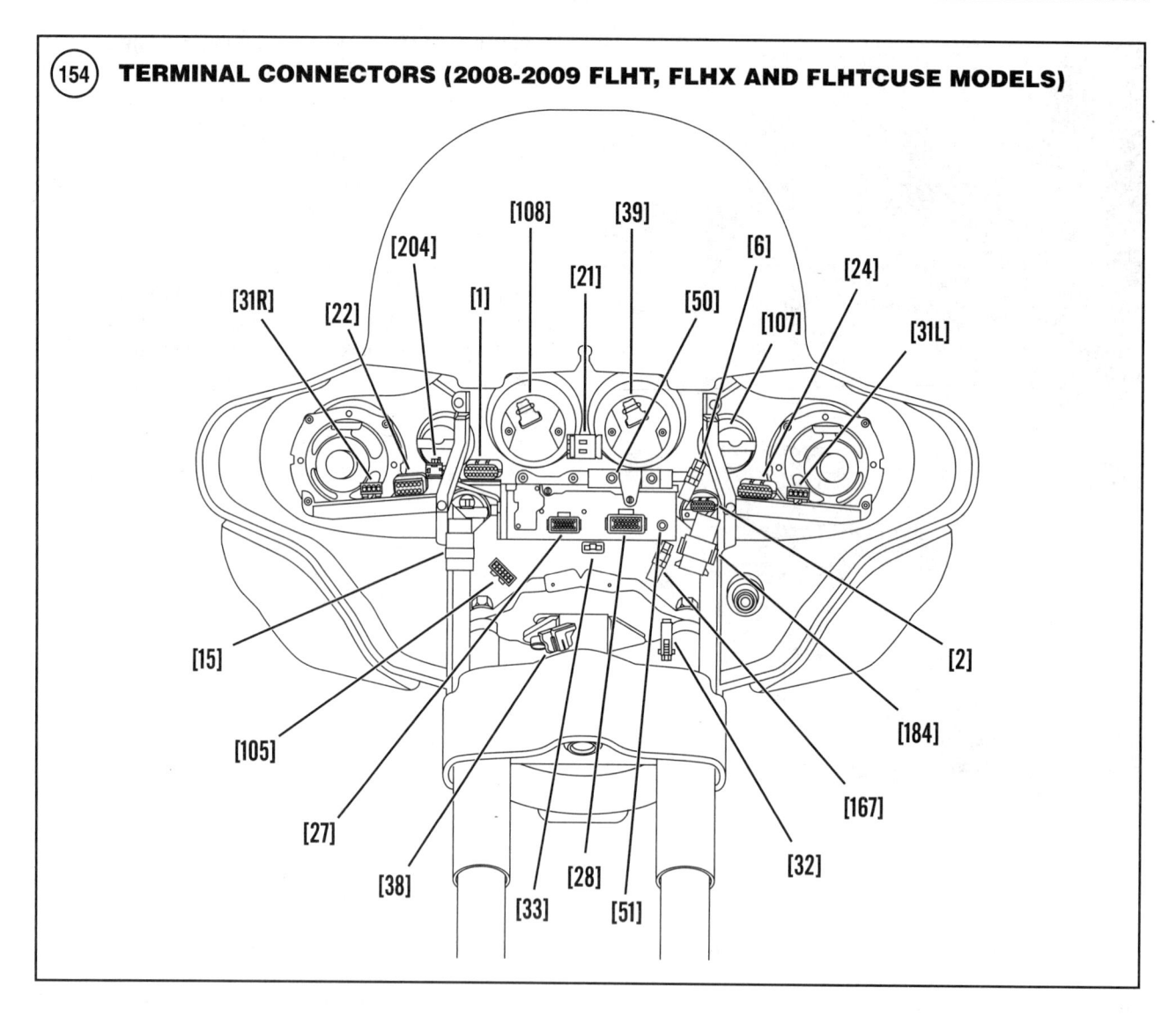

154 TERMINAL CONNECTORS (2008-2009 FLHT, FLHX AND FLHTCUSE MODELS)

[31R] [22] [204] [1] [108] [21] [39] [50] [6] [107] [24] [31L]
[15] [2]
[105] [184]
[27] [167]
[38] [28] [32]
[33] [51]

2-pin connector (**Figure 154**) is visible. Disconnect this electrical connector.
  e. Pull the connector housing and wire down through the opening in front of lower fork bracket.
2. Carefully cut the two cable straps and release the wheel sensor wire from the front brake hose and front fender tip lamp cables, if equipped.
3. Release the wheel sensor wire as follows:
  a. Push in on lip at the rear of clip (A, **Figure 155**) and release it.
  b. Rotate the ABS tab (B, **Figure 155**) toward the rear until the clip is perpendicular to the bracket. Remove the clip and move the cable out of the way.
4. Refer to Chapter Twelve and partially remove the front axle until the wheel sensor is free. Remove the wheel sensor and push the front axle back through the left side fork slider. Install the axle nut finger-tight.

Installation

1. Remove the front axle nut and withdraw front axle (Chapter Twelve) sufficiently to install the wheel sensor.

2. Move the ABS sensor into position adjacent to the left fork leg and align the front axle holes. Push the front axle in from the right side until it bottoms.
3. Rotate the ABS sensor *counterclockwise* until the index pin (**Figure 156**) makes contact with the left fork slider.
4. Refer to Chapter Twelve and complete the installation of the front axle and nut.
5A. On FLTR models, perform the following:
  a. Turn the front wheel to the full left fork stop.
  b. Locate the 2-pin connector next to the left side of the front fairing bracket.
  c. Reconnect the speed sensor wire connector. Push on the connector until locked into place.
  d. Install the outer front fairing as described in Chapter Seventeen.
5B. On FLHR models, perform the following:
  a. Turn the front wheel to the full right fork stop.
  b. Locate the 2-pin connector on the underside of the headlight nacelle at the left side of the steering head. Pull the connector down and reconnect the speed sensor wire connector. Push on the connector until locked into place.

BRAKES

8. Secure the wheel sensor wire as follows:
   a. Move the wire into position in the bracket.
   b. Rotate the ABS tab (B, **Figure 155**) toward the front until the clip is inline with the bracket. Press on the tab until the tab lip is engaged.
   c. Push in on lip at the rear of clip (A, **Figure 155**) and lock it in place.

Rear Wheel

Removal

1. Remove the right saddlebag and frame side cover as described in Chapter Seventeen.
2. On the right side of the electrical caddy, pull the anchor on the rear wheel sensor wire through the hole in the caddy.
3. Disconnect the electrical connector.
4. Insert a small flat blade screwdriver into the gap at the side of the clip. Gently rotate the screwdriver and open cable clip on T-stud on top of swing arm.
5. Refer to Chapter Twelve and partially remove the rear axle until the wheel sensor is free. Remove the wheel sensor and push the rear axle back through the right side of the swing arm. Install the axle nut finger-tight.

Installation

1. Remove the rear axle nut and withdraw the rear axle (Chapter Twelve) sufficiently to install the wheel sensor.
2. Move the ABS sensor into position adjacent to the rear brake caliper mounting bracket and align the front axle holes. Push the rear axle from the left side until it bottoms.
3. Refer to Chapter Twelve and complete the installation of the rear axle and nut.
4. Rotate the ABS sensor until the index pin (A, **Figure 157**) makes contact with the caliper bracket notch (B).

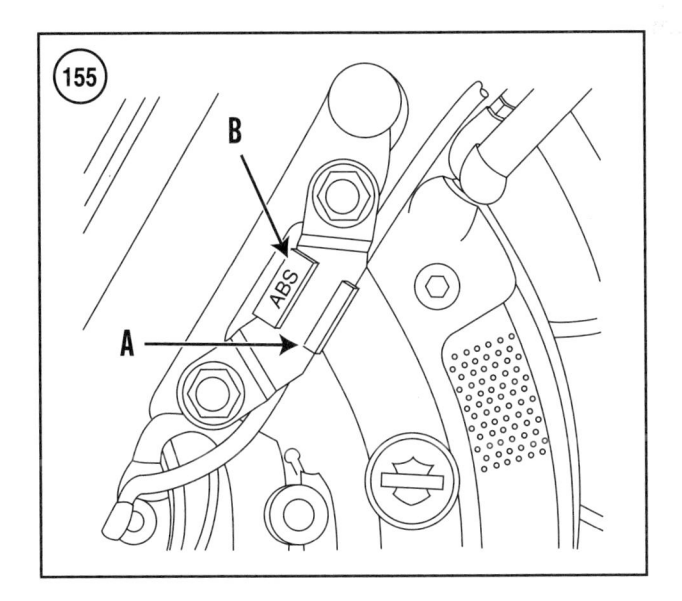

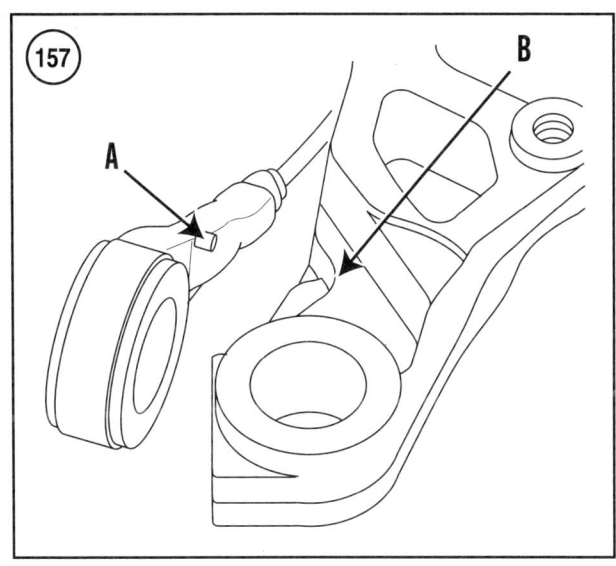

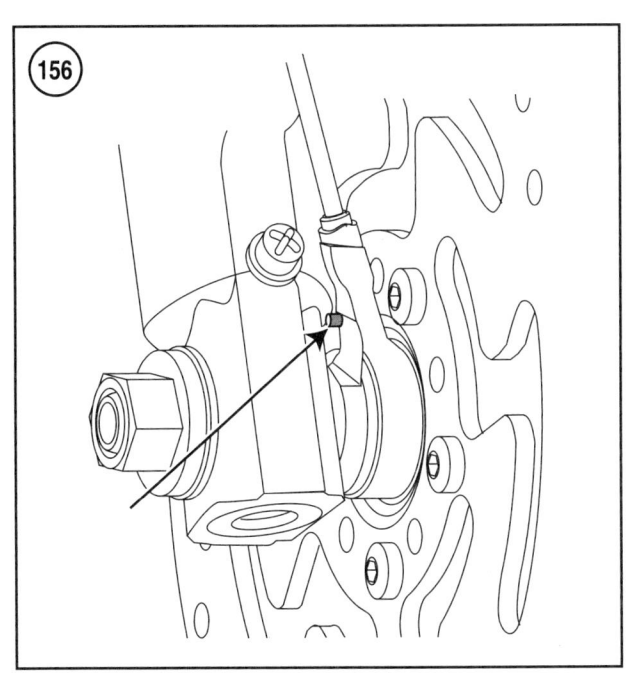

5C. On FLHT and FLHX models, perform the following:
   a. Turn the front wheel to the full right fork stop.
   b. Locate the 2-pin connector (**Figure 154**) on the underside of the fairing cap at the left side of the steering head. Pull the connector down and reconnect the speed sensor wire connector. Push on the connector until it locks into place.
   c. Install the outer front fairing as described in Chapter Seventeen.

6. Install a new cable strap 2.5 in. (63.5 mm) above the bottom of the brake hose crimp. Secure the front wheel sensor wire and front fender tip lamp electrical wires, if equipped.

7. Install a second new cable strap 2.5 in. (63.5 mm) above the top of the brake hose crimp. Secure the front wheel sensor wire and front fender tip lamp electrical wires, if equipped.

CHAPTER FIFTEEN

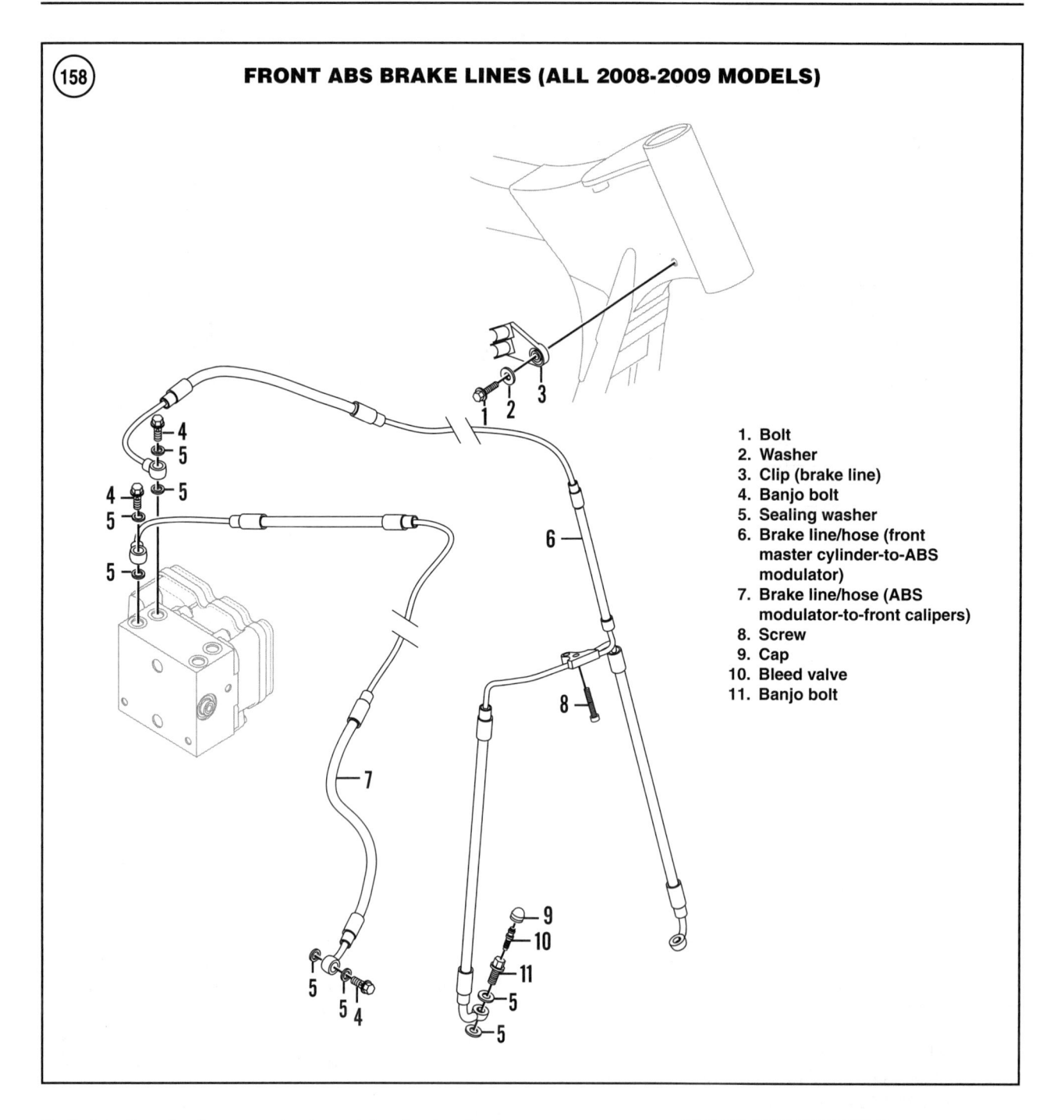

(158) FRONT ABS BRAKE LINES (ALL 2008-2009 MODELS)

1. Bolt
2. Washer
3. Clip (brake line)
4. Banjo bolt
5. Sealing washer
6. Brake line/hose (front master cylinder-to-ABS modulator)
7. Brake line/hose (ABS modulator-to-front calipers)
8. Screw
9. Cap
10. Bleed valve
11. Banjo bolt

5. Rotate the wheel sensor wire toward the front and outboard of the caliper bracket until it is parallel with the rear swing arm.
6. Place the wheel sensor wire and rear brake hose onto the cable clip on T-stud on top of the swing arm. Snap the clip closed.
7. Feed the sensor wire on the outboard side of the front frame rail down tube. Stay below the right side electrical caddy and reconnect the speed sensor wire connector. Push on the connector until locked into place.
8. Install the anchor on the rear wheel sensor through the hole in the electrical caddy.
9. Install the right saddlebag and frame side cover as described in Chapter Seventeen.

ABS BRAKE MODULE

Refer to **Figures 158-160**.

CAUTION
The ECU portion of the ABS module is sensitive to electrostatic discharge and can be easily damaged. Whenever handling the ABS module, or the ECU itself, ground yourself to the frame prior to touching the ABS module. Always touch the motorcycle frame or grounded surface before handling any portion of the ABS unit. This is especially true in areas with a very low air humidity index.

BRAKES

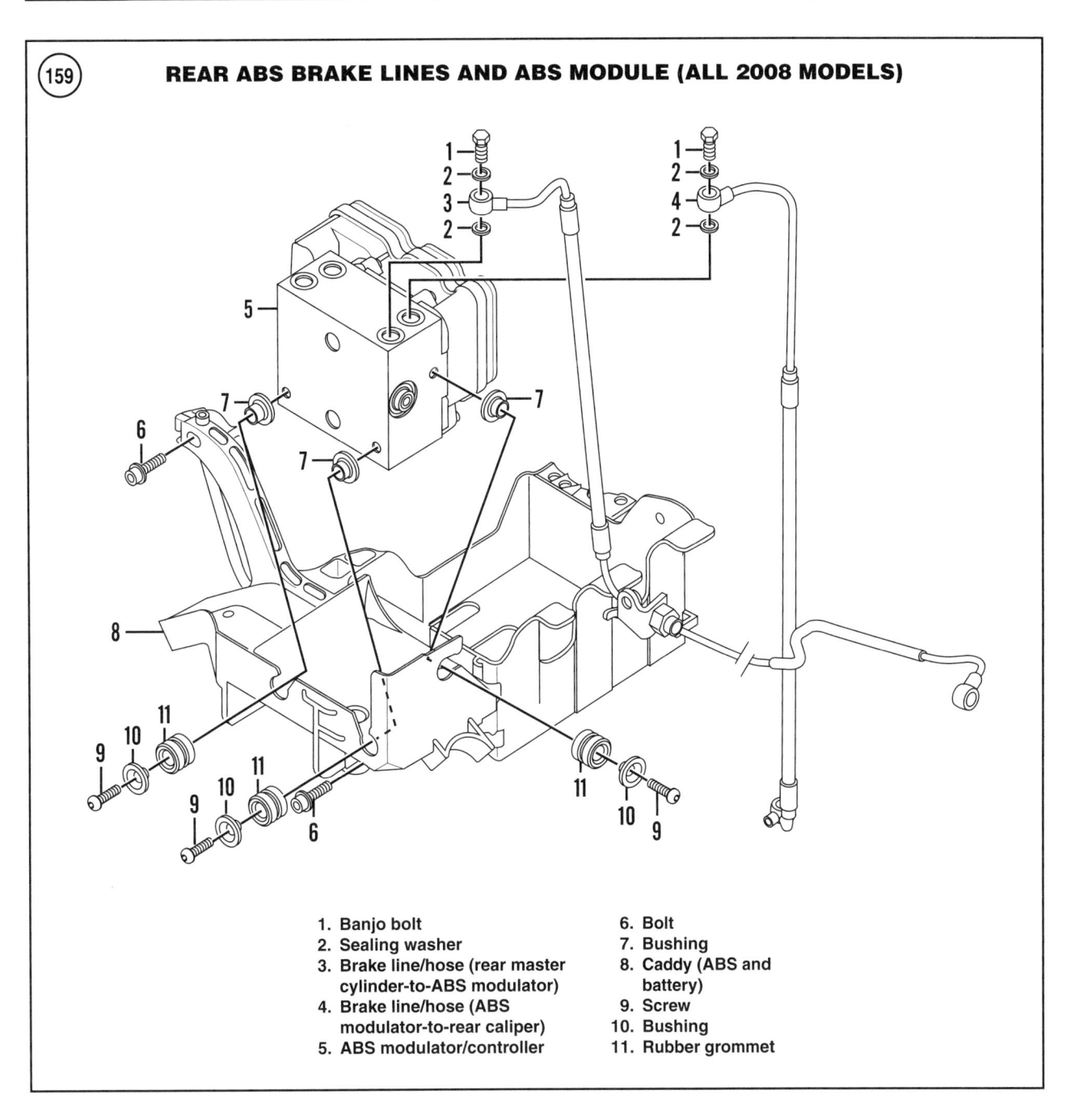

159 REAR ABS BRAKE LINES AND ABS MODULE (ALL 2008 MODELS)

1. Banjo bolt
2. Sealing washer
3. Brake line/hose (rear master cylinder-to-ABS modulator)
4. Brake line/hose (ABS modulator-to-rear caliper)
5. ABS modulator/controller
6. Bolt
7. Bushing
8. Caddy (ABS and battery)
9. Screw
10. Bushing
11. Rubber grommet

Removal

1. Support the motorcycle on level ground on a swing arm stand.
2. Block the front wheel so the motorcycle will not roll in either direction while the rear wheel is off ground.
3. Remove the right frame side cover and saddlebag as described in Chapter Seventeen.
4. Remove the battery as described in Chapter Eleven.
5. Drain the front and rear brake systems as described in *Brake Fluid Draining* (this chapter).

CAUTION
Ground yourself to the frame before handling the ABS module or connectors.

6. Disconnect the 20-pin connector from the ABS module.
7. Place several shop cloths under each brake line fitting to catch residual brake fluid when the fittings are disconnected.
8. Remove the banjo bolt and copper washers securing each fitting to the ABS module. Discard the copper washers if the ABS module assembly will not be reinstalled.
9. Remove the three Allen screws securing the ABS module to the caddy.
10. Carefully pull the ABS module up and out of the caddy and remove it.
11. If the ABS module assembly is going to be reinstalled, install the banjo bolts and old copper washers at each hose port to prevent the entry of foreign matter.

654								CHAPTER FIFTEEN

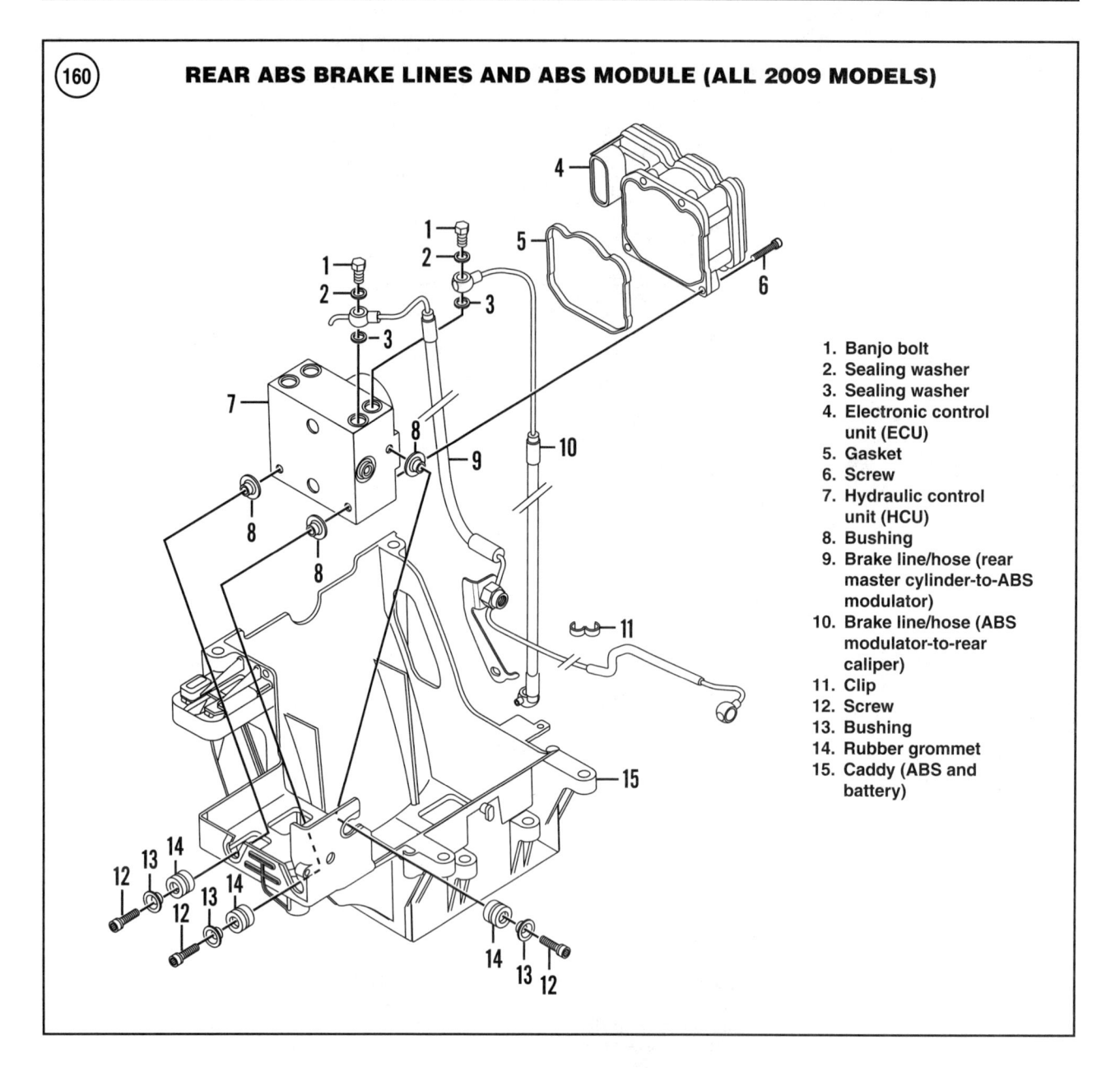

ⓘ60 REAR ABS BRAKE LINES AND ABS MODULE (ALL 2009 MODELS)

1. Banjo bolt
2. Sealing washer
3. Sealing washer
4. Electronic control unit (ECU)
5. Gasket
6. Screw
7. Hydraulic control unit (HCU)
8. Bushing
9. Brake line/hose (rear master cylinder-to-ABS modulator)
10. Brake line/hose (ABS modulator-to-rear caliper)
11. Clip
12. Screw
13. Bushing
14. Rubber grommet
15. Caddy (ABS and battery)

Installation

1. Inspect the rubber grommets for damage and deterioration. Replace as a set if one is damaged to ensure correct retention of the ABS module.
2. Make sure the bushing is in place on each side of the rubber grommets. Both bushings must be in place on each rubber grommet and the rubber grommet must be installed correctly in the caddy receptacles.

CAUTION
Ground yourself to the frame before handling the ABS module or connectors.

3. Position the ABS module with the brake hose ports on the right side, and carefully install the module assembly into the caddy. The caddy must sit flat and bottom in the caddy.
4. Install the three ABS module Allen screws and tighten alternately to 39-60 in.-lb. (4.4-6.8 N•m).
5. Remove the banjo bolts and *old* copper washers from the hose ports. Discard the copper washers.
6. The ABS module ports are marked to ensure correct placement of each banjo fitting as follows:
   a. To front brake calipers: F.
   b. To rear brake caliper: R.
   c. From front master cylinder: MF.
   d. From rear master cylinder: MR.
7. Position the fitting of each hose to the correct port on the ABS modulator. Route the front caliper brake line fittings beneath the front master cylinder brake line.
8. Install the banjo bolt with a *new* copper washer on each side of the fitting. Alternately tighten the ABS module banjo bolts to 12.5-14.5 ft.-lb. (17.0-19.7 N•m).
9. Connect the 20-pin connector onto the ABS modulator.
10. Install the battery as described in Chapter Eleven.

BRAKES

11. Fill both brake systems with DOT 4 brake fluid and bleed each of the systems as described in this chapter.
12. Install the right saddlebag and frame side cover as described in Chapter Seventeen.
13. The system must be checked by a dealership with the H-D digital technician to make sure the system is properly connected. This must be done for safety concerns as well as maintaining any applicable warranty.

Separation (2009 Models)

The hydraulic control unit (HCU) can be separated from the electronic control unit (ECU) if one of the units fails. Refer to **Figure 160**.

1. Remove the ABS module as described in this section and take unit to the workbench.

CAUTION
Ground yourself to the frame before proceeding.

2. Remove the four screws mating the ECU to the HCU and separate the two units.
3. Remove the gasket from the ECU, if necessary.
4. If removed, install the gasket into the groove in the ECU and make sure it seats correctly around the ECU.
5. Mate the HCU to the ECU and make sure they are correctly aligned.
6. Install the four mating screws and tighten to 35-45 in.-lb. (4.0-5.1 N•m).
7. Install the ABS module as described in this section.

ABS DIODE PACK

Replacement

1. Remove the left frame side cover as described in Chapter Seventeen.
2. Remove the diode pack from the clip on the base of the fuse panel.
3. Disconnect the 4-pin connector from the diode pack and remove diode pack.
4. Connect the 4-pin connector onto the diode pack and press it on until it bottoms.
5. Install the diode pack onto the clip on the base of the fuse panel.
6. Install the left frame side cover as described in Chapter Seventeen.

BRAKE LINE REPLACEMENT (ABS MODELS)

The master cylinders are connected to the calipers by a combination of steel and flexible brake line assemblies. Banjo bolts connect brake hoses to individual components and are sealed with copper washers on each side of the fitting.

Replace the brake line assembly if the flexible portion shows swelling, cracking or other damage. Likewise, replace the brake line assembly if the metal portion leaks or if there are dents or cracks.

Refer to **Figures 158-160**.

CAUTION
The ECU portion of the ABS module is sensitive to electrostatic discharge and can be easily damaged. Whenever handling the ABS module, or the ECU itself, ground your self prior to touching the ABS module. Always touch the motorcycle frame or grounded surface before handling any portion of the ABS unit. This is especially true in areas with a very low air humidity index.

Front Master Cylinder-to-ABS Module

Removal

1. Support the motorcycle on level ground on a swing arm stand.
2. Block the front wheel so the motorcycle will not roll in either direction while the rear wheel is off ground.
3. Remove the right frame side cover and saddlebag as described in Chapter Seventeen.
4. Remove the fuel tank as described in Chapter Ten.
5. Remove the top of the electrical caddy as described in Chapter Eleven.
6. On models so equipped, refer to Chapter Seventeen and remove all front fairing panels necessary to gain access to the front brake line where it attaches to the lower steering stem.
7. Before removing the brake line assembly, note the brake line routing from the master cylinder to the calipers.
8. Remove the bolt securing the brake hose mounting plate to the lower steering stem.
9. Release the brake line as follows:
    a. Cut cable strap securing front brake line to right side handlebar riser or right handlebar.
    b. Cut cable strap securing front brake lines to bracket on right side of handlebar.
    c. Cut cable strap securing front brake lines to narrow ledge at side of frame wiring trough.
    d. Remove three double sided clips and separate brake lines from frame backbone.
    e. Release brake lines from frame channel at front of wiring trough.
    f. On FLHTCU models, cut cable strap and release audio harness from upper right frame tube, if so equipped.
10. Remove the banjo bolt and washers securing the brake hose to each front brake caliper. Discard the copper washers.
11. Remove the banjo bolt and washers securing the brake hose to the front master cylinder. Discard the copper washers.
12. Remove the banjo bolt and washers securing the brake hose to the ABS module MF port. Discard the copper washers.
13. Cover the ends of the brake hoses to prevent brake fluid leaks.

14. Pull the front section of the brake line forward toward the upper fork bridge. Pull the brake line toward the rear and remove the brake line and hose assembly from the frame.

Installation

1. Position the brake line and hose assembly as follows:
   a. Place the assembly over the frame behind the steering head.
   b. Place the brake line along the right side of the frame wire trough with the rear banjo fitting adjacent to the ABS module.
   c. Insert the front section toward the front along the right side of the steering head.
   d. Move it up over the top fork bride and toward the rear following the right side of the handlebar to the front master cylinder.
2. Position the rear fitting onto the ABS modulator MF port. Install the banjo bolt and two *new* copper washers into the MF port, but do not tighten it yet.
3. Position the fitting onto the master cylinder port. Install the banjo bolt and two *new* copper washers into the master cylinder port, but do not tighten it yet.
4. Secure the brake line assembly as follows:
   a. On FLHT and FLHX series models, install a *new* cable strap 2.5 in. (63.5 mm) rear of the fairing cap opening. Secure the brake hose and the right side switch wiring to the right side handlebar riser. Secure the strap.
   b. On FLHR and FLTR series models, install a *new* cable strap and secure the brake hose and the right side switch wiring harness to the right side handlebar riser. Secure the strap.
   c. On all models, install a *new* cable strap and secure the brake hose and the bracket on the right side steering head. Secure the strap. Install a *new* cable strap and secure the brake hose from the master cylinder to the frame top channel and the brake hose to the calipers to the frame bottom channel.
   d. Press the brake line in the frame channel at front of wiring trough.
   e. Press the brake line on narrow ledge at side of wire trough. At the rear ledge, install a *new* cable strap and secure the brake line to the wire trough.
   f. Install the brake lines into the three double-sided clips at the following locations: one in front of the ignition coil bracket, one above wire trough through breakouts, and one in front of the fuel tank bracket threaded bolt receptacle.
   g. On FLHTCU models, install a *new* cable strap and secure the audio harness to the right side upper frame tube, if equipped.
5. Install the brake hose onto the front master cylinder. Install the banjo bolt with two *new* sealing washers.
6. Tighten all banjo bolts to 12.5-14.5 ft.-lb. (17.0-19.7 N•m).
7. Refill the front brake line circuit with clean DOT 4 brake fluid. Bleed the front brake system as described in this chapter.
8. On models so equipped, refer to Chapter Seventeen and install all front fairing panels that were removed.
9. Install the top of the electrical caddy as described in Chapter Eleven.
10. Install the fuel tank as described in Chapter Ten.
11. Install the right frame side cover and saddlebag as described in Chapter Seventeen.
12. Have the system checked by a dealership with the H-D digital technician to make sure the system is properly connected. This must be done for safety concerns as well as maintaining any applicable warranty.

ABS Module-to-Front Brake Calipers

Removal

1. Support the motorcycle on level ground on a swing arm stand.
2. Block the front wheel so the motorcycle will not roll in either direction while the rear wheel is off ground.
3. Remove the right frame side cover and saddlebag as described in Chapter Seventeen.
4. Remove the fuel tank as described in Chapter Ten.
5. Remove the top of the electrical caddy as described in Chapter Eleven.
6. On models so equipped, refer to Chapter Seventeen and remove all front fairing panels necessary to gain access to the front brake line where it attaches to the lower steering stem.
7. Before removing the brake line assembly, note the brake line routing from the master cylinder to the calipers.
8. On FLHR models, remove the left side of headlight nacelle as described in Chapter Eleven.
9. On FLHT and FLHX models, remove the following:
   a. Remove the outer front fairing and fairing cap as described in Chapter Seventeen.
   b. On FLHT models, remove the front passing lights as described in Chapter Eleven.
   c. On FLHX models, remove the front turn signals as described in Chapter Eleven.
10. On all models, remove the chrome skirt.
11. Cut two cable straps securing the front wheel sensor cable and front fender tip lamp electrical wires to the left caliper brake hose, if equipped.
12. Release the brake line as follows:
    a. Cut cable strap securing front brake line to right side handlebar riser or right handlebar.
    b. Cut cable strap securing front brake line to bracket on right side of steering head.
    c. Cut cable strap securing front brake lines to narrow ledge at side of frame wiring trough.
    d. Remove three double sided clips and separate brake lines from frame backbone.
    e. Release brake lines from frame channel at front of wiring trough.
    f. On FLHTCU models, cut cable strap securing the audio harness to the right upper frame tube.

BRAKES

13. Remove the Torx screw (T40) at base of lower fork bridge, and release brake line from bracket.
14. Remove the banjo bolt and washers securing the brake hose to each front brake caliper. Discard the copper washers.
15. Remove the banjo bolt and washers securing the brake hose to the ABS module MF port. Discard the copper washers.
16. Cover the ends of the brake hoses to prevent brake fluid leaks.
17. Pull the front section of the brake line forward toward the upper fork bridge. Pull the brake line toward the rear and remove the brake line and hose assembly from the frame.

Installation

1. Position the brake line and hose assembly as follows:
    a. Place the assembly over the frame behind the steering head.
    b. Place the brake line along the right side of the frame wire trough with the rear banjo fitting adjacent to the ABS module.
    c. Insert the front section toward the front along the right side of the steering head.
    d. Move it up over the top fork bridge and toward the rear following the right side of the handlebar to the front master cylinder.
2. Locate brake line bracket with the base of lower fork bridge and install the Torx screw (T40), but do not tighten it yet.
3. Position the rear fitting onto the ABS module MF port. Install the banjo bolt and two *new* copper washers into the MF port, but do not tighten it yet.
4. Position the fittings onto both front calipers. Install the banjo bolt and two *new* copper washers into each of the calipers, but do not tighten them yet.
5. Secure the brake line assembly as follows:
    a. On all models, install a *new* cable strap and secure the front brake line to the bracket on the right side of the steering head. Secure the strap. Install a *new* cable strap and secure the brake hose from the master cylinder to the frame top channel. Install a *new* cable strap and secure the brake hose from the calipers to the frame bottom channel.
    b. Press the brake line in the frame channel at front of wiring trough.
    c. Press the brake line onto narrow ledge at side of wire trough. At the rear ledge, install a *new* cable strap and secure the brake line to the wire trough.
    d. Install the brake lines into the three double-sided clips at the following locations: one in front of the ignition coil bracket, one above wire trough through breakouts, and one in front of the fuel tank bracket threaded bolt receptacle.
    e. On FLHTCU models, install a *new* cable strap and secure the audio harness to the right side upper frame tube, if equipped.
6. From the rear of the motorcycle, verify that the front brake lines are equal distance from their specific fork sliders. Tighten the brake line bracket Torx screw (T40) to 120-180 in.-lb. (13.6-20.3 N•m).
7. Tighten the ABS module MF port banjo bolt to 12.5-14.5 ft.-lb. (17.0-19.7 N•m).
8. On all models, tighten two *new* cable straps as follows:
    a. Install cable strap 2.5 in. (63.5 mm) above the bottom of the brake hose crimp and capture the front wheel sensor cable and front fender tip lamp electrical wires, on models so equipped.
    b. Install cable strap 2.5 in. (63.5 mm) above the top of the brake hose crimp and capture the front wheel sensor cable and front fender tip lamp electrical wires, on models so equipped.
9. Refill the front brake line circuit with clean DOT 4 brake fluid. Bleed the front brake system as described in this chapter.
10. On all models, install the chrome skirt.
11. On FLHT and FLHX series models, install the following:
    a. Install the outer front fairing and fairing cap as described in Chapter Seventeen.
    b. On FLHX models, install the front turn signals as described in Chapter Eleven.
    c. On FLHT models, install the front passing lights as described in Chapter Eleven.
12. On FLHR models, install the left side of headlight nacelle as described in Chapter Eleven.
13. Install the top of the electrical caddy as described in Chapter Eleven.
14. Install the fuel tank as described in Chapter Ten.
15. Install the right frame side cover and saddlebag as described in Chapter Seventeen.
16. Have the system checked by a dealership with the H-D digital technician to make sure the system is properly connected. This must be done for safety concerns as well as maintaining any applicable warranty.

Rear Master Cylinder-to-ABS Module

Removal

1. Support the motorcycle on level ground on a swing arm stand.
2. Block the front wheel so the motorcycle will not roll in either direction while the rear wheel is off ground.
3. Remove the exhaust system as described in Chapter Four.
4. Remove the right frame side cover and saddlebag as described in Chapter Seventeen.
5. Remove the right side footboards as described in Chapter Seventeen.
6. Before removing the brake line assembly, note the brake line routing from the master cylinder to the ABS module.
7. Cut the cable straps securing the brake line to the rubber saddles attached to the T-studs on the top of lower frame rail.

8. Disconnect the electrical connector from the rear brake light switch.

9. Remove the screw securing the rear brake light switch. Push on the bracket and release the locking tab from frame weldment.

10. On the right side next to the swing arm bracket, cut the cable strap in the middle frame down tube hole securing the brake line to the main wiring harness.

11. Remove the banjo bolt and washers securing the brake hose to the ABS module MR port. Discard the copper washers.

12. Remove the banjo bolt and washers securing the brake hose to the rear brake caliper. Discard the copper washers.

13. Remove the rear brake master cylinder and brake pedal assembly as described in this chapter.

14. Cover the ends of the brake hoses to prevent brake fluid leaks.

15. Remove the brake line and hose assembly from the frame.

Installation

1. Position the brake line and hose assembly as follows:
   a. Place the assembly onto the brake pedal shaft on frame.
   b. From bottom inboard side of rear exhaust header, feed the rear section of the brake line upward at front of frame middle down tube crossing, and under the rear of the down tube at the bottom of frame cross member.
   c. Move the front section inboard of the frame weldment at bottom of the frame down tube.

2. Position the rear fitting onto the ABS module MR port. Install the banjo bolt and two *new* copper washers into the MF port, but do not tighten it yet.

3. Install the rear master cylinder and brake pedal assembly as described in this chapter.

4. Position the fitting onto the rear caliper. Install the banjo bolt and two *new* copper washers into the caliper, but do not tighten it yet.

5. Engage the locating tab on the rear brake light switch onto the frame weldment and install the screw. Tighten the screw securely.

6. Connect the electrical connector to the rear brake light switch.

7. Position a *new* cable strap above the rubber saddles attached to the T-studs on the top of lower frame rail. Install the *new* cable strap securing the brake line to the main wiring harness.

8. Install a *new* cable strap through the middle frame down tube hole and secure the brake line to the main wiring harness.

9. Tighten the ABS module MR port banjo bolt to 12.5-14.5 ft.-lb. (17.0-19.7 N•m).

10. Refill the rear brake line circuit with clean DOT 4 brake fluid. Bleed the rear brake system as described in this chapter.

11. Install the exhaust system as described in Chapter Four.

12. Install the right side footboards as described in Chapter Seventeen.

13. Install the right frame side cover and saddlebag as described in Chapter Seventeen.

14. Have the system checked by a dealership with the H-D digital technician to make sure the system is properly connected. This must be done for safety concerns as well as maintaining any applicable warranty.

ABS Module-to-Rear Brake Caliper

Removal

1. Support the motorcycle on level ground on a swing arm stand.

2. Block the front wheel so the motorcycle will not roll in either direction while the rear wheel is off ground.

3. Remove the right frame side cover and saddlebag as described in Chapter Seventeen.

4. Remove the fuel tank as described in Chapter Ten.

5. Remove the right side electrical caddy as described in Chapter Eleven.

6. Before removing the brake line assembly, note the brake line routing from the ABS module to the calipers.

7. Open the two cable clips on the T-stud at the top of rear swing arm. Release the brake hose from the cable clips.

BRAKES

8. Cut cable strap securing the rear wheel sensor to the rear brake hose.
9. Remove the banjo bolt and washers securing the brake hose to the ABS module R port. Discard the copper washers.
10. Remove the banjo bolt and washers securing the brake hose to the rear brake caliper. Discard the copper washers.
11. Remove the brake line from the top and bottom sections of the front edge channel of the battery tray.
12. Cover the ends of the brake hoses to prevent brake fluid leaks.
13. Remove the brake line and hose assembly from the frame.

Installation

1. Position the brake line and hose assembly as follows:
   a. Place the assembly at top of swing arm with the rear banjo fitting adjacent to the rear caliper.
   b. Turn the forward portion of the assembly up toward the ABS module near the frame cross member.
2. Place the brake hose into the two cable clips on the T-stud at the top of rear swing arm.
3. Move the rear wheel speed sensor next to the brake hose and close the rear cable clip onto both components. Snap both cable clips closed.
4. Install the brake line onto the top and bottom sections of the front edge channel of the battery tray.
5. Position the rear fitting onto the ABS module R port. Install the banjo bolt and two *new* copper washers into the R port, but do not tighten it yet.
6. Position the fitting onto the rear caliper. Install the banjo bolt and two *new* copper washers into the caliper, but do not tighten it yet.
7. Tighten the ABS module R port banjo bolt to 12.5-14.5 ft.-lb. (17.0-19.7 N•m).
8. Tighten the brake caliper banjo bolt to 17-19 ft.-lb. (23.1-25.8 N•m).
9. Install cable strap 1.2 in. (30.48 mm) in front of the rear brake hose crimp and capture the rear wheel sensor cable and brake hose.
10. Install the right side electrical caddy as described in Chapter Eleven.
11. Install the fuel tank as described in Chapter Ten.
12. Install the right frame side cover and saddlebag as described in Chapter Seventeen.
13. Refill the rear brake line circuit with clean DOT 4 brake fluid. Bleed the rear brake system as described in this chapter.
14. Have the system checked by a dealership with the H-D digital technician to make sure the system is properly connected. This must be done for safety concerns as well as maintaining any applicable warranty.

BRAKE DISC

The front and rear brake discs can be inspected while installed on the motorcycle.

Small nicks on the disc are not important, but deep scratches or other marks may reduce braking effectiveness and increase brake pad wear. If these grooves are evident and the brake pads are wearing rapidly, replace the brake disc.

Refer to **Table 1** for brake disc specifications. Each disc is also marked with the minimum (MIN) thickness. If the specification marked on the brake disc differs from the one in **Table 1**, use the specification found on the brake disc.

1. Support the motorcycle with the wheel (front or rear) off the ground.
2. Measure the thickness (**Figure 161**) of the brake disc at several locations around the disc. Replace the disc if the thickness in any area is less than the minimum allowable specification stamped on the brake disc, or less than the service limit in **Table 1**.
3. Make sure the disc mounting bolts are tight.
4. Position the dial indicator stem against the brake disc (**Figure 162**). Zero the dial gauge and slowly turn the wheel and measure the runout. If the runout is excessive:
   a. Check for loose or missing fasteners.
   b. Remove the front and/or rear wheel and check the wheel bearing condition.
5. Clean the disc of any corrosion and wipe clean with brake cleaner. Never use an oil-based solvent that may leave an oily residue on the disc.

Removal/Installation

1. Remove the front or rear wheel as described in Chapter Twelve.
2. Mark the disc with a R (right side) and L (left side) prior to removal.
3. Remove the bolts (**Figure 163**) securing the brake disc to the hub and remove the disc. Discard the bolts as they cannot be reused.
4. Check the threaded brake disc bolt holes in the wheel hub for thread damage. Clean out with a tap if necessary.
5. Clean the disc and the disc mounting surface thoroughly with brake cleaner or contact cleaner. Allow the surfaces to dry before installation.

NOTE
On Screamin' Eagle models, front brake discs are symmetrical and can be installed on either side. When installing used discs, install them on the same side as noted during removal.

6. Install the disc onto the correct side of the wheel hub.
7. Install *new* Torx bolts and tighten to the following:
   a. Front wheel Torx bolt (T40): 16-24 ft.-lb. (21.7-32.5 N•m).
   b. Rear wheel Torx bolt (T45): 30-45 ft.-lb. (40.7-61.0 N•m).
8. Install the front or rear wheel as described in Chapter Twelve.

BRAKE BLEEDING

General Bleeding Tips

1. Clean the bleed valves and the area around the valves of all dirt and debris. Make sure the passageway in the end of the bleed valve is open and clear.
2. Use a box-end wrench to open and close the bleed valves. This prevents damage to the bleed valve hex-head. Replace bleed valves with damaged hex-heads. These are difficult to loosen and cannot be tightened fully.
3. Install the box-end wrench on the bleed valve before installing the catch hose. This allows operation of the wrench without having to disconnect the hose.
4. Use a clear catch hose to allow visual inspection of the brake fluid as it leaves the brake caliper. Air bubbles visible in the catch hose indicate there still may be air trapped in the brake system.
5. Depending on the amount of play at the bleed valve when it is loosened, it is possible to see air exiting through the catch hose even though there is no air in the brake system. A damaged catch hose can also cause air leaks. In both cases, air is being introduced into the bleed system at the bleed valve threads and catch hose connection and not from within the brake system itself. This condition can be misleading and can cause excessive brake bleeding when there is not air in the system.
6. Open the bleed valve just enough to allow fluid to pass through the screw and into the catch bottle. The farther the bleed valve is opened, the looser the valve becomes. This allows air to be drawn into the system from around the bleed valve threads.
7. If air is suspected of entering from around the bleed valve threads, remove the bleed valve and wrap a small amount of Teflon tape around the bleed valve threads to seal the threads. Install the bleed valve.
8. If the system is difficult to bleed, tap the banjo bolt on the master cylinder several times, it is not uncommon for air bubbles to become trapped in the hose connection where the brake fluid exits the master cylinder. When a number of bubbles appear in the master cylinder reservoir after tapping the banjo bolt, it means air was trapped in this area. Also, tap the other bolt and the line connections at the caliper and other brake units.

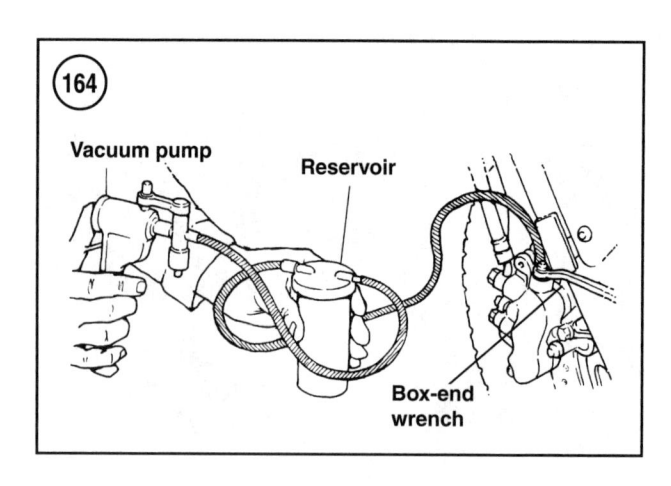

Vacuum Bleeding

Vacuum bleeding can be accomplished by using either a hand-operated bleeder or an air-tool bleeder powered by compressed air. The tools (**Figure 164**) described in this section can be used by one person to drain and bleed the brake system.

Hand-operated vacuum pump

1. Connect the catch hose between the bleed valve and catch bottle. Connect the other hose between the catch bottle and vacuum pump. Refer to the tool manufacturer's instructions for additional information.
2. Secure the vacuum pump to the motorcycle with a length of wire so it is possible to check and refill the master cylinder reservoir without having to disconnect the catch hose.
3. Remove the dust cap from the brake caliper bleed valve.
4. Place a clean shop cloth over the caliper to protect it from accidental brake fluid spills.
5. Clean all dirt and debris off the top of the master cylinder.
6. Remove the screws securing the master cylinder top cover. Remove the cover and diaphragm.
7. Fill the reservoir almost to the top with clean DOT 4 brake fluid and reinstall the diaphragm and cover. Leave the cover in place during this procedure to prevent the entry of dirt.
8. Operate the vacuum pump to create a vacuum in the catch hose connected to the bleed valve. Then, open the bleed valve with the wrench to allow the brake fluid to be drawn through the master cylinder, brake hoses and lines. Close the bleed valve before the brake fluid stops flowing from the system (no more vacuum in the line) or before the master cylinder reservoir runs empty.

NOTE
Do not allow the master cylinder reservoir to empty during the bleeding operation or more air will enter the system. If this occurs, the bleeding procedure must be repeated.

BRAKES

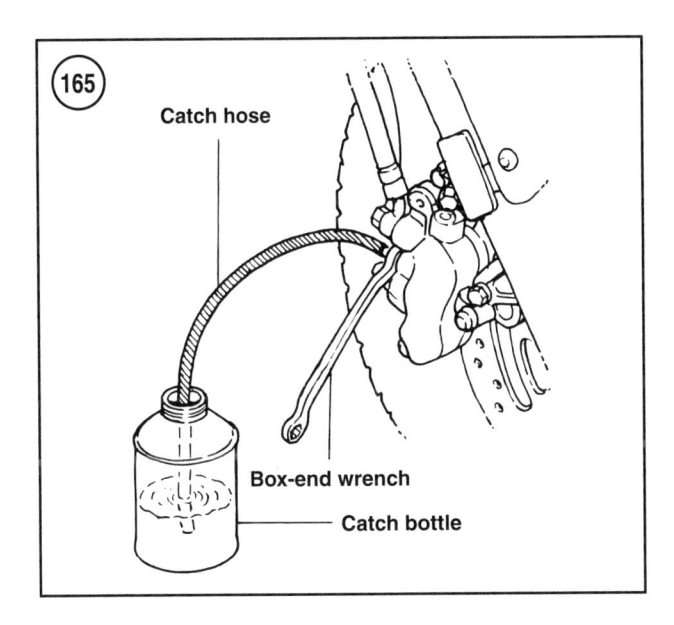

165
Catch hose
Box-end wrench
Catch bottle

9. Continue the bleeding process until the fluid running through the vacuum hose is a clear and solid stream without any air bubbles. Tighten the bleed valve and remove the brake bleeder assembly. Reinstall the bleed valve dust cap.

10A. If necessary, add fluid to correct the level in the front master cylinder reservoir. When topping off the front master cylinder, turn the handlebar until the reservoir is level. Add fluid until it is level is as follows:
   a. On 2006-2007 models, the brake fluid level should be 1/4 in. (6.4 mm) from the top edge of the master cylinder body (**Figure 27**).
   b. On 2008-2009 models, the brake fluid level should be flush with the top ledge cast into the front of the master cylinder body.

10B. If necessary, add fluid to correct the level in the rear master cylinder reservoir. When topping off the rear master cylinder, secure the motorcycle until the reservoir is level. Add fluid until it is level is as follows:
   a. On 2006-2007 models, the brake fluid level should be 1/4 in. (6.4 mm) from the top edge of the master cylinder body (**Figure 27**).
   b. On 2008-2009 models, the brake fluid level should be flush with the top ledge cast into the front of the master cylinder body.

11. Reinstall the reservoir diaphragm and cover. Install the screws and tighten to 6-8 in.-lb. (0.7-0.9 N•m).

12. Test the feel of the brake lever or pedal. It should be firm and offer the same resistance each time it is operated. If it feels spongy, there is probably still air in the system. Bleed the system again. After bleeding the system, check for leaks and tighten all fittings and connections as necessary.

Compressed air vacuum pump

NOTE
This system is highly recommended for models with ABS due to the number of brake lines and hoses.

1. Assemble the tool, following the manufacturer's instructions.
2. Connect the box-end wrench onto the bleed screw. Connect the vacuum hose onto the bleed valve.
3. Connect a compressed air source to the vacuum tool.

NOTE
Always close the bleed valve before releasing the lever on top of the pump.

4. Depress the lever on top of the pump and open the bleed valve slightly. As long as the lever is depressed, a vacuum is created in the canister and brake fluid will evacuate from the brake line. Releasing the lever stops the vacuum. Because this tool will drain the master cylinder rapidly, check the master cylinder fluid level often.

5. Continue until the brake fluid running through the vacuum hose is a clear and steady stream without bubbles. Air drawn in around the bleed valve will cause bubbles to form in the vacuum hose. While this is normal, it is misleading as it always appears there is air in the system, even when the system has been bled completely. If necessary, remove the bleed valve and wrap a small amount of Teflon tape around the bleed valve threads to seal the threads. Install the bleed valve.

Manual Bleeding

This is a one-person procedure that requires a reservoir bottle, length of clear hose (catch hose), wrench and the specified brake fluid (**Figure 165**).

1. Connect the catch hose to the bleed valve on the caliper. Submerge the other end of the hose into a bottle partially filled with clean DOT 4 brake fluid. This prevents air from being drawn into the catch hose and back into the brake system.
2. Apply the front brake lever or rear brake pedal until it stops and hold in this position.
3. Open the bleed valve with a wrench and let the lever or pedal move to the limit of its travel. Then, close the bleed valve; make sure to close the bleed valve before releasing the brake lever or pedal. This prevents air from being drawn back into the system on the lever's or pedal's return stroke if the bleed valve was left open.
4. Release the lever or pedal slowly, and then repeat the process until the brake fluid exiting the system is clear and air-free.

Brake Fluid Draining

Before disconnecting a brake hose from the front or rear brake component, drain the brake fluid as described in this section. Doing so reduces the amount of brake fluid that can spill out when disconnecting the brake hoses and lines from the system.

Front master cylinder line

1. Support the motorcycle on level ground on a swing arm sand.

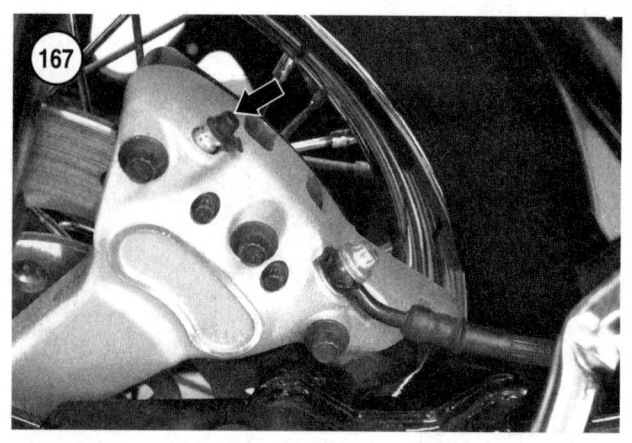

2. Block the front wheel so the motorcycle will not roll in either direction while on the swing arm stand.
3. Turn the handlebars to the straight ahead position to level the front master cylinder and remove the screws, cover and diaphragm.
4. Connect a brake bleeder to the front brake caliper bleed valve (**Figure 166**). Open the bleed valve and operate the brake bleeder until the fluid stops flowing. Tighten the bleed valve to 80-100 in.-lb. (9.0-11.3 N•m).
5. Repeat the process to drain the other caliper.
6. Disconnect the bleeder tool.

Rear master cylinder line

1. Support the motorcycle on level ground on a swing arm stand.
2. Block the front wheel so the motorcycle will not roll in either direction.
3. Remove the screws, cover and diaphragm from the reservoir.
4. Connect a brake bleeder to the rear brake caliper bleed valve (**Figure 167**). Open the bleed valve and operate the brake bleeder until the fluid stops flowing. Tighten the bleed valve.
5. Disconnect the bleeder tool.

Bleeding The System

Front brake line

1. Support the motorcycle on level ground on a swing arm stand.
2. Block the front wheel so the motorcycle will not roll in either direction while on the swing arm stand.
3. Turn the handlebars to the straight ahead position to level the front master cylinder and remove the screws, cover and diaphragm (**Figure 168**).
4. Connect a brake bleeder to the front brake caliper bleed valve (**Figure 166**). Open the bleed valve and operate the brake bleeder to bleed the brake line. Repeat until the brake fluid exiting the catch hose is clear and free of air. Tighten the bleed valve.

5. Repeat this process as necessary until the front brake lever feels firm when applying it there are not air bubbles in the catch hose.
6. Repeat the procedure to bleed the other front caliper.
7. After bleeding the system and making sure there are no air bubbles appearing in the catch hose, test the feel of the brake lever. It should be firm and should after the same resistance each time it is operated. If the brake lever feels spongy, air is still trapped in the system and the bleeding procedure must be continued.
8. Tighten the bleed valve to 80-100 in.-lb. (9.0-11.3 N•m).
9. Remove the brake bleeder.
10. If necessary, add clean DOT 4 brake fluid to correct the level in the master cylinder reservoir. Observe the brake fluid level (**Figure 169**) within the master cylinder body.
11. Install diaphragm and cover. Tighten the screws to 6-8 in.-lb. (0.7-0.9 N•m).

Rear brake line

1. Support the motorcycle on level ground on a swing arm stand.
2. Block the front wheel so the motorcycle will not roll in either direction while on the swing arm stand.
3. Remove the cover (**Figure 170**) and diaphragm from the reservoir.
4. Connect a brake bleeder to the rear brake caliper bleed valve (**Figure 167**). Open the bleed valve and operate the

BRAKES

brake bleeder to bleed the brake line. Repeat until the brake fluid exiting the catch hose is clear and free of air. Tighten the bleed valve securely.

5. After bleeding the bleed valves and the system so no air bubbles appear in the catch hose, test feel of the brake pedal. It should be firm and should offer the same resistance each time it is operated. If the brake pedal feels spongy, air is still trapped in the system and the bleeding procedure must be continued.

6. Tighten the bleed valve to 80-100 in.-lb. (9.0-11.3 N•m).

7. Remove the brake bleeder.

8. If necessary, add clean DOT 4 brake fluid to correct the level in the master cylinder reservoir as follows:
   a. 2006-2007 models, the correct level is 1/4 in. (6.4 mm) from the reservoir top ledge.
   b. 2008-2009 models, the correct level is flush with the top ledge cast into the front surface within the reservoir.

9. Install diaphragm and cover. Tighten the screws to 6-8 in.-lb. (0.7-0.9 N•m).

FLUSHING THE BRAKE SYSTEM

When flushing the brake system, use the recommended brake fluid as a flushing fluid. Flushing consists of pulling new brake fluid through the system until the new fluid appears at the caliper and without the presence of any air bubbles. To flush the brake system, follow one of the bleeding procedures described in this chapter.

Table 1 BRAKE SPECIFICATIONS

Item	Specification
Brake fluid type	DOT 4
Brake fluid height	
Front and rear reservoir	
2006-2007 models	1/4 in. (6.4 mm) from the top edge of the master body
2008-2009 models	Flush with top ledge cast into front of master cylinder body
Brake disc	
Lateral runout, maximum	0.008 in. (0.2 mm)
Warp, maximum	0.008 in. (0.2 mm)
Minimum thickness*	
Front disc	0.18 in. (4.6 mm)
Rear disc	0.25 in. (6.35 mm)
Brake pad minimum thickness	
2006-2007 models	
Front and rear pads	0.04 in. (1.02 mm)
2008-2009 models	
Front and rear pads	0.016 in. (0.4 mm)

*The minimum thickness is stamped on side of the disc.

Table 2 BRAKE TORQUE SPECIFICATIONS

Item	ft.-lb.	in.-lb.	N•m
ABS brake module (2008-2009 models)			
Allen mounting screws	–	39-60	4.4-6.8
Banjo bolts	12.5-14.5	–	17.0-19.7
ABS brake module/control unit (2009 models)			
Mating screws	–	35-45	4.0-5.1
ABS front brake line bracket Torx screws	–	120-180	13.6-20.3
Banjo bolt			
Front and rear master cylinder			
2006-2007 models	17-22	–	23.1-29.8
Front and rear caliper			
2006-2007 models	17-22	–	23.1-29.8
2008-2009 models	17-19	–	23.1-25.8
Front and rear master cylinder (2008-2009 models)			
Non-ABS equipped	12.5-14.5	–	17.0-19.7
ABS equipped	13-15	–	17.6-20.3
Banjo bleed bolt at front caliper			
2008-2009 models	17-19	–	23.1-25.8
Bleed valve (all models and years)	–	80-100	9.0-11.3
Brake disc Torx bolts			
Front wheel	16-24	–	21.7-32.5
Rear wheel	30-45	–	40.7-61.0
Brake pad pin bolt			
2006-2007 models	–	180-200	20.3-22.6
2008-2009 models	–	75-102	8.5-11.5
Front brake caliper mounting bolts	28-38	–	38.0-51.5
Front and rear brake caliper assembly bolts	23-38	–	38.0-51.5
Front brake master cylinder clamp bolt	–		
2006-2007 models	–	60-80	6.8-9.0
2008-2009 models	–	71-80	8.0-9.0
Master cylinder reservoir top cover screws (front and rear)	–	6-8	0.7-0.9
Rear brake caliper body mounting bolts			
2006-2007 models	28-38	–	38.0-51.5
Rear brake caliper mounting bolts			
2008-2009 models (to caliper mounting bracket)	43-48	–	58.3-65.1
Rear brake light switch	12-15	–	16.3-20.3
Rear brake master cylinder mount hex nut			
2006-2007 models	30-40	–	40.7-54.2
Rear brake master cylinder-to-frame mounting bolts 2008-2009 models	–	126-150	14.2-17.0
Rear brake pedal-to-frame pivot post locknut	15-20	–	20.3-27.1

CHAPTER SIXTEEN

CRUISE CONTROL

SYSTEM COMPONENTS AND OPERATION

On 2006-2007 models, the cruise control system consists of a cruise control module containing the stepper motor, switches and the related wiring. The stepper motor actuates the cruise control cable through a gear train and ribbon reel. The cruise control system on 2008-2009 models is controlled by the Electronic Control Module (ECM).

The cruise control module receives command signals from the cruise control SET/RESUME switch on the right side handlebar switch. The cruise control module receives information on operating conditions from the speedometer output signal.

The cruise control system will set and automatically maintain any speed between 30-85 mph (48-137 km/h). To set the cruise control, turn the cruise ON/OFF switch to the ON position. Power is then supplied to the cruise control module through the 15-amp fuse located in the fuse block under the frame left side cover.

After reaching the desired speed, momentarily push the cruise SET/RESUME switch to the SET position. The cruise control module receives a signal input from the speedometer output signal. The cruise control module sends a signal to the steeper motor to open or close the throttle via the cruise control cable. The cruise control module monitors both the engine rpm and the speedometer output signal to order the steeper motor to open or close the throttle to maintain the desired speed.

The cruise control is automatically disengaged whenever the cruise control module receives one of the following inputs:
1. The front or rear brake is applied.
2. The throttle is rolled back or closed.
3. The clutch is disengaged.
4. The cruise ON/OFF switch is moved to the OFF position.
5. The engine run/stop switch is moved to the OFF position.
6. The handlebar cruise SET/RESUME switch is moved to the SET position and held in that position until the motorcycle speed drops below 30 mph (48 km/h).

2006-2007 Models

The cruise control system uses mechanical and electrical components to maintain a selected speed set by the rider. This chapter covers service procedures for the factory cruise control system.

The cruise control system provides on-board diagnostics to help isolate any problems that may occur within the system. If a fault code within the cruise control system has been set, the cruise control engagement light (*C*) on the tachometer face will be used to retrieve the codes. During normal operation, the cruise control engagement light (C) is illuminated only when the cruise control is in operation.

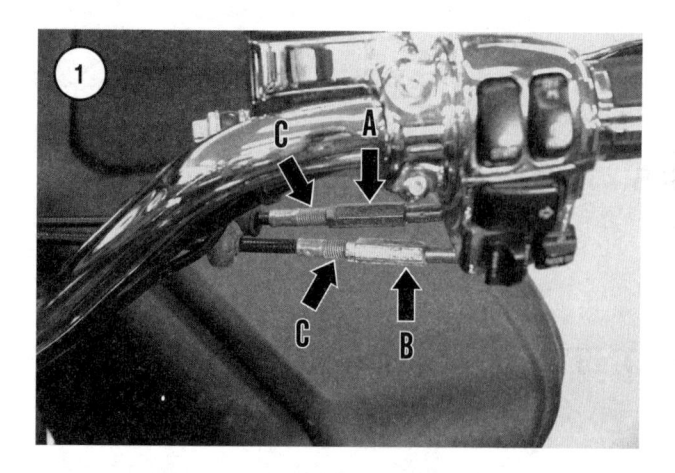

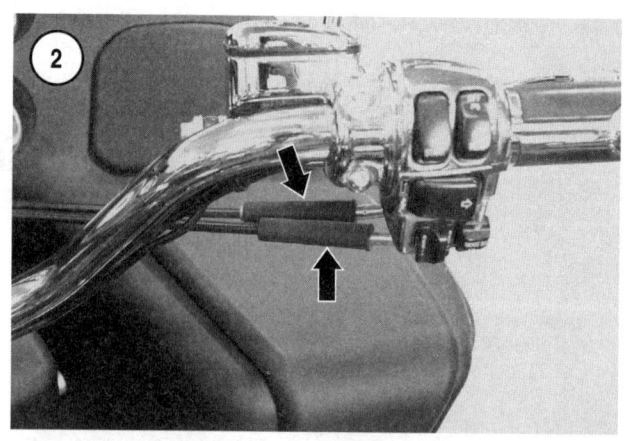

Refer to *Cruise Control System Diagnostic Trouble Codes (2006-2007 Models)* in Chapter Two to retrieve the diagnostic trouble codes (DTC).

2008-2009 Models

The cruise control system on 2008-2009 models is controlled by the Electronic Control Module (ECM). There is no cruise control module nor control cables since the throttle position is maintained electronically by the throttle control actuator.

Refer to *Cruise Control System Diagnostic Codes (2008-2009 Models)* in Chapter Two to retrieve the diagnostic trouble codes (DTC).

CONTROL CABLES ADJUSTMENT (2006-2007 MODELS)

NOTE
The ECM controls the throttle positioning on 2008-2009 models. There are no cables to adjust.

Throttle and Idle Cables Adjustment

There are two different throttle cables. At the throttle grip, the front cable (A, **Figure 1**) is the throttle control cable and the rear cable (B) is the idle control cable.

The throttle control cable must be adjusted first, and then the idle control cable.
1. Remove the air filter and backplate as described in Chapter Nine or Chapter Ten.
2. Slide the boots (**Figure 2**) off the cable adjusters.
3. At the handlebar, loosen both control cable adjuster locknuts. Then, turn the cable adjusters (C, **Figure 1**) *clockwise* as far as possible to increase cable slack.
4. Turn the handlebars so the front wheel points straight ahead.
5. Adjust the throttle control cable as follows:

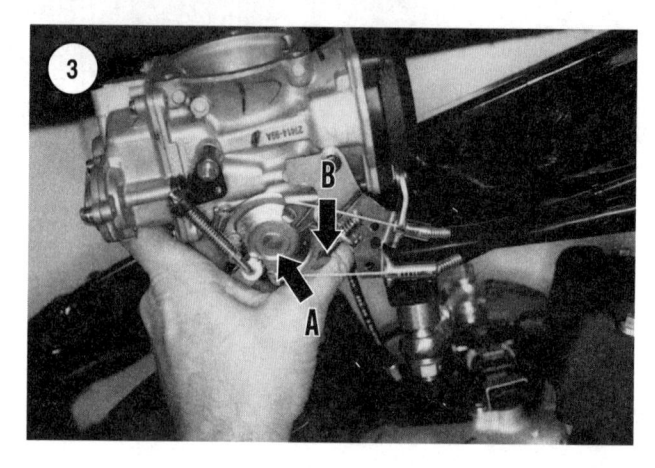

   a. Carefully rotate the throttle control *counterclockwise* to the wide open position and hold it in this position.
   b. On carbureted models, turn the throttle control cable adjuster *counterclockwise* until the throttle cam (A, **Figure 3**) stop just touches the stop boss (B) on the carburetor body.
   c. On fuel-injected models, turn the throttle control cable adjuster (C, **Figure 1**) *counterclockwise* until the throttle cam (A, **Figure 4**) stop just touches the stop boss (B, **Figure 4**) on the fuel induction module (C, **Figure 4**).
   d. Release the throttle grip, and turn the cable adjuster *counterclockwise* an additional 1/2 - 1 full turn. Tighten the adjuster locknut.

   NOTE
   If the throttle stop does not touch the idle stop, loosen the throttle cable just enough so that there is contact made through full lock-to-lock movement. Also check that the cruise cable has slack and is not opening the throttle. Loosen the cruise control cable if necessary.

   e. Rotate the throttle control *clockwise* to the full closed position, and check that the throttle cam stop just touches the idle stop boss on the carburetor body (B, **Figure 3**) or fuel induction module (D, **Figure 4**), while turning the handlebars from full lock-to-lock position.

CRUISE CONTROL

4

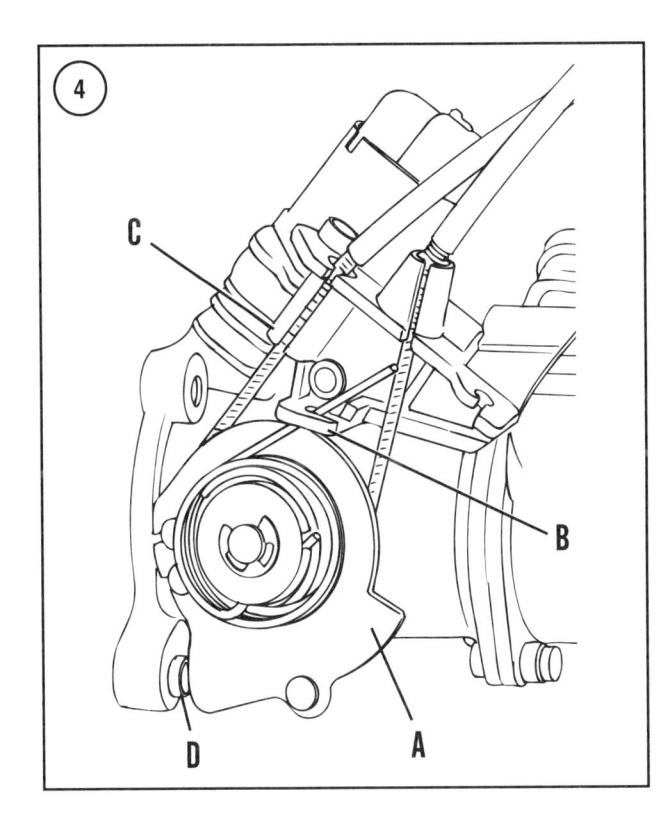

5

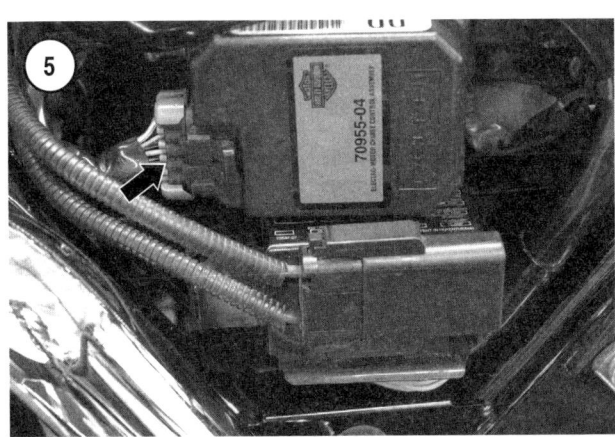

6 Rotational free play = 0.06 in. (1.5 mm)

e. Position the handlebar in the straight ahead position.
f. Adjust the idle control cable so there is approximately 0.06 in. (1.5 mm) rotational free play at the throttle grip (**Figure 6**).
g. Use light force, rotate the throttle grip toward the *closed* position. The ohmmeter must now read continuity. If not, decrease cable free play until continuity is present, while maintaining some cable free play.
h. Use light force, rotate throttle grip toward the *closed* position. Turn the handlebar from full lock-to-lock position. The ohmmeter must indicate continuity throughout handlebar movement.
i. Disconnect the ohmmeter and connect the 10-pin cruise control electrical connector (**Figure 5**) onto the module. Engage the catch to ensure full connection.
j. Position the handlebar in the straight ahead position. Rotate the throttle grip to the wide open position, and then release it. The throttle must return to the idle position freely.
k. Repeat this process with the handlebar in the full right position, and then the full left position. The throttle must return to the idle position freely. If the throttle will not return freely, loosen the cable adjuster slightly and repeat the adjustment procedure until this is achieved.
l. Install the left saddlebag and frame side cover as described in Chapter Seventeen.

Cruise Control Stepper Cable

The cruise control stepper cable only requires adjustment if the cruise control module or cruise control stepper cable were removed or replaced. If necessary, adjust the cruise control stepper cable using the *Cable Lash Initialization* procedure in this chapter.

Removal

1. Remove the fuel tank as described in Chapter Nine or Chapter Ten.
2. Remove the left frame side cover and saddlebag as described in Chapter Seventeen.

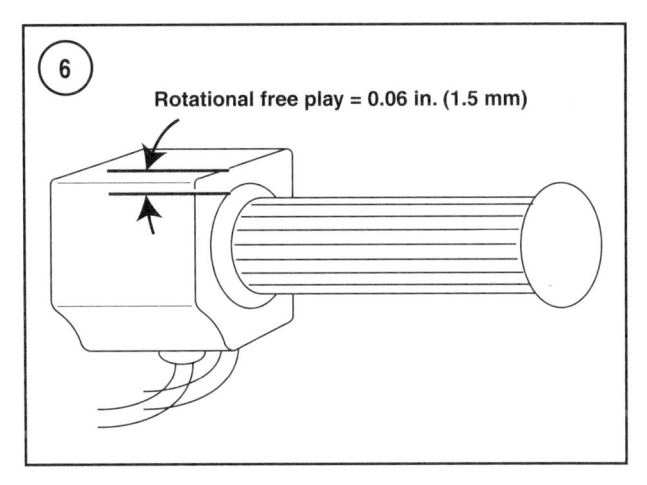

f. Carefully rotate the throttle control *counterclockwise* to the wide open position and release it. The throttle must return to the idle position freely. If it does not, check for improper cable routing, a damaged cable, or a binding throttle control.
6. Adjust the idle control cable as follows:
   a. Remove the left saddlebag and frame side cover as described in Chapter Seventeen.
   b. Lift the catch and disconnect the 10-pin cruise control electrical connector (**Figure 5**) from the module.
   c. Position the idle control cable adjusted to the *full slack* position.
   d. Connect an ohmmeter to the violet/yellow and orange/violet leads on the connector side. The reading must be infinity (switch contacts open). If there is continuity, there may be a short in the roll-off switch or the entire cable may be faulty and requires replacement. Do not disconnect the ohmmeter.

3. Remove the air filter and backplate as described in Chapter Nine or Chapter Ten.

4. Remove the E-clip and release the cable housing from the induction module.

5. At the outboard side the throttle cam pin wheel (A, **Figure 7**), push on the plastic end fitting (B) and remove it from the throttle cam pin wheel.

6. Remove the cruise cable (A, **Figure 8**) from the cable clip (B) on the frame.

7. Make a drawing or take a picture of the cable routing from the cruise control module through the frame to the induction module.

8. Carefully remove the cruise cable from under the fuel tank.

9. Rotate the cruise cable connector in a *counterclockwise* direction and detach it from the cruise control module.

10. Pull the cable out of the connector and remove the cable end bead from the ribbon end eyelet.

11. Pull the cruise control cable and connector from the hole (C, **Figure 8**) in the frame cross member and remove it from the frame.

Installation

1. On the left side, route the new cruise control cable forward over the top of the engine stabilizer, and then down between the cylinder heads to the induction module.

2. On the right side, position the new cruise control cable housing into the cable guide. Install a new E-clip on the cable housing and lock the cable into place.

3. Route the cruise control cable through the hole in the frame (C, **Figure 8**).

4. Position the hole in the ribbon end eyelet and the flat on the cable connector so they are facing outward. Insert the cable end bead into the ribbon end eyelet (**Figure 9**). Make sure it is secure in the eyelet.

5. Make sure the cable end bead, the eyelet and the ribbon are lined up correctly. At the induction end of the cable, gently pull on the end fitting to remove cable slack.

6. Insert the cruise control connector into the cruise control module. Rotate it *clockwise* until the connector tabs are fully engaged with the detents in the cruise control module. Carefully pull on the connector to make sure it securely correctly.

7. Attach the cruise cable (A, **Figure 8**) to the frame with a new cable clip (B).

8. Adjust the throttle and idle cables as described in this chapter.

9. Hold onto the cam lever assembly to prevent it from rotating. Install the cruise control cable and plastic end fitting (B, **Figure 7**) on the throttle cam pin wheel (A). Push the end fitting on until it locks into place.

10. Install the backplate and the air filter as described in Chapter Nine or Ten.

11. Install the frame left side cover and saddlebag.

12. Install the fuel tank as described in Chapter Nine or Ten.

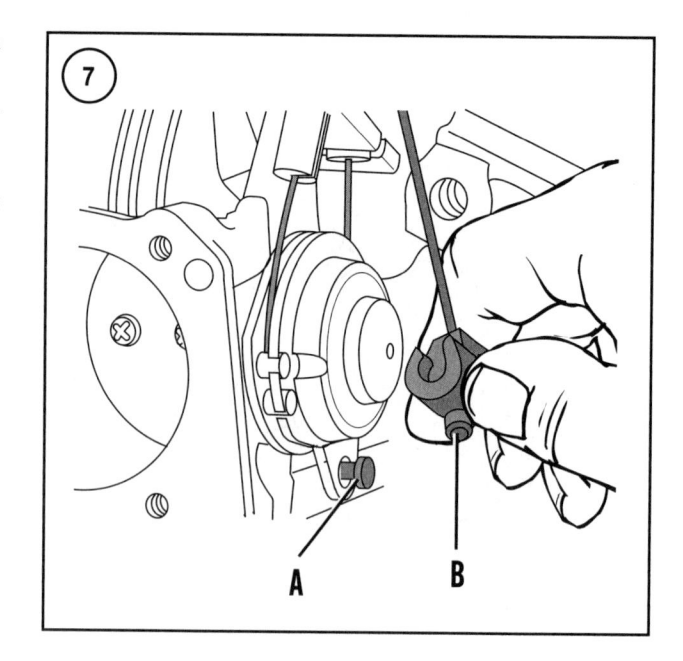

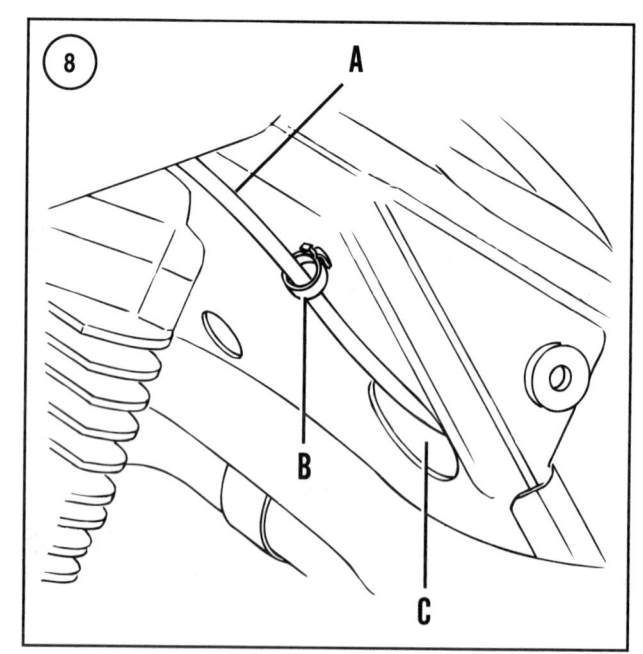

Cable lash initialization

This is not a routine adjustment and is only necessary if the cruise control module or cruise control stepper cable are removed or replaced.

1. Start the engine and allow it to reach normal operating temperature. Shut off the engine.

2. On the right side handlebar switch, push the cruise control SET/RESUME switch to the RESUME position and hold it on.

3. On the front fairing cap move the cruise control ON/OFF switch to the ON position.

4. Turn the ignition switch to IGN.

5. Start the engine and allow it to idle. The green cruise control engagement light (C) on the tachometer face will illuminate. Wait for three seconds for the lamp to go off.

CRUISE CONTROL

9

Ribbon end eyelet · Ribbon · Cruise cable connector · Flat · Cable end bead

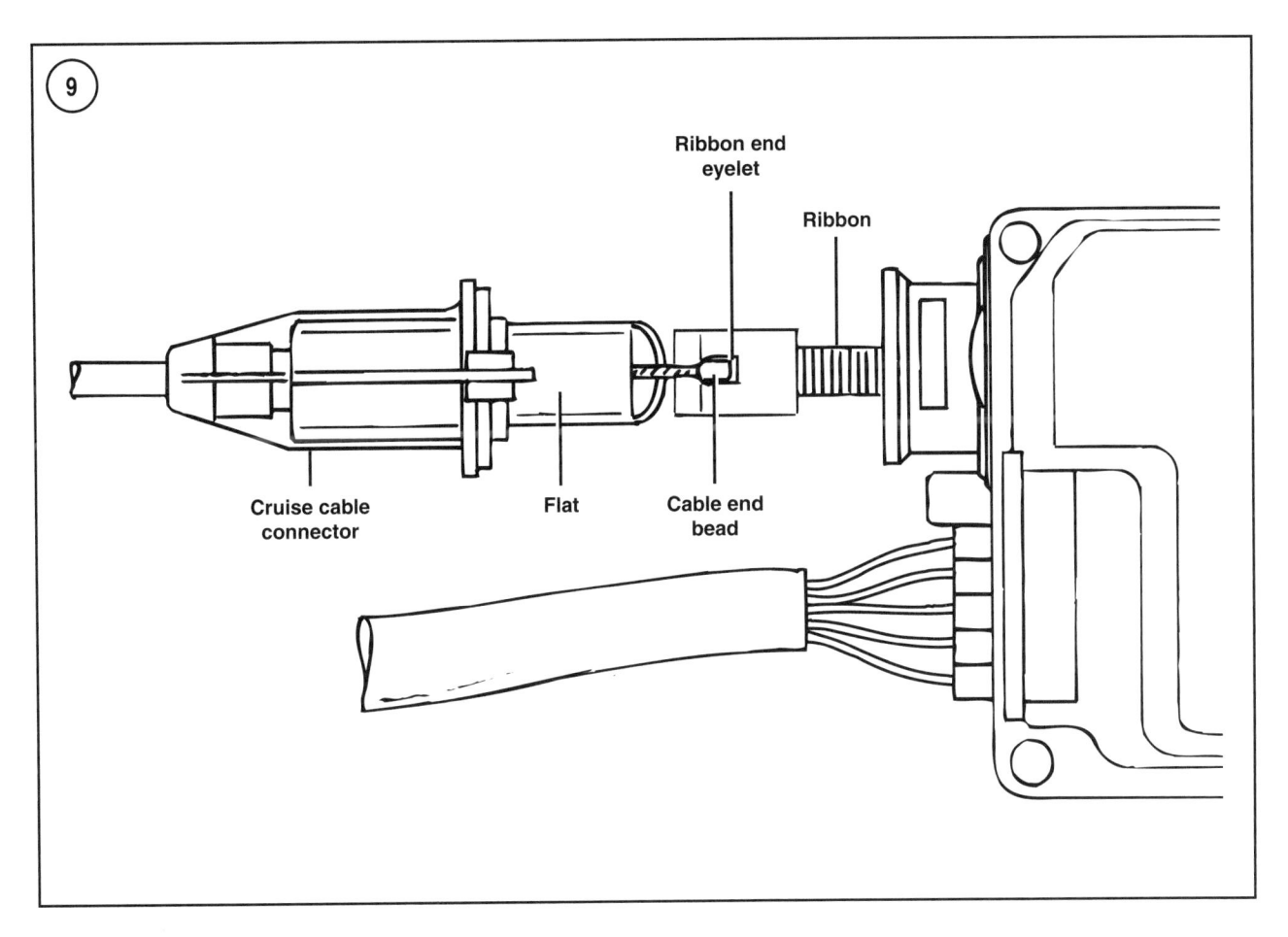

10

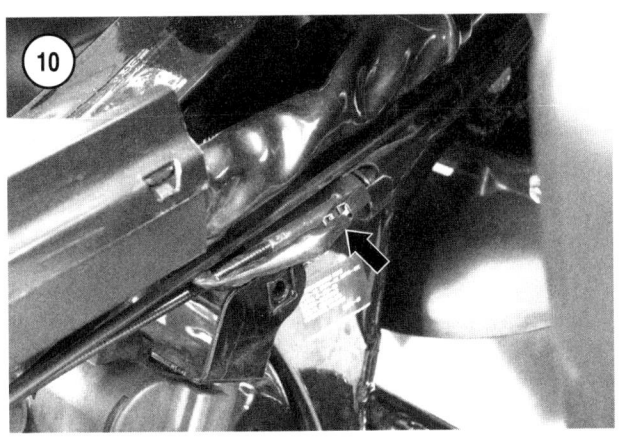

6. Release the SET/RESUME switch from the RESUME position.
7. On the right side handlebar switch, push the cruise control SET/RESUME switch to the RESUME position and hold it on.
8. Increase engine RPM and return to idle. The cruise control module will pull the cable in until a RPM change is detected. The number of motor steps is stored in the memory.
9. After the engine has returned to idle speed, and the green cruise control engagement light (*C*) is extinguished, release the SET/RESUME switch from the RESUME position.
10. Turn the ignition switch off.

CONTROL CABLES REPLACEMENT (2006-2007 MODELS)

Throttle and Idle Cables

NOTE
The 2008 models are not equipped with throttle or cruise control cables as the system is controlled electronically by the ECM.

Removal

1. Perform Steps 1-17 of *Throttle and Idle Cables (2006-2007 Non-Cruise Control Models), Removal* in Chapter Nine (carbureted models) or Steps 1-19 of *Throttle and Idle Cables (2006-2007 Non-Cruise Control Models), Removal* in Chapter Ten (EFI models).
2. On the right side of the motorcycle, locate the roll-off switch that is an integral part of the idle cable just behind the steering head.
3. Push the rubber boot (**Figure 10**) toward the front to expose the electrical connectors and remove the insulators from the spade terminals.
4. Use needle nose pliers, carefully disconnect both female spade connectors from the roll-off switch terminals (**Figure 11**).
5. Remove the cables from the frame.

①

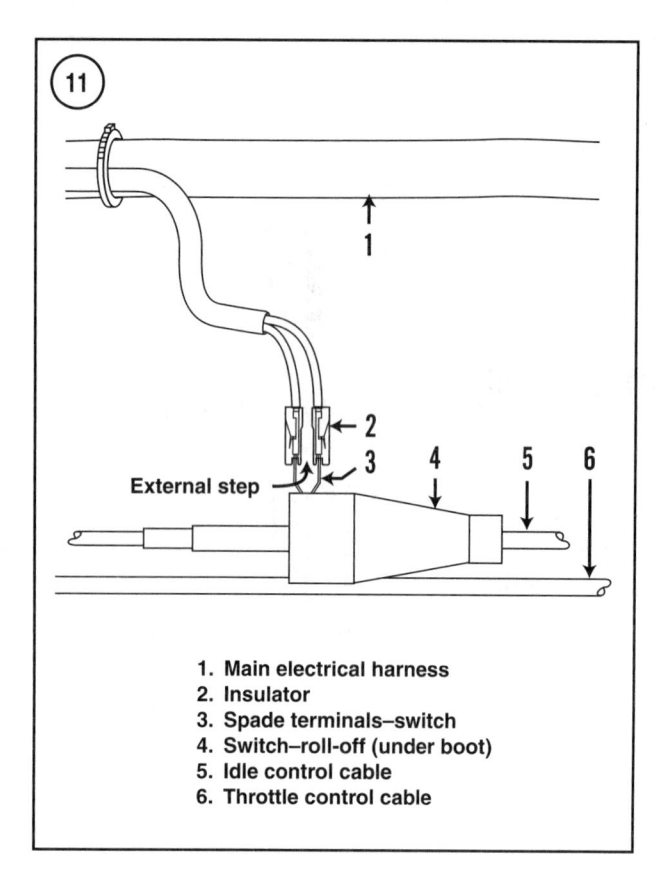

1. Main electrical harness
2. Insulator
3. Spade terminals–switch
4. Switch–roll-off (under boot)
5. Idle control cable
6. Throttle control cable

Installation

1. Perform Steps 1-14 of *Throttle and Idle Cables (2006-2007 Non-Cruise Control Models), Installation* in Chapter Nine (carbureted models) or Steps 1-13 of *Throttle and Idle Cables (2006-2007 Non-Cruise Control Models), Installation* in Chapter Ten (EFI models).
2. If necessary, straighten the switch terminals. The terminals must be parallel and line up perpendicular to the idle cable as shown in **Figure 11**.
3. Position the roll-off switch wires so the leads point straight down.
4. Position the idle cable so the switch spade terminals are at top.
5. Make sure the wires are not tangled and that the ends are free.
6. Connect both female spade connectors onto the roll-off switch terminals with the external step on the insulators facing each other. The connectors can be installed onto either switch terminal. Make sure the spade connectors are pushed on securely.
7. Slide the rubber boot over the cruise control roll-off switch with the oval cut located at the space terminal connections.
8. Position the throttle cable below the idle cable.
9. Perform Steps 16-24 of *Throttle and Idle Cables (2006-2007 Non-Cruise Control Models), Installation* in Chapter Nine (carbureted models) or Steps 15-21 of *Throttle and Idle Cables (2006-2007 Non-Cruise Control Models), Installation* in Chapter Ten (EFI models).
10. Adjust the cables as described in this chapter.

⑫ CRUISE CONTROL MODULE (2006-2007 MODELS)

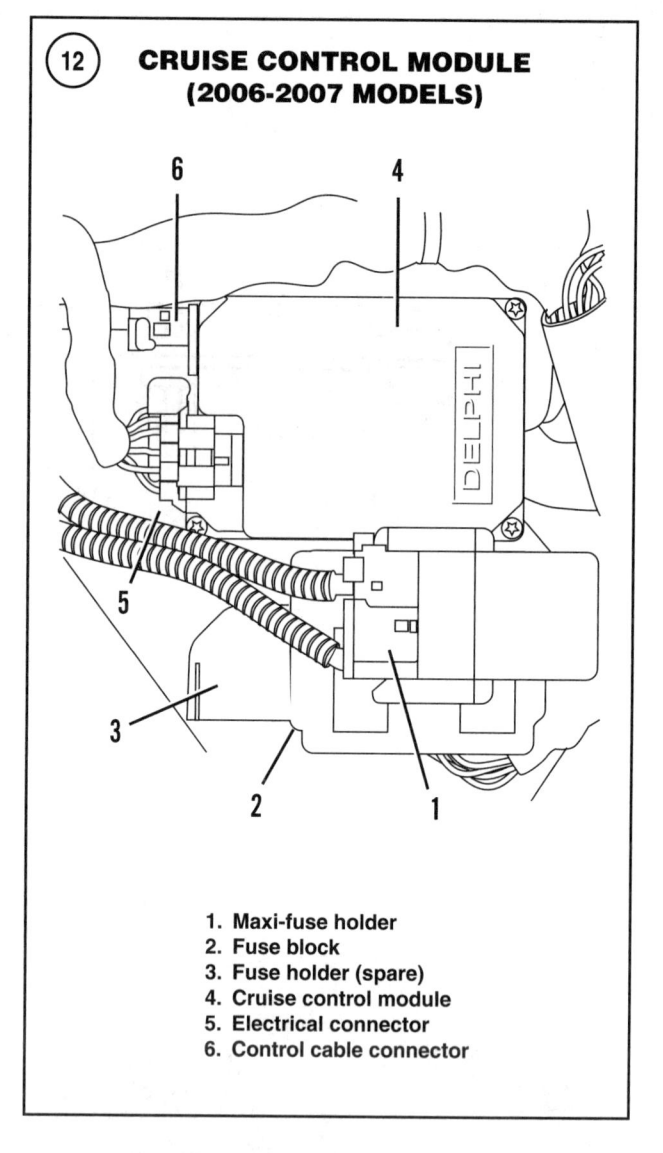

1. Maxi-fuse holder
2. Fuse block
3. Fuse holder (spare)
4. Cruise control module
5. Electrical connector
6. Control cable connector

CRUISE CONTROL MODULE (2006-2007 MODELS)

Removal/Installation

Refer to **Figure 12**.
1. Remove the battery as described in Chapter Eleven.
2. Disconnect the cruise control stepper cable from the module as described in this chapter.
3. Lift the lock and disconnect the 10-pin cruise control electrical connector (**Figure 5**) from the module.
4. Working within the battery box, remove the three flange nuts from the cruise control module mounting studs.
5. Carefully remove the cruise control module from the outer surface of the battery box. Do not lose the rubber grommet on each mounting stud.
6. Install by reversing the removal steps, while noting the following:
   a. Install the rubber grommet onto each mounting stud.
   b. Tighten the mounting flange nuts to 60-96 in.-lb. (6.8-10.8 N•m).

CRUISE CONTROL SWITCHES

ON/OFF Switch Replacement

1. Disassemble the left side switch assembly (**Figure 13**) as described in *Handlebar Switch Replacement* (Chapter Eleven).
2. Locate the switch and partially remove it from the switch housing.

NOTE
New replacement switches wires are cut to a length of 2 in. (50 mm) and the insulation partially stripped.

3. Cut the following wires about 1 1/2 inch from the old ON/OFF switch:
   a. 2006-2007 models: black, red/green and orange/violet.
   b. 2008-2009 models: black/green, red/green and orange/violet.
   c. Discard the old switch.
4. Slide a one-inch piece of dual wall heat shrink tubing, supplied with the new switch, over each wire.
5. Securely splice the new switch onto the existing wires and solder the connection.
6. Cover each splice with the dual wall heat shrink tubing.
7. Assemble the left side switch as described in Chapter Eleven.

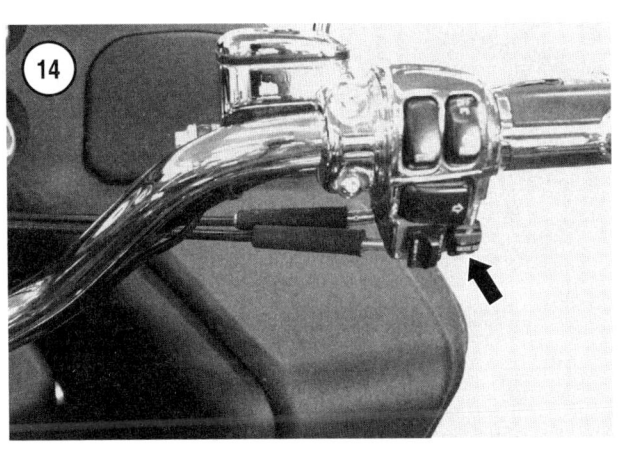

SET/RESUME Switch Replacement

1. Disassemble the right side switch assembly (**Figure 14**) as described in *Handlebar Switch Replacement* (Chapter Eleven).
2. Locate the switch and partially remove it from the switch housing.

NOTE
New replacement switches wires are cut to a length of 2 in. (50 mm) and the insulation partially stripped.

3. Cut the following wires about 1 1/2 inch from the old SET/RESUME switch:
   a. Blue/black, orange/white and white/blue.
   b. Discard the old switch.
4. Slide a one-inch piece of dual wall heat shrink tubing, supplied with the new switch, over each wire.
5. Securely splice the new switch onto the existing wires and solder the connection.
6. Cover the splice with the dual wall heat shrink tubing.
7. Assemble the right side switch as described in Chapter Eleven.

Table 1 CRUISE CONTROL TORQUE SPECIFICATIONS

Item	ft.-lb.	in.-lb.	N•m
Cruise control module mounting flange nuts	–	60-96	6.8-10.8

CHAPTER SEVENTEEN

BODY AND FRAME

This chapter describes the removal and installation of the body and frame components. Handle the body panels carefully to protect the finish and note that many are fragile. Once the component is removed, attach all loose mounting hardware to avoid misplacing them. If a component is going to be left off for a period of time, wrap it with a blanket or towel and place it in a safe location.

Table 1 is located at the end of this chapter.

SEATS

Removal/Installation

Refer to **Figure 1** and **Figure 2**.
1. Place the motorcycle on level ground on the jiffy stand.
2. On 2006-2007 FLHR models, perform the following:
   a. Remove the screw securing the back or the passenger seat to the top of the rear fender. Slightly lift up on the rear of the passenger seat, slide it toward the rear and remove it.
   b. Remove the two hex nuts securing the rear of the rider seat bracket to the mounting studs.
   c. Push the rider seat toward the rear and disengage the front bracket from the slot in the frame backbone. Remove the rider seat.
3. Observe the location of the passenger seat strap mounting bolt. Remove the saddlebag from that side as described in this chapter.
4. Remove the bolt and washer securing the passenger seat strap, on models so equipped. Pull on the strap and free it from the slot in the strap bracket. On models so equipped, carefully pull the strap through the slots in the seat.
5. Remove the screw (**Figure 3**) securing the rider seat bracket to the top of the rear fender.
6. Lift up on the rear (A, **Figure 4**) of the rider seat and pull toward the rear and disengage the front bracket from the slot in the frame backbone, or fuel tank bracket. On models with heated seats, disconnect the 4-pin electrical connector from the main harness on the right side. Remove the seat.
7. On FLHT models equipped with a backrest, remove the nut securing the backrest to the bracket and remove the backrest.
8. Inspect the screws securing the seat front mounting tab (**Figure 5**) and bracket (**Figure 6**). Replace if necessary.

WARNING
*Do not compress any of the fuel tank hoses (A, **Figure 7**) during seat installation.*

9. On models with heated seats, connect the 4-pin electrical connector to the main harness on the right side.
10. Place the seat on the frame. Firmly push down on the front of the seat and push it forward and engage the front bracket into the slot in the frame backbone, or fuel tank bracket (B, **Figure 7**). Push the seat down and install the screw securing the back of the passenger seat to the top of the rear fender.
11. Install the screw and washer (**Figure 3**) or hex nuts, securing the rear of the rider seat to the top of the rear fender. Tighten the screw or nuts securely.
12. Pull up on the front of the seat (B, **Figure 4**) to ensure the seat front hook is secured in place in the frame backbone, or fuel tank, slot.
13. Correctly position the seat strap onto the seat. Carefully insert the strap through the slots in the seat. On models so

BODY AND FRAME

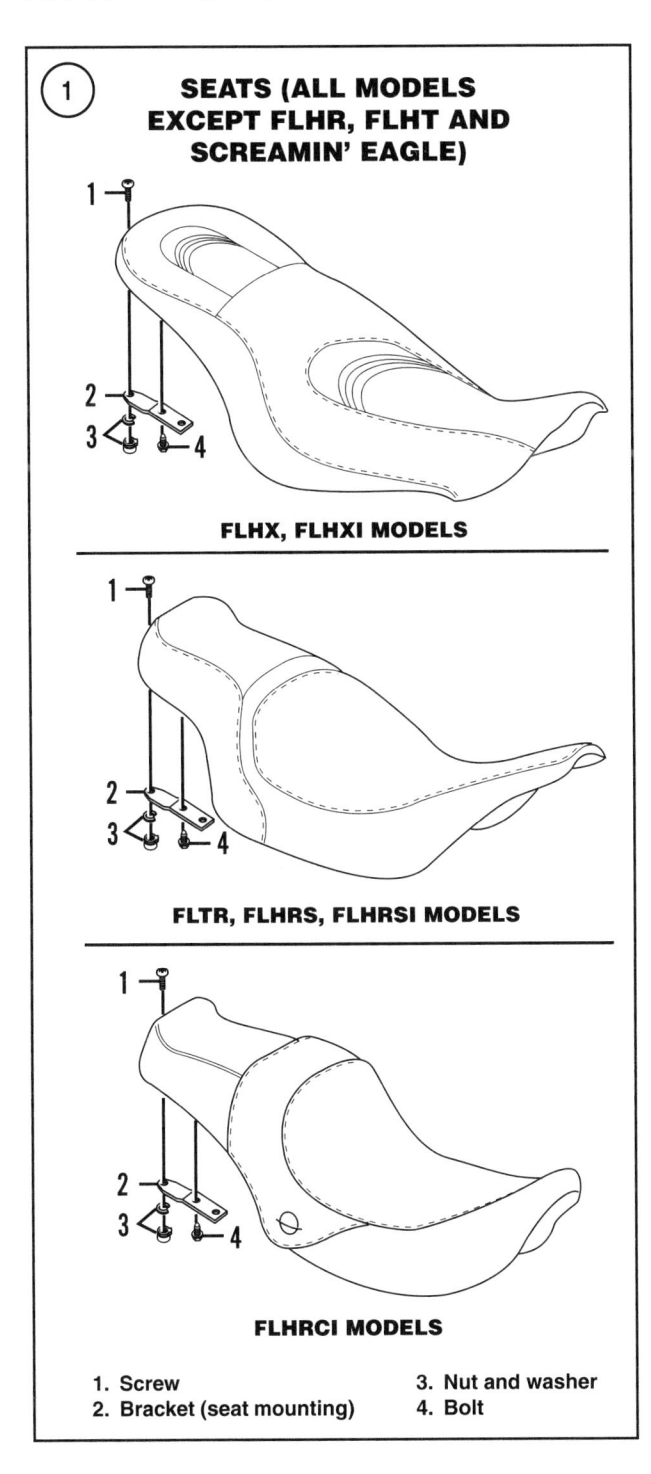

① SEATS (ALL MODELS EXCEPT FLHR, FLHT AND SCREAMIN' EAGLE)

FLHX, FLHXI MODELS

FLTR, FLHRS, FLHRSI MODELS

FLHRCI MODELS

1. Screw
2. Bracket (seat mounting)
3. Nut and washer
4. Bolt

② SEATS (SCREAMIN' EAGLE MODELS)

1. Screw
2. Backrest
3. Screw and washer
4. Grab strap
5. Seat
6. Bolt
7. Bracket (seat mounting)
8. Nut and washer
9. Locknut
10. Washer (nylon)
11. Bracket
12. Clip nut
13. Locknut
14. Mounting bracket

equipped, insert the strap into the slot in the strap bracket and make sure it is correctly seated.

14. Install the bolt and washer securing the passenger seat strap, on models so equipped. Tighten the bolt securely.

15. On FLHT models equipped with a backrest, install the backrest and tighten the nut securely.

16. On 2006-2007 FLHR models, perform the following:
    a. Install the passenger seat onto the top of the rear fender. Push it forward against the rider seat, install the mounting screw and tighten securely.
    b. Install the two hex nuts securing the rear of the rider seat bracket to the mounting studs and tighten securely.

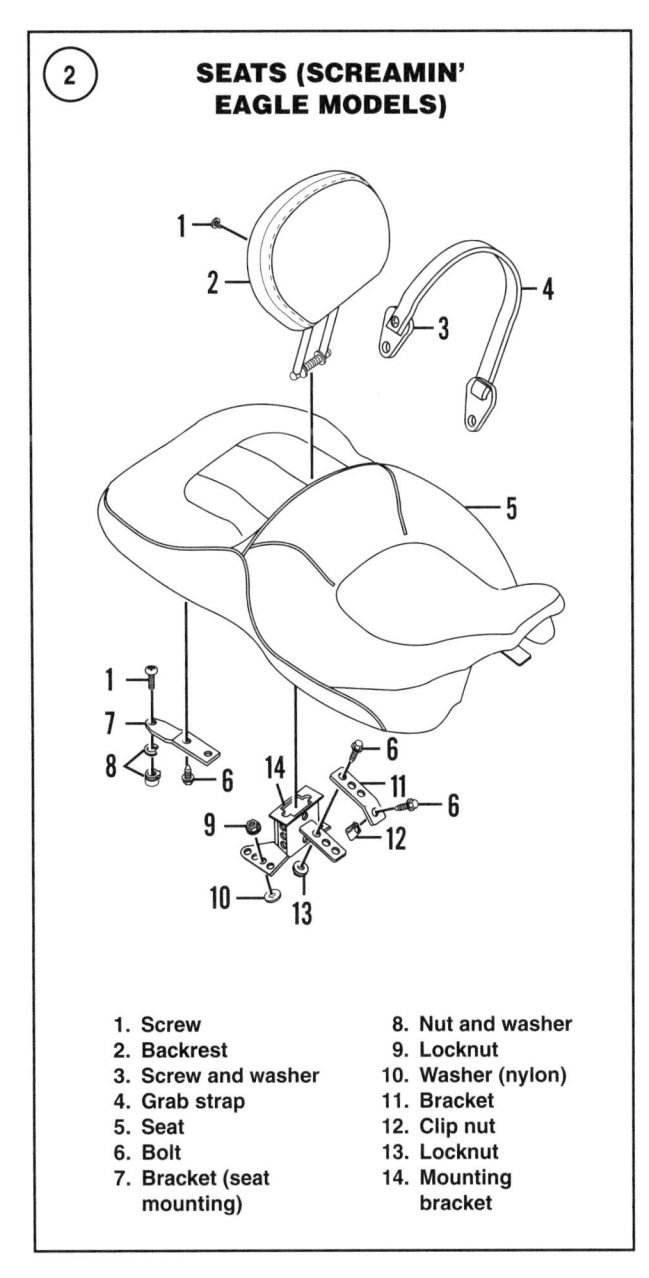

RIDER AND PASSENGER BACKRESTS

Rider Backrest and Bracket (2007-2008 FLHRSE Models)
Removal/Installation

Refer to **Figure 8**.

1. Spread the covering at the base of the backrest. Squeeze together the two spring-loaded backrest support arms.
2. Carefully pull straight up and remove the backrest from the mounting bracket.
3. Remove the rider seat as described in this chapter.
4. Remove the screw and frame clip securing the mounting bracket support.
5. Remove the screw and nut and separate the mounting bracket support from the backrest mounting bracket.
6. Remove the two flange nuts securing the backrest mounting bracket to the top of the rear fender.

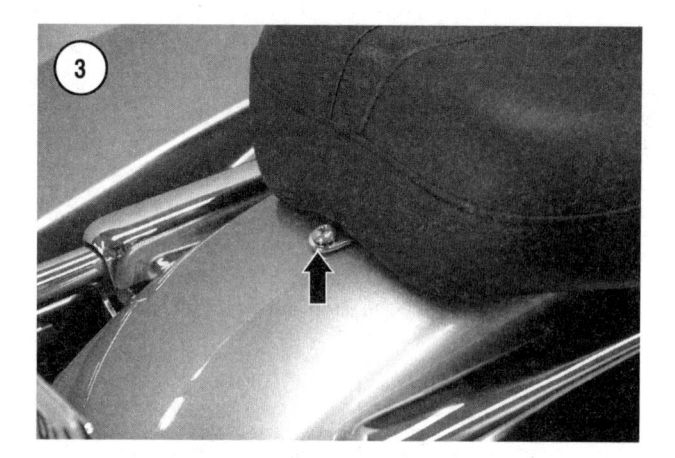

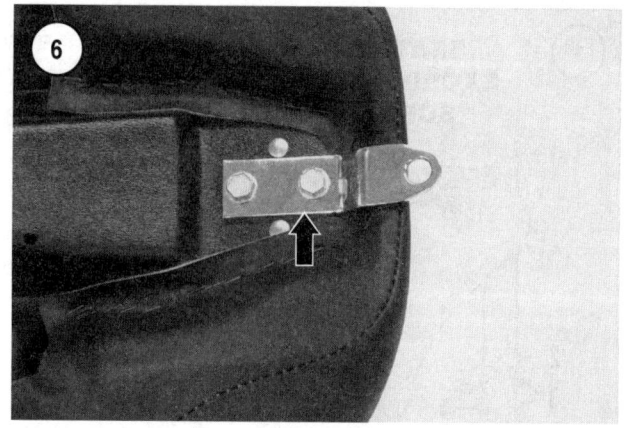

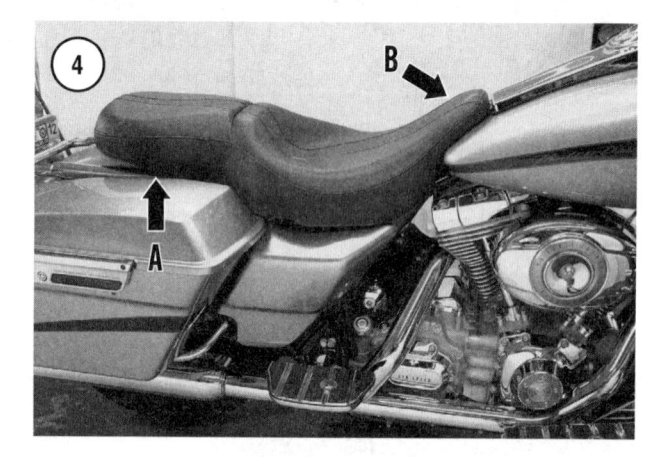

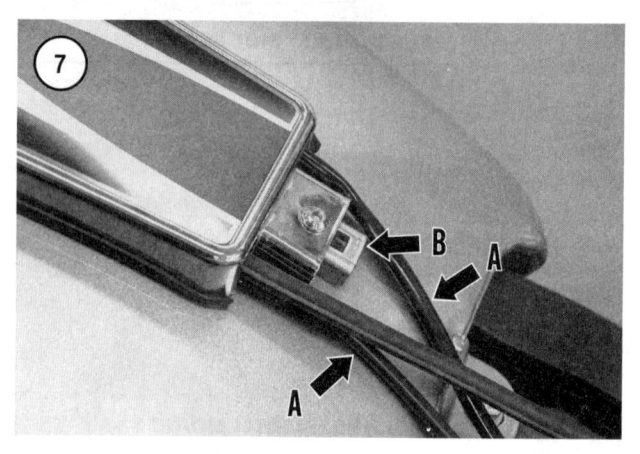

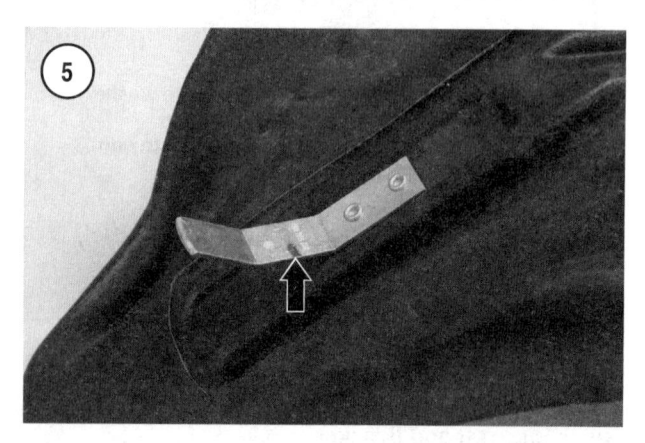

7. Remove the backrest mounting bracket and two nylon washers from the threaded studs on the stud plate.
8. Lower the rear wheel and remove the stud plate from the underside of the rear fender, if necessary.
9. Install by reversing the removal steps. Tighten the screws and flange nuts securely.

Passenger Backrest (2007-2008 FLHRSE Models) Removal/Installation

Refer to **Figure 9**.
1. Remove both saddlebags as described in this chapter.
2. Push in the spring-loaded latches and swivel the latches toward the rear on each side of the support.

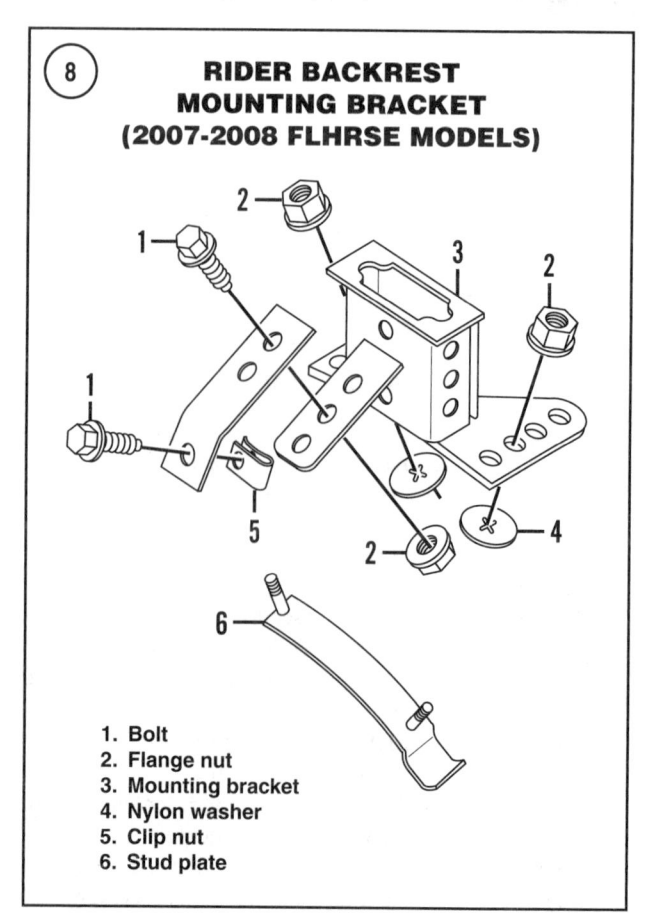

RIDER BACKREST MOUNTING BRACKET (2007-2008 FLHRSE MODELS)

1. Bolt
2. Flange nut
3. Mounting bracket
4. Nylon washer
5. Clip nut
6. Stud plate

BODY AND FRAME

PASSENGER BACKREST (2007-2008 FLHRSE MODELS)

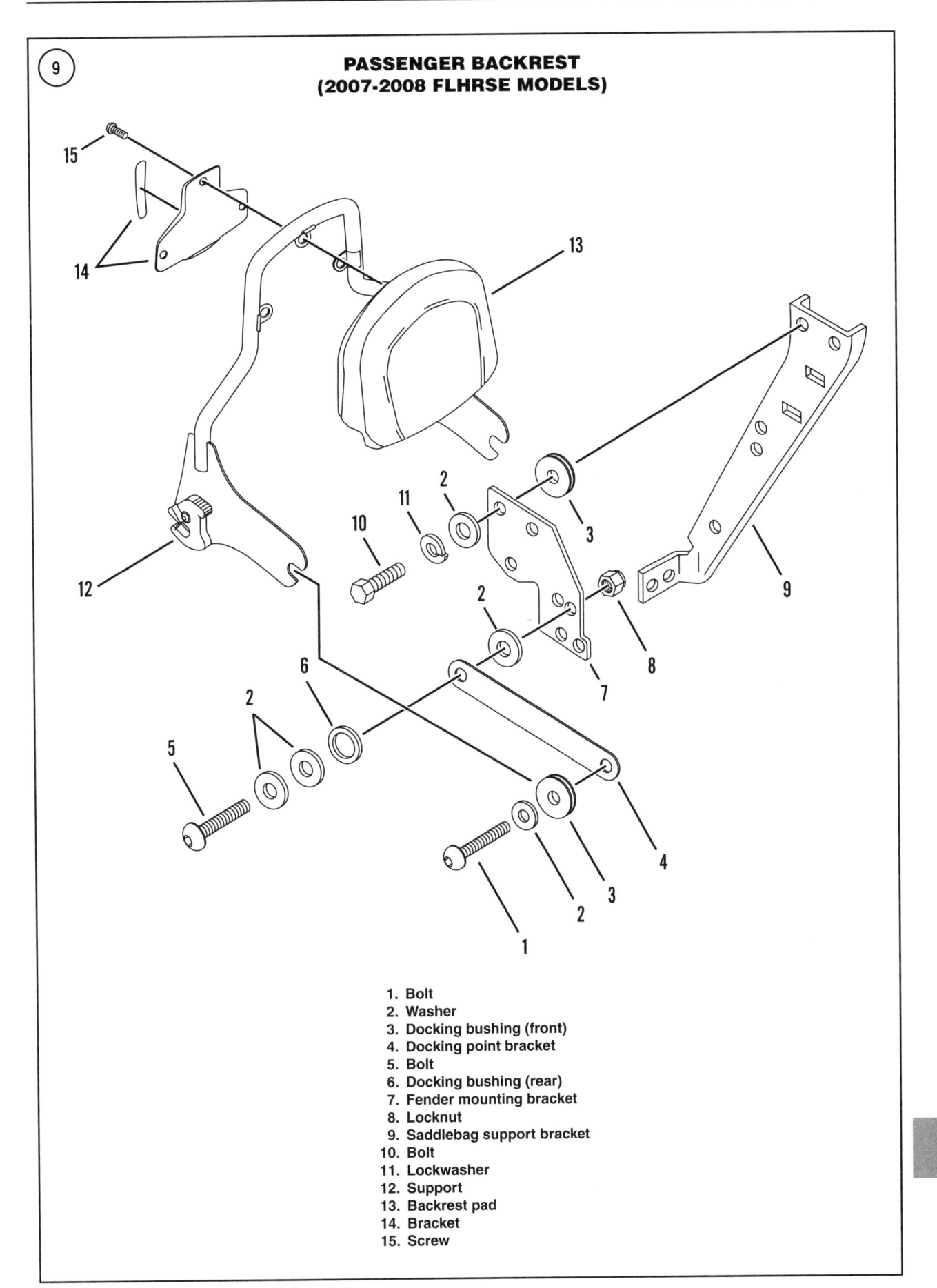

1. Bolt
2. Washer
3. Docking bushing (front)
4. Docking point bracket
5. Bolt
6. Docking bushing (rear)
7. Fender mounting bracket
8. Locknut
9. Saddlebag support bracket
10. Bolt
11. Lockwasher
12. Support
13. Backrest pad
14. Bracket
15. Screw

CHAPTER SEVENTEEN

PASSENGER BACKREST (2009 FLTRSE MODELS)

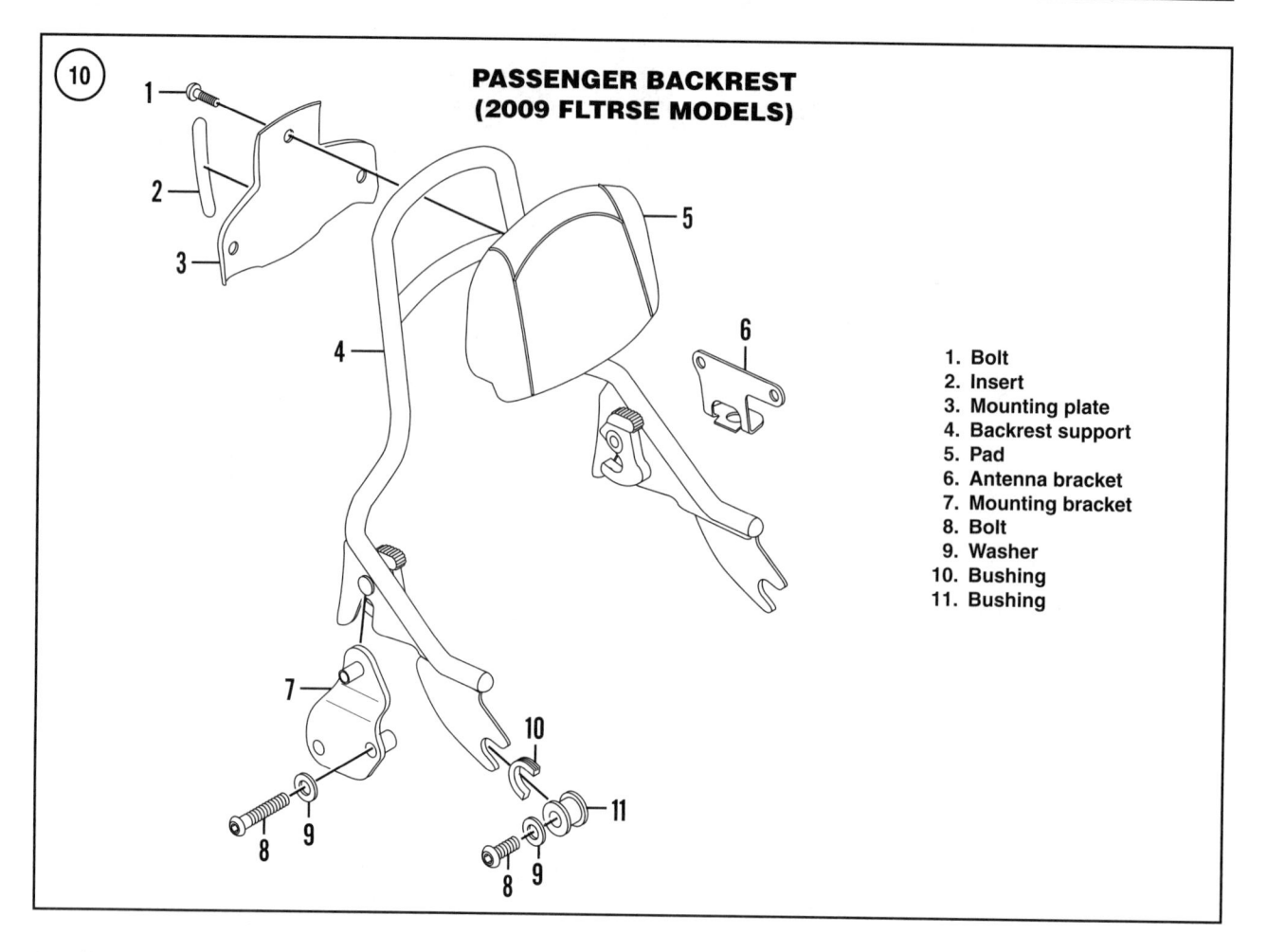

1. Bolt
2. Insert
3. Mounting plate
4. Backrest support
5. Pad
6. Antenna bracket
7. Mounting bracket
8. Bolt
9. Washer
10. Bushing
11. Bushing

3. Lift the backrest support up, and then move it toward the rear, unlocking the front of the backrest from the rear docking bushing. Remove the backrest from the frame.
4. Secure the nut behind the fender mounting bracket, and remove the bolt and washer securing the front docking point bushing, and then remove the bushing.
5. Remove the bolt and washer securing the rear docking point bushing, and then remove the docking point bracket.
6. Remove the top two bolts, lockwashers and washers securing the fender mounting bracket.
7. Cover the saddlebag filler strip to protect the finish, and remove the lower bolt and washer securing the fender mounting bracket.
8. Remove the fender mounting bracket assembly.
9. Install by reversing the removal steps, while noting the following:
   a. Tighten the fender mount bracket bolts to 15-20 ft.-lb. (20.3-27.1 N•m).
   b. Tighten the rear docking bolt to 15-20 ft.-lb. (20.3-27.1 N•m).

Passenger Backrest (2009 FLTRSE3 Models) Removal/Installation

Refer to **Figure 10**.

1. To remove the passenger backrest, perform the following:
   a. Push in on the spring-loaded locking latches, and pull the swivel latches toward the rear.
   b. Lift up on the backrest, and then move it toward the rear and release the backrest from the front docking point on the frame.
   c. Remove the passenger backrest from the frame.
2. To replace the front docking point bushing, remove the screw, washer and bushing from the frame. Repeat for the remaining side if necessary.
3. To replace the backrest brackets, perform the following:
   a. On the right side, remove the bolt and washer securing the bracket to the frame, and remove the bracket.
   b. On the left side, remove the bolt and washer securing the bracket and antenna bracket to the frame. Remove the bracket and antenna bracket.
4. Install the backrest, and antenna bracket, and tighten the screw to 16.7 ft.-lb. (22.6 N•m).
5. Install the backrest bushing assembly and tighten the screw to 120 in.-lb. (13.6 N•m).

REAR FRAME RAILS

Rear Frame Rails (2006-2008 Models) Removal/Installation

Refer to **Figure 11** and **Figure 12**.

BODY AND FRAME

SEAT AND REAR FRAME RAIL (2006-2008 FLHR MODELS)

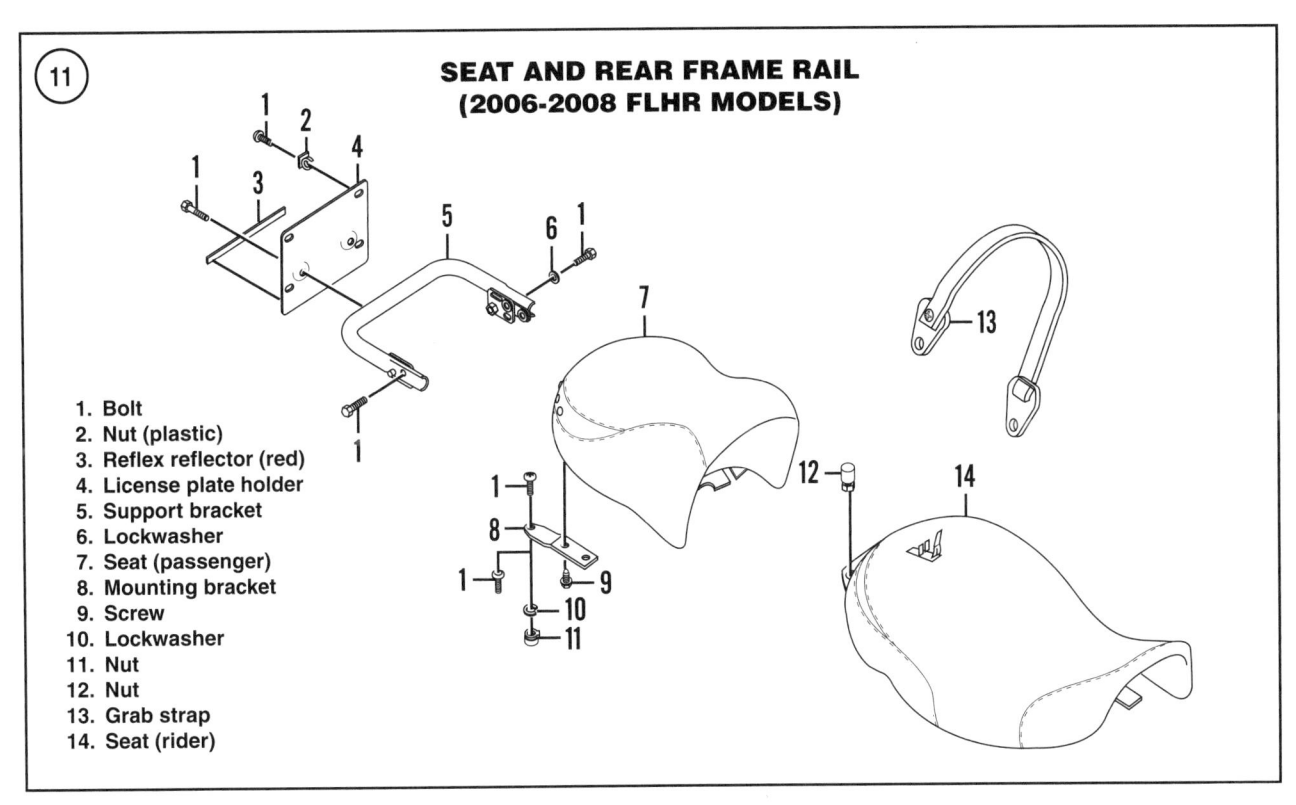

1. Bolt
2. Nut (plastic)
3. Reflex reflector (red)
4. License plate holder
5. Support bracket
6. Lockwasher
7. Seat (passenger)
8. Mounting bracket
9. Screw
10. Lockwasher
11. Nut
12. Nut
13. Grab strap
14. Seat (rider)

SEAT AND REAR FRAME RAIL (2006-2008 FLHT MODELS)

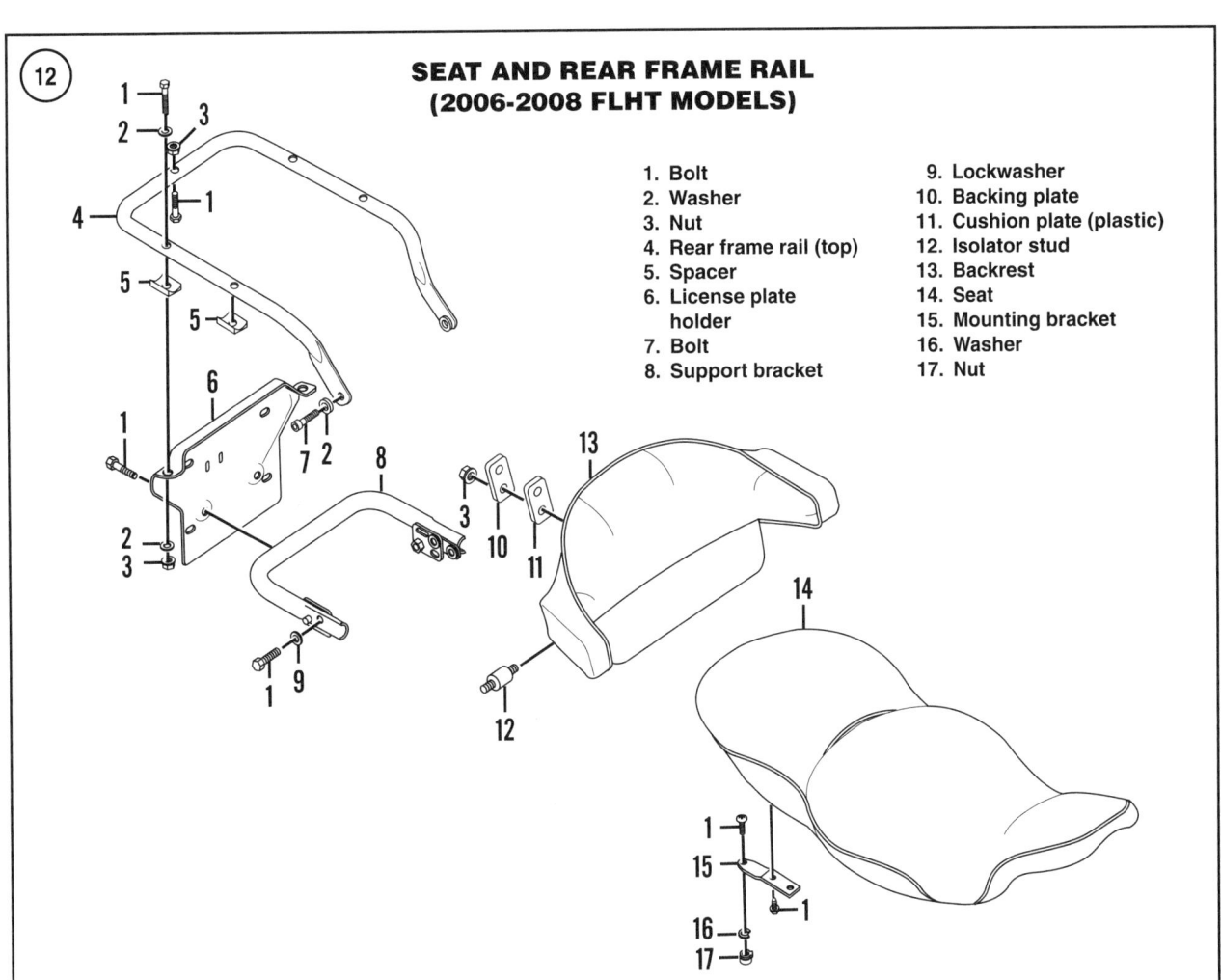

1. Bolt
2. Washer
3. Nut
4. Rear frame rail (top)
5. Spacer
6. License plate holder
7. Bolt
8. Support bracket
9. Lockwasher
10. Backing plate
11. Cushion plate (plastic)
12. Isolator stud
13. Backrest
14. Seat
15. Mounting bracket
16. Washer
17. Nut

17

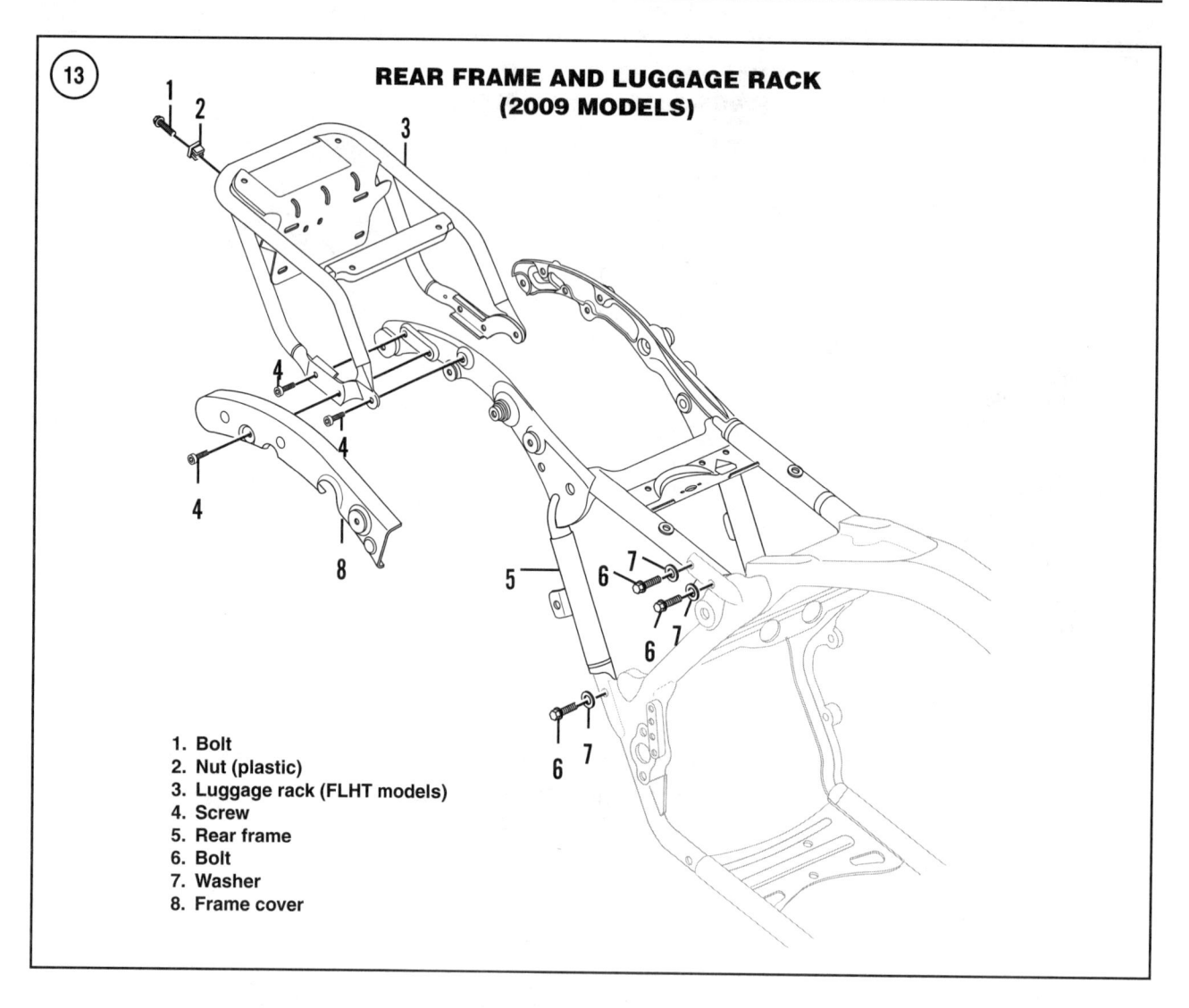

REAR FRAME AND LUGGAGE RACK (2009 MODELS)

⑬

1. Bolt
2. Nut (plastic)
3. Luggage rack (FLHT models)
4. Screw
5. Rear frame
6. Bolt
7. Washer
8. Frame cover

---

1. Remove the rider and passenger seats as described in this chapter.
2. Remove both saddlebags as described in this chapter.
3. Remove the Tour-Pak assembly as described in this chapter.
4. On models so equipped, remove the backrest as described in this chapter.
5A. On FLHR models, remove the bolts and lockwashers securing the support bracket to the frame. Then, remove the assembly.
5B. On FLHT models, do not separate the license plate holder from the supports brackets. Remove the bolts and lockwashers securing the top and bottom support bracket to the frame. Then, remove the assembly.
6. Install by reversing the removal steps. Tighten the screws securely.

Rear Frame/Luggage Rack (2009 Models)

Refer to **Figure 13**.

1. Support the motorcycle with the rear wheel off the ground.
2. Remove the rider and passenger seats as described in this chapter.
3. Remove the left frame side cover as described in this chapter.
4. Remove both saddlebags as described in this chapter.
5. Remove the Tour-Pak assembly as described in this chapter.
6. Remove the screws securing the top electrical caddy and move it out of the way as described in Chapter Eleven.
7. Remove the battery and battery tray as described in Chapter Eleven.
8. Note the location of the straps securing the wiring harness on each side of the rear frame. Cut the straps and move the wiring harnesses out of the way.
9. Remove both shock absorbers as described in Chapter Fourteen.
10. Remove the luggage rack as follows:
    a. Remove the bolts and washers securing the seat strap and forward saddlebag bracket. Remove the seat strap and the bracket.
    b. Remove the two bolts securing the frame cover and part of the luggage rack on each side. Then, remove the cover.

BODY AND FRAME

FRONT FENDER (ALL MODELS EXCEPT SCREAMIN' EAGLE)

1. Wiring harness
2. Clip
3. Bulb
4. Screw
5. Lens
6. Plug (HDI)
7. Grommet (wiring harness)
8. Front fender
9. Washer
10. Bolt
11. Lockplate
12. Bolt
13. Nut
14. Side trim
15. Trim skirt (models so equipped)
16. Nut
17. Nut
18. Reflex reflector (amber)
19. Locknut
20. Washer
21. Bracket (bumper)
22. Push nut
23. Bumper cushion (models so equipped)
24. Fender tip kit (models so equipped)
25. Bumper (models so equipped)
26. Light assembly

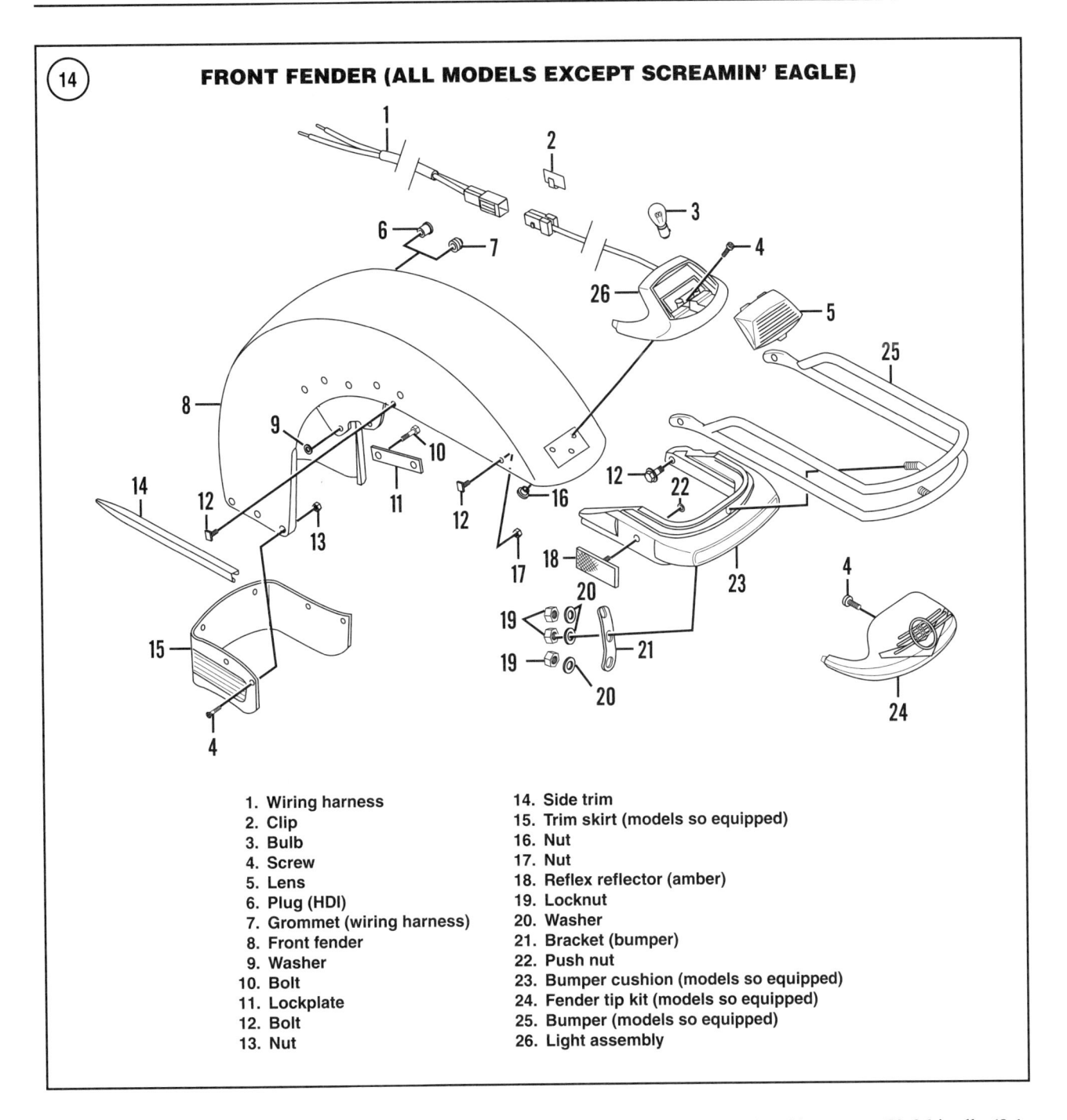

c. Remove the remaining two bolts on each side and remove the luggage rack.

11. Remove the two bolts securing the left side electrical caddy and move it out of the way as described in Chapter Eleven.

12. Remove the three bolts and hardened washers on each side securing the rear frame to the main frame. Carefully pull the rear frame toward the rear and remove it. Install the bolts and washers onto the rear frame to avoid misplacing them.

13. Install the rear frame and luggage by reversing the removal steps. Note the following bolt torque specifications:
   a. Rear frame bolts and hardened washers: 40-50 ft.-lb. (54.2-67.8 N•m).
   b. Left side electrical caddy screws: 72-96 in.-lb. (8.1-10.8 N•m).
   c. Battery tray screws: 72-96 in.-lb. (8.1-10.8 N•m).
   d. Luggage rack screws: 15-20 ft.-lb. (20.3-27.1 N•m).
   e. Seat strap and forward saddlebag bracket screw: 15-20 ft.-lb. (20.3-27.1 N•m).
   f. Top electrical caddy: 72-96 in.-lb. (8.1-10.8 N•m).

FRONT FENDER

Removal/Installation
(All Models Except Screamin' Eagle)

Refer to **Figure 14**.

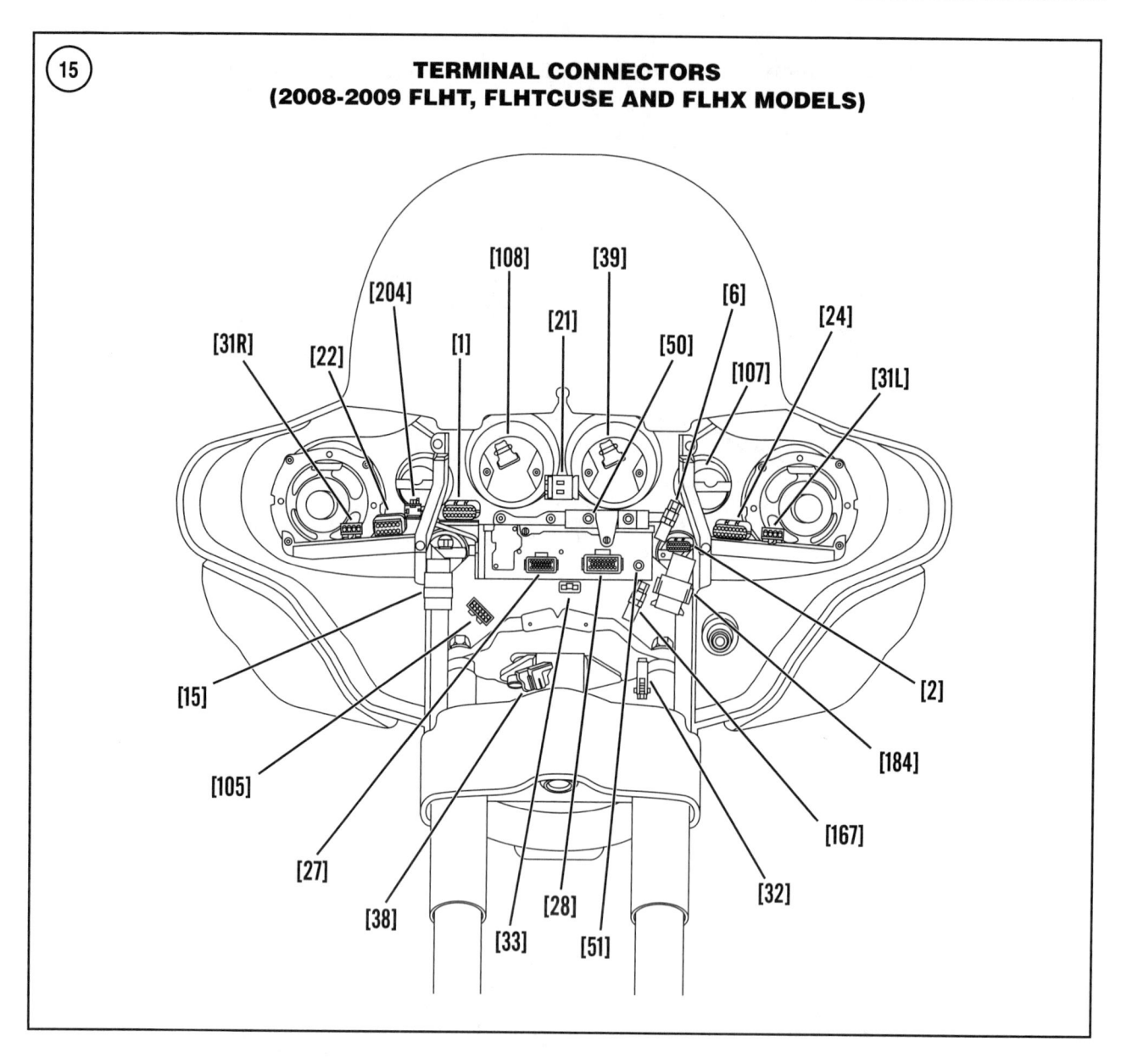

TERMINAL CONNECTORS (2008-2009 FLHT, FLHTCUSE AND FLHX MODELS)

1. Support the motorcycle with the front wheel off the ground as described in *Motorcycle Stands* (Chapter Twelve).

NOTE
Always disarm the optional TSSM/HFSM security system before disconnecting the battery or pulling the Maxi-Fuse so the siren will not sound.

2. Disconnect the negative battery cable as described in Chapter Eleven.
3A. On all FLHT, FLHTCUSE and FLHX models, perform the following:
   a. Remove the outer portion of the front fairing as described in this chapter.
   b. On the left side of the inner front fairing, locate and disconnect the 2-pin front fender tip lamp connector (**Figure 15**).
   c. Carefully pull the electrical connector free from the inner front fairing.
3B. On all FLHR models, perform the following:
   a. Remove the headlight unit as described in Chapter Eleven.
   b. Within the headlight case, locate and disconnect the 2-pin front fender tip lamp connector (**Figure 16**).
   c. Carefully pull the electrical connector free from within the headlight case.
4. On 2006-2007 models, carefully cut the cable strap securing the fender tip lamp wire to the front brake line.
5. Remove the front wheel as described in Chapter Twelve.
6. Straighten the locking tabs away from the front fender mounting bolts (**Figure 17**).
7. Remove the mounting bolts and lock plates securing the front fender to the fork sliders.
8. Remove the front fender (**Figure 18**) from the fork sliders. Be careful not scratch the paint.

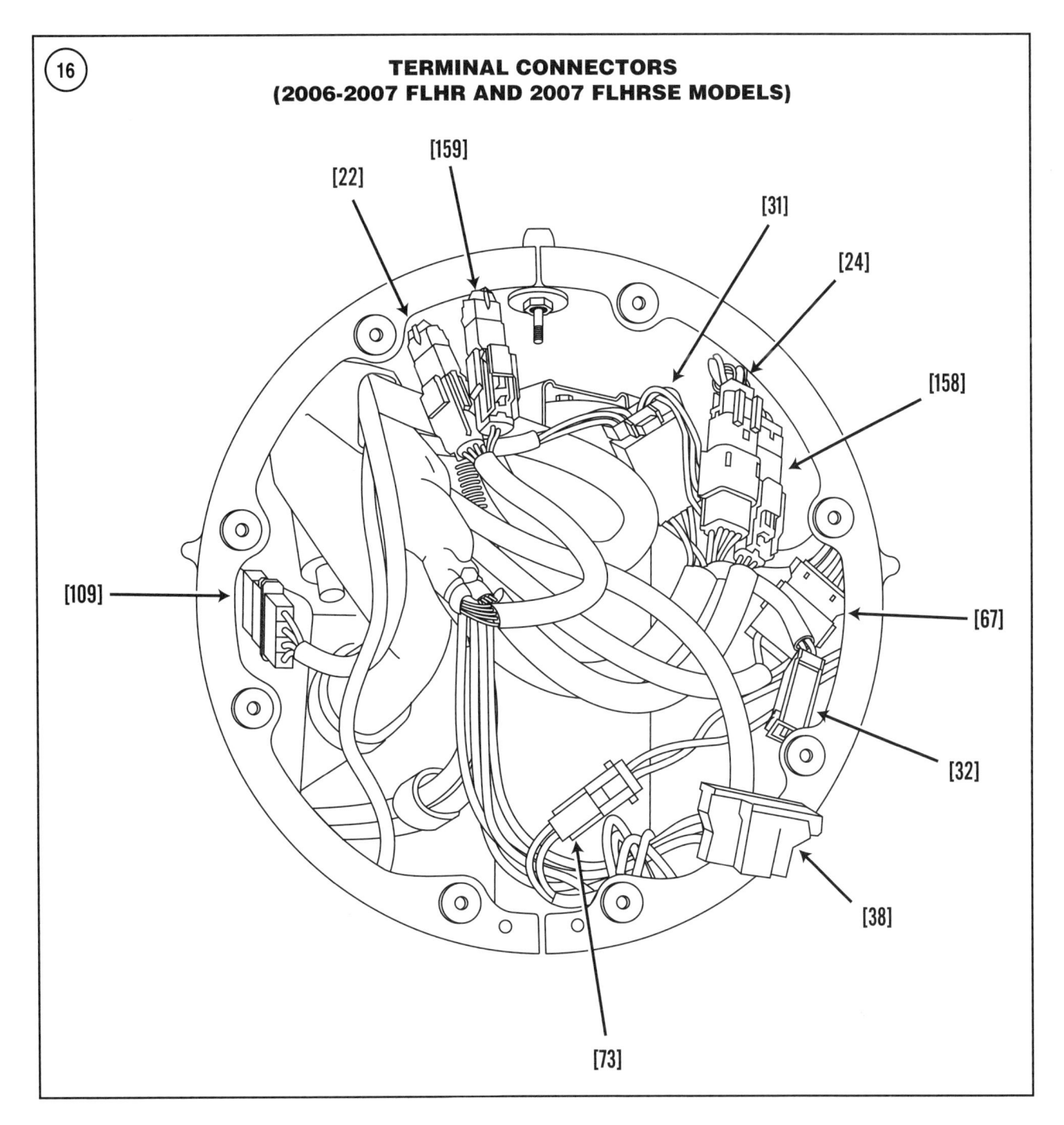

BODY AND FRAME 681

16 **TERMINAL CONNECTORS
(2006-2007 FLHR AND 2007 FLHRSE MODELS)**

[22] [159] [31] [24] [158] [109] [67] [32] [38] [73]

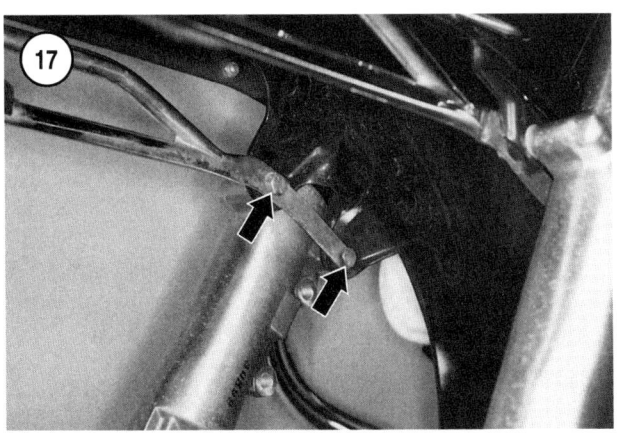

17

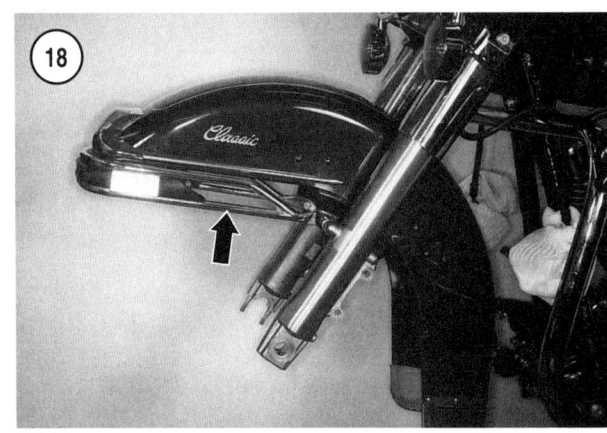

18

9. Install by reversing the removal steps. Note the following:
   a. Install the lock plates and tighten the bolts securely.
   b. Bend the locking tabs up against the bolt heads.

Removal/Installation (Screamin' Eagle Models)

Refer to **Figure 19** and **Figure 20**.

1. Support the motorcycle with the front wheel off the ground as described in *Motorcycle Stands* (Chapter Twelve.
2A. On 2007 FLHRSE3 models, perform the following:
   a. Remove the screws and nuts on each side securing the adapter to the front fender.
   b. Remove the front fender from the fork sliders. Be careful not scratch the paint.
   c. Remove the screws on each side securing the adapter to the fork legs and remove the adapter, if necessary.
2B. On all other models, perform the following:
   a. Straighten the locking tabs away from the front fender mounting bolts (**Figure 17**).
   b. Remove the mounting bolts and lock plates securing the front fender to the fork sliders.
   c. Remove the front fender from the fork sliders. Be careful not scratch the paint.
3. Install by reversing these removal steps while noting the following:
   a. Install the lock plates, on models so equipped, and install the front fender mounting bolts. Tighten the bolts securely.
   b. Bend the locking tabs, on models so equipped, up against the bolt heads.

REAR FENDER (ALL MODELS EXCEPT SCREAMIN' EAGLE)

Removal/Installation

Refer to **Figure 21**.

NOTE
Elevate the rear of the motorcycle sufficiently to allow the rear fender to roll back and over the rear wheel, as well as clear the frame rear cross member.

1. Support the motorcycle with the rear wheel slightly off the ground.

NOTE
Always disarm the optional TSSM/HFSM security system before disconnecting the battery or pulling the Maxi-Fuse so the siren will not sound.

2. Disconnect the negative battery cable as described in Chapter Eleven.
3. Remove the seat(s) as described in this chapter.
4. Remove both saddlebags as described in this chapter.

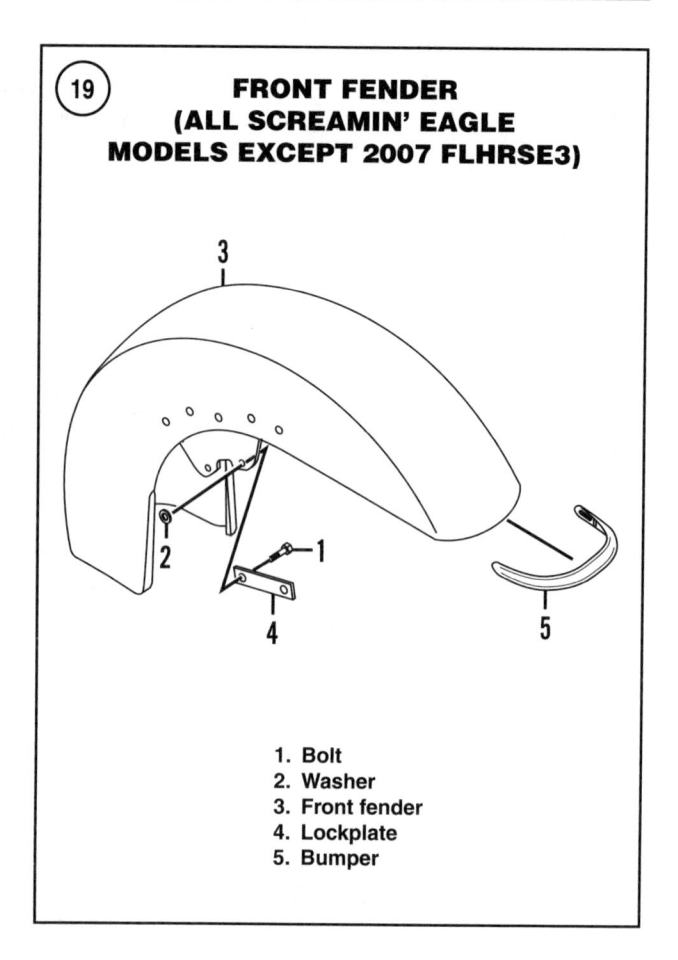

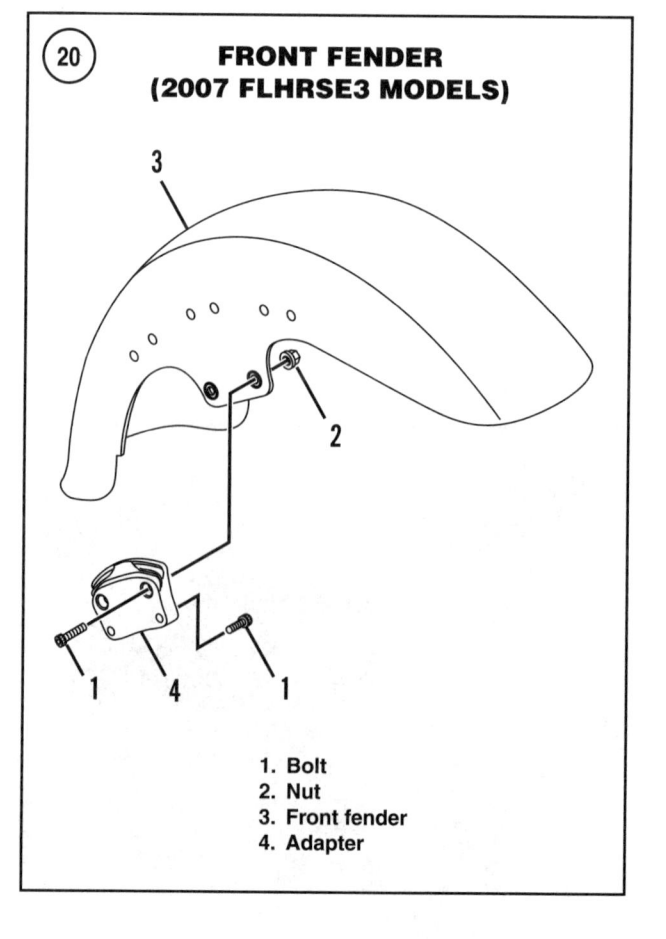

---

19 FRONT FENDER (ALL SCREAMIN' EAGLE MODELS EXCEPT 2007 FLHRSE3)

1. Bolt
2. Washer
3. Front fender
4. Lockplate
5. Bumper

20 FRONT FENDER (2007 FLHRSE3 MODELS)

1. Bolt
2. Nut
3. Front fender
4. Adapter

BODY AND FRAME 683

㉑ REAR FENDER (ALL MODELS EXCEPT SCREAMIN' EAGLE)

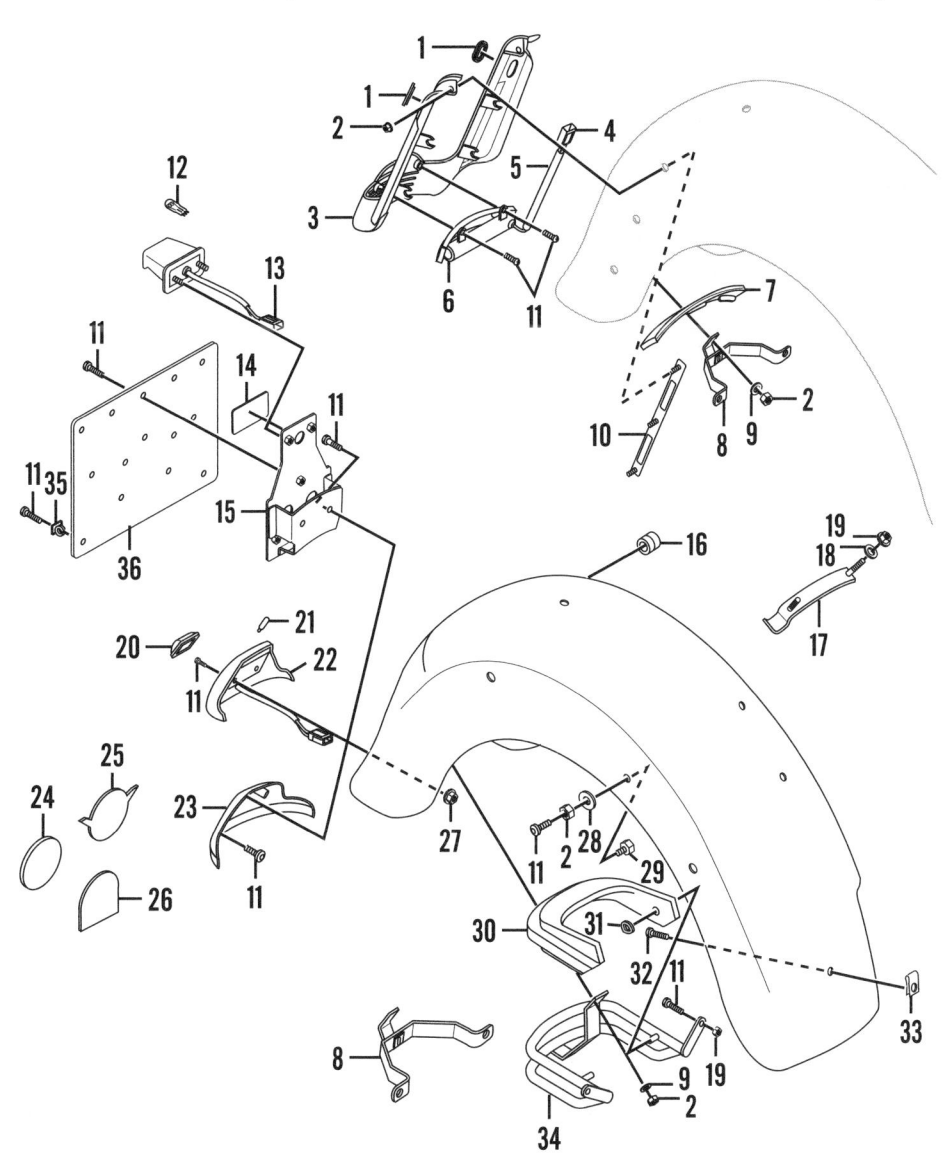

1. Grommet
2. Flange nut
3. Fascia trim (FLHX models)
4. Terminal housing
5. Wiring harness
6. Light assembly (FLHX models)
7. Support
8. Mounting bracket
9. Washer
10. Stud plate
11. Screw
12. Bulb
13. License plate light and wiring harness
14. Reflex reflector (red)
15. License plate mount (HDI models)
16. Grommet
17. Stud plate
18. Washer
19. Flange nut
20. Lens
21. Bulb
22. Lamp assembly (models so equipped)
23. Fender tip lamp assembly (models so equipped)
24. Emblem
25. Emblem
26. Emblem
27. Nut
28. Washer
29. Mounting boss
30. Bumper cushion
31. Nut
32. Screw
33. Clip nut
34. Bumper
35. Nut (plastic)
36. License plate bracket

17

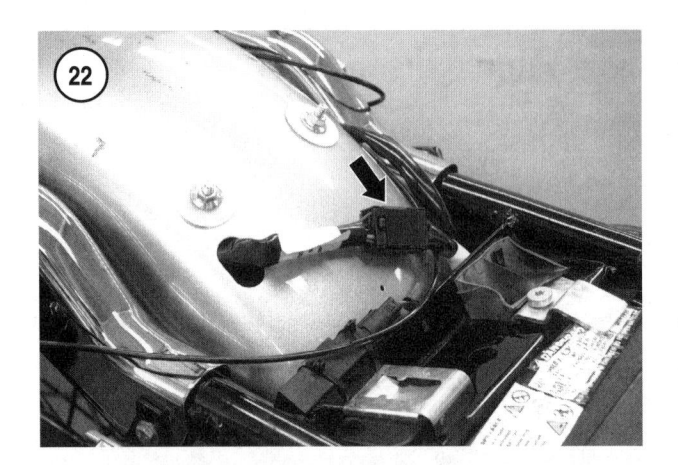

5. Remove both frame side covers as described in this chapter.
6. Remove the rear wheel as described in Chapter Twelve.
7. On FLHX models, remove the rear fascia as described in this chapter.
8. Disconnect the rear fender light connector (**Figure 22**) from the top of the rear fender. Release the connector anchor from the fender hole.
9. Remove the four hex screws and lockwasher securing the license plate bracket and remove it from the luggage rack.
10. On the left side of 2006-2007 models, remove the Torx screw (T40) securing the rear fender to the back of the battery box.

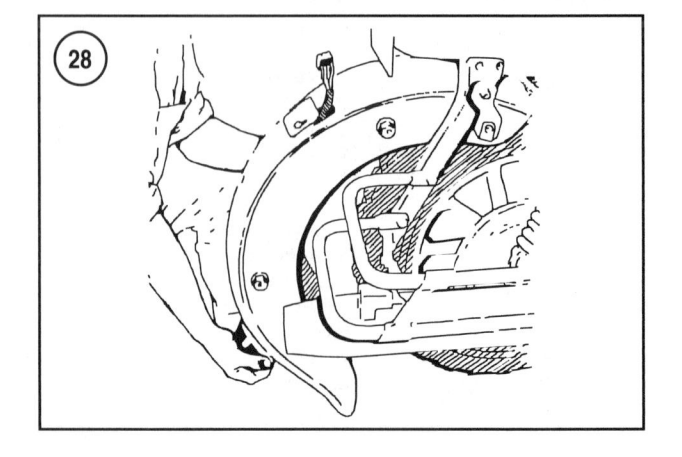

BODY AND FRAME

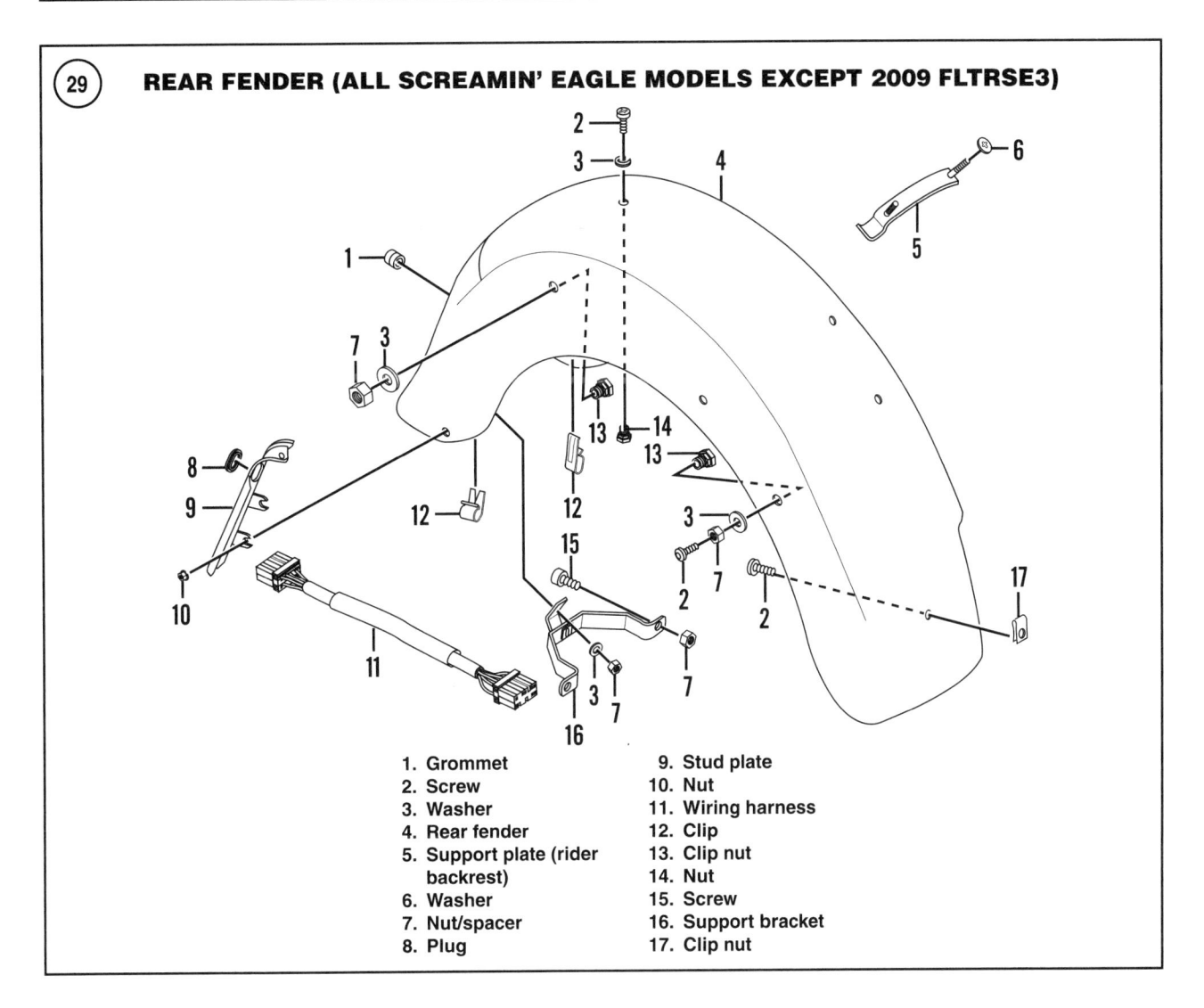

REAR FENDER (ALL SCREAMIN' EAGLE MODELS EXCEPT 2009 FLTRSE3)

1. Grommet
2. Screw
3. Washer
4. Rear fender
5. Support plate (rider backrest)
6. Washer
7. Nut/spacer
8. Plug
9. Stud plate
10. Nut
11. Wiring harness
12. Clip
13. Clip nut
14. Nut
15. Screw
16. Support bracket
17. Clip nut

11. At the rear of the rear fender, remove the inboard Torx bolt (**Figure 23**) and flange nut securing the rear bumper support rail to the saddlebag support bracket and saddlebag support rail. Repeat for the other side.

12. Working under the rear bumper, remove the flange nut with the flat washer and release the bumper bracket from the fender weld stud. Remove the rear bumper and rear bumper cushion.

13. Remove the Torx bolt (**Figure 24**; left side and **Figure 25**; right side) securing the fender to the clip nut below the frame side cover rubber grommet. Repeat for the other side.

14. Remove the rear bolt (A, **Figure 26** and A, **Figure 27**) securing the saddlebag support to the frame support. Repeat for the other side.

CAUTION
Hold onto the rear fender as it will drop down slightly when the following front bolt is removed.

15. Hold onto the rear fender and remove the front bolt (B, **Figure 26** and B, **Figure 27**) securing the saddlebag support to the frame support. Repeat for the other side.

16. Have an assistant spread the saddlebag supports outward. Slowly roll the rear fender back and off the rear wheel (**Figure 28**), staying away from the saddlebag supports and mufflers. Be careful not scratch the fender paint on any of the surrounding brackets.

17. Install by reversing the removal steps. Tighten all bolts and nuts as follows:
   a. Rear fender-to-battery box Torx bolt (T40) to 15-20 ft.-lb. (20.3-27.1 N•m).
   b. Saddlebag support bracket Torx bolt to 15-20 ft.-lb. (20.3-27.1 N•m).
   c. Fender side mounting Torx bolt to 15-20 ft.-lb. (20.3-27.1 N•m).
   d. Flange nut-to-weld stud to 45-85 in.-lb. (5.1-9.6 N•m).

REAR FENDER (SCREAMIN' EAGLE MODELS)

Removal/Installation (All Models Except 2009 FLTRSE3)

Refer to **Figure 29**.

NOTE
Elevate the rear of the motorcycle sufficiently to allow the rear fender to roll back and over the rear wheel, as well as clear the frame rear cross member.

1. Support the motorcycle with the rear wheel slightly off the ground.

NOTE
Always disarm the optional TSSM/HFSM security system before disconnecting the battery or pulling the Maxi-Fuse so the siren will not sound.

2. Disconnect the negative battery cable as described in Chapter Eleven.
3. Remove the seat as described in this chapter.
4. Remove both saddlebags as described in this chapter.
5. Remove both frame side covers as described in this chapter.
6. Remove the rear wheel as described in Chapter Twelve.
7. Remove the passenger's seat backrest as described in this chapter.
8. Remove the saddlebag support brackets as described in this chapter.
9. Remove the bolts and lockwashers on each side securing the luggage rack to the frame. Remove the luggage rack from the frame.
10. Remove the following components only if the rear fender is going to be replaced:
   a. Remove the rear fascia as described in this chapter.
   b. Remove the rider seat backrest as described in this chapter.
   c. Remove the rear turn signal assembly as described in Chapter Eleven.
   d. Remove the taillight assembly as described in Chapter Eleven.
11. At the rider backrest support, remove the screws securing the support strap to the mounting bracket. Remove the support strap.
12. Disconnect the rear lighting harness connector (**Figure 22**) and press the connector hold-down clip out of the rear fender.
13. Remove the locknut and washer securing the fender support bracket to the rear fender.
14. Remove the screw and clip nut securing the front of the rear fender to the frame.
15. Have an assistant support the rear fender, and remove the nuts/spacers and washers on each side.
16. Slowly roll the rear fender back and off the rear wheel (**Figure 28**), staying away from the saddlebag supports and mufflers. Be careful not scratch the fender paint on any of the surrounding brackets.
17. Install by reversing the removal steps. Note the following bolt torque specifications:
   a. Clip nut and bolt securing the front of fender-to-frame: 17-22 ft.-lb. (23.1-29.8 N•m).
   b. Passenger backrest support screws: 15-20 in.-lb. (20.3-27.1 N•m).
   c. Frame clip nut: 35-40 in.-lb. (4.0-4.5 N•m).
   d. Support bracket-to-fender locknut: 45-85 in.-lb. (5.1-9.6 N•m).

Removal/Installation (2009 FLTRSE3 Models)

Refer to **Figure 30**.

NOTE
Elevate the rear of the motorcycle sufficiently to allow the rear fender to roll back and over the rear wheel, as well as clear the frame rear cross member.

1. Support the motorcycle with the rear wheel slightly off the ground.

NOTE
Always disarm the optional TSSM/HFSM security system before disconnecting the battery or pulling the Maxi-Fuse so the siren will not sound.

2. Disconnect the negative battery cable as described in Chapter Eleven.
3. Remove the seat as described in this chapter.
4. Remove both saddlebags as described in this chapter.
5. Remove both frame side covers as described in this chapter.
6. Remove the rear wheel as described in Chapter Twelve.
7. Remove the passenger's seat backrest as described in this chapter.
8. Remove the saddlebag support guards as described in this chapter.
9. Remove the bolts and lockwashers on each side securing the luggage rack to the frame. Remove the luggage rack from the frame.
10. Remove the following components only if the rear fender is going to be replaced:
   a. Remove the rear fascia as described in this chapter.
   b. Remove the taillight/brake light/rear turn signal assembly from each side as described in Chapter Eleven.
   c. Remove the license plate bracket as described in this chapter.
11. At the rider backrest support, remove the screws securing the support strap to the mounting bracket. Remove the support strap.
12. Disconnect the air lines from both rear shock absorbers as described in Chapter Fourteen.
13. Disconnect the rear lighting harness connector (**Figure 22**) and press the connector hold-down clip out of the rear fender.
14. Remove the locknut and washer securing the fender support bracket to the rear fender.

BODY AND FRAME

REAR FENDER AND FASCIA (2009 FLTRSE3 MODELS)

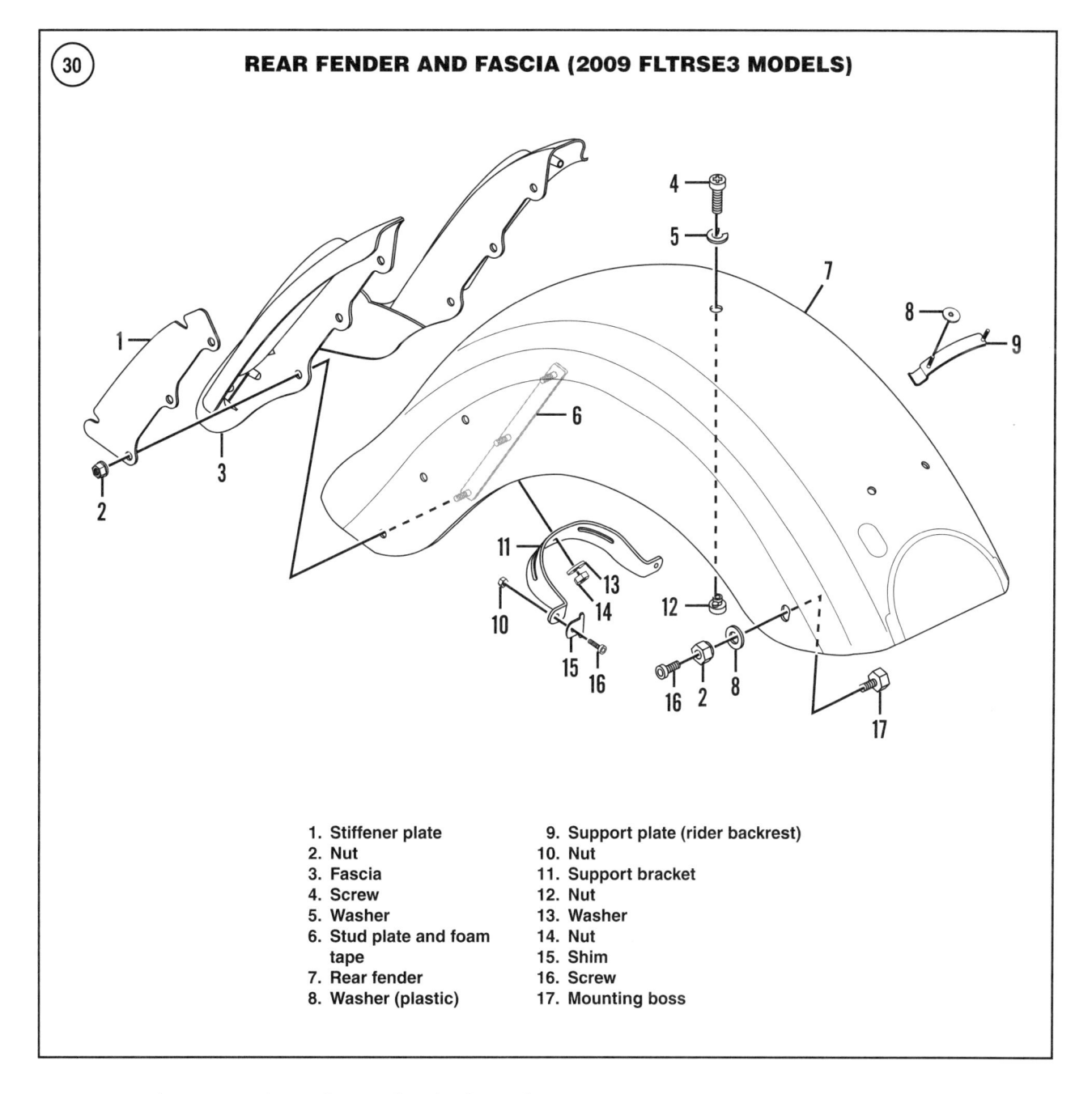

1. Stiffener plate
2. Nut
3. Fascia
4. Screw
5. Washer
6. Stud plate and foam tape
7. Rear fender
8. Washer (plastic)
9. Support plate (rider backrest)
10. Nut
11. Support bracket
12. Nut
13. Washer
14. Nut
15. Shim
16. Screw
17. Mounting boss

15. Remove the screw and nut slip securing the front of the rear fender to the frame.

16. Have an assistant support the rear fender, and remove the nut/spacers and washers on each side.

17. Slowly roll the rear fender back and off the rear wheel (**Figure 28**), staying away from the saddlebag supports and mufflers. Be careful not scratch the fender paint on any of the surrounding brackets.

18. Install by reversing the removal steps. Note the following bolt torque specifications:
   a. Bolts securing the front of fender to frame: 15-20 ft.-lb. (20.3-27.1 N•m).
   b. Saddlebag support-to-fender and frame: 15-20 ft.-lb. (20.3-27.1 N•m).
   c. Passenger backrest support screws: 16.7 ft.-lb. (22.6 N•m).

REAR FENDER FASCIA

Removal/Installation (FLHX Models)

1. Support the motorcycle with the rear wheel slightly off the ground.

NOTE
Always disarm the optional TSSM/HFSM security system before disconnecting the battery or pulling the Maxi-Fuse so the siren will not sound.

2. Disconnect the negative battery cable as described in Chapter Eleven.

3. Remove the seat as described in this chapter.

4. Remove both saddlebags as described in this chapter.
5. Along the side of the rear fender, remove the three flange nuts from the studs on each side.
6. On the left side, loosen the set screw and unscrew the radio antenna mast from the bracket.
7. Carefully open the conduit on the rear fascia lamp wires at the split line and release the wires.
8. Carefully spread the top sections of the rear fascia and release if from the studs on each side.
9. Carefully pull straight down and release the fascia from the rear fender. Gently wiggle the fascia if necessary. Be careful not scratch the fender paint.
10. Remove the two Torx screws (T20), and then remove the lamp assembly from the fascia, if necessary.
11. Install by reversing the removal steps, while noting the following:
    a. Apply a small dab of Loctite 243 (blue) threadlock to the studs.
    b. Tighten the flange nuts to 30-45 in.-lb. (3.4-5.1 N•m).

Removal/Installation (FLHRSE Models)

1. Support the motorcycle with the rear wheel slightly off the ground.
2. Along the side of the rear fender, remove the three flange nuts from the studs.
3. Pull straight out and remove the fascia from the studs.
4. Repeat the process to remove the remaining fascia, if necessary.
5. Remove the stud plate and double sided foam tape from the fender, if necessary.
6. If removed, scrape off old tape residue from the stud plate and fender. Clean off with isopropyl alcohol.
7. Apply two new foam tape strips onto the fascia and install. Press firmly to seat the foam tape.
8. Install by reversing the removal steps. Tighten the flange nuts to 30-45 in.-lb. (3.4-5.1 N•m).

Removal/Installation (2009 FLTRSE3 Models)

Refer to **Figure 30**.
1. Support the motorcycle with the rear wheel slightly off the ground.

NOTE
Always disarm the optional TSSM/HFSM security system before disconnecting the battery or pulling the Maxi-Fuse so the siren will not sound.

2. Disconnect the negative battery cable as described in Chapter Eleven.
3. Remove both saddlebags as described in this chapter.
4. Remove the taillight/brake light/rear turn signal assembly from each side as described in Chapter Eleven.

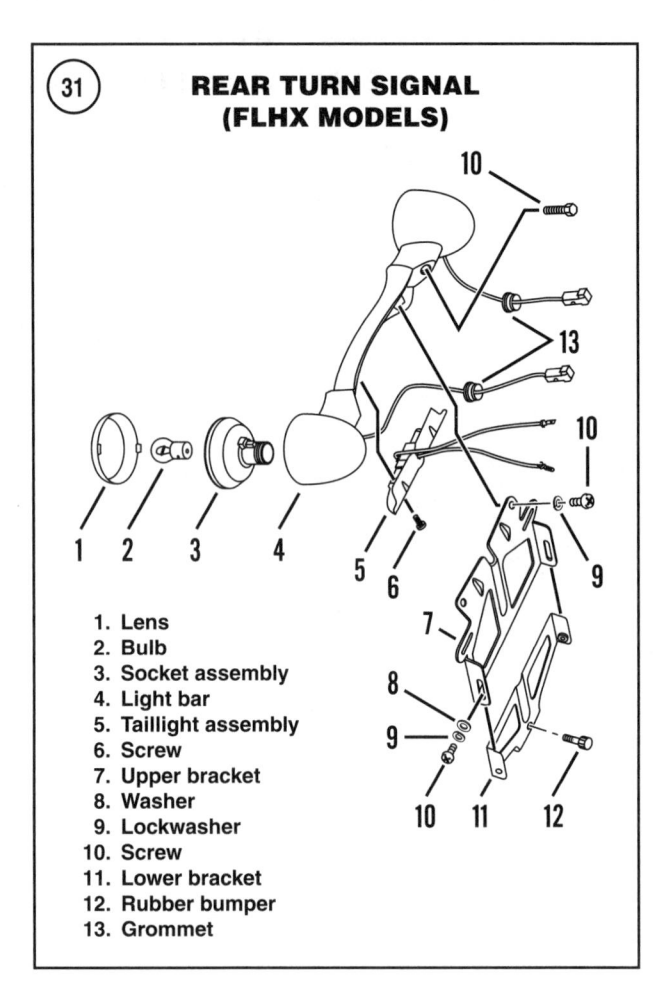

31 REAR TURN SIGNAL (FLHX MODELS)

1. Lens
2. Bulb
3. Socket assembly
4. Light bar
5. Taillight assembly
6. Screw
7. Upper bracket
8. Washer
9. Lockwasher
10. Screw
11. Lower bracket
12. Rubber bumper
13. Grommet

5. Remove the two lower flange nuts on each side securing the stiffener plate and rear fascia to the rear fender.
6. Secure the rear fascia and remove the upper flange nut on each side and remove the stiffener plates from each side.
7. Carefully pull one side of the rear fascia and remove it from the studs on that side stud plate. Then, repeat the process for the other side.
8. Carefully remove the rear fascia from the rear fender. Do not scratch the rear fender finish.
9. Remove the stud plate assembly from the inside of the rear fender, if necessary. Repeat for the other side, if necessary.
10. If the stud plate was removed, perform the following:
    a. Thoroughly scrape off all old foam tape residue from the stud plate and the underside of the fender where the stud plate was secured. Remove old foam tape residue with isopropyl alcohol.
    b. Apply two *new* sections of foam tape to the stud plate where it attaches to the under side of the rear fender.
    c. Install the stud plate onto the inner surface of the rear fender and press onto place to seat the foam tape. Repeat for the remaining stud plate, if necessary.
11. Carefully install the rear fascia onto the rear fender and the studs on each side.
12. Install the stiffener plates over the studs and install the six flange nuts. Tighten the flange nuts to 30-45 in.-lb. (3.4-5.1 N•m).

BODY AND FRAME

LICENSE PLATE BRACKET (2009 FLTRSE3 MODELS)

1. Reflex reflector (red [HDI])
2. Bracket (HDI)
3. Reflex reflector (red)
4. Bracket
5. Cover
6. Light assembly
7. Screw
8. Light bracket
9. Terminal housing
10. Gasket
11. Stud plate
12. Electrical connector
13. Connector cover
14. Nut

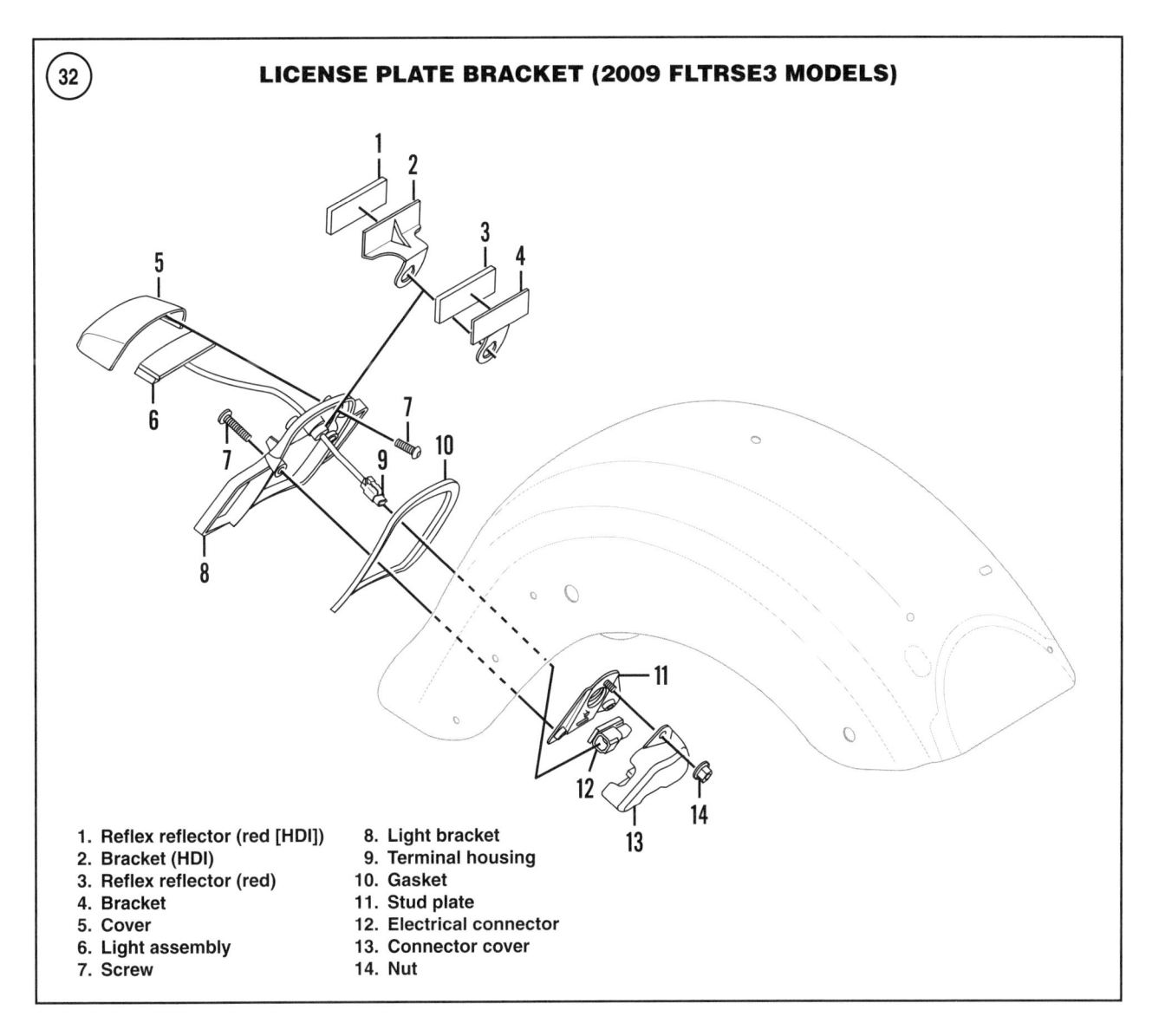

13. Install the taillight/brake light/rear turn signal assembly onto each side as described in Chapter Eleven.
14. Install both saddlebags as described in this chapter.
15. Connect the negative battery cable as described in Chapter Eleven.

LICENSE PLATE BRACKET

Removal/Installation (FLHX Models)

Refer to **Figure 31**.

1. Remove the license plate light assembly as described in Chapter Eleven.
2. Remove the two Allen screws and washers securing the bracket to the rear turn signal bracket.
3. Remove the two screws, lockwashers and washer securing the lower bracket to the upper bracket, if necessary. Separate the lower bracket from the upper bracket.
4. Install the lower bracket to the upper bracket and tighten the screws securely, if removed.
5. Install the license plate bracket onto the rear turn signal bracket. Install the two Allen screws and washers, and then tighten the screws securely.
6. Install the license plate light assembly as described in Chapter Eleven.

Removal/Installation (2009 FLTRSE3 Models)

Refer to **Figure 32**.

1. Remove the rear wheel as described in Chapter Twelve.

NOTE
Always disarm the optional TSSM/HFSM security system before disconnecting the battery or pulling the Maxi-Fuse so the siren will not sound.

2. Disconnect the negative battery cable as described in Chapter Eleven.

WINDSHIELD (FLHR MODELS) ㉝

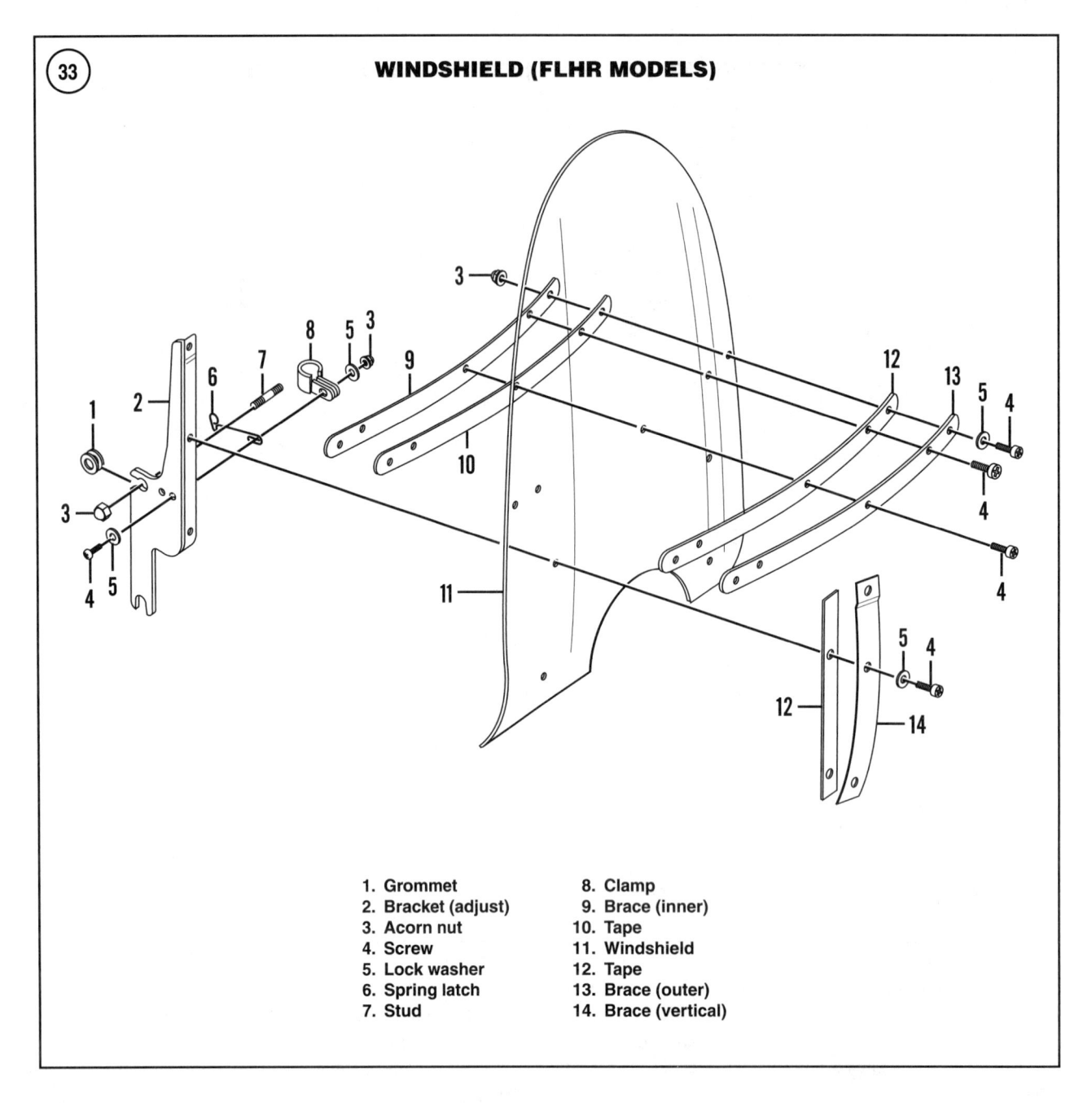

1. Grommet
2. Bracket (adjust)
3. Acorn nut
4. Screw
5. Lock washer
6. Spring latch
7. Stud
8. Clamp
9. Brace (inner)
10. Tape
11. Windshield
12. Tape
13. Brace (outer)
14. Brace (vertical)

3. Remove the flange nut, and then remove the electrical connector cover.
4. Disconnect the electrical connector from the main harness.
5. Separate the electrical connector and remove the terminals from the connector.
6. Secure the stud plate under the rear fender.
7. Remove the two screws securing the bracket assembly and stud plate to the rear fender. Remove the bracket assembly from the rear fender.
8. Remove the two screws securing the light assembly to the bracket and remove the light assembly.
9. Remove the gasket from the fear fender or from the light bracket.
10. Install by reversing the removal steps, while noting the following:

a. Install the screws securing the license plate light assembly to the plate bracket. Tighten the screws to 57-69 in.-lb. (6.4-7.8 N•m).
b. Install the screws securing the light assembly to the rear fender. Tighten the screws securely.
c. Install the electrical connector cover flange nut, and tighten it to 30-45 in.-lb. (3.4-5.1 N•m).

WINDSHIELD

FLHR and FLHRSE Models
Removal/Installation

Refer to **Figure 33** and **Figure 34**.

1. Place the motorcycle on level ground on the jiffy stand.

BODY AND FRAME

WINDSHIELD (FLHRSE MODELS)

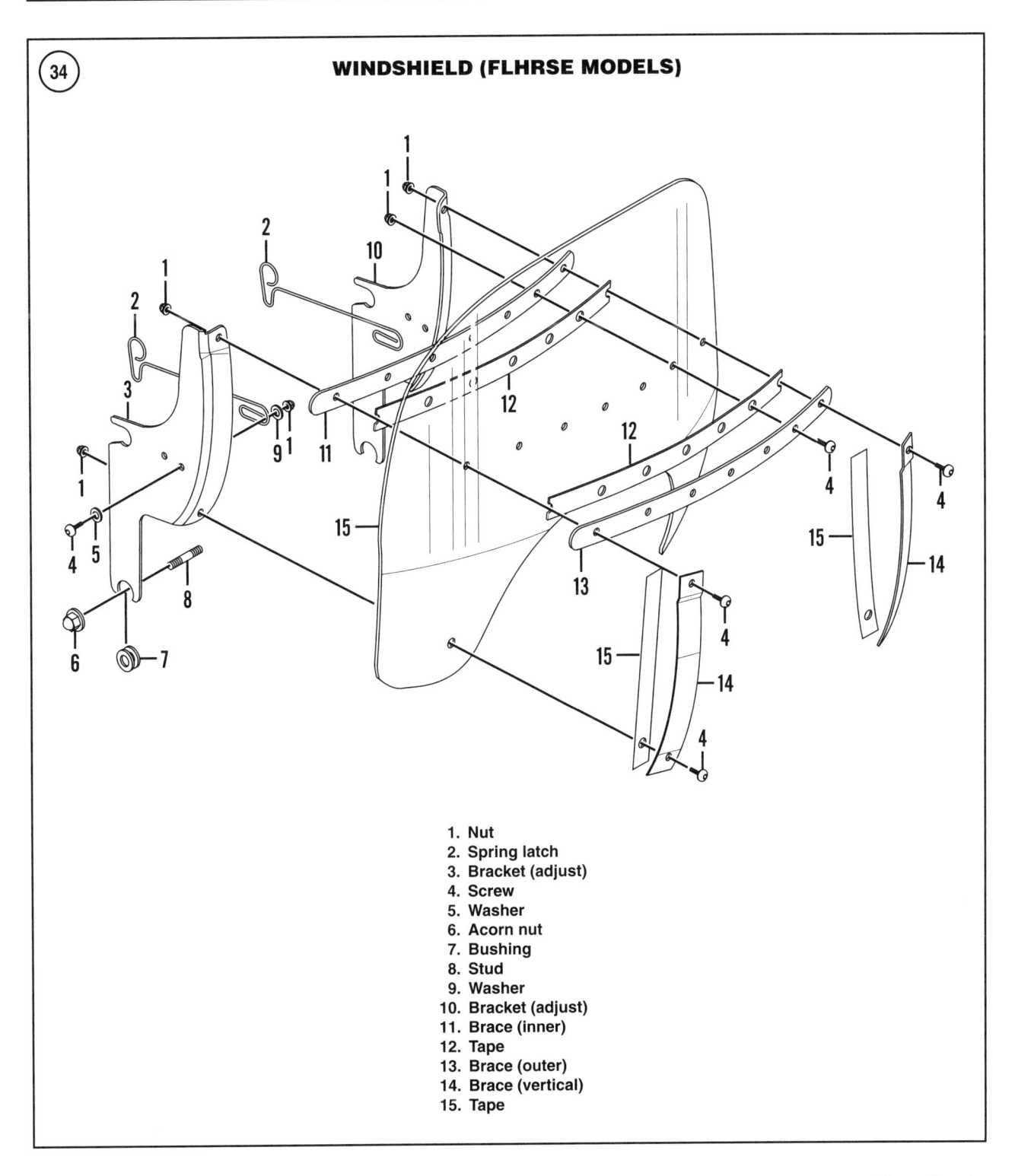

1. Nut
2. Spring latch
3. Bracket (adjust)
4. Screw
5. Washer
6. Acorn nut
7. Bushing
8. Stud
9. Washer
10. Bracket (adjust)
11. Brace (inner)
12. Tape
13. Brace (outer)
14. Brace (vertical)
15. Tape

2. Use a finger and lift up on the wire form latch spring on each side of the windshield next to the headlight nacelle.

3. Straddle the front wheel and hold onto the windshield. Gently pull straight up on the top of the windshield until the upper notches on the side brackets are free of the upper grommets on the passing light support.

4. Continue to raise the windshield until the side brackets lower notches are free from the lower grommets, and remove the windshield.

5. Install by reversing the removal steps while noting the following:
   a. Lower the windshield down until the latches are firmly seated on the grommet on each side.
   b. Push down on the wire form latch springs until they overhang the rubber grommets.
   c. To adjust, loosen the retaining screws and rotate the latch springs into the proper location.
   d. Make sure the windshield is securely in place prior to riding.

CHAPTER SEVENTEEN

(35) WINDSHIELD (2006-2008 FLTR MODELS)

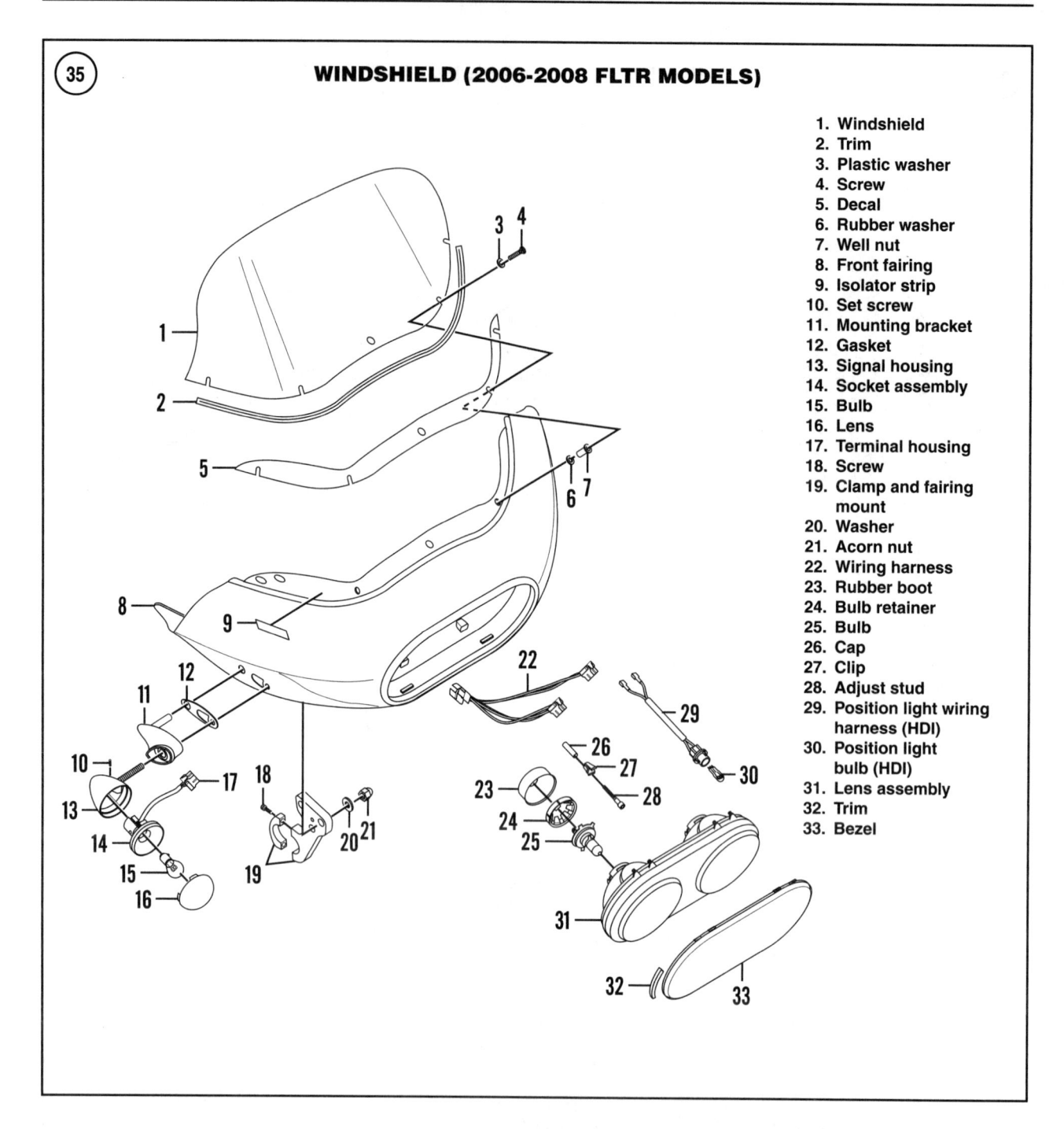

1. Windshield
2. Trim
3. Plastic washer
4. Screw
5. Decal
6. Rubber washer
7. Well nut
8. Front fairing
9. Isolator strip
10. Set screw
11. Mounting bracket
12. Gasket
13. Signal housing
14. Socket assembly
15. Bulb
16. Lens
17. Terminal housing
18. Screw
19. Clamp and fairing mount
20. Washer
21. Acorn nut
22. Wiring harness
23. Rubber boot
24. Bulb retainer
25. Bulb
26. Cap
27. Clip
28. Adjust stud
29. Position light wiring harness (HDI)
30. Position light bulb (HDI)
31. Lens assembly
32. Trim
33. Bezel

2006-2008 FLTR Models
Removal/Installation

Refer to **Figure 35**.

NOTE
If working with a non-OEM windshield, as shown in this procedure, follow the manufactures instructions.

1. Place the motorcycle on level ground using the jiffy stand.
2. At the front surface of the front outer fairing, located the five screws (A, **Figure 36**, typical) securing the windshield to the outer fairing. Using an alternating pattern, loosen and remove the five screws along with the plastic washers.

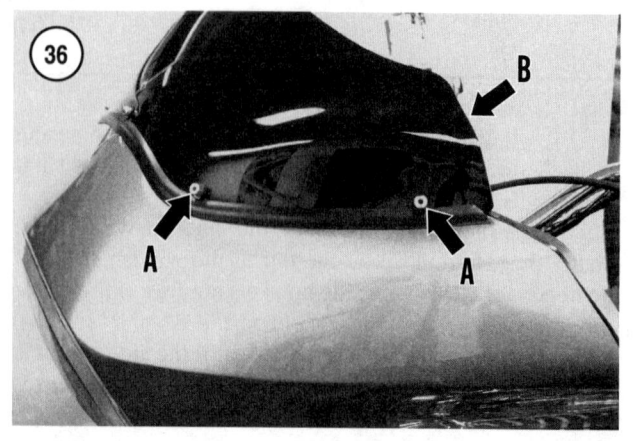

BODY AND FRAME

693

37 **FRONT FAIRING (2009 FLTR AND FLTRSE3 MODELS)**

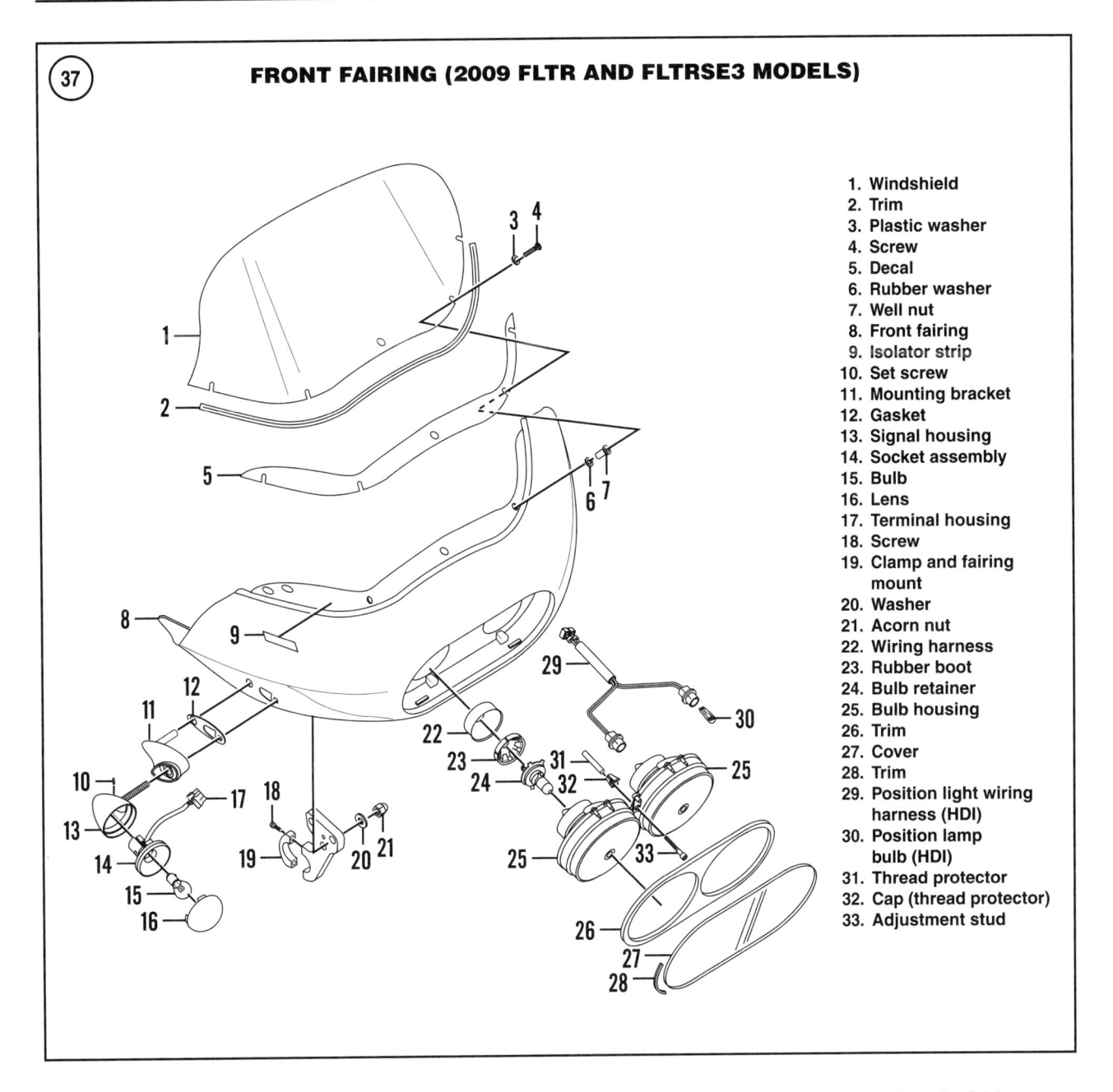

1. Windshield
2. Trim
3. Plastic washer
4. Screw
5. Decal
6. Rubber washer
7. Well nut
8. Front fairing
9. Isolator strip
10. Set screw
11. Mounting bracket
12. Gasket
13. Signal housing
14. Socket assembly
15. Bulb
16. Lens
17. Terminal housing
18. Screw
19. Clamp and fairing mount
20. Washer
21. Acorn nut
22. Wiring harness
23. Rubber boot
24. Bulb retainer
25. Bulb housing
26. Trim
27. Cover
28. Trim
29. Position light wiring harness (HDI)
30. Position lamp bulb (HDI)
31. Thread protector
32. Cap (thread protector)
33. Adjustment stud

3. Carefully pull the windshield (B, **Figure 36**, typical) and trim away from the outer fairing.

4. Carefully remove the well-nuts straight out from the outer fairing. Do not push them into the inner fairing during removal.

5. Inspect the well-nuts in the front outer fairing for wear, cuts or damage. Replace as a set if necessary.

6. If installing a new windshield, carefully poke holes for the screws in the decal from the inside surface. If poked from the outside surface the decal will be will be broken loose from the windshield and may tear.

7. Install the flat plastic washer onto the mounting screw.

8. Insert the screws through the windshield slots and the decal.

9. Partially screw the well nuts onto the screws.

10. At the front surface of the front outer fairing, position the five well nuts with the openings in the outer fairing. Carefully push the well-nuts into the fairing openings. Push the windshield onto the outer fairing until it is flush.

11. Starting with the center screw and alternating from side-to-side, tighten the five windshield screws to 6-13 in.-lb. (0.7-1.5 N•m). Do not overtighten the screw as the windshield area around the screw may fracture.

FRONT FAIRING (2009 FLTR AND FLTRSE3 MODELS)

Outer Front Fairing
Removal/Installation

Refer to **Figure 37**.

1. Place the motorcycle on level ground using the jiffy stand.

2. Remove the seat and windshield as described in this chapter.

NOTE
Always disarm the optional TSSM/HFSM security system before disconnecting the battery or pulling the Maxi-Fuse so the siren will not sound.

3. Disconnect the negative battery cable as described in Chapter Eleven.
4. Cover the front fender with towels or a blanket to protect the painted finish.
5. Remove the six Torx screws (T25) securing the outer fairing to the inner fairing in the following order:
   a. On the left side, remove the screw (A, **Figure 38**) at the edge of the fairing next to the left speaker.
   b. Loosen, but do not remove, the top left (B, **Figure 38**) and top right side screws outboard of the fuel and volt gauges.
   c. On the left side, remove the long screw (**Figure 39**) just below the left side glove box.
   d. On the right side, remove the screw at the edge of the fairing next to the right speaker.
   e. On the right side, remove the long screw just below the right side glove box.
6. Remove both turn signal assemblies as described in Chapter Eleven.
7. Have an assistant secure the outer fairing.
8. Remove the top left and top right fairing screws.

CAUTION
*The outer fairing is secured onto two radio-mounted brackets (**Figure 40**). The outer fairing mounting notches (**Figure 41**) can be easily damaged if the outer fairing is pulled on too hard during its release from the mounting brackets.*

9. Carefully lift the outer fairing up, move it slightly to the rear, and disengage it from the two radio mounting brackets (**Figure 40**).
10. Partially lower the outer fairing (**Figure 42**).
11. Working inside the outer fairing, disconnect the electrical connector (**Figure 43**) from the backside of the each headlight assembly.
12. Remove the outer front fairing and store it in a safe place.
13. Paint the outer tips of the radio mounting brackets (**Figure 44**) with a light color paint to easily locate the brackets during installation.
14. Move the outer fairing into position and connect the electrical connectors onto the backside of the headlights.
15. Carefully move the outer fairing part way into position (**Figure 42**). Look down into the fairing and locate the radio mounting brackets. Carefully hook the outer fairing notches (**Figure 41**) onto the radio mounting brackets (**Figure 44**). Do not force the outer fairing as damage to the notches will occur.

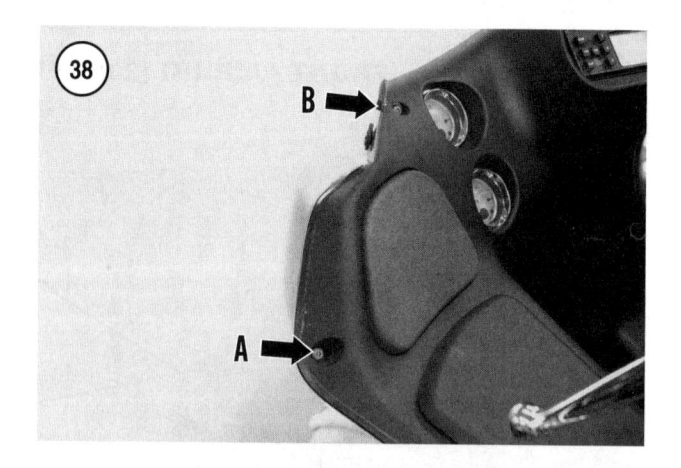

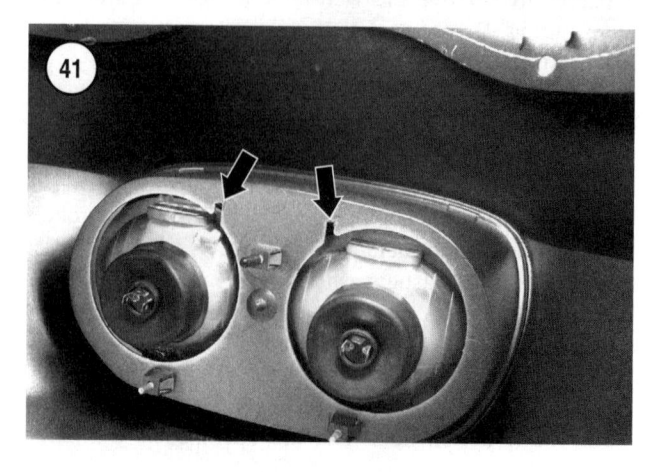

BODY AND FRAME

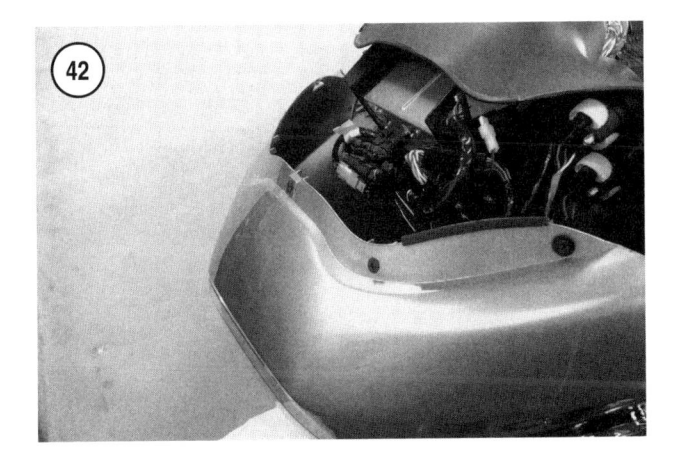

16. Align the tabs on the inner fairing to the outside of those on the outer fairing. Make sure this condition exists on both sides of the fairing (A, **Figure 45**).
17. Align the trim edge (B, **Figure 45**) between the two fairing panels.
18. Hold the fairing in position and install the top left (B, **Figure 38**) and top right side screws outboard of the fuel and volt gauges, but do not tighten them yet.
19. Install the screws (A, **Figure 38**) at the edge of the fairing next to the speakers on each side, but do not tighten them yet.
20. Install the long screw (**Figure 39**) just below the glove box on each side, but do not tighten them yet.
21. Using a crossing pattern, tighten the four short fairing screws to 6-12 in.-lb. (0.7-1.4 N•m).
22. Tighten the two long screws to 10-15 in.-lb. (1.1-1.7 N•m), alternating from side to side.

Do not overtighten as the plastic surrounding the screw hole may fracture.

23. Install the front turn signal light assembly as described in Chapter Eleven.

Instrument Bezel Housing Removal/Installation

Refer to **Figure 46**.

1. Place the motorcycle on level ground using the jiffy stand.
2. Remove the seat as described in this chapter.

NOTE
Always disarm the optional TSSM/HFSM security system before disconnecting the battery or pulling the Maxi-Fuse so the siren will not sound.

3. Disconnect the negative battery cable as described in Chapter Eleven.
4. Remove the instruments (A, **Figure 47**) and bezel as described in Chapter Eleven.
5. Remove the ignition switch knob (A, **Figure 48**), nut, collar and washer as described in *Switches* (Chapter Eleven).
6. Remove the clutch cable clip (**Figure 49**) from the hole on the left side of the instrument housing.
7. Remove the throttle cable clip (B, **Figure 47**) from the hole on the right side of the instrument housing.
8. Remove the two Torx screws (T25) and washers (B, **Figure 48**) securing the right and left side housing to the upper and lower fork bracket.
9. On the left side of the housing, unscrew the rubber boot from the odometer reset switch (C, **Figure 48**).
10. Partially remove the left side of the housing (D, **Figure 48**). Pull the odometer reset switch from the hole.
11. At the front portion of the instrument bezel housing, disconnect the 12-pin electrical connector (**Figure 50**) for the instrument switches from the interconnect harness.

INSTRUMENTS (FLTR AND FLTRSE3 MODELS)

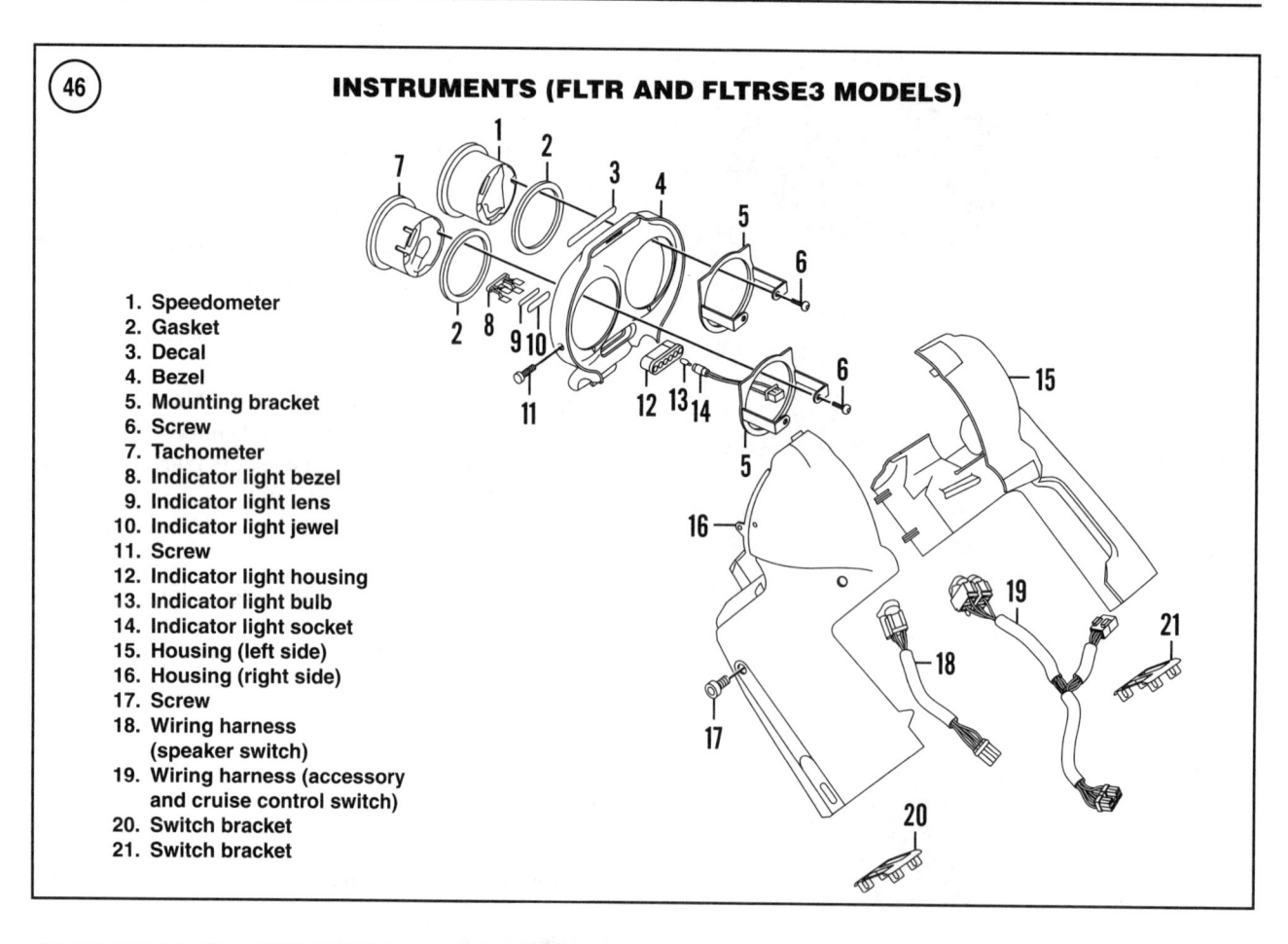

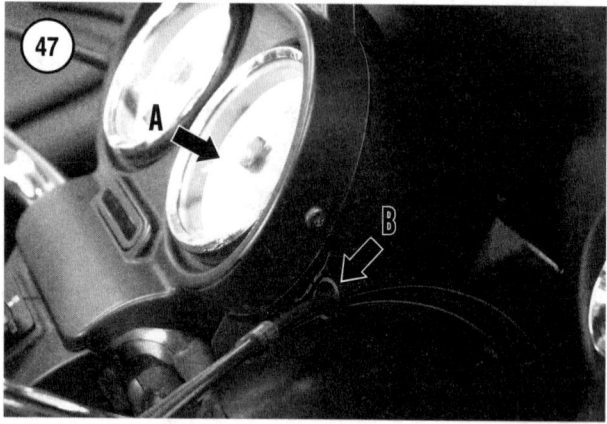

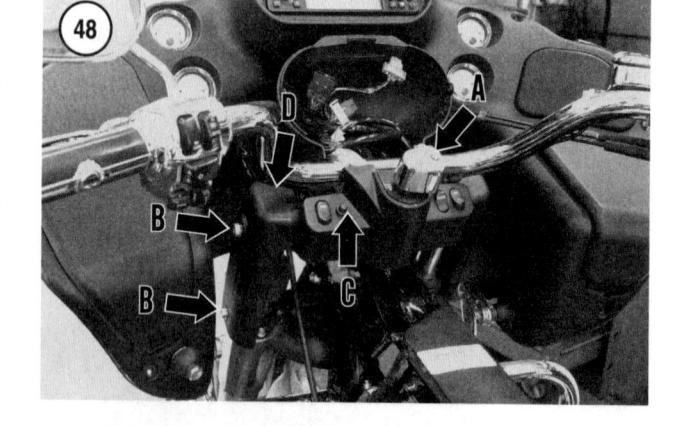

1. Speedometer
2. Gasket
3. Decal
4. Bezel
5. Mounting bracket
6. Screw
7. Tachometer
8. Indicator light bezel
9. Indicator light lens
10. Indicator light jewel
11. Screw
12. Indicator light housing
13. Indicator light bulb
14. Indicator light socket
15. Housing (left side)
16. Housing (right side)
17. Screw
18. Wiring harness (speaker switch)
19. Wiring harness (accessory and cruise control switch)
20. Switch bracket
21. Switch bracket

12. Carefully separate the instrument bezel and housing halves and remove each one from the frame. Store the panels in a safe place.

13. Install by reversing the removal steps. Tighten the Torx screws (T25) to 15-20 ft.-lb. (20.3-27.1 N•m).

Inner Front Fairing
Removal/Installation

Refer to **Figure 51** and **Figure 52**.

1. Place the motorcycle on level ground using the jiffy stand.
2. Remove the seat as described in this chapter.

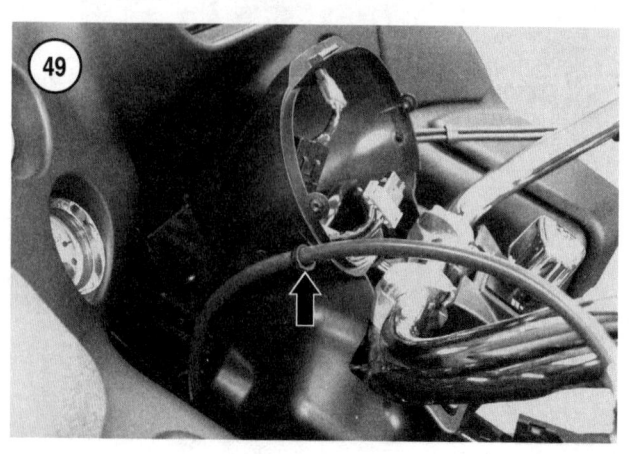

BODY AND FRAME 697

50 TERMINAL CONNECTORS (FLTR AND FLTRSE3 MODELS)

[21]
[39]
[105A/B]
[10B]
[105C/D]
[107]

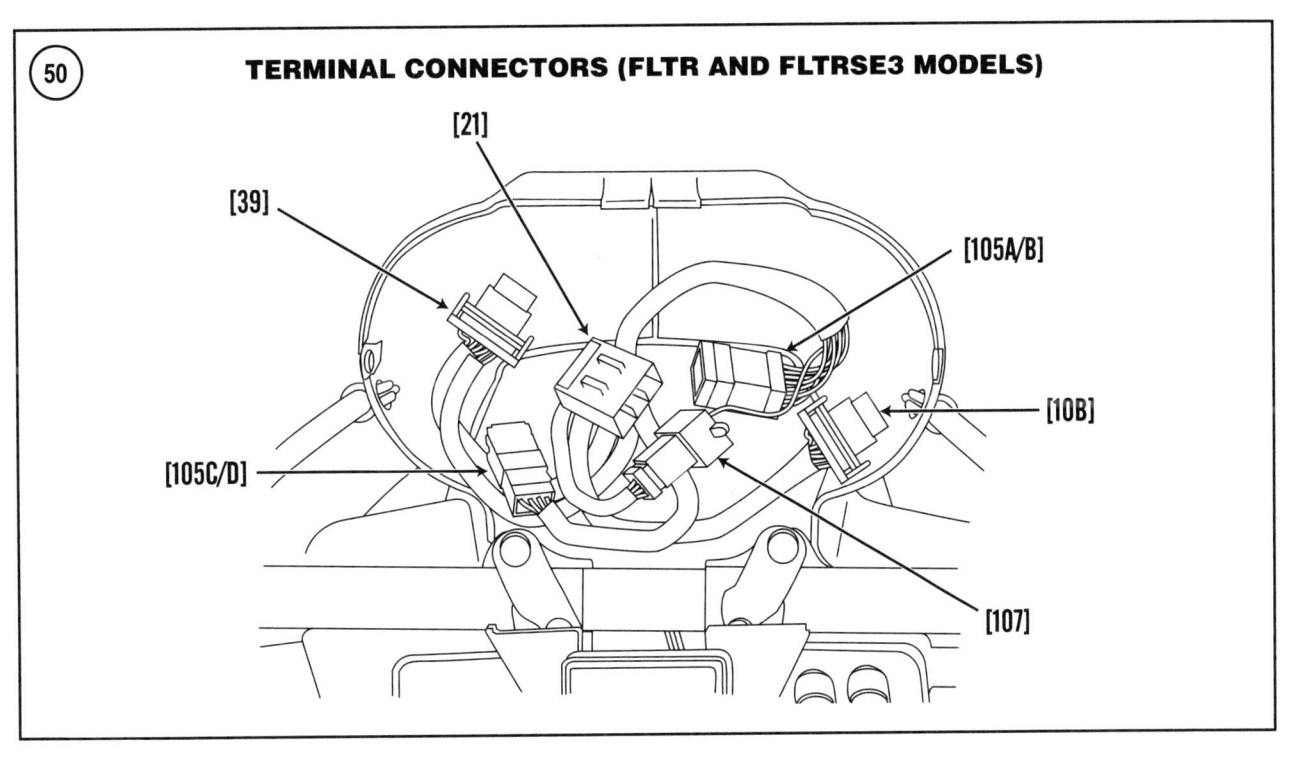

51 INNER FRONT FAIRING (FLTR AND FLTRSE3 MODELS)

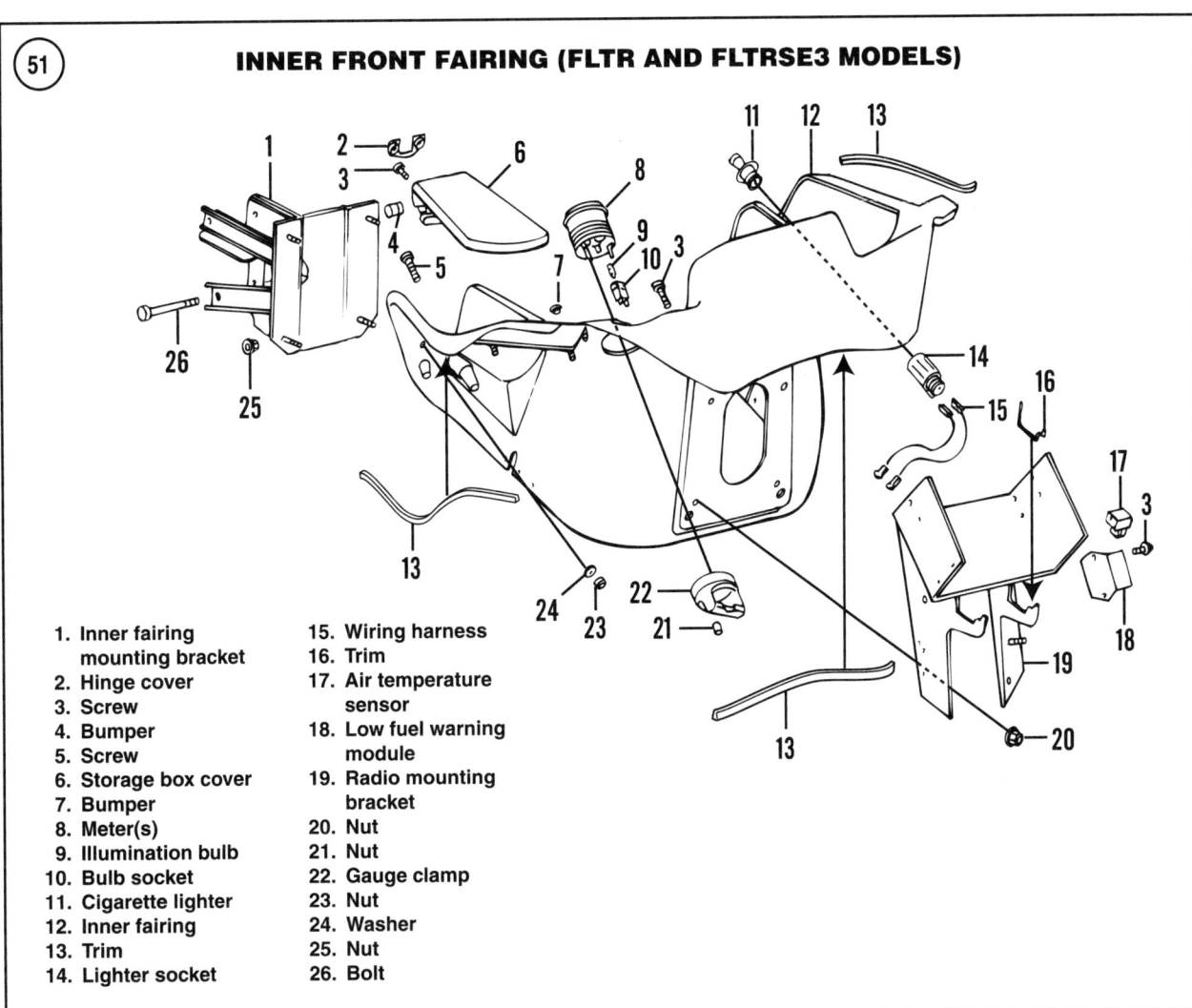

1. Inner fairing mounting bracket
2. Hinge cover
3. Screw
4. Bumper
5. Screw
6. Storage box cover
7. Bumper
8. Meter(s)
9. Illumination bulb
10. Bulb socket
11. Cigarette lighter
12. Inner fairing
13. Trim
14. Lighter socket
15. Wiring harness
16. Trim
17. Air temperature sensor
18. Low fuel warning module
19. Radio mounting bracket
20. Nut
21. Nut
22. Gauge clamp
23. Nut
24. Washer
25. Nut
26. Bolt

17

698 CHAPTER SEVENTEEN

52 **FAIRING TERMINAL CONNECTORS (FLTR AND FLTRSE3 MODELS)**

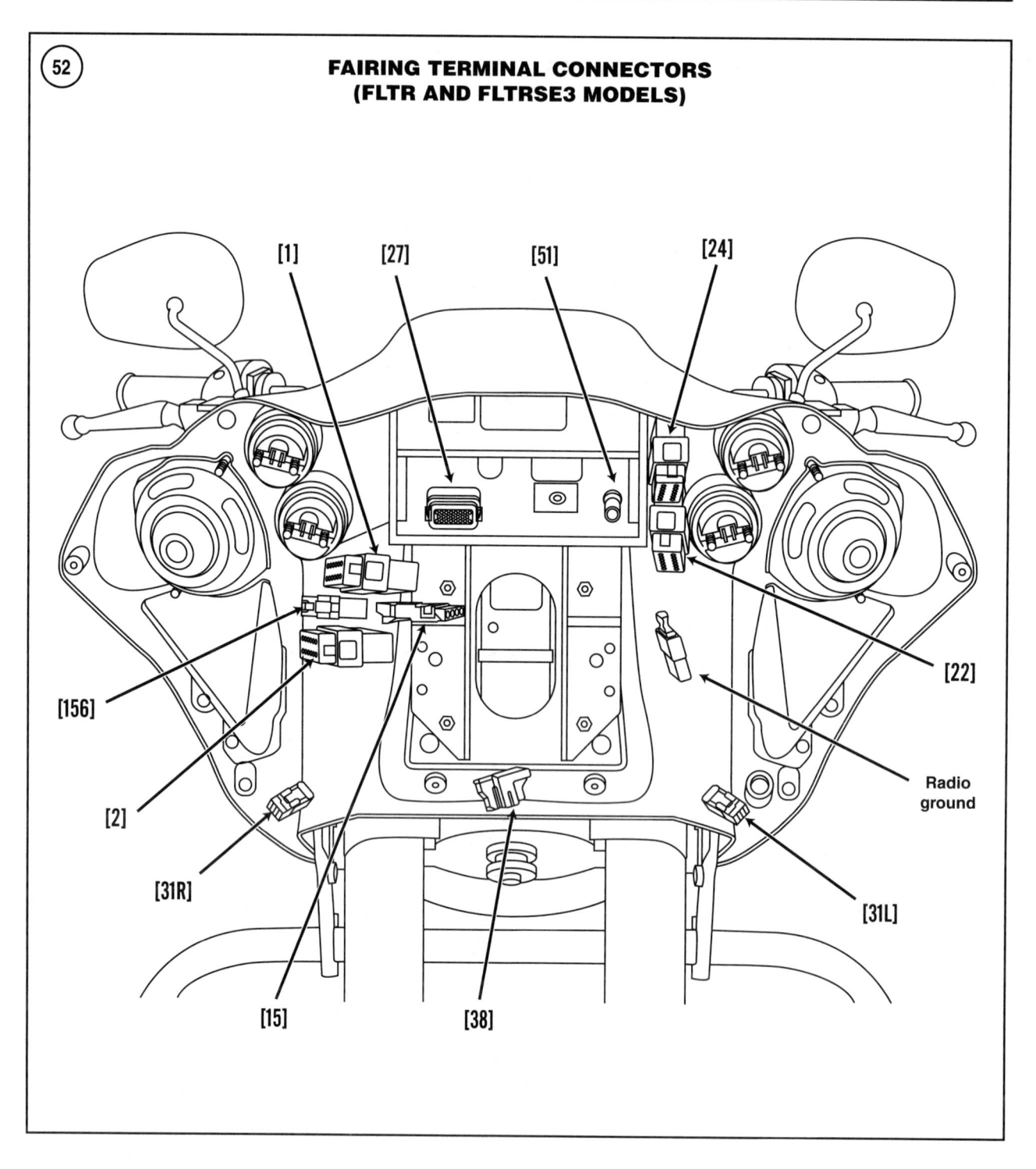

[1] [27] [51] [24]

[156]

[2]

[31R]

[15] [38]

[22]

Radio ground

[31L]

NOTE
Always disarm the optional TSSM/HFSM security system before disconnecting the battery or pulling the Maxi-Fuse so the siren will not sound.

3. Disconnect the negative battery cable as described in Chapter Eleven.
4. Cover the front fender with towels or a blanket to protect the painted finish.
5. Remove the instrument bezel housing as described in this section.

6. Remove the outer front fairing as described in this section.

NOTE
Due to the large number of electrical connectors to be disconnected in the following steps, be sure identify each mating half of the connectors to assist during installation.

7. Refer to **Figure 52** and to the wiring diagrams located on the CD inserted into the back cover of the manual. Disconnect the main harness from the interconnect harness electrical connectors as follows:

BODY AND FRAME

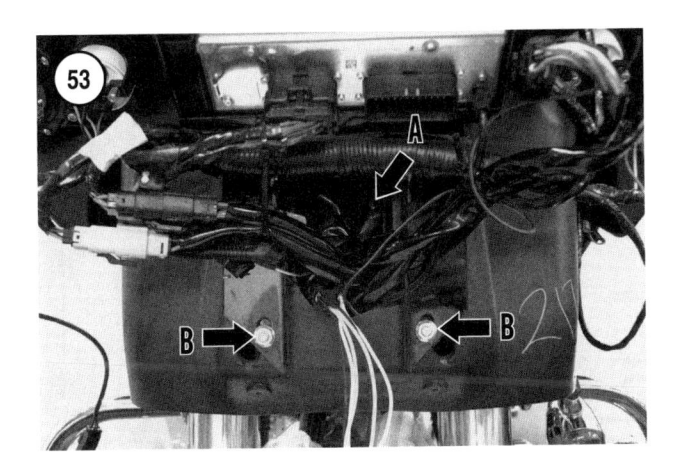

699

a. The black 16-pin interconnect harness connector located on the right side below the radio.
b. The gray 12-pin main harness to interconnect harness connector located on the right side below the radio.
c. The black 4-pin main power-to-interconnect harness connector located on the right side below the radio.

8. Refer to **Figure 52** and disconnect the radio cable and ground connectors as follows:
   a. The radio antenna cable connector located on the left side at the back of the radio.
   b. Radio ground, single spade and socket terminal located on the left side below the radio.

9. Disconnect the handlebar switch controls from the interconnect harness as follows:
   a. The gray 16-pin left side handlebar switch connector secured to the T-stud on the left side radio bracket.
   b. The black 12-pin right side handlebar switch connector secured to the T-stud on the right side radio bracket.
   c. The 6-pin front turn signal connector located on the right side below the radio.
   d. The radio ground single spade and socket terminal.

10. Carefully pull the main harness, handlebar switch conduit, radio ground wire and antenna cable as far forward as possible. Rest the connector of the longer harnesses on the front fender.

11. Refer to **Figure 50**, and disconnect the instrument nacelle switches and air temperature sensor from the interconnect harness as follows:
    a. The 12-pin instrument nacelle switch connector.
    b. 3-pin air temperature sensor connector.

12. Wrap the harness bundle tightly with shop cloths and secure them with tape or string. This bundle of wires must pass through the front opening (A, **Figure 53**) in the inner fairing and bracket tunnel.

13. Carefully pull the interconnect harness connectors from the instrument nacelle through the front fairing tunnel.

14. Disconnect the ignition switch as follows:
    a. Disconnect the 3-pin ignition switch connector at the front of the switch.
    b. Use the ignition switch connector remover (H-D part No. HD-45961). Gently insert the tool into the switch housing until it stops.
    c. Grasp the main harness conduit and the tool, and pull at the same time, releasing the socket from the ignition switch housing.

15. Pull the ignition switch branch of the main harness forward and out of the instrument nacelle. Pull it through the fairing bracket tunnel, toward the front of the inner fairing.

16. Separate all interconnect harness branches that may be tangled with the main wiring harness conduit. Let the interconnect harness hang down along the left side of the front fender.

17. Carefully gather and bundle all of the disconnected harnesses and electrical connectors. Wrap the harness bundle tightly with shop cloths and secure them with tape or string. This bundle of wires must pass through the front opening (A, **Figure 53**) in the inner fairing and bracket tunnel.

18. Hold onto the inner front fairing and remove the four locknuts (B, **Figure 53**) securing the inner front fairing and radio mounting bracket to the fairing mounting bracket.

19. Remove the inner front fairing and radio mounting bracket from the frame. Store it in a safe place.

20. Install by reversing the removal steps, while noting the following:
    a. Tighten the four locknuts to 96-144 in.-lb. (10.9-16.3 N•m).
    b. Correctly reconnect all electrical connectors by referring to the wiring diagrams located on the CD inserted into the back cover of the manual and to **Figure 52**.

FRONT FAIRING (FLHT, FLHTCUSE AND FLHX MODELS)

Outer Front Fairing Removal/Installation

Refer to **Figures 54-56**.

1. Place the motorcycle on level ground using the jiffy stand.
2. Remove the seat as described in this chapter.

NOTE
Always disarm the optional TSSM/HFSM security system before disconnecting the battery or pulling the Maxi-Fuse so the siren will not sound.

3. Disconnect the negative battery cable as described in Chapter Eleven.
4. Cover the front fender with towels or a blanket to protect the painted finish.
5. At the front of the outer front fairing, locate the three Torx screws (**Figure 57**) securing the windshield and the outer fairing to the inner fairing. Using an alternating pattern, loosen but do not remove, the screws at this time.

17

CHAPTER SEVENTEEN

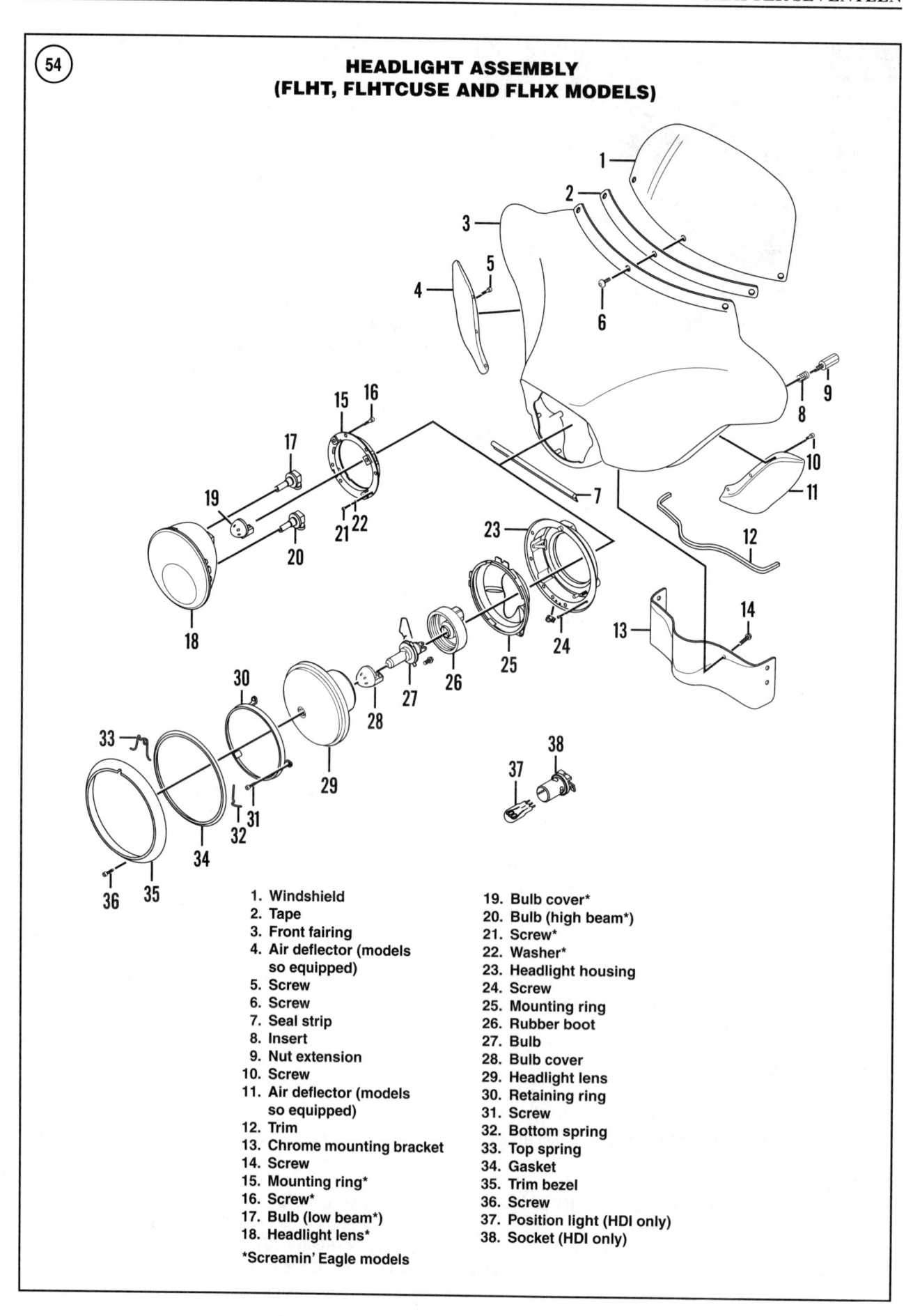

54 **HEADLIGHT ASSEMBLY
(FLHT, FLHTCUSE AND FLHX MODELS)**

1. Windshield
2. Tape
3. Front fairing
4. Air deflector (models so equipped)
5. Screw
6. Screw
7. Seal strip
8. Insert
9. Nut extension
10. Screw
11. Air deflector (models so equipped)
12. Trim
13. Chrome mounting bracket
14. Screw
15. Mounting ring*
16. Screw*
17. Bulb (low beam*)
18. Headlight lens*
19. Bulb cover*
20. Bulb (high beam*)
21. Screw*
22. Washer*
23. Headlight housing
24. Screw
25. Mounting ring
26. Rubber boot
27. Bulb
28. Bulb cover
29. Headlight lens
30. Retaining ring
31. Screw
32. Bottom spring
33. Top spring
34. Gasket
35. Trim bezel
36. Screw
37. Position light (HDI only)
38. Socket (HDI only)

*Screamin' Eagle models

BODY AND FRAME

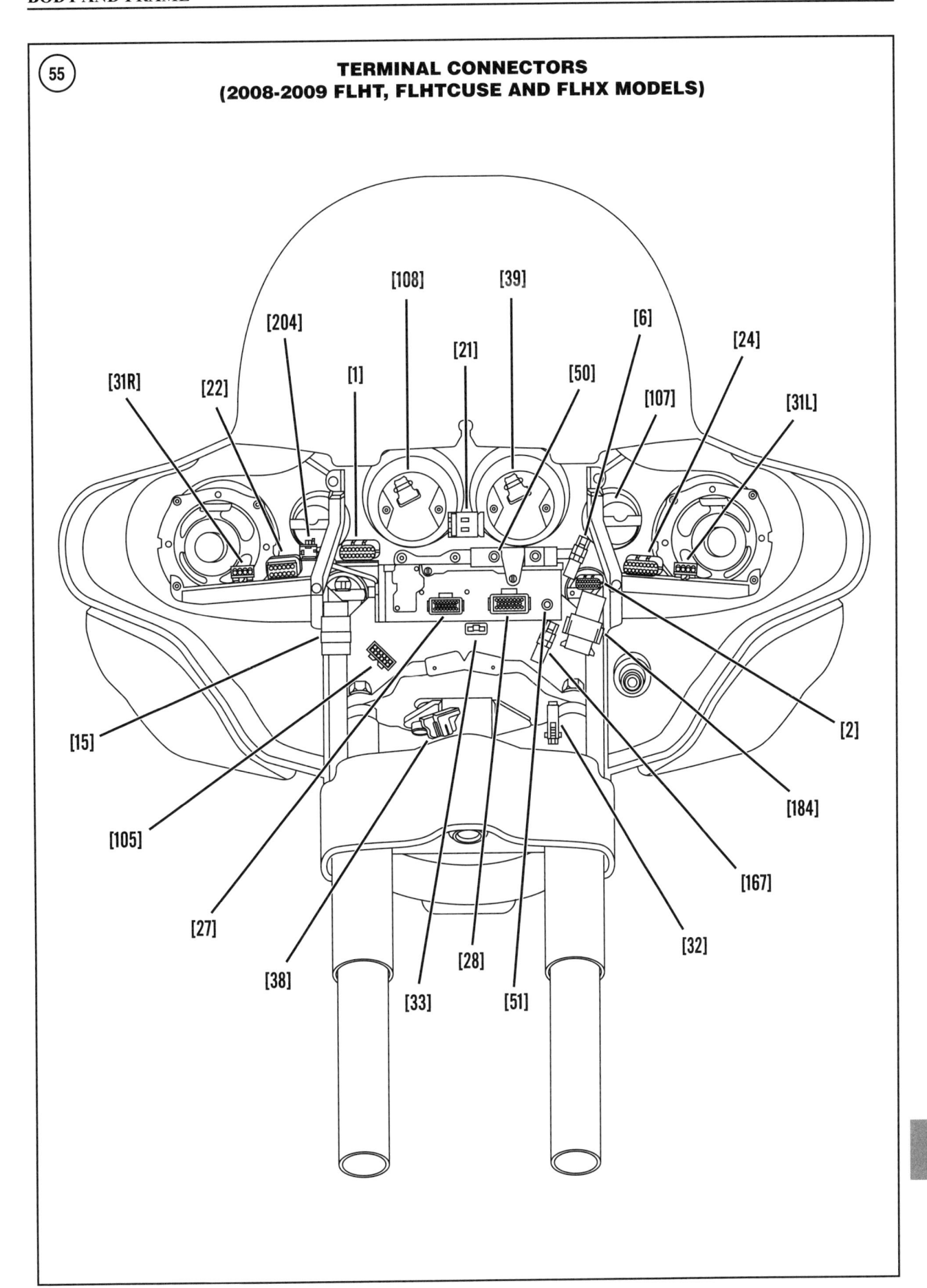

55

TERMINAL CONNECTORS
(2008-2009 FLHT, FLHTCUSE AND FLHX MODELS)

[31R] [22] [204] [1] [108] [21] [39] [50] [6] [107] [24] [31L]
[15]
[105]
[27]
[38]
[33]
[28]
[51]
[32]
[167]
[184]
[2]

CHAPTER SEVENTEEN

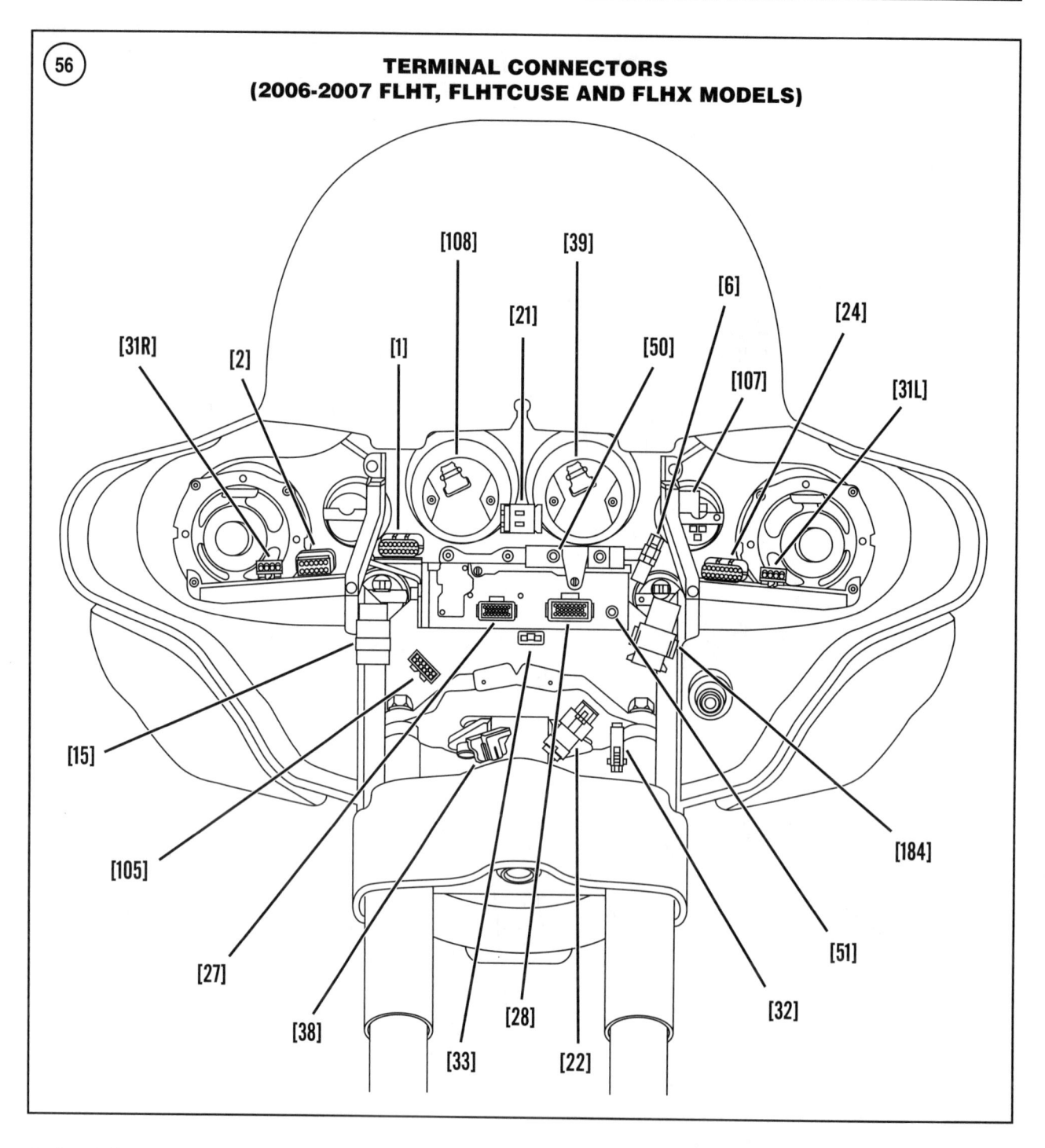

**(56) TERMINAL CONNECTORS
(2006-2007 FLHT, FLHTCUSE AND FLHX MODELS)**

6. Carefully raise the windshield from between the inner and outer front fairings.
7. While working on the inner fairing side, remove the Torx screw (T25) at corner (**Figure 58**) on each side of the inner fairing.
8. Turn the front wheel all the way to the left. Working below the fairing cap, remove the screw (**Figure 59**) securing the outer front fairing to the mounting bracket.

NOTE
On FLHX models, have an assistant hold onto the front outer fairing as it will be loose after removal of the fastener.

9. Turn the front wheel all the way to the right. Working below the fairing cap, remove the other screw securing the outer front fairing to the mounting bracket.
10. Remove the three loosened Torx screws and washers.
11. Tilt the outer front fairing forward and disconnect the headlight connector from the headlight assembly.
12. Remove the outer front fairing and windshield and store it in a safe place. Remove the windshield from the fairing if necessary.
13. Install by reversing the removal steps while noting the following:

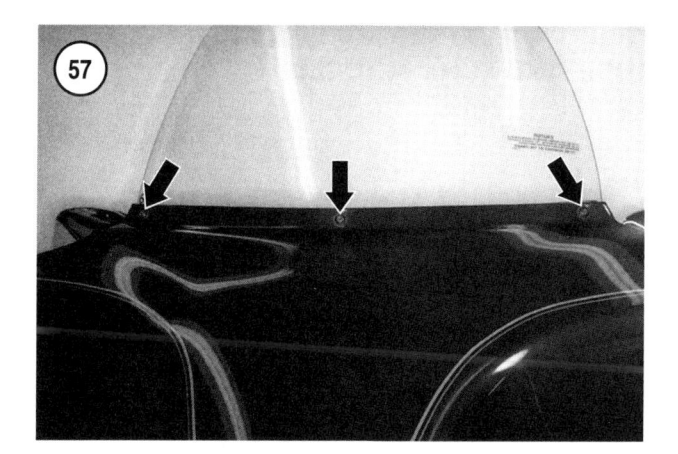

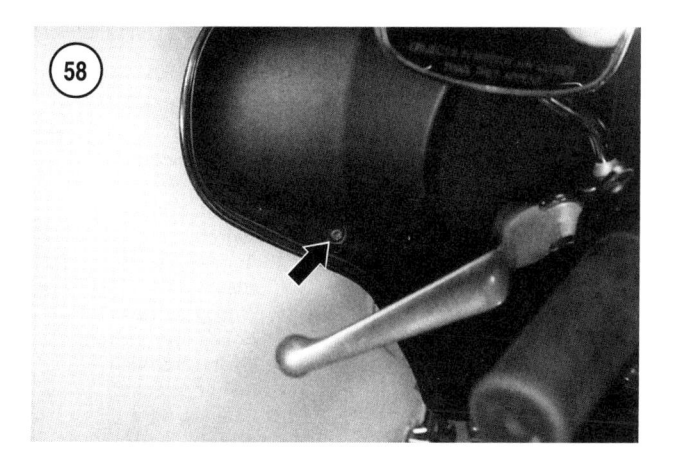

BODY AND FRAME

a. Tighten the Torx screw (T25) at corner (**Figure 58**) on each side of the inner fairing to 20-30 in.-lb. (2.3-3.4 N•m).
b. Tighten the screws (**Figure 59**) securing the outer front fairing to the mounting bracket to 20-30 in.-lb. (2.3-3.4 N•m).
c. Starting with the center screw and alternating from side-to-side, tighten the three Torx screws (**Figure 57**) securing the windshield to 25-30 in.-lb. (2.8-3.4 N•m). Do not overtighten as the area surrounding the screw may fracture.

Front Inner Fairing Cap Removal/Installation

Refer to **Figure 55**, **Figure 56** and **Figure 60**.
1. Place the motorcycle on level ground using the jiffy stand.
2. Remove the seat as described in this chapter.

NOTE
Always disarm the optional TSSM/HFSM security system before disconnecting the battery or pulling the Maxi-Fuse so the siren will not sound.

3. Disconnect the negative battery cable as described in Chapter Eleven. 
4. Partially remove ignition switch as described in Chapter Eleven.
5. Remove the two Torx screws (T27) and washers securing the fairing cap to the inner fairing.
6. Turn the front wheel to full left stop.
7. Reach behind the right side of the fairing cap and disconnect the black 12-pin fairing cap switch connector.
8. Carefully remove front inner fairing cap from the inner fairing.
9. Install by reversing the removal steps. Tighten the Torx screws (T27) to 25-30 in.-lb. (2.8-3.4 N•m).

Front Inner Fairing Removal/Installation

Refer to **Figure 55**, **Figure 56** and **Figure 60**.
1. Place the motorcycle on level ground using the jiffy stand.
2. Remove the outer front fairing and windshield as described in this section.
3. Disconnect both of the 4-pin front turn signal/passing light connectors from the T-studs located at the top, outboard side of both fairing support braces (A, **Figure 61**, typical).
4. Remove the passing light assembly as described in Chapter Eleven.
5. Remove the inner fairing cap as described in this section.
6. Remove the screws securing the chrome mounting skirt (**Figure 62**) and remove it.
7A. On all models except FLHTCUSE, perform the following:
   a. Disconnect the clutch cable from the clutch lever as described in *Clutch Cable Replacement* (Chapter Six).
   b. Withdraw the clutch cable from the inner fairing rubber grommet (**Figure 63**). Move the clutch cable forward and out of the way. Remove the rubber grommet.
7B. On FLHTCUSE models, remove the clutch master cylinder from the handlebar as described in Chapter Six.
8. Remove the front brake master cylinder from the handlebar as described in Chapter Fifteen.

⑥⓪ INNER FAIRING (FLHT, FLHTCUSE AND FLHX MODELS)

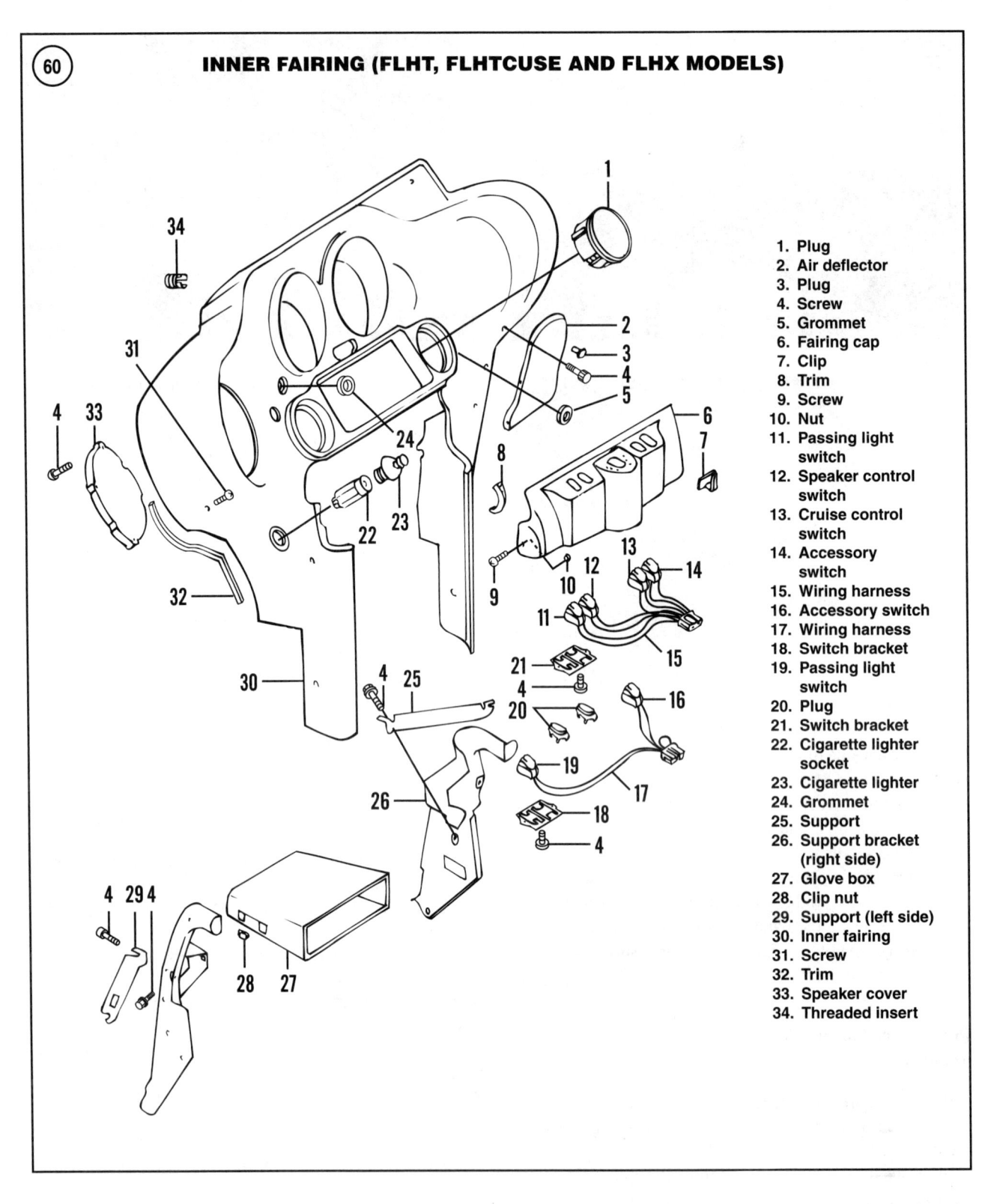

1. Plug
2. Air deflector
3. Plug
4. Screw
5. Grommet
6. Fairing cap
7. Clip
8. Trim
9. Screw
10. Nut
11. Passing light switch
12. Speaker control switch
13. Cruise control switch
14. Accessory switch
15. Wiring harness
16. Accessory switch
17. Wiring harness
18. Switch bracket
19. Passing light switch
20. Plug
21. Switch bracket
22. Cigarette lighter socket
23. Cigarette lighter
24. Grommet
25. Support
26. Support bracket (right side)
27. Glove box
28. Clip nut
29. Support (left side)
30. Inner fairing
31. Screw
32. Trim
33. Speaker cover
34. Threaded insert

9. Separate the right side handlebar switch housing as described in Chapter Eleven.
10. On 2006-2007 models, perform the following:
   a. Disconnect both the throttle and idle cables from the throttle grip as described in Chapter Nine or Chapter Ten.
   b. Withdraw the throttle and idle cables from the inner fairing rubber grommet. Move the idle and throttle cables forward and out of the way. Remove the rubber grommet.
11. Disconnect the spade terminals from the cigarette lighter (B, **Figure 61**). Hold the socket to keep if from rotating and unscrew the outer shell. Remove the socket from the inner fairing and reinstall the shell onto the socket.
12. Disconnect the spade terminals (C, **Figure 61**) from both speakers.

BODY AND FRAME

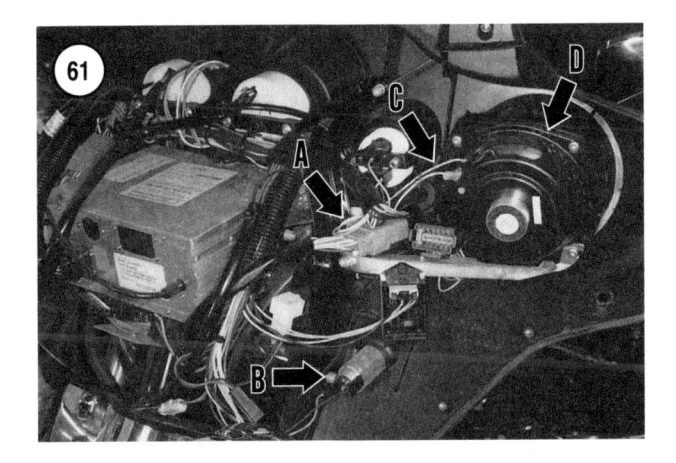

13. Remove the Torx screws (T25) securing the speaker adapter (D, **Figure 61**) to the inner fairing. Repeat for the remaining adapter.
14. On the left side of the inner fairing, unscrew the rubber boot and remove the odometer reset switch from the housing.
15. Disconnect the speedometer connector and tachometer connector from the instrument assembly.
16. Remove the Phillips screws securing the speedometer and tachometer (**Figure 64**) to the mounting brackets. Remove the speedometer and tachometer from the inner fairing. Leave the anchors on the interconnect harness installed on the outboard ears of the brackets. Push the gauges toward the rear of the motorcycle and remove both gauges from the inner fairing.
17. Disconnect the 10-pin indicator light connector.
18. Carefully cut the cable strap securing the indicator light connector between the speedometer and tachometer brackets.
19. Release the four paddles and free the indicator bulb housing from the lens assembly. Remove the lens assembly from the inner fairing.
20. Disconnect the voltmeter light connector and voltmeter connector.
21. Disconnect the fuel gauge light connector and fuel gauge connector.
22. Remove the four Allen bolts securing the inner fairing to the fairing mounting bracket.
23. Spread the bottom of the inner fairing and free it from the locating dowels in the lower fork bracket. Spread the bottom of the inner fairing bracket and release if from the same locating dowels.
24. Slightly raise the inner fairing and the support brackets further up to prevent the reengagement of the locating dowels. Raise the lower fairing and support brackets sufficiently high enough to gain access to the lower row of gauges.
25. On FLHTCU and FLHTCUSE models, disconnect the following electrical connectors:
    a. The oil pressure gauge light and oil pressure gauge connectors.
    b. The air temperature gauge light and air temperature gauge connectors.
26. Raise the inner fairing and fairing bracket together as an assembly. Pull the fairing bracket toward the front of the motorcycle and inner fairing toward the rear, and then separate them.
27. As the inner fairing is free of the radio, remove the inner fairing. Move it to the workbench and place it on towels or a blanket.
28. Reposition the fairing bracket, radio and interconnect harness onto the frame. Align the holes with the locating dowels in the lower fork bracket. Install the Allen screws and finger-tighten the screws at this time.
29. On all models, remove the hex nuts securing the voltmeter and fuel level gauges to the mounting brackets. Then, remove the voltmeter and fuel level gauge from the inner fairing, if necessary.
30. On FLHTCU and FLHTCUSE models, remove the hex nuts securing the oil pressure and air temperature gauges

CHAPTER SEVENTEEN

65 **LOWER FAIRING (FLHTCU AND FLHTCUSE MODELS)**

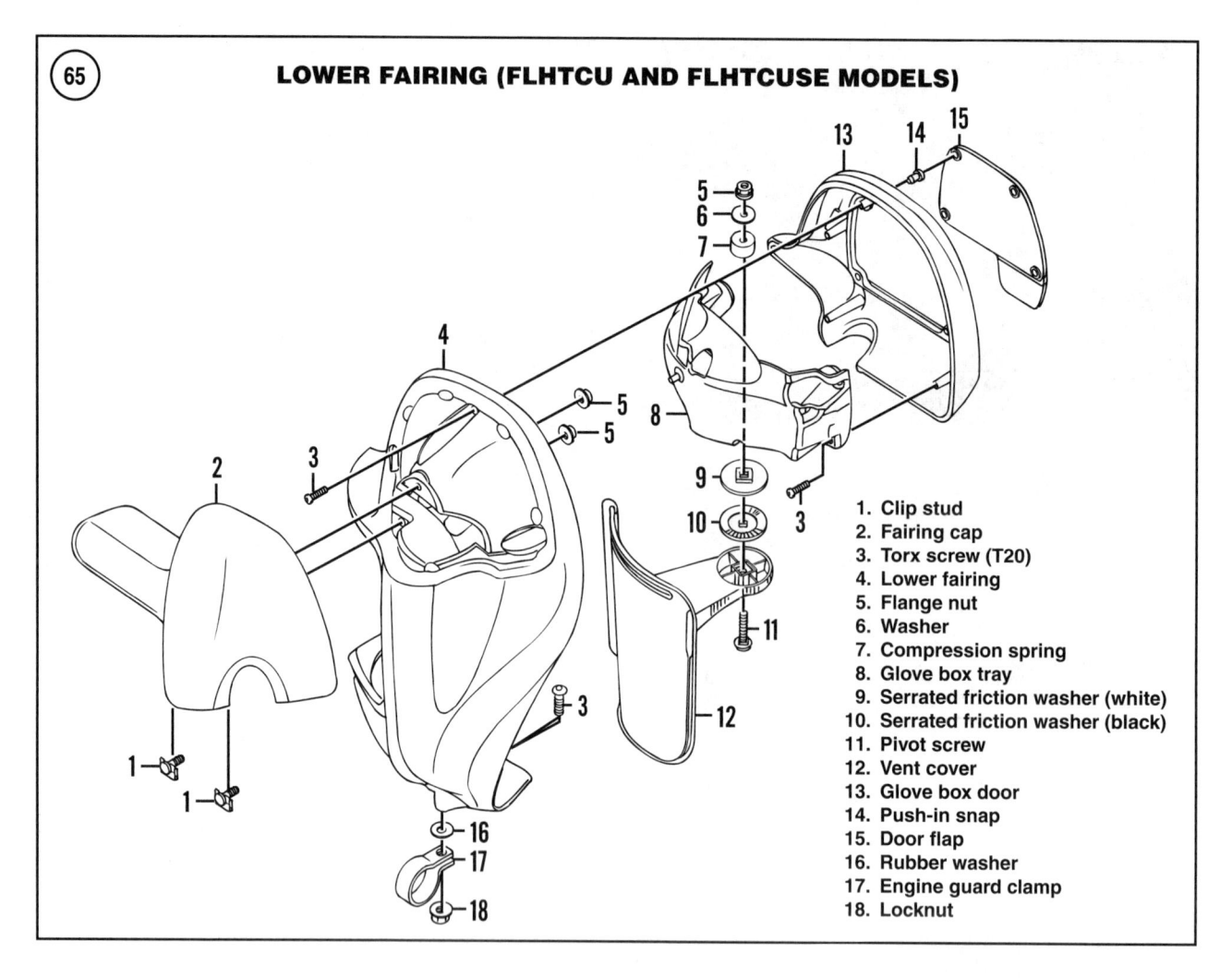

1. Clip stud
2. Fairing cap
3. Torx screw (T20)
4. Lower fairing
5. Flange nut
6. Washer
7. Compression spring
8. Glove box tray
9. Serrated friction washer (white)
10. Serrated friction washer (black)
11. Pivot screw
12. Vent cover
13. Glove box door
14. Push-in snap
15. Door flap
16. Rubber washer
17. Engine guard clamp
18. Locknut

to the mounting brackets. Remove the oil pressure and air temperature gauges from the inner fairing, if necessary.

31. Install by reversing the removal steps while noting the following:

   a. Install the two or four gauges into the inner fairing and slide the brackets over the threaded studs. Install the hex nuts and finger-tighten them. Correctly align the gauges and tighten the hex nuts to 10-20 in.-lb. (1.1-2.3 N•m).

   b. Install the speedometer and tachometer into the inner fairing. Install the Phillips screws finger-tight, correctly align the gauges, and then tighten the screws to 10-20 in.-lb. (1.1-2.3 N•m).

   c. Install both speaker adapters (D, **Figure 61**). Install the long Torx screws (T25) at the top and tighten to 35-50 in.-lb. (4.0-5.7 N•m). Install the short Torx screws (T25) at the bottom and tighten to 22-28 in.-lb. (2.5-3.2 N•m).

   d. On all models except FLHTCUSE, adjust the clutch as described in Chapter Three.

Air Deflectors (FLHTCU and FLHTCUSE Models) Removal/Installation

Refer to **Figure 60**.

1. Remove the three knurled thumb screws securing the air deflector to the lower fairing, and remove the deflector. Repeat for the remaining side if necessary.
2. Install the air deflector and the knurled thumb screws. Tighten the thumb screws to 25-30 in.-lb. (2.8-3.4 N•m).

Lower Fairing (FLHTCU and FLHTCUSE Models)

Removal

Refer to **Figure 65**.

1. Position the front wheel in the straight ahead position to protect finish on the fender and lower fairing during removal.
2. Carefully pull out and release the door flap push-in snaps. Release all four snaps and remove the door flap.
3. Reach into the glove box and remove the two flange nuts from the clip studs.
4. Push in on end of both studs. Carefully pull straight out and remove the fairing cap from the lower fairing. Do not twist the fairing cap during removal as it will be damaged.
5. Secure the upper portion of the lower fairing to the engine guard with tape or twine.

BODY AND FRAME

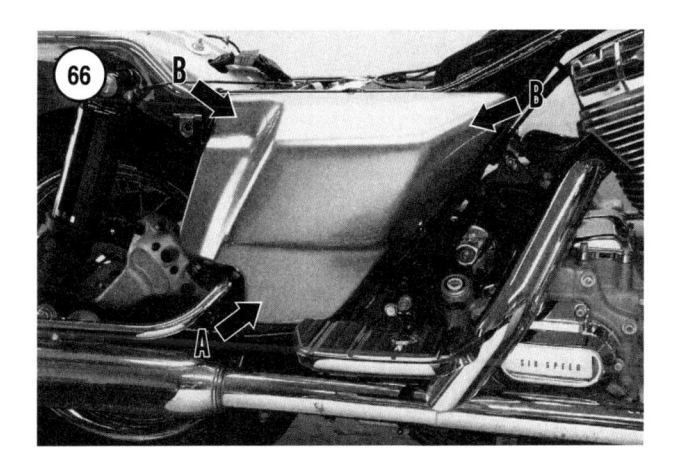

6. Secure the locknut below the engine guard clamp and remove the Torx screw (T40) securing the lower fairing to the engine guard.
7. Carefully remove the lower fairing from the engine guard.
8. Remove and discard the rubber washer located between the lower fairing and the clamp.
9. Repeat the procedure for the other side, if necessary.

Installation

1. Make sure the front wheel is in the straight ahead position.
2. Install the lower fairing onto the engine guard and secure it with tape or twine.
3. Install the Torx screw (T40) through the lower fairing, *new* rubber washer and engine guard clamp.
4. Install the locknut onto the Torx screw and finger-tighten the nut.
5. Make sure the clip studs are in place on the fairing cap.
6. Position the fairing cap against the engine guard and against the fairing lower while aligning the clips suds with the holes in the lower fairing.
7. Secure both parts and install the flange nuts onto the clip studs.
8. Make sure the lower fairing is centered on the engine guard, and alternately tighten the flange nuts to 35-40 in.-lb. (4.0-4.5 N•m).
9. Secure the locknut on the engine guard clamp and tighten the Torx screw (T40) to 90-100 in.-lb. (10.2-11.3 N•m).
10. Repeat the procedure for the other side, if necessary.

Disassembly

1. Remove the Torx screws (T20) securing the glove box door and tray to the lower fairing. Separate the parts.
2. Remove the Torx screws (T20) securing the glove box tray to the door. Separate the parts.
3. Remove the locknut, washer and compression spring (rubber sleeve) glove box tray and two serrated washers from the pivot screw in vent door arm.
4. Remove the pivot screw from the vent door arm.

Assembly

1. Slide threaded end of pivot screw up through hole in center of vent door arm and hold it in place with tape or other means.
2. Position the *new* black serrated friction washer with the teeth facing up and install it over the pivot screw.
3. Install the serrated friction washer's square shaped boss onto the square recess in the vent door arm, and seat it correctly.

NOTE
Always use two washers of different colors. If two black or two white washers are installed there will be a chirping sound when the lower fairing is adjusted.

4. Position the *new*, white, serrated friction washer with the teeth facing down, and install it over the pivot screw. The teeth on the two washers must engage.
5. Install the glove box tray over the pivot screw and engage the square boss of the white serrated washer. Engage the glove box tray's pin with the slot at the top of the vent door.
6. Install the compression spring, flat washer and locknut onto the pivot screw.
7. Tighten the locknut against the flat washer until it is snug against it. Do not allow the flat washer to rotate, and then tighten the locknut an additional 1 1/2 turns. Move the vent door and check for ease of movement. It is recommended that the compression spring should be compressed to a height of 0.420-0.460 in (10.7-11.7 mm). Readjust if necessary.
8. Install the glove box door onto the glove box tray. Align the two holes in the glove box tray with the two bosses in the glove box door and install the two Torx screws (T20). Alternately tighten the Torx screws (T20) to 20-25 in.-lb. (2.3-2.8 N•m). Do not overtighten the screws as the screw mounting posts may crack or strip out.
9. Install the glove box tray into the top of the lower fairing and align the three holes in the lower fairing with the holes in the glove box tray, and the bosses in the glove box door. Install the two Torx screws (T20). Alternately tighten the Torx screws (T20) to 20-25 in.-lb. (2.3-2.8 N•m). Do not overtighten the screws as the screw mounting posts may crack or strip out.
10. Install the anchor on draw string of glove box flap into the hole in the glove box door. Install the glove box door flap and fasten snaps.

FRAME SIDE COVERS

Removal/Installation

1. Carefully pull out on the bottom of the side cover (A, **Figure 66**). Then, pull on each corner of the top (B, **Figure 66**) and remove the side cover from the frame grommets.
2. Install the side cover onto the frame grommets and tap into place with the palm of hand. Make sure the side cover posts are completely engaged with the frame grommets.

CHAPTER SEVENTEEN

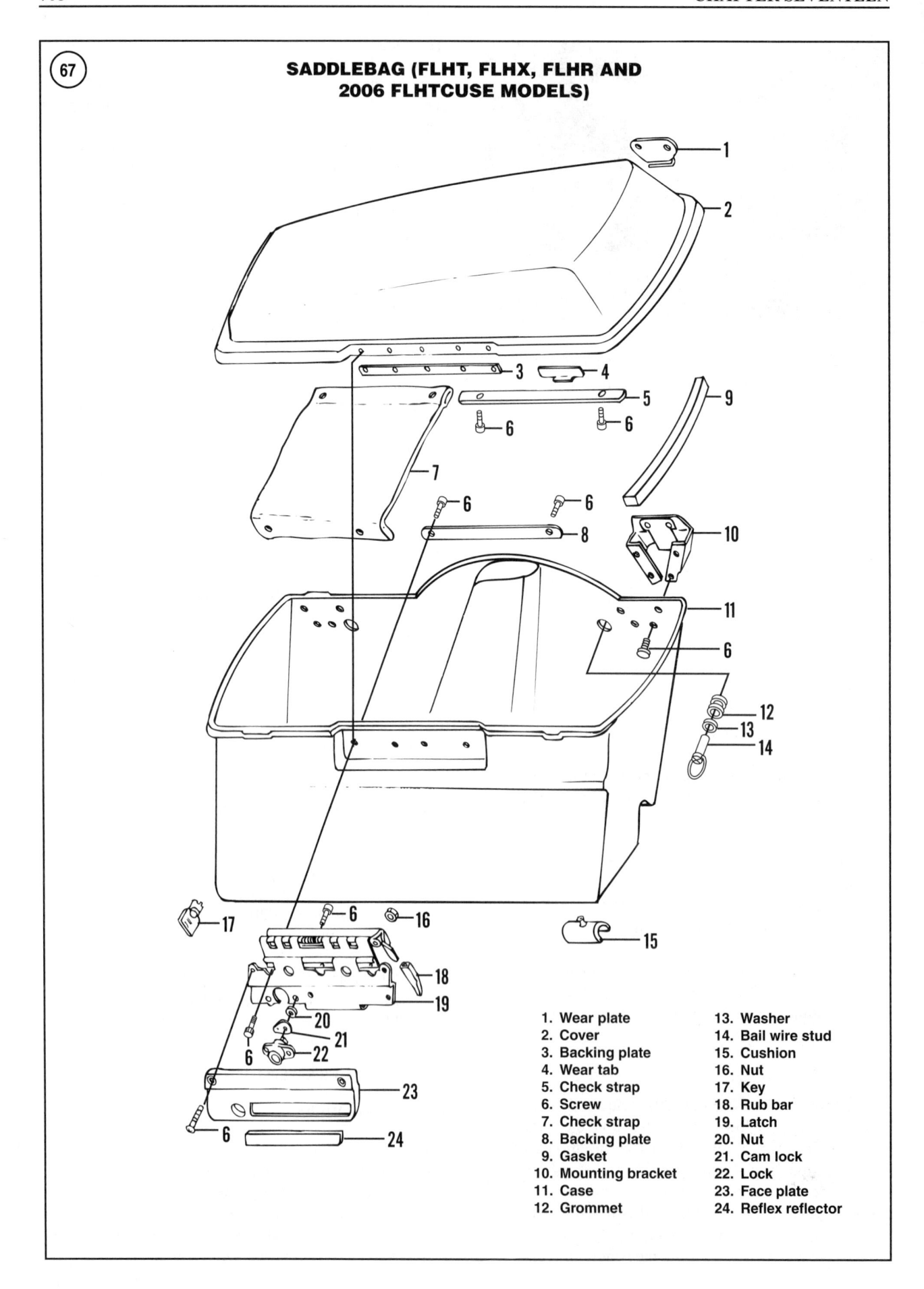

67 SADDLEBAG (FLHT, FLHX, FLHR AND 2006 FLHTCUSE MODELS)

1. Wear plate
2. Cover
3. Backing plate
4. Wear tab
5. Check strap
6. Screw
7. Check strap
8. Backing plate
9. Gasket
10. Mounting bracket
11. Case
12. Grommet
13. Washer
14. Bail wire stud
15. Cushion
16. Nut
17. Key
18. Rub bar
19. Latch
20. Nut
21. Cam lock
22. Lock
23. Face plate
24. Reflex reflector

BODY AND FRAME

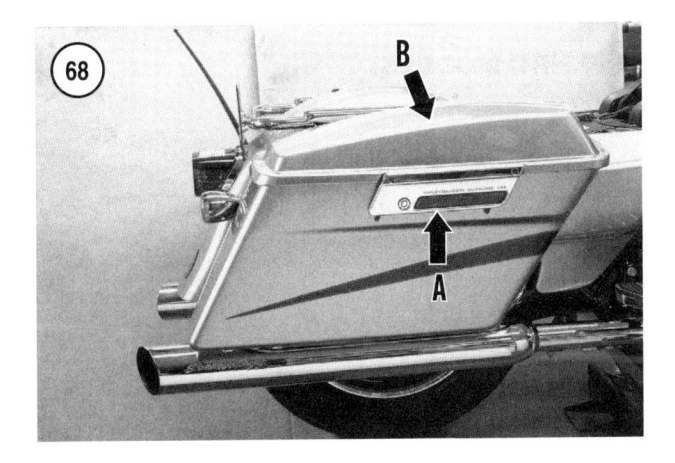

SADDLEBAGS

FLHT, FLHX, FLHR and 2006 FLHTCUSE Models

Removal/installation

Refer to **Figure 67**.
1. Place the motorcycle on level ground using the jiffy stand.
2. Unlock the handle latch.
3. Pull out on bottom of latch (A, **Figure 68**) and open the cover (B).
4. Within the saddlebag case, grasp the latch bail wire (**Figure 69**), rotate the latch stud 1/4 turn counterclockwise and release the stud from the mounting bracket (**Figure 70**). Repeat for the other latch stud.
5. Carefully pull the saddlebag up and out of the bracket or guards.
6. Inspect the latch mounting brackets (**Figure 71** and **Figure 72**) for damage.
7. Install by reversing the removal steps. Make sure the saddlebag is locked securely into place.

FLHRS, FLHRC and FLHRSE Models

Removal/installation

Refer to **Figures 73-75**.
1. Place the motorcycle on level ground using the jiffy stand.
2A. On FLHRC models, raise the decorative buckle and press on the tabs on both sides of the catch. Repeat for the remaining buckle and catch. Open the cover.
2B. On FLHRS and FLHRSE models, press on the button at the front inboard side of the saddlebag and open the cover.
3. Within the saddlebag case, grasp the latch bail wire (**Figure 69**), rotate the latch stud 1/4 turn counterclockwise and release the stud from the mounting bracket (**Figure 70**). Repeat for the remaining stud.
4. Carefully pull the saddlebag up and out of the bracket or guards.

CHAPTER SEVENTEEN

SADDLEBAG (2006-2009 FLHRC MODELS)

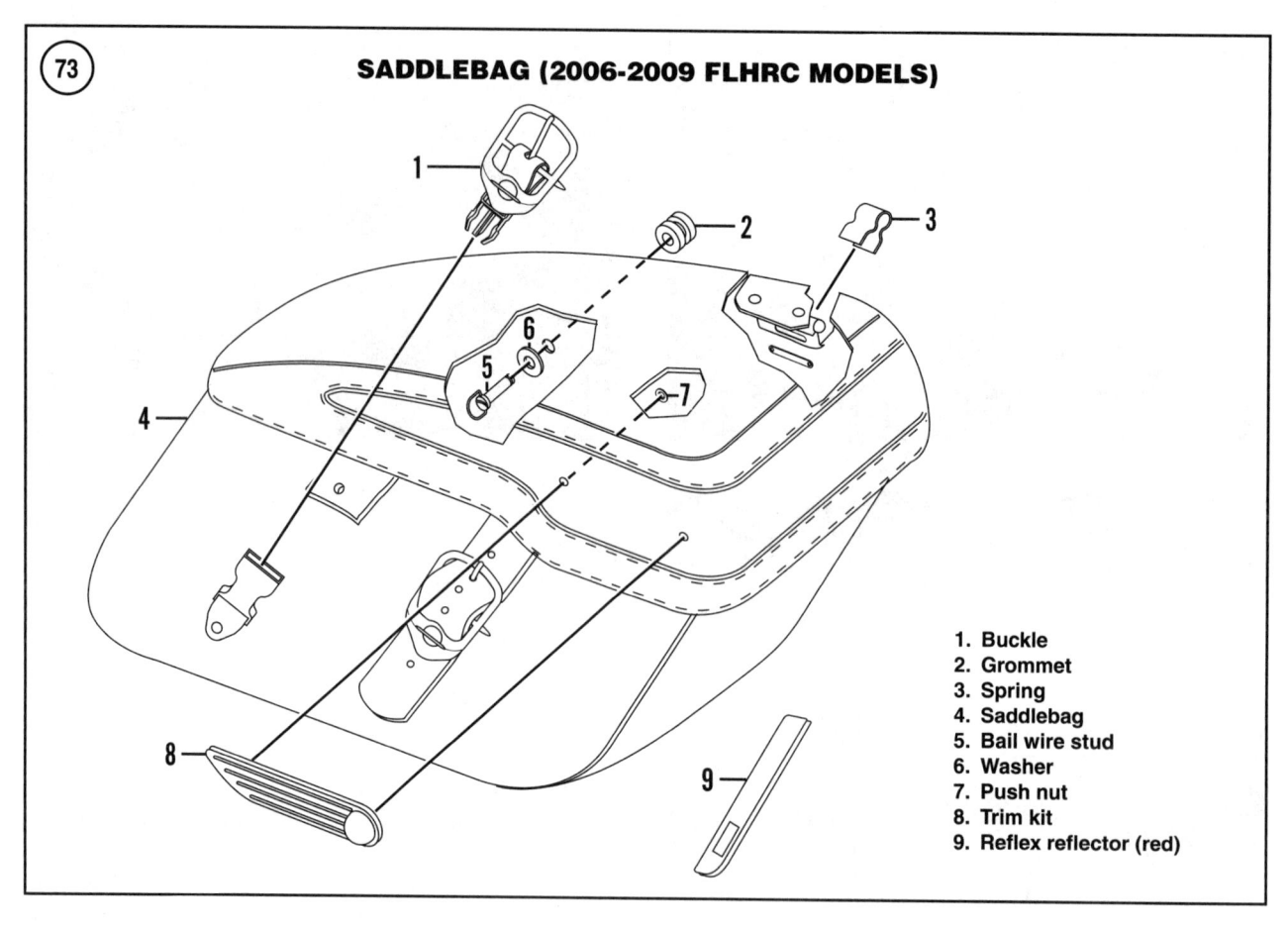

1. Buckle
2. Grommet
3. Spring
4. Saddlebag
5. Bail wire stud
6. Washer
7. Push nut
8. Trim kit
9. Reflex reflector (red)

SADDLEBAG (2006-2007 FLHRS MODELS)

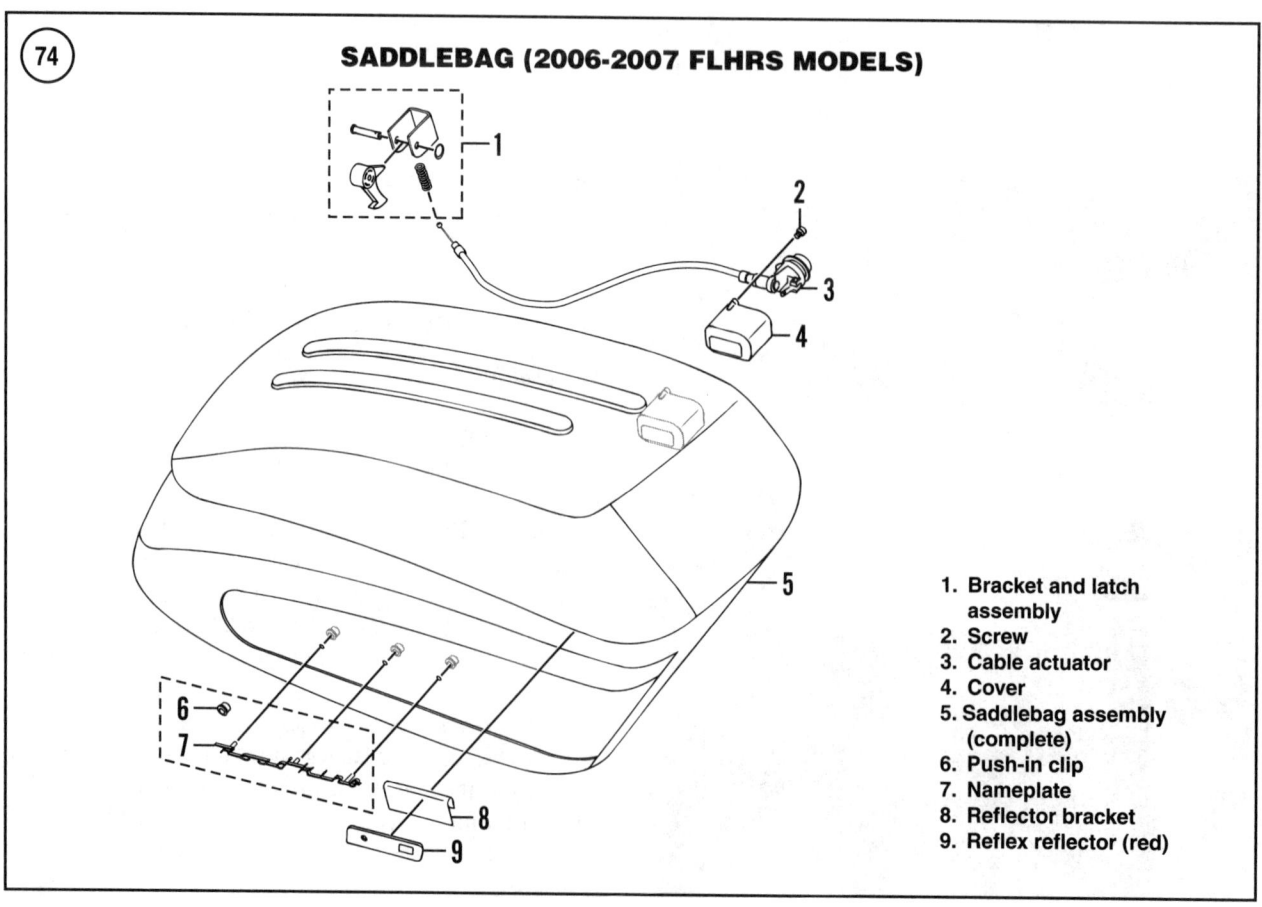

1. Bracket and latch assembly
2. Screw
3. Cable actuator
4. Cover
5. Saddlebag assembly (complete)
6. Push-in clip
7. Nameplate
8. Reflector bracket
9. Reflex reflector (red)

BODY AND FRAME

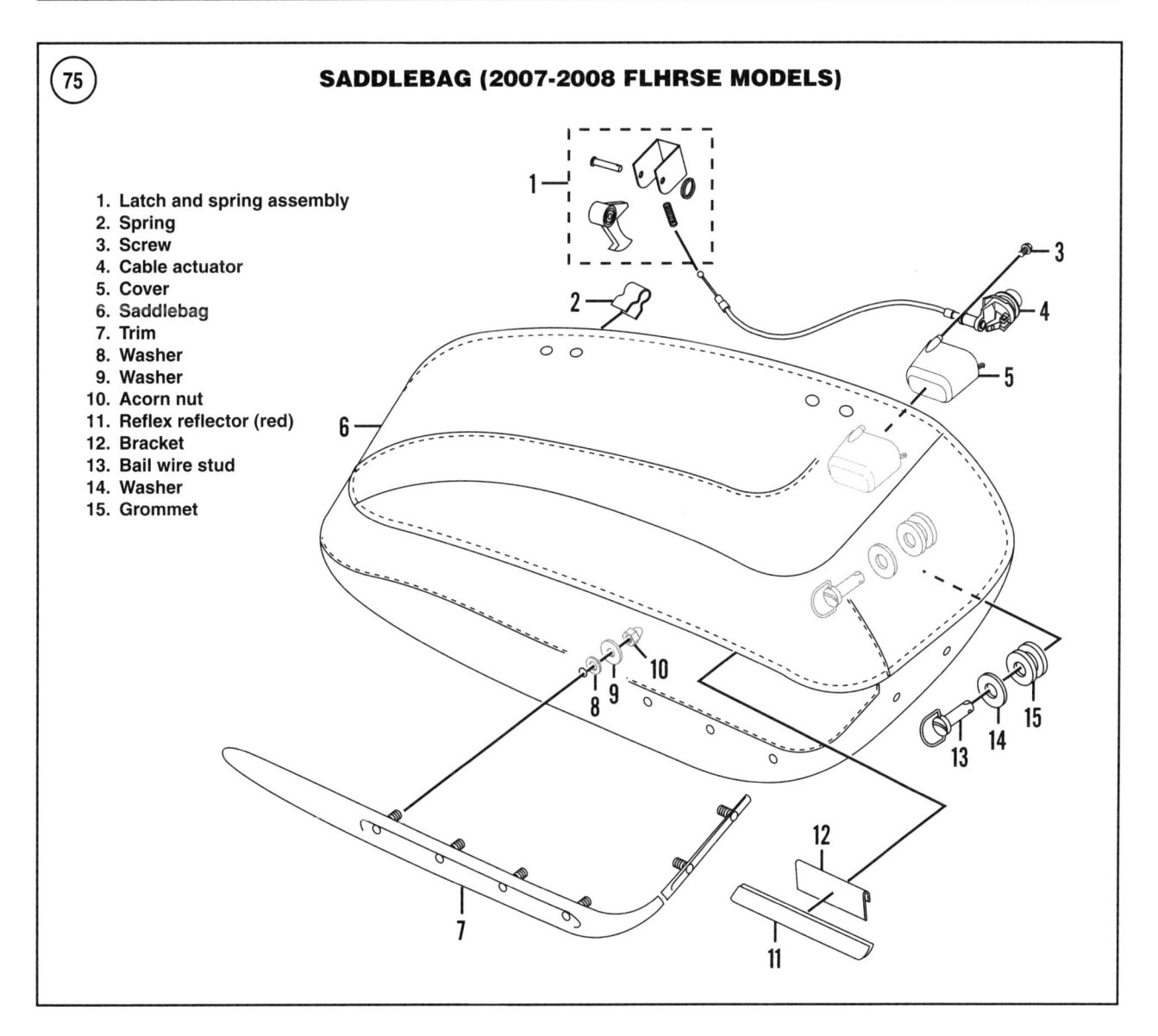

SADDLEBAG (2007-2008 FLHRSE MODELS)

1. Latch and spring assembly
2. Spring
3. Screw
4. Cable actuator
5. Cover
6. Saddlebag
7. Trim
8. Washer
9. Washer
10. Acorn nut
11. Reflex reflector (red)
12. Bracket
13. Bail wire stud
14. Washer
15. Grommet

5. Inspect the latch mounting brackets (**Figure 71** and **Figure 72**) for damage.
6. Install by reversing the removal steps. Make sure the saddlebag is locked securely into place.

Cable Assembly and Latch (FLHRS and FLHRSE Models)

Removal/installation

Refer to **Figure 74** and **Figure 75**.
1. Open the saddlebag cover as described in this section.
2. Remove the two screws on the inboard side of the saddlebag securing the plastic cover. Remove the cover.
3. Depress the wire form and pull button from opening in the saddlebag.
4. Remove sleeve from opening in the saddlebag.
5. On the inboard side of the saddlebag cover, remove the lock ring from the opening in the end of the latch pin.
6. Pull the latch pin from the metal shroud, the saddlebag bracket and the latch. Remove the metal shroud.

7. Depress the spring and pull on the cable ball end and remove from the slot in the latch. Remove the latch.
8. Remove the spring from the cable and remove the e-clip from the groove in the fitting in the end of the cable.
9. Pull the cable end fitting from the opening in the saddlebag bracket.
10. Pull the cable from the channel along the inboard edge of the saddlebag and remove it.
11. Install by reversing the removal steps.

Adjustment

1. Open the saddlebag cover as described in this section.
2. Remove the two screws on the inboard side of the saddlebag securing the plastic cover and remove the cover.
3. Loosen the locknut on the cable adjuster hex body.
4. Rotate the adjuster hex body in either direction until the closest part of the latch is approximately 3/8 in. (9.5 mm) from the inboard side of the saddlebag cover.
5. Tighten the locknut securely.

CHAPTER SEVENTEEN

⑦⑥ SADDLABAG TOP (FLHTCUSE MODELS)

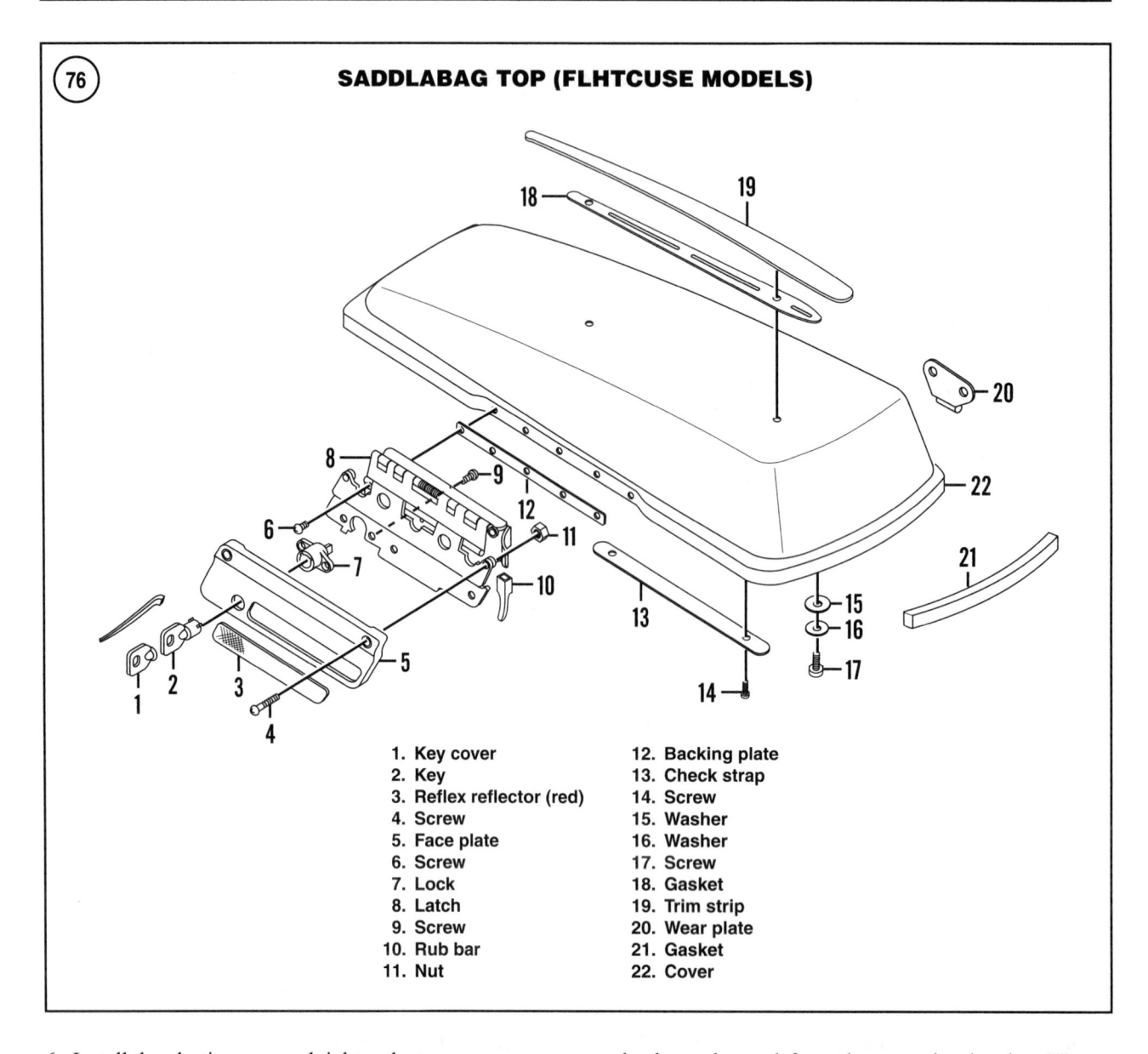

1. Key cover
2. Key
3. Reflex reflector (red)
4. Screw
5. Face plate
6. Screw
7. Lock
8. Latch
9. Screw
10. Rub bar
11. Nut
12. Backing plate
13. Check strap
14. Screw
15. Washer
16. Washer
17. Screw
18. Gasket
19. Trim strip
20. Wear plate
21. Gasket
22. Cover

6. Install the plastic cover and tighten the two screws.
7. Close and open the saddlebag cover several times to make sure it locks each time. Readjust if necessary.

FLHTCUSE Models

Removal/installation

Refer to **Figure 76** and **Figure 77**.
1. Place the motorcycle on level ground using the jiffy stand.
2. Pull out on bottom of latch (A, **Figure 68**) and open the cover (B).

CAUTION
Hold onto the saddlebag while removing the second latch to avoid damage to the wiring harness.

3. Within the saddlebag case, grasp the latch bail wire (**Figure 69**), rotate the latch stud 1/4 turn counterclockwise and release the stud from the mounting bracket (**Figure 70**). Repeat for the remaining stud.
4. Tilt the top of the saddlebag away from the guard and disconnect the electrical connector for the power lock.
5. Carefully pull the saddlebag up and out of the bracket or guards.
6. Install by reversing the removal steps. Make sure the saddlebag is locked securely into place.

Latch replacement

1. Place the motorcycle on level ground using the jiffy stand.
2. Unlock the handle latch.
3. Pull out on bottom of latch (A, **Figure 68**) and open the cover (B).
4. Pull straight up and remove the felt liner.
5. Remove the two screws from the check strap and the latch cover.

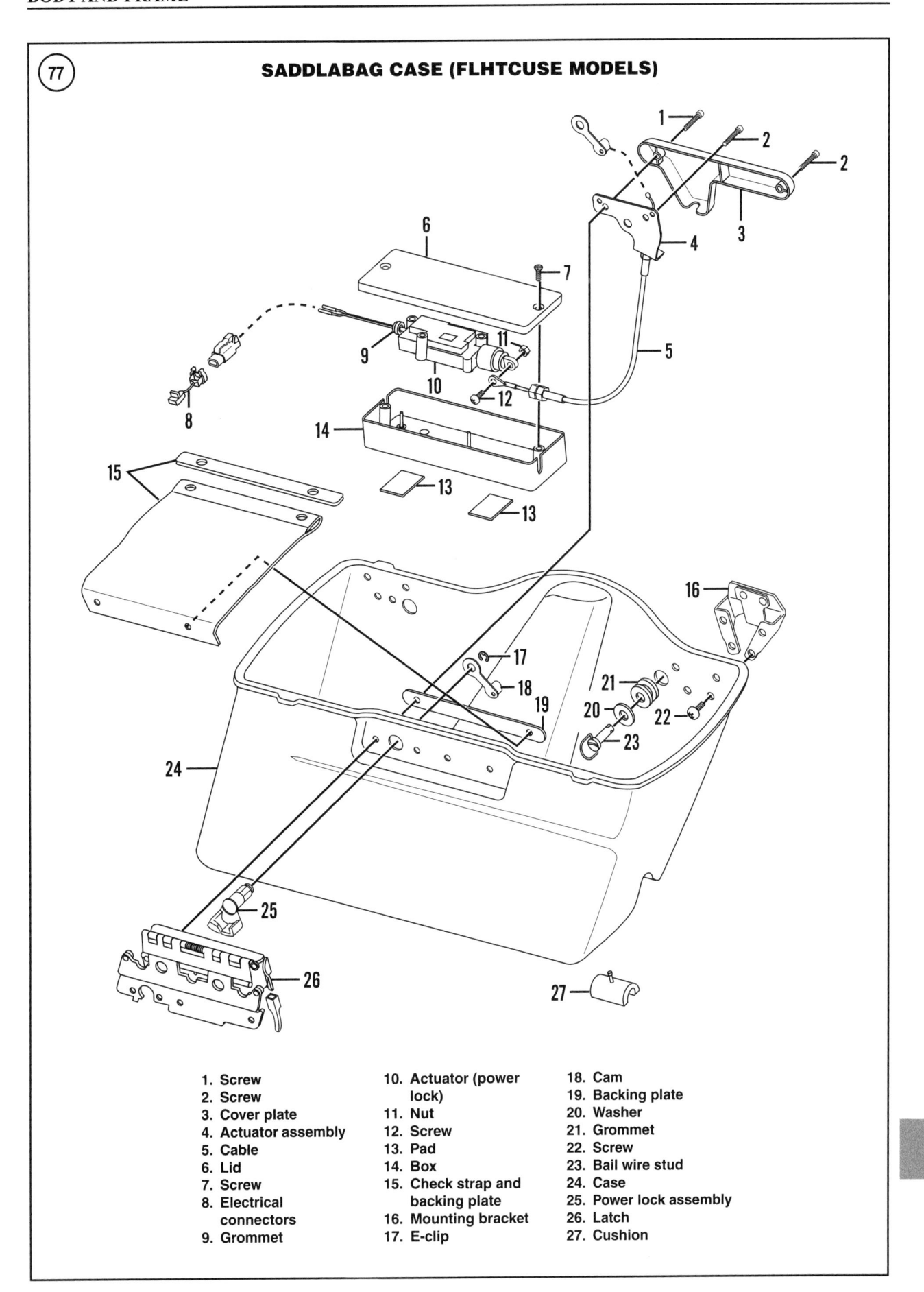

BODY AND FRAME

SADDLABAG CASE (FLHTCUSE MODELS)

1. Screw
2. Screw
3. Cover plate
4. Actuator assembly
5. Cable
6. Lid
7. Screw
8. Electrical connectors
9. Grommet
10. Actuator (power lock)
11. Nut
12. Screw
13. Pad
14. Box
15. Check strap and backing plate
16. Mounting bracket
17. E-clip
18. Cam
19. Backing plate
20. Washer
21. Grommet
22. Screw
23. Bail wire stud
24. Case
25. Power lock assembly
26. Latch
27. Cushion

CHAPTER SEVENTEEN

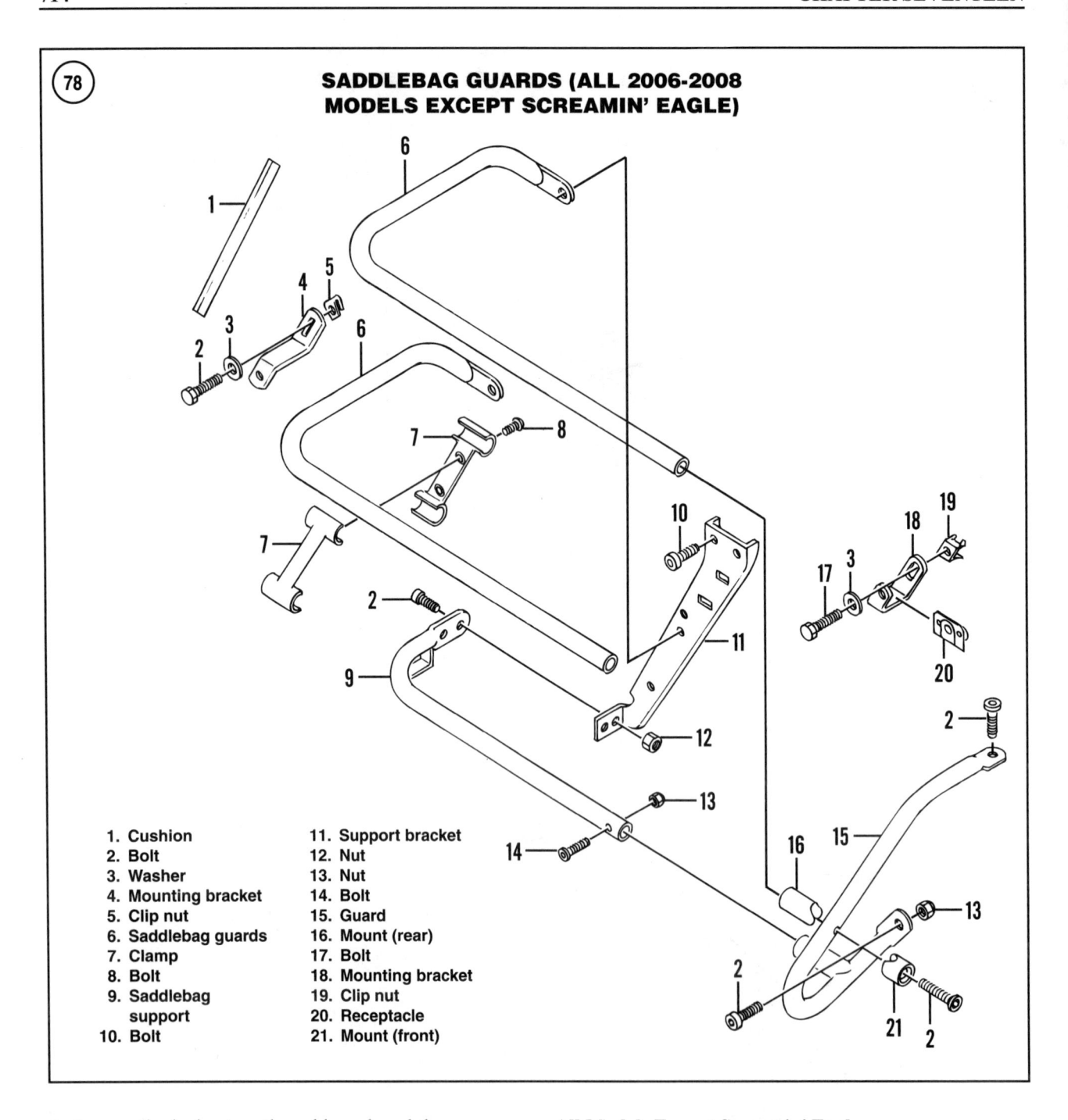

⑦⑧ SADDLEBAG GUARDS (ALL 2006-2008 MODELS EXCEPT SCREAMIN' EAGLE)

1. Cushion
2. Bolt
3. Washer
4. Mounting bracket
5. Clip nut
6. Saddlebag guards
7. Clamp
8. Bolt
9. Saddlebag support
10. Bolt
11. Support bracket
12. Nut
13. Nut
14. Bolt
15. Guard
16. Mount (rear)
17. Bolt
18. Mounting bracket
19. Clip nut
20. Receptacle
21. Mount (front)

6. Loosen the locknut on the cable end, and then remove the barrel and cable from the inner cam arm.
7. Remove the e-clip, spacer, spring, inner cam and outer cam.
8. Remove the two inner screws and remove the cam plate from the saddlebag.
9. Install by reversing the removal steps. Tighten the two inner screws to 25 in.-lb. (2.8 N•m).

SADDLEBAG SUPPORTS/GUARDS

The following procedures explain the complete removal and installation of the entire assembly. Follow the procedure only as far as necessary to reach the damaged part.

All Models Except Screamin' Eagle Removal/Installation

Refer to **Figure 78** and **Figure 79**.

Saddlebag lower support rail

1. Place the motorcycle on level ground using the jiffy stand.
2. Remove the saddlebag as described in this chapter.
3. Remove the bolts (**Figure 80**), lockwashers and nuts securing the rail to the frame bracket and rear fender.
4. Remove the bolts (**Figure 81**) securing the muffler to the support rail.

BODY AND FRAME 715

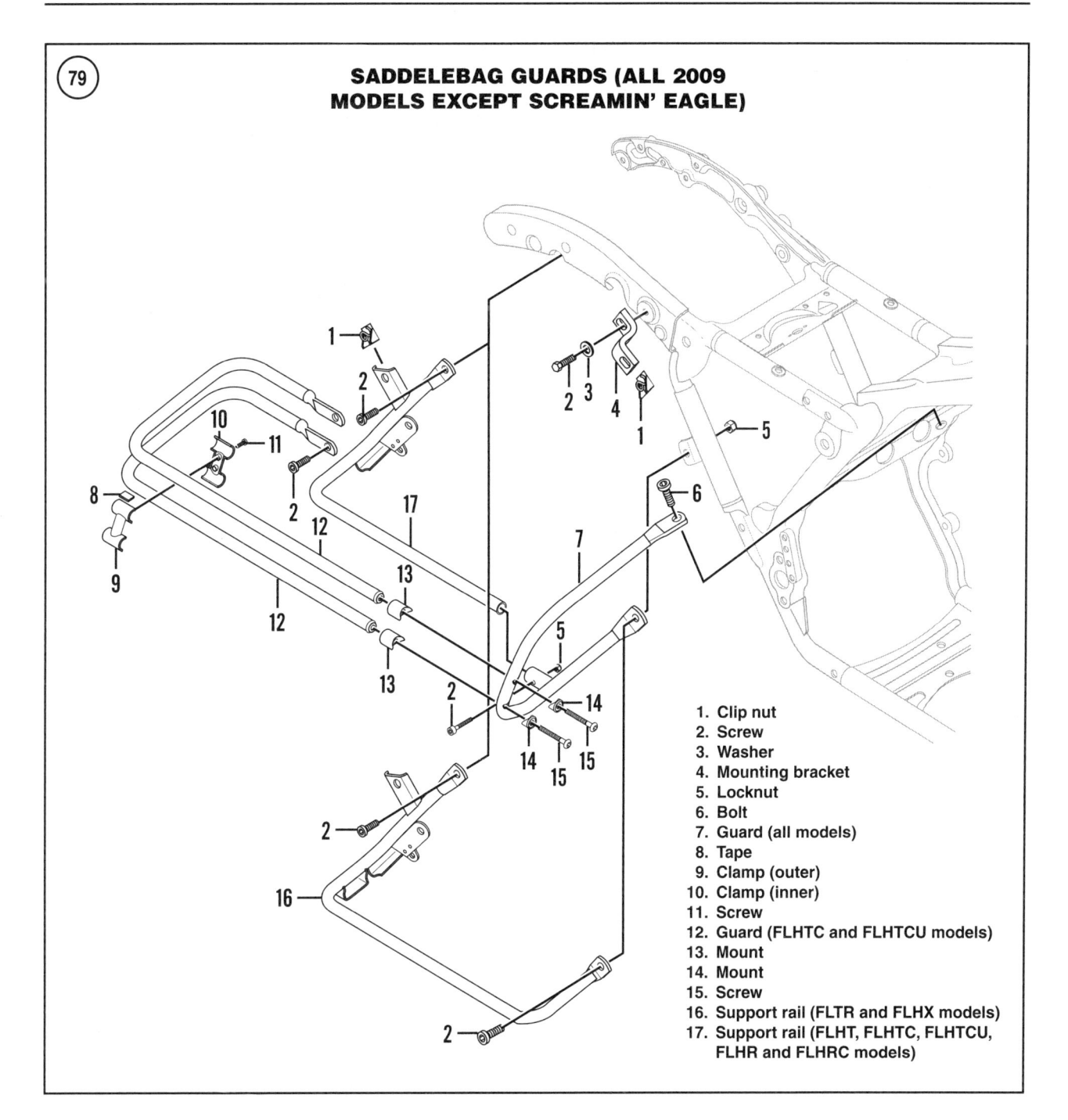

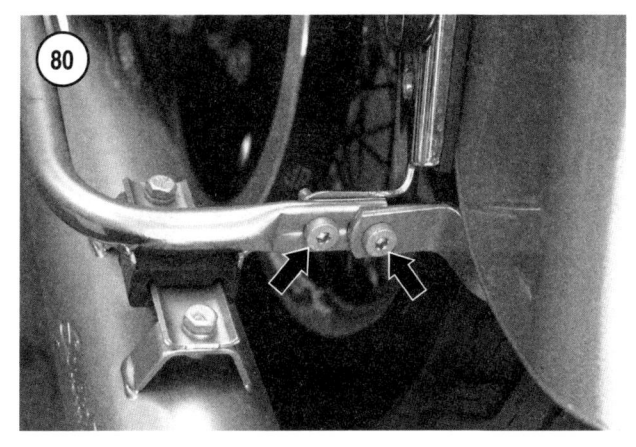

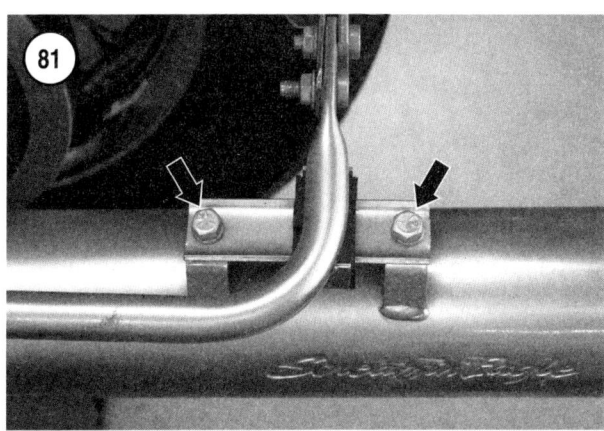

SADDLEBAG GUARDS (ALL 2009 MODELS EXCEPT SCREAMIN' EAGLE)

1. Clip nut
2. Screw
3. Washer
4. Mounting bracket
5. Locknut
6. Bolt
7. Guard (all models)
8. Tape
9. Clamp (outer)
10. Clamp (inner)
11. Screw
12. Guard (FLHTC and FLHTCU models)
13. Mount
14. Mount
15. Screw
16. Support rail (FLTR and FLHX models)
17. Support rail (FLHT, FLHTC, FLHTCU, FLHR and FLHRC models)

17

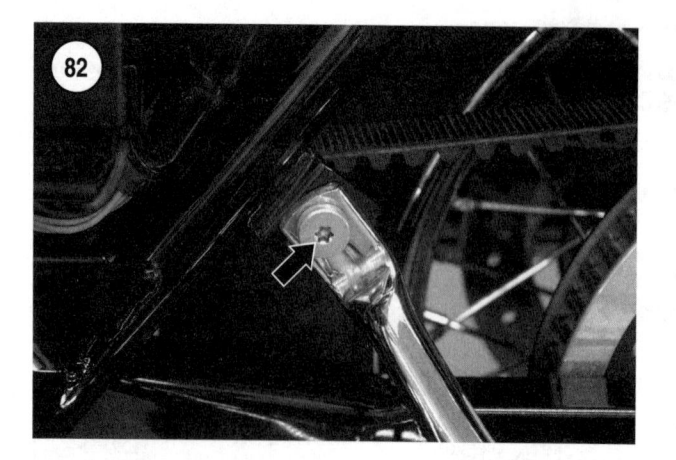

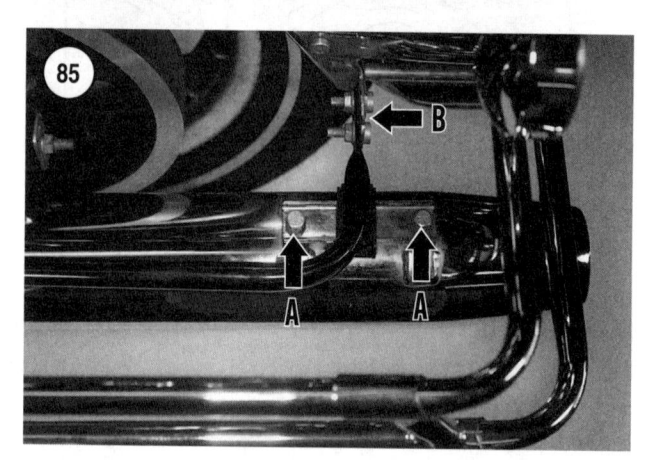

5. Support the rear of the muffler to the frame with a Bungee cord or rope.
6. Remove the Torx bolt (**Figure 82**) securing the support rail to the frame weldment and remove the support rail.
7. Remove the bolt and washer (A, **Figure 83**, typical) securing the support bracket (B), if necessary. Remove the bracket and spring plate assembly.
8. Install by reversing the removal steps. Tighten all bolts and nuts as follows:
   a. Saddlebag support rail-to-support bracket bolts: 15-20 ft.-lb. (20.3-27.1 N•m).
   b. Support rail to rear fender and frame bolt and nut: 15-20 ft.-lb. (20.3-27.1 N•m).
   c. Support rail to muffler bolts: 96-144 in.-lb. (10.8-16.3 N•m).
   d. Support bracket assembly bolt: 15-20 ft.-lb. (20.3-27.1 N•m).

Saddlebag support guards

1. Place the motorcycle on level ground using the jiffy stand.
2. Remove the saddlebag as described in this chapter.
3. Remove the front lower bolt (**Figure 84**) and locknut securing the guard to the frame.
4. Remove the bolts (A, **Figure 85**, typical) and lockwashers securing the saddlebag support rail to the muffler.

BODY AND FRAME

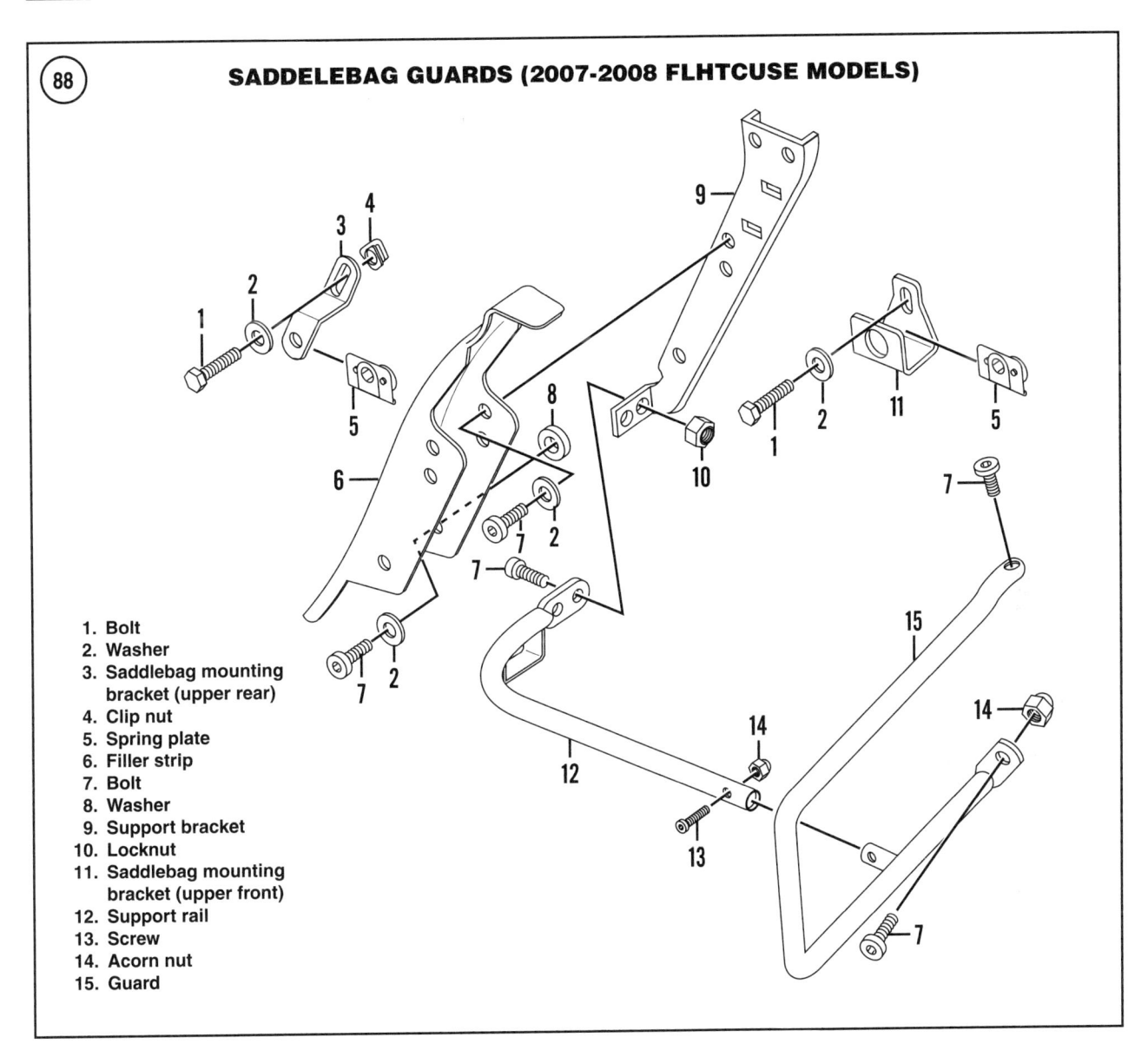

⑧ SADDLEBAG GUARDS (2007-2008 FLHTCUSE MODELS)

1. Bolt
2. Washer
3. Saddlebag mounting bracket (upper rear)
4. Clip nut
5. Spring plate
6. Filler strip
7. Bolt
8. Washer
9. Support bracket
10. Locknut
11. Saddlebag mounting bracket (upper front)
12. Support rail
13. Screw
14. Acorn nut
15. Guard

5. Remove one of the bolts (B, **Figure 85**) securing the rear support bracket to the frame bracket and rear fender. Loosen the other bolt at this time, but leave it in place.

6. Hold onto the saddlebag support and remove the front upper bolt (A, **Figure 86**) securing the front guard to the frame.

7. Remove the remaining bolt (B, **Figure 86**) securing the rear support bracket to the frame bracket.

8. Remove the saddlebag guard assembly (**Figure 87**) from the frame.

9. Support the rear of the muffler to the frame with a Bungee cord or rope.

10. Remove the bolt and washer (A, **Figure 83**, typical) securing the support bracket (B), if necessary. Remove the bracket and spring plate assembly.

11. Disassemble the assembly as necessary.

12. Install by reversing the removal steps. Tighten all bolts and nuts as follows:

   a. Saddlebag mounting bracket screws: 60-96 in.-lb. (6.8-10.8 N•m).

   b. Saddlebag support bracket bolts: 15-20 ft.-lb. (20.3-27.1 N•m).

   c. Saddlebag support rail-to-support bracket bolts: 15-20 ft.-lb. (20.3-27.1 N•m).

   d. Front guard-to-frame bolts, or bolts and nuts: 15-20 ft.-lb. (20.3-27.1 N•m).

   e. Support rail-to-guard screws: 70-100 in.-lb. (7.9-11.3 N•m).

   f. Front guard-to-saddlebag guard screws: 70-120 in.-lb. (7.9-13.6 N•m).

   g. Saddlebag guard-to-clamp screws: 30-50 in.-lb. (3.4-5.7 N•m).

Screamin' Eagle Models
Removal/Installation

Refer to **Figures 88-91**.

1. Remove both frame side covers as described in this chapter.

89 SADDLEBAG GUARDS (2007-2008 FLHRSE MODELS)

1. Bolt
2. Washer
3. Mounting bracket (upper rear)
4. Spring plate
5. Support bracket
6. Clip nut
7. Trim
8. Locknut
9. Mounting bracket (upper front)
10. Support rail
11. Bolt

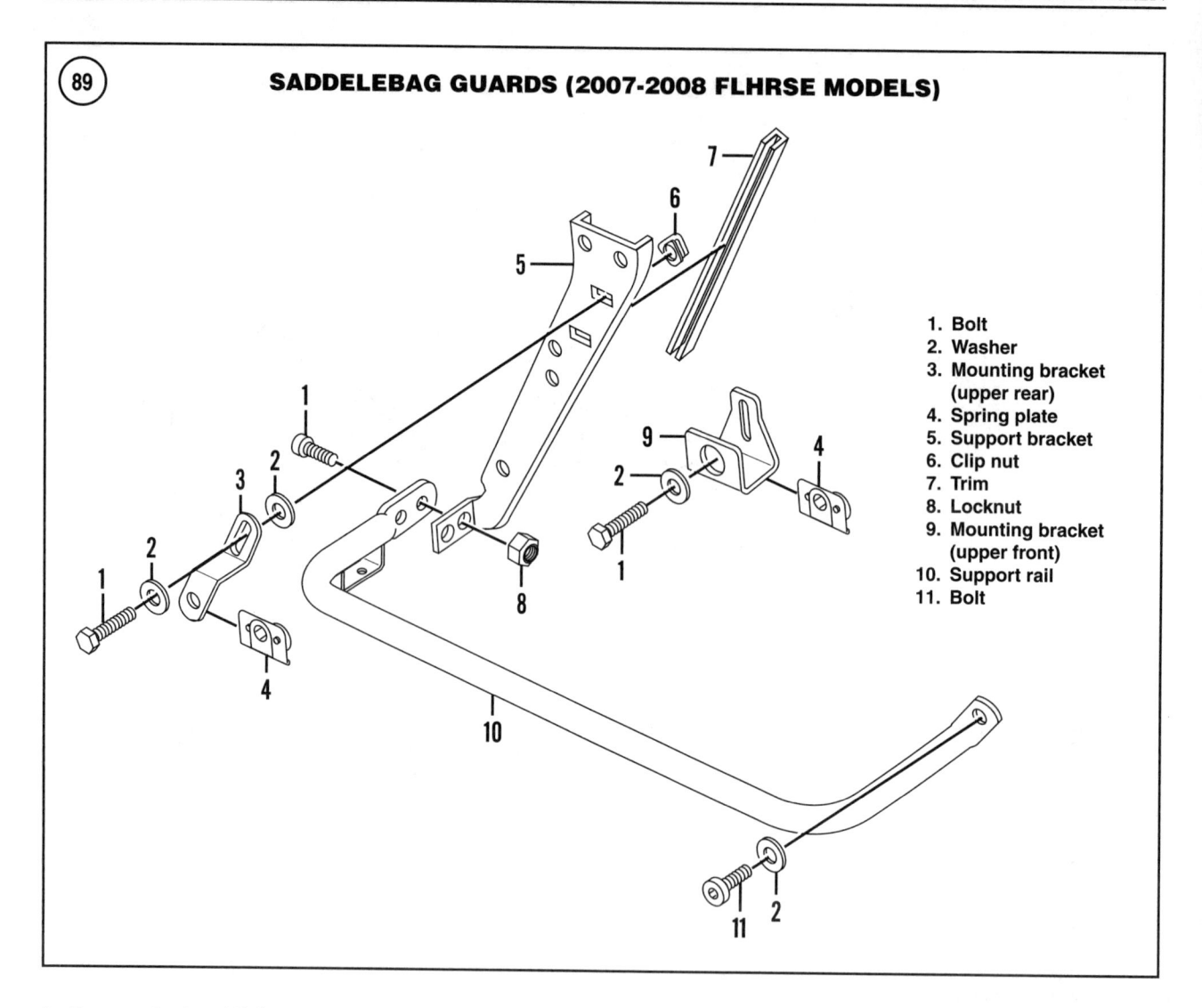

2. Remove both saddlebags as described in this chapter.
3A. On FLHTCUSE models, perform the following:
   a. Remove the two bolts, washers and spacers (locknuts on 2009 models) securing the filler panel to the support bracket, or support rail.
   b. Remove the two screws and lockwashers securing the support rail to the muffler. Remove the muffler mounting bracket and rubber mount from the support rail.
   c. On 2007-2008 models, remove the bolt and locknut securing the support rail to the support bracket.
   d. On 2009 models, remove the bolt securing the support rail to the frame.
   e. Remove the bolt and locknut securing the guard to the frame.
   f. Remove the support rail and guard assembly.
3B. On FLHRSE models, perform the following:
   a. Remove the front bolt and locknut securing the support rail to the frame.
   b. Remove the bolts and locknuts securing the support rail to the mounting bracket.
   c. Remove the support rail.
3C. On FLTRSE models, perform the following:

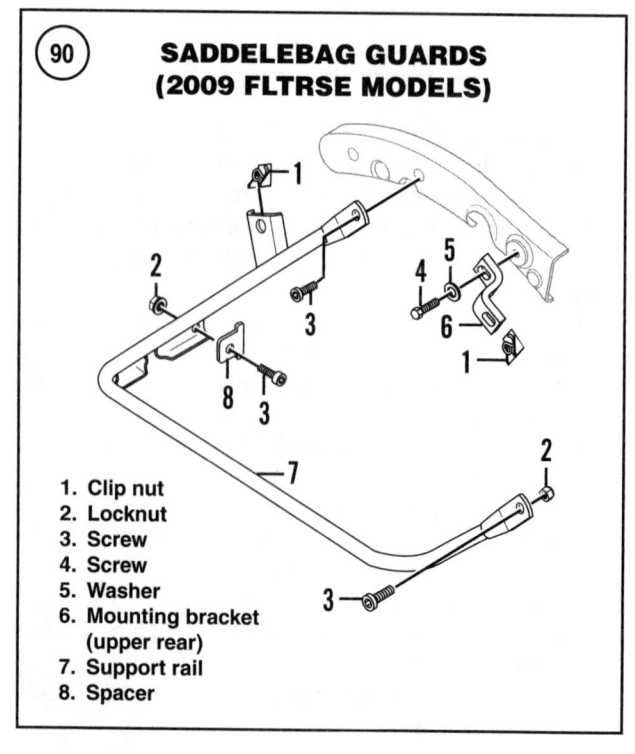

90 SADDLEBAG GUARDS (2009 FLTRSE MODELS)

1. Clip nut
2. Locknut
3. Screw
4. Screw
5. Washer
6. Mounting bracket (upper rear)
7. Support rail
8. Spacer

BODY AND FRAME

SADDLEBAG GUARDS (2009 FLHTCUSE)

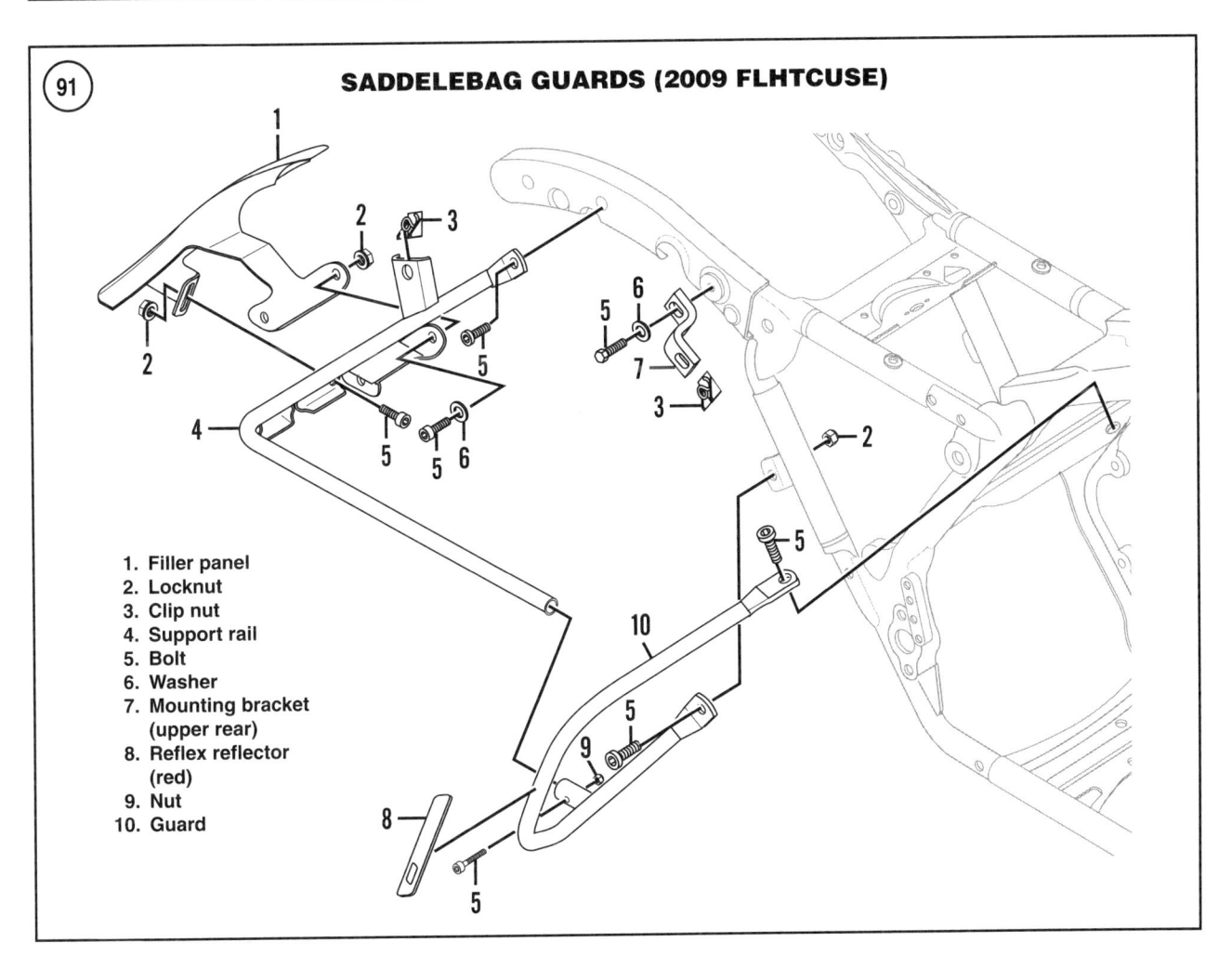

91

1. Filler panel
2. Locknut
3. Clip nut
4. Support rail
5. Bolt
6. Washer
7. Mounting bracket (upper rear)
8. Reflex reflector (red)
9. Nut
10. Guard

92

a. Remove the screws, spacers and locknuts securing the support rail to the rear mounting tab.
b. Remove the front screw and locknut securing the support rail to the frame.
c. Remove the rear screw securing the support to the frame.
d. Remove the support rail.

4. Install by reversing the removal steps. Tighten all bolts and nuts as follows:
   a. Tighten the bolts and nuts securing the support rail to the support bracket to 15-20 ft.-lb. (20.3-27.1 N•m).
   b. Tighten the bolts securing the guard to the frame to 15-20 ft.-lb. (20.3-27.1 N•m).
   c. Tighten the screw and nut securing the support rail to the guard to 70-100 in.-lb. (7.9-11.3 N•m).
   d. Tighten the remaining bolts securely.

Support Bracket (All Models)
Removal/Installation

1. Remove the radio antenna (A, **Figure 92**) as described in Chapter Eleven, on models so equipped.
2. Remove the saddlebag guards (B, **Figure 92**) attached to the support bracket, on models so equipped.
3. Remove the bolts and washers securing the support bracket and upper bracket (C, **Figure 92**) to the frame.
4. Remove the support bracket from the frame and rear fender.
5. Install by reversing the removal steps, while noting the following:
   a. Tighten the upper bracket bolt to 60-96 in.-lb. (6.8-10.8 N•m).
   b. Tighten the support bracket bolts to 15-20 ft.-lb. (20.3-27.1 N•m).

ENGINE GUARD

Removal/Installation

Refer to **Figure 93**.

1. Support the motorcycle with the front wheel off the ground as described in *Motorcycle Stands* (Chapter Twelve).
2. Cover the backside of the front fender with a towel or blanket to protect the finish.
3. On FLHTCU and FLHTCUSE models, remove the lower fairing assembly from each side as described in this chapter.
4. Remove the lower Torx bolt (T40) and locknut from the frame weldment on each side.
5. Remove the bolt, washer, mounting strap and washer securing the engine guard to the frame.
6. Carefully pull the engine guard forward and remove from the frame.
7. Install by reversing the removal steps. Tighten all mounting bolts and nuts to 15-20 ft.-lb. (20.3-27.1 N•m).

JIFFY STAND

Removal

Refer to **Figure 94**.

1. Support the motorcycle with the front wheel off the ground as described in *Motorcycle Stands* (Chapter Twelve).
2. The motorcycle must be raised sufficiently to allow room for full movement of the jiffy stand.
3. Move left side rider footboard up away from the jiffy stand.
4. Move the jiffy stand down to the full forward position.
5. Remove the return spring (A, **Figure 95**) from the jiffy stand leg and the hole in the frame weldment.
6. Remove the four bolts (B, **Figure 95**) and lockwashers securing the bracket and front footboard to the frame.
7. Inspect the jiffy stand leg and bracket as described in this section.

Installation

1. Install the bracket and the four bolts and lockwashers.
2. Align the rear of the bracket to the footboard and tighten the front bolts to 36-42 ft.-lb. (48.8-56.9 N•m).
3. Tighten the rear bracket bolts to 36-42 ft.-lb. (48.8-56.9 N•m).
4. Hook the return spring onto *front* of the frame weldment. If installed on the rear, the spring will rub on the leg when it is moved.
5. Hook the return spring onto the hole in the leg. Make sure return spring is secure on both the frame and leg.
6. Hold the leg in the normal down position.
7. Secure the leg in this position and check the tightness of the top hex bolt. Tighten the hex bolt to 15-20 ft.-lb. (20.3-27.1 N•m), if necessary.

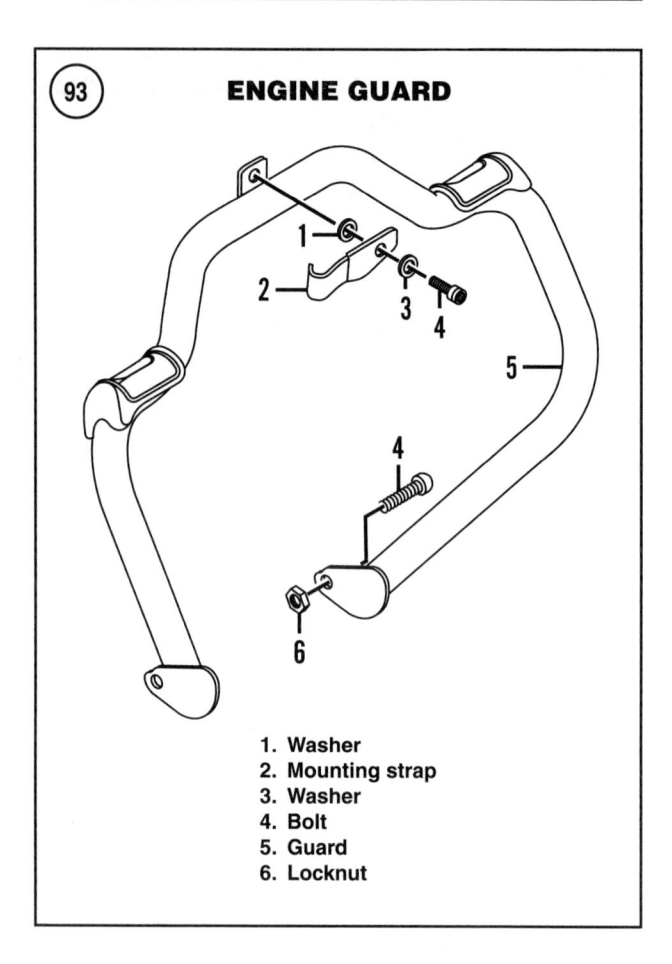

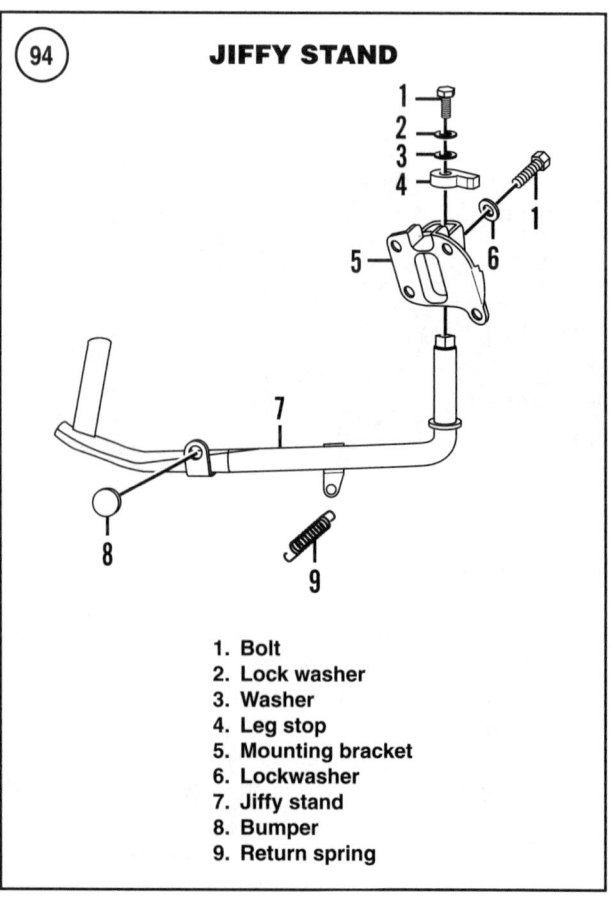

93 ENGINE GUARD

1. Washer
2. Mounting strap
3. Washer
4. Bolt
5. Guard
6. Locknut

94 JIFFY STAND

1. Bolt
2. Lock washer
3. Washer
4. Leg stop
5. Mounting bracket
6. Lockwasher
7. Jiffy stand
8. Bumper
9. Return spring

BODY AND FRAME

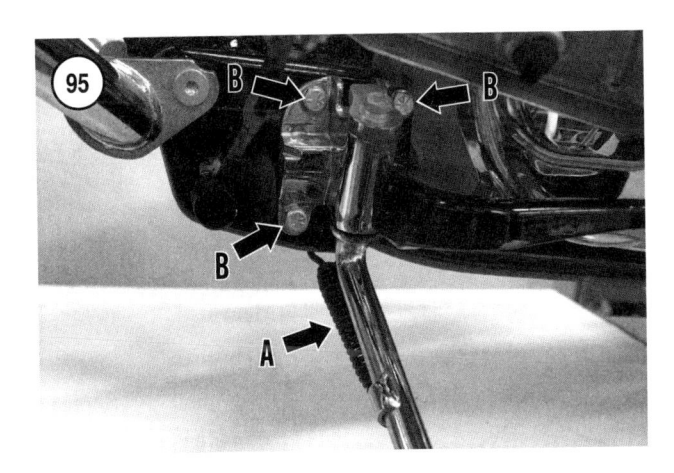

8. Extend and retract the leg several times to ensure proper operation. The jiffy stand must move freely from the fully extended to the fully retracted positions.
9. If removed, install the bumper onto the leg.
10. Remove the motorcycle from the stand.

Inspection

1. Thoroughly clean all old grease and road debris from the pivot point in the bracket and the pivot post of the leg.
2. Inspect the leg for cracks or other damage. Replace if necessary.
3. Inspect the threaded end of the leg for damage. Clean out with a thread tap if necessary.
4. Inspect the bracket mounting holes for damage and elongation. Replace as necessary.

Interlock Sensor
(2008-2009 HDI Models)
Replacement

1. At the jiffy stand bracket, locate the wiring harness to the base of the voltage regulator.
2. Remove the anchor on the interlock sensor connector from the hole in the front cross member.
3. Carefully cut the strap securing the wiring harness to the frame.
4. Disconnect the 3-pin interlock sensor connector.
5. Move the jiffy stand to the full forward (down) position.
6. Remove the Allen bolt, and then remove the sensor from the bracket.
7. Apply a small dab of Loctite Threadlocker 243 (Blue) to the Allen bolt prior to installation. Install the bolt and tighten to 96-120 in.-lb. (10.8-13.6 N•m).
8. Route the cable over the top of the frame weldment, behind the front down tube and toward the voltage regulator.
9. Connect the 3-pin sensor connector, and then push the anchor into the hole in the front frame cross member.
10. Install a new cable strap and secure the wiring harness.

TOUR-PAK

FLHT Models
Removal/Installation

Refer to **Figure 96** and **Figure 97**.
1. Place the motorcycle on level ground using the jiffy stand.
2. Remove the seat as described in this chapter.

NOTE
Always disarm the optional TSSM/HFSM security system before disconnecting the battery or pulling the Maxi-Fuse so the siren will not sound.

3. Disconnect the negative battery cable as described in Chapter Eleven.
4. Remove both saddlebags as described in this chapter.
5. Open the cover and remove the bottom liner. Leave the cover open for the remainder of this procedure.
6. On FLHTCU models, perform the following:
   a. Open the map pocket and remove the acorn nuts and flat washers securing the molded inner liner to the lower case. Remove the map pocket and molded liner.
   b. Depress the latch and rotate the housing and release the bulb socket from the left side of the lower case.
7. Rotate the knurled locking ring *counterclockwise* and disconnect the radio antenna cable pin and socket connector. Release the cable from the two clips on the base of the lower case.
8. Disconnect the 3-pin Tour-Pak connector. Pull the grommet into the lower case and remove it from the wire harness.
9. Feed the harness down and through the opening in the bottom of the lower case.
10. On FLHTCU models, perform the following:
   a. Release the headrest receptacle from the bottom of the left side speaker box.
   b. Remove the trim ring and carefully pull the wire harness out of the left side speaker box. Disconnect the 6-pin speaker and controller connector.
   c. On the right side, disconnect the CB antenna cable connector, and then release the cable from the two clips on the bottom of the lower case.
   d. Pull the grommet surrounding the CB antenna cable into the lower case and remove it from the cable.
   e. Feed the CB antenna down and through the opening in the bottom of the lower case.
   f. Remove the trim ring and carefully pull the wire harness out of the right and left side speaker housing. Disconnect the left and right 6-pin speaker and controller connectors.
11. Secure the locknut below each mounting bolt, and then remove the four bolts, washers and nuts securing the Tour-Pak lower case to the luggage rack. Remove the nuts and spacers from the luggage rack.

TOUR-PAK (FLHT MODELS)

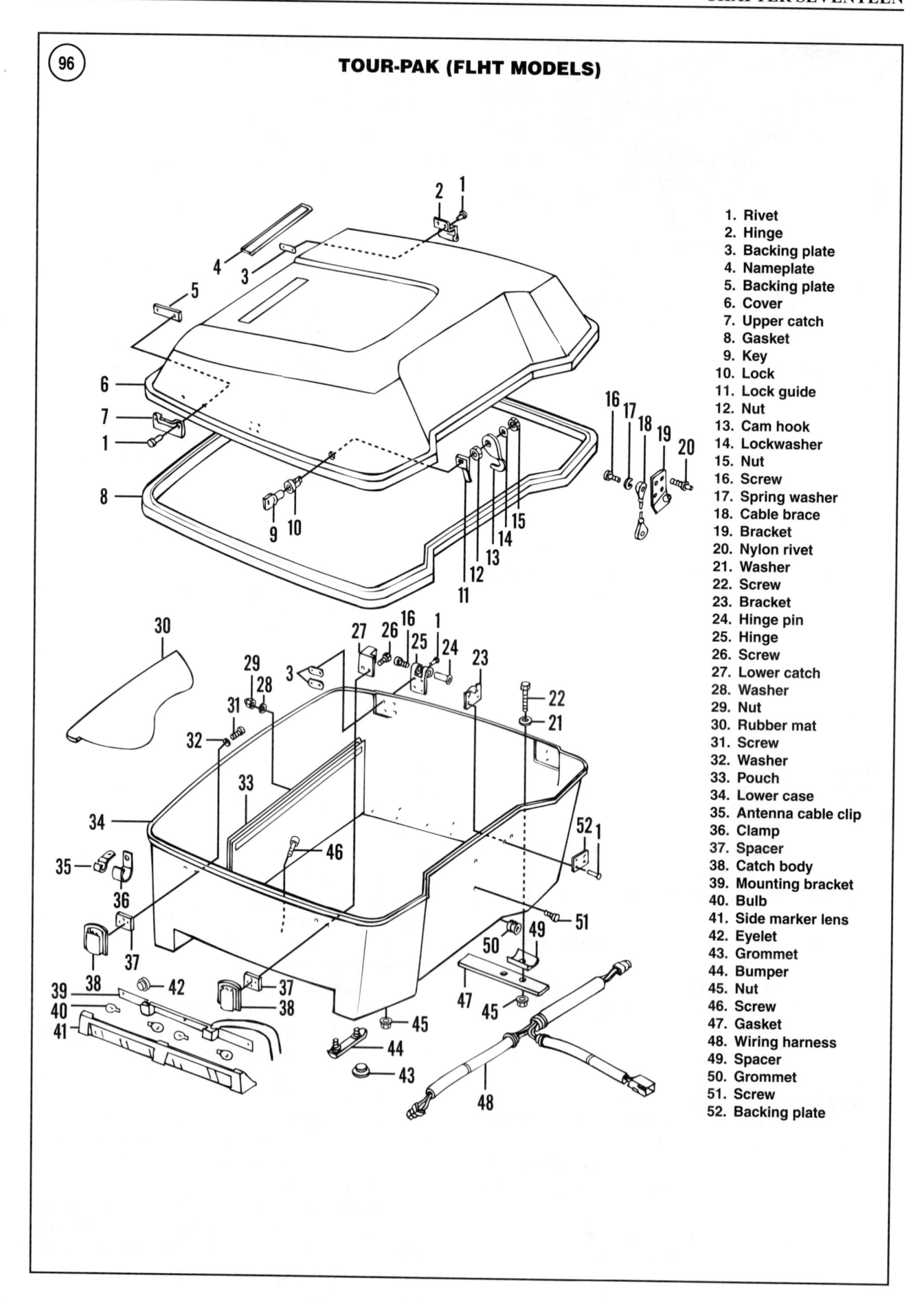

1. Rivet
2. Hinge
3. Backing plate
4. Nameplate
5. Backing plate
6. Cover
7. Upper catch
8. Gasket
9. Key
10. Lock
11. Lock guide
12. Nut
13. Cam hook
14. Lockwasher
15. Nut
16. Screw
17. Spring washer
18. Cable brace
19. Bracket
20. Nylon rivet
21. Washer
22. Screw
23. Bracket
24. Hinge pin
25. Hinge
26. Screw
27. Lower catch
28. Washer
29. Nut
30. Rubber mat
31. Screw
32. Washer
33. Pouch
34. Lower case
35. Antenna cable clip
36. Clamp
37. Spacer
38. Catch body
39. Mounting bracket
40. Bulb
41. Side marker lens
42. Eyelet
43. Grommet
44. Bumper
45. Nut
46. Screw
47. Gasket
48. Wiring harness
49. Spacer
50. Grommet
51. Screw
52. Backing plate

BODY AND FRAME

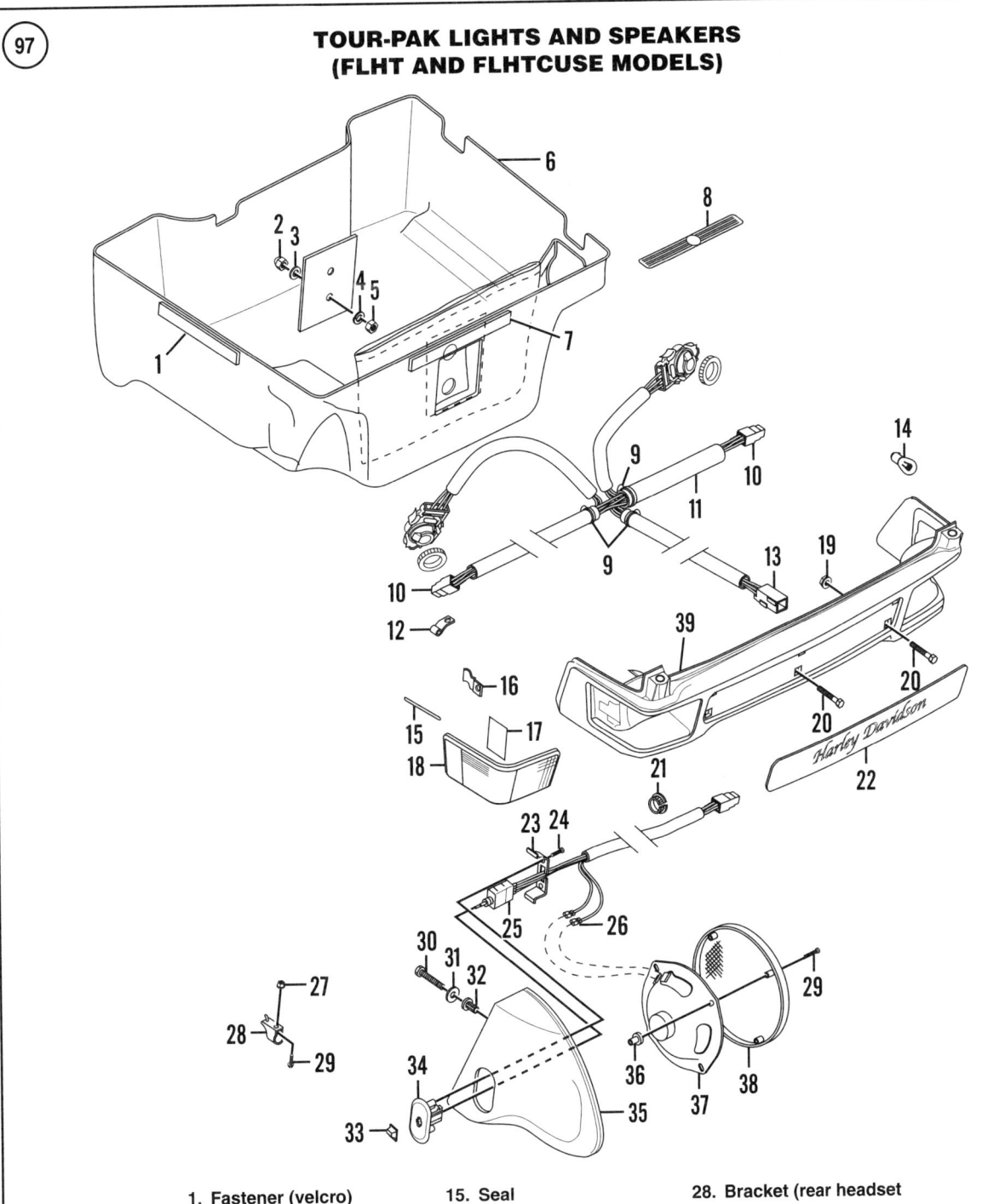

(97) **TOUR-PAK LIGHTS AND SPEAKERS (FLHT AND FLHTCUSE MODELS)**

1. Fastener (velcro)
2. Acorn nut
3. Washer
4. Lockwasher
5. Lockwasher
6. Tour-Pak molded liner
7. Pouch
8. Trim decal
9. Cable strap
10. Terminal housing
11. Wiring harness
12. Clip (antenna cable)
13. Terminal housing
14. Bulb
15. Seal
16. Clip
17. Reflector
18. Lens (left side)
19. Nut
20. Bolt
21. Grommet
22. Nameplate
23. Bracket (rear switch control housing)
24. Screw
25. Switch terminal housing
26. Terminal
27. Nut
28. Bracket (rear headset tether)
29. Screw
30. Bolt
31. Washer
32. Crimp nut
33. Select knob
34. Housing (rear control switch)
35. Speaker box (left side shown)
36. Nut (well)
37. Speaker
38. Grill
39. Light housing

NOTE
Have an assistant hold onto the Tour-Pak during removal of the last bolt and nut. The Tour-Pak is top heavy on the left side with the cover open.

12. Secure the remaining mounting bolt underneath the lower case. Remove nut and flat washer from the inside of the lower case. Remove the bolt and spacer from the luggage rack.
13. Remove the Tour-Pak from the luggage rack.
14 On FLHTCU models, to remove the speaker box, perform the following:
   a. Remove the trim ring and carefully pull the wire harness out of the right and left side speaker housing. Disconnect the 6-pin speaker and controller connectors.
   b. Open map pocket, remove the acorn nuts and washers, and then remove the map pocket.
   c. Remove the three bolts and washers securing the speaker housing. Pull straight out and remove the speaker housing from the lower case.
15. Install by reversing these removal steps. Tighten the Tour-Pak mounting bolts and nuts to 90-108 in.-lb. (10.2-12.2 N•m).

Screamin' Eagle Series Models Removal/Installation

Refer to **Figures 98-101**.
1. Place the motorcycle on level ground using the jiffy stand.
2. Remove the seat as described in this chapter.

NOTE
Always disarm the optional TSSM/HFSM security system before disconnecting the battery or pulling the Maxi-Fuse so the siren will not sound.

3. Disconnect the negative battery cable as described in Chapter Eleven.
4. Remove both saddlebags as described in this chapter.
5. Open the cover and remove the bottom liner. Leave the cover open for the remainder of this procedure.
6. Unscrew the AM/FM antenna cable connector from the antenna mount on the left rear corner. Disconnect the antenna cable from the clip on the bottom left side of the bottom case.
7. Disconnect the power lock connector at the left rear side of the bottom case, on models so equipped.
8. Unplug the interior lighting harness connectors.
9. Remove the split grommet from the exit hole in the left front side of the bottom case. Carefully feed the AM/FM antenna cable down and out through this exit hole.
10. Unplug the CB antenna cable connector at the bottom right side of the bottom case. Disengage the cable from the clips on the bottom right side of the bottom case.
11. Remove the split grommet from the exit hole in the right front side of the bottom case. Carefully feed the CB antenna cable down and out through this exit hole.

12. Carefully feed the speaker wiring harness out of the hole in the right and left speaker box. Disconnect the left and right 6-pin speaker and controller connectors.
13. Disconnect the 24-pin amplifier connector from the under the right side of the Tour-Pak.
14. Hold onto the passenger headset DIN connector and carefully pull it partially out from under the Tour-Pak. Carefully pull down on the wiring and release it from the cable clip.
15. Place a towel or small blanket on top of the rear fender to protect it during amplifier removal.
16. Note the location of which five mounting bolts are used to secure the lower case to the luggage rack as the location varies with different years.
17. Secure the locknut below each mounting bolt, and then remove the four bolts, washers and nuts securing the Tour-Pak lower case to the luggage rack. Remove the nuts and spacers from the luggage rack.
18. Slide the amplifier out the right side and lower it onto the rear fender.

NOTE
Have an assistant hold onto the Tour-Pak during removal of the last bolt and nut. The Tour-Pak is top heavy on the left side with the cover open.

19. Secure the remaining mounting bolt underneath the lower case. Remove nut, flat washer and antenna ground strap from the top of the lower case. Remove the bolt and spacer from the luggage rack.
20. Remove the Tour-Pak from the luggage rack.
21. To remove the speaker box, perform the following:
   a. Remove the trim ring and carefully pull the wire harness out of the right and left side speaker housing. Disconnect the 6-pin speaker and controller connectors.
   b. Open map pocket, remove the acorn nuts and washers, and then remove the map pocket.
   c. Remove the three bolts and washers securing the speaker housing. Pull straight out and remove the speaker housing from the lower case.
   d. Install speaker box by reversing the removal steps. Tighten the three mounting bolts to 25-35 in.-lb. (2.8-4.0 N•m).
22. Install Tour-Pak by reversing the removal steps. Tighten the bolts and nuts to 96-108 in.-lb. (10.8-12.2 N•m).

FOOTBOARDS AND HIGHWAY FOOT PEGS

Refer to **Figures 102-106**.

Rider Footboard

Removal/installation

1. Support the motorcycle with the front wheel off the ground as described in *Motorcycle Stands* (Chapter Twelve).

BODY AND FRAME

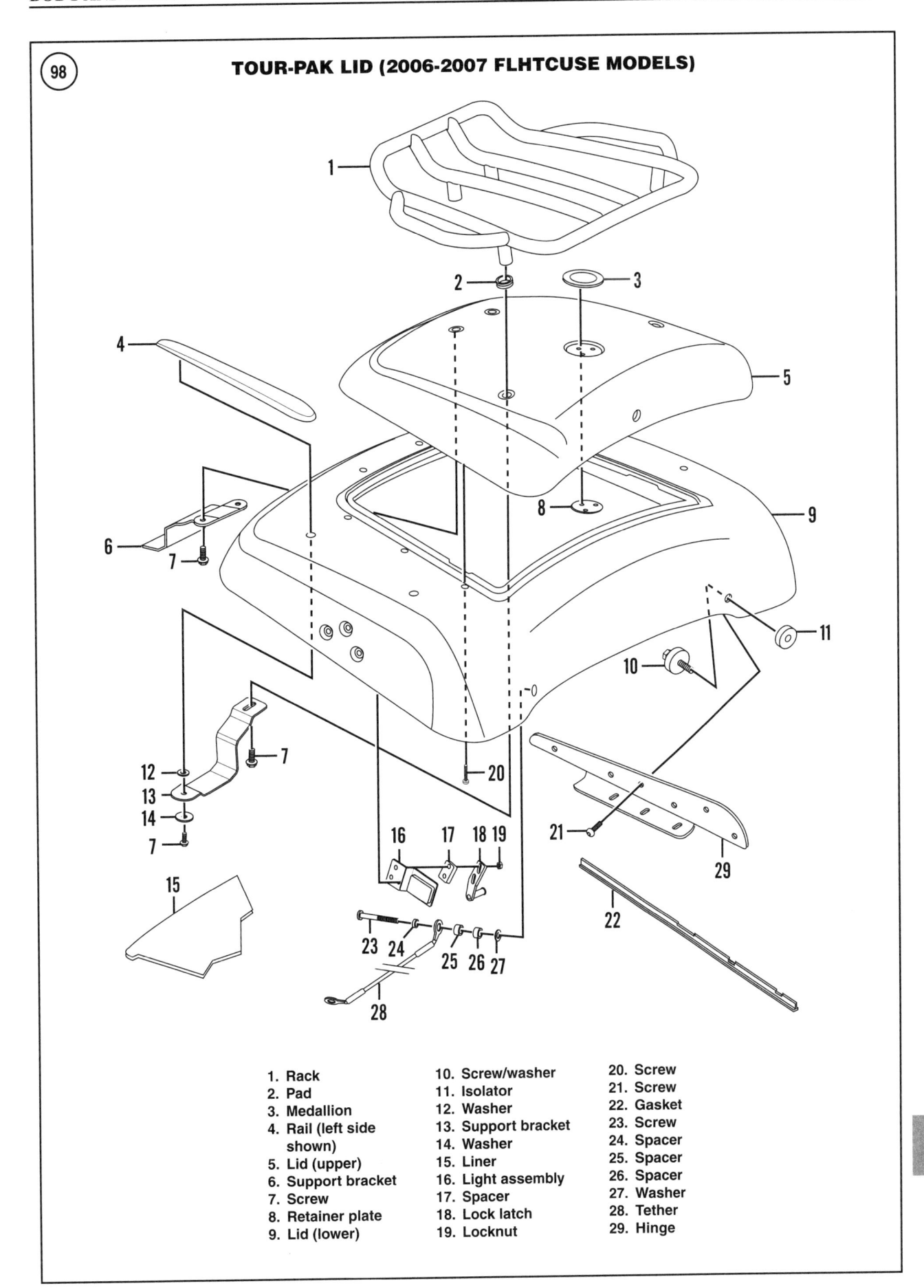

98 **TOUR-PAK LID (2006-2007 FLHTCUSE MODELS)**

1. Rack
2. Pad
3. Medallion
4. Rail (left side shown)
5. Lid (upper)
6. Support bracket
7. Screw
8. Retainer plate
9. Lid (lower)
10. Screw/washer
11. Isolator
12. Washer
13. Support bracket
14. Washer
15. Liner
16. Light assembly
17. Spacer
18. Lock latch
19. Locknut
20. Screw
21. Screw
22. Gasket
23. Screw
24. Spacer
25. Spacer
26. Spacer
27. Washer
28. Tether
29. Hinge

CHAPTER SEVENTEEN

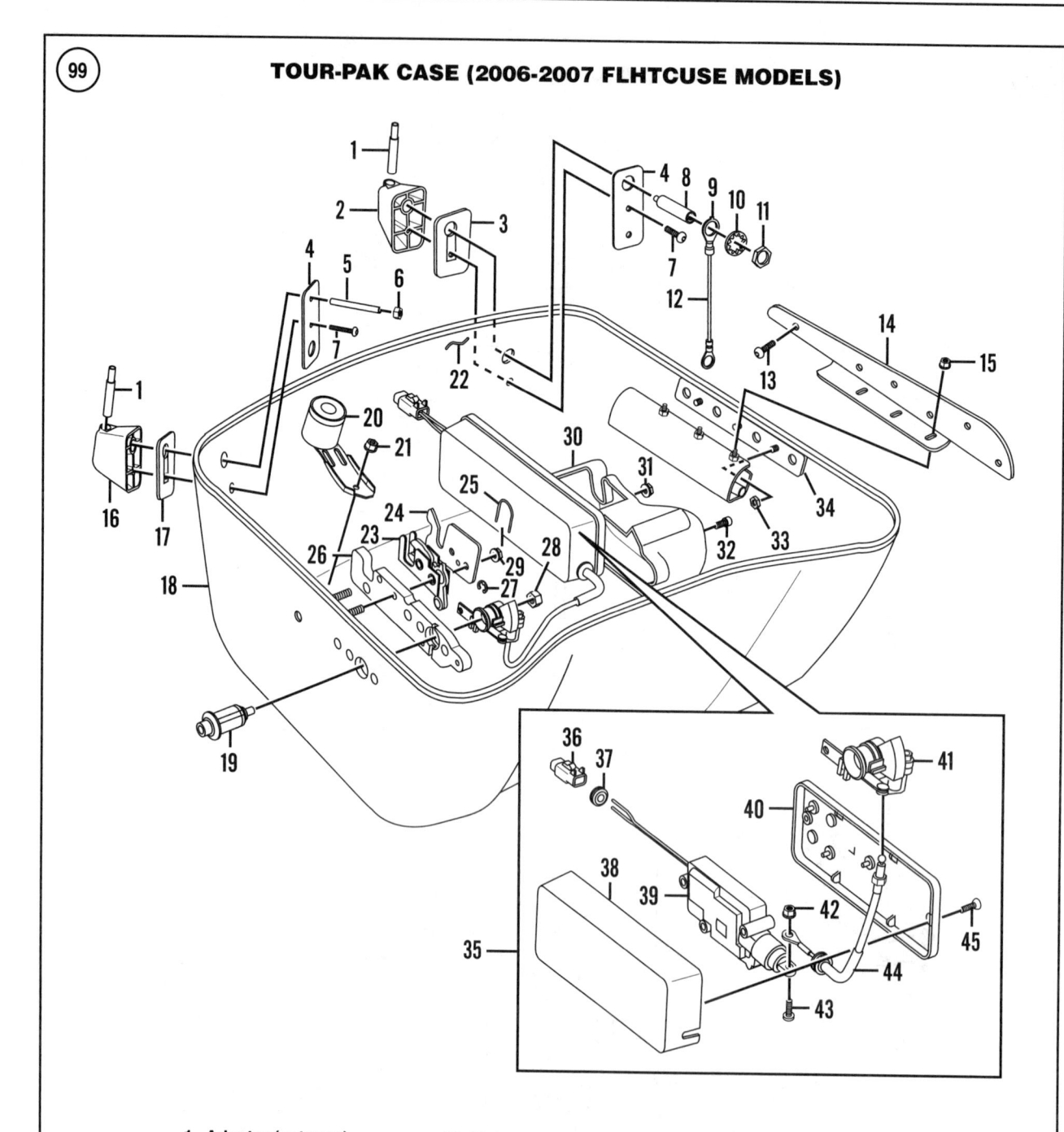

TOUR-PAK CASE (2006-2007 FLHTCUSE MODELS)

1. Adapter (antenna)
2. Antenna base (left side)
3. Gasket
4. Backup plate
5. Screw (cup point)
6. Nut
7. Screw
8. Antenna (coaxial jack)
9. Ring terminal (insulated)
10. Lockwasher
11. Nut
12. Cable assembly (AM/FM antenna ground)
13. Screw
14. Hinge
15. Nut
16. Antenna base (right side)
17. Gasket
18. Case
19. Lock
20. Loading coil assembly (CB antenna)
21. Nut
22. Liner
23. Latch mechanism
24. Latch (strike plate)
25. Locking clip
26. Spacer
27. E-clip
28. Locknut
29. Nut
30. Shroud
31. Nut
32. Screw
33. Nut
34. Stud plate
35. Power lock assembly
36. Terminal socket
37. Grommet
38. Base
39. Actuator
40. Cover
41. Housing (push button)
42. Locknut
43. Screw
44. Cable assembly
45. Screw

BODY AND FRAME

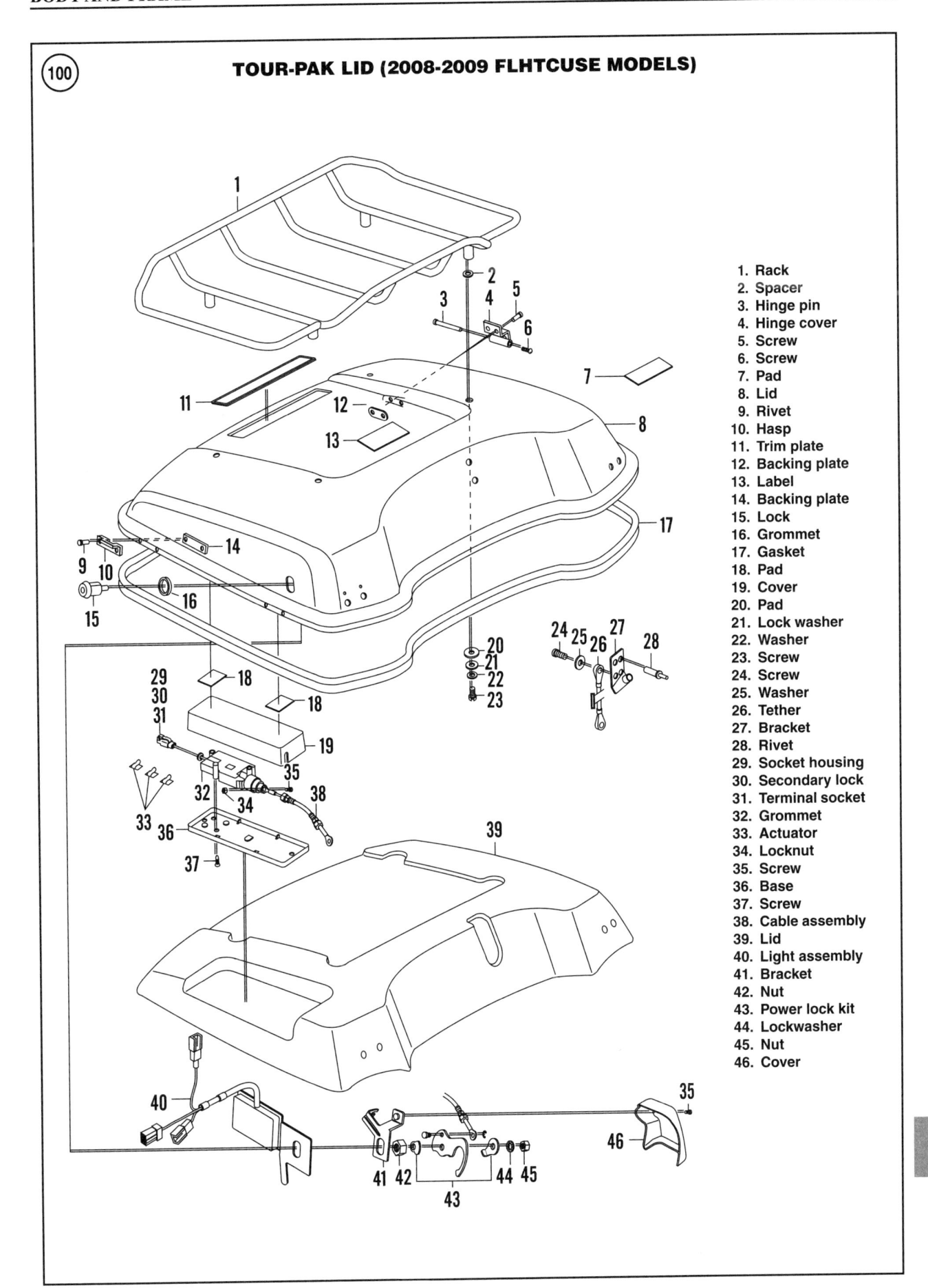

727

TOUR-PAK LID (2008-2009 FLHTCUSE MODELS)

1. Rack
2. Spacer
3. Hinge pin
4. Hinge cover
5. Screw
6. Screw
7. Pad
8. Lid
9. Rivet
10. Hasp
11. Trim plate
12. Backing plate
13. Label
14. Backing plate
15. Lock
16. Grommet
17. Gasket
18. Pad
19. Cover
20. Pad
21. Lock washer
22. Washer
23. Screw
24. Screw
25. Washer
26. Tether
27. Bracket
28. Rivet
29. Socket housing
30. Secondary lock
31. Terminal socket
32. Grommet
33. Actuator
34. Locknut
35. Screw
36. Base
37. Screw
38. Cable assembly
39. Lid
40. Light assembly
41. Bracket
42. Nut
43. Power lock kit
44. Lockwasher
45. Nut
46. Cover

17

TOUR-PAK CASE (2008-2009 FLHTCUSE MODELS)

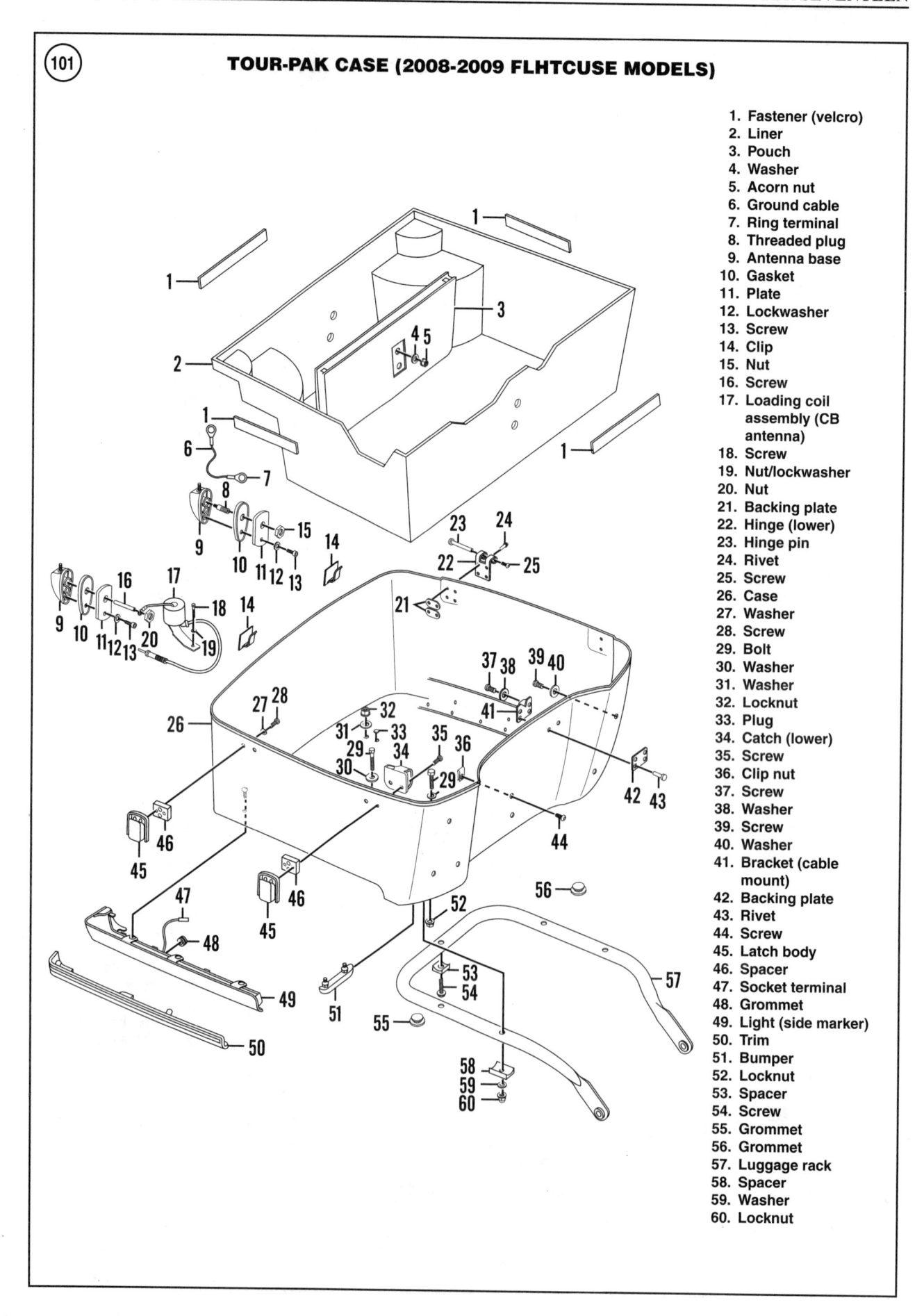

1. Fastener (velcro)
2. Liner
3. Pouch
4. Washer
5. Acorn nut
6. Ground cable
7. Ring terminal
8. Threaded plug
9. Antenna base
10. Gasket
11. Plate
12. Lockwasher
13. Screw
14. Clip
15. Nut
16. Screw
17. Loading coil assembly (CB antenna)
18. Screw
19. Nut/lockwasher
20. Nut
21. Backing plate
22. Hinge (lower)
23. Hinge pin
24. Rivet
25. Screw
26. Case
27. Washer
28. Screw
29. Bolt
30. Washer
31. Washer
32. Locknut
33. Plug
34. Catch (lower)
35. Screw
36. Clip nut
37. Screw
38. Washer
39. Screw
40. Washer
41. Bracket (cable mount)
42. Backing plate
43. Rivet
44. Screw
45. Latch body
46. Spacer
47. Socket terminal
48. Grommet
49. Light (side marker)
50. Trim
51. Bumper
52. Locknut
53. Spacer
54. Screw
55. Grommet
56. Grommet
57. Luggage rack
58. Spacer
59. Washer
60. Locknut

BODY AND FRAME

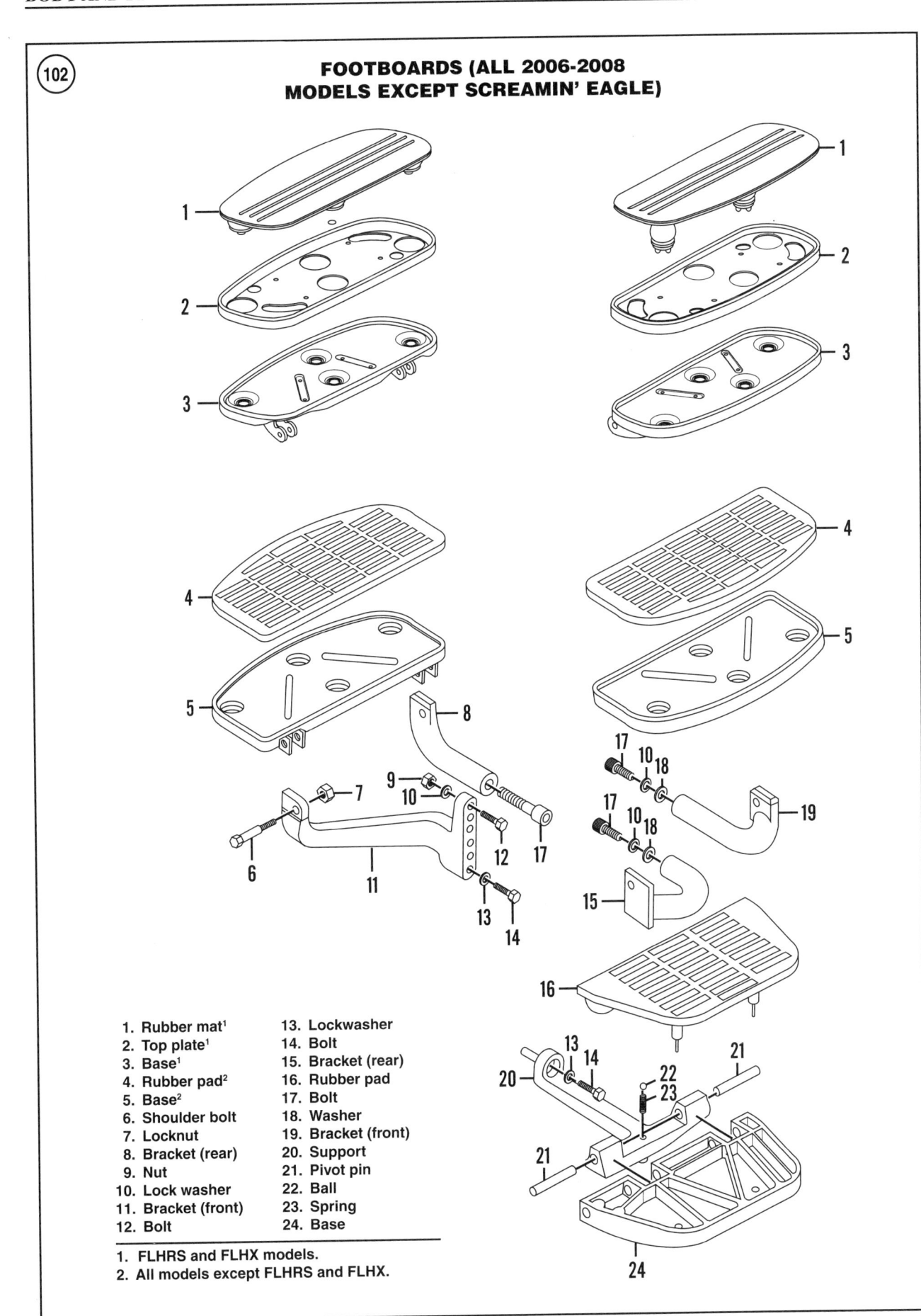

FOOTBOARDS (ALL 2006-2008 MODELS EXCEPT SCREAMIN' EAGLE)

1. Rubber mat[1]
2. Top plate[1]
3. Base[1]
4. Rubber pad[2]
5. Base[2]
6. Shoulder bolt
7. Locknut
8. Bracket (rear)
9. Nut
10. Lock washer
11. Bracket (front)
12. Bolt
13. Lockwasher
14. Bolt
15. Bracket (rear)
16. Rubber pad
17. Bolt
18. Washer
19. Bracket (front)
20. Support
21. Pivot pin
22. Ball
23. Spring
24. Base

1. FLHRS and FLHX models.
2. All models except FLHRS and FLHX.

CHAPTER SEVENTEEN

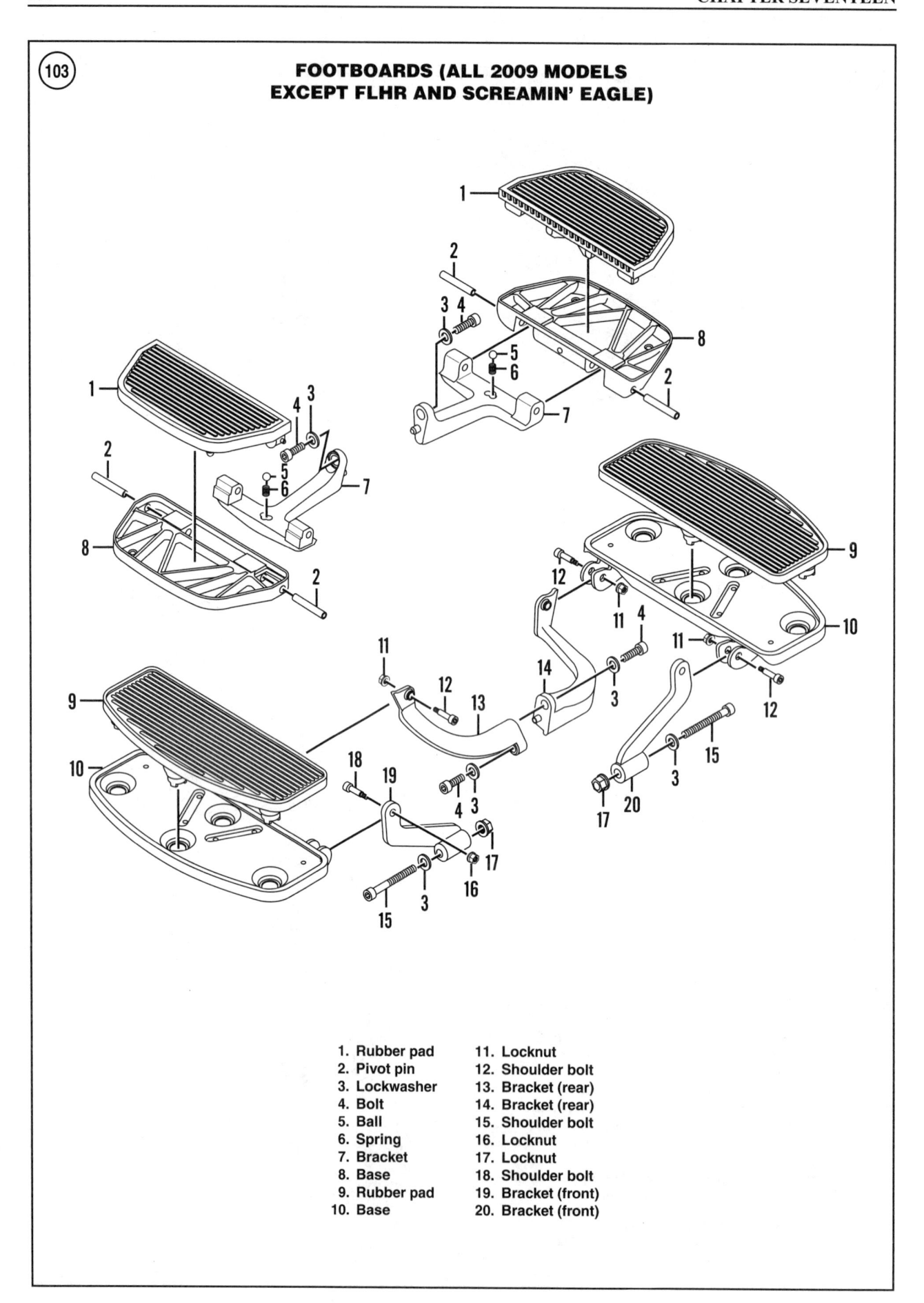

103

FOOTBOARDS (ALL 2009 MODELS EXCEPT FLHR AND SCREAMIN' EAGLE)

1. Rubber pad
2. Pivot pin
3. Lockwasher
4. Bolt
5. Ball
6. Spring
7. Bracket
8. Base
9. Rubber pad
10. Base
11. Locknut
12. Shoulder bolt
13. Bracket (rear)
14. Bracket (rear)
15. Shoulder bolt
16. Locknut
17. Locknut
18. Shoulder bolt
19. Bracket (front)
20. Bracket (front)

BODY AND FRAME

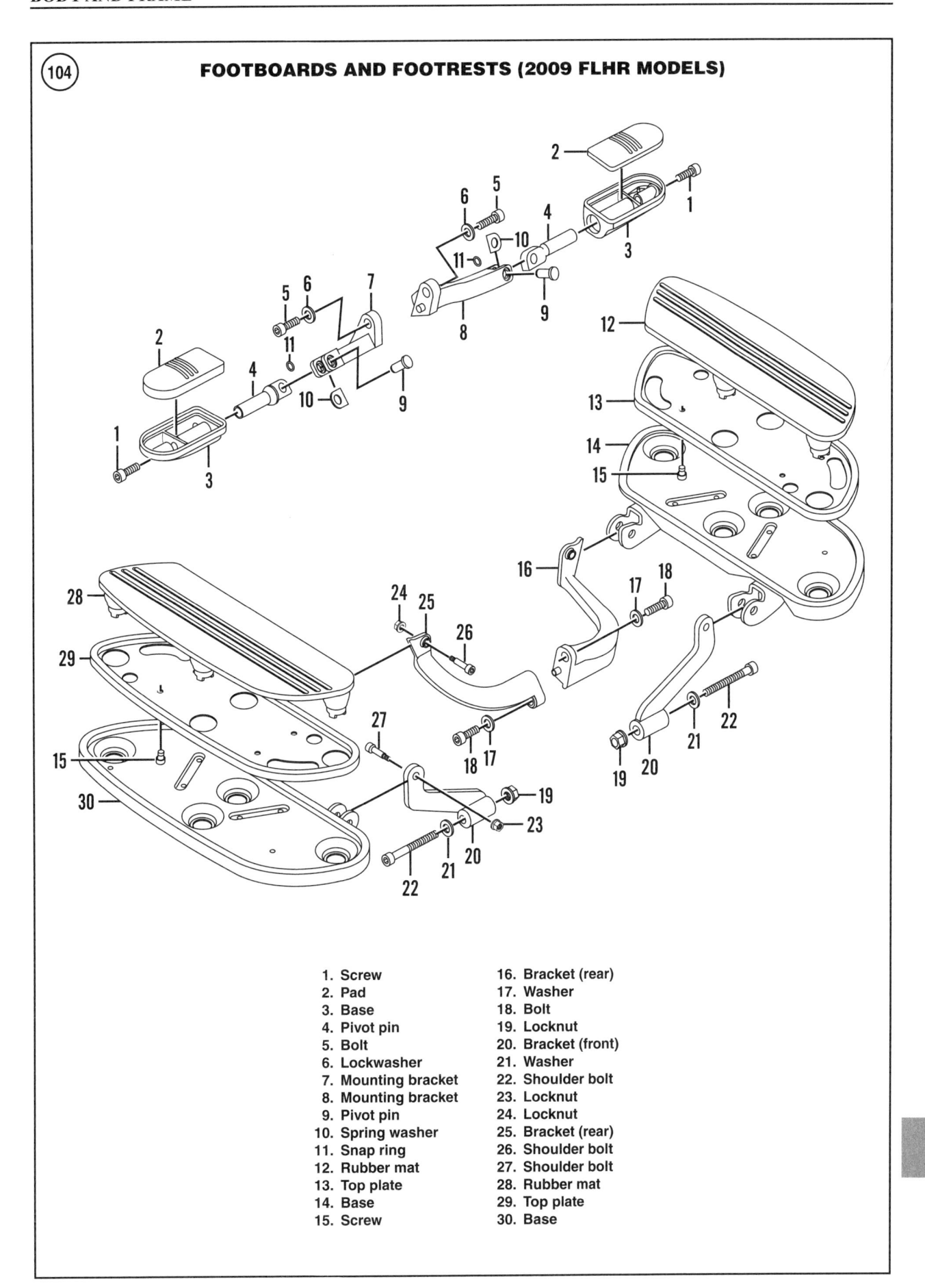

FOOTBOARDS AND FOOTRESTS (2009 FLHR MODELS)

(104)

1. Screw
2. Pad
3. Base
4. Pivot pin
5. Bolt
6. Lockwasher
7. Mounting bracket
8. Mounting bracket
9. Pivot pin
10. Spring washer
11. Snap ring
12. Rubber mat
13. Top plate
14. Base
15. Screw
16. Bracket (rear)
17. Washer
18. Bolt
19. Locknut
20. Bracket (front)
21. Washer
22. Shoulder bolt
23. Locknut
24. Locknut
25. Bracket (rear)
26. Shoulder bolt
27. Shoulder bolt
28. Rubber mat
29. Top plate
30. Base

CHAPTER SEVENTEEN

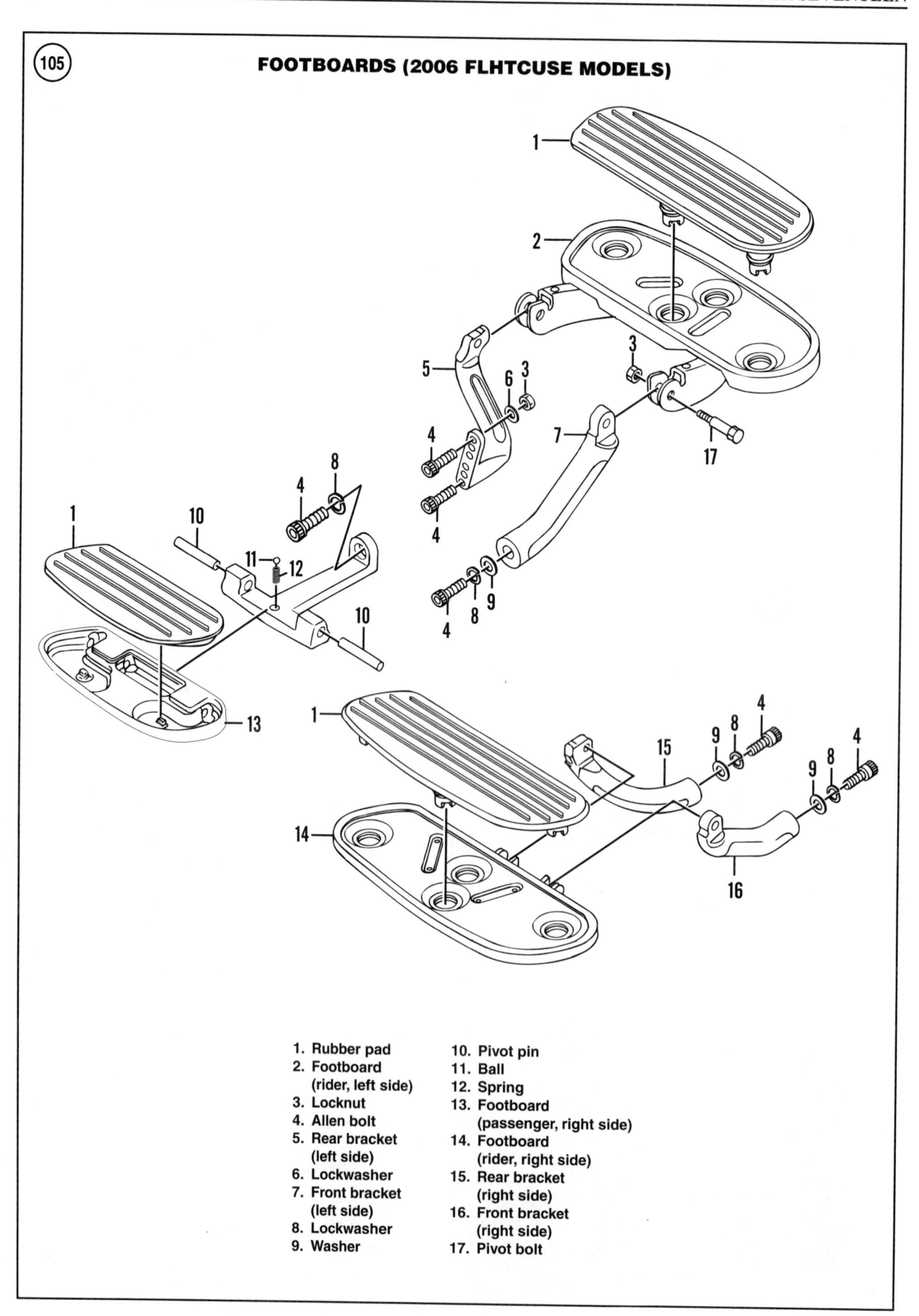

FOOTBOARDS (2006 FLHTCUSE MODELS)

1. Rubber pad
2. Footboard (rider, left side)
3. Locknut
4. Allen bolt
5. Rear bracket (left side)
6. Lockwasher
7. Front bracket (left side)
8. Lockwasher
9. Washer
10. Pivot pin
11. Ball
12. Spring
13. Footboard (passenger, right side)
14. Footboard (rider, right side)
15. Rear bracket (right side)
16. Front bracket (right side)
17. Pivot bolt

BODY AND FRAME

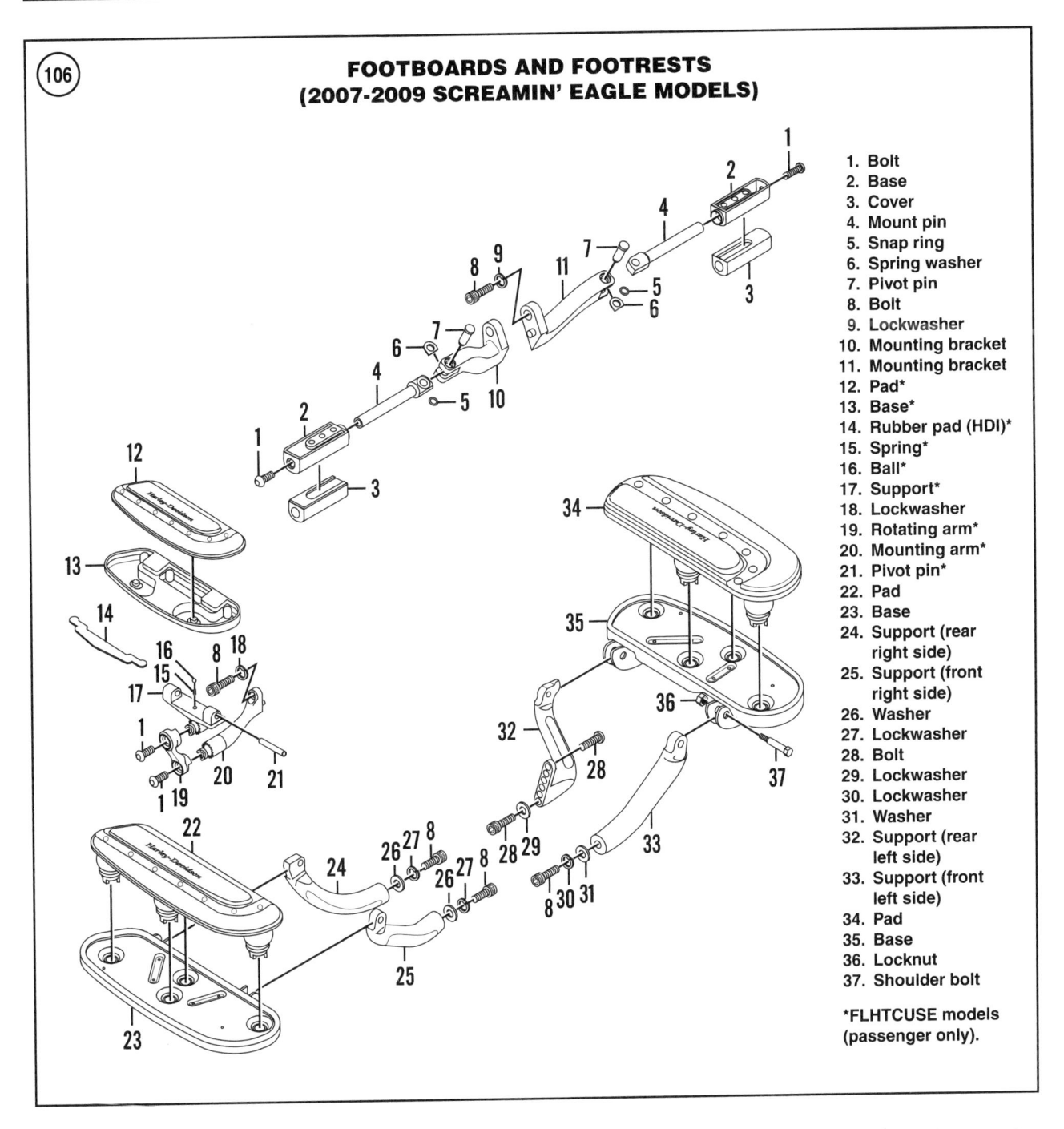

106 FOOTBOARDS AND FOOTRESTS (2007-2009 SCREAMIN' EAGLE MODELS)

1. Bolt
2. Base
3. Cover
4. Mount pin
5. Snap ring
6. Spring washer
7. Pivot pin
8. Bolt
9. Lockwasher
10. Mounting bracket
11. Mounting bracket
12. Pad*
13. Base*
14. Rubber pad (HDI)*
15. Spring*
16. Ball*
17. Support*
18. Lockwasher
19. Rotating arm*
20. Mounting arm*
21. Pivot pin*
22. Pad
23. Base
24. Support (rear right side)
25. Support (front right side)
26. Washer
27. Lockwasher
28. Bolt
29. Lockwasher
30. Lockwasher
31. Washer
32. Support (rear left side)
33. Support (front left side)
34. Pad
35. Base
36. Locknut
37. Shoulder bolt

*FLHTCUSE models (passenger only).

2. To remove the footboard only and leave the mounting brackets in place, perform the following:
   a. Remove the shoulder bolts (A, **Figure 107**) and washers, and then remove the footboard (B).
   b. Clean all oxidation and road debris from the shoulder bolts.
   c. Install the shoulder bolts and nuts and tighten to 60-80 in.-lb. (6.8-9.0 N•m).

3A. On the right side, perform the following:
   a. Working on the inner side of the frame side rail, loosen and remove the Allen bolt, lockwasher and washer securing the front mounting bracket to the frame.
   b. Working on the inner side of the frame side rail, loosen and remove the lower hex bolt and lock-

washer securing the rear mounting bracket to the frame.

3B. On the left side, working on the inner side of the frame side rail, loosen and remove the Allen bolt(s), lockwasher(s) and washer(s) securing the front (A, **Figure 108**) and rear mounting brackets (B) to the frame.

4. Remove the footboard assembly from the frame.

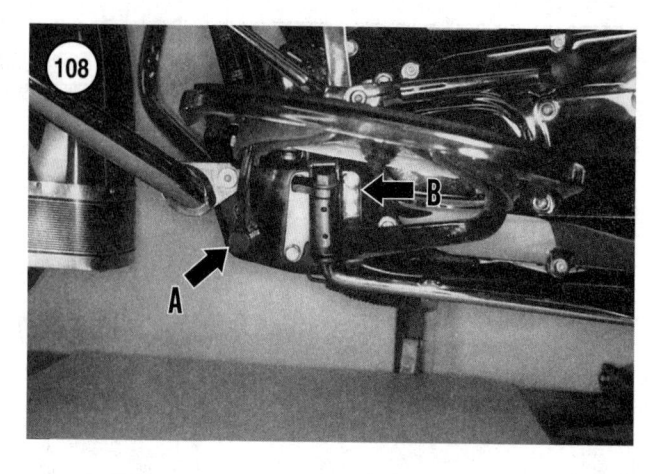

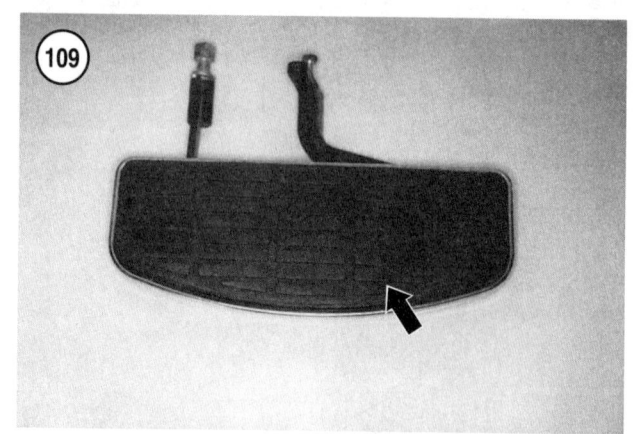

5. If necessary, remove the rubber pad (**Figure 109**) from the footboard and install a new one. Push the locating pins all the way through the footboard to secure the rubber pad in place.

6. Inspect the pivot bolts (**Figure 110**) and nuts for looseness. Replace if necessary.

7. Inspect the footboard and the mounting brackets for damage and fractures. Replace as necessary.

8A. On all models except Screamin' Eagle, install the footboard onto the frame and tighten the Allen and hex bolts as follows:

 a. 2006-2008 models, right side footboard Allen and hex bolts: 30-35 ft.-lb. (40.7-47.5 N•m).
 b. 2006-2008 models, left side front footboard Allen and hex bolts: 30-35 ft.-lb. (40.7-47.5 N•m).
 c. 2006-2008 models, left side rear footboard Allen bolts: 15-20 ft.-lb. (20.3-27.1 N•m).
 d. 2009 models (all bolts): 36-42 ft.-lb. (48.8-56.9 N•m).

8B. On all Screamin' Eagle models, install the footboard onto the frame and tighten the Allen bolts to 36-42 ft.-lb. (48.8-56.9 N•m).

Disassembly/assembly

1. Remove the footboard as described in this section.

2. From underside of footboard, use a large, flat-bladed screwdriver to push in on the pad's rubber anchors. Then, remove the pad from the footboard.

3. Remove the nut and pivot bolt, and then remove the mounting bracket from the base of the footboard. Repeat for the remaining bracket.

4. Install the bracket to the footboard. Install the pivot bolt so the nut will be located on the inboard side.

5. Apply a small amount of soapy water to the rubber anchors and place on footboard. Use pliers and pull the rubber anchors through the footboard receptacles until they bottom.

6. Install the nut and pivot bolt. On Screamin' Eagle models, tighten the fasteners to 60-80 in.-lb. (6.8-9.0 N•m).

Passenger Footboard

Removal/installation

1. Support the motorcycle with the front wheel off the ground as described in *Motorcycle Stands* (Chapter Twelve).

2. Remove the Allen bolt (A, **Figure 111**) and lockwasher securing the passenger footbaord (B) to the frame and remove it.

3. Repeat for the other side if necessary.

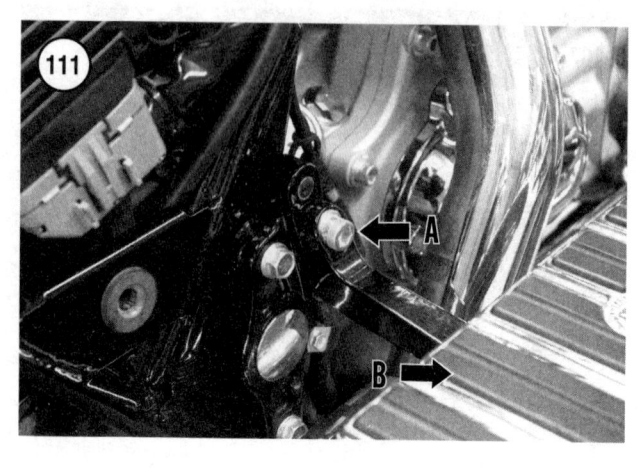

BODY AND FRAME

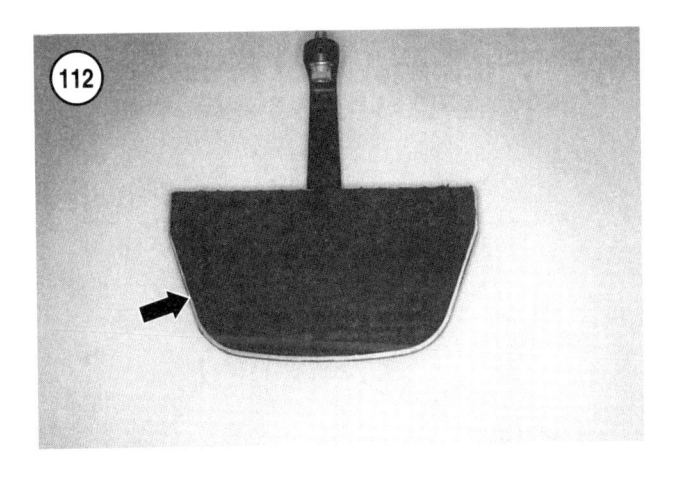

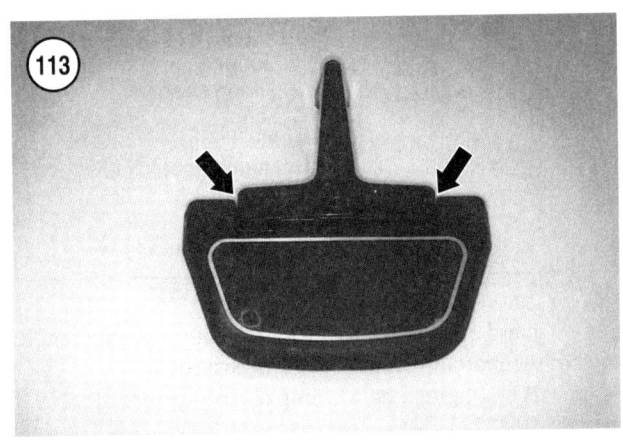

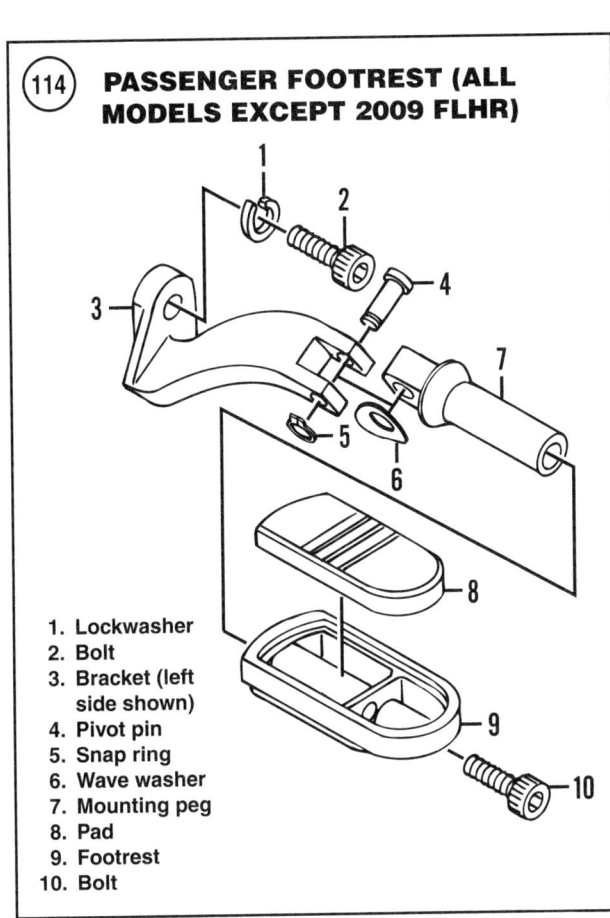

4. If necessary, remove the rubber pad (**Figure 112**) from the footboard and install a new one. Push the locating pins all the way through the footboard to secure the rubber pad in place.

5. Inspect the pivot pins (**Figure 113**) for looseness. Replace if necessary.

6. Install the footboard onto the frame and tighten the Allen bolt as follows:
   a. All 2006-2008 models and Screamin' Eagle: 30-35 ft.-lb. (40.7-47.5 N•m).
   b. All 2009 models and 2009 Screamin' Eagle: 36-42 ft.-lb. (48.8-56.9 N•m).

Disassembly/assembly

1. Remove the footboard as described in this section.
2. From underside of footboard, use a small, flat-bladed screwdriver to push in on the pad's rubber anchors and remove the pad from the footboard.
3. Turn the footboard upside down on shop cloths.
4. Tap the pivot pins toward the center of the footboard with a small drift punch and hammer.
5. Remove the footboard from the bracket and remove the small steel ball and spring from the bracket.
6. Inspect the pivot pins, steel ball and spring for wear or damage.
7. Turn the bracket upside down on shop cloths.
8. Install the spring into the bracket receptacle and place the steel ball on top of it.
9. Lower the footboard onto the bracket and make sure the steel ball remains in place.
10. Align the holes and install the pivot pins. Tap the pins into place until centered in the bracket lugs.
11. Apply a small amount of soapy water to the rubber anchors and place on footboard. Use pliers and pull the rubber anchors through the footboard receptacles until they bottom.

Passenger Footrest

Refer to **Figure 114**.

Removal/installation

1. Support the motorcycle with the front wheel off the ground as described in *Motorcycle Stands* (Chapter Twelve).
2. Remove the Allen bolt and lock washer securing the footrest to the frame. Then, remove the footrest.
3. Repeat for the other side if necessary.
4. Inspect the footrest for wear or damage.
5. Install the footrest onto the frame.
6. Tighten the Allen bolt as follows:
   a. All 2006-2008 models and Screamin' Eagle: 30-35 ft.-lb. (40.7-47.5 N•m).
   b. All 2009 models and 2009 Screamin' Eagle: 36-42 ft.-lb. (48.8-56.9 N•m).

---

114 PASSENGER FOOTREST (ALL MODELS EXCEPT 2009 FLHR)

1. Lockwasher
2. Bolt
3. Bracket (left side shown)
4. Pivot pin
5. Snap ring
6. Wave washer
7. Mounting peg
8. Pad
9. Footrest
10. Bolt

Disassembly/assembly

1. Remove the footrest as described in this section.
2. Remove the Allen bolt and slide the footrest assembly off the mounting peg.
3. Remove the snap ring from the pivot pin and remove the pivot pin.
4. Remove the pivot pin and wave washer, and remove mounting peg from mounting bracket.
5. From underside of footrest, use a small, flat-bladed screwdriver to push in on the pad's rubber anchor. Then, remove the pad from the footrest.
6. Inspect the footrest for wear or damage.
7. Apply a small amount of soapy water to the rubber anchor and place on footrest. Use pliers and pull the rubber anchor through the footrest receptacle until it bottoms.
8. Correctly position the convex side of the wave washer facing up toward the pivot pin. Hold it in this position.
9. Position the mounting peg with the flat surface facing down and install it onto the mounting bracket. Do not dislodge the spring washer.
10. Install the pivot down from the top and install a *new* snap ring. Make sure it seats correctly in the pivot pin groove.
11. Install the footrest assembly onto the mounting peg.
12. Apply a small dab of Loctite Threadlocker 243 (Blue) to the Allen bolt prior to installation. Install the Allen bolt and tighten to 15-20 ft.-lb. (20.3-27.1 N•m).

Highway Foot Pegs

Refer to **Figure 115**.

Removal/installation

1. Place the motorcycle on level ground using the jiffy stand.
2. Place a strip of masking tape above and below the foot peg bracket on the engine guard, if the foot peg location is satisfactory.
3. Remove the two screws securing the clamp bracket and separate it from the mounting bracket.
4. Remove the foot peg assembly from the engine guard.
5A. Install the foot peg in the same location as marked, unless a different location is required.
5B. Use a grease pencil and mark a line on the engine guard down 6.5 in. (165 mm) from the top of the upper rail as a beginning point, if a new location is desired.
6. Correctly position the mounting bracket so it will not contact the lower fairings.
7. Position the mounting bracket onto the engine guard with the pivot screw and mounting screws facing forward.
8. Match the flair on the clamp bracket with the bevel on the mounting bracket. Install the bracket and clamp on the engine guard at the new, or desired, location at a 25° angle toward the rear and secure it in this position.
9. Install and tighten both clamp screws to 14 ft.-lb. (19.0 N•m).

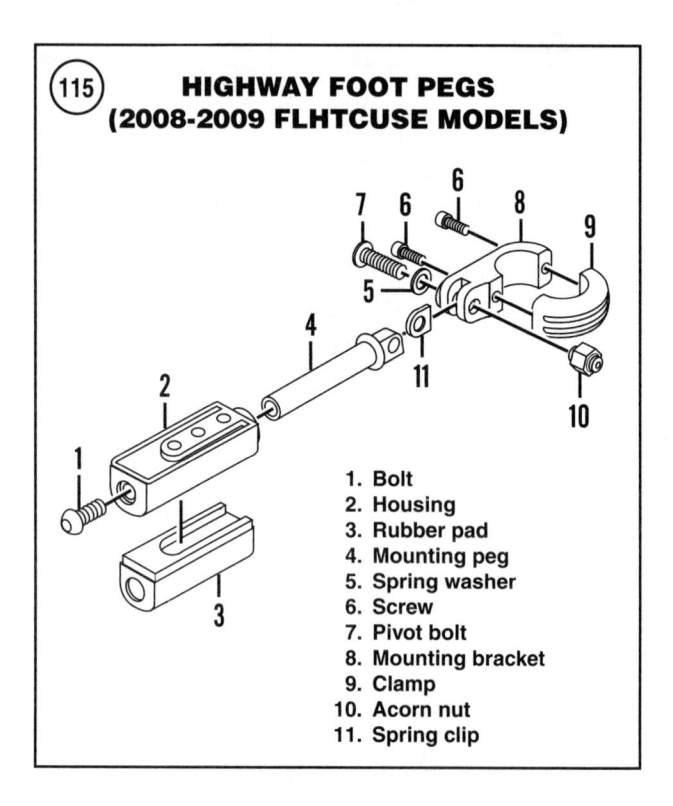

**HIGHWAY FOOT PEGS
(2008-2009 FLHTCUSE MODELS)**

1. Bolt
2. Housing
3. Rubber pad
4. Mounting peg
5. Spring washer
6. Screw
7. Pivot bolt
8. Mounting bracket
9. Clamp
10. Acorn nut
11. Spring clip

Disassembly/assembly

1. Place the motorcycle on level ground using the jiffy stand.
2. Remove the end screw and slide the rubber pad and housing off the mounting peg.
3. Remove the pivot bolt, washer and acorn nut.
4. Remove the mounting peg and spring washer from the mounting bracket.
5. Apply a small dab of Loctite 243 (blue) threadlock to the pivot screw.
6. Correctly position the square edge of the spring clip facing the mounting bracket slot, and insert it in the mounting bracket. Hold it in this position.
7. Position the mounting peg with the flat surface facing down and install it onto the mounting bracket. Do not dislodge the spring washer.
8. Install the pivot bolt, washer and acorn nut. Tighten the acorn nut to 14-19 ft.-lb. (19.0-25.8 N•m).
9. Install the housing and rubber pad onto the mounting peg. Push it on until it bottoms.
10. Apply a small dab of Loctite 243 (blue) threadlock to the end screw.
11. Install the end screw and tighten to 19 ft.-lb. (25.8 N•m).

BODY AND FRAME

Table 1 BODY AND FRAME TORQUE SPECIFICATIONS

Item	ft.-lb.	in.-lb.	N•m
Air deflector thumb screws (FLHTCU and FLHTCUSE Models)	–	25-30	2.8-3.4
Battery tray screws	–	72-96	8.1-10.8
Engine guard mounting bolts/nuts	15-20	–	20.3-27.1
Footboards (rider)			
Footboard shoulder bolts and nuts (removal only)	–	60-80	6.8-9.0
Footboard complete disassembly (all models except Screamin' Eagle)			
Right side footboard Allen bolt (2006-2008 models)	30-35	–	40.7-47.5
Left side footboard (2006-2008 models)			
Front Allen bolt	30-35	–	40.7-47.5
Rear Allen bolt	15-20	–	20.3-27.1
Right and left side all bolts (2009 models)	36-42	–	48.8-56.9
Rider footboard complete disassembly (Screamin' Eagle models)			
Allen and hex bolts	36-42	–	48.8-56.9
Footboard-to-mounting bracket pivot bolt and nut	–	60-80	6.8-9.0
Footboards (passenger)			
Allen bolts			
2009 all models and 2009 Screamin' Eagle models	36-42	–	48.8-56.9
All 2006-2008 models and Screamin' Eagle	30-35	–	40.7-47.5
Footrest (passenger)			
Allen bolts (removal/installation)			
2009 all models and 2009 Screamin' Eagle models	36-42	–	48.8-56.9
All 2006-2008 models and Screamin' Eagle	30-35	–	40.7-47.5
Allen bolt (disassembly/assembly)	15-20	–	20.3-27.1
Foot pegs (highway)			
Allen bolts (removal/installation)	14	–	19.0
Disassembly/assembly			
Pivot bolt and acorn nut	14-19	–	19.0-25.8
End screw	19	–	25.8
Front fairing (FLTR and FLTRSE3 models)			
Outer fairing			
Four short screws	–	6-12	0.7-1.4
Two long screws	–	10-15	1.1-1.7
Instrument bezel housing Torx screws	15-20	–	20.3-27.1
Inner fairing-to-radio mounting bracket locknuts	–	96-144	10.9-16.3
Front fairing (FLHT, FLHTCUSE and FLHX models)			
Outer fairing			
T25 Torx corner screw	–	20-30	2.3-3.4
Fairing-to-mounting bracket	–	20-30	2.3-3.4
Windshield Torx screws	–	25-30	2.8-3.4
Inner fairing cap-to-inner fairing Torx screws	–	25-30	2.8-3.4
Inner fairing			
Gauge-to-bracket hex nuts	–	10-20	1.1-2.3
Speedometer and tachometer mounting screws	–	10-20	1.1-2.3
Speaker adapter			
Long Torx screws (T25)	–	35-50	4.0-5.7
Short Torx screws (T25)	–	22-28	2.5-3.2
Jiffy stand			
Bracket-to-footboard bolt	36-42	–	48.8-56.9
Jiffy stand-to-bracket top hex bolt	15-20	–	20.3-27.1
Interlock Allen bolt (2008-2009 models)	–	96-120	10.8-13.6
License plate bracket (FLTRSE3 models)			
Connector cover flange nut	–	30-45	3.4-5.1
Light bracket screw	–	57-69	6.4-7.8
Lower fairing (FLHTCU and FLHTCUSE models)			
Engine guard clamp Torx screw (T40)	–	90-100	10.2-11.3
Glove box door Torx screw (T20)	–	20-25	2.3-2.8
Lower fairing-to-engine guard flange nut	–	35-40	4.0-4.5

(continued)

Table 1 BODY AND FRAME TORQUE SPECIFICATIONS (continued)

Item	ft.-lb.	in.-lb.	N•m
Passenger backrest			
FLHRSE (2007-2008) and FLTRSE3 (2009) models			
Backrest and antenna bracket mounting bolt	16.7	–	22.6
Backrest bushing assembly bolt	–	120	13.6
Fender mount bracket bolt	15-20	–	20.3-27.1
Rear docking bolt	15-20	–	20.3-27.1
Rear frame/luggage rack (2009 models)			
Battery tray screws	–	72-96	8.1-10.8
Electrical caddy (left side) and top caddy screws	–	72-96	8.1-10.8
Luggage rack screw	15-20	–	20.3-27.1
Rear frame bolts and washers	40-50	–	54.2-67.8
Seat strap and forward luggage bracket screw	15-20	–	20.3-27.1
Rear fender (all models except Screamin' Eagle)			
Fender side mounting Torx bolt	15-20	–	20.3-27.1
Flange nut-to-weld stud	–	45-85	5.1-9.6
Rear fender-to-battery box Torx bolt	15-20	–	20.3-27.1
Saddlebag support bracket Torx bolt	15-20	–	20.3-27.1
Rear fender (all Screamin' Eagle models except FLTRSE3)			
Backrest support screws	15-20	–	20.3-27.1
Fender-to-frame clip nut and bolt	17-22	–	23.1-29.8
Frame clip nut	–	35-40	4.0-4.5
Support bracket-to-fender locknut	–	45-85	5.1-9.6
Rear fender (FLTRSE3 models)			
Fender-to-frame bolt	15-20	–	20.3-27.1
Passenger backrest support screws	16.7	–	22.6
Saddlebag support-to-fender and frame	15-20	–	20.3-27.1
Rear fender fascia			
FLHX models flange nut	–	30-45	3.4-5.1
FLHRSE models flange nut	–	30-45	3.4-5.1
FLRSE models flange nut	–	30-45	3.4-5.1
FLTRSE3 models flange nut	–	30-45	3.4-5.1
Saddlebag (FLHTCUSE models)			
Latch mount inner screws	–	25	2.8
Saddlebag guards/supports (all models except Screamin' Eagle)			
Lower support rail			
Support rail-to-support bracket bolts	15-20	–	20.3-27.1
Support rail-to-rear fender and frame bolt and nut	15-20	–	20.3-27.1
Support rail-to-muffler bolt	–	96-144	10.8-16.3
Support bracket bolt	15-20	–	20.3-27.1
Support guards			
Saddlebag mounting bracket screw	–	60-96	6.8-10.8
Support bracket bolts	15-20	–	20.3-27.1
Support rail-to-support bracket bolt	15-20	–	20.3-27.1
Front guard-to-frame bolt and nut	15-20	–	20.3-27.1
Support guard-to-support rail screw	–	70-100	7.9-11.3
Front guard-to-saddlebag guard screw	–	70-120	7.9-13.6
Guard clamp screw	–	30-50	3.4-5.7
Saddlebag guards/supports (Screamin' Eagle models)			
Saddlebag support rail-to-support bracket	15-20	–	20.3-27.1
Saddlebag guard-to-frame bolt	15-20	–	20.3-27.1
Support rail-to-guard	–	70-100	7.9-11.3
Support bracket (all models)			
Upper bracket bolts	–	60-96	6.8-10.8
Bracket bolts	15-20	–	20.3-27.1
Tour-Pak			
FLHT models			
Mounting bolts and nuts	–	90-108	10.2-12.2
Screamin' Eagle models			
Speaker box mounting bolts	–	25-35	2.8-4.0
Mounting bolts and nuts	–	96-108	10.8-12.2
Windshield screws (FLTR models)	–	6-13	0.7-1.5

INDEX

A

ABS
  brake
    module 652-655
    system. 648-649
  diode pack. 655
  DTC priority, multiple
    troubleshooting 63-64
Active exhaust (2007-2009 HDI
  models, except Japan) 158-159
Air
  filter. 83-89
  and backplate
    carbureted models. . . . 348-350
    fuel-injected models
      2007 FLHRSE3 and 2009
        FLTRSE3 domestic
        models 384-385
      all models except 2007
        FLHRSE3 and 2009
        FLTRSE3 380-384
  pressure loss inspection . . 600-601
Alternator 448-451
Autofuse electrical
  connectors 537-538
Automatic compression release
  solenoid (2006-2009 Screamin'
  Eagle models) 503

B

Backrests
  rider and passenger 673-676
Battery. 440-443
  charging rates/times
    (approximate) 539
  tray 443-446

Body
  backrests 673-676
  engine guard 720
  fairing
    front
      FLHT, FLHTCUSE and
        FLHX models 699-707
      FLTR and FLTRSE3
        models. 693-699
  fender
    front 679-682
    rear
      all models except Screamin'
        Eagle. 682-685
      Screamin' Eagle
        models. 685-687
      fascia. 687-689
  footboards and highway
    foot pegs 724-736
  jiffy stand 720-721
  license plate bracket 689-690
  saddlebags 709-714
    supports/guards 714-719
  seats 672-673
  torque specifications 737-738
  Tour-Pak 721-724
  windshield. 690-693
Brakes
  ABS
    diode pack 655
    module 652-655
    system. 648-649
    wheel speed sensors 649-652
  bleeding 660-663
  caliper
    front
      2006-2007 models . . . 613-618

    2008-2009 models . . . 618-619
    rear
      2006-2007 models . . . 632-637
      2008-2009 models . . . 637-638
  disc 659-660
  flushing the brake system 663
  hose and line replacement
    (non-ABS models) 645-648
  line replacement
    (ABS models). 655-659
  master cylinder
    front
      2006-2007 models . . . 620-625
      2008-2009 models . . . 625-629
    rear
      and brake pedal
        (all models). 638-641
      service
        2006-2007 models . 641-643
        2008-2009 models . 643-645
  pad replacement
    front 610-613
    rear 630-632
  pedal, rear 638-641
  problems, troubleshooting . . 53-54
  service. 609-610
  specifications 663
    torque 664
  system. 79-81

C

Camshaft
  sprocket spacers, rear 222
  support plate 183-204
Carbureted models
  air filter and backplate . . . 348-350
  carburetor 350-361

Carbureted models (continued)
  fuel
    level sender (canopy) . . . 374-375
    shutoff valve 373-374
    specifications 379
      torque 379
    tank. 369-373
      console 365-369
  intake manifold 361-363
  starting enrichment valve
    (choke) cable replacement . . . 365
  throttle and idle cables . . . 363-365
CB module 517-518
Charging system 446-448
  troubleshooting 44-47
Choke cable
  adjustment 76
  replacement 365
Clutch
  adjustment 81-82
  and primary chaincase
    torque specifications 275-276
  assembly 234-240
  cable replacement 261-264
  compensating sprocket
    inspection 256-259
  hydraulic hose
    replacement 274-275
  lever assembly 264-265
  master cylinder 267-272
  pushrod and release plate
    inspection 240-241
  release cover
    all models except
      Screamin' Eagle 265-266
    Screamin' Eagle
      models 272-273
  secondary actuator 273-274
  service 267
  shell, hub and
    sprocket 249-255
  specifications and
    sprocket sizes 277
  sprocket alignment spacers 277
  starter jackshaft
    (2006 models) 259-261
  system 81-83
    bleeding 275-276
    draining 275
    flushing 275
    troubleshooting 52
Compensating sprocket
  inspection 256-259
Compression test 89-92
Control cables 74-75
  adjustment 666-669
  replacement 669-670
Conversion formulas 25

Crankcase
  and crankshaft 205-215
  bearing replacement 215-221
Cruise control
  cables
    adjustment 666-669
    replacement 669-670
  fuel-injected models 419
  inoperative diagnosis,
    troubleshooting 65-66
  trouble codes 57
  module (2006-2007 models) . . . 670
  specifications
    torque 671
  switches 671
  system components and
    operation 665-666
Cylinder 140-145
  head 121-128

D

Depressurizing the fuel
  system 385-386
Device part numbers,
  troubleshooting 65
Diagnostic flow charts . . . . . . See CD
Diagnostic trouble codes,
  troubleshooting . . . . 59-62, See CD
Dimensions 22-23
Drive belt 566-567
Driven sprocket assembly . . 563-566
DTC flow charts . . . . See CD

E

Electrical system
  alternator 448-451
  autofuse electrical
    connectors 537-538
  automatic compression release
    solenoid 503
  bulb specifications 539-540
  battery 440-443
    charging rates/times
      (approximate) 539
    tray 443-446
  CB module 517-518
  charging system 446-448
  component replacement 437
  connector
    location and identification . . . 521
    service 521-537
  electrical
    bracket 457-458
    caddies 458-460
  electronic control module (ECM)
    (fuel-injected models) . . . 456-457

fender tip light 496-497
front
  fairing speakers 516
  headset receptacle 516-517
fundamentals 15-16
fuses 437-438
  specifications (amperes) 539
headlight 475-485
horn 511-512
ignition
  coil 452-456
  control module (ICM)
    (carbureted models) 456
  system 451-452
instruments 500-503
license plate light 498
lighting system 475
Maxi-Fuse 438-440
passing lights and front
  turn signals 485-488
radio
  antenna 515-516
  storage box 515
rear
  fascia light 497-498
  passenger switches 517
  speakers 517
  relays 518-521
sealed butt connectors 538
security siren 514-515
sensors 460-462
specifications 538-539
  torque 540-542
  troubleshooting 57-58
starter 462-475
switches 503-511
taillight/brake light 494-496
testing, troubleshooting 34-38
Tour-Pak 498-500
turn signals 488-494
  security module (TSM,
    TSSM and HFSM 512-514
voltage regulator 451
wiring diagrams . . . . See CD
Electronic
  control module (ECM) . . . 456-457
  diagnostic system,
    troubleshooting 54-56
  fuel injection (EFI) 413-416
Engine 164-173
  break-in 221
  guard 720
  in-frame servicing 105
  lower end
    camshaft
      sprocket spacers, rear 222
      support plate 183-204
    crankcase and crankshaft . . 205-213

INDEX

crankcase bearing
   replacement 215-221
oil
   cooler, filter mount and
      thermostat 177-183
   filter mount 176-177
   pump 173-176
   specifications 221-222
   torque 222-223
lubrication troubleshooting.. 51-52
noises, troubleshooting 34
oil and filter 68-71
performance,
   troubleshooting 33-34
starting, troubleshooting 31-33
top end
   active exhaust 158-159
   cylinder 140-145
      head 121-128
   engine
      general specifications 160
      service precautions 105
      servicing in frame 105
   exhaust system 151-158
   pistons and piston
      rings 145-151
   pushrod and lifter location ... 163
   rocker arms, pushrods and valve
      lifters 105-121
   top end
      and exhaust torque
         specifications 163
   specifications
      all models except
         Screamin' Eagle .. 160-161
      general 160
      Screamin' Eagle
         models 161-162
   valves and valve
      components 128-140
   work methods 105
Evaporative emission control
   system
   carbureted and fuel-injected
      models 375-379
Excessive vibration
   troubleshooting 53
Exhaust system 151-158
   active exhaust 158-159
   upper end and exhaust torque
      specifications 163
External shift mechanism
   five speed transmission 279
   six speed transmission ... 310-312

F

Fascia light, rear 497-500

Fairing
   front
      FLHT, FLHTCUSE and
         FLHX models 699-707
      FLTR and FLTRSE3
         models 693-699
      speakers 516
Fasteners 3-6
Fender
   front 679-682
   rear
      all models except
         Screamin' Eagle 682-685
      fascia 687-689
      Screamin' Eagle models . 685-687
   tip light 496-497
Flow charts,
   troubleshooting .... See CD
Flushing the brake system 663
Footboards and highway foot
   pegs 724-736
Fork
   front 583-593
   oil filling and adjustment 593
   capacity and oil level
      specifications 599
Frame
   rails, rear 676-679
   side covers 707
Fuel
   engine and drive fluid
      capacities 102
   injected models
      air filter and backplate
         2007 FLHRSE3 and
            2009 FLTRSE3 domestic
            models 384-385
         all models except 2007
            FLHRSE3 and 2009
            FLTRSE3 380-384
      depressurizing the fuel
         system 385-386
      electronic fuel injection
         (EFI) 413-416
      induction module 422-428
      injectors 428-430
      level sender 403
      pressure test 403-405
      pump and fuel filter 400-403
      pump/level sender
         assembly 394-400
      supply check valve 394
      tank 386-394
         console 405-413
      sensors
         2006-2007 models ... 430-434
         2008-2009 models ... 434-435
      specifications 436

      torque 436
   throttle
      and idle cables 416-419
      twist grip sensor
         (TGS) 419-421
         jumper wire 421-422
   level sender (canopy),
      carbureted models 374-375
   shutoff valve, carbureted
      models 373-374
   system 81-83
   carbureted models
      specifications 379
      torque specifications 379
      troubleshooting 49-51
   electronic fuel injection,
      troubleshooting 51
   tank
      carbureted models 369-373
      fuel-injected models 386-394
      console
         carbureted models 365-368
         fuel-injected models .. 405-412
Fuses 437-438
   specifications (amperes) 539

G

General
   engine specifications 160
   information
      American tap drill sizes ... 26-27
      conversion formulas 25
      decimal and metric equivalents .. 24
      electrical system
         fundamentals 15-16
      fasteners 3-6
      general
         dimensions 22-23
         torque specifications 25
      measuring tools 11-15
      metric tap drill sizes 27
      model designations 22
      motorcycle weight 23-24
      serial numbers 3
      shop supplies 6-7
      storage 21
      technical abbreviations 25-26
      tools 7-11
         special 27-30

H

Handlebar
   all models except Screamin'
      Eagle 577-580
   Screamin' Eagle
      models 580-583

INDEX

Headlight 475-485
Headset receptacle, front . . . 516-517
Horn 511-512
Hubs, front and rear 548-563

I

Idle speed adjustment 94-95
Ignition
  coil 452-456
  control module (ICM) (carbureted
    models) 456
  system 451-452
    troubleshooting 47-49
  timing 94
Induction module 422-428
Instruments 500-503
Intake manifold 361-363

J

Jiffy stand 720-721

L

License plate
  bracket 689-690
  light 498
Lighting system 475
  troubleshooting 52
Lubrication
  and maintenance
    schedule 100-102
  control cables 74-76
  engine oil and filter 68-71
  front fork oil 74
  fuel, engine and drive fluid
    capacities 102
  primary chaincase oil 72-74
  recommended
    engine oil 102
    lubricants and fluids 103
  Screamin' Eagle 68
  transmission oil 71-72

M

Main drive gear
  five speed transmission . . . 301-305
  six speed transmission . . . 335-340
Maintenance
  and tune-up torque
    specifications 103-104
  air filter 83-89
  brake system 79-81
  clutch system 81-83
  compression test 89-92
  control cables 74-76
  fuel system 83
  idle speed adjustment 94-95
  ignition timing 94
  intervals 67
  pre-ride inspection 67-68
  primary chain and drive belt . 76-79
  schedule 100-102
  spark plugs 92-94
  specifications 103
  suspension and fasteners 89
  tires
    and wheels 68
    inflation pressure (cold) 102
  vehicle alignment 95-100
Maxi-fuse 438-440
Measuring tools 11-15
Metric tap drill sizes 27
Model designations 22
Motorcycle
  stands 543
  weight 23-24
Multiple DTC priority,
  troubleshooting 62-63

O

Odometer reset switch,
  removal 695
Oil
  cooler, filter mount and
    thermostat 177-182
  filter mount 176-177
  pan
    five speed
      transmission 308-309
    six speed transmission . . 345-346
  pump 173-176

P

Passenger switches, rear 517
Passing lights and front
  turn signals 485-488
Pistons and rings 145-151
Pre-ride inspection 67-68
Primary
  chain
    alignment 244-245
    and drive belt 76-79
    and tensioner inspection 256
  chaincase
    cover 224-228
    housing
      2006 models 228-231
      2007-2009 models . . . 231-233
    oil 72-74
  drive
    assembly
      2006 models 241-244
      2007-2009 models . . . 245-249
    chain
      alignment 244-245
      and tensioner inspection . . . 256
    chaincase
      and clutch torque
        specifications 277-278
      cover 224-228
      housing
        2006 models 228-231
        2007-2009 models . 231-233
Pushrod and lifter location 163

R

Radio
  antenna 515-516
  storage box 515
Relays 518-521
Rocker arms, pushrods and
  valve lifters 105-121

S

Saddlebags 709-714
  supports/guards 714-719
Safety 1-3
Sealed butt connectors 538
Seats 672-673
Security siren 514-515
Sensors 460-462
  fuel-injected models
    2006-2007 models 430-434
    2008-2009 models 434-435
Serial numbers 3
Servicing engine in frame 105
Shift
  arm assembly
    five speed transmission . 286-287
    six speed transmission . . 315-317
  assembly
    five speed transmission 279
    six speed transmission 312
  cam, five speed
    transmission 284-286
  forks
    and shift cam, six speed
      transmission 317-320
    five speed transmission . 287-288
Shock
  absorbers 601-603
  air pressure adjustment 600
  air pressure loss
    inspection 600-601
Side door
  bearings
    six speed transmission 335
      specifications 347

INDEX

five speed transmission 301
Spark plugs 92-94
   cables 49
Speakers, rear 517
Specifications
   ABS DTC priority 64-65
   battery charging rates/times ... 539
   body and frame torque ... 737-738
   brake 663
      torque 664
   bulb 539-540
   clutch
      and primary chaincase torque
         specifications 277-278
      and sprocket sizes 277
   conversion formulas 25
   cruise inoperative
      diagnosis 65-66
   decimal and metric
      equivalents 24
   device part numbers 65
   diagnostic trouble codes 59-62
   electrical system ... 57-58, 538-539
      torque specifications 540-542
   fork oil capacity and oil level .. 599
   fuel system
      carbureted models 379
         torque specifications 379
      engine and drive fluid
         capacities 102
      injected models 436
         torque specifications 436
   fuse specifications (amperes) .. 539
   general
      dimensions 22-23
      engine specifications 160
      torque recommendations 25
   headlight aim adjustments 540
   laced wheel offset 575
   lower end 221-222
      torque specifications 222-223
   maintenance 103
      and lubrication
         schedule 100-102
      and tune-up torque
         specifications 103-104
   metric tap and drill sizes 27
   model designations 22
   motorcycle weight 23-24
   multiple DTC priority 63-64
   push rod and lifter location 163
   rear
      camshaft sprocket spacers ... 222
      suspension
         air pressure 608
         torque specifications 608
   recommended
      engine oil 102

lubricants and fluids 102-103
special tools 27-30
suspension torque specifications,
   front 599
symptoms that do not set
   DTC codes 62-63
technical abbreviations 25-26
tire inflation pressure
   (cold) 102, 576
transmission
   five speed transmission
      general 309
      service 310
      torque specifications .. 310-311
   six speed
      side door bearings 347
      general 346
      service 346-347
      torque specifications 347
typical engine scan values (EFI
   models only) 59
upper end
   and exhaust torque
      specifications 163
   all models except Screamin'
      Eagle 160-161
   Screamin' Eagle
      models 161-162
wheel
   runout (maximum) 575
   torque specifications 576
U.S. tap and drill sizes 27
Starter 462-475
   jackshaft (2006 models) .. 259-261
Starting
   enrichment valve (choke) cable
      carbureted models
         adjustment 76
         replacement 365
   system 462
   troubleshooting 38-44
Steering
   handlebar
      all models except Screamin'
         Eagle 577-580
      Screamin' Eagle models. 580-583
   head
      and stem 593-596
      bearing race
         replacement 596-597
      play, inspection and
         adjustment 597-599
Storage 21
Suspension
   fasteners 89
   steering, troubleshooting 53
   front
      fork 583-593

oil capacity and oil level
   specifications 599
handlebar
   all models except Screamin'
      Eagle 577-580
   Screamin' Eagle
      models 580-583
   torque specifications 599
rear
   air pressure 608
   torque specifications 608
Swing arm, rear 603-607
Switches 503-511

T

Taillight/brake light 494-496
Technical abbreviations 25-26
TDC, locating 108
Throttle
   and idle cables non-cruise control
      models
      2006 and 2007 models
         fuel-injected models .. 415-419
         carbureted models 363-365
   control actuator (TCA) 419
   or twist grip sensor 419-422
Tires
   and wheels 68
   changing
      alloy wheels 573-574
      laced wheels 570-572
   inflation pressure (cold) .. 102, 576
   repairs 574-575
Tools 7-11
   special 27-30
Torque specifications
   body and frame 737-738
   brake 664
   clutch and primary chaincase .. 278
   electrical system 540-542
   five speed transmission ... 310-311
   fuel system
      carbureted models 379
      fuel-injected models 436
   general recommendations 25
   lower end 222-223
   maintenance and tune-up . 103-104
   six speed transmission 347
   suspension
      front 599
      rear 608
   upper end and exhaust 163
   wheel 576
Tour-Pak 498-500, 721-724
Transmission
   five speed
      case 306-308

Transmission (continued)
   cover.................. 281-284
   drive sprocket......... 305-306
   external shift mechanism.... 281
   general specifications....... 309
   main drive gear........ 301-305
   oil pan................ 308-309
   service specifications....... 310
   shafts................. 290-301
   shift
      arm assembly....... 286-287
      assembly............... 279
      cam................ 284-286
      forks.............. 287-288
   side door
      assembly........... 288-290
      bearings............... 301
   torque specifications.... 310-311
oil........................ 71-72
six speed
   case................. 341-345
   cover................ 314-315
   drive sprocket......... 340-341
   external shift
     mechanism.......... 312-314
   general specifications....... 346
   main drive gear........ 335-340
   oil pan................ 345-346
   service specifications... 346-347
   shafts................. 325-335
   shift
      arm assembly....... 315-317
      assembly............... 312
      forks and shift cam... 317-320
   side door
      assembly........... 320-325
      bearings............... 335
        specifications......... 347
   torque specifications........ 347
   troubleshooting.............. 52

Troubleshooting
   ABS DTC priority........ 64-65
   brake problems........... 53-54
   charging system.......... 44-47
   clutch..................... 52
   cruise control system
     diagnostic trouble codes...... 57
     inoperative diagnosis..... 65-66
     device part numbers.......... 65
   diagnostic trouble codes.... 59-61
   electrical
     system specifications..... 57-58
     testing.................. 34-38
   electronic diagnostic
     system.................. 54-56
   engine
     lubrication.............. 51-52
     noises...................... 34
     performance............. 33-34
     starting................. 31-33
   excessive vibration........... 53
   flow charts.............. See CD
   fuel system
     carbureted models....... 49-51
     electronic fuel injection...... 51
   ignition system.......... 47-49
   lighting system.............. 52
   multiple DTC priority...... 63-64
   starting system.......... 38-44
   suspension and steering,
     front...................... 53
   symptoms that do not set DTC
     codes.................. 62-63
   transmission................. 52
   typical engine scan values (EFI
     models only).............. 59
Tune-up
   and maintenance torque
     specifications......... 103-104
   air filter................. 83-89

   compression test.......... 89-92
   idle speed adjustment...... 94-95
   ignition timing.............. 94
   spark plug............... 92-94
   suspension and fasteners....... 89
   vehicle alignment (2006-2008
     models)............... 95-100
Turn signals............. 488-494
   security module (TSM, TSSM and
     HFSM).............. 512-514
Twist grip sensor jumper
   wire.................. 422-423

V

Valves and components.... 128-140
Vehicle alignment......... 95-100
Voltage regulator............. 451

W

Wheels
   balance............... 569-570
   front................. 543-546
   hubs
     front and rear......... 548-563
   laced wheel
     offset..................... 575
     service............... 567-569
   rear.................. 546-548
   runout..................... 575
   speed sensors.......... 649-652
   torque specifications......... 576
Wiggle test................... 37
Windshield.............. 690-693
Wiring diagrams........... See CD
WOW test.................... 56

MAINTENANCE LOG

Date	Miles	Type of Service

Check out clymer.com for our full line of powersport repair manuals.

BMW
M308	500 & 600cc Twins, 55-69
M502-3	BMW R50/5-R100GS PD, 70-96
M500-3	BMW K-Series, 85-97
M501-2	K1200RS, GT & LT, 98-08
M503-3	R850, R1100, R1150 & R1200C, 93-05
M309	F650, 1994-2000

HARLEY-DAVIDSON
M419	Sportsters, 59-85
M429-5	XL/XLH Sportster, 86-03
M427-2	XL Sportster, 04-09
M418	Panheads, 48-65
M420	Shovelheads, 66-84
M421-3	FLS/FXS Evolution, 84-99
M423-2	FLS/FXS Twin Cam, 00-05
M250	FLS/FXS/FXC Softail, 06-09
M422-3	FLH/FLT/FXR Evolution, 84-98
M430-4	FLH/FLT Twin Cam, 99-05
M252	FLH/FLT, 06-09
M426	VRSC Series, 02-07
M424-2	FXD Evolution, 91-98
M425-3	FXD Twin Cam, 99-05

HONDA
ATVs
M316	Odyssey FL250, 77-84
M311	ATC, TRX & Fourtrax 70-125, 70-87
M433	Fourtrax 90, 93-00
M326	ATC185 & 200, 80-86
M347	ATC200X & Fourtrax 200SX, 86-88
M455	ATC250 & Fourtrax 200/250, 84-87
M342	ATC250R, 81-84
M348	TRX250R/Fourtrax 250R & ATC250R, 85-89
M456-4	TRX250X 87-92; TRX300EX 93-06
M446-3	TRX250 Recon & Recon ES, 97-07
M215	TRX250EX, 01-05
M346-3	TRX300/Fourtrax 300 & TRX300FW/Fourtrax 4x4, 88-00
M200-2	TRX350 Rancher, 00-06
M459-3	TRX400 Foreman 95-03
M454-4	TRX400EX 99-07
M205	TRX450 Foreman, 98-04
M206	TRX500, 05-11
M210	TRX500 Rubicon, 01-04

Singles
M310-13	50-110cc OHC Singles, 65-99
M315	100-350cc OHC, 69-82
M317	125-250cc Elsinore, 73-80
M442	CR60-125R Pro-Link, 81-88
M431-2	CR80R, 89-95, CR125R, 89-91
M435	CR80R & CR80RB, 96-02
M457-2	CR125R, 92-97; CR250R, 92-96
M464	CR125R, 1998-2002
M443	CR250R-500R Pro-Link, 81-87
M432-3	CR250R, 88-91 & CR500R, 88-01
M437	CR250R, 97-01
M352	CRF250R, CRF250X, CRF450R & CRF450X, 02-05
M319-3	XR50R, CRF50F, XR70R & CRF70F, 97-09
M312-14	XL/XR75-100, 75-91
M222	XR80R, CRF80F, XR100R, & CRF100F, 92-09
M318-4	XL/XR/TLR 125-200, 79-03
M328-4	XL/XR250, 78-00; XL/XR350R 83-85; XR200R, 84-85; XR250L, 91-96
M320-2	XR400R, 96-04
M221	XR600R, 91-07; XR650L, 93-07
M339-8	XL/XR 500-600, 79-90
M225	XR650R, 00-07

Twins
M321	125-200cc Twins, 65-78
M322	250-350cc Twins, 64-74
M323	250-360cc Twins, 74-77
M324-5	Twinstar, Rebel 250 & Nighthawk 250, 78-03
M334	400-450cc Twins, 78-87
M333	450 & 500cc Twins, 65-76
M335	CX & GL500/650, 78-83
M344	VT500, 83-88
M313	VT700 & 750, 83-87
M314-3	VT750 Shadow Chain Drive, 98-06
M440	VT1100C Shadow, 85-96
M460-4	VT1100 Series, 95-07
M230	VTX1800 Series, 02-08
M231	VTX1300 Series, 03-09

Fours
M332	CB350-550, SOHC, 71-78
M345	CB550 & 650, 83-85
M336	CB650, 79-82
M341	CB750 SOHC, 69-78
M337	CB750 DOHC, 79-82
M436	CB750 Nighthawk, 91-93 & 95-99
M325	CB900, 1000 & 1100, 80-83
M439	600 Hurricane, 87-90
M441-2	CBR600F2 & F3, 91-98
M445-2	CBR600F4, 99-06
M220	CBR600RR, 03-06
M434-2	CBR900RR Fireblade, 93-99
M329	500cc V-Fours, 84-86
M349	700-1000cc Interceptor, 83-85
M458-2	VFR700F-750F, 86-97
M438	VFR800FI Interceptor, 98-00
M327	700-1100cc V-Fours, 82-88
M508	ST1100/Pan European, 90-02
M340	GL1000 & 1100, 75-83
M504	GL1200, 84-87

Sixes
M505	GL1500 Gold Wing, 88-92
M506-2	GL1500 Gold Wing, 93-00
M507-2	GL1800 Gold Wing, 01-05
M462-2	GL1500C Valkyrie, 97-03

KAWASAKI
ATVs
M465-2	Bayou KLF220 & KLF250, 88-03
M466-4	Bayou KLF300, 86-04
M467	Bayou KLF400, 93-99
M470	Lakota KEF300, 95-99
M385-2	Mojave KSF250, 87-04

Singles
M350-9	80-350cc Rotary Valve, 66-01
M444-2	KX60, 83-02; KX80 83-90
M448-2	KX80, 91-00; KX85, 01-10 & KX100, 89-09
M351	KDX200, 83-88
M447-3	KX125 & KX250, 82-91; KX500, 83-04
M472-2	KX125, 92-00
M473-2	KX250, 92-00
M474-3	KLR650, 87-07
M240	KLR650, 08-09

Twins
M355	KZ400, KZ/Z440, EN450 & EN500, 74-95
M360-3	EX500, GPZ500S, & Ninja 500R, 87-02
M356-5	Vulcan 700 & 750, 85-06
M354-3	Vulcan 800 & Vulcan 800 Classic, 95-05
M357-2	Vulcan 1500, 87-99
M471-3	Vulcan 1500 Series, 96-08

Fours
M449	KZ500/550 & ZX550, 79-85
M450	KZ, Z & ZX750, 80-85
M358	KZ650, 77-83
M359-3	Z & KZ 900-1000cc, 73-81
M451-3	KZ, ZX & ZN 1000 &1100cc, 81-02
M452-3	ZX500 & Ninja ZX600, 85-97
M468-2	Ninja ZX-6, 90-04
M469	Ninja ZX-7, ZX7R & ZX7RR, 91-98
M453-3	Ninja ZX900, ZX1000 & ZX1100, 84-01
M409	Concours, 86-04

POLARIS
ATVs
M496	3-, 4- and 6-Wheel Models w/250-425cc Engines, 85-95
M362-2	Magnum & Big Boss, 96-99
M363	Scrambler 500 4X4, 97-00
M365-4	Sportsman/Xplorer, 96-10
M366	Sportsman 600/700/800 Twins, 02-10
M367	Predator 500, 03-07

SUZUKI
ATVs
M381	ALT/LT 125 & 185, 83-87
M475	LT230 & LT250, 85-90
M380-2	LT250R Quad Racer, 85-92
M483-2	LT-4WD, LT-F4WDX & LT-F250, 87-98
M270-2	LT-Z400, 03-08
M343	LT-F500F Quadrunner, 98-00

Singles
M369	125-400cc, 64-81
M371	RM50-400 Twin Shock, 75-81
M379	RM125-500 Single Shock, 81-88
M386	RM80-250, 89-95
M400	RM125, 96-00
M401	RM250, 96-02
M476	DR250-350, 90-94
M477-3	DR-Z400E, S & SM, 00-09
M384-4	LS650 Savage/S40, 86-07

Twins
M372	GS400-450 Chain Drive, 77-87
M484-3	GS500E Twins, 89-02
M361	SV650, 1999-2002
M481-5	VS700-800 Intruder/S50, 85-07
M261	1500 Intruder/C90, 98-07
M260-2	Volusia/Boulevard C50, 01-08
M482-3	VS1400 Intruder/S83, 87-07

Triple
M368	GT380, 550 & 750, 72-77

Fours
M373	GS550, 77-86
M364	GS650, 81-83
M370	GS750, 77-82
M376	GS850-1100 Shaft Drive, 79-84
M378	GS1100 Chain Drive, 80-81
M383-3	Katana 600, 88-96 GSX-R750-1100, 86-87
M331	GSX-R600, 97-00
M264	GSX-R600, 01-05
M478-2	GSX-R750, 88-92; GSX750F Katana, 89-96
M485	GSX-R750, 96-99
M377	GSX-R1000, 01-04
M266	GSX-R1000, 05-06
M265	GSX1300R Hayabusa, 99-07
M338	Bandit 600, 95-00
M353	GSF1200 Bandit, 96-03

YAMAHA
ATVs
M499-2	YFM80 Moto-4, Badger & Raptor, 85-08
M394	YTM200, 225 & YFM200, 83-86
M488-5	Blaster, 88-05
M489-2	Timberwolf, 89-00
M487-5	Warrior, 87-04
M486-6	Banshee, 87-06
M490-3	Moto-4 & Big Bear, 87-04
M493	Kodiak, 93-98
M287	YFZ450, 04-09
M285-2	Grizzly 660, 02-08
M280-2	Raptor 660R, 01-05
M290	Raptor 700R, 06-09

Singles
M492-2	PW50 & 80 Y-Zinger & BW80 Big Wheel 80, 81-02
M410	80-175 Piston Port, 68-76
M415	250-400 Piston Port, 68-76
M412	DT & MX Series, 77-83
M414	IT125-490, 76-86
M393	YZ50-80 Monoshock, 78-90
M413	YZ100-490 Monoshock, 76-84
M390	YZ125-250, 85-87 YZ490, 85-90
M391	YZ125-250, 88-93 & WR250Z, 91-93
M497-2	YZ125, 94-01
M498	YZ250, 94-98; WR250Z, 94-97
M406	YZ250F & WR250F, 01-03
M491-2	YZ400F, 98-99 & 426F, 00-02; WR400F, 98-00 & 426F, 00-01
M417	XT125-250, 80-84
M480-3	XT350, 85-00; TT350, 86-87
M405	XT/TT 500, 76-81
M416	XT/TT 600, 83-89

Twins
M403	650cc Twins, 70-82
M395-10	XV535-1100 Virago, 81-03
M495-6	V-Star 650, 98-09
M281-4	V-Star 1100, 99-09
M283	V-Star 1300, 07-10
M282	Road Star, 99-05

Triple
M404	XS750 & XS850, 77-81

Fours
M387	XJ550, XJ600 & FJ600, 81-92
M494	XJ600 Seca II/Diversion, 92-98
M388	YX600 Radian & FZ600, 86-90
M396	FZR600, 89-93
M392	FZ700-750 & Fazer, 85-87
M411	XS1100, 78-81
M461	YZF-R6, 99-04
M398	YZF-R1, 98-03
M399	FZ1, 01-05
M397	FJ1100 & 1200, 84-93
M375	V-Max, 85-03
M374	Royal Star, 96-03

VINTAGE MOTORCYCLES
Clymer® Collection Series
M330	Vintage British Street Bikes, BSA 500–650cc Unit Twins; Norton 750 & 850cc Commandos; Triumph 500-750cc Twins
M300	Vintage Dirt Bikes, V. 1 Bultaco, 125-370cc Singles; Montesa, 123-360cc Singles; Ossa, 125-250cc Singles
M305	Vintage Japanese Street Bikes, Honda, 250 & 305cc Twins; Kawasaki, 250-750cc Triples; Kawasaki, 900 & 1000cc Fours